Glencoe Science Level Red
Contents in Brief

W9-AZW-156

Teacher Wraparound Edition

Correlations and Standards

Program Resources

Support for All Learners

Classroom Activities and Materials

Student Edition

SAFETY SYMBOLS

SAFETY SYMBOLS	HAZARD	EXAMPLES	PRECAUTION	REMEDY
DISPOSAL	Special disposal procedures need to be followed.	certain chemicals, living organisms	Do not dispose of these materials in the sink or trash can.	Dispose of wastes as directed by your teacher.
BIOLOGICAL	Organisms or other biological materials that might be harmful to humans	bacteria, fungi, blood, unpreserved tissues, plant materials	Avoid skin contact with these materials. Wear mask or gloves.	Notify your teacher if you suspect contact with material. Wash hands thoroughly.
EXTREME TEMPERATURE	Objects that can burn skin by being too cold or too hot	boiling liquids, hot plates, dry ice, liquid nitrogen	Use proper protection when handling.	Go to your teacher for first aid.
SHARP OBJECT	Use of tools or glassware that can easily puncture or slice skin	razor blades, pins, scalpels, pointed tools, dissecting probes, broken glass	Practice common-sense behavior and follow guidelines for use of the tool.	Go to your teacher for first aid.
FUME	Possible danger to respiratory tract from fumes	ammonia, acetone, nail polish remover, heated sulfur, moth balls	Make sure there is good ventilation. Never smell fumes directly. Wear a mask.	Leave foul area and notify your teacher immediately.
ELECTRICAL	Possible danger from electrical shock or burn	improper grounding, liquid spills, short circuits, exposed wires	Double-check setup with teacher. Check condition of wires and apparatus.	Do not attempt to fix electrical problems. Notify your teacher immediately.
IRRITANT	Substances that can irritate the skin or mucous membranes of the respiratory tract	pollen, moth balls, steel wool, fiberglass, potassium permanganate	Wear dust mask and gloves. Practice extra care when handling these materials.	Go to your teacher for first aid.
CHEMICAL	Chemicals that can react with and destroy tissue and other materials	bleaches such as hydrogen peroxide; acids such as sulfuric acid, hydrochloric acid; bases such as ammonia, sodium hydroxide	Wear goggles, gloves, and an apron.	Immediately flush the affected area with water and notify your teacher.
TOXIC	Substance may be poisonous if touched, inhaled, or swallowed	mercury, many metal compounds, iodine, poinsettia plant parts	Follow your teacher's instructions.	Always wash hands thoroughly after use. Go to your teacher for first aid.
OPEN FLAME	Open flame may ignite flammable chemicals, loose clothing, or hair	alcohol, kerosene, potassium permanganate, hair, clothing	Tie back hair. Avoid wearing loose clothing. Avoid open flames when using flammable chemicals. Be aware of locations of fire safety equipment.	Notify your teacher immediately. Use fire safety equipment if applicable.

 Eye Safety Proper eye protection should be worn at all times by anyone performing or observing science activities.

 Clothing Protection This symbol appears when substances could stain or burn clothing.

 Animal Safety This symbol appears when safety of animals and students must be ensured.

 Radioactivity This symbol appears when radioactive materials are used.

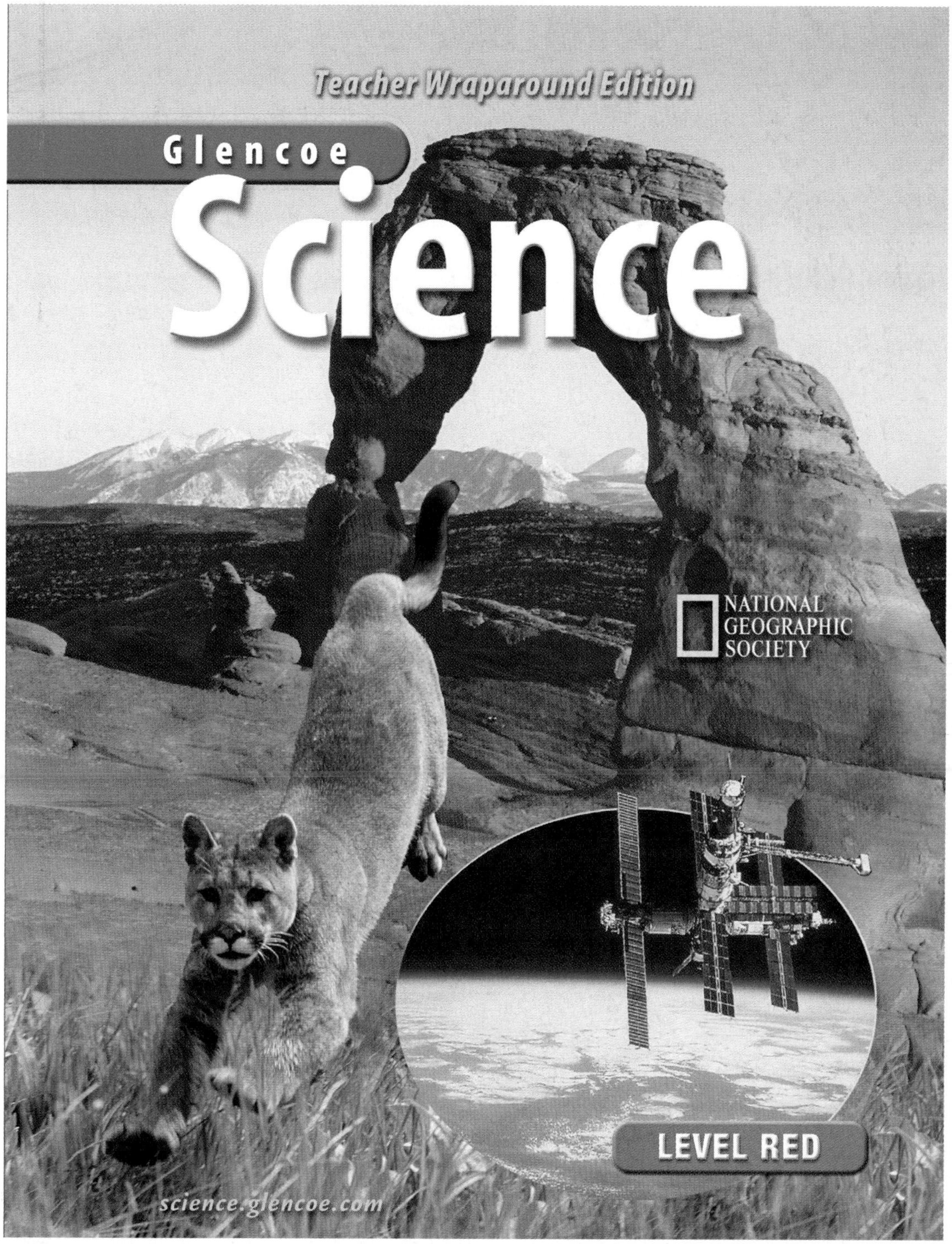

Glencoe Science

NATIONAL GEOGRAPHIC SOCIETY

LEVEL RED

science.glencoe.com

Glencoe McGraw-Hill

New York, New York   Columbus, Ohio   Woodland Hills, California   Peoria, Illinois

GLENCOE SCIENCE LEVEL RED

Student Edition
Teacher Wraparound Edition
Interactive Teacher Edition CD-ROM
Interactive Lesson Planner CD-ROM
Lesson Plans
Content Outline for Teaching
Directed Reading for Content Mastery
Foldables: Reading and Study Skills
Assessment
    Chapter Review
    Chapter Tests
    ExamView® Pro Test Bank CD-ROM
    Assessment Transparencies
    Performance Assessment in the Science Classroom
    The Princeton Review Test Practice Booklet
Directed Reading for Content Mastery in Spanish
Spanish Resources
English/Spanish Guided Reading Audio Program
Reinforcement

Enrichment
Activity Worksheets
Section Focus Transparencies
Teaching Transparencies
Laboratory Activities
Science Inquiry Labs
Critical Thinking/Problem Solving
Reading and Writing Skill Activities
Mathematics Skill Activities
Cultural Diversity
Laboratory Management and Safety in the Science Classroom
MindJogger Videoquizzes and Teacher Guide
Interactives CD-ROM with Presentation Builder
Vocabulary PuzzleMaker Software
Cooperative Learning
Environmental Issues in the Science Classroom
Home and Community Involvement
Using the Internet in the Science Classroom
Dinah Zike's Teaching Science with Foldables

THE PRINCETON REVIEW

"Test-Taking Tip," "Study Tip," and "Test Practice" features in this book were written by The Princeton Review, the nation's leader in test preparation. Through its association with McGraw-Hill, The Princeton Review offers the best way to help students excel on standardized assessments.

The Princeton Review is not affiliated with Princeton University or Educational Testing Service.

Glencoe/McGraw-Hill

A Division of The McGraw-Hill Companies

Copyright © 2003 by Glencoe/McGraw-Hill. All rights reserved. Except as permitted under the United States Copyright Act, no part of this publication may be reproduced or distributed in any form or by any means, or stored in a database or retrieval system, without prior written permission of the publisher.

The "Visualizing" features in each chapter and the unit opening pages of this textbook were designed and developed by National Geographic Society's Education Division, copyright © 2002 National Geographic Society. The name "National Geographic Society" and the yellow border rectangle are trademarks of the Society, and their use without prior written permission is strictly prohibited. All rights reserved.

The "Science and Society" and the "Science and History" features that appear in this book were designed and developed by TIME School Publishing, a division of TIME Magazine. TIME and the red border are trademarks of Time, Inc. All rights reserved.

Send all inquiries to:

    Glencoe/McGraw-Hill
    8787 Orion Place
    Columbus, OH 43240

ISBN 0-07-828239-X

Printed in the United States of America

4 5 6 7 8 9 10 071/055 10 09 08 07 06 05 04 03

Authors, Reviewers, and Consultants

for the *Teacher Wraparound Edition*

Authors

National Geographic Society
Education Division
Washington, D.C.

Alton Biggs
Biology Teacher
Allen High School
Allen, Texas

Lucy Daniel, EdD
Teacher/Consultant
Rutherford County Schools
Rutherfordton, North Carolina

Ralph M. Feather Jr., PhD
Science Department Chair
Derry Area School District
Derry, Pennsylvania

Norman G. Lederman, PhD
Professor of Science and Math Education
Oregon State University
Corvallis, Oregon

Peter Rillero, PhD
Professor of Science Education
Arizona State University West
Phoenix, Arizona

Susan Leach Snyder
Earth Science Teacher, Consultant
Jones Middle School
Upper Arlington, Ohio

Dinah Zike
Educational Consultant
Dinah-Might Activities, Inc.
San Antonio, Texas

Contributing Authors

Cathy Ezrailson
Science Department Head
Academy for Science and Health Professions
Conroe, Texas

Patricia Horton
Mathematics and Science Teacher
Summit Intermediate School
Etiwanda, California

Thomas McCarthy, PhD
Science Department Chair
St. Edwards School
Vero Beach, Florida

Reviewers

Sandra K. Enger, PhD
Coordinator
UAH Institute for Science Education
Huntsville, Alabama

Lee Meadows, PhD
Associate Professor of Science Education
University of Alabama
Birmingham, Alabama

Gilbert Naizer, PhD
Assistant Professor of Elementary Education
Texas A&M University
Commerce, Texas

Kimberly S. Roempler, PhD
Associate Director
Eisenhower National Clearinghouse for
Math and Science
The Ohio State University
Columbus, Ohio

Cultural Diversity Consultants

Nedaro Bellamy
Associate Director,
Rice Model Science Laboratory
Lanier Middle School, Houston ISD
Houston, Texas

Joyce Hilliard-Clark, PhD
Director, Imhotep Academy
North Carolina State University
Raleigh, North Carolina

Inclusion Strategies Consultant

Barry Barto
Special Education Teacher
John F. Kennedy Elementary School
Manistee, Michigan

National Science Education Standards

"The National Science Education Standards are premised on a conviction that all students deserve and must have the opportunity to become scientifically literate. The Standards look toward a future in which all Americans, familiar with basic scientific ideas and processes, can have fuller and more productive lives."

—*National Science Education Standards*

About the Standards

This book, published by the National Research Council, represents the contributions of thousands of educators and scientists, and offers a comprehensive vision of a scientifically literate society. The standards describe what all students should know at the end of grades 4, 8, and 12, and offer guidelines for science teaching and assessment.

How *Glencoe Science Level Red* Aligns with *The National Science Education Standards*

Content Standards

The correlations that follow show the close alignment between *Glencoe Science Level Red* and the grade-appropriate standards. *Glencoe Science Level Red* allows students to discover concepts within each of the content standards and gives students opportunities to make connections among the science disciplines. Hands-on activities and inquiry-based lessons reinforce the science processes emphasized in the standards.

Teaching Standards

Glencoe Science Level Red provides activities and discussions that allow students to discover science concepts through inquiry and to apply the knowledge they've constructed to their own lives. The *Teacher Wraparound Edition* supports this endeavor with an abundance of effective strategies for guiding students of different ability levels and interests as they explore science.

Assessment Standards

Glencoe Science Level Red provides many opportunities in many different formats to assess students' understanding of important concepts. Ideas for portfolios, performance activities, and written assessments accompany every section. Glencoe's Professional Series booklet *Performance Assessment in the Science Classroom* contains rubrics and Performance Task Assessment Lists. This booklet also contains information about evaluating cooperative work. Learning outcomes improve for students of all ability levels in a cooperative learning environment.

Correlation to
National Science Education Standards

The following chart illustrates how *Glencoe Science Level Red* addresses the National Science Education Standards.

Content Standard	Chapter and Section
(UCP) Unifying Concepts and Processes	
1. Systems, order, and organization	1-4, 2-1, 2-2, 4-1, 4-2, 5-1, 6-1, 6-2, 6-3, 6-4, 8-1, 11-1, 11-2, 11-3, 12-2, 12-3, 13-2, 17-2
2. Evidence, models, and explanation	1-1, 1-2, 1-3, 3-2, 8-3, 9-1, 9-2, 9-3, 9-4, 10-1, 11-3, 12-4, 13-3, 14-1, 14-2, 14-3, 15-3, 17-1, 18-1, 18-2, 21-1, 21-2, 21-3, 22-1, 22-2
3. Change, constancy, and measurement	10-2, 10-3, 11-2, 13-1, 13-3, 15-2, 16-1, 16-2, 19-1, 19-2, 19-3, 20-1, 20-3
4. Evolution and equilibrium	7-1, 7-2, 7-3, 7-4, 8-2, 12-1, 13-3, 17-3, 20-2
5. Form and function	3-1, 4-1, 4-2, 5-2, 5-3, 15-1
(A) Science as Inquiry	
1. Abilities necessary to do scientific inquiry	1-1, 1-4, 2-1, 2-2, 3-1, 3-2, 4-1, 4-2, 5-2, 5-3, 6-3, 6-4, 7-2, 7-3, 7-4, 8-1, 8-2, 8-3, 9-2, 9-3, 9-4, 10-1, 10-2, 10-3, 11-1, 11-3, 12-1, 12-2, 12-3, 12-4, 13-1, 13-2, 13-3, 14-2, 14-3, 15-1, 15-2, 15-3, 16-1, 16-2, 17-1, 17-3, 18-1, 18-2, 19-2, 19-3, 20-1, 10-2, 20-3, 21-2, 21-3, 22-1, 22-2
2. Understandings about scientific inquiry	1-1, 1-3, 1-4, 11-3
(B) Physical Science	
1. Properties and changes of properties in matter	1-1, 12-1, 12-2, 12-3, 13-1, 16-1, 16-2, 18-1, 18-2, 22-1, 22-2
2. Motion and forces	8-3, 10-3, 14-1, 14-2, 14-3, 17-2, 19-1, 19-2, 19-3, 22-1, 22-2
3. Transfer of energy	10-2, 14-1, 14-2, 14-3, 20-1, 20-2, 20-3, 21-1, 21-2, 21-3, 22-2
(C) Life Science	
1. Structure and function in living systems	1-2, 1-3, 1-4, 2-1, 2-2, 3-1, 4-1, 4-2, 5-1, 5-2, 5-3, 6-1, 6-2, 6-3, 6-4, 7-1, 7-2, 7-3, 7-4, 8-1, 9-3, 21-1
2. Reproduction and heredity	3-1, 4-2, 7-2
3. Regulation and behavior	2-1, 2-2, 3-1
4. Populations and ecosystems	1-2, 3-2, 6-3, 7-1, 7-2, 7-3, 7-4, 8-1, 8-2, 8-3, 12-4
5. Diversity and adaptations of organisms	3-1, 4-1, 4-2, 5-1, 5-2, 5-3, 6-1, 6-2, 6-3, 6-4, 7-1, 7-2, 7-3, 7-4, 12-4
(D) Earth and Space Science	
1. Structure of the Earth system	9-1, 9-2, 9-3, 9-4, 10-1, 10-2, 10-3, 11-1, 11-2, 11-3, 12-1, 12-2, 12-3, 13-1, 13-2, 13-3, 14-1, 14-2, 14-3, 15-1, 15-2, 15-3, 16-1, 16-2, 21-1
2. Earth's history	1-3, 7-4, 22-2
3. Earth in the solar system	10-1, 17-1, 17-2, 17-3
(E) Science and Technology	
1. Abilities of technological design	9-2, 11-3, 17-3, 19-3, 20-3
2. Understandings about science and technology	5-3, 9-1, 9-2, 9-3, 11-1, 11-3, 15-3, 19-3, 21-2, 21-3, 22-1
(F) Science in Personal and Social Perspectives	
1. Personal health	3-2, 14-3, 21-3
2. Populations, resources, and environments	9-1, 9-2, 9-3, 9-4, 16-1, 16-2
3. Natural hazards	11-1, 11-2, 14-3, 21-1
4. Risks and benefits	5-2, 9-1, 9-2, 11-3, 20-3
5. Science and technology in society	1-4, 2-2, 3-2, 4-2, 5-3, 9-1, 9-2, 9-3, 14-3, 15-2, 15-3, 19-3, 21-3, 22-2
(G) History and Nature of Science	
1. Science as a human endeavor	4-2, 7-4, 8-3, 9-4, 10-3, 11-3, 13-3, 16-2, 17-3, 19-3, 20-3, 22-2
2. Nature of science	1-4, 3-2, 5-3, 13-3, 14-3, 18-2, 21-3
3. History of science	1-3, 1-4, 15-3, 16-2, 18-2

National Council of Teachers of Mathematics
Principles and Standards for School Mathematics

Students often make personal, educational, and career choices on their own that can influence the rest of their lives. Throughout their school years, they acquire skills that help them make these decisions. The development of keen mathematical skills can ensure that students have a wide variety of life options.

Principles and Standards for School Mathematics of the National Council of Teachers of Mathematics describes the foundation of mathematical concepts and applications that can provide students with the necessary mathematical skills to help achieve their life goals.

The ten categories of mathematical concepts and applications, as shown in the table below, include a broad range of topics that build on previous knowledge. They also allow students to increase their abilities to visualize, describe, and analyze situations in mathematical terms.

In *Glencoe Science Level Red,* each Math Skill Activity and Problem-Solving Activity provides students with the opportunity to practice and apply some of the mathematical concepts and applications described in the Standards. These activities serve to reinforce mathematical skills in real-life situations, thus preparing students to meet their needs in an ever-changing world.

Correlation of
Glencoe Science Level Red to NCTM Standards Grades 6–8

Standard	Page
1. Number and Operations	11, 47, 199, 247, 286, 313, 358, 425, 503, 557, 558, 560, 566, 571, 597, 637, 640
2. Algebra	47, 313, 381, 425, 453, 503, 557, 558, 560, 566, 571, 597, 637, 640, 657
3. Geometry	657
4. Measurement	11, 47, 199, 247, 286, 313, 503, 545, 557, 558, 560, 566, 571, 597, 637, 640, 657
5. Data Analysis and Probability	11, 126, 230, 286, 358, 381, 503, 545, 597
6. Problem Solving	11, 47, 72, 97, 126, 162, 199, 230, 247, 286, 313, 358, 381, 425, 453, 479, 503, 545, 557, 558, 560, 566, 571, 597, 637, 640, 657
7. Reasoning and Proof	358, 381, 479, 503, 545, 597
8. Communication	11, 47, 72, 97, 126, 162, 199, 230, 247, 286, 313, 358, 381, 425, 453, 503, 545, 557, 558, 560, 566, 571, 597, 637, 640, 657
9. Connections	11, 47, 126, 199, 230, 247, 286, 313, 358, 381, 425, 453, 503, 545, 557, 558, 560, 566, 571, 597, 637, 640, 657
10. Representation	126, 230, 286, 358, 381, 453, 503, 597, 657

Benchmarks for Science Literacy

Benchmarks for Science Literacy is a publication by the American Association for the Advancement of Science that describes how students should progress toward science literacy. People who are science literate are "equipped with knowledge and skills they need to make sense of how the world works, to think critically and independently, and to lead interesting, responsible, and productive lives in a culture increasingly shaped by science and technology."

Benchmarks was the culmination of Project 2061, the work of scientists, mathematicians, engineers, and educators to develop benchmarks, or statements, of what *all* students should know or be able to do in science, mathematics, and technology by the end of grades 2, 5, 8, and 12.

Glencoe Science Level Red is aligned with *Benchmarks* in the following ways:

- Concepts are presented in ways that help students understand the how and why of science, not just requiring them to learn facts that they commit to short-term memory.

- Science concepts are related to students' daily experiences.

- Teachers are provided strategies for encouraging students in independent work and for addressing the needs of students of varied abilities.

- Specific strategies are provided for identifying and addressing student misconceptions.

IDENTIFYING Misconceptions

Educators are becoming increasingly aware of the importance of identifying and addressing misconceptions—prescientific or naïve ideas—that students may hold about science. Students often develop these from their experiences as a way to make sense of the world.

A one-page feature, Identifying Misconceptions, is found on the F interleaf pages preceding selected chapters in the *Teacher Wraparound Edition.* This feature provides specific teaching strategies to find out what students think about a particular concept, to help them understand the concept, and to assess the accuracy of their understanding after learning the concept. These strategies were developed by science education professors with a special interest in the field of student misconceptions. These professors are Norman G. Lederman, Ph.D., Professor of Science and Math Education at Oregon State University, and Peter Rillero, Ph.D., Professor of Science Education at Arizona State University.

Correlation to Benchmarks

Glencoe Science Level Red addresses many of the Benchmarks for Science Literacy.

Benchmark	Chapter(s)
4 The Physical Setting	
4A. The Universe	17
4B. The Earth	9, 10, 11, 12, 13, 14, 15, 16
4C. Processes That Shape the Earth	9, 11, 12, 14, 16
4D. Structure of Matter	18, 20
4E. Energy Transformation	8, 9, 10, 18, 19, 20, 21, 22
4F. Motion	10, 19
4G. Forces of Nature	10, 14, 16, 21, 22
5 The Living Environment	
5A. Diversity of Life	1, 2, 3, 4, 5, 6, 7, 12
5C. Cells	2, 3, 4
5D. Interdependence of Life	8, 12
5E. Flow of Matter and Energy	8
5F. Evolution of Life	1, 7
8 The Designed World	
8C. Energy Sources and Use	9, 20, 21, 22
10 Historical Perspectives	
10A. Displacing the Earth from the Center of the Universe	17
12 Habits of Mind	
12A. Values and Attitudes	1, All "Oops! Accidents in Science," "Science and History," and "Science and Language Arts" features
12B. Computation and Estimation	All chapters, 1–22
12D. Communication Skills	All Activities and Skill Builders

Planning Your Course

Glencoe Science Level Red is a flexible program that allows you to decide the pace at which you cover the content and which topics to present, based on the needs of your students and on district requirements. The **Glencoe Interactive Lesson Planner** integrates the **Teacher Classroom Resources** with an electronic lesson planner to make your job easier.

Pacing Options

Two approaches to covering all content are provided in the Planning Guide.

- A **traditional, full-year** course comprises 180 periods of approximately 45 minutes each.

- A **block scheduling** approach involves covering the same information in fewer days but in longer class periods.

Chapter Organizers

A two-page organizer (A–B pages) precedes every chapter in the teacher edition. These organizers include:

- pacing information and objectives.

- correlations to standards.

- lists of activities and the materials needed.

- lists of reproducible resources, assessments, and technologies with page or booklet references.

Interactive Lesson Planner

This easy-to-use CD-ROM allows you to:

- plan daily, weekly, monthly, or yearlong lessons in a versatile calendar format.

- select or customize a built-in plan, or make a new plan.

- print lesson plans.

- access all print components of the *Teacher Classroom Resources* through a convenient pop-up menu.

- print student pages and answer keys from the resource list or from the lesson plan.

Unit	Chapter	Single-Class (180 days*)	Block (90 days*)
1	**Life's Structure and Function**		
	1 Exploring and Classifying Life	9	4.5
	2 Cells—The Units of Life	7	3.5
	3 Bacteria	5	2.5
2	**Life's Diversity**		
	4 Protists and Fungi	7	3.5
	5 Plants	8	4
	6 Invertebrate Animals	9	4.5
	7 Vertebrate Animals	9	4.5
3	**Life and the Environment**		
	8 Interactions of Living Things	8	4
	9 Resources	9	4.5
4	**Earth's Air and Water**		
	10 Atmosphere	8	4
	11 Weather	8	4
	12 Oceans	10	5
5	**Earth and Space**		
	13 Rocks and Minerals	8	4
	14 Earthquakes	8	4
	15 Views of Earth	8	4
	16 Weathering and Erosion	7	3.5
	17 The Solar System and Beyond	8	4
6	**Matter, Forces, and Energy**		
	18 Properties and Changes of Matter	9	4.5
	19 Motion, Forces, and Simple Machines	10	5
	20 Energy	9	4.5
7	**Electricity and Magnetism**		
	21 Electricity	9	4.5
	22 Magnetism	7	3.5

The suggested number of days is the recommended maximum number of days needed to thoroughly cover a chapter. Individual planning will vary.

Student Edition Features

This table will help you choose from many options that will help you teach the chapter.

Feature	Location and Suggestions For Use
Design Your Own Experiment	• Find near end of chapter where concept is taught. • Promote inquiry learning through open-ended activities. • Reinforce understanding of scientific methods.
Use the Internet	• Find near end of chapter where concept is taught. • Strengthen skills in collecting, organizing, and sharing data. • Integrate the Internet into your class easily.
Model and Invent	• Find near end of chapter where concept is taught. • Reinforce the use of models to represent relationships or abstract ideas, and to predict outcomes. • Strengthen investigative skills.
Other Full-Length Activities	• Find near end of chapter where concept is taught. • Strengthen lab skills. • Reinforce understanding of science process.
Mini LAB / **TRY AT HOME Mini LAB**	• Find in every chapter. • Do as a demonstration. • Involve parents in the student's learning. • Reinforce that science is not restricted to the classroom.
EXPLORE ACTIVITY	• Find at beginning of each chapter. • Stimulate curiosity for the topic and focus students' attention.
Problem-Solving Skills / **Math Skills Activity**	• Find one in every chapter at the point where the concept is taught. • Use after reading or other work to strengthen critical thinking and math skills.
SCIENCE Online	• Find in every chapter. • Focus students' Internet time with predetermined links.

Feature	Location and Suggestions For Use
Skill Builders	• Find at the end of every Section Assessment. • Assign as homework or class work.
FOLDABLES Reading & Study Skills	• Find on every Chapter Opener and Chapter Study Guide. • Provide a purpose for reading with these fun, simple, hands-on activities. • Encourage students to use as a study tool for review of chapter content.
Interdisciplinary Connections **Oops! Accidents in Science** **Science and Language Arts** **Science Stats** **TIME Science & History** **TIME Science & Society**	• Find one of these five features in every chapter. • Stimulate students' interest by studying science-related events that are out of the ordinary. • Advance reading and writing skills through literature connected to science. • Show students the fun side of mathematics and how it is an integral part of science. • Illustrate how scientific phenomena, discoveries, and inventions shape history. • Connect science to people's everyday lives.
NATIONAL GEOGRAPHIC **Visualizing**	• Find in every chapter. • Use the discussion and activities to teach science content.
Career Connection	• Find in every Science & Language Arts feature. • Point out that people of all ages, ethnicities, and training work in science.
Field GUIDE	• Find in the back of the student text. • Promote interest and independent study. • Teach students how to use a classification key.
Science, Technology, and Math Skill Handbooks	• Find at the back of the student and teacher editions. • Use to teach students scientific processes. • Use to teach students how to organize information. • Refer students to handbooks for assistance.

Teacher Wraparound Edition Features

This table will help you locate features of the *Teacher Wraparound Edition* that will help you develop your lesson plans.

Component	Where and How Many	What It Provides
Teacher to Teacher	Every Unit Opener	Teaching tip that relates to teaching unit content or activities.
Chapter Organizer	A and B pages preceding every chapter	• Objectives • Occurrence of activities and other features within each section • List of materials needed for each activity • List of materials from the *Teachers Classroom Resources* box • List of technology resources
Science Content Background	In every chapter on E page and F page where an Identifying Misconceptions feature does not appear	• Helps you prepare for the lesson by giving you more information about each section • Assists you with questions the students might ask
IDENTIFYING Misconceptions	F page of some chapters	Strategies to • determine misconceptions students may hold • promote understanding of concept • assess understanding
Key to Teaching Strategies	B page preceding every chapter	Coding to assist in planning for individual needs
Three-Step Teaching Cycle **1 Motivate** **2 Teach** **3 Assess**	Every chapter	• Help for a first-year teacher • Help for experienced teacher in the first year in a new program
Resource Manager	C and D pages of every chapter Every two pages throughout each chapter	**C and D pages:** • List of transparencies • List of chapter teacher resources **Throughout chapter:** • List of reproducible resources • List of technology resources
Activity	Throughout all chapters in side wrap	Reinforces science concepts

Component	Where and How Many	What It Provides
Quick Demo	Throughout all chapters in side wrap	Idea to illustrate a concept; performed in a short amount of time, using available materials
LAB DEMONSTRATION	Throughout all chapters in bottom wrap	Teacher-performed activity, more complex than Quick Demo, often involving students
Extension	Throughout all chapters in side wrap	An activity idea for: • more advanced students • students who finish their work early • students who want to learn more about the topic
Teacher FYI	Throughout all chapters in side wrap	Additional information about a concept
Visual Learning	Throughout all chapters in side and bottom wrap	Idea for discussion or activity related to a graphic
Fun Fact	Throughout all chapters in side and bottom wrap	Interesting science content to share with students
Make a Model	Throughout all chapters in side wrap	Idea for model that students can make to clarify or illustrate abstract concepts
Use an Analogy	Throughout all chapters in side wrap	Way to make abstract concepts more concrete
Curriculum Connection	Throughout all chapters in bottom wrap	Way that science ties in with other curricular areas
Cultural Diversity	Throughout all chapters in bottom wrap	Current or historical background on a custom or belief associated with a science concept
Use Science Words	Throughout all chapters in side wrap	Strategies for students to learn word origins, meanings, and uses
Active Reading Strategies	Throughout all chapters in bottom wrap	Strategies to help students read and understand content
Science Journal	Throughout all chapters in bottom wrap	Writing exercises that promote writing and critical thinking skills
Assessment		
Section Assessment	First page of every section	• Location of Portfolio, Performance, and Content Assessments in the section
Chapter Assessment	Chapter Assessment page	• Ideas for Portfolio and Performance Assessments
Assessment Resources	Chapter Assessment page	• List of Reproducible Masters, CD-ROMs, and other technologies for assessment

Glencoe Science is also online at mhln.com

The McGraw-Hill Learning Network mhln.com

The Interactive E-Textbook that will change the way you teach!

The McGraw-Hill Learning network is an online learning space connecting parents, teachers, and students.

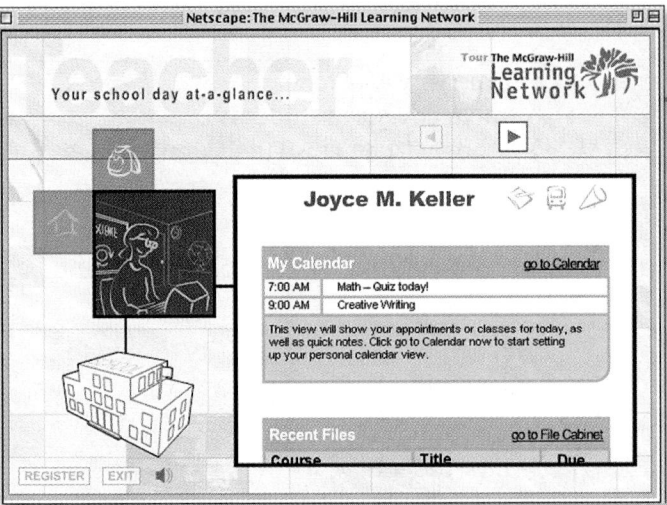

For Teachers

- Online Lesson Planner
- Calendar/Class Organizer
- Assignment Creator (Teachers can create, grade, and send assignments to students.)
- Grade Book/Class Roster
- And much more . . .

There's a ton of helpful tools, such as a Web site builder and thousands of educational Web links.

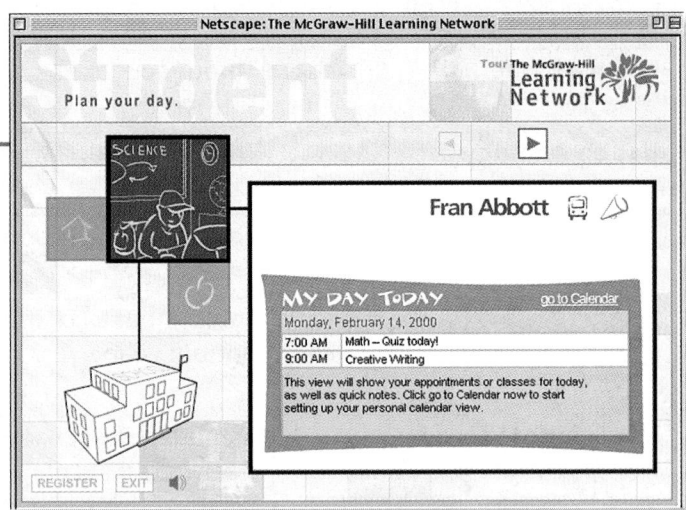

For Students

- Interactive games
- 24–hour homework help
- Online planner
- Instant feedback with diagnostic assessments
- Unlimited practice
- And much more . . . including movies, animations, sound, Web links, and an online encyclopedia

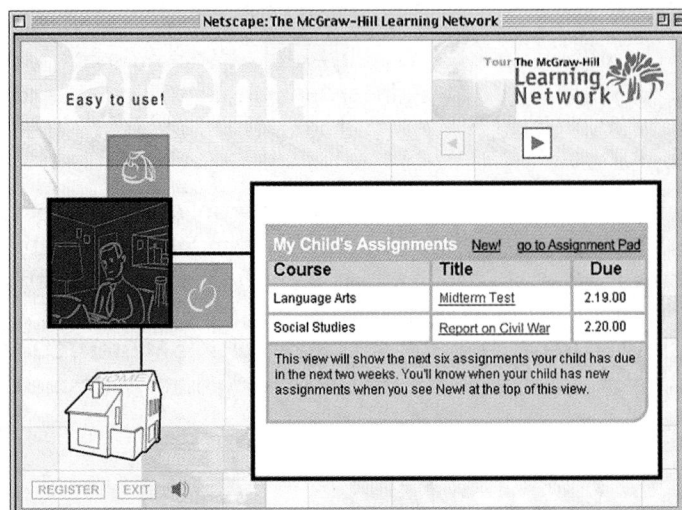

For Parents

- Tips to help their child succeed in school
- Instant access to textbooks, homework assignments, and progress reports

Online Science

The Glencoe Science Web site **science.glencoe.com** is an invaluable resource for all teachers and students.

Teachers can:
- share ideas on Teacher Bulletin Board.
- access current scientific information on textbook updates.

Students can:
- access the *Student Edition* online.
- access previewed Web links.
- record information on printable Internet log worksheets.
- review chapter content with the Interactive Tutor.
- prepare for tests using Interactive Quizzes.
- share data with students worldwide using our exclusive Internet Activities.

Teaching TODAY

Access *Teaching Today* at **teachingtoday.glencoe.com** for teaching tips, annotated Web resources, educational news, and more. New material is added each week to meet the diverse needs of secondary classroom teachers.

Interactive CD-ROM with Presentation Builder

Provides students the opportunity to:
- develop hypotheses.
- manipulate variables.
- build presentations.
- review content.
- think critically.

Program Resources

ExamView® Pro
Test Bank CD-ROM

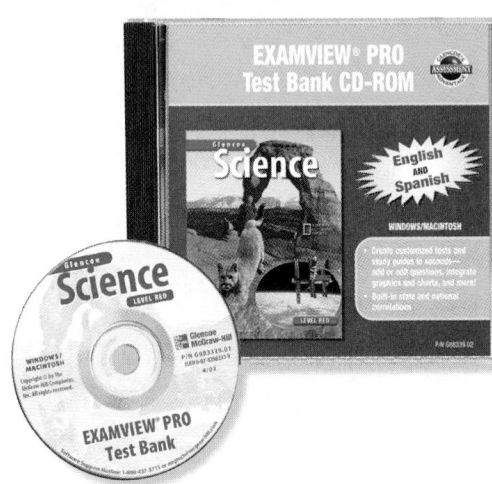

You can design and create your own test instruments in minutes, using Glencoe Science ExamView® Pro Test Bank CD-ROM. This versatile program allows you to create paper tests as well as tests that can be used on your school LAN system, or posted on your class Web site.

Interactive **Student Edition**

Give your students the option of carrying home a single CD-ROM instead of a book! With interactive assessments and many more exciting tools, the Interactive Student Editions become powerful learning resources.

Interactive **Lesson Planner**

Need help planning your lessons and organizing your resources? Glencoe's Interactive Lesson Planner is the perfect solution. All you need to do is to identify your length of course and number of class days and the program automatically places all the materials available for each day for each chapter into the calendar. Every page of your Teacher Classroom Resources is available to you at the click of a mouse.

Interactive **Teacher Edition**

Imagine having your entire Teacher Edition and all your Teacher Classroom Resources available to you on one CD-ROM. That is what the Interactive Teacher Edition provides for you. The program allows you to view all teacher material and the student

text on your computer screen. You can export all worksheet masters to your own word processor for editing.

MindJogger Videoquizzes

The interactive quiz-show format of the Glencoe Science MindJogger Videoquizzes provides fun for your students while reviewing key concepts for every chapter. The three levels of increasing difficulty add to the drama and excitement of the game, and help you assess your students' understanding of the concepts.

Guided Reading Audio Program
English/Spanish

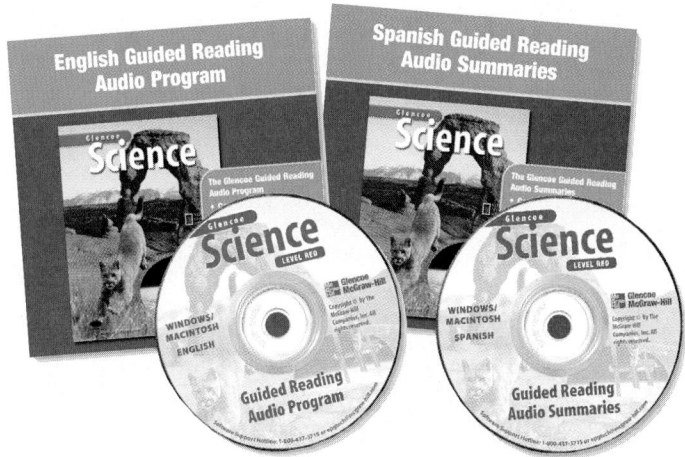

Complete chapter text read in English provides another way for students who are auditory learners, or for ELL students, to access chapter content. Students can listen individually in class or at home. They can also choose to read along with their texts to improve reading skills. Tie to the Directed Reading for Content Mastery in the *Chapter Resources* booklets to give students a way to check their understanding of the material. The Guided Reading program is provided in CD format.

Vocabulary PuzzleMaker Software

This software program allows you to create crossword puzzles, jumble puzzles, or word searches in minutes to review chapter vocabulary. The puzzles can be printed or played on the computer screen.

Teacher Classroom Resources

Chapter Resources

We've organized all of the materials you need for each chapter into chapter-based booklets. The cover of each booklet becomes a file folder to help you stay organized.

Program Resources

FAST FILE

Name

Activity

Lab Preview
Direction

Name   Class

LAB
1

Name

SECTION
1   **Enrichment**

Five of the planets in our
discovered thousands of ye
Mercury, Venus Mars, Satu
Neptune, and Uranus, on
discovered within about

The Discovery of Uran
The planet Uranus
William Herschel,
veying the ni
covery of
 one. O
ref

FOLD
Reading &
Skills

Directions: Use this

Comp

Inner Pla
Outer P

Mars
Saturn
Earth
Venus
Nept
Ura

Chapter Resources

CHAPTER
17   The Solar System and Beyond

FAST FILE

INCLUDES:

Reproducible Student Pages

ASSESSMENT
✓ Chapter Tests
✓ Chapter Review

HANDS-ON ACTIVITIES
✓ Activity Worksheets for each
  Student Edition Activity
✓ Two additional Laboratory
  Activities
✓ Foldables—Reading and Study
  Skills activity sheet

MEETING INDIVIDUAL NEEDS

Extension and Intervention
✓ Directed Reading for Content
  Mastery
✓ Directed Reading for Content
  Mastery in Spanish
✓ Reinforcement
✓ Enrichment
✓ Worksheets

Glencoe
Science

NATIONAL
GEOGRAPHIC
SOCIETY

Chapter 17   The Solar System and Beyond

3.
the

B. How the
b. All of

2. A clo
3. Sho
imb

1. Which two planets have the same period of rotati
   A Earth and Saturn
   B Mars and Jupiter
   C Earth and Jupiter

used by the rotation of Earth

Earth

Companies, Inc.

Each **Chapter Resources** booklet contains:

Reproducible Student Pages

Assessment
- Chapter Review
- Chapter Test

Hands-On Activities
- Activity Worksheets for each activity in the **Student Edition**
- Two additional laboratory activities
- Foldables: Reading and Study Skills

Meeting Individual Needs
(Extension and Intervention)
- Directed Reading for Content Mastery
- Directed Reading for Content Mastery *in Spanish*
- Reinforcement
- Enrichment
- Note-taking Worksheets

Transparency Activities
- Section Focus Activity
- Teaching Transparency Activity
- Assessment Transparency Activity

Teacher Support and Planning
- Content Outline for Teaching
- Spanish Resources
- Teacher Guide and Answers

Additional Resources

These resources are available as stand-alone booklets to give you the flexibility to decide when to use them.

Transparencies
   Section Focus Transparencies
   Teaching Transparencies
   Assessment Transparencies

Content Outline for Teaching

Lesson Plans

Laboratory Activities *SE*

Math Skill Activities
(SE and TE)

Reading and Writing Skill Activities
(SE and TE)

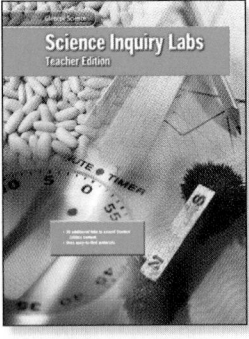

Science Inquiry Labs
(SE and TE)

Standardized Test Practice
(SE and TE)

Physical Science

Life Science

Earth Science

Home and Community Involvement

Laboratory Management and Safety

Dinah Zike's Teaching Science with Foldables

Guide to Using the Internet in the Science Classroom

Cooperative Learning

Cultural Diversity

Performance Assessment in the Science Classroom

Meeting Individual Needs

Each student brings his or her unique set of abilities, perceptions, and needs into the classroom. *Glencoe Science Level Red Teacher Wraparound Edition* offers you a variety of strategies so that your students can learn science concepts through many different methods.

Strategy	Designation
Ability Levels Activities are provided that accommodate students of all ability levels.	L1 Basic activities that reinforce the concepts for lower-ability students L2 Application activities that give all students an opportunity for practical application of concepts L3 Challenging activities that allow students to expand their perspectives on the basic concepts
English-Language Learners These strategies focus on overcoming a language barrier. It is important not to confuse ability in speaking/reading English with academic ability or "intelligence."	ELL These activities reinforce content and aid in the development of science vocabulary.
Learning Styles A variety of instructional strategies help students to learn science concepts through their preferred learning styles. Students generally display more than one of these styles. You may want to assign activities to students that accommodate their strongest learning styles, but assign other activities that help to develop their weaker styles.	LS Look for these bold-faced designations wherever you see this logo: • **Kinesthetic** learners learn through touch, movement, and manipulating objects. • **Visual-Spatial** learners think in terms of images, illustrations, and models. • **Logical-Mathematical** learners understand numbers easily and have highly-developed reasoning skills. • **Linguistic** learners write clearly and easily understand the written word. • **Auditory-Musical** learners remember spoken words and can create rhythms and melodies. • **Interpersonal** learners understand and work well with other people. • **Intrapersonal** learners can analyze their own strengths and weaknesses and may prefer to work on their own.

Strategy	Designation
Inclusion Strategies Inclusion strategies provide you with additional support for helping students with special needs.	Look for these bold-faced designations and strategies wherever you see the **Inclusion** Strategies • **Learning Disabled**—ideas for additional concept review • **Behaviorally Disordered**—activities for helping to keep students on task • **Physically Challenged**—tips for adjusting activities to accommodate students who have less mobility or dexterity than others • **Visually Impaired** or **Hearing Impaired**—ideas for aiding these students in grasping concepts • **Gifted**—challenging activities and research projects that extend chapter concepts
Cooperative Learning In cooperative learning, students work together in small groups to learn content and interpersonal skills. Group members learn that each is responsible for accomplishing an assigned group task as well as for learning the material. Cooperative learning fosters academic, personal, and social success for all students.	COOP LEARN Strategies with this designation are suitable for group work that will help students to: • develop positive attitudes toward science and school; • build respect for others, regardless of race, ethnic origin, or gender; and • increase their sensitivity to and tolerance of diverse perspectives.
Cultural Diversity Classrooms in the United States reflect the rich and diverse cultural heritage of the American people. Students come from different ethnic backgrounds and different cultural experiences into a common classroom that must assist all of them in learning.	 **Cultural Diversity** The Cultural Diversity features provide insights into unique ways in which different people have approached science or adapted to their environments. The intent of these features is to build awareness and appreciation for the global community in which we live.
Misconceptions Students have had many experiences outside the science classroom that have shaped their understandings of the natural world. Unfortunately, interpretations based on casual observation are not always accurate. For example, based on their observations, some students might think that the Sun moves around Earth. As a science teacher, you need strategies to help replace these naive conceptions with scientific facts.	 **Misconceptions** This one-page feature provides ideas about the types of misconceptions your students may have. It provides you with teaching strategies to uncover misconceptions and to help students understand concepts. You can find these preceding many chapters on the F interleaf pages of the Teacher Wraparound Edition. In addition, you will find several misconceptions stated, followed by the correct information, in the teacher wrap throughout each chapter.

Support for All Learners

Reading and Writing in the Content Area

Glencoe Science Level Red is designed to increase science literacy through improving reading comprehension and deepening students' understanding of ideas and concepts. The reading strategies are active, constructive, and engaging.

In the **Student Edition**

Reading Checks throughout each chapter stimulate quick recall to keep students focused on main ideas and important details.

> ✔ **Reading Check**
>
> *Which type of chemical reaction is burning?*

Caption Questions throughout each chapter help students to comprehend what they have read through interpreting the visual. This is especially useful for less proficient readers.

> **Figure 6**
> **After a golf ball is thrown, it follows a curved path toward the ground.** *How does this curved path show that the ball is accelerating?*

Skill Builder Activities in each Section Assessment often include questions that directly address reading and writing skills. Students are referred to the *Science Skill Handbook* for help.

> **Communicating** Watch carefully as you travel home from school or walk down your street. What examples of wave reflection and refraction do you notice? Describe each of these in your Science Journal and explain your reasons. **For more help, refer to the Science Skill Handbook.**

The Before You Read and After You Read Activities in every chapter set a purpose for reading and help students to construct a graphic organizer to use for learning content and as a study aide.

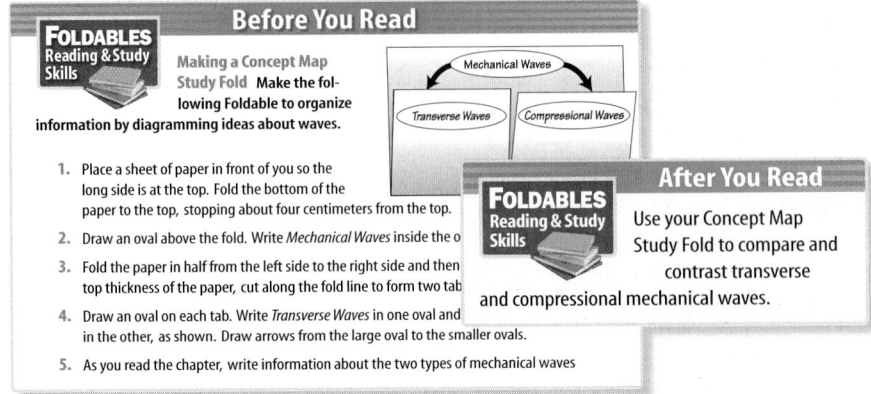

FOLDABLES
Reading & Study Skills

Before You Read

Making a Concept Map Study Fold Make the following Foldable to organize information by diagramming ideas about waves.

Mechanical Waves

Transverse Waves   Compressional Waves

1. Place a sheet of paper in front of you so the long side is at the top. Fold the bottom of the paper to the top, stopping about four centimeters from the top.

2. Draw an oval above the fold. Write *Mechanical Waves* inside the o

3. Fold the paper in half from the left side to the right side and then top thickness of the paper, cut along the fold line to form two tab

4. Draw an oval on each tab. Write *Transverse Waves* in one oval and in the other, as shown. Draw arrows from the large oval to the smaller ovals.

5. As you read the chapter, write information about the two types of mechanical waves

After You Read

FOLDABLES
Reading & Study Skills

Use your Concept Map Study Fold to compare and contrast transverse and compressional mechanical waves.

Print and Technology Resources to Promote Reading and Writing in the Content Area

Ancillaries

Chapter Resources

- Directed Reading for Content Mastery pages *(in English and Spanish)*
- Foldables: Reading and Study Skills Worksheets
- Note-taking Worksheets

Dinah Zike's Teaching Science with Foldables

Reading and Writing Skill Activities

Technology

Guided Reading Audio Program *(English and Spanish)*

MindJogger VideoQuizzes

Interactive CD-ROM

Vocabulary PuzzleMaker

Glencoe Science Online

Support for All Learners

Foldables: Improving Reading and Study Skills

Students love Foldables because they're fun. Teachers love them because they're effective.

What is a Foldable?

Foldables are three-dimensional, interactive graphic organizers. As students fold paper, cut tabs, write, and manipulate what they have made, they are kinesthetically involved in learning. These unique, hands-on tools for studying and reviewing were created exclusively for Glencoe Science by teaching specialist Dinah Zike.

Foldables are Useful!

Reading in the Content Area

Foldables help students develop ways of organizing information that are fun and creative. These useful activities help students practice basic writing skills, find and report main ideas, organize information, review key vocabulary terms, and much more!

Every chapter begins with a Foldable activity. Students make the physical structure of a Foldable that incorporates one of many prereading strategies. Then, as students read through the chapter and do the activities, students record information as they learn it in the appropriate part of the foldable. In the Chapter Study Guide, the After You Read feature gives students a strategy for using the fold they made to help them review the chapter concepts.

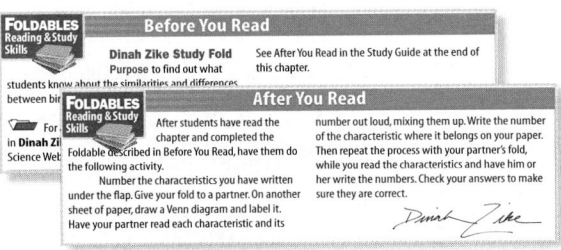

Review One advantage of Foldables is that they result in an organized study guide. The Foldables then can be used not only while preparing for the chapter test, but they can also be used for reviewing for unit tests, end of course exams, and even standardized tests.

Assessment Foldables present an ideal opportunity for you to probe the depth of your students' knowledge. You'll get detailed feedback on exactly what they know and what misconceptions they may have.

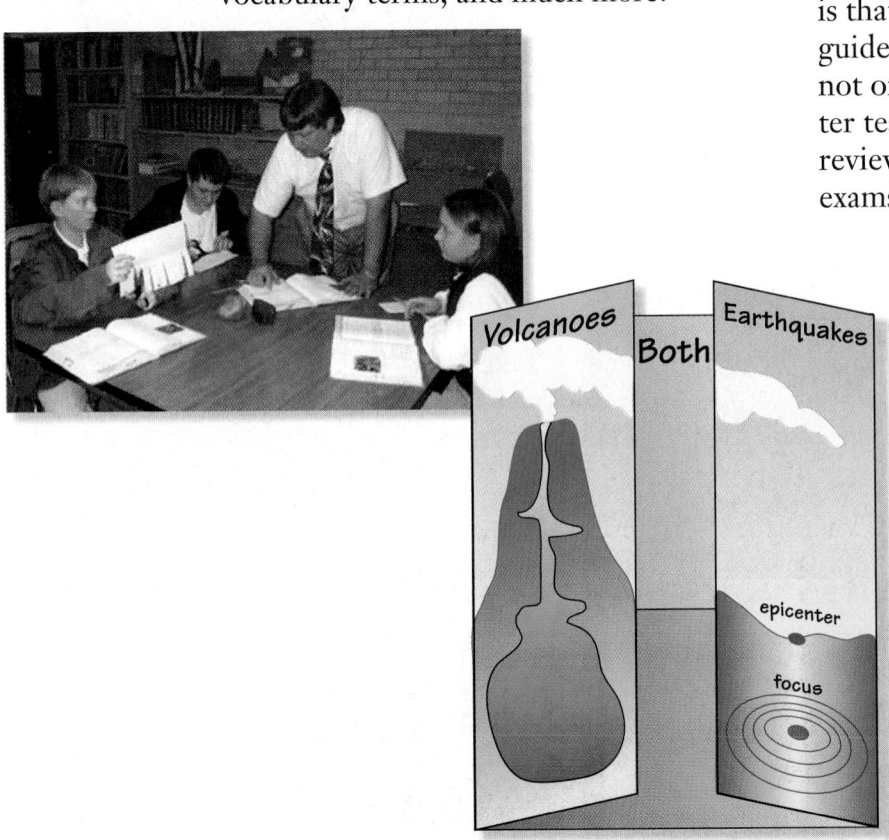

Foldables are Easy!

Anyone who has paper, scissors, and maybe a stapler or some glue can implement Foldables in the classroom. Glencoe's Foldables have been tested with teachers and middle school students to make sure the directions are easy for both students and teachers. After doing a couple of them, your class will quickly become seasoned experts. Don't be surprised if you find them inventing their own for use in projects and reports in all of their classes!

A message from **the creator of Foldables,** Dinah Zike

You might not know my name or me, but I bet you have seen at least one of my graphic organizers or folds used in supplemental programs or teacher workshops. Today, my graphic organizers and manipulatives are used internationally. I present workshops and keynote presentations to over 50,000 teachers a year, sharing the manipulatives I began inventing, designing, and adapting over thirty years ago. Around the world, students of all ages are using them as daily work, note-taking activities, student-directed projects, forms of alternative assessment, science lab journals, quantitative and qualitative observation books, graphs, tables, and more. But through all my years of teaching, designing, and publishing, my materials had never been featured in a middle school textbook. When Glencoe/McGraw-Hill approached me to share some of my three-dimensional, manipulative graphic organizers with you in this new and innovative science series, I was thrilled.

Working with Glencoe, we all had the vision that Foldables should be an integral part of the curriculum, not simply tacked on. What we ended up with was a strategy that will help students read and learn science concepts. One of the advantages of using the same manipulative repeatedly is that students are immersed in what they are learning. It is not out of sight and out of mind. How long is your average student actively involved with a duplicated activity sheet? Ten minutes? Fifteen? Students will use the Foldable at the beginning of each chapter, before reading the chapter, during reading, and after reading. That's a lot of immersion!

Dinah Zike

Reading and Writing in the Content Area

In the Teacher Edition

Science & Language Arts

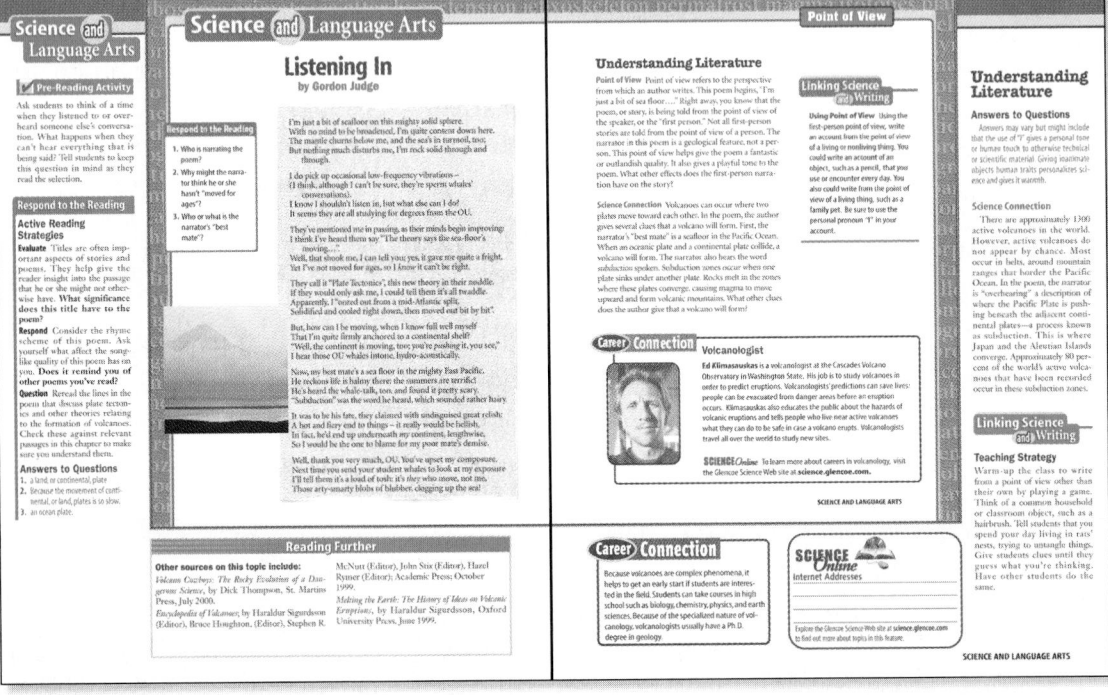

Pre-Reading Activity helps students draw upon their personal experience and sets a purpose for reading.

Respond to the Reading provides active reading strategies that provide a variety of ways for students to respond to the feature through listening, speaking, and writing activities. It also provides students with an opportunity to make connections to the theme.

Linking Science and Writing provides options that all students can use to respond in writing to the feature.

Use Science Words

Word Usage The distinction between distance and displacement can be confusing. Have students use each of these words correctly in a sentence. Possible response: When I go to school and then back home, my displacement is zero, even though the distance from home to school is 2 km.

 **L2** **IS** Linguistic

Use Science Words appears throughout each chapter and provides three types of reading strategies. Students structurally analyze root words (Word Origin), develop vocabulary (Word Meaning), or apply their knowledge of science terms (Word Usage).

Science Journal

Cathode-Ray Tube Ask students to pretend that they are coworkers with Crookes at the time of his experiments with a cathode-ray tube. Have students write letters in their Science Journals to a fellow scientist telling about the exciting results they obtained and how they interpreted the results. **L2** **IS** Linguistic

Science Journals throughout each chapter provide opportunities for students to write responses to questions that require critical thinking; to conduct research and write about it; or to practice creative writing skills.

Active Reading Strategies

A variety of active reading strategies are provided throughout the *Teacher Wraparound Edition*. These strategies utilize a variety of learning styles, and encourage cooperative learning and intrapersonal reflection on chapter content.

✔ Active Reading

Think-Pair Share This strategy encourages students to think first before discussing their ideas or thoughts about a topic. Ask students to respond to a question by writing a response. After thinking for a few minutes, partners share responses to the question. Finally, ask the students to share responses with the class. Have students become involved in a Think-Pair Share about cathode rays.

Making Concept Maps and Charts

Bubble Map Students brainstorm and organize words in clusters to describe concepts.

Double-Bubble Map Students compare concepts using two bubble maps.

Flow Chart Students logically analyze and draw a sequence of events.

Cause and Effect Chart Students visually represent the causes and effects of an event or process.

Supporting Idea Chart Students make a concept map to analyze the relationship between a whole and its parts.

Using the Science Journal

Double Entry Journal Students read and record ideas, then reflect on the text and respond to the ideas.

Metacognition Students analyze what and how they have learned.

Learning Journal Students write and reflect on notes about content.

Problem-Solution Journal Students analyze problems and suggest workable solutions.

Speculation About Effects/Prediction Journal Students examine events and speculate about their possible long-term effects.

Synthesis Journal Students reflect on a project, a paper, or a performance task and plan how to apply what they have learned to their own lives.

Reflective Journal Students identify what they learned in an activity and record responses.

Quickwrites Students use spontaneous writing to discover what they already know.

Collaborative Learning Strategies

Pair of Pairs Partners respond to a question and compare their response to that of other pairs and to the class.

Write-Draw-Discuss Students write about and draw a picture of a concept, then share it with the class.

Four-Corner Discussion The class works in four groups to debate a complex issue.

Jigsaw Students work in groups to become experts on a portion of text and share their expertise with their "home" group.

Buddy Interviews Students interview one another to find out what helps them to understand what they are reading.

Reciprocal Teaching Students take turns reading the text and retelling it in their own words, then asking one another questions.

News Summary Students are given several minutes to summarize, retell, or analyze an activity for a "TV" audience.

ReQuest The teacher reads aloud an article or story. Student pairs then construct discussion questions and review the content.

Support for All Learners

Concept Maps

Helping students understand concepts through visuals

Concept maps are visual representations or graphic organizers of relationships among particular concepts. Concept maps can be generated by individual students, small groups, or an entire class. Four types of concept maps that are most applicable to studying science are developed and reinforced in this program. Students can learn how to construct each of these types of concept maps by referring to the Skill Handbook in the *Student Edition*.

Concept maps can be used to increase understanding of science concepts, to strengthen reading skills, to promote cooperative learning, and to assess learning. When evaluating concept maps, look for the conceptual strength of student responses, not absolute accuracy.

- **Science Concepts** Concept mapping helps students to understand science concepts through analyzing relationships among ideas and reinforcing those relationships by visualizing them.

- **Reading Skills** Concept maps can help students preview a chapter's content by visually relating the concepts to be learned and aiding students to read with purpose. Students learn key science terms by choosing the terms to use, supplying connecting words, or by placing terms and connecting words when provided by the teacher. To further develop concept mapping skills, the *Chapter Resources* booklet for each chapter contains concept maps in the reproducible student pages Directed Reading for Content Mastery.

- **Cooperative Learning** Construction of concept maps using cooperative learning strategies allows students to practice interpersonal skills as they work together to build the map.

- **Review and Assessment** As a review, constructing concept maps reinforces main ideas and clarifies their relationships. As an assessment tool, concept maps can be constructed by students or students can fill in the terms. Look for concept mapping assessment in the Chapter Assessment section of every chapter.

Network Tree
- Order information from general to specific.
- Show a hierarchy.
- Use branching procedures.
- Explain relationships with connecting terms.

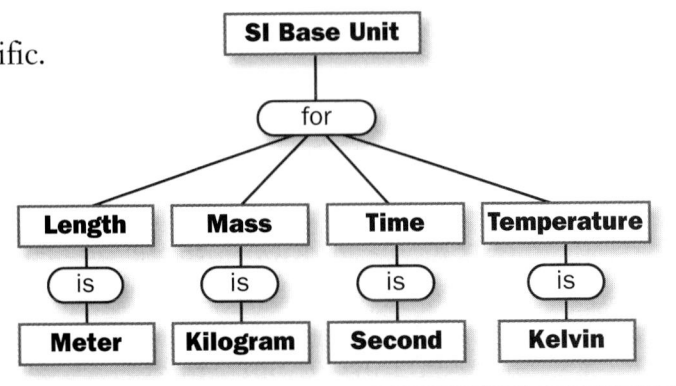

Events Chain

- Describe the stages of a process.
- Order the steps in a linear procedure.
- Show a sequence of events.

Initiating Event

| Determine the problem. |

↓

| Make a hypothesis. |

↓

| Test your hypothesis. |

↓

| Analyze the results. |

↓

| Draw conclusions. |

Cycle Concept Map

- Show how a series of events interact.
- Depict how the last event relates to the initiating event.

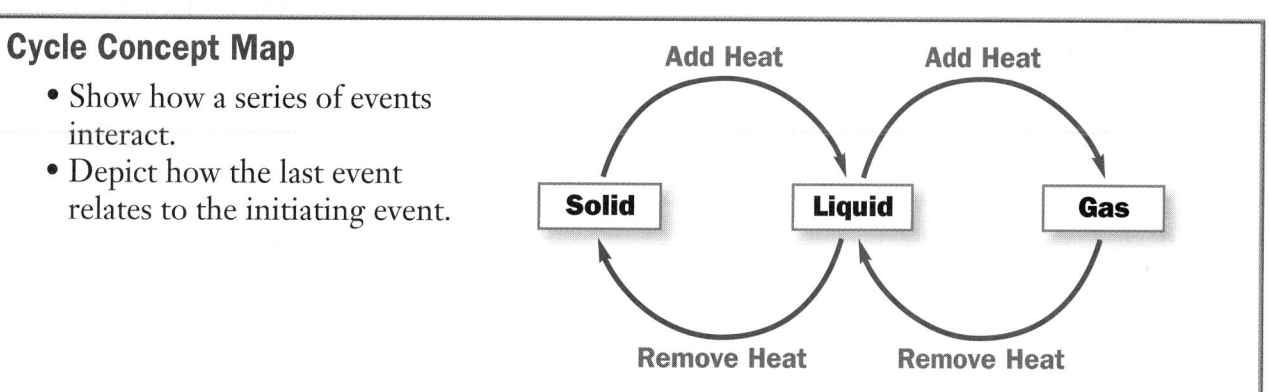

Spider Concept Map

- Use for brainstorming.
- Separate and group unrelated terms.
- Show relationship of nonrelated terms to a central idea.

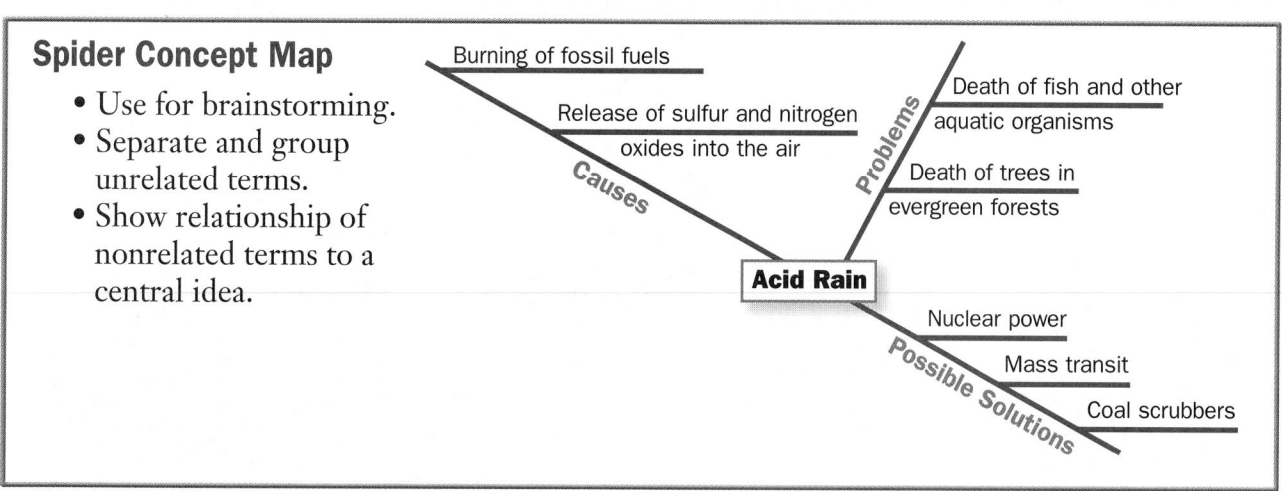

Assessment Support

Glencoe Science Level Red offers the Glencoe Assessment Advantage, a system of assessment options designed to give you the flexibility and tools to conduct standardized test preparation, and content and performance assessment.

Glencoe has partnered with *The Princeton Review*, a nationally renowned company that helps students prepare for state and national tests. This partnership has resulted in the Study Tips and Test Practice questions at the end of each Chapter Assessment in the *Student Edition.* Test practice booklets help prepare students for success on standardized tests.

Content Assessment

- **Section Assessment** questions and **Skill Builder Activities** appear in every chapter of the *Student Edition.*

- A **Study Guide** at the end of each chapter in the *Student Edition* allows you to determine whether reteaching is needed.

- The **Chapter Assessment** questions in the *Student Edition* help you evaluate students' knowledge and ability to apply science concepts.

- **Assessment—Chapter Tests** in the *Chapter Resources* booklets assess recognition, recall of vocabulary and facts, and ability to interpret information and relationships.

- **MindJogger Videoquizzes** offer interactive videos that provide a fun way for your students to review chapter concepts.

- The **Interactive CD-ROM** provides quizzes that can be used as a whole-class presentation or as a review for individual students. These materials also are available on the Glencoe Science Web site.

- **ExamView® Pro Test Bank CD-ROM (English/Spanish)** Software for Macintosh and Windows provides an easy way to make, edit, and print tests. You can add your own questions and graphics.

Performance Assessment

Performance Assessment refers to the strategies used to assess students' level of science literacy. Performance Assessment is based on judging the quality of a student's response to a performance task. A performance task is constructed to require the use of important concepts with supporting information, work habits important to science, and one or more of the elements of scientific literacy.

Performance Task Assessment Lists

Performance Assessments accompany **Activities** and **Chapter Assessments** in the *Glencoe Science Level Red Student Edition*. Task Assessment Lists are provided in Glencoe's *Performance Assessment in the Science Classroom*. Both the teacher and the student assess the work and assign points based on the well-defined categories and possible points for each category. These task lists were developed for the summative performance tasks included in the booklet.

Assessing Student Work with Rubrics

A rubric is a set of descriptions of the quality of a process and a product. The set of descriptions includes a continuum of quality from excellent to poor. Rubrics for various types of assessment products are provided in the Glencoe Professional Development Series booklet *Performance Assessment in the Science Classroom*. In addition to sample rubrics, blank rubric forms allow teachers to customize assessment methods. The booklet also

provides a step-by step model showing teachers how to use the materials most effectively.

Portfolios

Portfolio suggestions are featured throughout each chapter in the *Glencoe Science Level Red Teacher Wraparound Edition*. The Portfolio should help the student see the big picture of how he or she is performing in gaining knowledge and skills and how effective his or her work habits are. The performance portfolio is not a complete collection of all worksheets and other assignments but rather a collection that reflects the student's growth in concept attainment and skill development. Writings and drawings from the student's **Science Journal**, featured in the *Student Edition* and the *Teacher Wraparound Edition*, often are suggested to include in portfolios.

Group Assessment

All students benefit from a cooperative learning environment. Research has shown that student-learning outcomes improve for students of all ability levels. An example, along with information about evaluating cooperative work, is provided in the booklet *Performance Assessment in the Science Classroom*.

Lab Safety

The activities in *Glencoe Science Level Red* have been tested in the laboratory and have been reviewed by safety consultants. Even so, there are no guarantees against accidents. For additional help, refer to the *Laboratory Management and Safety* booklet, which contains safety guidelines and masters to test students' lab and safety skills.

General Guidelines

- Post safety guidelines, fire escape routes, and a list of emergency procedures in the classroom. Make sure students understand these procedures. Remind them at the beginning of *every* lab session.

  - Understand and make note of the Safety Symbols used in each activity.
  - Have students fill out a safety contract. Students should pledge to follow the rules, to wear safety attire, and to conduct themselves in a responsible manner.

- Know where emergency equipment is stored and how to use it.

- Supervise students at all times. Check assembly of all setups.

- Perform all activities before you allow students to do so.

- Instruct students to follow directions carefully.

- Make sure that all students are wearing proper safety attire. They should wear goggles at all times. They should secure long hair and loose clothing. Do not permit wearing contact lenses, even with safety glasses; splashing chemicals could infuse under a lens and cause eye damage.

Handling Chemicals

- Handle chemicals carefully at all times. Always wear safety goggles, gloves, and an apron when handling chemicals. Treat all chemicals as potentially dangerous.

- Never ingest chemicals. Use proper techniques to smell solutions.

- Use a fume hood when handling chemicals that are poisonous or corrosive or that give off a vapor.

- *Always add acids to water, never the reverse.*

- Prepare solutions by adding the solid to a small amount of distilled water and then diluting with water to the volume listed. If you use a hydrate that is different from the one specified in a particular preparation, you will need to adjust the amount of hydrate to obtain the correct concentration.

- Consider purchasing premixed solutions from a scientific supply house to reduce the amount of chemicals on hand.

- Maintain appropriate MSDS (Materials Safety Data Sheets) in the laboratory.

Chemical Storage and Disposal

The following are some commonly used guidelines for chemical storage and disposal, but your school or local government may have additional requirements for handling chemicals. It is your responsibility to be informed of the rules governing chemical storage and disposal in your area.

- Use wood shelving rather than metal. All shelving should be firmly attached to the wall and have antiroll edges.
- Store only those chemicals you intend to use. Do not store chemicals above eye level.
- Store chemicals in labeled containers that indicate the contents, concentration, source, date purchased (or prepared), safety precautions for handling, and expiration date.
- Separate chemicals by reaction type. Store acids in one place and bases in another. Oxidants should be stored away from easily oxidized materials, for example.
- Dispose of outdated or waste chemicals properly.
- Follow regulations for storing hazardous chemicals.

Disposal of Chemicals

Local, state, and federal laws regulate the disposal of chemicals. Consult these laws before attempting to dispose of any chemicals. The following resource provides some general guidelines for handling and disposing of chemicals: *Prudent Practices in the Laboratory: Handling and Disposal of Chemicals.* Washington, DC: National Academy Press, 1995. Current laws in your area supersede the information in this book.

Disclaimer

Glencoe/McGraw-Hill makes no claims to the completeness of this discussion of laboratory safety and chemical storage. The material presented is not all-inclusive, nor does it address all of the hazards associated with handling, storage, and disposal of chemicals, or with laboratory management.

Activity Materials

Glencoe Science Level Red makes it easy for you to plan and facilitate activities in your classroom.

- You'll find a variety of hands-on activities, from short to long, from directed to open-ended.
- Many activities use common, inexpensive materials.
- Activities are easy to manage, with clearly numbered steps and illustrations.
- All MiniLABS have been teacher tested.

All laboratory activities have been thoroughly reviewed by a safety expert.

All full-length labs were bench tested by Science Kit to ensure quality and safety.

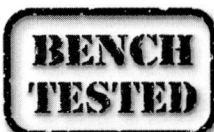

It's Quick and Easy to Order

Glencoe and Science Kit, Inc., have teamed up to make materials for *Glencoe Science Level Red* easier with an activity-materials folder. You can order materials and equipment for the program using the **Activity Materials List** master. Call Science Kit at 1-800-828-7777 to get your folder.

Materials Support Provided by

Science Kit® & Boreal®
   Laboratories
777 East Park Drive
Tonawanda, NY 14151-5003
Phone: 800-828-7777
Fax 800-828-3299
www.sciencekit.com

List of Activity Materials

It is assumed that laboratory aprons, goggles, tap water, metersticks, metric rulers, textbooks, scissors, calculators, paper, pencils, and pens are available.

Non-Consumables

Item	EXPLORE ACTIVITY Page	Mini LAB Page	Activity Chapter and 1-page or 2-page
Air Pump		287	
Aluminum pie pan	339	390	
Aquarium, 4 L			7-1
Balance		9, 125, 287	8-1, 16-2, 20-1
Ball	587	287, 495, 593	17-1, 18-1, 19-1, 20-1
Basin	465		12-2
Bathroom scale		564	
Batteries		638, 662	21-1, 22-2
Battery holders		662	21-1
Beaker(s)	587	68, 125, 381, 390, 544	12-1, 15-1, 16-1, 18-1, 20-2, 21-2
Binder clips			21-2
Boards, wooden			12-2, 22-2
Bottle, plastic, clear		254	12-2
Bowl(s)	339	195, 198, 352, 390	12-1, 18-2, 22-1
Box, clear plastic		349	10-2, 15-1
Bread pan	465		
Brick(s)	465		12-2
Broomsticks (2) or dowels		573	
Building blocks		426	
Can, metal	243	293, 312, 327	
Clock or watch with second hand	465		16-2, 21-2
Cloth, wool	623	632	
Coat		564	
Collection jar(s)			4-2
Comb		632	
Container, clear		131, 232, 602	
Container, flat, with cover		169	
Containers, plastic, with drainage holes			6-2
Containers, small planting			8-2
Containers, wide-mouthed		171	1-2
Dropper(s)	37	469, 602	2-1, 4-1
Fan, battery-operated			12-2
Fishnet, small			7-1
Flashlight	587	507	17-1
Flashlight bulb		638	

Non-Consumables *continued*

Item	EXPLORE ACTIVITY Page	Mini LAB Page	Activity Chapter and 1-page or 2-page
Funnel, plastic			21-2
Glasses, drinking	281	531	2-2
Graduated cylinder		125	18-1
Hammer			22-2
Hand lens	87, 375	96, 131, 226, 469, 544	1-1, 1-2, 4-2, 11-1, 13-2, 16-1
Hose clamp			21-2
Hot lamp	339		
Hot plate	309, 587		
Insect collection or collection of leaves	5		
Iron fillings		658	
Jar(s)		260	2-1, 3-2, 6-1, 7-1, 8-1
Knife, paring			18-2
Knife, putty			13-2
Light bulbs			21-1
Magnet(s)	653	381, 658	22-1, 22-2
Marble(s)	555		12-1, 19-1
Microscope		46	2-1, 3-1, 4-1, 4-2
Microscope slide(s)	37		2-1, 4-1, 4-2
Mini-bulb sockets			21-1
Model of landform			15-1
Nail(s)		662	22-2
Needle, sewing			22-1
Needle (steel knitting) or steel rod			22-2
Overhead light with reflector			10-2
Pails			16-2
Paint trays			16-2
Pans, metal, cooking	309		
Paper clips		662	
Pennies	527	352, 495	18-1
Petri dish(es)		658	22-1
Photo of furniture		25	
Plastic bags, self-sealing		198	20-2
Plate	59		
Prepared slide of *Anabaena* or photomicrograph			3-1

Non-Consumables *continued*

Item	EXPLORE ACTIVITY Page	Mini LAB Page	Activity Chapter and 1-page or 2-page
Prepared slide of *Gloeocapsa* or photomicrograph			3-1
Prepared slide of nitrogen-fixing bacteria		226	
Prepared slide of *Nostoc* or photomicrograph			3-1
Prepared slide of *Oscillatoria* or photomicrograph			3-1
Prepared slide of slime mold			4-1
Prepared slides of human cells		46	
Pressure gauge		287	
Reference-atlas	437		
Reference, book, *100 Topographic Maps*			15-2
Reference-books about planets			17-2
Reference-field guide to fungi or club fungi			4-2
Reference-field guide to minerals			13-2
Reference-globe	437		14-1
Reference-Mohs scale of hardness			13-2
Reference-US Geological Survey maps			15-2
Reference-US map, physical		440	
Reference-world map	437	445	
Ring stand with ring			10-2, 21-2
Rock/Mineral-calcite		381	
Rock/Mineral-fossil limestone		390	
Rock/Mineral-gneiss sample			13-1
Rock/Mineral-granite sample	375		13-1
Rock/Mineral-hornblende		381	
Rock/Mineral-igneous rock samples	375		
Rock/Mineral-limestone		469	
Rock/Mineral-magnetite		381	
Rock/Mineral-mineral samples			13-2
Rock/Mineral-quartz		381	
Rock/Mineral-rock	375		7-1, 12-2
Rolling pin			13-1
Rope, 3-m long		573	
Rubber bands	407	232, 426	6-1, 8-1
Sphere, plastic, hollow			18-1
Sponge	59	9, 169	
Spoon	339	349, 352	2-2, 8-1, 8-2, 12-1, 20-2, 22-1

Non-Consumables *continued*

Item	EXPLORE ACTIVITY Page	Mini LAB Page	Activity Chapter and 1-page or 2-page
Spray bottle			6-2, 15-2
Stereomicroscope			7-1, 16-1
Stirring rod		312	20-2
Stopwatch			19-1, 20-1, 21-2
Streak plate			13-2
Tablespoon		531, 544	
Thermal mitts	309		19-1
Thermometer(s)		312	7-1, 10-2, 20-2
Thermometer, non-mercury	243		
Thumbtacks		349	
Trowel			8-2
Tubing			21-2
Watch glass			7-1
Watering can			3-2
Wire		638, 662	21-1, 22-2
Wire cutters			22-2
Wood block(s)	465		16-2, 22-1

Consumables

Item	EXPLORE ACTIVITY Page	Mini LAB Page	Activity Chapter and 1-page or 2-page
Aluminum foil			3-2, 8-2
Art supplies			4-2
Balloons	623	160	
Branches of various conifers or illustrations of branches			5-1
Bottle, clear small plastic		254	
Buttons		42	
Candy wrapper, plastic			3-2
Cardboard	281, 555	42, 507, 593	20-1
Cheesecloth		125	6-1
Cloth, cotton		195	
Construction paper, black	243, 491	293, 507	
Construction paper, white	243		
Coverslips			2-1, 4-1, 4-2
Crayon, white	491		
Cups, paper		349	

Consumables *continued*

Item	EXPLORE ACTIVITY Page	Mini LAB Page	Activity Chapter and 1-page or 2-page
Drawing paper			17-1, 17-2
Envelopes, large	149		
Fertilizer, garden			8-1
Food coloring		131, 254, 349, 602	2-2, 15-1
Food-apples			3-2, 6-1, 18-2
Food-baking soda		531	
Food-bananas			3-2, 18-2
Food-beans, dried		68	
Food-bran or oatmeal			6-1
Food-bread (dry) or cookie crumbs			6-1
Food-candy	181		
Food-carrot			6-1
Food-celery			2-2
Food-corn oil			18-1
Food-corn syrup			18-1, 20-2
Food-green onion		131	
Food-lemons			18-2
Food-lettuce			7-1
Food-macaroni, dry		42, 390	
Food-mushrooms	87	103	
Food-onions	37		
Food-orange		593	
Food-pancake syrup or corn syrup			20-2
Food-pasta wheels	181		
Food-pears			18-2
Food-pepper		632	
Food-raisins		531	
Food-rice, uncooked	491		13-1
Food-salt, noniodized			1-2
Food-salt, table	339	349, 632	12-1
Food-scraps			6-2
Food-sugar		544	
Food-vegetable shortening		198	
Food-vinegar		381, 469, 531	
Food-yeast, dry		544	1-2
Gel, hair-styling	59		
Glue, white		42, 390	
Glycerin			18-1

Consumables *continued*

Item	EXPLORE ACTIVITY Page	Mini LAB Page	Activity Chapter and 1-page or 2-page
Graph paper			14-2, 19-1
Grass			11-2
Grass sod			16-2
Gravel			7-1, 12-2
Grid paper			9-2
Ice	309	198, 312	20-2
Index card(s)	37, 149		
Label(s)			1-2, 8-2
Leaves			3-2
Magazines	117, 149		
Marker(s)	555	232	7-2, 15-1, 17-2, 22-1
Modeling clay	587	42, 593	13-1
Newspaper	37	470	3-2, 6-2
Paper towels		312	6-1, 15-2
Pencils, colored	149		2-1, 7-2, 9-2, 10-2
Petroleum jelly		195	
Pipe cleaners	181	42	
Plastic wrap, clear	37	232	8-1, 12-1
Plates, paper		544, 632	
Poster board			7-2
Sand	339, 465		12-2, 15-2
Sandpaper	407		22-2
Seeds, 10 different kinds			1-1
Seeds, bean			8-2
Soil		250, 470	3-2, 6-2, 8-2, 10-2, 12-2, 16-1, 16-2
Sphagnum moss		125	
String		61	14-1
Sunscreens			10-1
Tape	37, 243, 407, 55	232, 260, 327, 507, 65	10-2, 12-1, 15-1, 22-1, 22-2
Tissue paper	623		
Toothpicks		352	
Water, distilled		68	1-2
Water, pond			2-1, 7-1, 8-1
Weighing paper			8-1
Yarn		42, 61	

Chemical Supplies

Item	EXPLORE ACTIVITY Page	Mini LAB Page	Activity Chapter and 1-page or 2-page
Hydrochloric acid, 5%		469	
Isopropyl (rubbing) alcohol			18-2

Live Organisms

Item	EXPLORE ACTIVITY Page	Mini LAB Page	Activity Chapter and 1-page or 2-page
Algae			2-1
Amoeba culture or prepared slide			4-1
Aquatic plants			7-1
Brine shrimp eggs			1-2
Elodea stalks or other aquatic plant			8-1
Euglena culture or prepared slide			4-1
Frog egg mass			7-1
Legume plant		226	
Mealworms			6-1
Nonlegume plant		226	
Paramecium culture or prepared slide			4-1
Physarum polycephaalum		96	
Sow bugs		169	
Spirogyra			4-1
Wiggle worms			6-2

Suppliers

Scientific Suppliers

Carolina Biological Supply Company
2700 York Road
Burlington, NC 27215
800-334-5551
www.carolina.com

Fisher Scientific Company
4500 Turnberry Drive
Hanover Park, IL 60103
800-766-7000
www.fishersci.com

Fisher Scientific Educational
485 South Frontage Road
Burr Ridge, IL 60521
800-955-1177
www.fisheredu.com

Flinn Scientific
P.O. Box 219
770 N. Raddant Road
Batavia, IL 60510
800-452-1261
www.flinnsci.com

Frey Scientific
100 Paragon Road
Mansfield, OH 44903
800-225-3739
www.freyscientific.com

Sargent-Welch/Cenco
P.O. Box 5229
911 Commerce Court
Buffalo Grove, IL 60089
800-727-4368
www.sargentwelch.com

Science Kit & Boreal Laboratories
777 East Park Drive
Tonawanda, NY 14150
800-828-7777
www.sciencekit.com

Ward's Natural Science Establishment, Inc.
P.O. Box 92912
5100 Henrietta Road
Rochester, NY 14692
800-962-2660
www.wardsci.com

Software Distributors

(AIT) Agency for Instructional Technology
Box A
Bloomington, IN 47402-0120
800-457-4509
www.ait.net

Educational Activities, Inc.
1937 Grand Avenue
Baldwin, NY 11510
800-645-3739
www.edact.com

IBM Educational Systems
Department PC
4111 Northside Parkway
Atlanta, GA 30327
800-426-4968
www.IBM.com

Microphys
12 Bridal Way
Sparta, NJ 07871
800-832-6591
www.microphys.com

Queue, Inc.
338 Commerce Drive
Fairfield, CT 06432
800-335-0906
www.queueinc.com

School Division of The Learning Company
6160 Summit Drive
Minneapolis, MN 55430
www.learningcompanyschool.com

Ventura Educational Systems
P.O. Box 425
Grover Beach, CA 93483
2782 Sevada
Arroyo, CA 93420
800-336-1022
www.venturaES.com

Audiovisual Distributors

Aims Multimedia
9710 Desoto Avenue
Chatsworth, CA 91311-4409
800-367-2467
www.aimsmultimedia.com

BFA Educational Media
2349 Chaffee Drive
St. Louis, MO 63146
800-221-1274
www.phoenixcoronet.com

CRM Films
2215 Faraday Avenue
Carlsbad, CA 92008
800-421-0833
www.crmfilms.com

Encyclopedia Britannica Educational Corp. (EBEC)
310 S. Michigan Avenue
Chicago, IL 60604
800-554-9862 ext. 7007
www.ebec.com

Hawkill Associates, Inc.
125 E. Gilman Street
Madison, WI 53703
800-422-4295
www.hawkill.com

Lumivision
877 Federal Boulevard
Denver, CO 80204
303-446-0400
www.lumivision.com

National Geographic School Publishing
P.O. Box 10579
Des Moines, IA 50340
17th and "M" Streets, NW
Washington, DC 20009
800-368-2728
www.nationalgeographic.com\education

Time-Life Education
P.O. Box 8502
Richmond, VA 23285
800-449-2010
www.timelifeedu.com

Video Discovery
Suite 600
1700 Westlake Avenue, N
Seattle, WA 98109
800-548-3472
www.videodiscovery.com

Glencoe
Science

NATIONAL GEOGRAPHIC SOCIETY

LEVEL RED

science.glencoe.com

Glencoe McGraw-Hill

New York, New York   Columbus, Ohio   Woodland Hills, California   Peoria, Illinois

Glencoe Science

LEVEL RED

Student Edition
Teacher Wraparound Edition
Interactive Teacher Edition CD-ROM
Interactive Lesson Planner CD-ROM
Lesson Plans
Content Outline for Teaching
Dinah Zike's Teaching Science with Foldables
Directed Reading for Content Mastery
Foldables: Reading and Study Skills
Assessment
   Chapter Review
   Chapter Tests
   ExamView Pro Test Bank Software
   Assessment Transparencies
   Performance Assessment in the Science Classroom
   The Princeton Review Standardized Test Practice Booklet
Directed Reading for Content Mastery in Spanish
Spanish Resources
English/Spanish Guided Reading Audio Program

Reinforcement
Enrichment
Activity Worksheets
Section Focus Transparencies
Teaching Transparencies
Laboratory Activities
Science Inquiry Labs
Critical Thinking/Problem Solving
Reading and Writing Skill Activities
Mathematics Skill Activities
Cultural Diversity
Laboratory Management and Safety in the Science Classroom
MindJogger Videoquizzes and Teacher Guide
Interactive CD-ROM with Presentation Builder
Vocabulary PuzzleMaker Software
Cooperative Learning in the Science Classroom
Environmental Issues in the Science Classroom
Home and Community Involvement
Using the Internet in the Science Classroom

"Study Tip," "Test-Taking Tip," and the "Test Practice" features in this book were written by The Princeton Review, the nation's leader in test preparation. Through its association with McGraw-Hill, The Princeton Review offers the best way to help students excel on standardized assessments.

The Princeton Review is not affiliated with Princeton University or Educational Testing Service.

Glencoe/McGraw-Hill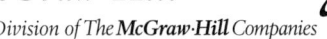

A Division of The **McGraw·Hill** Companies

The "Visualizing" features in this textbook were designed and developed by the National Geographic Society's Education Division, copyright ©2002 National Geographic Society. The name "National Geographic Society" and the yellow border rectangle are trademarks of the Society, and their use, without prior written permission, is strictly prohibited. All rights reserved.

The "Science and Society" and the "Science and History" features that appear in this book were designed and developed by TIME School Publishing, a division of TIME Magazine. TIME and the red border are trademarks of Time Inc. All rights reserved.

Cover Images: Delicate arch in Utah; puma jumping in field; Mir Space Station over the Pacific Ocean.

Send all inquiries to:
Glencoe/McGraw-Hill
8787 Orion Place
Columbus, OH 43240

ISBN 0-07-828238-1
Printed in the United States of America.
  4 5 6 7 8 9 10 071/055 06 05 04 03

Series Authors

National Geographic Society
Education Division
Washington, D.C.

Alton Biggs
Biology Teacher
Allen High School
Allen, Texas

Lucy Daniel, PhD
Science Teacher/Consultant
Rutherford County Schools
Rutherfordton, North Carolina

Ralph M. Feather Jr., PhD
Science Department Chair
Derry Area School District
Derry, Pennsylvania

Susan Leach Snyder
Earth Science Teacher, retired
Jones Middle School
Upper Arlington, Ohio

Dinah Zike
Educational Consultant
Dinah-Might Activities, Inc.
San Antonio, Texas

Contributing Authors

Dan Blaustein
Science Teacher
Evanston Intermediate School
Evanston, Illinois

Patricia Horton
Mathematics and Science Teacher
Summit Intermediate School
Etiwanda, California

Thomas McCarthy, PhD
Science Department Chair
St. Edwards School
Vero Beach, Florida

Cathy Ezrailson
Science Department Head
Academy for Science and Health Professions
Conroe, Texas

Deborah Lillie
Science Teacher
Sudbury Intermediate School
Sudbury, Massachusetts

Series Reading Consultants

Elizabeth Babich
Special Education Teacher
Mashpee Public Schools
Mashpee, Connecticut

Carol A. Senf, PhD
Associate Professor of English
Georgia Institute of Technology
Atlanta, Georgia

Nancy Woodson, PhD
Professor of English
Otterbein College
Westerville, Ohio

Barry Barto
Special Education Teacher
John F. Kennedy Elementary
Manistee, Michigan

Rachel Swaters
Science Teacher
Rolla Middle Schools
Rolla, Missouri

Series Reading Consultants

Malcolm Cheney, PhD
OSHA Chemical Safety Officer
Hall High School
West Hartford, Connecticut

Aileen Duc, PhD
Science II Teacher
Hendrick Middle School
Plano, Texas

Sandra West, PhD
Associate Professor of Biology
Southwest Texas State University
San Marcos, Texas

Series Math Consultants

Michael Hopper, D. Eng.
Manager of Aircraft Certification
Raytheon Company
Greenville, Texas

Teri Willard, EdD
Department of Mathematics
Montana State University
Belgrade, Montana

Content Consultants

Jack Cooper
Adjunct Faculty Math and Science
Navarro College
Corsicana, Texas

Stephen M. Letro
National Weather Service
Meteorologist in Charge
Jacksonville, Florida

Sandra K. Enger, PhD
Coordinator
UAH Institute for Science Education
Huntsville, Alabama

Lisa McGaw
Science Teacher
Hereford High School
Hereford, Texas

Leanne Field, PhD
Lecturer Molecular Genetics and Microbiology
University of Texas
Austin, Texas

Lee Meadows, PhD
University of Alabama at Birmingham
Education Department
Birmingham, Alabama

Jerry Jackson, PhD
Program Director Center for Science,
Mathematics, and Technology Education
Florida Gulf Coast University
Fort Meyers, Florida

Robert Nierste
Science Department Head
Hendrick Middle School
Plano, Texas

William C. Keel, PhD
Department of Physics and Astronomy
University of Alabama
Tuscaloosa, Alabama

Dominic Salinas, PhD
Middle School Science Supervisor
Caddo Parish Schools
Shreveport, Louisiana

Linda Knight, EdD
Associate Director
Rice Model Science Lab
Houston, Texas

Betsy Wrobel-Boerner
Department of Microbiology
Ohio State University
Columbus, Ohio

Carl Zorn, PhD
Staff Scientist
Jefferson Laboratory
Newport News, Virginia

Series Activity Testers

José Luis Alvarez, PhD
Math/Science Mentor Teacher
El Paso, Texas

Mary Helen Mariscal-Cholka
Science Teacher
William D. Slider Middle School
El Paso, Texas

Nerma Coats Henderson
Science Teacher
Pickerington Jr. High School
Pickerington, Ohio

José Alberto Marquez
TEKS for Leaders Trainer
El Paso, Texas

Science Kit and Boreal Laboratories
Tonawanda, New York

Reviewers

CONTENTS IN BRIEF

UNIT **1** Life's Structure and Function — 2

CONTENTS

Alabama Map Turtle,
Graptemys pulchra

CONTENTS

Contents

UNIT 5 Earth and Space — 372

CONTENTS

Contents

UNIT 7 Electricity and Magnetism — 620

Interdisciplinary Connections

NATIONAL GEOGRAPHIC Unit Openers

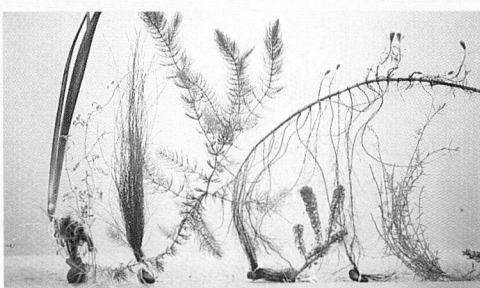

NATIONAL GEOGRAPHIC VISUALIZING

Interdisciplinary Connections

Activities

Feature Contents

Mini LAB

Activities

EXPLORE ACTIVITY

Problem-Solving Activities

Math Skills Activities

Activities

Skill Builder Activites

Science

Classifying: 26, 65, 233, 603

Communicating: 13, 26, 49, 123, 163, 191, 233, 256, 267, 289, 328, 350, 361, 391, 454, 471, 513, 576, 595, 630, 635, 659

Comparing and Contrasting: 18, 43, 107, 157, 163, 191, 299, 350, 384, 471, 546, 659

Concept Mapping: 49, 129, 152, 196, 261, 294, 317, 328, 391, 443, 496, 539

Drawing Conclusions: 21, 227, 396, 635

Forming Hypotheses: 123, 138, 186, 361, 411, 427

Interpreting Scientific Illustrations: 289, 447

Making and Using Graphs: 186, 317, 561, 595, 642

Making and Using Tables: 98, 576

Making Models: 454, 513

Measuring in SI: 73

Observing and Inferring: 608

Predicting: 170, 256, 419

Recognizing Cause and Effect: 248, 325, 344, 354, 481, 569, 630

Recording Observations: 221

Researching Information: 43, 201, 669

Math

Calculating Ratios: 669

Converting Units: 13

Solving One-Step Equations: 65, 157, 201, 227, 294, 344, 419, 427, 481, 496, 539, 546, 561, 603

Using Fractions: 129, 447

Using Percentages: 21, 384

Using Proportions: 107, 170, 248, 642

Technology

Developing Multimedia Presentations: 73, 505

Using a Database: 18, 221, 261

Using an Electronic Spreadsheet: 98, 196, 325, 396, 443, 505, 569

Using Graphics Software: 299, 411

Using a Word Processor: 138, 152, 267, 354, 608

Science
INTEGRATION

SCIENCE *Online*

THE PRINCETON REVIEW

UNIT 1

Unit Contents

✔ Pre-Reading Activity

Have students look through the unit for pictures of cells and identify differences among cells.

UNIT 1 Life Structure and Function

How Are Seaweed & Cell Cultures Connected?

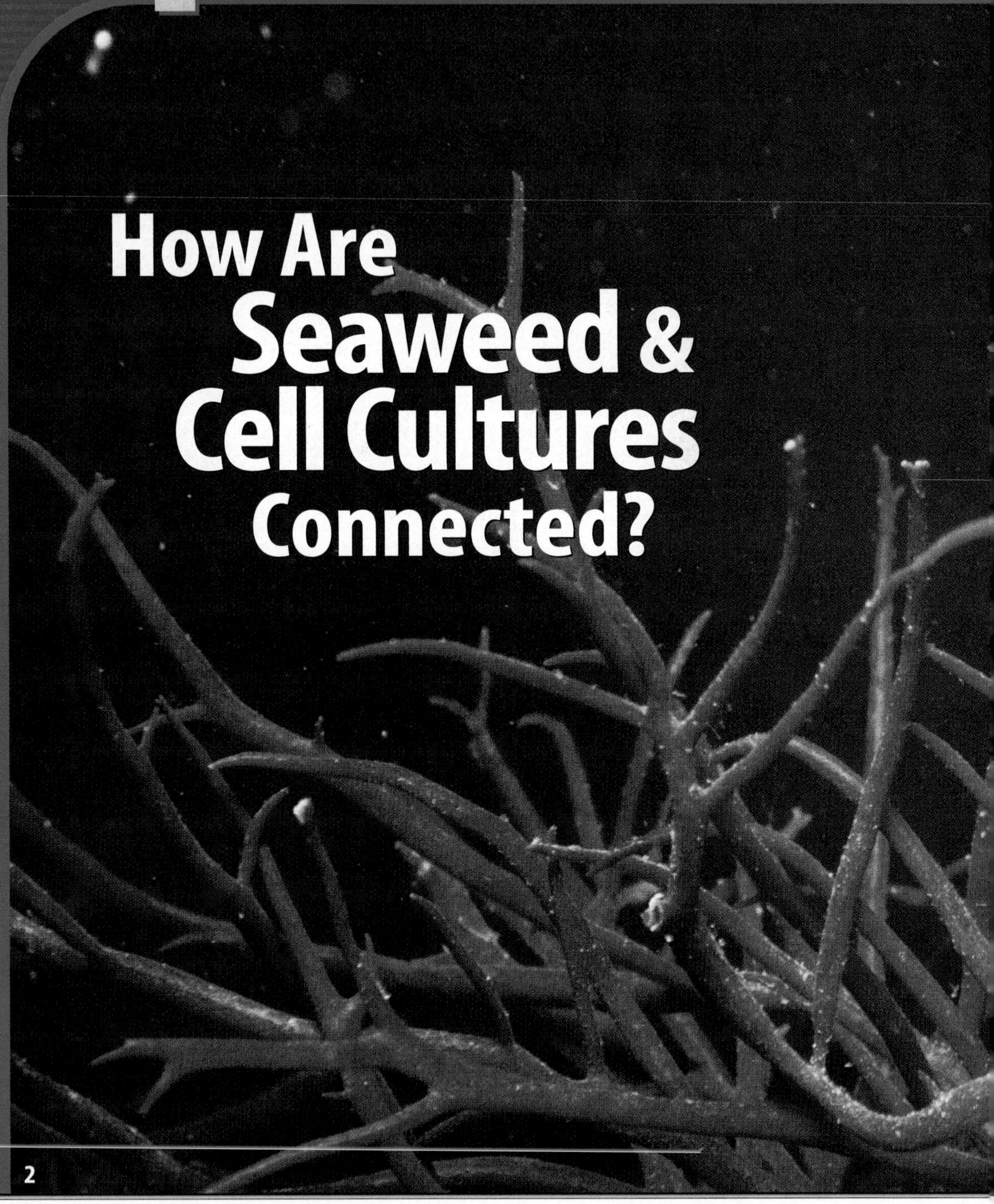

Teacher to Teacher

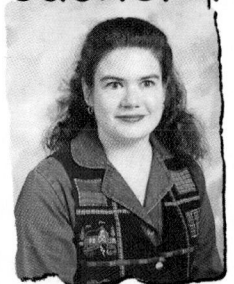

"Writing vocabulary words on large index cards and posting them above the chalkboard helps my learning disabled students. They can use these cards to spell the terms correctly on their tests and quizzes. It is like a word bank."

Catherine C. Walker, Teacher
Martin Middle School
Raleigh, NC

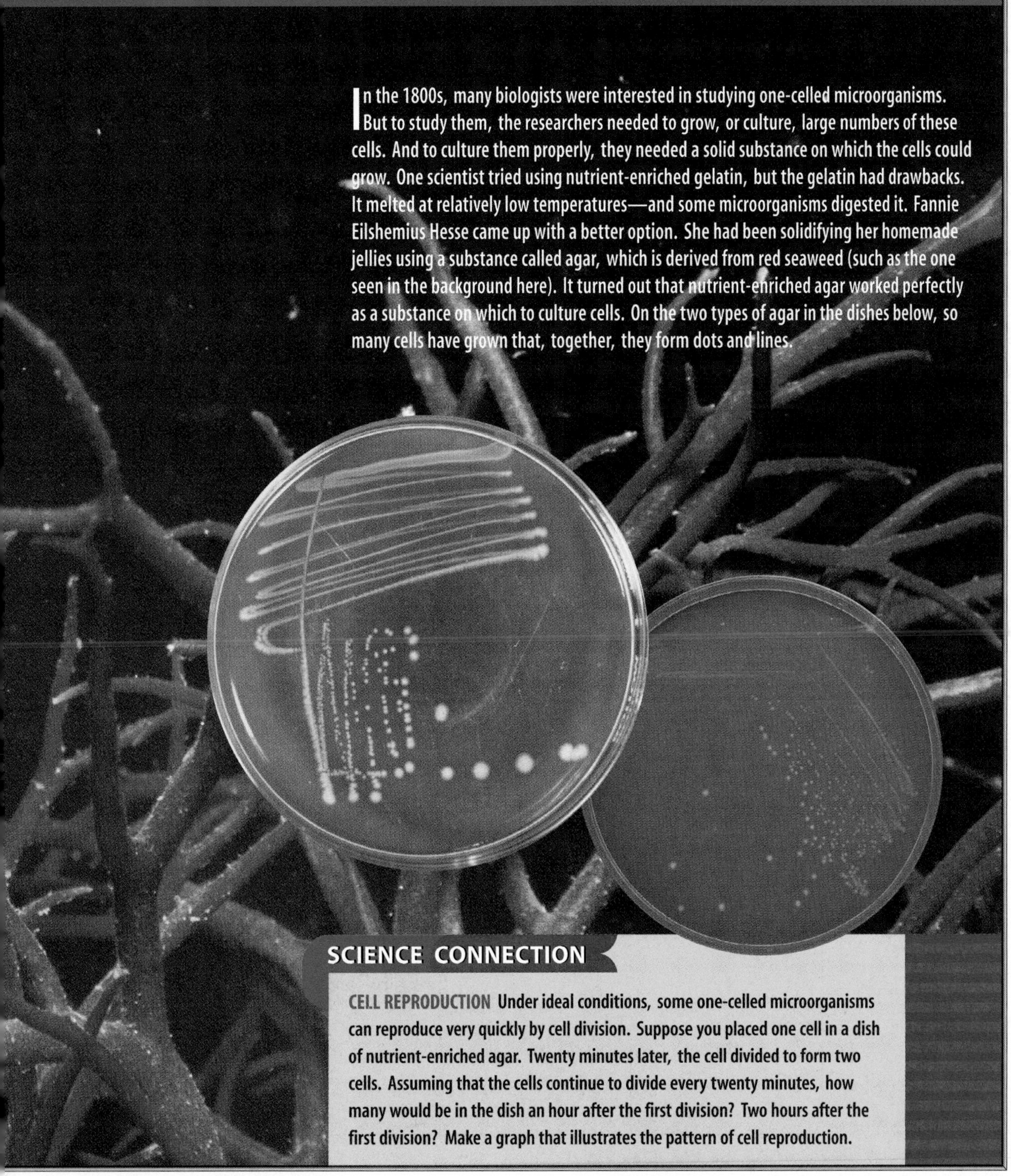

In the 1800s, many biologists were interested in studying one-celled microorganisms. But to study them, the researchers needed to grow, or culture, large numbers of these cells. And to culture them properly, they needed a solid substance on which the cells could grow. One scientist tried using nutrient-enriched gelatin, but the gelatin had drawbacks. It melted at relatively low temperatures—and some microorganisms digested it. Fannie Eilshemius Hesse came up with a better option. She had been solidifying her homemade jellies using a substance called agar, which is derived from red seaweed (such as the one seen in the background here). It turned out that nutrient-enriched agar worked perfectly as a substance on which to culture cells. On the two types of agar in the dishes below, so many cells have grown that, together, they form dots and lines.

SCIENCE CONNECTION

CELL REPRODUCTION Under ideal conditions, some one-celled microorganisms can reproduce very quickly by cell division. Suppose you placed one cell in a dish of nutrient-enriched agar. Twenty minutes later, the cell divided to form two cells. Assuming that the cells continue to divide every twenty minutes, how many would be in the dish an hour after the first division? Two hours after the first division? Make a graph that illustrates the pattern of cell reproduction.

Introducing the Unit

How Are Seaweed & Cell Cultures Connected?

AGAR, a gelatin-like product, is made primarily from the algae *Gelidium* and *Gracilaria* (red seaweeds). Best known as a solidifying component of bacteriological culture media, it is used also in cosmetics; in medicines; and in dentistry. It is also used as a clarifying agent in brewing and wine making; as a thickening agent in ice cream, pastries, desserts, and salad dressings; and as a wire-drawing lubricant.

Agar is isolated from the algae as an amorphous and translucent product sold as powder, flakes, or bricks. It is produced chiefly in Japan, New Zealand, Australia, the United States, and Russia. Although agar is insoluble in cold water, it absorbs as much as 20 times its own weight. It dissolves readily in boiling water; a dilute solution is still liquid at 42° C (108° F) but solidifies at 37° C into a firm gel.

In the natural state, agar occurs as a complex cell-wall constituent containing a complex carbohydrate (polysaccharide) with sulfate and calcium. It was in 1883 that Frau Hesse came up with this medium for culturing cells. Unlike gelatin, agar could be liquefied by only a few microorganisms and does not provide a food source, thus allowing better control of the nutrient content of the medium.

SCIENCE
Online
Internet Addresses

_____

_____

_____

_____

Explore the Glencoe Science Web site at **science.glencoe.com** to find out more about topics in this unit.

SCIENCE CONNECTION

Activity
If a cell divides every twenty minutes, students should find there would be eight cells at the end of one hour and 64 cells at the end of two hours. Have students compare their graphs with that of a partner.

Section/Objectives	Standards		Activities/Features
Chapter Opener	**National**	**State/Local**	**Explore Activity:** Use features to classify organisms, p. 5 **Before You Read,** p. 5
	See p. 5T for a Key to Standards.		
Section 1 What is science? 🕐 2 sessions 📦 1 block 1. **Apply** scientific methods to problem solving. 2. **Demonstrate** how to measure using scientific units.	National Content Standards: UCP2, A1, A2, B1, G1		**Science Online,** p. 8 **MiniLAB:** Analyzing Data, p. 9 **Problem-Solving Activity:** Does temperature affect the rate of bacterial reproduction?, p. 11
Section 2 Living Things 🕐 2 sessions 📦 1 block 1. **Distinguish** between living and nonliving things. 2. **Identify** what living things need to survive.	National Content Standards: UCP2, C1, C4		**Science Online,** p. 15 **Health Integration,** p. 17
Section 3 Where does life come from? 🕐 1 session 📦 0.5 block 1. **Describe** experiments about spontaneous generation. 2. **Explain** how scientific methods led to the idea of biogenesis. 3. **Examine** how chemical compounds found in living things might have formed.	National Content Standards: UCP2, A2, C1, D2, G3		**Visualizing the Origins of Life,** p. 20 **Earth Science Integration,** p. 21
Section 4 How are living things classified? 🕐 3 sessions 📦 1.5 blocks 1. **Describe** how early scientists classified living things. 2. **Explain** the system of binomial nomenclature. 3. **Demonstrate** how to use a dichotomous key.	National Content Standards: UCP1, A1, A2, C1, F5, G2, G3		**Science Online,** p. 23 **MiniLAB:** Communicating Ideas, p. 25 **Activity:** Classifying Seeds, p. 27 **Activity:** Using Scientific Methods, p. 28 **Science and Society:** Monkey Business, p. 30

NATIONAL GEOGRAPHIC

Teacher's Corner

PRODUCTS AVAILABLE FROM GLENCOE
To order call 1-800-334-7344:
Books
National Geographic Book of Mammals
Field Guide to the Birds of North America
CD-ROMs
Mammals: A Multimedia Encyclopedia

NGS PictureShow: Classifying Plants and Animals
Curriculum Kits
GeoKit: Cells and Organisms
GeoKit: Fish, Reptiles, and Amphibians
GeoKit: Plants
Transparency Set

NGS PicturePack: Classifying Plants and Animals

PRODUCTS AVAILABLE FROM NATIONAL GEOGRAPHIC SOCIETY
To order call 1-800-368-2728:
Video
Plant Classification

Activity Materials	Reproducible Resources	Section Assessment	Technology
Explore Activity: insect collection	**Chapter Resources Booklet** Foldables Worksheet, p. 15 Directed Reading Overview, p. 17 Note-taking Worksheets, pp. 33–35	GLENCOE'S ASSESSMENT ADVANTAGE	
MiniLAB: pan balance, sponge, water	**Chapter Resources Booklet** Transparency Activity, p. 44 MiniLAB, p. 3 Enrichment, p. 29 Reinforcement, p. 25 Lab Activity, pp. 9–10 Directed Reading, p. 18	Portfolio Science Journal, p. 7 Performance MiniLAB, p. 9 Problem-Solving Activity, p. 11 Skill Builder Activities, p. 13 Content Section Assessment, p. 13	Section Focus Transparency Interactive CD-ROM Guided Reading Audio Program
Need materials? Contact Science Kit at 1-800-828-7777 or www.sciencekit.com on the Internet.	**Chapter Resources Booklet** Transparency Activity, p. 45 Enrichment, p. 30 Reinforcement, p. 26 Directed Reading, p. 18	Portfolio Curriculum Connection, p. 16 Performance Skill Builder Activities, p. 18 Content Section Assessment, p. 18	Section Focus Transparency Interactive CD-ROM Guided Reading Audio Program
	Chapter Resources Booklet Transparency Activity, p. 46 Enrichment, p. 31 Reinforcement, p. 27 Directed Reading, p. 19	Portfolio Reteach, p. 21 Performance Skill Builder Activities, p. 21 Content Section Assessment, p. 21	Section Focus Transparency Interactive CD-ROM Guided Reading Audio Program
MiniLAB: magazine picture of a piece of furniture **Activity:** packets of seeds (10 different kinds), metric ruler, hand lens **Activity:** 3 500-mL, wide-mouthed containers; brine shrimp eggs; small plastic spoon; distilled water; weak salt solution; strong salt solution; 3 labels; hand lens	**Chapter Resources Booklet** Transparency Activity, p. 47 MiniLAB, p. 4 Enrichment, p. 32 Reinforcement, p. 28 Directed Reading, pp. 19, 20 Transparency Activity, pp. 49–50 Lab Activity, pp. 11–13 Activity Worksheets, pp. 5–6, 7–8 **Lab Management and Safety,** p. 65	Portfolio Assessment, p. 26 Performance MiniLAB, p. 25 Skill Builder Activities, p. 26 Content Section Assessment, p. 26	Section Focus Transparency Teaching Transparency Interactive CD-ROM Guided Reading Audio Program

End of Chapter Assessment

GLENCOE'S ASSESSMENT ADVANTAGE

Blackline Masters	Technology	Professional Series
Chapter Resources Booklet Chapter Review, pp. 37–38 Chapter Tests, pp. 39–42 **Standardized Test Practice by The Princeton Review,** pp. 11–14	MindJogger Videoquiz Interactive CD-ROM Vocabulary PuzzleMakers ExamView Pro Test Bank Interactive Lesson Planner Interactive Teacher Edition	Performance Assessment in the Science Classroom (PASC)

Transparencies

Section Focus

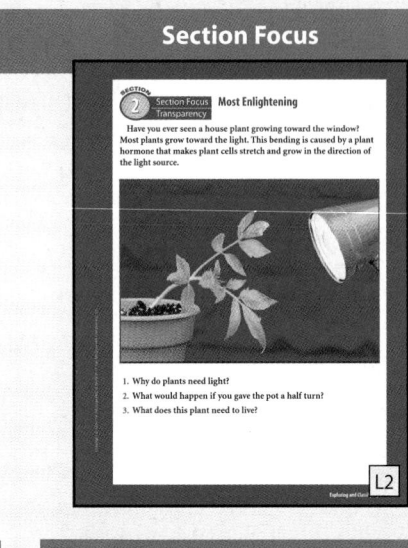

Assessment

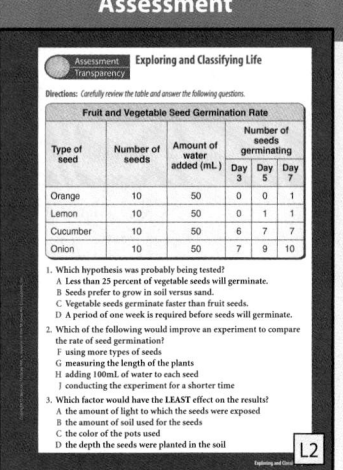

Teaching

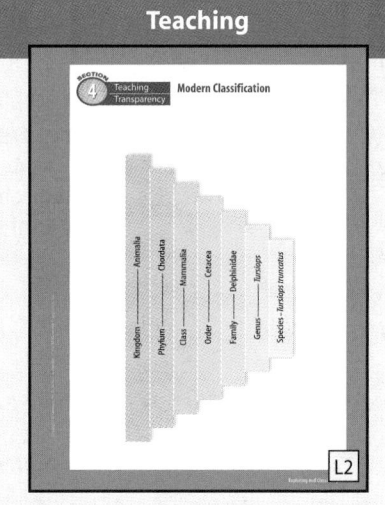

This is a representation of key blackline masters available in the Teacher Classroom Resources. See Resource Manager boxes within the chapter for additional information.

Key to Teaching Strategies

The following designations will help you decide which activities are appropriate for your students.

L1 Level 1 activities should be appropriate for students with learning difficulties.

L2 Level 2 activities should be within the ability range of all students.

L3 Level 3 activities are designed for above-average students.

ELL ELL activities should be within the ability range of English Language Learners.

COOP LEARN Cooperative Learning activities are designed for small group work.

LS Multiple Learning Styles logos, as described on page 22T, are used throughout to indicate strategies that address different learning styles.

P These strategies represent student products that can be placed into a best-work portfolio.

Hands-on Activities

Activity Worksheets

Laboratory Activities

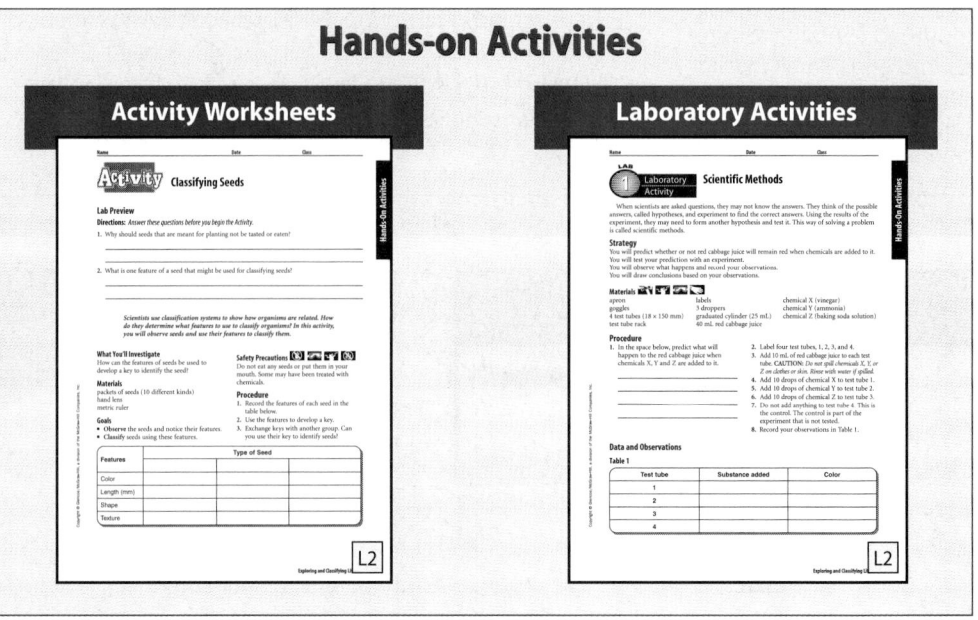

Meeting Different Ability Levels

Content Outline

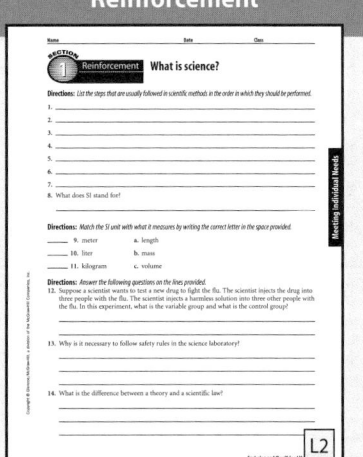

Reinforcement

Directed Reading

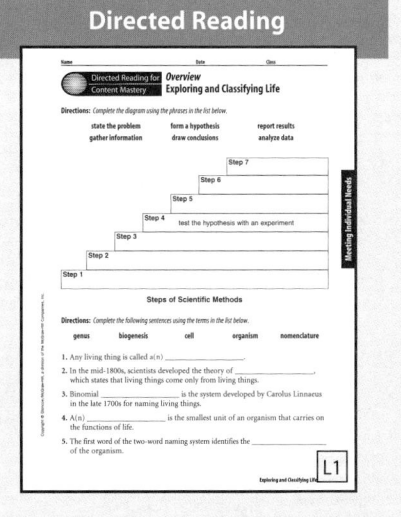

Assessment

Chapter Tests

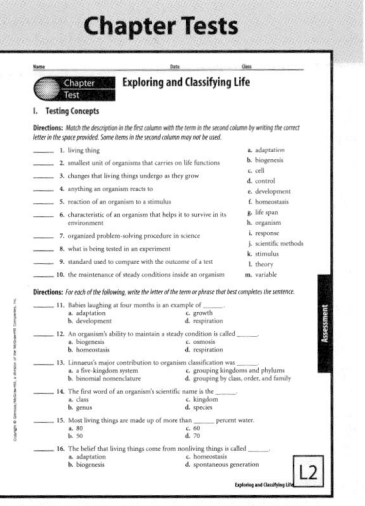

Enrichment

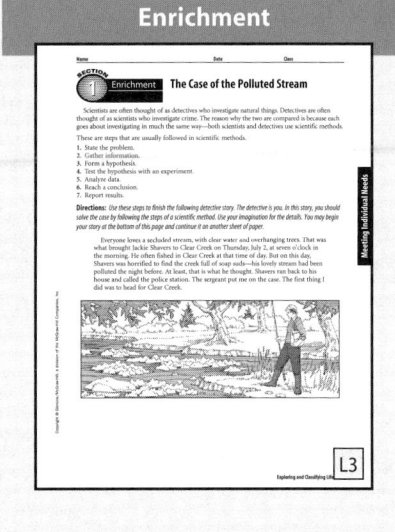

Spanish Directed Reading

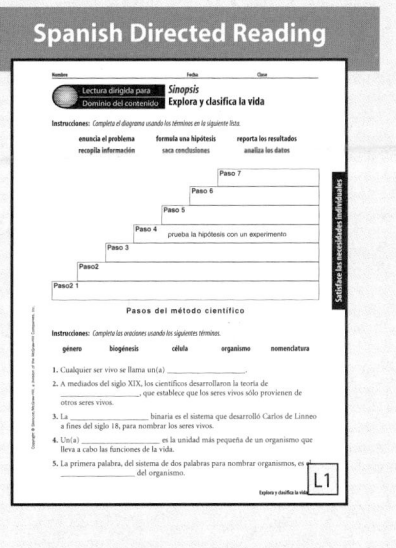

Test Practice Workbook

Chapter Review

Science Content Background

SECTION 2

Living Things
Living Versus Nonliving

Living organisms consist of highly organized systems that interact and are dependent upon one another. Living systems are open systems requiring a constant source of energy. All living organisms have a metabolic process by which the energy in carbohydrates is released for use. All living organisms respond to their environment in adaptive ways, including physiological responses as well as behaviors. Living organisms must also have a means of reproduction, growth, and development if their species is to continue.

Student Misconception

All things that move are alive.

Refer to the facing page for teaching strategies to address this misconception. Refer to pages 14–17 for content related to this topic.

SECTION 4

How are living things classified?
Modern Classification

This textbook uses a combination of phenetics and cladistics to classify organisms. Phenetics is based on particular features. Cladistics uses shared, derived characteristics to classify organisms. By comparing DNA nucleotide sequences between species and by measuring the amount of bonding between DNA from different species, taxonomists infer the degree of similarity between organisms. Scientists hypothesize that organisms with similar proteins are closely related. A comparison of the amino acid sequences between species' proteins provides objective, quantitative data for taxonomists because the structure of proteins is genetically determined.

Scientific Names

Most taxonomists currently divide the six-kingdom system into groups called domains. The three domains are Eubacteria, Archaea, and Eukarya. The domains Eubacteria and Archaea contain Kingdom Eubacteria and Kingdom Archaebacteria, respectively. Domain Eukarya contains four kingdoms—Kingdom Protista, Kingdom Fungi, Kingdom Plantae, and Kingdom Animalia.

The two kingdoms of prokaryotes, Kingdom Eubacteria and Kingdom Archaebacteria, differ. All eubacteria have muramic acid in their cell walls, but archaebacteria do not. The RNA sequences of eubacteria and archaebacteria are also different. Organisms that possess cells with membrane-bound organelles are eukaryotes. Several organelles—mitochondria, chloroplasts, and Golgi apparatus—are approximately the size of a prokaryotic cell.

Tools for Identifying Organisms

A system of classification avoids ambiguity among species, reflects the phylogeny (evolutionary history) of organisms, and provides clues about the organism's habits and possible features shared with similar organisms. The second word of a scientific name is called the specific epithet, usually an adjective that describes the organism, indicates the organism's place of origin, or is a Latinized surname to honor someone. Subspecies have two specific epithets. Today, species names are a mixture of Latin and Greek. At least 1.5 million species of organisms have been named.

SCIENCE *Online*

For additional content background on this topic, go to the Glencoe Science Web site at science.glencoe.com.

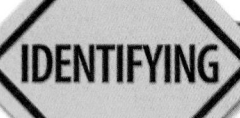 **IDENTIFYING** **Misconceptions**

Find Out What Students Think

Students may think that . . .

• **All things that move are alive.**

Students generally define "living" according to the characteristics of large animals. Hence they associate "living" with movement. Students often do not consider plants and fungi to be alive because they do not appear to move, but may classify rivers or clouds as living because they do move. Students may add other mammalian characteristics to their definitions of life such as eating, breathing, or the presence of a heartbeat.

Clouding the concept further is the confusion between "nonliving" and "dead." Students may classify both a dead animal and a rock as "nonliving" objects, even though they classify animals in general as alive.

Discussion

Place a rock, a houseplant, and a living animal (such as a caged hamster or a volunteer student) in view of the class. Ask students if they think any of the three items are alive. As students respond, ask them why the think the item is or is not alive. From this, generate a list of characteristics that students believe belong to all living organisms. Students will probably recognize that the animal is alive. Some will understand that the plant is alive, but have difficulty explaining why. Most will know that the rock is not alive.

Promote Understanding

Activity

Have the students read **Section 2** in this chapter, then review the list they generated in the discussion suggestion above. Ask the students if they want to change anything on the list.

Next, place a candle in full view of the class and light it. Ask students if they think the flame is alive. Then do the following:

• Blow gently on the flame to show that it responds.

• Light another candle or a match from the flame to show that the flame can reproduce.

• Point out that the wax of the candle is being consumed, showing that the flame uses energy.

Remind students that many nonliving things have some characteristics of living things.

• Ask the class what characteristics the candle flame lacks. Students should recognize that the flame is not highly organized, it is not made up of organic molecules, and it contains no cells.

Assess

After completing the chapter, see *Identifying Misconceptions* in the Study Guide.

Exploring and Classifying Life

Chapter Vocabulary

What do you think?

Science Journal The animals in the picture are tube sponges. Tube sponges remain attached to one place. They remove oxygen and food from water that flows through a series of canals in their bodies.

Exploring and Classifying Life

How many different living things do you see in this picture? Did your answer include the living coral? What do all living things have in common? How are they different? In this chapter, you will read the answers to these questions. You also will read how living things are classified. In the first part of the chapter, you will read how scientific methods may be used to solve many everyday and scientific problems.

What do you think?

Science Journal Look at the picture below with a classmate. Discuss what you think these might be. Here's a hint: *You could really clean up with these things.* Write your answer or best guess in your Science Journal.

4

Theme Connection

Systems and Interactions Scientists have devised systems for classifying organisms. These systems use an organism's traits, which have changed over time as a result of organisms' interactions with the environment.

Life scientists discover, describe, and name hundreds of organisms every year. How do they decide if a certain plant belongs to the iris or orchid family of flowering plants, or if an insect is more like a grasshopper or a beetle?

Use features to classify organisms

1. Observe the organisms on the opposite page or in an insect collection in your class.
2. Decide which feature could be used to separate the organisms into two groups, then sort the organisms into the two groups.
3. Continue to make new groups using different features until each organism is in a category by itself.

Observe

What features would you use to classify the living thing in the photo above? How do you think scientists classify living things? List your ideas in your Science Journal.

Before You Read

FOLDABLES
Reading & Study Skills

Making a Vocabulary Study Fold To help you study the interactions of life, make the following vocabulary Foldable. Knowing the definition of vocabulary words in a chapter is a good way to ensure you have understood the content.

1. Place a sheet of notebook paper in front of you so that the short side is at the top. Fold the paper in half from the left to the right side.
2. Through one thickness of paper, cut along every third line from the outside edge to the center fold, forming ten tabs as shown.
3. On the front of each tab, write a vocabulary word listed on the first page of each section in this chapter. On the back of each tab, write what you think the word means. Add to or change the definitions as you read.

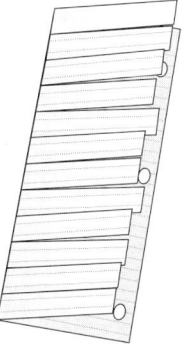

5

SECTION

What is science?

Bellringer Transparency

Display the Section Focus Transparency for Section 1. Use the accompanying Transparency Activity Master. L2

ELL

Tie to Prior Knowledge

Students use problem-solving skills daily. Discuss how they solve everyday problems, such as deciding what outfit to wear or how to manage homework with sports schedules. Relate solving everyday problems to scientific methods.

Text Question Answer

bacteria

SECTION

What is science?

What You'll Learn
- **Apply** scientific methods to problem solving.
- **Demonstrate** how to measure using scientific units.

Vocabulary

scientific methods	variable
hypothesis	theory
control	law

Why It's Important

Learning to use scientific methods will help you solve ordinary problems in your life.

The Work of Science

Movies and popcorn seem to go together. So before you and your friends watch a movie, sometimes you pop some corn in a microwave oven. When the popping stops, you take out the bag and open it carefully. You smell the mouthwatering, freshly popped corn and avoid hot steam that escapes from the bag. What makes the popcorn pop? How do microwaves work and make things hot? By the way, what are microwaves anyway?

Asking questions like these is one way scientists find out about anything in the world and the universe. Science is often described as an organized way of studying things and finding answers to questions.

Types of Science Many types of science exist. Each is given a name to describe what is being studied. For example, energy and matter have a relationship. That's a topic for physics. A physicist could answer most questions about microwaves.

On the other hand, a life scientist might study any of the millions of different animals, plants, and other living things on Earth. Look at the objects in **Figure 1.** What do they look like to you? A life scientist could tell you that some of the objects are living plants and some are just rocks. Life scientists who study plants are botanists, and those who study animals are zoologists. What do you suppose a bacteriologist studies?

Figure 1
Are all of these objects rocks?
Examine the picture carefully. Some of these objects are actually *Lithops* **plants. They commonly are called stone plants and are native to deserts in South Africa.**

6

Section ✓*Assessment* Planner

Critical Thinking

Whether or not you become a trained scientist, you are going to solve problems all your life. You probably solve many problems every day when you sort out ideas about what will or won't work. Suppose your CD player stops playing music. To figure out what happened, you have to think about it. That's called critical thinking, and it's the way you use skills to solve problems.

If you know that the CD player does not run on batteries and must be plugged in to work, that's the first thing you check to solve the problem. You check and the player is plugged in so you eliminate that possible solution. You separate important information from unimportant information—that's a skill. Could there be something wrong with the first outlet? You plug the player into a different outlet, and your CD starts playing. You now know that it's the first outlet that doesn't work. Identifying the problem is another skill you have.

Solving Problems

Scientists use the same types of skills that you do to solve problems and answer questions. Although scientists don't always find the answers to their questions, they always use critical thinking in their search. Besides critical thinking, solving a problem requires organization. In science, this organization often takes the form of a series of procedures called **scientific methods. Figure 2** shows one way that scientific methods might be used to solve a problem.

State the Problem Suppose a veterinary technician wanted to find out whether different types of cat litter cause irritation to cats' skin. What would she do first? The technician begins by observing something she cannot explain. A pet owner brings his four cats to the clinic to be boarded while he travels. He leaves his cell phone number so he can be contacted if any problems arise. When they first arrive, the four cats seem healthy. The next day however, the technician notices that two of the cats are scratching and chewing at their skin. By the third day, these same two cats have bare patches of skin with red sores. The technician decides that something in the cats' surroundings or their food might be irritating their skin.

Figure 2
The series of procedures shown below is one way to use scientific methods to solve a problem.

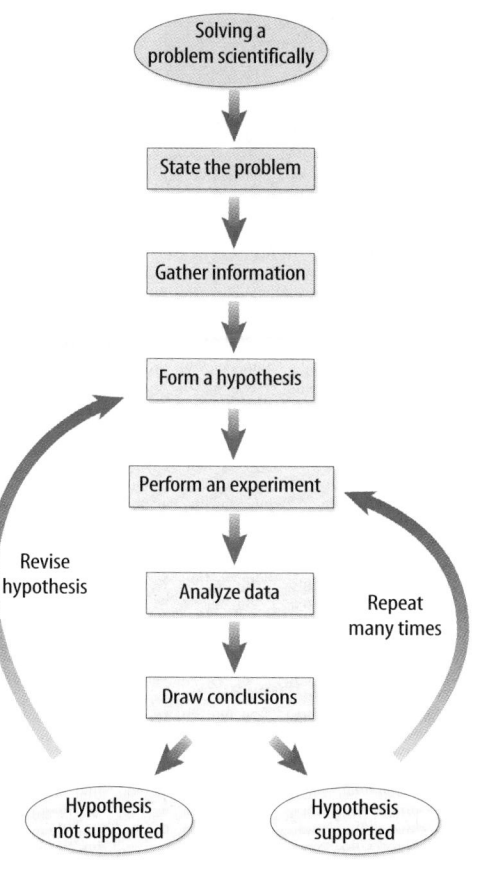

The Work of Science

Activity

Divide the class into small groups. Ask: **What do you think life scientists do? Where might they work?** Allow time for groups to discuss the questions and record their responses. Have each group use their results to write a Help Wanted advertisement seeking a life scientist. Ask groups to present their advertisements to the class. COOP LEARN
KS Interpersonal

Critical Thinking

IDENTIFYING
Misconceptions

Science is often thought of as a discipline out of reach of most people. Many believe that only well-educated or specially trained people can practice science. Explain that science is a process of understanding and that anyone can use the methods of science in daily life.

Solving Problems

Visual Learning

Figure 2 Are all the steps shown here always followed in the exact same sequence? No; if a hypothesis is not supported, the scientist starts over by forming a new hypothesis. Sometimes, only a few of the steps are used.

Resource Manager

Chapter Resources Booklet
  Transparency Activity, p. 44
  Directed Reading for Content Mastery, pp. 17, 18
  Note-taking Worksheets, pp. 33–35

Science Journal

Critical-Thinking Log Ask students to keep in their journals a log of instances in which they used critical thinking to solve problems. Logs should note the date, problem, and solution. At the end of one week, have students share their logs with classmates. Guide students in recognizing that critical thinking is a life skill.
L2 **KS** Interpersonal P

Quick Demo

Fill a 2-L clear container with pond water and place it in a well-lighted area. Have students hypothesize how the water will appear in ten days. Collect the written hypotheses. At the end of ten days, have students check their hypotheses against the conditions in the jar. L1

LS Linguistic

SCIENCE *Online*
Internet Addresses

_____

_____

_____

Explore the Glencoe Science Web site at **science.glencoe.com** to find out more about topics in this section.

Figure 3
Observations can be made in many different settings.

A Laboratory investigations

B Computer models

C Fieldwork

SCIENCE *Online*

Research Visit the Glencoe Science Web site at **science.glencoe.com** for more information about how scientists use controlled experiments. Communicate to your class what you learn.

Gather Information Laboratory observations and experiments are ways to collect information. Some data also are gathered from fieldwork. Fieldwork includes observations or experiments that are done outside of the laboratory. For example, the best way to find out how a bird builds a nest is to go outside and watch it. **Figure 3** shows some ways data can be gathered.

The technician gathers information about the problem by watching the cats closely for the next two days. She knows that cats sometimes change their behavior when they are in a new place. She wants to see if the behavior of the cats with the skin sores seems different from that of the other two cats. Other than the scratching and chewing, all four cats' behavior seems to be the same.

The technician calls the owner and tells him about the problem. She asks him what brand of cat food he feeds his cats. Because his brand is the same one used at the clinic, she decides that food is not the cause of the skin irritation. She decides that the cats probably are reacting to something in their surroundings. There are many things in the clinic that the cats might react to. How does she decide what it is?

During her observations she notices that the cats seem to scratch and chew themselves most after using their litter boxes. The cat litter used by the clinic contains a deodorant. The technician calls the owner and finds out that the cat litter he buys does not contain a deodorant.

Form a Hypothesis Based on this information, the next thing the veterinary technician does is form a hypothesis. A **hypothesis** is a prediction that can be tested. After discussing her observations with the clinic veterinarian, she hypothesizes that something in the cat litter is irritating the cats' skin.

Test the Hypothesis with an Experiment The technician gets the owner's permission to test her hypothesis by performing an experiment. In an experiment, the hypothesis is tested using controlled conditions. The technician reads the labels on two brands of cat litter and finds that the ingredients of each are the same except that one contains a deodorant.

8 CHAPTER 1 Exploring and Classifying Life

LAB DEMONSTRATION

Purpose to compare observations and inferences
Materials one red apple
Alternate Materials one purple grape for each student pair
Preparation Wash the fruit.

Procedure Have students record visual observations of the fruit and then classify the following statements as observations or inferences. 1. The apple's covering is red. 2. The apple is edible. 3. There are seeds inside the apple.
Expected Outcome 1 is an observation; 2 and 3 are inferences.

✔Assessment

How are observations and inferences different? Observations are information gathered through the senses. Inferences result from past observations and knowledge.

Controls The technician separates the cats with sores from the other two cats. She puts each of the cats with sores in a cage by itself. One cat is called the experimental cat. This cat is given a litter box containing the cat litter without deodorant. The other cat is given a litter box that contains cat litter with deodorant. The cat with deodorant cat litter is the control.

A **control** is the standard to which the outcome of a test is compared. At the end of the experiment, the control cat will be compared with the experimental cat. Whether or not the cat litter contains deodorant is the variable. A **variable** is something in an experiment that can change. An experiment should have only one variable. Other than the difference in the cat litter, the technician treats both cats the same.

 **Reading Check** *How many variables should an experiment have?*

Analyze Data The veterinary technician observes both cats for one week. During this time, she collects data on how often and when the cats scratch or chew, as shown in **Figure 4.** These data are recorded in a journal. The data show that the control cat scratches and chews more often than the experimental cat does. The sores on the skin of the experimental cat begin to heal, but those on the control cat do not.

Draw Conclusions The technician then draws the conclusion—a logical answer to a question based on data and observation—that the deodorant in the cat litter probably irritated the skin of the two cats. To accept or reject the hypothesis is the next step. In this case, the technician accepts the hypothesis. If she had rejected it, new experiments would have been necessary.

Although the technician decides to accept her hypothesis, she realizes that to be surer of her results she should continue her experiment. She should switch the experimental cat with the control cat to see what the results are a second time. If she did this, the healed cat might develop new sores. She makes an ethical decision and chooses not to continue the experiment. Ethical decisions, like this one, are important in deciding what science should be done.

Mini LAB

Analyzing Data
Procedure
1. Obtain a **pan balance.** Follow your teacher's instructions for using it.
2. Record all data in your **Science Journal.**
3. Measure and record the mass of a dry **sponge.**
4. Soak this sponge in **water.** Measure and record its mass.
5. Calculate how much water your sponge absorbed.
6. Combine the class data and calculate the average amount of water absorbed.

Analysis
What other information about the sponges might be important when analyzing the data from the entire class?

Figure 4
Collecting and analyzing data is part of scientific methods.

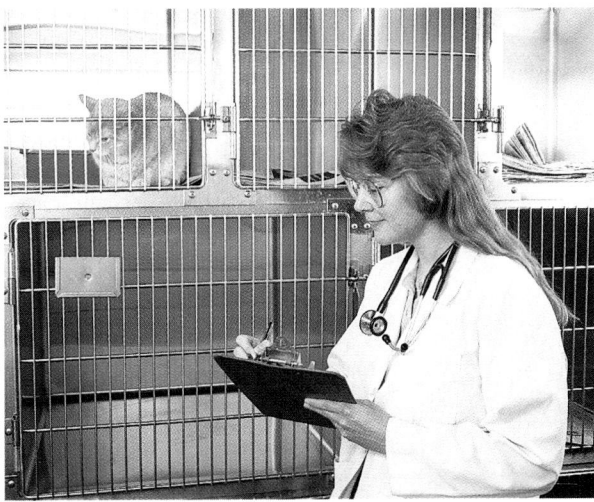

Discussion
Is it possible to form a hypothesis without first making observations? Explain. No; a hypothesis is formed from observations.

 **Reading Check**

Answer one

Mini LAB

Purpose to obtain data using a pan balance L1
IS Logical-Mathematical
Materials pan balance, sponge, water, Science Journal
Teaching Strategies
- Demonstrate the use of a balance.
- Review techniques for transporting a balance: be sure all riders are back to the zero point; place one hand under the balance and the other hand on the beam's support to carry the balance.

Analysis
Accept all reasonable answers. Students may suggest that the size of the sponges or how long each was soaked in water would affect results.

Assessment

Performance Have students use a meterstick to measure the length and width of their lab tables. Ask them to explain how they decided which units of measure to use. Use **PASC**, p. 97.

Resource Manager

Chapter Resources Booklet
MiniLAB, p. 3
Reinforcement, p. 25
Life Science Critical Thinking/Problem Solving, p. 4

Curriculum Connection

Language Arts Have students research a major discovery in life science and the person who made the discovery. Possible research subjects include Francesco Redi, William Harvey, Alexander Fleming, Barbara McClintock, and George Washington Carver. Have students use their findings to write newspaper articles describing their discoveries. L1 IS **Linguistic**

Developing Theories

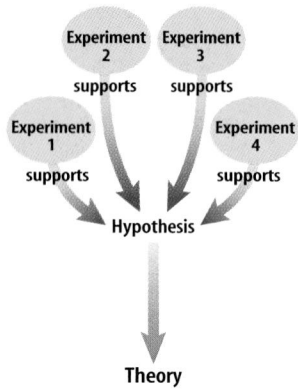
Figure 5
If data collected from several experiments over a period of time all support the hypothesis, it can finally be called a theory.

Report Results When using scientific methods, it is important to share information. The veterinary technician calls the cats' owner and tells him the results of her experiment. She tells him she has stopped using the deodorant cat litter.

The technician also writes a story for the clinic's newsletter that describes her experiment and shares her conclusions. She reports the limits of her experiment and explains that her results are not final. In science it is important to explain how an experiment can be made better if it is done again.

Developing Theories

After scientists report the results of experiments supporting their hypotheses, the results can be used to propose a scientific theory. When you watch a magician do a trick you might decide you have an idea or "theory" about how the trick works. Is your idea just a hunch or a scientific theory? A scientific **theory** is an explanation of things or events based on scientific knowledge that is the result of many observations and experiments. It is not a guess or someone's opinion. Many scientists repeat the experiment. If the results always support the hypothesis, the hypothesis can be called a theory, as shown in **Figure 5.**

✔ **Reading Check** *What is a theory based on?*

A theory usually explains many hypotheses. For example, an important theory in life sciences is the cell theory. Scientists made observations of cells and experimented for more than 100 years before enough information was collected to propose a theory. Hypotheses about cells in plants and animals are combined in the cell theory.

A valid theory raises many new questions. Data or information from new experiments might change conclusions and theories can change. Later in this chapter you will read about the theory of spontaneous generation and how this theory changed as scientists used experiments to study new hypotheses.

Laws A scientific **law** is a statement about how things work in nature that seems to be true all the time. Although laws can be modified as more information becomes known, they are less likely to change than theories. Laws tell you what will happen under certain conditions but do not necessarily explain why it happened. For example, in life science you might learn about laws of heredity. These laws explain how genes are inherited but do not explain how genes work. Due to the great variety of living things, laws that describe them are few. It is unlikely that a law about how all cells work will ever be developed.

Scientific Methods Help Answer Questions You can use scientific methods to answer all sorts of questions. Your questions may be as simple as "Where did I leave my house key?" or as complex as "Will global warming cause the polar ice caps to melt?" You probably have had to find the answer to the first question. Someday you might try to find the answer to the second question. Using these scientific methods does not guarantee that you will get an answer. Often scientific methods just lead to more questions and more experiments. That's what science is about—continuing to look for the best answers to your questions.

Problem-Solving Activity

Does temperature affect the rate of bacterial reproduction?

Some bacteria make you sick. Other bacteria, however, are used to produce foods like cheese and yogurt. Understanding how quickly bacteria reproduce can help you avoid harmful bacteria and use helpful bacteria. It's important to know things that affect how quickly bacteria reproduce. How do you think temperature will affect the rate of bacterial reproduction? A student makes the hypothesis that bacteria will reproduce more quickly as the temperature increases.

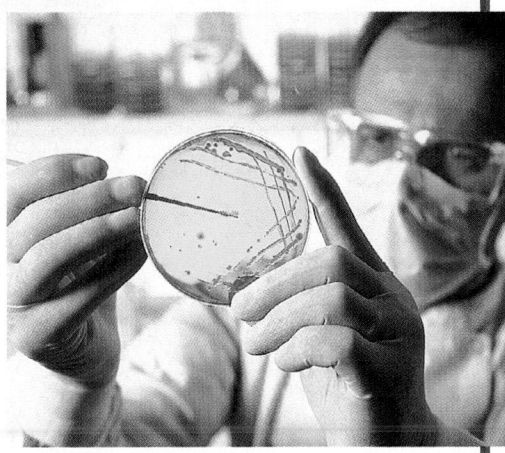

Identifying the Problem

The table below lists the reproduction-doubling rates at specific temperatures for one type of bacteria. A rate of 2.0 means that the number of bacteria doubled two times that hour (e.g., 100 to 200 to 400).

Bacterial Reproductive Rates	
Temperature (°C)	**Doubling Rate per Hour**
20.5	2.0
30.5	3.0
36.0	2.5
39.2	1.2

Look at the table. What conclusions can you draw from the data?

Solving the Problem

1. Do the data in the table support the student's hypothesis?
2. How would you write a hypothesis about the relationship between bacterial reproduction and temperature?
3. Make a list of other factors that might have influenced the results in the table.
4. Are you satisfied with these data? List other things that you wish you knew.
5. Describe an experiment that would help you test these other ideas.

SECTION 1 What is science? **11**

Measuring with Scientific Units

Quick Demo

Show students a nickel and a dime. Tell them the nickel has a mass of about 5 g and the dime is 1 mm thick. Using a triple-beam balance and calipers, have students determine the mass and thickness of other coins they may have.

Teacher FYI

The U.S. is the only industrialized country that has not officially adopted SI. This has caused difficulties in the area of trade and commerce. To successfully compete in world markets, many products made in the U.S. are labeled in both SI and customary units. Invite students to conduct an SI measurement hunt in their homes to find five items that are marked with both types of measures.

Figure 6
Your food often is measured in metric units.

A The label of this juice bottle shows you that it contains 473 mL of juice.

B Nutritional information on the label is listed in grams or milligrams.

Nutrition Facts
Serv. Size 8 fl oz (240 mL)
Servings 2

Amount Per Serving	
Calories 110	
	% Daily Value*
Total Fat 0g	0%
Sodium 25mg	1%
Potassium 480mg	14%
Total Carb 27g	9%
Sugars 24g	
Protein 0g	
Vitamin C 100% • Thiamin 8%	

Not a significant source of fat cal., sat. fat, cholest, fiber, vitamin A, calcium and iron.

*Percent Daily Values are based on a 2,000 calorie diet.

Measuring with Scientific Units

An important part of most scientific investigations is making accurate measurements. Think about things you use every day that are measured. Ingredients in your hamburger, hot dog, potato chips, or soft drink are measured in units such as grams and milliliters, as shown in **Figure 6.** The water you drink, the gas you use, and the electricity needed for a CD player are measured, too.

In your classroom or laboratory this year, you will use the same standard system of measurement scientists use to communicate and understand each other's research and results. This system is called the International System of Units, or SI. For example, you may need to calculate the distance a bird flies in kilometers. Perhaps you will be asked to measure the amount of air your lungs can hold in liters or the mass of an automobile in kilograms. Some of the SI units are shown in **Table 1.**

Table 1 Common SI Measurements

Measurement	Unit	Symbol	Equal to
Length	1 millimeter	mm	0.001 (1/1,000) m
	1 centimeter	cm	0.01 (1/100) m
	1 meter	m	100 cm
	1 kilometer	km	1,000 m
Volume	1 milliliter	mL	0.001 (1/1,000) L
	1 liter	L	1,000 mL
Mass	1 gram	g	1,000 mg
	1 kilogram	kg	1,000 g
	1 tonne	t	1,000 kg = 1 metric ton

12   CHAPTER 1 Exploring and Classifying Life

Resource Manager

Chapter Resources Booklet
   Lab Activity, pp. 9–10
Reading and Writing Skill Activities,
   pp. 17, 33

Cultural Diversity

Ancient Measurements The ancient Chinese system of weights and measures included an acoustical dimension. The quantity of content in a vessel was defined by both weight and by the pitch produced when the vessel was struck. Have students research and report on other measurement instruments and systems. Students might investigate the cubit and thermoscope or the history of the metric system.

Safety First

Doing science is usually much more interesting than just reading about it. Some of the scientific equipment that you will use in your classroom or laboratory is the same as what scientists use. Laboratory safety is important. In many states, a student can participate in a laboratory class only when wearing proper eye protection. Don't forget to wash your hands after handling materials. Following safety rules, as shown in **Figure 7,** will protect you and others from injury during your lab experiences. Symbols used throughout your text will alert you to situations that require special attention. Some of these symbols are shown below. A description of each symbol is in the Safety Symbols chart at the front of this book.

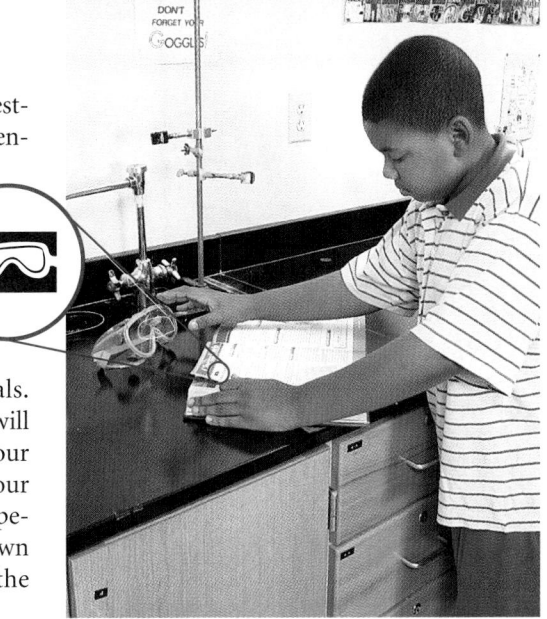

Figure 7
Proper eye protection should be worn whenever you see this safety symbol.

Section 1 Assessment

1. Identify steps that might be followed when using scientific methods.

2. Why is it important to test only one variable at a time during an experiment?

3. What SI unit would you use to measure the width of your classroom?

4. How is a theory different than a hypothesis?

5. **Think Critically** Can the veterinary technician in this section be sure that the deodorant caused the cats' skin problems? What could she change in her experiment to make it better?

Skill Builder Activities

6. **Communicating** Write a newsletter article that explains what the veterinary technician discovered from her experiment. **For more help, refer to the** Science Skill Handbook.

7. **Converting Units** Sometimes temperature is measured in Fahrenheit degrees. Normal human body temperature is 98.6°F. What is this temperature in degrees Celsius? Use the English-to-metric conversion chart at the back of this book. **For more help, refer to the** Math Skill Handbook.

Safety First

Discussion

What is the purpose of safety symbols? Each safety symbol alerts experimenters to a potential danger associated with a particular situation.

③ Assess

Reteach

Divide the class into groups. Give each student in a group a slip of paper labeled with a step of a scientific method. After all the papers have been distributed, have students arrange themselves in a line that shows the order in which the steps are often carried out. Have groups compare their results and discuss why each group may not necessarily have the steps in the same order.

Challenge

A scientist shares the results of her experiment with others. Three scientists repeat the experiment and get different results. **What might you conclude about the first scientist's experiment?** Possible answers: The experiment was not well designed, the procedure was not clearly stated, or variables exist that the first scientist did not identify.

✓ Assessment

Portfolio Safety is just as important at home as it is in the laboratory. For each safety symbol in the chart at the front of the book, have students write one safety rule to follow at home in the kitchen, bathroom, or outdoors. Use **Performance Assessment in the Science Classroom,** p. 157.

Bellringer Transparency

Display the Section Focus Transparency for Section 2. Use the accompanying Transparency Activity Master. L2

ELL

Tie to Prior Knowledge

Students will have ideas about characteristics and needs of all living things. Ask them to name traits and needs that all organisms share. Record responses on the board.

2 Living Things

As You Read

What You'll Learn
- **Distinguish** between living and nonliving things.
- **Identify** what living things need to survive.

Vocabulary
organism
cell
homeostasis

Why It's Important
All living things, including you, have many of the same traits.

Magnification: 106×

Muscle cells

Magnification: 2,000×

What are living things like?

What does it mean to be alive? If you walked down your street after a thunderstorm, you'd probably see earthworms on the sidewalk, birds flying, clouds moving across the sky, and puddles of water. You'd see living and nonliving things that are alike in some ways. For example, birds and clouds move. Earthworms and water feel wet when they are touched. Yet, clouds and water are nonliving things, and birds and earthworms are living things. Any living thing is called an **organism.**

Organisms vary in size from the microscopic bacteria in mud puddles to gigantic oak trees and are found just about everywhere. They have different behaviors and food needs. In spite of these differences, all organisms have similar traits. These traits determine what it means to be alive.

Living Things Are Organized If you were to look at almost any part of an organism, like a plant leaf or your skin, under a microscope, you would see that it is made up of small units called cells. A **cell** is the smallest unit of an organism that carries on the functions of life. Some organisms are composed of just one cell while others are composed of many cells. Cells take in materials from their surroundings and use them in complex ways. Each cell has an orderly structure and contains hereditary material. The hereditary material contains instructions for cellular organization and function. **Figure 8** shows some organisms that are made of many cells. All the things that these organisms can do are possible because of what their cells can do.

Nerve cells

Figure 8
Your body is organized into many different types of cells. Two types are shown.

Section ✓Assessment Planner

PORTFOLIO
Curriculum Connection, p. 16

PERFORMANCE ASSESSMENT
Skill Builder Activities, p. 18
See page 34 for more options.

CONTENT ASSESSMENT
Section, p. 18
Challenge, p. 18
Chapter, pp. 34–35

Living Things Respond Living things interact with their surroundings. Watch your cat when you use your electric can opener. Does your cat come running to find out what's happening even when you're not opening a can of cat food? The cat in **Figure 9** ran in response to a stimulus—the sound of the can opener. Anything that causes some change in an organism is a stimulus (plural, *stimuli*). The reaction to a stimulus is a response. Often that response results in movement, such as when the cat runs toward the sound of the can opener. To carry on its daily activity and to survive, an organism must respond to stimuli.

Living things also respond to stimuli that occur inside them. For example, water or food levels in organisms' cells can increase or decrease. The organisms then make internal changes to keep the right amounts of water and food in their cells. Their temperature also must be within a certain range. An organism's ability to keep the proper conditions inside no matter what is going on outside the organism is called **homeostasis.** Homeostasis is a trait of all living things.

 **Reading Check** *What are some internal stimuli living things respond to?*

Living Things Use Energy Staying organized and carrying on activities like homeostasis requires energy. The energy used by most organisms comes either directly or indirectly from the Sun. Plants and some other organisms use the Sun's energy and the raw materials carbon dioxide and water to make food. You and most other organisms can't use the energy of sunlight directly. Instead, you take in and use food as a source of energy. You get food by eating plants or other organisms that ate plants. Most organisms, including plants, also must take in oxygen in order to release the energy of foods.

Some bacteria live at the bottom of the oceans and in other areas where sunlight cannot reach. They can't use the Sun's energy to produce food. Instead, the bacteria use energy stored in some chemical compounds and the raw material carbon dioxide to make food. Unlike most other organisms, many of these bacteria do not need oxygen to release the energy that is found in their food.

Figure 9
Some cats respond to a food stimulus even when they are not hungry. *Why does a cat come running when it hears a can opener?*

Research Visit the Glencoe Science Web site at **science.glencoe.com** for more information about homeostasis. Communicate to your class what you learn.

❷ Teach

What are living things like?

Quick Demo
Responses in plants are usually less obvious than in animals. However, if you touch a mimosa plant, all the small leaflets on the branch fold upward. Obtain a mimosa plant to demonstrate this rapid response.

Caption Answer
Figure 9 The cat is responding to the stimulus of the can opener.

☑ **Reading Check**

Answer water and food levels, temperature

Use an Analogy
Compare the homeostasis that must be maintained by the body to the conditions necessary for a car to function. For example, a car must have fuel, oil, and other fluids in proper balance in order to run. In the same way, organisms must have fuel and other materials in order to remain alive.

SCIENCE
Online
Internet Addresses
_____
_____
_____
_____
Explore the Glencoe Science Web site at **science.glencoe.com** to find out more about topics in this section.

Discussion

How does an acorn grow and develop? An acorn sprouts and produces roots, stems, and leaves that continue to grow for years. As it grows, it takes in substances from the air and soil and changes those substances into living cells. It continues to add new cells and tissues to replace those that wear out.

IDENTIFYING Misconceptions

Students may think that all things that move are alive. Refer to page 4F for teaching strategies that address this misconception.

Teacher FYI

Nonliving things use energy just as living things do. Windmills, solar calculators, solar panels, and thunderclouds all use energy from their environments and change it into different forms. However, living things take in energy from their environments and use it for specialized purposes such as growth, development, and reproduction.

Figure 10
Complete development of an organism can take a few days or several years. The pictures below show the development of **A** a dog, **B** a human, **C** a pea plant, and **D** a butterfly.

Living Things Grow and Develop When a puppy is born, it might be small enough to hold in one hand. After the same dog is fully grown, you might not be able to hold it at all. How does this happen? The puppy grows by taking in raw materials, like milk from its female parent, and making more cells. Growth of many-celled organisms, such as the puppy, is mostly due to an increase in the number of cells. In one-celled organisms, growth is due to an increase in the size of the cell.

Organisms change as they grow. Puppies can't see or walk when they are born. In eight or nine days, their eyes open, and their legs become strong enough to hold them up. All of the changes that take place during the life of an organism are called development. **Figure 10** shows how four different organisms changed as they grew.

The length of time an organism is expected to live is its life span. Adult dogs can live for 20 years and a cat for 25 years. Some organisms have a short life span. Mayflies live only one day, but a land tortoise can live for more than 180 years. Some bristlecone pine trees have been alive for more than 4,600 years. Your life span is about 80 years.

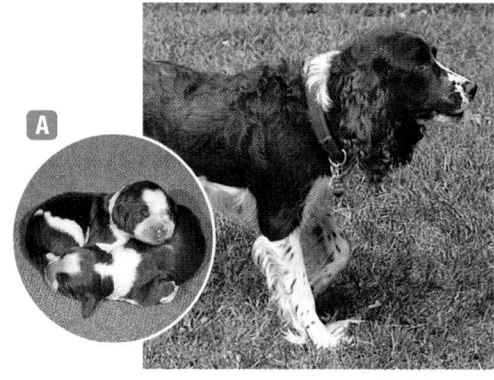

16 CHAPTER 1 Exploring and Classifying Life

Science Journal

Characteristics of Living Things Have students choose an animal that they have observed. In their Science Journals, have them write an essay explaining how their observations show that the animal is a living organism. L2
IS **Linguistic**

Curriculum Connection

Math Have students obtain data that illustrates how they have changed as they have grown older. Ask them to research their heights at three different ages. (If this information is not available at home, have students obtain the data from their school records.) Then have students work in pairs to measure their current heights. Ask students to present their results as bar graphs. L2 IS **Logical-Mathematical** P

Figure 11
Living things reproduce themselves in many different ways. **A** A *Paramecium* reproduces by dividing into two. **B** Beetles, like most insects, reproduce by laying eggs. **C** Every spore released by these puffballs can grow into a new fungus.

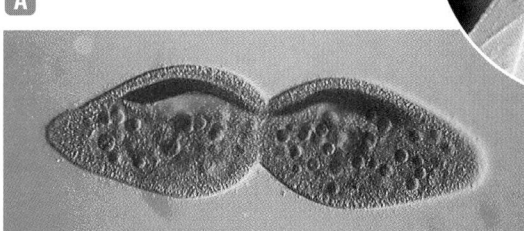

B

C

A

Magnification: 400×

Living Things Reproduce Cats, dogs, alligators, fish, birds, bees, and trees eventually reproduce. They make more of their own kind. Some bacteria reproduce every 20 minutes while it might take a pine tree two years to produce seeds. **Figure 11** shows some ways organisms reproduce.

Without reproduction, living things would not exist to replace those individuals that die. An individual cat can live its entire life without reproducing. However, if cats never reproduced, all cats soon would disappear.

 Reading Check *Why is reproduction important?*

What do living things need?

What do you need to live? Do you have any needs that are different from those of other living things? To survive, all living things need a place to live and raw materials. The raw materials that they require and the exact place where they live can vary.

A Place to Live The environment limits where organisms can live. Not many kinds of organisms can live in extremely hot or extremely cold environments. Most cannot live at the bottom of the ocean or on the tops of mountains. All organisms also need living space in their surroundings. For example, thousands of penguins build their nests on an island. When the island becomes too crowded, the penguins fight for space and some may not find space to build nests. An organism's surroundings must provide for all of its needs.

Health
INTEGRATION

Human infants can't take care of themselves at birth. Research to find out what human infants can do at different stages of development. Make a chart that shows changes from birth to one year old.

SECTION 2 Living Things **17**

Teacher FYI

All the characteristics of living things are needed for survival of the individual, except for reproduction. Reproduction is needed for survival of the species.

Resource Manager

Chapter Resources Booklet
  Enrichment, p. 30
  Reinforcement, p. 26
Cultural Diversity, pp. 7, 9

Visual Learning

Figure 11 How do these organisms reproduce? Beetles lay eggs, a fungus releases spores, and a paramecium undergoes cell division to become two organisms.

Reading Check

Answer Organisms must reproduce to replace members of their species that die, or the species will become extinct.

What do living things need?

Activity

Label five sheets of paper with one of the subheads in this section. Divide the class into five groups. Give each group a sheet of paper. Ask group members to cut pictures from magazines that illustrate the subhead, to paste the pictures on the paper, and write a caption for each picture. When all groups have finished their tasks, combine the pages into a booklet titled "How Living Things Are Alike." L1
COOP LEARN

Extension

Have students name the characteristics and needs of living things that can be observed in a classroom aquarium or terrarium. L2

Health
INTEGRATION

1 month: movements are clumsy, throaty sounds can be made; 3 months: can sit up with assisstance and laugh; 6 months: birth weight doubles, can roll over, sit alone and babble; 9 months: can crawl and repeat syllables; 1 year: birth weight triples, can walk and speak first words

What do living things need?, continued

Caption Answer

Figure 12 Plants take in water through their roots.

③ Assess

Reteach

Write the characteristics of living things on 3" x 5" cards. Have students draw a card and give an example of the characteristic. L1

Challenge

Which characteristic of life is important to survival of a species rather than to the organism itself? Explain. Reproduction; a living thing can survive without reproducing, but the species would not survive if none of its members reproduced.

✓Assessment

Process Have students heat water in a beaker and dissolve as much sugar in the beaker as they can. Tie a string around a stirring rod. Place the rod across the top of the beaker so the string is immersed in the cooled water. Leave the string in the beaker until sugar crystals begin to grow. Ask students why these crystals are not alive. They have none of the other characteristics of living things. Use **Performance Assessment in the Science Classroom,** p. 97.

Figure 12
You and a corn plant each take in and give off about 2 L of water in a day. Most of the water you take in is from water you drink or from foods you eat. *Where do plants get water to transport materials?*

Raw Materials Water is important for all living things. Plants and animals take in and give off large amounts of water each day, as shown in **Figure 12.** Organisms use homeostasis to balance the amounts of water lost with the amounts taken in. Most organisms are composed of more than 50 percent water. You are made of 60 to 70 percent water. Organisms use water for many things. For example, blood, which is about 90 percent water, transports digested food and wastes in animals. Plants have a watery sap that transports materials between roots and leaves.

Living things are made up of substances such as proteins, fats, and sugars. Animals take in most of these substances from the foods they eat. Plants and some bacteria make them using raw materials from their surroundings. These important substances are used over and over again. When organisms die, substances in their bodies are broken down and released into the soil or air. The substances can then be used again by other living organisms. Some of the substances in your body might once have been part of a butterfly or an apple tree.

At the beginning of this section, you learned that things such as clouds, sidewalks, and puddles of water are not living things. Now do you understand why? Clouds, sidewalks, and water do not reproduce, use energy, or have other traits of living things.

Section ② Assessment

1. What is the main source of energy used by most organisms?
2. List five traits most organisms have.
3. Why would you expect to see cells if you looked at a section of a mushroom cap under a microscope?
4. In order to survive, what things do most organisms need?
5. **Think Critically** Why is homeostasis important to organisms?

Skill Builder Activities

6. **Comparing and Contrasting** What are the similarities and differences between a goldfish and the flame of a burning candle? **For more help, refer to the** Science Skill Handbook.
7. **Using a Database** Use references to find the life span of ten animals. Use your computer to make a database. Then graph the life spans from shortest to longest. **For more help, refer to the** Technology Skill Handbook.

18 CHAPTER 1 Exploring and Classifying Life

Answers to Section Assessment

1. the Sun
2. Living things are organized, respond, take in and use energy, grow and develop, and reproduce.
3. All living things are made of cells.
4. Organisms need raw materials and a place to live.
5. Without homeostasis—the maintaining of proper conditions inside an organism regardless of external conditions—the organism would die.
6. The goldfish is made of cells, takes in and uses energy, responds, grows and develops, reproduces, and needs a place to live and raw materials. The candle flame moves, responds to wind, uses energy from the candle, gives off heat energy, produces waste products, and uses oxygen to burn.
7. Life spans will vary in different references. Sample data (in years): humans: 76; horses: 30; cows: 24; dogs: 15; cats: 12; turtles: 125; elephants: 60; penguins: 23; shrews: 1, snakes: 11; spiders: 3

Where does life come from?

Life Comes from Life

You've probably seen a fish tank, like the one in **Figure 13**, that is full of algae. How did the algae get there? Before the seventeenth century, some people thought that insects and fish came from mud, that earthworms fell from the sky when it rained, and that mice came from grain. These were logical conclusions at that time, based on repeated personal experiences. The idea that living things come from nonliving things is known as **spontaneous generation.** This idea became a theory that was accepted for several hundred years. When scientists began to use controlled experiments to test this theory, the theory changed.

✔ Reading Check *According to the theory of spontaneous generation, where do fish come from?*

Spontaneous Generation and Biogenesis From the late seventeenth century through the middle of the eighteenth century, experiments were done to test the theory of spontaneous generation. Although these experiments showed that spontaneous generation did not occur in most cases, they did not disprove it entirely.

It was not until the mid-1800s that the work of Louis Pasteur, a French chemist, provided enough evidence to disprove the theory of spontaneous generation. It was replaced with **biogenesis** (bi oh JEN uh suhs), which is the theory that living things come only from other living things.

As You Read

What You'll Learn
- **Describe** experiments about spontaneous generation.
- **Explain** how scientific methods led to the idea of biogenesis.
- **Examine** how chemical compounds found in living things might have formed.

Vocabulary
spontaneous generation
biogenesis

Why It's Important
You can use scientific methods to try to find out about events that happened long ago or just last week. You can even use them to predict how something will behave in the future.

Figure 13
The sides of this tank were clean and the water was clear when the aquarium was set up. Algal cells, which were not visible on plants and fish, reproduced in the tank. So many algal cells are present now that the water is cloudy.

SECTION 3   Where does life come from?   **19**

Where does life come from?

 **Motivate**

Bellringer Transparency

Display the Section Focus Transparency for Section 3. Use the accompanying Transparency Activity Master. L2
ELL

Tie to Prior Knowledge

Review the characteristics and needs of living things. Elicit from volunteers their ideas on where organisms possessing such characteristics and needs came from.

✔ Reading Check

Answer from mud

Resource Manager

Chapter Resources Booklet
Transparency Activity, p. 46
Directed Reading for Content Mastery, p. 19

Section ✔*Assessment* Planner

PORTFOLIO
Reteach, p. 21
PERFORMANCE ASSESSMENT
Skill Builder Activities, p. 21
See page 34 for more options.

CONTENT ASSESSMENT
Section, p. 21
Challenge, p. 21
Chapter, pp. 34–35

Visualizing the Origins of Life

Have students examine the pictures and read the captions. Then ask the following questions.

What are the similarities of Spallanzani's and Redi's work? Students should note that both Spallanzani and Redi did experiments that questioned the idea of spontaneous generation.

What must have been present in the neck of the S-necked flasks used by Pasteur in his experiments? The necks of the S-neck flasks must have contained microorganisms, which contaminated the broth when the flask was tilted.

Activity

Students should work in small groups to create and play a matching game based on the scientists in the this feature and their work. In the game, points should be awarded for correctly matching a scientist with his work. Have students explain the rules of their game to the class.

Extension

Have interested students research other world events that occurred in the years the experiments shown in this feature took place. These students can construct an expanded time line showing these other events, and shared their findings with the class.

Figure 14

For centuries scientists have theorized about the origins of life. As shown on this timeline, some examined spontaneous generation—the idea that nonliving material can produce life. More recently, scientists have proposed theories about the origins of life on Earth by testing hypotheses about conditions on early Earth.

1668 Francesco Redi put decaying meat in some jars, then covered half of them. When fly maggots appeared only on the uncovered meat (see below, left), Redi concluded that they had hatched from fly eggs and had not come from the meat.

John Needham heated broth in sealed flasks. When **1745** the broth became cloudy with microorganisms, he mistakenly concluded that they developed spontaneously from the broth.

Lazzaro Spallanzani broiled **1768** broth in sealed flasks for a longer time than Needham did. Only the ones he opened became cloudy with contamination.

Not contaminated   Contaminated

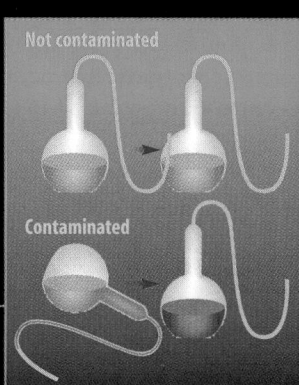

Not contaminated

Contaminated

1859 Louis Pasteur disproved spontaneous generation by boiling broth in S-necked flasks that were open to the air. The broth became cloudy (see above, bottom right) only when a flask was tilted and the broth was exposed to dust in the S-neck.

Gases of Earth's early atmosphere

Electric current

Oceanlike mixture forms

Cools

Materials in present-day cells

1924 Alexander Oparin hypothesized that energy from the Sun, lightning, and Earth's heat triggered chemical reactions early in Earth's history. The newly-formed molecules washed into Earth's ancient oceans and became a part of what is often called the primordial soup.

Stanley Miller and Harold Urey sent electric currents **1953** through a mixture of gases like those thought to be in Earth's early atmosphere. When the gases cooled, they condensed to form an oceanlike liquid that contained materials such as amino acids, found in present-day cells.

20 **CHAPTER 1** Exploring and Classifying Life

Resource Manager

Chapter Resources Booklet
Enrichment, p. 31
Reinforcement, p. 27

Earth Science Critical Thinking/Problem Solving, pp. 1, 12, 14

Visual Learning

Figure 14 Have students create a poster showing the progression of scientific thought on life origins, as evidenced by the experiments in this feature.

Life's Origins

Astronomy
INTEGRATION

If living things can come only from other living things, how did life on Earth begin? Some scientists hypothesize that about 5 billion years ago, Earth's solar system was a whirling mass of gas and dust. They hypothesize that the Sun and planets were formed from this mass. It is estimated that Earth is about 4.6 billion years old. Rocks found in Australia that are more than 3.5 billion years old contain fossils of once-living organisms. Where did these living organisms come from?

Oparin's Hypothesis In 1924, a Russian scientist named Alexander I. Oparin suggested that Earth's early atmosphere had no oxygen but was made up of the gases ammonia, hydrogen, methane, and water vapor. Oparin hypothesized that these gases could have combined to form the more complex compounds found in living things.

Using gases and conditions that Oparin described, American scientists Stanley L. Miller and Harold Urey set up an experiment to test Oparin's hypothesis in 1953. Although the Miller-Urey experiment showed that chemicals found in living things could be produced, it did not prove that life began in this way.

For many centuries, scientists have tried to find the origins of life, as shown in **Figure 14.** Although questions about spontaneous generation have been answered, some scientists still are investigating ideas about life's origins.

Earth Science
INTEGRATION

Scientists hypothesize that Earth's oceans originally formed when water vapor was released into the atmosphere from many volcanic eruptions. Once it cooled, rain fell and filled Earth's lowland areas. Identify five lowland areas on Earth that are now filled with water. Record your answer in your Science Journal.

Section 3 Assessment

1. Compare and contrast spontaneous generation and biogenesis.
2. Describe three controlled experiments that helped disprove the theory of spontaneous generation.
3. List one substance that was used in the Miller-Urey experiment.
4. What were the results of the Miller-Urey experiment?
5. **Think Critically** Why was Oparin's hypothesis about the origins of life important to Miller and Urey?

Skill Builder Activities

6. **Drawing Conclusions** It was thought that in the 1768 experiment some "vital force" in the broth was destroyed. Was it? Based on this experiment, what could have been concluded about where organisms come from? **For more help, refer to the** Science Skill Handbook.

7. **Using Percentages** Earth's age is estimated at 4.6 billion years old. It is estimated that life began 3.5 billion years ago. Life has been present for what percent of Earth's age? **For more help, refer to the** Math Skill Handbook.

---

2 Teach

Life's Origins

Earth Science
INTEGRATION

Students may list five of Earth's oceans and seas.

Teacher FYI

When Oparin first presented his hypotheses on the origins of life, they received a negative response. It was only after continued re-testing that his ideas began to be accepted.

3 Assess

Reteach

Have students make a three-column chart to summarize the experiments described in this section. Columns should be headed Experimenter, Summary of Experiment, and Conclusions. L2 P

Challenge

How did Pasteur's experiments lead to the development of pasteurization? He showed that heating could kill bacteria that caused food to spoil.

✔ Assessment

Performance Have students review the results of Redi's experiment and write their interpretation. The jars that were left open to the air attracted flies, and maggots appeared on the meat. Flies could not get to the meat in the jars that were covered, and no maggots appeared. Use **Performance Assessment in the Science Classroom**, p. 99.

Answers to Section Assessment

1. spontaneous generation: living things come from nonliving matter; biogenesis: living things come only from other living things of the same kind
2. Students should describe the experiments performed by Redi, Pasteur, and Spallanzani.
3. Possible answer: ammonia
4. The experiment showed that chemicals found in living things could be produced.
5. Miller and Urey used the chemicals suggested in Oparin's hypothesis.
6. By boiling the broth, the microorganisms present in it were destroyed. It

could have been concluded that organisms come from the air.
7. 76%

SECTION

4

How are living things classified?

1 Motivate

Bellringer Transparency

Display the Section Focus Transparency for Section 4. Use the accompanying Transparency Activity Master. L2

ELL

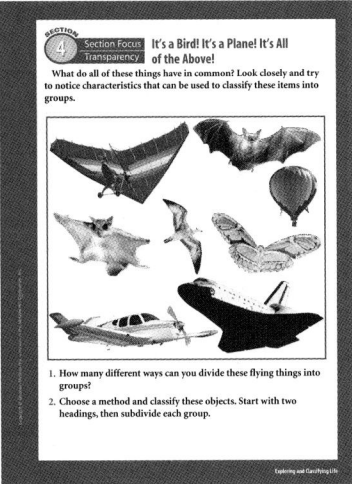

Tie to Prior Knowledge

Ask students to identify real-life situations in which they need to classify a group of items. Possible responses may include organizing a collection of tapes or CDs, arranging canned goods in a pantry, and sorting beads used to make jewelry. Have volunteers explain the process they use in these instances.

Caption Answer

Figure 15 Possible answer: amphibians and all invertebrates

As You Read

What You'll Learn
- **Describe** how early scientists classified living things.
- **Explain** the system of binomial nomenclature.
- **Demonstrate** how to use a dichotomous key.

Vocabulary
phylogeny
kingdom
binomial nomenclature
genus

Why It's Important
Knowing how living things are classified will help you understand the relationships that exist among all living things.

Figure 15
According to Aristotle's classification system, all animals without hair would be grouped together. *What other animals without hair would Aristotle have put in this group?*

Classification

If you go to a library to find a book about the life of Louis Pasteur, where do you look? Do you look for it among the mystery or sports books? You expect to find a book about Pasteur's life with other biography books. Libraries group similar types of books together. When you place similar items together, you classify them. Organisms also are classified into groups.

History of Classification When did people begin to group similar organisms together? Early classifications included grouping plants that were used in medicines. Animals were often classified by human traits such as courageous—for lions—or wise—for owls.

More than 2,000 years ago, a Greek named Aristotle observed living things. He decided that any organism could be classified as either a plant or an animal. Then he broke these two groups into smaller groups. For example, animal categories included hair or no hair, four legs or fewer legs, and blood or no blood. **Figure 15** shows some of the organisms Aristotle would have grouped together. For hundreds of years after Aristotle, no one way of classifying was accepted by everyone.

22 CHAPTER 1 Exploring and Classifying Life

Section ✓Assessment Planner

PORTFOLIO
Assessment, p. 26
PERFORMANCE ASSESSMENT
Try at Home MiniLAB, p. 25
Skill Builder Activities, p. 26
See page 34 for more options.

CONTENT ASSESSMENT
Section, p. 26
Challenge, p. 26
Chapter, pp. 34–35

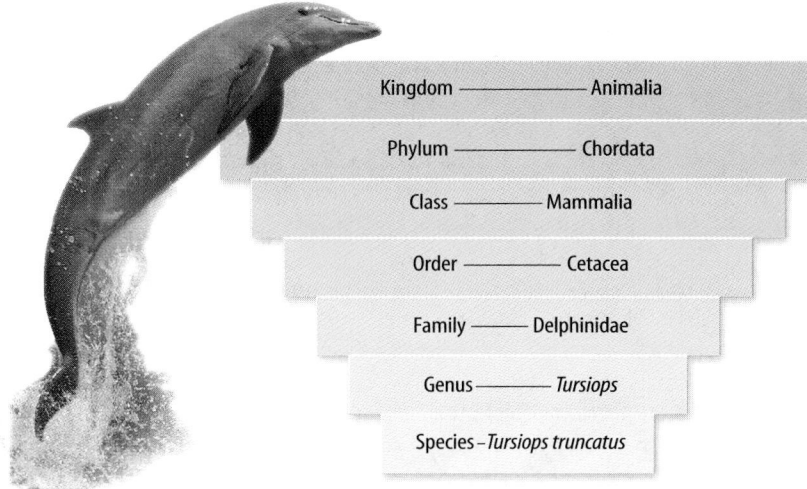

Figure 16
The classification of the bottle-nosed dolphin shows that it is in the order Cetacea. This order includes whales and porpoises.

Kingdom —————— Animalia
Phylum —————— Chordata
Class —————— Mammalia
Order —————— Cetacea
Family ——— Delphinidae
Genus ———— *Tursiops*
Species – *Tursiops truncatus*

Linnaeus In the late eighteenth century, Carolus Linnaeus, a Swedish naturalist, developed a new system of grouping organisms. His classification system was based on looking for organisms with similar structures. For example, plants that had similar flower structure were grouped together. Linnaeus's system eventually was accepted and used by most other scientists.

Modern Classification Like Linnaeus, modern scientists use similarities in structure to classify organisms. They also study fossils, hereditary information, and early stages of development. Scientists use all of this information to determine an organism's phylogeny. **Phylogeny** (fi LAH juh nee) is the evolutionary history of an organism, or how it has changed over time. Today, it is the basis for the classification of many organisms.

✔ Reading Check *What information would a scientist use to determine an organism's phylogeny?*

A classification system commonly used today groups organisms into six kingdoms. A **kingdom** is the first and largest category. Organisms are placed into kingdoms based on various characteristics. Kingdoms can be divided into smaller groups. The smallest classification category is a species. Organisms that belong to the same species can mate and produce fertile offspring. To understand how an organism is classified, look at the classification of the bottle-nosed dolphin in **Figure 16.** Some scientists propose that before organisms are grouped into kingdoms, they should be placed in larger groups called domains. One proposed system groups all organisms into three domains.

SCIENCE
Online

Data Update For an online update of domains, visit the Glencoe Science Web site at **science.glencoe.com** and select the appropriate chapter. Communicate to your class what you learn.

---

2 Teach

Classification

Quick Demo
Display a photo or an actual member of each of the six kingdoms to the class. Have students identify the kingdom each represents. L2 **Visual-Spatial**

Use Science Words
Word Meaning Have students compare the use of the word *kingdom* in the context of this chapter and in a Social Studies text. In science, a kingdom is the largest category of organisms. In social studies, it is a community or area governed by a king or queen. L2 **Linguistic**

Use an Analogy
Develop the idea that the classification system is similar to divisions that exist within your school. The entire school population is similar to all living things with each grade representing a kingdom, each classroom a phylum, and so on.

✔ Reading Check

Answer similar structures, fossils, hereditary information, and early stages of development

Discussion
Which classification group has the most members? Which has the fewest? Kingdom has the most; species has the fewest.

Resource Manager

Chapter Resources Booklet
Transparency Activity, p. 47
Directed Reading for Content Mastery, pp. 19, 20

SCIENCE *Online*
Internet Addresses
_____
_____
_____

Explore the Glencoe Science Web site at **science.glencoe.com** to find out more about topics in this section.

Scientific Names

Quick Demo

Use a world map or globe to point out the Roman Empire. Tell students that Latin originated there thousands of years ago. Explain that Latin was the basis of the Romance languages—Spanish, French, Italian, and Portuguese.

Use an Analogy

The two-word naming system is similar to the structure of Chinese names. The first word in a Chinese name is that of the family and the second and third words are those of the individual. American and European names represent the same idea in reverse order.

Extension

Challenge students to identify an organism from its scientific name. Use *Musca domestica* (housefly), *Equus zebra* (zebra), and *Camelus dromedarius* (dromedary camel). Have students find other scientific names to present to their classmates.

Caption Answer

Figure 17B Possible answers: Sea horses are not horses that live in the sea; wolverines are not small wolves.

Scientific Names

Using common names can cause confusion. Suppose that Diego is visiting Jamaal. Jamaal asks Diego if he would like a soda. Diego is confused until Jamaal hands him a soft drink. At Diego's house, a soft drink is called *pop*. Jamaal's grandmother, listening from the living room, thought that Jamaal was offering Diego an ice-cream soda.

What would happen if life scientists used only common names of organisms when they communicated with other scientists? Many misunderstandings would occur, and sometimes health and safety are involved. In **Figure 17,** you see examples of animals with common names that can be misleading. A naming system developed by Linnaeus helped solve this problem. It gave each species a unique, two-word scientific name.

Figure 17
Common names can be misleading.

A Sea lions are more closely related to seals than to lions.

B Jellyfish are neither fish nor jelly. *Do you know a misleading common name?*

Binomial Nomenclature The two-word naming system that Linnaeus used to name the various species is called **binomial nomenclature** (bi NOH mee ul • NOH mun klay chur). It is the system used by modern scientists to name organisms. The first word of the two-word name identifies the genus of the organism. A **genus** is a group of similar species. The second word of the name might tell you something about the organism—what it looks like, where it is found, or who discovered it.

In this system, the tree species commonly known as red maple has been given the name *Acer rubrum.* The maple genus is *Acer.* The word *rubrum* is Latin for red, which is the color of a red maple's leaves in the fall. The scientific name of another maple is *Acer saccharum.* The Latin word for sugar is *saccharum.* In the spring, the sap of this tree is sweet.

Curriculum Connection

Math Ask students to explain how numbers are classified. Answers may include real and imaginary, whole numbers and fractions, decimals and percents, and rational and irrational.

Teacher FYI

Aristotle's classification system remained in use for almost two thousand years. In the 16th and 17th centuries, there was renewed interest in classification when European explorers brought back unidentified plant and animal species from other lands. In the 17th century, John Ray classified plants according to the structure of their seeds.

A

B

 **Reading Check**

Answer to avoid mistakes, classify organisms with similar evolutionary histories together, give descriptive information about a species, help organize information about species

Uses of Scientific Names Scientific names are used for four reasons. First, they help avoid mistakes. Both of the lizards shown in **Figure 18** have the name *iguana*. Using binomial nomenclature, the green iguana is named *Iguana iguana*. Someone who studied this iguana, shown in **Figure 18A**, would not be confused by information he or she read about *Dispsosaurus dorsalis*, the desert iguana, shown in **Figure 18B**. Second, organisms with similar evolutionary histories are classified together. Because of this, you know that organisms in the same genus are related. Third, scientific names give descriptive information about the species, like the maples mentioned earlier. Fourth, scientific names allow information about organisms to be organized easily and efficiently. Such information may be found in a book or a pamphlet that lists related organisms and gives their scientific names.

 **Reading Check** *What are four functions of scientific names?*

Tools for Identifying Organisms

Tools used to identify organisms include field guides and dichotomous (di KAH tuh mus) keys. Using these tools is one way you and scientists solve problems scientifically.

Many different field guides are available. You will find some field guides at the back of this book. Most have descriptions and illustrations of organisms and information about where each organism lives. You can identify species from around the world using the appropriate field guide.

TRY AT HOME
Mini LAB

Communicating Ideas

Procedure
1. Find a **magazine picture of a piece of furniture** that can be used as a place to sit and to lie down.
2. Show the picture to ten people and ask them to tell you what word they use for this piece of furniture.
3. Keep a record of the answers in your **Science Journal.**

Analysis
1. In your Science Journal, infer how using common names can be confusing.
2. How do scientific names make communication among scientists easier?

TRY AT HOME
Mini LAB

Purpose Students ask people to give them the name of a common piece of furniture seen in a photo. [L2]

[LS] **Visual-Spatial**

Materials photo from magazine

Teaching Strategy Review how to collect and record data.

Analysis
1. More than one name might be used for the same object.
2. Each organism has a specific, unique name.

✔ *Assessment*

Oral To further assess students' abilities to identify characteristic features, ask them to list traits of other common objects. Use **Performance Assessment in the Science Classroom,** p. 89.

Tools for Identifying Organisms

Make a Model

Have students list the characteristics of several related objects such as shoes, animals, or foods. Then have students use their lists to make a model dichotomous key.

Visual Learning

Figure 18 What traits do the desert iguana and green iguana share? clawed toes, scaly skin

Resource Manager

Chapter Resources Booklet
Enrichment, p. 32
Reinforcement, p. 28
MiniLAB, p. 4
Transparency Activity, pp. 49–50

Tools for Identifying Organisms, continued

Activity

Pass out taxonomic keys or field guides. Ask students to describe how these tools are used. Have them use the keys to identify a particular organism. Note that students may try to skip steps in keys. Point out that skipping steps often leads to the wrong identification. L2

Text Question Answer

Microtus pinetorum

3 Assess

Reteach

Develop understanding of modern classification by asking students to name the lowest taxonomic category for the organisms described. Ask: **Which level contains a spider plant?** species **Which level contains all willow trees?** genus **Which level contains all plants?** kingdom

Challenge

Why do organisms in the same classification group have characteristics that are similar? Many probably evolved from a common ancestor.

✔Assessment

Performance Have students make a concept map to show how an address is like a classification system. The first step should be Country—United States. Use **Performance Assessment in the Science Classroom,** p. 161. P

Dichotomous Keys A dichotomous key is a detailed list of identifying characteristics that includes scientific names. Dichotomous keys are arranged in steps with two descriptive statements at each step. If you learn how to use a dichotomous key, you can identify and name a species.

Did you know many types of mice exist? You can use **Table 2** to find out what type of mouse is pictured to the left. Start by choosing between the first pair of descriptions. The mouse has hair on its tail, so you go to 2. The ears of the mouse are small, so you go on to 3. The tail of the mouse is less that 25 mm. What is the name of this mouse according to the key?

Table 2 Key to Some Mice of North America

1. Tail hair	**a.** no hair on tail; scales show plainly; house mouse, *Mus musculus* **b.** hair on tail, go to 2
2. Ear size	**a.** ears small and nearly hidden in fur, go to 3 **b.** ears large and not hidden in fur, go to 4
3. Tail length	**a.** less than 25 mm; woodland vole, *Microtus pinetorum* **b.** more than 25 mm; prairie vole, *Microtus ochrogaster*
4. Tail coloration	**a.** sharply bicolor, white beneath and dark above; deer mouse, *Peromyscus maniculatus* **b.** darker above than below but not sharply bicolor; white-footed mouse, *Peromyscus leucopus*

Section 4 Assessment

1. What is the purpose of classification?
2. What were the contributions of Aristotle and Carolus Linnaeus to classification of living things?
3. How can you identify a species using a dichotomous key?
4. Why can common names cause confusion?
5. **Think Critically** Would you expect a field guide to have common names as well as scientific names? Why or why not?

Skill Builder Activities

6. **Classifying** Create a dichotomous key that identifies types of cars. **For more help, refer to the** Science Skill Handbook.
7. **Communicating** Select a field guide for trees, insects, or mammals. Select two organisms in the field guide that closely resemble each other. Use labeled diagrams to show how they are different. **For more help, refer to the** Science Skill Handbook.

Answers to Section Assessment

1. to arrange or group things according to similarities and differences
2. Aristotle—two kingdoms: plants and animals; Linnaeus—binomial nomenclature
3. A dichotomous key contains a detailed list of identifying characteristics for species.
4. Two different organisms may have the same common name.
5. A field guide does not give as much scientific information as a key. It has pictures and descriptions that help you identify what you see, and often includes common as well as scientific names.
6. Keys will vary, but should be structured like the key shown in **Table 2.**
7. Students should be able to identify two organisms and state how they differ.

Classifying Seeds

Scientists use classification systems to show how organisms are related. How do they determine which features to use to classify organisms? In this activity, you will observe seeds and use their features to classify them.

What You'll Investigate
How can the features of seeds be used to develop a key to identify the seed?

Materials
packets of seeds (10 different kinds)
hand lens
metric ruler

Goals
- **Observe** the seeds and notice their features.
- **Classify** seeds using these features.

Safety Precautions

WARNING: Some seeds may have been treated with chemicals. Do not put them in your mouth. Wash your hands after you handle the seeds.

Procedure

1. Copy the following data table in your Science Journal and record the features of each seed. Your table will have a column for each different type of seed you observe.

Seed Data			
Feature	Type of Seed		
	corn	kidney bean	wheat
Color	yellow	dark brown	light brown
Length (mm)	10	17	5
Shape	triangle	oval	oval
Texture	smooth	smooth	smooth

2. Use the features to develop a key.
3. Exchange keys with another group. Can you use their key to identify seeds?

Conclude and Apply

1. How can different seeds be classified?
2. Which feature could you use to divide the seeds into two groups?
3. **Explain** how you would classify a seed you had not seen before using your data table.
4. Why is it an advantage for scientists to use a standardized system to classify organisms? What observations did you make to support your answer?

*C*ommunicating
Your Data

Compare your conclusions with those of other students in your class. **For more help, refer to the** Science Skill Handbook.

ACTIVITY 27

*C*ommunicating
Your Data

Comparisons may or may not result in agreement. If one group can use another group's key, the second group was successful.

Resource Manager

Chapter Resources Booklet
Activity Worksheets, pp. 5–6, 7–8
Lab Activity, pp. 11–13
Lab Management and Safety, p. 65

Activity

BENCH TESTED

Purpose Students observe seed features and then classify the seeds. [L2] [IS] **Kinesthetic**

Process Skills observing and inferring, classifying, forming operational definitions, communicating, making and using tables, comparing and contrasting

Time Required 45 minutes

Alternate Materials Any objects may be used, but biological specimens should be used if possible.

Safety Precautions Use only edible seeds, not seeds that have been treated for planting.

Teaching Strategy Prepare packets of ten different kinds of easily classified seeds, such as black-eyed peas, squash, beans (lima, kidney, pinto, black), green peas, popcorn, seed corn, and sunflower.

Answers to Questions

1. color, shape, size, texture, how they are attached to the plant
2. Answers will vary; color, shape, size, and texture are possibilities.
3. You would use the data table to categorize identifying characteristics of seeds.
4. Different classification systems could result in confusion. Answers should be based on the observation that students classified the same seeds in different ways.

✓*Assessment*

Performance Give students photocopies of ten different leaves. Have them devise and describe a classification system for the leaves. Use **PASC**, p. 121.

Activity

Recognize the Problem

Purpose
Design and carry out an experiment using scientific methods to infer why brine shrimp live in the ocean. L1 COOP LEARN
IS Interpersonal

Process Skills
observing and inferring, comparing and contrasting, recognizing cause and effect, interpreting data, hypothesizing, communicating, making and using tables, making and using graphs, designing an experiment, separating and controlling variables, measuring in SI

Time Required
50 minutes on Day 1, 5 minutes a day for 3 days, 30 minutes to summarize

Materials
Purchase brine shrimp eggs from a pet store or a biological supply house. Do not place too many brine shrimp eggs in each container. Brine shrimp are orange-colored and swim with a jerking motion. To maintain the brine shrimp, add a pinch of yeast to the container two or three times a week.

Safety Precautions
Students should use care when working with live animals.

Form a Hypothesis

Possible Hypothesis
Brine shrimp will best grow in a strong salt solution.

Activity — *Design Your Own Experiment*

Using Scientific Methods

Brine shrimp

Brine shrimp are relatives of lobsters, crabs, crayfish, and the shrimp eaten by humans. They are often raised as a live food source in aquariums. In nature, they live in the oceans where fish feed on them. They can hatch from eggs that have been stored in a dry condition for many years. In this investigation, you will use scientific methods to find what factors affect their hatching and growth.

Recognize the Problem

How can you use scientific methods to determine whether salt affects the hatching and growth of brine shrimp?

Form a Hypothesis

Based on your observations, state a hypothesis about how salt affects the hatching and growth of brine shrimp.

Goals
■ **Design** and carry out an experiment using scientific methods to infer why brine shrimp live in the ocean.
■ **Observe** the jars for one week and notice whether the brine shrimp eggs hatch.

Possible Materials
500-mL, widemouthed containers (3)
brine shrimp eggs
small, plastic spoon
distilled water (500 mL)
weak salt solution (500 mL)
strong salt solution (500 mL)
labels (3)
hand lens

Safety Precautions
Protect eyes and clothing. Be careful when working with live organisms.

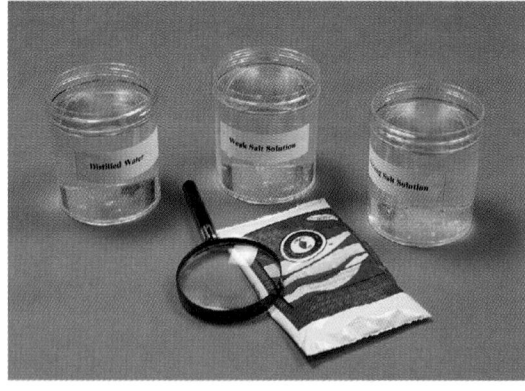

Test Your Hypothesis

Possible Procedures
The same amount of brine shrimp eggs can be added to the three solutions and observed.

Inclusion Strategies

Visually Impaired Have sighted students make paper or clay models of brine shrimp that visually impaired students can touch. Estimate the number of times the model has been enlarged so visually impaired students can have some idea of the size of brine shrimp.

Test Your Hypothesis

Plan

1. As a group, agree upon the hypothesis and decide how you will test it. Identify what results will confirm the hypothesis.

2. **List** the steps that you need to test your hypothesis. Be specific. Describe exactly what you will do in each step.

3. **List** your materials.

4. **Prepare** a data table in your Science Journal to record your data.

5. Read over your entire experiment to make sure that all planned steps are in logical order.

6. **Identify** any constants, variables, and controls of the experiment.

Do

1. Make sure your teacher approves your plan before you start.

2. Carry out the experiment as planned by your group.

3. While doing the experiment, record any observations and complete the data table in your Science Journal.

4. Use a bar graph to plot your results.

Analyze Your Data

1. **Describe** the contents of each jar after one week. Do they differ from one another? How?

2. What was your control in this experiment?

3. What were your variables?

Draw Conclusions

1. Did the results support your hypothesis? Explain.

2. **Predict** the effect that increasing the amount of salt in the water would have on the brine shrimp eggs.

3. **Compare** your results with those of other groups.

*C*ommunicating
Your Data

Prepare a set of instructions on how to hatch brine shrimp to use to feed fish. Include diagrams and a step-by-step procedure.

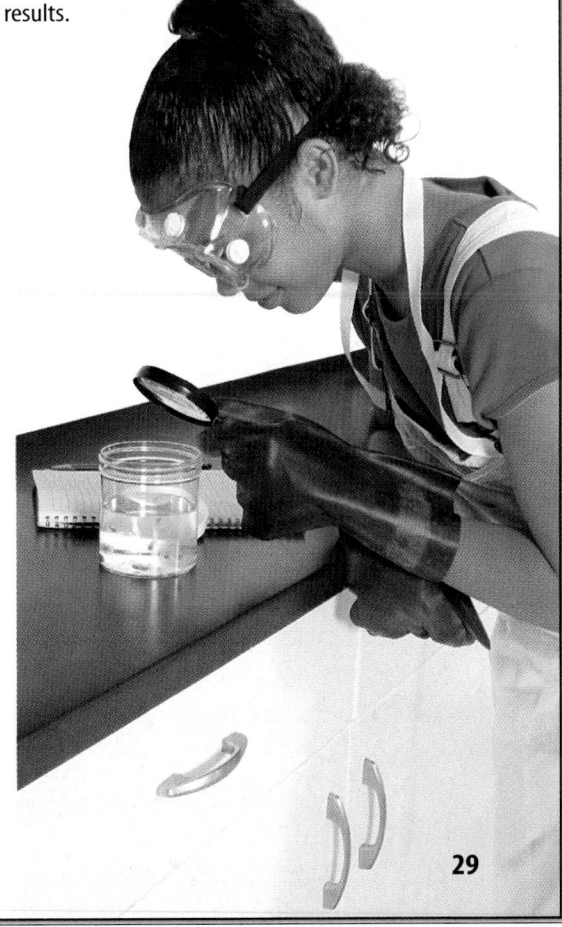

29

Teaching Strategies

Prepare the solutions as follows:

• Dechlorinated water: Allow tap water to stand for 48 hours.

• Weak salt solution: Add 20 mL noniodized salt to 4 L dechlorinated water. Stir until dissolved.

• Strong salt solution: Add 75 mL noniodized salt to 4 L dechlorinated water. Stir until dissolved.

Expected Outcome

Most results will reflect that the brine shrimp grew best in the strong salt solution.

Analyze Your Data

1. There were no shrimp in the distilled water or weak salt solution. There were many shrimp in the strong salt solution.

2. The dechlorinated water without salt was the control.

3. The amount of salt in the water was the variable.

Error Analysis

Have students compare their results and their hypotheses and explain any differences.

Draw Conclusions

1. Answers will be determined by students' hypotheses.

2. Answers will vary. Some may predict that more brine shrimp will hatch.

3. Results will vary.

*C*ommunicating
Your Data

Instructions should include information on the amount of salt to add to the water, light conditions, and so on. Students can use word-processing software programs to write their instructions.

✔*Assessment*

Performance Have students design an experiment to determine how ocean currents affect brine shrimp. Use **Performance Assessment in the Science Classroom,** p. 95.

Content Background

The rain forests of the world are home to fifty percent of all species of plants and animals. Some insect species evolve and become extinct without ever having been seen alive by humans. This is partly a function of the fact that most rain forest species live in the forest canopy between about 18 to 46 meters (60–150 ft) above the ground. Observing wildlife in this environment is extremely difficult, particularly over long periods of time. The need for extensive study of the rain forest canopy becomes more pressing as logging and slash and burn agriculture destroys more of the forest habitat.

One method being attempted to halt the incursion of uncontrolled agriculture is the development of ecotourism. Governments, corporations and environmental groups have fostered programs intended to preserve wild areas by attracting tourists. The idea is to build an economy based on service industries, thereby relieving some of the pressure to clear more land for farming. One version of ecotourism is the canopy tour effected by means ranging from climbing harnesses to walkways and aerial tramways. One of the benefits of these operations is the establishment of permanent platforms from which canopy research can be conducted.

A marmoset stands in a tree. It is about the size of a squirrel.

Manicore marmoset

Deep in the heart of the rain forest lives a small, furry animal. It swings from the trees, searches for food, and sleeps nestled high in the treetop canopy. What makes this animal unique is that it never had been seen by a human being. In fact, there is a whole world of creatures as yet undiscovered by humans. Many of them reside in the Amazon rain forest.

In 2000, a scientist from Brazil's Amazon National Research Institute came across two squirrel-sized monkeys in a remote and isolated corner of the rain forest, about 2,575 km from Rio de Janeiro.

It turns out that the monkeys had never been seen before, or even known to exist.

The new species were spotted by a scientist who named them after two nearby rivers the Manicore and the Acari, where the animals were discovered. Both animals are marmosets, which is a type of monkey found only in Central and South America. Marmosets have claws instead of nails, live in trees, and use their extraordinarily long tail like an extra arm or leg. Small and light, both marmosets measure about 23 cm in length with a 38 cm tail, and weigh no more than 0.4 kg.

The Manicore marmoset has a silvery-white upper body, a light-gray cap on its head, a yellow-orange underbody, and a black tail.

30

Resources for Teachers and Students

Tropical Rain Forest, by Arnold Newman, New York: Facts On File, Inc., 1990.

Rain Forests of the World: Water, Fire, Earth, Air, by Art Wolfe and Sir Ghillean Prance, New York: Crown Publishers, 1998.

"New study pinpoints rain-forest destruction" by Jeff Donn, The Associated Press, *Seattle Times,* Thursday, April 8, 1999.

key BUSINESS

The Amazon rain forest is home to animals waiting to be discovered

Acari marmoset

The Acari marmoset's upper body is snowy white, its gray back sports a stripe running to the knee, and its black tail flashes a bright-orange tip.

Amazin' Amazon

The Amazon Basin is a treasure trove of unique species. The Amazon River is Earth's largest body of freshwater, with 1,100 smaller tributaries. And more than half of the world's plant and animal species live in its rain forest ecosystems.

Many of these species are found nowhere else on Earth. Scientists believe that some animals, like the newly discovered marmosets, evolved differently from other marmosets because the rivers create natural barriers that separated the animals.

The discovery reminds people of how much we have to learn about Earth's diversity of life. Even among humans' closest relatives, the primates, there are still new species to be discovered.

CONNECTIONS Research and Report Working in small groups, find out more about the Amazon rain forest. Which plants and animals live there? What products come from the rain forest? How does what happens in the Amazon rain forest affect you? Prepare a multimedia presentation.

Online

For more information, visit science.glencoe.com

Discussion

What features of the rain forest make it possible for a large number species to remain unknown? Possible answer: The difficulty of travel and the remoteness of some areas make observation points difficult to get to. The fact that most of the species live in the canopy further complicates making accurate and wide-ranging surveys.

Activity

The Amazon is the largest river system by volume in the world, and the rain forest surrounding it regulates the flow of water into that system. Organize the class into groups and have each group construct a miniature river system, using flat disposable aluminum roasting pans, sand, and pieces of sod. Pour equal amounts of water on each group's "system" and have the group record results. Then have students remove portions of the sod and repeat the experiment. Use the results to discuss the effects of deforestation. COOP LEARN **Kinesthetic**

Investigate the Issue

Direct students to research the estimated number of plant and animal species worldwide and chart their distribution on a world map using colored pins. **How many species are in the rain forests? How will deforestation affect these species?**

CONNECTIONS As an extension, have students discuss the pros and cons of ecotourism in light of their research of current rain forest uses and conditions.

Online

Internet Addresses

_____

_____

_____

Explore the Glencoe Science Web site at **science.glencoe.com** to find out more about topics in this feature.

Reviewing Main Ideas

Preview

Students can answer the questions in their Science Journals. Discuss the answers as you go through the chapter. **LS Linguistic**

Review

Students can write their answers, then compare them with those of other students. **LS Interpersonal**

Reteach

Students can look at the illustrations and describe details that support the main ideas of the chapter. **LS Visual-Spatial**

Answers to Chapter Review

SECTION 1

1. Accept all reasonable answers.

SECTION 2

2. water

SECTION 3

2. from mosquitos

SECTION 4

3. It assigns a unique two-word name for every species of organism.

Chapter ① Study Guide

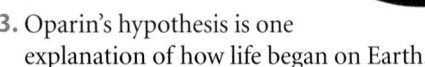

Reviewing Main Ideas

Section 1 What is science?

1. Scientists investigate observations about living and nonliving things with the help of problem-solving techniques. *What problem-solving methods would this scientist use to find out how dolphins learn?*

2. Scientists use SI measurements to gather measurable data.

3. Safe laboratory practices help you learn more about science.

Section 2 Living Things

1. Organisms are made of cells, use energy, reproduce, respond, grow, and develop.

2. Organisms need energy, water, food, and a place to live. *What raw material is limited for organisms living in a desert?*

Section 3 Where does life come from?

1. Controlled experiments over many years finally disproved the theory of spontaneous generation.

2. Pasteur's experiment proved biogenesis, which is the theory that life comes from life. *Where did the mosquito larvae in this pond come from?*

3. Oparin's hypothesis is one explanation of how life began on Earth.

Section 4 How are living things classified?

1. Classification is the grouping of ideas, information, or objects based on their similar characteristics.

2. Scientists today use phylogeny to group organisms into six kingdoms.

3. All organisms are given a two word scientific name using binomial nomenclature. *How would binomial nomenclature keep scientists from confusing these two beetles?*

4. Dichotomous keys are used to identify specific organisms.

FOLDABLES
Reading & Study Skills

After You Read

Trade vocabulary study Foldables with a classmate and quiz each other to see how many words you can define without looking under the tabs.

FOLDABLES
Reading & Study Skills

After You Read

After students have read the chapter and completed the Foldable described in Before You Read, have them do the activity on the student page.

Dinah Zike

Visualizing Main Ideas

Use the following terms to complete an events chain concept map showing the order in which you might use a scientific method: analyze data, perform an experiment, *and* form a hypothesis.

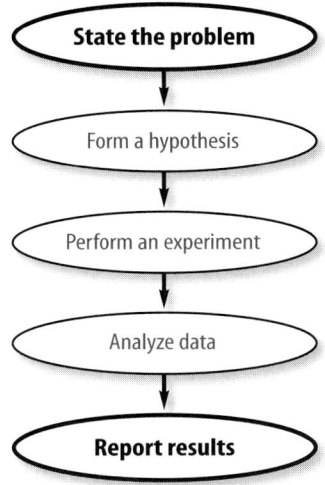

State the problem

↓

Form a hypothesis

↓

Perform an experiment

↓

Analyze data

↓

Report results

Vocabulary Review

Vocabulary Words

a. binomial nomenclature
b. biogenesis
c. cell
d. control
e. genus
f. homeostasis
g. hypothesis
h. kingdom

i. law
j. organism
k. phylogeny
l. scientific methods
m. spontaneous generation
n. theory
o. variable

> **THE PRINCETON REVIEW** **Study Tip**
>
> If you're not sure how terms in a question are related, try making a concept map of the terms. Ask your teacher to check your map.

Using Vocabulary

Explain the differences in the vocabulary words in each pair below. Then explain how they are related.

1. control, variable
2. law, theory
3. biogenesis, spontaneous generation
4. binomial nomenclature, phylogeny
5. organism, cell
6. kingdom, phylogeny
7. hypothesis, scientific methods
8. organism, homeostasis
9. kingdom, genus
10. theory, hypothesis

CHAPTER STUDY GUIDE   33

Chapter ① Study Guide

Visualizing Main Ideas

See student page.

Vocabulary Review

Using Vocabulary

1. variable—condition tested; control—standard used to compare with outcome of the test
2. Theory—explanation of things or events based on many observations; law—a statement about how things work in nature.
3. The theory of spontaneous generation (living things come from nonliving things) was replaced with the theory of biogenesis (living things come only from other living things).
4. Phylogeny is the evolutionary history of an organism; binomial nomenclature—a naming system based on phylogeny.
5. A cell is the smallest unit of an organism that carries out the functions of life. All organisms are made of cells.
6. Phylogeny is the basis for placing organisms into kingdoms.
7. Forming a hypothesis is an important part of solving a problem with scientific methods.
8. Homeostasis—keeping proper internal conditions no matter what external conditions are—is a trait of all organisms.
9. A genus is a subgroup of a kingdom.
10. If the results of repeated experiments always support the same hypothesis, the hypothesis may be called a theory.

◇ **IDENTIFYING** ▷ **Misconceptions**

Assess

Use the assessment as follow-up to page 4F after students have completed the chapter.

Assessment Show students several pictures of living and nonliving things, and have them record whether they think each item is living or nonliving and their reason. When responses are recorded, list their ideas on the board and generate a list of characteristics that students think describe living things. Compare this list to the characteristics of life listed in **Section 2** and ask the class if they would like to make any changes in their list.

Expected Outcome Some students may persist in listing only animal-like characteristics, but most students should be forming a more sophisticated definition that includes the characteristics given in the text. They should begin to recognize that their favorite "characteristic," movement, is simply one way that some living organisms respond to the environment.

Chapter 1 Assessment

Checking Concepts

1. D
2. D
3. A
4. D
5. C
6. D
7. A
8. B
9. D
10. B

Thinking Critically

11. Scientists can compare and repeat experiments; they have a common tool for measurement.
12. A bird is made up of cells, uses energy to fly and breathe, moves, responds to the environment, maintains a constant body temperature, reproduces young that grow and develop, and has a life span.
13. Binomial nomenclature is a two-word naming system. It is important because scientists assign a unique name to an organism that may have many common names. This allows accurate communication between scientists and others.
14. Redi's experiment used a variable and a control.
15. The name *odoratus* tells you that the sweet pea probably has an odor.

Chapter 1 Assessment

Checking Concepts

Choose the word or phrase that best answers the question.

1. What category of organisms can mate and produce fertile offspring?
   A) family
   B) class
   C) genus
   D) species

2. What is the closest relative of *Canis lupus*?
   A) *Quercus alba*
   B) *Equus zebra*
   C) *Felis tigris*
   D) *Canis familiaris*

3. What is the source of energy for plants?
   A) the Sun
   B) carbon dioxide
   C) water
   D) oxygen

4. What makes up more than 50 percent of all living things?
   A) oxygen
   B) carbon dioxide
   C) minerals
   D) water

5. Who finally disproved the theory of spontaneous generation?
   A) Oparin
   B) Aristotle
   C) Pasteur
   D) Miller

6. What gas do some scientists think was missing from Earth's early atmosphere?
   A) ammonia
   B) hydrogen
   C) methane
   D) oxygen

7. What is the length of time an organism is expected to live?
   A) life span
   B) stimulus
   C) homeostasis
   D) theory

8. What is the part of an experiment that can be changed called?
   A) conclusion
   B) variable
   C) control
   D) data

9. What does the first word in a two-word name of an organism identify?
   A) kingdom
   B) species
   C) phylum
   D) genus

10. What SI unit is used to measure the volume of liquids?
    A) meter
    B) liter
    C) gram
    D) degree

Thinking Critically

11. How does SI help scientists in different parts of the world?

12. Using a bird as an example, explain how it has all the traits of living things.

13. Explain what binomial nomenclature is and why it is important.

14. Explain how the experiment of 1668 correctly used scientific methods to test the theory of spontaneous generation.

15. What does *Lathyrus odoratus,* the name for a sweet pea, tell you about one of its characteristics?

Developing Skills

16. **Identifying and Manipulating Variables and Controls** Design an experiment to test the effects of fertilizer on growing plants. Identify scientific methods used in your experiment.

17. **Forming Hypotheses** A lima bean plant is placed under a green light, another is placed under a red light, and a third under a blue light. Their growth is measured for four weeks to determine which light is best for plant growth. What are the variables in this experiment? State a hypothesis for this experiment.

18. **Comparing and Contrasting** What characteristics do an icicle and a plant share? How can you tell that the plant is a living thing and the icicle is not?

Chapter ✓ Assessment Planner

Portfolio Encourage students to place in their portfolios one or two items of what they consider to be their best work. Examples include:
- Science Journal, p. 7
- Curriculum Connection, p. 16
- Reteach, p. 21
- Assessment, p. 26

Performance Additional performance assessments, Performance Task Assessment Lists, and rubrics for evaluating these activities can be found in Glencoe's **Performance Assessment in the Science Classroom.**

19. Interpreting Data Read the following hypothesis: Babies with a birth weight of 2.5 kg have the best chance of survival. Do the data in the following graph support this hypothesis? Explain.

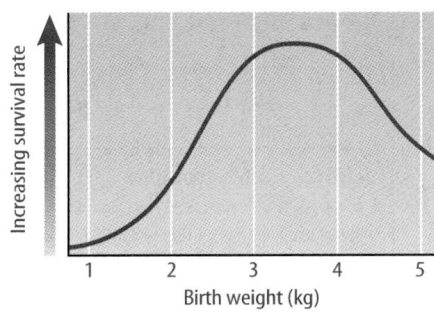

20. Classifying Which of these metric units—meter, kilometer, kilogram, or liter—is the best one to use when measuring each of the following?
A) your height
B) distance between two cities
C) how much juice is in a pitcher
D) your mass

Performance Assessment

21. Bulletin Board Interview people in your community whose jobs require a knowledge of life science. Make a Life Science Careers bulletin board. Summarize each person's job and what he or she had to study to prepare for that job.

TECHNOLOGY

 Go to the Glencoe Science Web site at **science.glencoe.com** or use the **Glencoe Science CD-ROM** for additional chapter assessment.

 **Test Practice**

A science class was learning about how living things respond to stimuli. Their experiment about the response of plants to light is shown below.

Study the experiment and answer the following questions.

1. Which hypothesis is probably being tested by this experiment?
A) Plants grow better in full light.
B) Plants prefer to grow in a box with one hole.
C) Plants can grow in any direction.
D) Plants grow toward the light.

2. After day 4, Fatima wanted to find out how plant 2 and plant 3 would grow in normal light. To do this, she would have to _____ .
F) use all new plants and boxes without holes
G) add water to all of the pots
H) remove the boxes over plant 2 and plant 3
J) put holes on all sides of the boxes

CHAPTER ASSESSMENT 35

 **Test Practice**

The Test-Taking Tip was written by The Princeton Review, the nation's leader in test preparation.
1. D
2. H

Developing Skills

16. An experiment should contain a hypothesis, observations, a variable, a control, and an interpretation of results.
17. variables: the different colors of light; hypothesis might be that the green light will cause the most favorable plant growth.
18. Both respond to their surroundings and grow in size. Unlike a plant, an icicle is not made of cells and cannot take in and use energy or reproduce.
19. No; babies with a birth weight of approximately 3.5 kg have the best chance of survival.
20. a. meter b. kilometer c. liter d. kilogram

Performance Assessment

21. Careers could include farmers, produce clerks, florists, veterinary technicians, health care workers, and teachers. Use **PASC**, p. 131.

✔Assessment Resources

📁 **Reproducible Masters**
Chapter Resources Booklet
Chapter Review, pp. 37–38
Chapter Tests, pp. 39–42
Assessment Transparency Activity, p. 51
Glencoe Science Web site
Interactive Tutor
Chapter Quizzes

Glencoe Technology
🖊 Assessment Transparency
💿 Interactive CD-ROM Chapter Quizzes
💿 ExamView Pro Test Bank
💿 Vocabulary PuzzleMaker Software
📼 MindJogger Videoquiz

Section/Objectives	Standards		Activities/Features
Chapter Opener	**National**	**State/Local**	**Explore Activity:** Observe onion cells, p. 37 **Before You Read,** p. 37
	See p. 7T for a Key to Standards.		
Section 1 The World of Cells 🕐 3 sessions 📦 1.5 blocks 1. **Discuss** the cell theory. 2. **Identify** the parts of animal and plant cells. 3. **Explain** the purpose of different cell parts.	National Content Standards: UCP1, A1, C1, C3		**Science Online,** p. 40 **Chemistry Integration,** p. 41 **MiniLAB:** Modeling a Cell, p. 42 **Activity:** Observing Algae, p. 44
Section 2 The Different Jobs of Cells 🕐 4 sessions 📦 2 blocks 1. **Discuss** how different cells have different jobs. 2. **Explain** the differences among tissues, organs, and organ systems.	National Content Standards: UCP1, A1, C1, C3, F5		**MiniLAB:** Analyzing Cells, p. 46 **Math Skills Activity:** Calculating Numbers of Blood Cells, p. 47 **Astronomy Integration,** p. 47 **Science Online,** p. 49 **Activity:** Water Movement in Plants, p. 50 **Science and Society:** Test Tube Tissue, p. 52

NATIONAL GEOGRAPHIC   Teacher's Corner

PRODUCTS AVAILABLE FROM GLENCOE
To order call 1-800-334-7344:
CD-ROMs
NGS PictureShow: The Cell; NGS Picture-Show: Plants: What It Means to Be Green
Curriculum Kit
GeoKit: Cells and Microorganisms

Transparency Sets
NGS PicturePack: The Cell; NGS Picture-Pack: What It Means to Be Green
PRODUCTS AVAILABLE FROM NATIONAL GEOGRAPHIC SOCIETY
To order call 1-800-368-2728:

Video
DNA: Laboratory Life

INDEX TO NATIONAL GEOGRAPHIC SOCIETY
The following articles may be used for research relating to this chapter:
"The Rise of Life on Earth," by Richard Monastersky, March 1998.

Activity Materials	Reproducible Resources	Section Assessment	Technology
Explore Activity: index card, scissors, plastic wrap, onion skin, microscope slide, water, dropper, tape, metric ruler, newspaper	**Chapter Resources Booklet** Foldables Worksheet, p. 17 Directed Reading Overview, p. 19 Note-taking Worksheets, pp. 31–32	GLENCOE'S **ASSESSMENT** ADVANTAGE	
MiniLAB: household materials (clay, yarn, cardboard, buttons, dry macaroni), glue, paper **Activity:** microscope, microscope slides, coverslips, large jars, pond water, algae, dropper, colored pencils *Need materials?* Contact Science Kit at 1-800-828-7777 or www.sciencekit.com on the Internet.	**Chapter Resources Booklet** Transparency Activity, p. 42 MiniLAB, p. 3 Enrichment, p. 29 Reinforcement, p. 27 Directed Reading, p. 20 Transparency Activity, pp. 45–47 Activity Worksheet, pp. 5–6 Lab Activity, pp. 9–12 **Home and Community Involvement,** p. 38 **Science Inquiry Labs,** pp. 3, 59	Portfolio Curriculum Connection, p. 39 Make a Model, p. 40 Performance MiniLAB, p. 42 Skill Builder Activities, p. 43 Content Section Assessment, p. 43	Section Focus Transparency Teaching Transparency Interactive CD-ROM Guided Reading Audio Program
MiniLAB: prepared slides of human cells, microscope **Activity:** fresh stalk of celery with leaves, clear drinking glass, scissors, red food coloring, water	**Chapter Resources Booklet** Transparency Activity, p. 43 MiniLAB, p. 4 Enrichment, p. 30 Reinforcement, p. 28 Directed Reading, pp. 21–22 Activity Worksheet, pp. 7–8 Lab Activity, pp. 13–16 **Mathematics Skill Activities,** p. 9 **Performance Assessment in the Science Classroom,** p. 61 **Lab Management and Safety,** p. 69	Portfolio Science Journal, p. 46 Performance MiniLAB, p. 46 Math Skills Activity, p. 47 Skill Builder Activities, p. 49 Content Section Assessment, p. 49	Section Focus Transparency Interactive CD-ROM Guided Reading Audio Program

GLENCOE'S **ASSESSMENT** ADVANTAGE

End of Chapter Assessment

Blackline Masters	Technology	Professional Series
Chapter Resources Booklet Chapter Review, pp. 35–36 Chapter Tests, pp. 37–40 **Standardized Test Practice by The Princeton Review,** pp. 11–14	MindJogger Videoquiz Interactive CD-ROM Vocabulary PuzzleMakers ExamView Pro Test Bank Interactive Lesson Planner Interactive Teacher Edition	Performance Assessment in the Science Classroom (PASC)

Transparencies

Section Focus

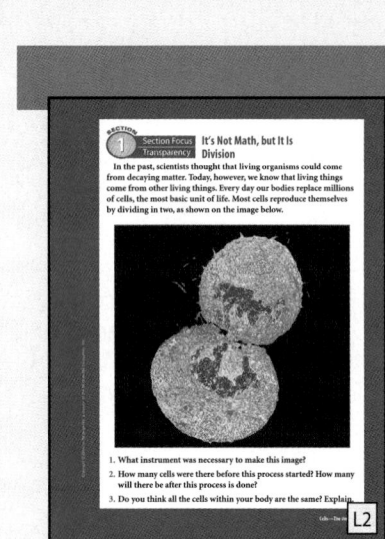

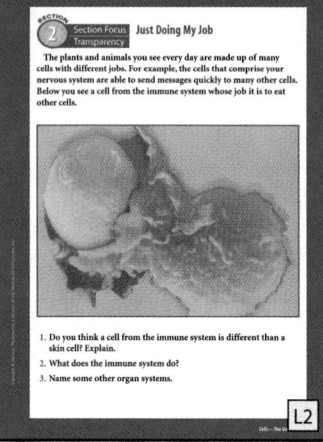

Assessment

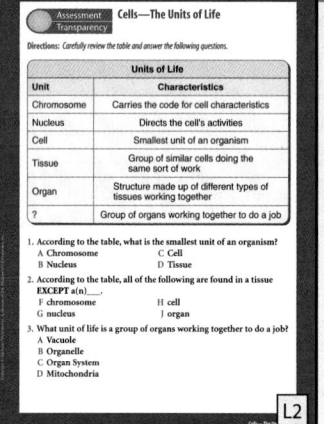

Teaching

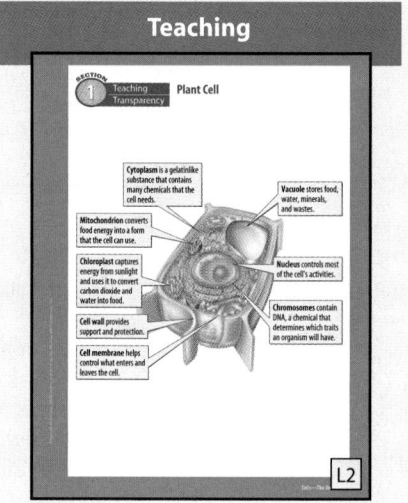

This is a representation of key blackline masters available in the Teacher Classroom Resources. See Resource Manager boxes within the chapter for additional information.

Key to Teaching Strategies

The following designations will help you decide which activities are appropriate for your students.

- **L1** Level 1 activities should be appropriate for students with learning difficulties.
- **L2** Level 2 activities should be within the ability range of all students.
- **L3** Level 3 activities are designed for above-average students.
- **ELL** ELL activities should be within the ability range of English Language Learners.
- **COOP LEARN** Cooperative Learning activities are designed for small group work.
- **LS** Multiple Learning Styles logos, as described on page 22T, are used throughout to indicate strategies that address different learning styles.
- **P** These strategies represent student products that can be placed into a best-work portfolio.

Hands-on Activities

Activity Worksheets

Laboratory Activities

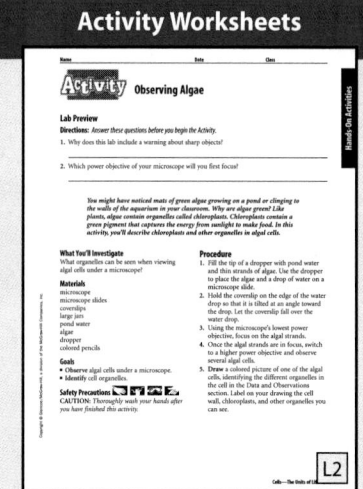

Meeting Different Ability Levels

Content Outline

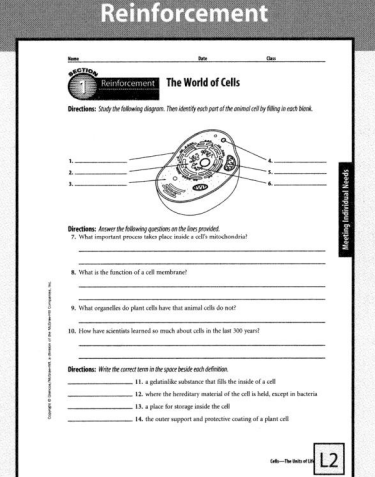

Reinforcement

Directed Reading

Assessment

Chapter Tests

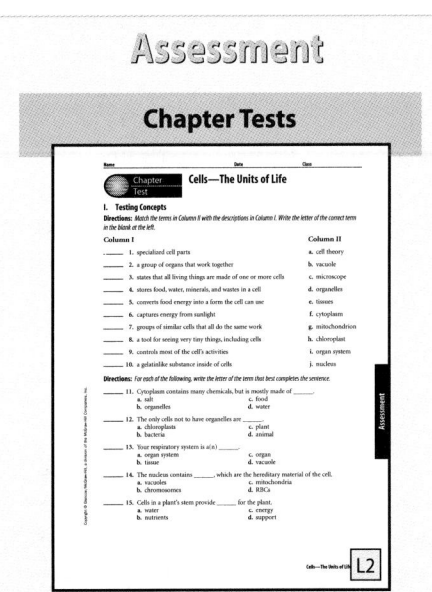

Enrichment

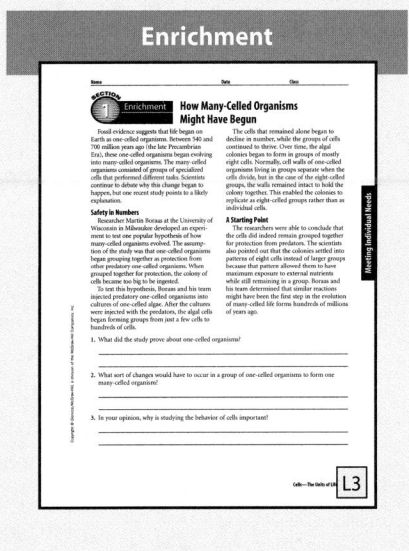

Spanish Directed Reading

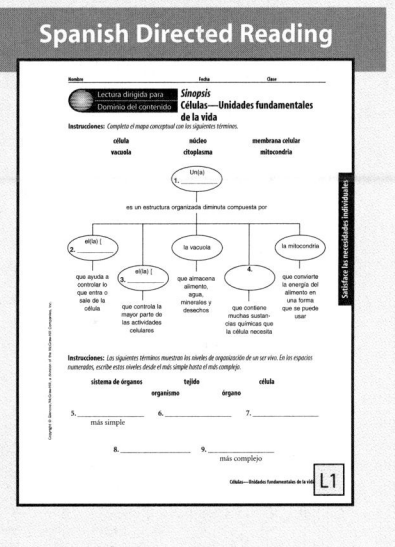

Test Practice Workbook

Chapter Review

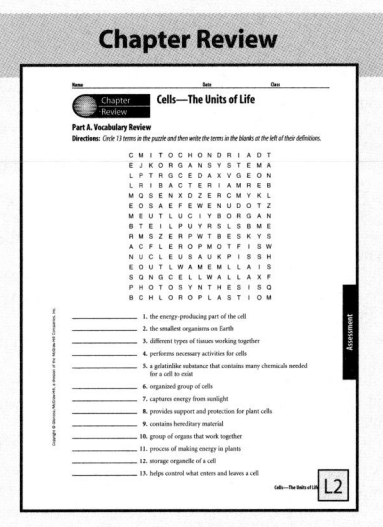

Science Content Background

The World of Cells

Cell Theory

Prior to the discovery of cells and the introduction of cell theory, people believed in the idea of spontaneous generation; that is, the idea that living things could spontaneously originate from nonliving material. For example, people believed that maggots could arise from decomposing organic material or that frogs and toads arose from rain or moist soil. Throughout the remainder of the seventeenth and eighteenth centuries, several scientists worked to disprove this idea. By the mid-1800s scientists had shown through a series of independent scientific experiments that living matter could not be spontaneously generated. It was not until this time that the concept of biogenesis, the idea that living cells can be produced only from already existing cells, and the other ideas of cell theory began to be widely accepted.

Fun Fact

The human body contains about 200 different types of cells that total more than 100 trillion cells in all.

Outside the Cell

One of the functions of the cell membrane is to control what substances pass into and out of the cell. Substances can move across the cell membrane by several processes. Diffusion of materials across the cell membrane is driven by a concentration gradient. In this process, substances move from areas of high concentration to areas of low concentration until equilibrium is reached. The rate of diffusion is affected by the thickness of the cell membrane. The thinner the membrane, the less time it takes for a substance to diffuse across it. The membranes of the alveoli in the lungs, the sites where oxygen and carbon dioxide are exchanged in breathing, are some of the thinnest in the body with a width of only 0.5 micrometers. Active transport is another way materials are moved across cell membranes. In active transport, energy is inputted to actively move materials against the concentration gradient. The sodium-potassium pump, which takes place in all body cells, is one example of active transport in which cells continually regulate the amount of sodium and potassium entering and leaving the cell. If the sodium-potassium pump ceases to function, cell death can result.

Organelles

Plants contain organelles called plastids. Plastids are enclosed by a double membrane. Chloroplasts are one example of a plastid that stores the pigment chlorophyll and manufactures glucose. Leukoplasts store sugar, which is produced during photosynthesis in chloroplasts, in the form of starch. Chromoplasts store different types of plant pigments, including the orange, yellow, and red pigments that give some fruits their color.

Cabisco/Visuals Unlimited

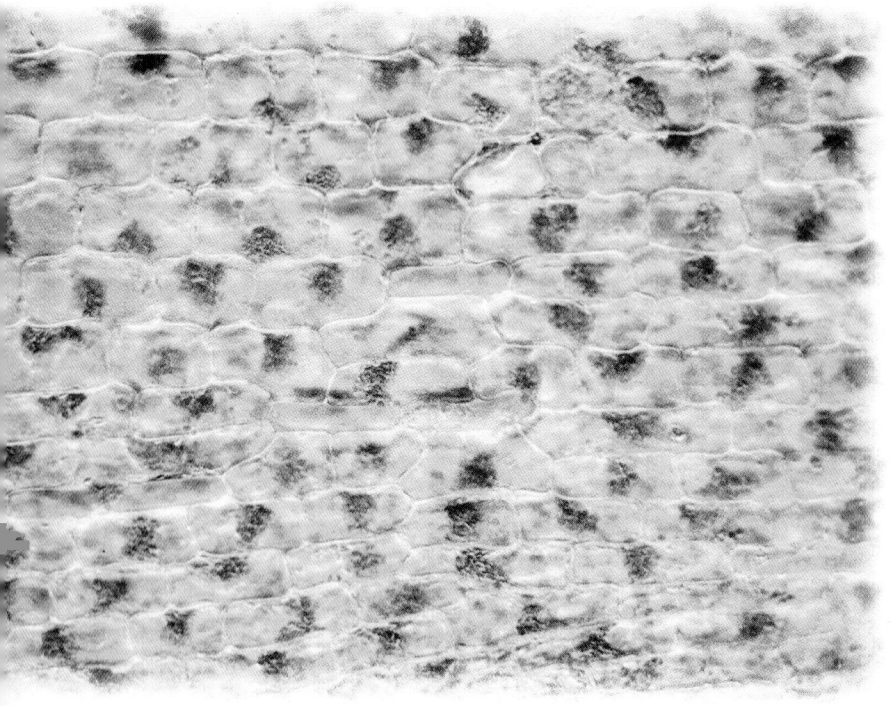

SECTION

2

The Different Jobs of Cells

Some Skin Cells

The epidermis, the upper layer of the skin, includes cells called keratinocytes. These cells manufacture the protein keratin. Keratin, which has a tough, fibrous consistency, provides protection from heat and chemicals. Keratinocytes also make skin waterproof. Melanocytes, another type of cell found in the skin, produce melanin, the pigment responsible for skin color. Melanin works to protect cells from overexposure to UV radiation by absorbing it as the rays penetrate the skin. Melanin granules gather over the nuclei of the skin cells in order to form a protective barrier and safeguard the DNA from the harmful rays.

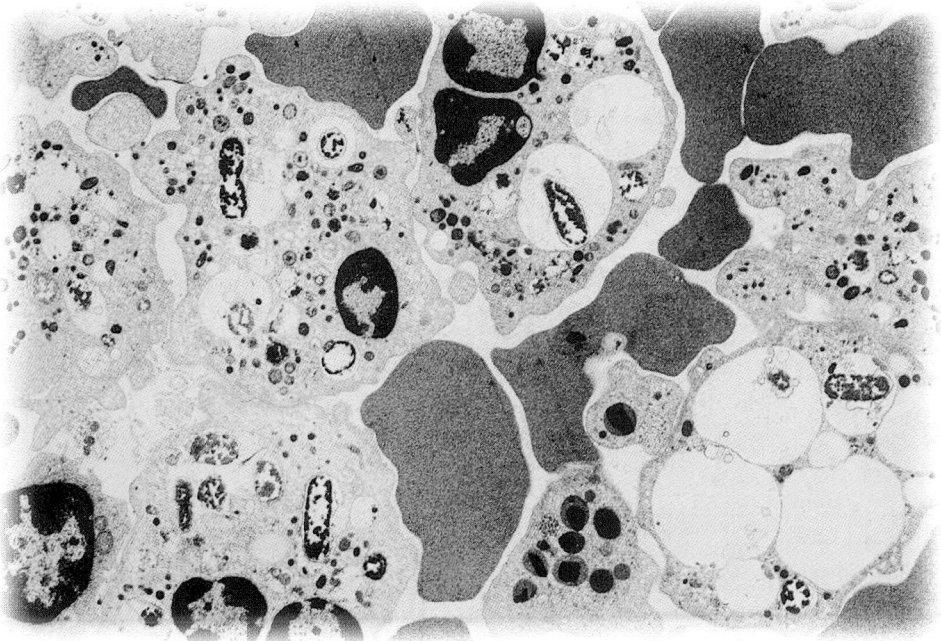

David M. Phillips/Visuals Unlimited

Tissues, Organs and Organ Systems

Some organs perform functions for more than one organ system. The pancreas functions as part of the endocrine system; it also performs an essential role in the digestive system. As an endocrine gland, the pancreas produces and releases the two major hormones that control blood glucose levels—insulin and glucagon. Insulin lowers blood glucose level by assisting glucose in moving into body cells. Glucagon has the opposite effect; it functions to raise blood glucose level. In the digestive system the pancreas produces and releases into the small intestine powerful digestive enzymes that work to break down carbohydrates, proteins, and fats.

The spleen, although it is located in the abdominal cavity, is not an organ of the digestive system. Instead it is the largest mass of lymphatic tissue in the body. The lymphatic system performs a range of functions including producing lymphocytes, which are types of white blood cells that fight infection and produce antibodies. The lymphatic system also is involved in moving lipids and some vitamins to the blood, after absorbing them in the small intestines. The spleen, the lymph nodes and fluid, and red bone marrow compose a major portion of the lymphatic system.

The appendix is located in the lower right section of the abdominal cavity very near the junction of the small and large intestines. If it becomes inflamed or infected it must be removed in a procedure called an appendectomy. The exact function of the appendix is uncertain.

Fun Fact

The largest and heaviest organ of the human body is the skin. The heaviest internal organ is the liver, weighing over 1 kg in adults.

SCIENCE *Online*

For additional content background on this topic, go to the Glencoe Science Web site at science.glencoe.com.

Cells—The Units of Life

Chapter Vocabulary

What do you think?

Science Journal The photo shows a bacterial cell being attacked by white blood cells. This response by the body protects the body from disease.

CHAPTER 2

Cells—The Units of Life

I f you look closely, you can see that these giraffes are made up of small, plastic building blocks. Similarly, living giraffes also are made up of small building blocks. The building block of all living things is the cell. In this chapter, you will learn about what makes up a cell and how cell parts work together to keep a cell alive. You also will learn about different types of cells and their functions in living things.

What do you think?

Science Journal Look at the picture below with a classmate and discuss what this might be or what is happening. Here's a hint. *It's an all-out attack inside your body.* Write your answer or best guess in your Science Journal.

36

Theme Connection

Scale and Structure On the most basic level of organization, all living things are composed of microscopic units called cells. Cells carry out important processes for organisms, such as releasing energy and producing important chemicals such as hormones.

An active world is inside you and in all other living things. It is an organized world so important that life couldn't exist without it. Yet it is a world that you usually can't see with just your eyes. Make the magnifier in the activity below to help you see how living things are organized.

Observe onion cells

1. Cut a 2-cm hole in the middle of an index card. Tape a piece of plastic wrap over the hole.

2. Turn down about 1 cm of the two shorter sides of the card, then stand it up.

3. Place a piece of onion skin on a microscope slide, then put it directly under the hole in the card.

4. Put a drop of water on the plastic wrap. Look through the water drop and observe the piece of onion. Draw what you see.

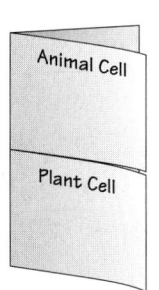

Observe

In your Science Journal, describe how the onion skin looked when viewed with your magnifier.

Before You Read

Making a Compare and Contrast Study Fold Make the following Foldable to help you see how animal and plant cells are similar and different.

1. Place a sheet of paper in front of you so the long side is at the top. Fold the paper in half from the left side to the right side. Fold top to bottom and crease. Then unfold.

2. Through the top thickness of paper, cut along the middle fold line to form two tabs as shown.

3. Label *Animal Cell* and *Plant Cell* on the tabs as shown.

4. Before you read the chapter, write what you know about each of these cells.

5. As you read the chapter, add to or correct what you have written under the tabs.

Purpose Students make and use a simple form of a microscope to examine onion skin cells. L2

ELL 🖐 **Kinesthetic**

Preparation Cut tiny pieces from the thin, transparent skin of an onion for each student group.

Materials dropper, water, index card, colorless plastic wrap, scissors, tape, onion skin, metric ruler, newspaper, microscope slide

Teaching Strategies

• Be sure adequate light is available to illuminate the object being observed.

• You may wish to have students examine other plant tissues, such as leaves or roots of common plants.

Observe

The onion skin appears bricklike.

Performance Have students use a microscope to observe the onion cells. Have them draw what they see and compare these drawings with the ones from the Explore activity. Use **Performance Assessment in the Science Classroom,** p. 127.

Before You Read

Dinah Zike Study Fold

Purpose Students make a Foldable to help them identify what they know about plant and animal cells and to organize new information about these cells as they read.

📁 For additional help, see Foldables Worksheet, p. 17 in **Chapter Resources Booklet,** or go to the Glencoe Science Web site at **science.glencoe.com.** See After You Read in the Study Guide at the end of this chapter.

SECTION

1

The World of Cells

Bellringer Transparency

Display the Section Focus Transparency for Section 1. Use the accompanying Transparency Activity Master. L2
ELL

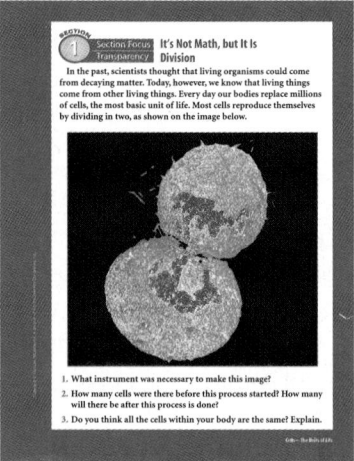

Tie to Prior Knowledge

Students may have used magnifying glasses, a telescope, or binoculars. Explain how a microscope magnifies in the same way.

As You Read

What You'll Learn

- **Discuss** the cell theory.
- **Identify** some of the parts of animal and plant cells.
- **Explain** the functions of different cell parts.

Vocabulary

bacteria	nucleus
cell membrane	vacuole
cell wall	mitochondria
cytoplasm	photosynthesis
organelle	chloroplast

Why It's Important

Cells carry out the activities of life.

Figure 1
Robert Hooke designed this microscope and drew the cork cells he observed.

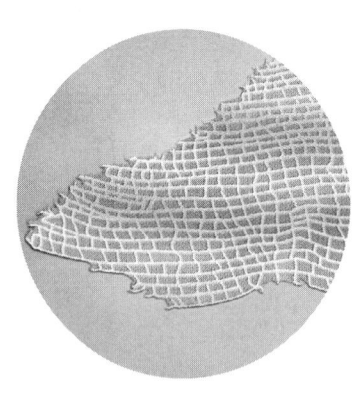

Importance of Cells

A cell is the smallest unit of life in all living things. Cells are important because they are organized structures that help living things carry on the activities of life, such as the breakdown of food, movement, growth, and reproduction. Different cells have different jobs in living things. Some plant cells help move water and other substances throughout the plant. White blood cells, found in humans and many other animals, help fight diseases. Plant cells, white blood cells, and all other cells are alike in many ways.

Cell Theory Because most cells are small, they were not observed until microscopes were invented. In 1665, scientist Robert Hooke, using a microscope that he made, observed tiny, boxlike things in a thin slice of cork, as shown in **Figure 1.** He called them cells because they reminded him of the small, boxlike rooms called cells, where monks lived.

Throughout the seventeenth and eighteenth centuries, scientists observed many living things under microscopes. Their observations led to the development of the cell theory. The three main ideas of the cell theory are:

1. All living things are made of one or more cells.

2. The cell is the basic unit of life in which the activities of life occur.

3. All cells come from cells that already exist.

Section ✔*Assessment* Planner

PORTFOLIO	**CONTENT ASSESSMENT**
Curriculum Connection, p. 39	Section, p. 43
Make a Model, p. 40	Challenge, p. 43
PERFORMANCE ASSESSMENT	Chapter, pp. 56–57
Try at Home MiniLAB, p. 42	
Skill Builder Activities, p. 43	
See page 56 for more options.	

The Microscopic Cell All the living things pictured in **Figure 2** are made up of cells. The smallest organisms on Earth are **bacteria.** They are one-celled organisms, which means they are made up of only one cell.

 **Reading Check** *How many cells does each bacterium have?*

Larger organisms are made of many cells. These cells work together to complete all of the organism's life activities. The living things that you see every day—trees, dogs, insects, people—are many-celled organisms. Your body contains more than 10 trillion (10,000,000,000,000) cells.

Microscopes Scientists have viewed and studied cells for about 300 years. In that time, they have learned a lot about cells. Better microscopes have helped scientists learn about the differences among cells. Some modern microscopes allow scientists to study the small features that are inside cells.

Physics INTEGRATION The microscope used in most classrooms is called a compound light microscope. In this type of microscope, light passes through the object you are looking at and then through two or more lenses. The lenses enlarge the image of the object. How much an image is enlarged depends on the powers of the eyepiece and the objective lens. The power—a number followed by an ✕—is found on each lens. For example, a power of 10✕ means that the lens can magnify something to ten times its actual size. The magnification of a microscope is found by multiplying the powers of the eyepiece and the objective lens.

Figure 2
All living things are made up of cells.

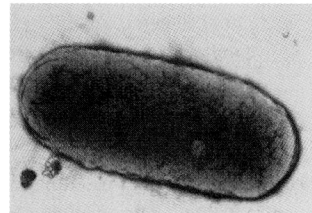

Magnification: 67,500✕

A *E. coli*—a bacterium—is a one-celled organism.

B Plant cells are different from animal cells.

C Human cells are similar to other animal cells like those in cats and turtles.

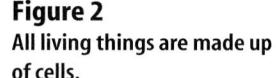

Importance of Cells

Teacher FYI

Hooke did not see cells; he saw the cell walls of dead cells from the bark of the cork tree. The cork tree is a type of oak. It is green year-round and grows abundantly in Portugal and Spain.

✔ **Reading Check**

Answer one

Resource Manager

Chapter Resources Booklet
Transparency Activity, p. 42
Directed Reading for Content Mastery, pp. 19, 20
Note-taking Worksheets, pp. 31–32

Curriculum Connection

Art Discuss the use of art before the camera was invented. Have students compare Hooke's drawing of cells with photographs throughout the chapter. Have students write their opinions of the advantages and disadvantages of using artwork and photography. L2 IN **Visual-Spatial** P

✔ Active Reading

Think-Pair-Share This strategy encourages students to think first before discussing their ideas or thoughts about a topic. After thinking for a few minutes, partners discuss responses to the question. Finally, the teacher asks the students to discuss responses with the class. Have students become involved in a Think-Pair-Share about cells.

What are cells made of?

Activity

Make a bulletin board showing unlabeled parts of an animal cell and a plant cell. As each cell part is studied, have a student place its label beside it on the bulletin board. ⬛ L1 ⬛ **Visual-Spatial**

Discussion

What color are cells? Living tissues are, for the most part, colorless. **Why are stains used?** Most cells can be seen only when stained a color.

Make a Model

Give groups of students small lumps of different-colored clay. As you teach about the parts of cells, have groups build model cells. Introduce and discuss the cell parts, and have students add clay parts to their own model cells. Have groups make small labels for each of the parts. Students can use toothpicks to place the labels on the model cells. ⬛ L1
ELL   COOP LEARN ⬛ **Kinesthetic**
P

Figure 3
These are some of the parts of an animal cell that perform the activities necessary for life.

What are cells made of?

As small as cells are, they are made of even smaller parts, each doing a different job. A cell can be compared to a bakery. The activities of a bakery are inside a building. Electricity is used to run the ovens and other equipment, power the lights, and heat the building. The bakery's products require ingredients such as dough, sugar, and fillings, that must be stored, assembled, and baked. The bakery's products are packaged and shipped to different locations. A manager is in charge of the entire operation. The manager makes a plan for every employee of the bakery and a plan for every step of making and selling the baked goods.

A living cell operates in a similar way. Like the walls of the bakery, a cell has a boundary. Inside this boundary, the cell's life activities take place. These activities must be managed. Smaller parts inside the cell can act as storage areas. The cell also has parts that use ingredients such as oxygen, water, minerals, and other nutrients. Some cell parts can release energy or make substances that are necessary for maintaining life. Some substances leave the cell and are used elsewhere in the organism.

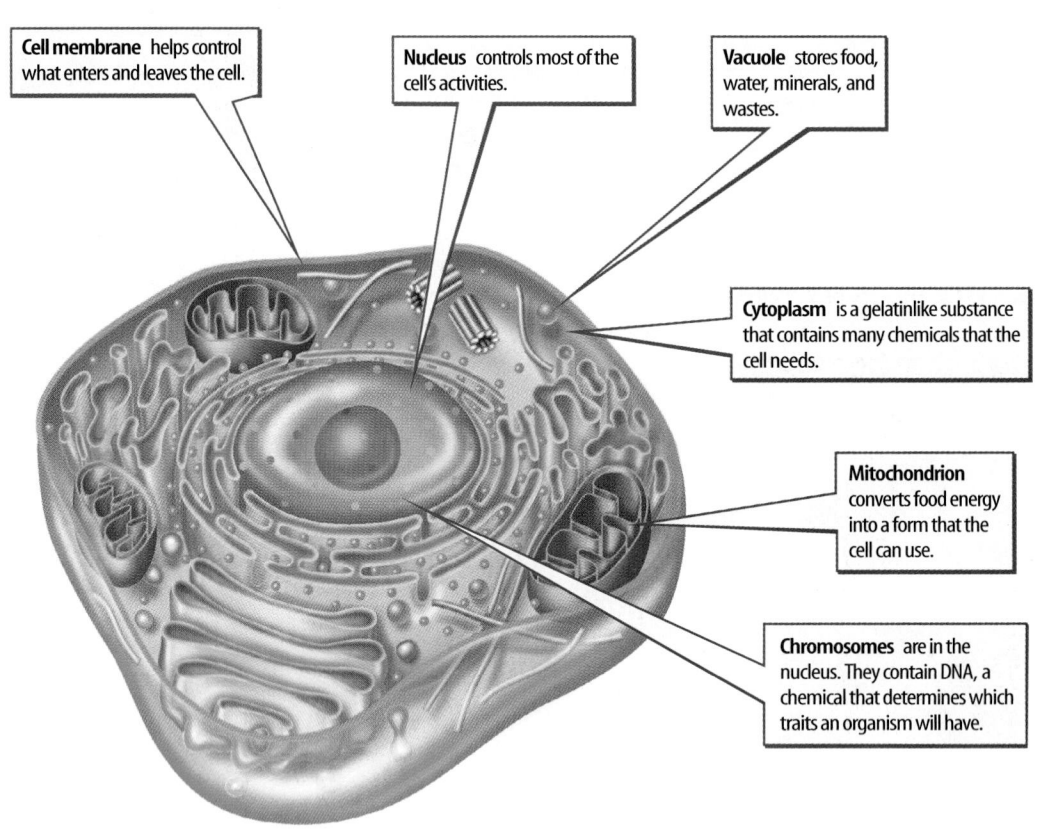

Cell membrane helps control what enters and leaves the cell.

Nucleus controls most of the cell's activities.

Vacuole stores food, water, minerals, and wastes.

Cytoplasm is a gelatinlike substance that contains many chemicals that the cell needs.

Mitochondrion converts food energy into a form that the cell can use.

Chromosomes are in the nucleus. They contain DNA, a chemical that determines which traits an organism will have.

Visual Learning

Figure 3 and **Figure 4** These drawings are illustrations of generalized cells. Discuss the meaning of the word *generalized*. Explain that cells don't really look like these illustrations. You also may wish to discuss the importance of scientific illustrations. Explain the value of illustrations for learning science, especially when microscopic structures, such as cells, are depicted. ELL

Inclusion Strategies

Visually Impaired Students with visual impairments may benefit from using and constructing models of cells. Some of the large, demonstration cell models sold by science-supply houses are excellent for this purpose. Such models are typically large, detailed, and three-dimensional. ⬛ L2 ⬛ **Kinesthetic**

Outside the Cell The **cell membrane**, shown in **Figure 3,** is a flexible structure that holds the cell together, similar to the walls of the bakery. The cell membrane forms a boundary between the cell and its environment. It also helps control what goes into and comes out of the cell. Some cells, like those in plants, algae, fungi, and many types of bacteria, also have a structure outside the cell membrane called a **cell wall,** shown in **Figure 4.** The cell wall helps support and protect these cells.

Inside the Cell The inside of a cell is filled with a gelatinlike substance called **cytoplasm** (SI tuh pla zum). It is mostly water but the cytoplasm also contains many chemicals that are needed by the cell. Like the work area inside the bakery, the cytoplasm is where the cell's activities take place.

Organelles Except for bacterial cells, cells contain **organelles** (or guh NELZ) like those in **Figure 3** and **Figure 4.** These specialized cell parts can move around in the cytoplasm and perform activities that are necessary for life. You could think of these organelles as the employees of the cell because each type of organelle does a different job. In bacteria, most cell activities occur in the cytoplasm.

Chemistry
INTEGRATION

The cell membrane is a double layer of complex molecules called phospholipids (fahs foh LIH pudz). Research to find the elements that are in these molecules. Find those elements on the periodic table at the back of this book.

Figure 4
Most plant cells contain the same types of organelles as in animal cells. Plant cells also have a cell wall and chloroplasts.

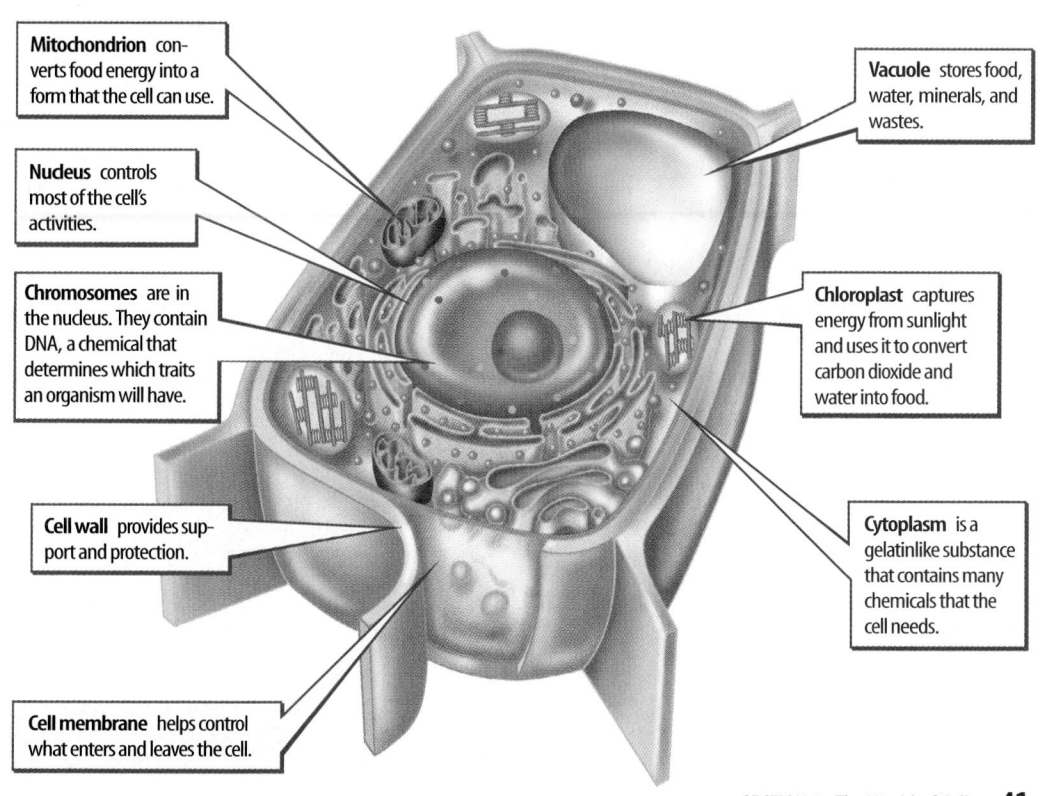

Mitochondrion converts food energy into a form that the cell can use.

Nucleus controls most of the cell's activities.

Chromosomes are in the nucleus. They contain DNA, a chemical that determines which traits an organism will have.

Cell wall provides support and protection.

Cell membrane helps control what enters and leaves the cell.

Vacuole stores food, water, minerals, and wastes.

Chloroplast captures energy from sunlight and uses it to convert carbon dioxide and water into food.

Cytoplasm is a gelatinlike substance that contains many chemicals that the cell needs.

Chemistry
INTEGRATION

the elements carbon (C), hydrogen (H), oxygen (O), phosphorus (P), and nitrogen (N)

Extension

Students who have mastered the content can construct more elaborate clay models of cells. Have them research cells and cell parts. Students can construct detailed models that display all of the important cell parts. L2 ELL COOP LEARN

Use an Analogy

You may wish to have students brainstorm a list of other possible analogies for living cells. For instance, one common analogy is that cells are like factories. Both produce things (cells produce energy, proteins, and other substances), and they have specialized areas where this production takes place. In addition, production operates within enclosed spaces, and wastes are removed during the process. After student groups are finished, ask individuals to present their ideas to class. Accept all reasonable answers. L2 ELL IS **Interpersonal**

Use Science Words

Word Usage Have students brainstorm several different meanings of the word *cell*. Have them compare the meanings and brainstorm a list that shows how all these cells have similar characteristics. L2 ELL IS **Linguistic**

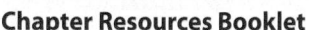

Resource Manager

Chapter Resources Booklet
Enrichment, p. 29
Reinforcement, p. 27
Lab Activity, pp. 9–12
Transparency Activity, pp. 45–47

Cultural **Diversity**

Ernest Everett Just Just, an African American biologist in the early 1900s, studied cells and how they function. His research showed that all parts of the cell influence its activities, not just the nucleus, as scientists then believed. This idea changed scientific opinion concerning the basis of life. Discuss how Ernest Just's research is important to the study of cells today.

What are cells made of?, continued

Purpose Students make models of cells. L2 N **Kinesthetic**

Materials clay, cardboard boxes, pipe cleaners, yarn, buttons, dry macaroni, paper

Teaching Strategies

- Have students supply the materials needed. Ask each student to bring in a small quantity of one item on the list.
- Instruct students to represent each cell part with a different item.

Safety Precautions Remind students not to eat any materials used in the lab.

Analysis

1. Answers will vary, but should agree with the textbook.
2. Answers will vary, but the cell parts should be easily identifiable.
3. Accept all reasonable answers.

Assessment

Process Have students compare and contrast one another's cell models. Instruct students to examine several of the models carefully. Next, ask them to report on how different students modeled cell parts. Use **PASC**, p. 123.

TRY AT HOME
Mini LAB

Modeling a Cell

Procedure

1. Collect **household materials such as clay, cardboard, yarn, buttons, dry macaroni,** or other objects.
2. Using the objects that you collected, make a three-dimensional model of an animal or plant cell.
3. On a separate sheet of **paper,** make a key to the materials in your cell model.

Analysis

1. What does each part of your cell model do?
2. Have someone look at your model. Which of the cell parts could they identify without using the key?
3. How could you improve your model?

Figure 5
Inside a mitochondrion, food energy is changed into a form of energy that a cell can use.

The Nucleus A bakery's manager follows a business plan to make sure that the business runs smoothly. A business plan describes how the business should operate. These plans could include how many donuts are made and what kinds of pies are baked.

The hereditary material of the cell is like the bakery's manager. It directs most of the cell's activities. In the cells of organisms except bacteria, the hereditary material is in an organelle called the **nucleus** (NEW klee us). Inside the nucleus are chromosomes (KROH muh zohmz). They contain a plan for the cell, similar to the bakery's business plan. Chromosomes contain an important chemical called DNA. It determines which traits an organism will have, such as the shape of a plant's leaves or the color of your eyes.

✔ **Reading Check** *Which important chemical determines the traits of an organism?*

Storage Pantries, closets, refrigerators, and freezers store food and other supplies that a bakery needs. Trash cans hold garbage until it can be picked up. In cells, food, water, and other substances are stored in balloonlike organelles in the cytoplasm called **vacuoles** (VA kyuh wohlz). Some vacuoles store wastes until the cell is ready to get rid of them. Plant cells usually have a large vacuole that stores water and other substances.

Energy and the Cell

Electrical energy or the energy in natural gas is converted to heat energy by the bakery's ovens. The heat then is used to bake the breads and other bakery products. Cells need energy, too. Cells, except bacteria, have organelles called **mitochondria** (mi tuh KAHN dree uh)(singular, *mitochondrion).* An important process called cellular respiration (SEL yuh lur • res puh RAY shun) takes place inside a mitochondrion as shown in **Figure 5.** Cellular respiration is a series of chemical reactions in which energy stored in food is converted to a form of energy that the cell can use. This energy is released as food and oxygen combine. Waste products of this process are carbon dioxide and water. All cells with mitochondria use the energy from cellular respiration to do all of their work.

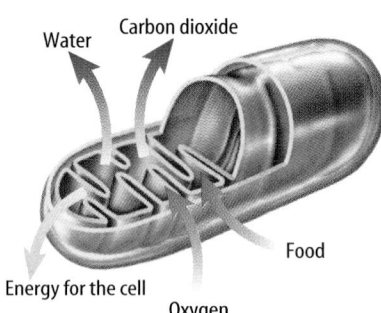

Water
Carbon dioxide
Energy for the cell
Oxygen
Food

LAB DEMONSTRATION

Purpose to demonstrate a by-product of cellular respiration

Materials bromothymol blue solution, glass jar, straw, graduated cylinder

Preparation Have the correct amount of solution measured out beforehand.

Procedure Place 50 mL of bromothymol blue solution in a glass jar. Using a straw, exhale into the solution. **CAUTION:** *Do not inhale any solution.*

Expected Outcome As carbon dioxide from the lungs reacts with the bromothymol blue solution, the solution will turn bluish green.

Assessment

What gas product was exhaled by your lungs and reacted with the bromothymol solution? carbon dioxide **Carbon dioxide is the by-product of what cellular process?** cellular respiration

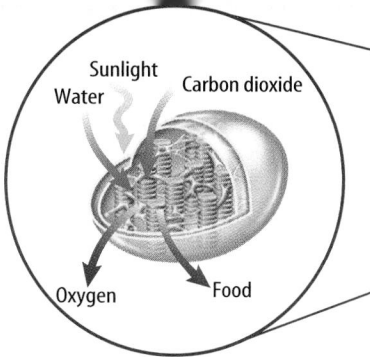

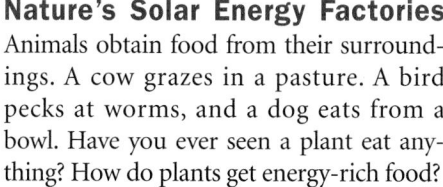

Sunlight
Water
Carbon dioxide

Oxygen
Food

Nature's Solar Energy Factories

Animals obtain food from their surroundings. A cow grazes in a pasture. A bird pecks at worms, and a dog eats from a bowl. Have you ever seen a plant eat anything? How do plants get energy-rich food?

Plants, algae, and many types of bacteria make food through a process called **photosynthesis** (foh toh SIHN thuh sus). Most photosynthesis in plants occurs in leaf cells. Inside these cells are green organelles called **chloroplasts** (KLOR uh plasts). Most leaves are green because their cells contain so many chloroplasts. During plant photosynthesis, as shown in **Figure 6,** chloroplasts capture light energy and combine carbon dioxide from the air with water to make food. Energy is stored in food. As the plant needs energy, its mitochondria release the food's energy. The captured light energy is passed to other organisms when they eat organisms that carry on photosynthesis.

Figure 6
Photosynthesis can take place inside the chloroplasts of plant cells.

Section 1 Assessment

1. What are the three main ideas of cell theory?
2. Why is the nucleus so important to the living cell?
3. How do cells get the energy they need to carry on their activities?
4. What is the purpose of a cell membrane?
5. **Think Critically** Suppose your teacher gave you a slide of an unknown cell. How would you tell whether the cell was from an animal or from a plant?

Skill Builder Activities

6. **Comparing and Contrasting** Compare and contrast the parts of animal cells and plant cells and the jobs that they do. **For more help, refer to the** Science Skill Handbook.
7. **Researching Information** In cooler regions, leaves of some trees lose their green color in autumn and turn shades of yellow, orange, or red. Find out how photosynthesis is affected when leaves change color in autumn. **For more help, refer to the** Science Skill Handbook.

③ Assess

Reteach

Place a large drawing of a compound microscope on the board. Write the functions of the parts on index cards. Have students select a card, name the part, and find it on the drawing.

Challenge

How has the development of different microscopes helped scientists study cells? Improved microscopes allow parts to be seen more clearly. Electron microscopes reveal structures not visible otherwise.

✔ *Assessment*

Content Have students prepare "game show"-type questions on cells. Collect all the questions and quiz the groups on the material. Use **Performance Assessment in the Science Classroom,** p. 91.

Answers to Section Assessment

1. All living things are made of one or more cells. The cell is the basic unit of life in which activities of life occur. All cells come from cells that already exist.
2. The nucleus controls most of the cell's activities.
3. The cell's mitochondria release energy by combining food molecules and oxygen during cellular respiration.
4. It holds the cell together and helps control what enters and leaves the cell.
5. Answers may vary, but students should indicate that most plant cells have chloroplasts and cell walls, and animal cells do not.
6. Students' answers should reflect the information in **Figure 3** and **Figure 4**.
7. Photosynthesis stops when leaves lose chlorophyll.

Resource Manager

Chapter Resources Booklet
MiniLAB, p. 3

Home and Community Involvement, p. 38

Activity

BENCH TESTED

Purpose Students use a microscope to observe organelles in algal cells. [L2] [IS] **Visual-Spatial**

Process Skills observing, classifying, drawing

Time Required 40 minutes

Safety Precautions Caution students never to drink or eat anything in the lab.

Teaching Strategy Make sure that students have focused well before they switch to high power.

Troubleshooting Remind students not to put too much algae and water on the microscope slide.

Answers to Questions

1. chloroplasts, nucleus, large vacuoles
2. Chloroplasts can capture energy from the Sun to make food. This makes algae and plants producers.
3. Algal cells are essential because they produce food from the energy of sunlight. Most organisms cannot produce their own food, so they need to have other sources of nutrients. Algal cells also released oxygen into the water.

✔ Assessment

Oral Have students explain why they were not able to view all organelles with the microscope. Large organelles were visible. Smaller organelles such as mitochondria are either too small or too thin to be seen. Use **PASC**, p. 89.

Activity

Observing Algae

You might have noticed mats of green algae growing on a pond or clinging to the walls of the aquarium in your classroom. Why are algae green? Like plants, algae contain organelles called chloroplasts. Chloroplasts contain a green pigment that captures the energy in light to make food. In this activity, you'll describe chloroplasts and other organelles in algal cells.

What You'll Investigate
What organelles can be seen when viewing algal cells under a microscope?

Materials
microscope
microscope slides
coverslips
large jars
pond water
algae
dropper
colored pencils

Goals
■ **Observe** algal cells under a microscope.
■ **Identify** cell organelles.

Procedure
1. Fill the tip of a dropper with pond water and thin strands of algae. Use the dropper to place the algae and a drop of water on a microscope slide.
2. Place a coverslip over the water drop and then place the slide on the stage of a microscope.

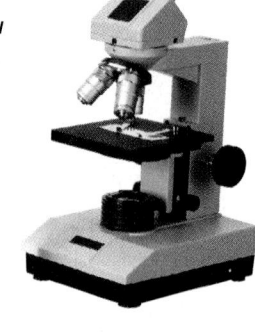

3. Using the microscope's lowest power objective, focus on the algal strands.
4. Once the algal strands are in focus, switch to a higher power objective and observe several algal cells.
5. **Draw** a colored picture of one of the algal cells, identifying the different organelles in the cell. Label on your drawing the cell wall, chloroplasts, and other organelles you can see.

Conclude and Apply
1. **List** the organelles you found in each cell.
2. **Explain** the function of chloroplasts.
3. **Infer** why algal cells are essential to all pond organisms.

WARNING: *Thoroughly wash your hands after you have finished this activity.*

Communicating Your Data
Work with three other students to create a collage of algal cell pictures complete with labeled organelles. Create a bulletin board display about algal cells.

44 **CHAPTER 2** Cells—The Units of Life

Communicating Your Data
Encourage students to include drawings or diagrams that show algal strands as well as algal cells. If computers are available, suggest that students use a computer drawing program and a word processor to make drawings and descriptive text for the bulletin board display.

Resource Manager
Chapter Resources Booklet
Activity Worksheet, pp. 5–6

The Different Jobs of Cells

Special Cells for Special Jobs

Choose the right tool for the right job. You might have heard this common expression. The best tool for a job is one that has been designed for that job. For example, you wouldn't use a hammer to saw a board in half, and you wouldn't use a saw to pound in a nail. You can think of your body cells in a similar way.

Cells that make up many-celled organisms, like you, are specialized. Different kinds of specialized cells work as a team to perform the life activities of a many-celled organism.

Types of Human Cells Your body is made up of many types of specialized cells. The same is true for other animals. **Figure 7** shows some human cell types. Notice the variety of sizes and shapes. A cell's shape and size can be related to its function.

As You Read

What **You'll Learn**
- **Discuss** how different cells have different jobs.
- **Explain** the differences among tissues, organs, and organ systems.

Vocabulary
tissue   organ system
organ

Why **It's Important**
Understanding how different types of cells work together will help you understand the importance of good health.

Figure 7
Human cells come in different shapes and sizes.

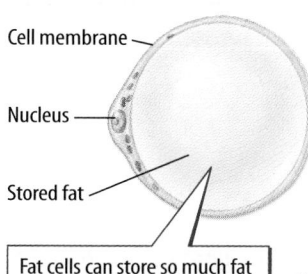

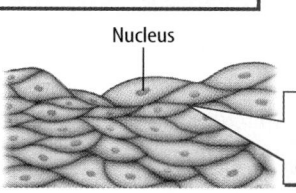

Cell membrane

Nucleus

Stored fat

Fat cells can store so much fat that the nucleus gets pushed against the cell membrane.

Nucleus

Skin cells are mostly flat and close together. They form a protective layer for your body.

Nucleus

Bone cell

Hardened bone

Bone cells are surrounded by a hard substance made of calcium and phosphorus.

Nucleus

Muscle cells are usually long and have many fibers that can contract and relax.

Nucleus

Nerve cells are long and have many branches. This allows them to receive and deliver messages quickly.

Cell branches

SECTION 2 The Different Jobs of Cells **45**

Section ✔*Assessment* Planner

PORTFOLIO
Science Journal, p. 46
PERFORMANCE ASSESSMENT
MiniLAB, p. 46
Skill Builder Activities, p. 49
See page 56 for more options.

CONTENT ASSESSMENT
Section, p. 49
Challenge, p. 49
Chapter, pp. 56–57

1 Motivate

Bellringer Transparency

Display the Section Focus Transparency for Section 2. Use the accompanying Transparency Activity Master. L2
ELL

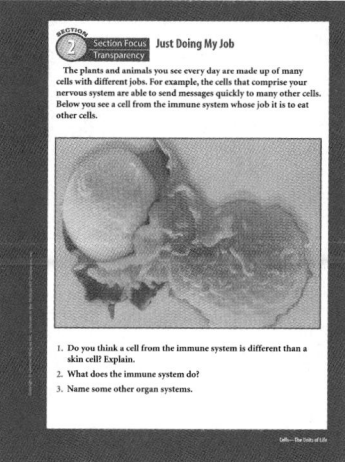

Tie to Prior Knowledge

Students should be familiar with tools such as hammers, screwdrivers, saws, chisels, and files. Have students make observations about how the structure of each tool is related to its function. Just as tools are shaped according to their functions, so too are the cells of many-celled organisms.

Purpose Students compare and contrast different human cells and hypothesize how cell shape and structure relate to function. L2 ELL

LS Visual-Spatial

Materials prepared slides of human muscle cells, nerve cells, blood cells, and skin cells; compound microscope

Teaching Strategy If slides are not available, you may wish to use high-quality photomicrographs of different types of cells.

Analysis

1. All of the cells are microscopic. With the exception of muscle cells, the cells are somewhat round in shape.
2. Students' answers should reflect information in **Figure 7.**

✔ Assessment

Process In the human body, structure is related closely to function. Have students use slides or photographs of cells (bone, blood, and other cell types) to prepare a presentation that explains how structure is related to function. Use **PASC,** p. 143.

✔ Reading Check

Answer form a system through which water, food, and other materials move in the plant

---

Figure 8
Plants, like animals, have specialized cells.

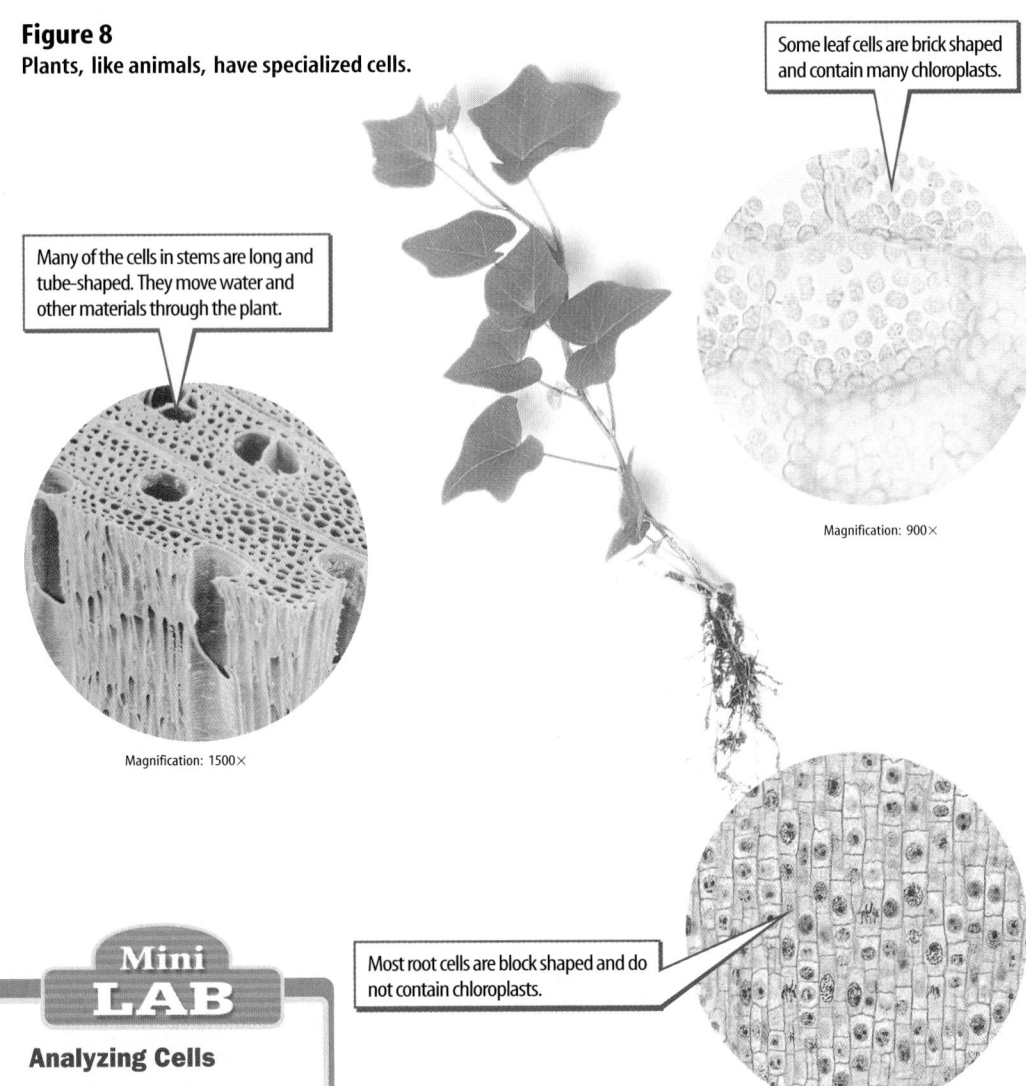

Many of the cells in stems are long and tube-shaped. They move water and other materials through the plant.

Magnification: 1500×

Some leaf cells are brick shaped and contain many chloroplasts.

Magnification: 900×

Most root cells are block shaped and do not contain chloroplasts.

Magnification: 450×

Mini LAB

Analyzing Cells

Procedure
1. Examine **prepared slides of human cells.**
2. Draw each type of cell that you observe in your **Science Journal.** Label cell parts that you can see.

Analysis
1. In what ways were the cells that you observed similar? How were they different?
2. Hypothesize how the cells' shapes relate to their jobs?

Types of Plant Cells Like animals, plants also are made of several different cell types, as shown in **Figure 8.** For instance, plants have different types of cells in their leaves, roots, and stems. Each type of cell has a specific job. Some cells in plant stems are long and tubelike. Together they form a system through which water, food, and other materials move in the plant. Other cells, like those that cover the outside of the stem, are smaller or thicker. They provide strength to the stem.

✔ **Reading Check** *What do long, tubelike cells do in plants?*

Science Journal

Form and Function Different types of eating utensils—forks, knives, and spoons— also are perfectly designed for their functions. Have students write in their Science Journals brief paragraphs about how the shapes of eating utensils match their functions. Have them relate this concept to cells. L2 **LS Linguistic** P

Visual Learning

Figure 8 Why do leaf cells contain so many chloroplasts? The primary reason is genetics. Secondary to genetics is environment because the number of chloroplasts can vary with the amount of light present.

Cell Organization

How well do you think your body would work if all the different cell types were just mixed together in no particular pattern? Could you walk if your leg muscle cells were scattered here and there, each doing its own thing, instead of being grouped together in your legs? How could you think if your brain cells weren't close enough together to communicate with each other? Many-celled organisms are not just mixed-up collections of different types of cells. Cells are organized into systems that, together, perform functions that keep the organism healthy and alive.

Astronomy
INTEGRATION

Systems are also found in space. The solar system is just one of many systems that make up the Milky Way Galaxy. Research to learn the planets and other parts of the solar system. As a class, create a bulletin board of your results.

Math Skills Activity

Calculating Numbers of Blood Cells

Example Problem

The human body has about 200 different types of cells. Red blood cells (RBCs) carry oxygen from your lungs to the rest of your cells. Each milliliter of blood contains 5 million RBCs. On average, an adolescent has about 3.5 L of blood. On average, how many RBCs are in an adolescent's body?

Solution

1 *This is what you know:*
number of RBCs per 1 mL
1,000 mL = 1 L
average volume of blood in the human body

2 *This is what you need to find:*
number of RBCs in the human body, N

3 *This is the equation you need to use:*
N = (number of RBCs/1 mL)(1,000 mL/1 L) (average volume of blood)

4 *Substitute the values:*
N = (5,000,000 RBCs/1mL)(1,000 mL/1L)(3.5 L of blood)

5 *Solve the equation:*
N = 17,500,000,000, or 17.5 billion red blood cells

Substitute your answer into the equation to see whether it is correct.

Magnification: 250×

Practice Problem

Each milliliter of blood contains approximately 7,500 white blood cells. How many white blood cells are in the average human body?

For more help, refer to the **Math Skill Handbook.**

Cell Organization

Astronomy
INTEGRATION

The solar system is made up of nine planets and their moons, comets, and asteroids rotating around the Sun. The planets are Mercury, Venus, Earth, Mars, Jupiter, Saturn, Uranus, Neptune, and Pluto.

Quick Demo

Use the microprojector to show slides of different plant and animal tissues. Point out that each type of tissue is made of similar cells, as is evident from the shape of the cells in the tissues. L1 [LS] **Visual-Spatial**

Math Skills Activity

National Math Standards

Correlation to Mathematics Objectives
1, 2, 4, 6, 8, 9

Answer to Practice Problem

3.5 L = 3,500 mL
3,500 mL × 7,500 = 26,250,000 white blood cells

Resource Manager

Chapter Resources Booklet
Transparency, p. 26
MiniLAB, p. 28
Directed Reading for Content Mastery, pp. 21, 22

Teacher FYI

Andreas Vesalius (1514–1564) conducted some of the most accurate and thorough examinations of the human body that had ever been done. Vesalius wrote a classic book about human anatomy that has become popular because of its extremely detailed anatomical drawings.

Cell Organization,
continued

Fun Fact

The largest artery in the body, called the aorta, is about the diameter of a garden hose. It takes ten capillaries to equal the thickness of a human hair.

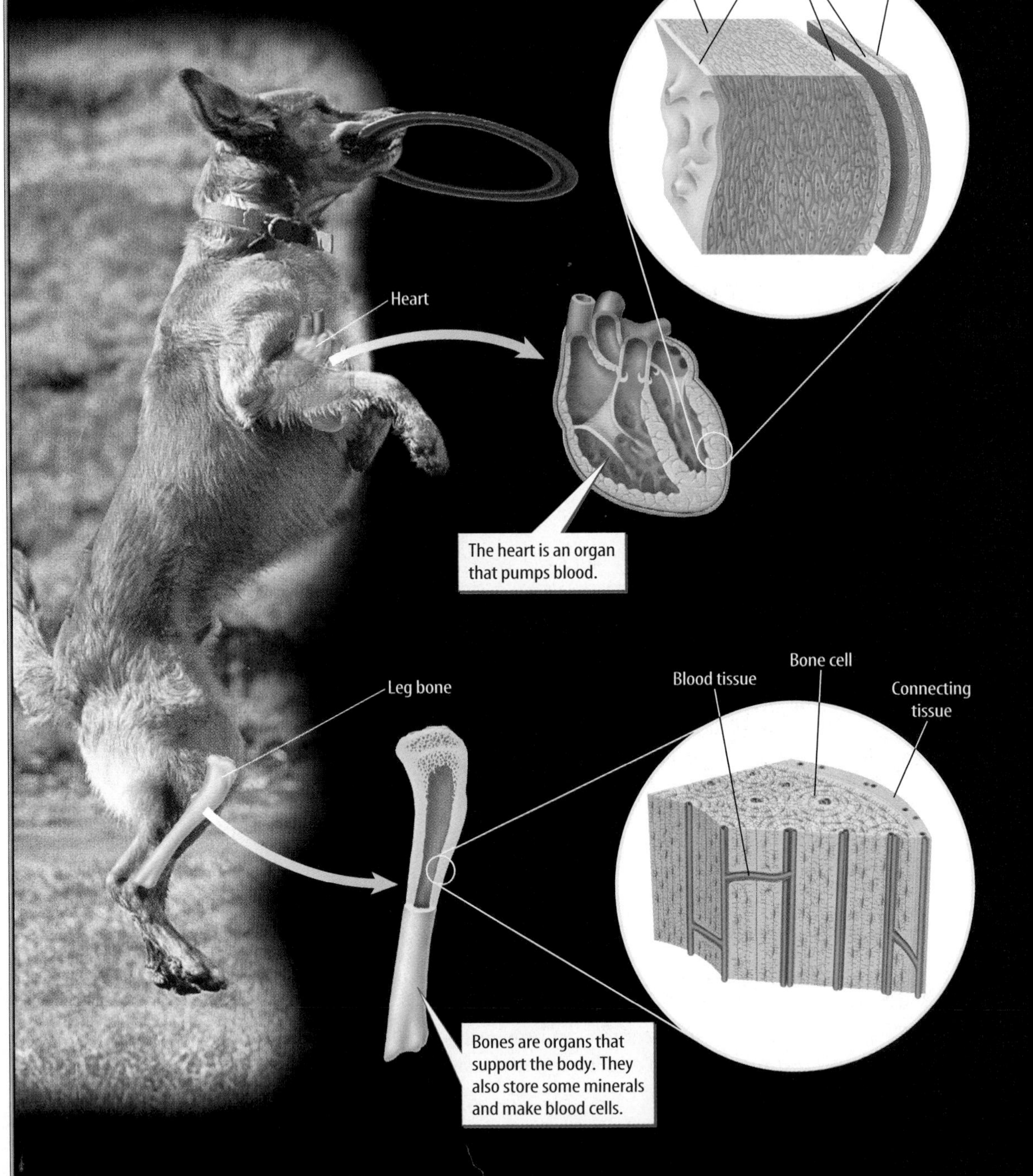

Figure 9
Organs are two or more tissue types that work together. An organ performs a task that no other organ performs.

Muscle tissue   Covering and lining tissue   Connecting tissue

Heart

The heart is an organ that pumps blood.

Leg bone

Bone cell

Blood tissue   Connecting tissue

Bones are organs that support the body. They also store some minerals and make blood cells.

48   **CHAPTER 2**   Cells——The Units of Life

Resource Manager

Chapter Resources Booklet
   Reinforcement, p. 28
   Enrichment, p. 30
   Lab Activity, pp. 13–16
   Activity Worksheet, pp. 7–8
Lab Management and Safety, p. 69

Inclusion Strategies

Learning Disabled Students who have difficulty understanding the levels of organization may benefit from making models. First, have them make a small model cell out of clay. Next, instruct students to make a few more of the same kind of cell. Have them join the individual cells to make a tissue. The other levels of organization can be studied in a similar fashion. L1
LS Kinesthetic

Tissues and Organs Cells that are alike are organized into tissues (TIH shewz). **Tissues** are groups of similar cells that all do the same sort of work. For example, animals with muscles have muscle tissue that mostly is made up of muscle cells. Bone tissue is made up of bone cells, and nerve tissue is made up of nerve cells. Blood, a liquid tissue, includes different types of blood cells.

As important as individual tissues are, they do not work alone. Different types of tissues working together can form a structure called an **organ** (OR gun). For example, the stomach is an organ that includes muscle tissue, nerve tissue, and blood tissue. All of these tissues work together and enable the stomach to perform its digestive functions. Other human organs include the heart and the kidneys.

✔ **Reading Check** *Which term means "two or more tissue types that work together"?*

Organ Systems A group of organs that work together to do a certain job is called an **organ system.** The stomach, mouth, intestines, and liver are involved in digestion. Together, these and several other organs make up the digestive system. Other organ systems found in your body include the respiratory system, the circulatory system, the reproductive system, and the nervous system.

Organ systems also work together, as shown in **Figure 9.** For example, the muscular system has more than 600 muscles that are attached to bones. The contracting cells of muscle tissue cause your bones, which are part of the skeletal system, to move.

SCIENCE *Online*

Research Visit the Glencoe Science Web site at **science.glencoe.com** to find out what types of organisms are made up of only one cell. Make a poster that includes images and gives information about five of these organisms.

Section 2 Assessment

1. Describe three types of cells found in the human body.
2. Compare and contrast the cells found in a plant's roots, stems, and leaves.
3. What is the difference between a cell and a tissue? What is the difference between a tissue and an organ?
4. Give an example of a human organ system, and name some of the organs in that system.
5. **Think Critically** Why must specialized cells work as a team?

Skill Builder Activities

6. **Concept Mapping** Make an events chain concept map of the different levels of cell organization from cell to organ system. Provide an example for each level of organization. **For more help, refer to the** Science Skill Handbook.
7. **Communicating** In terms of organization, organisms can be compared to a school band. Write a short paragraph in your Science Journal explaining how an organism is like a band. **For more help, refer to the** Science Skill Handbook.

Answers to Section Assessment

1. Descriptions may include information on fat, skin, bone, nerve, or muscle cells.
2. Answers should contain information from **Figure 8.**
3. Tissues are made up of cells. Organs are made up of tissues.
4. Answers will vary. The digestive system is made up of the mouth, stomach, intestines, and liver.
5. to perform the life activities of a many-celled organism
6. Possible answer: Cell (muscle cell) → Tissue (muscle) → Organ (heart) → Organ System (circulatory system)
7. A school band is made up of individuals who work together. Organisms are made up of different cells that must work together to keep an organism alive.

✔ **Reading Check**

Answer organ

3 Assess

Reteach

Have students make a chart with two columns. In one column, have them list the different levels of organization, beginning with the cell. In the other column, have students provide a real example for each different level. Have students choose an organism not discussed in the chapter.
IS Logical-Mathematical

Challenge

Have students make a poster listing the main organ systems of the human body and the main organs in each system. Allow students to do research if necessary.

✔ Assessment

Portfolio Have students design posters illustrating the levels of organization in living things. Posters should include a type of cell in the human body; groups of these cells together to show a particular tissue; how this tissue is incorporated in an organ; and the organ system that the organ belongs to. Use **PASC,** p. 147.

Activity

Recognize the Problem

Purpose
Students will observe where water moves in a plant and how long it takes for plants to absorb water. L2 ELL COOP LEARN

Visual-Spatial

Process Skills
forming a hypothesis, designing an experiment, making and using tables, observing and inferring, separating and controlling variables

Time Required
45 minutes

Materials
Use red food coloring. Blue, green, and yellow food coloring do not show up well in celery.

Safety Precautions
Caution students to avoid getting food coloring on clothing. Remind them not to eat food used in science labs.

Form a Hypothesis

Possible Hypotheses
- Plant stems are hollow and act like drinking straws.
- Plant stems contain thin, strawlike passageways for water to flow through.

Test Your Hypothesis

Possible Procedures
Put several ounces of water in the glass. Add a few drops of red food coloring and stir. Place the celery stalk in the glass, with the leaves at the top. Keep track of how long it takes for the celery to absorb the water. After all of the water is absorbed, cut the stalk crosswise.

Activity *Design Your Own Experiment*

Water Movement in Plants

When you are thirsty, you can sip water from a glass or drink from a fountain. Plants must get their water in other ways. In most plants, water moves from the soil into cells in the roots. How does this water get to other parts of the plant?

Recognize the Problem
Where does water travel in a plant?

Form a Hypothesis
Based on what you already know about how a plant functions, state a hypothesis about where you think water travels in a plant.

Goals
- ■ **Design** an investigation to show where water moves in a plant.
- ■ **Observe** how long it takes water to move in a plant.

Possible Materials
fresh stalk of celery with leaves
clear drinking glass
scissors
red food coloring
water

Safety Precautions
🥽 👕 ✂️

WARNING: Use care when handling sharp objects such as scissors. Avoid getting red food coloring on your clothing.

Sample Data Table:

Time	Observations
Start of activity	Celery is light green.
During the activity	Red streak moves up stalk.
End of activity	Celery stalk is red on the inside.

Teacher FYI
The shape of cells in a plant's stem are directly related to function. They are shaped somewhat like straws. Through capillary action, water is drawn upward by the stem's cells and carried to the plant's leaves.

Test Your Hypothesis

Plan

1. As a group, agree upon a hypothesis and decide how you will test it. Identify which results will support the hypothesis.

2. **List** the steps you will need to take to test your hypothesis. Be specific. Describe exactly what you will do in each step. List your materials.

3. Prepare a data table in your Science Journal to record your observations.

4. **Read** the entire investigation to make sure all steps are in logical order.

5. **Identify** all constants, variables, and controls of the investigation.

Do

1. Make sure your teacher approves your plan before you start.

2. Carry out the investigation according to the approved plan.

3. While doing the investigation, record your observations and complete the data tables in your Science Journal.

Analyze Your Data

1. **Compare** the color of the celery stalk before, during, and after the investigation.

2. **Compare** your results with those of other groups.

3. Make a drawing of the cut stalk. Label your drawing.

4. What was your control in this investigation? What were your variables?

Draw Conclusions

1. Did the results of this investigation support your hypothesis? Explain.

2. Why do you suppose that only some of the plant tissue is red?

3. What would you do to improve this investigation?

4. Predict if other plants have tissues that move water.

Communicating
Your Data

Write a report about your investigation. Include illustrations to show how the investigation was performed. **Present** your report to your class.

ACTIVITY 51

Teaching Strategies

- Have students relate this activity to plant cell types.
- To get maximum absorption, cut the celery diagonally and place stalks in water containing a high concentration of food coloring.

Expected Outcome

Most results will show vertical red lines on the stalk where the colored water traveled through the stalk.

Analyze Your Data

1. See Sample Data Table.
2. Students' results should be similar.
3. Students' drawings should show that the tissue that carries water inside the stem turned red.
4. The control was using the same plant; the variables were concentration of food coloring and time.

Error Analysis

Answers will vary, depending on the health of plant tissue and the amount of time it was kept in colored water.

Draw Conclusions

1. Answers will vary, depending on students' hypotheses and results.
2. Only the plant tissue that carried the water inside the stem turned red.
3. Possible answer: Keep the celery in the colored water for a longer period of time for better results.
4. Students should predict that all plants contain water-moving tissues.

✔Assessment

Content Have groups of students design a similar experiment to determine whether different plants absorb water in the same way. Have students write hypotheses to answer this question. Then have them plan and carry out experiments using fresh carrots instead of celery stalks to test the hypotheses. Use **Performance Assessment in the Science Classroom**, p. 105.

Communicating
Your Data

Class reports can be enhanced with visual aids such as overhead transparencies or computer slide show presentations. Have students write the key points of their presentations on index cards.

Content Background

Tissue and organ transplants are referred to with the following terms, depending on the source of the transplanted material. An *autograft* is a transplant from one part of the patient's body to another. A transplant from an identical twin is an *isograft*. A transplant of tissue from one person unrelated to the patient is an *allograft*. The first such operation was the transplant of a kidney from one dog to another in 1899. Transplants of tissue or organs from one species to a different species of animal are called *xenografts*. Corneas, kidneys, livers, lungs, cartilage and bone tissues, and skin have all been transplanted since that time. The more closely related a person is to the tissue donor, the greater the chance that the tissue will not be rejected by the recipient's immune system. Autografts clearly are the best option whenever possible. The new technology of tissue engineering increases the availability and success of autografts. In addition to growing samples of skin tissue from the skin of a burn victim, scientists are developing techniques that may allow the growth of entirely new organs to replace those damaged by injury or disease. The process involves building a scaffold of biodegradable proteins that will support a sample of a patient's own cells. As the cells replicate, the artificial structures will degrade, leaving behind only the natural tissues produced by the patient's body. Such artificially produced organs are called *neo-organs*. There is evidence to suggest that it will someday be possible to construct large and complex organs like livers, kidneys and intestines for use in transplantations.

TEST TUBE

In Chicago, a young woman named Kelly is cooking pasta on her stove. Her clothes catch fire from the gas flame and, in the blink of an eye, 80 percent of her body is severely burned. Will she survive?

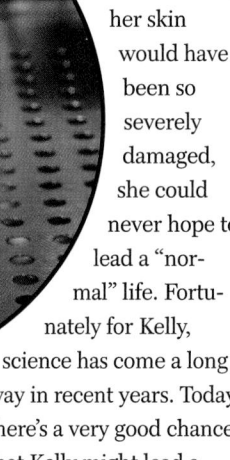

This artificial bladder was grown from cultured bladder cells in five weeks.

Just 15 years ago, the answer to this question probably would have been "no." Or if she lived, her skin would have been so severely damaged, she could never hope to lead a "normal" life. Fortunately for Kelly, science has come a long way in recent years. Today, there's a very good chance that Kelly might lead a long and healthy life.

Like the brain or the heart, the skin is an organ. In fact, it is the body's largest organ, about 1/12 of your total body weight. Composed of protective layers, skin keeps your internal structure safe from damage, infection, and temperature changes.

Without even the outer layer of skin, your body would dry out and would be susceptible to attacks from disease-causing invaders such as bacteria, fungi, and other pathogens.

Today, just as farmers can grow crops of corn and wheat, scientists can grow human skin. How?

Tissue Engineers

Scientists, called tissue engineers, take a piece of skin (no bigger than a quarter) from an undamaged part of the burn victim's body. The skin cells are isolated, mixed with special nutrients, and then they multiply in a culture dish.

After about two to three months, the tissue engineers can harvest sheets of new, smooth skin. These sheets, as large as postcards, are grafted onto the victim's damaged body and act like seeds that promote additional skin growth.

By grafting Kelly's own skin on her body rather than using donor skin—skin from another person or from an animal—doctors avoid at least three potential complications. First, donor skin may not even be available. Second, Kelly's body might perceive the new skin cells from another source to be a danger, and her immune system might reject—or destroy—the transplant. Finally, even if the skin produced from a foreign source is accepted, it may leave extensive scarring.

52

Resources for Teachers and Students

Scar No More by Diane Martindale, Scientific American, July 2000.

Growing New Organs by David J. Mooney and Antonios G. Mikos, Scientific American, September 1999.

Office of Public Affairs Food and Drug Administration
5600 Fishers Lane
Rockville, Maryland 20857

Growing A New Field, Tissue Engineering Comes Into Its Own by Gary Stix, Scientific American, September 1997.

TISSUE

Artificial cartilage is used to replace joints or rebuild features such as noses or ears.

Thanks to advances in science, skin tissue is being "grown" in laboratories

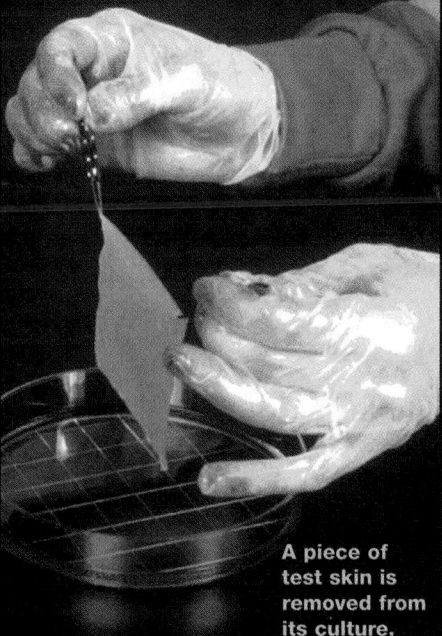

A piece of test skin is removed from its culture.

Tissue Testing

What else can tissue engineers grow? They produce test skin—skin made in the lab and used to test the effects of cosmetics and chemicals on humans. This skin is eliminating the use of animals for such tests. Also, tissue engineers are working on ways to replace other body parts such as livers, heart valves, and ears, that don't grow back on their own.

Of the over two million Americans who are treated for burns each year, 13,000 require some kind of skin graft. With this demand, tissue engineers are hard at work finding ways to save more people like Kelly.

CONNECTIONS **Safety List** Using the Glencoe Science Web site or your media center, learn about fire safety tips, including kitchen safety and escape routes in your home. Make a list of them and share it with your family.

Online

For more information, visit science.glencoe.com

CONNECTIONS Common fire safety tips include: placement and maintenance of smoke detectors on every floor of a residence; changing batteries in smoke detectors twice every year; insuring that every room in a residence has two exits in case of emergency; regular practice of fire escape routes by every family member.

Online

Internet Addresses

_____

_____

_____

_____

Explore the Glencoe Science Web site at **science.glencoe.com** to find out more about topics in this feature.

Discussion

Ask students to speculate about the kinds of injuries that might be treated because of new tissue engineering technology. **How would these treatments affect the lives of affected individuals?** Possible answers: spinal cord damage can result in paralysis. Advances in treatment of nerve tissue damage may be able to restore normal function and movement in many cases.

Activity

Have students write short science fiction stories or plays using tissue engineering as a theme. Create characters who put together new forms of life from various organs and tissues. They can use common diseases as themes also, creating characters that cure untreatable conditions. Remind students that events like heart transplants were once considered to be impossible.

Investigate the Issue

Have students research the appropriate first aid treatments for various burn injuries. What are the differences between first, second, and third degree burns? How should each type of burn be treated in an emergency situation before medical help arrives? Have students include this information in the safety list they share with their families.

Reviewing Main Ideas

Preview

Students can answer the questions in their Science Journals. Discuss the answers as you go through the chapter. ⬛ **Linguistic**

Review

Students can write their answers, then compare them with those of other students. ⬛ **Interpersonal**

Reteach

Students can look at the illustrations and describe details that support the main ideas of the chapter. ⬛ **Visual-Spatial**

Answers to Chapter Review

SECTION 1

2. The microscopes necessary to view small cells and protists were not invented yet.

4. The vacuole stores water and other substances.

SECTION 2

1. White blood cells help fight disease.

2. Tissues are made up of similar cells working together. Sports teams are made up of individual players who work together as a team.

Reviewing Main Ideas

Section 1 The World of Cells

1. Cell theory states that all living things are made of one or more cells, the cell is the basic unit of life, and all cells come from other cells.

2. The microscope is an instrument that enlarges the image of an object. *Why weren't cells, like these one-celled protists, described before the mid-1600s?*

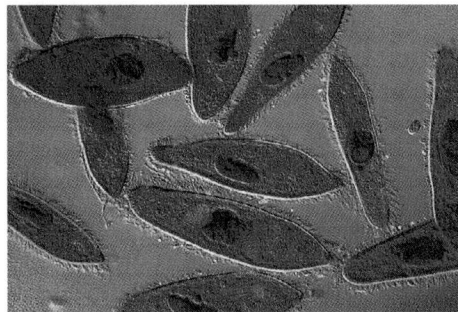

3. All cells are surrounded by a cell membrane and contain hereditary material and cytoplasm. Cells, except bacteria, contain organelles.

4. The nucleus directs the cell's activities. Chromosomes contain DNA that determines what kinds of traits an organism will have. Vacuoles store substances. *What does the large vacuole do in plant cells?*

5. In organelles called mitochondria, the process of cellular respiration combines food molecules with oxygen. This series of chemical reactions releases energy for the cell's activities and produces carbon dioxide and water as wastes.

6. The energy in light is captured and stored in food molecules during the process of photosynthesis. Plants, algae, and some bacteria make their own food by photosynthesis.

Section 2 The Different Jobs of Cells

1. Many-celled organisms are made up of different kinds of cells that perform different tasks. *What is the job of white blood cells?*

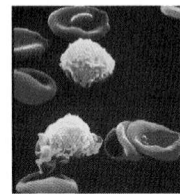

2. Many-celled organisms are organized into tissues, organs, and organ systems that perform specific jobs to keep an organism alive. *How is the organization of cells into tissues similar to the organization of a sports team?*

FOLDABLES
Reading & Study Skills

After You Read

Use your Compare and Contrast Study Fold to find the similarities and differences between an animal cell and a plant cell.

FOLDABLES
Reading & Study Skills

After You Read

After students have read the chapter and completed the Foldable described in Before You Read, have them do the activity on the student page.

Dinah Zike

Visualizing Main Ideas

Complete the following concept map on the parts of a plant cell.

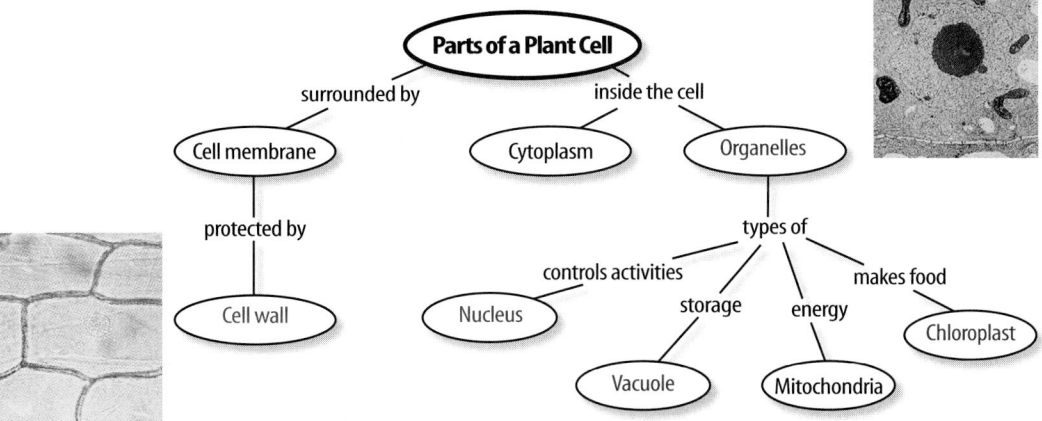

Vocabulary Review

Vocabulary Words

a. bacteria
b. cell membrane
c. cell wall
d. chloroplast
e. cytoplasm
f. mitochondria
g. nucleus
h. organ
i. organ system
j. organelle
k. photosynthesis
l. tissue
m. vacuole

Study Tip

Make a note of anything you don't understand so you'll remember to ask your teacher to clarify it.

Using Vocabulary

Explain the difference between the terms in the following sets.

1. mitochondria, chloroplast
2. tissue, organ
3. cell membrane, nucleus
4. organ, organ system
5. nucleus, organelle
6. cytoplasm, nucleus
7. vacuole, mitochondria
8. organ system, tissue
9. organelle, organ
10. cell wall, cell membrane

See student page.

Vocabulary Review

Using Vocabulary

1. Mitochondria convert food energy so that the cell can use it; chloroplasts capture energy from sunlight to convert carbon dioxide and water into food.
2. tissue—group of similar cells that all do the same sort of work; organ—group of two or more different types of tissues that work together
3. The cell membrane helps control what enters and leaves a cell; the nucleus controls the cell's activities.
4. organ—group of two or more different types of tissues that work together; organ system—a group of organs that work together
5. The nucleus is an organelle that controls the cell's activities; an organelle is a cell part that performs life activities.
6. Cytoplasm is a gelatinlike substance in all cells; the nucleus is found in cytoplasm of some cells and controls cell activities.
7. A vacuole is an organelle that stores food, water, minerals and wastes; mitochondria are organelles that convert food energy so that the cell can use it.
8. organ system—group of organs that work together; tissue—group of similar cells that work together
9. organelle—cell part that performs life activities for a cell; organ—two or more different types of tissues that work together to perform life activities for an organism
10. The cell wall provides support and protection for some cells; the cell membrane is found in all cells and holds the cell together.

Checking Concepts

1. B
2. B
3. A
4. C
5. A
6. B
7. A
8. D
9. B
10. D

Thinking Critically

11. The cell would die because it couldn't get water, food, or other materials, and it couldn't release wastes.
12. The cell would die because it would not have usable energy.
13. All of life's activities take place within the cell of one-celled organisms. In many-celled organisms, cells work together as a team to complete all of the activities necessary for life.
14. Cells with a lot of mitochondria present include cells with high energy requirements, such as muscle cells.
15. The presence of organelles would make it a plant cell. Bacterial cells do not have organelles.

Checking Concepts

Choose the word or phrase that best answers the question.

1. Which of the following controls what enters and leaves the cell?
   A) mitochondrion C) vacuole
   B) cell membrane D) nucleus

2. Which of the following are found inside the nucleus of the cell?
   A) vacuoles C) chloroplasts
   B) chromosomes D) mitochondria

3. What is the gelatinlike substance in a cell that contains water and chemicals?
   A) cytoplasm C) chromosome
   B) tissue D) mitochondrion

4. Which of the following terms best describes the stomach?
   A) organelle C) organ
   B) organ system D) tissue

5. What does photosynthesis make for a plant?
   A) food C) water
   B) organs D) tissues

6. What does DNA do?
   A) makes food
   B) determines traits
   C) converts food to energy
   D) stores substances

7. Which of the following terms best describes your blood?
   A) tissue C) organ
   B) cell D) organ system

8. Which of the following terms is the name of a human organ system?
   A) protective C) photosynthetic
   B) growth D) respiratory

9. What cell structure helps support plants?
   A) cell membrane C) vacuole
   B) cell wall D) nucleus

10. Which of these organisms is one cell?
    A) mouse C) snake
    B) cat D) bacteria

Thinking Critically

11. What would happen to a cell if the cell membrane were solid and waterproof?

12. What might happen to a cell if all its mitochondria were removed? Explain.

13. Why are cells called the units of life?

14. What kinds of animal cells might have a lot of mitochondria present?

15. How would you tell if a cell is a bacterium or a plant cell? Explain.

Developing Skills

16. **Comparing and Contrasting** Compare and contrast photosynthesis and cellular respiration.

17. **Making and Using Tables** Copy and complete this table about the functions of the following cell parts: *nucleus, cell membrane, mitochondrion, chloroplast,* and *vacuole.*

Functions of Cell Parts	
Cell Part	**Function**
Nucleus	See section
Cell membrane	1 of this
Mitochondrion	chapter
Chloroplast	for
Vacuole	answers

Chapter ✓*Assessment* Planner

Portfolio Encourage students to place in their portfolios one or two items of what they consider to be their best work. Examples include:
- Curriculum Connection, p. 39
- Make a Model, p. 40
- Science Journal, p. 46

Performance Additional performance assessments, Performance Task Assessment Lists, and rubrics for evaluating these activities can be found in Glencoe's **Performance Assessment in the Science Classroom.**

18. **Recognizing Cause and Effect** Why is the bricklike shape of some plant cells important?

19. **Identifying and Manipulating Variables and Controls** Describe an experiment you might do to determine whether water moves into and out of cells.

20. **Making and Using Graphs** Light is necessary for plants to make food. Using the graph below, determine which plant produced the most food. How much light was needed by the plant every day to produce the most food?

Food Production in Plants

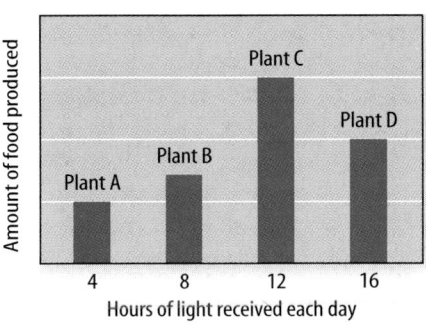

Performance Assessment

21. **Skit** Working with three or four classmates, develop a short skit about how a living cell works. Have each group member play the role of a different cell part.

TECHNOLOGY

Go to the Glencoe Science Web site at **science.glencoe.com** or use the **Glencoe Science CD-ROM** for additional chapter assessment.

A student was viewing different types of cells using a compound light microscope.

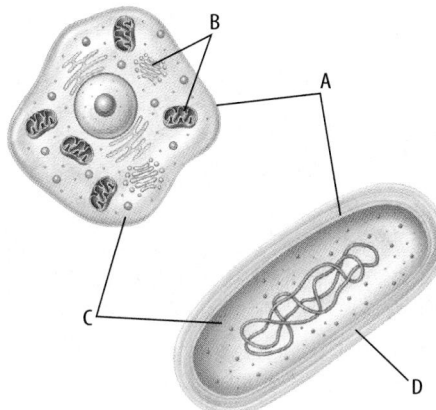

Study the pictures and answer the following questions.

1. Which of these is the major characteristic of all cells?
   A) They can be observed by the human eye.
   B) They are powered by vacuoles.
   C) They are organized structures.
   D) They have strong cell walls and organelles.

2. Organelles are specialized cell parts that perform specific activities. Which of these letters represents cell organelles?
   F) A
   G) B
   H) C
   J) D

The Test-Taking Tip was written by The Princeton Review, the nation's leader in test preparation.
1. C
2. G

Developing Skills

16. Possible answer: Photosynthesis and cellular respiration appear to be opposite processes. The starting materials of one process are the resulting materials of the other process.
17. See student page.
18. Answers may vary, but students should recognize that many plants are tall and need strong, rigid cells for support.
19. Students should describe an experiment that demonstrates osmosis. Variables and controls should be clearly defined, along with the process.
20. According to the graph, Plant C produced the most food. Twelve hours of light were needed every day.

Performance Assessment

21. Assess student skits by observing how detailed and informative the different characters' roles are. Use **Performance Assessment in the Science Classroom**, p. 147.

✓Assessment Resources

 Reproducible Masters

Chapter Resources Booklet
 Chapter Review, pp. 35–36
 Chapter Tests, pp. 37–40
 Assessment Transparency Activity, p. 47

Glencoe Science Web site
 Interactive Tutor
 Chapter Quizzes

Glencoe Technology
 Assessment Transparency
 Interactive CD-ROM Chapter Quizzes
 ExamView Pro Test Bank
 Vocabulary PuzzleMaker Software
 MindJogger Videoquiz

Section/Objectives	Standards		Activities/Features
Chapter Opener	**National**	**State/Local**	**Explore Activity:** Model a bacterium's slime layer, p. 59 **Before You Read,** p. 59
	See p. 5T for a Key to Standards.		
Section 1 What are bacteria? ⏱ 2 sessions 📦 1 block 1. **Identify** the characteristics of bacteria cells. 2. **Compare and contrast** aerobic and anaerobic organisms.	National Content Standards: UCP5, A1, C1, C2, C3, C5		**MiniLAB:** Modeling Bacteria Size, p. 61 **Science Online,** p. 63 **Earth Science Integration,** p. 64 **Activity:** Observing Cyanobacteria, p. 66
Section 2 Bacteria in Your Life ⏱ 3 sessions 📦 1.5 blocks 1. **Identify** some ways bacteria are helpful. 2. **Determine** the importance of nitrogen-fixing bacteria. 3. **Explain** how some bacteria can cause human disease.	National Content Standards: UCP2, A1, C4, F1, F5, G2		**MiniLAB:** Observing Bacterial Growth, p. 68 **Visualizing Nitrogen Fixing Bacteria,** p. 69 **Chemistry Integration,** p. 70 **Science Online,** p. 71 **Problem-Solving Activity:** Controlling Bacterial Growth, p. 72 **Activity:** Composting, p. 74 **Science Stats:** Unusual Bacteria, p. 76

NATIONAL GEOGRAPHIC   Teacher's Corner

PRODUCTS AVAILABLE FROM GLENCOE
To order call 1-800-334-7344:
CD-ROM
NGS PictureShow: The Cell
Curriculum Kit
GeoKit: Cells and Microorganisms

Transparency Set
NGS PicturePack: The Cell
Videodisc
STV: The Cell
PRODUCTS AVAILABLE FROM NATIONAL GEOGRAPHIC SOCIETY
To order call 1-800-368-2728:

Videos
Bacteria; Discovering the Cell

INDEX TO NATIONAL GEOGRAPHIC SOCIETY
The following articles may be used for research relating to this chapter: "Body Beasts" by Richard Coniff, December 1998.

Activity Materials	Reproducible Resources	Section Assessment	Technology
Explore Activity: synthetic kitchen sponge, water, hair-styling gel, plate, scissors	**Chapter Resources Booklet** Foldables Worksheet, p. 13 Directed Reading Overview, p. 15 Note-taking Worksheets, pp. 27–28	GLENCOE'S ASSESSMENT ADVANTAGE	
MiniLAB: meterstick, yarn or string **Activity:** prepared slides (or micrograph photos) of *Oscillatoria, Nostoc, Gloeocapsa,* and *Anabaena*; microscope	**Chapter Resources Booklet** Transparency Activity, p. 38 MiniLAB, p. 3 Enrichment, p. 25 Reinforcement, p. 23 Directed Reading, p. 16 Activity Worksheet, pp. 5–6 Lab Activity, pp. 9–10 Transparency Activity, pp. 41–43 **Home and Community Involvement,** p. 37 **Life Science Critical Thinking/ Problem Solving,** p. 1	Portfolio Science Journal, p. 63 Performance MiniLAB, p. 61 Skill Builder Activities, p. 65 Content Section Assessment, p. 65	Section Focus Transparency Teaching Transparency Interactive CD-ROM Guided Reading Audio Program
MiniLAB: 2–3 dried beans, distilled water, glass beaker **Activity:** 4 or more wide-mouth clear glass jars, soil, water, watering can, banana peel, apple core, scrap of newspaper, leaf, plastic candy wrapper, scrap of aluminum foil *Need materials?* Contact Science Kit at 1-800-828-7777 or www.sciencekit.com on the Internet.	**Chapter Resources Booklet** Transparency Activity, p. 39 MiniLAB, p. 4 Enrichment, p. 26 Reinforcement, p. 24 Directed Reading, pp. 17, 18 Lab Activity, pp. 11–12 Activity Worksheet, pp. 7–8 **Mathematics Skill Activities,** p. 19 **Reading and Writing Skill Activities,** p. 25 **Lab Management and Safety,** p. 58	Portfolio Cultural Diversity, p. 68 Science Journal, p. 72 Performance MiniLAB, p. 68 Problem Solving Activity, p. 72 Skill Builder Activities, p. 73 Content Section Assessment, p. 73	Section Focus Transparency Interactive CD-ROM Guided Reading Audio Program

End of Chapter Assessment		
Blackline Masters	**Technology**	**Professional Series**
Chapter Resources Booklet Chapter Review, pp. 31–32 Chapter Tests, pp. 33–36 **Standardized Test Practice by The Princeton Review,** pp. 35–38	MindJogger Videoquiz Interactive CD-ROM Vocabulary PuzzleMakers ExamView Pro Test Bank Interactive Lesson Planner Interactive Teacher Edition	Performance Assessment in the Science Classroom (PASC)

Transparencies

Section Focus

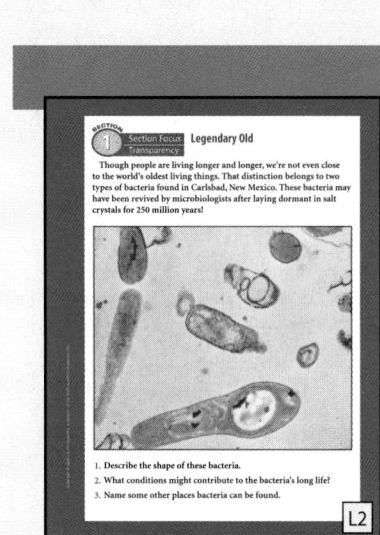

Section Focus Transparency 1 — Legendary Old

Though people are living longer and longer, we're not even close to the world's oldest living things. That distinction belongs to two types of bacteria found in Carlsbad, New Mexico. These bacteria may have been revived by microbiologists after laying dormant in salt crystals for 250 million years!

1. Describe the shape of these bacteria.
2. What conditions might contribute to the bacteria's long life?
3. Name some other places bacteria can be found.

L2

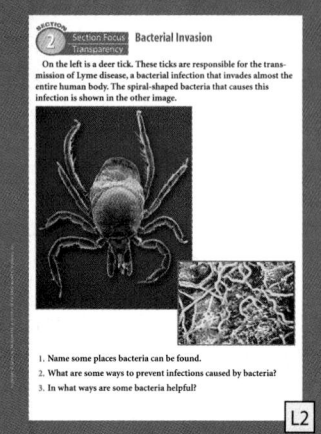

Section Focus Transparency 2 — Bacterial Invasion

On the left is a deer tick. These ticks are responsible for the transmission of Lyme disease, a bacterial infection that invades almost the entire human body. The spiral-shaped bacteria that causes this infection is shown in the other image.

1. Name some places bacteria can be found.
2. What are some ways to prevent infections caused by bacteria?
3. In what ways are some bacteria helpful?

L2

This is a representation of key blackline masters available in the Teacher Classroom Resources. See Resource Manager boxes within the chapter for additional information.

Key to Teaching Strategies

The following designations will help you decide which activities are appropriate for your students.

L1 Level 1 activities should be appropriate for students with learning difficulties.

L2 Level 2 activities should be within the ability range of all students.

L3 Level 3 activities are designed for above-average students.

ELL ELL activities should be within the ability range of English Language Learners.

COOP LEARN Cooperative Learning activities are designed for small group work.

LS Multiple Learning Styles logos, as described on page 22T, are used throughout to indicate strategies that address different learning styles.

P These strategies represent student products that can be placed into a best-work portfolio.

Assessment

Assessment Transparency — Bacteria

Directions: Carefully review the diagram and answer the following questions.

Test tube 1 · Test tube 2 · Test tube 3 · Test tube 4

1. Which hypothesis is probably being tested by this experiment?
   A Beef broth is a good substance for growing bacteria.
   B A cotton stopper will prevent bacteria from getting inside the test tubes.
   C Bacteria need nutrients in order to grow.
   D The more chemical X added, the less bacteria will grow.
2. About how much more liquid does Test tube 4 contain than Test tube 1?
   F 10 mL   G 15 mL   H 20 mL   J 25 mL
3. In a properly designed experiment, a control is set up exactly like the other setups except that the control does not contain the variable. According to this definition, which is the control in this experiment?
   A Test tube 1   C Test tube 3
   B Test tube 2   D Test tube 4

L2

Teaching

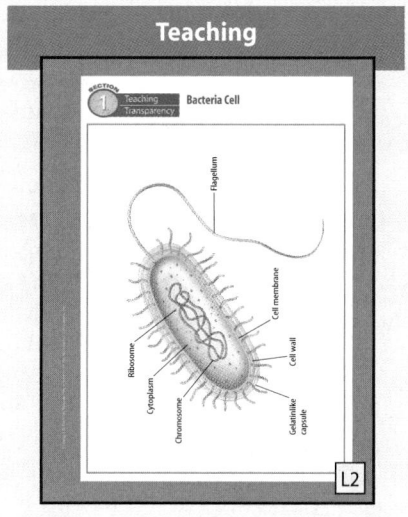

Teaching Transparency — Bacteria Cell

L2

Hands-on Activities

Activity Worksheets

Activity — Observing Cyanobacteria

Lab Preview
Directions: Answer these questions before you begin the Activity.
1. What safety symbols are associated with this activity?
2. Under what power of the microscope do you observe your slide?

You can obtain many species of cyanobacteria from ponds. When you look at these organisms under a microscope, you will find that they have many similarities and differences. In this activity, you will compare and contrast species of cyanobacteria.

What You'll Investigate
What do cyanobacteria look like?

Materials
micrograph photos of Oscillatoria and Nostoc
*prepared slides of Oscillatoria and Nostoc
prepared slides of Gloeocapsa and Anabaena
*micrograph photos of Anabaena and Gloeocapsa
microscope
*Alternate materials

Goals
• Observe several species of cyanobacteria.
• Describe the structure and function of cyanobacteria.

Safety Precautions
Procedure
1. Review the data table in the Data and Observations section. Record the presence or absence of each characteristic in the data table for each cyanobacterium you observe.
2. Observe prepared slides of Gloeocapsa and Anabaena under low and high power of the microscope. Notice the difference in the arrangement of the cells. Draw and label a few cells of each on a separate sheet of paper.
3. Observe photos of Nostoc and Oscillatoria. On a separate sheet of paper, draw and label a few cells of each.

L2

Laboratory Activities

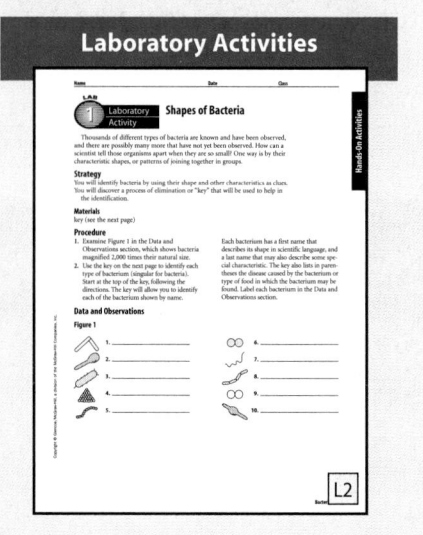

Laboratory Activity — Shapes of Bacteria

Thousands of different types of bacteria are known and have been observed, and there are possibly many more that have not yet been observed. How can a scientist tell these organisms apart when they are so small? One way is by their characteristic shapes, or patterns of joining together in groups.

Strategy
You will identify bacteria by using their shape and other characteristics as clues. You will discover a process of elimination or "key" that will be used to help in the identification.

Materials
key (see the next page)

Procedure
1. Examine Figure 1 in the Data and Observations section, which shows bacteria magnified 2,000 times their natural size.
2. Use the key on the next page to identify each type of bacterium (singular for bacteria). Start at the top of the key, following the directions. The key will allow you to identify each of the bacterium shown by name.

Each bacterium has a first name that describes its shape in scientific language, and a last name that may also describe some special characteristic. The key also lists in parentheses the disease caused by the bacterium or type of food in which the bacterium may be found. Label each bacterium in the Data and Observations section.

Data and Observations
Figure 1

L2

Meeting Different Ability Levels

Content Outline

Note-taking Worksheet — **Bacteria**

Section 1   What are bacteria?

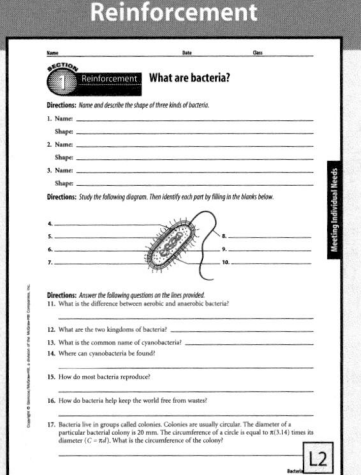

L2

Reinforcement

Reinforcement — **What are bacteria?**

L2

Directed Reading

Directed Reading for Content Mastery — *Overview* **Bacteria**

L1

Enrichment

Enrichment — **How Temperature Affects Bacterial Growth**

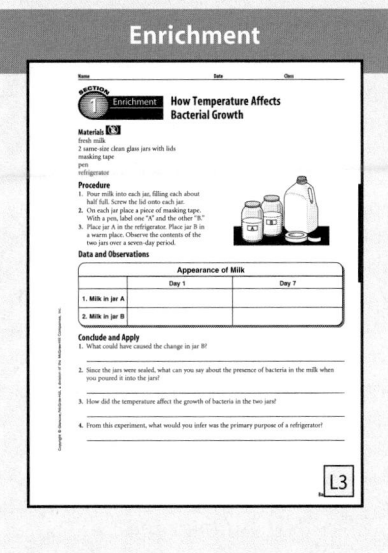

L3

Spanish Directed Reading

Lectura dirigida para Dominio del contenido — *Sinopsis* **Las bacterias**

L1

Assessment

Chapter Tests

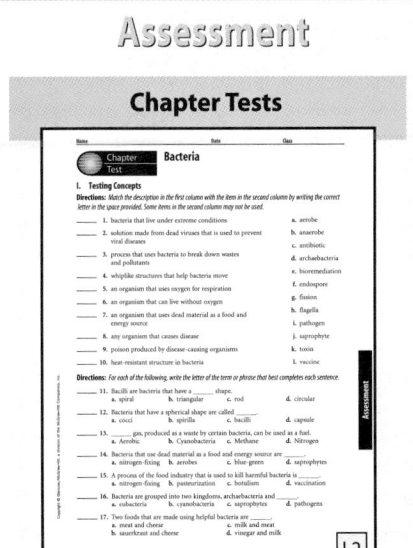

Chapter Test — **Bacteria**

I. Testing Concepts

L2

Test Practice Workbook

Standardized Test Practice
Teacher Edition

Glencoe **Science**

LEVEL RED

L2

Chapter Review

Chapter Review — **Bacteria**

Part A. Vocabulary Review

L2

Science Content Background

SECTION 1

What are bacteria?
Characteristics

The sizes of bacteria are genetically determined and are measured in microns—1 micron (mμ)= 0.001 mm. Most bacteria range from 0.2mμ to 2mμ in width and from 2 mμ to 8mμ in length. Bacteria generally have a rigid cell wall that maintains the shape of the organism. Bacterial cell walls prevent cells from bursting in environments where the pressure in the cell is greater than the pressure in the surrounding medium or fluid. Bacterial cells usually die in environments where the external pressure is greater than the pressure in the cell.

Bacteria have three basic shapes. Unlike the rod-shaped bacilli (singular, *bacillus*) and helical spirillia (singular, *spirillum*), the spherical cocci (singular, *coccus*) never possess flagella.

Fun Fact

In the late 1970s and 1980s, Carl Woese studied bacteria classification by examining sequences of genetic mutations. He determined that archaebacteria are more closely related to animals, plants, and fungi than to other bacteria.

Eubacteria

Most named bacteria are members of Kingdom Eubacteria. The five major phylogenetic groups of eubacteria are based on comparisons of their ribosomal RNA.

Cyanobacteria, formerly called blue-green algae, are bacteria that contain chlorophyll, enabling them to make their own food. This process is different from photosynthesis in plants. These organisms probably produced most of the original free oxygen in the atmosphere about 2.5 billion years ago. Cyanobacteria may be unicellular or colonial. Most live in freshwater, but some are symbiotic with fungi to form lichens.

Reproduction

Most bacteria reproduce by a process of cell division known as binary fission. In binary fission, the one or more circular chromosomes of the bacterial cell are duplicated. The duplicated chromosomes attach to the cell membrane. Continued growth of the cell separates the chromosomes, and the cell membrane eventually pinches in two as a cell wall is deposited between the daughter cells.

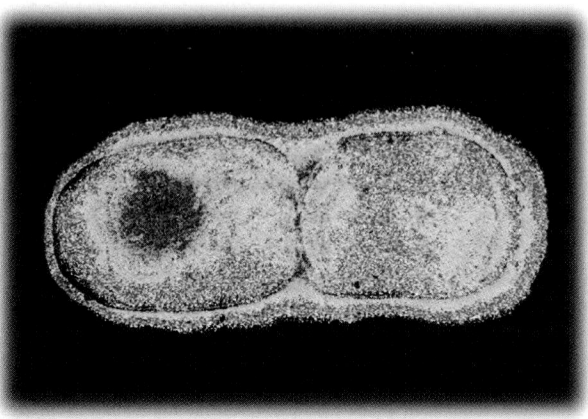

George Musil/Visuals Unlimited

SECTION 2

Bacteria in Your Life
Beneficial Bacteria

Prokaryotes have a large impact on ecology. They and fungi are the organisms primarily responsible for the decay and recycling of materials. Of these materials, carbon and nitrogen are essential.

Nitrogen gas can be used as a source of nitrogen only by some eubacteria, including cyanobacteria. These organisms not only remove nitrogen from the air for their own use, but also change the nitrogen into compounds other organisms can use. This is important, because nitrogen is necessary in order for plants and animals to make amino acids and nucleic acids. Because the nitrogen content of the environment varies considerably in quantity and kinds of nitrogen-containing compounds, it is not surprising that organisms have evolved the ability to utilize more than one nitrogen source.

Antibiotics and Vaccines

An antibiotic is a chemical that is able to kill or inhibit the growth of a microorganism. Thousands of antibiotics are known, but only a

Fun Fact

In 1939, Rene Dubos isolated the antibiotic tyrothricin from soil bacteria. This was the first antibiotic to be used successfully to treat a human disease.

few have practical uses. Many types of microorganisms including bacteria, protists, and fungi, produce antibiotics.

The action of an antibiotic is dependent on its chemical structure. Certain antibiotics affect cell wall synthesis or destroy cell membrane permeability. Others act by inhibiting protein synthesis by causing the wrong amino acid to be inserted into the growing polypeptide chain of proteins in ribosomes. Broad spectrum antibiotics act on many different kinds of organisms. Some antibiotics, such as penicillin, act only on prokaryotes. Other antibiotics, such as cycloheximide, are active against eukaryotes but not prokaryotes.

VCG/FPG International

Vaccines, on the other hand, are specific to certain bacteria or viruses. This is because a vaccine is made of damaged or killed bacterial cells or viruses. The white blood cells learn to recognize these pathogens and can respond quickly when they enter the body. It is important to note that antibiotics are taken after a bacterial pathogen enters the body, whereas a vaccine is a preventive measure.

tion does not kill all the microbes present and should not be confused with sterilization, which uses high heat and pressure to kill all bacteria. Although pasteurization was originally used to kill organisms that cause tuberculosis, typhoid, and brucellosis, today it is used to increase the shelf life of milk.

Pasteurization

Pasteurization is achieved by passing milk continuously through a heat exchanger where its temperature quickly is raised to 71.6°C, held at that temperature for 15 s, and then quickly cooled. The process, named for Louis Pasteur, was first used to control spoilage of wine and saved the wine industry in France. Pasteuriza-

SCIENCE Online

For additional content background on this topic, go to the Glencoe Science Web site at science.glencoe.com.

Bacteria

Chapter Vocabulary

What do you think?

Science Journal The photo shows bacteria on the surface of a protist. Bacteria live on surfaces or within the cells of organisms.

Bacteria

I magine a world of such small scale that a powerful microscope is needed to see the organisms that live there. What effects do these small organisms, some of which are bacteria, have on living things including you? In this chapter you will find the answer to this question. You also will read about many of the ways humans use bacteria, such as for composting. In addition, you will learn how the unique characteristics of bacteria help them live in almost every environment.

What do you think?

Science Journal Look at the picture below with a classmate. Discuss what you think this might be or what is happening. Here's a hint: *Bacteria can live on the surface of other organisms.* Write your answer or best guess in your Science Journal.

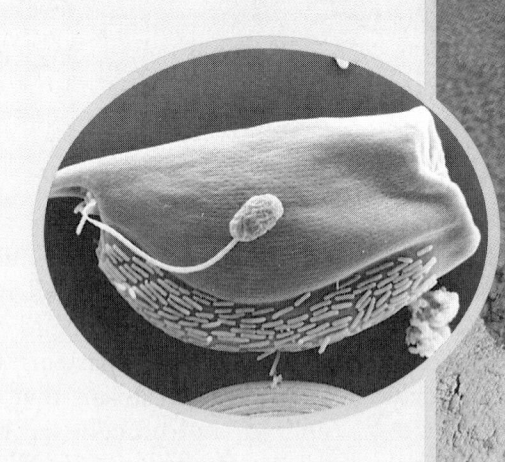

58

Theme Connection

Systems and Interactions The role of bacteria in maintaining a homeostatic balance is discussed. In addition to homeostasis, the ecological importance of bacteria is illustrated by using examples of niches filled by these organisms.

EXPLORE ACTIVITY

B acterial cells have a gelatinlike, protective coating on the outside of their cell walls. In some cases, the coating is thin and is referred to as a slime layer. A slime layer helps a bacterium attach to other surfaces. Dental plaque forms when bacteria with slime layers stick to teeth and multiply there. A slime layer also can reduce water loss from a bacterium. In this activity you will make a model of a bacterium's slime layer.

Model a bacterium's slime layer

1. Cut two 2-cm-wide strips from the long side of a synthetic kitchen sponge.
2. Soak both strips in water. Remove them from the water and squeeze out the excess water. Both strips should be damp.
3. Completely coat one strip with hair-styling gel. Do not coat the other strip.
4. Place both strips on a plate (not paper) and leave them overnight.

Observe

The next day, record your observations of the two sponge strips in your Science Journal. Infer how a slime layer protects a bacterial cell from drying out. What environmental conditions are best for survival of bacteria?

Before You Read

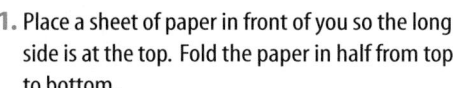

Making a Venn Diagram Study Fold **Make the following Foldable to compare and contrast the characteristics of bacteria.**

1. Place a sheet of paper in front of you so the long side is at the top. Fold the paper in half from top to bottom.
2. Fold both sides in. Unfold the paper so three sections show.

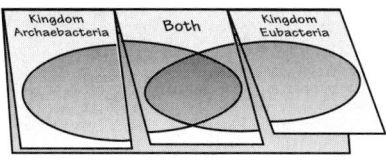

3. Through the top thickness of paper, cut along each of the fold lines to the topfold, forming three tabs. Label the tabs *Kingdom Archaebacteria, Both,* and *Kingdom Eubacteria.* Draw ovals on the front of the paper as shown.
4. As you read the chapter, list characteristics of each kingdom of bacteria under the tabs.

59

Purpose Use this Explore Activity to help students discover how the slime layer surrounding bacterial cells helps protect them from dehydration. [L2]

IS Kinesthetic

Preparation Collect kitchen sponges, plates, and hair styling gel. Locate areas where students can leave their sponges overnight.

Materials synthetic kitchen sponge; scissors; water; hair styling gel; plate

Teaching Strategy Have students do this activity the day before you introduce the topic of bacteria slime layers. Use the activity to demonstrate the properties of a slime layer.

Observe

Students should find that the gel-treated sponge is still damp and adheres to the plate. The untreated sponge will have dried out. A slime layer seals moisture inside the bacteria cell. Bacteria cells thrive in moist, damp environmental conditions.

Assessment

Process Ask students to infer how Earth's nutrient cycles would be affected if bacteria cells did not have slime layers. Bacteria decompose dead and decaying materials into nutrients. Slime layers allow bacteria to lie dormant during drier conditions. Without slime layers, fewer bacteria would survive dry conditions, which would result in fewer nutrients being recycled. Use **PASC,** p. 89.

Before You Read

FOLDABLES Reading & Study Skills

Dinah Zike Study Fold

Purpose Have students use a Foldable Venn diagram to determine what they know about bacteria in general and to record similarities and differences between the two kingdoms of bacteria.

For additional help, see Foldables Worksheet, p. 13 in **Chapter Resources Booklet,** or go to the Glencoe Science Web site at **science.glencoe.com.** See After You Read in the Study Guide at the end of this chapter.

1 Motivate

Bellringer Transparency

Display the Section Focus Transparency for Section 1. Use the accompanying Transparency Activity Master. **L2**
ELL

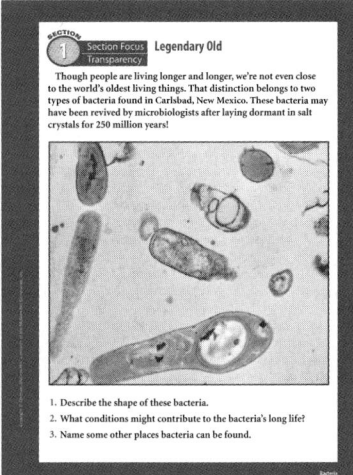

Tie to Prior Knowledge

Review with students the characteristics of living things. Emphasize that bacterial cells have all of these characteristics, although they are smaller than the more familiar cells of plants and animals.

Caption Answer

Figure 1 sphere, rod, and spiral

Resource Manager

Chapter Resources Booklet
Transparency Activity, p. 38
MiniLAB, p. 3
Directed Reading, pp. 15, 16

As You Read

What You'll Learn
- **Identify** the characteristics of bacterial cells.
- **Compare and contrast** aerobic and anaerobic organisms.

Vocabulary
flagella   aerobe
fission   anaerobe

Why It's Important
Bacteria are found in almost all environments and affect all living things.

Figure 1
A Coccus-, **B** bacillus-, and **C** spirillum-shaped bacteria can be found in almost any environment. *What common terms could be used to describe these cell shapes?*

Characteristics of Bacteria

For thousands of years people did not understand what caused disease. They did not understand the process of decomposition or what happened when food spoiled. It wasn't until the latter half of the seventeenth century that Antonie van Leeuwenhoek, a Dutch merchant, discovered the world of bacteria. Leeuwenhoek observed scrapings from his teeth using his simple microscope. Although he didn't know it at that time, some of the tiny swimming organisms he observed were bacteria. After Leeuwenhoek's discovery, it was another hundred years before bacteria were proven to be living cells that carry on all of the processes of life.

Where do bacteria live? Bacteria are almost everywhere—in the air, in foods that you eat and drink, and on the surfaces of things you touch. They are even found thousands of meters underground and at great ocean depths. A shovelful of soil contains billions of them. Your skin has about 100,000 bacteria per square centimeter, and millions of other bacteria live in your body. Some types of bacteria live in extreme environments where few other organisms can survive. Some heat-loving bacteria live in hot springs or hydrothermal vents—places where water temperature exceeds 100°C. Others can live in cold water or soil at 0°C. Some bacteria live in very salty water, like that of the Dead Sea. One type of bacteria lives in water that drains from coal mines, which is extremely acidic at a pH of 1.

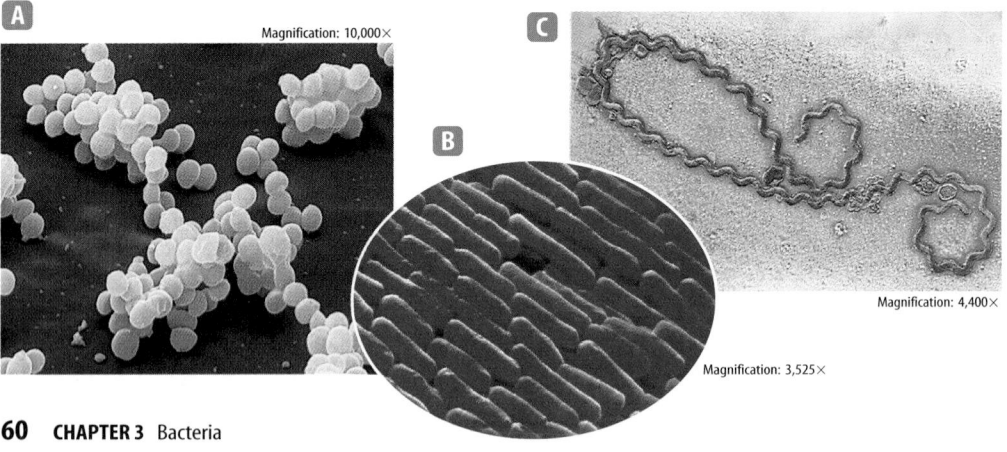

Magnification: 10,000×
Magnification: 4,400×
Magnification: 3,525×

60 CHAPTER 3 Bacteria

Section ✔*Assessment* Planner

PORTFOLIO
Science Journal, p. 63
PERFORMANCE ASSESSMENT
Try at Home MiniLAB, p. 61
Skill Builder Activities, p. 65
See page 80 for more options.

CONTENT ASSESSMENT
Section, p. 61
Challenge, p. 61
Chapter, pp. 80–81

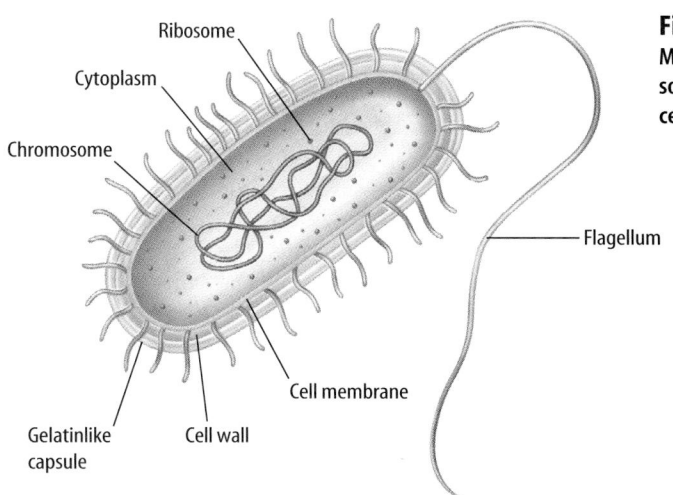

Ribosome

Cytoplasm

Chromosome

Gelatinlike capsule

Cell wall

Cell membrane

Flagellum

Figure 2
Most bacteria are about the size of some organelles found inside other cell types.

Structure of Bacterial Cells Bacteria normally have three basic shapes—spheres, rods, and spirals, as shown in **Figure 1.** Sphere-shaped bacteria are called cocci (KAH ki) (singular, *coccus*), rod-shaped bacteria are called bacilli (buh SIH li) (singular, *bacillus*), and spiral-shaped bacteria are called spirilla (spi RIH luh) (singular, *spirillum*). Bacteria are smaller than plant or animal cells. They are one-celled organisms that occur alone or in chains or groups.

A typical bacterial cell contains cytoplasm surrounded by a cell membrane and a cell wall, as shown in **Figure 2.** Bacterial cells are classified as prokaryotic because they do not contain a membrane-bound nucleus or other membrane-bound internal structures called organelles. Most of the genetic material of a bacterial cell is in its one circular chromosome found in the cytoplasm. Many bacteria also have a smaller circular piece of DNA called a plasmid. Ribosomes also are found in a bacterial cell's cytoplasm.

Special Features Some bacteria, like the type that causes pneumonia, have a thick, gelatinlike capsule around the cell wall. A capsule can help protect the bacterium from other cells that try to destroy it. The capsule, along with hairlike projections found on the surface of many bacteria, also can help them stick to surfaces. Some bacteria also have an outer coating called a slime layer. Like a capsule, a slime layer allows a bacterium to stick to surfaces and reduces water loss. Many bacteria that live in moist conditions also have whiplike tails called **flagella** to help them move.

✔ **Reading Check**   *How do bacteria use flagella?*

TRY AT HOME

Mini LAB

Modeling Bacteria Size

1. One human hair is about 0.1 mm wide. Use a **meterstick** to measure a piece of **yarn or string** that is 10 m long. This yarn represents the width of your hair.
2. One type of bacteria is 2 micrometers long (1 micrometer = 0.000001 m). Measure another piece of yarn or string that is 20 cm long. This piece represents the length of the bacterium.
3. Find a large area where you can lay the two pieces of yarn or string next to each other and compare them.

Analysis

1. How much smaller is the bacterium than the width of your hair?
2. In your **Science Journal** describe why a model is helpful to understand how small bacteria are.

---

2 Teach

Characteristics of Bacteria

Visual Learning

Figure 1 Emphasize that bacteria have three-dimensional shapes. Ask students to name common objects that are similar in shape to bacteria. Balls are similar to cocci, lengths of thick wire are similar to bacilli, and wire spirals on notebooks are similar to spirilla. **Figure 2** Emphasize that bacterial cells are small. Compare the size of a bacterium to another object you have studied. Chloroplasts and mitochondria are about the same size as a bacterium.

TRY AT HOME

Mini LAB

Purpose to model the size of bacterial cells ⃞ **Visual-Spatial**

Materials 11 m of yarn or string; meterstick

Teaching Strategy Have students compare the size of bacteria with viruses. The diameter of the average virus is 100 nm, or 0.0000001 m, which is 10 times smaller than the average bacteria.

Analysis

1. 50 times smaller
2. Using models for size comparison allows one to understand the actual size of a bacterium.

Curriculum Connection

Math Ask students whether they would rather have $10 every 20 minutes for 13 hours or start with one penny and have their money doubled every 20 minutes for 13 hours. $400 by arithmetic growth or more than $5 trillion by exponential growth Point out that the growth rate of bacteria is like that of the penny. L2 ⃞ **Logical-Mathematical**

✔ Assessment

Oral Explain how the size of bacteria contributes to the spread of infection. Their small size allows them to be transferred through the air when a person sneezes or coughs. Use **PASC**, p. 89.

✔ Reading Check

Answer to help them move

Fun Fact

Fission is also called binary fission. Binary fission is a quick and efficient means of producing many cells to utilize an energy resource.

Make a Model

Have students use objects from home to make a model of bacteria undergoing fission. For instance, two golf balls could be used to model fission in cocci. L1 IS **Kinesthetic**

Discussion

Have groups of students discuss the possible combinations of cocci, such as pairs (diplococci), strands (streptococci), and clusters (staphylococci). Explain that different species of bacteria assume all these shapes. L2 COOP LEARN
IS **Interpersonal**

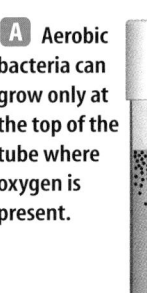

Magnification: 500×

Figure 3
Before dividing, these bacteria are exchanging DNA through the tubes that join them.

Reproduction Bacteria usually reproduce by fission. **Fission** is a process that produces two new cells with genetic material identical to each other and that of the original cell. It is the simplest form of asexual reproduction.

Some bacteria exchange genetic material through a process similar to sexual reproduction, as shown in **Figure 3.** Two bacteria line up beside each other and exchange DNA through a fine tube. This results in cells with different combinations of genetic material than they had before the exchange. As a result, the bacteria may acquire variations that give them an advantage for survival.

How Bacteria Obtain Food and Energy Bacteria obtain food in a variety of ways. Some make their food and others get it from the environment. Bacteria that contain chlorophyll or other pigments make their own food using energy from the Sun. Other bacteria use energy from chemical reactions to make food. Bacteria and other organisms that can make their own food are called producers.

Most bacteria are consumers. They do not make their own food. Some break down dead organisms to obtain energy. Others live as parasites of living organisms and absorb nutrients from their host.

Most organisms use oxygen when they break down food and obtain energy through a process called respiration. An organism that uses oxygen for respiration is called an **aerobe** (AY rohb). You are an aerobic organism and so are most bacteria. In contrast, an organism that is adapted to live without oxygen is called an **anaerobe** (AN uh rohb). Several kinds of anaerobic bacteria live in the intestinal tract of humans. Some bacteria, like those in **Figure 4B,** cannot survive in areas with oxygen.

Figure 4
Observing where bacteria can grow in tubes of a nutrient mixture shows you how oxygen affects different types of bacteria.

A Aerobic bacteria can grow only at the top of the tube where oxygen is present.

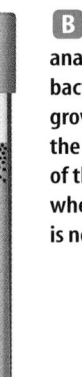

B Some anaerobic bacteria will grow only at the bottom of the tube where there is no oxygen.

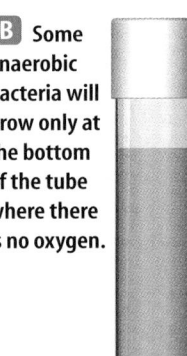

C Other anaerobic bacteria can grow in areas with or without oxygen.

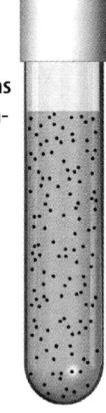

Inclusion Strategies

Learning Disabled Have pairs of students create flash cards that have the vocabulary for this chapter on one side and the definitions on the other. Allow students to practice using the vocabulary with their flash cards until they show proficiency with the terms. Students can also use flash cards to learn the names or structures of bacteria. L1 IS **Linguistic**

Teacher FYI

Leeuwenhoek was probably not the first person to observe bacteria, but he was the first to keep convincingly accurate records of his microscopic observations. He was also the first to show fission in cells.

Figure 5

Figure 5
Many different bacteria can live in the intestines of humans and other animals. They often are identified based on the foods they use and the wastes they produce.

Can they use lactose as a food?

No → Can they use citric acid as their only carbon source?

Yes → Can they use citric acid as their only carbon source?

No → Magnification: 3,500× — *Shigella*

Yes → Magnification: 6,000× — *Salmonella*

No → Magnification: 3,600× — *Escherichia*

Yes → Do they produce acetoin as a waste?

No → Magnification: 750× — *Citrobacter*

Yes → Magnification: 4,000× — *Enterobacter*

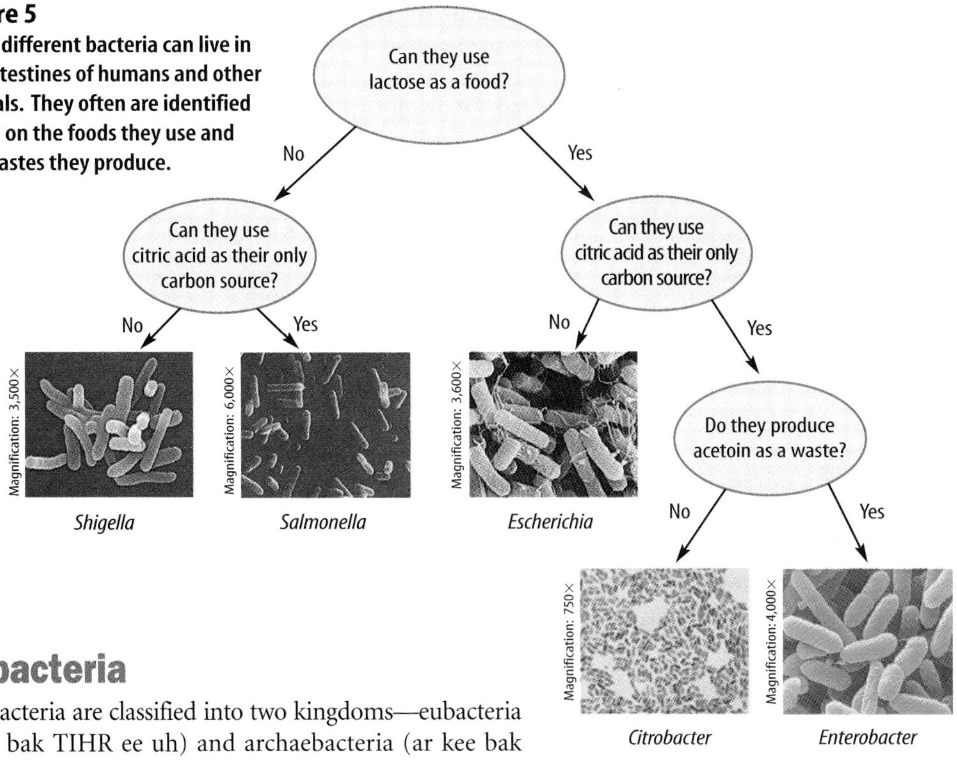

Eubacteria

Bacteria are classified into two kingdoms—eubacteria (yew bak TIHR ee uh) and archaebacteria (ar kee bak TIHR ee uh). Eubacteria is the larger of the two kingdoms. The organisms in this kingdom are diverse, and scientists must study many characteristics in order to classify eubacteria into smaller groups. Most eubacteria are grouped according to their cell shape and structure, the way they obtain food, the type of food they eat, and the wastes they produce, as shown in **Figure 5.** Other characteristics used to group eubacteria include the method used for cell movement and whether the organism is an aerobe or anaerobe. New information about their genetic material is changing how scientists classify this kingdom.

Producer Eubacteria One important group of producer eubacteria is the cyanobacteria (si an oh bak TIHR ee uh). They make their own food using carbon dioxide, water, and energy from sunlight. They also produce oxygen as a waste. Cyanobacteria contain chlorophyll and another pigment that is blue. This pigment combination gives cyanobacteria their common name—blue-green bacteria. However, some cyanobacteria are yellow, black, or red. The Red Sea gets its name from red cyanobacteria.

✔ Reading Check *Why are cyanobacteria classified as producers?*

SCIENCE Online

Research Not all producer eubacteria use photosynthesis. Visit the Glencoe Science Web site at **science. glencoe.com** for more information about the ways that producer bacteria make food. Communicate to your class what you learn.

SECTION 1 What are bacteria? **63**

Section 1 What are bacteria? **63**

Visual Learning

Figure 5 After discussing the phylogeny of bacteria, explain to students that phylogeny is based on the theory that organisms change over time and on their characteristics. Ask if these bacteria could ever be re-grouped. Yes, organisms are often re-classified as new information is gained.

Use Science Words

Word Usage Have students use the words *aerobe* and *anaerobe* in sentences. An aerobe is a bacterium that requires oxygen. An anaerobe is a bacterium that lives without oxygen.
L2 IS **Linguistic**

Eubacteria

Use Science Words

Word Origin The word *eubacteria* comes from the Greek words *eys*, meaning "good" and *bakterion*, meaning "staff." **Which group of eubacteria gave them their name?** bacilli

✔ Reading Check

Answer They make their own food.

SCIENCE Online
Internet Addresses

_____
_____
_____
_____

Explore the Glencoe Science Web site at **science.glencoe.com** to find out more about topics in this section.

Resource Manager

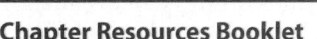

Chapter Resources Booklet
Enrichment, p. 25
Note-taking Worksheets, pp. 27–28
Transparency Activity, pp. 41–43

Science Journal

Bacteria in the News Ask students to find at least three newspaper or magazine articles that mention bacteria. Have them read the articles and then use **Figure 5** to classify the bacteria in the article. Have them write a paragraph about each bacteria, justifying their classification. L2
IS **Linguistic** P

Activity

Have students make a wet mount to observe *Oscillatoria*. Point out that swaying movements are made as the bacteria secrete a slimy substance from their cells. L2 IS **Visual-Spatial**

Earth Science
INTEGRATION

Ocean vents form where two of Earth's tectonic plates are splitting apart. The conditions are hypothesized to be similar to those on early Earth. Some organisms that live near ocean vents include tube worms, clams, mussels, and bacteria.

Caption Answer

Figure 7 thick if the cells are purple or thin if the cells are pink

Quick Demo

Demonstrate the classification of bacteria through staining by allowing students to view commercially prepared slides of gram-positive and gram-negative organisms. L2 IS **Visual-Spatial**

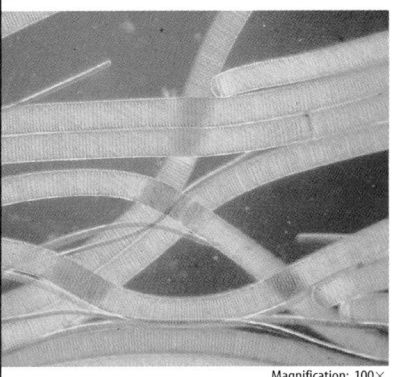

Magnification: 100×

Figure 6
These colonies of the cyanobacteria *Oscillatoria* can move by twisting like a screw.

Earth Science
INTEGRATION

Ocean vents are geysers on the floor of the ocean. Research and find out how ocean vents form and what conditions are like at an ocean vent. In your Science Journal, describe organisms that have been found living around ocean vents.

Figure 7
When stained with certain chemicals, bacteria with thin cell walls appear pink when viewed under a microscope. Those with thicker cell walls appear purple. *What type of cell walls do the coccus bacteria in this photo have?*

64 CHAPTER 3 Bacteria

Importance of Cyanobacteria Some cyanobacteria live together in long chains or filaments, as shown in **Figure 6.** Many are covered with a gelatinlike substance. This adaptation enables cyanobacteria to live in groups called colonies. They are an important source of food for some organisms in lakes, ponds, and oceans. The oxygen produced by cyanobacteria is used by all other aquatic organisms.

Cyanobacteria also can cause problems for aquatic life. Have you ever seen a pond covered with smelly, green, bubbly slime? When large amounts of nutrients enter a pond, cyanobacteria increase in number. Eventually the population grows so large that a bloom is produced. A bloom looks like a mat of bubbly green slime on the surface of the water. Available resources in the water are used up quickly and the cyanobacteria die. Other bacteria that are aerobic consumers feed on dead cyanobacteria and use up the oxygen in the water. As a result of the reduced oxygen in the water, fish and other organisms die.

Consumer Eubacteria Many of the consumer eubacteria are grouped by the type of cell wall produced—a thick cell wall or a thinner cell wall. This difference can be seen under a microscope after they are treated with certain chemicals that are called stains. As shown in **Figure 7,** thick-cell-walled bacteria stain a different color than thin-cell-walled bacteria.

The composition of the cell wall also can affect how a bacterium is affected by medicines given to treat an infection. Some medicines will be more effective against the type of bacteria with thicker cell walls than they will be against bacteria with thinner cell walls.

One group of eubacteria is unique because they do not produce cell walls. This allows them to change their shape. They are not described as coccus, bacillus, or spirillum. One type of bacteria in this group, *Mycoplasma pneumoniae*, causes a type of pneumonia in humans.

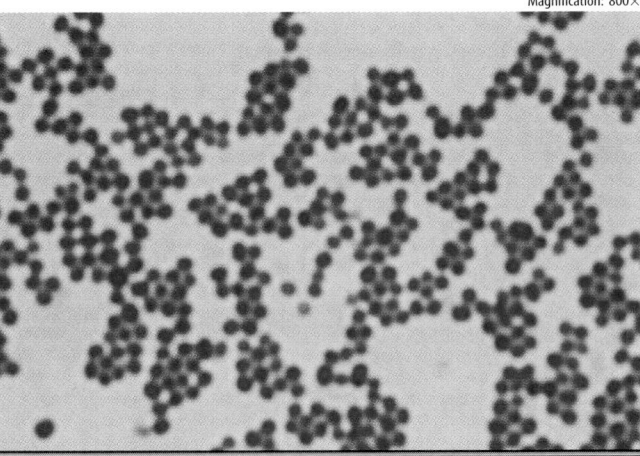

Magnification: 800×

Inclusion Strategies

Learning Disabled If possible, bring in some pond water that has a mat of cyanobacteria on it. Place the mat in the light and ask what the bubbles are that appear in the mat. They are oxygen bubbles produced by photosynthesis. Then ask how large numbers of cyanobacteria can cause problems. When cyanobacteria die and decompose, oxygen levels drop. This can cause other organisms, such as fish, to die. L1
IS **Visual-Spatial**

✔ Active Reading

Buddy Interviews This strategy helps students understand and clarify the reading. Have students interview one another to find out what helps them to understand what they are reading, how they find answers, and how they assimilate new vocabulary terms. Have students use Buddy Interviews to help them master concepts about bacteria.

Archaebacteria

Kingdom Archaebacteria contains certain kinds of bacteria that often are found in extreme conditions, such as hot springs. The conditions in which some archaebacteria live today are similar to conditions found on Earth during its early history. Archaebacteria are divided into groups based on where they live or how they get energy.

Salt-, Heat-, and Acid-Lovers One group of archaebacteria lives in salty environments such as the Great Salt Lake in Utah and the Dead Sea. Some of them require a habitat ten times saltier than seawater to grow.

Other groups of archaebacteria include those that live in acidic or hot environments. Some of these bacteria live near deep ocean vents or in hot springs where the temperature of the water is above 100°C.

Methane Producers Bacteria in this group of archaebacteria are anaerobic. They live in muddy swamps, the intestines of cattle, and even in you. Methane producers, as shown in **Figure 8,** use carbon dioxide for energy and release methane gas as a waste. Sometimes methane produced by these bacteria bubbles up out of swamps and marshes. These archaebacteria also are used in the process of sewage treatment. In an oxygen-free tank, the bacteria are used to break down the waste material that has been filtered from sewage water.

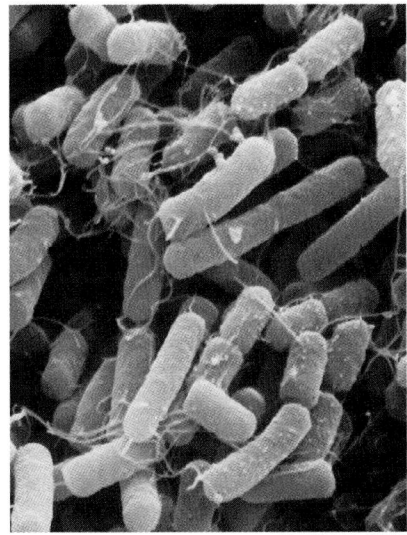

Magnification: 4,200×

Figure 8
Some methane-producing bacteria live in the digestive tracts of cattle. They help digest the plants that cattle eat.

Section ① Assessment

1. What are the characteristics common to all bacteria?
2. How do aerobic organisms and anaerobic organisms differ?
3. How do most bacteria reproduce?
4. Who is given credit for first discovering bacteria?
5. **Think Critically** A pond is surrounded by recently fertilized farm fields. What effect would rainwater runoff from the fields have on the organisms in the pond?

Skill Builder Activities

6. **Classifying** A scientist recently found bacteria that grow in boiling water. In what kingdom is the bacteria most likely classified? Why? **For more help, refer to the** Science Skill Handbook.
7. **Solving One-Step Equations** Some bacteria reproduce every 20 min. Suppose that you have one bacterium. How long would it take for the number of bacteria to increase to more than 1 million? **For more help, refer to the** Math Skill Handbook.

Answers to Section Assessment

1. one-celled; cytoplasm surrounded by cell membrane and cell wall; single circular chromosome; ribosomes in cytoplasm; plasmid; no membrane-bound organelles
2. Aerobic: require oxygen to live; anaerobic: can live without oxygen. Oxygen kills some anaerobes.
3. Fission; some bacteria also exchange

genetic material in a process similar to sexual reproduction.
4. Antonie van Leeuwenhoek
5. It could potentially kill the pond organisms as cyanobacteria flourish, die, and decompose.

6. Kingdom Archaebacteria; these organisms often live in harsh conditions.
7. 6 hours and 40 minutes (1,048,576 bacteria)

Purpose to observe and record the characteristics of several cyanobacteria L2 ELL

IS Naturalist

Process Skills observing, classifying, interpreting data

Time Required 50 minutes

Alternate Materials In addition to the cyanobacteria listed, many others can be found in biological supply house catalogs.

Teaching Strategy Having prepared slides for use will be more interesting and visually stimulating for students than having them look at pictures.

Troubleshooting If students have trouble seeing the jellylike layer of the capsule, have them reduce the amount of light coming through the microscope's diaphragm.

Answers to Questions

1. You can infer that they are producers that carry on photosynthesis.
2. Cyanobacteria contain chlorophyll, which makes them photosynthetic eubacteria.

Assessment

Performance Have students draw, label, and describe different cyanobacteria they observe. Use **Performance Assessment in the Science Classroom,** p. 127.

Activity

Observing Cyanobacteria

You can obtain many species of cyanobacteria from ponds. When you look at these organisms under a microscope, you will find that they have similarities and differences. In this activity, compare and contrast species of cyanobacteria.

What You'll Investigate
What do cyanobacteria look like?

Materials
micrograph photos of *Oscillatoria* and *Nostoc*
prepared slides of Oscillatoria *and* Nostoc
prepared slides of *Gloeocapsa* and *Anabaena*
micrograph photos of Anabaena *and* Gloeocapsa
microscope
Alternate materials

Goals
■ **Observe** several species of cyanobacteria.
■ **Describe** the structure and function of cyanobacteria.

Safety Precautions 🥽 👕 🔬

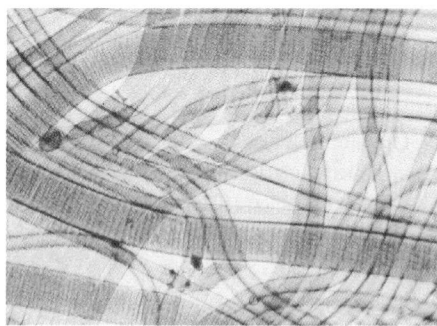

Cyanobacteria Observations

Structure	*Anabaena*	*Gloeocapsa*	*Nostoc*	*Oscillatoria*
Filament or Colony	filament	colony	filament	filament
Nucleus	no	no	no	no
Chlorophyll	yes	yes	yes	yes
Gel-Like Layer	yes	yes	yes	yes

Procedure

1. Copy the data table in your Science Journal. **Record** the presence or absence of each characteristic in the data table for each cyanobacterium you observe.

2. **Observe** prepared slides of *Gloeocapsa* and *Anabaena* under low and high power of the microscope. Notice the difference in the arrangement of the cells. In your Science Journal, draw and label a few cells of each.

3. **Observe** photos of *Nostoc* and *Oscillatoria.* In your Science Journal, draw and label a few cells of each.

Conclude and Apply

1. What can you infer from the color of each cyanobacterium?

2. How can you tell by observing that a cyanobacterium is a eubacterium?

Communicating
Your Data

Compare your data table with those of other students in your class. **For more help, refer to the** Science Skill Handbook.

Communicating
Your Data

Data tables should be the same for all students. Students who have differences should be prepared to explain them to others.

Resource Manager

Chapter Resources Booklet
Activity Worksheet, pp. 5–6

2 Bacteria in Your Life

Beneficial Bacteria

When most people hear the word *bacteria*, they probably associate it with sore throats or other illnesses. However, few bacteria cause illness. Most are important for other reasons. The benefits of most bacteria far outweigh the harmful effects of a few.

Bacteria That Help You Without bacteria, you would not be healthy for long. Bacteria, like those in **Figure 9,** are found inside your digestive system. These bacteria are found in particularly high numbers in your large intestine. Most are harmless to you, and they help you stay healthy. For example, the bacteria in your intestines are responsible for producing vitamin K, which is necessary for normal blood clot formation.

Some bacteria produce chemicals called **antibiotics** that limit the growth of other bacteria. For example, one type of bacteria that is commonly found living in soil produces the antibiotic streptomycin. Another kind of bacteria, *Bacillus,* produces the antibiotic found in many nonprescription antiseptic ointments. Many diseases in humans and animals can be treated with antibiotics.

As You Read

What You'll Learn
- **Identify** some ways bacteria are helpful.
- **Determine** the importance of nitrogen-fixing bacteria.
- **Explain** how some bacteria can cause human disease.

Vocabulary
antibiotic   toxin
saprophyte   endospore
nitrogen-fixing bacteria vaccine
pathogen

Why It's Important
Discovering the ways bacteria affect your life can help you understand biological processes.

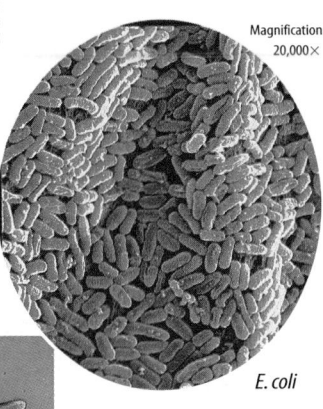

Magnification: 250×
Lactobacillus

Magnification: 11,000×
Klebsiella

Magnification: 20,000×

Proteus
Magnification: 1,000×

Fusobacterium
Magnification: 3,000×

E. coli

Figure 9
Many types of bacteria live naturally in your large intestine. They help you digest food and produce vitamins that you need.

SECTION 2 Bacteria in Your Life **67**

SECTION

2 Bacteria in Your Life

1 Motivate

Bellringer Transparency
Display the Section Focus Transparency for Section 2. Use the accompanying Transparency Activity Master. L2
ELL

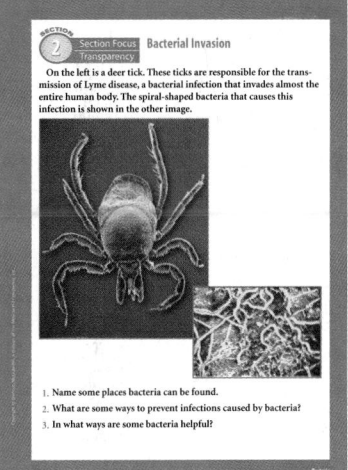

Tie to Prior Knowledge
Ask students if they have ever had a sore throat or eaten cheese. Explain that both of these experiences involve bacteria. In this section, they will learn about beneficial and harmful bacteria.

Section ✓Assessment Planner

PORTFOLIO
Cultural Diversity, p. 68
Science Journal, p. 72
PERFORMANCE ASSESSMENT
MiniLAB, p. 68
Skill Builder Activities, p. 73
See page 80 for more options.

CONTENT ASSESSMENT
Section, p. 73
Challenge, p. 73
Chapter, pp. 80–81

Beneficial Bacteria

Caption Answer

Figure 10 aerobes

☑ **Reading Check**

Answer an organism that uses dead material as a food and energy source

Mini LAB

Purpose to observe and infer the growth rate of bacteria [L1]
[ELL] [COOP LEARN] [IS] **Kinesthetic**

Materials dried beans, distilled water, glass beaker

Teaching Strategies

• You may want to soak the beans for 24 hours prior to doing the lab, as this makes it easier for students to break them apart.

• Point out that the water's cloudiness indicates bacterial growth.

Safety Precautions Tell students to wash their hands after handling the materials and not to eat any of them.

Troubleshooting To avoid odors, caution students not to leave the beans and water in the classroom for more than five days.

Analysis

1. It usually takes 3–4 days.
2. the beans

☑ *Assessment*

Process Have students hypothesize the doubling time of bacterial cells. Then have them design an experiment to test their hypothesis. Use **PASC**, p. 93.

Figure 10
Air is bubbled through the sewage in this aeration tank so that bacteria can break down much of the sewage wastes. *Are the bacteria that live in this tank aerobes or anaerobes?*

Mini LAB

Observing Bacterial Growth

Procedure 🥽 🧤 🚫

1. Obtain two or three **dried beans.**
2. Carefully break them into halves and place the halves into 10 mL of **distilled water** in a **glass beaker.**
3. Observe how many days it takes for the water to become cloudy and develop an unpleasant odor.

Analysis

1. How long did it take for the water to become cloudy?
2. What do you think the bacteria were using as a food source?

Bacteria and the Environment Without bacteria, there would be layers of dead material all over Earth deeper than you are tall. Consumer bacteria called saprophytes (SAP ruh fitz) help maintain nature's balance. A **saprophyte** is any organism that uses dead organisms as food and energy sources. Saprophytic bacteria help recycle nutrients. These nutrients become available for use by other organisms. As shown in **Figure 10,** most sewage-treatment plants use saprophytic aerobic bacteria to break down wastes into carbon dioxide and water.

☑ **Reading Check** *What is a saprophyte?*

Plants and animals must take in nitrogen to make needed proteins and nucleic acids. Animals can eat plants or other animals that contain nitrogen, but plants need to take nitrogen from the soil or air. Although air is about 78 percent nitrogen, neither animals nor plants can use it directly. **Nitrogen-fixing bacteria** change nitrogen from the air into forms that plants and animals can use. The roots of some plants such as peanuts and peas develop structures called nodules that contain nitrogen-fixing bacteria, as shown in **Figure 11.** It is estimated that nitrogen-fixing bacteria save U.S. farmers millions of dollars in fertilizer costs every year. Many of the cyanobacteria also can fix nitrogen and are important in providing nitrogen in usable forms to aquatic organisms.

Bioremediation Using organisms to help clean up or remove environmental pollutants is called bioremediation. One type of bioremediation uses bacteria to break down wastes and pollutants into simpler harmless compounds. Other bacteria use certain pollutants as a food source. Every year about five percent to ten percent of all wastes produced by industry, agriculture, and cities are treated by bioremediation. Sometimes bioremediation is used at the site where chemicals, such as oil, have been spilled. Research continues on ways to make bioremediation a faster process.

Teacher FYI

Bioremediation has been used on a wide variety of organic and toxic compounds. Cleanup of oil spills by bioremediation is likely to increase in the future.

Cultural Diversity

In a Pickle Pickling is a process of food preservation that depends on the chemical process of fermentation and the inhibition of bacterial growth in a highly acidic solution. It is found in the cuisine of many cultures. Have students research different pickling processes and prepare lists of how and what products are pickled in different cultures. [L2] [P]

Figure 11

Although 78 percent of Earth's atmosphere is nitrogen gas (N_2), most living things are unable to use nitrogen in this form. Some bacteria, however, convert N_2 into the ammonium ion (NH_4^+) that organisms can use. This process is called nitrogen fixation. Nitrogen-fixing bacteria in soil can enter the roots of plants, such as beans, peanuts, alfalfa, and peas, as shown in the background photo. The bacteria and the plant form a relationship that benefits both of them.

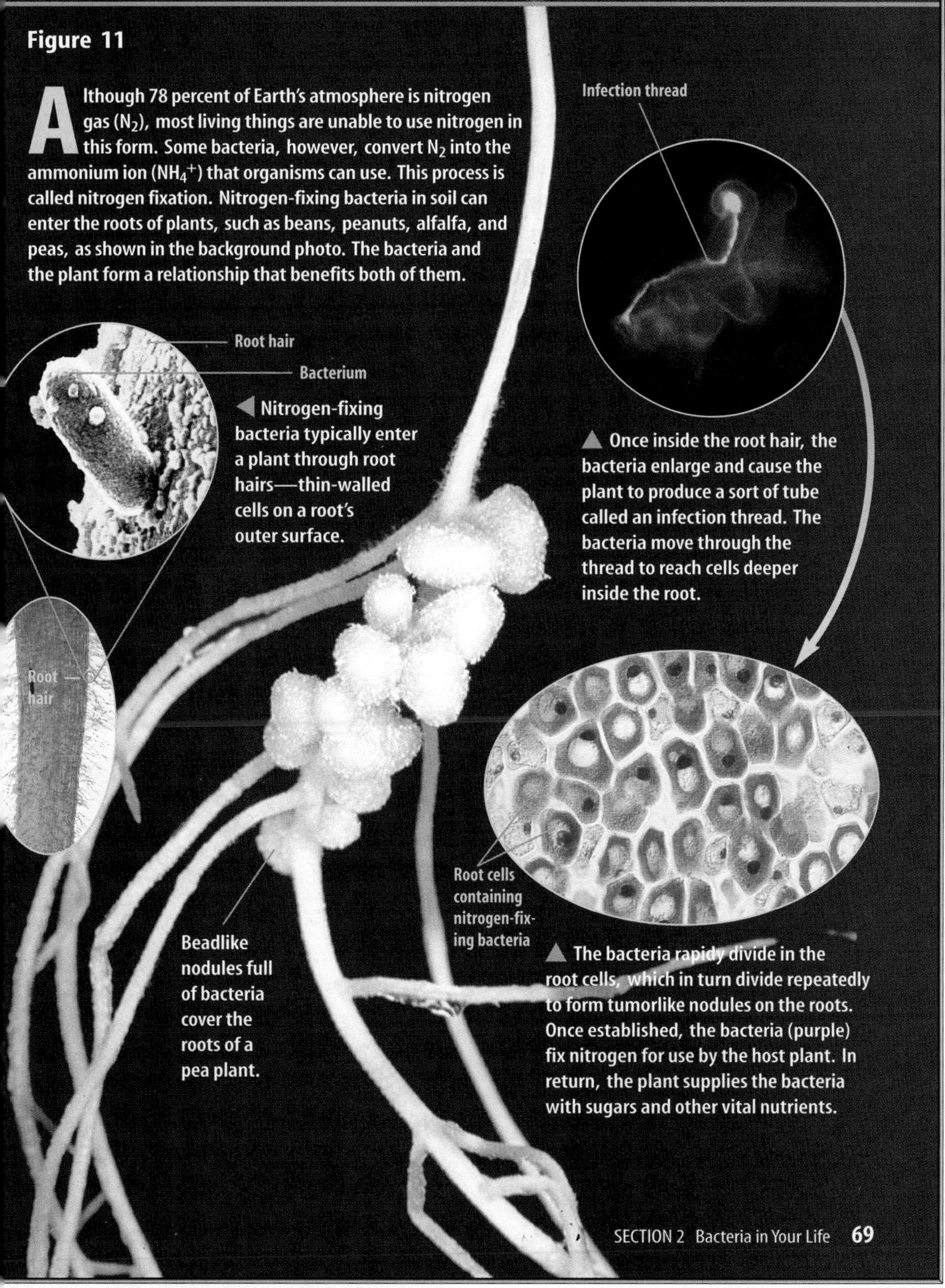

Infection thread

Root hair

Bacterium

◀ Nitrogen-fixing bacteria typically enter a plant through root hairs—thin-walled cells on a root's outer surface.

Root hair

▲ Once inside the root hair, the bacteria enlarge and cause the plant to produce a sort of tube called an infection thread. The bacteria move through the thread to reach cells deeper inside the root.

Beadlike nodules full of bacteria cover the roots of a pea plant.

Root cells containing nitrogen-fixing bacteria

▲ The bacteria rapidly divide in the root cells, which in turn divide repeatedly to form tumorlike nodules on the roots. Once established, the bacteria (purple) fix nitrogen for use by the host plant. In return, the plant supplies the bacteria with sugars and other vital nutrients.

Resource Manager

Chapter Resources Booklet
Transparency Activity, p. 39
MiniLAB, p. 4

Visualizing Nitrogen Fixing Bacteria

Have students examine the pictures and read the captions. Then ask the following questions.

What is the "cost" to a plant for having nitrogen-fixing bacteria in its root cells? The "cost" to the plant is that the carbohydrates it makes are used by the bacteria.

When pea plants are producing peas, the nitrogen fixation of the associated bacteria dips to a low level. What would be a logical explanation for this? When producing peas, the plant has little extra sugar for the bacteria to use, so nitrogen fixation slows.

Activity

Have students model the relationship between plants and nitrogen fixation. Designate each student as either a plant or a nitrogen-fixing bacterium. Plants should carry two index cards, one labeled "sugars" and one labeled "nutrients." Bacteria should carry two index cards, each labeled "NH_4^+." Explain that each student must have one sugar and nutrient card and one NH_4^+ card to survive. Have the students exchange cards to meet their needs. L1 IS **Interpersonal**

Extension

Direct interested students to examine the contents of different brands of garden and lawn fertilizer and infer why nitrogen is an ingredient in most of these products. Nitrogen is needed for plants to grow well. Nitrogen in the form provided by the fertilizers can be absorbed and used by plants.

Beneficial Bacteria,
continued

Chemistry
INTEGRATION

Answers will vary, but most bacteria require a slightly acidic pH.

Science Journal

A Mutualist Relationship
Have students explain in their Science Journals why "infection" of roots by nitrogen-fixing bacteria is beneficial for both plant and environment. Nitrogen gas in the atmosphere is unusable for most organisms. The bacteria fix nitrogen in a form that plants can use. After the plant dies, nitrogen is available for use by other organisms. L2 **IS** **Linguistic**

Visual Learning

Figure 12 Enhance the impact of the photo by having students taste cheese curds. You may also have students bring various cheeses from home to taste. Point out that these foods were prepared by using beneficial bacteria. Caution students who may have food allergies to avoid tasting the cheeses. L1 ELL
IS **Kinesthetic**

Reading Check

Answer methane

Chemistry
INTEGRATION

One condition that must be monitored in a bioreactor is pH, or how acidic the conditions are in the bioreactor. Research and find out what pH levels different bacteria require for growth. In your Science Journal, write a paragraph describing what you find out about bacteria and pH levels.

Figure 12
A When bacteria such as *Streptococcus lactis* are added to milk, it causes the milk to separate into curds (solids) and whey (liquids). **B** Other bacteria are added to the curds, which ripen into cheese. The type of cheese made depends on the bacterial species added to the curds.

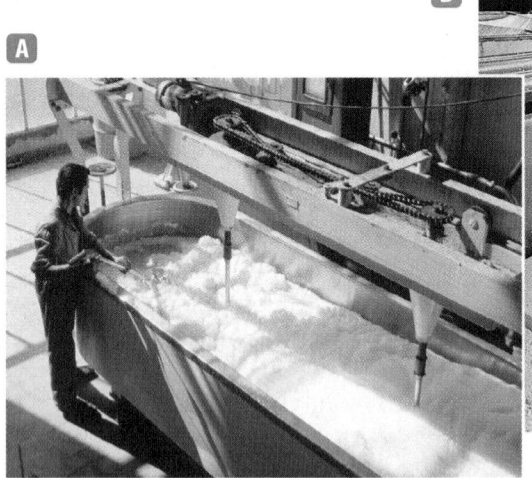
A

Bacteria and Food Have you had any bacteria for lunch lately? Even before people understood that bacteria were involved, they were used in the production of foods. One of the first uses of bacteria was for making yogurt, a milk-based food that has been made in Europe and Asia for hundreds of years. Bacteria break down substances in milk to make many dairy products. Cheeses and buttermilk also can be produced with the aid of bacteria. Cheese making is shown in **Figure 12.**

Other foods you might have eaten also are made using bacteria. Sauerkraut, for example, is made with cabbage and a bacterial culture. Vinegar, pickles, olives, and soy sauce also are produced with the help of bacteria.

Bacteria in Industry Many industries rely on bacteria to make many products. Bacteria are grown in large containers called bioreactors. Conditions inside bioreactors are carefully controlled and monitored to allow for the growth of the bacteria. Medicines, enzymes, cleansers, and adhesives are some of the products that are made using bacteria.

Methane gas that is released as a waste by certain bacteria can be used as a fuel for heating, cooking, and industry. In landfills, methane-producing bacteria break down plant and animal material. The quantity of methane gas released by these bacteria is so large that some cities collect and burn it, as shown in **Figure 13.** Using bacteria to digest wastes and then produce methane gas could supply large amounts of fuel worldwide.

Reading Check
What waste gas produced by some bacteria can be used as a fuel?

B

LAB DEMONSTRATION

Purpose to observe the activity of bacteria
Materials plastic wastebasket, soil, paper, grass clippings, leaves, small sticks, dried food, bacteria culture, water, thermometer
Preparation Provide materials for students to see. Have them write down their expectations for mixed materials.

Procedure Mix the materials, keeping the mixture as light as possible. Add small amounts of water. Take the temperature of the mixture every couple of days and stir the compost pile. You may want to continue adding materials.

Expected Outcome Students should observe the decay of organic materials.

✔*Assessment*

Why does the temperature rise above room temperature? As bacteria respire, they release heat. **What happens to the paper and other organic material?** It decays to form compost.

Harmful Bacteria

As mentioned earlier, not all bacteria are beneficial. Some bacteria are known as pathogens. A **pathogen** is any organism that causes disease. If you have ever had strep throat, you have had firsthand experience with a bacterial pathogen. Other pathogenic bacteria cause anthrax in cattle, as well as diphtheria, tetanus, and whooping cough in humans.

How Pathogens Make You Sick Bacterial pathogens can cause illness and disease by several different methods. They can enter your body through a cut in the skin, you can inhale them, or they can enter in other ways. Once inside your body, they can multiply, damage normal cells, and cause illness and disease.

Some bacterial pathogens produce poisonous substances known as **toxins**. Botulism—a type of food poisoning that can result in paralysis and death—is caused by a toxin-producing bacterium. Botulism-causing bacteria are able to grow and produce toxins inside sealed cans of food. However, when growing conditions are unfavorable for their survival, some bacterial pathogens like those that cause botulism can produce thick-walled structures called **endospores**. Endospores, shown in **Figure 14,** can exist for hundreds of years before they resume growth. If the endospores of the botulism-causing bacteria are in canned food, they can grow and develop into regular bacterial cells and produce toxins again. Commercially canned foods undergo a process that uses steam under high pressure, which kills bacteria and most endospores.

Research Visit the Glencoe Science Web site at **science.glencoe.com** for more information about pathogenic bacteria and antibiotics. Communicate to your class what you learn.

Figure 14
Bacterial endospores can survive harsh winters, dry conditions, and heat. *How can endospores be destroyed?*

Magnification: 47,500×

Harmful Bacteria,
continued

Use an Analogy

Some antibiotics bind to fat-like molecules found in cell membranes. Just like detergents break up food and grease on dirty dishes, these antibiotics break up the fatlike molecules and destroy the cell membranes of harmful bacteria.

Science Journal

Battling TB Have students write one-page reports in their Science Journals explaining why the battle with tuberculosis and other pathogens is becoming increasingly difficult. L2
LS **Linguistic** P

Figure 15
Pasteurization lowers the amount of bacteria in foods. Dairy products, such as ice cream and yogurt, are pasteurized.

Pasteurization Unless it has been sterilized, all food contains bacteria. But heating food to sterilizing temperatures can change its taste. Pasteurization is a process of heating food to a temperature that kills most harmful bacteria but causes little change to the taste of the food. You are probably most familiar with pasteurized milk, but some fruit juices and other foods, as shown in **Figure 15,** also are pasteurized.

Problem-Solving Activity

Controlling Bacterial Growth

Bacteria can be controlled by slowing or preventing their growth, or killing them. When trying to control bacteria that affect humans, it is often desirable just to slow their growth because substances that kill bacteria or prevent them from growing can harm humans. For example, bleach often is used to kill bacteria in bathrooms or on kitchen surfaces, but it is poisonous if swallowed. *Antiseptic* is the word used to describe substances that slow the growth of bacteria.

Identifying the Problem

Advertisers often claim that a substance kills bacteria, when in fact the substance only slows its growth. Many mouthwash advertisements make this claim. How could you test three mouthwashes to see which one is the best antiseptic?

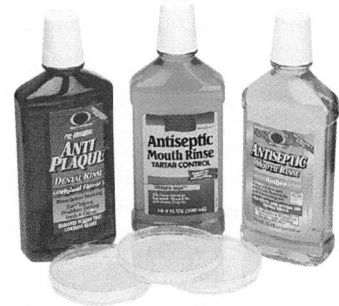

Solving the Problem

1. Describe an experiment that you could do that would test which of three mouthwash products is the most effective antiseptic.
2. What control would you use in your experiment?
3. Read the ingredients label on a bottle of mouthwash. List the ingredients in the mouthwash. What ingredient do you think is the antiseptic? Explain.

Curriculum Connection

Geography Have students show on a world map where each of the major diseases discussed in this section occurs with greatest incidence. L2
LS **Visual-Spatial**

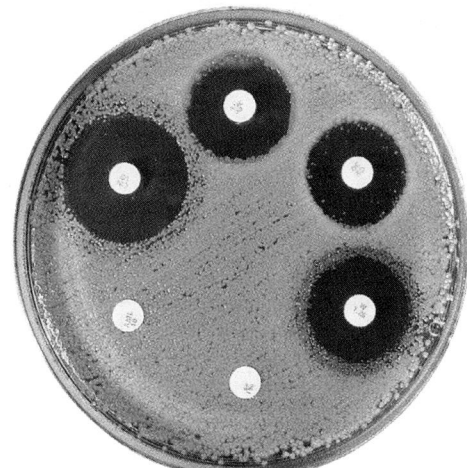

Figure 16
Each of these paper disks contains a different antibiotic. Clear areas where no bacteria are growing can be seen around some disks.
Which one of these disks would you infer contains an antibiotic that is most effective against the bacteria growing on the plate?

Health INTEGRATION

Treating Bacterial Diseases

Bacterial diseases in humans and animals usually are treated effectively with antibiotics. Penicillin, a well-known antibiotic, works by preventing bacteria from making cell walls. Without cell walls, certain bacteria cannot survive. **Figure 16** shows antibiotics at work.

Vaccines can prevent some bacterial diseases. A **vaccine** can be made from damaged particles taken from bacterial cell walls or from killed bacteria. Once the vaccine is injected, white blood cells in the blood recognize that type of bacteria. If the same type of bacteria enters the body at a later time, the white blood cells immediately attack them. Vaccines have been produced that are effective against many bacterial diseases.

Section 2 Assessment

1. Why are saprophytic bacteria helpful and necessary?
2. Why are nitrogen-fixing bacteria important?
3. List three uses of bacteria in food production and industry.
4. How do some bacteria cause disease?
5. **Think Critically** Why is botulism associated with canned foods and not fresh foods?

Skill Builder Activities

6. **Measuring in SI** Air can have more than 3,500 bacteria per cubic meter. How many bacteria might be in your classroom? **For more help, refer to the** Science Skill Handbook.

7. **Developing Multimedia Presentations** Prepare a presentation on how bacteria are used in industry to produce products you use. **For more help, refer to the** Technology Skill Handbook.

---

3 Assess

Reteach

Show students photographs of processes carried out by bacteria. Have students identify each process and its importance. L2
Visual-Spatial

Challenge

Have students demonstrate their understanding of the work of bacteria by bringing to class foods that are processed using bacteria or objects that show the effects of bacteria. L2

✔Assessment

Process Assess students' understanding of vaccines by having them make a concept map outlining what happens when someone receives a vaccination for a disease, and later is infected with that disease. The individual receives a vaccine, which allows their white blood cells to recognize and develop a defense against a particular disease-causing organism. When the organism later enters the individual's bloodstream, it is immediately recognized and killed by the white blood cells. Use **Performance Assessment in the Science Classroom,** p. 161.

Answers to Section Assessment

1. They recycle nutrients.
2. They change atmospheric nitrogen into a form that can be used by plants or animals.
3. Bacteria are used in making yogurt, sauerkraut, and other food products. Biotechnology industries use bacteria to produce medicines and other products. Methane gas can be produced in landfills.
4. Some bacteria produce toxins; others multiply in the body, damaging normal cells and causing illness and disease.
5. The bacteria that cause botulism are anaerobes, which grow in an oxygen-free environment, such as that in canned foods.
6. To calculate the answer, measure the length, width, and height of the classroom in meters. Multiply these numbers to find the volume of air in the classroom. Multiply the volume by 3,500 to obtain the number of bacteria per cubic meter.
7. Check students' work for accuracy.

Activity

BENCH TESTED

Recognize the Problem

Purpose

Students design an experiment to determine the types of materials that will decompose in a compost pile. [L2] [IS] **Visual-Spatial**

Process Skills

comparing, contrasting, predicting, describing, making a data table, interpreting data

Time Required

One 45-minute class period; three or four 20-minute observation periods over a period of four weeks

Form a Hypothesis

Possible Hypotheses

Most student hypotheses will reflect the knowledge that food items will decay most rapidly, but many students will not be able to identify all the biodegradable items in their experiments.

Test Your Hypothesis

Possible Procedure

Establish several compost piles in wide-mouthed jars or flat baking pans by burying food scraps, grass clippings, and leaf litter under 10 cm of soil. Water, turn, and add layers of soil to the containers regularly. After the compost is established, place test items flat on the compost and bury them under 10 cm of soil. Examine the items once a week for signs of decomposition.

Activity

Composting

Over time, landfills fill up and new places to dump trash become more difficult to find. One way to reduce the amount of trash that must be dumped in a landfill is to recycle. Composting is a form of recycling that changes plant wastes into reusable, nutrient-rich compost. How do plant wastes become compost? What types of organisms can assist in the process?

Recognize the Problem

What types of items can be composted and what types cannot?

Form a Hypothesis

Based on readings or prior knowledge, form a hypothesis about what types of items will decompose in a compost pile and which will not.

Safety Precautions 🥽 🧤 🧹

Be sure to wash your hands every time after handling the compost material.

Goals

■ **Predict** which of several items will decompose in a compost pile and which will not.

■ **Demonstrate** the decomposition, or lack thereof, of several items.

■ **Compare** and **contrast** the speed at which various items break down.

Possible Materials

widemouthed, clear glass jars (at least 4)
soil
water
watering can
banana peel
apple core
scrap of newspaper
leaf
plastic candy wrapper
scrap of aluminum foil

Teaching Strategies:

• Encourage students to use common items such as polystyrene cups, aluminum cans, notebook paper, glossy magazine paper, and articles of clothing made of both natural and artificial fibers as well as biodegradable food items.

• Encourage students to bring garden gloves to school to use when unearthing their items.

Test Your Hypothesis

Plan

1. **Decide** what items you are going to test. Choose some items that you think will decompose and some that you think will not.

2. **Predict** which of the items you chose will or will not decompose. Of the items that will, which do you think will decompose fastest? Slowest?

3. **Decide** how you will test whether or not the items decompose. How will you see the items? You may need to research composting in books, magazines, or on the Internet.

4. Prepare a data table in your Science Journal to record your observations.

5. **Identify** all constants, variables, and controls of the experiment.

Do

1. Make sure your teacher approves of your plan and your data table before you start.

2. Set up your experiment and collect data as planned.

3. While doing the experiment, record your observations and complete your data tables in your Science Journal.

Analyze Your Data

1. **Describe** your results. Did all of the items decompose? If not, which did and which did not?

2. Were your predictions correct? Explain.

3. Was there a difference in how fast items decomposed? If so, which items decomposed fastest and which took longer?

Draw Conclusions

1. What general statement(s) can you make about what types of items can be composted and which cannot? What about the speed of decomposition?

2. Do your results support your hypothesis?

3. What might happen to your compost pile if antibiotics were added to it? Explain.

4. **Describe** what you think happens in a landfill to items similar to those that you tested.

ℂommunicating
Your Data

Write a letter to the editor of the local newspaper describing what you have learned about composting and encouraging your neighbors to do more composting.

ACTIVITY 75

Expected Outcome

Student results should show various degrees of decay for the food items, natural fiber clothing, and paper. Nonbiodegradable items will not show significant signs of decay.

Analyze Your Data

1. Food items, paper, and clothing made of natural fibers will show various signs of decay, but nondegradable items will not.

2. Answers will vary with results.

3. The food items will decay most rapidly, followed by clothing made of natural fibers. Moist items will decay more rapidly than drier items.

Error Analysis

To avoid confusion when examining the composted items, students should use initially new items and make a record of the appearance of each item before it is composted.

Draw Conclusions

1. Materials made of natural ingredients can be composted, but artificial items will not compost. Aerating the soil and keeping the compost moist increases decay.

2. Answers will vary.

3. Bacteria are the primary decomposing agents in compost piles. Killing bacteria would slow or stop the decay process.

4. Landfill items are frequently buried more deeply, are exposed to less moisture, and receive little or no aeration. Thus items would decay more slowly in a landfill.

✔Assessment

Performance With permission, have students plan and construct a school compost pile in a corner of the school property. Use **Performance Assessment in the Science Classroom,** p. 105.

ℂommunicating
Your Data

Encourage students to access the Glencoe Science Web site to gather information on local landfills, compost sites, and recycling centers.

Science Stats

Content Background

There are many bacteria species that thrive in extreme environmental conditions. Thermophiles are bacteria that thrive at temperatures between 50°C to 60°C. Some can even live in hot springs and ocean hydrothermal vents, where temperatures can reach 110°C. Other bacteria, called psychrophiles, are most comfortable at temperatures of 15°C to 20°C. Psychrophiles that live in the soil and water of Arctic regions can survive temperatures as low as 0°C. Bacteria that live under extreme pressure are called barophiles. Barophiles that live on the ocean floor at a depth of 7 km cannot survive at atmospheric pressure. Some species of bacteria, called acidophiles, can survive in highly acidic environments. These bacteria can survive in a pH as low as 1 and are found in water that drains from coal mines, which contains high amounts of sulfuric acid and in hydrothermal vents.

Discussion

What advantages do unusual bacteria have over other types of bacteria? Possible answer: These bacteria can survive in extreme environmental conditions.

Activity

Have students research different methods of food preservation, such as refrigeration, pasteurization, sterilization, pH alteration, radiation, and chemical preservatives, and discuss how the form of preservation relates to the basic survival or environmental requirements of many bacteria.

Science Stats

Unusual Bacteria

Did you know...

...The hardiest bacteria, *Deinococcus radiodurans* (DE no KO kus·RA de oh DOOR anz), has a nasty odor, which has been described as similar to rotten cabbage. It might have an odor, but it can survive 3,000 times more radiation than humans because it quickly repairs damage to its DNA molecule. These bacteria were discovered in canned meat when they survived sterilization by radiation.

...The smallest bacteria, nanobes (NAN obes), are Earth's smallest living things. These miniature creatures live far below the ocean floor and are 20 to 150 nanometers long. That means, depending on their size, it would take about 6,500,000 to 50,000,000 nanobes lined up to equal 1 m!

...Nanobes were discovered in ancient stone about 5 km beneath the ocean floor in petroleum exploration wells near Australia. To understand just how deep this is, first picture the bottom of the ocean. Then imagine a hole in the bottom of the ocean that's deep enough to bury about 13 Empire State Buildings stacked on top of each other.

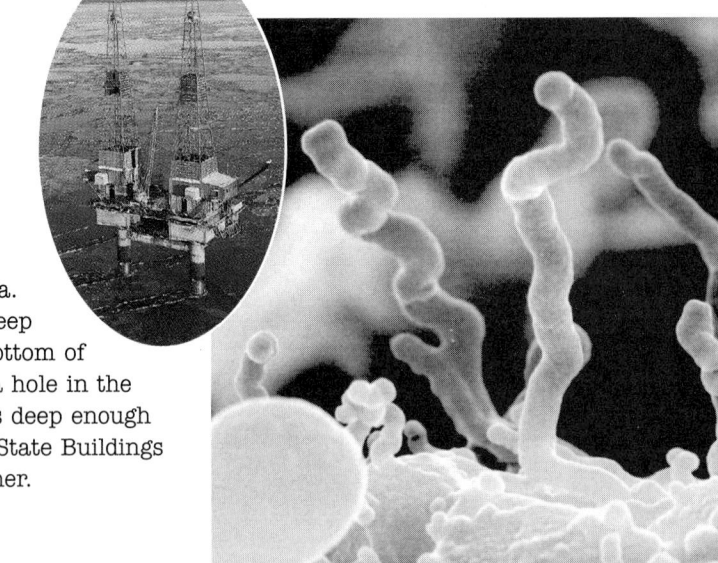

76 CHAPTER 3 Bacteria

SCIENCE Online
Internet Addresses

_____
_____
_____

Explore the Glencoe Science Web site at **science.glencoe.com** to find out more about topics in this feature.

...The largest bacterium on Earth,
Thiomargarita namibiensis (THE oh ma ga RE ta·nah ME be yen sis), is about the same size as the period at the end of this sentence. Its name means, "Sulfur Pearl of Namibia," and describes its appearance. The sulfur inside its cells reflects white light. The cells form strands that look like strings of pearls.

T. namibiensis

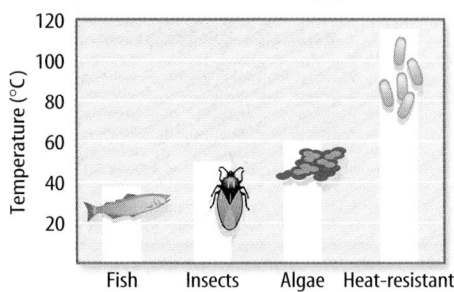

How hot can they get?

Temperature (°C) — Fish, Insects, Algae, Heat-resistant bacteria

Organisms

...Earth's oldest living bacteria are thought to be 250 million years old. These ancient bacteria were revived from a crystal of rock salt buried 579 m below the desert floor in New Mexico.

Do the Math

Teaching Strategies
- Have students recall how to convert km to m by multiplying km by 1000.
- Have students recall how to set up an equation to solve for an unknown variable.

Answers
1. smallest, 4421 m
2. 130 nanometers
3. 500 rads

Go Further
Have students list locations where halophiles can be found. ocean, Great Salt Lake, Dead Sea, salt licks, brine vats, salt flats Have students make a chart of the different types of halophiles, the salt concentration in which they can survive, and the number of times higher that is than the concentration in which nonhalophiles.
Logical-Mathematical

Do the Math

1. The smallest and the oldest bacteria were found beneath Earth's surface. Which was deeper? How many meters deeper was it found?
2. What is the difference in size between the smallest nanobe and the largest nanobe?
3. A rad is a unit for measuring radiation. *Deinococcus radiodurans* can withstand a maximum of 1.5 million rads of radiation. How many rads would be deadly to humans?

Go Further
Do library research about halophiles, the bacteria that can live in salty environments. What is the maximum salt concentration in which they can survive? How does this compare to the maximum salt concentration bacteria that are not halophiles can survive?

SCIENCE STATS 77

Visual Learning

How hot can they get? How much higher temperatures can heat-resistant bacteria withstand than insects? about 60°C What is the minimum temperature needed to sterilize foods such as canned goods against heat-resistant bacteria? 120°C

Chapter ③ Study Guide

Reviewing Main Ideas

Preview

Students can answer the questions in their Science Journals. Discuss the answers as you go through the chapter. **LS** **Linguistic**

Review

Students can write their answers, then compare them with those of other students. **LS** **Interpersonal**

Reteach

Students can look at the illustrations and describe details that support the main ideas of the chapter. **LS** **Visual-Spatial**

Answers to Chapter Review

SECTION 1

1. cocci

5. When cyanobacteria die, aerobic bacteria decompose them and use up all available oxygen in the water. Fish and other organisms die.

SECTION 2

1. Certain bacteria are able to use oil as an energy source. These bacteria could be sprayed on the spill in order to digest it.

3. Vaccinations protect you from the effects of pathogens.

Reviewing Main Ideas

Section 1 What are bacteria?

1. Bacteria can be found almost everywhere. They have three basic shapes—cocci, bacilli, and spirilli. *What shape of bacteria is shown here?*

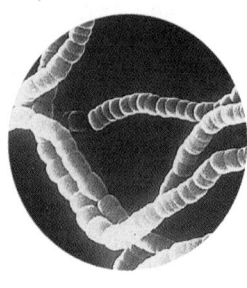

2. Bacteria are prokaryotic cells that usually reproduce by fission. All bacteria contain DNA, ribosomes, and cytoplasm but lack a membrane-bound nucleus.

3. Most bacteria are consumers, but some can make their own food. Anaerobes are bacteria that are able to live without oxygen, but aerobes need oxygen to survive.

4. Cell shape and structure, how they get food, if they use oxygen, and their waste products can be used to classify eubacteria.

5. Cyanobacteria are producer eubacteria. They are an important source of food and oxygen for some aquatic organisms. *How does a bloom of cyanobacteria affect other aquatic organisms?*

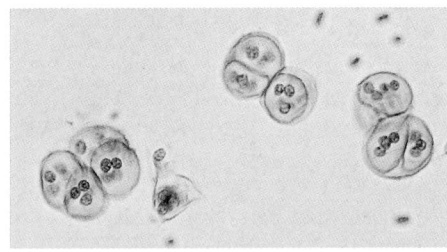

6. Archaebacteria are bacteria that often exist in extreme conditions, such as near ocean vents and in hot springs.

Section 2 Bacteria in Your Life

1. Most bacteria are helpful. They aid in recycling nutrients, fixing nitrogen, or helping in food production. They even can be used to break down harmful pollutants. *How could bacteria be used to clean up this oil spill?*

2. Some bacteria that live in your body help you stay healthy and survive.

3. Other bacteria are harmful because they can cause disease in the organisms they infect. *Why are vaccinations important to your health?*

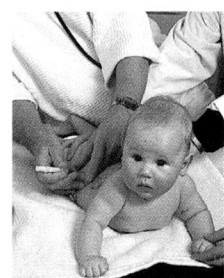

4. Pasteurization is one process that can prevent the growth of harmful bacteria in food.

FOLDABLES
Reading & Study Skills

After You Read

Using the information on your Foldable, write about the characteristics these two kingdoms of bacteria have in common under the *Both* tab.

FOLDABLES
Reading & Study Skills

After You Read

After students have read the chapter and completed the Foldable described in Before You Read, have them do the activity on the student page.

Dinah Zike

Visualizing Main Ideas

Complete the following concept map on how bacteria affect the environment.

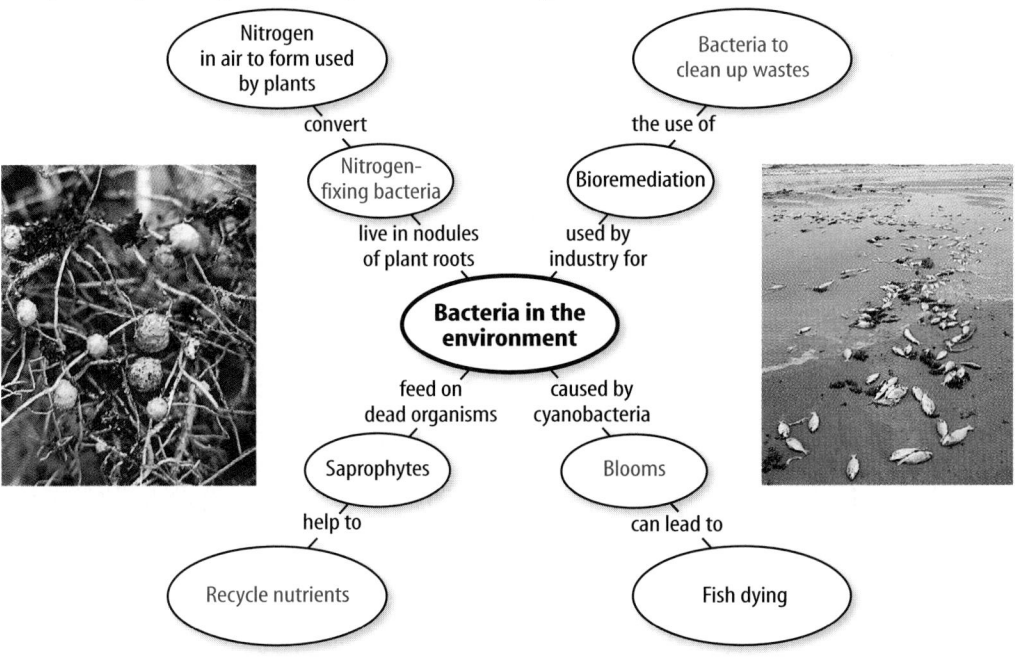

Nitrogen in air to form used by plants

— convert →

Nitrogen-fixing bacteria

— live in nodules of plant roots →

Bacteria to clean up wastes

— the use of →

Bioremediation

— used by industry for →

Bacteria in the environment

— feed on dead organisms →

Saprophytes

— help to →

Recycle nutrients

— caused by cyanobacteria →

Blooms

— can lead to →

Fish dying

Vocabulary Review

Vocabulary Words

a. aerobe
b. anaerobe
c. antibiotic
d. endospore
e. fission
f. flagella
g. nitrogen-fixing bacteria
h. pathogen
i. saprophyte
j. toxin
k. vaccine

THE PRINCETON REVIEW **Study Tip**

Make flash cards for new vocabulary words. Put the word on one side and the definition on the other. Then use them to quiz yourself.

Using Vocabulary

Replace the underlined words with the correct vocabulary word(s).

1. An <u>aerobe</u> uses dead organisms as a food source.

2. A <u>toxin</u> can prevent some bacterial diseases.

3. A <u>saprophyte</u> causes disease.

4. A bacterium that needs oxygen to carry out respiration is a(n) <u>pathogen</u>.

5. Bacteria reproduce using <u>flagella</u>.

6. <u>Anaerobes</u> are bacteria that convert nitrogen in the air to a form used by plants.

7. A(n) <u>flagella</u> can live without oxygen.

Chapter **3** Study Guide

Visualizing Main Ideas

See student page.

Vocabulary Review

Using Vocabulary

1. saprophyte
2. vaccine
3. pathogen
4. aerobe
5. fission
6. Nitrogen-fixing bacteria
7. anaerobe

CHAPTER STUDY GUIDE **79**

Checking Concepts

1. D
2. B
3. A
4. D
5. A
6. A
7. B
8. C
9. D
10. A

Thinking Critically

11. Nitrogen would no longer be available in a form that plants could use; therefore, the plants would die unless fertilizer was added.
12. Bacteria can reproduce quickly, have means of moving, and can form endospores to survive extreme conditions. They can also exchange DNA, providing the population with variations that may be helpful.
13. Crops like beans, peas, and peanuts have nitrogen-fixing bacteria. These crops help to increase soil fertility.
14. spheres
15. Using fresh foods and keeping them refrigerated, washing hands and all surfaces and utensils, and properly cooking foods are ways to prevent food poisoning.

Checking Concepts

Choose the word or phrase that best answers the question.

1. What is a way of cleaning up an ecosystem using bacteria to break down harmful compounds?
   A) landfill
   C) toxic waste dumps
   B) waste storage
   D) bioremediation

2. What do bacterial cells contain?
   A) nucleus
   C) mitochondria
   B) DNA
   D) four chromosomes

3. What pigment do cyanobacteria need to make food?
   A) chlorophyll
   C) plasmids
   B) chromosomes
   D) ribosomes

4. Which of the following terms describes most bacteria?
   A) anaerobic
   C) many-celled
   B) pathogens
   D) beneficial

5. What is the name for rod-shaped bacteria?
   A) bacilli
   C) spirilla
   B) cocci
   D) colonies

6. What structure allows bacteria to stick to surfaces?
   A) capsule
   C) chromosome
   B) flagella
   D) cell wall

7. What organisms can grow as blooms in ponds?
   A) archaebacteria
   C) cocci
   B) cyanobacteria
   D) viruses

8. Which of these organisms are recyclers in the environment?
   A) producers
   C) saprophytes
   B) flagella
   D) pathogens

9. Which of the following is caused by a pathogenic bacterium?
   A) an antibiotic
   C) nitrogen fixation
   B) cheese
   D) strep throat

10. Which organisms do not need oxygen to survive?
    A) anaerobes
    C) humans
    B) aerobes
    D) fish

Thinking Critically

11. What would happen if nitrogen-fixing bacteria could no longer live on the roots of some plants?

12. Why are bacteria capable of surviving in almost all environments of the world?

13. Farmers often rotate crops such as beans, peas, and peanuts with other crops such as corn, wheat, and cotton. Why might they make such changes?

14. One organism that causes bacterial pneumonia is called pneumococcus. What is its shape?

15. What precautions can be taken to prevent food poisoning?

Developing Skills

16. **Making and Using Graphs** Graph the data from the table below. Using the graph, determine where the doubling rate would be at 20°C.

Bacterial Reproduction Rates	
Temperature (°C)	Doubling Rate Per Hour
20.5	2.0
30.5	3.0
36.0	2.5
39.2	1.2

17. **Interpreting Data** What is the effect of temperature in question 16?

Chapter ✔Assessment Planner

Portfolio Encourage students to place in their portfolios one or two items of what they consider to be their best work. Examples include:
- Science Journal, p. 63
- Cultural Diversity, p. 68
- Science Journal, p. 72

Performance Additional performance assessments, Performance Task Assessment Lists, and rubrics for evaluating these activities can be found in Glencoe's **Performance Assessment in the Science Classroom.**

18. **Concept Mapping** Complete the following events-chain concept map about the events surrounding a cyanobacteria bloom.

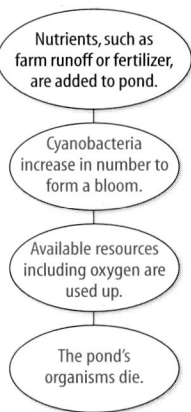

Nutrients, such as farm runoff or fertilizer, are added to pond.

↓

Cyanobacteria increase in number to form a bloom.

↓

Available resources including oxygen are used up.

↓

The pond's organisms die.

19. **Identifying and Manipulating Variables and Controls** How would you decide if a kind of bacteria could grow anaerobically?

20. **Communicating** Describe the nitrogen-fixing process in your own words, using numbered steps. You will probably have more than four steps.

Performance Assessment

21. **Poster** Create a poster that illustrates the effects of bacteria. Use photos from magazines and your own drawings.

22. **Poem** Write a poem that demonstrates your knowledge of the importance of bacteria to human health.

TECHNOLOGY

Go to the Glencoe Science Web site at **science.glencoe.com** or use the **Glencoe Science CD-ROM** for additional chapter assessment.

 **THE PRINCETON REVIEW** **Test Practice**

In science class, Melissa's homework assignment was to look up five diseases that are caused by bacteria. She was to find the name of the bacterium that causes the disease and how it is transmitted to humans. The results of her research are listed in the chart below.

Infectious Diseases

Disease	Source	Bacterium
Cholera	Contaminated water	*Vibrio cholerae*
Botulism	Improperly canned foods	*Clostridium botulinum*
Legionnaires' disease	Air vents	*Legionella pneumophila*
Lyme disease	Tick bites	*Borrelia burgdorferi*
Tuberculosis	Airborne from humans	*Mycobacterium tuberculosis*

Study the chart and answer the following questions.

1. According to the chart, which disease-causing bacterium can be transmitted to humans by a bite from another animal?
   A) *Vibrio cholerae*
   B) *Clostridium botulinum*
   C) *Borrelia burgdorferi*
   D) *Legionella pneumophila*

2. Based on the information in the chart, which disease can be prevented by purifying water that is used for drinking, cooking, or washing fruits and vegetables?
   F) cholera   H) Legionnaires'
   G) botulism   J) tuberculosis

CHAPTER ASSESSMENT 81

 **THE PRINCETON REVIEW** **Test Practice**

The Test-Taking Tip was written by The Princeton Review, the nation's leader in test preparation.
1. C
2. F

Developing Skills

16. Graph should increase until a peak is reached, then decrease. Doubling rate will be almost 2.0 at 20°C.

17. Doubling rate increases until an optimal temperature of approximately 30.5 °C is reached. After this temperature, the doubling rate decreases as the temperature increases.

18. See student page.

19. Place the organism in an environment without oxygen and measure its growth rate.

20. (1) Root hairs curl before infection by nitrogen-fixing bacteria. (2) Bacteria enter roots through an infection thread. (3) Pocketlike spaces within the root form and the cells begin to grow and divide. (4) Root nodules containing nitrogen-fixing bacteria form on the roots of legumes. (5) Atmospheric nitrogen is fixed and becomes available for other living things.

Performance Assessment

21. Posters should show beneficial and harmful effects of bacteria. Use **PASC**, p. 145.

22. Poems should demonstrate knowledge of the importance of bacteria to human health. Use **PASC**, p. 157.

✓Assessment Resources

 Reproducible Masters

Chapter Resources Booklet
Chapter Review, pp. 31–32
Chapter Tests, pp. 33–36
Assessment Transparency Activity, p. 43

Glencoe Science Web site
Interactive Tutor
Chapter Quizzes

Glencoe Technology
- Assessment Transparency
- Interactive CD-ROM Chapter Quizzes
- ExamView Pro Test Bank
- Vocabulary PuzzleMaker Software
- MindJogger Videoquiz

CHAPTER ASSESSMENT 81

Standardized Test Practice

Reading Comprehension

QUESTION 1: C

Students should refer back to the second paragraph to find the correct answer.

QUESTION 2: H

Students must decide what is the summary of the reading passage.

- **Choice F** No; this is a detail from the passage.
- **Choice G** No; this is a detail from the passage.
- **Choice H** Yes; this summarized many of the ideas in the passage.
- **Choice J** No; this is a detail from the passage.

QUESTION 3: B

Students must identify the main idea of the third paragraph of the reading passage.

- **Choice A** No; this is a detail from the paragraph.
- **Choice B** Yes; this is the main idea of the information in the third paragraph.
- **Choice C** No; this is a detail from the paragraph.
- **Choice D** No; this is a detail from the first paragraph.

THE PRINCETON REVIEW
All questions written and validated by The Princeton Review.

Read the passage. Then read each question that follows the passage. Decide which is the best answer to each question.

Life on Earth

The oldest rocks found on Earth have been estimated to be about 4.0 billion years old. But these rocks do not contain any fossil remains. The oldest rocks that have been found with any evidence of life are about 3.5 billion years old. These rocks have fossils of one-celled organisms that once lived in the oceans. No life could have survived on land at that time because so much ultraviolet radiation was reaching Earth's surface from the Sun.

Early bacteria made it possible for other species to inhabit Earth. Scientists hypothesize that little oxygen existed in Earth's early atmosphere. However, nearly 3 billion years ago, bacteria began producing oxygen during photosynthesis. This oxygen bubbled into the oceans, and eventually, entered the atmosphere.

This oxygen was important because as it entered the atmosphere, some of it absorbed energy from the Sun's radiation. The radiation caused chemical reactions, which produced ozone gas. This ozone acted as a protective shield, blocking Earth's surface from most of the incoming ultraviolet radiation. As a result, it became possible for life to survive on land without being damaged by ultraviolet radiation.

The fossil record provides clues about past life on Earth. The earliest multicellular organisms lived in the oceans during the late part of the Precambrian portion of Earth's history.

Fossil evidence indicates that animals did not inhabit land until much later.

Test-Taking Tip Number the paragraphs in the passage to make sure that you are referring to the correct paragraph when answering a question.

---

1. According to the passage, what type of organism added oxygen to Earth's early atmosphere?
   A) vertebrates
   B) mammals
   C) bacteria
   D) fungi

2. Which of these statements provides the best summary of this passage?
   F) The earliest organisms lived in the ocean.
   G) The oldest rocks that have been found with any evidence of life are about 3.5 billion years old.
   H) The production of oxygen by bacteria, which began nearly 3 billion years ago, helped make life on land possible.
   J) Oxygen can act like a protective shield, blocking Earth's surface from most of the incoming ultraviolet radiation.

3. What is the main idea of the third paragraph of this passage?
   A) Oxygen entered the atmosphere.
   B) The presence of oxygen was important.
   C) Oxygen absorbed radiation from the Sun to make ozone.
   D) The oldest rocks on Earth do not have any fossils in them.

Read each question and choose the best answer.

1. Which of these facts best explains why the oldest fossils have been discovered in sediments that were deposited in ancient oceans?
   A) Only aquatic animals leave fossils.
   B) Fossils from land organisms have been destroyed.
   C) The first life on Earth began in the oceans.
   D) All living organisms need water.

Test-Taking Tip Some answer choices might be true statements but might not be the best explanation for a particular question.

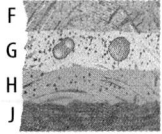
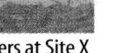
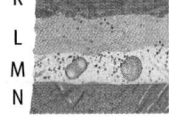

Rock layers at Site X   Rock layers at Site Z

2. Paleontologists study fossils to find out about environmental conditions on Earth long ago. The fossils that appear in rock layer G are the same species that appear in layer M. What might you infer about local conditions when these two rock layers were deposited?
   F) Conditions were similar.
   G) No other organisms were present.
   H) Conditions were different.
   J) A drought occurred.

Test-Taking Tip Organisms of the same species often require similar conditions.

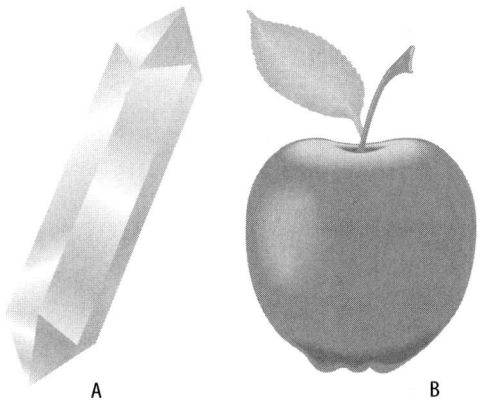

A   B

3. Item A above is different from item B because it _____.
   A) is not organized
   B) does not require energy for its formation
   C) is not composed of cells
   D) does not respond to changes in temperature or pressure

Test-Taking Tip Organization requires energy. Review the definition of living things.

Consider this question carefully before writing your answer on a separate sheet of paper.

4. Early in the twentieth century, Alexander Oparin suggested that the compounds that make up living organisms came from gases that were present in Earth's early atmosphere. Why is Oparin's idea still considered to be a hypothesis and not a theory or scientific law?

Test-Taking Tip Review the definitions of hypothesis, scientific theory, and scientific law.

QUESTION 4: Answers will vary.
Students should explain the difference between a hypothesis, a theory, and a scientific law. Oparin's hypothesis was strongly opposed at first, but has since received some experimental support. However, it has not yet received sufficient support to be considered a theory.

QUESTION 1: C
Students must use the clue *oldest fossils* in the question in order to identify the correct answer choice.
- **Choice A** No; this is an incorrect fact.
- **Choice B** No; this is an incorrect fact.
- **Choice C** Yes; this is accurate and explains why the oldest fossils have been discovered in ancient marine deposits.
- **Choice D** No; although this is an accurate fact, it is not related to fossil formation.

Teaching Tip

Students should use the process of elimination when some answer choices are clearly false statements.

QUESTION 2: F

Students must conclude that the identical fossils in the diagrams indicate similar conditions.

QUESTION 3: C

Students must understand cells to identify the difference between Item A and Item B. Only choice C, *is not composed of cells*, correctly identifies an attribute held by Item A but not Item B.

Teaching Tip

Make sure that students carefully consider information presented in diagrams.

UNIT 2

Unit Contents

✔ Pre-Reading Activity

Have students look for pictures of familiar organisms and list what they know about them.

UNIT 2 Life's Diversity

How Are Animals & Airplanes Connected?

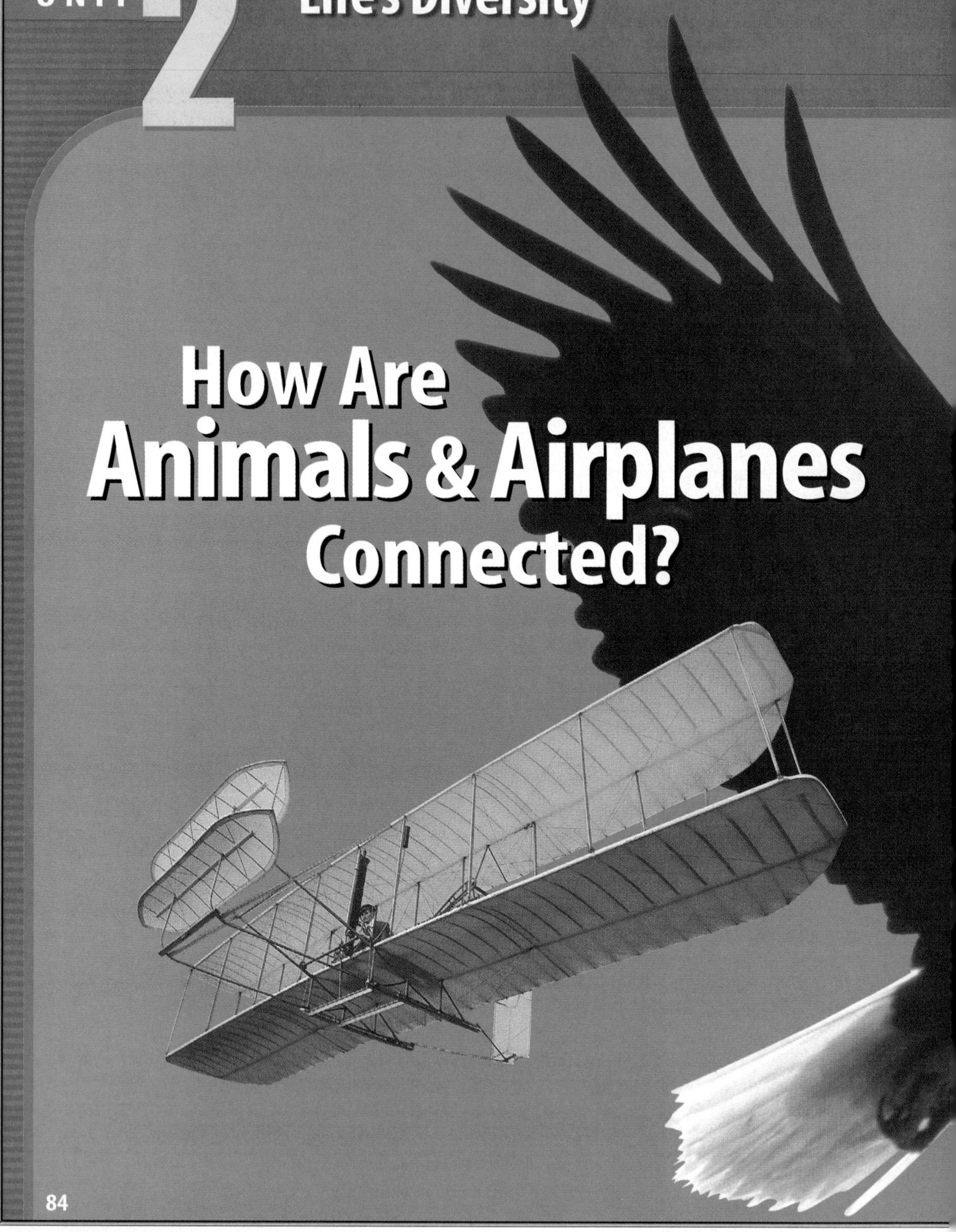

84

Teacher to Teacher

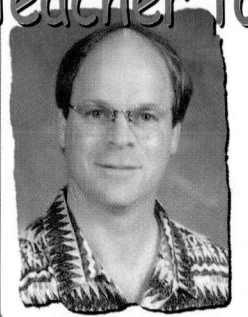

"Using everyday objects such as buttons, bolts, and letters of the alphabet is one way to introduce students to classifying. Students can easily divide objects into groups and describe the characteristics. Student-made keys help to introduce the dichotomous keys scientist use to identify plants and animals."

John E. Burns, Teacher
Ramona Junior High School
Chino, CA

For thousands of years, people dreamed of flying like birds. Detailed sketches of flying machines were made about 500 years ago. Many of these machines featured mechanical wings that were intended to flap like the wings of a bird. But human muscles are not powerful enough to make such wings flap. Later, inventors studied birds such as eagles, which often glide through the air on outstretched wings. Successful gliders were built in the 1800s. However, the gliders had no source of power to get them off the ground—and they were hard to control. Around 1900, two inventors studied bird flight more carefully and discovered that birds steer by changing the shape and position of their wings. The inventors built an engine-powered flying machine equipped with wires that could cause small changes in the shape and position of the wings. Though hardly as graceful as a soaring bird, the first powered, controlled flight took place in 1903, in the airplane seen here.

SCIENCE CONNECTION

FLYING ANIMALS Birds are not the only animals that fly. Bats and many insects also have wings. Investigate birds, bats, and flying insects, paying close attention to the shapes of their wings. Using black construction paper, draw and cut out "silhouettes" of 8 to 10 different flying animals with their wings outstretched. Create a mobile by suspending your silhouettes from a coat hanger or similar object with thread. In what ways are the wings similar and different?

SCIENCE CONNECTION

Activity

All living things, from one-celled bacteria to plants and animals, share a number of simple requirements for survival. In addition to comparing the wing structure of birds, bats, and flying insects, ask students to consider the diverse ways in which organisms meet their energy needs, reproduce, and grow and develop. While studying the diversity of organisms, have students identify the basic requirements common to all organisms, and the various adaptations organisms have for meeting them.

Introducing the Unit

How Are Animals & Airplanes Connected?

Wings are complex, specialized adaptations. They enable birds to use a part of the environment not accessible to most other organisms. Their mastery of flight is reflected in the anatomical structures that allow them to modify the shape and angle of their wings. Their ability to steer and soar through the air provides them with a means of preying on other animals and of escaping predation themselves. It also allows them access to safe places for nesting. Other animals have developed anatomical adaptations for flight. Their wings are different in structure, but these species achieve the same results as birds. Some, like bats, have further adaptations allowing them to navigate through the air in darkness. As they study each chapter, ask students to identify structures, behaviors, and other adaptations that each group of organisms exhibits that allows them to survive and reproduce in diverse environments.

SCIENCE Online
Internet Addresses

_____

_____

_____

Explore the Glencoe Science Web site at **science.glencoe.com** to find out more about topics in this unit.

Section/Objectives	Standards		Activities/Features
Chapter Opener	**National**	**State/Local**	**Explore Activity:** Dissect a mushroom, p. 87 **Before You Read,** p. 87
	See p. 5T for a Key to Standards.		
Section 1 Protists ⏱ 3 sessions 📦 1.5 blocks 1. **Describe** the characteristics shared by all protist. 2. **Compare and contrast** the three groups of protists. 3. **List** examples of each of the three protist groups. 4. **Explain** why protists are so difficult to classify.	National Content Standards: UCP1, UCP5, A1, C1, C5		**Science Online,** p. 92 **Health Integration,** p. 95 **MiniLAB:** Observing Slime Molds, p. 96 **Problem-Solving Activity:** Is it a fungus or a protist?, p. 97 **Activity:** Comparing Algae and Protozoans, p. 99
Section 2 Fungi ⏱ 4 sessions 📦 2 blocks 1. **Identify** the characteristics shared by all fungi. 2. **Classify** fungi into groups based on their methods of reproduction. 3. **Differentiate** between the imperfect fungi and all other fungi.	National Content Standards: UCP1, UCP5, A1, C1, C2, C5, F5, G1		**Science Online,** p. 101 **MiniLAB:** Interpreting Spore Prints, p. 103 **Visualizing Lichens as Air Quality Indicators,** p. 105 **Environmental Science Integration,** p. 106 **Activity:** Creating a Fungus Field Guide, p. 108 **Science and Society:** Chocolate SOS, p. 110

NATIONAL GEOGRAPHIC

Teacher's Corner

PRODUCTS AVAILABLE FROM GLENCOE
To order call 1-800-334-7344:
CD-ROM
NGS PictureShow: The Cell
Transparency Set
NGS PicturePack: The Cell

PRODUCTS AVAILABLE FROM NATIONAL GEOGRAPHIC SOCIETY
To order call 1-800-368-2728:
Videos
Protists: Threshold of Life
INDEX TO NATIONAL GEOGRAPHIC SOCIETY
The following articles may be used

for research relating to this chapter:
"Leafcutters: Gardeners of the Ant World," by Mark W. Moffet, July 1995.
"Slime Mold: The Fungus That Walks," by Douglas B. Lee, July 1981.
"The Wild World of Compost," by Cecil E. Johnson, August 1980.

Activity Materials	Reproducible Resources	Section Assessment	Technology
Explore Activity: mushroom, hand lens	**Chapter Resources Booklet** Foldables Worksheet, p. 15 Directed Reading Overview, p. 17 Note-taking Worksheets, pp. 29–30	GLENCOE'S **ASSESSMENT** ADVANTAGE	
MiniLAB: live specimen of *Physarum polycephaalum*, hand lens **Activity:** cultures of *Paramecium, Amoeba, Euglena,* and *Spirogyra*; prepared slide of slime mold, 4 microscope slides, 4 coverslips, microscope, dropper	**Chapter Resources Booklet** Transparency Activity, p. 40 MiniLAB, p. 3 Enrichment, p. 27 Reinforcement, p. 25 Directed Reading, p. 18 Transparency Activity, pp. 43–44 Activity Worksheet, pp. 5–6 **Cultural Diversity,** p. 3 **Science Inquiry Labs,** p. 3	Portfolio Science Journal, p. 90 Health Integration, p. 95 Performance MiniLAB, p. 96 Problem-Solving Activity, p. 97 Skill Builder Activities, p. 98 Content Section Assessment, p. 98	Section Focus Transparency Teaching Transparency Interactive CD-ROM Guided Reading Audio Program
MiniLAB: several grocery-store mushrooms, unlined white paper **Activity:** Collection jars, hand lens, microscope, microscope slides and coverslips, field guide to fungi or club fungi, art supplies *Need materials?* Contact Science Kit at 1-800-828-7777 or www.sciencekit.com on the Internet.	**Chapter Resources Booklet** Transparency Activity, p. 41 MiniLAB, p. 4 Enrichment, p. 28 Reinforcement, p. 26 Directed Reading, pp. 19, 20 Lab Activities, pp. 9–10, 11–13 Activity Worksheet, pp. 7–8 **Mathematics Skill Activities,** p. 5 **Reading and Writing Skill Activities,** p. 37 **Lab Management and Safety,** p. 58	Portfolio MiniLAB, p. 103 Performance MiniLAB, p. 103 Skill Builder Activities, p. 107 Content Section Assessment, p. 107	Section Focus Transparency Interactive CD-ROM Guided Reading Audio Program

End of Chapter Assessment

GLENCOE'S **ASSESSMENT** ADVANTAGE

Blackline Masters	Technology	Professional Series
Chapter Resources Booklet Chapter Review, pp. 33–34 Chapter Tests, pp. 35–38 **Standardized Test Practice by The Princeton Review,** pp. 39–42	MindJogger Videoquiz Interactive CD-ROM Vocabulary PuzzleMakers ExamView Pro Test Bank Interactive Lesson Planner Interactive Teacher Edition	Performance Assessment in the Science Classroom (PASC)

Transparencies

Section Focus

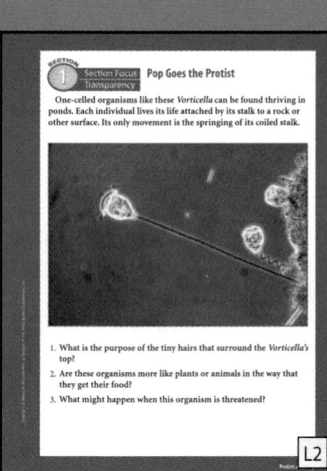

This is a representation of key blackline masters available in the Teacher Classroom Resources. See Resource Manager boxes within the chapter for additional information.

Key to Teaching Strategies

The following designations will help you decide which activities are appropriate for your students.

L1 Level 1 activities should be appropriate for students with learning difficulties.

L2 Level 2 activities should be within the ability range of all students.

L3 Level 3 activities are designed for above-average students.

ELL ELL activities should be within the ability range of English Language Learners.

COOP LEARN Cooperative Learning activities are designed for small group work.

LS Multiple Learning Styles logos, as described on page 22T, are used throughout to indicate strategies that address different learning styles.

P These strategies represent student products that can be placed into a best-work portfolio.

Assessment

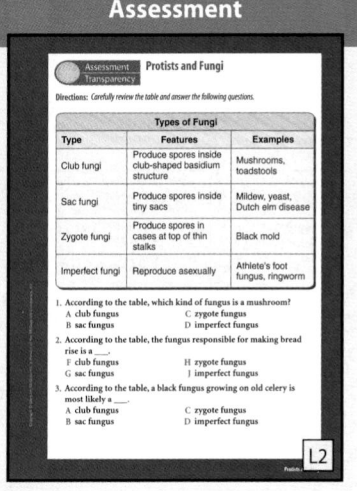

Teaching

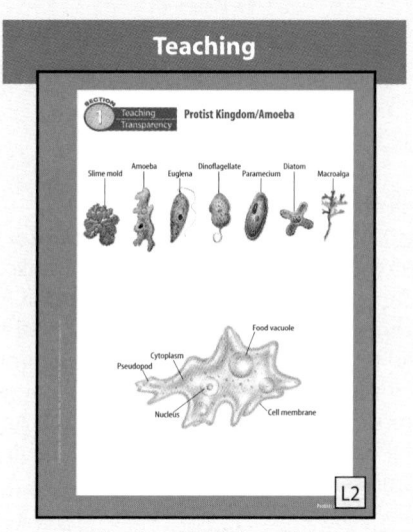

Hands-on Activities

Activity Worksheets

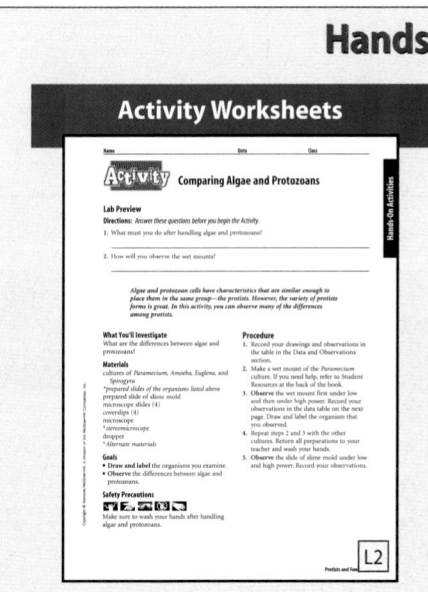

Laboratory Activities

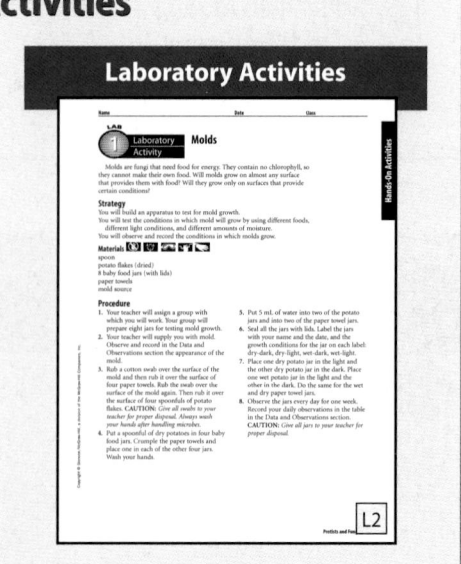

Meeting Different Ability Levels

Content Outline

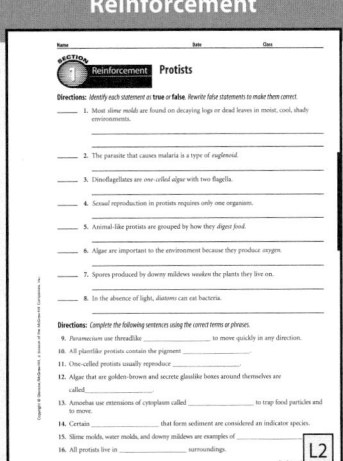

Reinforcement

Directed Reading

Assessment

Chapter Tests

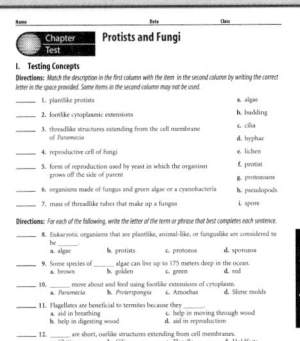

Enrichment

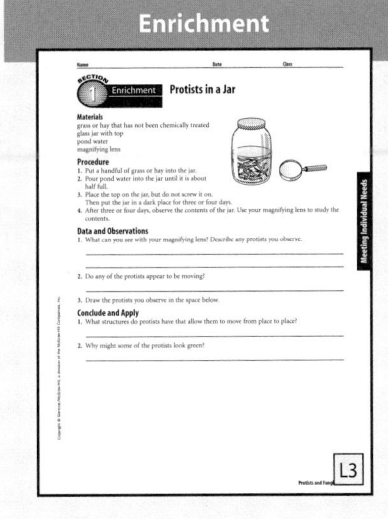

Spanish Directed Reading

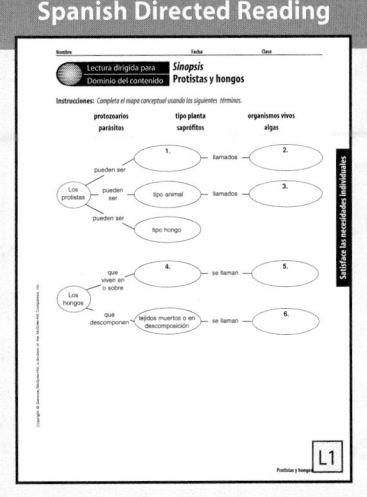

Test Practice Workbook

Chapter Review

Science Content Background

Protists

Evolution of Protists

Convenience is the primary reason for grouping all eukaryotes that are not animals, plants, or fungi into a single kingdom. Because the phyla of Kingdom Protista appear to have evolved independently from one another, protists pose several problems for taxonomists. One of the major theories of evolution explains how eukaryotic cells evolved. According to this theory, chloroplasts evolved from a cyanobacterium taken up by an ancestor. Mitochondria and other organelles are thought to have evolved from aerobic heterotrophic prokaryotes. In these cases, the prokaryotes evolved into the organelles through symbiotic relationships in which the smaller prokaryotes lived inside larger prokaryotes. These symbiotic relationships are somewhat similar to the symbiotic relationships that exist between humans and the anaerobic protists living in the human digestive tract.

> **Fun Fact**
>
> A plasmodial slime mold can reach several centimeters in length and contain many nuclei, although it is one cell. A slime mold often has a web-like appearance, which allows it to increase its surface area (increasing its contact with food, water, and oxygen) and helps distribute nutrients and oxygen to different parts of the slime mold.

Plantlike Protists

The chloroplasts of diatoms in the phylum Bacillariophyta most resemble those of the brown algae and dinoflagellates. Diatoms store their food reserves as a type of oil. This oil provides buoyancy to the diatoms, keeping them near the surface of the water, and thus near sunlight. Dinoflagellates are characterized by unique chromosomes and by an unusual form of mitosis that takes place within a nucleus whose nuclear membrane does not degenerate. Dinoflagellates are widespread as symbionts of corals. In this relationship, the dinoflagellates are responsible for much of the productivity of coral reefs.

The extreme diversity of the green algae in the phylum Chlorophyta is reflected by their abundance in marine, freshwater, and damp terrestrial environments, such as on tree trunks and in soil. Red algae lack centrioles and flagellated cells. For this reason, most taxonomists hypothesize that these organisms descended from the most ancient eukaryotes. Red algae have complex life cycles that involve alternation of generations. Brown algae also have alternating generations, with small gametophytes and large sporophytes.

> **Fun Fact**
>
> Phylum Oomycota, the oomycetes, occur in water or as plant parasites. A member of this phylum caused the Irish potato famine of the mid-nineteenth century. Oomycotes have a filamentous structure similar to that of fungi, and they exhibit alternation of generations.

Animal-like Protists

Most flagellates are nonparasitic. But some of the parasitic flagellates can be quite harmful to humans. These harmful parasites include *Trypanosoma*, which live in the bloodstreams of many vertebrates. These protozoans cause diseases such as sleeping sickness. They protect themselves from attack by the host's immune system by changing the molecular structure of their coats frequently.

Funguslike Protists

Phylum Myxomycota contains plasmodial slime molds. These slime molds form round spore-containing capsules under unfavorable environmental conditions such as starvation. These capsules then release spores that may undergo meiosis.

SCIENCE Online

For additional content background on this topic, go to the Glencoe Science Web site at science.glencoe.com.

SECTION 2 — Fungi

Club Fungi

Basidiomycota includes about 25,000 species of mushrooms, puffballs, shelf fungi, and rusts. Some species of this phylum form mycorrhizae. Others are plant parasites that cause considerable damage each year. Basidiomycotes are named for club-shaped structures that form the sexual spores.

Sac Fungi

Ascomycota is the largest group of fungi accounting for 75 percent of all described fungi. These fungi are named for the sac in which their sexual spores are produced. Yeast are sac fungi that are important in baking and brewing.

Zygote Fungi

Phylum Zygomycota is made up of about 600 species of fungi, including mycorrhizae, an important group that forms mutually beneficial relationships with the roots of most species of plants. Sexual reproduction in this group occurs when appropriate mating strains grow together and produce resistant spores called zoosporangia.

Imperfect Fungi

Fungal species with no known method of sexual reproduction are classified in the phylum Deuteromycota. Some members of this phylum are responsible for producing the colors and flavors of several types of cheese.

Fun Fact

Truffles grow underground and are associated with tree roots. They are one of the most prized of edible fungi. Truffle hunters have traditionally used pigs to hunt truffles because the pigs can smell them. In more recent times, the hunters have begun to train dogs to hunt truffles because, unlike pigs, dog don't try to eat the truffles.

Antman/The Image Works

Protists and Fungi

Chapter Vocabulary

protist, p. 88
algae, p. 89
flagellum, p. 90
protozoan, p. 93
cilia, p. 93
pseudopod, p. 94
hyphae, p. 100
saprophyte, p. 100
spore, p. 101
basidium, p. 102
ascus, p. 102
budding, p. 102
sporangium, p. 103
lichen, p. 104
mycorrhizae, p. 104

What do you think?

Science Journal The picture shows the surface of a diatom, a kind of photosynthetic protist called an alga. Diatoms have intricately etched walls made of silica.

Protists and Fungi

How many protists helped form this limestone cliff, and how did they do it? Did you know that fungi help to make hot dog buns? Some fungi can be seen only through a microscope but others are more than 100 m long. In this chapter, you will learn what characteristics separate protists and fungi from bacteria, plants, and animals. You also will learn why protists and fungi are important to you and the environment.

What do you think?

Science Journal Look at the picture below with a classmate. Discuss what you think this might be. Here's a hint: *This organism is visible only under a microscope.* Write your answer or best guess in your Science Journal.

86

Theme Connection

Systems and Interactions Changes over time and ecological relationships of protists and fungi are discussed.

I t is hard to tell by a mushroom's appearance whether it is safe to eat or is poisonous. Some edible mushrooms are so highly prized that people keep their location a secret for fear that others will find their treasure. Do the activity below to learn about the parts of mushrooms.

Dissect a mushroom 🥽 🧤 🚫 ✋

WARNING: *Wash your hands after handling mushrooms. Do not eat any lab materials.*

1. Obtain a mushroom from your teacher.

2. Using a magnifying glass, observe the underside of the mushroom cap where the stalk is connected to it. Then carefully pull off the cap and observe the gills, which are the thin, tissuelike structures. Hundreds of thousands of tiny reproductive structures called spores will form on these gills.

3. Use your fingers to pull the stalk apart lengthwise. Continue this process until the pieces are as small as you can get them.

Poisonous or edible?

Observe

In your Science Journal, write a description of the parts of the mushroom, and make a labeled drawing of the mushroom and its parts.

Before You Read

Making a Compare and Contrast Study Fold Make the following Foldable to help you see how protists and fungi are similar and different.

1. Place a sheet of paper in front of you so the short side is at the top. Fold the top of the paper down and the bottom up.

2. Open the paper and label the three rows *Protists, Protists and Fungi,* and *Fungi.*

3. As you read the chapter, write information about each type of organism in the appropriate row and information that they share in the middle row.

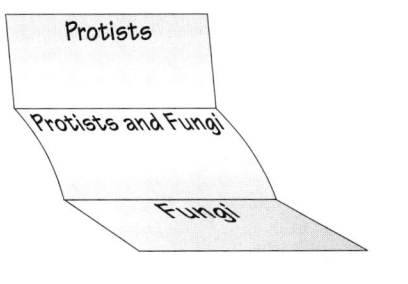

87

Purpose Use the Explore Activity to introduce students to fungi. They will learn more about fungi in this chapter. L1

ELL   COOP LEARN

IS Visual-Spatial

Preparation Buy enough mushrooms for each student to have one.

Materials mushroom, hand lens

Teaching Strategies

• The best mushrooms to use will be those that have the membrane of the cap just separated from the stalk as opposed to those that are still tightly closed.

• Encourage students to examine the mushroom gills thoroughly with the hand lens.

• Tell students not to eat anything used in the lab.

Observe

Parts identified are cap, gills, spores, and stalk. Drawings will vary, but should include all parts.

✔Assessment

Oral Have students hypothesize how fungi became so widespread in the environment. Their spores are light, numerous, and easily carried by air currents. Use **Performance Assessment in the Science Classroom,** p. 93.

Before You Read

Dinah Zike Study Fold

Purpose Students will make a Foldable for listing characteristics of protists and fungi during reading. They will use data collected to compare and contrast these forms of life after reading.

📁 For additional help, see Foldables Worksheet, p. 15 in **Chapter Resources Booklet,** or go to the Glencoe Science Web site at **science.glencoe.com.** See After You Read in the Study Guide at the end of this chapter.

SECTION

1

Protists

1 Motivate

Bellringer Transparency

Display the Section Focus Transparency for Section 1. Use the accompanying Transparency Activity Master. [L2] [ELL]

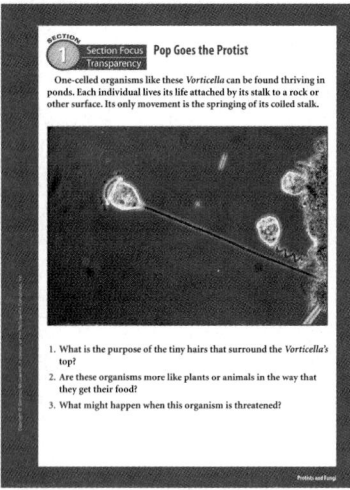

Tie to Prior Knowledge

Review classification with students. Explain that protists have some characteristics of animals, plants, and fungi.

SECTION

1

Protists

As You Read

What You'll Learn

- **Describe** the characteristics shared by all protists.
- **Compare and contrast** the three groups of protists.
- **List** examples of each of the three protist groups.
- **Explain** why protists are so difficult to classify.

Vocabulary

protist   protozoan
algae   cilia
flagellum   pseudopod

Why It's Important

Many protists are important food sources for other organisms.

What is a protist?

Look at the organisms in **Figure 1.** Do you see any similarities among them? As different as they appear, all of these organisms belong to one kingdom—the protist kingdom. A **protist** is a one- or many-celled organism that lives in moist or wet surroundings. All protists are made up of eukaryotic cells—cells that have a nucleus and other internal, membrane-bound structures. Some protists are plantlike. They contain chlorophyll and make their own food. Other protists are animal-like. They do not have chlorophyll and can move. Some protists have a solid or a shell-like structure on the outside of their bodies.

Protist Reproduction One-celled protists usually reproduce asexually. In protists, asexual reproduction requires only one parent organism and occurs by the process of cell division. During cell division, the hereditary material in the nucleus is duplicated before the nucleus divides. After the nucleus divides, the cytoplasm divides. The result is two new cells that are genetically identical. In asexual reproduction of many-celled protists, parts of the large organism can break off and grow into entire new organisms by the process of cell division.

Most protists also can reproduce sexually. During sexual reproduction, the process of meiosis produces sex cells. Two sex cells join to form a new organism that is genetically different from the two organisms that were the sources of the sex cells. How and when sexual reproduction occurs depends on the specific type of protist.

Figure 1
The protist kingdom is made up of a variety of organisms. Many are difficult to classify. *What characteristics do the organisms shown here have in common?*

| Slime mold | Amoeba | Euglena | Dinoflagellate | Paramecium | Diatom | Macroalga |

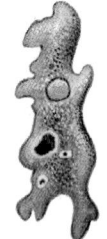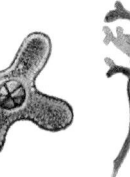

Section ✔ *Assessment* Planner

PORTFOLIO
Science Journal, p. 90
Health Integration, p. 95
PERFORMANCE ASSESSMENT
MiniLAB, p. 96
Skill Builder Activities, p. 98
See page 114 for more options.

CONTENT ASSESSMENT
Section, p. 98
Challenge, p. 98
Chapter, pp. 114–115

Classification of Protists

Not all scientists agree about how to classify the organisms in this group. Protists usually are divided into three groups—plantlike, animal-like, and funguslike—based on whether they share certain characteristics with plants, animals, or fungi. **Table 1** shows some of these characteristics. As you read this section, you will understand some of the problems of grouping protists in this way.

Evolution of Protists

Although protists that produce a hard outer covering have left many fossils, other protists lack hard parts so few fossils of these organisms have been found. But, by studying the genetic material and structure of modern protists, scientists are beginning to understand how they are related to each other and to other organisms. Scientists hypothesize that the common ancestor of most protists was a one-celled organism with a nucleus and other cellular structures. However, evidence suggests that protists with the ability to make their own food could have had a different ancestor than protists that cannot make their own food.

Plantlike Protists

Protists in this group are called plantlike because, like plants, they contain the pigment chlorophyll in chloroplasts and can make their own food. Many of them have cell walls like plants, and some have structures that hold them in place just as the roots of a plant do, but these protists do not have roots.

Plantlike protists are known as **algae** (AL jee) (singular, *alga*). As shown in **Figure 2,** some are one cell and others have many cells. Even though all algae have chlorophyll, not all of them look green. Many have other pigments that cover up their chlorophyll.

Table 1 Characteristics of Protist Groups

Plantlike	Animal-Like	Funguslike
Contain chlorophyll and make their own food using photosynthesis	Cannot make their own food; capture other organisms for food	Cannot make their own food; absorb food from their surroundings
Have cell walls	Do not have cell walls	Some organisms have cell walls; others do not
No specialized ways to move from place to place	Have specialized ways to move from place to place	Have specialized ways to move from place to place

Figure 2
Algae exist in many shapes and sizes. **A** Microscopic algae are found in freshwater and salt water. **B** You can see some types of green algae growing on rocks, washed up on the beach, or floating in the water.

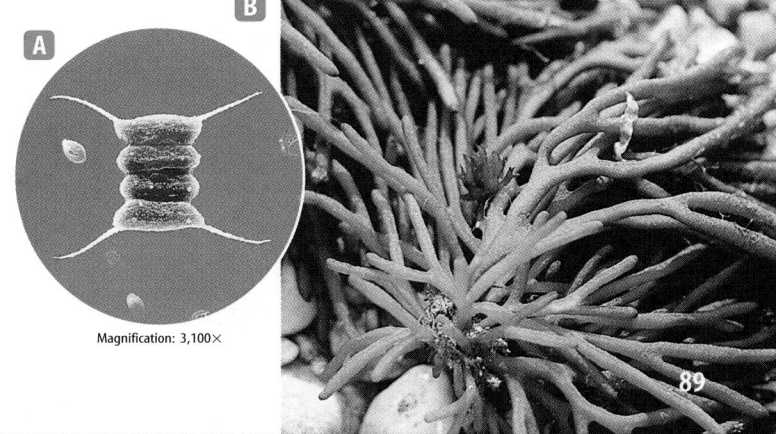

Magnification: 3,100×

2 Teach

What is a protist?

Caption Answer
Figure 1 All are eukaryotic and live in a moist or wet environment.

Visual Learning

Table 1 Use information presented here to lead a discussion of the characteristics of the groups of protists. Allow students to compare and contrast the groups using these characteristics.

Plantlike Protists

Activity

Have students bring in pond water. Allow students to observe wet-mount slides of the water. They should observe a variety of algae. Use a dichotomous key to identify the algae. [L2] ELL
Visual-Spatial

Make a Model

After students have looked at various algae under the microscope, have them make models to show what they look like. Materials for models might include clay, polystyrene, or plaster of paris. [L2] ELL
Kinesthetic

Figure 3 Point out to students that taxonomists use the markings on silica shells to identify individual species.

Figure 4 What advantage does having both an eyespot and a flagellum give *Euglena?* The eyespot would be useful in detecting light and the flagellum could be used to propel *Euglena* toward light.

Activity

Organize students into cooperative groups. Provide each group with about 40 buttons to arrange in a classification system. Relate this activity to the variety of protists and the difficulty in classifying them. L1

ELL   COOP LEARN

Logical-Mathematical

Caption Answer

Figure 4B Euglenoids are similar to animals because they do not have cell walls, they move, and they respond to light. They are similar to plants because they contain chloroplasts and can make their own food.

Fun Fact

When placed in the dark, euglenoids can lose their chloroplasts and become even more like protozoans.

Figure 3
The cell walls of diatoms contain silica, the main element in glass. The body of a diatom is like a small box with a lid. The pattern of dots, pits, and lines on the wall's surface is different for each species of diatom.

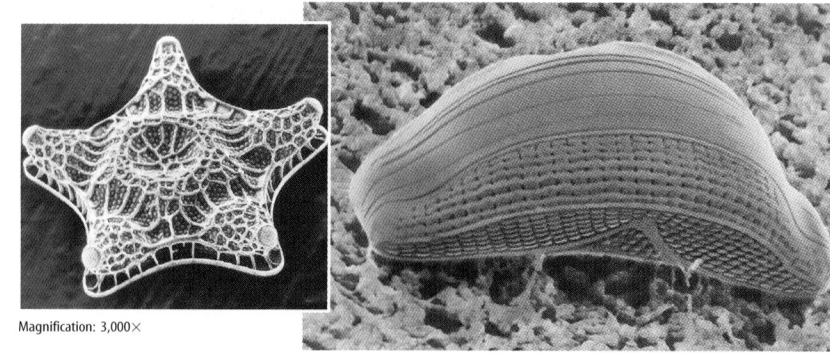

Magnification: 3,000×

Magnification: 2,866×

Diatoms Extremely large populations of diatoms exist. Diatoms, shown in **Figure 3,** are found in freshwater and salt water. They have a golden-brown pigment that covers up the green chlorophyll. Diatoms secrete glasslike boxes around themselves. When the organisms die, these boxes sink. Over thousands of years, they can collect and form deep layers.

Dinoflagellates Another group of algae is called the dinoflagellates, which means "spinning flagellates." Dinoflagellates, as shown in **Figure 4A,** have two flagella. A **flagellum** (plural, *flagella*) is a long, thin, whiplike structure used for movement. One flagellum circles the cell like a belt, and another is attached to one end like a tail. As the two flagella move, they cause the cell to spin. Because many of the species in this group produce a chemical that causes them to glow at night, they are known as fire algae. Almost all dinoflagellates live in salt water. While most contain chlorophyll, some do not and must feed on other organisms.

Euglenoids Protists that have characteristics of both plants and animals are known as the euglenoids (yew GLEE noydz). Many of these one-celled algae have chloroplasts, but some do not.

Figure 4
A Dinoflagellates usually live in the sea. Some are free living and others live in the tissues of animals like coral and giant clams.
B How are euglenoids similar to plants and animals?

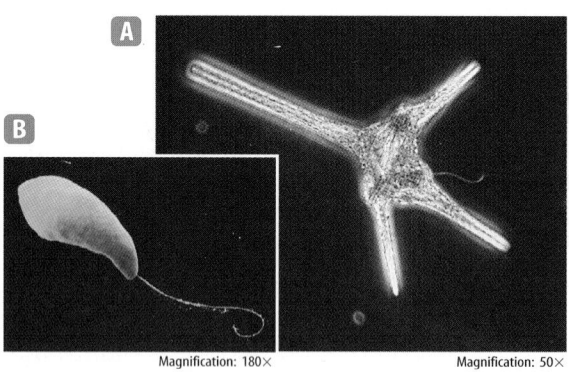

Magnification: 180×

Magnification: 50×

Those with chloroplasts, like *Euglena* shown in **Figure 4B,** can produce their own food. However, when light is not present, *Euglena* can feed on bacteria and other protists. Although *Euglena* has no cell wall, it does have a strong, flexible layer inside the cell membrane that helps it move and change shape. Many euglenoids move by whipping their flagella. An eyespot, an adaptation that is sensitive to light, helps photosynthetic euglenoids move toward light.

Teacher FYI

Overlapping protein fibers in many protists, such as *Euglena*, allow them to alter their shape considerably.

Science Journal

Euglenoids Have students write a fictional story in their Science Journals to describe a day in the life of *Euglena*. Tell students to use the plantlike and animal-like characteristics of the protist in their stories. L2 **Linguistic** P

Red Algae Most red algae are many-celled and, along with the many-celled brown and green algae, sometimes are called seaweeds. Red algae contain chlorophyll, but they also produce large amounts of a red pigment. Some species of red algae can live up to 200 m deep in the ocean. They can absorb the limited amount of light at those depths to carry out the process of photosynthesis. **Figure 5** shows the depths at which different types of algae can live.

Green Algae Due to the diversity of their traits, about 7,000 species of green algae have been classified. These algae, shown in **Figure 6A,** contain large amounts of chlorophyll. Green algae can be one-celled or many-celled. They are the most plantlike of all the algae. Because plants and green algae are similar in their structure, chlorophyll, and how they undergo photosynthesis, some scientists hypothesize that plants evolved from ancient, many-celled green algae. Although most green algae live in water, you can observe types that live in other moist environments, including on damp tree trunks and wet sidewalks.

Brown Algae As you might expect from their name, brown algae contain a brown pigment in addition to chlorophyll. They usually are found growing in cool, saltwater environments. Brown algae are many-celled and vary greatly in size. An important food source for many fish and invertebrates is a brown alga called kelp, as shown in **Figure 6B.** Kelp forms a dense mat of stalks and leaflike blades where small fish and other animals live. Giant kelp is the largest organism in the protist kingdom and can grow to be 100 m in length.

✔ Reading Check *What is kelp?*

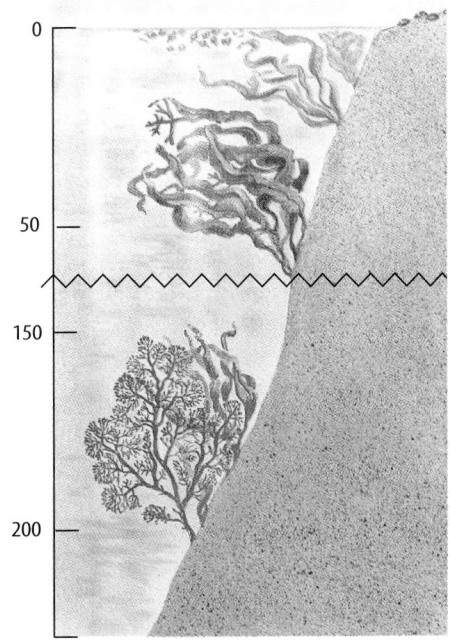

Figure 5
Green algae are found closer to the surface. Brown algae can grow from a depth of about 35 m. Red algae are found in the deepest water at 175 m to 200 m.

Figure 6
A Green algae often can be seen on the surface of ponds in the summer. **B** Giant kelp, a brown alga, can form forests like this one located off the coast of California. Extracts from kelp add to the smoothness and spreadability of products such as cheese spreads and mayonnaise.

SECTION 1 Protists **91**

Importance of Algae

Activity

Have students research how satellites are used to capture images of red tides. L3

SCIENCE *Online*

Internet Addresses

_____
_____
_____
_____

Explore the Glencoe Science Web site at **science.glencoe.com** to find out more about topics in this section.

Extension

Each year, more than 200,000 metric tons of diatomaceous earth is mined in a quarry in California. Ask students what this means in terms of the number of diatoms it took to accumulate such a deposit and where the ocean was located at one time. This indicates that, at one time, this area may have been under water.

✔ Reading Check

Answer Possible answer: algae is used in food and cosmetics.

SCIENCE *Online*

Research Visit the Glencoe Science Web site at **science.glencoe.com** for more information about red tides. Determine whether there is an area or time of year in which red tides occur more frequently. Communicate to your class what you learned.

Figure 7
Carrageenan, a substance extracted from the red alga Irish moss, is used for thickening dairy products such as chocolate milk.

92

Importance of Algae

Have you thought about how important grasses are as a food source for animals that live on land? Cattle, deer, zebras, and many other animals depend on grasses as their main source of food. Algae sometimes are called the grasses of the oceans. Most animals that live in the oceans eat either algae for food or other animals that eat algae. You might think many-celled, large algae like kelp are the most important food source, but the one-celled diatoms and dinoflagellates claim that title. Algae, such as *Euglena*, also are an important source of food for organisms that live in freshwater.

Algae and the Environment Algae are important in the environment because they produce oxygen as a result of photosynthesis. The oxygen produced by green algae is important for most organisms on Earth, including you.

Under certain conditions, algae can reproduce rapidly and develop into what is known as a bloom. Because of the large number of organisms in a bloom, the color of the water appears to change. Red tides that appear along the east and Gulf coasts of the United States are the result of dinoflagellate blooms. Toxins produced by the dinoflagellates can cause other organisms to die and can cause health problems in humans.

Algae and You People in many parts of the world eat some species of red and brown algae. You probably have eaten foods or used products made with algae. Carrageenan (kar uh JEE nuhn), a substance found in the cell walls of red algae, has gelatinlike properties that make it useful to the cosmetic and food industries. It is usually processed from the red alga Irish moss, shown in **Figure 7.** Carrageenan gives toothpastes, puddings, and salad dressings their smooth, creamy textures. Another substance, algin (AL juhn), found in the cell walls of brown algae, also has gelatinlike properties. It is used to thicken foods such as ice cream and marshmallows. Algin also is used in making rubber tires and hand lotion.

Ancient deposits of diatoms are mined and used in insulation, filters, and road paint. The cell walls of diatoms produce the sparkle that makes some road lines visible at night and the crunch you feel in toothpaste.

✔ **Reading Check** *What are some uses by humans of algae?*

Curriculum Connection

Geography Have students plot on a United States map the major areas where diatomite, or diatomaceous earth, is mined. Leading producers in the United States are California, Nevada, Arizona, Washington, and Florida. L2 ELL

Science **Journal**

News Item Have students write in their Science Journals an item that might appear on a news program to warn people about red tides. The item should contain information about the organisms that are causing the problem and health precautions to prevent poisoning. L2
IS Linguistic

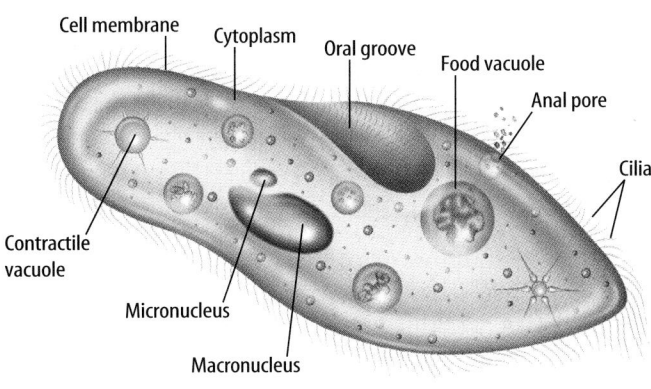

Cell membrane
Cytoplasm
Oral groove
Food vacuole
Anal pore
Cilia
Contractile vacuole
Micronucleus
Macronucleus

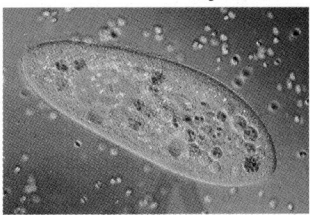

Magnification: 107×

Figure 8
Paramecium **is a typical ciliate found in many freshwater environments. These rapidly swimming protists consume bacteria.** *Locate the contractile vacuoles in the photo. What is their function?*

Animal-Like Protists

One-celled, animal-like protists are known as **protozoans.** Usually protozoans are classified by how they move. These complex organisms live in or on other living or dead organisms that are found in water or soil. Many protozoans have specialized vacuoles for digesting food and getting rid of excess water.

Ciliates As their name suggests, these protists have **cilia** (SIHL ee uh)—short, threadlike structures that extend from the cell membrane. Ciliates can be covered with cilia or have cilia grouped in specific areas on the surface of the cell. The cilia beat in a coordinated way. As a result, the organism moves swiftly in any direction. Organisms in this group include some of the most complex, one-celled protists and some of the largest, one-celled protists.

A typical ciliate is *Paramecium,* shown in **Figure 8.** *Paramecium* has two nuclei—a macronucleus and a micronucleus—another characteristic of the ciliates. The micronucleus is involved in reproduction. The macronucleus controls feeding, the exchange of oxygen and carbon dioxide, the amount of water and salts entering and leaving *Paramecium,* and other functions of *Paramecium.*

Ciliates usually feed on bacteria that are swept into the oral groove by the cilia. Once the food is inside the cell, a vacuole forms around it and the food is digested. Wastes are removed through the anal pore. Freshwater ciliates, like *Paramecium,* also have a structure called the contractile vacuole that helps get rid of excess water. When the contractile vacuole contracts, excess water is ejected from the cell.

Animal-Like Protists

Caption Answer

Figure 8 The contractile vacuoles are star-shaped. Their function is to eliminate excess water from the cell.

Use Science Words

Word Meaning Have students determine the meanings of the prefix *pro-* and the suffix *-zoa* in the word *protozoan*. Ask them how these relate to the meaning of the word. *Pro-* comes from the Greek word, meaning "before," and *-zoa* comes from the Greek word for "animal." So, a protozoan is an organism that probably evolved before animals.

Use an Analogy

To help students visualize the beating of cilia, show them a photograph of a rowing crew. All members move together so that their oars are all in the same position at the same time. This propels the boat through the water as cilia propel a paramecium or other ciliate through its watery medium.

IDENTIFYING Misconceptions

Point out that the use of the words *hairlike* and *threadlike* as they refer to flagella and cilia relate to how the organelles appear. They function more like oars or propellers.

Curriculum Connection

Math A paramecium may be about 0.1 cm long. Giant kelp may be 100 m long. **How many times larger is giant kelp than a paramecium?** 0.1 cm/paramecium × 1 m/100 cm × 1 giant kelp/100 m = 100,000 times larger L2 **Logical-Mathematical**

Quick Demo

Use model plant and animal cells to illustrate the organelles in common between algae and plants and between protozoans and animals. **IN Visual-Spatial**

Teacher FYI

Recent research suggests that some termite species can digest wood without their flagellated mutualists. However, wood digestion is more efficient with the mutualists than without them.

Discussion

Have groups of students research a particular parasitic protozoan such as *Plasmodium*, *Trypanosoma*, *Giardia*, or *Trichomona*. During class have them share their findings about location of outbreaks, numbers of cases, and disease symptoms. L2 COOP LEARN **IN Interpersonal**

Quick Demo

Squash a termite's abdomen in a saline solution that is isotonic for insects, making a wet mount. Allow students to observe the flagellates in the termite's gut.

Caption Answer

Figure 10 It is a one-celled consumer, has no cell wall, and moves by using pseudopods.

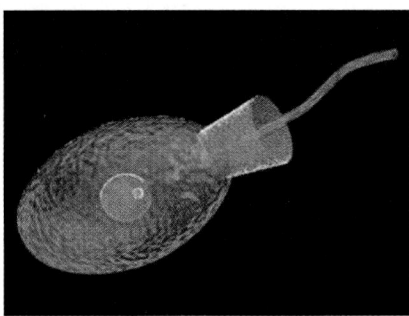

Figure 9
Proterospongia is a rare, freshwater protist. Some scientists hypothesize that it might share an ancestor with ancient animals.

Figure 10
In many areas of the world, a disease-causing species of amoeba lives in the water. If it enters a human body, it can cause dysentery—a condition that can lead to a severe form of diarrhea. *Why is an amoeba classified as a protozoan?*

Magnification: 2,866×

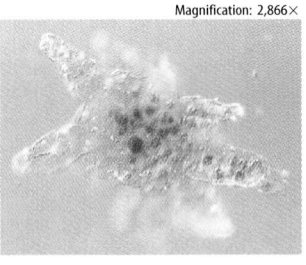

Flagellates Protozoans called flagellates move through their watery environment by whipping their long flagella. Many species of flagellates live in freshwater, though some are parasites that harm their hosts.

Proterospongia, shown in **Figure 9,** is a member of one group of flagellates that might share an ancestor with ancient animals. These flagellates often grow in colonies of many cells that are similar in structure to cells found in animals called sponges. Like sponge cells, when *Proterospongia* cells are in colonies, they perform different functions. Moving the colony through the water and dividing, which increases the colony's size, are two examples of jobs that the cells of *Proterospongia* carry out.

Movement with Pseudopods Some protozoans move through their environments and feed using temporary extensions of their cytoplasm called **pseudopods** (SEWD uh pahdz). The word *pseudopod* means "false foot." These organisms seem to flow along as they extend their pseudopods. They are found in freshwater and saltwater environments, and certain types are parasites in animals.

The amoeba shown in **Figure 10** is a typical member of this group. To obtain food, an amoeba extends the cytoplasm of a pseudopod on either side of a food particle such as a bacterium. Then the two parts of the pseudopod flow together and the particle is trapped. A vacuole forms around the trapped food. Digestion takes place inside the vacuole.

Although some protozoans of this group, like the amoeba, have no outer covering, others secrete hard shells around themselves. The white cliffs of Dover, England are composed mostly of the remains of some of these shelled protozoans. Some shelled organisms have holes in their shells through which the pseudopods extend.

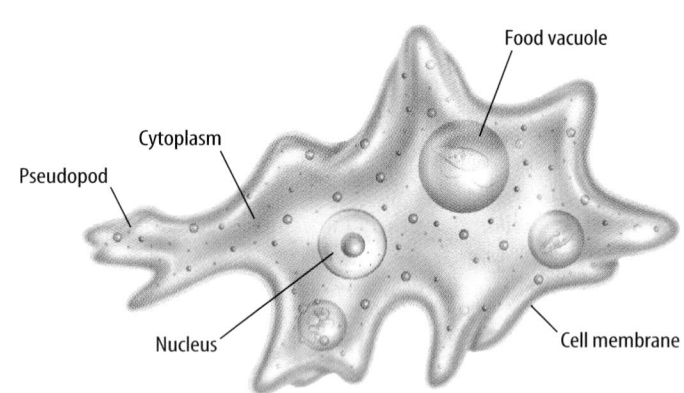

Food vacuole
Cytoplasm
Pseudopod
Nucleus
Cell membrane

LAB DEMONSTRATION

Purpose to observe how amoebas capture prey

Materials amoeba culture, small ciliates, projecting microscope, slide and coverslip, dropper

Preparation Have all necessary equipment set up before class starts. Pre-dyed amoebas and ciliates may be helpful to obtain.

Procedure A drop of amoeba and a drop of prey per slide are sufficient. Observe under low power, then high power with the projecting microscope.

Expected Outcome Students should observe amoebas extending pseudopodia and capturing prey in food vacuoles.

✔Assessment

When is the organism captured? when the pseudopod completely envelopes it **Is the prey still alive after capture?** The prey lives for some time before digestive fluids kill it.

Figure 11
Asexual reproduction takes place inside a human host. Sexual reproduction takes place in the intestine of a mosquito.

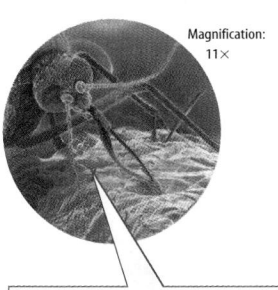

Magnification: 11×

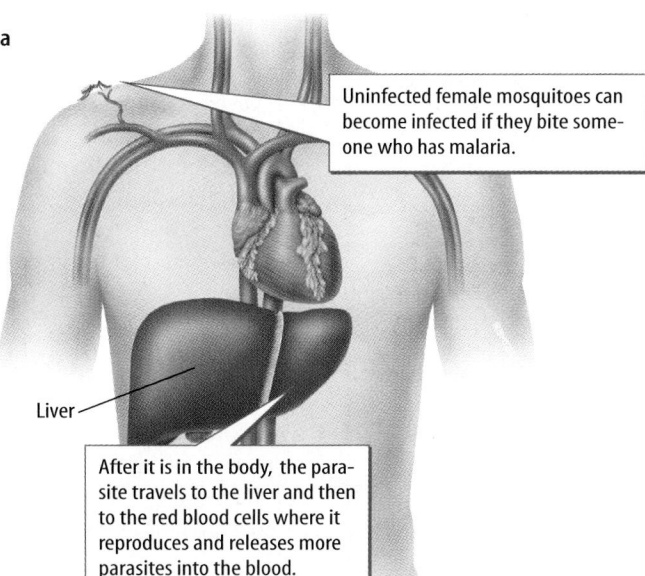

Uninfected female mosquitoes can become infected if they bite someone who has malaria.

Liver

Plasmodium lives in the salivary glands of certain female mosquitoes. The parasite can be transferred to a human's blood if an infected mosquito bites them.

After it is in the body, the parasite travels to the liver and then to the red blood cells where it reproduces and releases more parasites into the blood.

Other Protozoans One group of protozoans has no way of moving on their own. All of the organisms in this group are parasites of humans and other animals. These protozoans have complex life cycles that involve sexual and asexual reproduction. They often live part of their lives in one animal and part in another. The parasite that causes malaria is an example of a protozoan in this group. **Figure 11** shows the life cycle of the malaria parasite.

Importance of Protozoans

Like the algae, some protozoans are an important source of food for larger organisms. When some of the shelled protozoans die, they sink to the bottom of bodies of water and become part of the sediment. Sediment is a buildup of plant and animal remains and rock and mineral particles. The presence of these protists in sediments is used sometimes by field geologists as an indicator species. This tells them where petroleum reserves might be found beneath the surface of Earth.

✔ **Reading Check** *Why are shelled protozoans important?*

One type of flagellated protozoan lives with bacteria in the digestive tract of termites. Termites feed mainly on wood. These protozoans and bacteria produce wood-digesting enzymes that help break down the wood. Without these organisms, the termites would be unable to use the chemical energy stored in wood.

 Health INTEGRATION

The flagellate *Trypanosoma* is carried by the tsetse fly in Africa and causes African sleeping sickness in humans and other animals. It is transmitted to other organisms during bites from the fly. The disease affects the central nervous system. Research this disease and create a poster showing your results.

Importance of Protozoans

 Health INTEGRATION

African sleeping sickness is prevalent in sub-Saharan Africa. Some regions are uninhabitable because of the risk of becoming infected. There are several varieties, caused by different species of protozoa, which differ slightly in their symptoms and severity. Early symptoms usually include fever and inflammation of the lymph nodes. More advanced symptoms may include a sensation of pain, severe headaches, mental dullness and apathy, tremors, paralysis, chorea, and profound sleepiness. These symptoms are often followed by coma and death, though in some cases the individual develops a tolerance and lives for many years as a carrier. Posters may relate the numbers of cases each year, the number of deaths, the vector, and locations of infestations. Some students may research possible cures. P

✔ **Reading Check**

Answer The presence of these organisms in sediment can indicate where petroleum may be found.

Curriculum Connection

Math Have students analyze the following story by making a graph. A person who contracted malaria had the following body temperatures (°C) at the given times. Day 1: 1:00 P.M., 39.4° (chills); 6:00 P.M., 38.3° (sweating); Day 2: 1:00 A.M., 36.1°; 6:00 A.M., 36.7°; 1:00 P.M., 36.1°; 6:00 P.M, 37.2°; Day 3: 1:00 A.M., 38.3° (chills); 6:00 A.M., 39.4°; 1:00 P.M., 39.4°; 6:00 P.M., 38.3° (sweating). **When will the person have chills next?** The person will have the chills next at 1:00 P.M. on Day 5. L2 **IS Logical-Mathematical**

Resource Manager

Chapter Resources Booklet
Enrichment, p. 27
Transparency Activity, pp. 43–44

Funguslike Protists

Caption Answer

Figure 12 Slime molds move and behave like animal-like protists during part of their life cycle, but, like fungi, they are decomposers that reproduce with spores.

Figure 12
Slime molds come in many different forms and colors ranging from brilliant yellow or orange to rich blue, violet, pink, and jet black. *How are slime molds similar to protists and fungi?*

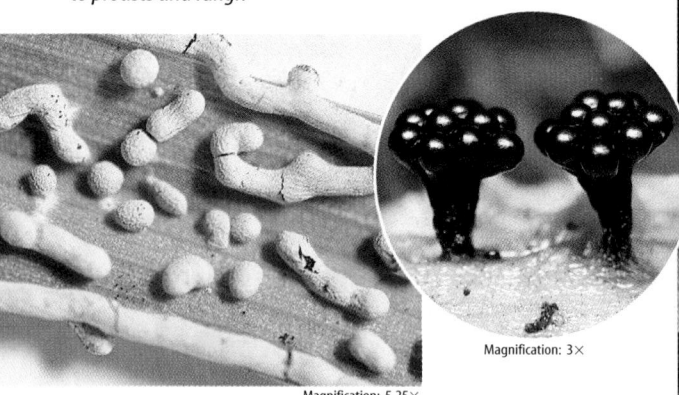

Magnification: 3×

Magnification: 5.25×

96   CHAPTER 4 Protists and Fungi

Disease in Humans The protozoans that are most important to you are the ones that cause diseases in humans. In tropical areas, flies or other biting insects transmit many of the parasitic flagellates to humans. A flagellated parasite called *Giardia* can be found in water that is contaminated with wastes from humans or wild or domesticated animals. If you drink water directly from a stream, you could get this diarrhea-causing parasite.

Some amoebas also are parasites that cause disease. One parasitic amoeba, found in ponds and streams, can lead to a brain infection and death.

Funguslike Protists

Funguslike protists include several small groups of organisms such as slime molds, water molds, and downy mildews. Although all funguslike protists produce spores like fungi, most of them can move from place to place using pseudopods like the amoeba. All of them must take in food from an outside source.

Slime Molds As shown in **Figure 12,** slime molds are more attractive than their name suggests. Slime molds form delicate, weblike structures on the surface of their food supply. Often these structures are brightly colored. Slime molds have some protozoan characteristics. During part of their life cycle, slime molds move by means of pseudopods and behave like amoebas.

Most slime molds are found on decaying logs or dead leaves in moist, cool, shady environments. One common slime mold sometimes creeps across lawns and mulch as it feeds on bacteria and decayed plants and animals. When conditions become less favorable, reproductive structures form on stalks and spores are produced.

Water Molds and Downy Mildews

Most members of this large, diverse group of funguslike protists live in water or moist places. Like fungi, they grow as a mass of threads over a plant or animal. Digestion takes place outside of these protists, then they absorb the organism's nutrients. Unlike fungi, the spores these protists produce have flagella. Their cell walls more closely resemble those of plants than those of fungi.

Some water molds are parasites of plants, and others feed on dead organisms. Most water molds appear as fuzzy, white growths on decaying matter. **Figure 13** shows a parasitic water mold that grows on aquatic organisms. If you have an aquarium, you might see water molds attack a fish and cause its death. Another important type of protist is a group of plant parasites called downy mildew. Warm days and cool, moist nights are ideal growing conditions for them. They can live on aboveground parts of many plants. Downy mildews weaken plants and even can kill them.

Figure 13
Water mold, the threadlike material seen in the photo, grows on a dead salamander. In this case, the water mold is acting as a decomposer. This important process will return nutrients to the water.

✔ Reading Check *How do water molds affect organisms?*

Problem-Solving Activity

Is it a fungus or a protist?

Slime molds, such as the pipe cleaner slime shown in the photograph to the right, can be found covering moist wood. They can be white or bright red, yellow, or purple. If you look at a piece of slime mold on a microscope slide, you will see that the cell nuclei move back and forth as the cytoplasm streams along. This streaming of the cytoplasm is how a slime mold creeps over the wood.

Identifying the Problem
Should slime molds be classified as protists or as fungi?

Solving the Problem
1. What characteristics do slime molds share with protists? How are slime molds similar to protozoans and algae?

2. What characteristics do slime molds share with fungi? What characteristics do slime molds have that are different from fungi?
3. What characteristics did you compare to decide what group slime molds should be classified in? What other characteristics could scientists examine to help classify slime molds?

SECTION 1 Protists **97**

Section 1 Protists **97**

Importance of the Funguslike Protists

Activity

Have students make a chart listing the positive and negative effects of funguslike protists.

③ Assess

Reteach

Have students examine photographs or illustrations of various protists and identify the life cycle phase of each. L2
IS Visual-Spatial

Challenge

What are the causes and effects of a red tide? A red tide is caused by a population explosion of dinoflagellates. Millions of these organisms cause the water to look red. Some species release a nerve toxin that can kill fish and humans.

✔Assessment

Performance Have students write a statement in their Science Journals comparing the environments of slime molds and water molds. Use **Performance Assessment in the Science Classroom,** p. 175.

Figure 14
Downy mildews can have a great impact on agriculture and economies when they infect potatoes, sugar beets, grapes, and melons like those above.

Importance of the Funguslike Protists

Some of the organisms in this group are important because they help break down dead organisms. However, most funguslike protists are important because of the diseases they cause in plants and animals. One species of water mold that causes lesions in fish can be a problem when the number of organisms in a given area is high. Fish farms and salmon spawning in streams can be greatly affected by a water mold spreading throughout the population. Water molds cause disease in other aquatic organisms including worms and even diatoms.

Economic Effects Downy mildews can have a huge effect on economies as well as social history. A downy mildew infection of grapes in France during the 1870s nearly wiped out the entire French wine industry. One of the most well-known members of this group is a downy mildew, which caused the Irish potato famine during the 1840s. Potatoes were Ireland's main crop and the primary food source for its people. When the potato crop became infected with downy mildew, potatoes rotted in the fields, leaving many people with no food. Downy mildews, as shown in **Figure 14,** continue to infect crops such as lettuce, corn, and cabbage, as well as tropical avocados and pineapples.

Section Assessment

1. What are the characteristics common to all protists?
2. Compare and contrast the different characteristics of animal-like, plantlike, and funguslike protists.
3. How are plantlike protists classified into different groups?
4. How are protozoans classified into different groups?
5. **Think Critically** Why are there few fossils of certain groups of protists?

Skill Builder Activities

6. **Making and Using Tables** Make a table of the positive and negative effects that protists have on your life and health. **For more help, refer to the** Science Skill Handbook.
7. **Using an Electronic Spreadsheet** Use a spreadsheet to make a table that compares the characteristics of the three groups of protozoans. Include *example organisms, method of transportation,* and *other characteristics.* **For more help, refer to the** Technology Skill Handbook.

Answers to Section Assessment

1. single-celled or many-celled organisms that live in moist or wet surroundings; possess membrane-bound nuclei; protists may be plantlike, animal-like, or funguslike
2. Algae are plantlike protists with chloroplasts and cell walls. Protozoans are single-celled animal-like protists

that lack cell walls and cannot produce their own food. Funguslike protists are all consumers that produce spores.
3. by their structure and the pigments they contain
4. by their method of movement

5. Protists are small and do not have hard parts that are fossilized easily. The protists decay rapidly, leaving no trace of their existence.
6. Check student tables for accuracy.
7. Tables should accurately display information from this section.

Activity

Comparing Algae and Protozoans

Magnification: 50×

A lgae and protozoans have characteristics that are similar enough to place them in the same group—the protists. However, the variety of protist forms is great. In this activity, you can observe many of the differences among protists.

What You'll Investigate
What are the differences between algae and protozoans?

Materials
cultures of *Paramecium, Amoeba, Euglena,* and *Spirogyra*
prepared slides of the organisms listed above
prepared slide of slime mold
microscope slides (4)
coverslips (4)
microscope
stereomicroscope
dropper
Alternate materials

Goals
■ **Draw and label** the organisms you examine.
■ **Observe** the differences between algae and protozoans.

Safety Precautions

Make sure to wash your hands after handling algae and protozoans.

Procedure
1. Copy the data table in your Science Journal.
2. Make a wet mount of the *Paramecium* culture. If you need help, refer to Student Resources at the back of the book.

Protist Observations		
Protist	Drawing	Observations
Paramecium		
Amoeba	Student drawings	
Euglena	should resemble group features	
Spirogyra	described in this section.	
Slime mold		

3. **Observe** the wet mount first under low and then under high power. Record your observations in the data table. Draw and label the organism that you observed.
4. **Repeat** steps 2 and 3 with the other cultures. Return all preparations to your teacher and wash your hands.
5. **Observe** the slide of slime mold under low and high power. Record your observations.

Conclude and Apply
1. Which structure was used for movement by each organism that could move?
2. Which protists make their own food? Explain how you know that they can make their own food.
3. **Identify** the protists you observed with animal-like characteristics.

*C*ommunicating
Your Data
Share the results of this activity with your classmates. **For more help,** refer to the **Science Skill Handbook.**

ACTIVITY   99

---

*C*ommunicating
Your Data
Students should have similar results. They may communicate by using drawings or written descriptions of their observations.

Activity

BENCH TESTED

Purpose to observe the differences between algae and protozoans [L2] [LS] **Visual-Spatial**

Process Skills observing and inferring, classifying, making and using tables, comparing and contrasting

Time Required 50 minutes

Materials Prepared slides of protozoans and algae may be used. All live specimens should be obtained from a reputable supply house. No parasitic forms should be used.

Safety Precautions Remind students to be careful when plugging and unplugging the microscope. Water should be kept away from the outlet.

Teaching Strategies
• Use a videotape of the organisms to prepare students for what they will see.
• Remind students that algae and protozoans are protists.

Troubleshooting Maintain separate cultures for each organism. Prevent students from using the same dropper for more than one culture.

Answers to Questions
1. Paramecia use cilia; amoebas use pseudopods; euglenas use flagella.
2. *Spirogyra* and *Euglena* make their own food; they contain chloroplasts for photosynthesis.
3. *Paramecium, Euglena, Amoeba,* slime mold

✓*Assessment*

Performance To further assess students' abilities to classify algae and protozoans, have them make and view wet mounts of scrapings from fish tanks. Use **PASC**, p. 121.

SECTION
2
Fungi

Bellringer Transparency

Display the Section Focus Transparency for Section 2. Use the accompanying Transparency Activity Master. L2 ELL

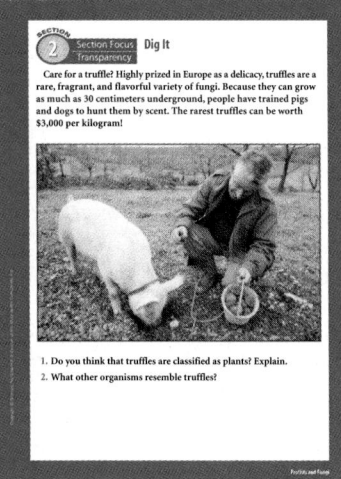

Tie to Prior Knowledge

Have students relate examples of fungi they know about. Students will likely know about toadstools and fungi used in food. Explain that fungi are in a kingdom separate from other organisms.

SECTION
2

Fungi

As You Read

What You'll Learn

- **Identify** the characteristics shared by all fungi.
- **Classify** fungi into groups based on their methods of reproduction.
- **Differentiate** between the imperfect fungi and all other fungi.

Vocabulary

hyphae	budding
saprophyte	sporangium
spore	lichen
basidium	mycorrhizae
ascus	

Why It's Important

Fungi are important sources of food and medicines, and they help recycle Earth's wastes.

Figure 15
The hyphae of fungi are involved in the digestion of food, as well as reproduction.

What are fungi?

Do you think you can find any fungi in your house or apartment? You have fungi in your home if you have mushroom soup or fresh mushrooms. What about that package of yeast in the cupboard? Yeasts are a type of fungus used to make some breads and cheeses. You also might find fungus growing on a loaf of bread or mildew fungus growing on your shower curtain.

Origin of Fungi Although fossils of fungi exist, most are not useful in determining how fungi are related to other organisms. Some scientists hypothesize that fungi share an ancestor with ancient, flagellated protists and slime molds. Other scientists hypothesize that their ancestor was a green or red alga.

Structure of Fungi Most species of fungi are many-celled. The body of a fungus is usually a mass of many-celled, thread-like tubes called **hyphae** (HI fee), as shown in **Figure 15.** The hyphae produce enzymes that help break down food outside of the fungus. Then, the fungal cells absorb the digested food. Because of this, most fungi are known as saprophytes. **Saprophytes** are organisms that obtain food by feeding on dead or decaying tissues of other organisms. Other fungi are parasites. They obtain their food directly from living things.

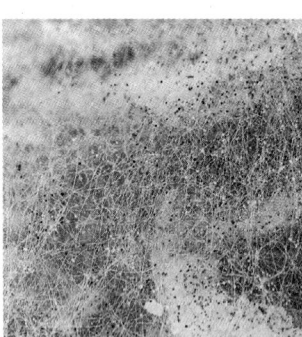

A The body of a fungus is visible to the unaided eye.

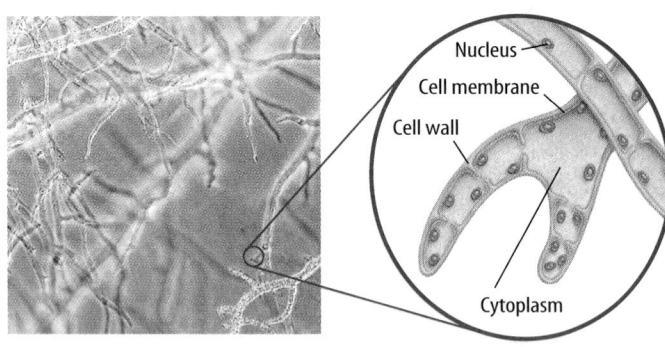

B Threadlike, microscopic hyphae make up the body of a fungus.

C The internal structure of hyphae.

Section ✓ Assessment Planner

PORTFOLIO
Try at Home MiniLAB, p. 103

PERFORMANCE ASSESSMENT
Try at Home MiniLAB, p. 103
Skill Builder Activities, p. 107
See page 114 for more options.

CONTENT ASSESSMENT
Section, p. 107
Challenge, p. 107
Chapter, pp. 114–115

Other Characteristics of Fungi What other characteristics do all fungi share? Because fungi grow anchored in soil and have a cell wall around each cell, fungi once were classified as plants. But fungi don't have the specialized tissues and organs of plants, such as leaves and roots. Unlike plants, fungi cannot make their own food because they don't contain chlorophyll.

Fungi grow best in warm, humid areas, such as tropical forests or between toes. You need a microscope to see some fungi, but in Michigan one fungus was found growing underground over an area of about 15 hectares. In the state of Washington, another type of fungus found in 1992 was growing throughout nearly 600 hectares of soil.

Reproduction Asexual and sexual reproduction in fungi usually involves the production of spores. A **spore** is a waterproof reproductive cell that can grow into a new organism. In asexual reproduction, cell division produces spores. These spores will grow into new fungi that are genetically identical to the fungus from which the spores came.

Fungi are not identified as either male or female. Sexual reproduction can occur when the hyphae of two genetically different fungi of the same species grow close together. If the hyphae join, a reproductive structure will grow, as shown in **Figure 16.** Following meiosis in these structures, spores are produced that will grow into fungi. These fungi are genetically different from either of the two fungi whose hyphae joined during sexual reproduction. Fungi are classified into three main groups based on the type of structure formed by the joining of hyphae.

✔ **Reading Check** *How are fungi classified?*

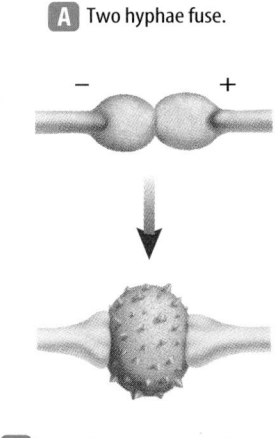

A Two hyphae fuse.

B Reproductive structure forms.

Figure 16

A When two genetically different fungi of the same species meet, **B** a reproductive structure, in this case a zygospore, will be formed. The new fungi will be genetically different from either of the two original fungi.

SCIENCE *Online*

Research Visit the Glencoe Science Web site at **science.glencoe.com** for more information about the gigantic fungus *Armillaria ostoyae* and other unusual fungi. Communicate to your class what you learned.

---

② Teach

What are fungi?

Activity

Mix some yeast suspension with flour and water and put it in a warm place. Ask students to predict what will happen over the course of the day. The dough will rise as the yeast's respiratory processes produce carbon dioxide. L2

Discussion

Have students discuss why fungi are no longer classified as plants. Unlike plants, fungi contain no chloroplasts.

Quick Demo

Show students some food that has mold growing on it. This is best done if the food can be kept under a plastic cover as in a freezer storage bag. **Caution:** *Before beginning, ask if any students have known allergies to fungal spores. Contact the school nurse if a student shows signs of an allergic reaction to fungal spores used in demonstrations during this section. It is rare, but some students may experience breathing difficulties in the presence of fungal spores.*

✔ **Reading Check**

Answer by the type of structure formed by the joining of hyphae

---

Resource Manager

Chapter Resources Booklet
Transparency Activity, p. 41
Directed Reading for Content Mastery, pp. 19, 20

SCIENCE *Online*

Internet Addresses

_____

_____

_____

Explore the Glencoe Science Web site at **science.glencoe.com** to find out more about topics in this section.

Sac Fungi

Figure 17

A Club fungi, like this mushroom, form a reproductive structure called a basidium. Each basidium produces four balloonlike structures called basidiospores. **B** Spores will be released from these as the final step in sexual reproduction.

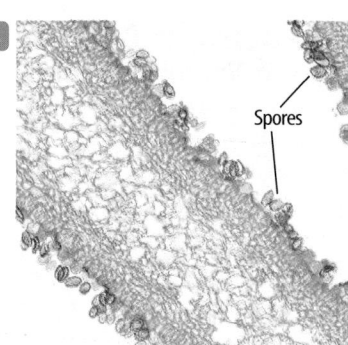

Spores

Club Fungi

The mushrooms shown in **Figure 17** are probably the type of fungus that you are most familiar with. The mushroom is only the reproductive structure of the fungus. Most of the fungus grows as hyphae in the soil or on the surface of its food source. These fungi commonly are known as club fungi. Their spores are produced in a club-shaped structure called a **basidium** (buh SIHD ee uhm) (plural, *basidia*).

Sac Fungi

Yeasts, molds, morels, and truffles are all examples of sac fungi—a diverse group containing more than 30,000 different species. The spores of these fungi are produced in a little, saclike structure called an **ascus** (AS kus), as shown in **Figure 18A.**

Although most fungi are many-celled, yeasts are one-celled organisms. Yeasts reproduce by forming spores and reproduce asexually by budding, as illustrated in **Figure 18B. Budding** is a form of asexual reproduction in which a new organism forms on the side of an organism. The two organisms are genetically identical.

Figure 18

A The spores of a sac fungus are released when the tip of an ascus breaks open.
B Yeasts can reproduce by forming buds off their sides. A bud pinches off and forms an identical cell.

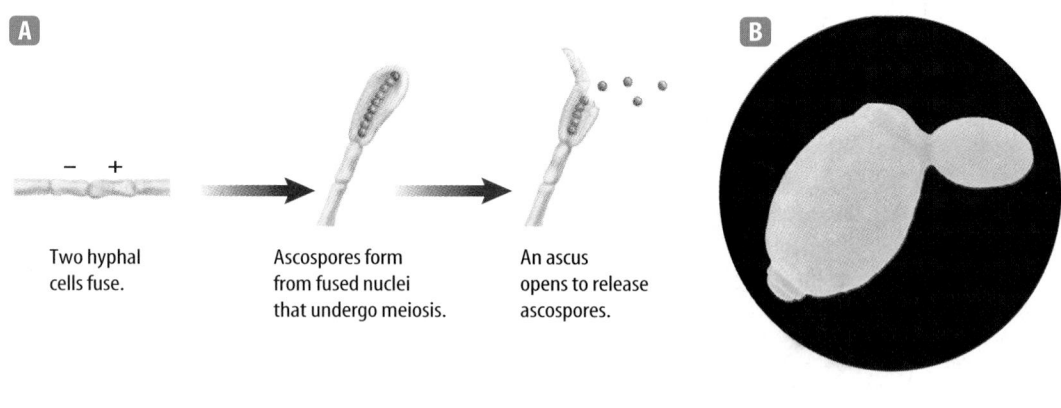

A

− +

Two hyphal cells fuse.

Ascospores form from fused nuclei that undergo meiosis.

An ascus opens to release ascospores.

B

Fun Fact

One of the largest organisms in the world is a fungus growing under acres of forest floor in Michigan. It is estimated to weigh at least 100 tons.

Curriculum Connection

Math The fairy ring toadstool (a type of mushroom) advances outward from the center at a rate of about 30 cm per year. One ring is estimated to be 150 years old. **How many meters in diameter is this fairy ring?** 150 years × 30 cm/year × 2 radii/diameter = 9,000 cm = 90 meters

L2 **IS** Logical-Mathematical

Figure 19
The black mold found growing on bread or fruit is a type of zygospore fungus.

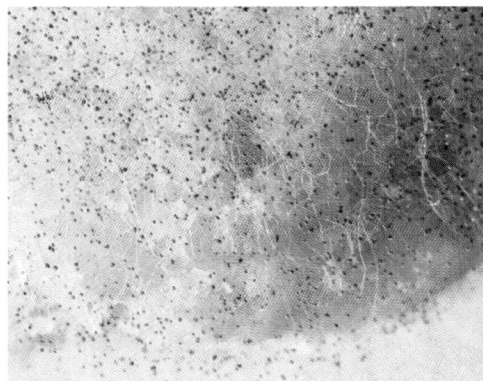

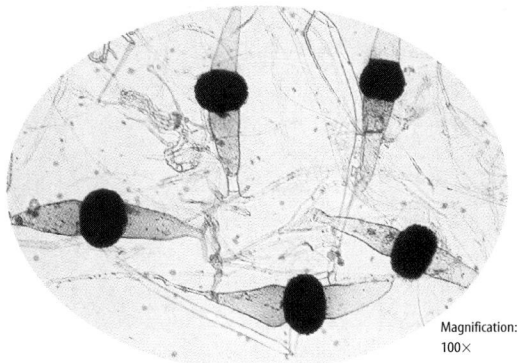

Magnification: 100×

B The zygospores shown here produce sporangia that hold the individual spores.

A This black mold produces zygospores during sexual reproduction.

Zygote Fungi and Other Fungi

The fuzzy black mold that you sometimes find growing on a piece of fruit or an old loaf of bread as shown in **Figure 19,** is a type of zygospore fungus. Fungi that belong to this group produce spores in a round spore case called a **sporangium** (spuh RAN jee uhm) (plural, *sporangia*) on the tips of upright hyphae. When each sporangium splits open, hundreds of spores are released into the air. Each spore will grow and reproduce if it lands in a warm, moist area that has a food supply.

✔ Reading Check *What is a sporangium?*

Some fungi either never reproduce sexually or never have been observed reproducing sexually. Because of this, these fungi are difficult to classify. They usually are called imperfect fungi because there is no evidence that their life cycle has a sexual stage. Imperfect fungi reproduce asexually by producing spores. When the sexual stage of one of these fungi is observed, the species is classified immediately in one of the other three groups.

Penicillium is a fungus that is difficult to classify. Some scientists classify *Penicillium* as an imperfect fungi. Others believe it should be classified as a sac fungus based on the type of spores it forms during asexual reproduction. Another fungus, which causes pneumonia, has been classified recently as an imperfect fungus. Like *Penicillium*, scientists do not agree about which group to place it in.

TRY AT HOME
Mini LAB

Interpreting Spore Prints

Procedure

1. Obtain several **mushrooms from the grocery store** and let them age until the undersides look brown.
2. Remove the stems. Place the mushroom caps with the gills down on a piece of **unlined white paper.** Wash your hands.
3. Let the mushroom caps sit undisturbed overnight and remove them from the paper the next day. Wash your hands.

Analysis
1. Draw and label the results in your **Science Journal.** Describe the marks on the page and what made them.
2. How could you estimate the number of new mushrooms that could be produced from one mushroom cap?

Zygote Fungi and Other Fungi

Make a Model

After students have observed bread mold with a dissecting microscope or hand lens, have them construct a model of the structures they observe. Students should show spores, hyphae, and so on. L2 [IS] **Kinesthetic**

✔ Reading Check

Answer a round spore case

TRY AT HOME
Mini LAB

Purpose to observe spore prints L1 ELL [IS] **Visual-Spatial** P

Materials mushrooms, unlined white paper

Teaching Strategy Caution students not to disturb the mushrooms while spore prints are being made.

Safety Precautions Remind students not to eat anything used in the lab.

Analysis
1. Sketches will vary. Brown lines will be parallel or concentric rings made by falling spores.
2. Count a few spores in one area and multiply by the total area of spore production.

✔ Assessment

Performance To further assess understanding of mushrooms, have students carefully tease apart a bit of gill from under the cap and make a wet mount of an extremely small piece. Students should draw and describe what they see in their Science Journals. Use **PASC,** p. 127.

Resource Manager

Chapter Resources Booklet
  MiniLAB, p. 4
Home and Community Involvement, p. 43

Inclusion Strategies

Learning Disabled Have students make flash cards with the name of a group of fungi and a picture on one side and the characteristics and an example on the other. Allow students to practice learning the fungi by using their flash cards. L1 [IS] **Linguistic**

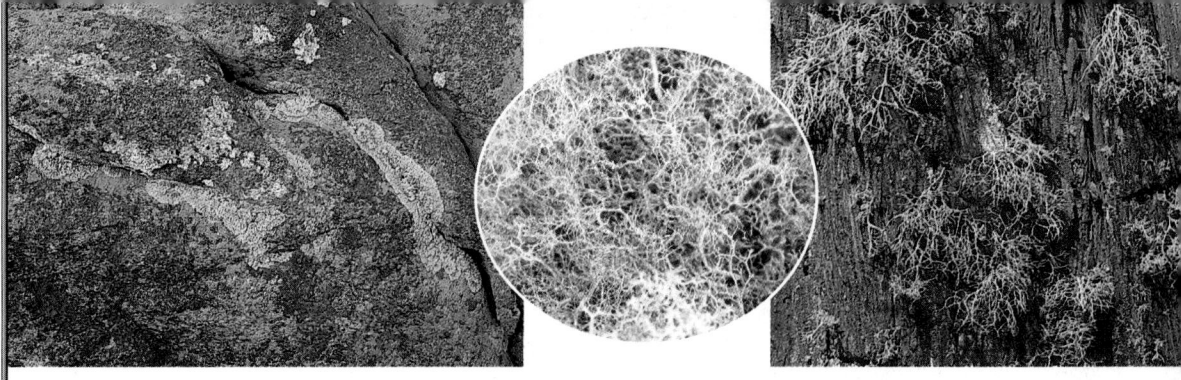

Lichens

Caption Answer

Figure 20 Possible answers: by the kind of photosynthetic cells they associate with or by their forms

Fungi and Plants

Visual Learning

Figure 22 Use the picture to point out that almost all orchid species require mycorrhizae in order to live. An important orchid to most students is the vanilla orchid. Have students research which part of the vanilla plant is useful to humans. The vanilla bean is the seedpod of the orchid plant.

✔ **Reading Check**

Answer The fungus helps the plant take in more nutrients than the plant can take in by itself or take in certain nutrients that the plant cannot take in without the fungus.

Figure 20
Lichens can look like a crust on bare rock, appear leafy, or grow upright. All three forms can grow near each other. *What is one way lichens might be classified?*

Figure 22
Many plants, such as these orchids, could not survive without mycorrhizae to help absorb water and important minerals from soil.

Lichens

The colorful organisms in **Figure 20** are lichens. A **lichen** (LI kun) is an organism that is made of a fungus and either a green alga or a cyanobacterium. These two organisms have a relationship in which they both benefit. The alga or cyanobacterium lives among the threadlike strands of the fungus. The fungus gets food made by the green alga or cyanobacterium. The green alga or cyanobacterium gets a moist, protected place to live.

Importance of Lichens For many animals, including caribou and musk oxen, lichens are an important food source.

Lichens also are important in the weathering process of rocks. They grow on bare rock and release acids as part of their metabolism. The acids help break down the rock. As bits of rock accumulate and lichens die and decay, soil is formed. This soil supports the growth of other species.

Scientists also use lichens as indicator organisms to monitor pollution levels, as shown in **Figure 21.** Many species of lichens are sensitive to pollution. When these organisms show a decline in their health or die quickly, it alerts scientists to possible problems for larger organisms.

Fungi and Plants

Some fungi interact with plant roots. They form a network of hyphae and roots known as **mycorrhizae** (mi kuh RI zee). About 80 percent of plants develop mycorrhizae. The fungus helps the plant absorb more of certain nutrients from the soil better than the roots can on their own, while the plant supplies food and other nutrients to the fungi. Some plants, like the lady's slipper orchids shown in **Figure 22,** cannot grow without the development of mycorrhizae.

✔ **Reading Check** *Why are mycorrhizae so important to plants?*

104 CHAPTER 4 Protists and Fungi

Science Journal

Erosion Have students research the importance of fungi in erosion and write a paragraph about it in their Science Journals. Wind, water, temperature changes, and living things such as fungi are the main forces of erosion. Explain that all landforms—mountains, rivers, valleys, and plains—show visible results of erosional forces. L2 IS **Linguistic**

Figure 21

Widespread, slow-growing, and long-lived, lichens come in many varieties. Lichens absorb water and nutrients mainly from the air rather than the soil. Because certain types are extremely sensitive to toxic environments, lichens make natural, inexpensive air-pollution detectors.

Can you see a difference between these two red alder tree trunks? White lichens cover one trunk but not the other. Red alders are usually covered with lichens such as those seen in the photo on the left. Lichens could not survive on the tree on the right because of air pollution.

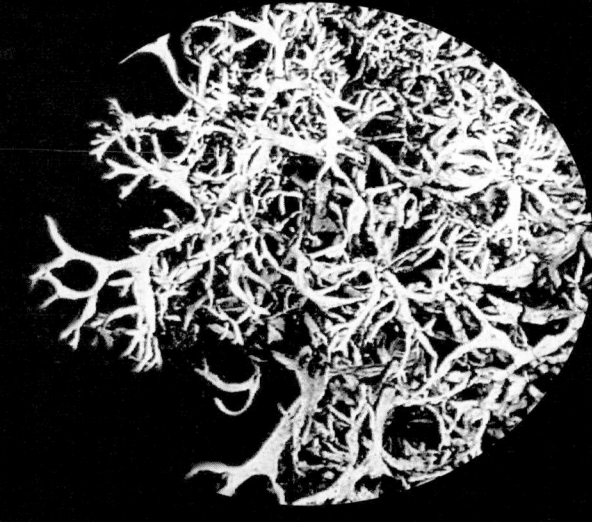

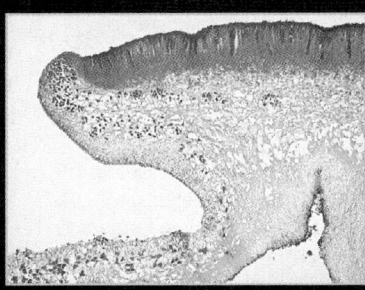

A lichen consists of a fungus and an alga or cyanobacterium living together in a partnership that benefits both organisms. In this cross section of a lichen (50x), reddish-stained bits of fungal tissue surround blue-stained algal cells.

Evernia lichens, left, sicken and die when exposed to sulfur dioxide, a common pollutant emitted by coal-burning industrial plants such as the one above.

SECTION 2 Fungi **105**

Visualizing Lichens as Air Quality Indicators

Have students examine the pictures and read the captions. Then ask the following questions.

If a tree has no lichens on its trunk, what does that indicate about the air quality in that area? Possible answer: The tree is in an area that has a source of air pollution.

Where do lichens get most of their nutrients? Lichens absorb water and nutrients from the air.

Activity

Have students make a map of the area surrounding the school. The area should encompass about 5 square km. Then have them indicate on the map which areas would most likely contain lichens. If there are no lichens in the area, have students discuss why that may be.

LS Naturalist

Extension

Many current studies are trying to determine the effect that air pollution has on lichens. Have students research several different species of lichens and determine whether the lichens are sensitive to certain types of air pollution.

Resource Manager

Chapter Resources Booklet
Enrichment, p. 28

Fungi and Plants,
continued

Earth Science
INTEGRATION

The fossilized fungus was mycorrhizae. In addition to providing evidence of how plants could have made the transition to land, the fossil also provided evidence of fungi that are scarce in the fossil record.

Importance of Fungi

Activity

Allow students to work in groups to develop and carry out interviews with local physicians concerning the role of fungi in the health field. Students will learn that fungi can cause infection in humans, but that some fungi are also used in the production of medicines. L2
COOP LEARN [LS] **Interpersonal**

Environmental Science
INTEGRATION

Some fungi form sticky nets that can be used to trap microscopic nematodes—roundworms that can be detrimental to plants.

Environmental Science
INTEGRATION

Although fungi can have negative effects on agriculture, they can be used to help farmers. Some farmers are using fungi as natural pesticides. Fungi can control a variety of pests including termites, rice weevils, tent caterpillars, aphids, and citrus mites.

Figure 23
A Rusts can infect the grains used to make many cereals including wheat, barley, rye, and oats. **B** Not all fungi are bad for agriculture. Some are natural pesticides. This grasshopper is infected with a fungal parasite.

Earth Science
INTEGRATION

Fossilized Fungus In 1999, scientists discovered a fossilized fungus in a 460 million-year-old rock. The fossil was a type of fungus that forms associations with plant roots. Scientists have known for many years that the first plants could not have survived moving from water to land alone. Early plants did not have specialized roots to absorb nutrients. Also, tubelike cells used for transporting water and nutrients to leaves were too simple.

Scientists have hypothesized that early fungi attached themselves to the roots of early plants, passing along nutrients taken from the soil. Scientists suggest that it was this relationship that allowed plants to move successfully from water onto land about 500 million years ago. Until the discovery of this fossil, no evidence had been found that this type of fungus existed at that time.

Importance of Fungi

As mentioned in the beginning of this chapter, some fungi are eaten for food. Cultivated mushrooms are an important food crop. However, wild mushrooms never should be eaten because many are poisonous. Some cheeses are produced using fungi. Yeasts are used in the baking industry. Yeasts use sugar for energy and produce alcohol and carbon dioxide as waste products. The carbon dioxide causes doughs to rise.

Agriculture Many fungi are important because they cause diseases in plants and animals. Many sac fungi are well known by farmers because they damage or destroy plant crops. Diseases caused by sac fungi are Dutch elm disease, apple scab, and ergot disease of rye. Smuts and the rust, shown in **Figure 23A,** are club fungi. They cause billions of dollars worth of damage to food crops each year.

✔ Active Reading

Quickwrites This strategy, sometimes called freewrites, lets students use spontaneous writing to discover what they already know. Have students write a list of ideas about a topic, then share these ideas with the class. Next, have students write their ideas freely in a paragraph without worrying about punctuation, spelling, and grammar. Have students use a Quickwrite to discover what they know about the importance of fungi.

Resource Manager

Chapter Resources Booklet
Reinforcement, p. 26
Lab Activities, pp. 9–10, 11–13

Health and Medicine Fungi are responsible for causing diseases in humans and animals. Ringworm and athlete's foot are two infections of the skin caused by species of imperfect fungi. Other fungi can cause respiratory infections. The effects of fungi on health and medicine are not all negative. Some species of fungi naturally produce antibiotics that keep bacteria from growing on or near them.

The antibiotic penicillin is produced by the imperfect fungi *Penicillium*. This fungus is grown commercially, and the antibiotic is collected to use in fighting bacterial infections. Cyclosporin, an important drug used to help fight the body's rejection of transplanted organs, also is derived from a fungus. There are many more examples of breakthroughs in medicine as a result of studying and discovering new uses of fungi. In fact, there is a worldwide effort among scientists who study fungi to investigate soil samples to find more useful drugs.

Decomposers As important as fungi are in the production of different foods and medicines, they are most important as decomposers that break down organic materials. Food scraps, clothing, and dead plants and animals are made of organic material. Often found on rotting logs, as shown in **Figure 24,** fungi break down these materials. The chemicals in these materials are returned to the soil where plants can reuse them. Fungi, along with bacteria, are nature's recyclers. They keep Earth from becoming buried under mountains of organic waste materials.

Figure 24
Fungi have an important role as decomposers in nature.

③ Assess

Reteach

Show students various illustrations of fungi. Ask them to identify the parts of each fungus. L2 [N] **Visual-Spatial**

Challenge

Why is it beneficial for fungi to reproduce both sexually and asexually? Asexual reproduction allows fungi to take full and rapid advantage of a food source. Sexual reproduction provides genetic variation for surviving in different environments.

✔ *Assessment*

Oral What has never been observed in any of the imperfect fungi? a sexual stage **How do the imperfect fungi reproduce if they don't have a sexual stage?** asexual spores Use **Performance Assessment in the Science Classroom,** p. 143.

Section ② Assessment

1. List characteristics common to all fungi.
2. How are fungi classified into different groups?
3. Differentiate between the imperfect fungi and all other fungi.
4. Why are lichens important to the environment?
5. **Think Critically** If an imperfect fungus were found to produce basidia under certain environmental conditions, how would the fungus be reclassified?

Skill Builder Activities

6. **Comparing and Contrasting** What are the similarities and differences among the characteristics of the four groups of fungi and lichens? **For more help, refer to the** Science Skill Handbook.

7. **Using Proportions** Of the 100,000 fungus species, approximately 30,000 are sac fungi. What percentage of fungus species are sac fungi? **For more help, refer to the** Math Skill Handbook.

Answers to Section Assessment

1. Fungi cannot make their own food. Most fungi are many-celled saprophytes with a body made of hyphae. They grow anchored in soil and have cell walls.
2. by the structure formed by the joining of hyphae
3. Imperfect fungi have no known sexual stage in their life cycle;

all other fungi do.
4. Lichens are an important food source for many animals, they help break down rocks into soil, and they are used to monitor pollution levels.
5. It would be reclassified as a club fungus belonging to division Basidiomycota.

6. Zygote fungi: round spore cases on upright stalks; sac fungi: spores grow in a protective sac; club fungi: spores grow in a club-shaped structure; imperfect fungi: no sexual stage has been observed; lichens: crusty, leafy or upright; closely associated with algae or cyanobacteria. See information in section 2 under: What are

fungi?; Club fungi; Sac Fungi; Zygote Fungi and other Fungi; Lichens
7. 30,000/100,000 $\times$ 100% = 30%

Activity

BENCH TESTED

Recognize the Problem

Purpose
Students identify fungi and design a field guide for fungi in their area. **Kinesthetic and Visual-Spatial**

Process Skills
identifying, classifying, analyzing, and designing

Time Required
three class periods

Thinking Critically

Discussion
Tell students to think about methods for observing fungi. Have them consider features in their field guides that they would want to use to make identifying fungi easier. How will they group the organisms in the book? What type of diagrams or photographs will they include? How can they waterproof the pages of the field guide? What size should the field guide be?

Possible Materials
Provide a wide selection of containers and other collection equipment. Provide students with detailed guidebooks to help them identify their discoveries. Encourage students to use a wide variety of art mediums including color pencils, markers, pastels, charcoal, paints, and photography.

Safety Precautions
Caution students never to eat any fungi they collect and to thoroughly wash their hands after handling fungi.

Activity — Model and Invent

Creating a Fungus Field Guide

Whether they are hiking deep into a rain forest in search of rare tropical birds, diving to coral reefs to study marine worms, or peering into microscopes to identify strains of bacteria, scientists all over the world depend on reliable field guides. Field guides are books that identify and describe certain types of organisms or the organisms living in a specific environment. Scientists find field guides for a specific area especially helpful. In this activity, you will create your own field guide for the club fungi found in your area.

Cross section of club fungus

Recognize the Problem

How could you create a field guide for the club fungi living in your area?

Thinking Critically

What information would you include in a field guide of club fungi?

Possible Materials
collection jars
magnifying glass
microscopes
microscope slides and coverslips
field guide to fungi or club fungi
art supplies

Goals
- **Identify** the common club fungi found in the woods or grassy areas near your home or school.
- **Create** a field guide to help future science students identify these fungi.

Data Source
SCIENCE *Online* Go to the Glencoe Science Web site at **science.glencoe.com** for more information about club fungi.

Safety Precautions
Be certain not to eat any of the fungi you collect. Wash your hands after handling any fungus collected. Do not touch your face during the activity.

108 **CHAPTER 4** Protists and Fungi

SCIENCE *Online*
Internet Addresses

_____

_____

_____

Explore the Glencoe Science Web site at **science.glencoe.com** to find out more about topics in this activity.

Resource Manager

Chapter Resources Booklet
   Activity Worksheet, pp. 7–8
Lab Management and Safety, p. 58

Planning the Model

1. Decide on the locations where you will conduct your search.

2. Select the materials you will need to collect and survey club fungi.

3. Design a data table in your Science Journal to record the fungi you find.

4. Decide on the layout of your field guide. What information about the fungi you will include? What drawings you will use? How will you group the fungi?

Check Model Plans

1. **Describe** your plan to your teacher and ask your teacher how it could be improved.

2. **Present** your ideas for collecting and surveying fungi, and your layout ideas for your field guide to the class. Ask your classmates to suggest improvements in your plan.

Making the Model

1. Search for samples of club fungi. **Record** the organisms you find in your data table. Use a fungus field guide to identify the fungi you discover. Do not pick or touch any fungi that you find unless you have permission.

2. Using your list of organisms, complete your field guide of club fungi as planned.

3. When finished, give your field guide to a classmate to identify a club fungus.

Analyzing and Applying Results

1. **Compare** the number of fungi you found to the total number of organisms listed in the field guide you used to identify the organisms.

2. **Infer** why your field guide would be more helpful to future science students in your school than the fungus field guide you used to identify organisms.

3. **Analyze** the problems you had while collecting and identifying your fungi. Suggest steps you could take to improve your collection and identification methods.

4. **Analyze** the problems you had while creating your field guide. Suggest ways your field guide could be improved.

𝒞ommunicating
Your Data

Compare your field guide with the field guides assembled by your classmates. Combine all the information on local club fungi compiled by your class to create a classroom field guide to club fungi.

ACTIVITY 109

Planning the Model

Teaching Strategies

- Assign each student a "buddy." Students should be responsible for staying with their buddies at all times.

- Review any poisonous fungi found in your area. Emphasize that students should not touch these organisms.

Making the Model

Expected Outcome Students will design and create a field guide that illustrates and identifies the types of fungi found in local woods and grassy areas.

Analyzing and Applying Results

Student answers will vary depending upon individual research. Accept all reasonable answers.

✔𝒜ssessment

Portfolio Ask students to draw a large colored picture of one of their fungi. Use **PASC**, p. 127.

𝒞ommunicating
Your Data

Offer students who are interested the opportunity to purchase color photocopies of the classroom field guide.

Content Background

The cacao tree is a perennial that yields several harvests annually. It was introduced to Europe in the sixteenth century after being cultivated in South America. On average the cacao stands 20 feet tall with 12-inch long shiny leaves. The cacao tree's pods contain beans with a high level of fat and are pulverized into a residue we commonly refer to as cocoa. Other uses for the cocoa bean include medication, cosmetics, and soap.

Of the three fungi mentioned, witches' broom is the most destructive. This fungus infects the pods, making them unusable. Brazil was once the top producer of cacao beans but because of this blight has fallen into eighth place in the last five years. Hard hit by this agricultural problem are the 5 to 6 million small farmers who depend heavily on production of the cacao tree for their financial survival. The Agricultural Research Service has developed new ways of combating the effects of fungi, including spraying with copper-based fungicides, breeding trees for resistance, pruning diseased trees, and cleaning up infected pods and branches.

Chocolate SOS

Can a fungus protect cacao trees under attack?

Chocolate is made from seeds (cocoa beans) that grow in the pods of the tropical cacao tree. To grow large crops more efficiently, farmers plant only a couple of the many varieties of cacao. They also use pesticides to protect the trees from destructive insect pests. These modern farming methods have produced huge crops of cocoa beans. But they also have helped destructive fungi sweep through cacao fields. There are fewer healthy cacao trees today than there were several years ago. And unless something stops the fungi that are destroying the trees, there could be a lot less chocolate in the future.

A cacao tree plantation

Pods contain dozens of beans.

Losing Beans

Three types of fungi (witches' broom, blackpod rot, and frosty pod rot) are now killing cacao trees. The monoculture (growing one type of crop) of modern fields helps fungi spread quickly. A disease that attacks one plant of a species in a monoculture will rapidly spread to all plants in the monoculture. If a variety of plant species is present, the disease won't spread as quickly or as far.

110

Resources for Teachers and Students

"Fighting a Fungal Siege on Cacao Farms." November 1999. *Agricultural Research*.

"No Fun Fungi." May 26, 2000. *St. Louis Post-Dispatch*.

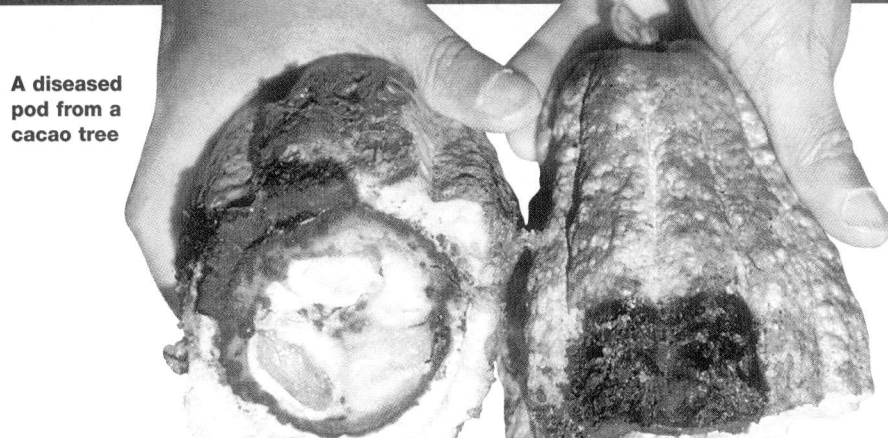

A diseased pod from a cacao tree

Since the blight began in the late 1980s and early 1990s, the world has lost 3 million tons of cocoa beans. Brazil was the top cocoa bean exporter in South America. In 1985, the United States alone bought 430,000 tons of cocoa beans from Brazil. In 1999, the whole Brazilian harvest contained just 130,000 tons, mostly because of the witches' broom fungus. The 2000 harvest was only 80,000 tons—the smallest in 30 years.

A Natural Cure

Farmers were using traditional chemical sprays to fight the fungus, but they were ineffective because in tropical regions, the sprays were washed away by rain. Now agriculture experts are working on a "natural" solution to the problem. They are using several types of "good" fungi to fight the "bad" fungi attacking the trees. When sprayed on infected trees, the good fungi (strains of *Trichoderma*) attack and stop the spread of the bad fungi. Scientists are already testing the fungal spray on trees in Brazil and Peru. The treatments have reduced the destruction of the trees by between 30 percent and 50 percent.

Don't expect your favorite chocolate bars to disappear from stores anytime soon. Right now, world cocoa bean supplies still exceed demand. But if the spread of the epidemic can't be stopped, those chocolate bars could become slightly more expensive and a little harder to find.

A fungus-infested cacao tree

CONNECTIONS Concept Map What are the steps in making chocolate—from harvesting cacao beans to packing chocolate products for sale? Use library and other sources to find out. Then draw a concept map that shows the steps. Compare your concept map with those of your classmates.

Online

For more information, visit science.glencoe.com

Discussion

What are farmers currently doing to fight the fungal attacks on the cacaos? Possible answer: Using "good" fungi called *Trichoderma* to stop the spread of the "bad" fungi that is destroying the cacao trees.

Activity

Use the Irish potato famine to illustrate how crop shortages can have devastating effects on a population. Use a team activity model. Have one group research the timetable for the famine. When did it start? Another group should focus on what caused the potatoes to become diseased and ultimately disappear as a resource. Another group should focus on the statistics of the famine. Who was affected? How many people died as a result? Another group should be responsible for an illustration representing the time period. Finally, after each group has presented, lead a discussion on how the two crop shortages are similar and how they differ.

Investigate the Issue

Lead a short discussion of the importance of each step that goes into cacao processing. To spur discussion, ask: **Would we still have easy access to chocolate bars if one group or part of the process was eliminated?**

CONNECTIONS Continue a dialogue asserting the necessity of each person in the process of making and distributing this product. Emphasize the role of the small farmers in the process. Try to convey their potential for loss if the amount of cacao that is diseased is great.

Online

Internet Addresses

_____
_____
_____

Explore the Glencoe Science Web site at **science.glencoe.com** to find out more about topics in this feature.

Reviewing Main Ideas

Preview

Students can answer the questions in their Science Journals. Discuss the answers as you go through the chapter. **IS** **Linguistic**

Review

Students can write their answers, then compare them with those of other students. **IS** **Interpersonal**

Reteach

Students can look at the illustrations and describe details that support the main ideas of the chapter. **IS** **Visual-Spatial**

Answers to Chapter Review

SECTION 1

2. Algae obtain energy through photosynthesis.

6. Downy mildews can kill plants, sometimes having a great economic impact.

SECTION 2

4. *Pencillium* does not appear to have a sexual stage, the primary characteristic used to classify fungi.

Reviewing Main Ideas

Section 1 Protists

1. Protists are one-celled or many-celled eukaryotic organisms. They can reproduce asexually, resulting in two new cells that are genetically identical. Protists also can reproduce sexually and produce genetically different organisms.

2. The protist kingdom has members that are plantlike, animal-like, and funguslike. *How do plantlike protists like the one shown below obtain food?*

3. Protists are thought to have evolved from a one-celled organism with a nucleus and other cellular structures.

4. Plantlike protists have cell walls and contain chlorophyll.

5. Animal-like protists can be separated into groups by how they move.

6. Funguslike protists have characteristics of protists and fungi. *What is the importance of funguslike protists such as the downy mildew shown below?*

Section 2 Fungi

1. Most species of fungi are many-celled. The body of a fungus consists of a mass of threadlike tubes.

2. Fungi are saprophytes or parasites—they feed off other things because they cannot make their own food.

3. Fungi reproduce using spores.

4. The three main groups of fungi are club fungi, sac fungi, and zygote fungi. Fungi that cannot be placed in a specific group are called imperfect fungi. Fungi are placed into one of these groups according to the structures in which they produce spores. *Why are fungi such as the* Penicillium *shown below so hard to classify?*

5. A lichen is an organism that consists of a fungus and a green alga or cyanobacterium.

FOLDABLES
Reading & Study Skills

After You Read

Using what you have learned, write about similarities and differences of protists and fungi on the back of your Compare and Contrast Study Fold.

FOLDABLES
Reading & Study Skills

After You Read

After students have read the chapter and completed the Foldable described in Before You Read, have them do the activity on the student page.

Dinah Zike

Visualizing Main Ideas

Complete the following concept map on a separate sheet of paper.

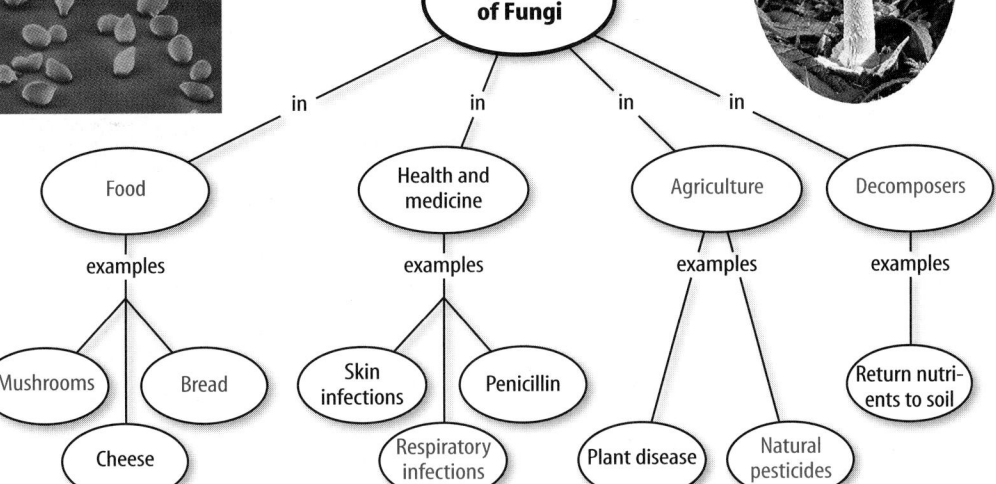

Importance of Fungi

in — **Food** — examples — **Mushrooms**, **Bread**, **Cheese**

in — **Health and medicine** — examples — **Skin infections**, **Penicillin**, **Respiratory infections**

in — **Agriculture** — examples — **Plant disease**, **Natural pesticides**

in — **Decomposers** — examples — **Return nutrients to soil**

Vocabulary Review

Vocabulary Words

a. algae
b. ascus
c. basidium
d. budding
e. cilia
f. flagellum
g. hyphae
h. lichen
i. mycorrhizae
j. protist
k. protozoan
l. pseudopod
m. saprophyte
n. sporangium
o. spore

Study Tip

THE PRINCETON REVIEW

Make sure to read over your class notes after each lesson. Reading them will help you better understand what you've learned, as well as prepare you for the next day's lesson.

Using Vocabulary

Write the vocabulary word that matches each of these descriptions.

1. reproductive cell of a fungus

2. organisms that are animal-like, plantlike, or funguslike

3. threadlike structures used for movement

4. plantlike protists

5. organism made up of a fungus and an alga or a cyanobacterium

6. reproductive structure made by sac fungi

7. threadlike tubes that make up the body of a fungus

8. structure used for movement formed by oozing cytoplasm

Visualizing Main Ideas

See student page.

Vocabulary Review

Using Vocabulary

1. spore
2. protist
3. cilia
4. algae
5. lichen
6. ascus
7. hyphae
8. pseudopod

Chapter 4 Assessment

Checking Concepts

1. D
2. B
3. D
4. D
5. B
6. A
7. D
8. B
9. B
10. C

Thinking Critically

11. no warmth, low humidity, low moisture
12. Accessory pigments help chlorophyll to be more efficient during photosynthesis.
13. Funguslike protists produce spores and take in food from an outside source like fungi. Unlike fungi, the funguslike protists usually move by using pseudopods.
14. When in association with certain mutualistic fungi, some plants are able to take in materials from their environment.
15. Fungi can digest food outside the organism. This mold secrets the enzymes, which help digest the fruit. Then the cells absorb the nutrients.

Checking Concepts

Choose the word or phrase that best answers the question.

1. Which of the following is an alga?
   A) *Paramecium* C) *Amoeba*
   B) lichen D) diatom

2. Which type of protist captures food, does not have cell walls, and can move from place to place?
   A) algae C) fungi
   B) protozoans D) lichens

3. Which of the following organisms cause red tides when found in large numbers?
   A) *Euglena* C) *Ulva*
   B) diatoms D) dinoflagellates

4. Algae are important for which of the following reasons?
   A) They are a food source for many aquatic organisms.
   B) Parts of algae are used in foods that humans eat.
   C) Algae produce oxygen as a result of the process of photosynthesis.
   D) all of the above

5. Which of the following moves using cilia?
   A) *Amoeba* C) *Giardia*
   B) *Paramecium* D) *Euglena*

6. Where would you most likely find funguslike protists?
   A) on decaying logs C) on dry surfaces
   B) in bright light D) on metal surfaces

7. Decomposition is an important role of which organisms?
   A) protozoans C) plants
   B) algae D) fungi

8. Where are spores produced in mushrooms?
   A) sporangia C) ascus
   B) basidia D) hyphae

9. Which of the following is used as an indicator organism?
   A) club fungus C) slime mold
   B) lichen D) imperfect fungus

10. Which of the following is sometimes classified as an imperfect fungus?
    A) mushroom C) *Penicillium*
    B) yeast D) lichen

Thinking Critically

11. What kind of environment is needed to prevent fungal growth?

12. Why do algae contain pigments other than just chlorophyll?

13. Compare and contrast the features of fungi and funguslike protists.

14. What advantages do some plants have when they form associations with fungi?

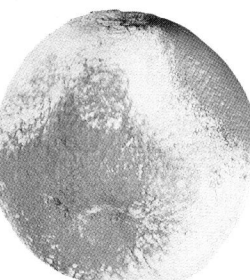

15. Explain the adaptations of fungi that enable them to get food. *How does this mold obtain food?*

Developing Skills

16. **Recognizing Cause and Effect** A leaf sitting on the floor of the rain forest will decompose in just six weeks. A leaf on the floor of a temperate forest, located in areas that have four seasons, will take up to a year to decompose. Explain how this is possible.

17. **Classifying** Classify these organisms based on their method of movement: *Euglena*, water molds, *Amoeba*, dinoflagellates, *Paramecium*, slime molds, and *Giardia*.

Chapter ✓Assessment Planner

Portfolio Encourage students to place in their portfolios one or two items of what they consider to be their best work. Examples include:
- Science Journal, p. 90
- Health Integration, p. 95
- Try at Home MiniLAB, p. 103

Performance Additional performance assessments, Performance Task Assessment Lists, and rubrics for evaluating these activities can be found in Glencoe's **Performance Assessment in the Science Classroom.**

18. **Comparing and Contrasting** Make a chart comparing and contrasting the different ways protists and fungi can obtain food.

19. **Making and Using Tables** Complete the following table that compares the different groups of fungi.

Fungi Comparisons		
Fungi Group	**Structure Where Sexual Spores Are Produced**	**Examples**
Club fungi	Basidium	Mushroom
Sac fungi	Ascus	Truffles
Zygospore fungi	Sporangium	Bread mold
Imperfect fungi	No sexual spores produced	*Penicillium*

20. **Identifying and Manipulating Variables and Controls** You find a new and unusual fungus growing in your refrigerator. Design an experiment to determine what fungus group it belongs to.

Performance Assessment

21. **Poster** Research the different types of fungi found in the area where you live. Determine to which group each fungus belongs. Create a poster to display your results and share them with your class.

22. **Poem** Write a poem about protists or fungi. Include facts about characteristics, types of movement, and ways of feeding.

TECHNOLOGY

Go to the Glencoe Science Web site at **science.glencoe.com** or use the **Glencoe Science CD-ROM** for additional chapter assessment.

Test Practice

Kingdom Protista includes a wide variety of organisms. Some can make their own food and others might get food from their environment. Two groups of protists are shown in the boxes below.

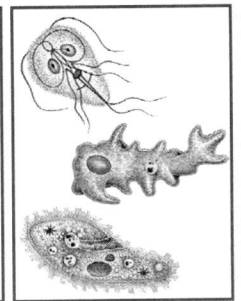

Group A   **Group B**

Study the pictures in the two boxes above and answer the following questions.

1. The protists in Group B are different from the protists in Group A because only the protists in Group B _____ .
   - **A)** have chlorophyll
   - **B)** are many-celled
   - **C)** can move
   - **D)** have a nucleus

2. Which of the following organisms would belong in Group A above?
   - **F)** bacteria **H)** grass
   - **G)** kelp **J)** fish

3. Which of the following is NOT characteristic of Group A?
   - **A)** cell membrane
   - **B)** contain chlorophyll
   - **C)** live in a watery environment
   - **D)** one-celled

Test Practice

The Test-Taking Tip was written by The Princeton Review, the nation's leader in test preparation.

1. C
2. G
3. D

Developing Skills

16. Warm, moist environments such as those found in the rain forest are ideal for the growth of fungi. Therefore, fungi decompose dead organic materials more rapidly in rain forests than in cooler, drier temperate forests.
17. flagella—*Euglena*, water molds, dinoflagellates, *Giardia*; pseudopods—*Amoeba*, slime molds; cilia—*Paramecium*.
18. Check charts for accuracy.
19. See student page.
20. Design will vary. Designs should include comparing the fungus with characteristics of different fungi and observing its sexual reproduction.

Performance Assessment

21. Posters will vary. Most will have photos or drawings of various mushrooms or slime molds. Posters should contain information about the groups of fungi. Use **PASC**, p. 145.
22. Poems will vary but should indicate characteristics and types of organisms studied in this chapter. Use **PASC**, p. 157.

✓Assessment Resources

📁 **Reproducible Masters**

Chapter Resources Booklet
Chapter Review, pp. 33–34
Chapter Tests, pp. 35–38
Assessment Transparency Activity, p. 45

Glencoe Science Web site
Interactive Tutor
Chapter Quizzes

Glencoe Technology
- Assessment Transparency
- Interactive CD-ROM Chapter Quizzes
- ExamView Pro Test Bank
- Vocabulary PuzzleMaker Software
- MindJogger Videoquiz

Section/Objectives	Standards		Activities/Features
Chapter Opener	**National**	**State/Local**	**Explore Activity:** Determine how you use plants, p. 117 **Before You Read,** p. 117
	See p. 5T for a Key to Standards.		
Section 1 An Overview of Plants 🕐 2 sessions 📦 1 block 1. **Identify** characteristics common to all plants. 2. **Explain** which plant adaptations make it possible for plants to survive on land. 3. **Compare and contrast** vascular and nonvascular plants.	National Content Standards: UCP1, C1, C5		**Chemistry Integration,** p. 120 **Visualizing Plant Classification,** p. 122
Section 2 Seedless Plants 🕐 2 sessions 📦 1 block 1. **Distinguish** between characteristics of seedless nonvascular plants and seedless vascular plants. 2. **Identify** the importance of some nonvascular and vascular plants.	National Content Standards: UCP5, A1, C1, C5, F4		**MiniLAB:** Measuring Water Absorption by a Moss, p. 125 **Science Online,** p. 126 **Problem-Solving Activity:** What is the value of rain forests?, p. 126
Section 3 Seed Plants 🕐 3 sessions 📦 1.5 blocks 1. **Identify** the characteristics of seed plants. 2. **Explain** the structures and functions of roots, stems, and leaves. 3. **Describe** the main characteristics and importance of gymnosperms and angiosperms. 4. **Compare** similarities and differences between monocots and dicots.	National Content Standards: UCP5, A1, C1, C5, E2, F5, G2		**MiniLAB:** Observing Water Moving in a Plant, p. 131 **Health Integration,** p. 133 **Science Online,** p. 137 **Activity:** Identifying Conifers, p. 139 **Activity:** Plants as Medicine, pp. 140–141 **Oops! Accidents in Science:** A Loopy Idea Inspires "Fasten-ating" Invention, pp. 142–143

■ NATIONAL GEOGRAPHIC

Teacher's Corner

PRODUCTS AVAILABLE FROM GLENCOE
To order call 1-800-334-7344:
CD-ROMs
NGS PictureShow: Plants: What It Means to Be Green
Curriculum Kit
GeoKit: Plants

Transparency Sets
NGS PicturePack: Plants: What It Means to Be Green
VideoDisc
STV: Plants

PRODUCTS AVAILABLE FROM NATIONAL GEOGRAPHIC SOCIETY
To order call 1-800-368-2728:
Videos
Plant Classification

Activity Materials	Reproducible Resources	Section Assessment	Technology
Explore Activity: old magazines, scissors	**Chapter Resources Booklet** Foldables Worksheet, p. 13 Directed Reading Overview, p. 15 Note-taking Worksheets, pp. 29–31	GLENCOE'S **ASSESSMENT** ADVANTAGE	
Need materials? Contact Science Kit at 1-800-828-7777 or www.sciencekit.com on the Internet.	**Chapter Resources Booklet** Transparency Activity, p. 40 Enrichment, p. 26 Reinforcement, p. 23 Directed Reading, p. 16 **Cultural Diversity,** p. 19 **Life Science Critical Thinking/ Problem Solving,** p. 9 **Earth Science Critical Thinking/ Problem Solving,** p. 17 **Performance Assessment in the Science Classroom,** p. 55	Portfolio Activity, p. 121 Performance Skill Builder Activities, p. 123 Content Section Assessment, p. 123	Section Focus Transparency Interactive CD-ROM Guided Reading Audio Program
MiniLAB: *sphagnum* moss, cheesecloth, spring scales, graduated cylinder, water, container for water	**Chapter Resources Booklet** Transparency Activity, p. 41 MiniLAB, p. 3 Enrichment, p. 27 Reinforcement, p. 24 Directed Reading, p. 17 **Home and Community Involvement,** p. 42 **Math Skill Activities,** p. 5	Portfolio Make a Model, p. 127 Performance MiniLAB, p. 125 Skill Builder Activities, p. 129 Content Section Assessment, p. 129	Section Focus Transparency Interactive CD-ROM Guided Reading Audio Program
MiniLAB: clear container, water, metric ruler, red food coloring, green onion, hand lens **Activity:** short branches of pine, cedar, spruce, Douglas fir, hemlock, fir, redwood, arborvitae, juniper **Activity:** no materials needed	**Chapter Resources Booklet** Transparency Activity, p. 42 MiniLAB, p. 4 Enrichment, p. 28 Reinforcement, p. 25 Directed Reading, pp. 17, 18 Activity Worksheets, pp. 5–6, 7–8 Transparency Activity, pp. 43–44 Lab Activities, pp. 9–10, 11–12 **Performance Assessment in the Science Classroom,** p. 61 **Lab Management and Safety in the Science Classroom,** p. 61	Portfolio Curriculum Connection, p. 133 Performance MiniLAB, p. 131 Skill Builder Activities, p. 138 Content Section Assessment, p. 138	Section Focus Transparency Teaching Transparency Interactive CD-ROM Guided Reading Audio Program

End of Chapter Assessment

GLENCOE'S **ASSESSMENT** ADVANTAGE

Blackline Masters	Technology	Professional Series
Chapter Resources Booklet Chapter Review, pp. 33–34 Chapter Tests, pp. 35–38 **Standardized Test Practice by The Princeton Review,** pp. 43–46	MindJogger Videoquiz Interactive CD-ROM Vocabulary PuzzleMakers ExamView Pro Test Bank Interactive Lesson Planner Interactive Teacher Edition	Performance Assessment in the Science Classroom (PASC)

Transparencies

Section Focus

SECTION 1 Section Focus Transparency A Lot Can Happen in 4,000 Years

Bristlecone pines live a very long time. The oldest one is thought to be over 4,600 years old. From the time the pyramids at Giza were built through this very moment, it has lived in a quiet spot in eastern California. Bristlecones are usually found at high altitudes where it is very dry.

1. Looking at the picture, describe the bristlecone pine's environment.
2. What might some advantages be to the bristlecone's habitat? What might be disadvantages?

L2

SECTION 2 Section Focus Transparency A Fresh Start

After a forest fire has burned out, what happens to the barren acres of land? Will lush vegetation ever thrive in these areas again? Probably. In fact, it could even be better than before!

1. What life can you identify in the top picture?
2. What life can you identify in the bottom picture? What function might these first plants serve?

L2

SECTION 3 Section Focus Transparency Rooted in Nature

Bonsai is an ancient method of growing trees or shrubs in small containers. The plants are kept small by pruning the branches and roots. Because some types of plants used for bonsai can live for more than 100 years, they are passed from generation to generation.

1. What are some advantages to having bonsai plants? What might some disadvantages be?
2. What qualities do you think would be important in practicing bonsai?

L2

This is a representation of key blackline masters available in the Teacher Classroom Resources. See Resource Manager boxes within the chapter for additional information.

Key to Teaching Strategies

The following designations will help you decide which activities are appropriate for your students.

L1 Level 1 activities should be appropriate for students with learning difficulties.

L2 Level 2 activities should be within the ability range of all students.

L3 Level 3 activities are designed for above-average students.

ELL ELL activities should be within the ability range of English Language Learners.

COOP LEARN Cooperative Learning activities are designed for small group work.

LS Multiple Learning Styles logos, as described on page 22T, are used throughout to indicate strategies that address different learning styles.

P These strategies represent student products that can be placed into a best-work portfolio.

Assessment

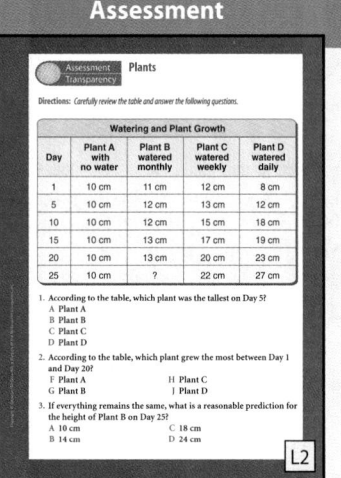

Assessment Transparency Plants

Directions: Carefully review the table and answer the following questions.

Watering and Plant Growth

Day	Plant A with no water	Plant B watered monthly	Plant C watered weekly	Plant D watered daily
1	10 cm	11 cm	12 cm	8 cm
5	10 cm	12 cm	13 cm	12 cm
10	10 cm	12 cm	15 cm	18 cm
15	10 cm	13 cm	17 cm	19 cm
20	10 cm	13 cm	20 cm	23 cm
25	10 cm	?	22 cm	27 cm

1. According to the table, which plant was the tallest on Day 5?
   A Plant A
   B Plant B
   C Plant C
   D Plant D
2. According to the table, which plant grew the most between Day 1 and Day 20?
   F Plant A   H Plant C
   G Plant B   J Plant D
3. If everything remains the same, what is a reasonable prediction for the height of Plant B on Day 25?
   A 10 cm   C 18 cm
   B 14 cm   D 24 cm

L2

Teaching

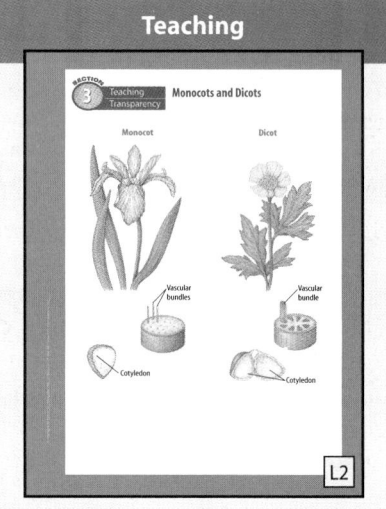

SECTION 3 Teaching Transparency Monocots and Dicots

L2

Hands-on Activities

Activity Worksheets

Laboratory Activities

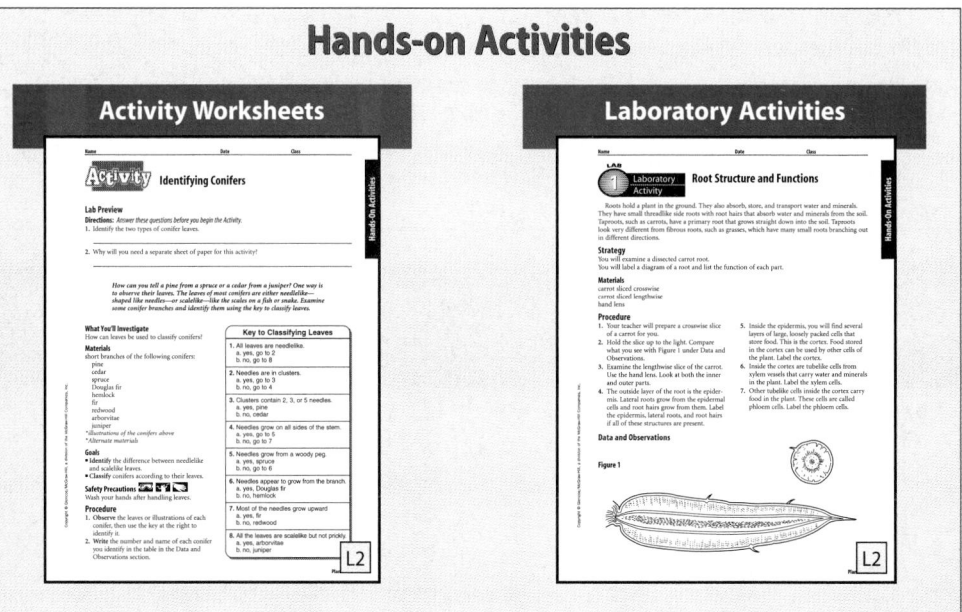

Meeting Different Ability Levels

Content Outline

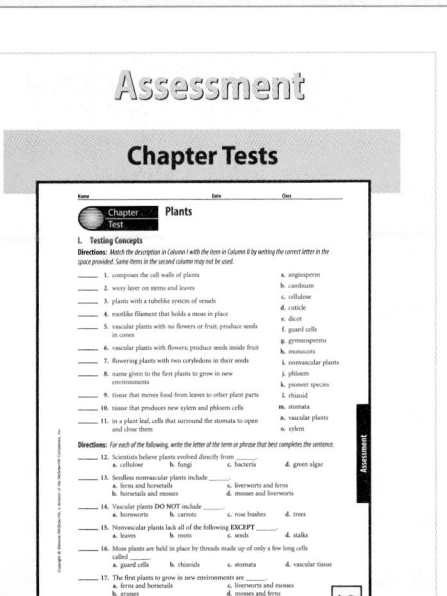

Note-taking Worksheet — Plants

L2

Reinforcement

Reinforcement 1 — An Overview of Plants

L2

Directed Reading

Directed Reading for Content Mastery — Overview Plants

L1

Assessment

Chapter Tests

Chapter Test — Plants

L2

Enrichment

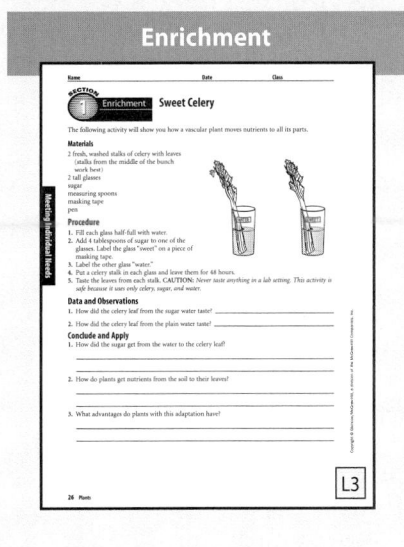

Enrichment 1 — Sweet Celery

L3

Spanish Directed Reading

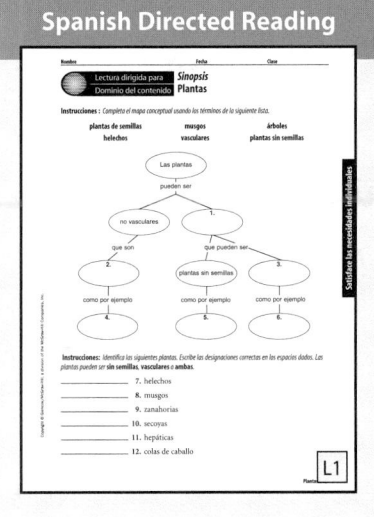

Lectura dirigida para Dominio del contenido — Sinopsis Plantas

L1

Test Practice Workbook

Standardized Test Practice — Teacher Edition

Glencoe Science

LEVEL RED

L2

Chapter Review

Chapter Review — Plants

L2

Science Content Background

An Overview of Plants
Origin and Evolution of Plants

Plants probably share an ancestor with multicellular Chlorophyta, the green algae. Common characteristics of plants and green algae include pigments such as chlorophyll a and b and carotenoids, cell walls that consist primarily of cellulose, starch as the primary food-storage product, and similar cell division. Some plants, including mosses, liverworts, and ferns, have free-swimming sperm and require water for fertilization—another feature they have in common with green algae.

Fun Fact

Luminous mosses glow with a greenish light. These mosses are found in caves and have cells shaped like tiny lenses that focus small amounts of light on the chloroplast.

Adaptations to Land

Fibers are long, slender cells that are found in the vascular tissue of some plants. They usually contain an organic substance called lignin that makes the walls tough and hard. Fibers add extra support to many terrestrial plants. People weave the fibers of some plants to make products such as rope and cloth.

Classification of Plants

Classification of plants traditionally has been based on morphological characteristics such as the number and arrangement of leaves and the structure of flowers and fruit. Recently, genetic studies have been used to make minor changes in the classification of some plants. However, derived characteristics such as vascular tissue and seed formation and similar, easily observable characteristics are reliable features for classification.

For many years plants have been separated into divisions, but in 1993 the International Botanical Congress made the term *phylum* an acceptable alternative. You may wish to introduce the alternate term to your students.

Seedless Plants
Less Familiar Plants

Liverworts and hornworts are leafy with creeping gametophyte forms. Mosses have distinct leaflike and stemlike structures, but because they do not contain vascular tissue, they are not homologous to the leaves and stems of vascular plants. Some liverworts produce structures called gemma cups on their surfaces. Groups of cells in these structures are washed out of the cup when it rains. These cells can grow into new liverwort plants.

Seedless vascular plants include whisk ferns (Psilophyta), club mosses (Lycopoda), horsetails (Sphenophyta), and ferns (Pterophyta). In each of these divisions, motile sperm require water to swim to the egg.

Pat Watson/The Image Works

SECTION 3

Seed Plants

Origins

Seed plants appeared suddenly about 65 million years ago at the beginning of the Cretaceous Period. These plants dominated the land. They developed sperm-containing pollen grains that could be transported from plant to plant without water. The development of an embryo inside a protective seed coat allowed seeds to survive harsh conditions for long periods. About 200,000 of the more than 260,000 species of plants in existence today are seed plants.

Vascular Tissue

The first vascular plants appeared no later than the early Silurian Period, some 430 million years ago. Early vascular plants had stems formed as a result of primary growth—growth from plant tips. Stems had vascular cylinders with conducting functions, as they do in modern vascular plants. Secondary growth, found in conifers and some dicots, is an important early development. It arises by mitotic divisions of cambium tissues and increases the plant's girth.

John Gerlach/Tom Stack & Associates

Fun Fact

An aphid drinks sap from plants by piercing the plant's phloem with its hollow mouthpart.

Xylem tissue is made of tracheids and vessel elements that carry water and dissolved minerals. Tracheids are found in all plants with vascular tissue, but vessel elements are limited almost exclusively to angiosperms. Both are long, tubelike cells that have thick cell walls. Small openings called pits allow water to seep through the cell walls from tracheid to tracheid. Vessels lack transverse end walls and are continuous pipelines through which water can flow.

Unlike xylem tissue, phloem tissue is living. It is composed mostly of sieve-tube elements and companion cells. Sieve-tube elements are cells that carry the products of photosynthesis throughout the plant. Their cell walls are thinner than those of cells found in xylem. Cytoplasm extends from one sieve-tube element to the next through structures called sieve plates. Since mature sieve-tube cells have no nuclei, companion cells help with their metabolism.

SCIENCE *Online*

For additional content background on this topic, go to the Glencoe Science Web site at science.glencoe.com.

Plants

What do you think?

Science Journal Indian pipe is the common name of the plant in this picture. Unlike most plants, Indian pipe plants are not green.

Plants

Go outside and look around. Where do you see plants? Plants cover almost every available surface in a tropical rain forest but only some areas of a desert. Plants are found nearly everywhere on Earth.

Take a close look at a plant. When you look at an animal, you expect to see eyes, a mouth, and maybe even legs. What do you expect to see when you look at a plant? Do all plants have leaves, roots, and flowers?

In this chapter, you'll learn what characteristics plants have and how they are classified. You'll also learn why plants are important.

What do you think?

Science Journal Look at the picture below with a classmate. Discuss what you think this might be or what is happening. Here's a hint: *Most of its relatives are green.* Write your answer or your best guess in your Science Journal.

116

Theme Connection

Stability and Change This chapter emphasizes plant adaptations that allow these organisms to adapt, survive, and reproduce in various environments.

Plants are just about everywhere—in parks and gardens, by streams, on rocks, in houses, and even on dinner plates. Do you use plants for things other than food? In the following activity, find out how plants are used. Then, in the pages that follow, learn about plant life.

Determine how you use plants

1. Brainstorm with two other classmates and make a list of everything that you use in a day that comes from plants.

2. Compare your list with those of other groups in your class.

3. Search through old magazines for images of the items on your list.

4. As a class, build a bulletin board of the magazine images.

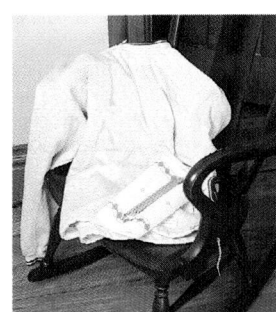

Observe

In your Science Journal, list things that were made from plants 100 years or more ago but today are made from plastics, steel, or some other material.

Before You Read

FOLDABLES
Reading & Study Skills

Making a Know-Want-Learn Study Fold It would be helpful to identify what you already know and what you want to know. Make the following Foldable to help you focus on reading about plants.

1. Place a sheet of paper in front of you so the long side is at the top. Fold the paper in half from top to bottom.

2. Fold both sides in to divide the paper into thirds. Unfold the paper so three columns show.

3. Through the top thickness of paper, cut along each of the fold lines to the top fold, forming three tabs.

4. Draw and label *Know, Want,* and *Learned* across the front of the paper as shown.

5. Before you read the chapter, write what you know under the left tab. Under the middle tab, write what you want to know.

6. As you read the chapter, write what you learn under the right tab.

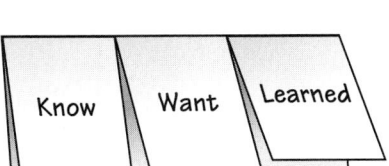

117

EXPLORE ACTIVITY

Purpose Use the Explore Activity to introduce students to the many uses of plants. L2
COOP LEARN IS **Interpersonal**

Preparation Provide books, magazines, and other resources from which students can get ideas.

Teaching Strategy Offer suggestions of additional items from plants to students who need help.

Observe

Examples include building materials, clothing fibers, dyes, paper, resins, paints, and inks.

✓ *Assessment*

Process Show students a picture of a desert succulent with plump water-filled leaves. Have them infer how desert animals might use this plant. The plant could provide water to animals in a dry environment. Use **Performance Assessment in the Science Classroom,** p. 89.

FOLDABLES
Reading & Study Skills

Before You Read

Dinah Zike Study Fold

Purpose This Foldable will provide students an opportunity to review what they know about plants and make them question what they would like to know. The Foldable can be used as an assessment tool at the end of the chapter to determine what students have learned.

📁 For additional help, see Foldables Worksheet, p. 13 in **Chapter Resources Booklet,** or go to the Glencoe Science Web site at **science.glencoe.com.** See After You Read in the Study Guide at the end of this chapter.

SECTION

1

An Overview of Plants

1 Motivate

Bellringer Transparency

Display the Section Focus Transparency for Section 1. Use the accompanying Transparency Activity Master. L2 ELL

SECTION 1 Section Focus Transparency

A Lot Can Happen in 4,000 Years

Bristlecone pines live a very long time. The oldest one is thought to be over 4,600 years old. From the time the pyramids at Giza were built through this very moment, it has lived in a quiet spot in eastern California. Bristlecones are usually found at high altitudes where it is very dry.

1. Looking at the picture, describe the bristlecone pine's environment.
2. What might some advantages be to the bristlecone's habitat? What might be disadvantages?

Tie to Prior Knowledge

Ask students to visualize a common plant and list its major parts. Students should know that most plants have the following parts in common: roots, stems, leaves, and often flowers and fruits. Display a common flowering plant, such as a geranium, and have students point out the parts they know.

As You Read

What You'll Learn

- **Identify** characteristics common to all plants.
- **Explain** which plant adaptations make it possible for plants to survive on land.
- **Compare and contrast** vascular and nonvascular plants.

Vocabulary
cuticle
cellulose
vascular plant
nonvascular plant

Why It's Important
Plants produce food and oxygen used by most organisms on Earth.

What is a plant?

What is the most common sight you see when you walk along nature trails in parks like the one shown in **Figure 1?** Maybe you've taken off your shoes and walked barefoot on soft, cool grass. Perhaps you've climbed a tree to see what things look like from high in its branches. In each instance, plants surrounded you.

If you named all the plants that you know, you probably would include trees, flowers, vegetables, fruits, and field crops like wheat, rice, or corn. Between 260,000 and 300,000 plant species have been discovered and identified. Scientists think more are still to be found, mainly in tropical rain forests. Some of these plants are important food sources to humans and other consumers. Without plants, most life on Earth as we know it would not be possible.

Plant Characteristics Plants range in size from microscopic water ferns to giant sequoia trees that are sometimes more than 100 m in height. Most have roots or rootlike structures that hold them in the ground or onto some other object like a rock or another plant. Plants are adapted to nearly every environment on Earth. Some grow in frigid, ice-bound polar regions and others grow in hot, dry deserts. All plants need water, but some plants cannot live unless they are submerged in either freshwater or salt water.

Figure 1
All plants are many-celled and nearly all contain chlorophyll. Grasses, trees, shrubs, mosses, and ferns are all plants.

Section ✔ *Assessment* Planner

PORTFOLIO
Activity, p. 121
PERFORMANCE ASSESSMENT
Skill Builder Activities, p. 123
See page 146 for more options.

CONTENT ASSESSMENT
Section, p. 123
Challenge, p. 123
Chapter, pp. 146–145

Plant Cells Like other living things, plants are made of cells. A plant cell has a cell membrane, a nucleus, and other cellular structures. In addition, plant cells have cell walls that make them different from animal cells. Cell walls provide structure and protection for plant cells.

Many plant cells contain the green pigment chlorophyll (KLOR uh fihl) so most plants are green. Plants need chlorophyll to make food using a process called photosynthesis. Chlorophyll is found in a cell structure called a chloroplast. Plant cells from green parts of the plant usually contain many chloroplasts.

Most plant cells have a large, membrane-bound structure called the central vacuole that takes up most of the space inside of the cell. This structure plays an important role in regulating the water content of the cell. Many substances are stored in the vacuole such as the pigments that make some flowers red, blue, or purple.

Origin and Evolution of Plants

Have plants always existed on land? The first plants that lived on land probably could survive only in damp areas. Their ancestors were probably ancient green algae that lived in the sea. Green algae are one-celled or many-celled organisms that use photosynthesis to make food. Today, plants and green algae have the same types of chlorophyll and carotenoids (kuh RAH tun oydz) in their cells. Carotenoids are red, yellow, or orange pigments that also are used for photosynthesis. This has led scientists to think that plants and green algae have a common ancestor.

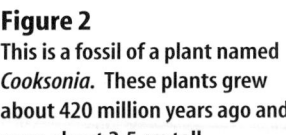 **Reading Check** *How are plants and green algae alike?*

Fossil Record The fossil record for plants is not like that for animals. Most animals have bones or other hard parts that can fossilize. Plants usually decay before they become fossilized. But, the oldest fossil plants are about 420 million years old. **Figure 2** shows *Cooksonia*, a fossil of one of these plants. Other fossils of early plants are similar to the ancient green algae. Scientists hypothesize that some of these kinds of plants evolved into the plants that exist today.

Cone-bearing plants, such as pines, probably evolved from a group of plants that grew about 350 million years ago. Fossils of these plants have been dated to about 300 million years ago. It is estimated that flowering plants did not exist until about 120 million years ago. However, the exact origin of flowering plants is not known.

Figure 2
This is a fossil of a plant named *Cooksonia*. These plants grew about 420 million years ago and were about 2.5 cm tall.

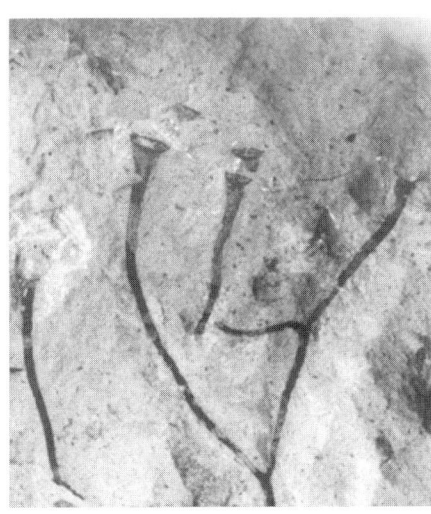

What is a plant?

Visual Learning
Figure 1 Which features of the organisms in the photo suggest they are plants? They are green, grow from soil, and have leaves and stems.

IDENTIFYING Misconceptions

Students may think that all plants produce seeds in flowers. Explain that some plants are seedless and do not make seeds, others produce seeds in cones.

Origin and Evolution of Plants

 **Reading Check**

Answer Both have similar chlorophyll and carotenoids.

Inclusion Strategies

Learning Disabled and Visually Impaired If possible, provide petrified wood or fossil casts of plants. Ask students what clues they have that these fossils were once living plants. The fossils may be shaped like plant stems or leaves. **Kinesthetic**

Resource Manager

Chapter Resources Booklet
    Note-taking Worksheets, pp. 29–31
    Transparency Activity, p. 40
Cultural Diversity, p. 19

Chemistry INTEGRATION

Long fibers of glucose in cellulose increase structural support.

Adaptations to Land

✔ Reading Check

Answer to slow the loss of water

Quick Demo

Use a spray mister to mist water onto a plant leaf that has a thick cuticle. Allow students to observe how the water beads up and runs off.

Activity

Set up stations around the class that contain different plant parts. Have students write the name of each plant part and important information about each as they move from one station to another. L1

IS **Visual-Spatial**

Chemistry INTEGRATION

Plant cell walls are made mostly of cellulose, which is made of long chains of glucose molecules ($C_6H_{12}O_6$). More than half of the carbon in plants is found in cellulose. Raw cotton is more than 90 percent cellulose. What physical property of cellulose makes it ideal for helping plants survive on land?

Figure 3
The alga *Spirogyra*, like all algae, must have water to survive. If the pool where it lives dries up, it will die.

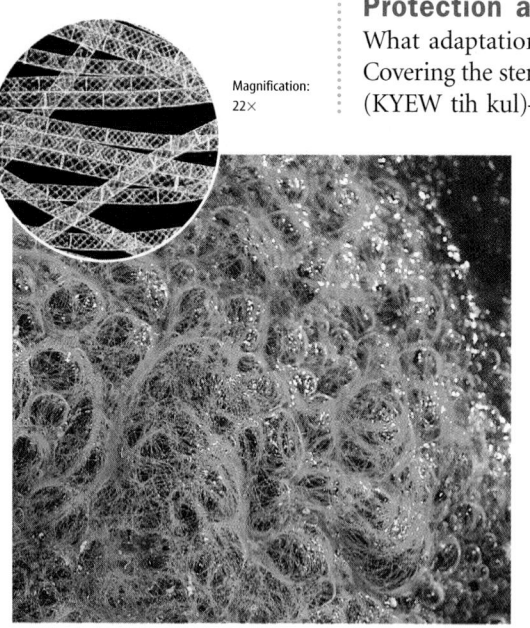

Magnification: 22×

Life on Land

Life on land has some advantages for plants. More sunlight and carbon dioxide—needed for photosynthesis—are available on land than in water. During photosynthesis, plants give off oxygen. Long ago, as more and more plants adapted to life on land, the amount of oxygen in Earth's atmosphere increased. This paved the way for organisms that depend on oxygen.

Adaptations to Land

What is life like for green algae, shown in **Figure 3,** as they float in a shallow pool? The water in the pool surrounds and supports them as the algae make their own food through the process of photosynthesis. Because materials can enter and leave through their cell membranes and cell walls, the algae cells have everything they need to survive as long as they have water.

Now, imagine a summer drought. The pool begins to dry up. Soon, the algae are on damp mud and are no longer supported by water. As long as the soil stays damp, materials can move in and out through the algae's cell membranes and cell walls. As the soil becomes drier and drier, the algae will lose water too because water moves through their cell membranes and cell walls from where there is more water to where there is less water. Without enough water in their environment, the algae will die.

Protection and Support Water is important for plants. What adaptations would help a plant conserve water on land? Covering the stems, leaves, and flowers of many plants is a **cuticle** (KYEW tih kul)—a waxy, protective layer secreted by cells onto the surface of the plant. The cuticle slows the loss of water. The cuticle and other adaptations shown in **Figure 4** enable plants to survive on land.

✔ Reading Check
What is the function of a plant's cuticle?

Supporting itself is another problem for a plant on land. Like all cells, plant cells have cell membranes, but they also have rigid cell walls outside the membrane. Cell walls contain **cellulose** (SEL yuh lohs), which is a chemical compound that plants can make out of sugar. Long chains of cellulose molecules form tangled fibers in plant cell walls. These fibers provide structure and support.

120 CHAPTER 5 Plants

Teacher FYI

Almost all of the oxygen in our atmosphere has been produced by the release of oxygen during photosynthesis. Plants also absorb carbon dioxide from the atmosphere during photosynthesis. Thus, the destruction of vast areas of tropical forest may negatively impact the balance of these gases in the atmosphere.

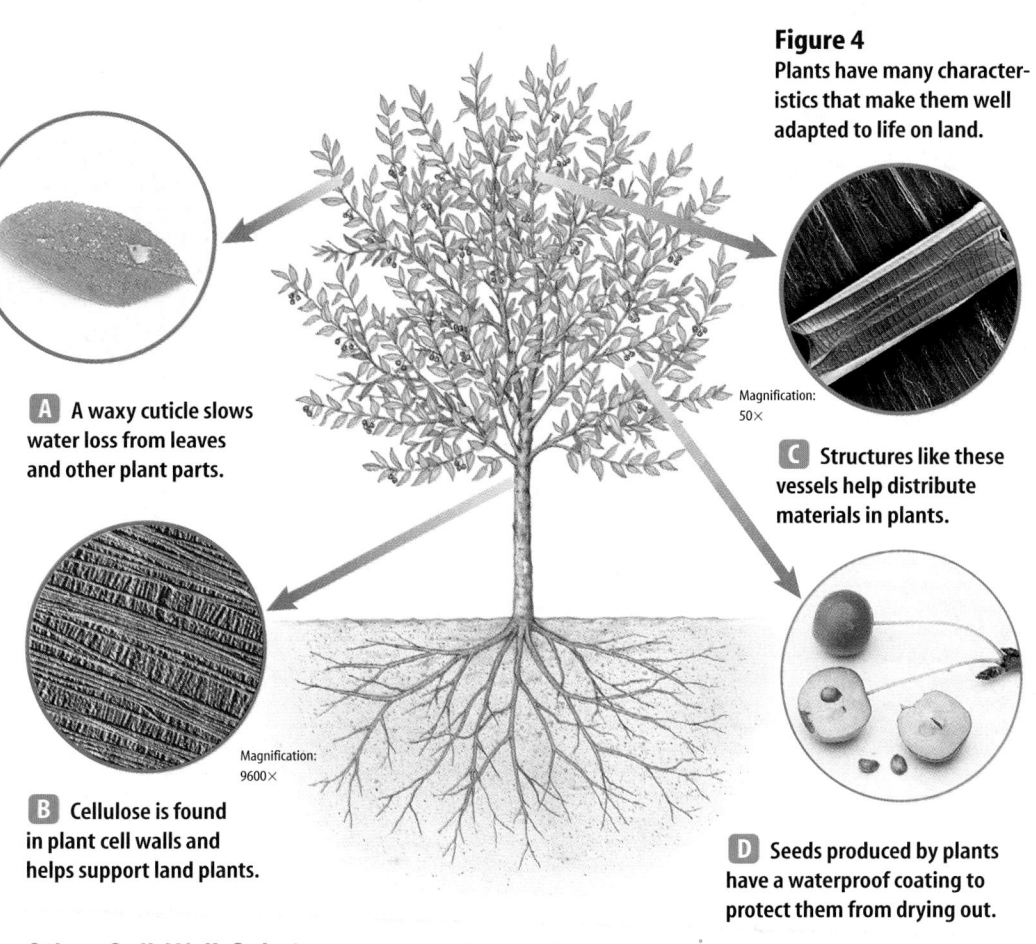

A A waxy cuticle slows water loss from leaves and other plant parts.

Magnification: 9600×

B Cellulose is found in plant cell walls and helps support land plants.

Magnification: 50×

C Structures like these vessels help distribute materials in plants.

D Seeds produced by plants have a waterproof coating to protect them from drying out.

Use Science Words

Word Meaning Have students compare the meaning of the word cuticle in relation to plants (protective layer on plant surface) and in relation to the human body (hardened skin at the base of nails). Both are derived from the Latin *cutis* meaning "skin." L2
IS Linguistic

Activity

Have students prepare posters that show examples of plant adaptations to life on land. L2
IS Visual-Spatial P

Use an Analogy

Explain that vascular tissue in plants is somewhat like the plumbing in a building. Some pipes, analogous to xylem, bring water up into the building. Other pipes, analogous to phloem, transport materials away. Reinforce that phloem does NOT carry water—it carries nutrients.

Other Cell Wall Substances Cells of some plants secrete other substances into the cellulose that make the cell wall even stronger. Trees, such as oaks and pines, could not grow without these strong cell walls. Wood can be used for construction mostly because of strong cell walls.

Life on land means that each plant cell is not surrounded by water. The plant cannot depend on water to move substances from one cell to the next. Through adaptations, structures developed in many plants that distribute water, nutrients, and food throughout the plant. These structures also help provide support for the plant.

Reproduction Changes in reproduction were necessary if plants were to survive on land. The presence of water-resistant spores helped some plants reproduce successfully. Other plants adapted by producing water-resistant seeds in cones or in flowers that developed into fruits.

SECTION 1 An Overview of Plants **121**

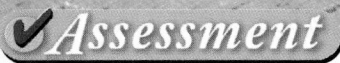
LAB DEMONSTRATION

Purpose to model the function of plant cuticles
Materials water, paper towels, wax paper, paper clips, string
Preparation Tie the string so it forms a line on which the towels can hang. Cut the towels and wax paper into 10-cm squares. Obtain a bowl of water for wetting the towels.

Procedure Wet three towel squares. Leave one uncovered. Cover one side of another with wax paper. Sandwich a third between two sheets of wax paper. Hang all three with clips. Have students observe how long it takes each towel to dry.
Expected Outcome Uncovered towels dry more quickly than covered towels.

✔Assessment

How are towels covered with wax paper like plant leaves with cuticles? Wax paper prevents the towel from drying, as the cuticle prevents water loss from plants.

Visualizing Plant Classification

Have students examine the pictures and read the captions. Then ask the following question.

How might an injury to the stem of a vascular plant affect the rest of the plant? Possible answer: Since the stem transports water and nutrients absorbed by the roots to the rest of the plant, an injury could result in the plant becoming dry or some leaves dying from lack of nutrients.

Activity

Provide students with hand lenses and the seeds of a variety of plants, such as sunflower, coconut, peanut, apple, orange, peach and common garden plants. Have students examine the samples to identify similarities and differences. If fern spores are available, have students compare and contrast these structures with seeds. L2
LS Visual-Spatial

Extension

Have students investigate how nonvascular plants transport food and water to cells. Nonvascular plants have rhizoids, root-like structures, that collect water and nutrients from soil. The plants transport the materials throughout the rest of the body in one of two ways. Water and nutrients spread by diffusion or are carried by simple conducting tissues. Because both of these methods are very slow, plant size is limited. Usually nonvascular plants are no more than 2 cm in height.

GEOGRAPHIC VISUALIZING PLANT CLASSIFICATION

Figure 5

Scientists group plants as either vascular—those with water- and food-conducting cells in their stems—or nonvascular. Vascular plants are further divided into those that produce spores and those that make seeds.

Sunflower

Vascular

Flowering

Seed vascular

Joint fir

Joint firs

Cycads

Seedless vascular

Nonvascular

Cycad

Conifers

Ginkgoes

Douglas fir

Ginkgo

Horsetail

Mosses

Liverworts

Hornworts

Hornwort

Horsetails

Ferns

Club mosses

Moss

Horsetail

Fern

Club moss

Liverwort

122

Resource Manager

Chapter Resources Booklet
   Reinforcement, p. 23
   Directed Reading for Content Mastery, pp. 15, 16

Performance Assessment in the Science Classroom, p. 55

Classification of Plants

The plant kingdom is classified into major groups called divisions. A division is the same as a phylum in other kingdoms. Another way to group plants is as vascular (VAS kyuh lur) or nonvascular plants, as illustrated in **Figure 5. Vascular plants** have tubelike structures that carry water, nutrients, and other substances throughout the plant. **Nonvascular plants** do not have these tubelike structures and use other ways to move water and substances.

Naming Plants Are biologists trying to show off when they call a pecan tree *Carya illinoiensis* or a white oak *Quercus alba*? Although it might seem so, they are just using words that accurately name the plant. In the third century B.C., most plants were grouped as trees, shrubs, or herbs and placed into smaller groups by leaf characteristics. This simple system survived until late in the eighteenth century when a Swedish botanist, Carolus Linnaeus, developed a new system. His new system used many characteristics to classify a plant. He also developed a way to name plants called binomial nomenclature (bi NOH mee ul • NOH mun klay chur). Under this system, every plant species is given a unique two-word name like the names above for the pecan tree and white oak and for the two daisies in **Figure 6.**

Shasta daisy, *Chrysanthemum maximum*

African daisy, *Dimorphotheca aurantiaca*

Figure 6
Although these two plants are called daisies, they are not the same species of plant. Using their binomial names helps eliminate the confusion that might come from using their common names.

3 Assess

Reteach

Obtain a sunflower with stem and leaves, or a large color photograph of one. Direct students to pick out the characteristics that would help this plant survive on land. thin cuticle that protects leaves and stem from drying out, tall stem supported by cellulose, vascular structures to distribute materials throughout the plant, seeds protected by hard covering L2

Challenge

How might animals have been affected if plants had not adapted to live on land? Life would probably not have been possible for animals on land, because plants are the foundation of all land food chains and they produce much of the atmospheric oxygen that land animals need to live.

✓ Assessment

Oral Have students write additional questions not included in the Section Assessment and quiz each other. Use **Performance Assessment in the Science Classroom,** p. 91.

Section 1 Assessment

1. List the characteristics of plants.
2. Compare and contrast vascular and nonvascular plants.
3. Name three adaptations that allow plants to survive on land.
4. Why is binomial nomenclature used to name plants?
5. **Think Critically** If you left a board lying on the grass for a few days, what would happen to the grass underneath the board? Why?

Skill Builder Activities

6. **Forming Hypotheses** Make a hypothesis about what adaptations land plants might undergo if they lived submerged in water instead of on land. **For more help, refer to the** Science Skill Handbook.

7. **Communicating** One of the oldest surviving plant species is *Ginkgo biloba*. Research the history of this species, then write about it in your Science Journal. **For more help, refer to the** Science Skill Handbook.

Answers to Section Assessment

1. eukaryotic cells with cell walls; pigments for photosynthesis; most have roots, stems, and leaves
2. Both have eukaryotic cells with cell walls and carry out photosynthesis. Vascular plants have tubelike structures to carry materials; nonvascular plants do not.
3. Adaptations listed may include the cuticle, vascular tissue, and seeds.
4. It gives every species of plant a unique two-word name.
5. The grass might die. Light is needed for photosynthesis.
6. Possible answers: A thicker cuticle or a system for pumping water from cells could be needed; some might have a long stem to raise leaves above the water.
7. Students' reports could include: The tree (also called the maidenhair tree) is the only surviving member of a group of plants that flourished millions of years ago. It is native to China.

Seedless Plants

1 Motivate

Bellringer Transparency

Display the Section Focus Transparency for Section 2. Use the accompanying Transparency Activity Master. L2

ELL

Tie to Prior Knowledge

Students may already be familiar with some seedless plants. Point out that wreaths often contain club mosses, gardeners use peat moss to keep young plants from drying out, and ferns are common as house plants.

As You Read

What You'll Learn

■ **Distinguish** between characteristics of seedless nonvascular plants and seedless vascular plants.
■ **Identify** the importance of some nonvascular and vascular plants.

Vocabulary
rhizoid
pioneer species

Why It's Important
Seedless plants are often the first to grow in damaged or disturbed environments.

Figure 7
The seedless nonvascular plants include mosses, liverworts, and hornworts.

Seedless Nonvascular Plants

If you were asked to name the parts of a plant, you probably would list roots, stems, leaves, and flowers. You also might know that many plants grow from seeds. However, some plants, called nonvascular plants, don't grow from seeds and they do not have all of these parts. **Figure 7** shows some common types of nonvascular plants.

Nonvascular plants are usually just a few cells thick and only 2 cm to 5 cm in height. Most have stalks that look like stems and green, leaflike growths. Instead of roots, threadlike structures called **rhizoids** (RI zoydz) anchor them where they grow. Most nonvascular plants grow in places that are damp. Therefore, water is absorbed and distributed directly through their cell membranes and cell walls. Nonvascular plants also do not have flowers or cones that produce seeds. They reproduce by spores. Mosses, liverworts, and hornworts are examples of nonvascular plants.

Mosses Most nonvascular plants are classified as mosses, like the ones in **Figure 7A.** They have green, leaflike growths arranged around a central stalk. Their rhizoids are made of many cells. Sometimes stalks with caps grow from moss plants. Reproductive cells called spores are produced in the caps of these stalks. Mosses often grow on tree trunks and rocks or the ground. Although they commonly are found in damp areas, some are adapted to living in deserts.

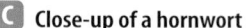

A Close-up of moss plants   **B** Close-up of a liverwort   **C** Close-up of a hornwort

Section ✔Assessment Planner

PORTFOLIO
Make a Model, p. 127
PERFORMANCE ASSESSMENT
MiniLab, p. 125
Skill Builder Activities, p. 129
See page 146 for more options.

CONTENT ASSESSMENT
Section, p. 129
Challenge, p. 129
Chapter, pp. 146–147

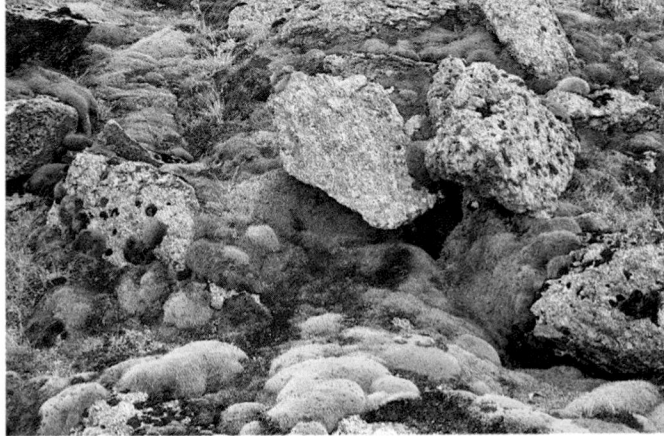

Figure 8
Mosses can grow in the thin layer of soil that covers these rocks.

Liverworts In the ninth century, liverworts were thought to be useful in treating diseases of the liver. The suffix -*wort* means "herb," so the word *liverwort* means "herb for the liver." Liverworts are rootless plants with flattened, leaflike bodies, as shown in **Figure 7B.** They usually have one-celled rhizoids.

Hornworts Most hornworts are less than 2.5 cm in diameter and have a flattened body like liverworts, as shown in **Figure 7C.** Unlike other nonvascular plants, almost all hornworts have only one chloroplast in each of their cells. Hornworts get their name from their spore-producing structures, which look like tiny horns of cattle.

Environmental Science
INTEGRATION

Nonvascular Plants and the Environment Mosses and liverworts are important in the ecology of many areas. Although they require moist conditions to grow and reproduce, many of them can withstand long, dry periods. They can grow in thin soil and in soils where other plants could not grow, as shown in **Figure 8.**

Spores of mosses and liverworts are carried by the wind. They will grow into plants if enough water is available and other growing conditions are right. Often, they are among the first plants to grow in new or disturbed environments, such as lava fields or after a forest fire. Organisms that are the first to grow in new or disturbed areas are called **pioneer species.** As pioneer plant species grow and die, decaying material builds up. This, along with the slow breakdown of rocks, builds soil. As a result, other organisms can move into the area.

✔ Reading Check *Why are pioneer plant species important in disturbed environments?*

Mini LAB

Measuring Water Absorption by a Moss
Procedure
1. Place a few teaspoons of *Sphagnum* **moss** on a piece of **cheesecloth.** Gather the corners of the cloth and twist, then tie them securely to form a ball.
2. Weigh the ball.
3. Put 200 mL of **water** in a **container** and add the ball.
4. After 15 min, remove the ball and drain the excess water into the container.
5. Weigh the ball and measure the amount of water left in the container.
6. Wash your hands after handling the moss.

Analysis
In your **Science Journal,** calculate how much water was absorbed by the *Sphagnum* moss.

---

2 Teach

Seedless Nonvascular Plants

Mini LAB

Purpose Students measure absorption capacity of *Sphagnum* moss. L2

IS Logical-Mathematical Materials *Sphagnum* moss, cheesecloth, scale, graduated cylinder, beaker, water

Teaching Strategies
• Remind students that 1 mL of water has a mass of 1 g.
• Have students predict how much water the moss will hold and then check their predictions at the end.

Analysis
1. *Sphagnum* moss will soak up about 100 g (100 mL) of water.

Performance Growers often root plants in a mix of equal parts clean sand to *Sphagnum* moss. Have students design an experiment to test this rooting method. Use **PASC,** p. 95.

✔ Reading Check

Answer They help form soil and create conditions that allow other plants to grow.

Curriculum Connection

History Because peat mosses contain chemicals that kill germs, they were used during World War I as dressings for wounds. Have students research mosses to find out some of their other uses in the past. Possible answer: Some Native Americans used peat mosses for diapers because of their absorbency. It has also been used for lamp wicks, bedding, and stable litter. L2

Resource Manager

Chapter Resources Booklet
Transparency Activity, p. 41
MiniLAB, p. 3
Home and Community Involvement, p. 42

Seedless Vascular Plants

Quick Demo

Show a variety of fern fronds. If possible, include some with sori. Have students note differences in color, size, and location among sori.

Extension

Have motivated students read natural history books to find out why ferns have such common names as Boston fern, maidenhair fern, staghorn fern, cinnamon fern, hay-scented fern, and bracken fern. These names have to do with the shapes or scents of their leaves. L3

Teacher FYI

The active ingredient in aspirin, the acetylsalicylic acid also found in willow bark, interferes with the body's production of prostaglandins. These hormonelike substances aid transmission of pain signals to the brain and help raise body temperature to fight infection. That is why taking aspirin helps dull pain and fight fever.

SCIENCE Online

Research Visit the Glencoe Science Web site at **science.glencoe.com** for more information about medicinal plants. In your Science Journal, list four medicinal plants and their uses.

Seedless Vascular Plants

The fern in **Figure 9** is growing next to some moss plants. Ferns and mosses are alike in one way. Both reproduce by spores instead of seeds. However, ferns are different from mosses because they have vascular tissue. The vascular tissue in the seedless vascular plants, like ferns, is made up of long, tubelike cells. These cells carry water, minerals, and food to cells throughout the plant. Why is having cells like these an advantage to a plant? Remember that nonvascular plants like the moss are usually only a few cells thick. Each cell absorbs water directly from its environment. As a result, these plants cannot grow large. Vascular plants, on the other hand, can grow bigger and thicker because the vascular tissue distributes water and nutrients.

Problem-Solving Activity

What is the value of rain forests?

Throughout history, cultures have used plants for medicines. Some cultures used willow bark to cure headaches. Willow bark contains salicylates (suh LIH suh layts), the main ingredient in aspirin. Heart problems were treated with foxglove, which is the main source of digitalis (dih juh TAH lus), a drug prescribed for heart problems. Have all medicinal plants been identified?

Identifying the Problem

Tropical rain forests have the largest variety of organisms on Earth. Many plant species are unknown. These forests are being destroyed rapidly. The map below shows the rate of destruction of the rain forests.

Some scientists estimate that most tropical rain forests will be destroyed in 30 years.

Solving the Problem

1. What country has the most rain forest destroyed each year?
2. Where can scientists go to study rain forest plants before the plants are destroyed?
3. Predict how the destruction of rain forests might affect research on new drugs from plants.

Deforested annually (km²)

- more than 15,000
- 2,000 to 14,800
- 100 to 1,900

126 CHAPTER 5 Plants

SCIENCE Online

Internet Addresses

_____

_____

_____

_____

Explore the Glencoe Science Web site at **science.glencoe.com** to find out more about topics in this section.

Inclusion Strategies

Visually Impaired Prepare samples of mosses, liverworts, and ferns for the class labeled with large print. Provide large magnifying glasses for closer observation of the plants.

Types of Seedless Vascular Plants

Besides ferns, seedless vascular plants include ground pines, spike mosses, and horsetails. About 1,000 species of ground pines, spike mosses, and horsetails are known to exist. Ferns are more abundant, with at least 12,000 known species. Many species of seedless vascular plants are known only from fossils. They flourished during the warm, moist period 360 million to 286 million years ago. Fossil records show that some horsetails grew 15 m tall, unlike modern species, which grow only 1 m to 2 m tall.

Ferns The largest group of seedless vascular plants is the ferns. They include many different varieties, as shown in **Figure 10.** They have stems, leaves, and roots. Fern leaves are called fronds. Ferns produce spores in structures that usually are found on the underside of their fronds. Thousands of species of ferns now grow on Earth, but many more existed long ago. From clues left in rock layers, scientists know that about 360 million years ago much of Earth was tropical. Steamy swamps covered large areas. The tallest plants were species of ferns. The ancient ferns grew as tall as 25 m—as tall as the tallest fern species alive today. The tallest modern tree ferns are about 3 m to 5 m in height, as shown in **Figure 10C,** and grow in tropical areas.

Figure 9
The mosses and ferns in this picture are seedless plants. *Why can the fern grow taller than the moss?*

Figure 10
Ferns come in many different shapes and sizes.

A The sword fern has a typical fern shape. Spores are produced in structures on the back of the frond.

B This fern grows on other plants, not in the soil. *Why do you think it's called the staghorn fern?*

C Tree ferns, like this one in Hawaii, grow in tropical areas.

Seedless Vascular Plants, continued

Discussion

How can you tell the difference between true mosses and club mosses? True mosses produce spores in capsules on stalks. Club mosses produce spores at the end of stems in structures that look like tiny pine cones.

Reading Check

Answer at the ends of stems in structures that look like pine cones

Quick Demo

Obtain horsetail plants. Demonstrate (and allow students to feel) how the grittiness of the silica in the plant's cell walls could be useful for scouring. L2 IS **Kinesthetic**

Caption Answer

Figure 12 in a conelike structure at the tips of some stems

Importance of Seedless Plants

Use Science Words

Word Usage Provide each student with a list of terms that can be used to describe nonvascular and seedless vascular plants. Have students write paragraphs that compare and contrast these plants using the terms given. Terms might include *nonvascular, vascular, moss, rhizoid, moist, liverwort, ferns, leaves, roots,* and *horsetails.* L2 IS **Linguistic**

Figure 11
Photographers once used the dry, flammable spores of club mosses as flash powder. It burned rapidly and produced the light that was needed to take photographs.

Figure 12
Most horsetails grow in damp areas and are less than 1 m tall. *Where would spores be produced on this plant?*

Club Mosses Ground pines and spike mosses are groups of plants that often are called club mosses. They are related more closely to ferns than to mosses. These seedless vascular plants have needle-like leaves. Spores are produced at the end of the stems in structures that look like tiny pine cones. Ground pines, shown in **Figure 11,** are found from arctic regions to the tropics, but never in large numbers. In some areas, they are endangered because they have been over collected to make wreaths and other decorations.

Reading Check *Where are spores in club mosses produced?*

Spike mosses resemble ground pines. One species of spike moss, the resurrection plant, is adapted to desert conditions. When water is scarce, the plant curls up and seems dead. When water becomes available, the resurrection plant unfurls its green leaves and begins making food again. The plant can repeat this process whenever necessary.

Horsetails The stem structure of horsetails is unique among the vascular plants. The stem is jointed and has a hollow center surrounded by a ring of vascular tissue. At each joint, leaves grow out from around the stem. In **Figure 12,** you can see these joints. If you pull on a horsetail stem, it will pop apart in sections. Like the club mosses, spores from horsetails are produced in a conelike structure at the tips of some stems. The stems of the horsetails contain silica, a gritty substance found in sand. For centuries, horsetails have been used for polishing objects, sharpening tools, and scouring cooking utensils. Another common name for horsetails is scouring rush.

Importance of Seedless Plants

When many ancient seedless plants died, they became submerged in water and mud before they decomposed. As this plant material built up, it became compacted and compressed and eventually turned into coal—a process that took millions of years.

Today, a similar process is taking place in bogs, which are poorly drained areas of land that contain decaying plants. The plants in bogs are mostly seedless plants like mosses and ferns.

Resource Manager

Chapter Resources Booklet
  Reinforcement, p. 24
  Directed Reading for Content Mastery, p. 17

Visual Learning

Figure 13 If possible, have students examine samples of peat and coal. Remind them that peat is the first stage of coal formation. **How does the appearance of peat differ from that of coal?** Peat is lighter in color and isn't as rocklike as coal.

Peat When plants die, the decay process is slow because waterlogged soil does not contain oxygen. Over time, these decaying plants are compressed into a substance called peat. Peat, which forms from the remains of sphagnum moss, is mined from bogs to use as a low-cost fuel in places such as Ireland and Russia, as shown in **Figure 13**. Peat supplies about one third of Ireland's energy requirements. Scientists hypothesize that over time, if additional layers of soil bury, compact, and compress the peat, it will become coal.

Uses of Seedless Vascular Plants Many people keep ferns as houseplants. Ferns also are sold widely as landscape plants for shady areas. Peat and sphagnum mosses also are used for gardening. Peat is an excellent soil conditioner, and sphagnum moss often is used to line hanging baskets. Ferns also are used for weaving material and basketry.

Although most mosses are not used for food, parts of many other seedless vascular plants can be eaten. The rhizomes and young fronds of some ferns are edible. The dried stems of one type of horsetail can be ground into flour. Seedless plants have been used as folk medicines for hundreds of years. For example, ferns have been used to treat bee stings, burns, fevers, and even dandruff.

Figure 13
Peat is cut from bogs and used for a fuel in some parts of Europe.

Section Assessment

1. What are the similarities and differences between mosses and ferns?
2. What do fossil records show us about some seedless plants?
3. Under what growing conditions would you expect to find pioneer plants such as mosses and liverworts?
4. What do vascular tissues provide for plants that have them?
5. **Think Critically** The electricity that you use every day might be produced by burning coal. What is the connection between electricity production and seedless nonvascular and seedless vascular plants?

Skill Builder Activities

6. **Concept Mapping** Make a concept map showing how seedless nonvascular and seedless vascular plants are related. Include these terms in the concept map: *plant kingdom, seedless nonvascular plants, seedless vascular plants, ferns, ground pines, horsetails, liverworts, hornworts, mosses,* and *spike mosses*. **For more help, refer to the** Science Skill Handbook.
7. **Using Fractions** Approximately 8,000 species of liverworts and 9,000 species of mosses exist today. Estimate what fraction of these seedless nonvascular plants are mosses. **For more help, refer to the** Math Skill Handbook.

SECTION

3

Seed Plants

1 Motivate

Bellringer Transparency

Display the Section Focus Transparency for Section 3. Use the accompanying Transparency Activity Master. L2

ELL

SECTION 3 Section Focus Transparency — Rooted in Nature

Bonsai is an ancient method of growing trees or shrubs in small containers. The plants are kept small by pruning the branches and roots. Because some types of plants used for bonsai can live for more than 100 years, they are passed from generation to generation.

1. What are some advantages to having bonsai plants? What might some disadvantages be?
2. What qualities do you think would be important in practicing bonsai?

Tie to Prior Knowledge

Invite students to brainstorm a list of plant seeds that they eat or see regularly. *Possible answers: any type of edible nut, sunflower seeds, sesame or poppy seeds, coconuts, seeds inside fruits*

SECTION

3 Seed Plants

As You Read

What You'll Learn

- **Identify** the characteristics of seed plants.
- **Explain** the structures and functions of roots, stems, and leaves.
- **Describe** the main characteristics and importance of gymnosperms and angiosperms.
- **Compare** similarities and differences between monocots and dicots.

Vocabulary

stomata	gymnosperm
guard cell	angiosperm
xylem	monocot
phloem	dicot
cambium	

Why It's Important

We depend on seed plants for food, clothing, and shelter.

Characteristics of Seed Plants

What foods from plants have you eaten today? Apples? Potatoes? Carrots? Peanut butter and jelly sandwiches? All of these foods and more come from seed plants.

Most of the plants you are familiar with are seed plants. Most seed plants have leaves, stems, roots, and vascular tissue. They produce seeds, which usually contain an embryo and stored food. The stored food is the source of energy for the embryo's early growth as it develops into a plant. Most of the plant species that have been identified in the world today are seed plants. Seed plants generally are classified into two major groups—gymnosperms (JIHM nuh spurmz) and angiosperms (AN jee uh spurmz).

Leaves Most seed plants have leaves—the organs of the plant where the food-making process—photosynthesis—usually occurs. Leaves come in many shapes, sizes, and colors. Examine the structure of a typical leaf, shown in **Figure 14.**

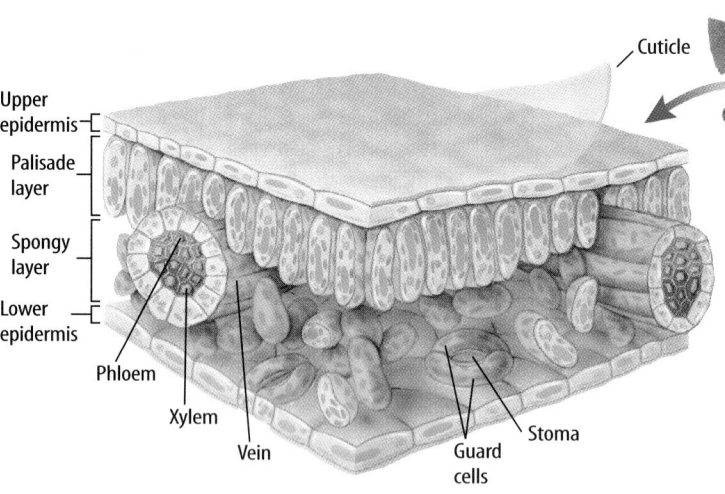

Upper epidermis
Palisade layer
Spongy layer
Lower epidermis
Phloem
Xylem
Vein
Guard cells
Stoma
Cuticle

Figure 14
The structure of a typical leaf is adapted for photosynthesis. *Why do cells in the palisade layer have more chloroplasts than cells in the spongy layer?*

Section ✓ *Assessment* Planner

PORTFOLIO
Curriculum Connection, p. 133

PERFORMANCE ASSESSMENT
Try at Home MiniLAB, p. 131
Skill Builder Activities, p. 138
See page 146 for more options.

CONTENT ASSESSMENT
Section, p. 138
Challenge, p. 138
Chapter, pp. 146–147

Leaf Cell Layers A typical leaf is made of different layers of cells. On the upper and lower surfaces of a leaf is a thin layer of cells called the epidermis, which covers and protects the leaf. A waxy cuticle coats the epidermis of some leaves. Most leaves have small openings in the epidermis called **stomata** (STOH muh tuh) (singular, *stoma*). Stomata allow carbon dioxide, water, and oxygen to enter into and exit from a leaf. Each stoma is surrounded by two **guard cells** that open and close it.

Just below the upper epidermis is the palisade layer. It consists of closely packed, long, narrow cells that usually contain many chloroplasts. Most of the food produced by plants is made in the palisade cells. Between the palisade layer and the lower epidermis is the spongy layer. It is a layer of loosely arranged cells separated by air spaces. In a leaf, veins containing vascular tissue are found in the spongy layer.

Stems The trunk of a tree is really the stem of the tree. Stems usually are located above ground and support the branches, leaves, and flowers. Materials move between leaves and roots through the vascular tissue in the stem. Stems also can have other specialized functions, as shown in **Figure 15.**

Plant stems are either herbaceous (hur BAY shus) or woody. Herbaceous stems usually are soft and green, like the stems of a tulip, while trees and shrubs have hard, rigid, woody stems. Lumber comes from woody stems.

Figure 15
Some plants have stems with special functions.

A These potatos are stems that grow underground and store food for the plant.

B The stems of this cactus store water and can carry on photosynthesis.

C Some stems of this grape plant help it climb on other plants.

Teacher FYI

Sweet potatoes are fleshy roots; white potatoes are fleshy underground stems (tubers). Both are structures that store food.

Quick Demo

Germinate some bean or corn seeds to demonstrate that the mass of the roots becomes larger than the rest of the plant very quickly.

Activity

Have students make posters that illustrate the different functions of roots and stems. For example, the roots of some orchids and the stems of cacti can photosynthesize. L2

IS Visual-Spatial

Caption Answer

Figure 16 to anchor the tree and to take in enough water and nutrients to support the above ground parts of the plant

✔ Reading Check

Answer Roots take in water and nutrients from soil, anchor the plant, and store food and water. Some plants have roots that take in oxygen from the air.

Figure 16
The root system of a tree is as long as the tree can be tall. *Why would the root system of a tree need to be so large?*

Roots Imagine a lone tree growing on top of a hill. What is the largest part of this plant? Maybe you guessed the trunk or the branches. Did you consider the roots? The root systems of most plants are as large or larger than the aboveground stems and leaves, as shown in **Figure 16.**

Roots are important to plants. Water and other substances enter a plant through its roots. Roots have vascular tissue in which water and dissolved substances move from the soil through the stems to the leaves. Roots also act as anchors, preventing plants from being blown away by wind or washed away by moving water. Each root system must support the other plant parts that are aboveground—the stem, branches, and leaves of a tree. Sometimes, part of or all of the roots are aboveground, too.

Roots can store food. When you eat carrots or beets, you eat roots that contain stored food. Plants that grow from year to year use this stored food to begin their growth in the spring. Plants that grow in dry areas often have roots that store water.

Root tissues also can perform functions such as absorbing oxygen that is used in the process of respiration. Because water does not contain as much oxygen as air does, plants that grow with their roots in water might not be able to absorb enough oxygen. Some swamp plants have roots that grow partially out of the water and take in oxygen from the air. In order to perform all these functions, the root systems of plants must be large.

 Reading Check *What are several functions of roots in plants?*

Resource Manager

Chapter Resources Booklet
Enrichment, p. 28
Transparency Activity, pp. 43–44

Visual Learning

Figure 16 How could planting a large tree such as this close to a building cause a problem? Students should infer that its extensive root system could interfere with the building's foundation or pipes leading into the building.

Vascular Tissue

Vascular Tissue Three tissues usually make up the vascular system in a seed plant. **Xylem** (ZI lum) tissue is made up of hollow, tubular cells that are stacked one on top of the other to form a structure called a vessel. These vessels transport water and dissolved substances from the roots throughout the plant. The thick cell walls of xylem are also important because they help support the plant.

Phloem (FLOH em) is a plant tissue also made up of tubular cells that are stacked to form structures called tubes. Tubes are different from vessels. Phloem tubes move food from where it is made to other parts of the plant where it is used or stored.

In some plants, a cambium is between xylem and phloem. **Cambium** (KAM bee um) is a tissue that produces most of the new xylem and phloem cells. The growth of this new xylem and phloem increases the thickness of stems and roots. All three tissues are illustrated in **Figure 17.**

Health INTEGRATION

Plants have vascular tissue, and you have a vascular system. Your vascular system transports oxygen, food, and wastes through blood vessels. Instead of xylem and phloem, your blood vessels include veins and arteries. In your Science Journal write a paragraph describing the difference between veins and arteries.

Figure 17
The vascular tissue of some seed plants includes xylem, phloem, and cambium.
Which of these tissues transports food throughout the plant?

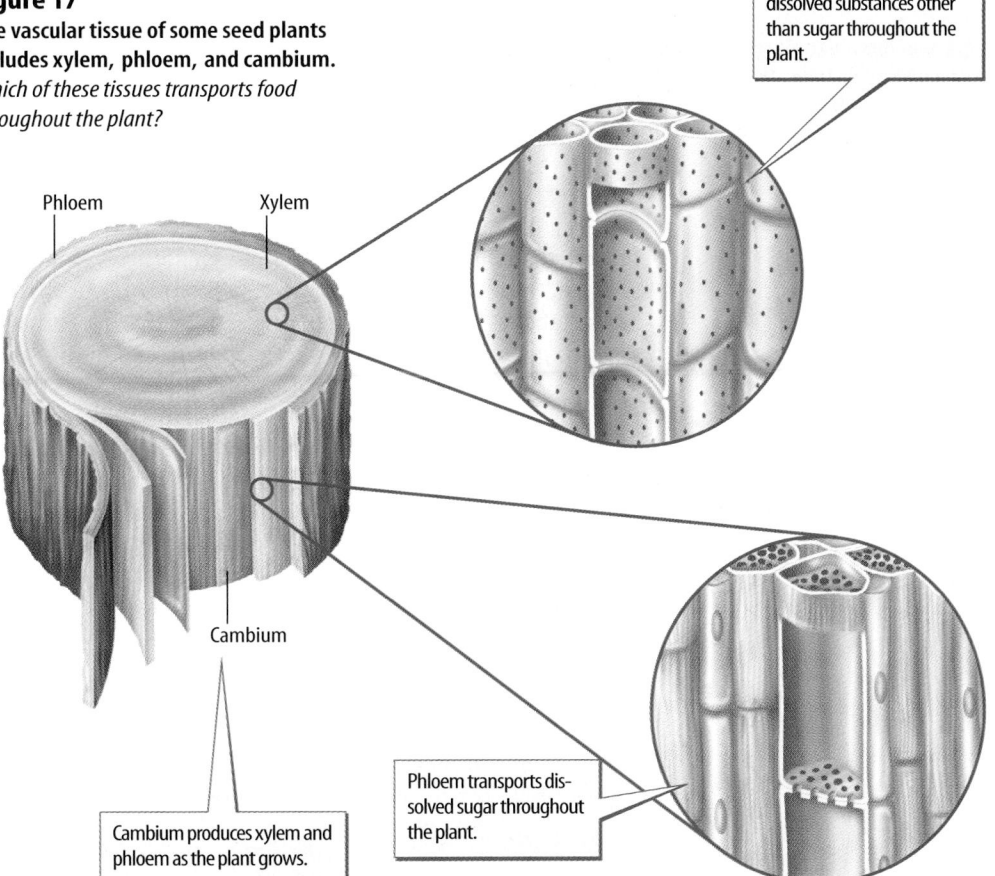

Xylem transports water and dissolved substances other than sugar throughout the plant.

Phloem   Xylem

Cambium

Cambium produces xylem and phloem as the plant grows.

Phloem transports dissolved sugar throughout the plant.

Quick Demo

Demonstrate the appearance of vascular tissue in woody plants by showing students a photo of a tree trunk cross-section, or by bringing a cut woody stem to class.

Extension

Foresters measure quantities of timber in board feet. Have students research the size of this unit. A board foot is a volume measure of lumber. A board measuring 12″ × 12″ × 1″ is one board foot. Challenge students to find out how many board feet of lumber are consumed by a common activity, such as building a house or producing pulp for a certain amount of newsprint. L3

Caption Answer

Figure 17 phloem

Curriculum Connection

History Theophrastus (ca. 372–ca. 287 B.C.) is known as the father of botany. His botanical works were so complete that nearly 1,800 years passed before any new discoveries were made. Have students research the name and contributions of other botanists and compile their findings into one time line. Bauhin, Linnaeus, Bailey, Gesner, Hales, Nageli, and Ray are botanists students may name. P

Teacher FYI

The pattern of rings in tree trunks provides information about a tree's life. Good growth years produce wide rings. Slower growth, due to less favorable conditions, forms a narrower ring. If there is an extended dry period between two wet periods, two rings will be produced. Rings are wider on the sunny side of a tree.

Gymnosperms

Discussion

Is an apple tree a gymnosperm? Explain. No, it has seeds encased in fruits. **Is a maple tree whose leaves turn golden and red in fall a gymnosperm? Explain.** No, its seeds are enclosed in a dry, winged fruit.

Activity

If possible, ask each student to find and bring to class a cone from a conifer in the area. Cones may be found in yards, in parks, and along routes to and from school. Have them compare and contrast the cones in class and make sketches and written descriptions of each type of cone. Discuss how the cones are alike and different. Although they have the same basic structure, they differ in size, color, and shape. L1
IS Visual-Spatial

Caption Answer

Figure 18D Most gymnosperms do not lose all of their leaves in the fall.

✔ Reading Check

Answer Cones are the reproductive structures of the plants; seeds develop on female cones.

Figure 18
The gymnosperms include four divisions of plants.

C About 100 species of cycads exist today. Only one genus is native to the United States.

B More than half of the 70 species of gnetophytes, such as this joint fir, are in one genus.

D The ginkgoes are represented by one living species. Ginkgoes lose their leaves in the fall. *How is this different from most gymnosperms?*

A Conifers are the largest, most diverse division. Most conifers are evergreen plants, such as this ponderosa pine.

Gymnosperms

The oldest trees alive are gymnosperms. A bristlecone pine tree in the White Mountains of eastern California is estimated to be 4,900 years old. **Gymnosperms** are vascular plants that produce seeds that are not protected by fruit. The word *gymnosperm* comes from the Greek language and means "naked seed." Another characteristic of gymnosperms is that they do not have flowers. Leaves of most gymnosperms are needlelike or scalelike. Many gymnosperms are called evergreens because some green leaves always remain on their branches.

Four divisions of plants—conifers, cycads, ginkgoes, and gnetophytes (NE tuh fites)—are classified as gymnosperms. **Figure 18** shows examples of the four divisions. You are probably most familiar with the division Coniferophyta (kuh NIH fur uh fi tuh), the conifers. Pines, firs, spruces, redwoods, and junipers belong to this division. It contains the greatest number of gymnosperm species. All conifers produce two types of cones—male and female. Both types usually are found on the same plant. Cones are the reproductive structures of conifers. Seeds develop on the female cone but not on the male cone.

✔ Reading Check
What is the importance of cones to gymnosperms?

Inclusion Strategies

Learning Disabled Bring branches from different conifers to class. Identify the branches and then have students feel the differences in texture and shape of the leaves. Encourage students to compare and contrast the smells and textures associated with each. L1 **IS Kinesthetic**

✔ Active Reading

Think-Pair-Share This strategy encourages students to think first before discussing their ideas or thoughts about a topic. Ask students to respond to a question. After recording ideas, have partners share responses to the question. Finally, ask students to share responses with the class. Have students become involved in a Think-Pair-Share about seed plants.

Angiosperms

When people are asked to name a plant, most name an angiosperm. An **angiosperm** is a vascular plant that flowers and has a fruit that contains one or more seeds, such as the peach in **Figure 19A.** The fruit develops from a part or parts of one or more flowers. Angiosperms are familiar plants no matter where you live. They grow in parks, fields, forests, jungles, deserts, freshwater, salt water, and cracks of sidewalks. You might see them dangling from wires or other plants, and one species of orchid even grows underground. Angiosperms make up the plant division Anthophyta (AN thoh fi tuh). More than half of the known plant species belong to this division.

Flowers The flowers of angiosperms vary in size, shape, and color. Duckweed, an aquatic plant, has a flower that is only 0.1 mm long. A plant in Indonesia has a flower that is nearly 1 m in diameter and can weigh 9 kg. Nearly every color can be found in some flower, although some people would not include black. Multicolored flowers are common. Some plants have flowers that are not recognized easily as flowers, such as those shown in **Figure 19B.**

Some flower parts develop into fruit. Most fruits contain seeds, like an apple, or have seeds on their surface, like a strawberry. If you think all fruits are juicy and sweet, there are some that are not. The fruit of the vanilla orchid, as shown in **Figure 19C,** contains seeds and is dry.

Angiosperms are divided into two groups—the monocots and the dicots—shortened forms of the words *monocotyledon* (mah nuh kah tul EE dun) and *dicotyledon* (di kah tul EE dun).

Figure 19
Angiosperms have a wide variety of flowers and fruits.

 The fruit of the vanilla orchid is the source of vanilla flavoring.

A The flowers and fruit of a peach tree are typical of many angiosperms.

B Ash flowers are not large and colorful. Their fruits are small and dry.

SECTION 3 Seed Plants **135**

Teacher FYI

Botanically, a fruit is any plant organ that grows from female flower parts. Therefore, tomatoes, green beans, squash, cucumbers, and peppers are fruit—although they're not necessarily sweet.

Science Journal

Nutritious Grains Have students research one of the major grains eaten in the United States and write a short report that includes what the plant looks like, what parts of it we eat, and where it is grown. Some students might also visit a supermarket to report on the number and kinds of foods containing the grain. Encourage students to include photos and diagrams in their reports, and to share their findings in class. Students could research corn, wheat, oats, or rice. L2
IS Linguistic

Cultural Diversity

Food for Thought People from different cultures rely on plants native to their part of the world for food. Have each student choose a country and prepare a poster that shows the main plants that are part of the diet there. After presenting each poster, encourage students to compare and contrast these foods with those that are commonly eaten in the United States.

Resource Manager

Chapter Resources Booklet
Directed Reading for Content Mastery, pp. 17, 18

Section 3 Seed Plants **135**

Angiosperms, continued

Activity

Prepare several lab stations to demonstrate different monocot or dicot characteristics. Have students rotate through the stations, making notes and sketches of each characteristic. When everyone has completed the activity, have students discuss how monocots and dicots are similar and different. L2

IS Interpersonal

Extension

Have students survey the plants they find at a home and garden store, a grocery store, or a florist shop. Tell them to sketch the leaves and flowers of one monocot and one dicot and bring the sketches to class. Remind them to write down the names of the plants on the back of each sketch and whether the plant is a monocot or dicot. Have each student present his or her two sketches in class. Quiz class members on whether the plants are monocots or dicots, and have students give reasons for their choices. L1

IS Visual-Spatial

Monocots and Dicots A cotyledon is part of a seed often used for food storage. The prefix *mono* means "one," and *di* means "two." Therefore, **monocots** have one cotyledon inside their seeds and **dicots** have two. The flowers, leaves, and stems of monocots and dicots are shown in **Figure 20**.

Many important foods come from monocots, including corn, rice, wheat, and barley. If you eat bananas, pineapple, or dates, you are eating fruit from monocots. Lilies and orchids also are monocots.

Dicots also produce familiar foods such as peanuts, green beans, peas, apples, and oranges. You might have rested in the shade of a dicot tree. Most shade trees, such as maple, oak, and elm, are dicots.

Figure 20
By observing a monocot and a dicot, you can determine their plant characteristics.

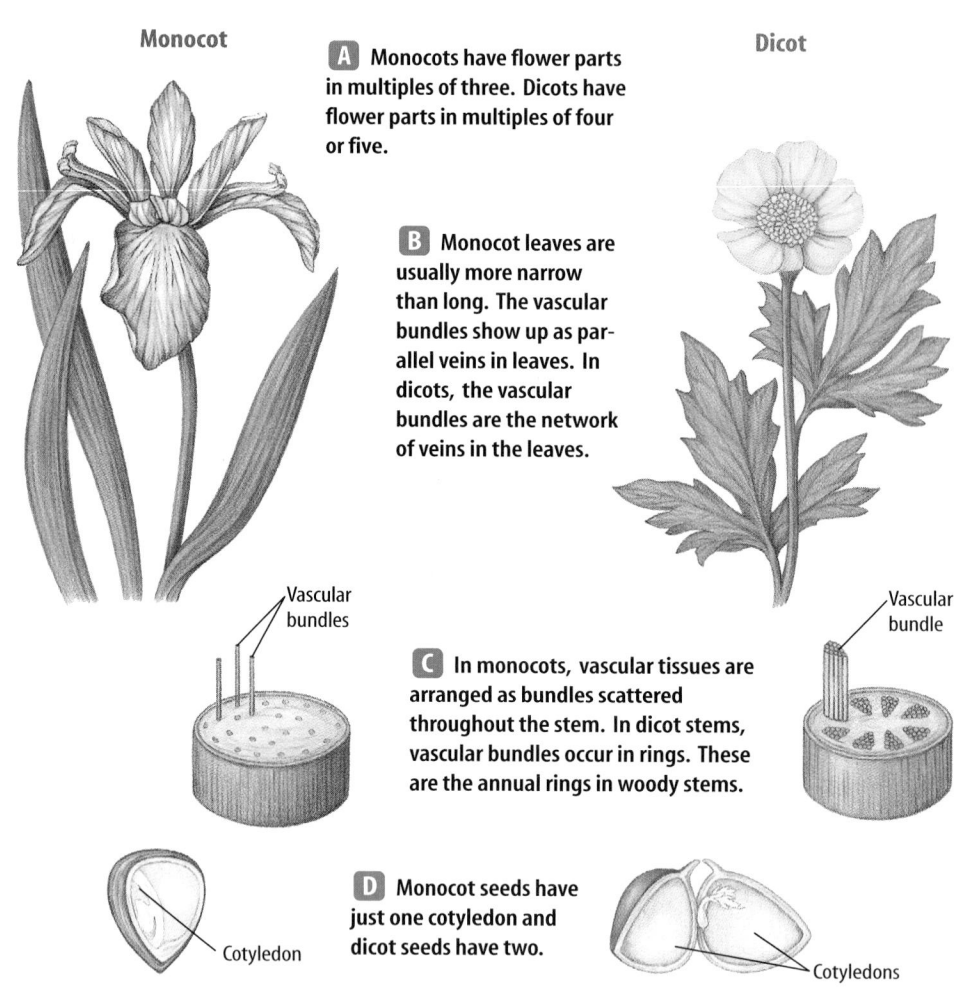

Monocot **Dicot**

A Monocots have flower parts in multiples of three. Dicots have flower parts in multiples of four or five.

B Monocot leaves are usually more narrow than long. The vascular bundles show up as parallel veins in leaves. In dicots, the vascular bundles are the network of veins in the leaves.

C In monocots, vascular tissues are arranged as bundles scattered throughout the stem. In dicot stems, vascular bundles occur in rings. These are the annual rings in woody stems.

Vascular bundles

Vascular bundle

D Monocot seeds have just one cotyledon and dicot seeds have two.

Cotyledon

Cotyledons

Life Cycles of Angiosperms Flowering plants vary greatly in appearance. Their life cycles are as varied as the kinds of plants, as shown in **Figure 21.** Some angiosperms grow from seeds to mature plants with their own seeds in less than a month. The life cycles of other plants can take as long as a century. If a plant's life cycle is completed within one year, it is called an annual. These plants must be grown from seeds each year.

Plants called biennials (bi EH nee ulz) complete their life cycles within two years. Biennials such as parsley store a large amount of food in an underground root or stem for growth in the second year. Biennials produce flowers and seeds only during the second year of growth. Angiosperms that take more than two years to grow to maturity are called perennials. Herbaceous perennials such as peonies appear to die each winter but grow and produce flowers each spring. Woody perennials such as fruit trees produce flowers and fruits on stems that survive for many years.

Importance of Seed Plants

What would a day at school be like without seed plants? One of the first things you'd notice is the lack of paper and books. Paper is made from pulp that comes from trees, which are seed plants. Are the desks and chairs at your school made of wood? They'll need to be made of something else if no seed plants exist. Clothing that is made from cotton would not exist because cotton comes from seed plants. When it's time for lunch, you'll have trouble finding something to eat. Bread, fruits, and potato chips all come from plants. Milk, hamburgers, and hot dogs all come from animals that eat seed plants. Unless you like to eat plants such as mosses and ferns, you'll go hungry. Without seed plants, your day at school would be different.

Figure 21
Life cycles of angiosperms include annuals, biennials, and perennials. A These petunias, which are annuals, complete their life cycle in one year.
B Parsley plants, which are biennials, do not produce flowers and seeds the first year.
C Perennials, such as this pecan tree, flower and produce fruits year after year.

SCIENCE *Online*

Research Visit the Glencoe Science Web site at **science.glencoe.com** for recent news or magazine articles about the timber industry's efforts to replant conifer trees. In your Science Journal, list the types of trees that are replanted.

SCIENCE *Online*
Internet Addresses

_____

_____

_____

Explore the Glencoe Science Web site at **science.glencoe.com** to find out more about topics in this section.

Reteach

Emphasize the important characteristics that distinguish gymnosperms from angiosperms, or monocots from dicots. Prepare flash cards with a written or visual characteristic of one of the groups on each one. Quiz students by having them quickly respond as you hold up each card. L2

Challenge

If you only know that a plant contains 12 petals, why can't you say for sure whether it is a monocot or dicot? Monocots have petals in multiples of three; dicots have petals in multiples of four or five. Since 12 is divisible by three and four, this characteristic alone won't provide the answer.

✓Assessment

Performance Assess students' abilities to classify food plants by plant part. Give them several common fruits and vegetables and have students classify them as roots, stems, leaves, fruits, or flowers. roots: yams, beets, carrots; stems: asparagus, white potatoes, ginger; leaves: spinach, lettuce; fruits: tomatoes, cherries; flowers: broccoli, cauliflower Use **Performance Assessment in the Science Classroom,** p. 121. ELL

Table 1 Some Products of Seed Plants

From Gymnosperms	From Angiosperms
lumber, paper, soap, varnish, paints, waxes, perfumes, edible pine nuts, medicines 	foods, sugar, chocolate, cotton cloth, linen, rubber, vegetable oils, perfumes, medicines, cinnamon, flavorings (toothpaste, chewing gum, candy, etc.), dyes, lumber 

Products of Seed Plants Conifers are the most economically important gymnosperms. Most of the wood used for construction and for paper production comes from conifers such as pines and spruces. Resin, a waxy substance secreted by conifers, is used to make chemicals found in soap, paint, varnish, and some medicines.

The most economically important plants on Earth are the angiosperms. They form the basis of diets for most animals. Angiosperms were the first plants that humans grew. They included grains, such as barley and wheat, and legumes, such as peas and lentils. Angiosperms are also the source of many of the fibers used in clothing. Besides cotton, linen fabrics come from plant fibers. **Table 1** shows just a few of the products of angiosperms and gymnosperms.

Section ③ Assessment

1. What are the characteristics of a seed plant?

2. Compare and contrast the characteristics of gymnosperms and angiosperms.

3. If you are looking at a flower with five petals, is it from a monocot or dicot?

4. Explain why the root system might be the largest part of a plant.

5. **Think Critically** The cuticle and epidermis of leaves are transparent. If they weren't, what might be the result?

Skill Builder Activities

6. **Forming Hypotheses** Examine the leaf diagram in **Figure 14** in this section. What cell structure is found in the guard cells but not in the other epidermal cells? Hypothesize about what guard cells might produce. **For more help, refer to the** Science Skill Handbook.

7. **Using a Word Processor** Use a word-processing program to outline the structures and functions that are associated with roots, stems, and leaves. **For more help, refer to the** Technology Skill Handbook.

138 CHAPTER 5 Plants

Answers to Section Assessment

1. Seed plants have roots, stems, leaves, vascular tissue, and produce seeds.
2. Gymnosperms produce seeds not protected by fruit; most have needle-like, evergreen leaves. Angiosperms produce flowers that become fruits that enclose seeds.
3. It is from a dicot.

4. Roots must absorb large amounts of water and nutrients and anchor plants.
5. Less light would reach the chloroplasts, which would reduce the rate of photosynthesis.
6. Chloroplasts; guard cells produce food (sugar).

7. Answers will vary. Partial sample outline:
   I. Roots
      A. Vascular Tissue
         1. Moves water.
         2. Moves minerals.

Activity

Identifying Conifers

How can you tell a pine from a spruce or a cedar from a juniper? One way is to observe their leaves. The leaves of most conifers are either needlelike—shaped like needles—or scalelike—like the scales on a fish or snake. Examine some conifer branches and identify them using the key to classifying leaves.

What You'll Investigate
How can leaves be used to classify conifers?

Materials
short branches of the following conifers:

pine	fir
cedar	redwood
spruce	arborvitae
Douglas fir	juniper
hemlock	

*illustrations of the conifers above
*Alternate materials

Goals
■ **Identify** the difference between needlelike and scalelike leaves.
■ **Classify** conifers according to their leaves.

Safety Precautions

Wash your hands after handling leaves.

Communicating Your Data

Use the information from the key to identify any conifers that grow on your school grounds. Draw a map that locates and identifies these conifers. Post the map for other students in your school to see. **For more help, refer to the** Science Skill Handbook.

Procedure

1. **Observe** the leaves or illustrations of each conifer, then use the key below to identify it.
2. **Write** the number and name of each conifer you identify in your Science Journal.

Conclude and Apply

1. What are two traits of hemlock leaves?
2. How are pine and cedar leaves alike?

Key to Classifying Conifer Leaves

1. All leaves are needlelike.
   a. yes, go to 2
   b. no, go to 8

2. Needles are in clusters.
   a. yes, go to 3
   b. no, go to 4

3. Clusters contain two, three, or five needles.
   a. yes, pine
   b. no, cedar

4. Needles grow on all sides of the stem.
   a. yes, go to 5
   b. no, go to 7

5. Needles grow from a woody peg.
   a. yes, spruce
   b. no, go to 6

6. Needles appear to grow from the branch.
   a. yes, Douglas fir
   b. no, hemlock

7. Most of the needles grow upward.
   a. yes, fir
   b. no, redwood

8. All the leaves are scalelike but not prickly.
   a. yes, arborvitae
   b. no, juniper

ACTIVITY 139

Activity

BENCH TESTED

Purpose Students observe and classify conifer leaves. L2 ELL
LS Logical-Mathematical
Process Skills observing, classifying, comparing and contrasting
Time Required 50 minutes
Safety Precautions Remind students not to eat any plant parts, and to wash their hands thoroughly after handling the leaves.
Teaching Strategy Provide hand lenses for students who want to have a closer look at the structures of the leaves.

Answers to Questions
1. Leaves are needlelike; needles grow on all sides of the stem.
2. Both have needlelike leaves with needles in clusters.

Process Direct students to come up with a classification chart similar to the one on this page to classify several broad leaves with very different characteristics. Have students test each other's classification systems. Use **Performance Assessment in the Science Classroom,** p. 121.

Resource Manager

Chapter Resources Booklet
Lab Activities, pp. 9–10, 11–12
Activity Worksheet, pp. 5–6

Communicating Your Data

If possible, have students use a software program to draw their maps. Students can also use a word processing program to make a table that lists the types of conifers and their locations in and around the school grounds.

Activity

Recognize the Problem

Internet Students will use Internet sites that can be accessed through the Glencoe Science Web site at **science. glencoe.com.** They will investigate plants that are used as medicine.

Non-Internet Sources Collect materials describing alternative medicines from nutritionists.

Time Required

three to six days

Preparation

Internet Access the Glencoe Science Web site at **science. glencoe.com** to run through the steps that the students will follow.

Non-Internet Collect books and brochures about plants used as medicine.

Form a Hypothesis

Possible Hypotheses

Students will identify plants that are used as medicine, then hypothesize about their effectiveness. For example, *Echinacea* eases common cold symptoms and peppermint helps an upset stomach.

Activity *Use the Internet*

Plants as Medicine

You may have read about using peppermint to relieve an upset stomach, or taking *Echinacea* to boost your immune system and fight off illness. But did you know that pioneers brewed a cough medicine from lemon mint? In this activity, you will explore plants and their historical use in treating illness, and the benefits and risks associated with using plants as medicine.

Echinacea

Recognize the Problem

How are plants used in maintaining good health?

Form a Hypothesis

How do you know that a particular plant helps you stay healthy? If there is conflicting data, how would you evaluate the use of that plant? Form a hypothesis about how to evaluate a plant's use as a medicine.

Goals

- **Identify** two plants that can be used as a treatment for illness or as a supplement to support good health.
- **Research** the cultural and historical use of each of the two selected plants as medical treatments.

- **Review** multiple sources to understand the effectiveness of each of the two selected plants as a medical treatment.
- **Compare and contrast** the research and form a hypothesis about the medicinal effectiveness of each of the two plants.

Data Source

SCIENCE*Online* Go to the Glencoe Science Web site at **science.glencoe.com** to get more information about plants that can be used for maintaining good health and for data collected by other students.

Monarda

Resource Manager

Chapter Resources Booklet
  Activity Worksheet, pp. 7–8
Lab Management and Safety, p. 61

Test Your Hypothesis

Plan

1. **Search** for information about plants that are used as medicine and identify two plants to investigate.

2. **Research** how these plants are currently recommended for use as medicine or to promote good health. Find out how each has been used historically.

3. **Explore** how other cultures used these plants as a medicine.

Do

1. Make sure your teacher approves your plan before you start.

2. **Record** data you collect about each plant in your Science Journal.

Mentha

Analyze Your Data

1. **Write** a description of how different cultures have used each plant as medicine.

2. How have the plants you investigated been used as medicine historically?

3. **Record** all the uses suggested by different sources for each plant.

4. **Record** the side effects of using each plant as a treatment.

Draw Conclusions

1. After conducting your research, what do you think are the benefits and drawbacks of using these plants as alternative medicines?

2. **Describe** any conflicting information about using each of these plants as medicine.

3. Based on your analysis, would you recommend the use of each of these two plants to treat illness or promote good health? Why or why not?

4. What would you say to someone who was thinking about using any plant-based, over-the-counter, herbal supplement?

*C*ommunicating
Your Data

SCIENCE *Online* Find this *Use the Internet* activity on the Glencoe Science Web site at **science. glencoe.com** Post your data for the two plants you investigated in the tables provided. **Compare** your data to those of other students. Review data that other students have entered about other plants that can be used as medicine.

ACTIVITY 141

*C*ommunicating
Your Data

Test Your Hypothesis

Teaching Strategies

Students should identify plants by common names and scientific names.

Troubleshooting Remind students that they may find conflicting information among their references.

Analyze Your Data

Answers will be subjective and based on students' individual research.

Draw Conclusions

Answers will be individualized and often based on students' opinions of their research. Look for depth and quality of research performed.

✔*Assessment*

Portfolio Have students create a guide describing each of the plants they investigated. The guide should include a picture of the plant, how they promote good health, and a summary of the plant's effectiveness. Use **PASC,** p. 129.

SCIENCE *Online*
Internet Addresses

_____

_____

_____

Explore the Glencoe Science Web site at **science.glencoe.com** to find out more about topics in this activity.

*C*ommunicating
Your Data

Suggest that students use a combination of their data and that obtained from others to draw their conclusions.

Content Background

Hook-and-loop tape was not quickly or easily accepted as a useful invention. George deMestral faced tremendous financial difficulty and great frustration while trying to promote hook-and-loop tape to clothing manufacturers, who saw the fastener as ugly. Astronauts were some of the first to use hook-and-loop tape. It was used to attach food pouches to the walls of spacecraft and astronaut's boots to the floor of the spacecraft. Hook-and-loop tape was slowly accepted as a useful addition to sportswear and equipment. Children's clothing manufacturers then began to view hook-and-loop tape as a useful and attractive material to use.

Discussion

After deMestral had his idea for a new fastener based on the properties of cockleburs, he experimented for years to design hook-and-loop tape. Have students hypothesize why it took years for the idea to become reality. Possible answers: Scientists and inventors must find a material to build their invention with, they might have another job that keeps them from devoting long hours to their project, and many details must be worked out of any design before it takes shape as a product.

Oops! Oops! Accidents in SCIENCE

SOMETIMES GREAT DISCOVERIES HAPPEN BY ACCIDENT!

A Loopy "Fasten-ating" Idea Inspires Invention

A wild cocklebur plant inspired the hook-and-loop fastener.

The idea for a hook-and-loop fastener comes from nature

142

Resources for Teachers and Students

Why Didn't I think of That?, by Allyn Freeman and Bob Golden, John Wiley & Sons, Inc., 1997.

Mistakes that Worked, by Charlotte Foltz Jones, Doubleday, 1991.

Inventing, Inventions and Inventors: A Teaching Resource Book, by Jerry D. Flack, Teacher Ideas Press, 1989.

Scientists often spend countless hours in the laboratory dreaming up useful inventions. Sometimes, however, the best ideas hit them in unexpected places at unexpected times. That's why scientists are constantly on the lookout for things that spark their curiosity.

One day in 1948, a Swiss inventor named George deMestral strolled through a field with his dog. When they returned home, deMestral discovered that the dog's fur was covered with cockleburs, parts of a prickly plant. These burs were also stuck to deMestral's jacket and pants. Curious about what made the burs so sticky, the inventor examined one under a microscope.

DeMestral noticed that the cocklebur was covered with lots of tiny hooks. By clinging to animal fur and fabric, this plant is carried to other places. While studying these burs, he got the idea to invent a new kind of fastener that could do the work of buttons, snaps, zippers, and laces—but better!

Hook-and-loop fasteners provide fun at some amusement parks. You can attach yourself to the sticky material!

After years of experimentation, deMestral came up with a strong, durable hook-and-loop fastener made of two strips of nylon fabric. One strip has thousands of small, stiff hooks; the other strip is covered with soft, tiny loops. Today, this hook-and-loop fastening tape is used on shoes and sneakers, watchbands, hospital equipment, space suits, clothing, book bags, and more. You may have one of those hook-and-loop fasteners somewhere on you right now. They're the ones that go rippppppppp when you open them.

So, if you ever get a fresh idea that clings to your mind like a hook to a loop, stick with it and experiment! Who knows? It may lead to a fabulous invention that changes the world!

This photo provides a close-up view of a hook-and-loop fastener.

CONNECTIONS

List Make a list of at least ten ways that hook-and-loop tape is used today. Think of three new uses for it. Since you can buy strips of hook-and-loop fastening tape in most hardware and fabric stores, you could even try out some of your favorite ideas.

SCIENCE Online

For more information, visit science.glencoe.com

Activity

Students should work in groups to examine a small sample of hook-and-loop tape with a hand lens. If possible, provide a cocklebur for the students to examine as well. Student groups should make a visual that describes the fastener with words or diagrams.

Analyze the Event

Ask students what characteristics allowed George deMestral to develop his hook-and-loop fastener. Possible answers: He was observant, he persevered through years of developing the invention, he was determined to have his invention accepted by clothing manufacturers. Stress that deMestral faced great personal difficulty while developing his product. It was financially very difficult, and many of his friends told him to give up his idea. Point out that the road from invention to finished product is not simple or easy.

Reviewing Main Ideas

Preview

Students can answer the questions in their Science Journals. Discuss the answers as you go through the chapter. **IS Linguistic**

Review

Students can write their answers, then compare them with those of other students. **IS Interpersonal**

Reteach

Students can look at the illustrations and describe details that support the main ideas of the chapter. **IS Visual-Spatial**

Answers to Chapter Review

SECTION 1

3. Possible answers: cuticle, vascular tissue, seeds, ability to store water, spines

SECTION 2

3. spores

SECTION 3

3. Needlelike leaves reduce water loss; seeds are produced in cones.

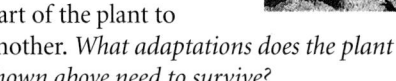

Chapter 5 Study Guide

Reviewing Main Ideas

Section 1 An Overview of Plants

1. Plants are made up of eukaryotic cells and vary greatly in size and shape.

2. Plants usually have some form of leaves, stems, and roots.

3. As plants evolved from aquatic to land environments, changes in structure and function occurred. Changes included how they reproduced, supported themselves, and moved substances from one part of the plant to another. *What adaptations does the plant shown above need to survive?*

4. The plant kingdom is classified into groups called divisions.

Section 2 Seedless Plants

1. Seedless plants include nonvascular and vascular types.

2. Seedless nonvascular plants have no true leaves, stems, or roots. Reproduction usually is by spores.

3. Club mosses, horsetails, and ferns are seedless vascular plants. They have vascular tissues that move substances throughout the plant. These plants may reproduce by spores. *What is produced in these fern structures?*

4. Many ancient forms of these plants underwent a process that resulted in the formation of coal.

Section 3 Seed Plants

1. Seed plants are adapted to survive in nearly every environment on Earth.

2. Seed plants produce seeds and have vascular tissue, stems, roots, and leaves. Vascular tissues transport food, water, and dissolved substances in the roots, stems, and leaves.

3. The two major groups of seed plants are gymnosperms and angiosperms. Gymnosperms generally have needlelike leaves and some type of cone. Angiosperms are plants that flower and are classified as monocots or dicots. *What is the importance of these structures to gymnosperms?*

4. Seed plants provide food, shelter, clothing, and many other products. They are the most economically important plants on Earth.

FOLDABLES Reading & Study Skills

After You Read

Use the information that you recorded in your Know-Want-Learned Study Fold to explain the characteristics of plants you see every day.

FOLDABLES Reading & Study Skills

After You Read

After students have read the chapter and completed the Foldable described in Before You Read, have them do the activity on the student page.

Dinah Zike

Visualizing Main Ideas

Complete the following concept map about the seed plants.

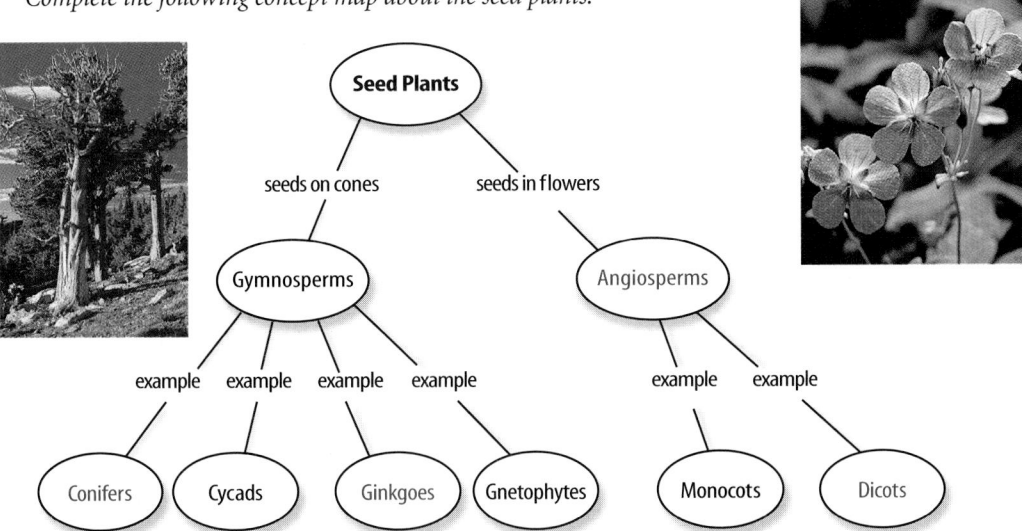

Visualizing Main Ideas

See student page.

Vocabulary Review

Using Vocabulary

1. gymnosperm
2. monocot
3. rhizoid
4. xylem
5. nonvascular plant
6. cuticle
7. pioneer species
8. cellulose

Vocabulary Review

Vocabulary Words

a. angiosperm
b. cambium
c. cellulose
d. cuticle
e. dicot
f. guard cell
g. gymnosperm
h. monocot
i. nonvascular plant
j. phloem
k. pioneer species
l. rhizoid
m. stomata
n. vascular plant
o. xylem

THE PRINCETON REVIEW **Study Tip**

Don't just memorize definitions. Write complete sentences using new vocabulary words to be certain you understand what they mean.

Using Vocabulary

Complete each analogy by providing the missing vocabulary word.

1. Angiosperm is to flower as _____ is to cone.

2. Dicot is to two seed leaves as _____ is to one seed leaf.

3. Root is to fern as _____ is to moss.

4. Phloem is to food transport as _____ is to water transport.

5. Vascular plant is to horsetail as _____ is to liverwort.

6. Cellulose is to support as _____ is to protect.

7. Fuel is to ferns as _____ is to bryophytes.

8. Cuticle is to wax as _____ is to fibers.

Checking Concepts

1. C
2. A
3. C
4. B
5. D
6. C
7. A
8. D
9. C
10. A

Thinking Critically

11. The plant might lose so much water that it would wilt or die.
12. Flowering plants all have vascular tissue.
13. Succulents grow naturally in dry environments.
14. They must grow in moist environments because they don't have vascular tissue for water or nutrient transport. All of their cells must absorb water from the environment.
15. Pioneer species help to break down rocks and make small pockets of soil needed by other, larger plants.

Chapter 5 Assessment

Checking Concepts

Choose the word or phrase that best answers the question.

1. Which of the following is a seedless vascular plant?
   A) moss   C) horsetail
   B) liverwort   D) pine

2. What are the small openings in the surface of a leaf surrounded by guard cells called?
   A) stomata   C) rhizoids
   B) cuticles   D) angiosperms

3. What are the plant structures that anchor the plant called?
   A) stems   C) roots
   B) leaves   D) guard cells

4. Where is most of a plant's new xylem and phloem produced?
   A) guard cell   C) stomata
   B) cambium   D) cuticle

5. What group has plants that are only a few cells thick?
   A) gymnosperms   C) ferns
   B) cycads   D) mosses

6. Which of the following plant parts is found only on gymnosperms?
   A) flowers   C) cones
   B) seeds   D) fruit

7. What kinds of plants have structures that move water and other substances?
   A) vascular   C) nonvascular
   B) protist   D) bacterial

8. In what part of a leaf does most photosynthesis occur?
   A) epidermis   C) stomata
   B) cuticle   D) palisade layer

9. Which one of the following do ferns have?
   A) cones   C) spores
   B) rhizoids   D) seeds

10. Which of these is an advantage to life on land for plants?
    A) more direct sunlight
    B) less carbon dioxide
    C) greater space to grow
    D) less competition for food

Thinking Critically

11. What might happen if a land plant's waxy cuticle were destroyed?

12. On a walk through the woods with a friend, you find a plant neither of you has seen before. The plant is herbaceous and has yellow flowers. Your friend says it is a vascular plant. How does your friend know this?

13. Plants called succulents store large amounts of water in their leaves, stems, and roots. In what environments would you expect to find succulents growing naturally?

14. Explain why mosses are usually found in moist areas.

15. How do pioneer species change environments so that other plants can grow there?

Developing Skills

16. **Interpreting Data** What do the data in this table tell you about where gas exchange occurs in each plant leaf?

Stomata (per mm²)		
Plant	Upper Surface	Lower Surface
Pine	50	71
Bean	40	281
Fir	0	228
Tomato	12	13

17. **Making and Using Graphs** Make two circle graphs using the table in question 16.

Chapter ✓Assessment Planner

Portfolio Encourage students to place in their portfolios one or two items of what they consider to be their best work. Examples include:
- Activity, p. 121
- Make a Model, p. 127
- Curriculum Connection, p. 133

Performance Additional performance assessments, Performance Task Assessment Lists, and rubrics for evaluating these activities can be found in Glencoe's **Performance Assessment in the Science Classroom.**

18. Concept Mapping Complete this map for the seedless plants of the plant kingdom.

Seedless Plants

No transport tissue → Nonvascular plants → examples → Mosses, liverworts, and hornworts

Transport tissue → Vascular plants → example: Ferns, example: Horsetails, example: Club mosses

19. Interpreting Scientific Illustrations Using **Figure 20** in this chapter, compare and contrast the number of cotyledons, bundle arrangement in the stem, veins in leaves, and number of flower parts for monocots and dicots.

20. Concept Mapping Put the following events in order to show how coal is formed from plants: *living seedless plants, coal is formed, dead seedless plants decay,* and *peat is formed.*

Performance Assessment

21. Poem Choose a topic in this chapter that interests you. Look it up in a reference book, in an encyclopedia, or on a CD-ROM. Write a poem to share what you learn.

TECHNOLOGY

Go to the Glencoe Science Web site at **science.glencoe.com** or use the **Glencoe Science CD-ROM** for additional chapter assessment.

Test Practice

Maria and Josh are studying how different environmental factors affect the growth of plants. They set up four pots. Each pot contains a different plant growing in a standard potting soil. They record their data in the following table.

Plant Growth Data			
Type of Plant	**Hours of Light**	**Amount of Water (mL)**	**Percent Growth**
Moss	0	100	2%
Lettuce	4	100	15%
Tree Seedling	8	100	40%
Grape Vine	12	100	65%

Study the table and answer the following questions.

1. According to this information, which is the most likely cause of the differences in plant growth?
   A) light
   B) water
   C) plant type
   D) soil

2. How could this experiment be improved?
   F) Vary the amount of water each plant receives.
   G) Record plant growth in cm.
   H) Use only one kind of plant.
   J) Expose each plant to the same number of hours of light.

Test Practice

The Test-Taking Tip was written by The Princeton Review, the nation's leader in test preparation.
1. A
2. H

Developing Skills

16. Gas exchange for pine and tomato leaves is nearly the same on both the upper and lower surfaces because the number of stomata on each are about equal. Most of the gas exchange for bean leaves occurs on the lower surface. All gas exchange for fir needles happens on the lower surface.

17. The upper-surface graph should show 177° for pine, 141° for bean, and 42° for tomato. The lower-surface graph should show 43° for pine, 171° for bean, 138° for fir, and 8° for tomato.

18. See student page.

19. Monocots have one seed leaf, scattered vascular bundles, parallel veins in leaves, and flower parts in multiples of three. Dicots have two seed leaves, vascular bundles in rings, a network of veins in leaves, and flower parts in multiples of four or five.

20. Living seedless plants, dead seedless plants decay, peat is formed, coal is formed.

Performance Assessment

21. Have students share their poems with the class. Use **PASC,** p. 157.

✔Assessment Resources

📁 **Reproducible Masters**

Chapter Resources Booklet
   Chapter Review, pp. 33–34
   Chapter Tests, pp. 35–38
   Assessment Transparency Activity, p. 45

Glencoe Science Web site
   Interactive Tutor
   Chapter Quizzes

Glencoe Technology
   🖌 Assessment Transparency
   💿 Interactive CD-ROM Chapter Quizzes
   💿 ExamView Pro Test Bank
   💿 Vocabulary PuzzleMaker Software
   📼 MindJogger Videoquiz

Section/Objectives	Standards		Activities/Features
Chapter Opener	National	State/Local	**Explore Activity:** Organize animal groups, p. 149 **Before You Read,** p. 149
	See p. 6T for a Key to Standards.		
Section 1 What is an animal? 🕐 1 session 📦 .5 block 1. **Identify** the characteristics of animals. 2. **Differentiate** between vertebrates and invertebrates. 3. **Explain** how the symmetry of animals differs.	National Content Standards: UCP1, C1, C5		
Section 2 Sponges, Cnidarians, Flatworms, and Roundworms 🕐 2 sessions 📦 1 block 1. **Describe** structures that make up sponges and cnidarians. 2. **Compare** how sponges and cnidarians get food and reproduce. 3. **Differentiate** between flatworms and roundworms.	National Content Standards: UCP1, C1, C5		**Chemistry Integration,** p. 154
Section 3 Mollusks and Segmented Worms 🕐 2 sessions 📦 1 block 1. **Identify** the characteristics of mollusks. 2. **Compare** the similarities and differences between an open and a closed circulatory system. 3. **Describe** the characteristics of segmented worms. 4. **Explain** the digestive process of an earthworm.	National Content Standards: UCP1, A1, C1, C3, C5		**Astronomy Integration,** p. 159 **MiniLAB:** Modeling Cephalopod Propulsion, p. 160 **Problem-Solving Activity:** How does soil management affect earthworms?, p. 162
Section 4 Arthropods and Echinoderms 🕐 4 sessions 📦 2 blocks 1. **List** the features used to classify arthropods. 2. **Explain** how the structure of the exoskeleton relates to its function. 3. **Identify** features of echinoderms.	National Content Standards: UCP1, A1, C1, C5		**Science Online,** p. 165 **Visualizing Arthropod Diversity,** p. 166 **MiniLAB:** Observing Sow Bugs, p. 169 **Activity:** Observing Complete Metamorphosis, p. 171 **Activity:** Garbage-Eating Worms, p. 172 **Science Stats:** Squid Power, p. 174

Teacher's Corner

PRODUCTS AVAILABLE FROM GLENCOE
To order call 1-800-334-7344:
CD-ROMs
NGS PictureShow: Classifying Plants and Animals; NGS PictureShow: Structure of Invertebrates

Transparency Sets
NGS PicturePack: Classifying Plants and Animals; NGS PicturePack: Structure of Invertebrates

INDEX TO NATIONAL GEOGRAPHIC SOCIETY
The following articles may be used for research relating to this chapter:

"The Gift of Gardening," by William S. Ellis, May 1992.
"Deception: Formula for Survival," by Robert F. Sisson, March 1980.
"Consider the Sponge," by Michael E. Long, March 1977.

Activity Materials	Reproducible Resources	Section Assessment	Technology
Explore Activity: large envelopes, index cards, colored pencils, magazines with animal pictures	**Chapter Resources Booklet** Foldables Worksheet, p. 17 Directed Reading Overview, p. 17 Note-taking Worksheets, pp. 35–37	*GLENCOE'S* **ASSESSMENT** *ADVANTAGE*	
	Chapter Resources Booklet Transparency Activity, p. 46 Enrichment, p. 31 Reinforcement, p. 27 Directed Reading, p. 20 **Science Inquiry Labs,** p. 3	Portfolio Explore Activity, p. 149 Performance Skill Builder Activities, p. 152 Content Section Assessment, p. 152	🔦 Section Focus Transparency ⊙ Interactive CD-ROM 🎧 Guided Reading Audio Program
Need materials? Contact Science Kit at 1-800-828-7777 or www.sciencekit.com on the Internet.	**Chapter Resources Booklet** Transparency Activity, p. 47 Enrichment, p. 32 Reinforcement, p. 28 Directed Reading, p. 20	Portfolio Make a Model, p. 155 Performance Skill Builder Activities, p. 157 Content Section Assessment, p. 157	🔦 Section Focus Transparency ⊙ Interactive CD-ROM 🎧 Guided Reading Audio Program
MiniLAB: balloon	**Chapter Resources Booklet** Transparency Activity, p. 48 MiniLAB, p. 3 Enrichment, p. 33 Reinforcement, p. 29 Directed Reading, p. 21 Lab Activity, pp. 9–12	Portfolio Assessment, p. 160 Performance MiniLAB, p. 160 Problem-Solving Activity, p. 162 Skill Builder Activities, p. 163 Content Section Assessment, p. 163	🔦 Section Focus Transparency ⊙ Interactive CD-ROM 🎧 Guided Reading Audio Program
MiniLAB: flat container with cover, 6 sow bugs, damp sponge **Activity:** wide-mouthed jar, bran or oatmeal, cookie crumbs, flour, apple or carrot, paper towel, cheesecloth, rubber band, mealworms **Activity:** red wiggler worms, 4-L plastic containers (2), soil, shredded newspaper, spray bottle, chopped food scraps	**Chapter Resources Booklet** Transparency Activity, p. 49 MiniLAB, p. 4 Enrichment, p. 34 Reinforcement, p. 30 Directed Reading, pp. 21, 22 Activity Worksheet, pp. 5–6, 7–8 Lab Activity, pp. 13–16 Transparency Activity, pp. 51–52 **Lab Management and Safety,** p. 73	Portfolio Extension, p. 168 Performance MiniLAB, p. 169 Skill Builder Activities, p. 170 Content Section Assessment, p. 170	🔦 Section Focus Transparency 🔦 Teaching Transparency ⊙ Interactive CD-ROM 🎧 Guided Reading Audio Program

GLENCOE'S **ASSESSMENT** *ADVANTAGE*	End of Chapter Assessment		
Blackline Masters	**Technology**	**Professional Series**
Chapter Resources Booklet Chapter Review, pp. 39–40 Chapter Tests, pp. 41–44 **Standardized Test Practice by The Princeton Review,** pp. 27–30	📼 MindJogger Videoquiz 🌐 Interactive CD-ROM 🌐 Vocabulary PuzzleMakers 🌐 ExamView Pro Test Bank 🌐 Interactive Lesson Planner 🌐 Interactive Teacher Edition	Performance Assessment in the Science Classroom (PASC)

Transparencies

Section Focus

Section Focus Transparency 1 — Jelly Sea

Jellyfish are interesting animals whose bodies are comprised mostly of water. They drift with the currents, but they are also able to move by expelling a jet of water.

1. How are jellyfish similar to you? How are they different?
2. Describe a jellyfish's shape.
3. Why are jellyfish classified as animals?

L2

Section Focus Transparency 2 — Rub-a-dub-dub

When you clean something with a sponge, you may be using the skeleton of a sea animal. People harvest sponges in areas like the Mediterranean Sea and the Gulf of Mexico. Most sponges you buy in stores, however, aren't animals at all; they're artificial sponges.

1. Why might scientists have originally thought sponges were plants?
2. How do animals get food? How do plants get food?

L2

Section Focus Transparency 3 — I'll Have One for Dinner

One thing these animals have in common is they're occasionally served as dinner. Food is one way people use them, but they are also important for other reasons. For example, some of these creatures live in the sea near the shore and filter large amounts of water each day.

1. What similarities do these three animals share?
2. Describe some of the differences among the three animals.

L2

Assessment

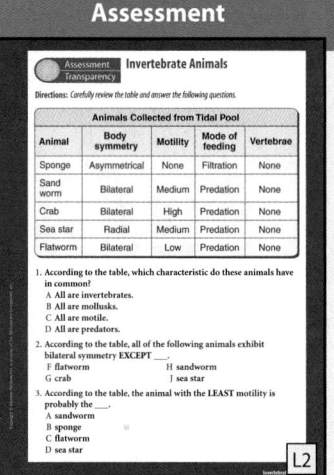

Assessment Transparency — Invertebrate Animals

Directions: *Carefully review the table and answer the following questions.*

Animals Collected from Tidal Pool

Animal	Body symmetry	Motility	Mode of feeding	Vertebrae
Sponge	Asymmetrical	None	Filtration	None
Sand worm	Bilateral	Medium	Predation	None
Crab	Bilateral	High	Predation	None
Sea star	Radial	Medium	Predation	None
Flatworm	Bilateral	Low	Predation	None

1. According to the table, which characteristic do these animals have in common?
   A All are invertebrates.
   B All are mollusks.
   C All are motile.
   D All are predators.
2. According to the table, all of the following animals exhibit bilateral symmetry EXCEPT ____.
   F flatworm   H sandworm
   G crab   J sea star
3. According to the table, the animal with the LEAST motility is probably the ____.
   A sandworm
   B sponge
   C flatworm
   D sea star

L2

Teaching

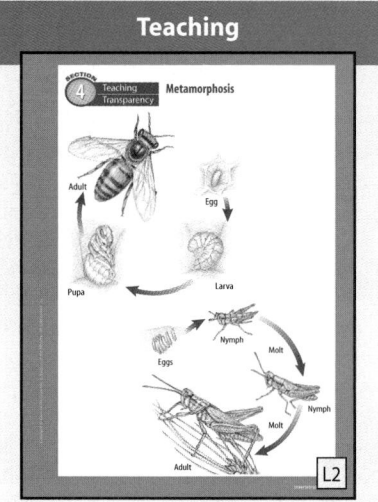

Section Focus Transparency 4 — Metamorphosis

L2

This is a representation of key blackline masters available in the Teacher Classroom Resources. See Resource Manager boxes within the chapter for additional information.

Key to Teaching Strategies

The following designations will help you decide which activities are appropriate for your students.

L1 Level 1 activities should be appropriate for students with learning difficulties.

L2 Level 2 activities should be within the ability range of all students.

L3 Level 3 activities are designed for above-average students.

ELL ELL activities should be within the ability range of English Language Learners.

COOP LEARN Cooperative Learning activities are designed for small group work.

LS Multiple Learning Styles logos, as described on page 22T, are used throughout to indicate strategies that address different learning styles.

P These strategies represent student products that can be placed into a best-work portfolio.

Hands-on Activities

Activity Worksheets

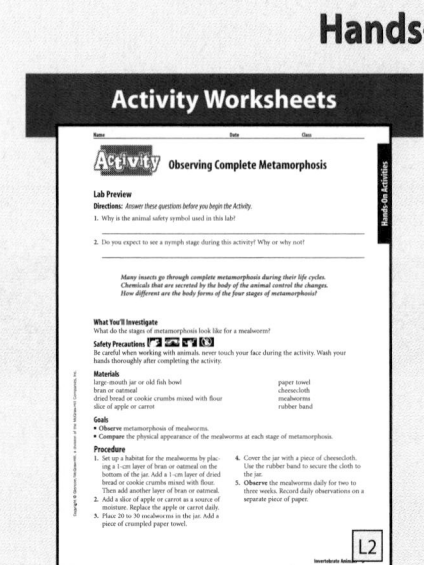

Activity — Observing Complete Metamorphosis

Lab Preview

Directions: *Answer these questions before you begin the Activity.*

1. Why is the animal safety symbol used in this lab!

2. Do you expect to see a nymph stage during this activity! Why or why not!

Many insects go through complete metamorphosis during their life cycles. Chemicals that are secreted by the body of the animal control the changes. How different are the body forms of the four stages of metamorphosis!

What You'll Investigate
What do the stages of metamorphosis look like for a mealworm?

Safety Precautions
Be careful when working with animals; never touch your face during the activity. Wash your hands thoroughly after completing the activity.

Materials
large-mouth jar or old fish bowl
bran or oatmeal
dried bread or cookie crumbs mixed with flour
slice of apple or carrot
paper towel
cheesecloth
mealworms
rubber band

Goals
• Observe metamorphosis of mealworms.
• Compare the physical appearance of the mealworms at each stage of metamorphosis.

Procedure
1. Set up a habitat for the mealworms by placing a 1-cm layer of bran or oatmeal on the bottom of the jar. Add a 1-cm layer of dried bread or cookie crumbs mixed with flour. Then add another layer of bran or oatmeal.
2. Add a slice of apple or carrot as a source of moisture. Replace the apple or carrot daily.
3. Place 20 to 30 mealworms in the jar. Add a piece of crumpled paper towel.
4. Cover the jar with a piece of cheesecloth. Use the rubber band to secure the cloth to the jar.
5. Observe the mealworms daily for two to three weeks. Record daily observations on a separate piece of paper.

L2

Laboratory Activities

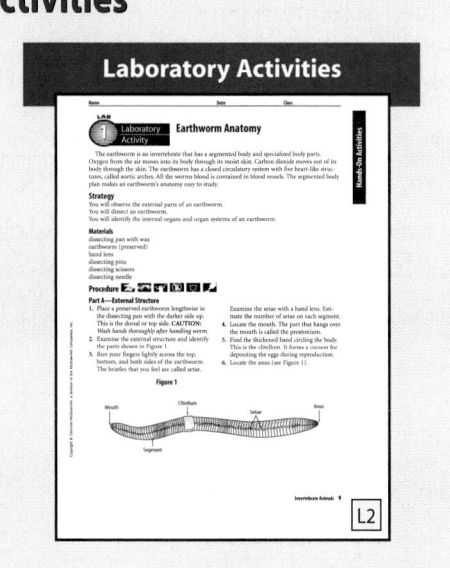

Laboratory Activity 1 — Earthworm Anatomy

The earthworm is an invertebrate that has a segmented body and specialized body parts. Oxygen from the air moves into its body through its moist skin. Carbon dioxide moves out of its body through the skin. The earthworm has a closed circulatory system with five heart-like structures, called aortic arches. All the worm's blood is contained in blood vessels. The segmented body plan makes an earthworm's anatomy easy to study.

Strategy
You will observe the external parts of an earthworm.
You will identify the internal organs and organ systems of an earthworm.

Materials
dissecting pan with wax
earthworm (preserved)
hand lens
dissecting pins
dissecting scissors
dissecting needle

Procedure

Part A—External Structure
1. Place a preserved earthworm lengthwise in the dissecting pan with the darker side up. This is the dorsal or top side. CAUTION: Wash hands thoroughly after handling worm.
2. Examine the external structure and identify the parts shown in Figure 1.
3. Run your fingers lightly across the top, bottom, and both sides of the earthworm. The bristles that you feel are called setae.
4. Locate the mouth. The part that hangs over the mouth is called the prostomium.
5. Find the thickened band circling the body. This is the clitellum. It forms a cocoon for depositing the eggs during reproduction.
6. Locate the anus (see Figure 1).

Examine the setae with a hand lens. Estimate the number of setae on each segment.

Figure 1

Mouth   Clitellum   Setae   Anus

Segment

L2

Meeting Different Ability Levels

Content Outline

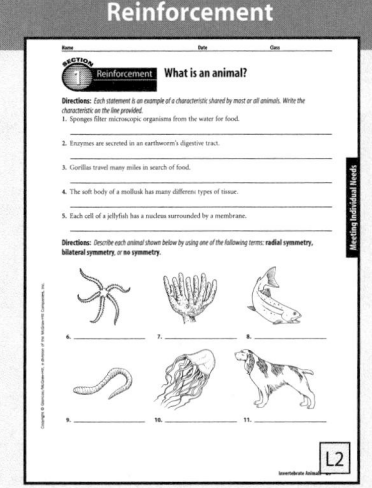

L2

Reinforcement

L2

Directed Reading

L1

Assessment

Chapter Tests

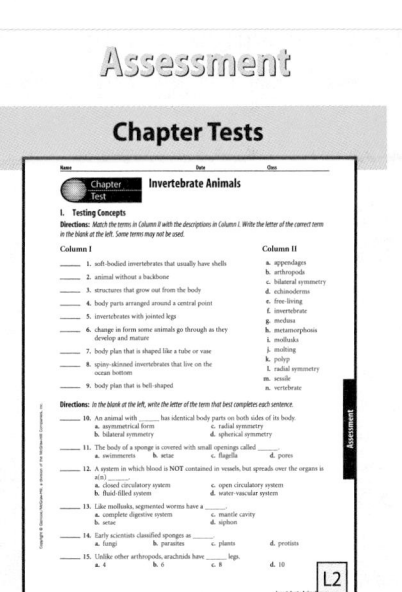

L2

Enrichment

L3

Spanish Directed Reading

L1

Test Practice Workbook

L2

Chapter Review

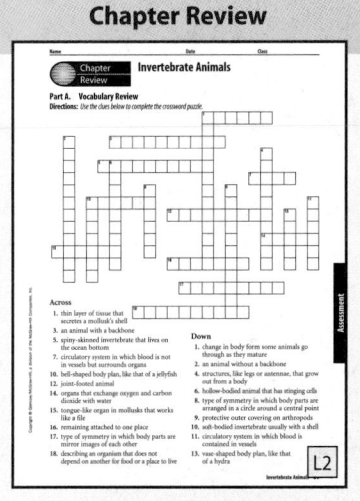

L2

Science Content Background

SECTION 1

What is an animal?
All About Animals

Scientists hypothesize that single-celled protozoan ancestors gave rise to multicellular animals. These protozoans left no fossils, making it impossible to trace the animal kingdom through its origins. The transition from single-celled protozoan to multicellular animal most likely occurred more than once. Certain sponge cells are almost identical to a specific type of flagellated protozoa—choanoflagellate—leading some zoologists to reason that protists gave rise to modern sponges.

Some important features that help distinguish animal phyla from one another are symmetry, body cavities, digestive cavities, and segmentation. An animal's symmetry often provides insight into how the organism survives in its environment. With food and other sensory information coming from all directions, animals with radial symmetry often are either sessile or slow moving. An important aspect of organisms exhibiting bilateral symmetry is cephalization—the tendency for sense organs to be concentrated in the head region and focused toward the direction in which the organism moves.

Sponges, cnidarians, and flatworms are, for the most part, masses of cells and do not have body cavities in which internal organs are found. Other organisms—roundworms, mollusks, segmented worms, arthropods, and echinoderms—do have body cavities. Most animals have a digestive cavity that collects food and secretes digestive enzymes. The digestive cavity may be a one-way sac, as in the sea anemone, or it may be a tube with two openings, as in segmented worms.

Segmentation—the repeating of parts that contain similar organs—is a characteristic of three of the largest animal phyla: annelids (segmented worms), arthropods, and chordates (vertebrates).

SECTION 2

Sponges, Cnidarians, Flatworms, and Roundworms
Sponges

Sponges—phylum Porifera—are the least complex of all the major animal phyla. They do not have nerve cells or sense organs. Their body cells are not even organized into tissues. Although food is taken into the central cavity of a sponge, the cavity is not a digestive cavity. Digestion of the food takes place in either collar cells or amoeboid cells.

Cnidarians

All cnidarians are carnivorous. Their stinging cells contain a coiled thread that is discharged when a "trigger" on the cell is touched by prey. The threads in some species contain paralyzing toxins. Cnidarians' outer tissue layer is the epidermis, and their inner layer is the gastrodermis. Between these two layers of tissue is a jellylike layer. Cnidarians lack true organs. Cells exchange oxygen and wastes with their environment by diffusion.

Flatworms

Flatworms—phylum Platyhelminthes—are the simplest organisms with bilateral symmetry.

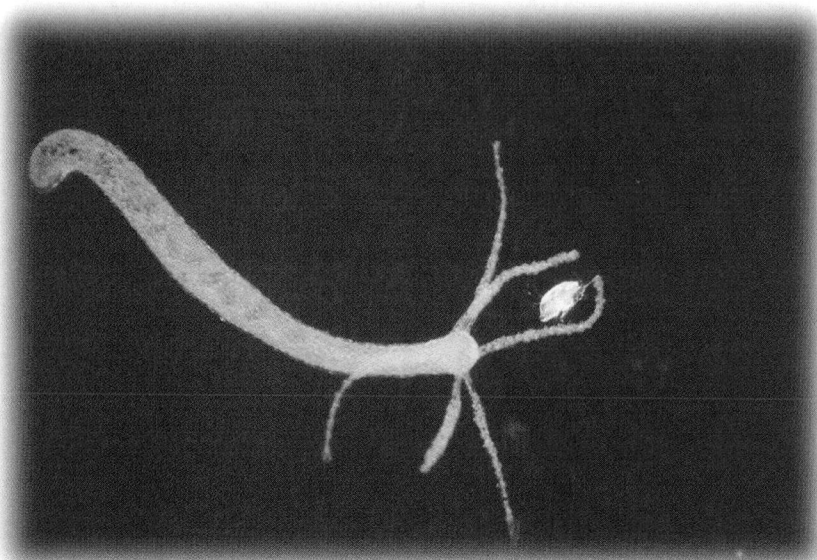

Larry Stepanowicz/Visuals Unlimited

The brain and nerve cords that run the length of the body are considered to be the evolutionary forerunners of a central nervous system. The middle layer of the flatworm contains muscle tissue used for locomotion. Flatworms also have complex reproductive and digestive systems. Although many flatworms are parasites, freshwater planaria are free-living and easily studied in the classroom.

Roundworms

Roundworms belong to the phylum Nematoda. The disease elephantiasis occurs when the roundworm *Wuchereria* blocks lymphatic vessels.

Mollusks and Segmented Worms

Mollusks

Mollusks are the second largest animal phyla, with more than 100,000 identified species. Segmented worms of the phylum Annelida comprise about 10,000 species and are divided into three major classes: oligochaetes (earthworms), polychaetes (marine bristleworms and tubeworms), and hirudineans (leeches).

Segmented Worms

Earthworm aeration of the soil is so beneficial that their presence in hundreds or thousands per hectare is a characteristic of a productive farm. Earthworms survive in thin films of water in slightly moist soil, but if the soil becomes flooded, they can drown.

Arthropods and Echinoderms

Arthropods

Arthropods are the most diverse group of animals on Earth. More than one million species have been identified. Flight is an important adaptation that helps insects find food and mates, escape predators, and spread to new areas.

Echinoderms

Echinoderms, such as sea stars and sea urchins, have a number of traits that set them apart from other invertebrates. The radial symmetry of these organisms is fivefold, or pentamerous. Fossil evidence indicates that early echinoderms were bilaterally symmetrical and only later developed radial symmetry suited for a sessile, or slow-moving, organism. The larvae of echinoderms are bilaterally symmetrical.

Fun Fact

A parasitic isopod (a crustacean) consumes most of the tongue of a fish called the spotted rose snapper. It then hooks itself to the mouth of the fish and takes over the role of the tongue, helping the fish get prey and also getting bits of food for itself.

SCIENCE *Online*

For additional content background on this topic, go to the Glencoe Science Web site at science.glencoe.com.

Invertebrate Animals

Chapter Vocabulary

symmetry, p. 151
invertebrate, p. 152
cnidarian, p. 154
polyp, p. 155
medusa, p. 155
mollusk, p. 158
mantle, p. 158
gill, p. 158
radula, p. 159
open circulatory system, p. 159
closed circulatory system, p. 160
arthropod, p. 164
appendage, p. 164
exoskeleton, p. 164
metamorphosis, p. 165

What do you think?

Science Journal The animal in this picture is a flat bark bug. Flat bark bugs feed on the fungus that grows on tree bark. As you can see, the bug appears to be a lichen growing on the tree. This camouflage would provide excellent protection from predators.

Invertebrate Animals

What characteristics do the sea stars and sea anemones in this picture have in common with a dog or a horse? What makes these animals different? How do scientists use these similarities and differences to classify animals? In this chapter, you will learn the differences between vertebrates and invertebrates. You also will learn about the different groups of invertebrate animals.

What do you think?

Science Journal Look at the picture below with a classmate. Discuss what you think this might be or what is happening. Here's a hint: *It cannot make its own food.* Write your answer in your Science Journal.

148

Theme Connection

Stability and Change The groups of animals from invertebrates to vertebrates show a trend toward increasing complexity. Many animals in both groups exhibit adaptations to the environment around them. Others have characteristics that enable them to meet the challenges of an ever-changing environment.

Scientists have identified at least 1.5 million different kinds of animals. In the following activity, you will learn about organizing animals by building a bulletin board display.

Organize animal groups

1. Write the names of different groups of animals on large envelopes and attach them to a bulletin board.

2. Choose an animal group to study. Make an information card about each animal with its picture on one side and characteristics on the other side.

3. Place your finished cards inside the appropriate envelope.

4. Select an envelope from the bulletin board for a different group of animals. Using the information on the cards, sort the animals into groups.

Observe

What common characteristics do these animals have? What characteristics did you use to classify them into smaller groups? Record your answers in your Science Journal.

Before You Read

Making a Venn Diagram Study Fold As you prepare to read this chapter, make the following Foldable to find out what you know about invertebrates. The figure below is a Venn Diagram. It can be used to compare and contrast the characteristics of invertebrates.

1. Place a sheet of paper in front of you so the long side is at the top. Fold the paper in half from top to bottom.

2. Draw overlapping ovals and label *Water Invertebrates, Both,* and *Land Invertebrates* across the front of the paper, as shown.

3. Fold both sides in to divide the paper into thirds. Unfold the paper.

4. Through the top thickness of paper, cut along each of the fold lines to the top fold, forming three tabs.

5. Before you read the chapter, list as many land and water invertebrates as you can on the front of the tabs. As you read the chapter, list new characteristics under each tab.

Purpose Use the Explore Activity to introduce the characteristics all animals share. Explain to students that they will learn more about animal characteristics and how scientists classify animals into groups with similar characteristics. L2 COOP LEARN

LS Visual-Spatial

Preparation Clear bulletin board space for the placement of animal group envelopes.

Materials 20 large envelopes, 4×6 index cards, colored pencils, magazines with animal pictures

Teaching Strategy Ask students which animals they are most familiar with. They will probably say dogs, cats, hamsters, fish, and other pets or vertebrates.

Observe

Possible response: similar body shapes and coverings; Possible response: similar methods of movement and food gathering

Portfolio Have students make extra cards of their favorite animals from the groups they worked with to place into their portfolios. Use **Performance Assessment in the Science Classroom,** p. 131. P

FOLDABLES Reading & Study Skills

Before You Read

Dinah Zike Study Fold

Purpose Use this activity to determine what students know about invertebrates. Students will investigate similarities and differences between land and water invertebrates by using a Venn diagram Foldable.

📁 For additional help, see Foldables Worksheet, p. 17 in **Chapter Resources Booklet,** or go to Glencoe Science Web site at **science.glencoe.com**.
See After You Read in the Study Guide at the end of this chapter.

SECTION

1 **What is an animal?**

1 Motivate

Bellringer Transparency

Display the Section Focus Transparency for Section 1. Use the accompanying Transparency Activity Master. L2

ELL

Tie to Prior Knowledge

Students will be familiar with many animal characteristics from observing pets. Remind students that animals cannot make their own food and are made of many nucleated cells.

As You Read

What You'll Learn
- **Identify** the characteristics of animals.
- **Differentiate** between vertebrates and invertebrates.
- **Explain** how the symmetry of animals differs.

Vocabulary
symmetry
invertebrate

Why It's Important
All animals have characteristics in common.

Figure 1
Animals come in a variety of shapes and sizes.

A The lion's mane jellyfish can be found in the cold, arctic water and the warm water off the coasts of Florida and Mexico. Their tentacles can be up to 30 m long.

Animal Characteristics

If you asked ten people for a characteristic common to all animals, you might get ten different answers or a few repeated answers. Look at the animals in **Figure 1.** What are their common characteristics? What makes an animal an animal?

1. Animals are many-celled organisms that are made of different kinds of cells. These cells might digest food, get rid of wastes, help in reproduction, or be part of systems that have these functions.

2. Most animal cells have a nucleus and organelles surrounded by a membrane. This type of cell is called a eukaryotic (yew KER ee oht ic) cell.

3. Animals cannot make their own food. Some animals eat plants to supply their energy needs. Some animals eat other animals, and some eat both plants and animals.

4. Animals digest their food. Large food particles are broken down into smaller substances that their cells can use.

5. Most animals can move from place to place. They move to find food, shelter, and mates, and to escape from predators.

B Monarch butterflies in North America migrate up to 5,000 km each year.

C The platypus lives in Australia. It is an egg-laying mammal.

150 CHAPTER 6 Invertebrate Animals

Section ✓Assessment Planner

PERFORMANCE ASSESSMENT
Skill Builder Activities, p. 152
See page 178 for more options.

CONTENT ASSESSMENT
Section, p. 152
Challenge, p. 152
Chapter, pp. 178–179

Figure 2
Most animals have radial or bilateral symmetry.
Only a few animals are asymmetrical.

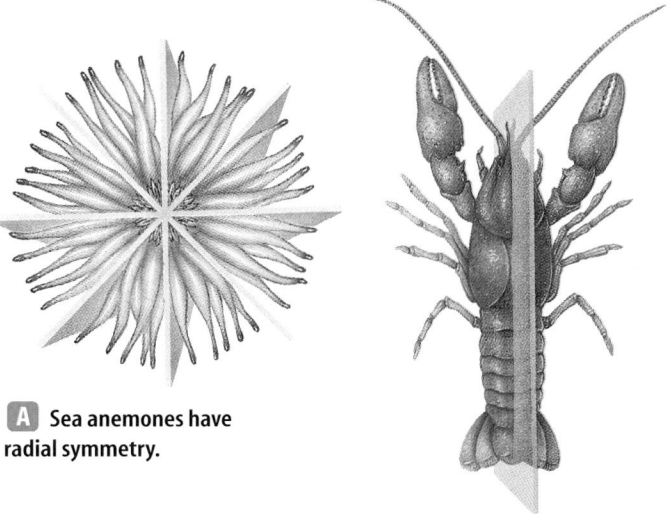

A Sea anemones have radial symmetry.

C Many sponges are asymmetrical.

B Lobsters have bilateral symmetry.

Symmetry As you study the different groups of animals, you will look at their symmetry (SIH muh tree). **Symmetry** refers to the arrangement of the individual parts of an object.

Most animals have either radial symmetry or bilateral symmetry. Animals with body parts arranged in a circle around a central point have radial symmetry. Can you imagine being able to locate food and gather information from all directions? Aquatic animals with radial symmetry, such as jellyfish, sea urchins, and the sea anemone shown in **Figure 2A,** can do that. On the other hand, animals with bilateral symmetry have parts that are mirror images of each other. A line can be drawn down the center of their bodies to divide them into two similar parts. Grasshoppers, lobsters, shown in **Figure 2B,** and humans are bilaterally symmetrical.

Some animals have no definite shape. They are called asymmetrical (AY suh meh trih kul). Their bodies cannot be divided into matching halves. Many sponges, like those in **Figure 2C,** are asymmetrical. As you learn more about invertebrates, notice how their body symmetry is related to how they gather food and do other things.

✔ **Reading Check** *What is symmetry?*

Teacher FYI

Animals constitute over 75% of Earth's species. The mobility of animals allows them great diversity. The ability to move provides flexibility in feeding, defense, and reproduction. Because animals can move to find food, escape predators, or search for a mate, they have adapted to nearly every environment on Earth.

Resource Manager

Chapter Resources Booklet

Transparency Activity, p. 46

Directed Reading for Content Mastery, pp. 19, 20

Note-taking Worksheets, pp. 35–37

② Teach

Animal Characteristics

Quick Demo

Compare symmetrical and asymmetrical objects. Use rocks, chalk, and other classroom objects.

Activity

Show students pictures of radially symmetrical animals (i.e. sea anemones, jellyfish). Challenge them to indicate the head of the animal. Explain that most animals with radial symmetry do not have a definite head. Have students examine pictures of animals such as dogs or cats that have bilateral symmetry. Again challenge them to indicate the location of the head. Point out that in animals with bilateral symmetry, sensory organs tend to be located in the head. Note that it is difficult to see the "head" in some bilaterally symmetrical animals, like roundworms. [L1] [IS] **Visual-Spatial**

IDENTIFYING Misconceptions

Many students do not think of invertebrates as animals. Elicit student help in writing a list of familiar invertebrates on the board. Stress that the animals listed are grouped together by the absence of a structural characteristic—a backbone—rather than the presence of a characteristic.

✔ **Reading Check**

Answer the arrangement of the individual parts of an object

Visual Learning

Figure 3 What animal groups are classified as invertebrates? sponges, cnidarians, flatworms, round-worms, mollusks, annelids, arthropods, and echinoderms L1 [IS] **Visual-Spatial**

3 Assess

Reteach

Have students look through magazines to find pictures of animals. Then have them work in groups to identify each animal's type of body symmetry. L1 COOP LEARN [IS] **Visual-Spatial**

Challenge

How does having a head help an animal? The head is the site of many sensory organs and brain structures that process sensory information. An animal moving headfirst can perceive the environment before its body enters, giving the animal a chance to retreat if necessary. L3 [IS] **Logical-Mathematical**

✓Assessment

Performance Have students formulate additional categories for classifying animals after identifying an animal's symmetry and whether it has a backbone. Use **PASC**, p. 121. L3

Animal Classification

Deciding whether an organism is an animal is only the first step in classifying it. Scientists place all animals into smaller, related groups. They can begin by separating animals into two distinct groups—vertebrates and invertebrates. Vertebrates (VUR tuh bruts) are animals that have a backbone. **Invertebrates** (ihn VUR tuh bruts) are animals that do not have a backbone. About 97 percent of all animals are invertebrates.

Scientists classify the invertebrates into smaller groups, as shown in **Figure 3.** The animals within each group share similar characteristics. These characteristics indicate that the animals within the group may have had a common ancestor.

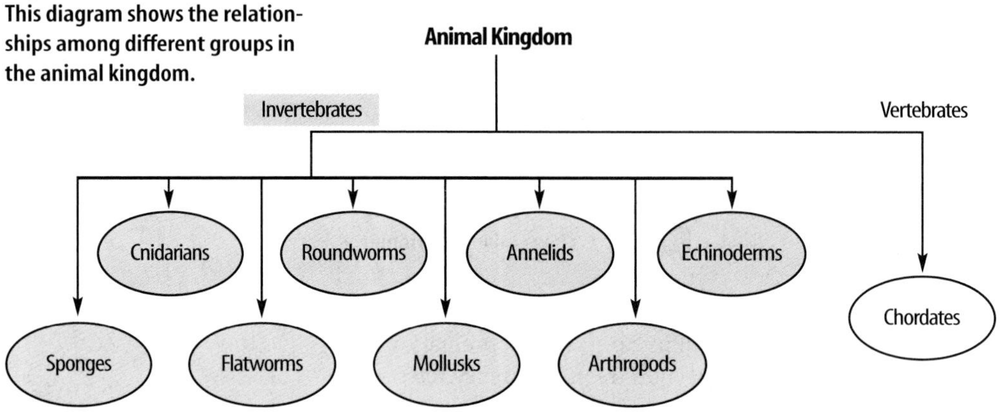

Figure 3
This diagram shows the relationships among different groups in the animal kingdom.

Animal Kingdom

Invertebrates — Cnidarians, Roundworms, Annelids, Echinoderms, Sponges, Flatworms, Mollusks, Arthropods

Vertebrates — Chordates

Section 1 Assessment

1. What are the characteristics of animals?
2. How are invertebrate animals different from vertebrate animals?
3. What are the types of symmetry? Name an animal that has bilateral symmetry.
4. Can animals with radial symmetry be divided in half? How?
5. **Think Critically** Most animals do not have a backbone. They are called invertebrates. What are some advantages that invertebrate animals might have over vertebrate animals?

Skill Builder Activities

6. **Concept Mapping** Using the information in this section, make a concept map showing the steps a scientist might use to classify a newly discovered animal. **For more help, refer to the** Science Skill Handbook.
7. **Using a Word Processor** Create a table that you will use as you complete this chapter. Label the following columns: *animal, group,* and *body symmetry.* Create ten rows to enter animal names. **For more help, refer to the** Technology Skill Handbook.

152 CHAPTER 6 Invertebrate Animals

Resource Manager

Chapter Resources Booklet
Enrichment, p. 31
Reinforcement, p. 27
Science Inquiry Labs, p. 3

Answers to Section Assessment

1. They are consumers, they digest their food, most have means of movement, and they are made up of many different cells that contain a nucleus.
2. Invertebrates lack a backbone; vertebrates have a backbone.
3. radial, bilateral, and asymmetrical; possible response: dog
4. They can be divided into equal halves by a line drawn through any body plane. Students may reference **Figure 2A.**
5. Accept all reasonable answers.
6. Concept maps should show the identification of the animal as a vertebrate or invertebrate, then the determination of

its symmetry, and finally a comparison with other organisms.
7. Students can choose animals from pictures found in magazines to go into their table. As they read the chapter, they should be able to fill in the information on each animal's symmetry and the group each animal is in.

2 Sponges, Cnidarians, Flatworms, and Roundworms

Sponges

Can you tell the difference between an animal and a plant? Sounds easy, doesn't it? But for a long time, even scientists didn't know how to classify sponges. Originally they thought sponges were plants because they don't move to search for food. Sponges, however, can't make their own food as most plants do. Sponges are animals. Adult sponges are sessile (SES ul), meaning they remain attached to one place. More than 5,000 species of sponges have been identified.

Filter Feeders Most species of sponges live in the ocean, but some live in freshwater. Sponge bodies, shown in **Figure 4,** are made of two layers of cells. All sponges are filter feeders. They filter food out of the water that flows through their bodies. Microscopic organisms and oxygen are carried with water into the central cavity through pores of the sponge. The inner surface of the central cavity is lined with collar cells. Thin, whiplike structures, called flagella (flah JE luh), extend from the collar cells and keep the water moving through the sponge. Other specialized cells digest the food, carry nutrients to all parts of the sponge, and remove wastes.

Body Support and Defense Not many animals eat sponges. The soft bodies of many sponges are supported by sharp, glasslike structures called spicules (SPIHK yewlz). Other sponges have a material called spongin. Spongin is similar to foam rubber because it makes sponges soft and elastic. Some sponges have both spicules and spongin to protect their soft bodies.

As You Read

What You'll Learn
- **Describe** the structures that make up sponges and cnidarians.
- **Compare** how sponges and cnidarians get food and reproduce.
- **Differentiate** between flatworms and roundworms.

Vocabulary
cnidarian
polyp
medusa

Why It's Important
Studying the body plans in sponges, cnidarians, flatworms, and roundworms helps you understand the complex organ systems in other organisms.

Figure 4
Red beard sponges grow where the tide moves in and out quickly.

153

SECTION

2 Sponges, Cnidarians, Flatworms, and Roundworms

1 Motivate

Bellringer Transparency
Display the Section Focus Transparency for Section 2. Use the accompanying Transparency Activity Master. L2 ELL

Tie to Prior Knowledge
Review cell structure, function, and tissue organization so students will understand differences in body structure of organisms in this section.

Section ✓Assessment Planner

PORTFOLIO
Make a Model, p. 155
PERFORMANCE ASSESSMENT
Skill Builder Activities, p. 157
See page 178 for more options.

CONTENT ASSESSMENT
Section, p. 157
Challenge, p. 157
Chapter, pp. 178–179

2 Teach

Sponges

Activity

Randomly arrange pictures of sponges, cnidarians, flatworms, roundworms, mollusks, and annelids on the bulletin board along with tags that name each phylum, or group. Have students place the pictures under the appropriate phylum, or group heading, as the animals in each group are studied. L1

 **Kinesthetic**

Chemistry
INTEGRATION

from the water, which contains calcium and silica

Cnidarians

Discussion

Why are there no sessile animals on land? Sessile animals must get nourishment from food that passes by. Food that swims or is suspended in water is more easily accessible than food that flies or is suspended in air.
L2 **Logical-Mathematical**

Chemistry
INTEGRATION

Sponge spicules of "glass" sponges are composed of silica. Other sponges have spicules made of calcium carbonate. Where do organisms get the silica and calcium carbonate that these spicules are made of? Write your prediction in your Science Journal.

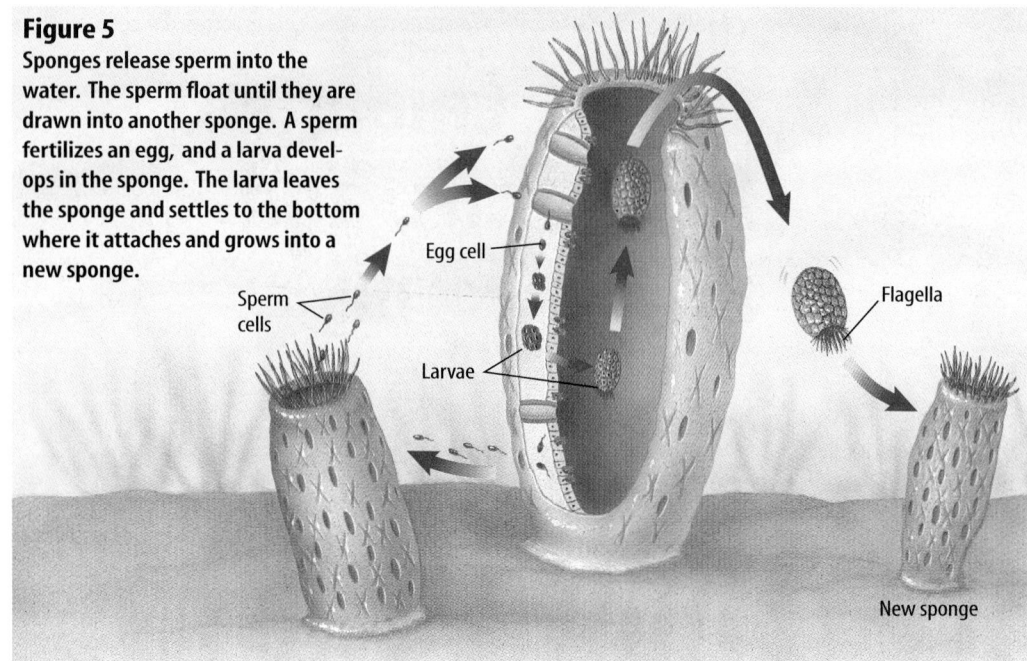

Figure 5
Sponges release sperm into the water. The sperm float until they are drawn into another sponge. A sperm fertilizes an egg, and a larva develops in the sponge. The larva leaves the sponge and settles to the bottom where it attaches and grows into a new sponge.

Egg cell
Sperm cells
Flagella
Larvae
New sponge

Sponge Reproduction Sponges can reproduce asexually and sexually. Asexual reproduction occurs when a bud on the side of the parent sponge develops into a small sponge. The small sponge breaks off, floats away, and attaches itself to a new surface. New sponges also may grow from pieces of a sponge. Each piece grows into a new, identical sponge.

Most sponges that reproduce sexually are hermaphrodites (hur MA fruh dites). This means that one sponge produces both eggs and sperm, as shown in **Figure 5.**

Cnidarians

Cnidarians (nih DAR ee uns), such as jellyfish, sea anemones, hydra, and corals, have tentacles surrounding their mouth. The tentacles shoot out stinging cells called nematocysts (NE muh tuh sists) to capture prey, similar to casting a fishing line into the water to catch a fish. Because they have radial symmetry, they can locate food that floats by from any direction.

Cnidarians are hollow-bodied animals with two cell layers that are organized into tissues. The inner layer forms a digestive cavity where food is broken down. Oxygen moves into the cells from the surrounding water, and carbon dioxide waste moves out of the cells. Nerve cells work together as a nerve net throughout the whole body.

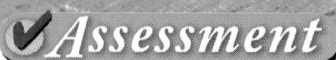 **LAB DEMONSTRATION**

Purpose to observe sponge structure
Materials natural or preserved sponge, magnifying lens, microscope, prepared slide of sponge cross-section
Preparation If using a preserved sponge, rinse with water before observations are made. Set up the microscopes and slides around the room.

Procedure Have students draw what they see when they examine the sponge with a magnifying lens, and label the pores. Then, have students examine the slides, note cell types, and label the central cavity and spicules.
Expected Outcome Students will observe pores, different cell types, and the body cavity.

Assessment

Describe the texture of the sponge. Texture will vary depending upon the type of sponge spicules. **What traits does a sponge have for living in water?** pores for taking in water and food, and spicules (or spongin) for support

Body Forms Cnidarians have two different body forms. The vase-shaped body of the sea anemone and the hydra is called a **polyp** (PAH lup). Although hydras are usually sessile, they can twist to capture prey. They also can somersault to a new location.

Jellyfish have a free-swimming, bell-shaped body that is called a **medusa** (mih DEW suh). Jellyfish are not strong swimmers. Instead, they drift with the ocean currents. Some cnidarians go through both a polyp and a medusa stage during their life cycles.

Cnidarian Reproduction Cnidarians reproduce asexually and sexually. Polyp forms of cnidarians, such as hydras, reproduce asexually by budding, as shown in **Figure 6.** The bud eventually falls off of the parent organism and develops into a new polyp. Some polyps also can reproduce sexually by releasing eggs or sperm into the water. The eggs are fertilized by sperm and develop into new polyps. Medusa forms of cnidarians, such as jellyfish, have a two-stage life cycle as shown in **Figure 7.** A medusa reproduces sexually to produce polyps. Then each of these polyps reproduces asexually to form new medusae.

Figure 6
Polyps, like these hydras, reproduce asexually by budding.

Figure 7
Cnidarians that spend most of their life as a medusa have a sexual (medusa) stage and an asexual (polyp) stage.

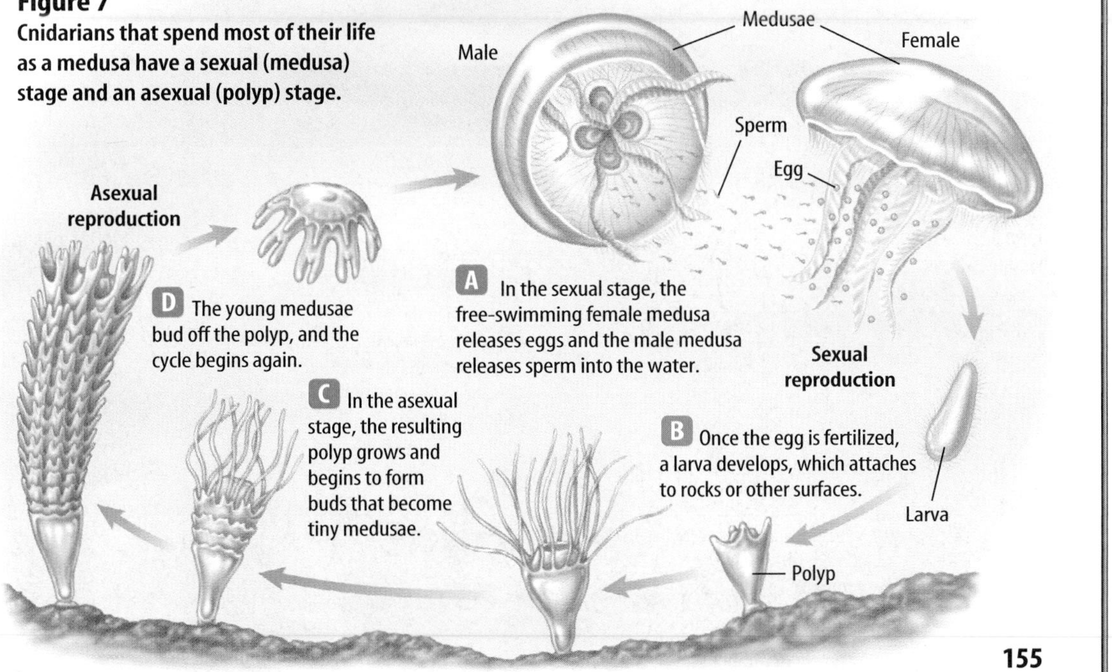

Medusae

Male

Female

Sperm

Egg

Asexual reproduction

D The young medusae bud off the polyp, and the cycle begins again.

A In the sexual stage, the free-swimming female medusa releases eggs and the male medusa releases sperm into the water.

C In the asexual stage, the resulting polyp grows and begins to form buds that become tiny medusae.

Sexual reproduction

B Once the egg is fertilized, a larva develops, which attaches to rocks or other surfaces.

Larva

Polyp

155

Make a Model

Provide students with modeling clay and have them make models of polyps and medusas. Have students compare the shapes and symmetry. The polyp is vase-shaped and the medusa is bell-shaped. Both have radial symmetry. L1
 Kinesthetic P

Teacher FYI

The jellyfish *Chironex fleckeri*, also known as the Australian box jellyfish, or sea wasp, is found along sandy bottoms off the coast of Australia. It is one of the most venomous animals in the sea. The poison found in its stinging cells can kill a human within five minutes, depending on the age of the victim and the severity of the stings. Although antivenom is available, it has not been proven to save lives.

Visual Learning

Figure 7 Use this figure to review with students the differences between sexual and asexual reproduction. L1 **Visual-Spatial**

Extension

Have students research the Great Barrier Reef off the coast of Australia. There are at least 350 species of coral that make up the reef. Have students research the other kinds of invertebrates living there and write a report of their findings. L1 **Linguistic**

Curriculum Connection

Language Arts The hydra was named for a giant mythical water monster with nine heads. Hercules, a Greek hero, was supposed to slay the monster, but each time he cut off one head, it grew two more to take its place. Have students do research to discover how the real hydra is like the mythical one. A real hydra can be cut into pieces, and each piece that has enough cells or tissue will generate a new hydra. L2 **Linguistic**

Resource Manager

Chapter Resources Booklet
   Transparency Activity, p. 47
   Directed Reading for Content Mastery, p. 20

Life Science Critical Thinking/Problem Solving, p. 10

Flatworms

Activity

Tapeworms as long as 9 m have been found in humans. Have students use a meterstick to measure 9 m of string, so they can observe a tapeworm's length. L1 IS **Kinesthetic**

Use Science Words

Word Meaning Flatworms belong to the phylum *Platyhelminthes*. Ask students to find the meaning of the prefix *platy-*. flat or platelike Then ask them to find other words with this prefix and their meanings. Possible responses: platypus—a small aquatic mammal that has a flattened tail; platyrrhine—an adjective that means to have a short broad nose L2 IS **Linguistic**

Extension

Explain that animals, including dogs and cats, commonly have tapeworms and flukes. Have each student choose an animal and find out how flukes and tapeworms affect it. Students can present their findings in oral presentations. L2 IS **Linguistic**

Roundworms

Teacher FYI

Over 1.4 billion people are currently estimated to be infected with intestinal round-worms alone.

Flatworms

Unlike sponges and cnidarians, flatworms search for food. Flatworms are invertebrates with long, flattened bodies and bilateral symmetry. Their soft bodies have three layers of tissue organized into organs and organ systems. Planarians are free-living flatworms that have a digestive system with one opening. They don't depend on one particular organism for food or a place to live. However, most flatworms are parasites that live in or on their hosts. A parasite depends on its host for food and shelter.

Tapeworms One type of parasitic flatworm is the tapeworm. To survive, it lives in the intestines of its host, including human hosts. The tapeworm lacks a digestive system so it absorbs nutrients from digested material in the host's intestine. In **Figure 8A,** you can see the hooks and suckers on a tapeworm's head that attach it to the host's intestine.

A tapeworm grows by adding sections directly behind its head. Each body segment has both male and female reproductive organs. The eggs and sperm are released into the segment. After it is filled with fertilized eggs, the segment breaks off.

Figure 8
Tapeworms are intestinal parasites that attach to a host's intestines with hooks and suckers. Their life cycle is shown here.

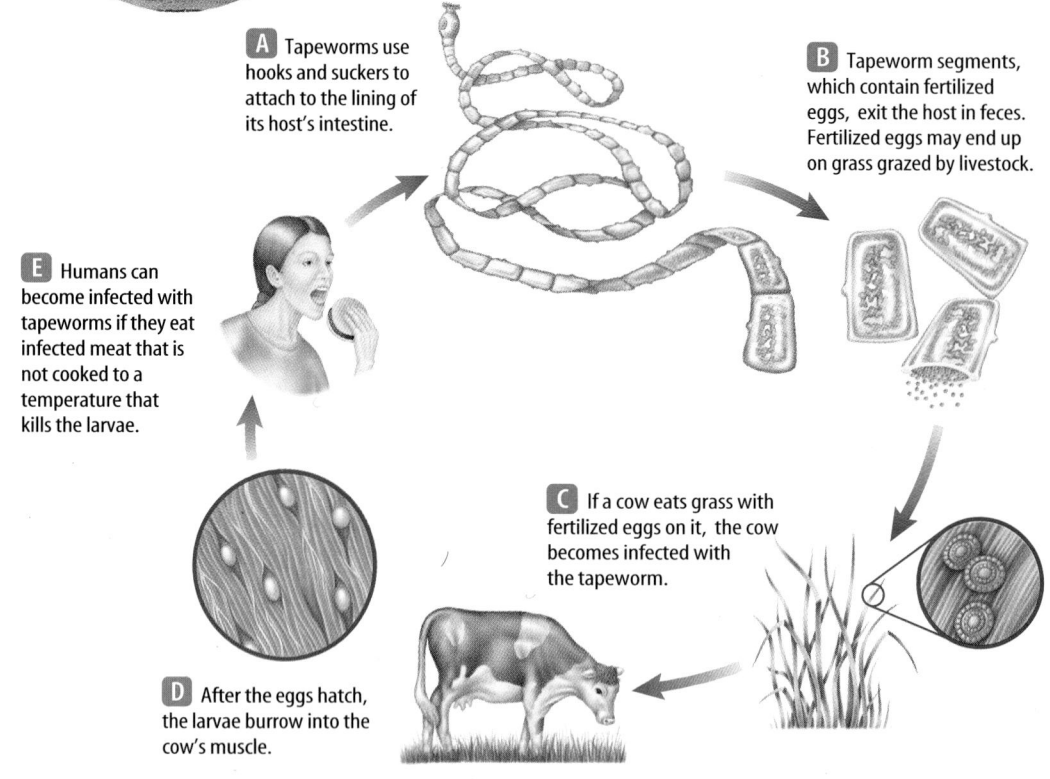

A Tapeworms use hooks and suckers to attach to the lining of its host's intestine.

B Tapeworm segments, which contain fertilized eggs, exit the host in feces. Fertilized eggs may end up on grass grazed by livestock.

C If a cow eats grass with fertilized eggs on it, the cow becomes infected with the tapeworm.

D After the eggs hatch, the larvae burrow into the cow's muscle.

E Humans can become infected with tapeworms if they eat infected meat that is not cooked to a temperature that kills the larvae.

156 CHAPTER 6 Invertebrate Animals

Resource Manager

Chapter Resources Booklet
Enrichment, p. 32
Reinforcement, p. 28

Inclusion Strategies

Learning Disabled Have students select one type of animal described in this chapter. Have them design and construct a detailed, three-dimensional model of the animal and use the model to demonstrate the characteristics of animals. L1 IS **Kinesthetic**

The segment passes with wastes out of the host's body. If another host eats a fertilized egg, it hatches and develops into a tapeworm. Tapeworm segments aren't ingested directly by humans. Most flatworms have an intermediate, or middle host. For example, **Figure 8C** shows how cattle are the intermediate host for tapeworms that infect humans.

 Reading Check *How can flatworms get into humans?*

Roundworms

If you have a dog, you may know already that heartworm disease, shown in **Figure 9,** can be fatal to dogs. In most areas of the United States, it's necessary to give dogs a monthly medicine to prevent heartworm disease. Heartworms are just one kind of the many thousands of roundworms that exist. Roundworms are the most widespread animal on Earth. Billions can live in an acre of soil. Many people confuse earthworms and roundworms. You will study earthworms in the next section.

A roundworm's body is described as a tube within a tube, with a fluid-filled cavity in between the two tubes. The cavity separates the digestive tract from the body wall. Roundworms are more complex than flatworms because their digestive tract has two openings. Food enters through the mouth, is digested in a digestive tract, and wastes exit through the anus.

Roundworms are a diverse group. Some roundworms are decomposers and others are predators. Some roundworms, like the heartworm, are parasites of animals. Other roundworms are parasites of plants.

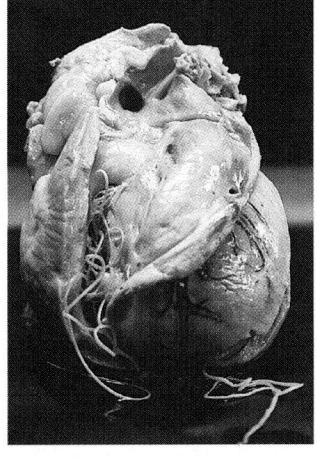

Figure 9
This dog heart is infested with heartworms. Heartworms are carried by mosquitoes. A heartworm infection can clog a dog's heart and cause death.

✔ **Reading Check**

Answer If humans eat infected, under-cooked meat

Quick Demo

Obtain preserved specimens of male and female *Ascaris* worms in sealed tubes from a biological supply house. Display them so students can see their round bodies and note that females are larger, with a hooked posterior end.

③ Assess

Reteach

Have students compare and contrast polyp and medusa forms of cnidarians in their Science Journals. They should include a drawing of each with labels. L1 **Visual-Spatial**

Challenge

Why could it be a reproductive advantage for a cnidarian to produce both polyp and medusa forms? The cnidarian can use the form best suited to the environment in which it finds itself. L2 **Logical-Mathematical**

✔ Assessment

Oral The presence of freshwater sponges indicates an environment with little pollution. Why? Sponges are filter feeders that take in food from the surrounding water. In water with high levels of pollution, they would die. Use **PASC**, p. 89. L2 **Naturalist**

Section ② Assessment

1. How do sponges and cnidarians get food?
2. What are three common characteristics of flatworms and roundworms?
3. Compare the body plan of flatworms to the body plan of roundworms.
4. Why would spongin and spicules discourage predators from eating sponges?
5. **Think Critically** Some types of sponges and cnidarians reproduce asexually. Why is this beneficial to them?

Skill Builder Activities

6. **Comparing and Contrasting** Compare and contrast sponges and jellyfish. **For more help, refer to the** Science Skill Handbook.
7. **Solving One-Step Equations** A sponge is 1 cm in diameter and 10 cm tall. It can move 22.5 L of water through its body in a day. Calculate the volume of water it pumps through its body in 1 min. **For more help, refer to the** Math Skill Handbook.

Answers to Section Assessment

1. Sponges filter food out of the water as it comes to them; cnidarians actively capture prey with their tentacles that have stinging cells.
2. Both types of worms are invertebrates with soft bodies, bilateral symmetry, and three distinct tissue layers organized into organs and organ systems.
3. Flatworms have flattened bodies with one opening—a mouth; roundworms have a tube-within-a-tube arrangement with fluid in between and two openings—a mouth and an anus.
4. Spicules are sharp and glasslike; spongin is like foam rubber; both would be hard to eat.
5. Because these organisms are sessile, sometimes it may be difficult to be near another organism of the same species for sexual reproduction. Being able to reproduce asexually helps ensure survival of their species.
6. Sponges are sessile and asymmetrical; jellyfish are mobile, radially symmetrical predators; both live in water, have soft bodies, and can reproduce sexually or asexually.
7. The sponge will move 15.625 mL (0.015625 L) of water in 1 minute.

SECTION

3

Mollusks and Segmented Worms

Mollusks and Segmented Worms

1 Motivate

Bellringer Transparency

Display the Section Focus Transparency for Section 3. Use the accompanying Transparency Activity Master. L2

ELL

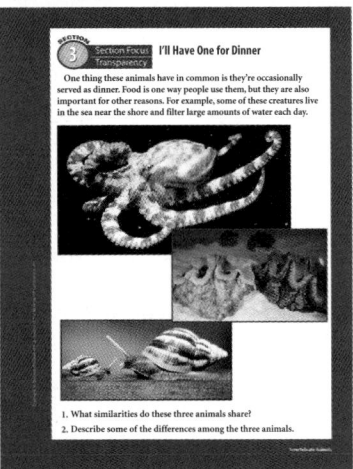

Tie to Prior Knowledge

Most students will be familiar with mollusks such as oysters, clams, squid, garden snails, and octopuses. Discuss how these organisms are alike and different.

As You Read

What You'll Learn
- **Identify** the characteristics of mollusks.
- **Compare** the similarities and differences between an open and a closed circulatory system.
- **Describe** the characteristics of segmented worms.
- **Explain** the digestive process of an earthworm.

Vocabulary
mollusk
mantle
gill
radula
open circulatory system
closed circulatory system

Why It's Important
Organ systems and specialized structures allow mollusks and segmented worms to live in varied environments.

Figure 10
At low tide, many mollusks can be found along a rocky seashore.

Mollusks

Imagine yourself walking along an ocean beach at low tide. On the rocks, you see small snails with conelike shells. In a small tidal pool, one arm of a shy octopus can be seen at the opening of its den. The blue-black shells of mussels are exposed along the shore as shown in **Figure 10.** How are these different animals related? What do they have in common?

Common Characteristics In many places snails, mussels, and octopuses—all mollusks (MAH lusks)—are eaten by humans. **Mollusks** are soft-bodied invertebrates that usually have a shell. They also have a mantle and a large, muscular foot. The **mantle** is a thin layer of tissue that covers the mollusk's soft body. If the mollusk has a shell, it is secreted by the mantle. The foot is used for moving or for anchoring the animal.

Between the mantle and the soft body is a space called the mantle cavity. Water-dwelling mollusks have gills in the mantle cavity. **Gills** are organs in which carbon dioxide from the animal is exchanged for oxygen in the water. In contrast, land-dwelling mollusks have lungs in which carbon dioxide from the animal is exchanged for oxygen in the air.

Section ✔️*Assessment* Planner

PORTFOLIO
Assessment, p. 160
PERFORMANCE ASSESSMENT
Skill Builder Activities, p. 163
Try at Home MiniLAB, p. 160
See page 178 for more options.

CONTENT ASSESSMENT
Section, p. 163
Challenge, p. 163
Chapter, pp. 178–179

A Many species of conchs are on the verge of becoming threatened species because they are overharvested for food.

B Scallops are used to measure an ecosystem's health because they're sensitive to water quality.

Figure 11
Many kinds of mollusks are a prized source of food for humans.

Body Systems Mollusks have a digestive system with two openings. Many mollusks also have a scratchy, tonguelike organ called the **radula.** The radula (RA juh luh) has rows of fine, teethlike projections that the mollusk uses to scrape off small bits of food.

Some mollusks have an **open circulatory system,** which means they do not have vessels to contain their blood. Instead, the blood washes over the organs, which are grouped together in a fluid-filled body cavity.

Types of Mollusks

Does the animal have a shell or not? This is the first characteristic that scientists use to classify mollusks. Then they look at the kind of shell or they look at the type of foot. In this section, you will learn about three kinds of mollusks.

Gastropods **Figure 11A** shows an example of a gastropod. Gastropods are the largest group of mollusks. Most gastropods, such as the snails and conchs, have one shell. Slugs also are gastropods, but they don't have a shell. Gastropods live in water or on land. All move about on a large, muscular foot. A secretion of mucus allows them to glide across objects.

Bivalves How many shells do you think a bivalve has? Think of other words that start with *bi-*. The scallop shown in **Figure 11B** is a bivalve. It is an organism with two shell halves joined by a hinge. Large, powerful muscles open and close the shell halves. Bivalves are water animals that also are filter feeders. Food is removed from water that is brought into and filtered through the gills.

Astronomy
INTEGRATION

Many types of mollusks live in tidal pools that form along seashores during low tide. Tides are daily changes in the water level of the oceans that are caused by the gravitational pull of the Moon and the Sun on Earth. Two high tides and two low tides occur each day. Research to find when the high and low tides will occur for a coastal city sometime next week. Report to your class what you learn.

SCIENCE Online

Research Visit the Glencoe Science Web site at **science.glencoe.com** for recent news or magazine articles about red tides and mollusks. Communicate to your class what you learn.

SECTION 3 Mollusks and Segmented Worms **159**

2 Teach

Mollusks

Activity

Collect snails from a local pond or purchase them from a pet shop. Have student groups observe how snails move. Have them give lettuce to the snails and observe their feeding with a magnifying lens. Be sure to obtain permission from the owner or proper authority before collecting snails from a pond. L2 ELL

Astronomy
INTEGRATION

Responses will vary depending upon the coastal area selected and day of the week. Tide times should be approximately 12 hours apart.

Types of Mollusks

SCIENCE Online
Internet Addresses

_____

_____

_____

Explore the Glencoe Science Web site at **science.glencoe.com** to find out more about topics in this section.

Resource Manager

Chapter Resources Booklet
Transparency Activity, p. 48
Directed Reading for Content Mastery, p. 21
Cultural Diversity, p. 3

✔ Active Reading

Quickwrites Have students write a list of ideas about a topic, then share these ideas with the class. Next, have students write their ideas freely in a paragraph without worrying about punctuation, spelling, and grammar. Have students use a Quickwrite to share ideas during or after learning about mollusks and segmented worms.

Types of Mollusks,
continued

Figure 12
A Living species of *Nautilus* are found in the western Pacific Ocean. **B** The chambered nautilus, squid, and other cephalopods are able to move quickly using a water-propulsion system as shown.

TRY AT HOME
Mini LAB

Modeling Cephalopod Propulsion

Procedure 🥽
1. Blow up a **balloon.** Hold the end closed, but don't tie it.
2. Let go of the balloon.
3. Repeat steps 1 and 2 three more times.

Analysis
1. In your **Science Journal,** describe how the balloon moved when you let go.
2. If the balloon models an octopus or a squid as it swims through the water, infer how cephalopods can escape from danger.

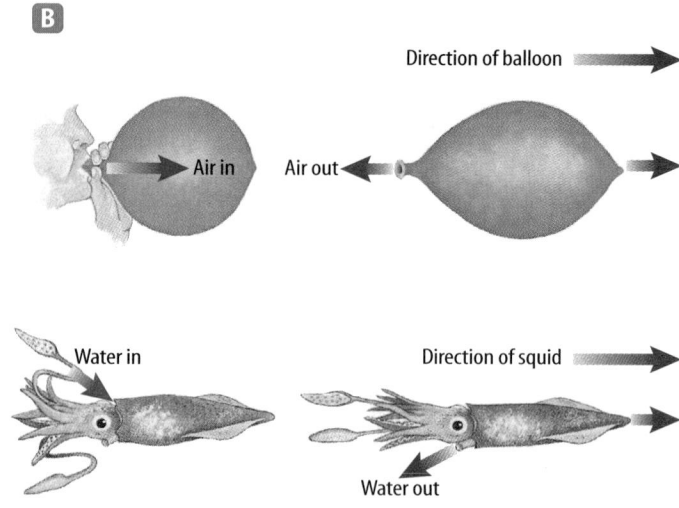

Direction of balloon

Air in   Air out

Water in   Direction of squid

Water out

Cephalopods The most complex type of mollusks are cephalopods (SE fah lah pawdz). The chambered nautilus, shown in **Figure 12A,** octopuses, squid, and cuttlefish are cephalopods. Most cephalopods have an internal plate instead of a shell. They have a well-developed head and a "foot" that is divided into tentacles with strong suckers. They have a **closed circulatory system** in which blood is carried through blood vessels instead of surrounding the organs.

Cephalopods are adapted for quick movement in the ocean. They have a muscular envelope, called the mantle, surrounding their internal organs. Water enters the space between the mantle and the other body organs. When the mantle closes around the collar of the cephalopod, the water is squeezed rapidly through a funnel-like structure called a siphon. **Figure 12B** shows how the rapid expulsion of water from the siphon causes the animal to move in the opposite direction of the stream of water.

Segmented Worms

When you hear the word *worm,* you probably think of an earthworm. Earthworms, leeches, and marine worms are segmented worms, or annelids (A nul idz). Their body is made of repeating segments or rings that make these worms flexible. Each segment has nerve cells, blood vessels, part of the digestive tract, and the coelom (SEE lum). The coelom, or internal body cavity, separates the internal organs from the body wall. Annelids have a closed circulatory system and a complete digestive system with two body openings.

160   CHAPTER 6 Invertebrate Animals

Earthworms When did you first encounter earthworms? Maybe it was on a wet sidewalk or in a garden, as shown in **Figure 13.** Earthworms have more than 100 body segments. Each segment has external bristlelike structures called setae (SEE tee). Earthworms use the setae to grip the soil while two sets of muscles move them through the soil. As earthworms move, they take soil into their mouths. Earthworms get the energy they need to live from organic matter found in the soil. From the mouth the soil moves to the crop, where it is stored. Behind the crop is a muscular structure called the gizzard. Here, the soil and food are ground. In the intestine, the food is broken down and absorbed by the blood. Undigested soil and wastes leave the worm through the anus.

✔ Reading Check *What is the function of setae?*

Examine the earthworm shown in **Figure 14.** Notice the lack of gills and lungs. Carbon dioxide passes out and oxygen passes in through its mucous-covered skin. It's important not to pick up earthworms with dry hands because if this thin film of mucus is removed, the earthworm may suffocate.

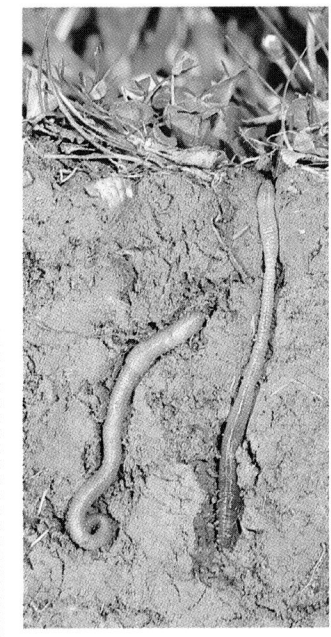

Figure 13
Earthworms are covered with a thin layer of mucus, which keeps them moist. Setae help them move through the soil.

Figure 14
Earthworms and other segmented worms have many organ systems including circulatory, reproductive, excretory, digestive, and muscular systems.

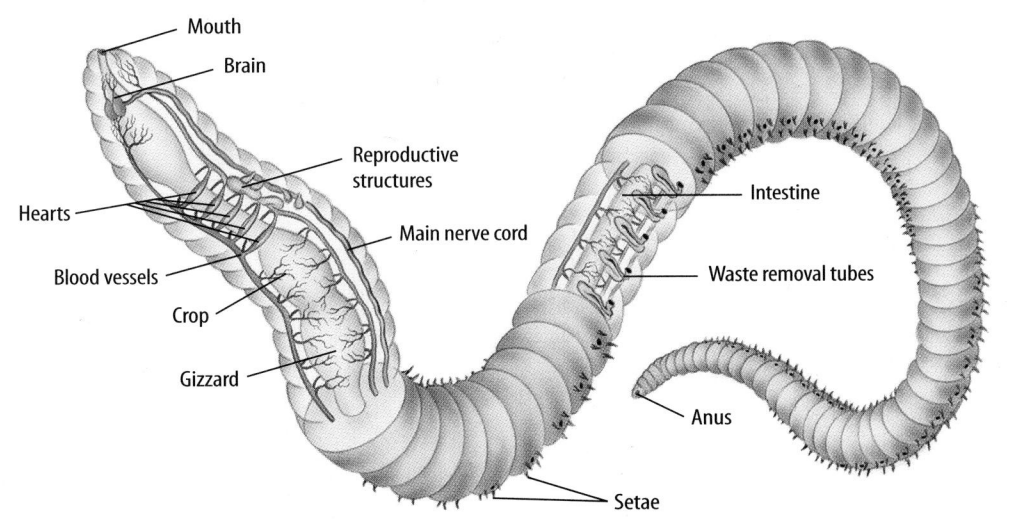

Mouth
Brain
Reproductive structures
Hearts
Intestine
Main nerve cord
Blood vessels
Waste removal tubes
Crop
Gizzard
Anus
Setae

Segmented Worms

Activity
Have students observe the body segments, bilateral symmetry, and setae of a living earthworm. Have students keep their hands moist while handling the earthworms and wash their hands afterwards. [L2] **⎣S⎦ Kinesthetic**

✔ Reading Check

Answer to help the worm move through and hold onto the soil

Quick Demo
Dissect a preserved earthworm and have students examine its digestive, excretory, circulatory, reproductive, and nervous systems.

Visual Learning

Figure 14 How many hearts, or aortic arches, does the earthworm have? five **What sensory organs are shown?** brain and nerve cord **How many blood vessels does the earthworm have?** two **What makes up the excretory system?** waste removal tubes [L1] **⎣S⎦ Visual-Spatial**

Extension
Ask students to investigate ways earthworms are important to farmers and gardeners. Earthworms help to aerate and fertilize soil and thus enhance plant growth. [L1] **⎣S⎦ Naturalist**

Curriculum Connection

Literature Read the poem "The Chambered Nautilus" by Oliver Wendell Holmes. Provide students with a nautilus shell to examine. Have them draw the shell and write a report in their journals about how the shell forms. [L2] **⎣S⎦ Linguistic**

Inclusion Strategies

Learning Disabled Have students make papier-mâché models of all the major invertebrates in this section. Attach a card to each with the reasons why they are important animals in the ecosystem. [L1] **⎣S⎦ Visual-Spatial**

Segmented Worms, continued

 **Reading Check**

Answer with sucking disks on both ends of their bodies

Problem-Solving Activity

Teaching Strategies

Question two can provide discussion on the knowledge required to make choices such as the use of sludge as fertilizer. Should tests be done on the sludge before its use as a fertilizer? Whose responsibility is it to test the sludge—the farmer accepting it or the municipality donating it? Is the amount of heavy metals and organic poisons found in birds enough to cause concern?

Answers to Questions

1. Earthworms are part of the food chain. Since they break down the sludge and can store high levels of poisons, other predators that feed on them, such as birds, can become poisoned.

2. The use of sludge as a fertilizer can be a benefit. It provides nutrients for earthworms that tillage by farmers has removed. However, the municipality must be aware of what can be present in the sludge. If there are poisonous substances that can accumulate in the earthworm and pass up through the food chain contaminating other critters, then the use of sludge as a fertilizer may not be a wise choice.

Figure 15
Leeches attach to fish, turtles, snails, and mammals and remove blood and other body fluids.

Leeches Leeches can be found in freshwater, marine waters, and on land in mild and tropical regions. These segmented worms have flat bodies from 5 mm to 460 mm long with sucking disks on both ends. They use these disks to attach themselves to an animal, as shown in **Figure 15,** and remove blood. Some leeches can store as much as ten times their own weight in blood. It can be stored for months and released a little at a time into the digestive system. Although leeches prefer a diet of blood, most of them can survive indefinitely on small aquatic animals.

 **Reading Check** *How do leeches attach themselves to an animal?*

Marine Worms The animals in **Figure 16** are polychaetes (PAH lee keets), the largest and most diverse group of annelids. Of the 10,000 named species of annelids, more than 8,000 of them are marine worms. The word *polychaete* means "many bristles." Most marine worms have bristles, or setae, along the sides of their body. Because of these bristles, marine worms are sometimes called bristle worms. Bristles are used for walking, swimming, or digging, depending on the type of marine worm.

Problem-Solving Activity

How does soil management affect earthworms?

Some earthworms tunnel through the soil about 30 cm below the soil surface. Earthworms called night crawlers dig deep, permanent tunnels that are up to 1.8 m long. Earthworms' tunnels loosen the soil, which allows better root growth by plants. It also increases air and water movement in the soil. As they tunnel, earthworms take in soil that contains organic matter such as plant material, microorganisms, and animal remains. This is their source of food. Microorganisms break down earthworms' wastes, which adds nutrients to the soil. Earthworms are a food source for frogs, snakes, birds, and other animals.

Identifying the Problem

As earthworms tunnel through the soil, they also take in other substances found there. High levels of pesticides and heavy metals can build up in the bodies of earthworms.

Solving the Problem

1. One soil management technique is to place municipal sludge on farmland as fertilizer. The sludge might contain heavy metals and harmful organic substances. Predict how this could affect birds.

2. Is the use of sludge as a fertilizer a wise choice? Explain your answer.

162 CHAPTER 6 Invertebrate Animals

Resource Manager

Chapter Resources Booklet
Enrichment, p. 33
Reinforcement, p. 29
Performance Assessment in the Science Classroom, p. 55

Curriculum Connection

History Ask students to research and report on the uses of leeches in medicine in the 1800s and through the 1900s. They were used for bloodletting, applied to the temples for headaches, and used to treat mental illness, gout, skin disease, and whooping cough. They are still used to produce the anticoagulant hirudin and to increase the flow of blood to reattached body parts. L2
IS Linguistic

Figure 16
More than 8,000 species of marine worms exist.

A Some polychaetes, like this fireworm, move around in search of food.

B Polychaetes, like this sea mouse, have long bristles that look like hair.

C Some polychaetes, like this tubeworm, cannot move around in search of food. Instead, they use their featherlike bristles to filter food from the water.

Body Types Some marine worms are filter feeders. They either burrow into the mud or build their own tube cases and use their featherlike bristles to filter food from the water. Some marine worms move around eating plants or decaying material. Other marine worms are predators or parasites. The many different lifestyles of marine worms explain why there are so many different body types.

Although annelids do not look complex, they are more complex than sponges and cnidarians. In the next section, you will learn how they compare to the most complex invertebrates.

Section 3 Assessment

1. Name the three groups of mollusks and identify a member from each group.
2. What are the characteristics of annelids?
3. Describe how an earthworm feeds and digests its food.
4. What type of circulatory system does a cephalopod have?
5. **Think Critically** Why would it be beneficial to a leech to be able to store blood for months and release it slowly?

Skill Builder Activities

6. **Comparing and Contrasting** Compare and contrast an open circulatory system with a closed circulatory system. **For more help, refer to the** Science Skill Handbook.
7. **Communicating** Choose a mollusk or annelid and write about it in your Science Journal. Describe its appearance, how it gets food, where it lives, and other interesting facts. **For more help, refer to the** Science Skill Handbook.

Answers to Section Assessment

1. gastropod—snail; bivalve—oyster; cephalopod—squid
2. bodies consist of repeating segments, coelom separates internal organs from the body wall, closed circulatory system, complete digestive tract with two openings
3. As earthworms move, they take soil in through their mouths. Soil moves through the crop, gizzard, and intestine, and the waste goes out the anus.
4. Cephalopods have a closed circulatory system.
5. It would have to feed less often.
6. closed circulatory system: blood contained in vessels; open circulatory system: blood bathes the body's organs; both bring needed blood and oxygen to organs
7. Answers will vary depending on which mollusk or annelid the student chooses.

Teacher FYI

Leech is a term that applies to any annelid in the class *Hirudinea*. There are about 300 known species. *Hirudo medicinalis*, the leech used in medicine, feeds primarily on mammalian blood, but it also sucks blood from amphibians, reptiles, and fish. Within the mouth are three jaws with sharp teeth that make a Y-shaped incision in the skin of the host. Once the leech has fed, it detaches from its host.

Discussion

How do marine worms and leeches differ? Marine worms have setae and live only in marine environments; leeches have suckers and live in a variety of environments. **Why are both classified as segmented worms?** Both have a body cavity and a segmented body.

3 Assess

Reteach

Have students make a table to compare the structures, ways of life (free-living or parasitic), and environments of flatworms, mollusks, and segmented worms. L1
Visual-Spatial

Challenge

How is a mollusk shell an adaptation? It provides protection, camouflage, and conserves water. L3
Logical-Mathematical

Assessment

Process Contrast the muscular foot of bivalves and gastropods. Gastropod—the foot spreads out under its body and a rippling motion moves it along; bivalve—the foot is normally hidden inside the two shells; some bivalves move by hooking the foot into the sand and pulling themselves along. Use **PASC**, p. 89. L2 **Naturalist**

SECTION

4

Arthropods and Echinoderms

Arthropods and Echinoderms

1 Motivate

Bellringer Transparency

Display the Section Focus Transparency for Section 4. Use the accompanying Transparency Activity Master. [L2]

[ELL]

Tie to Prior Knowledge

Many students will be familiar with shrimp and lobsters. All should have knowledge of insects and spiders. Use their knowledge of arthropods to identify common characteristics.

✔ Reading Check

Answer It protects and supports the body and reduces water loss.

As You Read

What You'll Learn

- **List** the features used to classify arthropods.
- **Explain** how the structure of the exoskeleton relates to its function.
- **Identify** features of echinoderms.

Vocabulary

arthropod
appendage
exoskeleton
metamorphosis

Why It's Important

Arthropods and echinoderms show great diversity and are found in many different environments.

Figure 17
About 8,000 species of ants are found in the world. Ants are social insects that live cooperatively in colonies.

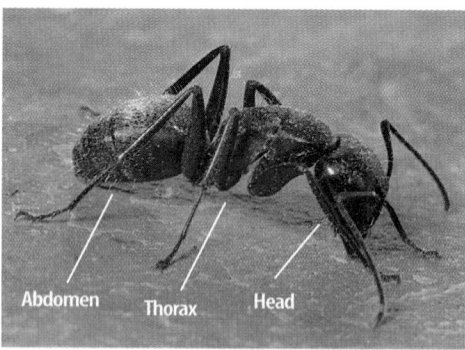

Abdomen   Thorax   Head

Arthropods

More than a million species of arthropods (AR thruh pahdz) have been discovered. They are the largest and most diverse group of animals. The term *arthropod* comes from *arthros,* meaning "jointed," and *poda,* meaning "foot." **Arthropods** are animals that have jointed appendages (uh PEN dihj uz). **Appendages** are structures such as claws, legs, and antennae that grow from the body.

Arthropods have a rigid body covering called an **exoskeleton.** It protects and supports the body and reduces water loss. The weight of the outer covering increases as the size of the animal increases. As the animal grows, the exoskeleton must be shed because it doesn't grow with the animal. This process is called molting. Weight and hardness of the exoskeleton could make it difficult to move, but the jointed appendages solve part of this problem.

✔ Reading Check   *What is the function of the exoskeleton?*

Arthropods have bilateral symmetry and segmented bodies similar to annelids. In most cases, arthropods have fewer, more specialized segments. Instead of setae, they have appendages.

Insects If asked to name an insect, you might say bee, fly, beetle, or butterfly. Insects make up the largest group of arthropods. More than 700,000 species of insects have been classified, and scientists discover and describe more of them each year.

Insects, like the ant in **Figure 17,** have three body regions—head, thorax, and abdomen. Well-developed sensory organs, including the eyes and antennae, are located on the head. The thorax has three pairs of jointed legs and usually one or two pairs of wings. The wings and legs of insects are highly specialized. The abdomen is divided into segments and has neither wings nor legs attached, but reproductive organs are located there.

164   CHAPTER 6 Invertebrate Animals

Section ✔ *Assessment* Planner

PORTFOLIO
Extension, p. 168
PERFORMANCE ASSESSMENT
Skill Builder Activities, p. 170
MiniLAB, p. 169
See page 178 for more options.

CONTENT ASSESSMENT
Section, p. 170
Challenge, p. 170
Chapter, pp. 178–179

Circulatory System Insects have an open circulatory system. Oxygen is not transported by blood in the system, but food and waste materials are. Oxygen is brought directly to the insect's tissues through small holes called spiracles (SPIHR ih kulz) located along the sides of the thorax and abdomen.

Metamorphosis The young of many insects don't look anything like the adults. This is because many insects completely change their body form as they mature. This change in body form is called **metamorphosis** (met uh MOR fuh sus). The two kinds of insect metamorphosis, complete and incomplete, are shown in **Figure 18.**

Butterflies, ants, bees, and beetles are examples of insects that undergo complete metamorphosis. Complete metamorphosis has four stages—egg, larva, pupa (PYEW puh), and adult. Notice how different each stage is from the others. Some insects, such as grasshoppers, cockroaches, termites, aphids, and dragonflies, undergo incomplete metamorphosis. They have only three stages—egg, nymph, and adult. A nymph looks similar to its parents, only smaller. A nymph molts as it grows until it reaches the adult stage. All the arthropods shown in **Figure 19** on the next two pages molt many times during their life.

SCIENCE
Online

Research Visit the Glencoe Science Web site at **science.glencoe.com** for more information about butterflies. Communicate to your class what you learned.

Figure 18
Metamorphosis occurs in two ways.

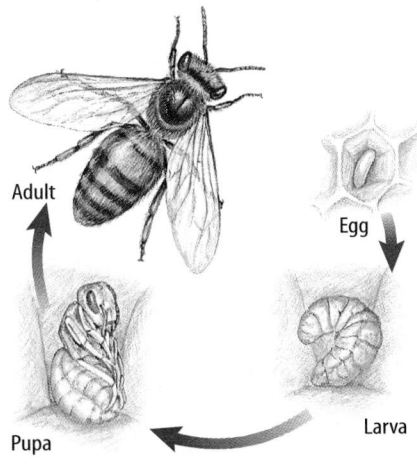

A Bees and many other insects undergo the four stages of complete metamorphosis.

Adult

Egg

Pupa

Larva

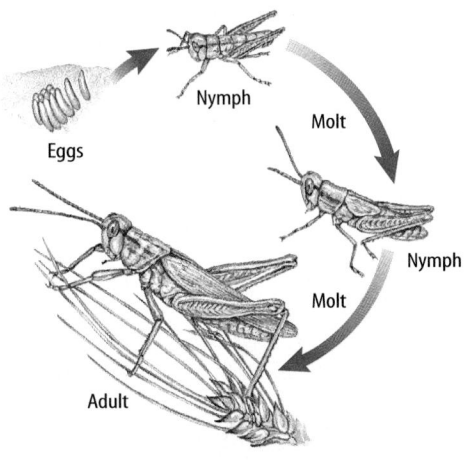

B Insects like the grasshopper undergo incomplete metamorphosis.

Nymph

Molt

Eggs

Nymph

Molt

Adult

SECTION 4 Arthropods and Echinoderms **165**

②Teach

Arthropods

Discussion

Why would molting be a dangerous time for arthropods? They would be unprotected until they grew a new exoskeleton. [L2]
IS Logical-Mathematical

Activity

Provide student groups with live or preserved specimens of insects, crayfishes, spiders, and other arthropods. Ask students to compare and contrast their exoskeletons and appendages. [L2] COOP LEARN **IS** Kinesthetic

Use an Analogy

Compare the limitations of the arthropod exoskeleton to a person wearing a suit of armor.

Visual Learning

Figure 18 Have students make an events chain concept map for each type of metamorphosis shown. Complete: egg, larva, pupa, adult; Incomplete: egg, nymph, adult

Resource Manager

Chapter Resources Booklet
Transparency Activity, p. 49
Directed Reading for Content Mastery, pp. 21, 22

SCIENCE
Online
Internet Addresses

_____

_____

_____

Explore the Glencoe Science Web site at **science.glencoe.com** to find out more about topics in this section.

Visualizing Arthropod Diversity

Make a Model

Provide construction paper, modeling clay, craft sticks, cardboard tubes, and other materials for students to construct a model of an arachnid, centipede, millipede, crustacean, or insect.
L1 LS **Kinesthetic**

Activity

Some insects can be helpful to humans while others can cause disease or devastate crops. Have students give three examples of how insects can be helpful and three examples of how insects can be harmful to humans. Possible answers: Insects pollinate many plants that are important to humans such as apples, grapes, cotton, and oranges. Bees make honey. Some insects help control other insect numbers such as ladybugs preying on aphids. Insects can be harmful when they destroy crops and trees. They can transmit diseases such as malaria, yellow fever, and typhoid. Bees can sting and termites can destroy wooden structures.

Extension

Have students research the motions of the insect wings and mechanisms involved during flight. They could compare and contrast the wing motions of a fast insect such as a wasp to that of a slower insect such as a dragonfly. Have students make a poster to show results.

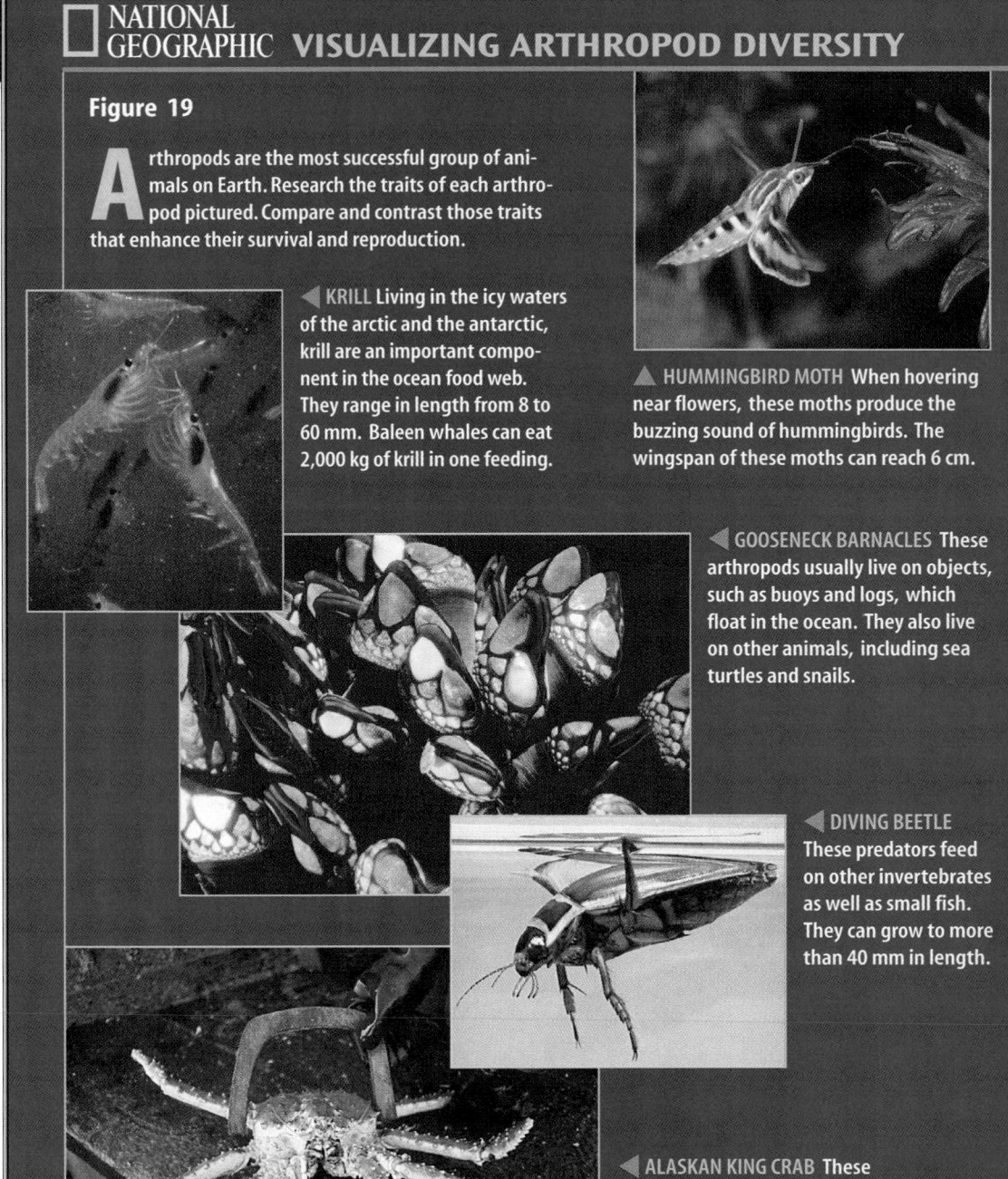

NATIONAL GEOGRAPHIC VISUALIZING ARTHROPOD DIVERSITY

Figure 19

Arthropods are the most successful group of animals on Earth. Research the traits of each arthropod pictured. Compare and contrast those traits that enhance their survival and reproduction.

KRILL Living in the icy waters of the arctic and the antarctic, krill are an important component in the ocean food web. They range in length from 8 to 60 mm. Baleen whales can eat 2,000 kg of krill in one feeding.

HUMMINGBIRD MOTH When hovering near flowers, these moths produce the buzzing sound of hummingbirds. The wingspan of these moths can reach 6 cm.

GOOSENECK BARNACLES These arthropods usually live on objects, such as buoys and logs, which float in the ocean. They also live on other animals, including sea turtles and snails.

DIVING BEETLE These predators feed on other invertebrates as well as small fish. They can grow to more than 40 mm in length.

ALASKAN KING CRAB These crabs live in the cold waters of the north Pacific. Here, a gauge of about 18 cm measures a crab too small to keep; Alaskan king crabs can stretch 1.8 m from tip to tip.

166 CHAPTER 6 Invertebrate Animals

Fun Fact

Some crabs camouflage themselves by placing sand, pieces of seaweed, and shells on their outer carapace. These crabs are commonly called decorator crabs.

NATIONAL GEOGRAPHIC

Visualizing Arthropod Diversity

Content Background

Insects are an especially successful group of arthropods. Scientists have identified 850,000 species of insects and feel there are many more not yet discovered. There are several characteristics that scientists attribute to their success. Their small size makes many habitats more accessible to them. The ability to fly allows insects to escape predators and disperse over greater distances to look for habitats and food. The waterproof exoskeleton provides hard mouthparts with which to extract and grind food, as well as protection from predation and desiccation. Their short life cycle and ability to undergo metamorphosis allows insects to exploit several different habitats in a single life time. Insects can be found in all habitats on Earth, including harsh environments such as those found in Antarctica and in the hot dry deserts.

▲ HORSESHOE CRAB More closely related to spiders than to crabs, horseshoe crabs dig their way into the sand near the shore to feed on small invertebrates.

◀ BUMBLEBEE A thick coat of hair and the ability to shiver their flight muscles to produce heat allow bumblebees to fly in cold weather.

▶ PILL BUG Many people think that pill bugs—also known as sow bugs, rolypolies, or wood lice—are insects. Actually, they are crustaceans that live on land.

▶ AMERICAN COCKROACH This arthropod, which can grow to a length of almost 5 cm, is the largest house-infesting roach. It is common in urban areas around the world.

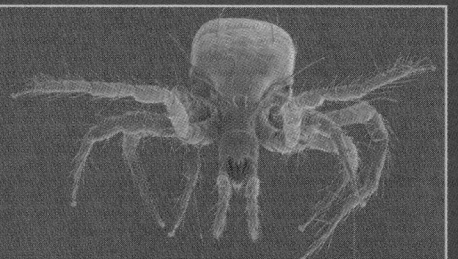

▲ SPIDER MITE These web-spinning arachnids are serious pests because they suck the juices out of plants. They damage houseplants, landscape plants, and crops. The spider mite above is magnified 14 times its normal size.

▲ DADDY LONGLEGS Moving on legs that can be as much as 20 times longer than their bodies, these arachnids feed on small insects, dead animals, and plant juices. Although they look like spiders, they belong to a different order of arachnids.

SECTION 4 Arthropods and Echinoderms **167**

Resource Manager

Chapter Resources Booklet
　　Enrichment, p. 34
　　Transparency Activity, pp. 51–52
Cultural Diversity, p. 7

Caption Answer

Figure 20B Possible answer: Having eyes on both the face and the top of the head increases the jumping spider's chances of locating prey.

Teacher FYI

The black widow, *Latrodectus mactans*, and the brown recluse, *Loxosceles reclusa*, are two of the spiders in the United States whose venom is dangerous to humans. The black widow has a red hourglass-shaped spot on the abdomen. The brown recluse has a dark violin-shaped marking on its cephalothorax.

Extension

Have students prepare an illustrated report on the various hunting methods of spiders. Include the jumping spider, wolf spider, and trap-door spider. L2 IS Linguistic P

Text Question Answer

Centipedes are predators; millipedes eat plants.

A
B
C

Figure 20
A This orb weaver spider uses its web to catch prey. Then it wraps the prey in silk to eat later.
B Jumping spiders have four large eyes on their face and four smaller eyes on the top of their head. *What advantage do all their eyes give them?*
C Scorpions usually hide during the day and hunt for their prey at night.

Figure 21
A Centipedes can have more than 100 segments.
B When a millipede feels threatened, it will curl itself into a spiral.

Arachnids Spiders, ticks, and mites often are confused with insects. However, these animals, along with scorpions, belong to a group of arthropods known as arachnids (uh RAK nudz). Arachnids have only two body regions—a cephalothorax (se fuh luh THOR aks) and an abdomen—instead of three. The cephalothorax is made of the fused head and thorax regions. All arachnids have four pairs of legs attached to the cephalothorax.

Spiders are predators. A spider uses a pair of fanglike appendages near its mouth to inject venom into its prey to paralyze it. The spider releases substances into its prey that digest the victim and turn it into a liquid. The spider then drinks its food. Some spiders, like the one in **Figure 20A**, weave a web to trap their prey. Other spiders, like the jumping spider in **Figure 20B**, chase and catch their prey. Other arachnids, like the scorpion in **Figure 20C**, paralyze their prey with venom from their stinger. Some types of ticks carry diseases—Rocky Mountain spotted fever and Lyme disease—which are threatening to humans.

Centipedes and Millipedes As shown in **Figure 21**, centipedes and millipedes are long, thin, segmented animals. These arthropods have pairs of jointed legs attached to each segment. Centipedes have one pair of jointed legs per segment, and millipedes have two pairs. Centipedes are predators that use poisonous venom to capture their prey. Millipedes eat plants. Besides the number of legs, how else is the centipede different from the millipede?

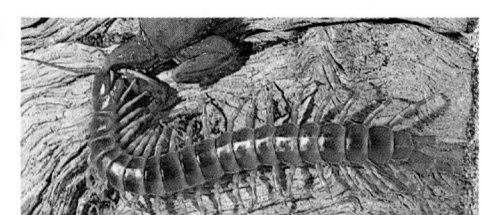

A
B

Science Journal

Have each student choose an arachnid in this section and write about it in his or her Science Journal. Journal entries should reflect the characteristics of the organism, its environment, its way of life, and other information. L2 IS Linguistic

Cultural Diversity

Controlling Pests Zhoa Jing Zhao, a university vice president in China, helped develop a technique for protecting crops from insects by using spiders. He discovered that using spiders to kill harmful insects in cotton fields reduced the need to use pesticides by 80%–90%. Have students discuss advantages of using spiders to control insect population in crop fields. Using spiders decreases the need for chemical pesticides.

Crustaceans Think about where you can lift the most weight—is it on land or in water? An object seems to weigh less in water because water pushes up against the pull of gravity. Therefore, a large, heavy exoskeleton is less limiting in water than on land. The group of arthropods called crustaceans includes some of the largest arthropods. However, most crustaceans are small marine animals that make up the majority of zooplankton. Zooplankton refers to the tiny, free-floating animals that are food for other marine animals.

Examples of crustaceans include crabs, crayfish, lobsters, shrimp, barnacles, water fleas, and sow bugs. Their body structures vary greatly. Crustaceans usually have two pairs of antennae attached to the head, three types of chewing appendages, and five pairs of legs. Many water-living crustaceans also have appendages called swimmerets on their abdomen. Swimmerets force water over the feathery gills where carbon dioxide from the crustacean is exchanged for oxygen in the water.

Echinoderms

Most people know what a starfish is. However, today they also are known as sea stars. Sea stars belong to a varied group of animals called echinoderms (ih KI nuh durmz). Echinoderms have radial symmetry and are represented by sea stars, brittle stars, sea urchins, sand dollars, and sea cucumbers. The name *echinoderm* means "spiny skin." Some echinoderms are predators, some are filter feeders, and others feed on decaying matter. As shown in **Figure 22,** echinoderms have spines of various lengths that cover the outside of their bodies. Most echinoderms are supported and protected by an internal skeleton made up of bonelike plates. A thin, spiny skin covers these plates. Echinoderms have a simple nervous system but don't have heads or brains.

Mini LAB

Observing Sow Bugs

Procedure

1. Place six **sow bugs** in a clean, **flat container.**

2. Put a damp **sponge** at one end of the container.

3. Cover the container for 60 s. Remove the **cover** and observe where the sow bugs are. Record your observations in your **Science Journal.**

Analysis

1. What type of habitat do the sow bugs seem to prefer?

2. Where do you think you could find sow bugs near your home?

Figure 22

A Sun stars have up to twelve arms instead of five like many other sea stars.

B Sea urchins are covered with protective spines.

C Sand dollars have tube feet on their undersides.

Mini LAB

Purpose to observe and identify sow bug reactions to wet and dry conditions L1

IS Kinesthetic

Materials flat container, 6 sow bugs, damp sponge, dark colored cover for container

Teaching Strategies

• Direct students to handle sow bugs gently and to wash their hands when done.

• Try not to use the same sow bugs over and over if they are used for more than one period in a day. The sow bugs will respond less or not at all.

Analysis

1. damp

2. under rocks or decaying pieces of wood where it is damp

✓ *Assessment*

Content Have students do research to discover why sow bugs live in damp places. Crustaceans have gills and need moisture for gas exchange. Use **PASC,** p. 97.

Echinoderms

Discussion

Why do you think scientists now refer to starfish as sea stars? The name is more accurate, since sea stars are not fish. L2

IS Logical-Mathematical

Resource Manager

Chapter Resources Booklet
MiniLAB, p. 4
Reinforcement, p. 30
Home and Community Involvement, p. 32

Inclusion Strategies

Visually Impaired and Learning Disabled Provide students with dried specimens of sea stars, sand dollars, and other echinoderms. Students who are visually impaired can observe their shapes and textures by touching them. L1

IS Kinesthetic

Echinoderms, continued

(3) Assess

Reteach

Have students explain why arthropods molt several times during their lifetime and why echinoderms have few predators. The exoskeleton of an arthropod does not grow with the animal, so it must be shed to allow a new, larger, one to form. The tough, spiny skin of echinoderms makes them difficult for other animals to eat. L2

Challenge

Why are there no insects as large as elephants? Exoskeletons that would be strong enough to support much weight on land would have to be extremely thick and heavy. If an ant were as large as an elephant, it would collapse under its own weight.

✓Assessment

Content Ask students to write in their Science Journals about how incomplete and complete metamorphosis are similar and how they are different. Both are a series of changes. In complete metamorphosis, the young look very different from the adults. Use **Performance Assessment in the Science Classroom,** p. 157. L1
IS **Linguistic**

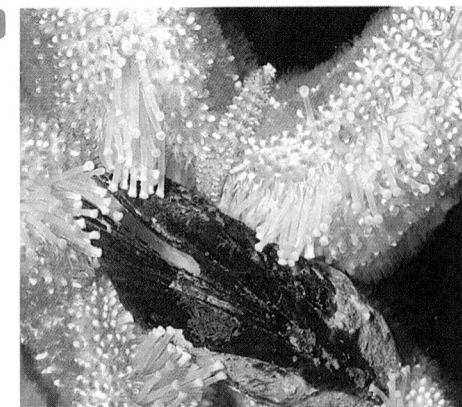

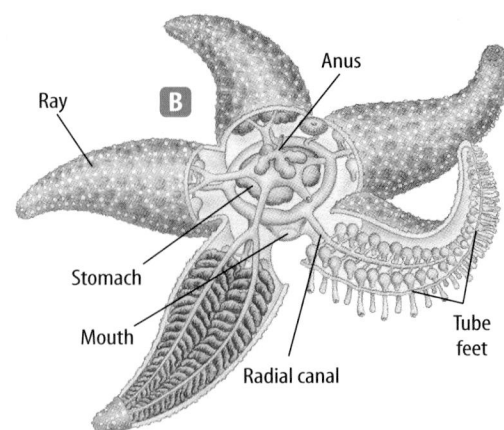

Ray · Anus · Stomach · Mouth · Radial canal · Tube feet

Figure 23
A Echinoderms use their tube feet to move. Sea stars also use their tube feet to capture prey and pull apart the shells.
B Tube feet are connected to an internal system of canals and are able to act like suction cups.

Water-Vascular System All echinoderms have a water-vascular system. It is a network of water-filled canals and thousands of tube feet. The tube feet work like suction cups to help the sea star move and capture prey. **Figure 23** shows how these tube feet are used to pull open their prey. Sea stars have a unique way of eating. The sea star pushes its stomach out of its mouth and into the opened shell of its prey, where the prey's body is digested.

Like some other invertebrates, sea stars can regenerate damaged parts. In an attempt to reduce the population of sea stars that ate their oysters, oyster farmers once captured sea stars, cut them into pieces, and threw them back into the bay. Within a short time, the sea star population was five times larger than before because of regeneration. The oyster beds were destroyed—not saved.

Section 4 Assessment

1. Name three characteristics found in all arthropods.
2. What are the advantages and disadvantages of an exoskeleton?
3. Describe the characteristics that set echinoderms apart from other invertebrates.
4. Why aren't spiders and ticks insects?
5. **Think Critically** What might happen to the sea star population after oyster beds are destroyed? Explain.

Skill Builder Activities

6. **Predicting** Observe the echinoderms pictured in **Figure 22.** Make a prediction about why they are slow moving. **For more help, refer to the** Science Skill Handbook.
7. **Using Proportions** A flea that is 4 mm in length can jump 25 cm from a resting position. If this flea were as tall as you are, how far could it jump? **For more help, refer to the** Math Skill Handbook.

Answers to Section Assessment

1. jointed legs, segmented bodies, exoskeleton
2. Advantages: it provides protection and supports the body; disadvantages: the body outgrows the exoskeleton, its weight limits the size a land invertebrate can grow
3. spiny skin, a water-vascular system, internal skeleton of bone-like plates
4. They have two body regions and four pairs of legs. Insects have three body regions and three pairs of legs.
5. The sea star population would decline, as their food source would be destroyed.
6. Most of the echinoderms pictured have no means of movement except their tube feet, which cannot move rapidly.
7. Answers will vary. Sample response: A flea measuring 160 cm could jump 10,000 cm (100 m).

Activity

Observing Complete Metamorphosis

Many insects go through complete metamorphosis during their life cycles. Chemicals that are secreted by the body of the animal control the changes. How different are the body forms of the four stages of metamorphosis?

What You'll Investigate
What do the stages of metamorphosis look like for a mealworm?

Safety Precautions
Be careful when working with animals. Never touch your face during the activity. Wash your hands thoroughly after completing the activity.

Materials
large-mouth jar or old fish bowl
bran or oatmeal
dried bread or cookie crumbs mixed with flour
slice of apple or carrot
paper towel
cheesecloth
mealworms
rubber band

Goals
■ **Observe** metamorphosis of mealworms.
■ **Compare** the physical appearance of the mealworms at each stage of metamorphosis.

Procedure
1. Set up a habitat for the mealworms by placing a 1-cm layer of bran or oatmeal on the bottom of the jar. Add a 1-cm layer of dried bread or cookie crumbs mixed with flour. Then add another layer of bran or oatmeal.

2. Add a slice of apple or carrot as a source of moisture. Replace the apple or carrot daily.
3. Place 20 to 30 mealworms in the jar. Add a piece of crumpled paper towel.
4. Cover the jar with a piece of cheesecloth. Use the rubber band to secure the cloth to the jar.
5. **Observe** the mealworms daily for two to three weeks. Record daily observations in your Science Journal.

Conclude and Apply
1. In your Science Journal, draw and describe the mealworms' metamorphosis to adults.
2. What are some of the advantages of an insect's young being different from the adults?
3. Infer where you might find mealworms or adult darkling beetles in your house.

*C*ommunicating Your Data
Draw a cartoon showing the different stages of metamorphosis from mealworm to adult darkling beetle. **For more help, refer to the Science Skill Handbook.**

ACTIVITY 171

Activity

BENCH TESTED

Purpose to observe the stages of complete metamorphosis L2
ELL COOP LEARN **Visual-Spatial**

Process Skills observing, communicating, interpreting data

Time Required one 45-minute class period; daily observation for two to three weeks

Teaching Strategy Find a warm place in the classroom to maintain an optimal environment for metamorphosis of the insect. Mealworms can stay in the larval stage for up to two years, depending on the environment.

Answers to Questions
1. Answers will vary.
2. Larval forms often eat different things than the adults, so they don't have to compete with adults for food.
3. kitchen cabinets

✔ *Assessment*

Performance Have students observe the metamorphosis of a fruit fly and compare it with that of a mealworm. Both are complete metamorphoses. The stages of fruit fly metamorphosis are shorter than those of the mealworm. Use **Performance Assessment in the Science Classroom**, p. 89. L2 IS **Visual-Spatial**

Resource Manager

Chapter Resources Booklet
  Activity Worksheet, pp. 5–6
  Lab Activity, pp. 13–16

*C*ommunicating Your Data
Students should use data from the activity to draw their cartoons.

Activity

Recognize the Problem

Purpose

Students will determine whether the presence of earthworms affects soil quality. L2 COOP LEARN ELL

IS **Naturalist**

Process Skills

designing an experiment, forming a hypothesis, observing and inferring, communicating, recognizing cause and effect, separating and controlling variables, interpreting data

Time Required

two 45-minute periods; twice-weekly observations for three weeks

Materials

Purchase *Eisenia foetida* or *Lumbricus rubella* (common names are red wigglers, brandlings, or manure worms) from a bait shop.

Possible containers: plastic shoe box or gallon jug with top cut off. Container must be at least 10 cm deep. Drill six to ten drainage holes in the bottom.

The ratio of food scraps to worms is 1:2 based on weight. Make sure that all food scraps are finely ground.

Safety Precautions

Caution students to wash their hands after handling worms or soil.

Activity *Design Your Own Experiment*

Garbage-Eating Worms

Susan knows that soil conditions can influence the growth of plants. She is trying to decide what factors might improve the soil in her backyard garden. A friend suggests that earthworms improve the quality of the soil. How could Susan find out if the presence of earthworms has any value in improving soil conditions?

Recognize the Problem

How does the presence of earthworms change the condition of the soil?

Form a Hypothesis

Based on your reading and observations, state a hypothesis about how earthworms might improve the conditions of soil.

Goals
- **Design** an experiment that compares the condition of soil in two environments—one with earthworms and one without.
- **Observe** the change in soil conditions for two weeks.

Safety Precautions

Be careful when working with live animals. Always keep your hands wet when handling earthworms. Don't touch your face during the activity. Wash your hands thoroughly after the activity.

Possible Materials

worms (red wigglers)
4-L plastic containers with
    drainage holes (2)
soil (7 L)
shredded newspaper
spray bottle
chopped food scraps including fruit
    and vegetable peels, pulverized
    eggshells, tea bags, and coffee
    grounds. Avoid meat and fat scraps.

Form a Hypothesis

Possible Hypothesis

Student hypotheses should reflect that worms will digest the food scraps and produce healthier soil.

Test Your Hypothesis

Possible Procedures

Fill two identical containers with 7.5 cm of loose soil. Do not pack soil down. Add worms to one container. Place a thin layer of finely chopped food scraps over the surface of each container and cover with shredded newspapers. Keep the newspaper moist by spraying it with water as needed. Observe each container for three weeks.

Test Your Hypothesis

Plan

1. As a group, agree upon a hypothesis and decide how you will test it. Identify what results will support the hypothesis.

2. List the steps you will need to take to test your hypothesis. Be specific. Describe exactly what you will do in each step. List your materials.

3. Prepare a data table in your Science Journal to record your observations.

4. Read over the entire experiment to make sure that all the steps are in a logical order.

5. **Identify** all constants, variables, and controls of the experiment.

Do

1. Make sure your teacher approves your plan before you start.

2. Carry out the experiment according to the approved plan.

3. While doing the experiment, record your observations and complete the data table in your Science Journal.

Analyze Your Data

1. **Compare** the changes in the two sets of soil samples.

2. **Compare** your results with those of other groups.

3. What was used as your control in this experiment?

4. What were your variables?

Draw Conclusions

1. Did the results support your hypothesis? Explain.

2. **Describe** what effect you think rain would have on the soil and worms.

ommunicating
Your Data

Write an informational pamphlet on how to use worms to improve garden soil. Include diagrams and a step-by-step procedure.

ommunicating
Your Data

Review the information for relevance and correctness.

Resource Manager

Chapter Resources Booklet
  Activity Worksheet, pp. 7–8
Mathematics Skill Activities, p. 29
Lab Management and Safety, p. 73

Teaching Strategy

Tie to Prior Knowledge Most students know that worms improve soil.

Expected Outcome

Most results will show that the worms ate the food scraps, and the resulting soil has a dark, rich-looking appearance.

Analyze Your Data

1. There should be fewer food scraps in the container with the worms, and the soil should have a darker appearance.
2. Student results should be similar to those of other groups.
3. The control in this experiment was the container filled with soil, chopped food, and shredded newspapers. It was treated in the same manner as the container with the worms in it.
4. The variable was the presence of worms in one container.

Error Analysis

Have students compare their results and their hypotheses and explain why differences occurred.

Draw Conclusions

1. Answers will be determined by student hypotheses.
2. Rain would compact the soil, and too much rain could drown the worms.

Oral Have students explain the relationship between worms and soil fertility. Worms break down organic matter and disperse it throughout the soil; they also dig tunnels that allow air and water to penetrate the soil more deeply. Use **PASC,** p. 89. L2
Linguistic

Content Background

Squid are cephalopods, the largest of the invertebrates. *Cephalopod* is a term that means head-foot. It refers to the fact that the foot of the ancestral species has evolved to become the head of the cephalopod. There are many types of squid, but one of the most fascinating and mysterious is the giant squid. Very few giant squid have ever been sighted, and giant squid have never been examined alive in their natural habitat. All of the information that scientists have gathered about giant squid has come from the examination of dead animals washed up on beaches or captured in fishing nets. Several teams of scientists are actively engaged in a search for giant squid to observe. Imagine being the first to see a living giant squid!

Discussion

Are young squid more or less independent than human babies? How do you know? Possible answer: Young squid are more independent than are human babies. This answer can be inferred from the information that states that the females of many species of squid die immediately after laying their eggs.

Activity

Research the characteristics of one type of squid. Prepare a poster that illustrates and explains the unique qualities of that species of squid.

LS Visual-Spatial

Science Stats

Squid Power

Did you know...

... Squid can light up like a multicolored neon sign because of chemical reactions inside their bodies. They do this to lure prey into their grasp or to communicate with other squid. These brilliantly-colored creatures, often called fire squid, can produce blue-, red-, yellow-, and white-colored flashes in 0.3-s bursts every 5 s.

... The scariest-looking squid is the vampire squid. It can wrap its webbed, spiked arms around itself like a cloak. Its fins look like pointed ears and its body is covered with light-producing organs that blink on and off. Imagine seeing that eerie sight in the dark depths of the ocean, nearly 1 km below the surface of the sea.

... The giant squid is the largest invertebrate on Earth. This torpedo-shaped creature can grow to a length of more than 17 m, which is about the length of two school buses. This amazing animal can weigh up to 900 kg. That's the weight of some small cars.

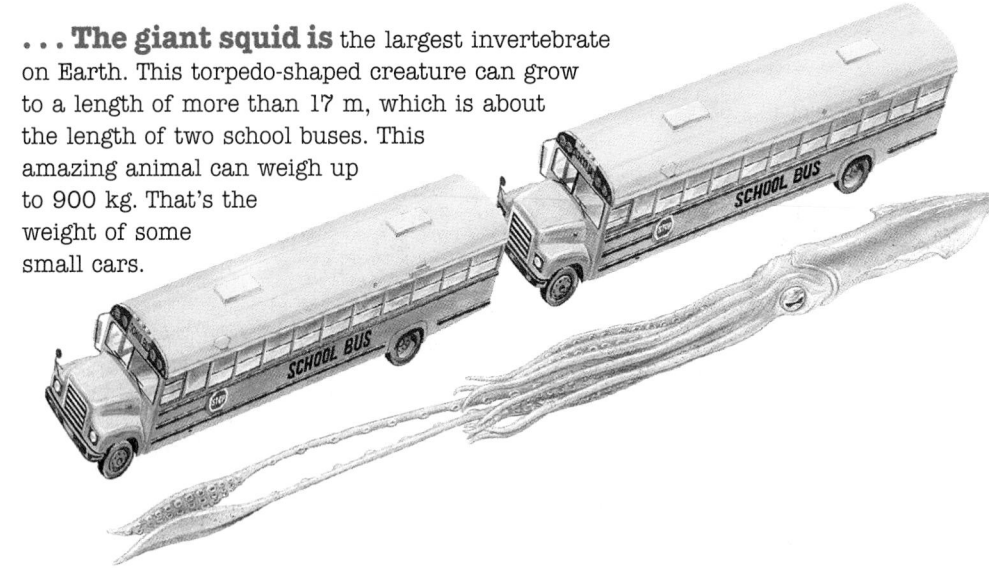

174 CHAPTER 6

SCIENCE Online

Internet Addresses

_____

_____

_____

Explore the Glencoe Science Web site at **science.glencoe.com** to find out more about topics in this feature.

Giant squid eyeball   Hubcap   Baseball   Golf ball

. . . The giant squid has the largest eyes in the animal kingdom. They can be about 38 cm in diameter—as big as a car's hubcaps. Like all squid, the giant squid is thought to have excellent eyesight but is probably color-blind.

. . . Squid have blue blood because their oxygen is transported by a blue copper compound not by bright-red hemoglobin like in human blood.

. . . Females of many species of squid die just after they lay eggs. In 1984, a giant squid washed ashore in Scotland, carrying more than 3,000 eggs.

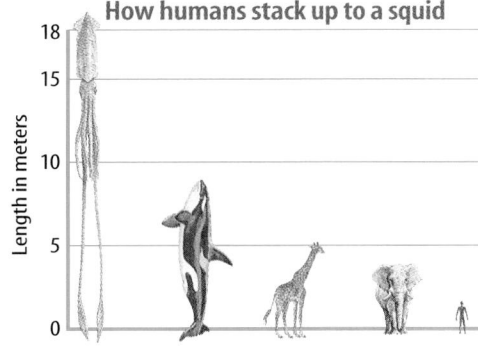

How humans stack up to a squid

Length in meters: 18, 15, 10, 5, 0

Do the Math

1. The best-preserved specimen of a giant squid is at the American Museum of Natural History. It is about 8 m long and has a mass of 114 kg. Its mass is only a fraction of the largest specimen ever found. What is the fraction?
2. Scientists estimate that the adult vampire squid, which grows to about 15 cm in length, can swim at the rate of two body lengths per second. How fast is that in centimeters per second? In kilometers per hour?
3. How tall would a man have to be to have a body that is in proper proportion to 40-cm-diameter eyes like the giant squid's? Assume that the man is 1.9 m tall and has eyes that are 3 cm in diameter.

Go Further

Scientists have never seen a living giant squid. Where would you look? At what depth? What kind of equipment would you use? To research these questions, go to the Glencoe Science Web site at **science.glencoe.com.**

SCIENCE STATS 175

Do the Math

Teaching Strategies

- Review fractions for the first question in Do the Math. Remind students to reduce fractions to the lowest possible terms.
- Remind students of the meaning of the metric prefixes *centi-* (1/100) and *kilo-* (1,000) to help them convert units in the second Do the Math problem.
- Remind students how to set up a proportion. Instruct them to look at their answer and check that it makes sense—a man with 40-cm eyes would have to be taller than a man with 3-cm eyes to be in the same proportion.

Answers

1. 114 kg/900 kg = 19/150
2. 30 cm/sec, or 1.08 km/hour
3. 25.3 m.

Go Further

Have students research the habitat of the giant squid to decide in which oceans and at what depths they would begin their squid search.

Visual Learning

How humans stack up to a squid—About how many humans would it take to equal the length of the giant squid? Students should estimate between 9 and 10 humans to equal the length of the giant squid. Have students use the measurements on the graph to cut a strip of paper the length of a giant squid. Have them use the paper strip to compare the length of the giant squid to objects in the classroom.

Chapter 6 Study Guide

Reviewing Main Ideas

Preview

Students can answer the questions in their Science Journals. Discuss the answers as you go through the chapter. **Linguistic**

Review

Students can write their answers, then compare them with those of other students. **Interpersonal**

Reteach

Students can look at the illustrations and describe details that support the main ideas of the chapter. **Visual-Spatial**

Answers to Chapter Review

SECTION 1

3. bilateral

SECTION 3

3. Cephalopods move by jet propulsion. Water is ejected through the funnel or siphon in one direction, which moves the animal in the opposite direction.

SECTION 4

1. two—cephalothorax and abdomen

Chapter 6 Study Guide

Reviewing Main Ideas

Section 1 What is an animal?

1. Animals are many-celled organisms that must find and digest their own food.

2. Invertebrates are animals without backbones, and vertebrates have backbones.

3. Symmetry is the way that animal body parts are arranged. The three types of symmetry are bilateral, radial, and asymmetrical. *What kind of symmetry does the animal in the photo have?*

Section 2 Sponges, Cnidarians, Flatworms, and Roundworms

1. Sponge cells are not organized as tissues, organs, or organ systems.

2. Adult sponges are sessile and obtain food and oxygen by filtering water through pores.

3. Cnidarian bodies have tissues and are radially symmetrical. Most have tentacles with stinging cells to get food.

4. Organisms replace lost or damaged parts, or reproduce asexually, by regeneration.

5. Flatworms and roundworms have bilateral symmetry. They have parasitic and free-living members.

Section 3 Mollusks and Segmented Worms

1. Mollusks are soft-bodied animals that usually have a shell and an open circulatory system.

2. Mollusks with one shell are gastropods. Mollusks with two shells are bivalves.

3. Cephalopods have a foot divided into tentacles, no outside shell, and a closed circulatory system. *How are octopuses and other cephalopods adapted for swimming?*

4. Annelids have a segmented body. Their body cavity separates their internal organs from their body wall.

Section 4 Arthropods and Echinoderms

1. Arthropods have exoskeletons that cover, protect, and support their bodies. They are classified by the number of body segments and appendages. *How many segments does this crab have?*

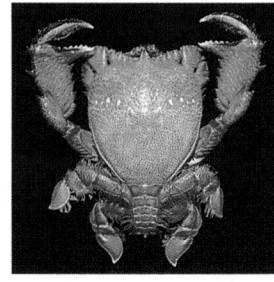

2. Arthropods develop either by complete metamorphosis or by incomplete metamorphosis.

3. Echinoderms such as sea stars are spiny-skinned invertebrates.

4. Echinoderms are the only animals that have a water-vascular system.

FOLDABLES
Reading & Study Skills

After You Read

Use your Venn Diagram Study Fold to determine what characteristics land and water invertebrates have in common.

FOLDABLES
Reading & Study Skills

After You Read

After students have read the chapter and completed the Foldable described in Before You Read, have them do the activity on the student page.

Dinah Zike

Visualizing Main Ideas

Complete the following concept map about the symmetry and movement of some invertebrates.

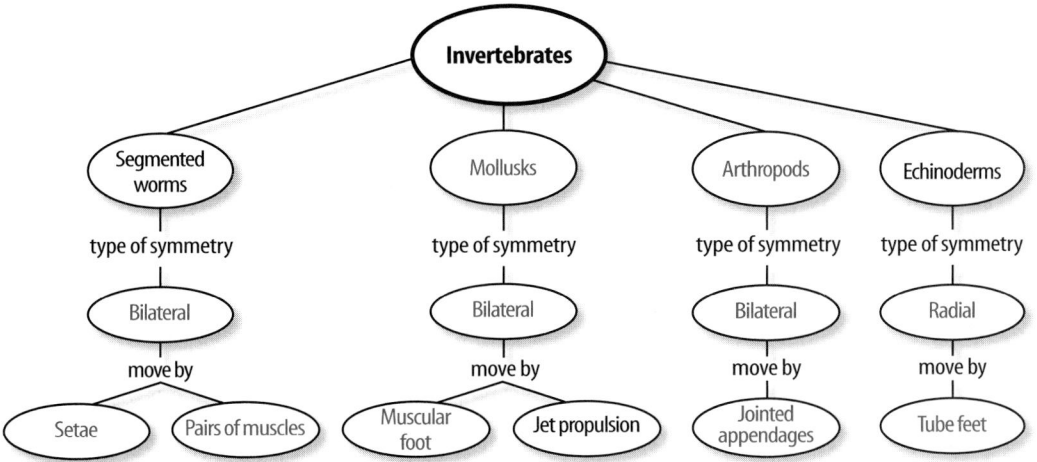

Vocabulary Review

Vocabulary Words

a. appendage
b. arthropod
c. closed circulatory system
d. cnidarian
e. exoskeleton
f. gill
g. invertebrate
h. mantle
i. medusa
j. metamorphosis
k. mollusk
l. open circulatory system
m. polyp
n. radula
o. symmetry

> **THE PRINCETON REVIEW** **Study Tip**
>
> Look for science-related news in the newspaper or on television. This will help you more thoroughly understand and remember what you are learning.

Using Vocabulary

For each set of vocabulary words below, explain the relationship that exists.

1. medusa, polyp
2. closed circulatory system, open circulatory system
3. vertebrate, invertebrate
4. arthropod, mollusk
5. exoskeleton, mantle
6. arthropod, appendage
7. cnidarian, invertebrate
8. mollusk, mantle
9. polyp, symmetry
10. medusa, cnidarian

Visualizing Main Ideas

See student page.

Vocabulary Review

Using Vocabulary

1. Both are forms the cnidarian takes on during its life cycle; medusa is the bell-shaped, free-floating form, and polyp is the vase-shaped, usually sessile form.
2. In a closed circulatory system, the blood is contained in vessels; in an open circulatory system, blood is not contained in vessels.
3. Vertebrates have a backbone; invertebrates do not.
4. Both arthropods and mollusks are invertebrates. Arthropods have an exoskeleton for protection, and mollusks have a shell.
5. Both are means of protection. An exoskeleton is composed of chitin and covers an arthropod; a mantle is a thin layer of tissue covering the soft body of a mollusk.
6. Arthropods have jointed appendages; an appendage is a structure such as a claw, leg, or antenna that grows from the body.
7. A cnidarian is a hollow-bodied invertebrate (animal without a backbone) that has tentacles and stinging cells.
8. The mantle is a thin layer of tissue that covers the soft body of a mollusk, an invertebrate that usually has a shell, mantle, and a large muscular foot.
9. Symmetry is the arrangement of the individual parts of an object. A polyp is the vase-shaped body of a radially symmetrical hydra.
10. A medusa is the free-swimming, bell-shaped body of a cnidarian.

Checking Concepts

1. B
2. D
3. C
4. B
5. C
6. A
7. A
8. C
9. B
10. C

Thinking Critically

11. Their larva is flagellated.
12. So they can respond to changing conditions; this diversity allows them to survive in adverse conditions.
13. Cnidarian tentacles have stinging cells for stunning prey; cephalopod tentacles have suckers for grasping prey.
14. Budding is a type of asexual reproduction in which a new organism develops. Regeneration involves replacing lost body parts.
15. They have jointed appendages, or legs, attached to each segment; worms do not. Centipedes have one pair of legs per segment; millipedes have two pairs of legs per segment.

Chapter 6 Assessment

Checking Concepts

Choose the word or phrase that best answers the question.

1. What symmetry do animals have if they can be divided in half along a single line?
   A) asymmetry
   C) radial
   B) bilateral
   D) anterior

2. Which of the following do not belong to the same group?
   A) snails
   C) octopuses
   B) oysters
   D) sea stars

3. Marine worms can live in all but which of the following?
   A) mud burrows
   C) soil
   B) tube cases
   D) salt water

4. The body plans of cnidarians are polyp and which of the following?
   A) larva
   C) pupa
   B) medusa
   D) bud

5. Which of the following is a parasite?
   A) sponge
   C) tapeworm
   B) planarian
   D) jellyfish

6. Which of the following groups of animals molt?
   A) crustaceans
   C) sea stars
   B) earthworms
   D) flatworms

7. Which of these organisms has a closed circulatory system?
   A) octopus
   C) oyster
   B) snail
   D) sponge

8. Radial symmetry is common in which group of invertebrates?
   A) annelids
   C) echinoderms
   B) mollusks
   D) arthropods

9. What structures help protect sponges from predators?
   A) thorax
   C) collar cells
   B) spicules
   D) tentacles

10. Which of the following organisms has two body regions?
    A) insect
    C) arachnid
    B) mollusk
    D) annelid

Thinking Critically

11. Which aspect of sponge reproduction would be evidence that they are more like animals than plants?

12. Why is it an advantage for organisms to have more than one means of reproduction?

13. Compare and contrast the tentacles of cnidarians and cephalopods.

14. What are the main differences between budding and regeneration?

15. Centipedes and millipedes have segments. Why are they not classified as worms?

Developing Skills

16. **Comparing and Contrasting** Compare and contrast the feeding habits of sponges and cnidarians.

17. **Identifying and Manipulating Variables and Controls** Design an experiment to test the sense of touch in planarians.

18. **Classifying** Complete the table below by listing the following arthropods under the correct heading: *spider, grasshopper, ladybug, beetle, crab, scorpion, lobster, butterfly, tick,* and *shrimp.*

Arthropod Groups		
Insects	**Arachnids**	**Crustaceans**
grasshopper	spider	crab
ladybug	scorpion	lobster
beetle	tick	shrimp
butterfly		

Chapter ✔Assessment Planner

Portfolio Encourage students to place in their portfolios one or two items of what they consider to be their best work. Examples include:
- Make a Model, p. 155
- Assessment, p. 160
- Extension, p. 168

Performance Additional performance assessments, Performance Task Assessment Lists, and rubrics for evaluating these activities can be found in Glencoe's **Performance Assessment in the Science Classroom.**

19. Drawing Conclusions Observe **Figure 11A.** Infer why gastropods are sometimes called univalves? Use examples in your answer.

20. Concept Mapping Complete the concept map below of classification about cnidarians.

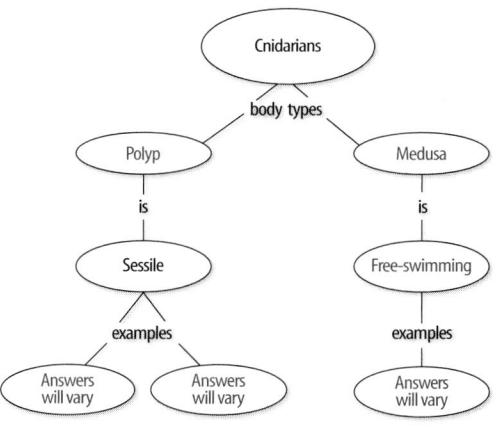

Performance Assessment

21. Poem Write a poem or a song about a group of animals that you studied in this chapter. Include information about their appearance, where they live, and how they get food.

22. Diary Pretend you are an earthworm. Write a diary with at least ten entries describing your daily life. Include how you move, how you get food, and where you live.

TECHNOLOGY

Go to the Glencoe Science Web site at **science.glencoe.com** or use the **Glencoe Science CD-ROM** for additional chapter assessment.

 **Test Practice**

A group of students on a field trip sketched the animals they observed. Their pictures are shown below.

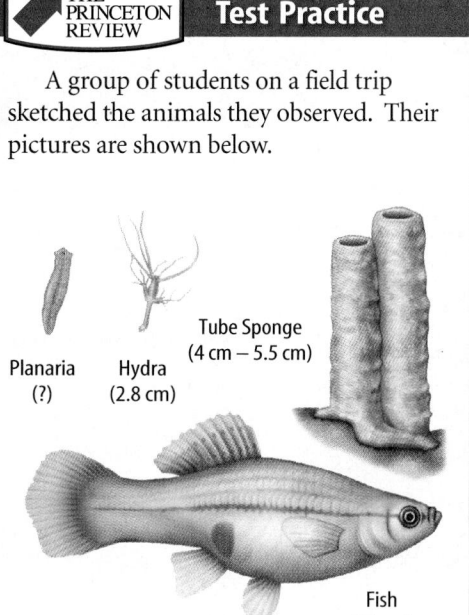

Planaria (?) Hydra (2.8 cm) Tube Sponge (4 cm – 5.5 cm) Fish (10 cm)

Study the pictures and answer the following questions.

1. Which of the animals in the picture above is **NOT** an invertebrate?
A) hydra
B) sponge
C) fish
D) planaria

2. According to the drawings, which of the following is the approximate length of the planaria?
F) 5.5 cm
G) 2 cm
H) 8 cm
J) 1 cm

 **Test Practice**

The Test-Taking Tip was written by The Princeton Review, the nation's leader in test preparation.
1. C
2. G

Developing Skills

16. Sponges filter microscopic materials out of the water. Collar cells help move water through the sponge. Cnidarians use stinging cells on their tentacles to paralyze prey; the tentacles pull prey into the mouth.
17. Students should suggest an experiment that involves touching the planarian with natural objects and observing its response.
18. See student page.
19. Gastropods have only one shell. Examples will vary.
20. See student page.

Performance Assessment

21. Students may write about sponges, cnidarians, flatworms, roundworms, mollusks, annelids, arthropods or echinoderms.
22. The earthworm diary should indicate that earthworms use setae to move through the soil and that they get food from the soil, which they take in as they move through it.

✓Assessment Resources

 Reproducible Masters
Chapter Resources Booklet
Chapter Review, pp. 39–40
Chapter Tests, pp. 41–44
Assessment Transparency Activity, p. 53
Glencoe Science Web site
Interactive Tutor
Chapter Quizzes

Glencoe Technology
Assessment Transparency
Interactive CD-ROM Chapter Quizzes
ExamView Pro Test Bank
Vocabulary PuzzleMaker Software
MindJogger Videoquiz

Section/Objectives	Standards		Activities/Features
Chapter Opener	**National**	**State/Local**	**Explore Activity:** Model a backbone, p. 181 **Before You Read,** p. 181
	See p. 6T for a Key to Standards.		
Section 1 Chordate Animals 🕐 1 session 📦 0.5 block 1. **Identify** the major characteristics of chordates. 2. **List** the major characteristics common to all vertebrates. 3. **Explain** the difference between ectotherms and endotherms. 4. **Name** the characteristics of the three classes of fish.	National Content Standards: UCP4, C1, C4, C5		**Physics Integration,** p. 184 **Visualizing Fish Diversity,** p. 185
Section 2 Amphibians and Reptiles 🕐 2 sessions 📦 1 block 1. **Describe** how amphibians have adapted to live in water and on land. 2. **Explain** what happens during frog metamorphosis. 3. **Identify** the adaptations that allow reptiles to live on land.	National Content Standards: UCP4, A1, C1, C2, C4, C5		**Science Online,** p. 194 **Health Integration,** p. 190 **Activity:** Frog Metamorphosis, p. 192
Section 3 Birds 🕐 2 sessions 📦 1 block 1. **Identify** the characteristics of birds. 2. **Describe** the adaptations birds have for flight. 3. **Explain** the function of feathers.	National Content Standards: UCP4, A1, C1, C4, C5		**Science Online,** p. 188 **MiniLAB:** Observing What Feathers Do, p. 195
Section 4 Mammals 🕐 4 sessions 📦 2 blocks 1. **Identify** the characteristics common to all mammals. 2. **Explain** how mammals are adapted to the different environments on Earth. 3. **Distinguish** among monotremes, marsupials, and placentals.	National Content Standards: UCP4, A1, C1, C4, C5, D2, G1		**MiniLAB:** Inferring How Blubber Insulates, p. 198 **Math Skills Activity:** Working with Percentages, p. 199 **Activity:** Homes for Endangered Animals, p. 202 **Oops! Accidents in Science:** Cosmic Dust and Dinosaurs, p. 204

NATIONAL GEOGRAPHIC — Teacher's Corner

PRODUCTS AVAILABLE FROM GLENCOE
To order call 1-800-334-7344:
CD-ROM: *Mammals: A Multimedia Encyclopedia; NGS PictureShow: Classifying Plants and Animals; NGS PictureShow: Structure of Vertebrates 1; NGS PictureShow: Structure of Vertebrates 2*

Curriculum Kit: *GeoKit: Fish, Reptiles, and Amphibians*
Transparency Sets: *NGS PictureShow: Classifying Plants and Animals; NGS PictureShow: Structure of Vertebrates 1; NGS PictureShow: Structure of Vertebrates 2*
Videodisc: *STV: Animals*

PRODUCTS AVAILABLE FROM NATIONAL GEOGRAPHIC SOCIETY
To order call 1-800-368-2728:
Book: *National Geographic Book of Mammals*
Video: *Reptiles and Amphibians*

Activity Materials	Reproducible Resources	Section Assessment	Technology
Explore Activity: pasta wheels, soft candy circles, long pipe cleaners	**Chapter Resources Booklet** Foldables Worksheet, p. 15 Directed Reading Overview, p. 17 Note-taking Worksheets, pp. 33–36	*GLENCOE'S* **ASSESSMENT** *ADVANTAGE*	
Need materials? Contact Science Kit at 1-800-828-7777 or www.sciencekit.com on the Internet.	**Chapter Resources Booklet** Transparency Activity, p. 46 Enrichment, p. 29 Reinforcement, p. 25 Directed Reading, p. 18 Transparency Activity, pp. 51–52 Lab Activity, pp. 9–11	Portfolio Activity, p. 183 Performance Skill Builder Activities, p. 186 Content Section Assessment, p. 186	Section Focus Transparency Teaching Transparency Interactive CD-ROM Guided Reading Audio Program
Activity: 4-L aquarium or jar, frog egg mass, lake or pond water, stereoscopic microscope, watch glass, small fishnet, aquatic plants, washed gravel, lettuce (previously boiled), large rock	**Chapter Resources Booklet** Transparency Activity, p. 47 Enrichment, p. 30 Reinforcement, p. 26 Directed Reading, p. 18 Activity Worksheet, pp. 5–6	Portfolio Activity, p. 190 Performance Skill Builder Activities, p. 191 Content Section Assessment, p. 191	Section Focus Transparency Interactive CD-ROM Guided Reading Audio Program
MiniLAB: cotton cloth, petroleum jelly, water, Science Journal	**Chapter Resources Booklet** Transparency Activity, p. 48 MiniLAB, p. 3 Enrichment, p. 31 Reinforcement, p. 27 Directed Reading, p. 19 Lab Activity, pp. 13–14	Portfolio Visual Learning, p. 193 Performance MiniLAB, p. 195 Skill Builder Activities, p. 196 Content Section Assessment, p. 196	Section Focus Transparency Interactive CD-ROM Guided Reading Audio Program
MiniLAB: self-sealing plastic bags (2), vegetable shortening, ice water **Activity:** poster board, markers or colored pencils, materials with which to make a scale model	**Chapter Resources Booklet** Transparency Activity, p. 49 MiniLAB, p. 4 Enrichment, p. 32 Reinforcement, p. 28 Directed Reading, pp. 19, 20 Activity Worksheet, pp. 7–8 **Lab Management and Safety,** p. 58	Portfolio Curriculum Connection, p. 198 Performance MiniLAB, p. 198 Skill Builder Activities, p. 201 Content Section Assessment, p. 201	Section Focus Transparency Interactive CD-ROM Guided Reading Audio Program

End of Chapter Assessment

GLENCOE'S **ASSESSMENT** *ADVANTAGE*

Blackline Masters	Technology	Professional Series
Chapter Resources Booklet Chapter Review, pp. 39–40 Chapter Tests, pp. 41–44 **Standardized Test Practice by The Princeton Review,** pp. 31–34	MindJogger Videoquiz Interactive CD-ROM Vocabulary PuzzleMakers ExamView Pro Test Bank Interactive Lesson Planner Interactive Teacher Edition	Performance Assessment in the Science Classroom (PASC)

Transparencies

Section Focus

Section Focus Transparency 1 — Do they have tests?

These colorful little fish live in warm, tropical waters. A group of fish swimming together like this is called a school. Fish swim in schools for protection as well as for feeding and breeding purposes.

1. What do fish and mammals have in common?
2. What are some characteristics of fish?

L2

Section Focus Transparency 2 — On Second Thought, Let's Eat Something Else

Usually, this animal stays hidden, but when it is threatened, it twists its body and puffs out its belly to show its brilliant red color. Its flashy colors warn other animals that it would make a dangerous—even deadly—meal!

1. What kind of environment do you think this animal lives in?
2. How is this creature different from a fish? A lizard?

L2

Section Focus Transparency 3 — Maybe the Scientists Were a Hoax!

This bird, called a kiwi, is the national bird of New Zealand. It's so unusual that when it was first brought to the attention of scientists, they thought it was a hoax. It has no tail and only stubby wings hidden by hair-like feathers. Flightless, the nocturnal kiwi lives in burrows and tends to be shy.

1. Why might scientists have thought the kiwi a hoax?
2. Why do you think the kiwi is classified as a bird?

L2

This is a representation of key blackline masters available in the Teacher Classroom Resources. See Resource Manager boxes within the chapter for additional information.

Key to Teaching Strategies

The following designations will help you decide which activities are appropriate for your students.

L1 Level 1 activities should be appropriate for students with learning difficulties.

L2 Level 2 activities should be within the ability range of all students.

L3 Level 3 activities are designed for above-average students.

ELL ELL activities should be within the ability range of English Language Learners.

COOP LEARN Cooperative Learning activities are designed for small group work.

LS Multiple Learning Styles logos, as described on page 22T, are used throughout to indicate strategies that address different learning styles.

P These strategies represent student products that can be placed into a best-work portfolio.

Assessment

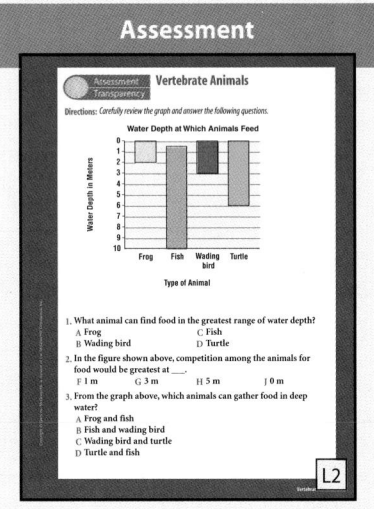

Assessment Transparency — Vertebrate Animals

Directions: Carefully review the graph and answer the following questions.

Water Depth at Which Animals Feed

1. What animal can find food in the greatest range of water depth?
   A Frog   C Fish
   B Wading bird   D Turtle
2. In the figure shown above, competition among the animals for food would be greatest at ___.
   F 1 m   G 3 m   H 5 m   J 0 m
3. From the graph above, which animals can gather food in deep water?
   A Frog and fish
   B Fish and wading bird
   C Wading bird and turtle
   D Turtle and fish

L2

Teaching

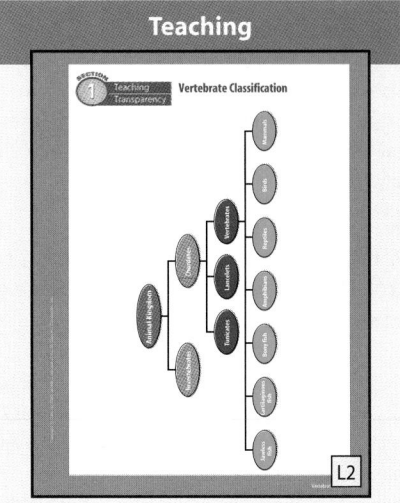

Teaching Transparency 1 — Vertebrate Classification

L2

Hands-on Activities

Activity Worksheets

Activity — Frog Metamorphosis

Lab Preview
Directions: Answer these questions before you begin the Activity.

1. Why does this activity contain the animal safety symbol?

2. How do you use the lettuce in this activity?

Frogs and other amphibians use external fertilization to reproduce. Female frogs lay hundreds of jellylike eggs in water. Male frogs then fertilize these eggs. Once larvae hatch, the process of metamorphosis begins. Over a period of time, young tadpoles develop into adult frogs.

What You'll Investigate
What changes occur as a tadpole goes through metamorphosis?

Materials
4-L aquarium or jar   watch glass   washed gravel
frog egg mass   small fishnet   lettuce (previously boiled)
lake or pond water   aquatic plants   large rock
stereoscopic microscope

Safety Precautions

Goals
• Observe how body structures change as a tadpole develops into an adult frog.
• Determine how long metamorphosis takes.

Procedure
1. As a class, use the aquarium, pond water, gravel, rock, and plants to prepare a water habitat for the frog eggs.
2. Place the egg mass in the water of the aquarium. Use the fishnet to separate a few eggs from the mass. Place these eggs in the watch glass. The eggs should have the dark side up. CAUTION: Handle the eggs with care.
3. Observe the eggs twice a week. Record your observations in the data table.
4. Continue observing the tadpoles twice a week after they hatch. Identify the mouth, eyes, gill cover, gills, nostrils, fin on the back, hind legs, and front legs. Observe how tadpoles eat boiled lettuce that has been cooked.

L2

Laboratory Activities

Laboratory Activity — Fish Dissection

Most fish are bony fish—bass, cod, salmon, and halibut are good examples. Most bony fish are covered with smooth, slimy scales, have a swim bladder, and have well-developed fins. Humans depend on bony fish as a high-protein, low-fat food source.

Strategy
You will dissect a bony fish, locating the swim bladder and the gills.
You will determine the age of the fish using the rings of its scales.

Materials
whole preserved fish (perch or trout work well)
tray
scalpel
dissecting scissors
magnifying lens

Procedure
1. Put the fish on a clean tray. Note its shape, color, and size in the data table in the Data and Observations section.
2. Examine the gills. Describe them in the data table in the Data and Observations section.

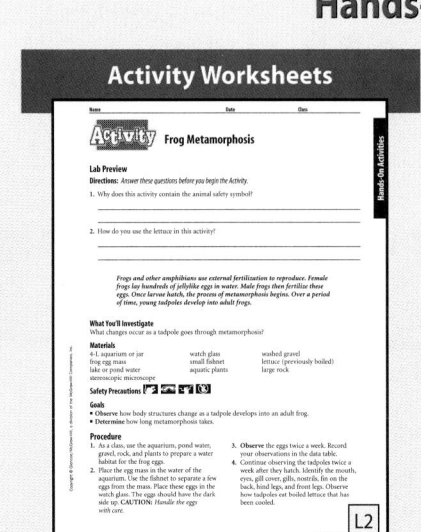

3. Insert the scalpel blade into the anus, or vent, of the fish. This is located just in front of the anal fin on the lower side of the fish.
4. Cut in a straight line along the fish's belly toward the head.
5. Use scissors to cut through the bones encountered along the midline. Keep cutting until you reach the area directly below the gills.
6. Now pull apart the two walls of the fish's body cavity to expose the internal organs.
7. The swim bladder is located roughly in the center of the fish. Pull the pinkish-red organs and tissue forward until you see the pinkish-silver swim bladder.
8. Use the scalpel scissors to remove the internal organs. This will allow better access to the swim bladder. Describe the bladder in the data table below.
9. Examine the scales of the fish. The number of rings on a scale tells you the age of the fish. Remove one scale and look at it with the magnifying lens. Count the rings on the scale to determine the age of the fish. Record this number in the data table on the next page.

L2

Meeting Different Ability Levels

Content Outline

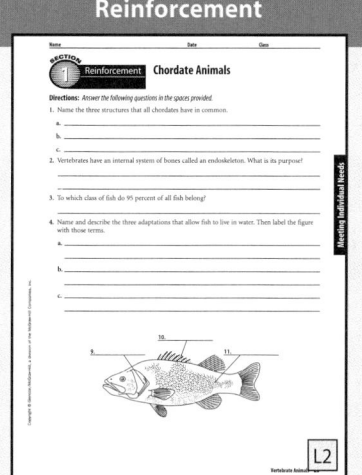

L2

Reinforcement

L2

Directed Reading

L1

Assessment

Chapter Tests

L2

Enrichment

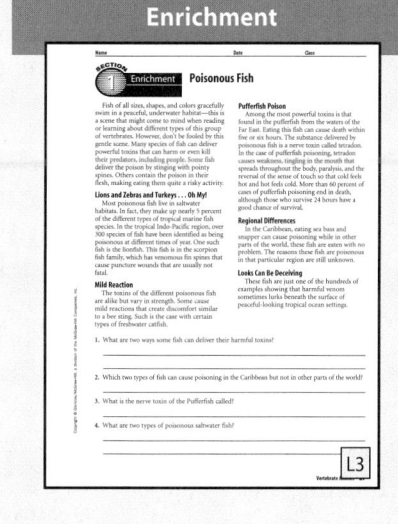

L3

Spanish Directed Reading

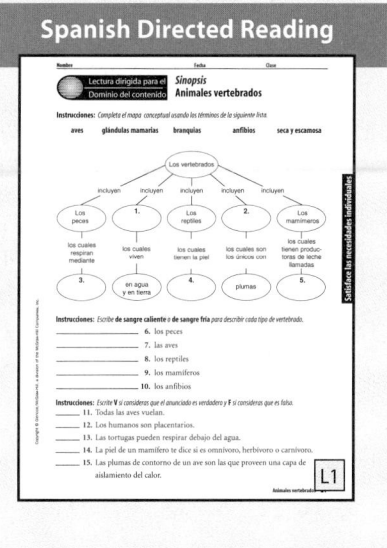

L1

Test Practice Workbook

L2

Chapter Review

L2

Science Content Background

SECTION 1

Chordate Animals

Vertebrates

Vertebrates have similar organ systems. Fish have a two-chambered heart and gills for the exchange of oxygen and carbon dioxide. In the gills the blood in the capillaries has lost nearly all its pressure, which seriously reduces the efficiency of the entire circulatory system. Amphibians have a three-chambered heart with two atria that separate systemic and pulmonary circulation. Even with only one ventricle, studies have shown that there is little mixing of oxygenated and deoxygenated blood. Reptiles have an incomplete four-chambered heart. The atria are completely separated, but the septum of the right and left ventricles is incomplete. Birds and mammals have four-chambered hearts that completely separate blood into systemic and pulmonary circulation.

Fish

Some fish are considered warm-blooded, but are not truly endotherms. Bluefin tuna are able to maintain a body temperature as much as 14°C higher than that of the surrounding water. Blood is heated in the swimming muscles that run down the center of the body and are well insulated. Blood vessels carrying cold blood from the gills to the body have contact with blood vessels carrying warm blood from the body to the gills. Cold blood coming from the gills is warmed before reaching the inside of the body, and blood from the body is cooled on its way to the gills. Thus, the fish retain precious body heat while swimming in cold water.

Bony Fish

The importance of the swim bladder can be seen in fish with swim bladder disease, a disease that primarily affects goldfish with rounded bodies. Some fish, including goldfish, have a special duct that allows them to adjust buoyancy by letting air out through the digestive tract. Some scientists suggest that the disease is caused by food blocking this duct. Goldfish with the disease cannot control their buoyancy and may float near the surface or stay on the bottom and have difficulty rising.

Fun Fact

Scientists think they have found the fossilized heart of a 66 million year old dinosaur from South Dakota. CAT scans of the fossil indicate it might have had four chambers, like endotherms.

Fun Fact

The jaw of the cownose ray is made of cartilage braced with mineral deposits. The ray uses its jaws like a nutcracker to crush the shells of the clams and oysters it eats.

SECTION 2

Amphibians and Reptiles

Amphibians

Because they live on land and reproduce in water, amphibians are affected by chemical changes in the terrestrial and the aquatic environment. Soil erosion and water pollution can adversely affect amphibians and, because they absorb gases through their skin, they are susceptible to air pollutants. Their sensitivity could explain why there have been such dramatic declines of amphibians in some areas.

Roland Seitre/Peter Arnold, Inc.

Fun Fact

Sometimes, a snake's prey is too heavy for the snake to lift and then swallow it. If this happens, the snake swallows its prey and crawls forward at the same time.

Reptiles

Reptiles live on every continent except Antarctica and in all the oceans except those in polar regions. Giant pythons 10 m in length can swallow deer whole. Some sea turtles have a mass of almost one metric ton and can swim faster than most humans can run. Three-horned lizards have movable eye sockets and tongues as long as their bodies.

SECTION 3

Birds

Archaeopteryx

In 1861 in a limestone quarry in Bavaria, Germany, one of the world's best-known fossils was found. The skeleton suggested that it was a small, bipedal, insect-eating dinosaur. Upon further study, the unmistakable imprint of wings and feathers was discovered. Feathers are one of the defining characteristics of all birds. The animal was given the name *Archaeopteryx lithographica*. Unlike modern birds, *Archaeopteryx* had teeth, a long tail, free-floating ribs, and wings with claws attached to movable fingers. Except for wings, these are all characteristics of small dinosaurs. *Archaeopteryx* is considered one of the intermediary species linking reptiles and birds.

SECTION 4

Mammals

Body Systems

The digestive system of mammals varies according to the kind of food each type of animal eats. Carnivores have short digestive systems compared with those of herbivores because meat is more easily digested than plant material. Herbivores need long digestive systems to help break down the carbohydrate called cellulose found in plants.

Walter Bibikow/FPG International

SCIENCE Online

For additional content background on this topic, go to the Glencoe Science Web site at **science.glencoe.com**.

Fun Fact

Scientists have made unspecialized mouse embryo cells transform into bone tissue. This research could be used to repair diseased bone in the future.

Vertebrate Animals

Chapter Vocabulary

chordate, p. 182
ectotherm, p. 183
endotherm, p. 183
cartilage, p. 184
hibernation, p. 187
estivation, p. 187
amniotic egg, p. 191
contour feather, p. 195
down feather, p. 195
herbivore, p. 198
carnivore, p. 198
omnivore, p. 198
monotreme, p. 199
marsupial, p. 200
placental, p. 200

What do you think?

Science Journal The photograph shows an infant human skull. At birth, a baby's skull is joined by sutures. These sutures allow portions of the skull to glide over one another during birth. As the baby grows, these sutures become immovable joints.

Vertebrate Animals

An eagle soars through the summer sky while many meters below, a salmon hurls its body at a roaring waterfall. Along the river's edge, a grizzly bear eats blackberries, and a snake suns itself on a rock. Nearby, a toad crawls through damp leaf litter searching for insects. Although these animals are different, they and humans share a common trait—an internal skeleton. In this chapter, you will learn about the wide variety of vertebrate animals and their individual traits.

What do you think?

Science Journal Look at the picture below with a classmate. Discuss what you think this might be. Here's a hint: *This had more parts and pieces when you were an infant.* Write your answer or best guess in your Science Journal.

180

Theme Connection

Stability and Change Like other organisms, fish, amphibians, reptiles, birds, and mammals have adaptations that allow each species to maintain a stable existence in its own unique environment.

A s you read in the Chapter Opener, an internal skeleton is common to many animals. Skeletons are made of bones or cartilage of various sizes and shapes. They give your body its overall shape and work with your muscles to help move your body. In the following activity, you will learn more about the structure of bones by modeling a backbone.

Model a backbone

WARNING: *Do not eat or drink anything in the lab.*

1. Use pasta wheels, soft-candy circles, and long pipe cleaners to make a model of a backbone.

2. On a pipe cleaner, string in an alternating pattern the pasta wheels and the soft-candy circles until the string is about 10 cm long.

3. Fold over each end of the pipe cleaner so the pasta and candy do not slide off.

Observe

Slowly bend the model. Does it move easily? How far can you bend it? What do you think makes up your backbone? Write your observations and answers in your Science Journal.

Before You Read

Making an Organizational Study Fold When information is grouped into clear categories, it is easier to make sense of what you are learning. Make the following Foldable to help you organize your thoughts about vertebrate animals before you begin reading.

1. Stack three sheets of paper in front of you so the short side of all sheets is at the top.

2. Slide the top sheet up so that about 4 cm of the middle sheet show. Slide the bottom sheet down so that about 4 cm of it shows.

3. Fold the sheets top to bottom to form six tabs and staple along the top fold as shown.

4. Label the flaps *Vertebrates, Fish, Amphibians, Reptiles, Birds,* and *Mammals,* as shown. Before you read the chapter, write what you know about each group under the tabs.

5. As you read the chapter, add to or change the information you wrote under the tabs.

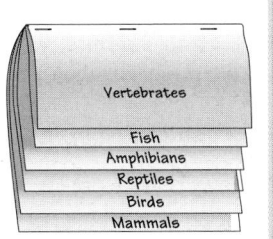

Vertebrates
Fish
Amphibians
Reptiles
Birds
Mammals

181

EXPLORE ACTIVITY

Purpose Use the Explore Activity to introduce students to vertebrates. Students will build a model of a backbone.

Preparation Purchase pasta wheels, soft candy circles, and pipe cleaners.

Materials pasta wheels, soft candy circles, pipe cleaners

Teaching Strategy Place materials for each group in a self-sealing plastic bag.

Observe

The model moves easily but can only be bent so far. Student responses will vary. The backbone is made of bone and flexible material (cartilage). Answers will vary but should include a good description of the model.

✓ Assessment

Process Have students make a model using beads instead of soft candy circles and compare the two models. **Which model allows for greater movement? Explain.** The first model; the soft candy circles increase flexibility. Use **Performance Assessment in the Science Classroom,** p. 123.

Before You Read

Dinah Zike Study Fold

Purpose Use a Foldable to determine what students know about vertebrate animals before reading the chapter. The Foldable will provide a place for recording and organizing notes on fish, amphibians, reptiles, birds, and mammals.

📁 For additional help, see Foldables Worksheet, p. 15 in **Chapter Resources Booklet,** or go to the Glencoe Science Web site at **science.glencoe.com.** See After You Read in the Study Guide at the end of this chapter.

SECTION

Chordate Animals

1 Motivate

Bellringer Transparency

Display the Section Focus Transparency for Section 1. Use the accompanying Transparency Activity Master. L2

ELL

Tie to Prior Knowledge

Ask students to describe vertebrae. They are bony or cartilaginous segments that make up the spinal column. **Have them infer what vertebrates are.** animals with a backbone **Ask them to name as many kinds of vertebrates as they can.** possible answers: horses, humans, cats, dogs, fish, mice, birds

---

Chordate Animals

As You Read

What You'll Learn

- **Identify** the major characteristics of chordates.
- **List** the major characteristics common to all vertebrates.
- **Explain** the difference between ectotherms and endotherms.
- **Name** the characteristics of the three classes of fish.

Vocabulary

chordate   endotherm
ectotherm   cartilage

Why It's Important

You and other vertebrate animals have an internal skeleton that supports and protects your internal organs.

What is a chordate?

Suppose you asked your classmates to list their pets. Dogs, cats, birds, snakes, and fish probably would appear on the list. Animals that are familiar to most people are animals with a backbone. These animals belong to a larger group of animals called chordates (KOR dayts). As shown in **Figure 1,** three characteristics of all **chordates** are a notochord, a nerve cord, and gill slits at some time during their development. The notochord is a flexible rod that extends along the length of the developing organism. Gill slits are slitlike openings between the body cavity and the outside of the body. They are present only during the early stages of the organism's development. In most chordates, one end of the nerve cord develops into the organism's brain.

Vertebrates Scientists classify the 42,500 species of chordates into smaller groups, as shown in **Figure 2.** The animals within each group share similar characteristics, which may indicate that they have a common ancestor. Vertebrates, which include humans, are the largest group of chordates.

Vertebrates have an internal system of bones called an endoskeleton. *Endo-* means "within." The vertebrae, skull, and other bones of the endoskeleton support and protect internal organs. For example, vertebrae surround and protect the nerve cord. Many muscles attach to the skeleton and make movement possible.

Figure 1
The 23 species of lancelets are filter feeders that live in the ocean. The body of a lancelet is up to 7 cm long.

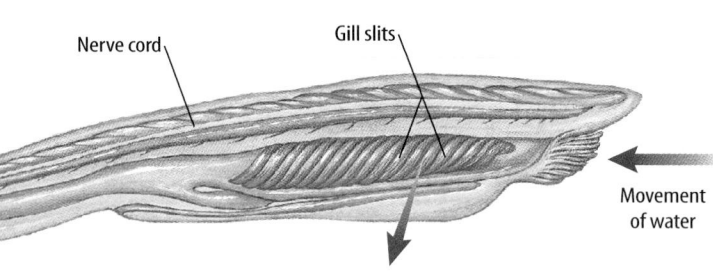

Nerve cord   Gill slits

Notochord

Movement of water

182 CHAPTER 7 Vertebrate Animals

Section ✓Assessment Planner

PORTFOLIO
Activity, p. 183
PERFORMANCE ASSESSMENT
Skill Builder Activities, p. 186
See page 208 for more options.

CONTENT ASSESSMENT
Section, p. 186
Challenge, p. 186
Chapter, pp. 208–209

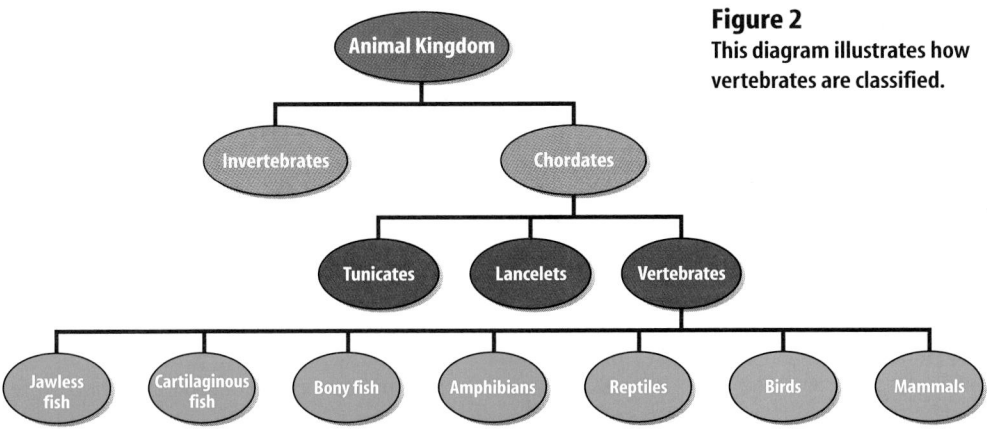

Figure 2
This diagram illustrates how vertebrates are classified.

Body Temperature Most vertebrate body temperatures change as the surrounding temperature changes. These animals are **ectotherms** (EK tuh thurmz), or cold-blooded animals. Fish are examples of ectotherms.

Humans and many other vertebrates are **endotherms** (EN duh thurmz), or warm-blooded animals. Their body temperature doesn't change with the surrounding temperature. Your body temperature is usually about 37°C, but it can vary by about 1°C, depending on the time of day. Changes of more than a degree or two usually indicate an infection or overexposure to extreme environmental temperatures.

☑ **Reading Check** *Are humans endotherms or ectotherms?*

Fish

The largest group of vertebrates—fish—lives in water. Fish are ectotherms that can be found in warm desert pools and the subfreezing Arctic Ocean. Some species are adapted to swim in shallow freshwater streams and others in salty ocean depths.

Fish have fleshy filaments called gills, shown in **Figure 3,** where carbon dioxide and oxygen are exchanged. Water with oxygen flows over the gills. When blood is pumped into the gills, the oxygen in the water moves into the blood. At the same time, carbon dioxide moves out of the blood in the gills and into the water.

Most fish have pairs of fanlike fins. The top and the bottom fins stabilize the fish. Those on the sides steer and move the fish. The tail fin propels the fish through the water.

Most fish have scales. Scales are thin structures made of a bony material that overlap like shingles on a house to cover the skin.

Figure 3
Fish gills are made of gill arches and gill filaments. Gas exchange occurs in the gill filaments.

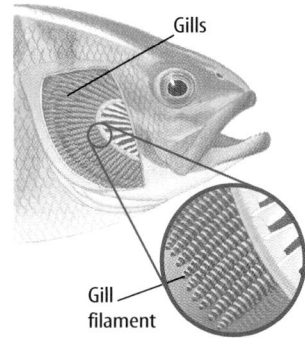

Gills

Gill filament

SECTION 1 Chordate Animals **183**

Quick Demo

To help students understand ectotherms, use two rocks of the same size and temperature. Place one rock in a cold place and the other one on a warm, sunny ledge for half an hour. Ask students to touch each rock and explain how it has changed.

Fish

Activity

Have students examine fish scales using a stereomicroscope. Ask them to draw the scales they observe. Explain that the age of some types of fish can be determined by counting the rings on the scales. [L2] [ELL] [LS] **Visual-Spatial** [P]

Cultural **Diversity**

Commercial Fishing Fish are a vital source of food for many people in the world. Fishing is important to the economies of many countries. **Have students research the fishing industry and mark on a world map which countries were the biggest importers and exporters of fish in 1997.** importers: Japan, US, China, Spain, France; exporters: Norway, China, US, Denmark, Thailand [L3]

Resource Manager

Chapter Resources Booklet
Transparency Activity, p. 46
Directed Reading for Content Mastery, pp. 17, 18
Note-taking Worksheets, pp. 33–36

Types of Fish

Quick Demo

Half-fill three 10-oz. plastic glasses with water. Have students observe as you drop a marble into one container, a tablespoon of cooking oil into another container, and a small inflated balloon into the third container. The marble sinks, but the oil and balloon float. Explain that sharks store large amounts of oil in their bodies, which gives them buoyancy in water. Most bony fish have gas-filled sacs that enable them to float.

Caption Answer

Figure 5 These fish all are adapted to a similar environment.

Physics
INTEGRATION

Submarines pump water into and out of special chambers, which causes the submarine to sink or rise. In a similar way, gases move into and out of a fish's swim bladder. This allows the fish to sink or rise in the water. How do fish without swim bladders move up and down in the water? Write your answer in your Science Journal.

Figure 5
The many types of bony fish range in size from a few millimeters to many meters in length. *Why might all bony fish have the same basic body plan?*

Types of Fish

Scientists classify fish into three groups—bony, jawless, and cartilaginous (kar tuh LA juh nuhs)—which are illustrated in **Figure 4** on the opposite page. Bony fish have skeletons made of bone, while jawless fish and cartilaginous fish have endoskeletons made of cartilage. **Cartilage** (KAR tuhl ihj) is a tough, flexible tissue that is similar to bone but is not as hard or brittle. Your external ears and the tip of your nose are made of cartilage.

Bony Fish About 95 percent of all fish have skeletons made of bone. Goldfish, trout, bass, and marlins are examples of bony fish. The body structure of a typical bony fish is shown in **Figure 5.** As a bony fish swims, water easily flows over its body because its scales are covered with slimy mucus.

If you've ever watched fish in a tank, you know that they rise and sink to different levels in the water. An important adaptation in most bony fish is the swim bladder. This air sac helps control the depth at which the fish swims. The swim bladder inflates and deflates as gases—mostly oxygen in deep-water fish and nitrogen in shallow-water fish—move between the swim bladder and the blood. As the swim bladder fills with gas, the fish rises in the water. When the gas leaves the bladder, it deflates and the fish sinks lower in the water.

Most bony fish use external fertilization (fur tul uh ZAY shun) to reproduce. External fertilization means that the eggs are fertilized outside the female's body. Females release large numbers of eggs into the water. Then, a male swims over the eggs, releases the sperm into the water, and many eggs are fertilized.

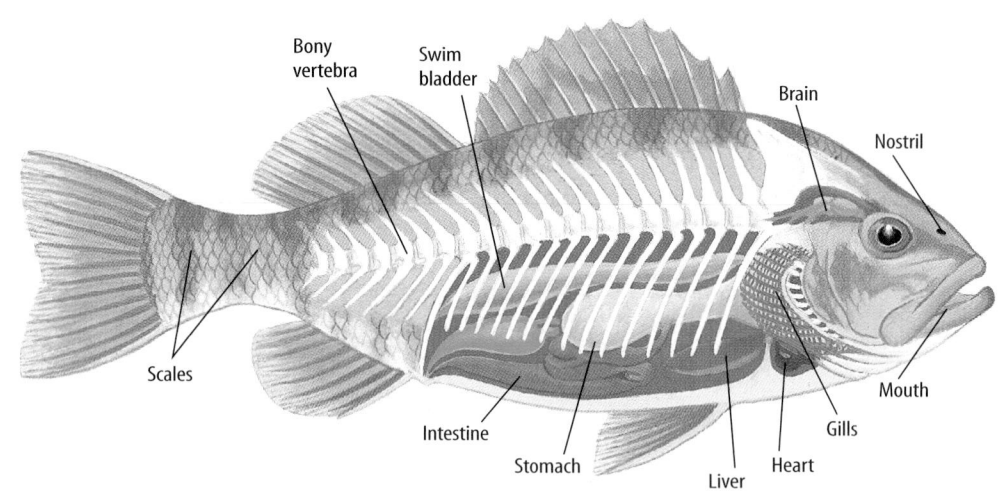

Bony vertebra / Swim bladder / Brain / Nostril / Scales / Intestine / Stomach / Liver / Heart / Gills / Mouth

---

✔ Active Reading

Write-Draw-Discuss This strategy encourages students to actively participate in reading and lectures, assimilating content creatively. Have students write about an idea, clarify it, then make an illustration or drawing. Ask students to share responses with the class and display several examples. Have students Write-Draw-Discuss about a concept in this chapter.

Inclusion Strategies

Learning Disabled Have students make a mobile of the different types of fish in this section (jawless, cartilaginous, and bony). As they read, have them write the information they find most interesting about each type beneath it on the mobile. The students can use this information to construct a concept map in their Science Journals. [L1] **Kinesthetic and Linguistic**

Figure 4

Fish are the most numerous and varied of all vertebrates, with more than 20,000 living species. These species can be organized into three groups—jawless, cartilaginous, and bony. Jawless fish are the most primitive and form the smallest group. Cartilaginous fish include more than 600 species, nearly all of them predators. Bony fish are the most numerous and diverse group. This page features photos of fish from each group.

Sturgeon

Wolf Eel

Whale Shark

Ratfish

BONY FISH The bodies of bony fish vary. The fins of the coelacanth below have jointed bones, like the legs of many land animals. Amphibians may have evolved from ancestors of coelacanths.

Angelfish

CARTILAGINOUS FISH The cartilage that gives these fish their shape is a lightweight material that is softer than bone. The hammerhead shark below has been known to use the cartilage in its hammer-shaped head to pin down stingrays, one of its favorite meals, before it devours them.

Electric Ray

Coelacanth

Hagfish

JAWLESS FISH Only about 70 species make up the jawless group of fish. Jawless fish are often parasitic. The hagfish, right, often crawls into fish trapped in nets and eats them from the inside out.

Hammerhead shark

185

Visualizing Fish Diversity

Have students examine the pictures and read the captions. Then ask the following questions.

Give a possible explanation for why jawless fish are often parasites. Possible answer: Because the fish do not have a jaw and cannot chew, this may make it difficult for the fish to be predatory.

How does the shape and coloring of an electric ray help it live near the bottom? Possible answer: The flattened body allows them to lie on the bottom and bury themselves in sand very easily. Their coloring allows them to blend with the sandy bottom.

Activity

Have students complete a Venn diagram comparing the characteristics of the organisms in the three groups. The diagram should show the characteristics the groups have in common and those that separate the groups from each other. L2
IS Visual-Spatial

Extension

Have students research information about fish that are adapted to live in the deep ocean where there is high pressure, cold water temperature, no light, and very little food. Direct students to make posters illustrating the adaptations of these fish. L2
IS Visual-Spatial

Resource Manager

Chapter Resources Booklet
Enrichment, p. 29
Transparency Activity, pp. 51–52
Lab Activity, pp. 9–11

Types of Fish, continued

Extension

Scientists thought an extinct fish called the coelacanth had died out 70 million years ago until a fisherman caught one in 1938 in the Indian Ocean. Have students research the coelacanths and write a report on their evolution, natural history, anatomy, and rediscovery. L2
IS Linguistic

3 Assess

Reteach

Have students explain how their own lungs can act like a fish's swim bladder. L2

Challenge

Why are there more fish than any other type of vertebrate? There is great variety in aquatic environments, from freshwater to saltwater, very shallow to extreme depth, and warm to frigid.

Assessment

Process Have students make a table comparing the characteristics of the three types of fish. Use **Performance Assessment in the Science Classroom,** p. 109.

B The inside of a lamprey's mouth contains structures that are used to attach to larger fish.

Figure 6

A Lampreys are specialized predators that attach to fish like salmon and trout. In places such as the Great Lakes, lampreys have caused a decrease in some fish populations.

Jawless and Cartilaginous Fish Only a few species of fish are classified as jawless fish, like the one in **Figure 6.** Jawless fish have scaleless, long, tubelike bodies; an endoskeleton made of cartilage; and a round, muscular mouth without a jaw. But the mouth has sharp, toothlike structures. One type of jawless fish, the lamprey, attaches itself to a larger host fish using its strong mouth and toothlike structures. Its tongue has sharp ridges that scrape through the host fish's skin. The lamprey obtains nutrients by feeding on the host fish's blood.

Sharks, skates, and rays are cartilaginous fish. They have skeletons made of cartilage just like the jawless fish. However, cartilaginous fish have rough, sandpaperlike scales and movable jaws. Many sharks have sharp teeth made from modified scales. Most cartilaginous fish are predators.

Section ① Assessment

1. What are two characteristics all chordates have in common?
2. Name the three groups of fish. What material makes up the skeleton of each of the three groups of fish?
3. Compare and contrast ectothermic animals and endothermic animals.
4. What are the major characteristics that are found in vertebrates?
5. **Think Critically** In one lake, millions of fish eggs are laid and fertilized annually. Why doesn't the lake become overcrowded with fish?

Skill Builder Activities

6. **Forming Hypotheses** Sharks don't have swim bladders and must move constantly or they sink. Hypothesize about the amount of food that a shark must eat compared to the amount eaten by a bony fish that is about the same size. **For more help, refer to the** Science Skill Handbook.
7. **Making and Using Graphs** Make a circle graph of the number of fish species currently classified: *jawless fish—70; cartilaginous fish—820;* and *bony fish—23,500.* **For more help, refer to the** Science Skill Handbook.

Resource Manager

Chapter Resources Booklet
Reinforcement, p. 25

Performance Assessment in the Science Classroom, p. 55

Answers to Section Assessment

1. a notochord and gill slits at some point in development
2. bony fish—bone; jawless and cartilaginous fish—cartilage
3. The body temperature of ectotherms changes with their surroundings. The body temperature of endotherms remains nearly constant.

4. An endoskeleton; muscles attached to bones for movement; some are ectotherms, others are endotherms.
5. Many eggs are not fertilized; some eggs and young fish are eaten by predators.
6. Sharks need more energy, and food provides this energy. Sharks have to

eat a greater amount of food than fish of a similar size that have swim bladders.
7. 0.3% of the circle graph (about 1°) represents jawless fish; 96.4% (about 347°) represents bony fish; 3.4% (about 12°) represents cartilaginous fish.

Amphibians and Reptiles

Amphibians

A spy might lead a double life, but what about an animal? Amphibians (am FIH bee unz) are animals that spend part of their lives in water and part on land. In fact, the term *amphibian* comes from the Greek word *amphibios,* which means "double life." Frogs, toads, newts, and salamanders, such as the red spotted salamander pictured in **Figure 7,** are examples of amphibians.

Amphibian Adaptations Living on land is different from living in water. Think about some of the things an amphibian must deal with in its environment. Temperature changes more quickly and more often in air than in water. More oxygen is available in air than in water. However, air doesn't support body weight as well as water does. Amphibians are adapted for survival in these different environments.

Amphibians are ectotherms. They adjust to changes in the temperature of their environment. In northern climates where the winters are cold, amphibians bury themselves in mud or leaves and remain inactive until the warmer temperatures of spring and summer arrive. This period of cold weather inactivity is called **hibernation.** Amphibians that live in hot, dry environments move to cooler, more humid conditions underground and become inactive until the temperature cools down. This period of inactivity during hot, dry summer months is called **estivation** (es tuh VAY shun).

As You Read

What You'll Learn
- **Describe** how amphibians have adapted to live in water and on land.
- **Explain** what happens during frog metamorphosis.
- **Identify** the adaptations that allow reptiles to live on land.

Vocabulary
hibernation
estivation
amniotic egg

Why It's Important
The sensitivity of amphibians to environmental changes may indicate problems that could affect humans.

Figure 7
Amphibians have many adaptations that allow for life on land and in the water. This red-spotted salamander spends most of its life on land. *Why must they return to the water?*

SECTION 2 Amphibians and Reptiles **187**

Amphibians and Reptiles

1 Motivate

Bellringer Transparency

Display the Section Focus Transparency for Section 2. Use the accompanying Transparency Activity Master. L2
ELL

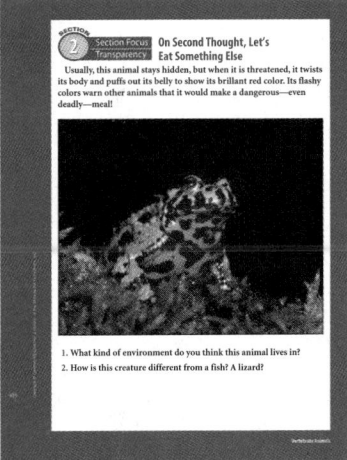

Tie to Prior Knowledge

Ask students to list adaptations a fish would need to survive on land. lungs, ability to move on land, ability to get food, and so on This will lead into the discussion of amphibian adaptations to life on land.

Caption Answer

Figure 7 Amphibians lay their eggs in the water.

Section ✓*Assessment* Planner

PORTFOLIO
Activity, p. 190
PERFORMANCE ASSESSMENT
Skill Builder Activities, p. 191
See page 208 for more options.

CONTENT ASSESSMENT
Section, p. 191
Challenge, p. 191
Chapter, pp. 208–209

Amphibians

Use Science Words

Word Origin Hibernation comes from the Latin word *hibernare*, which means "to pass the winter." Estivation is derived from the Latin word *aestas*, meaning "summer." Ask students to use each word in a sentence. L2

IS Linguistic

SCIENCE *Online*

Internet Addresses

_____

_____

_____

_____

Explore the Glencoe Science Web site at **science.glencoe.com** to find out more about topics in this section.

✔ Reading Check

Answer lungs, tympanums, strong legs, large eyes, long sticky tongues

Quick Demo

Place a live frog in an aquarium at the front of the classroom. Have students observe the frog to determine its adaptations. From student responses, make a table on the board that lists the adaptations a frog has for living on land and in the water. L2 **IS Visual-Spatial**

Fun Fact

Frogs use their teeth to hold food in place, not to chew. Amphibians usually swallow prey whole.

SCIENCE *Online*

Research Visit the Glencoe Science Web site at **science. glencoe. com** for recent news or magazine articles about the environment and amphibians. Communicate to your class what you learn.

Figure 8

Most young amphibians, like these tadpoles, look nothing like their parents when they hatch. The larvae go through metamorphosis in the water and eventually develop into adult frogs that live on land.

Amphibian Characteristics Amphibians are vertebrates with a strong endoskeleton made of bones. The skeleton helps support their body while on land. Adult frogs and toads have strong hind legs that are used for swimming and jumping.

Adult amphibians use lungs instead of gills to exchange oxygen and carbon dioxide. This is an important adaptation for survival on land. However, because amphibians have three-chambered hearts, the blood carrying oxygen mixes with the blood carrying carbon dioxide. This mixing makes less oxygen available to the amphibian. Adult amphibians also exchange oxygen and carbon dioxide through their skin which increases their oxygen supply. Amphibians can live on land, but they must stay moist so this exchange can occur.

Amphibian hearing and vision also are adapted to a life on land. The tympanum (TIHM puh nuhm), or eardrum, vibrates in response to sound waves and is used for hearing. Large eyes assist some amphibians in capturing their prey.

✔ Reading Check

What amphibian senses are adapted for life on land?

Land environments offer a great variety of insects as food for adult amphibians. A long, sticky tongue extends quickly to capture an insect and bring it into the waiting mouth.

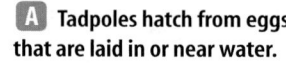

A Tadpoles hatch from eggs that are laid in or near water.

B Tadpoles use their gills for gas exchange.

Curriculum Connection

Math Many people are wary of reptiles. Have students write questions about reptiles to find out how people feel about these animals. They can give the survey to their classmates and others in the school. Have students graph the results and share them in class. L3 **IS Interpersonal and Logical-Mathematical**

Teacher FYI

Biologists divide amphibians into three orders: *Urodela*, the salamanders; *Anura*, the frogs and toads; and *Apoda*, the worm-like caecilians. There are about 400 species of salamanders in the world. Most are found in North America.

Amphibian Metamorphosis Young animals such as kittens and calves are almost miniature versions of their parents, but young amphibians do not look like their parents. A series of body changes called metamorphosis (me tuh MOR fuh sus) occurs during the life cycle of an amphibian. Most amphibians go through a metamorphosis, as illustrated in **Figure 8.** Most eggs are laid in water and hatch into larvae. Most adult amphibians live mainly on land.

The young larval forms of amphibians are dependent on water. They have no legs and breathe through gills. They develop body structures needed for life on land, including legs and lungs. The rate at which metamorphosis occurs depends on the species, the water temperature, and the amount of available food. If food is scarce and the water temperature is cool, then metamorphosis will take longer.

Like fish, most amphibians have external fertilization and require water for reproduction. Although most amphibians reproduce in ponds and lakes, some take advantage of other sources of water. For example, some species of rain forest tree frogs lay their eggs in rainwater that collects in leaves. Even more unusual is the Surinam toad shown in **Figure 9.** The fertilized eggs are placed on the mother's back. Her skin swells and covers the eggs to keep them moist. After metamorphosis occurs, fully formed toads emerge from under her skin.

Figure 9
Surinam toads live along the Amazon River. A female carries 60 to 100 fertilized eggs on her back. Complete metamorphosis takes 12 to 20 weeks. *What advantage would this provide for young Surinam toads?*

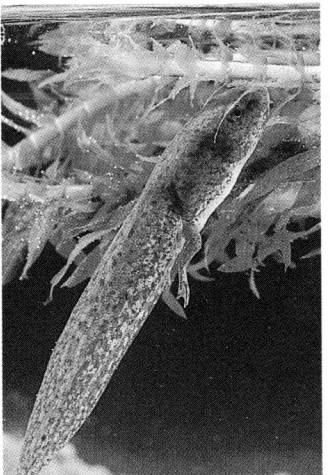

C Legs begin to develop. Soon, the tail will disappear.

D An adult frog uses lungs and skin for gas exchange.

Resource Manager

Chapter Resources Booklet
Transparency Activity, p. 47
Directed Reading for Content Mastery, p. 18
Enrichment, p. 30

Caption Answer
Figure 9 They are protected by their mother so a greater percentage of them survive.

Activity
Have students make a poster that shows the stages in the frog life cycle. Have them describe the characteristics of each stage.
L2 IS **Visual-Spatial**

Discussion
How could having two different forms in the life cycle help species survive? Answers may include that one form may be better adapted to seasonal conditions.

IDENTIFYING
Misconceptions

Students may think that people get warts from toads. This is not true, but a person should wash his or her hands after handling a toad because toads release a substance that can cause discomfort if it gets into the eyes or mouth. Also, many reptiles harbor certain strains of bacteria that can cause illness if they get into the mouth.

Discussion
Why do frogs and toads seem to suddenly appear after a rain? Because of the moisture present everywhere after a rain, frogs and toads can travel over a greater area to hunt for food. Frogs and toads breathe through their skin, which must be kept moist for them to survive.

Reptiles

Activity

Have students work in groups to make posters about ancient reptiles, including dinosaurs. Suggest that each poster have an ancient reptile on it with the adaptations listed that helped it survive in its environment. Make sure some posters feature ancient reptiles that were not dinosaurs.

L2 COOP LEARN IS **Visual-Spatial and Interpersonal** P

Fun Fact

Snakes use their tongues to detect chemicals in the air. Many snakes are poisonous, but few are deadly to humans.

Teacher FYI

Rattlesnakes inject their prey with poison and let them go. They follow the scent of their own poison to find the prey after it has died, and eat it at their leisure.

Health
INTEGRATION

Wash hands with soap and water.

Figure 10
Reptiles have different body plans.

A The rubber boa is one of only two species of boas in North America. Rubber boas have flexible jaws that enable them to eat prey that is larger than their head.

C Sea turtles, like this logger-head turtle, are threatened around the world because of pollution, loss of nesting habitat, drowning in nets, and lighted beaches.

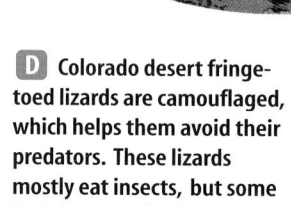

B Crocodiles and American alligators like this one build their nests on land near a body of water. They protect their eggs while they wait for them to hatch.

D Colorado desert fringe-toed lizards are camouflaged, which helps them avoid their predators. These lizards mostly eat insects, but some include plants in their diet.

Health
INTEGRATION

Every year, about 2 million reptiles are sold as pets. However, many reptiles carry a type of bacteria called *Salmonella*. *Salmonella* can make people sick if they touch their mouth after handling a pet reptile. What are some ways to prevent getting sick after handling a pet reptile? Write your answer in your Science Journal.

Reptiles

Reptiles come in many shapes, sizes, and colors. Snakes, lizards, turtles, and crocodiles are reptiles. Reptiles are ectothermic vertebrates with dry, scaly skin. Because reptiles do not depend on water for reproduction, most are able to live their entire lives on land. They have several other adaptations for life on land.

Types of Reptiles As shown in **Figure 10,** reptilian body plans vary. Turtles are covered with a hard shell, into which they withdraw for protection. Turtles eat insects, worms, fish, and plants.

Alligators and crocodiles are predators that live in and near water. These large reptiles live in warmer climates such as those found in the southern United States.

Lizards and snakes make up the largest group of reptiles. They have a highly developed sense of smell. An organ in the roof of the mouth senses molecules collected by the tongue. The constant in-and-out motion of the tongue allows a snake or lizard to smell its surroundings. Lizards have movable eyelids and external ears, and most lizards have legs with clawed toes. Snakes don't have eyelids, ears, or legs. Instead of hearing sounds, they feel vibrations in the ground.

190 CHAPTER 7 Vertebrate Animals

LAB DEMONSTRATION

Purpose to infer how a snake hears

Materials tuning fork, hard piece of rubber

Preparation Demonstrate how to use a tuning fork. Tuning forks should not be struck on anything hard such as wood or metal. Do not touch the prongs after hitting the fork on the hard piece of rubber, such as a shoe sole.

Procedure Tap the tuning fork on rubber and hold it next to a student's ear. Tap the fork again and press the stem hard against the student's chin. Snakes receive similar vibrations from the environment, which their brains interpret as sound.

Expected Outcome Students will observe and feel vibrations.

✔ Assessment

How are vibrations interpreted as sound? The vibrations travel through the bones in the student's jaw and skull, and into the fluid of the inner ear. There, they are changed into nerve impulses, which the brain interprets as sound.

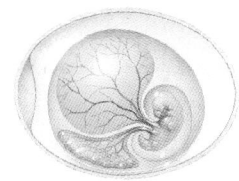

Figure 11
Young reptiles hatch from amniotic eggs.

Reptile Adaptations A thick, dry, waterproof skin is an adaptation that reptiles have for life on land. The skin is covered with scales that reduce water loss and help prevent injury.

✔ **Reading Check** *What are two functions of a reptile's skin?*

All reptiles have lungs for exchanging oxygen and carbon dioxide. Even sea snakes and sea turtles, which can stay submerged for long periods of time, must eventually come to the surface to breathe.

Two adaptations enable reptiles to reproduce successfully on land—internal fertilization and laying shell-covered, amniotic (am nee AH tihk) eggs. During internal fertilization, sperm are deposited directly into the female's body. Water isn't necessary for reptilian reproduction.

The embryo develops within the moist protective environment of the **amniotic egg,** as shown in **Figure 11.** The yolk supplies food for the developing embryo, and the leathery shell protects the embryo and yolk. When eggs hatch, young reptiles are fully developed. In some snake species, the female does not lay eggs. Instead, the eggs are kept within her body, where they incubate and hatch. The young snakes leave her body soon after they hatch.

Section Assessment

1. List the adaptations amphibians have for living in water and on land.
2. Sequence the steps of a frog's two-stage metamorphosis.
3. What adaptations do reptiles have for living on land?
4. Why is internal fertilization efficient?
5. **Think Critically** Some nonpoisonous snakes' patterns are similar to those of poisonous snakes. How is this coloring an advantage for a nonpoisonous snake?

Skill Builder Activities

6. **Comparing and Contrasting** Compare and contrast the exchange of oxygen and carbon dioxide in adult amphibians and reptiles. **For more help, refer to the** Science Skill Handbook.
7. **Communicating** In your Science Journal, write an explanation of why it is important for amphibians to live in moist or wet environments. **For more help, refer to the** Science Skill Handbook.

Reteach

Prepare a quiz game with descriptions of lizards, turtles, alligators, crocodiles, snakes, frogs, toads, and salamanders. Let students classify the animals as amphibians or reptiles. amphibians: frog, toad, salamander; reptiles: lizards, turtles, alligators, crocodiles, snakes L2

Challenge

Are reptiles or amphibians more likely to be affected by acid rain and ozone depletion? Amphibians; they respire through their skin, as well as their lungs, so they would absorb poisonous gases and chemicals along with oxygen; they lay their eggs in water.

 **Assessment**

Performance Have students create a Venn diagram of fish, reptile, and amphibian characteristics. Use **Performance Assessment in the Science Classroom,** p. 167.

Resource Manager

Chapter Resources Booklet
Reinforcement, p. 26

Life Science Critical Thinking/ Problem Solving, p. 7

Answers to Section Assessment

1. water: moist and smooth skin, larvae have gills, tails for swimming; land: lungs, strong skeleton, legs for jumping
2. Tadpoles hatch from eggs and use gills for gas exchange; tadpoles develop legs and lose tail; adult frog uses lungs and skin for gas exchange.
3. internal fertilization; shell-covered, amniotic egg or live births; thick, dry waterproof skin; scales; lungs
4. More eggs are fertilized since sperm don't have to move through water to get to them.
5. Predators think they are poisonous snakes and leave them alone.
6. amphibian—through lungs and skin; reptiles—through lungs only
7. Amphibians breathe through their skin, so they must keep their skin wet in order to survive.

Activity

BENCH TESTED

Purpose to observe tadpole metamorphosis and study the life cycle of a frog [L2] [ELL] [COOP LEARN] [IS] **Visual-Spatial**

Process Skills observing and inferring, classifying, sequencing, forming operational definitions

Time Required 30 minutes on Day 1, 10 minutes of observations twice weekly

Alternate Materials Tap water aged for 48 hours can be used instead of pond water.

Safety Precautions Caution students to use extreme care when working with live animals.

Teaching Strategy Field-collected eggs can be shipped from biological supply houses in January, February, and March. Peeper and toad eggs develop rapidly.

Troubleshooting The eggs must be handled carefully if they are to hatch. Make sure the temperature of the water remains at 20° C.

Answers to Questions

1. Answers will range from 8 to 20 days. Legs develop in approximately four weeks, depending on the species.
2. the hind legs
3. It protects the eggs and keeps them from drying out.
4. Young tadpoles—eyes are on each side of the head; older tadpoles—eyes are close to the top of the head.
5. 2–4 months

✔Assessment

Oral Have students sequence the events that occur as a frog develops from an egg into an adult. Use **PASC,** p. 163.

Activity

Frog Metamorphosis

Frogs and other amphibians use external fertilization to reproduce. Female frogs lay hundreds of jellylike eggs in water. Male frogs then fertilize these eggs. Once larvae hatch, the process of metamorphosis begins.

Materials

4-L aquarium or jar	aquatic plants
frog egg mass	washed gravel
lake or pond water	lettuce
stereoscopic microscope	(previously boiled)
watch glass	large rock
small fishnet	

What You'll Investigate

What changes occur as a tadpole goes through metamorphosis?

Safety Precautions 🐸 🥽 👕 ⚠

WARNING: *Handle the eggs with care.*

Goals

- **Observe** how body structures change as a tadpole develops into an adult frog.
- **Determine** how long metamorphosis takes.

Procedure

1. Copy the data table in your Science Journal.
2. As a class, use the aquarium, pond water, gravel, rock, and plants to prepare a water habitat for the frog eggs.

Frog Metamorphosis	
Date	**Observations**
	Answers will vary.

192   **CHAPTER 7** Vertebrate Animals

3. Place the egg mass in the aquarium's water. Use the fishnet to separate a few eggs from the mass and place them on the watch glass. Observe the eggs using the microscope. Record all observations in your data table. Return the eggs to the aquarium.
4. **Observe** the eggs twice a week until hatching begins. Then observe the tadpoles twice weekly. Identify the mouth, eyes, gill cover, gills, nostrils, back fin, and legs.
5. In your Science Journal, write a description of how tadpoles eat cooled, boiled lettuce.

Conclude and Apply

1. How long does it take for the eggs to hatch and the tadpoles to develop legs?
2. Which pair of legs appears first?
3. **Explain** why the jellylike coating around the eggs is important.
4. **Compare** the eyes of young tadpoles with the eyes of older tadpoles.
5. **Calculate** how long it takes for a tadpole to change into a frog.

𝒞ommunicating **Your Data**

Draw the changes you observe as the egg hatches and the tadpole goes through metamorphosis. **For more help, refer to the Science Skill Handbook.**

𝒞ommunicating **Your Data**

Suggest students organize their drawings in an events chain concept map.

Resource Manager

Chapter Resources Booklet
   Activity Worksheet, pp. 5–6

Life Science Critical Thinking/Problem Solving, p. 11

Birds

Characteristics of Birds

Ostriches have strong legs for running, and pelicans have specialized bills for scooping fish. Penguins can't fly but are excellent swimmers, and house wrens and hummingbirds are able to perch on branches. These birds are different, but they, and all birds, have common characteristics. Birds are endothermic vertebrates that have two wings, two legs, and a bill or beak. Birders, or bird-watchers, can tell where a bird lives and what it eats by looking at the type of wings, feet, and beak or bill it has. Birds are covered mostly with feathers—a feature unique to birds. They lay hard-shelled eggs and sit on these eggs to keep them warm until they hatch. Besides fish, birds are the most numerous vertebrates on Earth. **Figure 12** illustrates some of the more than 8,600 species of birds and their adaptations.

As You Read

What You'll Learn
- **Identify** the characteristics of birds.
- **Describe** the adaptations birds have for flight.
- **Explain** the function of feathers.

Vocabulary
contour feather
down feather

Why It's Important
Humans modeled flight of airplanes after birds.

Figure 12

A Emus can't fly but they have strong legs and feet that are adapted for running.

B Horned puffins can fly and their sleek bodies and small, pointed wings also enable them to "fly" underwater.

C With a wingspan of 3.5 m, an albatross glides in the air.

D Birds of prey, like this osprey, have sharp, strong talons that enable them to grab their prey.

SECTION 3 Birds **193**

Section ✓ Assessment Planner

PORTFOLIO
Visual Learning, p. 193
PERFORMANCE ASSESSMENT
Try at Home MiniLAB, p. 195
Skill Builder Activities, p. 196
See page 208 for more options.

CONTENT ASSESSMENT
Section, p. 196
Challenge, p. 196
Chapter, pp. 208–209

Birds

1 Motivate

Bellringer Transparency

Display the Section Focus Transparency for Section 3. Use the accompanying Transparency Activity Master. L2

ELL

Maybe the Scientists Were a Hoax!

This bird, called a kiwi, is the national bird of New Zealand. It's so unusual that when it was first brought to the attention of scientists, they thought it was a hoax. It has no tail and only stubby wings hidden by hair-like feathers. Flightless, the nocturnal kiwi lives in burrows and tends to be shy.

1. Why might scientists have thought the kiwi a hoax?
2. Why do you think the kiwi is classified as a bird?

Tie to Prior Knowledge

Have students compare reptile and bird characteristics, such as different skin coverings, and method of reproduction.

Visual Learning

Figure 12 Have students make a list of adaptations each bird has for its particular lifestyle, including those mentioned in the caption. P

Adaptations for Flight

Activity

Divide the class into pairs. Have one student keep time and count while the other holds his or her arms straight out and flaps them up and down. See how many times a student can flap his or her arms in one minute and how long it takes for the student to tire. Explain that just as our leg muscles are well developed for walking, the chest muscles of most birds are well developed for flying. L1 ELL COOP LEARN **Kinesthetic and Interpersonal**

✔ Reading Check

Answer They make the bird lighter so it can fly more easily.

Use Science Words

Word Origin Birds belong to the class Aves. *Avis* is the Latin word for bird and is the root of many bird-related words. **Ask students to find words with this root and explain their meanings.** aviator—pilot or member of an aircraft crew; avian—relating to birds; aviary—enclosure for breeding and rearing birds L2 **Linguistic**

Use an Analogy

Birds and mammals are endotherms. An endotherm is like a furnace that burns fuel to produce energy. In the case of animals, respiration and oxidation of food are similar to the burning of fuel in a furnace. Have students breathe onto their hands and observe that their breath is warm. L1

Figure 13
Wings provide an upward force called lift in both birds and airplanes.

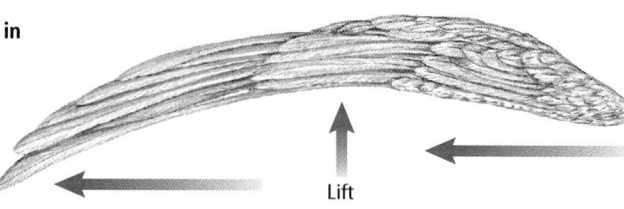
Lift

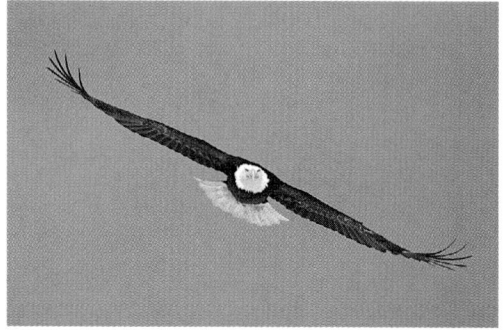
A Bald eagles are able to soar for long periods of time because their wings have a large surface area to provide lift.

B The glider gets lift from its wings the same way a bald eagle gets lift.

Adaptations for Flight

The bodies of most birds are designed for flight. They are streamlined and have light yet strong skeletons. The inside of a bird's bone is almost hollow. Internal crisscrossing structures strengthen the bones without making them as heavy as mammal bones are. Because flying requires a rigid body, a bird's tail vertebrae are joined together to provide the needed rigidity, strength, and stability.

✔ Reading Check
What advantage do birds' bones give them for flight?

Flight requires a lot of energy and oxygen. Birds eat insects, nectar, fish, meats, or other high-energy foods. They also have a large, efficient heart and a specialized respiratory system. A bird's lungs connect to air sacs that provide a constant supply of oxygen to the blood and make the bird more lightweight.

Slow-motion video shows that birds beat their wings up and down as well as forward and back. **Figure 13** illustrates how wing shape and surface area, and air speed and angle combine with wing movements to provide an upward push for flight. Inventors of the first flying machines used the body plan of birds as a model for flight.

SCIENCE Online

Research Visit the Glencoe Science Web site at **science.glencoe.com** for more information about wing designs of different aircraft. Communicate to your class what you learn.

SCIENCE Online
Internet Addresses

_____

_____

_____

Explore the Glencoe Science Web site at **science.glencoe.com** to find out more about topics in this section.

Science Journal

Bird Diary Ask students to draw or take pictures of different birds found around school or their home. They should identify the birds and start a bird diary in their Science Journals. Have them note the time of day they saw each bird, its location, and any other interesting observations. L2 **Visual-Spatial and Linguistic**

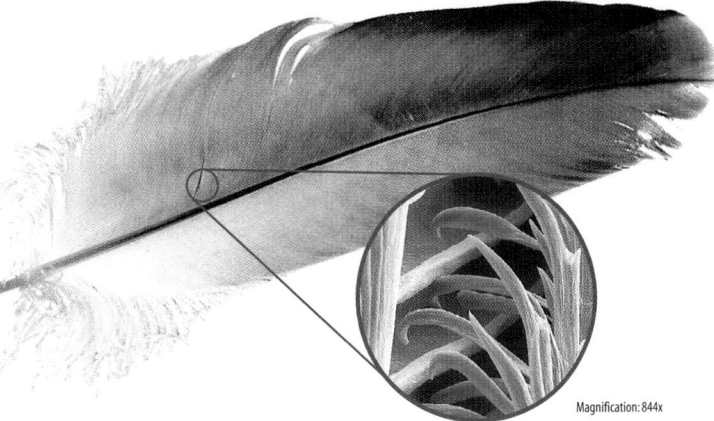

Figure 14
Microscopic barbs, located along contour feathers, keep the feathers smooth by holding the individual parts of the feather together.

Magnification: 844x

Functions of Feathers

Birds are the only animals with feathers. They have two main types of feathers—contour feathers and down feathers. Strong, lightweight **contour feathers** give adult birds their stream-lined shape and coloring. A close look at the contour feather in **Figure 14** shows the parallel strands, called barbs, that branch off the main shaft. Outer contour feathers help a bird move through the air or water. It is these long feathers on the wings and tail that help the bird steer and keep it from spinning out of control. Feather colors and patterns can help identify species. They also are useful in attracting mates and protecting birds from predators because they can be a form of camouflage.

Have you ever noticed that the hair on your arm stands up on a cold day? This response is one way your body works to trap and keep warm air close to your skin. Birds have **down feathers** that trap and keep warm air next to their bodies. These fluffy feathers, as shown in **Figure 15,** provide an insulating layer under the contour feathers of adult birds and cover the bodies of some young birds.

✓ **Reading Check**   *What are two ways feathers protect birds?*

TRY AT HOME

Mini LAB

Observing What Feathers Do

Procedure
1. Cut two 15-cm × 15-cm pieces of **cotton cloth.**
2. Apply a small amount of **petroleum jelly** to one piece of the cloth.
3. Wet both pieces of cloth with **water.**

Analysis
1. Compare the two pieces of cloth after they have been wet. In your **Science Journal,** describe what you observe.
2. Infer why birds do not have to find shelter from the rain.

Figure 15
Some species of birds, like chickens and these pheasants, are covered with feathers when they hatch. *Why might this be an advantage?*

SECTION 3 Birds **195**

Functions of Feathers

TRY AT HOME

Mini LAB

Purpose to discover how oil helps waterproof bird feathers
L2 Kinesthetic

Materials two 15 cm × 15 cm pieces of cotton cloth, bowl of water, petroleum jelly, Science Journal

Teaching Strategy Have students use only a small amount of jelly.

Analysis
1. The water soaks into the cloth without the petroleum jelly; it runs off the cloth covered with petroleum jelly.
2. Oil on the feathers keeps the bird dry and holds in body heat.

✓ Assessment

Oral Ask students to explain why waterbirds are more likely to preen than birds that live in trees. Use **PASC,** p. 89.

✓ **Reading Check**

Answer Contour feathers can provide camouflage; down feathers provide insulation.

Caption Answer
Figure 15 The feathers help keep the young chicks warm.

Teacher FYI

Airplanes are designed to use an airfoil similar to that of birds. Lift enables both to fly. The amount of lift produced is determined by wing area, shape, and speed. Airplanes extend flaps and slats to increase lift at low speeds. Similarly, birds increase their lift by flapping their wings, extending a feather, and spreading wing and tail feathers.

Resource Manager

Chapter Resources Booklet
　Transparency Activity, p. 48
　Directed Reading for Content Mastery, p. 19
　MiniLAB, p. 3

Reteach

Have students discuss how the area near your school can be made into a more favorable habitat for birds. L2

Challenge

Infer why birds are scarce in the fossil record. The bones of birds are lightweight and small, so they often disintegrate before they become fossils.

✔Assessment

Process Assess students' abilities to compare and contrast by having them examine the beaks and feet of birds indigenous to your area. Have students make a model of a hypothetical bird's foot and describe the bird's lifestyle. Use **Performance Assessment in the Science Classroom,** p. 93.

Resource Manager

Chapter Resources Booklet
Lab Activity, pp. 13–14
Enrichment, p. 31
Reinforcement, p. 27

Figure 16
Cormorants' feathers get wet when they go underwater to catch fish. When they return to their roost, they have to hold their wings out to dry.

Care of Feathers Your clothes can keep you warm only if they're dry and in good condition. In much the same way, feathers keep birds dry, warm, and able to fly only when the feathers are in good condition. Birds preen to reorganize their feathers and close breaks or gaps in them. For most birds, preening also makes feathers water-repellent. The bird rubs its beak or bill against an oil gland found at the base of the tail. Then, it applies the oil to its feathers. Making sure that the feathers stay water-repellent is important. Most water-soaked birds can't fly or maintain their body temperature. The cormorant, like the one in **Figure 16,** is an example of a bird that doesn't have water-repellent feathers and must air dry them.

Section Assessment

1. List four characteristics shared by all birds and a characteristic that is unique to birds.
2. Describe how a bird's skeletal system, respiratory system, and circulatory system all work together and enable a bird to fly.
3. Distinguish between contour feathers and down feathers.
4. How does the shape of a bird's wing help a bird fly?
5. **Think Critically** Explain why birds can reproduce in Antarctica when temperatures are below 0°C.

Skill Builder Activities

6. **Concept Mapping** Make a network tree concept map of birds using the following terms: *birds, adaptations for flight, air sacs, beaks, eggs, feathers, bones, wing, heart,* and *endotherm.* **For more help, refer to the** Science Skill Handbook.
7. **Using an Electronic Spreadsheet** During every 10 s of flight, a crow beats its wings 20 times, a robin 23 times, a chickadee 270 times, and a hummingbird 700 times. Use a spreadsheet to find out how many times the wings of each bird beat during a 5-min flight. **For more help, refer to the** Technology Skill Handbook.

Answers to Section Assessment

1. endothermic vertebrates, have feathers, lay and incubate eggs with a hard shell, have bills or beaks; feathers are unique to birds
2. skeletal system: hollow bones make the bird lighter; respiratory system: contains inflated air sacs to make birds lighter and provide oxygen; circulatory system: large, efficient hearts that supply blood to bird's organs
3. Contour feathers give adult birds their streamlined shape and color; down feathers trap and keep warm air next to a bird's body to provide insulation.
4. The shape of the wing provides an upward force called lift.
5. Birds are endotherms and incubate their eggs.
6. Concept maps should show a simple network tree beginning with birds, then adaptations for flight (include hollow bones, feathers, heart, maintaining a constant body temperature despite their environment, and they have air sacs). Eggs, beaks, endotherm, and wings should be on level with adaptations for flight.
7. Student spreadsheets should show: crow—600 times, robin—690 times, chickadee—8,100 times, and hummingbird—21,000 times.

Mammals

Mammal Characteristics

How many different kinds of mammals can you name? Moles, dogs, bats, dolphins, horses, and people are all mammals. They live in water and in many different climates on land. They burrow through the ground and fly through the air.

Mammals are endothermic vertebrates. They have mammary glands in their skin. In females, mammary glands produce milk that nourishes the young. A mammal's skin usually is covered with hair that insulates its body from cold and heat. It also protects the animal from wind and water. Some mammals, such as bears, are covered with thick fur. Others, like humans, have only patches of thick hair while the rest of their body is sparsely covered with hair. Still others, like the dolphins shown in **Figure 17C**, have little hair. Wool, spines, quills, and certain horns are modified hair. What function do you think quills and spines serve?

Mammary Glands Mammals put a great deal of time and energy into the care of their young, even before birth. When female mammals are pregnant, the mammary glands increase in size. After birth, milk is produced and released from these glands. For the first weeks or months of a young mammal's life, the milk provides all of the nutrition that the young mammal needs.

As You Read

What You'll Learn
- **Identify** the characteristics common to all mammals.
- **Explain** how mammals are adapted to the different environments on Earth.
- **Distinguish** among monotremes, marsupials, and placentals.

Vocabulary

herbivore	monotreme
carnivore	marsupial
omnivore	placental

Why It's Important
All mammals have similar body structures.

Figure 17
The type of hair mammals have varies from species to species.

A Porcupines have fur next to their skin but sharp quills on the outside. Quills are modified hairs.

B The long fur of a tree sloth appears to be greenish because blue-green algae grows on it.

C Dolphins do not have much hair on their bodies. A layer of fat under the skin acts as insulation.

SECTION 4 Mammals **197**

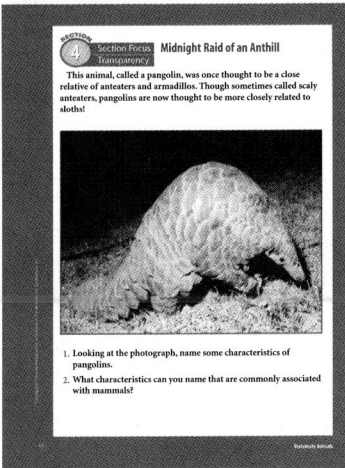

Mammal Characteristics

Figure 18 Have students draw a concept map in which they sort mammals as herbivores, carnivores, or omnivores. They should describe the teeth of each (both appearance and function) and give several examples of mammals in each group.

✔ Reading Check

Answer Herbivores eat only plants, carnivores eat only meat, and omnivores eat both plants and meat.

Mini LAB

Purpose Students model how blubber insulates. [L2]

[IS] Kinesthetic

Materials 2 self-sealing plastic bags, one-third cup of vegetable shortening, ice water

Teaching Strategy Demonstrate how to place the shortening in the self-sealing plastic bag and zip one bag inside the other. One bag will have to be turned inside out.

Analysis
1. the bare hand
2. Blubber is an insulator—it traps air and protects against cold.

✔ Assessment

Performance Have students repeat the experiment using polyester batting or wool fabric. Use **PASC**, p. 105.

Figure 18

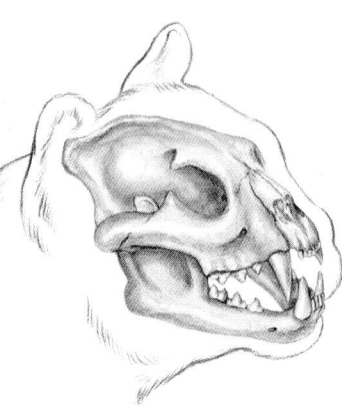

A Mountain lions are carnivores. They have sharp canines that are used to rip and tear flesh.

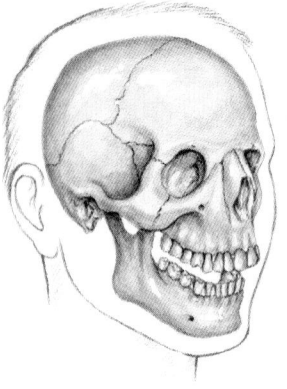

B Humans are omnivores. They have incisors that cut vegetables, premolars that are sharp enough to chew meat, and molars that grind food.

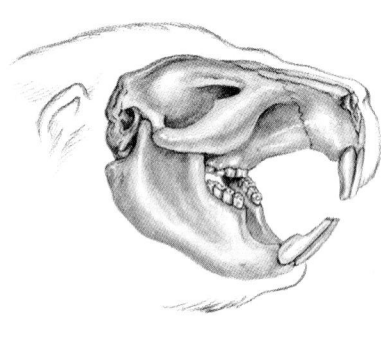

C Herbivores, like this beaver, have incisors that cut vegetation and large, flat molars that grind it.

Mini LAB

Inferring How Blubber Insulates

Procedure
1. Fill a **self-sealing plastic bag** about one-third full with solid **vegetable shortening.**
2. Turn another **self-sealing plastic bag** inside out. Place it inside the first bag so you are able to zip one bag to the other. This is a blubber mitten.
3. Put your hand in the blubber mitten. Place your mittened hand in **ice water** for 5 s. Remove the blubber mitten when finished.
4. Put your other bare hand in the same bowl of ice water for 5 s.

Analysis
1. Which hand seemed colder?
2. Infer the advantage a layer of blubber would give in the cold.

Different Teeth Mammals have teeth that are specialized for the type of food they eat. Plant-eating animals are called **herbivores.** Animals that eat meat are called **carnivores,** and animals that eat plants and animals are called **omnivores.** As shown in **Figure 18,** you usually can tell from the kind of teeth a mammal has whether it eats plants, other animals, or both. The four types of teeth are incisors, canines, premolars, and molars.

✔ Reading Check *How are herbivores, carnivores, and omnivores different?*

Body Systems Mammals live active lives. They run, swim, climb, hop, and fly. Their body systems must interact and be able to support all of these activities.

Mammals have well-developed lungs made of millions of microscopic sacs called alveoli, which enable the exchange of carbon dioxide and oxygen during breathing. They also have a complex nervous system and are able to learn and remember more than many other animals. The brain of a mammal is usually larger than the brain of other animals of the same size.

All mammals have internal fertilization. After an egg is fertilized, the developing mammal is called an embryo. Most mammal embryos develop inside a female organ called the uterus. Mammals can be divided into three groups based on how their embryos develop. The three groups of mammals are monotremes, marsupials, and placentals.

🌍 Cultural Diversity

Mammals Around the World Display a wall map of the world. Ask students to affix drawings and magazine pictures of mammals to the map to show where each mammal is commonly found. Students can visit a local zoo to take pictures of mammals to add to the map. [L2] **[IS] Visual-Spatial**

Curriculum Connection

Language Arts Ask students to make a list of expressions that draw an analogy between the behavior of a mammal and the behavior of a person. Some examples include quiet as a mouse, busy as a beaver, blind as a bat, eats like a pig, sly as a fox, and slothful. Each group of students can choose one to research and determine whether the expression is accurate. [L2] **[IS] Linguistic** [P]

Mammal Types

The duck-billed platypus, shown in **Figure 19,** along with two species of echidnas (ih KID nuhs)—spiny anteaters—belong to the smallest group of mammals called the monotremes. They are different from other mammals because **monotremes** lay eggs with tough, leathery shells instead of having live births. The female incubates the eggs for about ten days. Monotremes differ from other mammals because their mammary glands lack nipples. The milk seeps through the skin onto their fur. The young monotremes nurse by licking the milk from the fur surrounding the mammary glands. Duck-billed platypuses and spiny anteaters are found in New Guinea and Australia.

Figure 19
Duck-billed platypuses and spiny anteaters are the only species of mammals that lay eggs.

Math Skills Activity

Working with Percentages

Example Problem

It is estimated that during the four months elephant seals spend at sea, 90 percent of their time is spent underwater. On a typical day, how much of the time between the hours of 10:00 A.M. and 3:00 P.M. does the elephant seal stay at the surface?

1 *This is what you know:*   Total time: From 10:00 A.M. to 3:00 P.M. is 5 h.
1 h = 60 min, so $5 \times 60 = 300$ min
% of time on surface = $100\% - 90\% = 10\% = 0.10$

2 *This is what you need to know:*   How much time is spent on the surface?

3 *This is the equation you need to use:*   surface time = (total time)(% of time on surface)

4 *Substitute the known values:*   surface time = (300 min)(0.10) = 30 min

Check your answer by dividing your answer by the total time. Is the answer equal to 10 percent?

Practice Problems

On a typical day during those four months, how much time do elephant seals spend underwater from 9:00 A.M. until 6:00 P.M.?

For more help, refer to the Math Skill Handbook.

Curriculum Connection

Language Arts Have students work in groups of three to prepare a picture dictionary for younger children. They can use wildlife and nature magazines to cut out illustrations or they can draw pictures themselves. Have students illustrate only one mammal on a page, so that alphabetizing the names will be easy later. [L2]
COOP LEARN [IS] **Interpersonal and Visual-Spatial**

Resource Manager

Chapter Resources Booklet
Transparency Activity, p. 49
Directed Reading for Content Mastery, pp. 19, 20
Enrichment, p. 32
MiniLAB, p. 4

Mammal Types

Activity

Have students draw a mammal and label its parts, indicating the specialized adaptations that make it a mammal and help it survive. They should include information about how the mammal reproduces, what kind of skin and teeth it has, how it moves, how its lungs and heart function, and so on. [L2]
[IS] **Visual-Spatial**

Quick Demo

Arrange visits of mammals such as gerbils, rabbits, hamsters, or guinea pigs to the classroom for a day. Plan ahead to have all necessary supplies to care for them. Have students observe them carefully and write down their observations. [L2]
[IS] **Visual-Spatial and Linguistic**

Teacher FYI

Monotremes and marsupials make up only five percent of all mammals. Monotremes live in Australia and its nearby islands in various habitats.

Math Skills Activity

National Math Standards

Correlation to Mathematics Objectives
1, 4, 6, 8, 9

Answer to Practice Problem

total time = 9 hours
9 hours = 540 minutes
% of time underwater = 90% = 0.9
underwater time = (total time) $\times$ (% of time underwater)
underwater time = (540 min.) $\times$ (0.9) = 486 min. (8 hours 6 min.)

Mammal Types, continued

Discussion

What advantages do developing young marsupials have compared with developing young monotremes? They are usually protected in the female parent's pouch. Young monotremes are left alone while the parents seek food, making them more vulnerable to predators.

Answer The young marsupials finish developing in the female mammal's pouch.

IDENTIFYING Misconceptions

Students may not think of themselves as animals. To help them realize that humans are animals and are classified as mammals, list the specific characteristics of mammals on the chalkboard (*endothermic, hair, mammary glands, oil glands, sweat glands, specialized teeth, well-developed body systems*). Invite volunteers to circle each characteristic possessed by humans.

Extension

Place illustrations of the three types of mammals in the room for students to observe. Caption illustrations with simple, definitive sentences such as *monotremes lay eggs, marsupials have pouches,* and *placentals give birth to well-developed young.* L1
⓪ Visual-Spatial

Figure 20

A Marsupials are born before they are completely developed. They make the journey to a nipple that is usually in the mother's pouch where they will finish developing.

B Opossums can have up to 14 babies in a litter.

Marsupials Most **marsupials** carry their young in a pouch. Their embryos develop for only a few weeks within the uterus. When the young are born, they are without hair, blind, and not fully formed, like the ones shown in **Figure 20A.** Using their sense of smell, the young crawl toward a nipple and attach themselves to it. Here they feed and complete their development. Most marsupials—such as kangaroos, koalas, Tasmanian devils, and wallabies—live in Australia, Tasmania, and New Guinea. The opossum, shown in **Figure 20B,** is the only marsupial that lives in North America.

✔ **Reading Check** *Why do most marsupials have a pouch?*

Figure 21
Placental embryos rely on the umbilical cord to bring nutrients and to remove wastes. Your belly button is where your umbilical cord was connected to you.

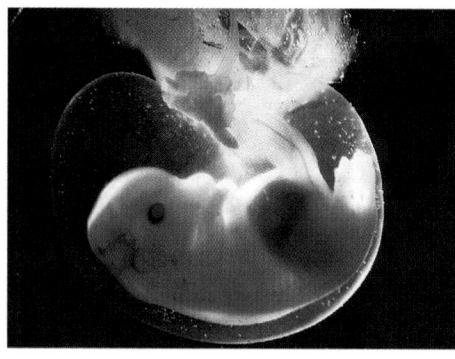

Placentals The largest number of mammals belongs to a group called placentals. **Placentals** are named for the placenta, which is a saclike organ that develops from tissues of the embryo and uterus. In the placenta food, oxygen, and wastes are exchanged between the mother's blood and the embryo's blood, but their bloods do not mix. An umbilical cord, as seen in **Figure 21,** connects the embryo to the placenta. Food and oxygen are absorbed from the mother's blood for the developing young. Blood vessels in the umbilical cord carry food and oxygen to the developing young, then take away wastes. In the placenta, the mother's blood absorbs wastes from the developing young. This time of development, from fertilization to birth, is called the gestation period. Mice and rats have a gestation period of about 21 days. Human gestation lasts about 280 days. The gestation period for elephants is about 616 days, almost two years.

200 CHAPTER 7 Vertebrate Animals

Cultural Diversity

Animal Gossip In many cultures, human interest in animals' abilities to communicate with each other and with humans has been a source of literature and legend. With the help of the school librarian, put together a collection of literature and let students investigate a story about an animal's ability to communicate. Have students retell a story that they found interesting. L2 **⓪ Linguistic**

Mammals Today

More than 4,000 species of mammals exist on Earth today. Mammals can be found on every continent, from cold arctic regions to hot deserts. Each kind of mammal has certain adaptations that enable it to live successfully within its environment.

Mammals, like all other groups of animals, have an important role in maintaining a balance in the environment. Large carnivores, such as wolves, help control populations of herbivores, such as deer and elk, thus preventing overgrazing. Bats and other small mammals such as honey possums help pollinate flowers. Other mammals unknowingly pick up plant seeds in their fur and distribute them. However, mammals and other animals are in trouble today because their habitats are being destroyed. They are left without enough food, shelter, and space to survive as millions of acres of wildlife habitat are damaged by pollution or developed for human needs. The grizzly bear, pictured in **Figure 22,** lives in North America and Europe and is an endangered species—a species in danger of becoming extinct—in most of its range because of habitat destruction.

Figure 22
Grizzly bears, sometimes called brown bears, used to range all over the western half of the United States. Now, because of human settlement, habitat loss, and overhunting, grizzly bears are found only in Alaska, Montana, Wyoming, Idaho, and Washington.

Section 4 Assessment

1. Describe five mammal characteristics and explain how they enable mammals to survive in different environments.

2. Discuss the differences among monotremes, marsupials, and placentals.

3. Why are animals in trouble today?

4. Give examples of how the teeth of mammals are specialized.

5. **Think Critically** Compare and contrast the development of embryos in placentals and marsupials.

Skill Builder Activities

6. **Researching Information** The monotremes are the smallest group of mammals. Using library resources, research to find more information about this group. **For more help, refer to the** Science Skill Handbook.

7. **Solving One-Step Equations** The tallest mammal is the giraffe at 5.6 m. Calculate your height in meters and determine how many of you it would take to be as tall as a giraffe. **For more help, refer to the** Math Skill Handbook.

Mammals Today

Discussion

Why are mammals important to people today? We get meat, milk, hides, and fur from from them; we make them into pets, use them for recreation, labor, and scientific research; they are also a critical part of the food web. They are sometimes used to help people with disabilities (i.e. guide dogs, capuchin monkeys).

 Assess

Reteach

Have students group the following characteristics under the headings *Mammals, Birds,* and *Both Mammals and Birds:* the most fully developed brains, endothermic, hollow bones, hair, feathers, shelled eggs, nurse their young, give birth to live young, extended parental care. L2

Challenge

In what ways are birds and mammals similar? Birds and mammals are endothermic vertebrates, provide extended periods of care for their young, and can live in and adapt to nearly any environment found on Earth.

✓ Assessment

Content Have students work in groups of three to write a poem or song distinguishing each of the three types of mammal. Use **PASC,** p. 151.

Answers to Section Assessment

1. All mammal characteristics allow them to adapt to most environments. They are endothermic, have hair, have mammary glands that produce milk to feed young, have teeth, have well-developed lungs, have a large brain, and reproduce sexually.

2. Monotremes lay eggs with tough leathery shells that the female incubates. Milk seeps through the skin into the fur. Marsupials carry their young in a pouch until they are fully developed. Placentals are well developed at birth. Marsupials and placentals have nippled mammary glands.

3. Wildlife habitat is being destroyed.

4. Incisors are sharp, chisel-shaped teeth used for biting and cutting food; canine teeth are used to stab, grip, and tear flesh; flat molars are used for grinding food.

5. Young marsupials are naked, blind, and not fully formed at birth. Most crawl to the pouch of the female parent and develop there. Placentals develop in the placenta of the female parent until they are fully formed.

6. Answers will vary. Accept all that are reasonable.

7. If a student is about 1.5 m tall, it would take 4 students to equal the height of a giraffe.

Activity

Recognize the Problem

Purpose

Students will determine the best environment for raising an endangered vertebrate species in captivity.

Process Skills

researching, designing and making a model, predicting, analyzing data

Time Required

45 minutes

Thinking Critically

Discussion

Tell students that they will select an endangered vertebrate species. **What groups of animals are vertebrates?** Fish, amphibians, reptiles, birds, and mammals. Ask students to name some vertebrate species they know are endangered. Possible answers: Tiger, elephants, gorilla, giant panda, manatee, California condor, whooping crane, American crocodile, leatherback turtle, tiger salamander

Teaching Strategies

- In order to make sure that no more than one group selects the same species, you may want to write a list of species from which groups can choose on the chalkboard. As each group informs you of their choice, cross that animal off the list and have remaining groups select from those still listed.

- Encourage some groups to select animals other than mammals.

Activity Model and Invent

Homes for Endangered Animals

Zoos, animal parks, and aquariums are safe places for endangered animals. Years ago, captive animals were kept in small cages or behind glass windows. The animals were on display like artwork in a museum. Now, some captive animals are kept in exhibit areas that closely resemble their natural habitats. These areas provide suitable environments for the animals so that they can reproduce, raise young, and have healthier and longer lives.

Recognize the Problem

What types of environments are best suited for raising animals in captivity?

Thinking Critically

How can endangered animals be rescued?

Goals

- ■ **Research** the natural habitat and basic needs of one endangered vertebrate species.
- ■ **Research and model** an appropriate zoo, animal park, or aquarium environment for this animal. Working cooperatively with your classmates, design an entire zoo or animal park.

Possible Materials

poster board
markers or colored pencils
materials with which to make a scale model

Data Source

SCIENCE *Online* Go to the Glencoe Science Web site at **science.glencoe.com** for more information about existing zoos, animal parks, and aquariums.

202 **CHAPTER 7** Vertebrate Animals

Inclusion Strategies

Learning Disabled Assign these students the task of locating and gathering pictures of the animal in its natural environment.

SCIENCE *Online*
Internet Addresses

_____
_____
_____
_____

Explore the Glencoe Science Web site at **science.glencoe.com** to find out more about topics in this activity.

Planning the Model

1. Choose an endangered animal to research. Find out where this animal is found in nature. What does it eat? Who are its natural predators? Does it exhibit unique territorial, courtship, or other types of social behavior? How is this animal adapted to its natural environment?

2. Why is this animal considered to be endangered.

3. **Design** a model of your proposed habitat in which this animal can live successfully.

Check the Model Plans

1. **Research** how a zoo, animal park, or aquarium provides a habitat for this animal. This information can be obtained by contacting a zoo, animal park, or aquarium.

2. **Present** your design to your class in the form of a poster, slide show, or video. Compare your proposed habitat with that of the animal's natural environment. Make sure you include a picture of your animal in its natural environment.

Making the Model

1. Using all of the information you have gathered, create a model exhibit area for your animal.

2. Indicate which other plants and animals might be present in the exhibit area.

Analyzing and Applying Results

1. **Decide** whether all of the endangered animals studied in this activity could exist in the same zoo or wildlife preserve.

2. **Predict** which animals could be grouped together in exhibit areas.

3. **Determine** how much land your zoo or wildlife preservation needs. Which animals require the largest habitat?

4. Using the information provided by all your classmates, design a zoo or wildlife preserve for the majority of endangered animals you've studied.

5. **Analyze** which type of problems might exist in your design.

Communicating
Your Data

Give an oral presentation on endangered animals and wildlife conservation to another class of students using your model. Use materials from zoos to supplement your presentation.

ACTIVITY 203

Troubleshooting

Discuss with the class how to make a scale model. Have them agree upon a scale to be used for all models so that all groups' models can be combined to make an entire zoo or animal park.

Making the Model
Expected Outcome

Most models should result in a habitat that closely resembles the animal's natural environment.

Analyzing and Applying Results

1. They probably could not all exist in the same wildlife preserve because their natural environments would be too different. They probably could all exist in the same zoo, since different areas of the zoo could be designed to match the habitats of the animals living there.

2. Predictions will depend on the animals selected. For example, elephants and rhinoceroses could be placed together, but a predator like a cheetah could not be placed with a prey animal like an antelope.

3. Answers will depend on the species included. For example, a blue whale would need a much larger saltwater tank than would a leatherback sea turtle.

4. Designs will vary depending on the animals chosen and their space and habitat requirements.

5. Answers will vary, but might include not including ponds or moats for animals' water supplies, barriers to prevent animals from escaping, or placing predators too close to prey animals.

✔ Assessment

Process Provide students with pictures of endangered species other than those chosen in the activity. Ask them to describe what they would do to determine the best environment for that species in a zoo. Use **Performance Assessment in the Science Classroom,** p. 89.

Communicating
Your Data

Students could use the Internet to find additional information about specific zoos to include in their presentations.

Content Background

Throughout Earth's history there have been about six mass extinctions. Several were more catastrophic than the mass extinction at the end of the Cretaceous Period when the dinosaurs died out.

Scientists still have many questions about the end of the Cretaceous Period. For example, the fossil record shows a sudden change in plant life at the end of the Cretaceous Period, but only in the northern hemisphere. The southern hemisphere shows a gradual pattern of change in plant life. What might have caused these differences?

There is also evidence that many marine species were in severe decline before the time of the hypothesized impact. Did this mean that a mass extinction was on its way as a result of a different and undetermined cause? Scientists do not all agree with the Alvarez hypothesis of an asteroid impact causing the dinosaurs' extinction.

Discussion

Hypothesize what allowed some species of animals and plants to survive the mass extinction 65 million years ago. Possible answers: Some species are able to adapt quickly to changes; others may be able to become dormant until conditions become more favorable.

Oops! Accidents in SCIENCE

SOMETIMES GREAT DISCOVERIES HAPPEN BY ACCIDENT!

Cosmic Dust and Dinosaurs

What killed the dinosaurs? Here is one theory.

Tiny bits of dust from comets and asteroids constantly sprinkle down on Earth. This cosmic dust, so fine it can scarcely be measured, led scientists Luis and Walter Alvarez to an Earth-shattering hypothesis about one of science's most intriguing mysteries: What caused the extinction of dinosaurs?

Their hypothesis: An asteroid collided with Earth.

Before exploring the steps that led to this idea, let's explore the mystery itself. It began some 65 million years ago when a mass extinction wiped out 60 percent of all species alive on Earth, including the dinosaurs. Scientists had long puzzled over why these species died out.

Walter Alvarez, a geologist, did not set out to solve this intriguing puzzle. He and his father, physicist and Nobel prize winner Luis Alvarez, were working together on a geology expedition in Italy. Luis Alvarez was helping his son analyze a layer of sedimentary rock. Using dating techniques, they were able to determine that this layer was deposited at roughly the same time that the dinosaurs became extinct. The younger Alvarez theorized that the rock might hold some clue to the mass extinction.

Luis (right) and Walter Alvarez— a father-son science team

204

Resources for Teachers and Students

Dinosaurs: Opposing Viewpoints, by Wendy Stein, Greenhaven Press, Inc., 1994.

The Search for the Killer Asteroid, by Gregory L. Vogt, The Millbrook Press, 1994.

"The Day the Dinosaurs Died," by Ron Cowen, *Astronomy*, April 1996.

The Alvarezes proposed that the sedimentary rock be analyzed for the presence of the element iridium. Iridium is a dense and rare metal that can be found in very low concentrations in Earth's core. At most, the two scientists expected to find a small amount of iridium. To their surprise, the sedimentary rock contained unusually high levels of iridium. What could account for this?

An asteroid, Walter Alvarez decided, was the answer. High concentrations of iridium are common in comets and asteroids. If a huge asteroid collided with Earth, its impact would send tons of dust, debris, and iridium high into the atmosphere.

For years afterward, life-giving sunlight would be blocked from the surface of the planet. Global temperatures would decrease. Most plants would die. Many animals that ate the plants would starve. In short, a mass extinction would occur. And when the dust settled, iridium would fall to the ground as evidence of the catastrophe.

The Alvarez hypothesis, published in 1980, is still debated. However, it has since been supported by other research, including the discovery of a huge, ancient crater in Mexico. Scientists theorize that this crater was formed by the impact of an asteroid as big as Mount Everest.

Did asteroids kill the dinosaurs? An artist drew this picture to show how Earth might have looked.

CONNECTIONS Write Imagine that an asteroid has impacted Earth. You are one of the few human survivors. Write a five-day journal describing the events that take place.

SCIENCE *Online*

For more information, visit science.glencoe.com

Reviewing Main Ideas

Preview

Students can answer the questions in their Science Journals. Discuss the answers as you go through the chapter. **Ⓛ Linguistic**

Review

Students can write their answers, then compare them with those of other students. **Ⓛ Interpersonal**

Reteach

Students can look at the illustrations and describe details that support the main ideas of the chapter. **Ⓛ Visual-Spatial**

Answers to Chapter Review

SECTION 1

3. cartilaginous

SECTION 3

2. swimming

SECTION 4

2. incisors, canines, premolars, and molars

Reviewing Main Ideas

Section 1 Chordate Animals

1. All chordates at some time in their development have a notochord and gill slits.

2. Endothermic animals maintain an internal body temperature. Ectothermic animals have body temperatures that change with the temperature of their surroundings.

3. The three classes of fish are jawless, cartilaginous, and bony. All fish are ectotherms. *What class of fish does the manta ray in the photo belong to?*

Section 2 Amphibians and Reptiles

1. Amphibians include frogs, toads, newts, and salamanders. They are ectothermic vertebrates that spend part of their lives in water and part on land. Most amphibians go through a metamorphosis, which includes water-living larva and land-living adult stages.

2. Reptiles include turtles, crocodiles, alligators, snakes, and lizards. They are ectothermic land animals that have dry, scaly skin.

3. Most reptiles lay eggs with a leathery shell.

Section 3 Birds

1. Birds are endotherms with feathers, and they lay eggs enclosed in hard shells. Most birds keep their eggs warm until they hatch.

2. Wings, feathers, and a light, strong skeleton are adaptations that allow birds to fly. *The penguins in the photo can't fly. What are their wings and feathers adapted for?*

Section 4 Mammals

1. Mammals are endotherms that have mammary glands. All mammals have some hair.

2. Mammals have specialized teeth that mostly determine what foods they eat. *What types of teeth do adult humans have?*

3. There are three groups of mammals. Monotremes lay eggs, and most marsupials have pouches in which embryos develop. Placentals have a placenta, and the embryos develop within the female's uterus.

4. Mammals have a variety of adaptations that allow them to live in different types of environments.

FOLDABLES Reading & Study Skills

After You Read

Look at the labels on the tabs of your Foldable. Explain why the groups of vertebrates are usually listed in this order.

FOLDABLES Reading & Study Skills

After You Read

After students have read the chapter and completed the Foldable described in Before You Read, have them do the activity on the student page.

Dinah Zike

**Chapter 7
Study Guide**

Visualizing Main Ideas

Complete the following table comparing the characteristics of fish, amphibians, and reptiles.

Vertebrate Characteristics			
Characteristic	Fish	Amphibians	Reptiles
Body Temperature	ectotherm	ectotherm	ectotherm
Body Covering	scales	skin	scales
Respiratory Organs	gills	lungs & skin	lungs
Method of Movement	fins	legs	most have legs
Fertilization	external	external	internal
Kind of Egg	lacks shell	lacks shell	amniotic

Vocabulary Review

Vocabulary Words

a. amniotic egg
b. carnivore
c. cartilage
d. chordate
e. contour feather
f. down feather
g. ectotherm
h. endotherm
i. estivation
j. herbivore
k. hibernation
l. marsupial
m. monotreme
n. omnivore
o. placental

THE PRINCETON REVIEW **Study Tip**

Without looking back at your textbook, write a summary of each section of a chapter after you've read it. If you write it in your own words, you will remember it better.

Using Vocabulary

Using complete sentences, explain how the vocabulary words in each pair listed below are alike and how they are different.

1. contour feather, down feather
2. ectotherm, endotherm
3. chordate, cartilage
4. estivation, hibernation
5. carnivore, herbivore
6. marsupial, monotreme
7. amniotic egg, monotreme
8. down feather, endotherm
9. omnivore, carnivore
10. placental, marsupial

Visualizing Main Ideas

See student page.

Vocabulary Review

Using Vocabulary

Student answers should contain the following information in complete sentences.

1. contour feather—strong, light-weight, used in flight; down feather—soft, fluffy, used to insulate
2. An ectotherm's body temperature changes with its environment; an endotherm's body temperature remains constant.
3. chordate—has a notochord and gill slits at some point in its development; cartilage—a tough flexible tissue found between vertebrae and which makes up the notochord
4. estivation—period of inactivity during hot summer months; hibernation—period of inactivity during cold winter months
5. carnivore—a meat-eating animal; herbivore—a plant-eating animal
6. monotreme—an egg-laying mammal; marsupial—a mammal that gives birth to immature offspring that develop in the female's pouch
7. An amniotic egg contains a yolk that supplies the developing embryo with food. Young monotremes develop in an amniotic egg.
8. A down feather insulates the bird's body. A bird is an endotherm with a constant body temperature.
9. An omnivore eats plants and meat; a carnivore eats only meat.
10. The young develop in the uterus of both; in marsupials, young are born prematurely and develop in the female's pouch.

Checking Concepts

1. D
2. D
3. C
4. C
5. A
6. A
7. A
8. C
9. A
10. B

Thinking Critically

11. Answers may include the fact that their skin absorbs all gases and chemicals in the area, including the poisonous ones.

12. internal fertilization for reproduction; amniotic egg; thick, dry, waterproof skin

13. Whales are insulated with large amounts of fat, called blubber.

14. It most likely has long, pointed canine teeth to stab, grip, and tear flesh. Its premolars would be sharp to cut and shred flesh.

15. The amniotic egg with its leathery shell provides a developing embryo with protection from drying out and from being eaten easily. Reptile eggs can be laid anywhere on land, thus freeing reptiles from relying on water for reproduction.

Chapter 7 Assessment

Checking Concepts

Choose the word or phrase that best answers the question.

1. Which of the following animals have fins, scales, and gills?
   A) amphibians
   C) reptiles
   B) crocodiles
   D) fish

2. What fish structure is used for steering and balancing?
   A) cartilage
   C) bone
   B) endoskeleton
   D) fin

3. Which of these is an example of a cartilaginous fish?
   A) trout
   C) shark
   B) bass
   D) goldfish

4. Which of the following has a swim bladder?
   A) shark
   C) trout
   B) lamprey
   D) skate

5. Which of the following is an adaptation that helps a bird fly?
   A) lightweight bones
   C) hard-shelled eggs
   B) webbed feet
   D) large beaks

6. Which of the following animals has skin without scales?
   A) dolphin
   C) lizard
   B) snake
   D) fish

7. Lungs and moist skin are characteristics of which of the following vertebrates?
   A) amphibians
   C) reptiles
   B) fish
   D) lizards

8. Which of these are mammals that lay eggs?
   A) carnivores
   C) monotremes
   B) marsupials
   D) placentals

9. To what group of mammals do animals with pouches belong?
   A) marsupials
   C) monotremes
   B) placentals
   D) amphibians

10. Which of the following animals eat only plant materials?
    A) carnivores
    C) omnivores
    B) herbivores
    D) endotherms

Thinking Critically

11. Give an explanation for the fact that there are fewer species of amphibians on Earth than any other type of vertebrate.

12. What important adaptation allows a reptile to live and reproduce on land while an amphibian must return to water to reproduce and complete its life cycle?

13. Whales do not have much hair. How do they stay warm in cold ocean water?

14. You observe a mammal in a field catching and eating a rabbit. What kind of teeth does this animal probably have? Explain how it uses its teeth.

15. Explain how the development of the amniotic egg led to the early success of reptiles on land.

Developing Skills

16. **Identifying and Manipulating Variables and Controls** Design an experiment to find out the effect of water temperature on frog egg development.

17. **Making and Using Graphs** Make a line graph from the data in the table to the right.

Bull Trout Population	
Year	Number per 100 m² Section
1996	4
1997	7
1998	5
1999	3
2000	4

Chapter ✓Assessment Planner

Portfolio Encourage students to place in their portfolios one or two items of what they consider to be their best work. Examples include:
- Activity, p. 183
- Activity, p. 190
- Visual Learning, p. 193
- Curriculum Connection, p. 198

Performance Additional performance assessments, Performance Task Assessment Lists, and rubrics for evaluating these activities can be found in Glencoe's **Performance Assessment in the Science Classroom.**

18. Comparing and Contrasting Compare and contrast the teeth of herbivores, carnivores, and omnivores. How is each tooth type adapted to the animal's diet?

19. Drawing Conclusions How can a bird like the arctic tern stand on ice and not lose too much body heat?

20. Concept Mapping Complete the concept map describing groups of mammals.

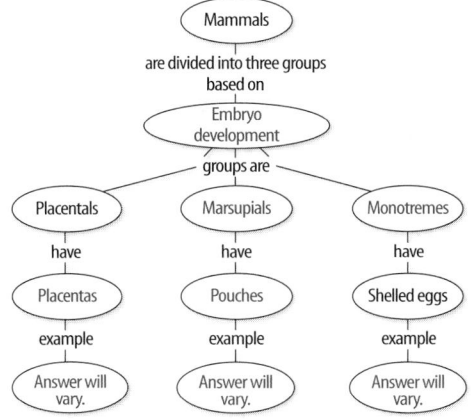

Performance Assessment

21. Debate Reptiles are often portrayed as dangerous and evil in fairy tales, folktales, and other fictional stories. Nonfiction information about reptiles presents another view. What is your opinion? Use library or online references to find evidence to support your position. Debate this issue with a classmate who has an opposing opinion.

TECHNOLOGY

Go to the Glencoe Science Web site at **science.glencoe.com** or use the **Glencoe Science CD-ROM** for additional chapter assessment.

Test Practice

Wyatt studied different types of vertebrates. He organized what he learned using the chart shown below.

Characteristics of Some Vertebrates

Animal	Characteristic
Fish	Swim under water
Amphibians	Live in water and on land
Birds	Flight
Mammals	Maintain body temperature

Use the chart to answer the following questions.

1. According to the chart, humans are adapted to _____ .
   A) swim underwater
   B) live on water and land
   C) flight
   D) maintain body temperature

2. Which characteristic do these animals have in common?
   F) maintain nearly constant body temperatures
   G) hibernate underground during the summer
   H) have hollow bones
   J) have internal skeletons

Test Practice

The Test-Taking Tip was written by The Princeton Review, the nation's leader in test preparation.
1. D
2. J

Developing Skills

16. Student designs should include a control with a set temperature and independent variables with higher and lower temperatures. The dependent variable for each will be egg development.
17. Check student graphs for accuracy.
18. herbivores: large incisors for cutting grass, molars to grind plants; carnivores: small incisors, large canine teeth to grip and tear food; omnivores: canines, incisors, and molars to feed on plants and animals
19. Arctic terns are endotherms with down feathers.
20. See student page.

Performance Assessment

21. Use Task Assessment List for Oral Presentations in **Performance Assessment in the Science Classroom**, p.143.

✔Assessment Resources

📁 Reproducible Masters

Chapter Resources Booklet
   Chapter Review, pp. 39–40
   Chapter Tests, pp. 41–44
   Assessment Transparency Activity, p. 53

Glencoe Science Web site
   Interactive Tutor
   Chapter Quizzes

Glencoe Technology
   🔖 Assessment Transparency
   💿 Interactive CD-ROM Chapter Quizzes
   💿 ExamView Pro Test Bank
   💿 Vocabulary PuzzleMaker Software
   📼 MindJogger Videoquiz

Reading Comprehension

Question 1: A

Students must read carefully the context surrounding the underlined word. The fact that *there are fewer than twenty living specimens of these plants now* implies that the species is in danger of dying out. Therefore, choice A, *death of species*, is the correct answer.

Teaching Tip

Students should number the paragraphs as they go through a reading passage.

Question 2: H

Students must identify the main idea of the second paragraph.

- **Choice F** No; this is a detail in the third paragraph.
- **Choice G** No; this is a detail from the second paragraph.
- **Choice H** Yes; this is the main idea of the information in the second paragraph.
- **Choice J** No; this is a detail from the second paragraph.

Reading Comprehension

Read the passage carefully. Then read the question that follows the passage. Decide which is the best answer to each question.

Medicine Plants

As part of his job, Paul Alan Cox, the director of the National Tropical Botanical Garden in Hawaii, leads teams of brave young people as they rappel down steep cliffs, hang from helicopters, and perform other daring feats. Are these people competing in an extreme sport? No, they are botanists, and they perform these daring acts with Cox in order to collect seeds from the nearly ninety Hawaiian plant species that are threatened with <u>extinction</u>. There are fewer than twenty living specimens of each of these plants now.

Why is Cox interested in saving plants from extinction? He knows that many plants contain medicinal, or healing, properties. For the past fifteen years, Cox has traveled all over the world to learn about the unique ways that people have been using plants to treat illnesses and to survive harsh environments. When Cox started this research, some of his colleagues thought he was throwing away his career as a scientist. Why, they wanted to know, would he be interested in what they considered nonscientific knowledge and folklore? Cox soon proved the value of his research.

Cox went to Western Samoa to record the practices of a 73-year-old woman, Epenesa Mauigoa. Epenesa gave him a detailed account of 121 herbal remedies she made from 90 different species of plants. One of those remedies she described especially caught Cox's attention. It was a preparation to fight hepatitis made from the mamala tree *Homolanthus nutans*.

The Samoan herbal remedy has since become the basis for an antiviral drug, prostratin. It is being studied as a drug to treat type 1 HIV. In 1994, a study found that there are 119 substances derived from plants in use worldwide as medicines. Cox is on the hunt to find more.

Test-Taking Tip Consider the actions of the people in the passage.

Dr. Cox holds a branch of the mamala tree from which the antiviral drug, prostratin, is obtained.

1. What is the meaning of <u>extinction</u> in the context of this passage?
   A) death of species
   B) survival
   C) ethnobotany
   D) herbal medicine

2. What is the main idea of the second paragraph?
   F) Cox discovered a preparation that could be used to fight hepatitis.
   G) Cox's colleagues thought he was throwing his career away.
   H) Cox decided to research how people use plants to treat illnesses and to survive harsh environments.
   J) Cox's colleagues thought Cox was interested in nonscientific knowledge.

Reasoning and Skills

Read each question and choose the best answer.

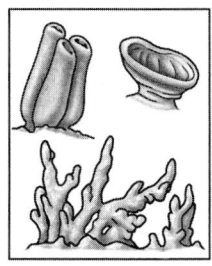 

Group A	Group B

1. The animals in Group A are different from the animals in Group B because only the animals in Group A _____.
   A) live under water
   B) reproduce asexually
   C) feed by filtering water
   D) reproduce by budding

> **Test-Taking Tip** Think about the different characteristics of sponges and cnidarians.

```
JAWLESS
CARTILAGE
SCALELESS
```

2. Which of the following animals have all of the characteristics that are listed above?
   F) shark
   G) tuna
   H) lamprey eel
   J) goldfish

> **Test-Taking Tip** Review the three classes of fish: bony, jawless, and cartilaginous.

3. Bacteria are one-celled organisms. The presence of bacteria in the human body could benefit human health by _____.
   A) decreasing the body's absorption of food
   B) decreasing the growth of other bacteria
   C) decreasing the production of vitamins
   D) increasing the rate of cell division

> **Test-Taking Tip** Consider what you know about antibiotics.

4. Protozoans are complex one-celled organisms that can feed on other organisms. The four major groups of protozoans can be classified according to _____.
   F) the presence of chlorophyll
   G) their method of locomotion
   H) the presence of food vacuoles
   J) the types of human disease they cause

> **Test-Taking Tip** Consider what you know about protozoans.

Consider this question carefully before writing your answer on a separate sheet of paper.

5. Consider what you have learned about the evolution of plants. Explain how the similarities and differences between plants and algae suggest that plants originally came from the sea. You might wish to begin by making a table that summarizes characteristics of plants and algae.

> **Test-Taking Tip** Consider the important characteristics of plants and algae before you begin writing.

Reasoning and Skills

QUESTION 1: C
Students must understand that sponges (Group A) feed passively by filtering water, whereas cnidarians (Group B) use stinging cells to capture prey.

> **Teaching Tip**
>
> Students should realize that, in questions like this one, they can eliminate the choices that both groups have in common. In this question, those would be choices A, B, and D.

QUESTION 2: H
Students must understand the characteristics of the different classes of fish.
- **Choice F** No; sharks have jaws.
- **Choice G** No; bony fishes have skeletons made of bone, not cartilage.
- **Choice H** Yes; lampreys are jawless, get support from cartilage, and have smooth skin.
- **Choice J** No; goldfish are bony fish.

QUESTION 3: B
Students need to remember how bacteria *benefit* human health.
- **Choice A** No; this does not benefit human health.
- **Choice B** Yes; this is a beneficial effect.
- **Choice C** No; some bacteria produce vitamin K in the intestine.
- **Choice D** No; this is not what students should know about bacteria.

QUESTION 4: G
Students must understand that protozoans can be classified as flagellates, amoeboids, and ciliates according to how they move.

QUESTION 5: Answers will vary.
Students should mention that plants had to adapt to survive on land. These adaptations were the result of random mutations and natural selection.

UNIT 3

Unit Contents

✔ Pre-Reading Activity

Have students find photographs or illustrations of plants and animals and speculate on the type of environment in which each lives.

UNIT 3 Life and the Environment

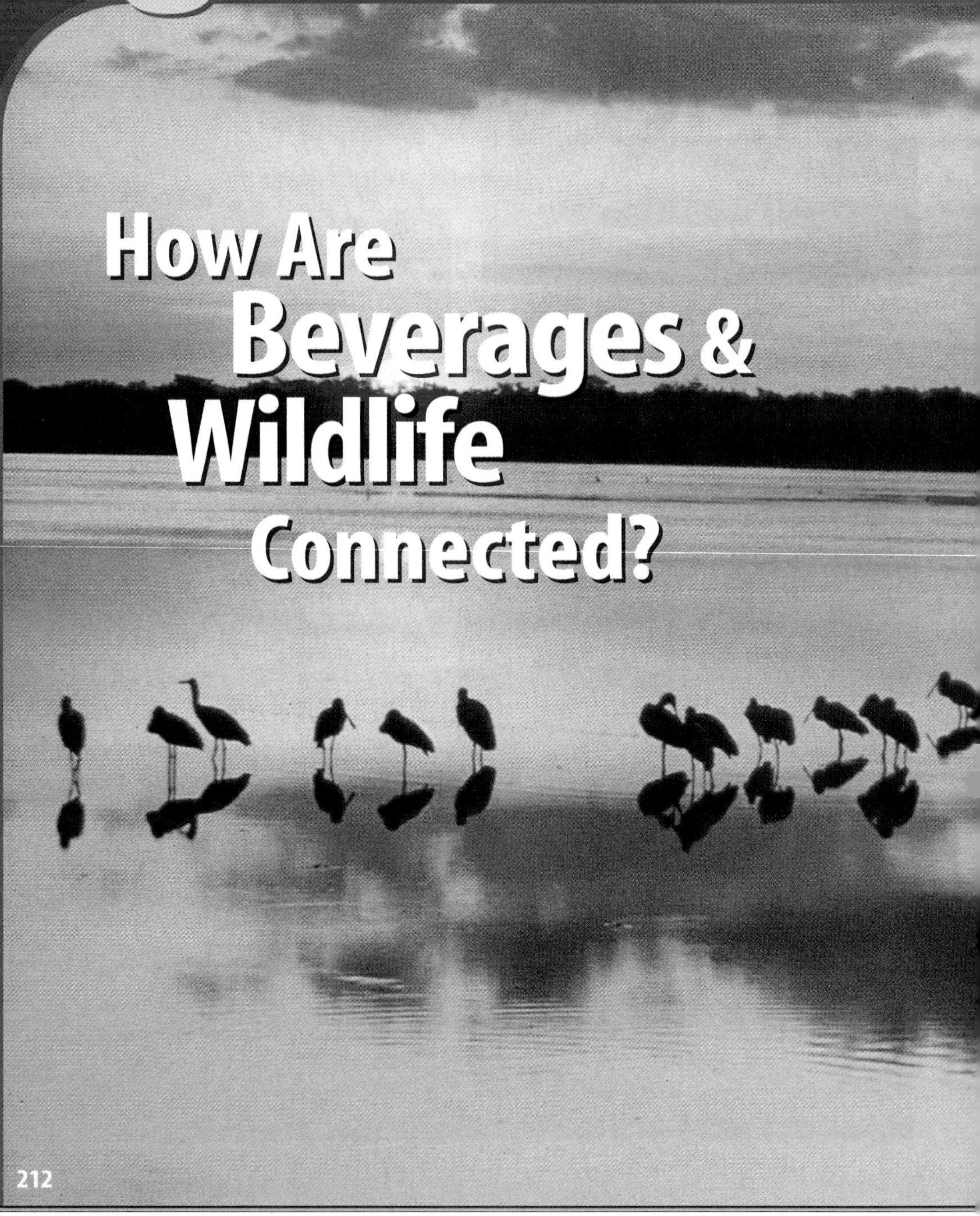

How Are Beverages & Wildlife Connected?

212

Teacher to Teacher

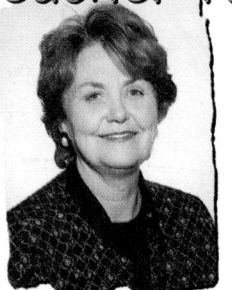

"At the beginning of our ecosystems unit, I assign each biome to a group of students. On bulletin boards, they create a 3-D mural of their biome, complete with cutouts and pictures of appropriate plants, animals, land features, climate, and so forth. The murals grow as their understanding increases."

Maureen E. Allen, Science Resource Specialist
Brywood Elementary School
Irvine, CA

In ancient times, people transported beverages in clay jars and animal skins. Around 100 BC, hand-blown glass bottles began to be used to hold liquids. In 1903, the invention of the automatic glass bottle-blowing machine made it possible to mass-produce bottles. They were used for everything from milk to soda. Consumers returned the empty bottles to be refilled. In 1929, companies began experimenting with cans for beverages. Cans were stackable, non-breakable, and fast cooling—and consumers didn't have to return them. The plastic six-pack yoke came along with the popular use of cans for beverages. This device bound cans together for easy carrying. Unfortunately, the yokes bound more than cans. Millions of yokes found their way into the environment where they entangled thousands of birds, fish, and marine animals. Today, animals are still being harmed—in some cases they are killed—by plastic six-pack yokes.

Introducing the Unit

How Are Beverages & Wildlife Connected?

The dumping of trash in the ocean was common practice for merchant and military ships until the practice was outlawed in 1988. It is uncertain how strictly the law is enforced, but it has alleviated some of the problem.

There is still a large amount of plastic debris that finds its way into the rivers and oceans. While sea animals do get caught in six-pack yokes, this is only part of the problem. Ingested plastic bags and balloons have killed sea turtles and whales because these items are indigestible. Drift nets entangle a wide array of marine animals, causing them to drown or starve.

The features that make plastics so useful also make them dangerous to animals that come across them in the wild. Plastics are durable and strong. It may take a synthetic plastic 400 years to completely disintegrate. The addition of biodegradable starches to some plastics was ineffective because it simply allowed the plastic to break into smaller pieces of plastic. Part of the problem is that ocean currents tend to concentrate floating debris in the same way they concentrate nutrients—in areas that become feeding and spawning grounds for many marine animals.

SCIENCE CONNECTION

REDUCE, REUSE, RECYCLE Look at the packaging on the things you eat, your crafts or hobbies, or the products used in your home. Work with a partner to design a more eco-friendly package for one of these products. Make a drawing of your new packaging and write a paragraph telling why your package is environmentally friendly. Share your drawings and paragraphs with your school or community through a bulletin board.

SCIENCE Online
Internet Addresses

_____

_____

_____

_____

Explore the Glencoe Science Web site at **science.glencoe.com** to find out more about topics in this unit.

SCIENCE CONNECTION
Activity

Place a large appliance box in a corner of the classroom. Request that students place the wrappers and bags from everything that they use for one week in the box. Use the resulting contents to illustrate the problem of proper disposal of packaging.

Section/Objectives	Standards		Activities/Features
Chapter Opener	**National**	**State/Local**	**Explore Activity:** Measure space, p. 215 **Before You Read,** p. 215
	See p. 6T for a Key to Standards.		
Section 1 The Environment 🕐 2 sessions 📦 1 block 1. **Identify** biotic and abiotic factors in an ecosystem. 2. **Describe** the different levels of biological organizations. 3. **Explain** how ecology and the environment are related.	National Content Standards: UCP1, A1, C1, C4, F2		**Earth Science Integration,** p. 218 **Science Online,** p. 220 **Activity:** Delicately Balanced Ecosystems, p. 222
Section 2 Interactions Among Living Organisms 🕐 2 sessions 📦 1 block 1. **Identify** the common characteristics of populations. 2. **Examine** the different types of relationships in a community. 3. **Determine** the habitat and niche of a species in a community.	National Content Standards: UCP4, A1, C4		**Science Online,** p. 224 **MiniLAB:** Observing Symbiosis, p. 226
Section 3 Matter and Energy 🕐 3 sessions 📦 1.5 blocks 1. **Explain** the difference between a food chain and a food web. 2. **Describe** how energy flows through ecosystems. 3. **Examine** how materials such as water, carbon, and nitrogen are used repeatedly.	National Content Standards: UCP2, A1, B3, C4, G1		**Visualizing a Food Chain,** p. 229 **Problem-Solving Activity,** p. 230 **Chemistry Integration,** p. 231 **MiniLAB:** Modeling the Water Cycle, p. 232 **Activity:** Identifying a Limiting Factor, p. 234 **Science and Language Arts:** The Solace of Open Spaces, p. 236

NATIONAL GEOGRAPHIC

Teacher's Corner

PRODUCTS AVAILABLE FROM GLENCOE
To order call 1-800-334-7344:
CD-ROMs
NGS Picture Show: Looking at Ecosystems
NGS Picture Show: Looking at Living Things
Poster
Water

Transparency Sets
NGS PicturePack: Looking at Ecosystems
NGS PicturePack: Looking at Living Things
Videodiscs
STV: Habitats
STV: Water

PRODUCTS AVAILABLE FROM NATIONAL GEOGRAPHIC SOCIETY
To order call 1-800-368-2728:
Videos
Ecosystem: A Struggle for Survival
Pond-Life: Food Web
Web of Life

Activity Materials	Reproducible Resources	Section Assessment	Technology
Explore Activity: meterstick	**Chapter Resources Booklet** Foldables Worksheet, p. 17 Directed Reading Overview, p. 19 Note-taking Worksheets, pp. 33–35	GLENCOE'S ASSESSMENT ADVANTAGE	

Activity: 4 large jars of equal size, clear-plastic wrap, 8 stalks of *Elodea*, garden fertilizer, 4 rubber bands, pond water, triple-beam balance, weighing paper, spoon, metric ruler	**Chapter Resources Booklet**
	Transparency Activity, p. 44
	Enrichment, p. 30
	Reinforcement, p. 27
	Directed Reading, p. 20
	Activity Worksheet, pp. 5–6
	Lab Activity, pp. 9–12
	Science Inquiry Labs, p. 7
	**Life Science Critical Thinking/
	  Problem Solving,** p. 13
	**Performance Assessment in the
	  Science Classroom,** p. 48
		Portfolio
		Curriculum Connection, p. 219
		Performance
		Skill Builder Activities, p. 221
		Content
		Section Assessment, p. 221
			Section Focus Transparency
			Interactive CD-ROM
			Guided Reading Audio
			  Program

MiniLAB: legume, plant, nonlegume plant, hand lens *Need materials?* Contact Science Kit at 1-800-828-7777 or www.sciencekit.com on the Internet.	**Chapter Resources Booklet** Transparency Activity, p. 45 MiniLAB, p. 3 Enrichment, p. 31 Reinforcement, p. 28 Directed Reading, p. 20 Lab Activity, pp. 13–15	Portfolio Curriculum Connection, p. 225 Performance MiniLAB, p. 226 Skill Builder Activities, p. 227 Content Section Assessment, p. 227	Section Focus Transparency Interactive CD-ROM Guided Reading Audio Program

MiniLAB: marker, plastic cup, water, plastic wrap, tape, rubber band
Activity: bean seeds, small planting containers, soil, water, label, trowel, aluminum foil, sunny window, refrigerator or oven
	Chapter Resources Booklet
	Transparency Activity, p. 46
	MiniLAB, p. 4
	Enrichment, p. 32
	Reinforcement, p. 29
	Directed Reading, pp. 21, 22
	Activity Worksheet, pp. 7–8
	Transparency Activity, pp. 47–48
	Lab Management and Safety
	  p. 39
		Portfolio
		Assessment , p. 233
		Performance
		MiniLAB, p. 232
		Skill Builder Activities, p. 233
		Content
		Section Assessment, p. 233
			Section Focus Transparency
			Teaching Transparency
			Interactive CD-ROM
			Guided Reading Audio
			  Program

End of Chapter Assessment

GLENCOE'S ASSESSMENT ADVANTAGE

Blackline Masters	Technology	Professional Series
Chapter Resources Booklet Chapter Review, pp. 37–38 Chapter Tests, pp. 39–42 **Standardized Test Practice by The Princeton Review,** pp. 35–38	MindJogger Videoquiz Interactive CD-ROM Vocabulary PuzzleMakers ExamView Pro Test Bank Interactive Lesson Planner Interactive Teacher Edition	Performance Assessment in the Science Classroom (PASC)

Transparencies

Section Focus

① Section Focus Transparency — The Way of the Vine

Kudzu is a vine that was introduced to the United States from Japan in 1876. In the 1930s and 1940s, kudzu was planted throughout the southeastern states as a means to control soil erosion. It turns out, however, that kudzu likes the southeast a little too much. The climate is ideal for the vine, and its natural insect pests stayed in Japan.

1. What do plants need to be healthy?
2. How is excessive kudzu growth harmful?
3. Could the original kudzu-eating insects from Japan be imported to solve this problem? Why or why not?

L2

② Section Focus Transparency — Night Lights

This photograph shows Earth at night as it is seen from space. It's not night everywhere at once, of course; the image was made specially so you could see over all of Earth at the same time. Even though it's dark, you can still identify many places because of all the electric lights.

1. What parts of Earth can you identify in this image?
2. What do you think the amount of electric lights indicates about the number of people living in an area?
3. Why are some areas more populated than others?

L2

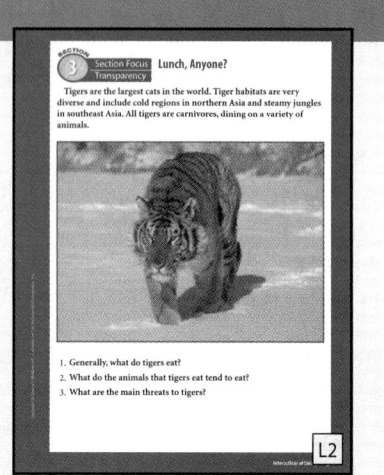

③ Section Focus Transparency — Lunch, Anyone?

Tigers are the largest cats in the world. Tiger habitats are very diverse and include cold regions in northern Asia and steamy jungles in southeast Asia. All tigers are carnivores, dining on a variety of animals.

1. Generally, what do tigers eat?
2. What do the animals that tigers tend to eat?
3. What are the main threats to tigers?

L2

This is a representation of key blackline masters available in the Teacher Classroom Resources. See Resource Manager boxes within the chapter for additional information.

Assessment

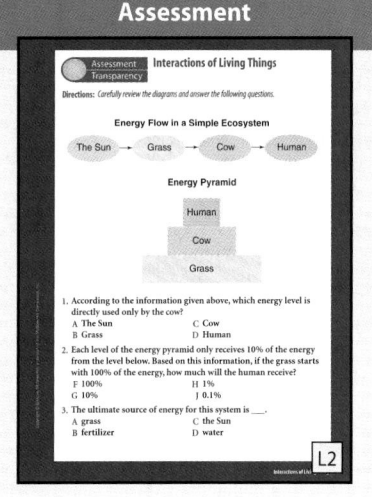

Assessment Transparency — Interactions of Living Things

Directions: Carefully review the diagrams and answer the following questions.

Energy Flow in a Simple Ecosystem

The Sun → Grass → Cow → Human

Energy Pyramid

Human
Cow
Grass

1. According to the information given above, which energy level is directly used only by the cow?
   A The Sun   C Cow
   B Grass   D Human
2. Each level of the energy pyramid only receives 10% of the energy from the level below. Based on this information, if the grass starts with 100% of the energy, how much will the human receive?
   F 100%   H 1%
   G 10%   J 0.1%
3. The ultimate source of energy for this system is ___.
   A grass   C the Sun
   B fertilizer D water

L2

Teaching

③ Teaching Transparency — Water Cycle/Carbon Cycle

Condensation Precipitation
Transpiration
Runoff
Evaporation

Plants remove carbon dioxide from the air and use it to make carbohydrates.

After the ... is returned ... atmosphere ... cycle beg...

The carbo... are eaten by other organisms...

The carbon fr... carbohydrates ... to the atmosphere through respi... combustion, ...

L2

Key to Teaching Strategies

The following designations will help you decide which activities are appropriate for your students.

L1 Level 1 activities should be appropriate for students with learning difficulties.

L2 Level 2 activities should be within the ability range of all students.

L3 Level 3 activities are designed for above-average students.

ELL ELL activities should be within the ability range of English Language Learners.

COOP LEARN Cooperative Learning activities are designed for small group work.

LS Multiple Learning Styles logos, as described on page 22T, are used throughout to indicate strategies that address different learning styles.

P These strategies represent student products that can be placed into a best-work portfolio.

Hands-on Activities

Activity Worksheets

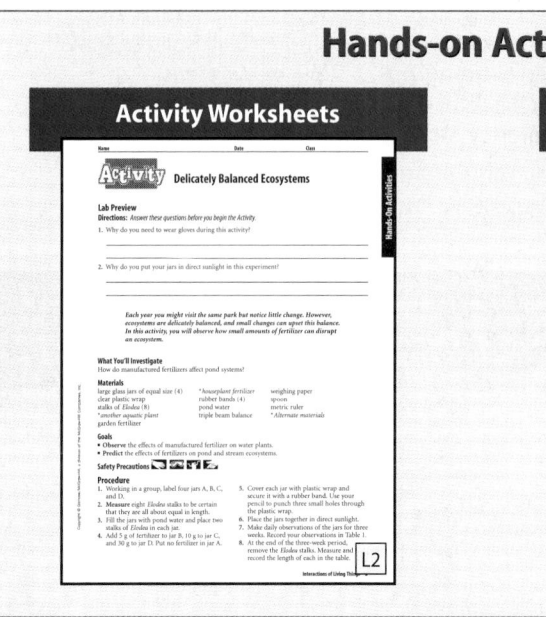

Activity — Delicately Balanced Ecosystems

Lab Preview
Directions: Answer these questions before you begin the Activity.

1. Why do you need to wear gloves during this activity?

2. Why do you put your jars in direct sunlight in this experiment?

Each year you might visit the same park but notice little change. However, ecosystems are delicately balanced, and small changes can upset this balance. In this activity, you will observe how small amounts of fertilizer can disrupt an ecosystem.

What You'll Investigate
How do manufactured fertilizers affect pond systems?

Materials
large glass jars of equal size (4)   *Aquaplant fertilizer
clear glass container   rubber bands (4)
stalks of *Elodea* (8)   pond water
*another aquatic plant   triple beam balance
garden fertilizer

Goals
• **Observe** the effects of manufactured fertilizer on water plants.
• **Predict** the effects of fertilizers on pond and stream ecosystems.

Safety Precautions 🧤

Procedure
1. Working in a group, label four jars A, B, C, and D.
2. Measure eight *Elodea* stalks to be certain that they are all about equal in length.
3. Fill the jars with pond water and place two stalks of *Elodea* in each jar.
4. Add 5 g of fertilizer to jar B, 10 g to jar C, and 30 g to jar D. Put no fertilizer in jar A.
5. Cover each jar with plastic wrap and secure it with a rubber band. Use your pencil to punch three small holes through the plastic wrap.
6. Place the jars together in direct sunlight.
7. Make daily observations of the jars for three weeks. Record your observations in Table 1.
8. At the end of the three-week period, remove the *Elodea* stalks. Measure and record the length of each in the table.

L2

Laboratory Activities

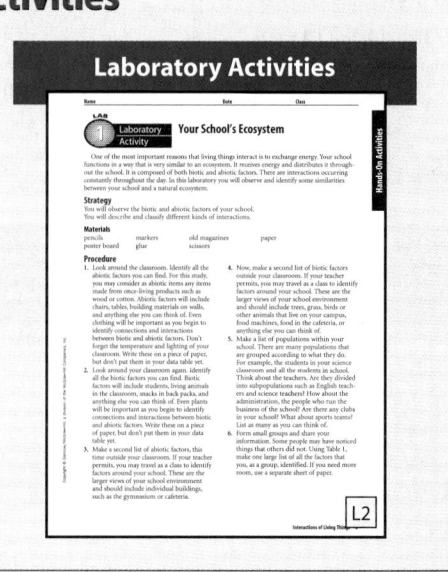

Laboratory Activity — Your School's Ecosystem

One of the most important reasons that living things interact is to exchange energy. Your school functions in a way that is very similar to an ecosystem. It receives energy and distributes it throughout the school. It is composed of both biotic and abiotic factors. There are interactions occurring constantly throughout the day. In this laboratory you will observe and identify some similarities between your school and a natural ecosystem.

Strategy
You will observe the biotic and abiotic factors of your school.
You will describe and classify different kinds of interactions.

Materials
pencils   markers   old magazines   paper
poster board   glue   scissors

Procedure
1. Look around the classroom. Identify all the biotic factors you can find. For this study, you may consider as abiotic items any items made from once-living products such as wood or cotton. Abiotic factors will include chairs, tables, building materials on walls, and anything else you can think of. Even clothing will be important as you begin to identify connections and interactions between biotic and abiotic factors. Don't forget the temperature and lighting of your classroom. Write these on a piece of paper, but don't put them in your data table set.
2. Look around your classroom again. Identify all the biotic factors you can find. Biotic factors will include students, living animals in the classroom, snacks in back packs, and anything else you can think of. Even plants will be important as you begin to identify connections and interactions between biotic and abiotic factors. Write these on a piece of paper, but don't put them in your data table set.
3. Make a second list of abiotic factors, this time outside your classroom. If your teacher permits, you may travel as a class to identify factors around your school. These are the larger views of your school environment and should include individual buildings, such as the gymnasium or cafeteria.
4. Now, make a second list of biotic factors outside your classroom. If your teacher permits, you may travel as a class to identify factors around your school. These are the larger views of your school environment and should include trees, grass, birds or other animals that live on your campus, food machines, food in the cafeteria, or anything else you can think of.
5. Make a list of populations within your school. There are many populations in your school. For example, the students in your science classroom and all the teachers in your school. Think about the teachers. Are they divided into subpopulations such as English teachers and science teachers? How about the administration, the people who run the business of the school? Are there any clubs in your school? What about sports teams? List as many as you can think of.
6. Form small groups and share your information. Some people may have noticed things that others did not. Using Table 1, make one large list of all the factors that you, as a group, identified. If you need more room, use a separate sheet of paper.

L2

Meeting Different Ability Levels

Content Outline

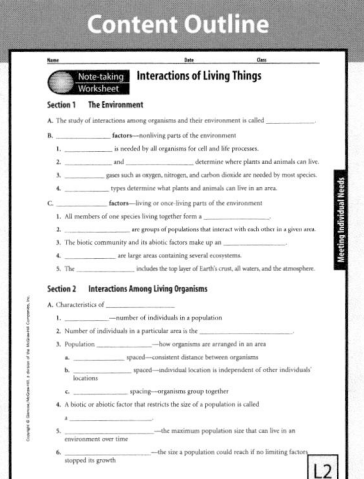

Reinforcement

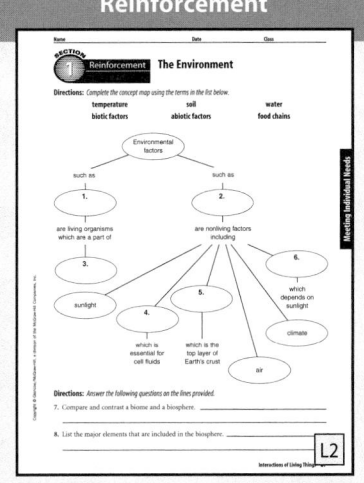

Directed Reading

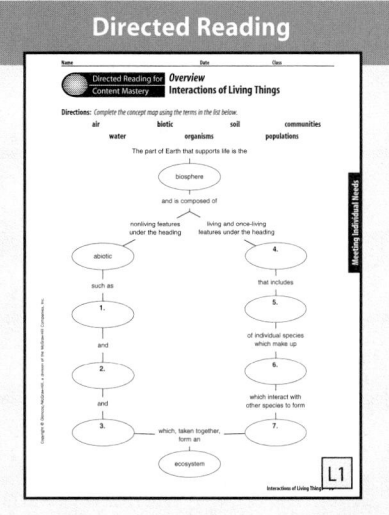

Assessment

Chapter Tests

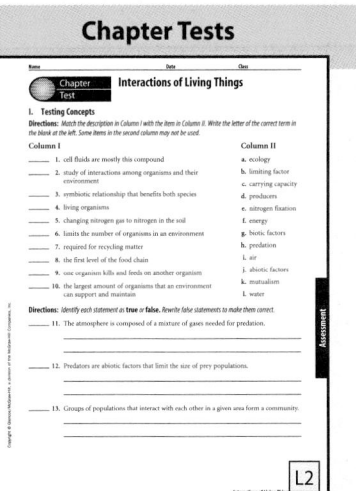

Enrichment

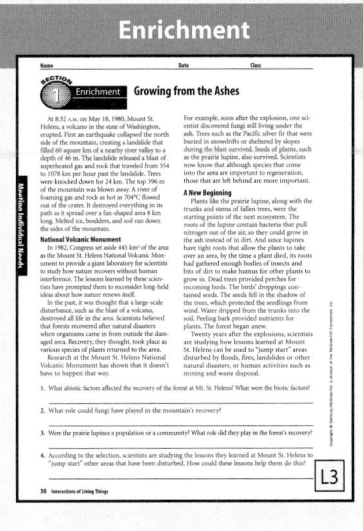

Spanish Directed Reading

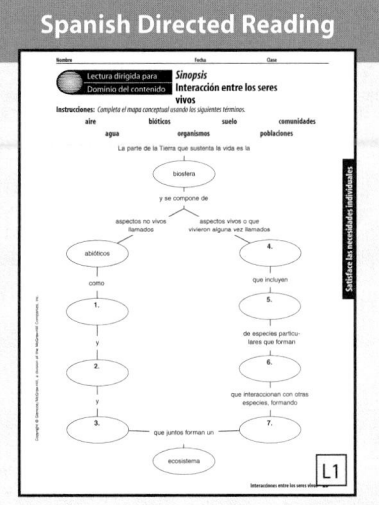

Test Practice Workbook

Chapter Review

Science Content Background

SECTION 1

Interactions of Living Things

Abiotic Factors

The interactions of biotic and abiotic factors determine what kinds of organisms live in various environments. Biotic and abiotic factors are not independent of each other. Abiotic factors include air currents, temperature, moisture, light, and soil. The importance of each factor varies from environment to environment and over time.

Soil

Soil, a mixture of humus, decayed organic matter, and particles of weathered rock, sand, silt, and clay, forms as rocks are weathered and eroded. Clay is an important component of soil because it helps hold water in the soil and contains nutrients that plants need for growth. The types of minerals found in clays are largely dependent on the climate. Humus is equally important because it helps separate clay and sand particles, allowing more water and air to enter the soil. It also provides food for soil organisms as well as nutrients for plants.

Biotic Factors

Ecologists study interactions among organisms at several different levels. They study individual organisms, interactions among organisms of the same species, and interactions among organisms of different species. They also study how abiotic factors affect groups of interacting species.

Ecological Systems

Hundreds of different systems interact within an ecosystem. An individual organism is a member and interacts with other members of the same species, or population, living in that area. Each population interacts with other populations that live in the same area, forming a community. The size of each population or community is dependent upon the availability of food, shelter, and space.

SECTION 2

Interactions Among Living Organisms

Characteristics of Populations

Population size can be difficult to measure. Animal population size can be influenced by the amount of food and space available. Natural populations cannot increase forever. Population density measures how crowded a population is and is expressed as the number of individuals per unit area or volume.

Dispersion is the spatial distribution of individuals within a population. The three patterns of dispersion are recognized: even, clumped, and random. The dispersion pattern sometimes depends on how the population is observed. Waterbirds that live near the shore may appear evenly spaced. However, if the entire island is observed, the birds may appear clumped near the water's edge.

Carrying Capacity

When a population arrives at the point at which its size is no longer increasing, it has reached the carrying capacity of the environment. The carrying capacity is the greatest number of individuals in a certain population that a given environment can support under a

> ### Fun Fact
> Mold, bacteria, beetles, centipedes, and worms are all busy recyclers. Without their help, dead plants and animals would just keep piling up. These decomposers break down the residue into rich soil for new plants to grow.

SCIENCE Online

For additional content background on this topic, go to the Glencoe Science Web site at science.glencoe.com.

specific set of conditions. The carrying capacity may vary with the time of the year, as conditions change. At carrying capacity the number of organisms born or produced in a given period of time balances the number of organisms that die during that same time. When this happens, the size of the population remains fairly stable.

SECTION 3 Matter and Energy

Energy Flow Through Ecosystems

The flow of energy through ecosystems is illustrated by food chains, food webs, ecological pyramids, and energy pyramids.

Food Chains

Food chains illustrate how energy flows from organism to organism in a community. The main parts of a food chain are the Sun, producers, consumers, and decomposers. The Sun produces energy used by living beings. Producers are green plants, protists, and bacteria that make their own food. A producer is the first step in the food chain. Decomposers are bacteria, fungi, and other organisms that break down dead organisms. They release carbon and nitrogen into the environment.

Food Webs

The feeding relationships among organisms in a community are called a food web, which illustrates energy flow. A food web is made up of interconnected food chains.

Steve Kaufman/DRK Photo

Interactions of Living Things

Chapter Vocabulary

What do you think?

Science Journal The photo shows a euphausiid shrimp, commonly known as krill. These tiny (less than 1 cm) animals cluster together in great clouds and are fed upon by everything from huge whales, to seabirds, to salmon.

CHAPTER 8

Interactions of Living Things

How do Alaskan brown bears and salmon interact? The relationship between these two species is clear to see. However, the Alaskan brown bear also depends on every species of insect and fish that the salmon eats, and many nonliving parts of the environment, too. In this chapter, you will learn how all living things depend on the living and nonliving factors in the environment for survival.

What do you think?

Science Journal Look at the picture below with a classmate. Discuss what you think this might be. Here's a hint: *This species and salmon interact.* Write your answer or best guess in your Science Journal.

214

Theme Connection

Systems and Interactions In learning about relationships among living and nonliving things in populations, communities, and ecosystems, students will discover how all living and nonliving things on Earth are connected.

I magine that you are in a crowded elevator. Every-one jostles and bumps each other. The temperature increases and ordinary noises seem louder. What a relief you feel when the doors open and you step out. Like people in an elevator, plants and animals in an area interact. How does the amount of space available to each organism affect its interaction with other organisms?

Measure space

1. Use a meterstick to measure the length and width of the classroom.

2. Multiply the length by the width to find the area of the room in square meters.

3. Count the number of individuals in your class. Divide the area of the classroom by the number of individuals. In your Science Journal, record how much space each person has.

Observe

Write a prediction in your Science Journal about what might happen if the number of students in your classroom doubled.

Before You Read

FOLDABLES
Reading & Study Skills

Making a Cause and Effect Study Fold Make this Foldable to help you understand the cause and effect relationship of biotic and abiotic things.

1. Place a sheet of paper in front of you so the long side is at the top. Fold the paper in half from the left side to the right side. Fold top to bottom and crease. Then unfold.

2. Through the top thickness of paper, cut along the middle fold line to form two tabs as shown. Label the tabs *Biotic*, which means living, and *Abiotic*, which means nonliving, as shown.

3. Before you read the chapter, list examples of biotic and abiotic things around you on the tabs. As you read, write about each under the tabs.

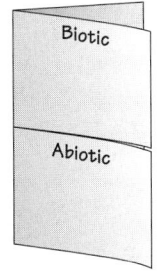
Biotic

Abiotic

215

EXPLORE ACTIVITY

Purpose Use the Explore Activity to give students firsthand experience in determining population density. L2 ELL COOP LEARN
LS Logical-Mathematical
Preparation Pair students to work together.
Materials meterstick
Teaching Strategy One student can measure and the other can record. They can find the answers to the questions together.

Observe

If the student population is 30 and the classroom size is 240 m^2, then each student would have 8 m^2. If the number of students in the classroom is doubled, each person would have only 4 m^2. To calculate population density, divide the number of individuals in a population by the area to get individuals per unit area. In this case, the population density would be:

30 students/240 m^2 = 0.125 students per m^2

Assessment

Performance Provide students with the total number of students and staff in the school and the area of the school building. Have them calculate the population density. Use **Performance Assessment in the Science Classroom,** p. 101.

Before You Read

FOLDABLES
Reading & Study Skills

Dinah Zike Study Fold

Purpose Students should make and use a Foldable to examine the biotic and abiotic factors in an environment. Students can use this information to examine common cause-and-effect relationships between biotic and abiotic factors.

📁 For additional help, see Foldables Worksheet, p. 17 in **Chapter Resources Booklet,** or go to the Glencoe Science Web site at **science.glencoe.com.** See After You Read in the Study Guide at the end of this chapter.

SECTION

The Environment

1 Motivate

Bellringer Transparency

Display the Section Focus Transparency for Section 1. Use the accompanying Transparency Activity Master. L2

ELL

Section Focus Transparency

The Way of the Vine

Kudzu is a vine that was introduced to the United States from Japan in 1876. In the 1930s and 1940s, kudzu was planted throughout the southeastern states as a means to control soil erosion. It turns out, however, that kudzu likes the southeast a little too much. The climate is ideal for the vine, and its natural insect pests stayed in Japan.

1. What do plants need to be healthy?
2. How is excessive kudzu growth harmful?
3. Could the original kudzu-eating insects from Japan be imported to solve this problem? Why or why not?

Tie to Prior Knowledge

Ask students to name organisms from their own environment. Ask how these organisms interact in their environment.

The Environment

As You Read

What You'll Learn

- **Identify** biotic and abiotic factors in an ecosystem.
- **Describe** the different levels of biological organization.
- **Explain** how ecology and the environment are related.

Vocabulary

ecology
abiotic factor
biotic factor
population

community
ecosystem
biosphere

Why It's Important

Abiotic and biotic factors interact to make up your ecosystem. The quality of your ecosystem can affect your health. Your actions can affect the health of the ecosystem.

Ecology

All organisms, from the smallest bacteria to a blue whale, interact with their environment. **Ecology** is the study of the interactions among organisms and their environment. Ecologists, such as the one in **Figure 1,** are scientists who study these relationships. Ecologists divide the environmental factors that influence organisms into two groups. **Abiotic** (ay bi AH tihk) **factors** are the nonliving parts of the environment. Living or once-living organisms in the environment are called **biotic** (bi AH tihk) **factors.**

✔ Reading Check *Why is a rotting log considered a biotic factor in the environment?*

Abiotic Factors

In a forest environment, birds, insects, and other living things depend on one another for food and shelter. They also depend on the abiotic factors that surround them, such as water, sunlight, temperature, air, and soil. All of these factors and others are important in determining which organisms are able to live in a particular environment.

Figure 1
Ecologists study biotic and abiotic factors in an environment and the relationships among them. Many times, ecologists must travel to specific environments to examine the organisms that live there.

Section ✔ *Assessment* Planner

PORTFOLIO
Curriculum Connection, p. 219

PERFORMANCE ASSESSMENT
Skill Builder Activities, p. 221
See page 240 for more options.

CONTENT ASSESSMENT
Section, p. 221
Challenge, p. 221
Chapter, pp. 240–241

The seas and oceans are home to thousands of different species.

This stream is a freshwater environment. It is home to many species of plants and animals.

Water All living organisms need water to survive. The bodies of most organisms are 50 percent to 95 percent water. Water is an important part of the cytoplasm in cells and the fluid that surrounds cells. Respiration, photosynthesis, digestion, and other important life processes can only occur in the presence of water.

More than 95 percent of Earth's surface water is found in the oceans. The saltwater environment in the oceans is home to a vast number of species. Freshwater environments, like the one in **Figure 2,** also support thousands of types of organisms.

Light and Temperature The abiotic factors of light and temperature also affect the environment. The availability of sunlight is a major factor in determining where green plants and other photosynthetic organisms live, as shown in **Figure 3.** By the process of photosynthesis, energy from the Sun is changed into chemical energy that is used for life processes. Most green algae live near the water's surface where sunlight can penetrate. On the other hand, little sunlight reaches the forest floor, so very few plants grow close to the forest floor.

The temperature of a region also determines which plants and animals can live there. Some areas of the world have a fairly consistent temperature year round, but other areas have seasons during which temperatures vary. Water environments throughout the world also have widely varied temperatures. Plant and animal species are found in the freezing cold Arctic, in the extremely hot water near ocean vents, and at almost every temperature in between.

Figure 2
Salt water accounts for 97 percent of the water on Earth. It is found in the seas and oceans. Only three percent of Earth's water is freshwater.

Figure 3
Flowers that grow on the forest floor, such as these bluebells, grow during the spring when they receive the most sunlight.

SECTION 1 The Environment **217**

Teacher FYI

Biotic factors affect abiotic factors. The trees in a rain forest hold the topsoil with their roots and shade the soil with their leaves; fallen leaves return organic matter to the soil; and leaves return water to the atmosphere by evaporation and transpiration. Trees, therefore, influence soil composition, temperature, and humidity.

---

2 Teach

Ecology

✔ **Reading Check**

Answer It was once living.

Use Science Words

Word Origin Have students look up *ecology* in the dictionary and write its definition, based on its two parts, *oikos*, meaning "house," and *-logy*, meaning "the study of." Ecology is the study of where we live. L2 IS **Linguistic**

Discussion

What happens to plants when rainfall in an area changes from season to season? During times of little rainfall, plants are smaller and fewer and may die. New plants come back when it rains again.

Abiotic Factors

Quick Demo

Show students an aquarium with live fish and aquatic plants. **What nonliving things influence a fish's life?** water quality, temperature, light, the presence of oxygen **What living things influence the life of a fish?** plants, bacteria, other fish, snails

Discussion

Which abiotic factors relate to climate? temperature, wind, soil, light, water

Use Science Words

Word Meaning Write *biosphere*, *biotic*, and *abiotic* on the board. Ask students to find the meanings of their parts in the dictionary. *bio:* "life;" *sphere:* "area;" and *-tic:* "relating to" L2 IS **Linguistic**

Abiotic Factors, continued

Activity

Have students make a list of the ways humans have changed the environment through pollution. Students may list thermal pollution by heating waters, water pollution by disposing of detergents and fertilizers, air pollution by acid rain and smog, and the ozone hole from release of CFCs. Ask students to list organisms that have been affected by these changes and then discuss changes that have occurred in their neighborhood. L2

Earth Science
INTEGRATION

Possible answer: Sonora desert

✔ Reading Check

Answer Only species that can tolerate air pollution remain. Some species may die out and others may move out of the area.

Discussion

Why is topsoil fertile? It contains humus, which is made up of the decayed remains of organisms.

Biotic Factors

Fun Fact

Earth can be thought of as four spheres—the lithosphere, or land; the hydrosphere, or water; the atmosphere, or gases that surround Earth; and the biosphere, or parts of the other spheres that can support life.

Figure 4
Air pollution can come from many different sources. Air quality in an area affects the health and survival of the species that live there.

Earth Science
INTEGRATION

When soil that receives little rain is damaged, a desert can form. This process is called desertification. Use reference materials to find where desertification is occurring in the United States. Record your findings in your Science Journal.

Figure 5
Soil provides a home for many species of animals.

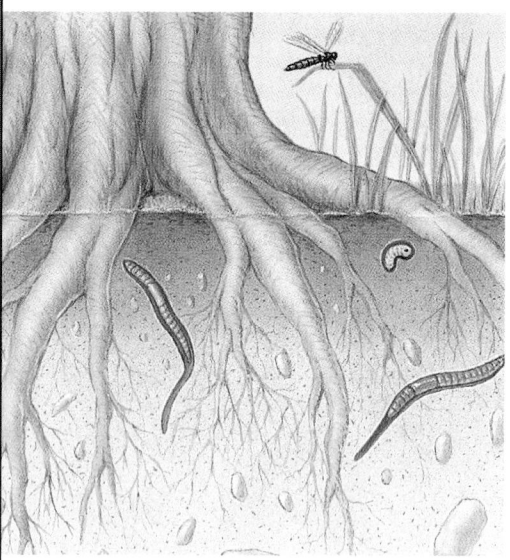

Air Although you can't see the air that surrounds you, it has an impact on the lives of most species. Air is composed of a mixture of gases including nitrogen, oxygen, and carbon dioxide. Most plants and animals depend on the gases in air for respiration. The atmosphere is the layer of gases and airborne particles that surrounds Earth. Polluted air, like the air in **Figure 4,** can cause the species in an area to change, move, or die off.

Clouds and weather occur in the bottom 8 km to 16 km of the atmosphere. All species are affected by the weather in the area where they live. The ozone layer is 20 km to 50 km above Earth's surface and protects organisms from harmful radiation from the Sun. Air pressure, which is the weight of air pressing down on Earth, changes depending on altitude. Higher altitudes have less air pressure. Few organisms live at extreme air pressures.

✔ Reading Check
How does air pollution affect the species in an area?

Soil From one enviroment to another, soil, as shown in **Figure 5,** can vary greatly. Soil type is determined by the amounts of sand, silt, and clay it contains. Various kinds of soil contain different amounts of nutrients, minerals, and moisture. Different plants need different kinds of soil. Because the types of plants in an area help determine which other organisms can survive in that area, soil affects every organism in an environment.

Biotic Factors

Abiotic factors do not provide everything an organism needs for survival. Organisms depend on other organisms for food, shelter, protection, and reproduction. How organisms interact with one another and with abiotic factors can be described in an organized way.

Inclusion Strategies

Learning Disabled Provide photographs from magazines to students who may require reinforcement of the concepts of biotic and abiotic factors. Ask students to identify all the biotic factors in each photograph and explain why they identified these factors as biotic. L1 **ELL**
IS **Visual-Spatial**

Science Journal

Area Survey Ask students to observe the natural environment of the area in which they live, and make a table in their Science Journal in which they list the biotic and abiotic factors of their area. Have them summarize the importance of the biotic factors listed in their tables. Then have students summarize the importance of the abiotic factors. L2 **IS** **Linguistic**

Levels of Organization The living world is highly organized. Atoms are arranged into molecules, which in turn are organized into cells. Cells form tissues, tissues form organs, and organs form organ systems. Together, organ systems form organisms. Biotic and abiotic factors also can be arranged into levels of biological organization, as shown in **Figure 6.**

Figure 6
The living world is organized in levels.

A **Organism** An organism is one individual from a population.

B **Population** All of the individuals of one species that live in the same area at the same time make up a population.

C **Community** The populations of different species that interact in some way are called a community.

D **Ecosystem** All of the communities in an area and the abiotic factors that affect them make up an ecosystem.

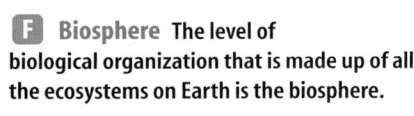

E **Biome** A biome is a large region with plants and animals well adapted to the soil and climate of the region.

F **Biosphere** The level of biological organization that is made up of all the ecosystems on Earth is the biosphere.

SECTION 1 The Environment **219**

Resource Manager

Chapter Resources Booklet
Lab Activity, pp. 9–12

Life Science Critical Thinking/Problem Solving, p. 13

Curriculum Connection

Art Have students create a visual illustrating the levels of organization within the biosphere. Have them include all applicable vocabulary words in their visual. L2 **Visual-Spatial and Kinesthetic** P

Visual Learning

Figure 6 Have student groups create a concept map showing the differences among organisms, populations, communities, ecosystems, and biomes. Make sure students include abiotic factors and their role.

Figure 6B Have students identify other populations. Possible answers: oak trees and grasses L2
COOP LEARN **Interpersonal**

IDENTIFYING
Misconceptions

Students may think that the location of a particular biome on Earth is permanent, not realizing that a change in climate would cause the biome to change. To help students understand that biomes and climate change over time, explain that evidence suggests that Earth's average temperature has increased over the past century. Ask them to speculate how a global temperature increase would affect climates and biomes.

Teacher FYI

The exponential model of population growth describes a population that increases rapidly after only a few generations. The larger a population gets, the faster it grows. This is called exponential growth. The logistic model of population growth builds on the exponential model but accounts for the influence of limiting factors.

Biotic Factors,
continued

Discussion

What factors distinguish one biome from another? precipitation, temperature, plant and animal life

SCIENCE *Online*
Internet Addresses

_____
_____
_____
_____

Explore the Glencoe Science Web site at **science.glencoe.com** to find out more about topics in this section.

Figure 7
Members of a penguin population compete for resources.

SCIENCE *Online*

Research Visit the Glencoe Science Web site at **science.glencoe.com** for more information about Earth's biomes. Make a poster to communicate to your class what you learn.

Populations All the members of one species that live together make up a **population.** For example, all of the catfish living in a lake at the same time make up a population. Part of a population of penguins is shown in **Figure 7.** Members of a population compete for food, water, mates, and space. The resources of the environment and the ways the organisms use these resources determine how large a population can become.

Communities Most populations of organisms do not live alone. They live and interact with populations of other types of organisms. Groups of populations that interact with each other in a given area form a **community**. For example, a population of penguins and all of the species that they interact with form a community. Populations of organisms in a community depend on each other for food, shelter, and other needs.

Ecosystem In addition to interactions among populations, ecologists also study interactions among populations and their physical surroundings. An **ecosystem** like the one in **Figure 8A** is made up of a biotic community and the abiotic factors that affect it. Examples of ecosystems include coral reefs, forests, and ponds. You will learn more about the interactions that occur in ecosystems later in this chapter.

Biomes Scientists divide Earth into different regions called biomes. A biome (BI ohm) is a large region with plant and animal groups that are well adapted to the soil and climate of the region. Many different ecosystems are found in a biome. Examples of biomes include mountains, as shown in **Figure 8B,** tropical rain forests, and tundra.

Figure 8
Biomes contain many different ecosystems. **A** This mountaintop ecosystem is part of the **B** mountain biome.

Cultural **Diversity**

Eco-Sensitivity Some changes can help maintain an ecosystem. Fires help maintain a prairie by eliminating trees. Native Americans understood the importance of controlled fires and were successful in maintaining prairies by setting fires as needed. Life was abundant and diverse on the prairie until the early settlers came and disturbed the balance of nature.

Resource Manager

Chapter Resources Booklet
   Enrichment, p. 30
   Reinforcement, p. 27
Science Inquiry Labs, p. 7

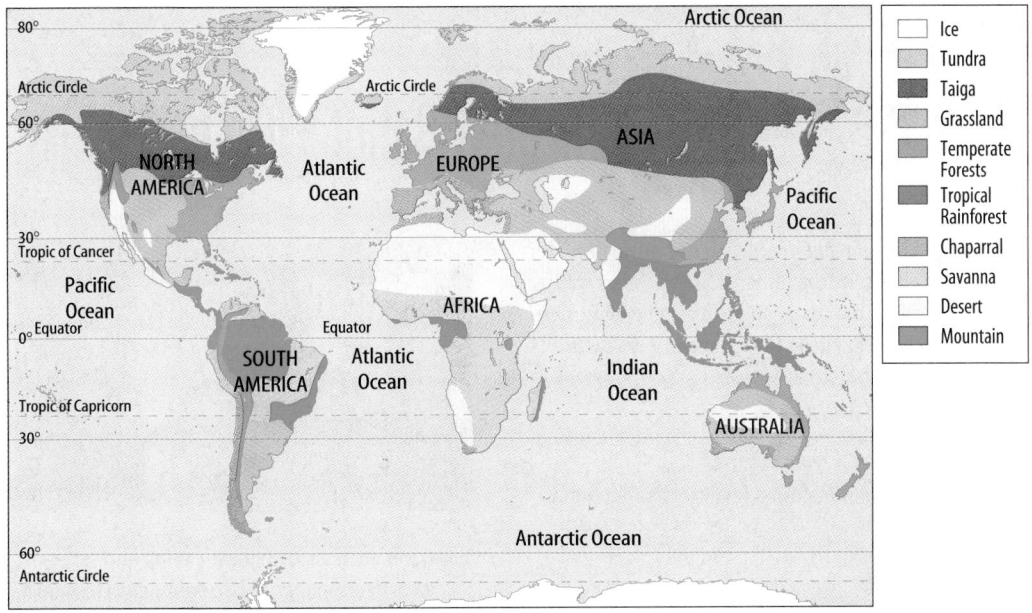

80° Arctic Ocean

Arctic Circle
60°

NORTH
AMERICA   Atlantic   EUROPE   ASIA
               Ocean

Arctic Circle

Pacific
Ocean

30°
Tropic of Cancer

Pacific
Ocean   AFRICA

0° Equator   Equator

SOUTH   Atlantic   Indian
AMERICA   Ocean   Ocean

Tropic of Capricorn

30°   AUSTRALIA

Antarctic Ocean

60°
Antarctic Circle

	Ice
	Tundra
	Taiga
	Grassland
	Temperate Forests
	Tropical Rainforest
	Chaparral
	Savanna
	Desert
	Mountain

The Biosphere Where do all of Earth's organisms live? Living things can be found 11,000 m below the surface of the ocean and on mountains as high as 9,000 m. The part of Earth that supports life is the **biosphere** (BI uh sfihr). The biosphere includes the top part of Earth's crust, all the waters that cover Earth's surface, the surrounding atmosphere and all biomes, as shown in **Figure 9.** The biosphere seems huge, but it is only a small part of Earth. If you used an apple as a model of Earth, the thickness of Earth's biosphere could be compared to the thickness of the apple's skin.

Figure 9
This map shows some of the major biomes of the world. *What biome do you live in?*

 Assess

Reteach

Have students write paragraphs in their Science Journals explaining the relationships among population, community, and ecosystem then share their paragraphs in small groups. Emphasize that populations interact to make a community and that communities and non-living things make up an ecosystem. L1 IS Linguistic

Challenge

What happens to vegetation when rainfall amounts gradually decrease over centuries? Plant species either adapt or they die out. New plant species may enter the area. The ecosystem may change from forest to grassland to desert over time.

✔Assessment

Portfolio Have students cut out magazine pictures that illustrate soil formation, and make a poster using the pictures. Be sure they include all stages. Use **PASC,** p. 145.

Section 1 Assessment

1. What is the difference between an abiotic factor and a biotic factor? Give five examples of each that are in your ecosystem.
2. Contrast a population and a community.
3. What is an ecosystem?
4. How are the terms *ecology* and *environment* related?
5. **Think Critically** Explain how biotic factors change in an ecosystem that has flooded.

Skill Builder Activities

6. **Recording Observations** Each person lives in a population as part of a community. Describe your population and community. **For more help, refer to the** Science Skill Handbook.
7. **Using a Database** Use a database to research biomes. Find the name of the biome that best describes where you live. **For more help, refer to the** Technology Skill Handbook.

Answers to Section Assessment

1. Biotic factors are living. Abiotic factors are nonliving. Biotic factors are bacteria, protists, fungi, plants, and animals; abiotic factors include soil, temperature, light, water, and wind.
2. A population is all the organisms of one species living together in the same place at the same time. A community is made up of groups of populations.

3. all of the communities in an area and the abiotic factors that affect them
4. Ecology is the study of the interactions among organisms and their environment.
5. Organisms that do not live in water would die. Other water organisms might move into the ecosystem.

6. A student's population includes the human beings in the area where he or she lives. A student's community includes all other living organisms in the area where he or she lives.
7. Answers will vary.

Activity

BENCH TESTED

Purpose Students will observe the effects of various artificial fertilizers on the organisms comprising a pond ecosystem.

L2 | IN | **Kinesthetic**

Process Skills observing, predicting, comparing, and inferring

Time Required 40 minutes; 5 minutes daily observation for three weeks; 40 minutes observation at end

Teaching Strategies

• This activity works best in the early fall or late spring.

• Have guidebooks to pond life available for students during their microscope observation period.

Troubleshooting Be certain students check the water levels in the jars daily and refill evaporated water with fresh pond water.

Answers to Questions

1. control: Jar A (no fertilizer); variables: amount of fertilizer added to Jars B, C, and D

2. Jars B and C should have shown more *Elodea* growth than Jar A. Jar D likely suffered from eutrophication, causing the *Elodea* to die off.

3. Possible answer: The slow addition of fertilizer may make the *Elodea* grow at a steady rate.

✔Assessment

Portfolio Ask students to draw diagrams of the organisms they find in their pond ecosystems. Use **PASC**, p. 127.

Activity
Delicately Balanced Ecosystems

Each year you might visit the same park, but notice little change. However, ecosystems are delicately balanced, and small changes can upset this balance. In this activity, you will observe how small amounts of fertilizer can disrupt an ecosystem.

What You'll Investigate
How do manufactured fertilizers affect pond systems?

Materials
large glass jars of   rubber bands (4)
  equal size (4)   pond water
clear plastic wrap   triple beam balance
stalks of *Elodea* (8)   weighing paper
*another aquatic plant   spoon
garden fertilizer   metric ruler
*houseplant fertilizer   *Alternate materials

Goals
■ **Observe** the effects of manufactured fertilizer on water plants.
■ **Predict** the effects of fertilizers on pond and stream ecosystems.

Safety Precautions

Procedure

1. Working in a group, label four jars A, B, C, and D.

2. **Measure** eight *Elodea* stalks to be certain that they are all about equal in length.

3. Fill the jars with pond water and place two stalks of *Elodea* in each jar.

4. Add 5 g of fertilizer to jar B, 10 g to jar C, and 30 g to jar D. Put no fertilizer in jar A.

222   CHAPTER 8 Interactions of Living Things

---

5. Cover each jar with plastic wrap and secure it with a rubber band. Use your pencil to punch three small holes through the plastic wrap.

6. Place all jars in a well-lit area.

7. Make daily observations of the jars for three weeks. Record your observations in your Science Journal.

8. At the end of the three-week period, remove the *Elodea* stalks. Measure and record the length of each in your Science Journal.

Conclude and Apply

1. **List** the control and variables you used in this experiment.

2. **Compare** the growth of *Elodea* in each jar.

3. **Predict** what might happen to jar A if you added 5 g of fertilizer to it each week.

Communicating
Your Data

Compare your results with the results of other students. Research how fertilizer runoff from farms and lawns has affected aquatic ecosystems in your area. **For more help, refer to the** Science Skill Handbook.

Communicating
Your Data

Make a data table on the board to record each group's final *Elodea* lengths for the different jars. This will be a good way to quickly compare student results.

Resource Manager

Chapter Resources Booklet
  Activity Worksheet, pp. 5–6

Performance Assessment in the Science Classroom, p. 48

---

2 Interactions Among Living Organisms

Characteristics of Populations

You, the person sitting next to you, everyone in your class, and every other organism on Earth is a member of a specific population. Populations can be described by their characteristics such as spacing and density.

Population Size The number of individuals in the population is the population's size, as shown in **Figure 10.** Population size can be difficult to measure. If a population is small and made up of organisms that do not move, the size can be determined by counting the individuals. Usually individuals are too widespread or move around too much to be counted. The population size then is estimated. The number of organisms of one species in a small section is counted and this value is used to estimate the population of the larger area.

Suppose you spent several months observing a population of field mice that live in a pasture. You probably would observe changes in the size of the population. Older mice die. Mice are born. Some are eaten by predators, and some mice wander away to new nests. The size of a population is always changing. The rate of change in population size varies from population to population. In contrast to a mouse population, the number of pine trees in a mature forest changes slowly, but a forest fire could reduce the pine tree population quickly.

As You Read

***What* You'll Learn**
■ **Identify** the characteristics that describe populations.
■ **Examine** the different types of relationships that occur among populations in a community.
■ **Determine** the habitat and niche of a species in a community.

Vocabulary
population density   niche
limiting factor   habitat
symbiosis

***Why* It's Important**
You must interact with other organisms to survive.

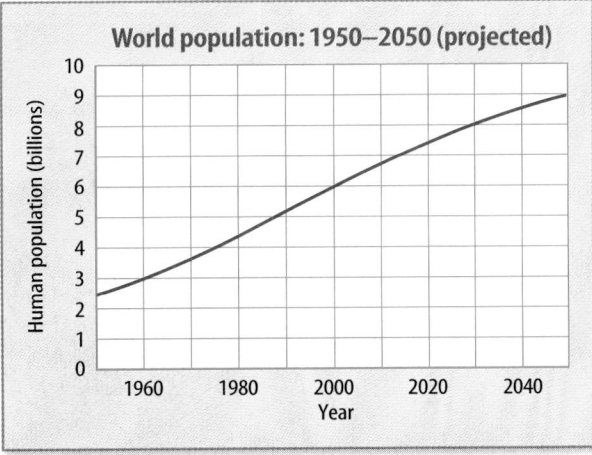

World population: 1950–2050 (projected)

Human population (billions) vs. Year (1960, 1980, 2000, 2020, 2040)

Source: U.S. Census Bureau, International Data Base 5-10-00.

Figure 10
The size of the human population is increasing each year. By the year 2050, the human population is projected to be more than 9 billion.

---

2 Interactions Among Living Organisms

1 Motivate

Bellringer Transparency
Display the Section Focus Transparency for Section 2. Use the accompanying Transparency Activity Master. L2 ELL

Tie to Prior Knowledge
Have students recall the needs of living things. Knowing what living things need to grow and reproduce will be helpful in understanding population size, density, spacing, and limiting factors.

Section ✓*Assessment* Planner

PORTFOLIO
Curriculum Connection, p. 225
PERFORMANCE ASSESSMENT
MiniLAB, p. 226
Skill Builder Activities, p. 227
See page 240 for more options.

CONTENT ASSESSMENT
Section, p. 227
Challenge, p. 227
Chapter, pp. 240–241

Characteristics of Populations

Visual Learning

Figure 11 Test students' abilities to interpret scientific illustrations by having them list two states in each population density color level. See if they can determine what area of the country has the most northern bobwhite birds.

SCIENCE Online
Internet Addresses
_____
_____
_____
_____

Explore the Glencoe Science Web site at **science.glencoe.com** to find out more about topics in this section.

Make a Model

Provide groups of students with a plain sheet of paper, glue or tape, and a self-sealing plastic bag that contains small squares cut from colored construction paper. Tell students that the paper represents a habitat and each square represents an individual member of a population. Have students glue or tape the squares to the paper to illustrate one of the types of population spacing. Display each group's habitat, and have the class identify the type of spacing each represents. |L2| COOP LEARN
[S] **Interpersonal and Kinesthetic**

Figure 11
Population density can be shown on a map. This map uses different colors to show varying densities of a population of northern bobwhite birds.

SCIENCE Online

Research Visit the Glencoe Science Web site at **science.glencoe.com** for recent news about the size of the human population. Communicate to your class what you learn.

Figure 12
In some populations, such as creosote bushes in the desert, individuals usually are spaced uniformly throughout the area.

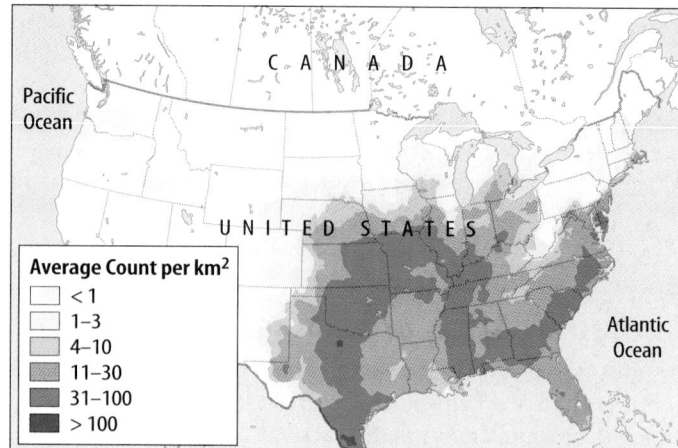

Population Density At the beginning of this chapter, when you figured out how much space is available to each student in your classroom, you were measuring another population characteristic. The number of individuals in a population that occupy a definite area is called **population density.** For example, if 100 mice live in an area of one square kilometer, the population density is 100 mice per square kilometer. When more individuals live in a given amount of space, as seen in **Figure 11,** the population is more dense.

Population Spacing Another characteristic of populations is spacing, or how the organisms are arranged in a given area. They can be evenly spaced, randomly spaced, or clumped together. If organisms have a fairly consistent distance between them, as shown in **Figure 12,** they are evenly spaced. In random spacing, each organism's location is independent of the locations of other organisms in the population. Random spacing of plants usually results when wind or birds disperse seeds. Clumped spacing occurs when resources such as food or living space are clumped. Clumping results when animals gather in herds, flocks, or other groupings.

Teacher FYI
Population density is often an important consideration for conservationists. Certain animals, like the grizzly bear, need a large amount of undisputed territory in order to survive.

✔ **Active Reading**

Think-Pair-Share This strategy encourages students to think first before discussing their ideas or thoughts about a topic. Ask students to respond to a question in writing. After thinking for a few minutes, partners share responses. Finally, ask pairs to share their responses with the class. Have students become involved with a Think-Pair-Share as they study populations.

Limiting Factors Populations cannot continue to grow larger forever. All ecosystems have a limited amount of food, water, living space, mates, nesting sites, and other resources. A **limiting factor,** as shown in **Figure 13,** is any biotic or abiotic factor that limits the number of individuals in a population. A limiting factor also can affect other populations in the community indirectly. For example, a drought might reduce the number of seed-producing plants in a forest clearing. Fewer plants means that food can become a limiting factor for deer that eat the plants and for a songbird population that feeds on the seeds of these plants. Food also could become a limiting factor for hawks that feed on the songbirds.

 **Reading Check** *What is an example of a limiting factor?*

Competition is the struggle among organisms to obtain the resources they need to survive and reproduce, as shown in **Figure 14.** As population density increases, so does competition among individuals for the resources in their environment.

Carrying Capacity Suppose a population increases in size year after year. At some point, food, nesting space, or other resources become so scarce that some individuals are not able to survive or reproduce. When this happens, the environment has reached its carrying capacity. Carrying capacity is the largest number of individuals of a species that an environment can support and maintain for a long period of time. If a population gets bigger than the carrying capacity of the environment, some individuals are left without adequate resources. They will die or be forced to move elsewhere.

Figure 13
These antelope and zebra populations live in the grasslands of Africa. *What limiting factors might affect the plant and animal populations shown here?*

What insect populations live in your area? To find out more about insects, see the **Insect Field Guide** at the back of the book.

Figure 14
During dry summers, the populations of animals at existing watering holes increase because some watering holes have dried up. This creates competition for water, a valuable resource.

Activity

Have groups of students observe 1-L containers of soil, leaf litter, and pill bugs. Each container should have a different number of pill bugs. Ask students to calculate the density of the pill bug population in each container. L2
IS **Logical-Mathematical**

Using an Analogy

Fill a beaker with water. Add water one drop at a time until the beaker overflows. Explain that the beaker has exceeded its water-holding capacity. Ecosystems also have a point at which they reach their capacity to support more organisms.

Reading Check

Answer any biotic or abiotic factor that limits the number of individuals in a population—water, food, living space

Caption Answer

Figure 13 food, water, living space, competition

Activity

Have students make lists of limiting factors for human population growth. Factors could include food, living space, pollution, and disease. L2
IS **Intrapersonal**

Curriculum Connection

Art Have students research populations that live in areas with extreme factors that restrict the kinds of organisms that can live there. Have them create a collage that shows several different populations, such as penguins and cacti. L2
IS **Visual-Spatial and Kinesthetic** P

Symbiosis and Other Interactions

Purpose Students compare the roots of a legume and a non-legume. L2 **Kinesthetic**

Materials legume plant (clover, alfalfa), nonlegume plant (geranium, coleus), prepared slide of nitrogen-fixing bacteria, beaker of water, magnifying glass.

Teaching Strategy A hand lens can be used to observe the nodules on the legume.

Analysis
1. The legume has nodules that contain nitrogen-fixing bacteria.
2. Mutualism; the bacteria make nitrogen available to the plant roots and the plant gives the bacteria food.

✓ Assessment

Performance Have students conduct research about symbiotic relationships. They should record the information in their Science Journals. Use **PASC**, p. 175.

Use Science Words

Word Meaning *Symbiosis* comes from a Greek word meaning "living together." Have students find words that begin with *sym-* and discuss their meanings. symbol, symmetry, sympathy, symphony, symposium L2 **Linguistic**

✓ Reading Check

Answer flatworms living in gills of horseshoe crabs, mistletoe growing on trees, yucca plant and yucca moth

---

Mini LAB

Observing Symbiosis

Procedure 🥽 👕 ✋

1. Carefully wash and examine the roots of a **legume plant** and a **nonlegume plant**.
2. Use a **magnifying glass** to examine the roots of the legume plant.

Analysis

1. What differences do you observe in the roots of the two plants?
2. Bacteria and legume plants help one another thrive. What type of symbiotic relationship is this?

Figure 15
The partnership between the desert yucca plant and the yucca moth is an example of mutualism.

Biotic Potential What would happen if a population's environment had no limiting factors? The size of the population would continue to increase. The maximum rate at which a population increases when plenty of food and water are available, the weather is ideal, and no diseases or enemies exist, is its biotic potential. Most populations never reach their biotic potential, or they do so for only a short period of time. Eventually, the carrying capacity of the environment is reached and the population stops increasing.

Symbiosis and Other Interactions

In ecosystems, many species of organisms have close relationships that are needed for their survival. **Symbiosis** (sihm bee OH sus) is any close interaction between two or more different species. Symbiotic relationships can be identified by the type of interaction between organisms. A symbiotic relationship that benefits both species is called mutualism. **Figure 15** shows one example of mutualism.

Commensalism is a form of symbiosis that benefits one organism without affecting the other organism. For example, a species of flatworms benefits by living in the gills of horseshoe crabs, eating scraps of the horseshoe crab's meals. The horseshoe crab is unaffected by the flatworms.

Parasitism is a symbiotic relationship between two species in which one species benefits and the other species is harmed. Some species of mistletoe are parasites because their roots grow into a tree's tissue and take nutrients from the tree.

✓ Reading Check   *What are some examples of symbiosis?*

The yucca depends on the moth to pollinate its flowers.

The moth depends on the yucca for protected place to lay its eggs and a source of food for its larvae.

Science Journal

Organism Interaction Have students explain the relationship between symbiosis and mutualism. Symbiosis includes several kinds of relationships. Mutualism is a type of symbiosis in which both species benefit. Have students find pictures in magazines or references that illustrate symbiosis and mutualism. L2 **Linguistic and Visual-Spatial**

Resource Manager

Chapter Resources Booklet
   MiniLAB, p. 3
   Enrichment, p. 31
   Reinforcement, p. 28

Predation One way that population size is regulated is by predation (prih DAY shun). Predation is the act of one organism hunting, killing, and feeding on another organism. Owls are predators of mice, as shown in **Figure 16.** Mice are their prey. Predators are biotic factors that limit the size of the prey population. Availability of prey is a biotic factor that can limit the size of the predator population. Because predators are more likely to capture old, ill, or young prey, the strongest individuals in the prey population are the ones that manage to reproduce. This improves the prey population over several generations.

Habitats and Niches In a community, every species plays a particular role. For example, some are producers and some are consumers. Each also has a particular place to live. The role, or job, of an organism in the ecosystem is called its **niche** (NICH). What a species eats, how it gets its food, and how it interacts with other organisms are all parts of its niche. The place where an organism lives is called its **habitat.** For example, an earthworm's habitat is soil. An earthworm's niche includes loosening, aerating, and enriching the soil.

Figure 16
Owls use their keen senses of sight and hearing to hunt for mice in the dark.

Use an Analogy

Use the analogy of two friends and basketball game tickets to discuss types of symbiosis. A friend offers to buy you a ticket if you will give him or her a ride to the game (mutualism). A friend with a free ticket gives it to you (commensalism). A friend sells you a ticket and you later find out he or she charged you much more than the ticket was worth (parasitism).

Extension

Have students list as many predator-prey relationships as they can. Write all contributions on the board. Have students determine which prey have more than one predator. L2

3 Assess

Reteach

Have students make a list of symbiotic relationships with which they are familiar and identify the organisms in each. L1

Challenge

What advantages does a population that feeds on several kinds of organisms have? Feeding on several kinds of organisms ensures a food supply for the population if one food source becomes unavailable.

✔Assessment

Performance Have students research data about population growth or decline of a threatened or endangered species. Then ask students to graph the data, with number of individuals on the *y*-axis and year on the *x*-axis. Students should describe the growth curve. Use **PASC,** p. 111.

Section 2 Assessment

1. Name three characteristics of populations.
2. Describe how limiting factors can affect the organisms in a population.
3. Explain the difference between a habitat and a niche.
4. Describe and give an example of two symbiotic relationships that occur among populations in a community.
5. **Think Critically** A parasite can obtain food only from its host. Most parasites weaken but do not kill their hosts. Why?

Skill Builder Activities

6. **Drawing Conclusions** Explain how sound could be used to relate the size of the cricket population in one field to the cricket population in another field. **For more help, refer to the Science Skill Handbook.**

7. **Solving One-Step Equations** A 15-m^2 wooded area has the following: 30 ferns, 150 grass plants, and 6 oak trees. What is the population density per m^2 of each species? **For more help, refer to the Math Skill Handbook.**

Answers to Section Assessment

1. size, spacing, and density
2. Limiting factors such as food, habitat, drought, and competition can cause a population to become smaller or limit its growth.
3. The place where an organism lives is its habitat. The way an organism interacts with its surroundings is its niche.

4. Possible answer: Commensalism—benefits one organism and does not harm the other; parasitism—benefits one organism and the other is harmed; examples will vary.
5. If a parasite kills its host, the parasite is likely to die because its food supply will disappear.

6. The loudest population will probably be the one with the most organisms.
7. 15-m^2 area = 225 m^2,
   ferns = 0.13
   grass = 0.67
   oak trees = 0.03

SECTION

3

Matter and Energy

1 Motivate

Bellringer Transparency

Display the Section Focus Transparency for Section 3. Use the accompanying Transparency Activity Master. [L2] [ELL]

Tie to Prior Knowledge

Remind students that animals get their energy from the food they eat. Have them speculate where plants get their energy from. Plants get their energy from the Sun through the process of photosynthesis.

Activity

Have students use **Figure 17** to construct a decomposition food chain to illustrate interactions of matter and energy in the decay of biomass. Students should label the organisms as biomass and show energy transfers with arrows.

leaves → mushrooms → bacteria

As You Read

What You'll Learn
- **Explain** the difference between a food chain and a food web.
- **Describe** how energy flows through ecosystems.
- **Examine** how materials such as water, carbon, and nitrogen are used repeatedly.

Vocabulary

food chain   water cycle
food web

Why It's Important
You are dependent upon the recycling of matter and the transfer of energy for survival.

Figure 17
These mushrooms are decomposers. They obtain needed energy for life when they break down organic material.

228

Energy Flow Through Ecosystems

Life on Earth is not simply a collection of independent organisms. Even organisms that seem to spend most of their time alone interact with other members of their species. They also interact with members of other species. Most of the interactions among members of different species occur when one organism feeds on another. Food contains nutrients and energy needed for survival. When one organism is food for another organism, some of the energy in the first organism (the food) is transferred to the second organism (the eater).

Producers are organisms that take in and use energy from the Sun or some other source to produce food. Some use the Sun's energy for photosynthesis to produce carbohydrates. For example, plants, algae, and some one-celled, photosynthetic organisms are producers. Consumers are organisms that take in energy when they feed on producers or other consumers. The transfer of energy does not end there. When organisms die, other organisms called decomposers, as shown in **Figure 17,** take in energy as they break down the remains of organisms. This movement of energy through a community can be diagrammed as a food chain or a food web.

Food Chains A **food chain,** as shown in **Figure 18,** is a model, a simple way of showing how energy, in the form of food, passes from one organism to another. When drawing a food chain, arrows between organisms indicate the direction of energy transfer. An example of a pond food chain follows.

small water plants → insects → bluegill → bass

Food chains usually have three or four links. This is because the available energy decreases from one link to the next link. At each transfer of energy, a portion of the energy is lost as heat due to the activities of the organisms. In a food chain, the amount of energy left for the last link is only a small portion of the energy in the first link.

Section ✓Assessment Planner

PORTFOLIO
Assessment, p. 233
PERFORMANCE ASSESSMENT
Try at Home MiniLAB, p. 232
Skill Builder Activities, p. 233
See page 240 for more options.

CONTENT ASSESSMENT
Section, p. 233
Challenge, p. 233
Chapter, pp. 240–241

Figure 18

In nature, energy in food passes from one organism to another in a sequence known as a food chain. All living things are linked in food chains, and there are millions of different chains in the world. Each chain is made up of organisms in a community. The photographs here show a food chain in a North American meadow community.

E The last link in many food chains is a top carnivore, an animal that feeds on other animals, including other carnivores. This great horned owl is a top carnivore.

D The fourth link of this food chain is a garter snake, which feeds on toads.

A The first link in any food chain is a producer—in this case, grass. Grass gets its energy from sunlight.

B The second link of a food chain is usually an herbivore like this grasshopper. Herbivores are animals that feed only on producers.

C The third link of this food chain is a carnivore, an animal that feeds on other animals. This woodhouse toad feeds on grasshoppers.

SECTION 3 Matter and Energy **229**

Visualizing A Food Chain

Have students examine the pictures and read the captions. Then ask the following questions.

What makes the first link in a food chain different from all of the other links? In the first step of a food chain the energy comes from the Sun, in all other cases the energy is obtained by eating another organism.

An omnivore can eat plants or animals. Where in a food chain could you find an omnivore? any spot occupied by an herbivore or carnivore in the feature, that is, any spot except the first link

Would the garter snake be classified as a producer, an herbivore, or a carnivore? The garter snake would be classified as a carnivore, an animal that feeds on other animals.

Activity

Have students make a poster that diagrams a food chain with themselves at the top. Have the students consider a food they have eaten recently, and show the food chain that led up to them consuming that particular food. [L2] [IS] **Visual-Spatial**

Extension

Have students consider the effect of a recent local event on local food chains. Some examples might be trees cut down to build a road, or a wetland drained to construct a parking lot. Have the students share their conclusion with the class.

Visual Learning

Figure 18 Have students practice interpreting scientific illustrations by writing a paragraph in which they summarize the relationships seen in this figure. [L2] [IS] **Linguistic and Visual-Spatial**

② Teach

Energy Flow Through Ecosystems

Activity

Mount magazine pictures of plants, animals, and fungi on construction paper. Give each group of four students seven to ten pictures. Have them develop a food chain using the pictures. Then have the groups use their food chains to make a food web. L2

ELL COOP LEARN **Interpersonal**

Food Webs Food chains are too simple to describe the many interactions among organisms in an ecosystem. A **food web** is a series of overlapping food chains that exist in an ecosystem. A food web provides a more complete model of the way energy moves through an ecosystem. They also are more accurate models because food webs show how many organisms are part of more than one food chain in an ecosystem.

Humans are a part of many different food webs. Most people eat foods from several different levels of a food chain. Every time you eat a hamburger, an apple, or a tuna fish sandwich, you have become a link in a food web. Can you picture the steps in the food web that led to the food in your lunch?

Problem-Solving Activity

How do changes in Antarctic food webs affect populations?

The food webs in the icy Antarctic Ocean are based on phytoplankton, which are microscopic algae that float near the water's surface. The algae are eaten by tiny, shrimp-like krill, which are consumed by baleen whales, squid, and fish. Toothed whales, seals, and penguins eat the fish and squid.

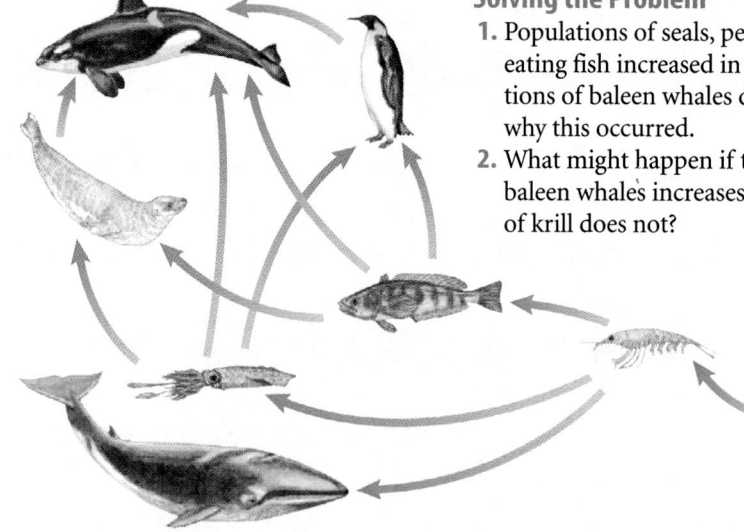

How would changes in any of these populations affect the other populations?

Identifying the Problem

Worldwide, the hunting of baleen whales has been illegal since 1986. It is hoped that the baleen whale population will increase. How will an increase in the whale population affect this food web?

Solving the Problem

1. Populations of seals, penguins, and krill-eating fish increased in size as populations of baleen whales declined. Explain why this occurred.
2. What might happen if the number of baleen whales increases but the amount of krill does not?

230 CHAPTER 8 Interactions of Living Things

LAB DEMONSTRATION

Purpose to demonstrate the niches in a mini-ecosystem

Materials terrarium including producers and consumers (salamanders, lizards, turtles).

Preparation Prepare a terrarium. Place a layer of charcoal under the soil to keep the soil "sweet." Include a pond area by burying a small plastic container in the soil. Use rocks to make a "ladder" for animals to use to enter and leave the pond. Cover the terrarium with a screen.

Procedure Have students identify the producers and consumers in the terrarium.

Expected Outcome Students observe the interactions in a mini-ecosystem.

Are there decomposers in the terrarium? Explain. Decomposers (bacteria and fungi) are found in the soil.

Ecological Pyramids Most of the energy in the biosphere comes from the Sun. Producers take in and transform only a small part of the energy that reaches Earth's surface. When an herbivore eats a plant, some of the energy in the plant passes to the herbivore. However, most of it is given off into the atmosphere as heat. The same thing happens when a carnivore eats a herbivore. An ecological pyramid models the number of organisms at each level of a food chain. The bottom of an ecological pyramid represents the producers of an ecosystem. The rest of the levels represent successive consumers.

✔ **Reading Check** *What is an ecological pyramid?*

Energy Pyramid The flow of energy from grass to the hawk in **Figure 19** can be illustrated by an energy pyramid. An energy pyramid compares the energy available at each level of the food chain in an ecosystem. Just as most food chains have three or four links, a pyramid of energy usually has three or four levels. Only about ten percent of the energy at each level of the pyramid is available to the next level. By the time the top level is reached, the amount of energy available is greatly reduced.

Chemistry INTEGRATION

Certain bacteria take in energy through a process called chemosynthesis. In chemosynthesis, the bacteria produce food using the energy in chemical compounds. In your Science Journal predict where these bacteria are found.

Figure 19
An energy pyramid illustrates that available energy decreases at each successive feeding step. *Why doesn't an energy pyramid have more levels?*

The Cycles of Matter

TRY AT HOME

Mini LAB

Purpose to model the water cycle L2 ELL LS **Kinesthetic**

Materials marker, clear plastic cup, water, plastic wrap, rubber band or tape

Teaching Strategy Remind students to observe their model for three days and record their observations.

Analysis

1. condensation, evaporation, and precipitation
2. It decreased.

Assessment

Performance Have students diagram the water cycle in their Science Journals. Use **PASC**, p. 127.

IDENTIFYING Misconceptions

Make sure students understand that the same water does not fall in a given area over and over. In fact, water moves great distances through the air all over Earth. Water in lakes, rivers, and streams is always moving. Currents in the oceans are constantly moving. Groundwater may also move great distances.

Caption Answer

Figure 20 Students should recognize all labeled paths.

TRY AT HOME

Mini LAB

Modeling the Water Cycle

Procedure

1. With a **marker**, make a line halfway up on a **plastic cup**. Fill the cup to the mark with **water**.
2. Cover the top with **plastic wrap** and secure it with a **rubber band or tape**.
3. Put the cup in direct sunlight. Observe the cup for three days. Record your observations.
4. Remove the plastic wrap and observe the cup for seven more days.

Analysis

1. What parts of the water cycle did you observe during this activity?
2. How did the water level in the cup change after the plastic wrap was removed?

Figure 20
A water molecule that falls as rain can follow several paths through the water cycle. *How many of these paths can you identify in this diagram?*

232

The Cycles of Matter

The energy available as food is constantly renewed by plants using sunlight. However, think about the matter that makes up the bodies of living organisms. The law of conservation of mass states that matter on Earth is never lost or gained. It is used over and over again. In other words, it is recycled. The carbon atoms in your body might have been on Earth since the planet formed billions of years ago. They have been recycled billions of times. Many important materials that make up your body cycle through the environment. Some of these materials are water, carbon, and nitrogen.

Chemistry INTEGRATION

Water Cycle Water molecules on Earth constantly rise into the atmosphere, fall to Earth, and soak into the ground or flow into rivers and oceans. The **water cycle** involves the processes of evaporation, condensation, and precipitation.

Heat from the Sun causes water on Earth's surface to evaporate, or change from a liquid to a gas, and rise into the atmosphere as water vapor. As the water vapor rises, it encounters colder and colder air and the molecules of water vapor slow down. Eventually, the water vapor changes back into tiny droplets of water. It condenses, or changes from a gas to a liquid. These water droplets clump together to form clouds. When the droplets become large and heavy enough, they fall back to Earth as rain or other precipitation. This process is illustrated in **Figure 20.**

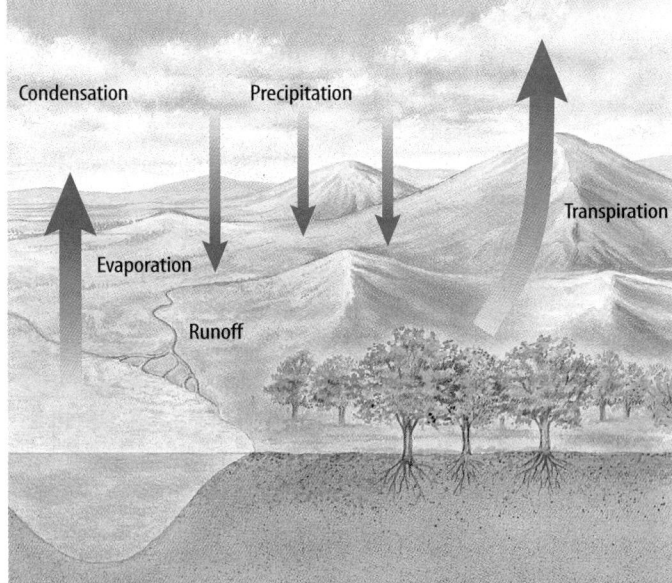

Condensation   Precipitation

Transpiration

Evaporation

Runoff

Cultural Diversity

Fertile Soil Native Americans taught early European settlers to bury pieces of fish with the corn seeds they planted, to ensure a good harvest. It worked because decomposers broke down nitrogen compounds in the fish and released ammonia that remained in the soil to be used by nitrifying bacteria. The soil ammonia and nitrates released by the bacteria are absorbed by the corn roots.

Resource Manager

Chapter Resources Booklet
 MiniLAB, p. 4
 Reinforcement, p. 29
 Activity Worksheet, pp. 7–8

Lab Management and Safety, p. 39

Other Cycles in Nature What do you have in common with all organisms? All organisms contain carbon. Earth's atmosphere contains about 0.03 percent carbon in the form of carbon dioxide gas. The movement of carbon through Earth's biosphere is called the carbon cycle, as shown in **Figure 21.**

Nitrogen is an element used by organisms to make proteins and nucleic acids. The nitrogen cycle begins with the transfer of nitrogen from the atmosphere to producers then to consumers. The nitrogen then moves back to the atmosphere or directly into producers again.

Phosphorus, sulfur, and other elements needed by living organisms also are used and returned to the environment. Just as you recycle aluminum, glass, and paper products, the materials that organisms need to live are recycled continuously in the biosphere.

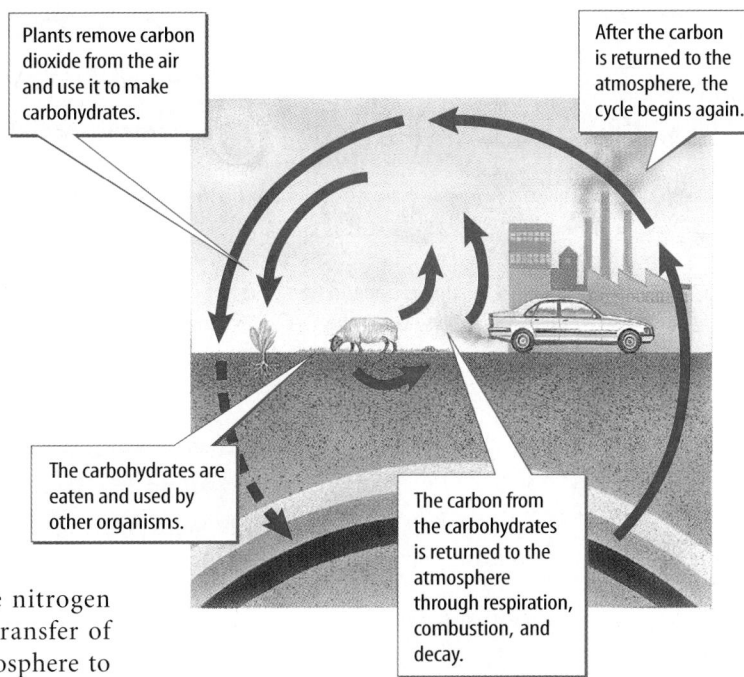

Plants remove carbon dioxide from the air and use it to make carbohydrates.

After the carbon is returned to the atmosphere, the cycle begins again.

The carbohydrates are eaten and used by other organisms.

The carbon from the carbohydrates is returned to the atmosphere through respiration, combustion, and decay.

Figure 21
Carbon can follow several different paths through the carbon cycle. Some carbon is stored in Earth's biomass.

Section 3 Assessment

1. Compare a food chain and a food web.
2. What are the differences among producers, consumers, and decomposers?
3. What is an energy pyramid?
4. How does carbon flow through ecosystems?
5. **Think Critically** Use your knowledge of food chains and the energy pyramid to explain why fewer lions than gazelles live on the African plains.

Skill Builder Activities

6. **Classifying** Look at the food chain in **Figure 18.** Classify each organism as a producer or a consumer. **For more help, refer to the** Science Skill Handbook.
7. **Communicating** In your Science Journal, write a short essay about how the *water cycle, carbon cycle,* and *nitrogen cycle* are important to living organisms. **For more help, refer to the** Science Skill Handbook.

---

3 Assess

Reteach
Play a food web game. List producers, consumers, and decomposers in a food web on separate index cards. Give a card to each student. Give each producer a ball of colored yarn. Have producers roll the ball to their primary consumers, then each subsequent consumer, until each chain is complete and creates a food web. L2 ELL COOP LEARN Kinesthetic

Challenge
Do all organisms remain in the same place in the food chain throughout their lives? Explain. No; tadpoles are herbivores, and frogs and toads are carnivores. Many insect larvae are herbivores and then become carnivores as adults.

✔Assessment

Performance Place a picture of an underwater pond scene on the overhead projector. Have students identify the producers, consumers, and decomposers. Then, have students diagram a possible food chain or web in their Science Journals. Use **Performance Assessment in the Science Classroom,** p. 127. P

Answers to Section Assessment

1. A food chain shows how energy from food passes from one organism to another. A food web is a series of overlapping food chains.
2. Producers capture and use energy from the Sun to produce carbohydrates. Consumers are organisms that obtain energy when they feed on producers or other consumers.

Decomposers obtain energy as they break down the remains of organisms.
3. a model showing the energy available at each level of a food chain in an ecosystem
4. Plants remove carbon dioxide from the air and use it to make carbohydrates. The carbohydrates are eaten and used by other organisms. The

carbon from the carbohydrates is returned to the atmosphere through respiration, decomposition, and decay. Then the cycle begins again.
5. Gazelles are lower in the food chain and energy pyramid, lions are higher; therefore there are fewer lions.

6. Check student answers against **Figure 18.**
7. Check to make sure answers are consistent with information in the text.

Activity

Recognize the Problem

Purpose

Students determine how abiotic factors affect the germination of seeds. L2 ELL COOP LEARN
IS Interpersonal

Process Skills

observing and inferring, communicating, making and using tables, comparing and contrasting, recognizing cause and effect, forming a hypothesis, designing an experiment, using numbers, separating and controlling variables, interpreting data

Time Required

50 minutes for setup; 10 minutes every three to four days for data collection for a period of about two weeks

Materials

Square milk cartons may be used for planters.

Alternate Materials

Other kinds of seeds, such as pea seeds or flower seeds, may be used.

Form a Hypothesis

Possible Hypothesis

Students may hypothesize that seeds will not germinate in the dark, in the refrigerator, or without water.

Activity

Design Your Own Experiment

Identifying a Limiting Factor

Organisms depend upon many biotic and abiotic factors in their environment to survive. When these factors are limited or are not available, it can affect an organism's survival. By experimenting with some of these limiting factors, you will see how organisms depend on all parts of their environment.

Recognize the Problem

How do abiotic factors such as light, water, and temperature affect the germination of seeds?

Form a Hypothesis

Based on what you have learned about limiting factors, make a hypothesis about how one specific abiotic factor might affect the germination of a bean seed. Be sure to consider factors that you can change easily.

Safety Precautions

Wash hands after handling soil and seeds.

Goals

■ **Observe** the effects of an abiotic factor on the germination and growth of bean seedlings.
■ **Design** an experiment that demonstrates whether or not a specific abiotic factor limits the germination of bean seeds.

Possible Materials

bean seeds
small planting containers
soil
water
label
trowel
*spoon
aluminum foil
sunny window
*other light source
refrigerator or oven
*Alternate materials

Data Table

Sample Data based on planting 10 seeds						
Number of Seeds That Germinate						
Days since planting	Sunlight	No sunlight	7.2°C	21.1°C	No water	20 mL water per day
3 days	0	0	0	0	0	0
6 days	3	0	0	3	0	3
9 days	6	0	0	6	0	6
12 days	10	0	0	10	0	10
15 days	10	0	0	10	0	10

Test Your Hypothesis

Plan

1. As a group, agree upon and write out a hypothesis statement.
2. **Decide** on a way to test your group's hypothesis. Keep available materials in mind as you plan your procedure. List your materials.
3. **Design** a data table in your Science Journal for recording data.
4. Remember to test only one variable at a time and use suitable controls.
5. Read over your entire experiment to make sure that all steps are in logical order.
6. **Identify** any constants, variables, and controls in your experiment.
7. Be sure the factor that you will test is measurable.

Do

1. Make sure your teacher approves your plan before you start.
2. Carry out the experiment according to the approved plan.
3. While the experiment is going on, record any observations that you make and complete the data table in your Science Journal.

Analyze Your Data

1. **Compare** the results of this experiment with those of other groups in your class.
2. **Infer** how the abiotic factor you tested affected the germination of bean seeds.
3. **Graph** your results in a bar graph that compares the number of bean seeds that germinated in the experimental container with the number of seeds that germinated in the control container.

Draw Conclusions

1. **Identify** which factor had the greatest effect on the germination of the seeds.
2. **Determine** whether or not you could change more than one factor in this experiment and still have germination of seeds.

*C*ommunicating

Write a set of instructions that could be included on a packet of this type of seeds. Describe the best conditions for seed germination.

ACTIVITY   235

*C*ommunicating

Instructions should include the results of the data collected.

✔*Assessment*

Performance Have students design an experiment to test the effect of the same variable on another kind of seed. Use **Performance Assessment in the Science Classroom,** p. 95.

Test Your Hypothesis

Possible Procedures

Plant the same number of seeds in each of two planters and keep all conditions the same, except for the variable. For example, place one planter in a refrigerator and another in a closed cabinet at room temperature. Give each the same amount of water. Observe the results.

Teaching Strategies

Troubleshooting Caution students not to plant the seeds too deep in the soil and not to over-water the seeds.

Expected Outcome

Most results will reflect that seeds need water and the proper temperature to germinate.

Analyze Your Data

1. Results should be consistent with those of other groups using the same variable.
2. Answers will vary based on the abiotic factor tested.
3. The graph will be determined by the number of seeds used in the experiment.

Error Analysis

Have students compare their results and their hypotheses and explain why any differences occurred.

Draw Conclusions

1. Answers will vary depending on the abiotic factor tested.
2. Each different type of abiotic factor is necessary for seeds to germinate.

The Solace of Open Spaces
a novel by Gretel Ehrlich

✔ **Pre-Reading Activity**

In groups, students should research how animals are used in work places or at home to help people overcome difficulties. They should consider how animals might assist people in performing tasks or how pets enrich people's lives.

Respond to the Reading

Active Reading Strategies

Evaluate Have students follow the writer's thoughts throughout the selection. Ask students why the writer interacts with the horses the way she does, and why she responds to the horse's behavior the way she does. Tell students to think about how the writer's feelings and opinions influence the selection.

Answers to Questions
1. a rancher
2. People and animals rely on each other. Both give and take in a relationship based on respect.
3. The author writes that horses are mischievous and dependable, as well as cunning enough to catch us off guard.

Respond to the Reading

1. From reading this passage, can you guess the occupation of the narrator?
2. Describe the relationship between people and animals in this passage.
3. What words does the author use to indicate that horses are intelligent?

Animals give us their constant, unjaded[1] faces and we burden them with our bodies and civilized ordeals. We're both humbled by and imperious[2] with them. We're comrades who save each other's lives. The horse we pulled from a boghole this morning bucked someone off later in the day; one stock dog refuses to work sheep, while another brings back a calf we had overlooked. . . . What's stubborn, secretive, dumb, and keen[3] in us bumps up against those same qualities in them. . . .

Living with animals makes us redefine our ideas about intelligence. Horses are as mischievous as they are dependable. Stupid enough to let us use them, they are cunning enough to catch us off guard. . . .

We pay for their loyalty; They can be willful, hard to catch, dangerous to shoe and buck on frosty mornings. In turn, they'll work themselves into a lather cutting cows, not for the praise they'll get but for the simple glory of outdodging a calf or catching up with an errant steer. . . .

[1] *Jaded* means "to be weary with fatigue," so *unjaded* means "not to be weary with fatigue."
[2] domineering or overbearing
[3] intellectually smart or sharp

Reading Further

Other works by this author include:
Horse: The Complete Guide, by Mary Gordon Watson, R. Russell Lyons, and Sue Montgomery, Team Media, Ltd., 1999.

Other sources on this topic include:
All Creatures Great and Small, by James Herriot, St. Martin's Press, 1972.

Polar Dreams, by Helen Thayer, Simon & Schuster, Inc., 1992.

Understanding Literature

Informative Writing The passage that you have just read is from a work of nonfiction and is based on facts. The passage is informative because it describes the real relationship between people and animals on a ranch in Wyoming. The author speaks from her own point of view, not from the point of view of a disinterested party. She uses her own experience to explain to readers that animals and people depend on each other for survival. For example, she writes, "Living with animals makes us redefine our ideas about intelligence." The language puts her firmly in the story—she is not only telling the story, but living it, too. How might this story have been different if it had been told from the point of view of a visiting journalist?

Science Connection Animals and ranchers are clearly dependent on each other. Ranchers provide nutrition and shelter for animals on the ranch and, in turn, animals provide food and perform work for the ranchers. You might consider the relationship between horses and ranchers to be a symbiotic one. Symbiosis (sihm bee OH sus) is any close interaction among two or more different species.

Career Connection

Large-Animal Veterinarian

Dave Garza works to keep horses healthy. Dave spends about 20 percent of his workday in his clinic. He goes there first thing in the morning to perform surgeries and take care of horses that have been brought to him. The rest of the day, he drives to local farms to examine patients. Dave vaccinates horses against rabies, the flu, and the encephalitis virus. He gives them tetanus shots and medication to prevent worms. He also cares for their teeth, replaces their shoes, and helps them deliver their foals in the spring.

SCIENCE *Online* To learn more about careers in veterinary medicine, visit the Glencoe Science Web site at **science.glencoe.com.**

Career Connection

A high school student interested in the field of veterinary science should emphasize science courses, especially biology. The rigorous veterinary degree program requires a minimum of six years of college. Veterinarians must be licensed, which requires passing a written state board of proficiency examination.

SCIENCE *Online*
Internet Addresses

_____

_____

_____

Explore the Glencoe Science Web site at **science.glencoe.com** to find out more about topics in this feature.

Understanding Literature

Answers to Questions

A journalist would offer an objective and concise reporting of the facts. Instead of a subjective look at the relationship between people and animals, a news article would present a concise, informative angle regarding the who, what, where, when, why, and how of life on a ranch.

Science Connection

Symbiosis is a biological term, but it can easily be applied to human relationships as well. Symbiosis usually applies to a dependent relationship that is beneficial to both members. This is called mutualism. Another kind of relationship is commensalism, in which one member benefits and the other is neither helped nor harmed. On the other hand, parasitism is a relationship in which one member depends upon the other and may even injure its host.

Linking Science and Writing

Teaching Strategies

With the students, make a chart that compares and contrasts human and animal traits. Students can then use these observations to write in their Science Journals why they think humans have the dominant role in the animal kingdom and what responsibilities come with that role.

Reviewing Main Ideas

Preview

Students can answer the questions in their Science Journals. Discuss the answers as you go through the chapter. **[IS] Linguistic**

Review

Students can write their answers, then compare them with those of other students. **[IS] Interpersonal**

Reteach

Students can look at the illustrations and describe details that support the main ideas of the chapter. **[IS] Visual-Spatial**

Answers to Chapter Review

SECTION 1

3. Accept all reasonable answers.

SECTION 2

4. The two species may nest at different levels on the tree, and one species may feed on insects while the other feeds on seeds.

SECTION 3

3. Energy decreases at each level of an energy pyramid.

Reviewing Main Ideas

Section 1 The Environment

1. Ecology is the study of interactions among organisms and their environment.

2. The nonliving features of the environment are abiotic factors, and the organisms in the environment are biotic factors.

3. Populations and communities make up an ecosystem. *What populations and communities might be present in this ecosystem?*

4. The region of Earth and its atmosphere in which all organisms live is the biosphere.

Section 2 Interactions Among Living Organisms

1. Characteristics that can describe populations include size, spacing, and density.

2. Any biotic or abiotic factor that limits the number of individuals in a population is a limiting factor.

3. A close relationship between two or more species is a symbiotic relationship. A symbiotic relationship that benefits both species is called mutualism. A relationship in which one species benefits and the other is unaffected is called commensalism.

4. The place where an organism lives is its habitat, and its role in the environment is its niche. *How could two similar species of birds live in the same area and nest in the same tree without occupying the same niche?*

Section 3 Matter and Energy

1. Food chains and food webs are models that describe the feeding relationships among organisms in a community.

2. At each level of a food chain, organisms lose energy as heat. Energy on Earth is renewed constantly by sunlight.

3. An ecological pyramid models the number of organisms at each level of a food chain in an ecosystem. *Why is each level of this energy pyramid smaller than the one below it?*

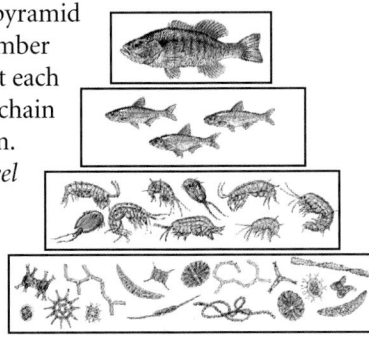

4. Matter on Earth is never lost or gained. It is used over and over again, or recycled.

FOLDABLES
Reading & Study Skills

After You Read

Using your Foldable, explain the cause and effect relationship between specific abiotic and biotic organisms around you.

FOLDABLES
Reading & Study Skills

After You Read

After students have read the chapter and completed the Foldable described in Before You Read, have them do the activity on the student page.

Dinah Zike

Visualizing Main Ideas

Complete the following concept map on the biosphere.

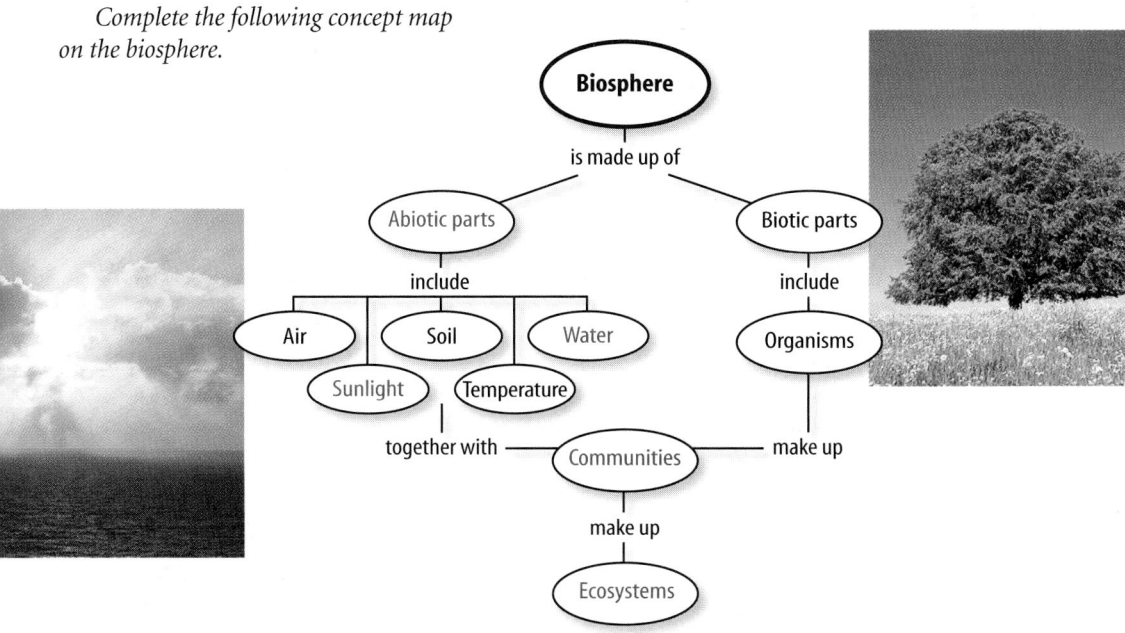

Vocabulary Review

Vocabulary Words

a. abiotic factor
b. biosphere
c. biotic factor
d. community
e. ecology
f. ecosystem
g. food chain
h. food web
i. habitat
j. limiting factor
k. niche
l. population
m. population density
n. symbiosis
o. water cycle

 **THE PRINCETON REVIEW** | **Study Tip**

Use tables to organize ideas. For example, put the levels of biological organization in a table. Tables help you review concepts quickly.

Using Vocabulary

Replace the underlined words with the correct vocabulary words.

1. A(n) <u>abiotic factor</u> is any living thing in the environment.

2. A series of overlapping food chains makes up a(n) <u>nitrogen cycle</u>.

3. The size of a population that occupies an area of definite size is its <u>carrying capacity</u>.

4. Where an organism lives in an ecosystem is its <u>niche</u>.

5. The part of Earth that supports life is the <u>limiting factor</u>.

6. Any close relationship between two or more species is <u>habitat</u>.

Vocabulary Review

Using Vocabulary

1. biotic factor
2. food web
3. population density
4. habitat
5. biosphere
6. symbiosis

Chapter 8 Assessment

Checking Concepts

1. B
2. D
3. C
4. D
5. C
6. D
7. B
8. B
9. A
10. B

Thinking Critically

11. Possible answers: populations—cactus, scorpion; ecosystems—ravine, near a water source; accept all reasonable responses.
12. The virus benefits, and the host is harmed.
13. The carrying capacity of the environment limits population size. Biotic potential is the largest size the population can reach under the best possible conditions. Carrying capacity usually prevents populations from reaching biotic potential.
14. They break down dead organisms and make the nutrients contained in the organisms' bodies available for plants to use.
15. Answers will vary. Habitat is the student's home. Niche includes food, ways of getting food and water, relationships with other organisms, and daily activities.

Checking Concepts

Choose the word or phrase that best answers the question.

1. Which of the following is NOT cycled in the biosphere?
   A) nitrogen
   B) soil
   C) water
   D) carbon

2. What are coral reefs, forests, and ponds examples of?
   A) niches
   B) habitats
   C) populations
   D) ecosystems

3. What is made up of all populations in an area?
   A) niche
   B) habitat
   C) community
   D) ecosystem

4. What is the term for the total number of individuals in a population occupying a certain area?
   A) clumping
   B) size
   C) spacing
   D) density

5. Which of the following is an example of a producer?
   A) wolf
   B) frog
   C) tree
   D) rabbit

6. Which level of the food chain has the most energy?
   A) consumer
   B) herbivores
   C) decomposers
   D) producers

7. What is a relationship called in which one organism is helped and the other is harmed?
   A) mutualism
   B) parasitism
   C) commensalism
   D) consumer

8. Which of the following is a model that shows the amount of energy available as it flows through an ecosystem?
   A) niche
   B) energy pyramid
   C) carrying capacity
   D) food chain

9. Which of the following is a biotic factor?
   A) animals
   B) air
   C) sunlight
   D) soil

10. What are all of the individuals of one species that live in the same area at the same time called?
    A) community
    B) population
    C) biosphere
    D) organism

Thinking Critically

11. What are two different populations that might be present in a desert biome? Two different ecosystems? Explain.

12. Why are viruses considered parasites?

13. What does carrying capacity have to do with whether or not a population reaches its biotic potential?

14. Why are decomposers vital to the cycling of matter in an ecosystem?

15. Write a paragraph that describes your own habitat and niche.

Developing Skills

16. **Classifying** Classify the following as the result of either evaporation or condensation.
    a. A puddle disappears after a rainstorm.
    b. Rain falls.
    c. A lake becomes shallower.
    d. Clouds form.

17. **Concept Mapping** Use the following information to draw a food web of organisms living in a goldenrod field. *Aphids eat goldenrod sap, bees eat goldenrod nectar, beetles eat goldenrod pollen and goldenrod leaves, stinkbugs eat beetles, spiders eat aphids,* and *assassin bugs eat bees.*

Chapter ✔Assessment Planner

Portfolio Encourage students to place in their portfolios one or two items of what they consider to be their best work. Examples include:
- Curriculum Connection, p. 219
- Curriculum Connection, p. 225
- Assessment, p. 233

Performance Additional performance assessments, Performance Task Assessment Lists, and rubrics for evaluating these activities can be found in Glencoe's **Performance Assessment in the Science Classroom.**

18. Making and Using Graphs Use the following data to graph the population density of a deer population over the years. Plot the number of deer on the *y*-axis and years on the *x*-axis. Predict what might have happened to cause the changes in the size of the population.

Arizona Deer Population	
Year	Deer Per 400 Hectares
1905	5.7
1915	35.7
1920	142.9
1925	85.7
1935	25.7

19. Recording Observations A home aquarium contains water, an air pump, a light, algae, a goldfish, and algae-eating snails. What are the abiotic factors in this environment?

20. Comparing and Contrasting Compare and contrast the role of producers, consumers, and decomposers in an ecosystem.

Performance Assessment

21. Poster Use your own observations or the results of library research to develop a food web for a nearby park, pond, or other ecosystem. Make a poster display illustrating the food web.

22. Oral Presentation Research the steps in the phosphorous cycle. Find out what role phosphorus plays in the growth of algae in ponds and lakes. Present your findings to the class.

TECHNOLOGY

 Go to the Glencoe Science Web site at **science.glencoe.com** or use the **Glencoe Science CD-ROM** for additional chapter assessment.

 **Test Practice**

Biologists want to estimate the total number of fish in a lake. They plan to tow a sampling device from one side of the lake to the other a single time. They discuss the sampling strategies shown below.

1  **3**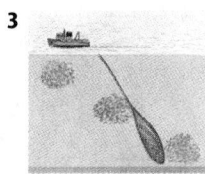

2 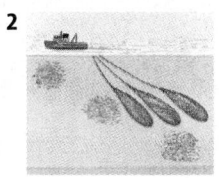 **4**

Use the diagrams to answer the following questions.

1. Which strategy is likely to provide the most accurate estimate of the number of fish in the lake?
- **A)** diagram 1
- **B)** diagram 2
- **C)** diagram 3
- **D)** diagram 4

2. How can the biologists improve their investigation?
- **F)** tow the sampling device very quickly
- **G)** tow the sampling device very slowly
- **H)** tow the sampling device more then once
- **J)** tow the sampling device around the edge of the lake

CHAPTER ASSESSMENT **241**

 **Test Practice**

The Test-Taking Tip was written by The Princeton Review, the nation's leader in test preparation.
1. D
2. H

Developing Skills

16. (a) evaporation, (b) condensation, (c) evaporation, (d) condensation

17.

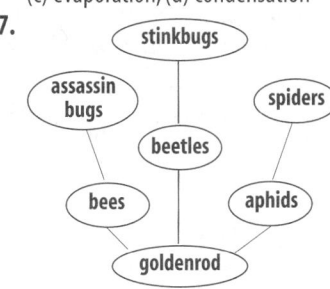

18. Possible answer: The deer population became so large that the deer consumed all the available food, and some deer starved. Check student graphs.

19. water, light, and air pump

20. Producers capture and transfer the Sun's energy into chemical energy. Consumers obtain energy by feeding on producers or other consumers. Decomposers obtain energy from the remains of organisms.

Performance Assessment

21. The poster should illustrate the concepts presented in this chapter. Use **PASC**, p. 145.

22. Excess phosphorus causes an increase in the growth of algae. When algae die, their decomposition removes much of the oxygen from the pond, affecting all other organisms in the pond. Use **PASC**, p. 143.

✓*Assessment* Resources

📁 Reproducible Masters

Chapter Resources Booklet
Chapter Review, pp. 37–38
Chapter Tests, pp. 39–42
Assessment Transparency Activity, p. 49

Glencoe Science Web site
Interactive Tutor
Chapter Quizzes

Glencoe Technology
- Assessment Transparency
- Interactive CD-ROM Chapter Quizzes
- ExamView Pro Test Bank
- Vocabulary PuzzleMaker Software
- MindJogger Videoquiz

Section/Objectives	Standards		Activities/Features
Chapter Opener	**National**	**State/Local**	**Explore Activity:** Observe solar energy, p. 243 **Before You Read,** p. 243
	See p. 7T for a Key to Standards.		
Section 1 Energy Resources ⏰ 1 session 🧊 0.5 block 1. **Describe** the advantages and disadvantages of using fossil fuels. 2. **Identify** nonrenewable resources.	National Content Standards: UCP2, D1, E2, F2, F4, F5		**Health Integration,** p. 245 **Math Skills Activity:** Estimating Car Pool Benefits, p. 247
Section 2 Alternative Energy Resources ⏰ 2 sessions 🧊 1 block 1. **List** different kinds of renewable resources. 2. **Describe** the advantages and disadvantages of using alternative energy resources.	National Content Standards: UCP2, A1, D1, E1, E2, F2, F4, F5		**Visualizing Solar Power Plants,** p. 250 **Life Science Integration,** p. 252 **MiniLAB:** Modeling the Effects of Heat, p. 254 **Science Online,** p. 255
Section 3 Water ⏰ 2 sessions 🧊 1 block 1. **Explain** how important water is to living things. 2. **Identify** different sources of water. 3. **Describe** how the location of water affects where humans live.	National Content Standards: UCP2, A1, C1, D1, F2, F4, F5		**Science Online,** p. 259 **MiniLAB:** Observing How Water Is Cleaned, p. 260 **Activity:** Using Water, p. 262
Section 4 Land ⏰ 4 sessions 🧊 2 blocks 1. **Explain** why land is a renewable resource. 2. **Explain** why trees are renewable resources but many forests are not. 3. **Describe** how mineral resources are used.	National Content Standards: UCP2, A1, D1, F2, G1		**Activity:** Using Land, pp. 268–269 **Science and Language Arts:** A Walk in the Woods, p. 270–271

NATIONAL GEOGRAPHIC

Teacher's Corner

PRODUCTS AVAILABLE FROM GLENCOE
To order call 1-800-334-7344:
Curriculum Kit
GeoKit: Pollution
Posters
Energy
Pollution

Water
Videodisc
STV: Water

PRODUCTS AVAILABLE FROM NATIONAL GEOGRAPHIC SOCIETY
To order call 1-800-368-2728:
Videos

Energy: The Fuels and Man
Energy: The Problems and the Future
Fossils: Clues to the Past
Nuclear Energy: The Question Before Us
Pollution: World at Risk; Rain Forest
Water: A Precious Resource

Activity Materials	Reproducible Resources	Section Assessment	Technology
Explore Activity: 2 empty tin cans, both black and white construction paper, water, 2 non-mercury thermometers, tape, scissors	**Chapter Resources Booklet** Foldables Worksheet, p. 13 Directed Reading Overview, p. 15 Note-taking Worksheets, pp. 31–34	*GLENCOE'S* **ASSESSMENT** *ADVANTAGE*	
Need materials? Contact Science Kit at 1-800-828-7777 or www.sciencekit.com on the Internet.	**Chapter Resources Booklet** Transparency Activity, p. 44 Enrichment, p. 27 Reinforcement, p. 23 Directed Reading, p. 16 Lab Activity, pp. 9–10 **Cultural Diversity,** p. 45	Portfolio Health Integration, p. 245 Performance Math Skills Activity, p. 247 Skill Builder Activities, p. 248 Content Section Assessment, p. 248	Section Focus Transparency Interactive CD-ROM Guided Reading Audio Program
MiniLAB: glass beaker, water (both hot and cold), small clear plastic bottle, food coloring	**Chapter Resources Booklet** Transparency Activity, p. 45 MiniLAB, p. 3 Enrichment, p. 28 Reinforcement, p. 24 Directed Reading, p. 16 **Cultural Diversity,** pp. 41, 53	Portfolio Life Science Integration, p. 252 Performance MiniLAB, p. 254 Skill Builder Activities, p. 256 Content Section Assessment, p. 256	Section Focus Transparency Interactive CD-ROM Guided Reading Audio Program
MiniLAB: glass jar with tight-fitting lid, water, soil, measuring scoop **Activity:** calculator	**Chapter Resources Booklet** Transparency Activity, p. 46 MiniLAB, p. 4 Enrichment, p. 29 Reinforcement, p. 25 Directed Reading, p. 17 Transparency Activity, pp. 49–50 Activity Worksheet, pp. 5–6	Portfolio Science Journal, p. 260 Performance MiniLAB, p. 260 Skill Builder Activities, p. 261 Content Section Assessment, p. 261	Section Focus Transparency Teaching Transparency Interactive CD-ROM Guided Reading Audio Program
Activity: grid paper (10 squares by 10 squares), colored pencils	**Chapter Resources Booklet** Transparency Activity, p. 47 Enrichment, p. 30 Reinforcement, p. 26 Directed Reading, pp. 17, 18 Lab Activity, pp. 11–12 Activity Worksheet, pp. 7–8	Portfolio Science Journal, p. 266 Performance Skill Builder Activities, p. 267 Content Section Assessment, p. 267	Section Focus Transparency Interactive CD-ROM Guided Reading Audio Program

GLENCOE'S **ASSESSMENT** *ADVANTAGE*

End of Chapter Assessment

Blackline Masters	Technology	Professional Series
Chapter Resources Booklet Chapter Review, pp. 37–38 Chapter Tests, pp. 39–42 **Standardized Test Practice by The Princeton Review,** pp. 39–42	MindJogger Videoquiz Interactive CD-ROM Vocabulary PuzzleMakers ExamView Pro Test Bank Interactive Lesson Planner Interactive Teacher Edition	Performance Assessment in the Science Classroom (PASC)

Transparencies

Section Focus

Section Focus Transparency 1 City Aglow

You can't see the city in this picture, but you know it's there because of the glow coming from all the electric lights. While you're probably familiar with many forms of pollution, did you ever consider the polluting effect of light itself? Many people want to reduce the amount of light we send into the skies.

1. How might the glow from a city interfere with the observations of professional and amateur astronomers?
2. How might the production of electricity generate pollution?
3. What could you do to reduce light pollution?

L2

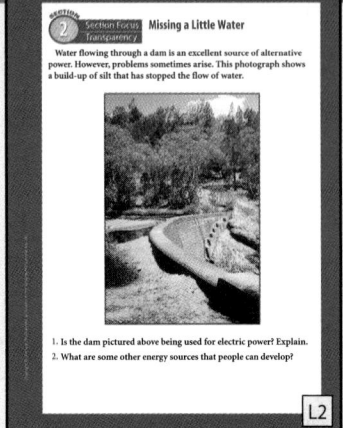

Section Focus Transparency 2 Missing a Little Water

Water flowing through a dam is an excellent source of alternative power. However, problems sometimes arise. This photograph shows a build-up of silt that has stopped the flow of water.

1. Is the dam pictured above being used for electric power? Explain.
2. What are some other energy sources that people can develop?

L2

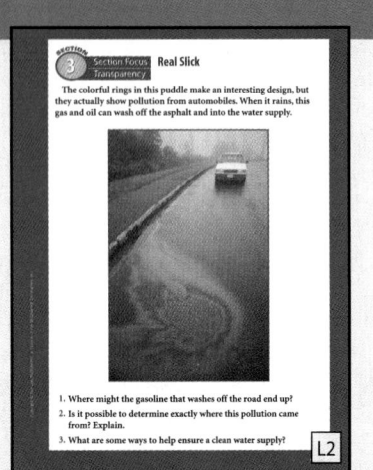

Section Focus Transparency 3 Real Slick

The colorful rings in this puddle make an interesting design, but they actually show pollution from automobiles. When it rains, this gas and oil can wash off the asphalt and into the water supply.

1. Where might the gasoline that washes off the road end up?
2. Is it possible to determine exactly where this pollution came from? Explain.
3. What are some ways to help ensure a clean water supply?

L2

This is a representation of key blackline masters available in the Teacher Classroom Resources. See Resource Manager boxes within the chapter for additional information.

Key to Teaching Strategies

The following designations will help you decide which activities are appropriate for your students.

L1 Level 1 activities should be appropriate for students with learning difficulties.

L2 Level 2 activities should be within the ability range of all students.

L3 Level 3 activities are designed for above-average students.

ELL ELL activities should be within the ability range of English Language Learners.

COOP LEARN Cooperative Learning activities are designed for small group work.

LS Multiple Learning Styles logos, as described on page 22T, are used throughout to indicate strategies that address different learning styles.

P These strategies represent student products that can be placed into a best-work portfolio.

Assessment

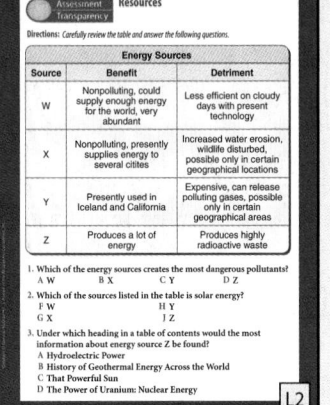

Assessment Transparency Resources

Directions: Carefully review the table and answer the following questions.

Energy Sources		
Source	Benefit	Detriment
W	Nonpolluting, could supply enough energy for the world, very abundant	Less efficient on cloudy days with present technology
X	Nonpolluting, presently supplies energy to several cities	Increased water erosion, wildlife disturbed, possible only in certain geographical locations
Y	Presently used in Iceland and California	Expensive, can release polluting gases, possible only in certain geographical areas
Z	Produces a lot of energy	Produces highly radioactive waste

1. Which of the energy sources creates the most dangerous pollutants?
   A W   B X   C Y   D Z
2. Which of the sources listed in the table is solar energy?
   F W   H Y
   G X   J Z
3. Under which heading in a table of contents would the most information about energy source Z be found?
   A Hydroelectric Power
   B History of Geothermal Energy Across the World
   C That Powerful Sun
   D The Power of Uranium: Nuclear Energy

L2

Teaching

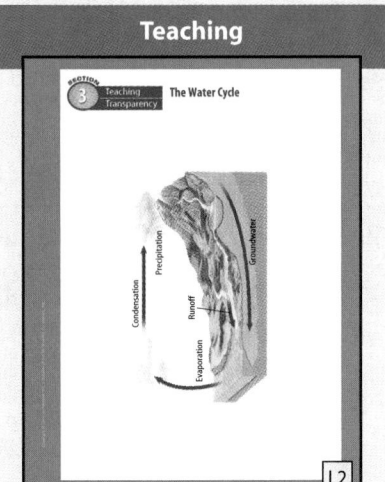

Teaching Transparency 3 The Water Cycle

L2

Hands-on Activities

Activity Worksheets

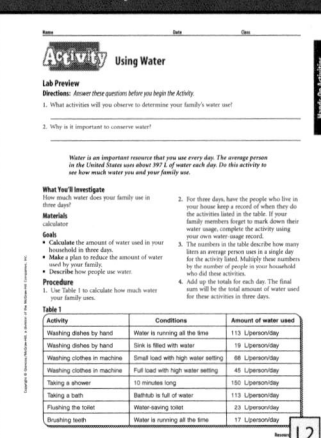

Activity Using Water

Lab Preview
Directions: Answer these questions before you begin the Activity.

1. What activities will you observe to determine your family's water use?

2. Why is it important to conserve water?

Water is an important resource that you use every day. The average person in the United States uses about 397 L of water each day. Do this activity to see how much water you and your family use.

What You'll Investigate
How much water does your family use in three days?

Materials
calculator

Goals
• **Calculate** the amount of water used in your household in three days.
• **Make** a plan to reduce the amount of water used by your family.
• **Describe** how people save water.

Procedure
1. Use Table 1 to calculate how much water your family uses.

Table 1

Activity	Conditions	Amount of water used
Washing dishes by hand	Water is running all the time	113 L/person/day
Washing dishes by hand	Sink is filled with water	19 L/person/day
Washing clothes in machine	Small load with high water setting	68 L/person/day
Washing clothes in machine	Full load with high water setting	45 L/person/day
Taking a shower	10 minutes long	180 L/person/day
Taking a bath	Bathtub is full of water	113 L/person/day
Flushing the toilet	Water-saving toilet	23 L/person/day
Brushing teeth	Water is running all the time	17 L/person/day

2. For three days, have the people who live in your house keep a record of when they do the activities listed in the table. If your family members forget to mark down their water usage, complete the activity using your own water-usage record.
3. The numbers in the table describe how many liters an average person uses in a single day for the activity listed. Multiply these numbers by the number of people in your household who did these activities.
4. Add up the totals for each day. The final sum will be the total amount of water used for these activities in three days.

L2

Laboratory Activities

Laboratory Activity Conservation—Recycling

You can do a lot to cut down on the waste of limited resources. For example, you can use electricity wisely and dispose of household wastes properly. You can also recycle, or reuse, materials instead of throwing them away.

Strategy
You will work with your class to collect waste materials.
You will find out what businesses reuse such materials.
You will interview a representative of a business and learn how that business recycles or conserves materials.

Materials
reference books on recycling   brush, soft   poster paint
telephone directory   poster board   water

Procedure
1. Research methods of recycling for several different materials including glass, rubber, and paper and the resources that are conserved with each.
2. Look in the phone book to find out who in your area will accept materials for recycling projects. If there is no recycling project in your area, your class may want to start your own.
3. Make a poster to tell the public that your group will collect material for recycling. It should be large enough to be placed in a business or store window.

   It should include that students will collect materials once a week and take them to a recycling center.
4. Survey your neighborhood and promote the collecting project.
5. At home keep a special container for glass and one for aluminum. Collect items used in your home that are made from these materials. Flatten the aluminum cans to save space. Once a week, deliver these containers to a collection center.

Data and Observations

Waste	Biodegradable (breaks down naturally)	Metal	Nonmetal	Synthetic

L2

Meeting Different Ability Levels

Content Outline

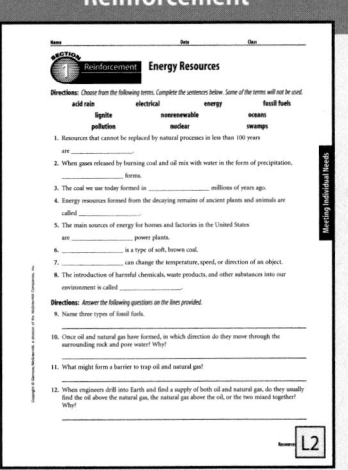

Reinforcement

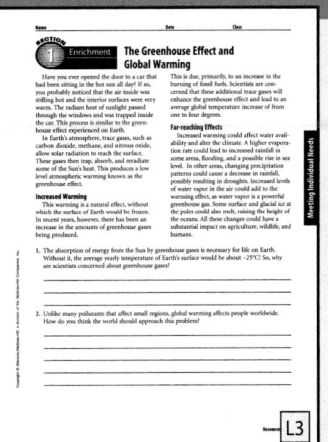

Directed Reading

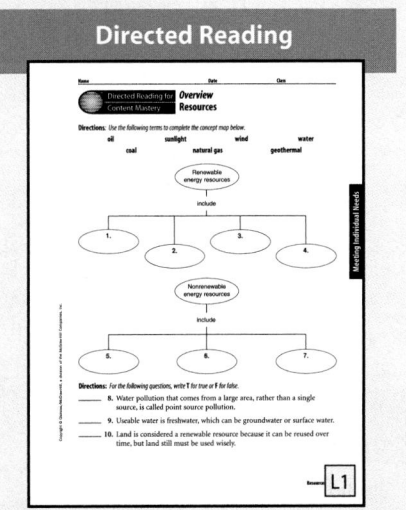

Assessment

Chapter Tests

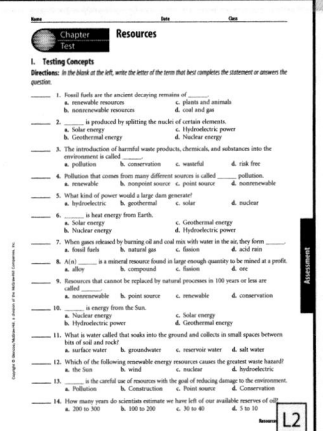

Enrichment

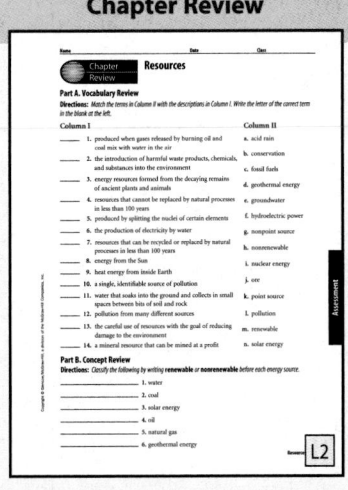

Spanish Directed Reading

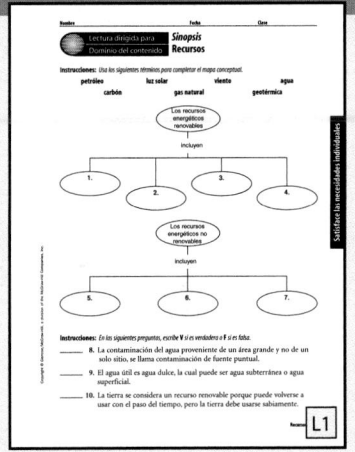

Test Practice Workbook

Chapter Review

Science Content Background

SECTION 1

Energy Resources
Coal

Carbon compounds are the source of the heat that is generated when coal is burned. The compounds in coal react with oxygen in the burning process to produce carbon dioxide and water. This reaction releases heat energy.

Peat is the first stage in coal formation. Composed of water and decaying twigs, leaves, and branches, peat contains up to 50 percent carbon. As peat becomes buried under sediment, it changes into lignite. This soft, brown coal is about 70 percent carbon and contains less moisture than peat.

> ## Fun Fact
>
> The first oil wells were dug in eastern Europe in the 1850s. Prior to this, petroleum often infiltrated wells being dug for water.

VCG/FRG International

As burial under sediments continues, bituminous coal, or soft coal, forms. Bituminous coal is commonly used as an energy resource. When burned, it provides a good deal of heat energy, but also pollutes the air. Bituminous coal is dense, black, and brittle, and is about 85 percent carbon. If heat and pressure are applied to bituminous coal, it changes into anthracite coal. The cleanest burning of all coals, anthracite coal is about 90 percent carbon.

SECTION 2

Alternative Energy Resources
Solar Energy

Electricity is generated through a similar process using a variety of energy resources. Heat is released and is used to turn water into steam; the steam is used to turn a turbine in a generator. Exceptions to this are hydroelectric power, wind power, and some types of solar power. Solar energy can be used in the heating process described above, or it can be used in a chemical process employing solar cells. Solar energy can also be used to heat water or air directly, which in turn can be used to heat buildings.

Nuclear Energy

A small uranium fuel pellet can produce a great deal of energy. One kilogram of fuel can generate 18.7 million kilowatt hours of heat. The heat is used to convert water into steam, which turns the turbine in a generator.

Nuclear fusion, the energy source of the Sun, has been achieved on Earth, but controlling the reaction has proved to be difficult. If fusion reactions become practical in the future, they will be a limitless source of energy. The fuel used is deuterium, which is a type of hydrogen found in ocean water. Fusion reactions release tremendous amounts of energy without the radioactive by-products that result from fission reactions.

3 Water

Usable Water

Salt water, which is abundant on Earth, can be processed into freshwater, but it is very expensive. Worldwide, there are about 4,000 desalination plants in operation producing up to 13 billion liters (3,500 million gallons) of freshwater a day. Research on less expensive purification methods may lead to greater use of this process as water demands increase.

Cleaning Up Water

The 1986 Safe Drinking Water Act set quality standards for drinking water in the United States. In 1996, however, a report indicated that about 30 million Americans still drank from potentially unsafe water supplies. The law was amended in 1996. New provisions overhauled the process used for setting standards, placing greater responsibility on the states. The amendment included a procedure to help state governments obtain funds to improve drinking water systems and also granted states greater flexibility in meeting federal regulations. New standards set by the amended act are subject to cost analysis whereby the costs of compliance are weighed against the obtainable benefits.

Fun Fact

In 1967, Key West, Florida, opened a desalination plant and became the first U.S. city to draw its fresh water from the ocean.

Grant Heilman Photography, Inc.

that temperatures are increasing due to an enhanced greenhouse effect resulting from the burning of fossil fuels. Greenhouse gases, such as carbon dioxide and water vapor are given off during the burning of fossil fuels. The amount of carbon dioxide in the atmosphere increased 20–30% during the last century and it has been estimated that it may increase by another 40% during the current century.

4 Land

Resource Use

The greenhouse effect is a natural process that has allowed Earth to remain warm; without it Earth would be a frozen world. Some scientists hypothesize

SCIENCE Online

For additional content background on this topic, go to the Glencoe Science Web site at science.glencoe.com.

Resources

Chapter Vocabulary

fossil fuel, p. 244
pollution, p. 246
acid rain, p. 246
nonrenewable, p. 248
renewable, p. 249
solar energy, p. 249
hydroelectric power, p. 253
geothermal energy, p. 254
nuclear energy, p. 255
groundwater, p. 258
point source, p. 259
nonpoint source, p. 259
conservation, p. 265
ore, p. 266

What Do You Think?

Science Journal A layer of dried peat is shown. Peat is an early step in the formation of coal and also can be considered a fossil fuel.

CHAPTER 9

Resources

When you toast a piece of bread for breakfast, do you realize that the bread started out as grains of wheat? What water source is used to irrigate the wheat fields? Where does the energy used to run the farm equipment come from? In this chapter you'll learn more about Earth's resources. You'll read that some resources are limited like coal and oil, and others are inexhaustible such as solar power. Finally, you'll read that natural resources such as water and land need to be managed carefully.

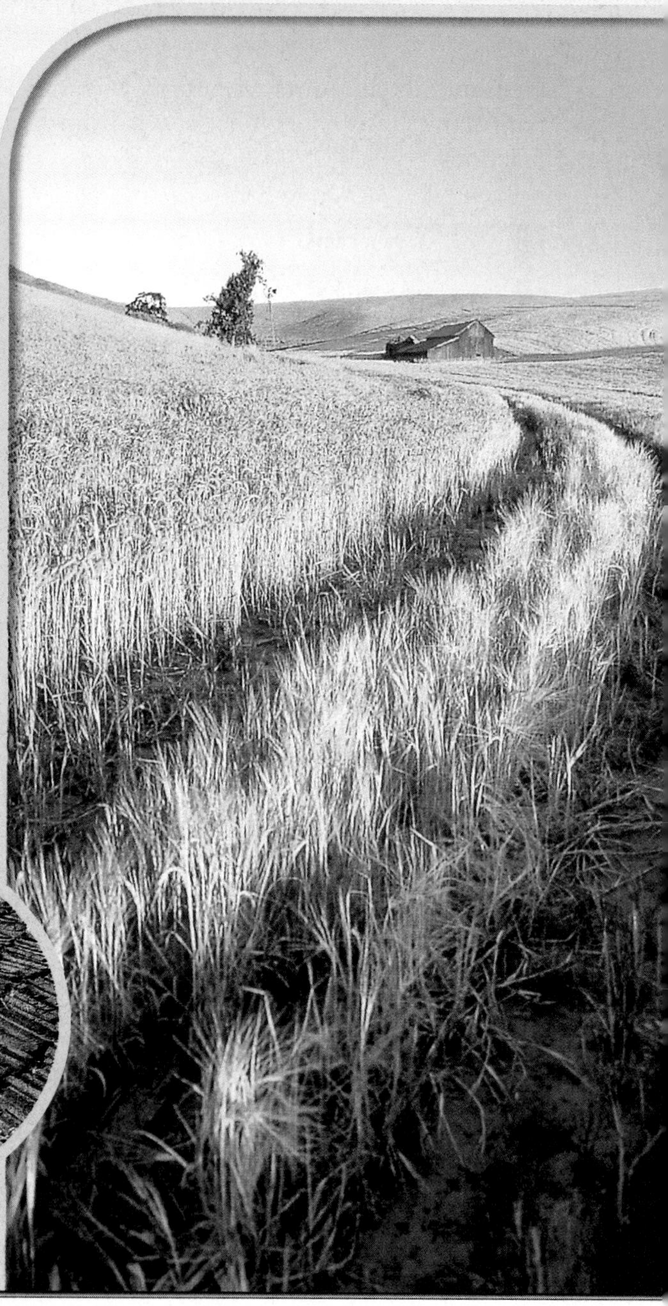

What do you think?

Science Journal Look at the picture below with a classmate. Discuss what you think this might be. Here's a hint: *It often is found in swampy areas and is dried and burned for fuel in some areas of the world.* Write your best guess in your Science Journal.

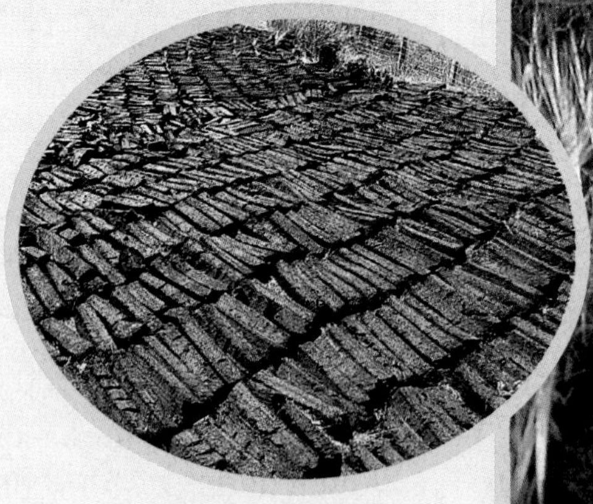

Theme Connection

Energy/Systems and Interactions This chapter explores energy from fossil fuels, the Sun, wind, water, and atoms. Interactions between humans and the environment are also presented.

 **EXPLORE ACTIVITY**

Do you know that you use resources 24 h per day? Even when you are asleep, resources are used to power streetlights and heat your home. Where do humans get the resources to meet their energy needs? Sometimes people harness energy from wind, water, and the Sun.

Observe solar energy

1. Get two empty tin cans from your teacher. Paint the outside of one can black or wrap it in black construction paper. Paint the outside of the other can white or wrap it in white construction paper.

2. Fill both cans with cool tap water. Record the temperature of the water in each can. Don't use a mercury thermometer.

3. Tape a piece of black construction paper over the top of the black can. Tape a piece of white construction paper over the top of the white can. Place both cans in direct sunlight.

4. After an hour, record the temperature of the water in both cans.

Observe

Which had the greater increase in temperature—the water in the black can or the water in the white can? How does the color of an object affect the way it absorbs the Sun's energy? Answer these questions in your Science Journal.

 **FOLDABLES**
Reading & Study Skills

Before You Read

Making a Compare and Contrast Study Fold Make the following Foldable to help you better understand advantages and disadvantages of different renewable and nonrenewable resources.

1. Place a sheet of paper in front of you so the long side is at the top. Fold the paper in half from the left side to the right side. Fold top to bottom and crease. Then unfold.

2. Through the top thickness of paper, cut along the middle fold line to form two tabs as shown.

3. Label *Nonrenewable Resources* and *Renewable Resources* across the front of the paper as shown.

4. Before you read the chapter, write what you know about the advantages and disadvantages of using nonrenewable resources and renewable resources.

5. As you read the chapter, list advantages and disadvantages for each type of resource discussed in the chapter.

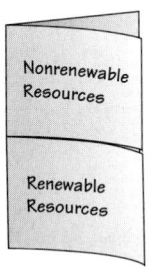
Nonrenewable Resources

Renewable Resources

243

EXPLORE ACTIVITY

Purpose Use this Explore Activity to help students analyze solar-energy absorption in different-colored materials. [L2] ELL COOP LEARN **Visual-Spatial**

Preparation Several days before you begin this chapter, remove any sharp edges on the cans.

Materials 2 tin cans, 2 non-mercury thermometers, scissors, black paper, white paper, masking tape, water, white paint, black paint, paintbrushes.

Teaching Strategy Have students compare their results with those of others. Discuss differences and similarities.

Safety Precautions Caution students to handle the cans with care.

Observe

The water in the black can had a higher temperature. Thus, the black can absorbed more solar radiation. Objects with darker colors absorb more solar energy.

 **Assessment**

Performance Cover a can with aluminum foil, fill it with water, take the temperature of the water, then place the can in sunlight. Ask students to predict what will happen to the temperature of the water. The aluminum foil will reflect most of the sunlight; thus, water temperature will stay nearly the same. Use **Performance Assessment in the Science Classroom,** p. 89.

FOLDABLES
Reading & Study Skills

Before You Read

Dinah Zike Study Fold

Purpose Students will make a foldable to examine before, during, and after reading the advantages and disadvantages of different types of resources.

📁 For additional help, see Foldables Worksheet, p. 13 in **Chapter Resources Booklet,** or go to the Glencoe Science Web site at **science.glencoe.com.** See After You Read in the Study Guide at the end of this chapter.

SECTION

1

Energy Resources

1 Motivate

Bellringer Transparency

Display the Section Focus Transparency for Section 1. Use the accompanying Transparency Activity Master. L2
ELL

Tie to Prior Knowledge

Point out various items in the classroom that were produced using fossils fuels. The metal desk frame or doorknob, for example, was probably manufactured in a factory that used fossil fuels to generate power. The wood in the desks or windowsills came from trees that were transported to lumber mills by trucks that used fossil fuels for power. Lead students into a discussion about how the use of one resource may affect another.

Energy Resources

As You Read

What You'll Learn
- **Describe** the advantages and disadvantages of using fossil fuels.
- **Identify** nonrenewable resources.

Vocabulary
fossil fuel
pollution
acid rain
nonrenewable

Why It's Important
Energy resources provide the electricity you use.

Figure 1
Coal is formed from the remains of ancient swamp vegetation.

Generating Energy

Does your day start like this? You wake up to the BEEP-BEEP of the alarm clock. You switch on the light and stumble toward the bathroom. You take a hot shower, then head back to your bedroom to dress. You flip on the radio to hear the weather report so you know what to wear. Your day has hardly begun and already you've used electricity at least four times. Have you ever wondered where your electricity comes from?

Fossil Fuels In the United States, electrical power plants are the main sources of energy for homes and factories. Energy is the ability to change things, such as the temperature, speed, or direction of an object. When energy is used to change things, energy itself often changes from one form to another. Wood, for instance, contains chemical energy. As wood is burned, its chemical energy is changed into heat and light energy. Most power plants produce electricity by burning fossil fuels. A **fossil fuel** is an energy resource formed from the decayed remains of ancient plants and other organisms. Coal, oil, and natural gas are examples of fossil fuels. Next you will take a closer look at how these important energy resources are formed.

A Over time, dead vegetation accumulated in swamps and was converted to peat.

B The peat was covered by layers of sediment. Heat and pressure caused the peat to form into a solid layer of lignite coal.

Section ✔Assessment Planner

PORTFOLIO
Health Integration, p. 245
PERFORMANCE ASSESSMENT
Math Skills Activity, p. 247
Skill Builder Activities, p. 248
See page 274 for more options.

CONTENT ASSESSMENT
Section, p. 248
Challenge, p. 248
Chapter, pp. 274–275

Coal The coal people use today began to form millions of years ago in swampy regions where huge, fernlike plants grew in abundance. When the plants died and fell into the swamp, they were covered by sediment such as mud, sand, and other dead plants. Layer upon layer of sediment piled up. Over time, microorganisms changed the plant material into a dark, organic substance called peat. The weight of sediment pressed down on the peat. Burial and decay generated heat. The combination of heat and pressure changed the decayed material into a soft, brown coal called lignite. Over time, more and more layers of sediment piled on top of the lignite, and further changes occurred in the coal, as shown in **Figure 1**.

Oil and Natural Gas Most geologists agree that oil and natural gas form over millions of years from the decay of algae and other microscopic ocean organisms called plankton. The process begins when these organisms die and fall to the seafloor. Over long periods of time, these decaying organisms accumulate in ocean sediment. Eventually, thick layers of sand and mud are deposited over the decayed organisms in the same way that coal is buried by sediment. As with coal, the combination of pressure and heat causes chemical reactions to occur. The decayed material eventually forms the liquid you know as oil and the gases known as natural gas.

Health INTEGRATION

Black lung, a disease that causes damage to the lungs, results from long-term inhalation of coal dust. Before the effects of inhaling coal dust were known, coal miners worked unprotected in mines, breathing in high amounts of dust. Find out more information about black lung and what preventative measures are used in coal mines today. Record what you find out in your Science Journal.

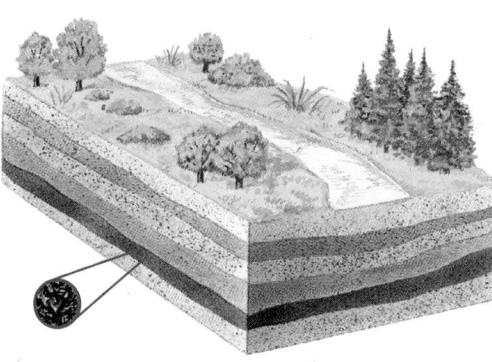

 **C** More layers of sediment piled up on top of the lignite and compressed it even further. Temperatures increased, and lignite became bituminous coal.

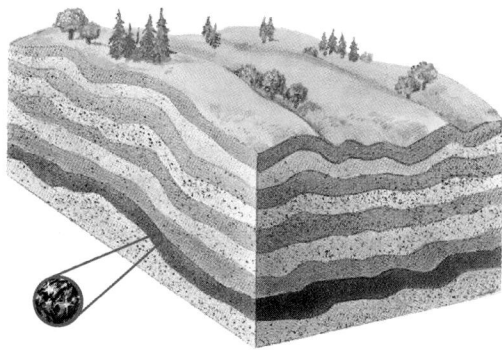

D When layers of bituminous coal were severely compressed and heated by forces within Earth, the layers changed into anthracite coal—the hardest of all coals.

SECTION 1 Energy Resources **245**

Resource Manager

Chapter Resources Booklet
Directed Reading for Content Mastery, pp. 15, 16
Note-taking Worksheets, pp. 31–34
Transparency Activity, p. 44

---

2 Teach

Generating Energy

Health INTEGRATION

Black lung disease seldom develops in mine workers who have worked in the mines for less than ten years. It requires long-term exposure to coal dust. The disease cannot be cured, but may be prevented through using respiratory protection and by enforcing standards for maximum permitted dust levels in occupational settings.
L2 P

Teacher FYI

The first coal mines in North America began operating in the 1740s. Deep seams of coal are mined through a network of tunnels and shafts. Strip mining is used when coal is near the surface. Layers of soil and rock above the coal are removed and piled to one side. The exposed coal is removed and the soil and rock are returned to the open pit and covered with topsoil.

Discussion

Using a variety of techniques, new sources of oil are being found beneath the ocean's floor. These reserves of oil appear to be large, but will be difficult to develop. Have students discuss potential problems in developing these resources. Possible answer: Oil could leak into the ocean or difficulties may exist with obtaining the oil. L2

Generating Energy,
continued

Use Science Words

Word Origin Petroleum is a thick, flammable mixture of substances made from hydrogen and carbon. It forms when marine organisms decompose in an oxygen-free environment. Have students look up the roots of the word *petroleum* in a dictionary. The word petroleum comes from the Latin words *petra* meaning "rock" and *oleum* meaning "oil."

Pollution and Fossil Fuels

Visual Learning

Figure 2 Geologists study the structure of underlying rock layers in an area when they think that conditions favorable for oil and natural gas to form previously existed. **Why do oil and natural gas collect at the top of folded rock layers?** Oil and natural gas are forced upward and collect at the highest parts of a folded rock layer if it is overlain by an impermeable rock layer.

Activity

Have students place flat paper plates coated with petroleum jelly in various locations around the school grounds. Place rocks on the plates to hold them in place. The next day, collect the plates and have students discuss potential sources for the dust, soot, or other evidence of air pollution found on the plates.
L2 ELL COOP LEARN
Kinesthetic

Reading Check

Answer Gases released by burning oil and coal mix with water in the air to form acid rain.

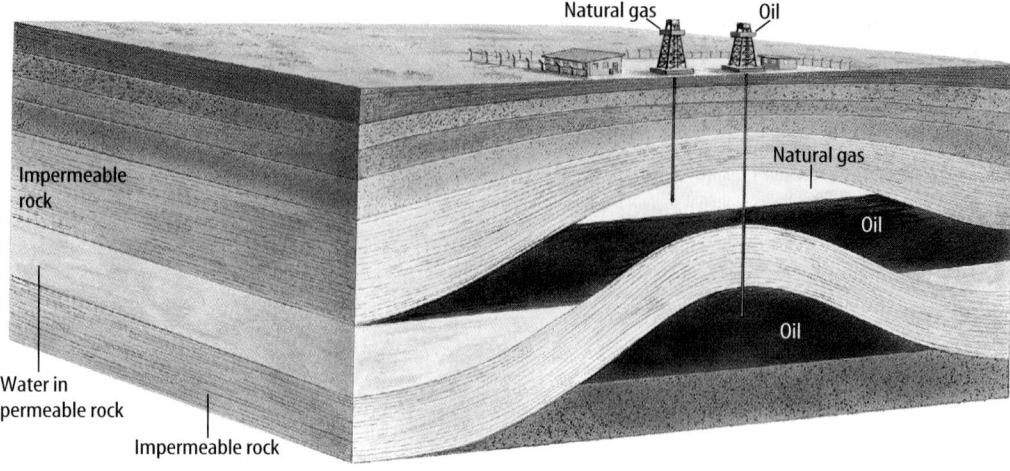

Figure 2
Engineers drill through layers of rock to reach underground deposits of oil and natural gas.

Finding Oil and Natural Gas Once oil and natural gas have formed, they will begin to move upward because they are less dense than the surrounding rock and pore water contained within small spaces in the rock. At some point the oil and natural gas might reach a barrier of impermeable rock and become trapped. Because natural gas is even less dense than oil, it usually is found above oil when drilling. **Figure 2** shows how engineers reach the oil and natural gas stored in Earth.

Pollution and Fossil Fuels

Fossil fuels are important resources. However, when they are burned to produce energy, environmental problems can occur. When fossil fuels are burned in cars, power plants, homes, and factories, gases such as nitrogen oxide and sulfur oxide and tiny bits of soot and dust are released into the air. These substances contribute to pollution. **Pollution** is harmful waste products, chemicals, and substances found in the environment.

Air pollution can make your throat feel dry or your eyes sting. Many people have trouble breathing when air pollution levels are high. For the elderly and people with lung or heart problems, air pollution can be deadly. In the United States, about 60,000 deaths each year are linked to air pollution.

People aren't the only living things that are harmed by air pollution. **Acid rain** is produced when gases released by burning oil and coal mix with water in the air to form acidic rain or snow. When acid rain reaches the soil, the growth of plants and trees is affected and many die. When acid rain falls into rivers and lakes, it can kill fish and other aquatic life such as frogs.

✔ **Reading Check** *How is acid rain produced?*

Curriculum Connection

Geography Have students find information on global coal reserves and coal use. Have them make a bar graph showing the five leading nations in terms of coal reserves. Have them make another bar graph showing the five leading nations in terms of coal use. Discuss patterns between the graphs. Do nations with the largest coal reserves tend to be the largest users of coal?
L3

Spare the Air The best solution for air pollution is prevention. Reducing the number of pollutants released into the air is easier to do than cleaning up pollutants that are already in the air. Today, cars have catalytic converters, shown in **Figure 3,** that reduce the amount of pollutants released in car exhaust. Governments around the world also are working together to find ways to reduce the amount of air pollutants that are released by factories.

Are fossil fuels running out?

Problems with fossil fuels aren't limited to pollution alone. People could find themselves running out of these energy resources in the future. Can this happen? Many people think so. Remember that the process of fossil fuel formation can take millions of years. Plants and other organisms that die today won't become fossil fuels for millions of years. Are people using fossil fuels faster than they are being replaced?

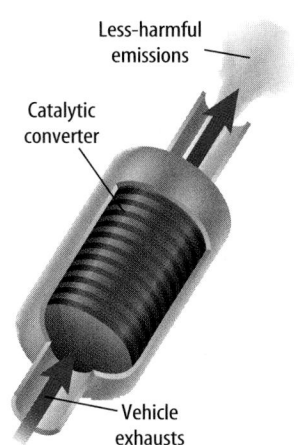

Figure 3
Catalytic converters work by converting pollutants into less harmful compounds.

Are fossil fuels running out?

Activity

Have students brainstorm about the conditions that might exist on Earth if fossil fuels were no longer available. Use the board to list conditions that students discuss. Have students work in teams of two to write an original poem or song about what Earth and human civilization would be like if fossil fuels did not exist.  **Auditory-Musical**

Math Skills Activity

Estimating Car Pool Benefits

Example Problem
Sally and Tania each drive 60 km round-trip to work five days a week, 50 weeks a year. It costs 20 cents per kilometer for gasoline and maintenance. How much money could each driver save yearly if they carpooled?

Solution

1 *This is what we know:*
Distance per person = 60 km per day
Cost per person = 20 cents or 0.2 dollars per km

2 *This is what we need to find out:*
Savings for each person per year if carpooling

3 *This is how you solve the problem:*
1) Total distance per person = 60 km/day × 5 days/week × 50 weeks/year = 15,000 km/year
2) Total cost per person = 15,000 km/year × $0.2/km = $3,000/year
3) Cost if carpooling = $3,000/year ÷ 2 = $1,500/year
4) Savings per person = $3,000/year − $1,500/year = $1,500/year

Practice Problems
What would be the savings for each driver if a third driver joined the carpool?

For more help, refer to the Math Skill Handbook.

Math Skills Activity

National Math Standards
Correlation to Mathematics Objectives
1, 4, 6, 8, 9

Answer to Practice Problem

- This is what we know:
  Distance per person = 60 km per day
  Cost per person = 20 cents or 0.2 dollars per km
- This is what we need to find out:
  Savings for each person per year if carpooling
- This is how to solve the problem:
  1) Total distance per person = 60 km/d × 5 d/wk × 50 wk/yr = 15,000 km/yr
  2) Total cost per person = 15,000 km/yr × $0.2/km = $3,000/yr
  3) Total cost per person if carpooling = $3,000/yr ÷ 3 = $1,000
  4) Total savings per person = $3,000 − $1,000 = $2,000

Resource Manager

Chapter Resources Booklet
Enrichment, p. 27
Reinforcement, p. 23
Lab Activity, pp. 9–10
Mathematics Skill Activities, p. 5

Curriculum Connection

Health Air pollution causes many people to develop bronchitis. Ask students to research which organs are inflamed when a person has bronchitis and describe the symptoms of bronchitis. The inflammation is in the bronchi and bronchioles of the lungs. Symptoms include a painful cough and muscle spasms that constrict airways.

Are fossil fuels running out?, continued

✔ **Reading Check**

Answer Natural processes cannot replace them in less than 100 years.

Caption Answer

Figure 4 Possible answer: Turn off TV when not watching.

3 Assess

Reteach

Have students brainstorm slogans urging people to reduce pollution through reduction of fossil fuel consumption. Encourage students to make posters displaying their slogans.

Challenge

In what way is the use of fossil fuels actually the use of solar energy? When plants are alive on Earth, they convert solar energy to chemical energy. The energy becomes stored as the plant's remains change to coal. Burning the coal releases this stored energy.

✔ Assessment

Process Assess students' abilities to make a concept map on the formation of oil and natural gas. Maps should include the following events: ocean organisms die and accumulate in ocean sediment; decayed organisms are covered by more sediment; chemical reactions form oil and natural gas. Use **Performance Assessment in the Science Classroom**, p. 161.

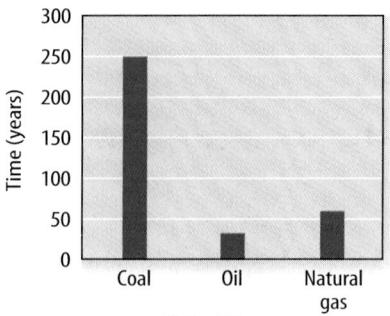

Figure 4
This graph shows available reserves of coal, oil, and natural gas. *What might you do at home to help reduce the use of fossil fuels?*

Nonrenewable Resources If you answered yes to the question on the previous page, you're right. Some energy resources are being used faster than natural processes can replace them. Resources that cannot be replaced by natural processes in less than about 100 years are **nonrenewable.** Fossil fuels are nonrenewable. This means that humans could run out of these important sources of energy someday. The question is when.

✔ **Reading Check** *Why are fossil fuels considered to be nonrenewable?*

How much is left? At current levels of usage, coal provides about 26 percent of the world's energy needs, and oil and natural gas provide almost 64 percent. As **Figure 4** shows, scientists estimate that there are enough coal reserves to last 200 to 300 years at present rates of usage. The available reserves of oil could be used up within 30 to 40 years. It is estimated that natural gas reserves will last about 60 more years.

How can this problem be solved? Conserving electricity helps reduce the use of fossil fuels. It also helps reduce pollution. Can you think of other ways to help? For example, you can use other energy resources in addition to fossil fuels to meet your energy needs. In the next section, you'll learn about alternative sources of energy that can be used again and again.

Section 1 Assessment

1. Why is coal considered a nonrenewable resource? Give two other examples of nonrenewable resources.
2. Describe the advantages and disadvantages associated with using the fossil fuels coal, oil, and natural gas.
3. Explain how acid rain forms and why it is considered harmful.
4. Why are coal, oil, and natural gas called fossil fuels?
5. **Think Critically** Why are you likely to find natural gas and oil deposits together, but less likely to find coal deposits at the same location?

Skill Builder Activities

6. **Recognizing Cause and Effect** Explain how keeping a television on overnight has an impact on the environment. Relate your answer to use of fossil fuels. **For more help, refer to the Science Skill Handbook.**
7. **Using Proportions** The United States has 5,630 cars for every 10,000 people. Cambodia, a country in Southeast Asia, has only one car for every 10,000 people. The population of the United States is about 276 million; the population of Cambodia is nearly 12 million. How many cars are in each country? **For more help, refer to the Math Skill Handbook.**

Answers to Section Assessment

1. Natural processes cannot replace coal in less than 100 years; natural gas, oil.
2. advantages—easy to obtain, found in great quantities; disadvantages—causes pollution, nonrenewable
3. Materials released by burning oil and coal mix with water in the air to form acid rain. Acid rain kills plants and fish and causes damage to structures.
4. They formed from the decayed remains of ancient organisms.
5. Natural gas and oil form when organisms die and are buried on the bottom of the ocean. Coal forms from buried plant material in a swamp.
6. Energy is wasted. This energy was most likely produced from burning fossil fuels, which produces pollution.

Thus, wasting energy adds pollution to the environment.
7. United States: 276,000,000/10,000 × 5630 = 155,388,000; Cambodia: 12,000,000/10,000 × 1 = 1,200 cars

Alternative Energy Resources

Other Sources of Energy

When you sit in the Sun, walk in the wind, or row against a river's current, you are feeling the power of resources that can be used to meet your energy needs. But unlike fossil fuels, the Sun, wind, and water are energy resources that can be used again and again. They are constant—the Sun has shone for billions of years and will shine for billions more. Energy resources that can be recycled or replaced by natural processes in less than about 100 years are considered **renewable.** Some renewable energy resources include the Sun, wind, water, and geothermal energy.

Solar Energy

Suppose you're a scientist trying to find a single source of energy to meet all the world's needs. You might look to the Sun for a solution. Energy from the Sun is renewable, and it doesn't cause pollution. Plus, enough energy from the Sun reaches Earth in an hour to supply all the energy the world uses in one year. Currently, we do not have the technology to harness all of the Sun's energy. But we do use energy from the Sun, called **solar energy,** for many things. One example is shown in **Figure 5.** This towering structure of flat mirrors is located outside the town of Odeillo, France. The mirrors are positioned to focus energy from the Sun on one part of the tower. The heat is used to run a solar furnace inside the tower, where temperatures can reach as high as 3,300°C. **Figure 6** shows how solar energy, through the use of solar panels, can be used to generate electricity.

Figure 5
The mirrors on this tower in France collect energy from the Sun. The solar furnace provides the high temperatures necessary for some types of research.

As You Read

What You'll Learn
- **List** different kinds of renewable resources.
- **Describe** the advantages and disadvantages of using alternative energy resources.

Vocabulary
renewable
solar energy
hydroelectric power
geothermal energy
nuclear energy

Why It's Important
Many alternative sources of energy are renewable.

SECTION

2

Alternative Energy Resources

1 Motivate

Bellringer Transparency
Display the Section Focus Transparency for Section 2. Use the accompanying Transparency Activity Master. [L2]
ELL

Section Focus Missing a Little Water

Water flowing through a dam is an excellent source of alternative power. However, problems sometimes arise. This photograph shows a build-up of silt that has stopped the flow of water.

1. Is the dam pictured above being used for electric power? Explain.
2. What are some other energy sources that people can develop?

Tie to Prior Knowledge
Ask students to describe the feel of wind. Tell them that air moves from regions of high pressure to regions of low pressure, creating wind—a renewable energy resource.

Kinesthetic

Section ✓Assessment Planner

PORTFOLIO
Life Science Integration, p. 252
PERFORMANCE ASSESSMENT
MiniLAB, p. 254
Skill Builder Activities, p. 256
See page 274 for more options.

CONTENT ASSESSMENT
Section, p. 256
Challenge, p. 256
Chapter, pp. 274–275

Resource Manager

Chapter Resources Booklet
Transparency Activity, p. 45
Directed Reading for Content Mastery, p. 16

Visualizing Solar Panels

Have students examine the pictures and read the captions. Then ask the following questions.

Why are the heliostats arranged in a circle? Possible answer: The circular arrangement reflects the Sun's rays toward the receiving tower from different mirrors throughout the day as Earth rotates.

When would it be necessary to use the stored hot liquid? Possible answer: During times of peak demand, such as in the morning when everyone is getting ready for school or work.

Activity

Have students paint the inside of a shoebox with black paint. Place a small dish of water in the bottom of the box. Record the temperature of the water. Cover with a piece of plastic wrap. Record the temperature of the water after placing the shoebox in the Sun for one hour. [L2] **IS Kinesthetic**

Extension

Challenge students to investigate areas of the United States where solar power plants may not be feasible. Have students research the average days of cloud cover for various United States cities and relate their results to the length of time that the hot liquid can be stored. [L2]
IS Logical-Mathematical

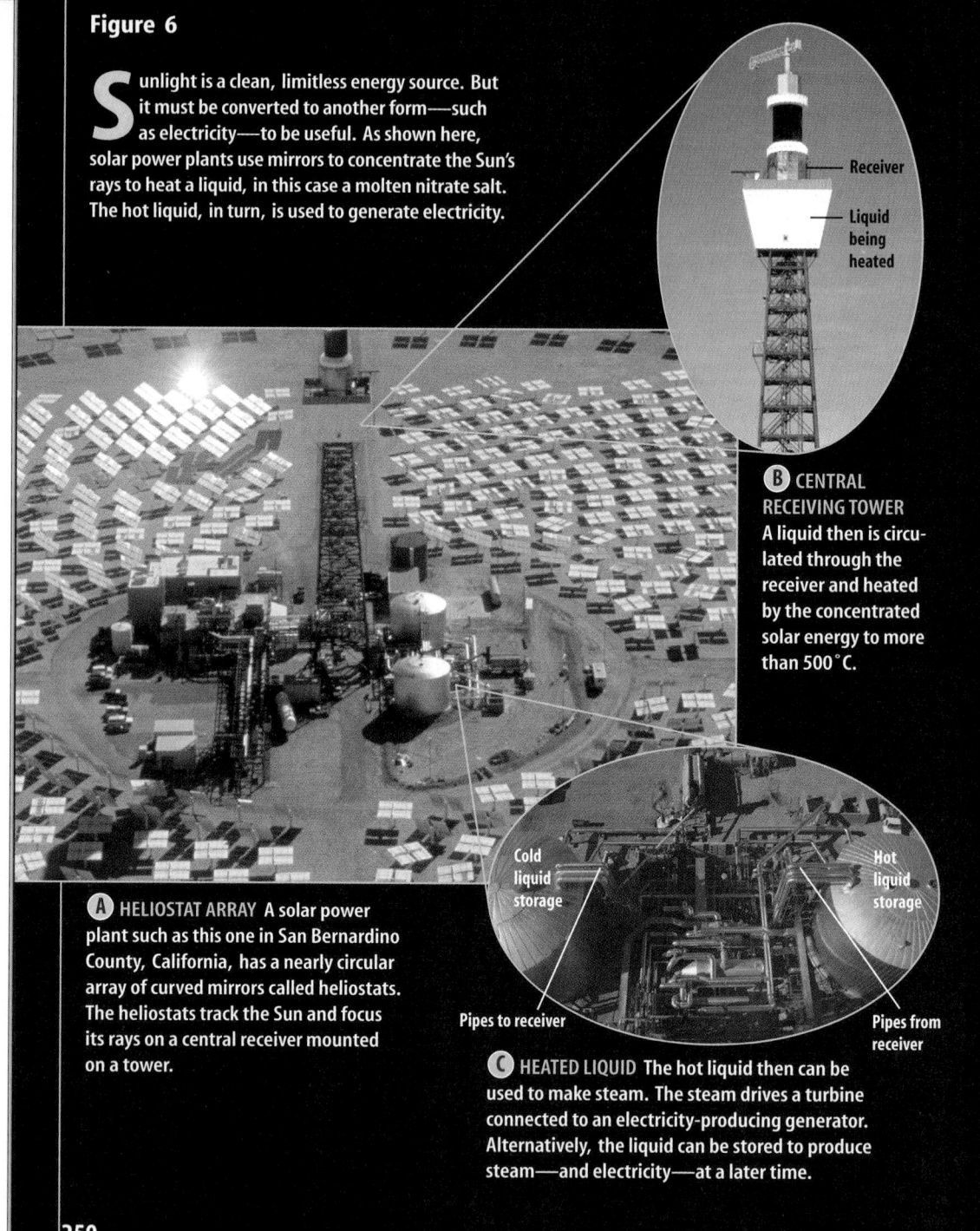

Figure 6

Sunlight is a clean, limitless energy source. But it must be converted to another form—such as electricity—to be useful. As shown here, solar power plants use mirrors to concentrate the Sun's rays to heat a liquid, in this case a molten nitrate salt. The hot liquid, in turn, is used to generate electricity.

Receiver

Liquid being heated

B CENTRAL RECEIVING TOWER A liquid then is circulated through the receiver and heated by the concentrated solar energy to more than 500°C.

Cold liquid storage

Hot liquid storage

Pipes to receiver

Pipes from receiver

A HELIOSTAT ARRAY A solar power plant such as this one in San Bernardino County, California, has a nearly circular array of curved mirrors called heliostats. The heliostats track the Sun and focus its rays on a central receiver mounted on a tower.

C HEATED LIQUID The hot liquid then can be used to make steam. The steam drives a turbine connected to an electricity-producing generator. Alternatively, the liquid can be stored to produce steam—and electricity—at a later time.

250

✔ Active Reading

News Summary The strategy helps students to explain and make connections to their study of science. Students are assigned the job of being television reporters. They are given several minutes to summarize, retell, or analyze the information about solar panels for their "television" audience. Have students prepare a News Summary of what they have learned about solar panels.

Solar Cells Other types of solar-energy technology are much simpler than the example shown in **Figure 6.** For instance, you might have used a solar calculator to complete your homework assignments. Solar calculators, such as the one shown in **Figure 7,** are powered by solar cells, which collect light and change it into electricity. In a solar cell, thin layers of silicon—a hard, dark-colored element—are sandwiched together and attached to tiny wires. As light strikes the different layers, it produces an electric current. On a larger scale, solar cells are used to supply electricity to remote areas. They also provide the power for the call boxes on the highways of North America. Solar cells are expensive and, to date, they have not been developed for wide-spread use.

Is solar energy the answer? Nonpolluting, renewable, and abundant—solar energy sounds like a wonderful way to generate energy, doesn't it? So why don't people rely on solar energy to meet all of their energy needs? Solar energy has some serious drawbacks. It's available only when the Sun is shining, so solar cells can't work at night. In addition, different parts of Earth receive different amounts of solar energy. If you live in an area that is cloudy much of the time, it's doubtful that solar energy can meet all of your energy needs because solar cells work less efficiently on cloudy days. At this point, scientists don't have the technology to harness and store effectively an adequate amount of the Sun's vast energy. Until that time, some scientists think that the best solution to energy problems might be to use fossil fuels and solar energy in combination with other energy sources. You'll read about these next.

Reading Check *What is one problem with solar energy use?*

Figure 7
The panels, car and calculator shown here receive their power from the Sun. *What are solar cells?*

Solar Energy

Caption Answer
Figure 7 A solar cell is a device that converts light from the Sun into electricity.

Discussion
Encourage students to discuss ways to use solar energy at home. *Possible answer:* Students may decide to raise curtains and blinds to let more sunlight enter during cold weather. Tea can be made by placing a jar of water with a tea bag in it in sunlight to "brew."

Quick Demo
Use a hand lens, a foil pie pan, and a ball of tissue paper to demonstrate the potential of focused sunlight. Hold the hand lens in the sunlight to focus the rays on the ball of tissue paper. Within a few minutes, the paper should begin to burn. Discuss why the paper burns. Have students consider how solar energy could be collected and focused for use in heating buildings. **CAUTION:** *Warn students that they should NOT repeat this demonstration.*

Reading Check

Answer The use of solar energy depends on cloud cover and the number of daylight hours.

Teacher **FYI**
In August 1980, the first human-piloted, solar-powered aircraft, *Gossamer Penguin*, flew 3.1 km at an altitude of 4.6 meters. A total of 3,920 solar cells powered this aircraft. The solar cells converted sunlight to electricity, which powered a motor driving a propeller.

Resource Manager

Chapter Resources Booklet
   Enrichment, p. 28

Earth Science Critical Thinking/Problem Solving, pp. 2, 10

Energy from Wind

Students should ask their parent or guardian to allow them to examine the monthly electricity bill. The amount of energy used for that month should be listed. [L2]

[IS] **Linguistic** [P]

Extension

Have students research the problem of shadow flicker that people would experience if a wind turbine were built close to their homes. They should consider the possibility that their neighbor has decided to install a wind turbine in order to generate electricity. Have students devise and produce drawings of a plan of implementation that would help their neighbor decide where to place the wind turbine in order to minimize problems caused by the shadow produced by a spinning turbine.

[IS] **Logical-Mathematical**

Physics

INTEGRATION

Energy usually is measured in units called *joules.* Another unit used to express energy is the *kilowatt-hour.* One kilowatt-hour is equal to 3,600,000 joules. Find out how many kilowatt-hours of energy are used in your home in a month's time.

Figure 8
This wind farm in California uses energy from the wind to generate electricity.

Energy from Wind

Imagine this. Outside, the sky is a clear shade of blue and the wind scatters fallen leaves across the street. Inside, a kite hangs in your closet. Can you think of a good way to spend the day?

A windy day is perfect for flying a kite. A strong wind can lift a kite high in the sky and whip it all around. When you fly a kite, you use energy from the wind. Energy from wind was and still is used to send sailboats skimming across the ocean. In the past windmills used wind energy to grind corn and pump water. The first large-scale use of wind energy was developed in Vermont during World War II. Today windmills are used to generate electricity worldwide. In the United States, regions of the Northeast, the Midwest, the Great Plains, and the West have been identified as having wind conditions best suited to using wind power. European countries such as Denmark and Finland also use wind power to their advantage. When a large number of windmills are placed in one area for the purpose of generating electricity, the area is called a wind farm. **Figure 8** shows a wind farm in California.

Like all forms of energy, energy from the wind has advantages and disadvantages. Wind is nonpolluting. It does not harm the environment or produce waste. However, only a few regions of the world have winds strong enough to generate electricity on a large scale. Also, wind isn't steady. Sometimes it blows too hard, and sometimes it stops altogether.

 **LAB DEMONSTRATION**

Purpose to observe wind energy in operation

Materials toy plastic pinwheel, fan

Procedure Set up the fan. Hold the pinwheel in front of the fan turning at low speed. Once the pinwheel is spinning, increase the speed of the fan. Be sure students can see what happens to the pinwheel when the fan speed is increased.

Help students see that the spinning pinwheel could be used to do work.

Expected Outcome Students should see that the wheel portion of the pinwheel spins around in the wind. Also, the faster the wind blows, the faster the pinwheel spins.

✓ **Assessment**

How does the action of the pinwheel model a windmill? Wind causes the blade of the windmill to turn just as wind from the fan causes the pinwheel to spin.

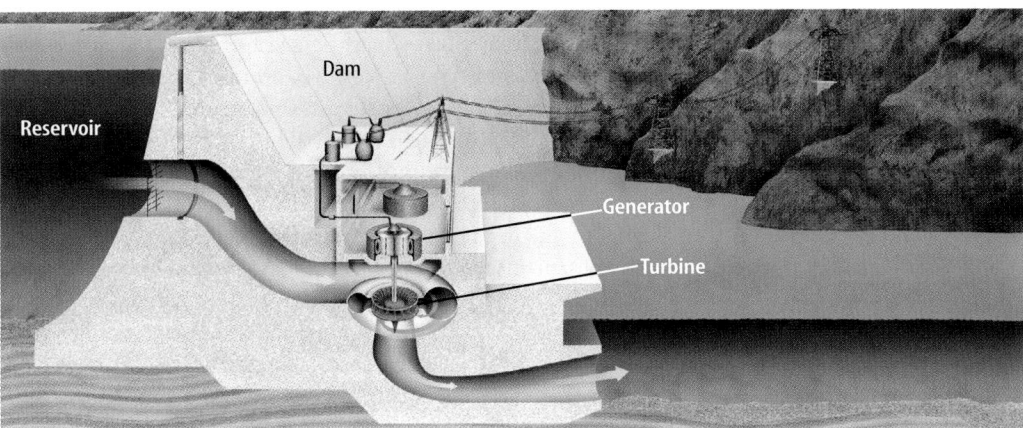

A The pipes lead to the turbines. Because of the weight of the water in the reservoir, the water in the pipes is under great pressure as it falls to the turbines.

B The pressure of the water turns the turbines that drive the electric generators in the plant.

Dam

Reservoir

Generator

Turbine

Make a Model

Have students build a model of a dam. Use the model to reinforce problems associated with hydroelectric energy. Students should explain how upstream lakes fill with sediment or how downstream erosion increases. Students also should discuss habitat loss above the dam. [L3]
ELL COOP LEARN **Visual-Spatial**

Visual Learning

Figure 9 When a dam is built, erosion of the stream bed increases below the dam. Have students research why this happens and report to the class. Possible answer: When a dam is built, the stream's gradient behind the dam is reduced and sediment is deposited. Because water coming through the dam does not carry much sediment, more erosion than deposition occurs downstream from the dam.

Hydroelectric Power

If you've ever watched a river flow, you've seen an energy resource in action. Energy from moving water also can generate electricity. The production of electricity using water is called **hydroelectric power.** People in southern Canada and the eastern United States use the water in Niagara Falls to generate hydroelectric power for a number of large cities. In other places that have no natural waterfalls, people have built concrete dams to produce hydroelectricity. The Shasta Dam on California's Sacramento River is one of the tallest structures of its type in the world. What happens to water of the Sacramento River behind the dam?

The river water that backs up behind a dam creates a reservoir, or large reserve, of water. Many reservoirs are big enough to be considered lakes. Lake Shasta, the reservoir created by the dam on the Sacramento River, is 56 km long. Look at **Figure 9** to see how a dam and a hydroelectric power plant work to generate electricity.

Hydroelectric Power Problems Like solar power and energy from the wind, hydroelectric power doesn't cause pollution and it's renewable. But this energy resource has its problems. When dams are built, the reservoir located behind the dam can fill with sediment, and increased erosion can occur downstream. Land above the dam is flooded and wildlife habitats are disturbed. In addition, dams and power plants already have been built near most rivers suitable for generating hydroelectricity. Other places can't use hydroelectric power because they're not located near flowing water.

Figure 9
Water in the reservoir is released through gateways into pipes near the base of the dam.

Science Journal

Tidal Power With a great enough difference between high and low tides, a dam could be built to generate tidal power. Have students research tidal power and write a summary of their findings in their Science Journals. They should describe the process involved in generating tidal power and explain why few areas use this alternative energy resource.

Resource Manager

Chapter Resources Booklet
Reinforcement, p. 24

Physical Science Critical Thinking/Problem Solving, pp. 17, 20

Mini LAB

Purpose Students will observe currents caused by differences in temperature. L2 ELL COOP LEARN IS **Visual-Spatial**

Materials glass beaker; small, clear bottle; food coloring

Safety Precautions Caution students to handle hot water carefully. Have them wear aprons, gloves, and safety goggles. Water should not be hot enough to cause burns.

Analysis

1. The cold water remained in the small bottle. The hot, colored water was forced out of the bottle by the cooler, denser water in the beaker.

2. Hot water in the bottle is less dense than the surrounding cooler water. Therefore, a parcel of hot water in the bottle has less mass above it and it rises. Expansion of water in a fracture also reduces the mass of water above. However, to produce a geyser the water flashes to steam and is forced to the surface.

Mini LAB

Modeling the Effects of Heat

Procedure

1. Fill a **glass beaker** with **cold water.**
2. Fill a small, clear **plastic bottle** nearly full of cold water. Add several drops of **food coloring** to the bottle.
3. Carefully lower the small bottle into the beaker so that the bottle is upright underwater. Hold the bottle in place, if necessary. Observe what happens to the colored liquid that is inside the bottle.
4. Repeat the experiment, but this time fill the bottle with **hot water.** Observe what happens to the colored liquid inside the bottle.

Analysis

1. How did heat affect the movement of the colored liquid inside the bottle?
2. Changes in heat and pressure force hot water under Earth's surface to rise. How is the movement of the colored liquid in the bottle similar to the movement of hot water under Earth? How is it different?

Figure 10
Geysers, such as this one in New Zealand, erupt because of geothermal energy.

254 CHAPTER 9 Resources

Energy from Earth

Another renewable energy resource exists beneath Earth's surface near bodies of hot, molten rock called magma. The heat from the magma and hot rock that surrounds it, called **geothermal energy,** can be used to generate electricity. **Figure 10** shows a geyser in New Zealand that erupts because of geothermal energy. A geyser forms when groundwater is heated by hot rocks and turns to steam. The steam, along with hot groundwater, is forced up in powerful spurts through openings in Earth's crust. This is an effect of geothermal energy from magma that is located close to Earth's surface. People in Iceland and California use the hot water and steam from geysers to heat their homes.

Sometimes magma is not found close to Earth's surface, but engineers can drill wells to reach heated rock. Groundwater or water injected into the rock then can turn to steam and rise to Earth's surface. This rising steam is used to generate electricity.

✔ **Reading Check** *How can geothermal energy be used to generate electricity?*

Geothermal Energy Problems As you've been learning, the use of each type of energy resource has advantages and disadvantages. Geothermal energy is no exception. Using geothermal energy can release hot, salty water at Earth's surface, which can be harmful to nearby plants and animals. In addition, only a few places have magma near Earth's surface. To generate geothermal power elsewhere, deep wells must be drilled. This process is expensive and can disrupt natural habitats near the well.

✔ Assessment

Performance Have students illustrate the movement of the hot, colored water in the beaker. Use **PASC,** p. 127.

Inclusion Strategies

Physically Challenged To help these students better understand the MiniLAB, have other students who can manipulate the small bottle work with them. In their group, perhaps the physically challenged student could be the recorder, another student could be the reader, and a third student the equipment controller.

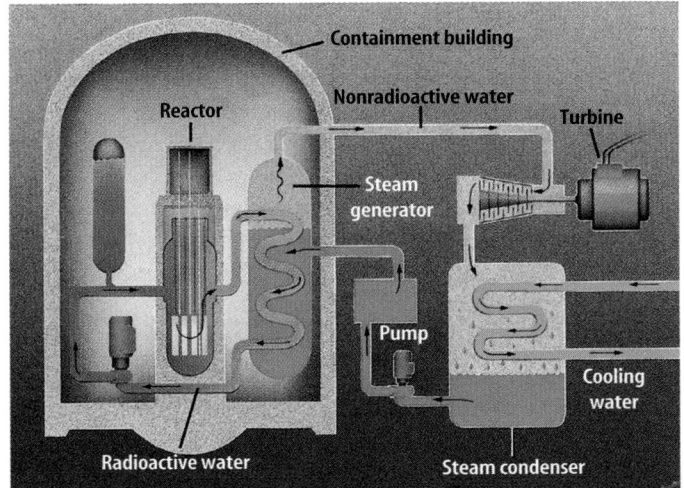

Nuclear Energy

Figure 11
Heat energy is generated by fission within the nuclear reactor. This heat is used to change water into steam. The steam moves the turbine, which is connected to a generator that produces electrical energy.

SCIENCE *Online*
Internet Addresses

_____

_____

_____

Explore the Glencoe Science Web site at **science.glencoe.com** to find out more about topics in this section.

Nuclear Energy

Atoms are the basic units of matter, and each atom contains a nucleus. All nuclei (singular, *nucleus*) have energy. Scientists have found a way to extract energy from atoms. This is called nuclear energy. **Nuclear energy** is produced by splitting the nuclei of certain elements. In this process, known as fission, energy is released. The energy is used to change water into steam. The steam then is used to drive a turbine and generate electricity for homes and industries, as shown in **Figure 11.**

The most commonly used fuel in nuclear power plants is uranium. Uranium has a nucleus that can be split easily. Once uranium ore is mined, it's refined and placed in long, metal pipes called fuel rods. The fuel rods sit in a pool of cooling water within a nuclear reactor. Energy is released when neutrons given off by the uranium split the nuclei of other uranium atoms, which in turn release more neutrons and more energy. This process is known as a chain reaction.

Nuclear Energy Problems Nuclear energy produces more than electricity. It also produces highly radioactive nuclear waste. This waste contains materials that can cause cancer or have other harmful effects on living things. Some of the waste will remain radioactive for more than 10,000 years. Nuclear waste must be handled and stored carefully to keep it from harming living things and from entering the environment. As you might have guessed, this is a major drawback in using nuclear power.

SCIENCE *Online*

Research Visit the Glencoe Science Web site at **science.glencoe.com** for more information about nuclear energy. Communicate to your class what you learn.

Use an Analogy

Ask students to imagine a small room full of mousetraps loaded with table-tennis balls. Each trap is set to spring when hit. A table-tennis ball sits in each trap, ready to shoot through the air if the trap snaps. Ask students to describe what would happen if a single ball were thrown into the room. Relate this action to a chain reaction in a nuclear power plant. L2
Ⓛ **Visual-Spatial**

✓ Reading Check

Answer p. 254 Water is heated to produce steam, which then turns turbines that run generators to produce electricity.

Science Journal

Chemistry Have students research fusion and explain its promise as a potential alternative energy source. Have students write a report of their research in their Science Journals. When atomic nuclei of light elements unite to form heavier nuclei, fusion occurs. Fusion produces an enormous amount of energy. With hydrogen fusion, the product (helium) is both useful and not radioactive.

Resource Manager

Chapter Resources Booklet
 MiniLAB, p. 3

Cultural Diversity, pp. 41, 53

Performance Assessment in the Science Classroom, p. 35

Caption Answer

Figure 12 85 percent

3 Assess

Reteach

Have students make a table listing the advantages and disadvantages of solar, wind, water, geothermal, and nuclear power.

Challenge

Have students research biomass fuel. Encourage them to discuss biomass fuel as a possible alternate energy source. **Possible answer:** Biomass fuel is produced from organic material. Biomass fuel includes wood, garbage, methane gas, and alcohol.

✓Assessment

Process Have students hypothesize why the United States does not rely more heavily on renewable energy sources. Possible answers: We lack the technology needed to use renewable energy resources to their fullest. Fossil fuels are easier to obtain. Use **Performance Assessment in the Science Classroom,** p. 89.

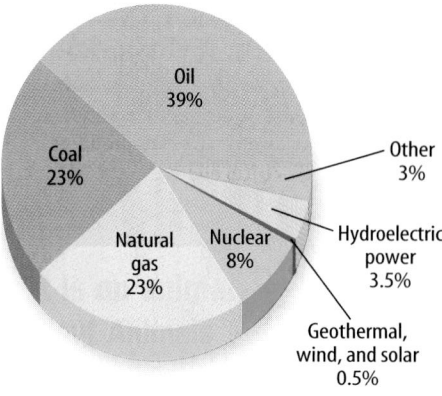

Energy Use in the United States, 1998

Oil 39%

Coal 23%

Natural gas 23%

Nuclear 8%

Other 3%

Hydroelectric power 3.5%

Geothermal, wind, and solar 0.5%

Figure 12
The use of different energy sources in the United States is shown above. *What percentage of energy came from fossil fuels?*

Nuclear Energy Use Because of potential problems in storing nuclear waste, nuclear energy has seen limited use in the United States. Electricity generated from nuclear power makes up only eight percent of the total energy used in the United States. Worldwide, about 30 countries use nuclear energy to generate electricity. Countries such as France and Japan lead the world in nuclear energy use. Almost 80 percent of France's energy needs are met by nuclear power.

Currently, the use of nuclear energy and renewable energy resources is limited. But improvements in technology might enable these resources, particularly the Sun, to be major sources of energy in the future.

Energy Use In 1998, the United States met eighty-five percent of its energy needs using fossil fuels. **Figure 12** shows the percentage of energy obtained from different sources in the United States. These numbers closely match global percentages of usage of nonrenewable and renewable energy resources. Ninety percent of the world's energy is supplied by fossil fuels. Nuclear and hydroelectric power provide seven percent and three percent of world energy needs, respectively. That leaves less than one percent for the remaining sources of energy—solar, geothermal, and wind combined.

Section 2 Assessment

1. What is a renewable resource? How is it different from a nonrenewable resource?

2. What are some advantages and disadvantages of solar energy, wind energy, and hydroelectric energy?

3. What are some disadvantages of using nuclear energy?

4. What are some disadvantages of geothermal energy?

5. **Think Critically** A well is drilled into hot rock to produce electricity. Explain how energy changes from one form to another during this process.

Skill Builder Activities

6. **Predicting** The world's energy demands are increasing. Oil could be depleted within 50 years. How do you think the use of alternative energy resources will change in your lifetime? **For more help, refer to the** Science Skill Handbook.

7. **Communicating** In your Science Journal, develop a plan to meet your town's energy needs. Describe at least three different energy sources that will provide electricity to buildings and homes. **For more help, refer to the** Science Skill Handbook.

Answers to Section Assessment

1. one that can be replaced by natural processes in less than 100 years
2. Advantages: solar, wind, and hydroelectric energy are renewable; disadvantages: solar—Sun doesn't always shine; wind—may not be strong enough; hydroelectric—reservoirs fill with sediment.
3. radioactive waste, nuclear accidents
4. release of hot, salty water
5. The thermal energy of the hot rock is used to heat water and produce steam. The steam is used to turn turbines, changing thermal energy to mechanical energy. The generator changes the mechanical energy of

the turbines to electrical energy.
6. Possible answer: The use of solar energy will increase. Electrically driven cars will be used more.
7. Possible answer: Coal, solar energy and hydrothermal energy will provide electricity for homes and other buildings.

Water—A Vital Resource

Have you ever seen a picture of Earth from space, such as the one shown in **Figure 13A?** Earth has a vast amount of water. In fact, about 70 percent of Earth is covered by water. This water continually moves through the water cycle, which is shown in **Figure 13B.** Water helps shape Earth's surface through the processes of erosion and deposition. Most importantly, water is needed by all living organisms to stay alive. Without water, living organisms could not carry out important life processes, such as growth and waste removal. Water could be Earth's most valuable resource. That's why it's important to know how much water is available and where it comes from.

Usable Water Only a small portion of Earth's water is available for use by humans. Approximately 97 percent of the world's total water supply is salt water in the oceans. That leaves only three percent in the form of freshwater, and more than three-fourths of that is frozen in glaciers and ice caps. Thus, less than one percent of Earth's total water supply is available for humans to use. This small percentage is found underground or in lakes, streams, and rivers.

As You Read

What **You'll Learn**
- **Explain** how important water is to living things.
- **Identify** different sources of water.
- **Describe** how the location of water affects where humans live.

Vocabulary
groundwater
point source
nonpoint source

Why **It's Important**
When water becomes polluted, it affects all living things.

Figure 13
All living things need clean water to survive.

A **About 70 percent of Earth is covered by water.** *How much is available for humans to use?*

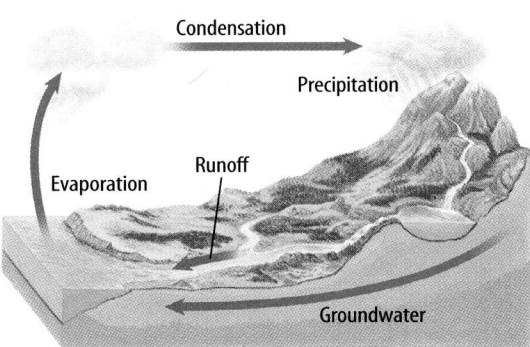

B **The water cycle shows how water moves through the atmosphere and returns to Earth's surface.**

Condensation

Precipitation

Evaporation

Runoff

Groundwater

Section ✓*Assessment* Planner

PORTFOLIO
Science Journal, p. 260
PERFORMANCE ASSESSMENT
Try at Home MiniLAB, p. 260
Skill Builder Activities, p. 261
See page 274 for more options.

CONTENT ASSESSMENT
Section, p. 261
Challenge, p. 261
Chapter, pp. 274–275

---

1 Motivate

Bellringer Transparency

Display the Section Focus Transparency for Section 3. Use the accompanying Transparency Activity Master. L2 ELL

Tie to Prior Knowledge

Show students photographs of polluted water. Ask them if they have ever seen polluted streams or lakes. Have them brainstorm sources of water pollution. When they have finished reading this section, ask them to revise their lists.

Resource Manager

Chapter Resources Booklet
Transparency Activity, p. 46
Directed Reading for Content Mastery, p. 17

Water—A Vital Resource

Caption Answer

Figure 13 less than one percent

Groundwater

Caption Answer

Figure 14 by drilling wells

Visual Learning

Figure 14 Groundwater is replenished by water that falls on Earth's surface. **What can happen to water when it falls on Earth's surface?** It can flow over the surface as runoff, evaporate, or become groundwater by infiltration.

✔ Reading Check

Answer Groundwater is water that soaks into the ground and collects in small spaces between bits of soil and rock.

Use Science Words

Word Meaning Soil and rock are permeable if water can pass through them. Ask students to define an *aquifer*. An aquifer is a layer of permeable rock that transmits water freely. Groundwater passes through aquifers. A layer of rock is impermeable if water cannot pass through it. Ask students to find out why this layer is called an *aquiclude*. An aquiclude is a layer of impermeable rock that does not transmit water.

Figure 14
Groundwater is found under Earth's surface in small spaces between bits of soil and rock.
How do people reach groundwater?

Groundwater

When you turn on a faucet, water flows out. Where does this water come from? One major source of freshwater is groundwater that lies under Earth's surface. **Groundwater** is water that soaks into the ground and collects in small spaces between bits of soil and rock, as shown in **Figure 14**. If the small spaces are connected, the water can flow through layers of rock and soil. People drill down into these layers to make wells. They then pump the water to the surface for use as drinking water, in factories, and in agriculture.

✔ Reading Check

What is groundwater?

In the United States, groundwater provides 40 percent of public water supplies. Industries and farms also use groundwater. In many agricultural areas, groundwater is the only source of water available. Is this important resource renewable or nonrenewable? Some people consider groundwater renewable because it is part of the water cycle, which recycles water constantly. However, it takes a long time for groundwater to move through rock layers. Therefore, it can take a long time to clean groundwater if it becomes polluted. Because of this, clean, usable groundwater should be considered a nonrenewable resource.

Surface Water Not all places get their water from underground. Surface water comes from streams, rivers, ponds, lakes, and reservoirs—it's the water you can see easily on Earth's surface. Do you use surface water or groundwater to meet your water needs? If you don't know, find out. Ask your teacher or another adult, or check with your city water department.

Water Use Your body needs water to survive, but people also depend on water for recreational uses such as swimming and fishing. People also need water to bathe and cook food.

Water is used by industries to manufacture products. Boats are used to transport these products and people across oceans or along rivers. Farmers use water to irrigate crops.

Many plants and animals live in oceans, lakes, or rivers. They spend their entire lives in water. What do you think would happen to these living things if the water they live in were polluted?

Inclusion Strategies

Behaviorally Disordered Ask students to record the number of glasses of water they drink during one day. Assuming each glass contains 240 mL (8 ounces) of water, have students calculate how much water they drink in one year. Possible answer: Students should multiply 240 mL by the number of glasses of water they drink in one day and then multiply that number by the number of days in one year. For example, if a student drinks eight glasses of water each day, he or she would drink 700,800 mL (700.8 L) per year. Ask students to consider other ways that they use water each day. Compile a list of these uses and have students estimate how much water they use during one year for all listed uses. **Logical-Mathematical**

Water Pollution

Have you ever seen water in the same condition as the water shown in **Figure 15A?** The chemicals found in the water are an example of water pollution. Water pollution occurs when harmful debris, chemicals, or biological materials are added to water. These pollutants lower its quality. Some pollution comes from a single, identifiable source called a **point source.** If an oil tanker such as the one shown in **Figure 15B** begins leaking, a skim of oil is released into the sea and pollutes the water directly. You can see the pollution occurring. Have you ever seen examples of this type of pollution near your home or school?

Most types of pollution are hard to trace to a single source. A **nonpoint source** is a source of pollution that cannot be traced back to an exact location. Nonpoint sources can be industries, homes, or farms. How can a farm pollute water? Chemical fertilizers are used to increase crop yields. These fertilizers enter streams, lakes, and wetlands where they can damage the environment. Some of these chemicals seep into the ground and can pollute groundwater supplies. Can you think of any way that you might cause water pollution? If you spill gasoline in your driveway, the gasoline will be carried away by runoff. It can enter the city sewage system or a stream and eventually make its way into a drinking water supply.

SCIENCE Online

Research Visit the Glencoe Science Web Site at **science.glencoe.com** for more information about ways to reduce water pollution. Communicate to your class what you learn.

✔ **Reading Check** *Why is the origin of nonpoint source pollution difficult to trace?*

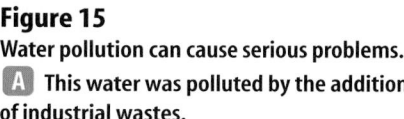

Figure 15
Water pollution can cause serious problems.
A This water was polluted by the addition of industrial wastes.

 This oil spill, the dark color leaking from the tanker, could threaten marine organisms and nearby beaches.

IDENTIFYING Misconceptions

Students may think that if a particular pollutant is no longer added to a lake, it will disappear from the lake over time. However, this is not true of some pollutants. A group of chemicals called polychlorinated biphenyls (PCBs) were banned in the United States in 1979. More than two decades later, they remain in high concentrations at the bottom of many lakes, where they have become trapped in the mud and continue to pass through food chains.

SCIENCE Online
Internet Addresses

_____

_____

_____

_____

Explore the Glencoe Science Web site at **science.glencoe.com** to find out more about topics in this section.

✔ **Reading Check**

Answer Nonpoint source pollution may enter the groundwater or flow into streams from many locations. Since there may not be a single source of the pollution, it is difficult to trace.

Teacher FYI

Water treatment plants use flocculation to remove impurities in water. Lime and alum are added to the water causing particles to stick together and settle out. The water then is filtered through beds of fine sand. The water then may be treated with chlorine for further purification.

Resource Manager

Chapter Resources Booklet
Transparency Activity, pp. 49–50
Enrichment, p. 29
Reinforcement, p. 25

Purpose Students model and observe the settling process in a water-purification plant. L2

ELL LS **Visual-Spatial**

Materials empty glass jar with lid, soil, water, measuring scoop

Teaching Strategies Have students label their jars with masking tape.

Safety Precautions Caution students to handle the jars with care.

Analysis

1. The soil gradually settled out of the water and collected at the bottom of the jar. The water became clear of visible sediment.

2. This experiment models the settling process of a water-purification plant, which occurs after chemicals have been added to the water and the water has been thoroughly mixed. Once mixed, the water lies in the settling basin so that gravity can work to separate impurities from the water. Any dissolved impurities, such as chemicals, would not be removed.

✔Assessment

Performance Have students hypothesize additional treatments that could further purify the water in the jars. Filters, for example, could be used to remove microscopic particles suspended in the water. Use **Performance Assessment in the Science Classroom,** p. 89.

Observing How Water Is Cleaned

Procedure

1. Fill a clean, empty **glass jar** two-thirds full of **water.**
2. Add a scoop of **soil** to the jar.
3. Put the **lid** on the jar, close it tightly, and then shake the jar until the water becomes muddy.
4. Put the jar aside and let it stand for two days.

Analysis

1. What happened to the soil in the jar? What happened to the water?
2. Which part of the water-purification process did you model? Which types of impurities would not be removed by the processes modeled in this activity?

Figure 16
Water is made safe for drinking at water purification plants such as the one shown here.

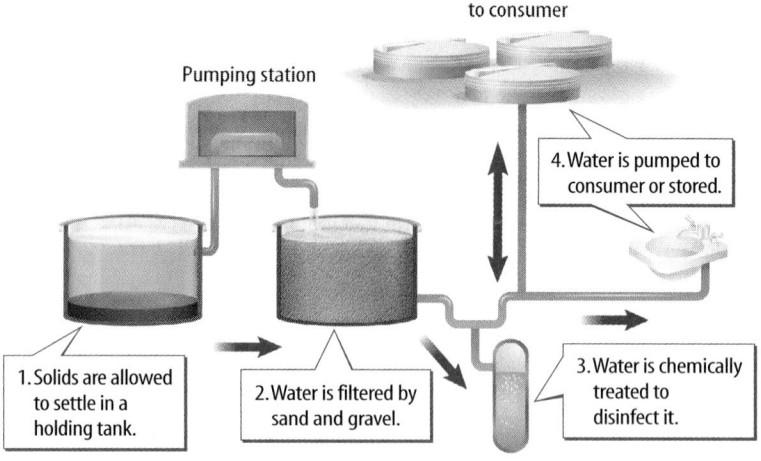

Storage tanks to consumer

Pumping station

4. Water is pumped to consumer or stored.

1. Solids are allowed to settle in a holding tank.

2. Water is filtered by sand and gravel.

3. Water is chemically treated to disinfect it.

Cleaning Up Water

Many countries are working together to reduce the amount of water pollution. For example, the United States and Canada cooperate to clean up the pollution in Lake Erie, which borders both countries. The U.S. government also has passed several laws to keep water supplies clean. The Safe Drinking Water Act is a set of government standards designed to ensure safe drinking water. The Clean Water Act gives money to states to build water-treatment plants, such as the one shown in **Figure 16.** Water is cleaned at such plants before being used for drinking and other purposes.

Water Purification In the first stage of water purification, water is run through a settling basin. Large particles of sediment settle out. Smaller particles are filtered out by sand and gravel. Water then is pumped into a tank where chemicals are added to kill microorganisms. In most water purification plants, chlorine is used to treat the water. Some treatment plants use alternative methods such as exposing the water to ultraviolet light to disinfect it. After it has been purified, the clean water is pumped to consumers.

Water Distribution

As you have learned, water is vital to the survival of all living things. Take a look at the map shown in **Figure 17.** Do you see a relationship between the location of major centers of population and major bodies of water? People usually build cities near shorelines and along large rivers. As you can see from the map, desert areas generally don't support large populations.

Resource Manager

Chapter Resources Booklet
 MiniLAB, p. 4
 Activity Worksheet, pp. 5–6

Science Journal

Effects of Pollution Globally, amphibian populations are decreasing at a rapid rate. Have students write a report in their Science Journals that explains why these animals seem particularly susceptible to pollution. Amphibians usually spend their juvenile life in water and the majority of their adult life on land. Because of their varied habitats, they are exposed to both water and air pollution. P

Managing Water Resources Recall that less than one percent of Earth's water is available for human use. In an effort to better manage water resources many countries have passed laws to reduce water pollution and to monitor the quality of the water supply. Water is a valuable resource, necessary for the survival of organisms as well as for use in everyday life. It is every bit as valuable as the energy resources you studied earlier. Next, you will read about another important resource—land.

Figure 17
This map shows that most of the world's population is centered around large bodies of water. The darker areas indicate densely-populated regions. The darker the area is, the more dense the population is.

Section 3 Assessment

1. Why is water considered one of the most valuable resources?

2. List three ways that humans use water. Describe where the water comes from for each of these uses.

3. Why are cities usually built near large bodies of water?

4. What is the difference between point source and nonpoint source pollution?

5. **Think Critically** Some cities are located near desert areas. How do you think they might meet their demands for water?

Skill Builder Activities

6. **Concept Mapping** Make an events-chain concept map that shows how soap chemicals in a bucket of water might end up as pollution in a local stream. **For more help, refer to the Science Skill Handbook.**

7. **Using a Database** Visit the Glencoe Science Web site at **science.glencoe.com** for more information about the Clean Water Act. Write a summary of how this legislation supports water-quality standards in the United States. **For more help, refer to the** Technology Skill Handbook.

Reteach
Divide the class into two groups. One group will represent city residents who want to divert water from a distant lake to supply their city with water. The other group will represent people who live near the lake and do not want the natural habitat disturbed. Have students debate the issue. They should role-play various people involved in the issue, such as city officials, farmers, industrial leaders, homeowners, environmentalists, and wildlife managers.
L2 COOP LEARN **Interpersonal**

Challenge
Have students study photographs of polluted oceans, lakes, or streams. Have them determine whether point sources or nonpoint sources may have caused the pollution.
L3 **Visual-Spatial**

Assessment

Oral Have students work in groups of three to write a poem about one of the following topics: surface water, water use, or water pollution. Use **Performance Assessment in the Science Classroom,** p. 151.

Answers to Section Assessment

1. Water keeps all living things alive. Without water, living things could not carry out important life processes.

2. Possible answer: People use water for drinking, cleaning, and recreation. water for drinking and cleaning—surface water or groundwater; water for recreation—oceans, lakes, and rivers.

3. The body of water provides an easily-tapped water source. Some students may also mention availability of water transportation.

4. Point source pollution originates from one location, whereas nonpoint source pollution cannot be traced to one location.

5. Possible answer: Cities can pipe water from areas with a surplus. Students may also mention drilling for groundwater

6. Possible answer: soapy water dumped in yard or street; runoff carries water away; water enters stream system.

7. The Clean Water Act provides money to states to build water-treatment plants.

Activity

Purpose Students estimate the amount of water used by their families. **L2** **ELL** **COOP LEARN** **LS** **Logical-Mathematical**

Process Skills observing and inferring, measuring in SI, collecting and organizing data, interpreting data, making and using tables, using numbers, recognizing cause and effect

Time Required three days for observations, 35 minutes to complete report

Teaching Strategies

- Have students meet with their families to describe the nature of the experiment and to ask for their help and cooperation.
- If family members forget to record water usage, allow students to list only their own water use.

Answers to Questions

1. Answers will vary depending on the size of the family and how many people participated in the study.
2. Answers will vary. Possible answer: Students may suggest that they should not let the water run continuously while washing dishes.
3. Student plans will vary, but might include turning off the water while washing dishes or brushing teeth, or taking baths instead of showers.

Activity

Using Water

Water is an important resource that you use every day. The average person in the United States uses about 626 L of water each day. Do this activity to see how much water you and your family use.

What You'll Investigate
How much water does your family use in three days?

Materials
calculator

Goals
- **Calculate** the amount of water used in your household in three days.
- **Make** a plan to reduce the amount of water used by your family.
- **Describe** how people use water.

Water Use		
Activity	**Conditions**	**Water Used (L/person/day)**
Washing dishes by hand	Water is running all the time	113
Washing dishes by hand	Sink is filled with water	19
Washing clothes in machine	Small load with high water setting	68
Washing clothes in machine	Full load with high water setting	45
Taking a shower	10 minutes long	150
Taking a bath	Bathtub is full of water	113
Flushing the toilet	Water-saving toilet	23
Brushing teeth	Water is running all the time	17

Procedure

1. Use the table on this page to calculate how much water your family uses.
2. For three days, have the people who live in your house keep a record of when they do the activities listed in the table. If your family members forget to mark down their water usage, complete the activity using your own water-usage record.
3. The numbers in the table describe how many liters an average person uses in a single day for the activity listed. Multiply these numbers by the number of people in your household who did these activities.
4. Add up the totals for each day. The final sum will be the total amount of water used for these activities in three days.

Conclude and Apply

1. How much water did your family use in three days?
2. **Study** the activities listed in the table. Do you see any ways to reduce the amount of water used?
3. **Develop** a detailed plan to reduce the amount of water your family uses.

*C*ommunicating

Share the results of this activity with your classmates. **For more help, refer to the Science Skill Handbook.**

✓ *Assessment*

Performance Have students propose a schedule of water usage by members of their families. Suggest they write the schedule in the form of a letter to their families. Use **Performance Assessment in the Science Classroom**, p. 139.

*C*ommunicating
Your Data

Have students use computer software to prepare the table in which they will record data. Ask students to begin by filling out the table with examples of data similar to those they will obtain at home. Encourage students to discuss the project with family members so they become active participants.

4 Land

Land as a Resource

Has your neighborhood changed lately? How about the outskirts of your town? Perhaps a grassy field has been turned into a parking lot or some nearby farmland has become a place where new homes were built. These changes, shown in **Figure 18,** are examples of the different ways land is used as a resource. How else do people use land?

Land Use Think about where your food comes from. Land is used to raise the crops and animals humans use for food. A simple peanut butter-and-jelly sandwich requires land to grow the wheat needed to make bread, land to grow peanuts for the peanut butter, and land to grow the sugarcane and fruit for the jelly. A hamburger? Land is needed to raise cattle and to grow the grain the cattle eat.

Think about your home, your school, and other places you go, like a park or a shopping mall. The things that you buy in the shopping mall come from factories. All these buildings take up space. This means that every time a house, a mall, or a factory is built, more land is used. Land is a renewable resource because it usually can be used over and over again. But one look at a globe will show you that the amount of usable land is limited. Therefore, wise choices need to be made when it comes to land use.

As You Read

What You'll Learn
- **Explain** why land is a renewable resource.
- **Explain** why trees are renewable resources but many forests are not.
- **Describe** how mineral resources are used.

Vocabulary
conservation
ore

Why It's Important
Resources are used to make some of the things you use every day.

Figure 18
This farmland soon will be a new housing development. *What are some other ways that land is used?*

---

1 Motivate

Bellringer Transparency

Display the Section Focus Transparency for Section 4. Use the accompanying Transparency Activity Master. L2 ELL

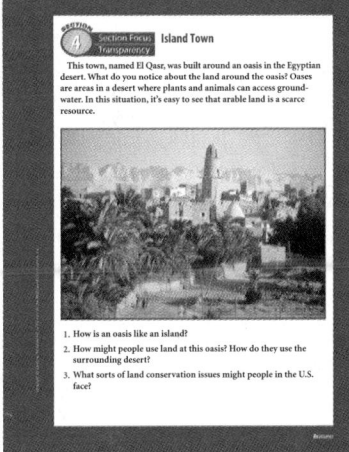

Tie to Prior Knowledge

Have students recall the last time they were asked to take out the garbage. Ask them whether they have ever considered where all the garbage goes. Much of the solid waste is collected and placed in landfills. Tell students that landfills are one of many ways people use land.

Section ✔*Assessment* Planner

PORTFOLIO
Science Journal, p. 266
PERFORMANCE ASSESSMENT
Skill Builder Activities, p. 267
See page 274 for more options.

CONTENT ASSESSMENT
Section, p. 267
Challenge, p. 267
Chapter, pp. 274–275

Resource Manager

Chapter Resources Booklet
Transparency Activity, p. 47
Directed Reading for Content Mastery, pp. 17, 18

Land as a Resource

Caption Answer

Figure 18 Possible answer: Land may be used for factories, stores, and parks.

Activity

Obtain a map of the local town or city and surrounding area. Ask students to study the use of land in and around your school. Encourage them to speculate as to whether they think the land has been used wisely. Ask them to explain how they might better use the land for all people living in or around your local town or city. L2
IS Visual-Spatial

Make a Model

Have students research the use of land for a landfill. Ask students to make a model of a sanitary landfill. Students might wish to use a large plastic container in which to build their model landfill. **IS Kinesthetic**

Resources from Land

Extension

Ask students to select a product they often use, then research and write in their Science Journals about how the product is manufactured. They should list the natural resources used to make the product, including those used in obtaining and transporting raw materials. They should describe the step-by-step process that is followed from the time the natural resource is obtained, through the time when the final product is placed in the store.

Figure 19
People are working to protect natural habitats in many areas, such as this tropical rain forest in Costa Rica.

Figure 20
A Improper use of rangeland can cause soil erosion, as seen in this photo taken in Brazil.

Using Land Wisely People need food, clothing, jobs, and a place to live, and each of these things takes space. But preserving natural habitats, such as the one shown in **Figure 19,** is also important. Recall that a habitat is the place where organisms live. Ponds, wetlands, and forests are examples of natural habitats. If a wetland is filled in to construct an apartment building, an important natural habitat is lost.

Laws help control habitat loss and help people use land wisely. Before major construction can take place in a new area, the land must be studied to determine the impact construction will have on the living things, the soil, and the water in the area. If endangered plants or animals live in the area, construction might not be allowed.

Problems also can arise when people use land for farming or grazing animals. If these activities are not done properly, soil can be eroded, causing its quality to be reduced. **Figure 20B** shows how farmers and ranchers work to reduce soil erosion problems.

Resources from Land

People use land to grow crops, to raise animals, and to live on. In addition to meeting human needs for food and shelter, land provides two other important resources—forests and minerals.

B Water belts, such as this one in Kentucky, help reduce water runoff and soil erosion by slowing the runoff and trapping soil.

✔ Active Reading

Double Entry Journal In this strategy, the student takes notes and adds his or her own reflections while reading the text. Students are encouraged to explore ideas, make responses, and take risks in giving opinions about the reading. Have them divide a sheet of paper in half, lengthwise. On the left, they should identify a particular passage of significance about resources from the land and conservation. Direct them to record anything luminous, enigmatic, stimulating, or disturbing. On the right, have the reader respond, question, elaborate, make personal connections, evaluate, reflect, analyze, or interpret. Have students make a Double Entry Journal for a passage in this section.

Forests Look around your classroom. Do you see books, paper, desks, and pencils? These products are made of wood. Wood comes from trees in a forest that were cut down and taken to a lumberyard to be processed into boards and other wooden products.

In addition to providing much-needed wood, forests have an important effect on Earth's atmosphere. In the process of photosynthesis, trees and other plants use carbon dioxide, water, and sunlight to produce oxygen and carbohydrates. As forests grow, they take in carbon dioxide and store carbon. If a forest is cut down, it can no longer take in carbon dioxide; therefore, more of this gas is left in the atmosphere. Increases in atmospheric carbon dioxide might cause global warming, which is a rise in temperatures around the world. Global warming could lead to changes in climate that would impact natural habitats all over Earth.

Forest Conservation

Because forests are such a valuable resource, they must be used with care. That's why many states now have forest conservation laws. **Conservation** is the careful use of resources with the goal of reducing damage to the environment. You can compare two methods of harvesting forests in **Figure 21.**

In select-cutting, shown in **Figure 21A,** a limited number of trees are cut, and new trees are planted in their place. The young saplings grow among the older trees. By the time all of the original trees are cut, a new forest has gradually grown.

In clear-cutting, shown in **Figure 21B,** all the trees in a specific area are cut down and the cleared area is replanted with new trees. One advantage of this method is that trees in a specific area of a forest are of the same age and can be removed more easily. But this method has drawbacks. Look again at **Figure 21B.** How do you think clear-cutting affected the plants and wildlife that lived in that area of the forest?

 *How do select-cutting and clear-cutting differ?*

Figure 21
Forests are valuable resources that must be used carefully.
A In select-cutting certain trees in a forest are cut down and new trees are planted in their place.
B Clear-cutting removes trees in a specific area and the entire area is replanted with new trees.

Forest Conservation

Teacher **FYI**

Conservation of forests helps maintain biodiversity. Biodiversity, in turn, helps maintain ecological stability. For example, many species are dependent upon one another for food, shelter, and other needs. The extinction of one species because of habitat loss can negatively affect other species in an ecosystem.

Visual Learning

Figure 21 Single trees are considered renewable resources, but entire forests are considered nonrenewable resources. **Why is this true?** When a single tree is cut, it can be replaced within 100 years. However, when a forest is completely removed by clear-cutting, it may take more than 100 years to reestablish a complete and complex forest ecosystem.

✔ Reading Check

Answer In select-cutting, a limited number of trees are cut down and new trees are planted in their place. In clear-cutting, all the trees in a specific area are cut down and the cleared area is replanted with new trees.

SECTION 4 Land **265**

Resource Manager

Chapter Resources Booklet
   Enrichment, p. 30
   Reinforcement, p. 26

Text Question Answer

The plants of this wildlife habitat have been destroyed. Because animal and plant species depend on each other, all wildlife from that particular habitat could die. At the least, they will have to move to another area, which could have a devastating effect on another habitat.

Mineral Resources

Quick Demo

Display various items that are classified as or made from natural resources. Items to show might include a container of oil, a wooden log, a stereo speaker wire, a glass of water, apples and oranges, and a car tire. Demonstrate that all items you are showing either are natural resources or are made from them. 🅛🅢 **Visual-Spatial**

Teacher FYI

Underwater submersibles have found potato-sized nuggets of iron, copper, nickel, cobalt, and manganese on the ocean's floor. The nuggets precipitate slowly from seawater.

Activity

Obtain samples of magnetite (iron ore), bauxite (aluminum ore), and chalcopyrite (copper ore). Inform students that magnetite is strongly magnetic. Give students the three samples described above and a magnet. Have them determine which of the minerals is an iron ore. *Magnetite will attract a magnet.*

🅛🅢 **Kinesthetic**

✔ Reading Check

Answer a mineral resource that can be mined at a profit

Renewable or Nonrenewable? If you've ever planted a tree, you know that it takes time for a tree to grow. Some trees take many years to mature. However, trees can be viewed as a renewable resource because as one tree is cut, another can be planted in its place.

Some forests, on the other hand, are nonrenewable. Why? Individual trees can be replanted, but forests are complex ecosystems that support countless living things. These ecosystems can take a long time to develop. If many or all of the trees are removed from a forest, it could take centuries for the forest ecosystem to develop again.

Mineral Resources

Take a moment to look around the classroom again. List three or four items that you use every day. Now try to decide what resources they were made from. It's easy if the item is made of wood. But what about the metal in your desk, in the door handle, or surrounding the windows? Metal objects come from mineral resources, which are found in rocks. So minerals are another type of resource that is obtained from land.

No matter which type of rock you pick up, it's likely made up of a number of minerals. Generally, it costs more to get those minerals out of the rock than the minerals are worth. But sometimes large deposits of valuable minerals are found in one place. These minerals can be classified as ores. An **ore** is a mineral resource that can be mined at a profit. **Figure 22** shows common uses for iron ore.

✔ **Reading Check** *What is an ore?*

Figure 22
Motorcycle parts and saw blades are two of the many products made from the iron extracted from the ore hematite.

Hematite

Resource Manager

Chapter Resources Booklet
Activity Worksheet, pp. 7–8
Lab Activity, pp. 11–12

Science Journal

Renewable or Nonrenewable? Have students write a report in their Science Journals about how forests can be used as a renewable resource. Encourage students to describe different methods of forest conservation. Also, ask students to describe when a forest should be classified as a nonrenewable resource. Have students discuss the current use of rain forests. P

Problems with Using Ores Ores, like fossil fuels, are resources found under Earth's surface. To get to ores, large quantities of soil and rock often must be moved. This process is called mining. Mines can look unsightly, and the waste rock produced by mines can pollute surface water. Air pollution also is produced when large industrial plants process the ores, generating dust and soot particles. Thus, the use of ores, like fossil fuels, affects the environment. Care must be taken to mine and use the ores in ways that do not harm water resources, living things, and natural habitats.

Resource Use As you have learned, using each type of resource has advantages and disadvantages. In addition, the way one resource is used often impacts another. For instance, burning too many fossil fuels can cause air and water pollution, as shown in **Figure 23.** Trees can be replanted to conserve a forest, but the trees might die if they're exposed to acid rain caused by burning fossil fuels. A farmer can manage a farm carefully to lessen soil erosion, but if the water supply is polluted from chemical runoff caused by mines, the crops will suffer regardless. Successful resource management is possible only if everyone uses all of Earth's resources wisely.

Figure 23
Industrial plants, such as the one shown here in Ohio, can create air pollution when they burn fossil fuels to generate electricity or to manufacture products.

Section 4 Assessment

1. Earth has only a limited amount of land, yet land is a renewable resource. Why?
2. Trees are renewable resources, but some forests are not. Why?
3. Compare and contrast minerals and ores.
4. How could using ores contribute to an increase in air pollution?
5. **Think Critically** About 117,000 km² of tropical rain forests are cut down each year. Why should people everywhere be concerned about the loss of forests located in the tropics?

Skill Builder Activities

6. **Using a Word Processor** Using a word processor, compile a list of do's and don'ts for forest conservation. **For more help, refer to the Technology Skill Handbook.**

7. **Communicating** Research one of the resources discussed in this section. Describe an environmental problem associated with its use. In your Science Journal, write a report that includes explanations of possible solutions to this problem. **For more help, refer to the Science Skill Handbook.**

Reteach

Have students list at least five items that are made from wood. Ask them to consider how those items would be made if trees were not readily available. Possible answer: Pencils could be made from plastic.

Challenge

Open pit mining is one way to remove an ore from the ground. **What are the steps necessary to successfully operate an open-pit mine today?** Possible answer: Remove vegetation and wildlife. Remove layers of soil and rock to expose ore to be mined. Remove ore. Fill open pit with waste rock and sediment. Cover with topsoil, plant new vegetation, and relocate wildlife.

Assessment

Oral Have students formulate additional questions about renewable and nonrenewable resources and then quiz each other aloud. Use **Performance Assessment in the Science Classroom,** p. 91.

Answers to Section Assessment

1. In most cases, land can be used over and over again.
2. Trees are renewable because one can be planted to replace one that is cut down. A forest can be nonrenewable because it may take over 100 years for a complete forest ecosystem to develop.
3. Minerals and ores are resources obtained from rocks. A mineral is an ore if it contains a useful substance that can be mined at a profit.
4. Processing of ore by industrial plants releases pollution into the air.
5. The trees take in carbon dioxide and release oxygen into the atmosphere. Cutting down trees may interrupt this cycle.
6. Students may list replanting and select-cutting under "Dos." Clear-cutting forests and destruction of crucial habitats may be listed under "Don'ts."
7. Student should deal with an environmental problem concerning land use, forests, or mineral resources.

Activity
Design Your Own Experiment

Using Land

Imagine planning a small town. Your job in this activity is to draw up a master plan to decide how 100 square units of land can be turned into a town.

Recognize the Problem

Purpose

Students plan a small town and demonstrate the need for wise land-use policies.

L2 ELL COOP LEARN

IS Logical-Mathematical

Process Skills

classifying, observing and inferring, comparing and contrasting, formulating hypotheses, designing an experiment to test a hypothesis, making models, recognizing cause and effect, measuring in SI, interpreting scientific illustrations, making and using tables

Time Required

40 minutes

Materials

Obtain or make grid paper (10 squares by 10 squares).

Form a Hypothesis

Possible Hypotheses

Land resources will be shared among living areas, recreational areas, commercial areas, schools, and landfills. Living areas should be planned first, followed by commercial areas.

Test Your Hypothesis

Possible Procedures

First, zone the plan into areas for living quarters. Then, zone office buildings and commercial areas. Finally, zone other parts of the town.

Recognize the Problem

How should land resources be used?

Form a Hypothesis

People need homes in which to live, places to work, and stores from which to buy things. Children need to attend schools and have parks in which to play. How can all of these needs be met when planning a small town?

Possible Materials

grid paper (10 squares by 10 squares)
colored pencils

Goals

■ **Design** a plan in which 100 square units of land can be turned into a small town.

Parts of Your Town	Number of Blocks Needed
Office buildings	6 blocks in one group
Industrial plant	6 blocks in one group
School	1 block
Landfill for garbage	4 blocks in one group
Houses and apartments	44 blocks—can be broken up
Stores and businesses	19 blocks—can be broken up
Park	20 blocks—can be broken up

SCIENCE Online
Internet Addresses

_____

_____

_____

Explore the Glencoe Science Web site at **science.glencoe.com** to find out more about topics in this activity.

Inclusion Strategies

Gifted Have these students use computer programs on city planning to produce their town plans. Have them present their work to the class. Then ask them to work with others to modify the plans in order to produce the most efficient use of the land. L3 COOP LEARN

Test Your Hypothesis

Plan

1. Make a square graph 10 blocks across and 10 blocks down. The graph represents a 100-square-unit piece of land.

2. The table on the previous page shows the different parts of a town that need to be included in your plan. The office buildings and industrial plant are each 6 blocks in size. These blocks must be treated as one group—they cannot be divided. The landfill is 4 blocks in size. It, too, cannot be broken up.

3. All other town parts can be broken up as needed. Stores and businesses are areas in which shops are located, as well as medical offices, restaurants, and churches.

4. As a group, discuss how the different parts of the town might be put together. Should the park be in the center of town or near the edge of town? Should the school be near the offices or near the houses? Where should the landfill go?

5. How will you show the different town parts on your grid paper?

Do

1. Make sure your teacher approves your plan before you start.

2. As a group, plan your town. Check over your plan to make sure that all town parts are accounted for.

Analyze Your Data

1. Where did you place the office buildings and the industrial plant? Why were they placed there? Where did you place the houses, school, and businesses? Explain why you placed each one as you did.

2. Did you make one park or many parks? What are the advantages of the location(s) of your park(s)?

Draw Conclusions

1. Where did you place the landfill? Will any of the towns-people be upset by its location? To answer this question, it might help to know what direction the wind usually blows from in your town.

2. Where would you put an airport in this town? Keep in mind safety issues, noise levels, and transportation needs.

Communicating Your Data

Share the results of this activity with your classmates. **For more help, refer to the Science Skill Handbook.**

ACTIVITY **269**

✔ Assessment

Performance Have students design an urban area and a suburban area. Discuss the different arrangements and needs of each. Ask students to make a model of each using monopoly parts or clay, or simply have them draw their plans and color them. Use **Performance Assessment in the Science Classroom,** p. 123.

Communicating Your Data

Students can use computer software to display their city plans. Students should compare their city plans with those of other students in the class. They should consider why other students may have designed a different plan and whether they could incorporate other ideas into their plans.

Teaching Strategies

- Have students determine wind direction in their model town. This may affect where factories and landfills are located.

- Students do not have to place their 100 squares in a 10 × 10 grid. A 4 × 25 grid of 100 squares or an irregular shape of 100 squares can be used to plot the town.

Tie to Prior Knowledge Discuss what students like and dislike about where they live, where their school is, and where their parents work.

Troubleshooting No allowances are made for roads, highways, or railroads, although these could be included in the model town.

Expected Outcome

Students' plans will show areas for office buildings and commerce; houses and apartments; parks; schools; roads; and landfills.

Analyze Your Data

1. Accept all reasonable explanations.
2. Answers should indicate that the locations of the parks are in areas easily accessible by all residents.

Error Analysis

Where is the landfill placed in relation to living areas and commercial areas? Is it downwind of these areas?

Draw Conclusions

1. Landfills should be placed downwind from most stores, businesses, and homes. People living near the landfill will be upset.
2. Ideally, an airport should be placed far away from schools and homes but located close to businesses, shopping malls, and hotels.

Science (and) Language Arts

A Walk in the Woods:
Rediscovering America on the Appalachian Trail by Bill Bryson

Respond to the Reading

Active Reading Strategies

Response After reading the selection, ask students to consider their response to it. What surprises them about the claims the author makes?

Question The author is a travel writer and not a geologist or climatologist. Ask students whether that changes their perception of the passage. Does it make his observations more or less authentic or accurate?

Connect Ask students to connect what they have learned in this passage about global warming with the claims the author makes. Are the author's claims similar to popular hypotheses on global warming?

Review Review the selection. Think about how climate has affected the area known as the Appalachian Trail.

Answers to Questions

1. It runs along the Eastern seaboard of the United States.
2. 20,000 years ago
3. warming temperatures

Respond to the Reading

1. Where is the Appalachian Trail?
2. When was the peak of the last ice age?
3. What does the author speculate was the cause of the last ice age?

Bill Bryson is a travel writer who enjoys hiking. Mr. Bryson writes in his book—A Walk in the Woods—of his attempt to walk the entire length of the Appalachian Trail, from Georgia to Maine, a length of more than 3,381 km! In the following passage, the author writes about the climatic changes that historically have affected the eastern seaboard of the United States along which the Appalachian Trail runs.

Imagine it—a wall of ice nearly half a mile high, and beyond it for tens of thousands of square miles nothing but more ice, broken only by the peaks of a very few of the loftiest mountains. What a sight that must have been. And here is a thing that most of us fail to appreciate: we are still in an ice age, only now we experience it for just part of the year. Snow and ice and cold are not really typical features of earth. Taking the long view, Antarctica is actually a jungle. (It's just having a chilly spell.) At the very peak of the last ice age 20,000 years ago, 30 percent of the earth was under ice. Today 10 percent still is. . . .

No one knows much of anything about the earth's many ice ages—why they came, why they stopped, when they may return. One interesting theory, given our present day concerns with global warming, is that the ice ages were caused not by falling temperatures but by warming ones. Warm weather would increase precipitation, which would increase cloud cover, which would lead to less snow melt at higher elevations. You don't need a great deal of bad weather to get an ice age.

Important Sites on the Appalachian Trail

1. Springer Mountain
2. Hiawassee
3. Franklin
4. Smoky Mountains National Park
5. Roanoke
6. Waynesboro
7. Rockfish Gap
8. Shenandoah
9. Skyland
10. Front Royal
11. Harpers Ferry
12. Centralia
13. Delaware Water Gap
14. Pittsfield
15. Williamstown
16. Manchester
17. Mount Killington
18. Hanover
19. Mount Washington
20. Manson
21. Mount Katahdin

Reading Further

Other works by this author include:

I'm a Stranger Here Myself: Notes on Returning to America After 20 Years Away, by Bill Bryson, Reprint edition Broadway Books, June 6, 2000.

The Lost Continent: Travels in Small Town America, by Bill Bryson, Harper Collins, 1990.

The Best American Travel Writing 2000, edited by Bill Bryson, Cambridge University Press, February 2001.

Understanding Literature

Travel Writing Bill Bryson's book is in the tradition of travel writing, which is one of the earliest forms of writing. Early travel writers such as Marco Polo and Christopher Columbus kept written records of their expeditions. Today, travel writing takes on many forms, such as guidebooks, how-to's, tales of adventure, scientific accounts, nature books, and travel memoirs.

Science Connection In this passage, the author reports on scientific research concerning climatic changes that have affected the Appalachian Trail. During ice ages, temperatures were much colder than they are now. The theory Bryson discusses says that to trigger these cold temperatures, the temperatures first had to warm up. Some of the effects of former ice ages linger along the East Coast of the United States, such as the Finger Lakes. What other topographical features of this area might show the effects of an ice age? How does Bryson's theory about global warming differ from some of the theories that are popular today? Think about what would happen if his theory is accurate—that ice ages are caused not by cooling trends, but by warming ones.

Linking Science and Writing

Travel Writing Write a travel memoir about a trip you have taken into nature. You might write about a walk you took in the woods or a family camping vacation you went on. Research the climate in the area where you traveled or explored. Even if you only have taken a walk in the woods or a field near your home, research the area's climate. Include your research in your personal account of your trip.

Career Connection

Climatologist

Tamara Ledley has spent much of her professional career out in the cold—the polar regions of Alaska and Antarctica. She studies the polar regions to see how they have helped change the world's climate over thousands of years. Climatologists use natural evidence to study climate. They find natural history in tree rings and glacial ice-core samples. Computer-based climate models help climatologists test their hypotheses. Ledley has worked with NASA and government agencies to study climate. She also educates students and teachers about climate.

SCIENCE*Online* To learn more about careers in climatology, visit the Glencoe Science Web site at **science.glencoe.com**.

Career Connection

Climatologists differ from meteorologists in that meteorologists focus on studying the day-to-day changes in weather. Climatologists are concerned with how the same region's atmosphere changes over time. They also are interested in why climate differs across the globe and how it interacts with other aspects of the natural environment.

Internet Addresses

_____

_____

_____

Explore the Glencoe Science Web site at **science.glencoe.com** to find out more about topics in this feature.

Understanding Literature

Science Connection

The Pleistocene Epoch is often referred to as the Great Ice Age. It is the most recent episode of glacial activity to affect much of the globe and is characterized by major climate changes. During this time, great sheets of ice covered much of North America and northwestern Europe and Asia. There was a major climatic cooling during this time.

Glaciers formed basins in the Northern Hemisphere creating lakes such as the Finger Lakes.

Along the central Appalachian Trail, glaciers made it only to the Ohio Valley region where they helped to form the Great Lakes. In this area, the movement of ice sheets out of the region deepened a valley.

Glaciers are responsible for some topographical features of the Appalachian Trail, particularly in New England where glaciers contributed to the shapes of certain mountain peaks.

Linking Science and Writing

Teaching Strategies

Ask students to write a list of all the factors that influence a region's climate. This could include the place's latitude and longitude, whether or not it is near an ocean or mountains, and so on. Tell students to keep these factors in mind when writing their travel memoirs.

Chapter 9 Study Guide

Reviewing Main Ideas

Preview

Students can answer the questions in their Science Journals. Discuss the answers as you go through the chapter. **Linguistic**

Review

Students can write their answers, then compare them with those of other students. **Interpersonal**

Reteach

Students can look at the illustrations and describe details that support the main ideas of the chapter. **Visual-Spatial**

Answers to Chapter Review

SECTION 1

2. Gases released by burning oil and coal mix with water in the air to form acid rain.

SECTION 2

2. Only a few regions have winds strong enough to generate electricity. Also, wind is not steady. Sometimes it blows too hard. Sometimes it blows too weakly or stops.

SECTION 3

2. Some water is polluted.

SECTION 4

2. Possible answer: Use select cutting, a method in which a limited number of trees are cut down and new trees are planted in their place.

Reviewing Main Ideas

Section 1 Energy Resources

1. Fossil fuels such as coal, oil, and gas are nonrenewable energy resources. They are being used faster than Earth is able to replace them.

2. Fossil fuels provide much-needed energy, but certain problems are associated with their use. *What is acid rain?*

Section 2 Alternative Energy Resources

1. Alternative energy resources, such as solar energy, energy from the wind, hydroelectric power, and geothermal energy, are constant and will not run out. For this reason, they are considered renewable.

2. Though some of these resources do not cause pollution, certain drawbacks are associated with their use. *Why can't wind energy be used to meet all of the world's energy needs?*

Section 3 Water

1. Less than one percent of Earth's total water supply is available for people to use. People use water to meet their basic needs and in industry and agriculture.

2. Clean water can become a nonrenewable resource if water supplies are overused or polluted. *Why is some water on Earth unusable as drinking water or for agriculture?*

Section 4 Land

1. Land is a valuable resource used for food, shelter, and other needs. Wood and minerals are two other important resources that come from land.

2. All of Earth's resources must be managed wisely. If one resource is polluted or overused, other resources can be affected as well. *Give an example of a way to harvest trees that conserves forests.*

FOLDABLES
Reading & Study Skills

After You Read

Circle the resources that have the fewest disadvantages on your Foldable. How do you think your resource use might change in the future?

FOLDABLES
Reading & Study Skills

After You Read

After students have read the chapter and completed the Foldable described in Before You Read, have them do the activity on the student page.

Dinah Zike

Visualizing Main Ideas

Complete the following concept map on resources.

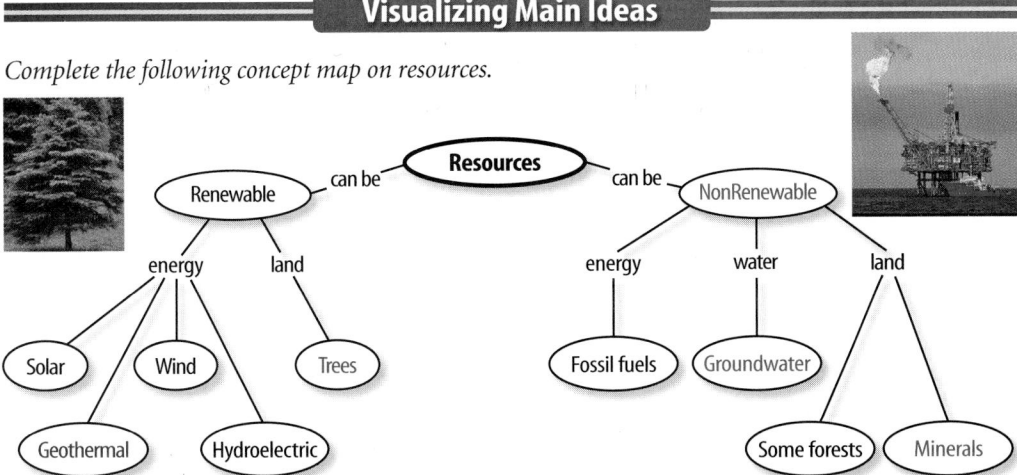

Vocabulary Review

Vocabulary Words

a. acid rain
b. conservation
c. fossil fuel
d. geothermal energy
e. groundwater
f. hydroelectric power
g. nonpoint source
h. nonrenewable
i. nuclear energy
j. ore
k. point source
l. pollution
m. renewable
n. solar energy

THE PRINCETON REVIEW **Study Tip**

Find a quiet place to study—whether at home, at school, or at the library. With no distractions, give your full attention to your lessons.

Using Vocabulary

Each of the following sentences is false. Make the sentence true by replacing the italicized word with a word from the list.

1. *Geothermal energy* is energy that comes from the Sun.

2. Careful use of resources with the goal of reducing damage to the environment is called *pollution.*

3. *Nuclear energy* forms from the remains of dead plants and animals.

4. Water that soaks into the ground and collects in the small spaces between bits of rock and soil is called *acid rain.*

5. Harmful waste products, chemicals, and substances found in the environment are called *conservation.*

6. When pollution can be traced directly to its point of origin, it is referred to as *nonpoint source* pollution.

Chapter 9 Study Guide

Visualizing Main Ideas

See student page.

Vocabulary Review

Using Vocabulary

1. Solar energy
2. conservation
3. Fossil fuel
4. groundwater
5. pollution
6. point source

Checking Concepts

1. C
2. B
3. C
4. B
5. D
6. C
7. A
8. C
9. A
10. D

Thinking Critically

11. As trees are cut down to make paper products from wood, new trees are planted to take their place.
12. Some heavily populated countries use fewer resources than countries with far fewer people. For example, in some heavily populated countries many people use bicycles for transportation instead of cars.
13. The pesticides used on farms were washed into streams. Streams carried the polluted water to the sea.
14. An earthquake could cause the containers holding the nuclear waste to rupture. Nuclear waste from the ruptured containers could enter the groundwater supply and harm the environment.
15. Not necessarily; if the value of the useful substance goes down, it may not be possible to mine it at a profit. If this occurs, the mineral resource is no longer considered an ore.

Chapter ⑨ Assessment

Checking Concepts

Choose the word or phrase that best answers the question.

1. What does nuclear energy produce?
   - A) solar energy
   - B) conservation
   - C) radioactive waste
   - D) nonrenewable resources

2. What is water in rivers, streams, lakes, and reservoirs called?
   - A) peat
   - B) surface water
   - C) groundwater
   - D) natural gas

3. Which of the following is an example of a fossil fuel?
   - A) wind
   - B) water
   - C) natural gas
   - D) uranium

4. Approximately what percentage of the energy used in the United States is from coal?
   - A) 12
   - B) 23
   - C) 32
   - D) 52

5. What kind of mineral resource can be mined for a profit?
   - A) solar cell
   - B) wind
   - C) dam
   - D) ore

6. What kind of energy is generated by large dams built on rivers?
   - A) wind
   - B) nuclear
   - C) hydroelectric
   - D) solar

7. When many windmills are located in one place in order to generate electricity, what do they form?
   - A) wind farm
   - B) dam
   - C) oil well
   - D) nuclear reactor

8. What is the source of energy used by geothermal power plants?
   - A) water
   - B) atoms
   - C) heated rocks
   - D) wind

9. When gases released by burning coal or oil mix with water that is in the air, what can they form?
   - A) acid rain
   - B) fission
   - C) conservation
   - D) groundwater

10. A nonrenewable resource can't be replaced in less than about how many years?
    - A) 5
    - B) 10
    - C) 50
    - D) 100

Thinking Critically

11. With all of the paper products that people use every day, why doesn't Earth run out of trees?

12. Some heavily populated countries cause less environmental damage than countries with far fewer people. Why?

13. A shark that lives at sea is found dead. It has chemicals in its body that can be traced to pesticides used on farms. How can this happen?

14. Why shouldn't nuclear wastes be stored near an area prone to earthquakes?

15. Once a mineral resource is classified as an ore, will it always remain an ore? Explain your answer.

Developing Skills

16. **Predicting** If a well were drilled into a rock layer that contains oil, natural gas, and water, which substance would be encountered first? Explain.

17. **Communicating** Make an outline that explains how nuclear energy is used to produce electricity.

Chapter ✔Assessment Planner

Portfolio Encourage students to place in their portfolios one or two items of what they consider to be their best work. Examples include:
- Health Integration, p. 245
- Life Science Integration, p. 252
- Science Journal, p. 260
- Science Journal, p. 266

Performance Additional performance assessments, Performance Task Assessment Lists, and rubrics for evaluating these activities can be found in Glencoe's **Performance Assessment in the Science Classroom.**

18. **Comparing and Contrasting** Compare and contrast solar energy and wind energy. Include information on availability and environmental effects.

19. **Interpreting Scientific Illustrations** The figure below shows a water-purification plant. In your own words, describe the path water takes from a stream to your faucet.

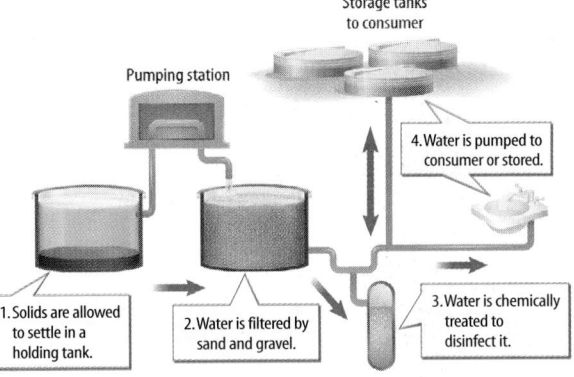

Storage tanks to consumer

Pumping station

4. Water is pumped to consumer or stored.

1. Solids are allowed to settle in a holding tank.

2. Water is filtered by sand and gravel.

3. Water is chemically treated to disinfect it.

20. **Making and Using Tables** Make a table showing the different ways water can be used as a resource.

Performance Assessment

21. **Design a Poster** Research water sources and how they are used in your area. Make a poster that shows your results. Display this poster for your class.

22. **Write a Poem** Write a poem about land as a resource. Include reasons why land is important and the different ways land can be used as a resource.

TECHNOLOGY

Go to the Glencoe Science Web site at **science.glencoe.com** or use the **Glencoe Science CD-ROM** for additional chapter assessment.

THE PRINCETON REVIEW **Test Practice**

The figure below compares the amount of energy used in certain areas of the world over a ten-year period.

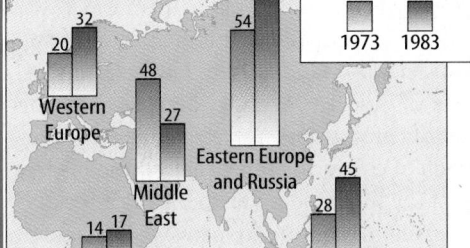

Energy production in quadrillion Btu
1973 1983

32
20
Western Europe

48
27
Middle East

54
74
Eastern Europe and Russia

14 17
Africa

28 45
Far East & Oceania

Study the map and answer the following questions.

1. According to the figure, which area had the largest increase in energy production during the ten-year period?
   A) Far East and Oceania
   B) Western Europe
   C) Eastern Europe and Russia
   D) Africa

2. According to the figure, which area experienced a decrease in energy production during the ten-year period?
   F) Far East and Oceania
   G) Middle East
   H) Africa
   J) Western Europe

THE PRINCETON REVIEW **Test Practice**

The Test-Taking Tip was written by The Princeton Review, the nation's leader in test preparation.
1. C
2. G

Developing Skills

16. Natural gas would be found first, followed by oil, and then water. The materials would form in layers according to their density.

17. Nuclear fission generates heat that is used to change water into steam. The steam is used to drive a turbine and generate electricity. Check students' outlines.

18. Solar energy and wind energy are nonpolluting alternative energy sources. Both are limited by weather and geographic location. Solar energy is also limited by the length of the day.

19. Water in the stream is collected in the water-purification plant, where it is treated to remove impurities. The water is then stored or piped to homes.

20. Tables may vary. Tables could list the type of use (for example industrial, recreational, home use) and what the water would be used for in those applications. Check student's work.

Application	Use
Industrial	coolant for machinery, ingredient in product
Home	cooking, bathing, drinking
Recreation	swimming, boating, fishing
Agriculture	water for livestock, irrigation

Performance Assessment

21. Posters should show how water resources are used in your area. Use **PASC**, p. 145.

22. Poems may be of any type as long as they show how land is used as a resource. Use **PASC**, p. 151.

✓ Assessment Resources

Reading Comprehension

QUESTION 1: B

Students must use the information in the reading passage in order to identify the best-supported conclusion.

- **Choice A** No; this is not supported by the passage.
- **Choice B** Yes; the passage mentions that Lavoisier knew that nothing (matter) had left or entered the flask.
- **Choice C** No; this is not supported by the passage.
- **Choice D** No; this is not supported by the passage.

QUESTION 2: J

Students can determine the meaning of the word from context. Students can use clues such as *served his country* and *to his nation* in order to identify choice J, *serves a country*, as the correct answer choice.

Teaching Tip

As students read through a passage, they should underline important words.

THE PRINCETON REVIEW
All questions written and validated by The Princeton Review.

REVIEW

Reading Comprehension

Read the passage. Then read each question that follows the passage. Decide which is the best answer to each question.

Antoine Laurent Lavoisier

Many scientists assisted in the development of modern chemistry. Among them was a French scientist named Antoine Laurent Lavoisier (1743–1794). He is known as the father of modern chemistry because of his theories of combustion, his development of a new system of chemical nomenclature, and his writing of the first modern textbook of chemistry. He served his country in many ways, including as a tax collector, an economist, and the director of France's gunpowder-making facility. Many considered him to be a great <u>patriot</u> to his nation.

Lavoisier's experiments were some of the first chemistry experiments that used measurements to support a hypothesis. He performed chemical reactions inside sealed flasks. In his most famous experiment, a sealed flask was filled with air and mercury. Lavoisier weighed the flask and then heated it for several days until the mercury turned red. The altered appearance of the mercury indicated that the air and mercury had reacted chemically to produce a different substance. Once he observed this color change, Lavoisier weighed the flask again and found that it weighed the same as it did before.

Lavoisier's experiment showed that the matter that exists at the start of a chemical reaction exists at the end of the chemical reaction, even if the matter's properties have changed. Because the flask weighed the same before and after the chemical reaction, Lavoisier knew that nothing had left or entered

---

the flask. The heat caused the atoms trapped inside to rearrange and form a new substance. Although it took many years for Lavoisier's explanation of what he observed to be accepted by everyone, it eventually was recognized as correct. His work helped scientists understand chemical reactions including those that occur in living organisms and in the environment.

Test-Taking Tip As you read the passage, underline or circle key words. Refer back to these key words as you answer the questions.

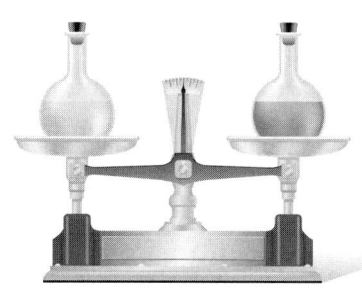

The two flasks were weighed before and after the chemical reaction occurred.

1. The passage best supports which of the following conclusions?
   A) Energy is neither created nor destroyed.
   B) Matter is neither created nor destroyed.
   C) Only heat and time create matter.
   D) Glass and heat make new substances.

2. You can tell from the passage that a <u>patriot</u> is someone who _____.
   F) makes gunpowder
   G) reacts chemically
   H) convinces other people
   J) serves a country

Reasoning and Skills

Read each question and choose the best answer.

1. Water exists in different states. Cells contain mostly water. Which of the following best represents the way that water is found in cells?

A)

B)

C)

D)

Test-Taking Tip Think about what you would find in your own cells.

Percentage of Elements that Make Up Organisms			
Element	Bacteria (%)	Alfalfa (%)	Human (%)
Carbon	12	11	19
Nitrogen	3	1	3
Oxygen	74	78	65
Phosphorus	1	1	1
Hydrogen	10	9	10

2. Elements come together in different combinations to make the many substances in your body. According to the information above, which element is most abundant in humans?

F) carbon
G) nitrogen
H) oxygen
J) phosphorus

Test-Taking Tip Use key words from the question, such as *in humans*, to direct your attention to the correct column in the table.

Experiments in Plant Growth			
Plant	Days Grown	Type of Light-bulb (watts)	Height (cm)
1	68	100	35
2	68	100	27.5

3. Above is a picture showing how an experiment on plant growth was performed. Data from the experiment also could have included the _____.
A) type of flower pot that was used
B) size of the laboratory
C) day of week that the data were recorded
D) amount of water given to the plants

Test-Taking Tip Think about which of the answer choices can affect a plant's growth.

Consider this question carefully before writing your answer on a separate sheet of paper.

4. Governments have started to talk about reducing the amount of pollution their countries release into oceans and air. Why would pollution from one country bother another, faraway country?

Test-Taking Tip Think about how pollutants might move through water or air. Then, carefully write your answer.

Reasoning and Skills

QUESTION 1: C
Students should infer that living cells contain liquid water.

QUESTION 2: H
Students must use information from the chart to identify choice H as the correct answer.

Teaching Tip

When using data from a table or chart to identify the correct answer, students should read the question carefully to decide what area of the chart is being asked about.

QUESTION 3: D
Students should consider each answer choice carefully.

- **Choice A** No; the type of flower pot would most likely not affect plant growth.
- **Choice B** No; the size of the laboratory would most likely not affect plant growth.
- **Choice C** No; the day the data was recorded would not affect plant growth.
- **Choice D** Yes; the amount of water given to the plants would affect plant growth.

QUESTION 4: Answers will vary.
Students should mention that air pollution might be carried great distances by wind or clouds (acid rain). Moreover, water pollution might be carried hundreds of miles by rivers and ocean currents.

Unit Contents

✔ Pre-Reading Activity

Have students read the objectives for each section and search for charts and pictures that relate to each objective.

How Are Air & Advertising Connected?

278

Teacher to Teacher

"I have students do a semester-long project on tracking high/low temperatures in a major city of the United States. The finished product is a tri-fold advertisement brochure to attract tourism to the city. Data collection, graphing, reading, persuasive writing, and art are integrated in this project."

Leonard G. Rodríguez, Assistant Principal
First Avenue Middle School
Pasadena, CA

HAND LAUNDRY

In the late 1800s, two scientists were studying the composition of air when they discovered an element that hadn't been known before. They named it "neon," and soon this new element, represented by the chemical symbol Ne, had been assigned a spot in the periodic table (right). It took a few years for people to figure out something useful to do with neon! In 1910, a French engineer experimented with passing an electrical current through neon gas in a vacuum tube. The result was a spectacular orange-red light. Neon's advertising possibilities were quickly realized, and soon the first neon sign blazed on a boulevard in Paris. Today, neon signs in a wide range of colors advertise shops and services all over the world. The other colors are made by mixing neon with other gases and by using tinted tubes.

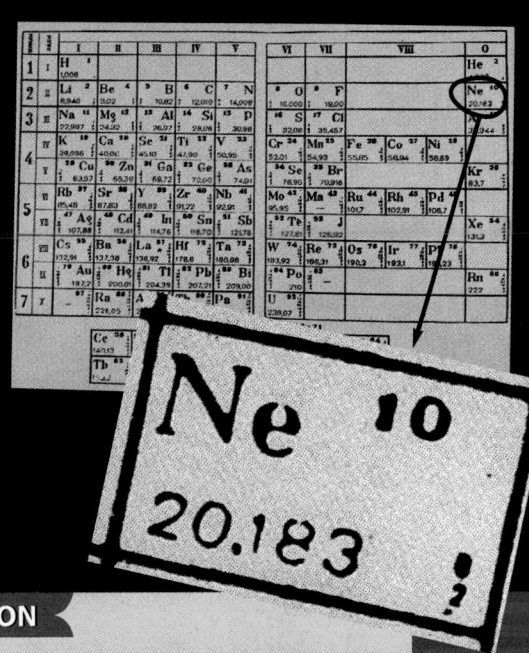

SCIENCE CONNECTION

NOBLE GASES Neon is one of six elements known as the noble gases. These gases make up a tiny fraction of the atmosphere. Conduct research to find out more about this group. What other gases belong to the group? What do they all have in common? Why are they called "noble"? Create a chart that shows when each of the noble gases was discovered and what distinctive characteristics and uses it has.

SCIENCE Online
Internet Addresses

_____

_____

_____

Explore the Glencoe Science Web site at **science.glencoe.com** to find out more about topics in this unit.

Introducing the Unit

How Are Air & Advertising Connected?

Although the noble gases make up only a small percentage of the atmosphere, the atmosphere as a whole is a unique feature that helps maintain the temperate conditions necessary for life.

Besides providing protection from harmful solar radiation, the atmosphere also drives the energy transfer between the oceans and large air masses.

Wind and clouds are created through differential heating of these air masses. The movement of these air masses produces global weather patterns.

These weather patterns, in combination with local geographical conditions, create the various climates found throughout the world.

Ask students to hypothesize why the atmosphere is 78% nitrogen and only 21% oxygen, despite the fact that oxygen is more important for life than nitrogen.

SCIENCE CONNECTION
Activity
Construct a chart with four columns and seven rows. In the top row list: name, discovered, characteristic, and use. In the first column, list the noble gases: helium, neon, argon, krypton, xenon, and radon. Divide the students into six groups; assign each group a noble gas to research. Have students complete their own chart as each group presents its findings to the class.

Section/Objectives	Standards		Activities/Features
Chapter Opener	**National**	**State/Local**	**Explore Activity:** Observe air pressure, p. 281
	See p. 5T for a Key to Standards.		**Before You Read,** p. 281
Section 1 Earth's Atmosphere ⏱ 2 sessions 📦 1 block 1. **Identify** the gases in Earth's atmosphere. 2. **Describe** the structures of Earth's atmosphere. 3. **Explain** what causes air pressure.	National Content Standards: UCP2, A1, D1, D3		**Science Online,** p. 284 **Problem-Solving Activity:** How does altitude affect air pressure?, p. 286 **MiniLAB:** Determining if air has mass, p. 287 **Life Science Integration,** p. 288 **Activity:** Evaluating Sunscreens, p. 290
Section 2 Energy Transfer in the Atmosphere ⏱ 2 sessions 📦 1 block 1. **Describe** what happens to the energy Earth receives from the Sun. 2. **Compare and contrast** radiation, conduction, and convection. 3. **Explain** the water cycle.	National Content Standards: UCP3, A1, B3, D1		**Physics Integration,** p. 292 **MiniLAB:** Modeling Heat Transfer, p. 293
Section 3 Air Movement ⏱ 3 sessions 📦 1.5 blocks 1. **Explain** why different latitudes on Earth receive different amounts of solar energy. 2. **Describe** the Coriolis effect. 3. **Locate** doldrums, trade winds, prevailing westerlies, polar easterlies, and jet streams.	National Content Standards: UCP3, A1, B2, D1, G1		**Science Online,** p. 296 **Visualizing Global Winds,** p. 297 **Activity:** The Heat Is On, pp. 300–301 **Science and Language Arts:** Song of the Sky Loom, pp. 302–303

NATIONAL GEOGRAPHIC

Teacher's Corner

PRODUCTS AVAILABLE FROM GLENCOE
To order call 1-800-334-7344:
Curriculum Kit
GeoKit: Weather
Videodisc
STV: Atmosphere

PRODUCTS AVAILABLE FROM NATIONAL GEOGRAPHIC SOCIETY
To order call 1-800-368-2728:
Videos
Atmosphere: On the Air
The Sun: Earth's Star
Ozone: Protecting the Invisible Shield

INDEX TO NATIONAL GEOGRAPHIC SOCIETY
The following articles may be used for research relating to this chapter:
"Antarctica: A Land of Isolation No More," by Bryan Hodgson, April 1990.

Activity Materials	Reproducible Resources	Section Assessment	Technology
Explore Activity: cardboard cereal box, glass, water, metric ruler, scissors	**Chapter Resources Booklet** Foldables Worksheet, p. 13 Directed Reading Overview, p. 15 Note-taking Worksheets, pp. 29–31	GLENCOE'S **ASSESSMENT** ADVANTAGE	
MiniLAB: pan balance, inflatable balls, air pump, pressure gauge **Activity:** several different brands of sunscreen	**Chapter Resources Booklet** Transparency Activity, p. 40 MiniLAB, p. 3 Enrichment, p. 26 Reinforcement, p. 23 Directed Reading, p. 16 Activity Worksheet, pp. 5–6 Lab Activity, pp. 9–10	Portfolio Extension, p. 285 Performance Problem-Solving Activity, p. 286 MiniLAB, p. 287 Skill Builder Activities, p. 289 Content Section Assessment, p. 289	🔦 Section Focus Transparency ⊙ Interactive CD-ROM ∩ Guided Reading Audio Program
MiniLAB: empty soup can, black construction paper, tape, cold water *Need materials?* Contact Science Kit at 1-800-828-7777 or www.sciencekit.com on the Internet.	**Chapter Resources Booklet** Transparency Activity, p. 41 MiniLAB, p. 4 Enrichment, p. 27 Reinforcement, p. 24 Directed Reading, p. 16 Lab Activity, pp. 11–12 Transparency Activity, pp. 43–44	Portfolio Science Journal, p. 293 Performance MiniLAB, p. 293 Skill Builder Activities, p. 294 Content Section Assessment, p. 294	🔦 Section Focus Transparency 🔦 Teaching Transparency ⊙ Interactive CD-ROM ∩ Guided Reading Audio Program
Activity: ring stand, soil, metric ruler, water, masking tape, 2 clear-plastic boxes, overhead light with reflector, 4 thermometers, 4 colored pencils	**Chapter Resources Booklet** Transparency Activity, p. 42 Enrichment, p. 28 Reinforcement, p. 25 Directed Reading, pp. 17, 18 Activity Worksheet, pp. 7–8 **Lab Management and Safety,** p. 71	Portfolio Extension, p. 297 Curriculum Connection, p. 297 Assessment, p. 299 Performance Skill Builder Activities, p. 299 Content Section Assessment, p. 299	🔦 Section Focus Transparency ⊙ Interactive CD-ROM ∩ Guided Reading Audio Program

GLENCOE'S **ASSESSMENT** ADVANTAGE

End of Chapter Assessment

Blackline Masters	Technology	Professional Series
Chapter Resources Booklet Chapter Review, pp. 33–34 Chapter Tests, pp. 35–38 **Standardized Test Practice by The Princeton Review,** pp. 67–70	▭ MindJogger Videoquiz ⊙ Interactive CD-ROM ⊙ Vocabulary PuzzleMakers ⊙ ExamView Pro Test Bank ⊙ Interactive Lesson Planner ⊙ Interactive Teacher Edition	Performance Assessment in the Science Classroom (PASC)

Transparencies

Section Focus

Section Focus Transparency 1 — Cosmic Impact

You might think you have to live on the Moon to find a large impact crater such as the one in this photo. Not so. This impact crater in Australia is one of the world's largest. However, unlike the Moon where impact craters are quite common, impact craters on Earth are pretty rare.

1. What does a meteor shower look like? What do you think is happening in a meteor shower?
2. Why is the surface of the Moon struck by objects from space so much more frequently than the surface of Earth?
3. What affect do you think the impact of the meteorite shown above had on the atmosphere?

L2

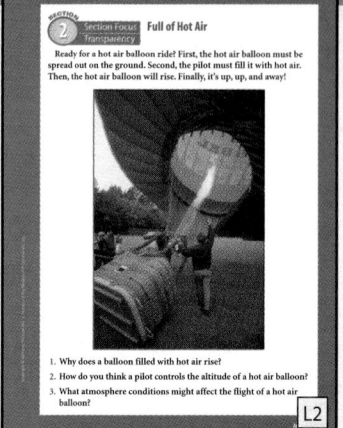

Section Focus Transparency 2 — Full of Hot Air

Ready for a hot air balloon ride? First, the hot air balloon must be spread out on the ground. Second, the pilot must fill it with hot air. Then, the hot air balloon will rise. Finally, it's up, up, and away!

1. Why does a balloon filled with hot air rise?
2. How do you think a pilot controls the altitude of a hot air balloon?
3. What atmosphere conditions might affect the flight of a hot air balloon?

L2

Section Focus Transparency 3 — The Growth of a Mountain

Did you know that Mount Everest, the world's highest point, is two meters higher than previously thought? Researchers on a 1999 expedition sponsored by the National Geographic Society used sophisticated satellite equipment to measure the peak's height. They found the elevation to be 8,850 m (29,035 feet), instead of 8,848 m (29,028 feet)—a measurement that had been accepted since 1954.

1. In general, what do you think conditions are like at the top of Mount Everest compared to the base?
2. What causes the plume coming off the summit of Mount Everest?
3. How do winds affect air travel?

L2

Assessment

Assessment Transparency — Atmosphere

Directions: Carefully review the diagram and answer the following questions.

1. The water in the lake evaporated in response to ___.
   A the Sun
   B the wind
   C the clouds
   D precipitation
2. Which of these facts best explains why water vapor condenses back into water drops?
   F Sunlight heats the water, causing it to turn into vapor.
   G Water vapor rises into the air and then cools again, forming clouds.
   H Rain falls back onto the ground from the clouds.
   J The water cycle needs the Sun.
3. Many types of chemicals are dumped into lakes and rivers from large factories. This practice could affect the environment by ___.
   A decreasing the amount of rain
   B decreasing the water level in lakes
   C increasing the temperature of the air
   D increasing the amount of pollution in rain

L2

Teaching

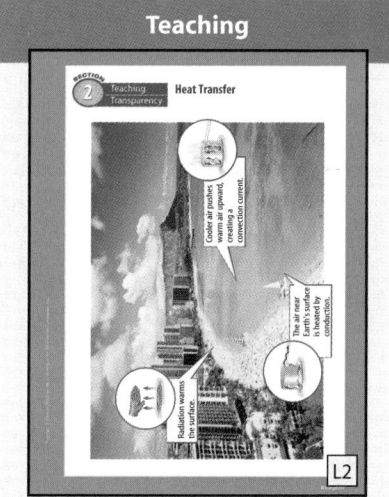

Teaching Transparency 2 — Heat Transfer

L2

This is a representation of key blackline masters available in the Teacher Classroom Resources. See Resource Manager boxes within the chapter for additional information.

Key to Teaching Strategies

The following designations will help you decide which activities are appropriate for your students.

L1 Level 1 activities should be appropriate for students with learning difficulties.

L2 Level 2 activities should be within the ability range of all students.

L3 Level 3 activities are designed for above-average students.

ELL ELL activities should be within the ability range of English Language Learners.

COOP LEARN Cooperative Learning activities are designed for small group work.

LS Multiple Learning Styles logos, as described on page 22T, are used throughout to indicate strategies that address different learning styles.

P These strategies represent student products that can be placed into a best-work portfolio.

Hands-on Activities

Activity Worksheets

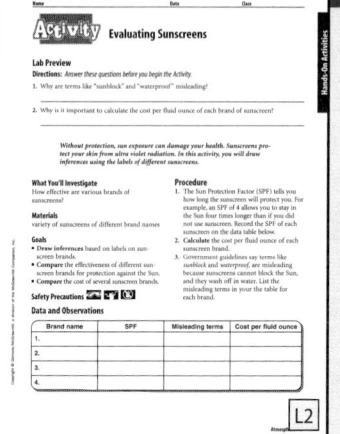

Activity — Evaluating Sunscreens

Lab Preview
Directions: Answer these questions before you begin the Activity!

1. Why are terms like "sunblock" and "waterproof" misleading?

2. Why is it important to calculate the cost per fluid ounce of each brand of sunscreen?

Without protection, sun exposure can damage your health. Sunscreens protect your skin from ultra violet radiation. In this activity, you will draw inferences using the labels of different sunscreens.

L2

Laboratory Activities

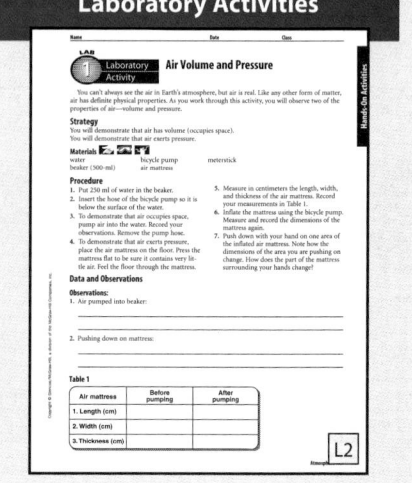

Laboratory Activity — Air Volume and Pressure

L2

Meeting Different Ability Levels

Content Outline

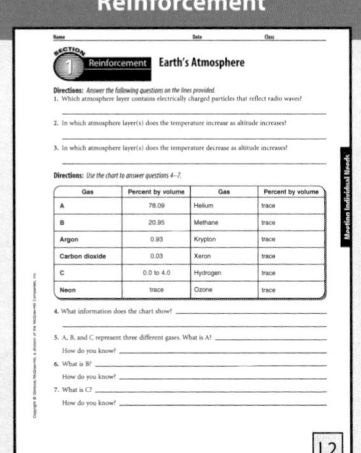

L2

Reinforcement

L2

Directed Reading

L1

Assessment

Chapter Tests

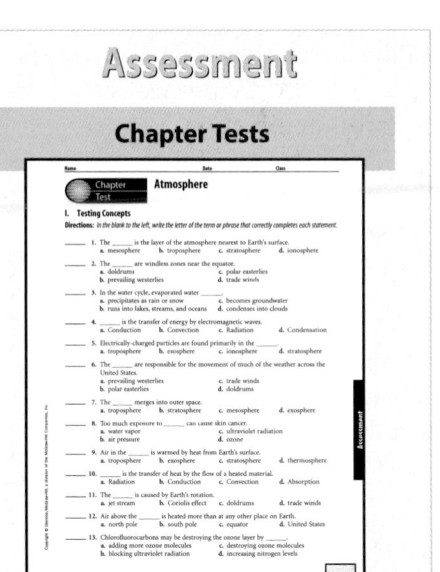

L2

Enrichment

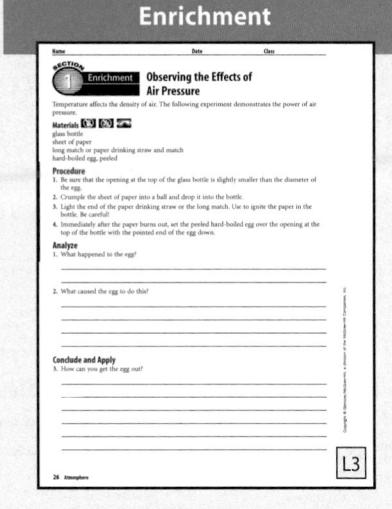

L3

Spanish Directed Reading

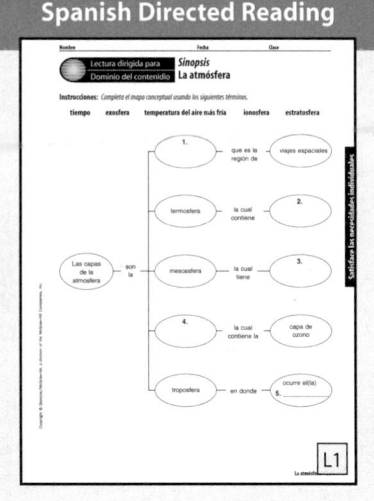

L1

Test Practice Workbook

L2

Chapter Review

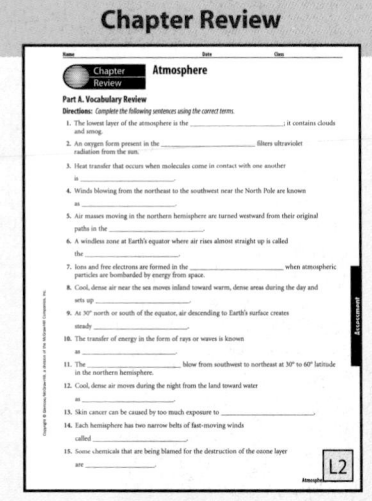

L2

Science Content Background

SECTION 1

Earth's Atmosphere
Makeup of the Atmosphere

Earth's original atmosphere was probably composed mostly of hydrogen and helium. This primitive atmosphere changed over geologic time as the lighter elements escaped Earth's gravity into space, and erupting volcanoes emitted gases such as water vapor, carbon dioxide, methane, ammonia, and nitrogen. As Earth continued to cool, the water vapor condensed and absorbed most of the carbon dioxide. Oxygen was probably formed from the dissociation of water vapor molecules and by photosynthetic bacteria.

SECTION 2

Energy Transfer in the Atmosphere
Energy from the Sun

Transfer of energy by radiation does not involve matter. Convection currents distribute energy until equilibrium is reached. On Earth, however, equilibrium is never attained. The tropics always receive more radiant energy than the rest of Earth. Therefore, energy transfer is always occurring in the atmosphere.

About 90% of the water vapor in our atmosphere comes from the evaporation of ocean water. The greater the amount of solar energy, the greater the amount of water vapor that is evaporated. Solar energy also keeps water vapor molecules in constant motion. Our atmosphere is unique because its temperature range enables water to exist as liquid, gas (water vapor), and solid (ice).

SECTION 3

Air Movement
Forming Wind

The Sun heats the troposphere unevenly, activating a system of winds that move energy from one area of Earth to another. Whenever air pressure increases or decreases rapidly in relation to nearby areas, winds increase in velocity. Winds can be either horizontal or vertical in direction.

Student Misconception

Wind is caused by something in the sky, such as a cloud, that blows very hard.

Refer to the facing page for teaching strategies to address this misconception. Refer to page 296 for content related to this topic.

Global Winds

The doldrums are areas of permanent low pressure that occur in zones of maximum solar heating with a weak horizontal pressure gradient. The trade winds are relatively steady winds. Westerlies and easterlies are more complex because their flows are impeded by mountains and valleys. Friction between land and air creates local eddies that slow wind movement.

E.R. Degginger/Photo Researchers, Inc.

For additional content background on this topic, go to the Glencoe Science Web site at science.glencoe.com.

IDENTIFYING > Misconceptions

Students may think that . . .

• **Wind is caused by something in the sky, such as a cloud, that blows very hard.**

Students often think that wind is caused by an external force. This has been reinforced by story books that picture winds as a cloud blowing air. Adding to this idea is the use of fans to move air. Taking these ideas together, some students have come to believe that some entity or device makes the wind. In fact, wind is caused by the uneven heating of Earth and its atmosphere.

Discussion

Bring a fan to class, plug it in, and turn it on.

• As students observe the fan, have them discuss what is causing the air to move. In this case electricity is running a motor that causes the fan blades to move. As the blades turn, they move the air.

Sunstar Photography/International Stock

• Organize the class into small groups. Ask each group to discuss how they think the outside air moves. Is there a "fan" that makes the wind blow? Have students write down their ideas, and then discuss them with the group. Have each group share their favorite ideas as well as the explanations they think are most correct.

Demonstration

Use this demonstration to develop the idea that air movements in nature are caused by uneven heating and cooling of Earth's surface.

• Use tape to attach a lunch bag, open end down, to each end of a meterstick. Balance the meterstick on the back of a chair.

• Carefully place a small electric heater under the open end of one of the bags. **CAUTION:** *Make sure the heater does not touch the bag.* Have students observe what happens.

• Explain to students that what they have just observed happens in the atmosphere. The Sun warms Earth's surface. This heat is transferred to the air directly above the surface. This warm air is less dense than the colder, surrounding air. It is pushed upward, which is what caused the bag to rise. As the warm air is pushed up, it is replaced with colder air. This trading places of warm and cold air in the atmosphere is what causes wind.

Assess

After completing the chapter, see *Identifying Misconceptions* in the Study Guide.

CHAPTER 10

Atmosphere

Chapter Vocabulary

atmosphere, p. 282
troposphere, p. 284
ionosphere, p. 285
ozone layer, p. 288
ultraviolet radiation, p. 288
chlorofluorocarbon, p. 288
radiation, p. 292
conduction, p. 292
convection, p. 292
hydrosphere, p. 293
condensation, p. 293
Coriolis effect, p. 296
jet stream, p. 298
sea breeze, p. 299
land breeze, p. 299

What do you think?

Science Journal The photo shows an eardrum. When there is a rapid change in air pressure outside the ear (as when a plane takes off), an air pressure difference develops between the middle and outer ear. The eardrum (between the middle and outer ear) bulges outward because the pressure in the middle ear is greater than the air pressure in the plane. Eventually, the pressures become equalized. As pressure changes, a person feels a popping sensation in the ear.

CHAPTER 10

Atmosphere

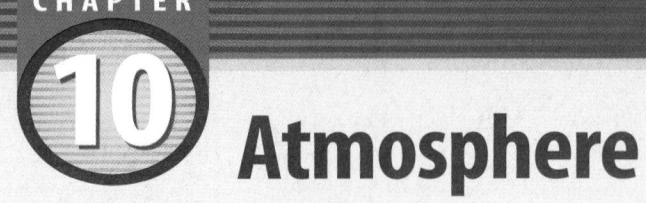

Why is it difficult to breathe at high elevations? Why are some mountain peaks permanently covered with snow? These mountain climbers aren't supplementing oxygen just because the activity is physically demanding. At elevations like this, the amount of oxygen available in the air is so small that the climbers' bodily functions might not be supported. In this chapter, you'll learn about the composition and structure of the atmosphere. You also will learn how energy is transferred in the atmosphere. In addition, you'll examine the water cycle and major wind systems.

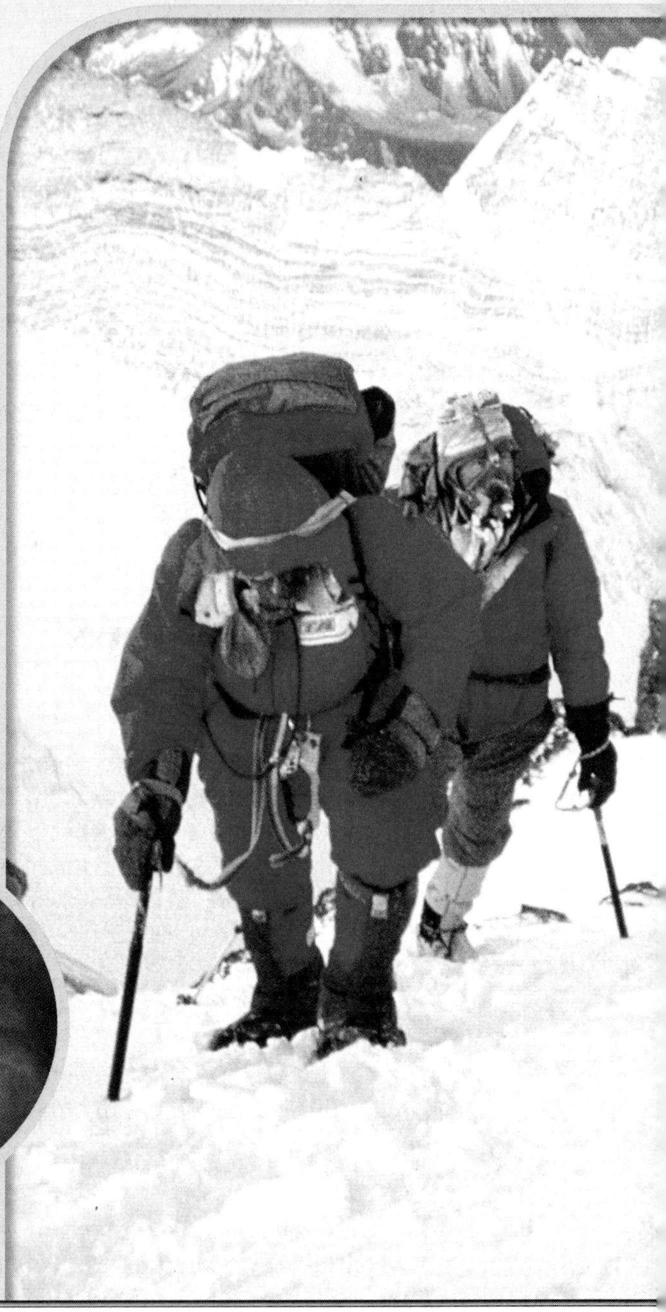

What do you think?

Science Journal Look at the picture below with a classmate. Discuss what this might be. Here's a hint: *It "pops" in thin air.* Write your answer or best guess in your Science Journal.

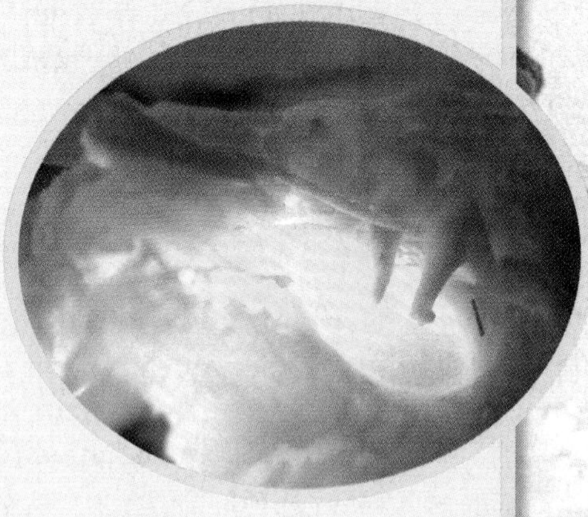

Theme Connection

Energy The Sun provides most of the energy that heats Earth's atmosphere, drives the water cycle, and (because of unequal heating) drives global wind systems.

The air around you is made of billions of molecules. These molecules are constantly moving in all directions and bouncing into every object in the room, including you. Air pressure is the result of the billions of collisions of molecules into these objects. Because you usually do not feel molecules in air hitting you, do the activity below to see the effect of air pressure.

Observe air pressure

1. Cut out a square of cardboard about 10 cm on a side from a cereal box.
2. Fill a glass to the brim with water.
3. Hold the cardboard firmly over the top of the glass, covering the water, and invert the glass.
4. Slowly remove your hand holding the cardboard in place and observe.

Observe

Write a paragraph in your Science Journal describing what happened to the cardboard when you inverted the glass and removed your hand. How does air pressure explain what happened?

Before You Read

FOLDABLES
Reading & Study Skills

Making a Sequence Study Fold Make the following Foldable to help you visualize the layers of Earth's atmosphere.

1. Stack three sheets of paper in front of you so the short sides are at the top.
2. Slide the top sheet up so that about four centimeters of the middle sheet show. Slide the middle sheet up so that about four centimeters of the bottom sheet show.
3. Fold the sheets top to bottom to form six tabs and staple along the topfold. Turn the Foldable so the staples are at the bottom.
4. Label the flaps *Earth's Atmosphere, Troposphere, Stratosphere, Mesosphere, Thermosphere,* and *Exosphere,* as shown.
5. As you read the chapter, write information about each layer of Earth's atmosphere under the tabs.

> Exosphere
> Thermosphere
> Mesosphere
> Stratosphere
> Troposphere
> Earth's Atmosphere

281

Purpose Students will observe the force exerted by air pressure.

Preparation Collect cereal boxes and cut the sides from the boxes for students to use. Ask students to bring in cereal boxes from home to be certain you have enough.

Materials cereal box side, metric ruler, scissors, drinking glass, and water for each pair of students

Teaching Strategy Inspect the cardboard and glass of water of each pair before they turn the glass over. Be certain there is no gap between the water level and the cardboard. Have students turn their glasses upside down over a sink.

Observe

The cardboard will stick to the glass, trapping the water inside. Air pressure presses on the cardboard allowing it to adhere to the rim of the glass.

Assessment

Process Ask students to make a hypothesis about how their experiment would differ if they could conduct it in a vacuum. Without air to supply pressure on the cardboard, the cardboard square would fall and the water would spill out. Use **Performance Assessment in the Science Classroom**, p. 93

Before You Read

FOLDABLES
Reading & Study Skills

Dinah Zike Study Fold
Purpose Determine what students know about Earth's atmosphere before reading the chapter by providing a Foldable for recording and organizing notes on the layers of the atmosphere as they read.

For additional help, see Foldables Worksheet, p. 13 in **Chapter Resources Booklet**, or go to the Glencoe Science Web site at **science.glencoe.com.** See After You Read in the Study Guide at the end of this chapter.

1 Motivate

Bellringer Transparency

Display the Section Focus Transparency for Section 1. Use the accompanying Transparency Activity Master. L2 ELL

Tie to Prior Knowledge

Ask students to name a major gas in Earth's atmosphere. Most students will name oxygen. Tell students oxygen is a major gas but not the most abundant gas in the air we breathe. In this section, they will learn what the most abundant gas is (nitrogen) and what other substances are in the atmosphere.

As You Read

What You'll Learn

- **Identify** the gases in Earth's atmosphere.
- **Describe** the structure of Earth's atmosphere.
- **Explain** what causes air pressure.

Vocabulary

atmosphere   ozone layer
troposphere   ultraviolet radiation
ionosphere   chlorofluorocarbon

Why It's Important

The atmosphere makes life on Earth possible.

Figure 1
Earth's atmosphere, as viewed from space, is a thin layer of gases. The atmosphere keeps Earth's temperature in a range that can support life.

Importance of the Atmosphere

Earth's **atmosphere,** shown in **Figure 1,** is a thin layer of air that forms a protective covering around the planet. If Earth had no atmosphere, days would be extremely hot and nights would be extremely cold. Earth's atmosphere maintains a balance between the amount of heat absorbed from the Sun and the amount of heat that escapes back into space. It also protects life-forms from some of the Sun's harmful rays.

Makeup of the Atmosphere

Earth's atmosphere is a mixture of gases, solids, and liquids that surround the planet. It extends from Earth's surface to outer space. The atmosphere is much different today from what it was when Earth was young.

Earth's early atmosphere, produced by erupting volcanoes, contained nitrogen and carbon dioxide, but little oxygen. Then, more than 2 billon years ago, Earth's early organisms released oxygen into the atmosphere as they made food with the aid of sunlight. These early organisms, however, were limited to layers of ocean water deep enough to be shielded from the Sun's harmful rays, yet close enough to the surface to receive sunlight. Eventually, a layer rich in ozone (O_3) that protects Earth from the Sun's harmful rays formed in the upper atmosphere. This protective layer eventually allowed green plants to flourish all over Earth, releasing even more oxygen. Today, a variety of life forms, including you, depends on a certain amount of oxygen in Earth's atmosphere.

Section ✓Assessment Planner

PORTFOLIO
Extension, p. 285
PERFORMANCE ASSESSMENT
Problem-Solving Activity, p. 286
MiniLab, p. 287
Skill Builder Activities, p. 289
See page 306 for more options.

CONTENT ASSESSMENT
Section, p. 289
Challenge, p. 289
Chapter, pp. 306–307

Gases in the Atmosphere Today's atmosphere is a mixture of the gases shown in **Figure 2.** Nitrogen is the most abundant gas, making up 78 percent of the atmosphere. Oxygen actually makes up only 21 percent of Earth's atmosphere. As much as four percent of the atmosphere is water vapor. Other gases that make up Earth's atmosphere include argon and carbon dioxide.

The composition of the atmosphere is changing in small but important ways. For example, car exhaust emits gases into the air. These pollutants mix with oxygen and other chemicals in the presence of sunlight and form a brown haze called smog. Humans burn fuel for energy. As fuel is burned, carbon dioxide is released as a by-product into Earth's atmosphere. Increasing energy use may increase the amount of carbon dioxide in the atmosphere.

Solids and Liquids in Earth's Atmosphere In addition to gases, Earth's atmosphere contains small, solid particles such as dust, salt, and pollen. Dust particles get into the atmosphere when wind picks them up off the ground and carries them along. Salt is picked up from ocean spray. Plants give off pollen that becomes mixed throughout part of the atmosphere.

The atmosphere also contains small liquid droplets other than water droplets in clouds. The atmosphere constantly moves these liquid droplets and solids from one region to another. For example, the atmosphere above you may contain liquid droplets and solids from an erupting volcano thousands of kilometers from your home, as illustrated in **Figure 3.**

Argon (0.93%)
Carbon dioxide (0.03%)

Neon
Helium
Methane
Krypton — Trace 1%
Xenon
Hydrogen
Ozone

21% Oxygen

78% Nitrogen

Figure 2
This graph shows the percentages of the gases, excluding water vapor, that make up Earth's atmosphere.

Figure 3
Solids and liquids can travel large distances in Earth's atmosphere, affecting regions far from their source.

A On June 12, 1991, Mount Pinatubo in the Philippines erupted, causing liquid droplets to form in Earth's atmosphere.

 **B** Droplets of sulfuric acid from volcanoes can produce spectacular sunrises.

SECTION 1 Earth's Atmosphere **283**

Fun Fact

The thickness of the troposphere varies with latitude, being thickest over the equator. At other latitudes, it thickens in summer and thins in winter.

Discussion

Why do you think rain and clouds occur mostly in the troposphere? because most of the water vapor exists in that layer

Caption Answer

Figure 4 troposphere

IDENTIFYING
Misconceptions

Looking at **Figure 4,** students may infer that there is a thick concentration of ozone molecules in the stratosphere. Inform students that the ozone layer in the stratosphere is a layer where there is a greater concentration of ozone molecules than elsewhere in the atmosphere.

SCIENCE
Online

Research Visit the Glencoe Science Web site at **science.glencoe.com** for more information about layers of Earth's atmosphere. Communicate to your class what you learn.

Figure 4
Earth's atmosphere is divided into five layers. *Which layer of the atmosphere do you live in?*

Layers of the Atmosphere

What would happen if you left a glass of chocolate milk on the kitchen counter for a while? Eventually, you would see a lower layer with more chocolate separating from upper layers with less chocolate. Like a glass of chocolate milk, Earth's atmosphere has layers. There are five layers in Earth's atmosphere, each with its own properties, as shown in **Figure 4.** The lower layers include the troposphere and stratosphere. The upper atmospheric layers are the mesosphere, thermosphere, and exosphere. The troposphere and stratosphere contain most of the air.

Lower Layers of the Atmosphere You study, eat, sleep, and play in the **troposphere,** which is the lowest of Earth's atmospheric layers. It contains 99 percent of the water vapor and 75 percent of the atmospheric gases. Rain, snow, and clouds occur in the troposphere, which extends up to about 10 km.

The stratosphere, the layer directly above the troposphere, extends from 10 km above Earth's surface to about 50 km. As **Figure 4** shows, a portion of the stratosphere contains higher levels of a gas called ozone. Each molecule of ozone is made up of three oxygen atoms bonded together. Later in this section you will learn how ozone protects Earth from the Sun's harmful rays.

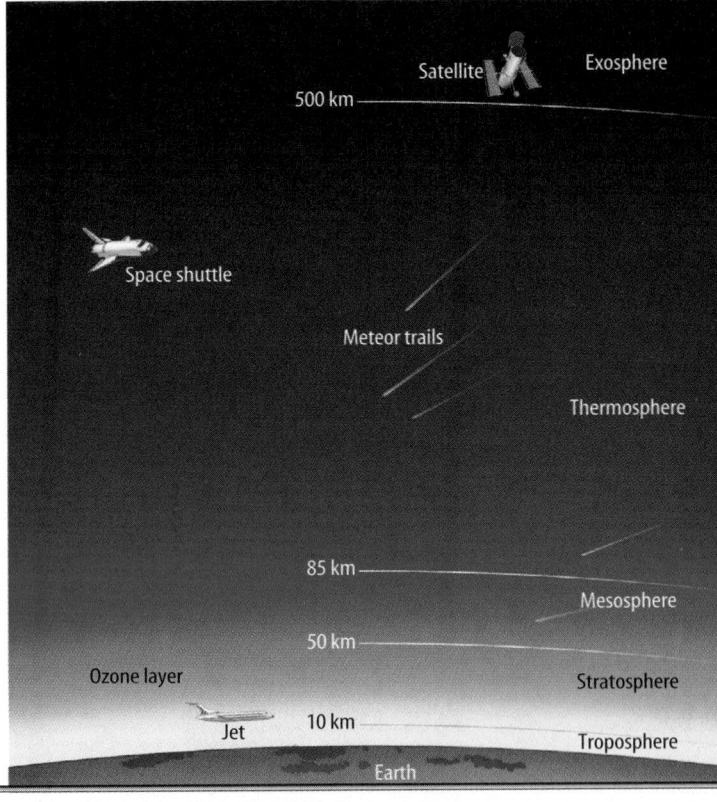

Exosphere
Satellite
500 km
Space shuttle
Meteor trails
Thermosphere
85 km
Mesosphere
50 km
Ozone layer
Stratosphere
Jet   10 km
Troposphere
Earth

Inclusion Strategies

Gifted Scientists have been measuring the characteristics of Earth's atmosphere for centuries. Have students research the history of atmospheric study, finding out how people studied the upper atmosphere before there were airplanes and other sophisticated instruments. In the 19th century, some scientists took weather instruments up in hot air balloons to study the upper atmosphere.

SCIENCE
Online
Internet Addresses

_____
_____
_____

Explore the Glencoe Science Web site at **science.glencoe.com** to find out more about topics in this section.

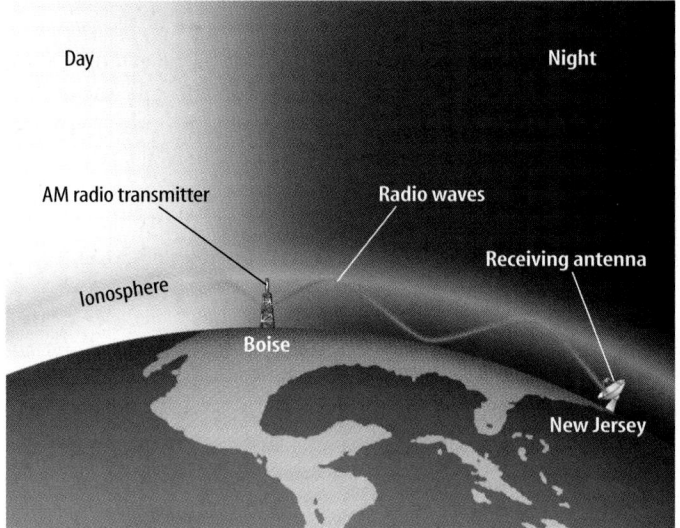

Upper Layers of the Atmosphere Beyond the stratosphere are the mesosphere, thermosphere, and exosphere. The mesosphere extends from the top of the stratosphere to about 85 km above Earth. If you've ever seen a shooting star, you might have witnessed a meteor in the mesosphere.

The thermosphere is named for its high temperatures. This is the thickest atmospheric layer and is found between 85 km and 500 km above Earth's surface.

Within the mesosphere and thermosphere is a layer of electrically charged particles called the **ionosphere** (i AHN uh sfir). If you live in New Jersey and listen to the radio at night, you might pick up a station from Boise, Idaho. The ionosphere allows radio waves to travel across the country to another city, as shown in **Figure 5.** During the day, energy from the Sun interacts with the particles in the ionosphere, causing them to absorb AM radio frequencies. At night, without solar energy, AM radio transmissions reflect off the ionosphere, allowing radio transmissions to be received at greater distances.

The space shuttle in **Figure 6** orbits Earth in the exosphere. In contrast to the troposphere, the layer you live in, the exosphere has so few molecules that the wings of the shuttle are useless. In the exosphere, the spacecraft relies on bursts from small rocket thrusters to move around. Beyond the exosphere is outer space.

 *How does the space shuttle maneuver in the exosphere?*

Figure 6
Wings help move aircraft in lower layers of the atmosphere. The space shuttle can't use its wings to maneuver in the exosphere because so few molecules are present.

Teacher FYI

The exosphere, extending from about 500 km outward, marks the transition from Earth's atmosphere to the void of space. The gas particles of the exosphere are so far apart that they rarely collide with one another.

Extension

Have students research the effects that solar flares have on the atmosphere. Have them write a brief report about their findings. L2 IS **Linguistic** P

Activity

After students have studied **Figure 5,** have them contrast the reception of a distant AM station during daylight hours and at night. Have them listen for three days at the same time during the daytime and at night. (Some AM stations power down at night, making reception difficult. Be sure students have not chosen a station that powers down.) Have students keep a record of their observations. Discuss how much farther radio signals travel at night as you discuss the results in class. L2 IS **Auditory-Musical**

✔ Reading Check

Answer with short bursts from rocket thrusters

Resource Manager

Chapter Resources Booklet
   Enrichment, p. 26

Physical Science Critical Thinking/Problem Solving, p. 5

Teacher FYI

The ionosphere is that part of Earth's upper atmosphere that contains free electrons and ions. It extends from about 90 km to about 600 km in altitude. The orbits of many satellites are within the ionosphere.

Atmospheric Pressure

Quick Demo

Display a barometer in the classroom. Demonstrate to students how to observe it each day to record pressure differences. Have students contrast pressure readings in fair and rainy weather. Readings will be lower during periods of precipitation. L2

 **Visual-Spatial**

Extension

Have students write brief reports explaining how an aneroid barometer called an altimeter is used to determine an airplane's altitude. L3

 **Linguistic**

✔ Reading Check

Answer in the troposphere

Problem-Solving Activity

National Math Standards

Correlation to Mathematics Objectives
1, 4, 5, 6, 8–10

1. The air pressure at 5 km is about 450 millibars.
2. Air pressure decreases quickly from 0 km to 12 km (lower altitudes), but above 12 km the pressure decreases at a much slower rate.

Figure 7
Air pressure decreases as you go higher in Earth's atmosphere.

Atmospheric Pressure

Imagine you're a football player running with the ball. Six players tackle you and pile one on top of the other. Who feels the weight more—you or the player on top? Like molecules anywhere else, atmospheric gases have mass. Atmospheric gases extend hundreds of kilometers above Earth's surface. As Earth's gravity pulls the gases toward its surface, the weight of these gases presses down on the air below. As a result, the molecules nearer Earth's surface are closer together. This dense air exerts more force than the less dense air near the top of the atmosphere. Force exerted on an area is known as pressure.

Like the pile of football players, air pressure is greater near Earth's surface and decreases higher in the atmosphere, as shown in **Figure 7**. People find it difficult to breathe in high mountains because fewer molecules of air exist there. Jets that fly in the stratosphere must maintain pressurized cabins so that people can breathe.

✔ **Reading Check** *Where is air pressure greater—in the exosphere or in the troposphere?*

Problem-Solving Activity

How does altitude affect air pressure?

Atmospheric gases extend hundreds of kilometers above Earth's surface, but the molecules that make up these gases are fewer and fewer in number as you go higher. This means that air pressure decreases with altitude.

Identifying the Problem

The graph on the right shows these changes in air pressure. Note that altitude on the graph goes up only to 50 km. The troposphere and the stratosphere are represented on the graph, but other layers of the atmosphere are not. By examining the graph, can you understand the relationship between altitude and pressure?

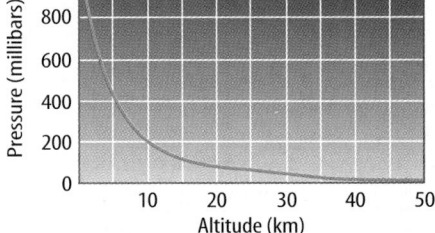

Air Pressure Changes with Altitude

Solving the Problem

1. Estimate the air pressure at an altitude of 5 km.
2. Does air pressure change more quickly at higher altitudes or at lower altitudes?

 LAB DEMONSTRATION

✔*Assessment*

Purpose to observe the effects of temperature on air pressure

Materials aluminum soda can, water, hot plate, bucket of cold water, hot pad or tongs

Preparation Review the term *density* with students.

Procedure Pour a small amount of water into the can. Heat the can over the hot plate until the water boils. Using tongs or the hot pad, submerge the can upside down in the bucket of cold water.

Expected Outcome The can will collapse.

Why did the can collapse? When put into the cold water, air inside the can cooled. The molecules lost energy and exerted less outward pressure on the walls of the can. The greater air pressure outside the can caused it to collapse.

Temperature in Atmospheric Layers

The Sun is the source of most of the energy on Earth. Before it reaches Earth's surface, energy from the Sun must pass through the atmosphere. Because some layers contain gases that easily absorb the Sun's energy while other layers do not, the various layers have different temperatures, illustrated by the red line in **Figure 8.**

Molecules that make up air in the troposphere are warmed mostly by heat from Earth's surface. The Sun warms Earth's surface, which then warms the air above it. When you climb a mountain, the air at the top is usually cooler than the air at the bottom. Every kilometer you climb, the air temperature decreases about 6.5°C.

Molecules of ozone in the stratosphere absorb some of the Sun's energy. Energy absorbed by ozone molecules raises the temperature. Because more ozone molecules are in the upper portion of the stratosphere, the temperature in this layer rises with increasing altitude.

Like the troposphere, the temperature in the mesosphere decreases with altitude. The thermosphere and exosphere are the first layers to receive the Sun's rays. Few molecules are in these layers, but each molecule has a great deal of energy. Temperatures here are high.

Temperature of the Atmosphere at Various Altitudes

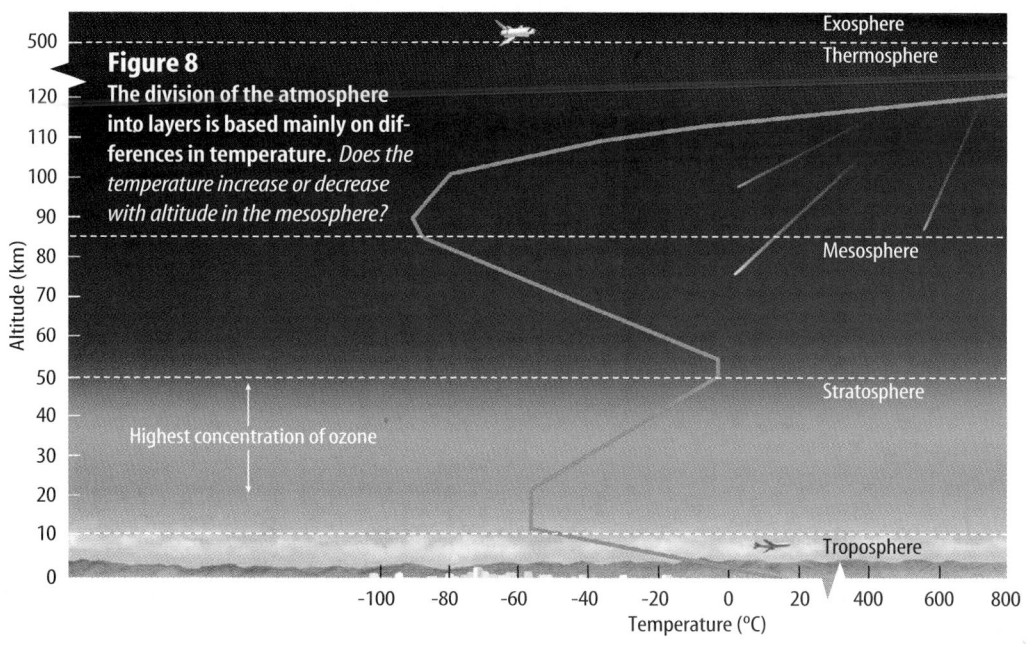

Figure 8
The division of the atmosphere into layers is based mainly on differences in temperature. *Does the temperature increase or decrease with altitude in the mesosphere?*

Temperature in Atmospheric Layers

Mini LAB

Purpose Students observe that air has mass. [L2] [ELL]
[IS] **Visual-Spatial**

Materials inflatable balls such as footballs or volleyballs; air pump with ball inflation needle; pressure gauge; pan balances

Teaching Strategy Review the use of the balance with students before starting the activity.

Safety Precautions Warn students to avoid overinflating the ball.

Troubleshooting Perform the activity in advance to make sure the ball is large enough to cause a detectable change in mass when air is added.

Analysis
1. The mass increases.
2. Air has mass.

✔Assessment

Process Have students write a lab report describing the activity. The report should include a Purpose, Materials, Procedure, and Conclusion. Students with access to computers can write the report using a word processing program. Use **PASC,** p. 119

Caption Answer
Figure 8 Decrease

Teacher FYI

The upper part of the mesosphere has the lowest average temperature in the atmosphere—about −95°C. Although clouds form mostly in the troposphere, the frigid temperatures of the upper mesosphere cause the small amount of water vapor available to condense into clouds of ice crystals that are called noctilucent clouds.

The Ozone Layer

Life Science INTEGRATION

The level of oxygen might decrease.

Make a Model

Have students use small polystyrene balls and toothpicks to make models of ozone and chlorofluorocarbon molecules. Each polystyrene ball will represent an atom. The ozone molecule will have three oxygen atoms. The chlorofluorocarbon molecule will have one carbon atom, one fluorine atom, and three chlorine atoms. Have students use their models to demonstrate how a chlorine atom from the chlorofluorocarbon molecule destroys an ozone molecule as shown in Figure 9. L3 IS **Visual-Spatial**

Discussion

If chlorofluorocarbons harm the ozone layer, why were they produced at all? Students should infer that the harm CFCs do to the ozone layer wasn't known when they were originally produced. When the harm was discovered, it took time for bans to be put into place by some countries, and for companies that use CFCs to switch to ozone-friendly substitutes. Inform students that CFCs are still being used in some places and in some products.

Life Science INTEGRATION

Algae are organisms that use sunlight to make their own food. This process releases oxygen to Earth's atmosphere. Some scientists suggest that growth is reduced when algae are exposed to ultraviolet radiation. Infer what might happen to the oxygen level of the atmosphere if increased ultraviolet radiation damages some algae.

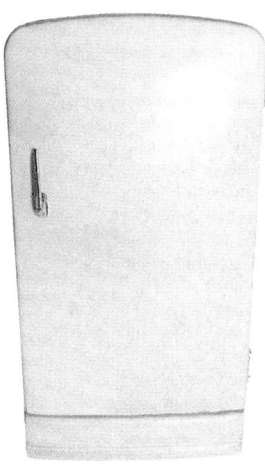

Figure 9
Chlorofluorocarbon (CFC) molecules were used in refrigerators and air conditioners. Each CFC molecule has three chlorine atoms. One atom of chlorine can destroy approximately 100,000 ozone molecules.

The Ozone Layer

Within the stratosphere, about 19 km to 48 km above your head, lies an atmospheric layer called the **ozone layer.** Ozone is made of oxygen. Although you cannot see the ozone layer, your life depends on it.

The oxygen you breathe has two atoms per molecule, but an ozone molecule is made up of three oxygen atoms bound together. The ozone layer contains a high concentration of ozone and shields you from the Sun's harmful energy. Ozone absorbs most of the ultraviolet radiation that enters the atmosphere. **Ultraviolet radiation** is one of the many types of energy that come to Earth from the Sun. Too much exposure to ultraviolet radiation can damage your skin and cause cancer.

CFCs Evidence exists that some air pollutants are destroying the ozone layer. Blame has fallen on **chlorofluorocarbons** (CFCs), chemical compounds used in some refrigerators, air conditioners, and aerosol sprays, and in the production of some foam packaging. CFCs can enter the atmosphere if these appliances leak or if they and other products containing CFCs are improperly discarded.

Recall that an ozone molecule is made of three oxygen atoms bonded together. Chlorofluorocarbon molecules, shown in **Figure 9,** destroy ozone. When a chlorine atom from a chlorofluorocarbon molecule comes near a molecule of ozone, the ozone molecule breaks apart. One of the oxygen atoms combines with the chlorine atom, and the rest form a regular, two-atom molecule. These compounds don't absorb ultraviolet radiation the way ozone can. In addition, the original chlorine atom can continue to break apart thousands of ozone molecules. The result is that more ultraviolet radiation reaches Earth's surface.

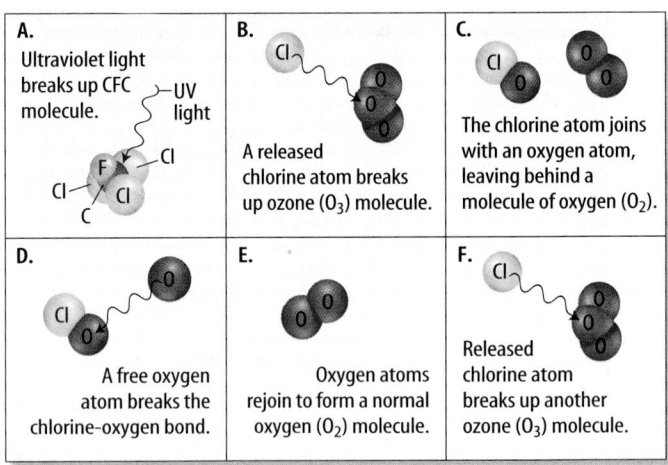

A. Ultraviolet light breaks up CFC molecule. —UV light

B. A released chlorine atom breaks up ozone (O_3) molecule.

C. The chlorine atom joins with an oxygen atom, leaving behind a molecule of oxygen (O_2).

D. A free oxygen atom breaks the chlorine-oxygen bond.

E. Oxygen atoms rejoin to form a normal oxygen (O_2) molecule.

F. Released chlorine atom breaks up another ozone (O_3) molecule.

Cultural **Diversity**

Changing Fashion Increased UV exposure because of thinning ozone has led to changing fashions in Australia. Baggy shorts, long sleeves, and hats are common on some beaches. Some cultures, such as those in northern Africa, traditionally wear clothing that protects them from the Sun. Have students research the traditional clothing of those cultures and explain why this style of clothing makes scientific sense.

Resource Manager

Chapter Resources Booklet
Lab Activity, pp. 9–10
Science Inquiry Labs, p. 25

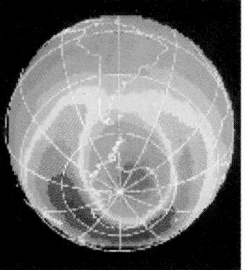 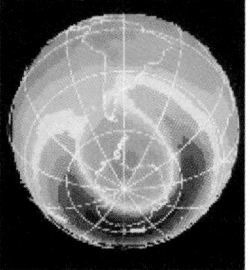 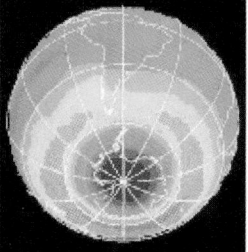 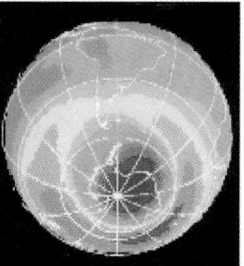

| October 1980 | October 1988 | October 1990 | September 1999 |

Ozone Holes Each year, more than 1.3 million Americans develop skin cancer, and more than 9,500 die from it. Exposure to ultraviolet radiation can cause skin cancer. If the ozone layer disappeared, skin cancer rates might increase. In 1986, scientists found areas in the stratosphere with extremely low amounts of ozone. One large hole was found over Antarctica. A smaller hole was discovered over the north pole. **Figure 10** shows how the ozone layer has thinned and developed holes.

In the mid 1990s, many governments banned the production and use of CFCs. Perhaps over time, the areas where the ozone layer is thinning will recover.

Figure 10
These images of Antarctica were produced using data from a NASA satellite. The purple color shows how the ozone hole has grown bigger over time.

Section 1 Assessment

1. Earth's early atmosphere had little oxygen. How did oxygen come to make up 21 percent of Earth's present atmosphere?

2. List the layers of the atmosphere in order beginning at Earth's surface.

3. While hiking in the mountains, you notice that it is harder to breathe as you climb higher. Explain why this is so.

4. What are some effects from a thinning ozone layer?

5. **Think Critically** During the day, the radio only receives AM stations from a city near you. At night, you are able to listen to an AM radio station from a distant city. Explain why this is possible.

Skill Builder Activities

6. **Interpreting Scientific Illustrations** Using **Figure 2**, determine the total percentage of nitrogen and oxygen in the atmosphere. What is the total percentage of argon and carbon dioxide? **For more help, refer to the** Science Skill Handbook.

7. **Communicating** The names of the atmospheric layers end with the suffix *-sphere* a word that means "ball." Use a dictionary to find out what *tropo-, meso-, thermo-,* and *exo-* mean. In your Science Journal, write the meaning of these prefixes and explain if the layers are appropriately named. **For more help, refer to the** Science Skill Handbook.

3 Assess

Reteach

Have students make tables that list the layers of the atmosphere and one or two characteristics of each layer. IS **Visual-Spatial** P

Challenge

Challenge students to determine if CFCs are still being produced and used in the U.S. If so, in which types of products? Has the government restricted CFC use at all? If so, how? If not, why not? Direct students to include information on substitutes for CFCs and what people can do to avoid using CFCs. L3
IS **Logical-Mathematical**

Performance Have groups of students write skits about how the depletion of the ozone layer might affect different organisms. The organisms could discuss the changes they are experiencing and their concerns for the future. Have students perform the skits for the class. Use **Performance Assessment in the Science Classroom,** p. 147.

Answers to Section Assessment

1. Early organisms released it into the air. Water vapor molecules were split apart.
2. troposphere, stratosphere, mesosphere, thermosphere, exosphere
3. There are fewer molecules of oxygen per liter of air in the mountains.
4. Possible answers: Increased UV radiation reaches Earth, causing more

cases of skin cancer; organisms such as algae could be damaged, resulting in the release of less oxygen into the atmosphere.
5. At night sunlight no longer interacts with particles in the ionosphere. This allows AM radio transmissions to be reflected back to Earth at greater distances.

6. 99 percent; 0.96 percent
7. The terms come from Greek and Latin. *Tropo-* means change, *strato-* comes from a word meaning to stretch out as in a layer, *meso-* means in the middle, *thermo-* means heat, and *exo-* means outside. Troposphere has some relevance, since temperature and pressure change with altitude and weather

changes constantly. Stratosphere just means layer. Mesosphere and exosphere describe the positions of the layers. The thermosphere is named for its high temperature.

Activity

BENCH TESTED

Purpose Students evaluate the effectiveness of various sunscreens. L2

[I] Logical-Mathematical

Process Skills comparing and contrasting, observing, making and using tables, inferring, using numbers

Time Required about 45 minutes

Materials To get a large variety of sunscreens, ask students to bring in products from home.

Teaching Strategy In order to keep the time needed to one class period, have each student evaluate no more than three brands of sunscreen.

Answers to Questions

1. Sunscreen blocks harmful UV radiation from the Sun.
2. Answers will vary depending on SPF of brands chosen.
3. Sunscreens that cost the least per milliliter and provide adequate protection without misleading claims on the label should be considered the best buys.

✔ Assessment

Process Have the class look at their results together to find the percentage of sunscreens evaluated that are considered good buys, as opposed to those that are overpriced or misleading in their claims. Use **Performance Assessment in the Science Classroom,** p. 115.

Activity

Evaluating Sunscreens

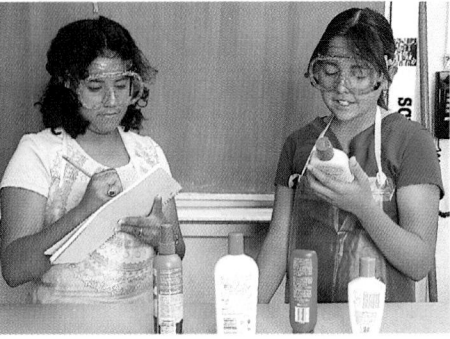

Without protection, sun exposure can damage your health. Sunscreens protect your skin from ultraviolet radiation. In this activity, you will draw inferences using the labels of different sunscreens.

What You'll Investigate
How effective are various brands of sunscreens?

Materials
variety of sunscreens of different brand names

Goals
- ■ **Draw inferences** based on labels on sunscreen brands.
- ■ **Compare** the effectiveness of different sunscreen brands for protection against the Sun.
- ■ **Compare** the cost of several sunscreen brands.

Safety Precautions

🥽 👕 🚫

Procedure

1. Make a data table in your Science Journal using the following terms: *brand name, SPF, misleading terms,* and *cost per milliliter.*

2. The Sun Protection Factor (SPF) tells you how long the sunscreen will protect you. For example, an SPF of 4 allows you to stay in the Sun four times longer than if you did not use sunscreen. Record the SPF of each sunscreen on your data table.

3. **Calculate** the cost per milliliter of each sunscreen brand.

4. Government guidelines say that terms like *sunblock* and *waterproof* are misleading because sunscreens cannot block the Sun, and they wash off in water. List the misleading terms in your data table for each brand.

Sunscreen Assessment			
Brand Name			
SPF	Answers will vary.		
Cost per Milliliter			
Misleading Terms			

Conclude and Apply

1. **Explain** why you need to use sunscreen.

2. A minimum of SPF 15 is considered adequate protection for a sunscreen. Sunscreens with an SPF greater than 30 are considered by government guidelines to be misleading because sunscreens will wash or wear off. Evaluate the SPF of each brand of sunscreen.

3. Considering the cost and effectiveness of all the sunscreen brands, discuss which brand you consider to be the best buy.

𝒞ommunicating Your Data

Create a poster on the proper use of sunscreens, and provide guidelines for selecting the safest product. **For more help, refer to the** Science Skill Handbook.

𝒞ommunicating Your Data

Direct students to choose one of the following subjects for the poster: (1) tips for the proper use of sunscreen; (2) what to look for when buying sunscreen; (3) why people should use sunscreen. P

Resource Manager

Chapter Resources Booklet
   Activity Worksheet, pp. 5–6
   Reinforcement, p. 23
Reading and Writing Skill Activities, p. 27

Energy Transfer in the Atmosphere

Energy from the Sun

The Sun provides most of the energy on Earth. This energy drives winds and ocean currents and allows plants to grow and produce food, providing nutrition for many animals. When Earth receives energy from the Sun, three different things can happen to that energy, as shown in **Figure 11.** Some energy is reflected back into space by clouds, atmospheric particles, and Earth's surface. Some is absorbed by the atmosphere. The rest is absorbed by land and water on Earth's surface.

Heat

Heat is energy that flows from an object with a higher temperature to an object with a lower temperature. Energy from the Sun reaches Earth's surface and heats objects such as roads, rocks, and water. Heat then is transferred through the atmosphere in three ways—radiation, conduction, and convection, as shown in **Figure 12.**

As You Read

What You'll Learn
- **Describe** what happens to the energy Earth receives from the Sun.
- **Compare and contrast** radiation, conduction, and convection.
- **Explain** the water cycle.

Vocabulary
radiation   hydrosphere
conduction   condensation
convection

Why It's Important
The Sun provides energy to Earth's atmosphere, allowing life to exist.

Figure 11
The Sun is the source of energy for Earth's atmosphere. Thirty-five percent of incoming solar radiation is reflected back into space. *How much is absorbed by Earth's surface and atmosphere?*

6% reflected by the atmosphere

25% reflected from clouds

15% absorbed by the atmosphere

4% reflected from Earth's surface

50% directly or indirectly absorbed by Earth's surface

291

1 Motivate

Bellringer Transparency

Display the Section Focus Transparency for Section 2. Use the accompanying Transparency Activity Master. L2
ELL

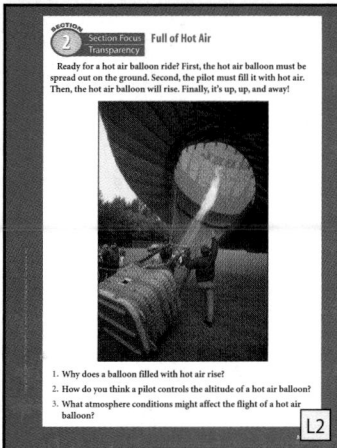

Tie to Prior Knowledge

Tell students that the air near the ground is heated mostly by Earth's surface, not directly by the Sun. Ask students to think of examples from their own experience that show Earth's surface absorbs the Sun's energy. Accept all reasonable answers, such as feeling hot road pavement or hot beach sand on a sunny day. Tell students that they will learn how the Sun heats the ground and the air in this section.

Caption Answer
Figure 11 65 percent

Section ✓Assessment Planner

PORTFOLIO
Science Journal, p. 293
PERFORMANCE ASSESSMENT
Try at Home MiniLAB, p. 293
Skill Builder Activities, p. 294
See page 306 for more options.

CONTENT ASSESSMENT
Section, p. 294
Challenge, p. 294
Chapter, pp. 306–307

Heat

Discussion
How can the Sun continue to heat the atmosphere at night? If the Sun has warmed the surface during the day, its heat can still warm the air in contact with the ground by conduction after sunset.

 **Reading Check**

Answer by radiation

 **Physics**
INTEGRATION

Water; it does not heat up as fast as land does.

Using Science Words
Word Meaning Have students look up the words *conduction*, *convection*, and *radiation* in the dictionary and write a sentence about how the meaning of each word reflects its root. The words come from the Latin roots *conducere* (to lead or escort), *convehere* (to bring together), and *radius* (ray), respectively.

Use an Analogy
The behavior of air molecules in atmospheric convection currents is analogous to the principle used to control a hot air balloon. When air inside a hot air balloon is heated, the molecules spread apart and the air becomes less dense. The balloon then rises through the denser air around it. When air cools inside the balloon, the molecules cluster closer together, the air density increases, and the balloon descends.

Radiation warms the surface.

The air near Earth's surface is heated by conduction.

Cooler air pushes warm air upward, creating a convection current.

Figure 12
Heat is transferred within Earth's atmosphere by radiation, conduction, and convection.

 **Physics**
INTEGRATION

Specific heat is the amount of heat required to change the temperature of a substance one degree. Substances with high specific heat absorb a lot of heat for a small increase in temperature. Land warms faster than water does. Infer whether soil or water has a higher specific heat value.

292 CHAPTER 10 Atmosphere

Radiation Sitting on the beach, you feel the Sun's warmth on your face. How can you feel the Sun's heat even though you aren't in direct contact with it? Energy from the Sun reaches Earth in the form of radiant energy, or radiation. **Radiation** is energy that is transferred in the form of rays or waves. Earth radiates some of the energy it absorbs from the Sun back toward space. Radiant energy from the Sun warms your face.

 **Reading Check** *How does the Sun warm your skin?*

Conduction If you walk barefoot on a hot beach, your feet heat up because of conduction. **Conduction** is the transfer of energy that occurs when molecules bump into one another. Molecules are always in motion, but molecules in warmer objects move faster than molecules in cooler objects. When objects are in contact, energy is transferred from warmer objects to cooler objects.

Radiation from the Sun heated the beach sand, but direct contact with the sand warmed your feet. In a similar way, Earth's surface conducts energy directly to the atmosphere. As air moves over warm land or water, molecules in air are heated by direct contact.

Convection After the atmosphere is warmed by radiation or conduction, the heat is transferred by a third process called convection. **Convection** is the transfer of heat by the flow of material. Convection circulates heat throughout the atmosphere. How does this happen?

Teacher FYI
The Sun is the source of almost all energy on Earth. Some energy is generated by the radioactive decay of atoms contained in Earth's rocks and magma.

Resource Manager

Chapter Resources Booklet
   Transparency Activities, pp. 41, 43–44
   MiniLAB, p. 4
   Enrichment, p. 27
   Reinforcement, p. 24
   Directed Reading, p. 16
   Lab Activity, pp. 11–12

When air is warmed, the molecules in it move apart and the air becomes less dense. Air pressure decreases because fewer molecules are in the same space. In cold air, molecules move closer together. The air becomes more dense and air pressure increases. Cooler, denser air sinks while warmer, less dense air rises, forming a convection current. As **Figure 12** shows, radiation, conduction, and convection together distribute the Sun's heat throughout Earth's atmosphere.

The Water Cycle

Hydrosphere is a term that describes all the water on Earth's surface. Water moves constantly between the atmosphere and the hydrosphere in the water cycle, shown in **Figure 13.**

If you watch a puddle in the Sun, you'll notice that over time the puddle gets smaller and smaller. Energy from the Sun causes the water in the puddle to change from a liquid to a gas by a process called evaporation. Water that evaporates from lakes, streams, and oceans enters Earth's atmosphere.

If water vapor in the atmosphere cools enough, it changes back into a liquid. This process of water vapor changing to a liquid is called **condensation.**

Clouds form when condensation occurs high in the atmosphere. Clouds are made up of tiny water droplets that can collide to form larger drops. As the drops grow, they fall to Earth as precipitation, which completes the cycle by returning water to the hydrosphere.

TRY AT HOME
Mini LAB

Modeling Heat Transfer

Procedure
1. Cover the outside of an empty **soup can** with **black construction paper.**
2. Fill the can with **cold water** and feel it with your fingers.
3. Place the can in sunlight for 1 h then pour the water over your fingers.

Analysis
1. Does the water in the can feel warmer or cooler after placing the can in sunlight?
2. What types of heat transfer did you model?

Figure 13
In the water cycle, water moves from Earth to the atmosphere and back to Earth again.

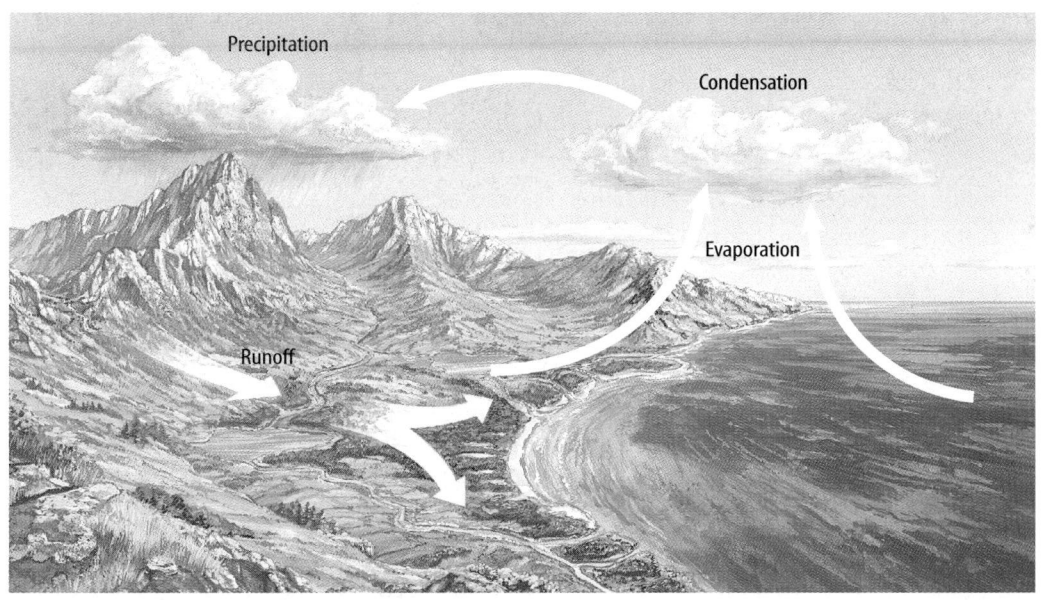

Precipitation

Condensation

Evaporation

Runoff

SECTION 2 Energy Transfer in the Atmosphere **293**

The Water Cycle

IDENTIFYING
Misconceptions

Some students may think that new water forms constantly. Explain that the water in the hydrosphere is continuously cycled between liquid water, water vapor, and ice.

TRY AT HOME
Mini LAB

Purpose Students model the transfer of heat.

Materials empty soup can, black construction paper, cold water

Teaching Strategy If the weather is cloudy, place the covered can under an incandescent light bulb.

Answers to Analysis
1. The water in the can felt warmer after placing it in the Sun.
2. The types of heat transfer modeled were radiation and conduction.

Science Journal

Water Cycle Have students write a poem that describes the water cycle. They should include all parts of the cycle in their poems. Challenge some students to write in Haiku, a Japanese poetic form consisting of 17 syllables arranged in three lines of 5, 7, and 5 syllables each. Have volunteers share their poems with the class. L2 IS **Auditory-Musical** P

✔Assessment

Oral Ask students to explain how rain is formed in clouds. When evaporated water rises and cools, the vapor condenses into water droplets, which can coalesce to form rain. Use **PASC**, p. 93.

Section 2 Energy Transfer in the Atmosphere **293**

Earth's Atmosphere Is Unique

Answer Earth's atmosphere

③ Assess

Reteach

Have students draw an events cycle concept map that describes the steps in the water cycle. [L1]
LS Visual-Spatial

Challenge

Explain that worldwide, about 500,000 km³ of water evaporates each year. About 110,000 km³ of this falls as precipitation on land. **What probably happens to the rest of the water?** It falls into bodies of water, such as the ocean. **What happens to the water that falls on land?** Possible answers: Some is absorbed by plants, some seeps into soil, some becomes runoff that eventually flows to the ocean or evaporates into the atmosphere.

✔ Assessment

Process Predict what would happen to the water cycle if Earth were covered by dense clouds that blocked the Sun's radiation. The cycle would not work; the Sun's energy is needed to drive the water cycle. Use **Performance Assessment in the Science Classroom,** p. 89.

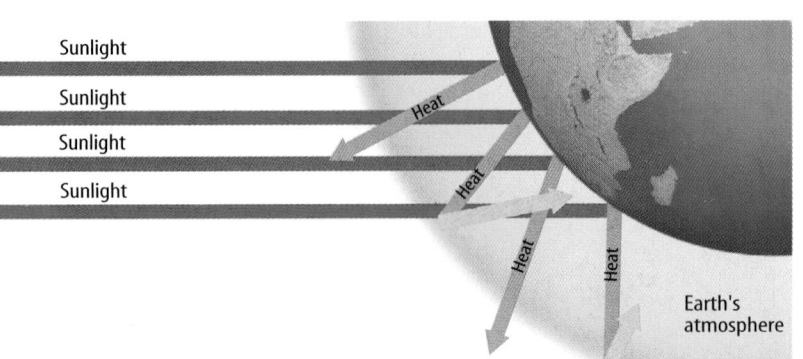

Sunlight
Sunlight
Sunlight
Sunlight

Heat
Heat
Heat
Heat

Earth's atmosphere

Figure 14
Earth's atmosphere creates a delicate balance between energy received and energy lost.

Earth's Atmosphere is Unique

On Earth, radiation from the Sun can be reflected into space, absorbed by the atmosphere, or absorbed by land and water. Once it is absorbed, heat can be transferred by radiation, conduction, or convection. Earth's atmosphere, shown in **Figure 14,** helps control how much of the Sun's radiation is absorbed or lost.

✔ **Reading Check** *What helps control how much of the Sun's radiation is absorbed on Earth?*

Why doesn't life exist on Mars or Venus? Mars is a cold, lifeless world because its atmosphere is too thin to support life or to hold much of the Sun's heat. Temperatures on the surface of Mars range from 35°C to –170°C. On the other hand, gases in Venus's dense atmosphere trap heat coming from the Sun. The temperature on the surface of Venus is 470°C. Living things would burn instantly if they were placed on Venus's surface. Life on Earth exists because the atmosphere holds just the right amount of the Sun's energy.

Section ② Assessment

1. How does the Sun transfer energy to Earth?
2. How is Earth's atmosphere different from the atmosphere on Mars?
3. How is heat transferred from the stove to the water when you boil a pot of water?
4. Briefly describe the steps included in the water cycle.
5. **Think Critically** What would happen to temperatures on Earth if the Sun's heat were not distributed throughout the atmosphere?

Skill Builder Activities

6. **Concept Mapping** Make a concept map that explains what happens to radiant energy that reaches Earth. **For more help, refer to the Science Skill Handbook.**

7. **Solving One-Step Equations** Earth is about 150 million km from the Sun. The radiation coming from the Sun travels at 300,000 km/s. How long does it take for radiation from the Sun to reach Earth? **For more help, refer to the Math Skill Handbook.**

Answers to Section Assessment

1. radiation
2. Earth's atmosphere is denser, so it holds in more of the Sun's heat.
3. Conduction from the burner to the pot and from the pot to the water
4. Water evaporates from Earth's surface, condenses into clouds, and falls back to Earth as precipitation.

5. It would be hotter near Earth's equator and colder near Earth's poles.

6. Concept maps should summarize the information provided in **Figure 11.**
7. 150,000,000 km/300,000 km/s = 500 s or 8.3 minutes

SECTION 3 Air Movement

Forming Wind

Uneven heating of Earth's surface by the Sun causes some areas to be warmer than others. Recall from Section 2 that warmer air expands, becoming less dense than colder air. This causes air pressure to be generally lower where air is heated. Wind is the movement of air from an area of higher pressure to an area of lower pressure.

Heated Air Areas of Earth receive different amounts of radiation from the Sun because Earth is curved. **Figure 15** illustrates why the equator receives more radiation than areas to the north or south. The heated air at the equator is less dense, so it is displaced by denser, colder air, creating convection currents.

This cold, denser air comes from the poles, which receive less radiation from the Sun, making air at the poles much cooler. The resulting dense, high-pressure air sinks and moves along Earth's surface. However, dense air sinking as less-dense air rises does not explain everything about wind.

As You Read

What You'll Learn

- **Explain** why different latitudes on Earth receive different amounts of solar energy.
- **Describe** the Coriolis effect.
- **Locate** doldrums, trade winds, prevailing westerlies, polar easterlies, and jet streams.

Vocabulary

Coriolis effect   sea breeze
jet stream   land breeze

Why It's Important

Wind systems determine major weather patterns on Earth.

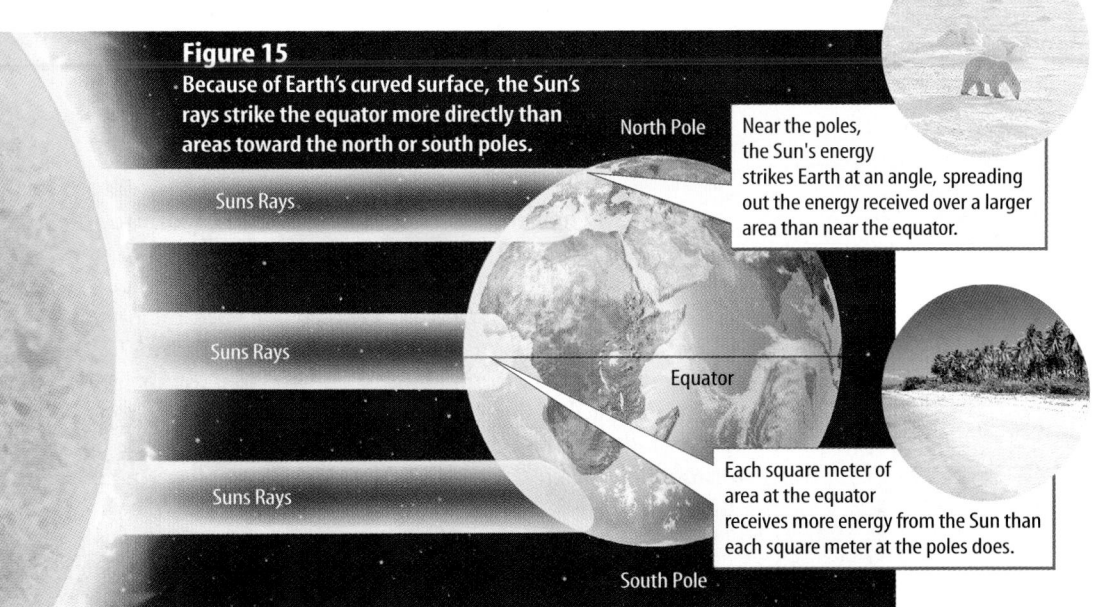

Figure 15
Because of Earth's curved surface, the Sun's rays strike the equator more directly than areas toward the north or south poles.

Near the poles, the Sun's energy strikes Earth at an angle, spreading out the energy received over a larger area than near the equator.

Each square meter of area at the equator receives more energy from the Sun than each square meter at the poles does.

North Pole

Suns Rays

Suns Rays

Equator

Suns Rays

South Pole

SECTION 3 Air Movement **295**

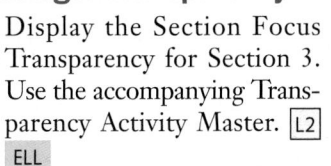

Bellringer Transparency

Display the Section Focus Transparency for Section 3. Use the accompanying Transparency Activity Master. L2
ELL

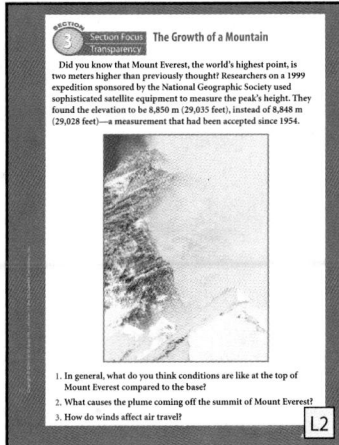

Tie to Prior Knowledge

Ask for a show of hands for students who have experienced a windy day. Now ask students to speculate on why wind forms. List their responses on the board. Tell students they will learn the answer in this section. Return to the list later to check the accuracy of the responses.

Section ✔Assessment Planner

PORTFOLIO
Extension, p. 297
Curriculum Connection, p. 297
Assessment, p. 299

PERFORMANCE ASSESSMENT
Skill Builder Activities, p. 299
See page 306 for more options.

CONTENT ASSESSMENT
Section, p. 299
Challenge, p. 299
Chapter, pp. 306–307

Resource Manager

Chapter Resources Booklet
Transparency Activity, p. 42
Enrichment, p. 28

Home and Community Involvement, p. 23

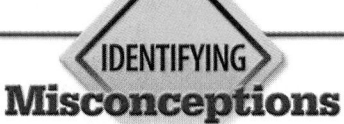

2 Teach

Forming Wind

IDENTIFYING Misconceptions

Students may think that wind is caused by something in the sky, such as a cloud, that blows very hard. Refer to page 280F for teaching strategies that address this misconception.

Quick Demo

Use this activity to introduce the Coriolis effect. Tape a sheet of white paper to a phonograph turntable. On top of the paper, tape a sheet of carbon paper, carbon side down. Turn on the phonograph. While the turntable is rotating, roll a steel ball bearing straight across the carbon paper. Remove the carbon paper and have students observe the mark on the white paper. Have them compare it to what they observed. Although the ball bearing rolls in a straight line, it traces a curved path across the paper. L2 ELL LS **Visual-Spatial**

Global Winds

Use Science Words

Word Meaning Have students explain why the term *doldrums* is a good description of the air near the equator. Doldrums are a state of inactivity, stagnation, or slump. Air in the doldrums seems motionless. L2 LS **Linguistic**

 **Reading Check**

Answer a windless, rainy zone near the equator

Figure 16
The Coriolis effect causes moving air to turn to the right in the northern hemisphere and to the left in the southern hemisphere.

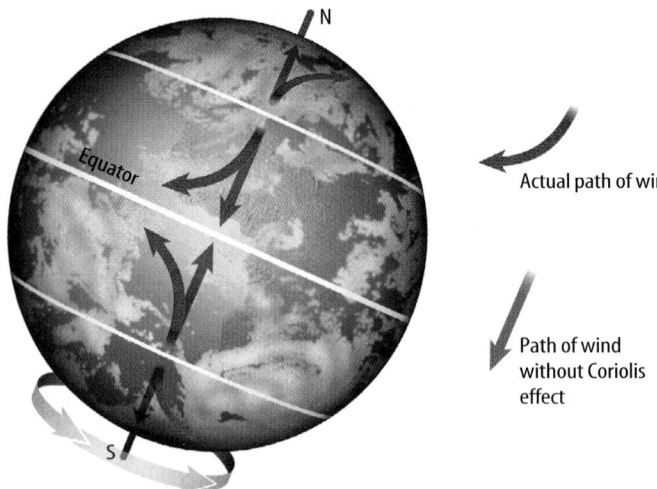

Actual path of wind

Path of wind without Coriolis effect

The Coriolis Effect What would happen if you threw a ball to someone sitting directly across from you on a moving merry-go-round? Would the ball go to your friend? By the time the ball got to the opposite side, your friend would have moved and the ball would appear to have curved.

Like the merry-go-round, the rotation of Earth causes moving air and water to appear to turn to the right north of the equator and to the left south of the equator. This is called the **Coriolis** (kohr ee OH lus) **effect.** It is illustrated in **Figure 16.** The flow of air caused by differences in the amount of solar radiation received on Earth's surface and by the Coriolis effect creates distinct wind patterns on Earth's surface. These wind systems not only influence the weather, they also determine when and where ships and planes travel most efficiently.

Global Winds

How did Christopher Columbus get from Spain to the Americas? The *Nina,* the *Pinta,* and the *Santa Maria* had no source of power other than the wind in their sails. Early sailors discovered that the wind patterns on Earth helped them navigate the oceans. These wind systems are shown in **Figure 17.**

Sometimes sailors found little or no wind to move their sailing ships near the equator. It also rained nearly every afternoon. This windless, rainy zone near the equator is called the doldrums. Look again at **Figure 17.** Near the equator, the Sun heats the air and causes it to rise, creating low pressure and little wind. The rising air then cools, causing rain.

✔ **Reading Check** *What are the doldrums?*

SCIENCE Online

Research Visit the Glencoe Science Web site at **science.glencoe.com** to learn more about global winds. Communicate to your class what you've learned.

SCIENCE Online
Internet Addresses
_____
_____
_____
Explore the Glencoe Science Web site at **science.glencoe.com** to find out more about topics in this section.

Visual Learning

Figure 16 Have students trace the path of the curving winds. **How does the movement of the westerly winds affect northern Europe?** They can bring warm, moist air from tropical areas.

Figure 17

The Sun's uneven heating of Earth's surface forms giant loops, or cells, of moving air. The Coriolis effect deflects the surface winds to the west or east, setting up belts of prevailing winds that distribute heat and moisture around the globe.

A WESTERLIES Near 30° north and south latitude, Earth's rotation deflects air from west to east as air moves toward the polar regions. In the United States, the westerlies move weather systems, such as this one along the Oklahoma-Texas border, from west to east.

B DOLDRUMS Along the equator, heating causes air to expand, creating a zone of low pressure. Cloudy, rainy weather, as shown here, develops almost every afternoon.

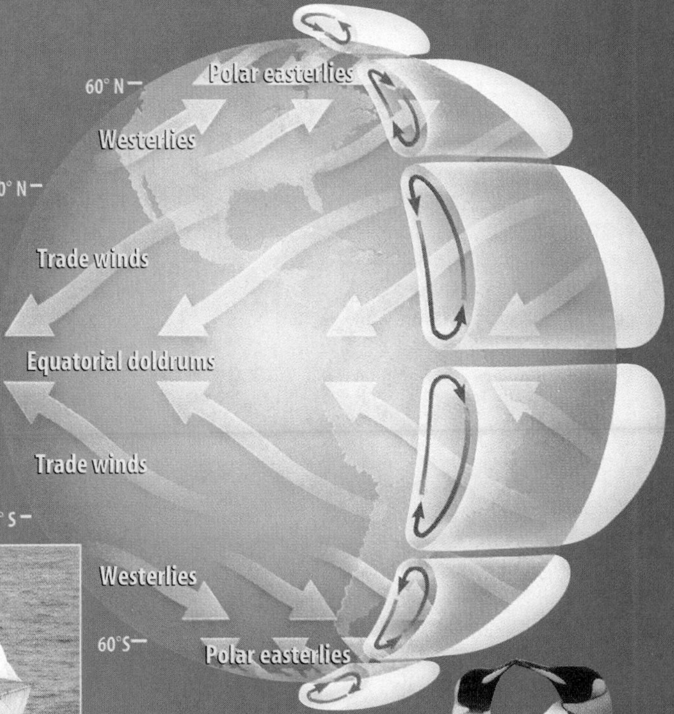

C TRADE WINDS Air warmed near the equator travels toward the poles but gradually cools and sinks. As the air flows back toward the low pressure of the doldrums, the Coriolis effect deflects the surface wind to the west. Early sailors, in ships like the one above, relied on these winds to navigate global trade routes.

D POLAR EASTERLIES In the polar regions, cold, dense air sinks and moves away from the poles. Earth's rotation deflects this wind from east to west.

60° N — Polar easterlies
Westerlies
30° N —
Trade winds
0° — Equatorial doldrums
Trade winds
30° S —
Westerlies
60° S — Polar easterlies

Resource Manager

Chapter Resources Booklet

Directed Reading for Content Mastery, pp. 17, 18

Activity Worksheet, pp. 7, 8

Science Inquiry Labs, p. 41

Curriculum Connection

History The trade winds were used by ships to sail from Europe to the Americas. Have students draw maps showing the routes that early explorers took to cross the oceans. Then have them compare these routes with the wind systems shown in **Figure 16.** [L2] [ELL] [IS] **Visual-Spatial** [P]

NATIONAL GEOGRAPHIC

Visualizing Global Winds

Have students examine the pictures and read the captions. Then ask the following questions.

Why did sailors in past centuries sail kilometers away from a direct route to reach the trade winds? The strong winds with a regular path helped them sail faster.

Suppose Earth did not rotate. How would this affect the movement of global winds? Global winds would move in straight paths from areas of high pressure to areas of low pressure.

Activity

Have pairs of students draw a dot in the center of a piece of paper and label it *North Pole.* Have one student slowly turn the paper counterclockwise (the direction Earth rotates when viewed from above the north pole) while the other student tries to draw a straight line away from the dot southward. Then have the other student start at the bottom edge of the paper and try to draw a straight line toward the dot as his or her partner turns the paper. Ask students to describe what happened in both cases. Relate this to how Earth's rotation deflects global winds.

Extension

Have students research the advantages of combining wind power and diesel power on fishing boats, cargo vessels, and oil tankers. Ask students to prepare posters illustrating one type of sail-assisted vessel and explaining how it operates. [L2] [IS] **Visual-Spatial** [P]

Global Winds,
continued

Teacher **FYI**

Jet streams were discovered during World War II, when American pilots flew their bombers higher than normal to avoid anti-aircraft fire. At those high altitudes, their ground speeds (that is, the speed of the plane in relation to the ground) increased by more than 240 km/h in some areas. The only plausible explanation was that the planes had entered a stream of swiftly moving air.

Local Wind Systems

Activity

Have students determine the wind direction near the school by using handmade wind vanes. Have groups of students submit designs, then make the wind vanes from easily-obtained materials. L1 ELL IS **Naturalist**

Extension

Have students research and describe other local winds, such as mountain breezes, foehn or chinook winds, and katabatic winds. L2 IS **Naturalist**

Figure 18
A strong current of air, called the jet stream, forms between cold, polar air and warm, tropical air.

A Flying from Boston to Seattle may take 30 min longer than flying from Seattle to Boston.

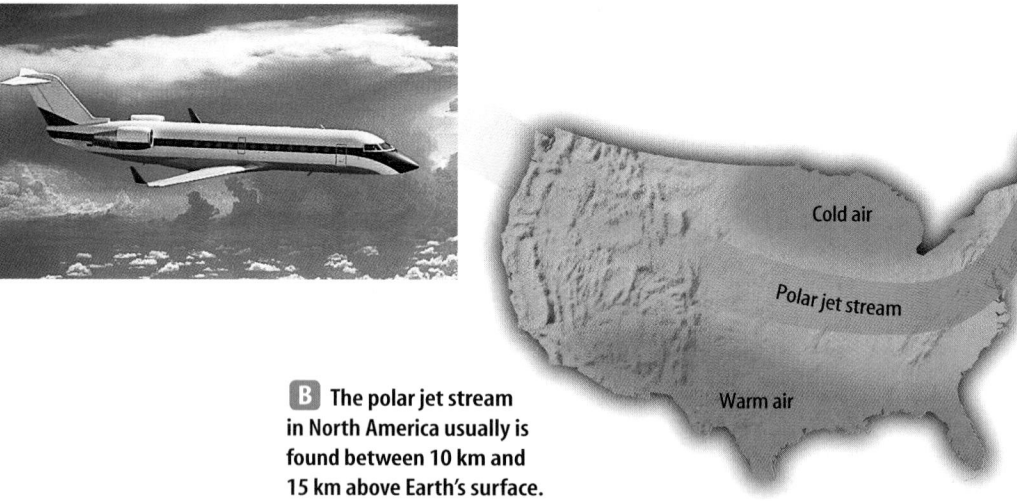

B The polar jet stream in North America usually is found between 10 km and 15 km above Earth's surface.

Surface Winds Air descending to Earth's surface near 30° north and south latitude creates steady winds that blow in tropical regions. These are called trade winds because early sailors used their dependability to establish trade routes.

Between 30° and 60° latitude, winds called the prevailing westerlies blow in the opposite direction from the trade winds. Prevailing westerlies are responsible for much of the movement of weather across North America.

Polar easterlies are found near the poles. Near the north pole, easterlies blow from northeast to southwest. Near the south pole, polar easterlies blow from the southeast to the northwest.

Winds in the Upper Troposphere Narrow belts of strong winds, called **jet streams,** blow near the top of the troposphere. The polar jet stream forms at the boundary of cold, dry polar air to the north and warmer, more moist tropical air to the south, as shown in **Figure 18.** The jet stream moves faster in the winter because the difference between cold air and warm air is greater. The jet stream helps move storms across the country.

Jet pilots take advantage of the jet streams. When flying eastward, planes save time and fuel. Going west, planes fly at different altitudes to avoid the jet streams.

Local Wind Systems

Global wind systems determine the major weather patterns for the entire planet. Smaller wind systems affect local weather. If you live near a large body of water, you're familiar with two such wind systems—sea breezes and land breezes.

Inclusion Strategies

Learning Disabled Have students keep track of the type of wind each day and the weather that accompanies it. Work with these students to help them make a chart for recording their data, and to help them look for patterns in their collected data. Provide copies of maps of North America. Have students draw arrows showing the direction of trade winds, prevailing westerlies, and polar easterlies. L1 IS **Naturalist**

Resource Manager

Chapter Resources Booklet
  Reinforcement, p. 25
Lab Management and Safety, p. 71

A

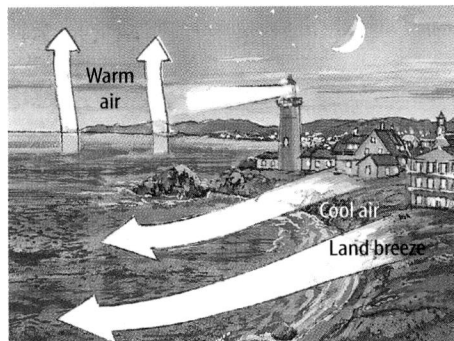

B

Sea Breezes Convection currents over areas where the land meets the sea can cause wind. A **sea breeze,** shown in **Figure 19,** is created during the day because solar radiation warms the land more than the water. Air over the land is heated by conduction. This heated air is less dense and has lower pressure. Cooler, denser air over the water has higher pressure and flows toward the warmer, less dense air. A convection current results, and wind blows from the sea toward the land.

 Reading Check *How does a sea breeze form?*

Land Breezes At night, land cools much more rapidly than ocean water. Air over the land becomes cooler than air over the ocean. Cooler, denser air above the land moves over the water, as the warm air over the water rises. Movement of air toward the water from the land is called a **land breeze.**

Figure 19
These daily winds occur because land heats up and cools off faster than water does. **A** During the day, cool air from the water moves over the land, creating a sea breeze. **B** At night, cool air over the land moves toward the warmer air over the water, creating a land breeze.

Section 3 Assessment

1. Why do some parts of Earth's surface, such as the equator, receive more of the Sun's heat than other regions?
2. How does the Coriolis effect influence wind circulation on Earth?
3. Why does little wind and lots of afternoon rain occur in the doldrums?
4. Which wind system helped early sailors navigate Earth's oceans?
5. **Think Critically** How does the jet stream help move storms across North America?

Skill Builder Activities

6. **Comparing and Contrasting** Compare and contrast sea breezes and land breezes. **For more help, refer to the** Science Skill Handbook.
7. **Using Graphics Software** Use graphics software and **Figure 17** to draw the wind systems on Earth. Make a separate graphic of major wind circulation cells shown by black arrows. On another graphic, show major surface winds. Print your graphics and share them with your class. **For more help, refer to the** Technology Skill Handbook.

Answer During the day, solar radiation warms the land more than water. The air over the land warms by conduction, becomes less dense, and is replaced by cooler, denser air moving inland from the ocean. Thus, wind blows from the sea toward the land.

③ Assess

Reteach

Have students indicate the locations of the doldrums, trade winds, prevailing westerlies, and polar easterlies on a world globe. L2 Ⓘ **Visual-Spatial**

Challenge

Challenge students to write a couple of paragraphs to explain why early sailors chose to travel across the Atlantic between latitudes 0° and 30° while going east to west, but chose to travel between latitudes 30° and 60° to go west to east. The trade winds blow from east to west between the equator and 30°, which would help sailors sail west. The prevailing westerlies blow from west to east between 30° and 60°, which would aid sailors sailing east.

✔ *Assessment*

Content Have students draw a diagram showing the directions winds blow during the day and at night in areas that experience land and sea breezes. Use **Performance Assessment in the Science Classroom,** p. 127. Ⓟ

Answers to Section Assessment

1. Earth's curved surface causes solar energy to strike Earth at different angles. The more direct the angle, the greater the energy received.
2. Air masses in the northern hemisphere are deflected to the right, while those in the southern hemisphere are deflected to the left.
3. As air at the equator is warmed it is lifted and cooled. This causes clouds and precipitation most afternoons.
4. trade winds
5. Storm systems are steered by the current of air in the polar jet stream.
6. Both occur near bodies of water. Sea breezes blow from the sea toward the land during the day when air over land is warmer than air over water.

Land breezes blow from the land toward the sea at night when conditions reverse.
7. Graphics should show three cells in each hemisphere where warm air rises and cooler air sinks. Major winds would be polar easterlies, westerlies, and trade winds. There should be two major jet streams in each hemisphere.

Activity

BENCH TESTED

Recognize the Problem

Purpose

Students observe how water and soil differ in their abilities to absorb and release heat. L2 ELL COOP LEARN ⅃Ⓢ **Visual-Spatial**

Process Skills

communicating, relating cause and effect, forming a hypothesis, using numbers, designing an experiment to test a hypothesis, identifying and manipulating variables, comparing and contrasting, interpreting data

Time Required

30 minutes to make and check the plan, 40 minutes to do the experiment, 30 minutes to analyze data and draw conclusions

Safety Precautions

Caution students to avoid touching the overhead light and to keep the electric cord away from the water.

Form a Hypothesis

Possible Hypothesis

Soil absorbs and releases heat faster than water.

Test Your Hypothesis

Possible Procedures

Tape one thermometer inside each box with the bulb 2 cm from the bottom. Tape another thermometer 8 cm from the bottom. Fill one box with 5 cm of water and the other with 5 cm of soil. Attach the light to the ring stand and suspend it above the boxes. Record the temperature of all thermometers

Activity — *Design Your Own Experiment*

The Heat Is On

Sometimes, a plunge in a pool or lake on a hot summer day feels cool and refreshing. Why does the beach sand get so hot when the water remains cool? A few hours later, the water feels warmer than the land does. In this activity, you'll explore how water and land absorb heat.

Recognize the Problem

How do soil and water compare in their abilities to absorb and emit heat?

Form a Hypothesis

Form a hypothesis about how soil and water compare in their abilities to absorb and release heat. Write another hypothesis about how air temperatures above soil and above water differ during the day and night.

Safety Precautions

WARNING: *Be careful when handling the hot overhead light. Do not let the light or its cord make contact with water.*

Possible Materials

ring stand	clear plastic boxes (2)
soil	overhead light
metric ruler	with reflector
water	thermometers (4)
masking tape	colored pencils (4)

Goals

■ **Design** an experiment to compare heat absorption and release for soil and water.

■ **Observe** how heat release affects the air above soil and above water.

before turning on the light. After the light is turned on, record the temperature every minute for 15 minutes. When the light is turned off, record the temperature for an additional 15 minutes.

Sample Data Table:

Time (minutes)	Light on (temperature °C)			
	thermometer			
	in soil	above soil	in water	above water
0	25	25	24	25
2	27	27	25	27

Time (minutes)	Light off (temperature °C)			
0	34	33	32	33
2	31	30	32	30

Test Your Hypothesis

Plan

1. As a group, agree upon and write your hypothesis.

2. **List** the steps that you need to take to test your hypothesis. Include in your plan a description of how you will use your equipment to compare heat absorption and release for water and soil.

3. **Design** a data table in your Science Journal for both parts of your experiment—when the light is on and energy can be absorbed and when the light is off and energy is released to the environment.

Do

1. Make sure your teacher approves your plan and your data table before you start.

2. Carry out the experiment as planned.

3. During the experiment, record your observations and complete the data table in your Science Journal.

4. Include the temperatures of the soil and the water in your measurements. Also compare heat release for water and soil. Include the temperatures of the air immediately above both of the substances. Allow 15 min for each test.

Teaching Strategy

Have students graph data for each thermometer with a different colored pencil.

Expected Outcome

When the light is on, the soil and the air above it heats up faster than the water. When the light is turned off, soil loses heat faster than water.

Analyze Your Data

1. Graphs should show that energy absorption and release by soil is faster.

2. soil

3. Air above the land cooled faster.

Error Analysis

If students do not get the expected outcome, they may have made an error in reading thermometers or may have skipped a temperature reading.

Analyze Your Data

1. Use your colored pencils and the information in your data tables to make line graphs. Show the rate of temperature increase for soil and water. Graph the rate of temperature decrease for soil and water after you turn the light off.

2. **Analyze** your graphs. When the light was on, which heated up faster—the soil or the water?

3. **Compare** how fast the air temperature over the water changed with how fast the temperature over the land changed after the light was turned off.

Draw Conclusions

1. Answers will vary depending on results.

2. soil

3. When the light was first turned off, the temperature above the soil was higher. After several minutes, the temperature above the water was higher. Soil absorbs and releases heat more quickly than water.

Draw Conclusions

1. Were your hypotheses supported or not? Explain.

2. **Infer** from your graphs which cooled faster—the water or the soil.

3. **Compare** the temperatures of the air above the water and above the soil 15 minutes after the light was turned off. How do water and soil compare in their abilities to absorb and release heat?

𝒞ommunicating
Your Data

Make a poster showing the steps you followed for your experiment. Include graphs of your data. **Display** your poster in the classroom. **For more help, refer to the Science Skill Handbook.**

✔𝒜ssessment

Oral Have students explain why in the summer a swimming pool can feel cool in the daytime and warm at night. More heat from the Sun is required to raise the temperature of water than of land. At night the land cools off faster. The water temperature doesn't change as fast as the land temperature does. Use **Performance Assessment in the Science Classroom**, p. 89.

𝒞ommunicating

Your Data

Suggest that students use word processing programs and electronic spreadsheets to make their posters.

Science and Language Arts

Song of the Sky Loom[1]

Brian Swann, ed.

Have students research the craft of weaving. Have them write a definition of a term related to this craft with which they are unfamiliar.

Respond to the Reading

Active Reading Strategies

Respond Ask students to reread the poem out loud as a group. Ask them if reading it orally changes their understanding of it. **How was your understanding different the second time?**

Evaluate Tell students to consider the form the poem takes. **What might account for the way the poem broadens at the top, narrows in the center, and then broadens again at the bottom?**

Question Ask students to whom they think the poem is written.

Respond to the Reading

1. Student answers will vary but might include how Mother Earth and Father Sky appear to surround the song in the same way a mother and father shelter or take care of their children.

2. Student answers will vary but might suggest that a garment keeps you warm and protects you against harsh weather.

Respond to the Reading

1. Why do the words *Mother Earth* and *Father Sky* appear on either side and above and below the rest of the words?

2. Why does the song use the image of a garment to describe Earth's atmosphere?

This Native American prayer probably comes from the Tewa-speaking Pueblo village of San Juan, New Mexico. The poem is actually a chanted prayer used in ceremonial rituals.

Mother Earth   Father Sky

we are your children

With tired backs we bring you gifts you love

Then weave for us a garment of brightness
its warp[2] the white light of morning,
weft[3] the red light of evening,
fringes the falling rain,
its border the standing rainbow.

Thus weave for us a garment of brightness
So we may walk fittingly where birds sing,
So we may walk fittingly where grass is green.

Mother Earth   Father Sky

[1] a machine or device from which cloth is produced

[2] threads that run lengthwise in a piece of cloth

[3] horizontal threads interlaced through the warp in a piece of cloth

302   **CHAPTER 10**   Atmosphere

Reading Further

Other sources on this topic include:

Weather Legends: Native American Lore and the Science of Weather by Carole Barbuny Vogel, September 2000.

Earthmaker's Tales (North American Indian Stories) by Gretchen Will Mayo, Walker & Co, reprint edition, February 1991.

Watching Weather (Accidental Scientist) by Tom Murphree, Mary K. Miller, Exploratorium, Owl Books, August 1998.

Metaphor

Understanding Literature

Metaphor A metaphor is a figure of speech that compares seemingly unlike things. Unlike a simile, a metaphor does not use the connecting words *like* or *as*. For instance, in the song you just read, Father Sky is a loom. A loom is a machine or device that weaves cloth. The song describes the relationship between Earth and sky as being a woven garment. Lines such as "weave for us a garment of brightness" serve as metaphors for how Mother Earth and Father Sky together create an atmosphere in which their "children," or humans, can thrive.

Science Connection In this chapter, you learned about the composition of Earth's atmosphere. The atmosphere maintains the proper balance between the amount of heat absorbed from the Sun and the amount of heat that escapes back into space. You also learned about the water cycle and how water evaporates from Earth's surface back into the atmosphere. Using metaphor instead of scientific facts, the Tewa song conveys to the reader how the relationship between Earth and its atmosphere is important to all living things.

Linking Science and Writing

Creating a Metaphor Write a four-line poem that uses a metaphor to describe rain. You can choose to write about a gentle spring rain or a thunderous rainstorm. Remember that a metaphor does not use the words *like* or *as*. Therefore, your poem should begin with something like "Rain is ..." or "Heavy rain is ..."

Career Connection

Meteorologist

Kim Perez is an on-air meteorologist for The Weather Channel, a national cable television network. She became interested in the weather when she was living in Cincinnati, Ohio. There, in 1974, she witnessed the largest tornado on record. Ms. Perez now broadcasts weather reports to millions of television viewers. Meteorologists study computer models of Earth's atmosphere. These models help them predict short-term and long-term weather conditions for the United States and the world.

SCIENCE *Online* To learn more about careers in meteorology, visit the Glencoe Science Web site at **science.glencoe.com.**

SCIENCE AND LANGUAGE ARTS **303**

Understanding Literature

Science Connection

The atmosphere of Earth has evolved over time and is constantly changing. It changes as human and organic activities change the ecosphere. For example, scientists believe that part way through the history of Earth, oxygen was emitted into the atmosphere as a result of photosynthesis from algae in the ocean. Today, oxygen is one of the atmosphere's primary elements.

The atmosphere continues to change based on human and organic activity. For example, human activities are having a potentially catastrophic effect on the stratosphere. Complex chemical reactions involving chlorofluorocarbons that have been released to the atmosphere have been blamed for causing temporary holes in the ozone layer.

Linking Science and Writing

Teaching Strategies

Tell students that they will do a prewriting activity to help write a poem using metaphor. On a sheet of paper have students make two columns. Tell students to write nouns in one column that are elements or objects found in nature, such as plants or animals. Tell students to write other nouns in the second column directly across from the nouns in the first column that remind them of those words. For example, if a student writes "weeping willow tree" in one column, he or she might write the words "crying man" in the second column.

Career Connection

Atmospheric scientists are commonly called meteorologists. They study the characteristics, motions, and processes of Earth's atmosphere. Most predict the weather. However, other atmospheric scientists solve problems dealing with air-pollution control, air and sea transportation, global warming, droughts, or ozone depletion.

Internet Addresses

Explore the Glencoe Science Web site at **science.glencoe.com** to find out more about topics in this feature.

SCIENCE AND LANGUAGE ARTS **303**

Reviewing Main Ideas

Preview

Students can answer the questions in their Science Journals. Discuss the answers as you go through the chapter. **Linguistic**

Review

Students can write their answers, then compare them with those of other students. **Interpersonal**

Reteach

Students can look at the illustrations and describe details that support the main ideas of the chapter. **Visual-Spatial**

Answers to Chapter Review

SECTION 1
3. Chlorine atoms from CFC molecules detach oxygen atoms from ozone molecules, destroying the ozone molecules.

SECTION 2
3. condensation

SECTION 3
4. Soil and water absorb and release heat at different rates. During the day, land heats more quickly than water, causing a sea breeze to move from water to land. During the night, land cools more quickly than water, causing a land breeze to move from land to water.

Reviewing Main Ideas

Section 1 Earth's Atmosphere

1. Earth's atmosphere is made up mostly of gases, with some suspended solids and liquids. The unique atmosphere allows life on Earth to exist.

2. The atmosphere is divided into five layers with different characteristics.

3. The ozone layer protects Earth from too much ultraviolet radiation, which can be harmful. *How do chlorofluorocarbon molecules destroy ozone?*

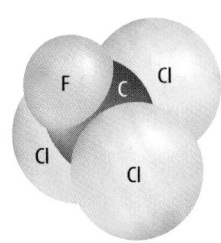

Section 2 Energy Transfer in the Atmosphere

1. Earth receives its energy from the Sun. Some of this energy is reflected back into space, and some is absorbed.

2. Heat is distributed in Earth's atmosphere by radiation, conduction, and convection.

3. Energy from the Sun powers the water cycle between the atmosphere and Earth's surface. *Clouds form during which part of the water cycle?*

4. Unlike the atmosphere on Mars or Venus, Earth's unique atmosphere maintains a balance between energy received and energy lost that keeps temperatures mild. This delicate balance allows life on Earth to exist.

Section 3 Air Movement

1. Because Earth's surface is curved, not all areas receive the same amount of solar radiation. This uneven heating causes temperature differences at Earth's surface.

2. Convection currents modified by the Coriolis effect produce Earth's global winds.

3. The polar jet stream is a strong current of wind found in the upper troposphere. It forms at the boundary between cold, polar air and warm, tropical air.

4. Land breezes and sea breezes occur near the ocean. *Why do winds change direction from day to night?*

FOLDABLES
Reading & Study Skills

After You Read

Draw pictures on the front of your Foldable of things that you might find in each layer of Earth's atmosphere.

FOLDABLES
Reading & Study Skills

After You Read

After students have read the chapter and completed the Foldable described in Before You Read, have them do the activity on the student page.

Dinah Zike

Visualizing Main Ideas

Complete the following cycle map on the water cycle.

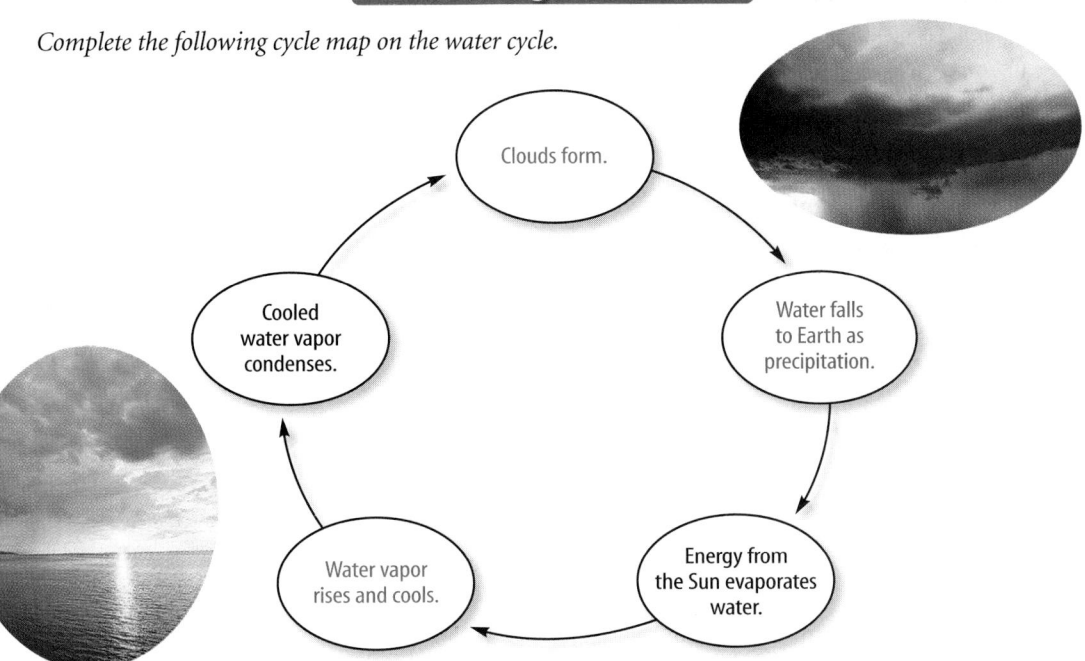

Clouds form.

Cooled water vapor condenses.

Water falls to Earth as precipitation.

Water vapor rises and cools.

Energy from the Sun evaporates water.

Visualizing Main Ideas

See student page.

Vocabulary Review

Using Vocabulary

1. Chlorofluorocarbons are dangerous because they destroy the ozone layer.
2. Narrow belts of strong winds called jet streams blow near the top of the troposphere.
3. The thin layer of air that surrounds Earth is called the atmosphere.
4. Heat energy transferred in the form of waves is called radiation.
5. The ozone layer helps protect us from ultraviolet radiation.

Vocabulary Review

Vocabulary Review

a. atmosphere
b. chlorofluorocarbon
c. condensation
d. conduction
e. convection
f. Coriolis effect
g. hydrosphere
h. ionosphere
i. jet stream
j. land breeze
k. ozone layer
l. radiation
m. sea breeze
n. troposphere
o. ultraviolet radiation

Study Tip

Describe ways that you might design an experiment to prove scientific principles.

Using Vocabulary

The sentences below include terms that have been used incorrectly. Change the incorrect terms so that the sentence reads correctly.

1. Chlorofluorocarbons are dangerous because they destroy the hydrosphere.

2. Narrow belts of strong winds called sea breezes blow near the top of the troposphere.

3. The thin layer of air that surrounds Earth is called the troposphere.

4. Heat energy transferred in the form of waves is called condensation.

5. The ozone layer helps protect us from the Coriolis effect.

IDENTIFYING ▷ Misconceptions

Assess

Use the assessment as follow-up to page 280F after students have completed the chapter.

Demonstration Take students outside to a large open area. Take a kite with you. Launch the kite and, while flying it, have students discuss what causes the kite to stay up in the sky.

Expected Outcome Students will begin to realize that the movement of air (wind) is caused by uneven heating of Earth's surface.

Reinforcement Discuss with students what color clothes you would want to wear on a hot, sunny day compared to a cold, sunny day. Relate this to the uneven heating of Earth's surface.

Chapter 10 Assessment

Checking Concepts

1. D
2. C
3. C
4. A
5. A
6. C
7. D
8. C
9. C
10. B

Thinking Critically

11. There is little or no water vapor available to form clouds.
12. The ozone layer prevents UV radiation, which is generally harmful to living organisms, from reaching Earth's surface. Early organisms living in the oceans were protected from UV by the water.
13. Sea breezes occur when the air over the water is cooler than the air over the land. This occurs during the day, when solar radiation is greatest.
14. It condenses. Students may also say it forms clouds.
15. With an increase in altitude, fewer and fewer molecules push against one another to cause air pressure.

Developing Skills

16. See student page.
17. During the afternoon, the ground warmed and heated the air above it through conduction. After sunset, the ground was no longer receiving solar energy and could no longer provide as much heat to the air above it.
18. Average global temperature might increase.

Checking Concepts

Choose the word or phrase that best answers the question.

1. What is the most abundant gas in the atmosphere?
A) oxygen   **C)** argon
B) water vapor   **D)** nitrogen

2. What causes a brown haze near cities?
A) conduction   **C)** car exhaust
B) mud   **D)** wind

3. Which is the uppermost layer of the atmosphere?
A) troposphere   **C)** exosphere
B) stratosphere   **D)** thermosphere

4. What layer of the atmosphere has the most water?
A) troposphere   **C)** mesosphere
B) stratosphere   **D)** exosphere

5. What protects living things from too much ultraviolet radiation?
A) the ozone layer **C)** nitrogen
B) oxygen   **D)** argon

6. Where is air pressure least?
A) troposphere   **C)** exosphere
B) stratosphere   **D)** thermosphere

7. How is energy transferred when objects are in contact?
A) trade winds   **C)** radiation
B) convection   **D)** conduction

8. Which surface winds are responsible for most of the weather movement across the United States?
A) polar easterlies **C)** prevailing westerlies
B) sea breeze   **D)** trade winds

9. What type of wind is a movement of air toward water?
A) sea breeze   **C)** land breeze
B) polar easterlies **D)** trade winds

10. What are narrow belts of strong winds near the top of the troposphere called?
A) doldrums   **C)** polar easterlies
B) jet streams   **D)** trade winds

Thinking Critically

11. Why are there few or no clouds in the stratosphere?

12. It is thought that life could not have existed on land until the ozone layer formed about 2 billion years ago. Why does life on land require an ozone layer?

13. Why do sea breezes occur during the day but not at night?

14. Describe what happens when water vapor rises and cools.

15. Why does air pressure decrease with an increase in altitude?

Developing Skills

16. Concept Mapping Complete the cycle concept map below using the following phrases to explain how air moves to form a convection current: *Cool air moves toward warm air, warm air is lifted and cools,* and *cool air sinks.*

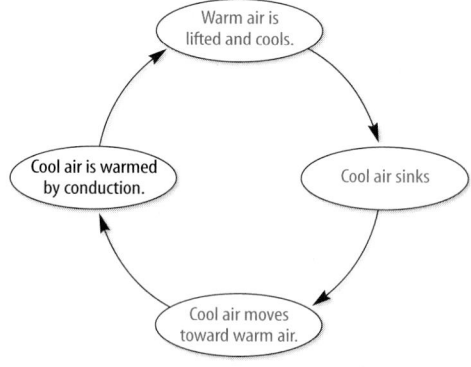

Warm air is lifted and cools.

Cool air is warmed by conduction.

Cool air sinks.

Cool air moves toward warm air.

Chapter ✓Assessment Planner

17. Drawing Conclusions In an experiment, a student measured the air temperature 1 m above the ground on a sunny afternoon and again in the same spot 1h after sunset. The second reading was lower than the first. What can you infer from this?

18. Forming Hypotheses Carbon dioxide in the atmosphere prevents some radiation from Earth's surface from escaping to space. Hypothesize how the temperature on Earth might change if more carbon dioxide were released from burning fossil fuels.

19. Identifying and Manipulating Variables and Controls Design an experiment to find out how plants are affected by differing amounts of ultraviolet radiation. In the design, use filtering film made for car windows. What is the variable you are testing? What are your constants? Your controls?

20. Recognizing Cause and Effect Why is the inside of a car hotter than the outdoor temperature on a sunny summer day?

Performance Assessment

21. Poster Illustrate or find magazine photos of convection currents that occur in everyday life.

22. Experiment Design and conduct an experiment to find out how different surfaces such as asphalt, soil, sand, and grass absorb and reflect solar energy. Share the results with your class.

TECHNOLOGY

Go to the Glencoe Science Web site at **science.glencoe.com** or use the **Glencoe Science CD-ROM** for additional chapter assessment.

THE PRINCETON REVIEW — Test Practice

Each layer of Earth's atmosphere has a unique composition and temperature. The four layers closest to Earth's surface are shown in the diagram below.

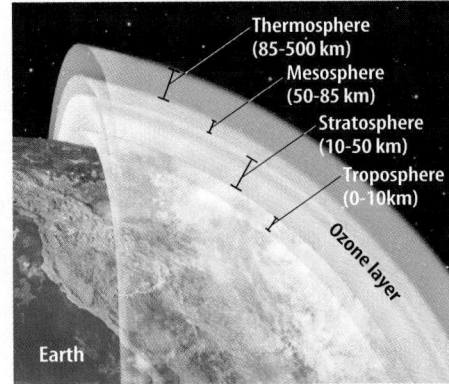

Thermosphere (85–500 km)
Mesosphere (50–85 km)
Stratosphere (10–50 km)
Troposphere (0–10km)
Ozone layer
Earth

Study the diagram and answer the following questions.

1. In which part of the atmosphere is ozone located.
  A) Thermosphere **C)** Stratosphere
  B) Troposphere **D)** Mesosphere

2. According to the diagram, how far does the mesosphere extend above Earth's surface?
  F) 10 km **H)** 50 km
  G) 85 km **I)** 60 km

3. What is the correct order of atmospheric layers that the space shuttle goes through when landing on Earth?
  A) Mesosphere **C)** Stratosphere
  Stratosphere Troposphere
  Troposphere Mesosphere
  B) Troposphere **D)** Mesosphere
  Stratosphere Troposphere
  Mesosphere Stratosphere

THE PRINCETON REVIEW — Test Practice

The Test-Taking Tip was written by The Princeton Review, the nation's leader in test preparation.
1. C
2. G
3. A

Developing Skills

19. Accept all reasonable designs. The variable is the amount of ultraviolet light that the plants receive. The constants are identical plants, pots, watering, soil, and placement of the pots. The controls are the plants that receive ultraviolet radiation without filtering.

20. Solar energy passes through the glass windows, where it is absorbed by the car interior. The interior reradiates the energy as heat. The glass windows trap the heat, which builds up inside as long as the car sits in the Sun.

Performance Assessment

21. Possible visual: liquids such as soups or water cooking or boiling on a stove burner, or weather systems, since convection distributes heat. Have students mount their drawings or photos on poster board. Display the posters in the classroom. Use **PASC**, p. 145.

22. As part of the experiment setup, students might lay a thermometer on each surface and suspend another one above each surface to collect temperature readings. Thermometers should be suspended at the same height. Use **PASC**, p. 95.

✓Assessment Resources

📁 **Reproducible Masters**
Chapter Resources Booklet
  Chapter Review, pp. 33–34
  Chapter Tests, pp. 35–38
  Assessment Transparency Activity, p. 45

Glencoe Science Web site
  Interactive Tutor
  Chapter Quizzes

Glencoe Technology
  🖌 Assessment Transparency
  💿 Interactive CD-ROM Chapter Quizzes
  💿 ExamView Pro Test Bank
  💿 Vocabulary PuzzleMaker Software
  📼 MindJogger Videoquiz

Section/Objectives	Standards		Activities/Features
Chapter Opener	**National**	**State/Local**	**Explore Activity:** Demonstrate how rain forms, p. 309 **Before You Read,** p. 309
	See p. 5T for a Key to Standards.		
Section 1 What is weather? ⏱ 2 sessions 📦 1 block 1. **Explain** how solar heating and water vapor in the atmosphere affect weather. 2. **Discuss** how clouds form and how they are classified. 3. **Describe** how rain, hail, sleet, and snow develop.	National Content Standards: UCP1, A1, D1, E2, F3		**Life Science Integration,** p. 311 **MiniLAB:** Determining Dew Point, p. 312 **Math Skills Activity,** Calculating the Amount of Dew, p. 313
Section 2 Weather Patterns ⏱ 2 sessions 📦 1 block 1. **Describe** how weather is associated with fronts and high- and low-pressure areas. 2. **Explain** how tornadoes develop from thunderstorms. 3. **Discuss** the dangers of severe weather.	National Content Standards: UCP1, UCP3, D1, F3		**Science Online,** p. 319 **Science Online,** p. 322 **Visualizing Tornadoes,** p. 323 **Environmental Science Integration,** p. 324
Section 3 Weather Forecasts ⏱ 3 sessions 📦 1.5 blocks 1. **Explain** how data are collected for weather maps and forecasts. 2. **Identify** the symbols used in a weather station model.	National Content Standards: UCP1, UCP2, A1, A2, D1, E1, E2, F5, G1		**MiniLAB:** Measuring Rain, p. 327 **Activity:** Reading a Weather Map, p. 329 **Activity:** Measuring Wind Speed, pp. 330–331 **Science and Society:** Rainmakers, pp. 332–333

NATIONAL GEOGRAPHIC   Teacher's Corner

PRODUCTS AVAILABLE FROM GLENCOE
To order call 1-800-334-7344:
CD-ROM *NGS PictureShow: Introduction to Weather*
Curriculum Kit *GeoKit: Weather*
Transparency Set *NGS PicturePack: Introduction to Weather*

PRODUCTS AVAILABLE FROM NATIONAL GEOGRAPHIC SOCIETY
To order call 1-800-368-2728:
Videos
Telling the Weather
Weather: Come Rain, Come Shine

Activity Materials	Reproducible Resources	Section Assessment	Technology
Explore Activity: 2 metal pans, water, hot plate, ice	**Chapter Resources Booklet** Foldables Worksheet, p. 17 Directed Reading Overview, p. 19 Note-taking Worksheets, pp. 33–35	GLENCOE'S ASSESSMENT ADVANTAGE	
MiniLAB: metal can, paper towels, thermometer, stirring rod, crushed ice, water	**Chapter Resources Booklet** Transparency Activity, p. 44 MiniLAB, p. 3 Enrichment, p. 30 Reinforcement, p. 27 Directed Reading, p. 20 Lab Activities, pp. 9–11, 13–15 **Mathematics Skill Activities,** p. 7 **Physical Science Critical Thinking/Problem Solving,** p. 16	Portfolio Life Science Integration, p. 311 Performance MiniLAB, p. 312 Math Skills Activity, p. 313 Skill Builder Activities, p. 317 Content Section Assessment, p. 317	Section Focus Transparency Interactive CD-ROM Guided Reading Audio Program
Need materials? Contact Science Kit at 1-800-828-7777 or www.sciencekit.com on the Internet.	**Chapter Resources Booklet** Transparency Activity, p. 45 Enrichment, p. 31 Reinforcement, p. 28 Directed Reading, p. 21 **Reading and Writing Skill Activity,** pp. 3, 45 **Science Inquiry Labs,** p. 27	Portfolio Use Science Words, p. 319 Performance Skill Builder Activities, p. 325 Content Section Assessment, p. 325	Section Focus Transparency Interactive CD-ROM Guided Reading Audio Program
MiniLAB: soup or coffee can, ducttape, ruler **Activity:** hand lens **Activity:** paper, scissors, confetti, grass clippings, meterstick	**Chapter Resources Booklet** Transparency Activity, p. 46 MiniLAB, p. 4 Enrichment, p. 32 Reinforcement, p. 29 Directed Reading, pp. 21, 22 Activity Worksheet, pp. 5–6, 7–8 Transparency Activity, pp. 47–48 **Lab Management and Safety,** p. 4	Portfolio Challenge, p. 328 Performance MiniLAB, p. 327 Skill Builder Activities, p. 328 Content Section Assessment, p. 328	Section Focus Transparency Teaching Transparency Interactive CD-ROM Guided Reading Audio Program

End of Chapter Assessment

GLENCOE'S ASSESSMENT ADVANTAGE

Blackline Masters	Technology	Professional Series
Chapter Resources Booklet Chapter Review, pp. 37–38 Chapter Tests, pp. 39–42 **Standardized Test Practice by The Princeton Review,** pp. 71–74	MindJogger Videoquiz Interactive CD-ROM Vocabulary PuzzleMakers ExamView Pro Test Bank Interactive Lesson Planner Interactive Teacher Edition	Performance Assessment in the Science Classroom (PASC)

Transparencies

Section Focus

Section Focus Transparency 1 Valley Mist

This Chinese painting depicts a mountain and valley scene. Mountains with fog hanging in the valleys are common elements in this style of painting.

1. What do you think the weather in this picture is like?
2. Describe how fog or mist feels.
3. How are fog and clouds similar?

L2

Section Focus Transparency 2 Cloud Walking

If you've ever hiked up a mountain, you may have noticed that it is often cooler at higher elevations. Sometimes, however, the air at the top of a mountain is noticeably warmer than the air at the bottom. The warm air traps the colder surface air.

1. How can you tell that there is not a lot of air movement in this picture?
2. What will happen when the Sun warms the lower air?
3. What would happen if there were pollutants near the ground?

L2

Section Focus Transparency 3 Whither wanders the weather?

For many people, knowing what the weather will be like is important. Farmers schedule planting, irrigation, or harvesting based on weather conditions. Weather can change travel schedules or even make travel unsafe. Many people like to know whether they should carry an umbrella.

1. Which of these items would you use if you wanted to know how much snow fell last night? Which item displays the path of a storm?
2. How has weather prediction changed in the last century?

L2

This is a representation of key blackline masters available in the Teacher Classroom Resources. See Resource Manager boxes within the chapter for additional information.

Assessment

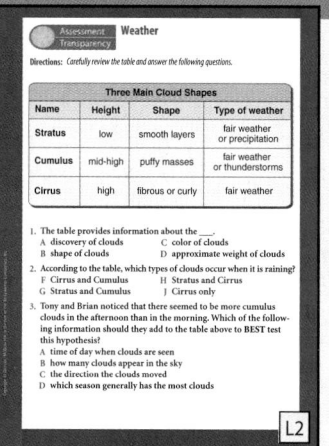

Assessment Transparency Weather

Directions: *Carefully review the table and answer the following questions.*

Three Main Cloud Shapes			
Name	**Height**	**Shape**	**Type of weather**
Stratus	low	smooth layers	fair weather or precipitation
Cumulus	mid-high	puffy masses	fair weather or thunderstorms
Cirrus	high	fibrous or curly	fair weather

1. The table provides information about the ____.
   A discovery of clouds   C color of clouds
   B shape of clouds   D approximate weight of clouds
2. According to the table, which types of clouds occur when it is raining?
   F Cirrus and Cumulus   H Stratus and Cirrus
   G Stratus and Cumulus   J Cirrus only
3. Tony and Brian noticed that there seemed to be more cumulus clouds in the afternoon than in the morning. Which of the following information should they add to the table above to BEST test this hypothesis?
   A time of day when clouds are seen
   B how many clouds appear in the sky
   C the direction the clouds moved
   D which season generally has the most clouds

L2

Teaching

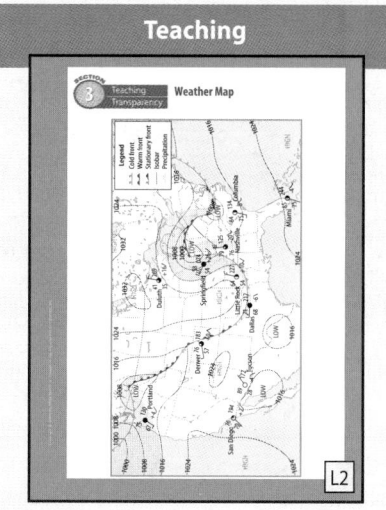

Teaching Transparency 3 Weather Map

L2

Key to Teaching Strategies

The following designations will help you decide which activities are appropriate for your students.

L1 Level 1 activities should be appropriate for students with learning difficulties.

L2 Level 2 activities should be within the ability range of all students.

L3 Level 3 activities are designed for above-average students.

ELL ELL activities should be within the ability range of English Language Learners.

COOP LEARN Cooperative Learning activities are designed for small group work.

LS Multiple Learning Styles logos, as described on page 22T, are used throughout to indicate strategies that address different learning styles.

P These strategies represent student products that can be placed into a best-work portfolio.

Hands-on Activities

Activity Worksheets

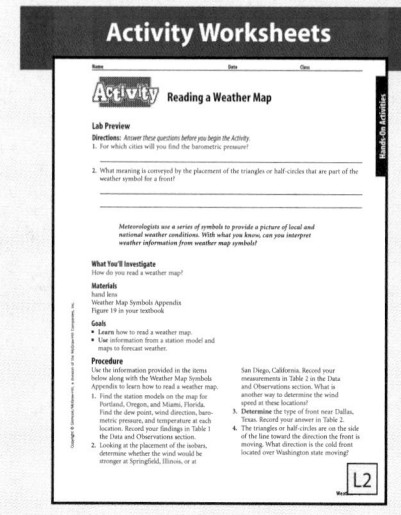

Activity Reading a Weather Map

Lab Preview

Directions: *Answer these questions before you begin the Activity.*
1. For which cities will you find the barometric pressure?

2. What meaning is conveyed by the placement of the triangles or half-circles that are part of the weather symbol for a front?

Meteorologists use a series of symbols to provide a picture of local and national weather conditions. With what you know, can you interpret weather information from weather map symbols?

What You'll Investigate
How do you read a weather map?

Materials
hand lens
Weather Map Symbols Appendix
Figure 19 in your textbook

Goals
• Learn how to read a weather map.
• Use information from a station model and maps to forecast weather.

Procedure
Use the information provided in the items below along with the Weather Map Symbols Appendix to learn how to read a weather map.
1. Find the station models on the map for Portland, Oregon, and Miami, Florida. Find the dew point, direction, barometric pressure, and temperature at each location. Record your findings in Table 1 the Data and Observations section.
2. Looking at the placement of the isobars, determine whether the wind would be stronger at Springfield, Illinois, or at

San Diego, California. Record your measurements in Table 2 in the Data and Observations section. What is another way to determine the wind speed at these locations?
3. **Determine** the type of front near Dallas, Texas. Record your answer in Table 2.
4. The triangles or half-circles are on the side of the line toward which the front is moving. What direction is the cold front located over Washington state moving?

L2

Laboratory Activities

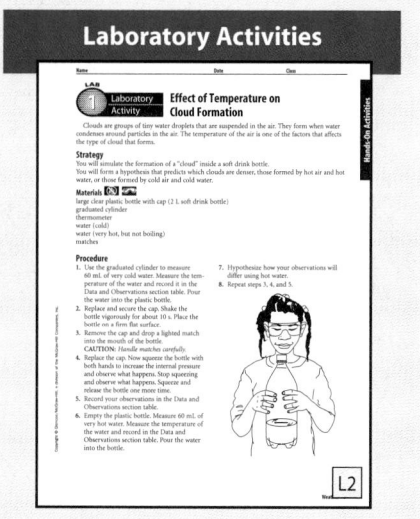

Laboratory Activity 1 Effect of Temperature on Cloud Formation

Clouds are groups of tiny water droplets that are suspended in the air. They form when water condenses around particles in the air. The temperature of the air is one of the factors that affect the type of cloud that forms.

Strategy
You will simulate the formation of a "cloud" inside a soft drink bottle. You will form a hypothesis that predicts which clouds are denser, those formed by hot air and hot water, or those formed by cold air and cold water.

Materials
large clear plastic bottle with cap (2 L soft drink bottle)
graduated cylinder
thermometer
water (cold)
water (very hot, but not boiling)
matches

Procedure
1. Use the graduated cylinder to measure 60 mL of very cold water. Measure the temperature of the water and record it in the Data and Observations section. Pour the water into the plastic bottle.
2. Replace and secure the cap. Shake the bottle vigorously for about 10 s. Place the bottle on a firm flat surface.
3. Remove the cap and drop a lighted match into the mouth of the bottle. CAUTION: *Handle matches carefully.*
4. Replace the cap. Now squeeze the bottle with both hands to increase the internal pressure and observe what happens. Stop squeezing and observe what happens. Squeeze and release the bottle one more time.
5. Record your observations in the Data and Observations section table.
6. Empty the plastic bottle. Measure 60 mL of very hot water. Measure the temperature of the water and record it in the Data and Observations section table. Pour the water into the bottle.
7. Hypothesize how your observations will differ using hot water.
8. Repeat steps 3, 4, and 5.

L2

Meeting Different Ability Levels

Content Outline

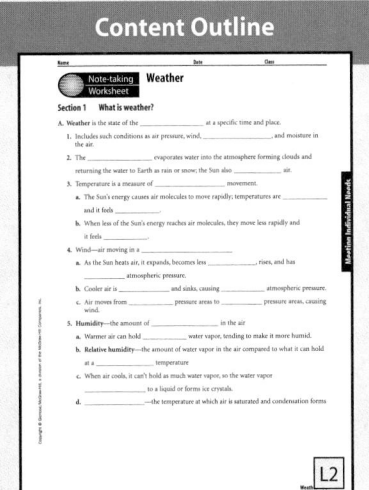

Reinforcement

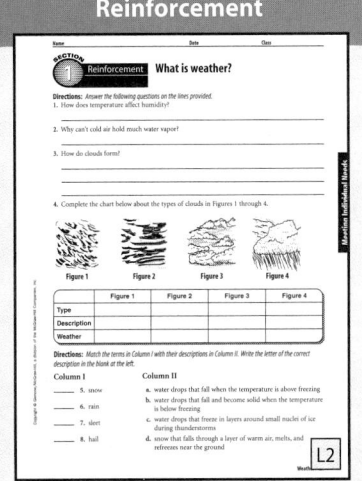

Directed Reading

Assessment

Chapter Tests

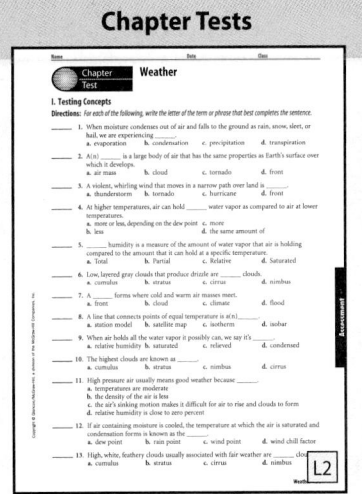

Enrichment

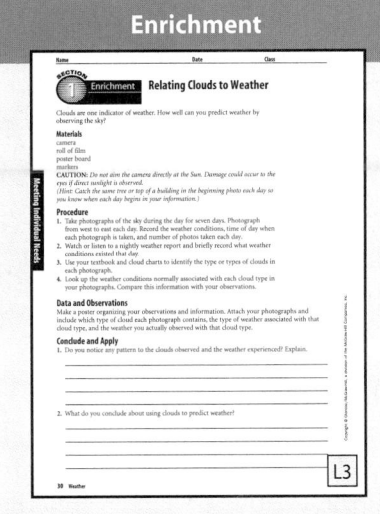

Spanish Directed Reading

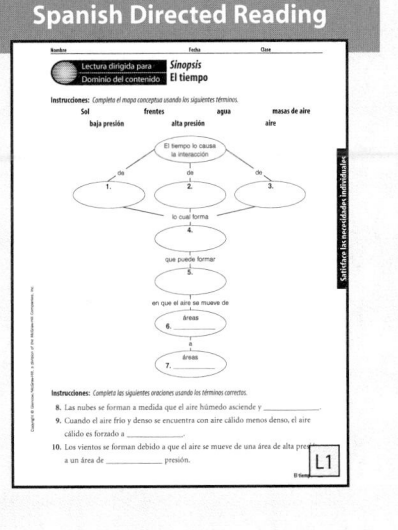

Test Practice Workbook

Chapter Review

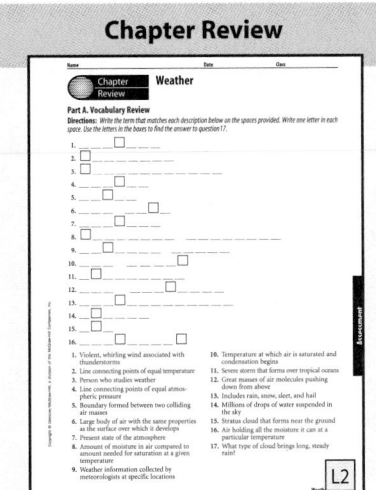

Science Content Background

What is weather?

Weather Factors

Relative humidity is measured using a hygrometer or a psychrometer. An early hygrometer used paper disks that absorbed water vapor from the air. As the paper absorbed more water vapor, its weight caused a pointer to rise, indicating the humidity level on a scale. Today hygrometers use human hair. Hair is more flexible under humid conditions. The hair lengthens in high humidity and contracts when dry, causing a dial to move.

A psychrometer is made of a wet-bulb and a dry-bulb thermometer. The wet-bulb thermometer has its tip wrapped in gauze and dipped into water. Once removed from the water, if the relative humidity of the air is less than 100 percent, water evaporates from the gauze. As this happens, the temperature of the thermometer drops. The dry bulb measures the actual air temperature. By comparing the temperatures of the two thermometers and using a chart, the relative humidity is determined.

Forming Clouds

A cloud is made of hundreds of millions of tiny ice crystals and droplets of water that condense around solids suspended in the air. If the temperature is above 0°C, water vapor condenses to form a liquid. At temperatures below 0°C, water vapor may sublimate, or turn directly into ice crystals. Clouds that form at high altitudes contain ice crystals. At lower altitudes, clouds are made up mostly of water droplets. At middle altitudes, clouds contain a mixture of ice crystals, supercooled water droplets, and water droplets. The type of cloud that forms depends on the amount of air moisture, the uplift of the air, and the stability of the atmosphere.

Classifying Clouds

Luke Howard developed the current cloud classification system in 1803. This classification is based on the most common cloud shapes. Howard used Latin words to describe the shapes of the clouds. *Cumulus* means "heap"; *stratus*, "layer"; *cirrus*, "lock of hair"; and *nimbus*, "rain-bearing." His classification system allows for the combination of names to describe more specific cloud types.

Corbis

Fun Fact

The largest temperature change in a 24-hour period occurred in Browning, Montana, in 1916. The temperature dropped from 44°F on January 23 to −56°F on January 24. That's a change of 100°F in only 24 hours!

SECTION 2 — Weather Patterns

Weather Changes

The stability of an air mass is one of the factors that determine the weather of an area. Warm, moist air masses are said to be unstable. Because the warm air at the surface is less dense than the cooler air above it, it will tend to be forced aloft, producing clouds, precipitation, and storms. Cold, dry air masses are stable because cold air is denser than warmer air and thus is not pushed aloft. In addition, cold air tends to contain less moisture than does warm air.

Thunderstorms

Hail forms in cumulonimbus clouds, where strong updrafts exist. Water droplets can freeze as they are tossed upward or ice crystals can form directly from vapor. Each time an ice crystal falls and is caught in an updraft, a new layer is added to the hail stone.

Tornadoes also form in cumulonimbus clouds. A tornado can develop in less than an hour and can destroy property and kill people within a matter of minutes. Although tornadic wind speed has been clocked at nearly 500 km/h, most tornadoes generate winds of less than 80 km/h.

Gene Moore/Phototake/Picturequest

Hurricanes

Hurricanes have been known to sustain winds of 250 km/h and gusts up to 300 km/h. A hurricane can last for weeks and cover thousands of kilometers. A well-developed hurricane has bands of cumulonimbus clouds spiraling around a calm eye. A hurricane can contain hundreds of cumulonimbus clouds and can measure 970 km in diameter.

Fun Fact

The average hurricane produces 3 trillion joules of energy per second. You would need to light 30 billion 100-watt light bulbs simultaneously to use that much energy!

SECTION 3 — Weather Forecasts

Weather Observations

Cameras on satellites take photographs of Earth's atmosphere and send the data to ground stations via microwave transmissions. Satellites gather visible and infrared data to help determine the temperature differences and locate cloudy and clear areas. Satellite photos are important to weather forecasters because the data they provide about cloud movements enable forecasters to locate low-pressure areas and fronts.

Forecasting Weather

In addition to surface weather maps, meteorologists use upper-air charts that show the movement of air at various altitudes to help them make forecasts. Since the early 1950s, meteorologists around the world have exchanged information to help with forecasting. Today, computer technology provides a global network for the exchange of information to help make more accurate short-range and long-range forecasts.

SCIENCE *Online*

For additional content background on this topic, go to the Glencoe Science Web site at science.glencoe.com.

Weather

Chapter Vocabulary

What do you think?

Science Journal The photograph shows a hurricane with a well-formed eye at its center. Although strong winds rage around the eye, the winds inside the eye are calm.

CHAPTER 11

Weather

It's summer and you've gone to your aunt's house in the country. You're playing baseball with your cousins, getting ready to bat, when suddenly you feel a strange sensation. The hot, humid air has suddenly turned cooler, and a strong breeze has kicked up. To the west, tall, black clouds are rapidly advancing. You see a flash of lightning and hear a loud clap of thunder. In this chapter, you'll learn how to measure weather conditions, interpret weather information, and make predictions.

What do you think?

Science Journal Look at the picture below with a classmate. Discuss what this might be or what is happening. Here's a hint: *It's calm in the center and rough around the edges.* Write your answer or best guess in your Science Journal.

308

Theme Connection

Systems and Interactions In this chapter, students see how the interaction of solar energy, Earth's atmosphere, and Earth's waters form dynamic weather systems.

How can it rain one day and be sunny the next? Powered by heat from the Sun, the air that surrounds you stirs and swirls. This constant mixing produces storms, calm weather, and everything in between. What causes rain and where does the water come from? Do the activity below to find out.

Demonstrate how rain forms

WARNING: *Boiling water and steam can cause burns.*

1. Bring a pan of water to a boil on a hot plate.

2. Carefully hold another pan containing ice cubes about 20 cm above the boiling water. Be sure to keep your hands and face away from the steam.

3. Keep the pan with the ice cubes in place until you see drops of water dripping from the bottom.

Observe

In your Science Journal, describe how the droplets formed. Infer where the water on the bottom of the pan came from.

Before You Read

FOLDABLES
Reading & Study Skills

Making an Organizational Study Fold **When information is grouped into clear categories, it is easier to make sense of what you are learning. Make the following Foldable to help you organize your thoughts about weather.**

1. Stack two sheets of paper in front of you so the short side of both sheets is at the top.

2. Slide the top sheet up so that about 4 cm of the bottom sheet shows.

3. Fold both sheets top to bottom to form four tabs and staple along the top fold, as shown.

4. Label the flaps *Weather, What is Weather?, Weather Patterns,* and *Forecasting Weather,* as shown.

5. As you read the chapter, list what you learn under the appropriate flaps.

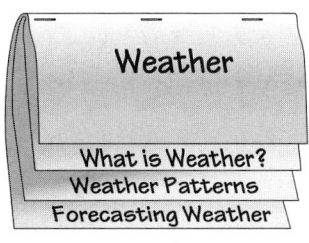

309

EXPLORE ACTIVITY

Purpose Use the Explore Activity to model parts of the water cycle. L2 ELL **Kinesthetic**

Preparation Bring in ice. Have students bring in aluminum pans.

Materials small pot, water, hot plate, aluminum pan, six ice cubes, oven mitts, goggles, apron

Teaching Strategy To save time, have students put the pots of water on to boil before starting the Activity.

Troubleshooting Make sure students hold the pan 20 cm above the boiling water. If it is held too far away, water droplets may not form.

Safety Precaution Students should use mitts and aprons and wear goggles when holding pans over hot water.

Observe

Water evaporated from the pot. It rose and condensed into droplets when it contacted the cold surface of the pan.

✓ **Assessment**

Oral Have students explain why ice was used in the top pan. Ice cooled the pan and the air below it. As warm air containing water vapor rose under the pan, the water vapor cooled, causing it to condense and form water droplets on the pan's bottom surface. Use **Performance Assessment in the Science Classroom,** p. 89.

FOLDABLES
Reading & Study Skills

Before You Read

Dinah Zike Study Fold

Purpose Use this activity to determine what students know about weather before reading the chapter. Students can use the Foldable for recording and organizing notes from each of the three sections of the chapter as they read.

For additional help, see Foldables Worksheet, p. 17 in **Chapter Resources Booklet,** or go to the Glencoe Science Web site at **science.glencoe.com.** See After You Read in the Study Guide at the end of this chapter.

SECTION

1

What is weather?

1 Motivate

Bellringer Transparency

Display the Section Focus Transparency for Section 1. Use the accompanying Transparency Activity Master. L2

ELL

Tie to Prior Knowledge

Ask students what they think of when someone says "weather." Record their responses on the board. Return to the list after students have read this section. Discuss how accurate they were in their initial assessment of what constitutes weather.

Caption Answer

Figure 1 Students' answers will vary; encourage them to notice concentrations of clouds and swirling patterns in the image.

As You Read

What You'll Learn

- **Explain** how solar heating and water vapor in the atmosphere affect weather.
- **Discuss** how clouds form and how they are classified.
- **Describe** how rain, hail, sleet, and snow develop.

Vocabulary

weather
humidity
relative humidity
dew point
fog
precipitation

Why It's Important

Weather changes affect your daily activities.

Weather Factors

It might seem like small talk to you, but for farmers, truck drivers, pilots, and construction workers, the weather can have a huge impact on their livelihoods. Even professional athletes, especially golfers, follow weather patterns closely. You can describe what happens in different kinds of weather, but can you explain how it happens?

Weather refers to the state of the atmosphere at a specific time and place. Weather describes conditions such as air pressure, wind, temperature, and the amount of moisture in the air.

The Sun provides almost all of Earth's energy. Energy from the Sun evaporates water into the atmosphere where it forms clouds. Eventually, the water falls back to Earth as rain or snow. However, the Sun does more than evaporate water. It is also a source of heat energy. Heat from the Sun is absorbed by Earth's surface, which then heats the air above it. Weather, as shown in **Figure 1,** is the result of heat and Earth's air and water.

Figure 1
The Sun provides the energy that drives Earth's weather.
Can you find any storms in this image?

310 CHAPTER 11 Weather

Section ✓Assessment Planner

A When air is heated, it expands and becomes less dense. This creates lower pressure.

B Molecules making up air are closer together in cooler temperatures, creating high pressure. Wind blows from higher pressure toward lower pressure.

Air Temperature During the summer when the Sun is hot and the air is still, a swim can be refreshing. But would a swim seem refreshing on a cold, winter day? The temperature of air influences your daily activities.

Air is made up of molecules that are always moving randomly, even when there's no wind. Temperature is a measure of the average amount of motion of molecules. When the temperature is high, molecules in air move rapidly and it feels warm. When the temperature is low, molecules in air move less rapidly, and it feels cold.

Wind Why can you fly a kite on some days but not others? Kites fly because air is moving. Air moving in a specific direction is called wind. As the Sun warms the air, the air expands and becomes less dense. Warm, expanding air has low atmospheric pressure. Cooler air is denser and tends to sink, bringing about high atmospheric pressure. Wind results because air moves from regions of high pressure to regions of low pressure. You may have experienced this on a small scale if you've ever spent time along a beach, as in **Figure 2.**

Many instruments are used to measure wind direction and speed. Wind direction can be measured using a wind vane. A wind vane has an arrow that points in the direction from which the wind is blowing. A wind sock has one open end that catches the wind, causing the sock to point in the direction toward which the wind is blowing. Wind speed can be measured using an anemometer (a nuh MAH muh tur). Anemometers have rotating cups that spin faster when the wind is strong.

Figure 2
The temperature of air can affect air pressure. Wind is air moving from high pressure to low pressure.

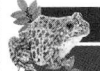 **Life Science**
INTEGRATION

Birds and mammals maintain a fairly constant internal temperature, even when the temperature outside their bodies changes. On the other hand, the internal temperature of fish and reptiles changes when the temperature around them changes. Infer from this which group is more likely to survive a quick change in the weather.

Weather Factor

Quick Demo

To demonstrate the movement of molecules of warm and cold air, half-fill a large, clear plastic bag with table tennis balls, popcorn, or packing "peanuts." Set a hand-held hair dryer on low and use it to blow cool air into the bag. Then increase the speed to high. The slower-moving objects represent molecules of cool air. The more rapidly-moving objects represent molecules of warmer air, which move faster and spread farther apart. L2 IN **Visual-Spatial**

 **Life Science**
INTEGRATION

Birds and mammals are more likely to survive. Because they maintain a certain internal temperature, sudden weather changes would not affect them as much. Have students research and write a short report about the physical and behavioral adaptations of fish and reptiles that help them contend with temperature extremes. Estivation is a dormant state that helps some animals deal with extreme heat and dryness, the way hibernation helps other animals survive cold. L2 IN **Linguistic** P

Teacher FYI

The highest wind speed ever recorded was 372 km/h, registered on New Hampshire's Mount Washington in 1934. At 56 km/h, the average wind speed on top of Mount Washington is the highest in the United States. These high winds occur when the prevailing westerlies accelerate as they flow up and over the mountain.

Resource Manager

Chapter Resources Booklet
  Transparency Activity, p. 44
  Note-taking Worksheet, pp. 33–35
  Directed Reading for Content Mastery, pp. 19, 20

Weather Factors, continued

Answer At warmer temperatures, water vapor molecules move too quickly to condense.

Purpose Students determine dew point. L2 ELL
IS Kinesthetic

Materials metal can, paper towels, thermometer, stirring rod, crushed ice, water

Teaching Strategy Have students start with 2/3 cup of water before adding ice.

Safety Precautions Caution students not to use the thermometers as stirring rods.

Troubleshooting Ice must be added to the water slowly.

Analysis

1. The amount of moisture in the air.
2. No, the dew point will not change unless moisture is added to or removed from the air.

✔Assessment

Performance Have students determine the dew point at two different locations. Use **PASC,** p. 97.

Mini LAB

Determining Dew Point

Procedure

1. Partially fill a **metal can** with room-temperature **water.** Dry the outer surface of the can.
2. Place a **stirring rod** in the water.
3. Slowly stir the water and add small amounts of **ice.**
4. On a data table in your **Science Journal,** with a thermometer, note the exact water temperature at which a thin film of moisture first begins to form on the outside of the metal can.
5. Repeat steps 1 through 4 two more times.
6. The average of the three temperatures at which the moisture begins to appear is the dew point temperature of the air surrounding the metal container.

Analysis

1. What determines the dew point temperature?
2. Will the dew point change with increasing temperature if the amount of moisture in the air doesn't change? Explain.

Figure 3
Warmer air can have more water vapor than cooler air can because water vapor doesn't easily condense in warm air.

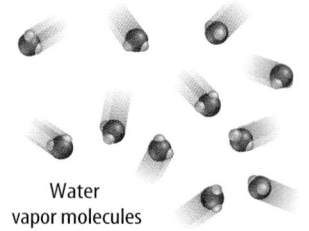

Water vapor molecules

Water droplets

A Water vapor molecules in warm air move rapidly. The molecules can't easily come together and condense.

B As air cools, water molecules in air move closer together. Some of them collide, allowing condensation to take place.

Humidity Heat evaporates water into the atmosphere. Where does the water go? Water vapor molecules fit into spaces among the molecules that make up air. The amount of water vapor present in the air is called **humidity.**

Air doesn't always contain the same amount of water vapor. As you can see in **Figure 3,** more water vapor can be present when the air is warm than when it is cool. At warmer temperatures, the molecules of water vapor in air move quickly and don't easily come together. At cooler temperatures, molecules in air move more slowly. The slower movement allows water vapor molecules to stick together and form droplets of liquid water. The formation of liquid water from water vapor is called condensation. When enough water vapor is present in air for condensation to take place, the air is saturated.

Why can more water vapor be present in warm air than in cold air?

Relative Humidity On a hot, sticky afternoon, the weather forecaster reports that the humidity is 50 percent. How can the humidity be low when it feels so humid? Weather forecasters report the amount of moisture in the air as relative humidity. **Relative humidity** is a measure of the amount of water vapor present in the air compared to the amount needed for saturation at a specific temperature.

If you hear a weather forecaster say that the relative humidity is 50 percent, it means that the air contains 50 percent of the water needed for the air to be saturated.

As shown in **Figure 4,** air at 25°C is saturated when it contains 22 g of water vapor per cubic meter of air. The relative humidity is 100 percent. If air at 25°C contains 11 g of water vapor per cubic meter, the relative humidity is 50 percent.

 **LAB DEMONSTRATION**

Purpose to observe changes in relative humidity using a chemical indicator
Materials relative humidity indicator paper
Procedure *Caution: Students should not put relative humidity paper in their mouths. Follow all manufacturer's safety precautions.* Obtain relative humidity indicator paper from a school supplier. Put strips of the paper in different areas inside and outside of the classroom. Have students record the color of the paper for several days.

Expected Outcome The paper's color changes over time with changing relative humidity. Pink indicates high relative humidity; blue indicates low relative humidity.

Assessment
At which locations and on which days was the relative humidity highest? Lowest? Answers will vary with local weather and location of paper strips.

Dew Point

When the temperature drops, less water vapor can be present in air. The water vapor in air will condense to a liquid or form ice crystals. The temperature at which air is saturated and condensation forms is the **dew point.** The dew point changes with the amount of water vapor in the air.

You've probably seen water droplets form on the outside of a glass of cold milk. The cold glass cooled the air next to it to its dew point. The water vapor in the surrounding air condensed and formed water droplets on the glass. In a similar way, when air near the ground cools to its dew point, water vapor condenses and forms dew. Frost may form when temperatures are near 0°C.

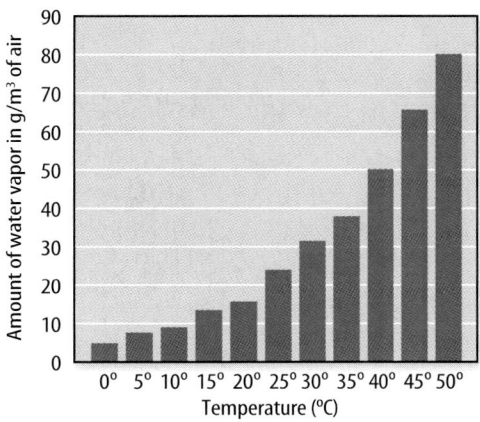

Figure 4
This graph shows that as the temperature of air increases, more water vapor can be present in the air.

Math Skills Activity

Calculating Whether Dew Will Form

Example Problem

One summer day, the relative humidity is 80 percent and the temperature is 35°C. Will the dew point be reached if the temperature falls to 25°C?

Solution

1 *This is what you know:*

From Figure 4

Air Temperature (°C)	Amount of Water Vapor Needed for Saturation (g/m³)
35	37
25	22

2 *This is what you need to find:* x = amount of water vapor in 35°C air at 80 percent relative humidity. Is $x > 22$ g/m³ or is $x < 22$ g/m³?

3 *This is how you solve the problem:* $x = .80 (37$ g/m³$)$
$x = 29.6$ g/m³ of water vapor
29.6 g/m³ > 22 g/m³, so the dew point is reached and dew will form.

Practice Problem

If the relative humidity is 50 percent and the air temperature is 30°C, will the dew point be reached if the temperature falls to 20°C?

SECTION 1 What is weather? **313**

Resource Manager

Chapter Resources Booklet
MiniLAB, p. 3
Lab Activity, pp. 9–11
Mathematics Skill Activities, p. 7

Discussion

Explain that a computer room and a science room are the same size and have the same humidity. The computer room is colder. **Which room has the higher relative humidity?** The water vapor in the air of the computer room represents a greater percentage of the water vapor needed for saturation. Thus, the computer room has a greater relative humidity.

Math Skills Activity

National Math Standards

Correlation to Mathematics Objectives
1, 2, 4, 6, 8, 9

Teaching Strategy

Use **Figure 4** to help solve the problem.

Answer to Practice Problem

- What you know: at 30°C you need 31g/m³ of water vapor to reach saturation. At 20°C, you need 15g/m³.
- You need to find: x = amount of water vapor in 30°C air at 50 percent relative humidity. Is $x > 15$g/m³ or is $x < 15$g/m³?
- Solve the problem:
  $x = 0.50(31$g/m³$)$
  $x = 15.5$g/m³ of water vapor
  15.5g/m³ > 15g/m³, so the dew point is reached and dew will form.

Curriculum Connection

Math Have students solve the following problem. At 20°C, 15 g of water vapor will saturate 1 m³ of air. If only 4 g are present, what is the relative humidity? (4 g ÷ 15 g) × 100 = 26.7%

 ELL

Forming Clouds

Classifying Clouds

Extension

Have students use a video camera to take stop-frame pictures of clouds as they form. Have them take one picture every minute for thirty minutes. Then, have them show their tapes to the class at regular speed. Have students classify the clouds. L2 ELL Visual-Spatial

Caption Answer

Figure 5C It condenses.

Visual Learning

Figure 5C Have students note that the leading edge of the clouds is high in the air, and well in front of most of the warm air mass. **Why do you think that high clouds can sometimes forecast a change in the weather?** These high clouds may be ahead of coming warm air which slides over the top of a cooler air mass and may eventually replace the cool air near the ground.

Forming Clouds

Why are there clouds in the sky? Clouds form as warm air is forced upward, expands, and cools. **Figure 5** shows several ways that warm, moist air forms clouds. As the air cools, the amount of water vapor needed for saturation decreases and the relative humidity increases. When the relative humidity reaches 100 percent, the air is saturated. Water vapor soon begins to condense in tiny droplets around small particles such as dust and salt. These droplets of water are so small that they remain suspended in the air. Billions of these droplets form a cloud.

Classifying Clouds

Clouds are classified mainly by shape and height. Some clouds extend high into the sky, and others are low and flat. Some dense clouds bring rain or snow, while thin, wispy clouds appear on mostly sunny days. The shape and height of clouds vary with temperature, pressure, and the amount of water vapor in the atmosphere.

Figure 5
Clouds form when moist air is lifted and cools. This occurs where air is heated, at mountain ranges, and where cold air meets warm air.

A Rays from the Sun heat the ground and the air next to it. The warm air rises and cools. If the air is moist, some water vapor condenses and forms clouds.

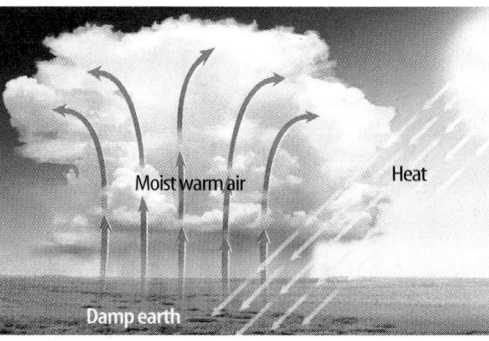

B As moist air moves over mountains, it is lifted and cools. Clouds formed in this way can cover mountains for long periods of time.

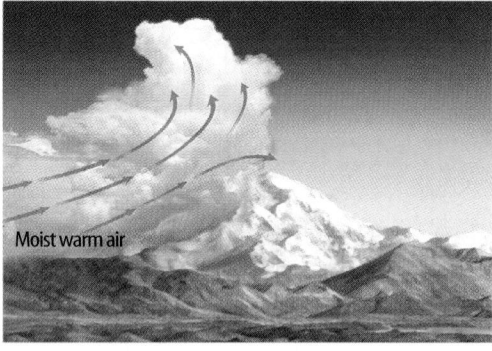

C When cool air meets warm, moist air, the warm air is lifted and cools. *What happens to the water vapor when the dew point is reached?*

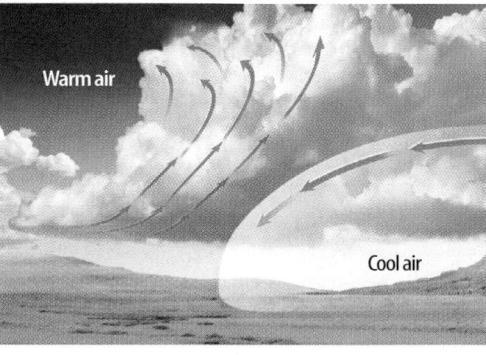

✔ Active Reading

ReQuest To improve listening skills have students listen carefully as you read an interesting piece or story aloud. After the reading, have students construct discussion questions. Assign students to read the story and participate in the questioning with other students. Have students participate in a ReQuest with the chapter feature, "Rain," or another interesting piece related to weather.

Science Journal

Animal Behavior Some animals react to changes in air pressure and humidity. Before a storm, birds and bats fly lower and frogs croak more frequently. Have students research and write short reports on other ways that animals react to weather changes. L2 Linguistic

Shape The three main cloud types are stratus, cumulus, and cirrus. Stratus clouds form layers, or smooth, even sheets in the sky. Stratus clouds usually form at low altitudes and may be associated with fair weather or rain or snow. When air is cooled to its dew point near the ground, it forms a stratus cloud called **fog**, as shown in **Figure 6.**

Cumulus (KYEW myuh lus) clouds are masses of puffy, white clouds, often with flat bases. They sometimes tower to great heights and can be associated with fair weather or thunderstorms.

Cirrus (SIHR us) clouds appear fibrous or curly. They are high, thin, white, feathery clouds made of ice crystals. Cirrus clouds are associated with fair weather, but they can indicate approaching storms.

Height Some prefixes of cloud names describe the height of the cloud base. The prefix *cirro-* describes high clouds, *alto-* describes middle-elevation clouds, and *strato-* refers to clouds at low elevations. Some clouds' names combine the altitude prefix with the term *stratus* or *cumulus.*

Cirrostratus clouds are high clouds, like those in **Figure 7.** Usually, cirrostratus clouds indicate fair weather, but they also can signal an approaching storm. Altostratus clouds form at middle levels. If the clouds are not too thick, sunlight can filter through them.

Figure 6
Fog surrounds the Golden Gate Bridge, San Francisco. Fog is a stratus cloud near the ground.

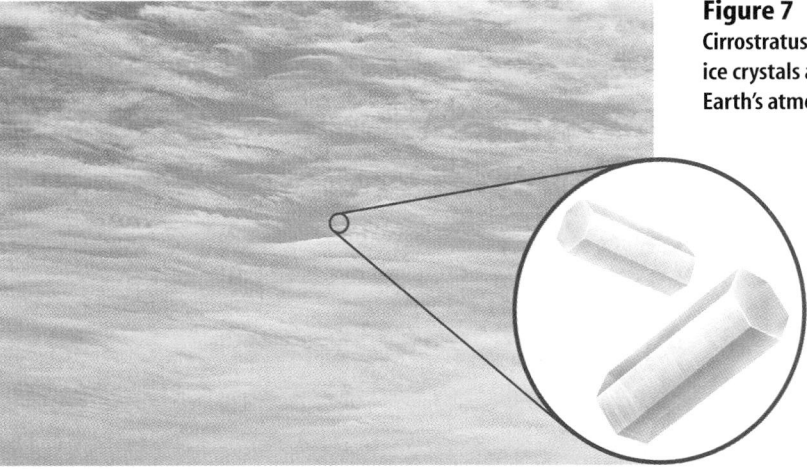
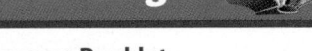

Figure 7
Cirrostratus clouds are made of ice crystals and form high in Earth's atmosphere.

Use Science Words
Word Origins In 1803, Luke Howard classified clouds using the Latin terms *cirrus, cumulus, stratus,* and *nimbus.* Have students use a dictionary and other reference sources to find how the meanings of these words relate to cloud descriptions. *Cirrus* comes from a word meaning "lock of hair"; *cumulus* from "heap"; *stratus* from "layer"; and *nimbus* from "rain bearing."

IDENTIFYING
Misconceptions

Students may wonder why clouds don't fall. Remind them that cloud droplets are tiny. They should infer that they are so small and light that they stay suspended. Students might suggest that fog falls to the ground. But actually fog forms near the ground.

Discussion

What is the difference between an altocumulus and a stratocumulus cloud? The difference is cloud height. An altocumulus is a middle-elevation cumulus cloud; a stratocumulus is a low-elevation cumulus cloud.

Resource Manager

Chapter Resources Booklet
Enrichment, p. 30
Physical Science Critical Thinking/Problem Solving, p. 16

Curriculum Connection

History Before satellites and radar, people used observations of nature to predict weather. They didn't know why things happened, but they noted patterns. For example, they knew rain often follows a halo around the moon. The reason? The ice crystals in cirrus clouds cause the halo, and cirrus clouds often mean coming rain. Have students research other weather folklore and make posters describing what they find.

Classifying Clouds

Teacher FYI

The succession of clouds that appears overhead as a warm front approaches can warn you it's on the way. A few days before the front arrives, high cirrus clouds appear. Cirrus clouds gradually give way to mid-level sheets of thin altostratus. When these clouds thicken enough to block the Sun, light rain or snow begins to fall. A day or so before the front passes over, clouds lower and thicken into a gray sheet of nimbostratus that bring steady precipitation. Skies clear after the front passes.

Precipitation

Discussion

Remind students that when the dew point is below 0° C, water vapor freezes on vegetation, forming frost. In some rural areas, frost is called "baby snow." **Is frost a type of precipitation? Explain.** No; it doesn't fall from clouds.

Fun Fact

The wettest inhabited city on Earth is Buenaventura, Colombia, with an average yearly rainfall of 674.3 cm. The driest inhabited city is Aswan, Egypt, with an annual average precipitation of 0.05 cm.

✔ Reading Check

Answer rain, snow, sleet, hail

Figure 8
Water vapor in air collects on particles to form water droplets or ice crystals. The type of precipitation that is received on the ground depends on the temperature of the air.

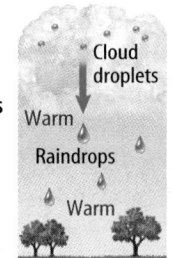

A When the air is warm, water vapor forms raindrops that fall as rain.

B When the air is cold, water vapor forms snowflakes.

Rain- or Snow-Producing Clouds Clouds associated with rain or snow often have the word nimbus attached to them. The term *nimbus* is Latin for "dark rain cloud" and this is a good description, because the water content of these clouds is so high that little sunlight can pass through them. When a cumulus cloud grows into a thunderstorm, it is called a cumulonimbus (kyew myuh loh NIHM bus) cloud. These clouds can tower to nearly 18,000 km. Nimbostratus clouds are layered clouds that can bring long, steady rain or snowfall.

Precipitation

Water falling from clouds is called **precipitation.** Precipitation occurs when cloud droplets combine and grow large enough to fall to Earth. The cloud droplets form around small particles, such as salt and dust. These particles are so small that a puff of smoke can contain millions of them.

You might have noticed that raindrops are not all the same size. The size of raindrops depends on several factors. One factor is the strength of updrafts in a cloud. Strong updrafts can keep drops suspended in the air where they can combine with other drops and grow larger. The rate of evaporation as a drop falls to Earth also can affect its size. If the air is dry, the size of raindrops can be reduced or they can completely evaporate before reaching the ground. Air temperature determines whether water forms rain, snow, sleet, or hail—the four main types of precipitation. **Figure 8** shows these different types of precipitation. Drops of water falling in temperatures above freezing fall as rain. Snow forms when the air temperature is so cold that water vapor changes directly to a solid. Sleet forms when raindrops pass through a layer of freezing air near Earth's surface, forming ice pellets.

✔ Reading Check *What are the four main types of precipitation?*

👥 Cultural **Diversity**

Changing the Weather For centuries, during periods of drought, people have tried to make it rain. In the Soyal festival, the Hopi Nation of the southwestern U.S. perform a dance for the purpose of bringing rain. Have students research other traditional customs for changing weather. Possible answer: The Hurocs of northern California hammer on a rain stone carved from soapstone to prevent excessive rain.

Resource Manager

Chapter Resources Booklet
Lab Activity, pp. 13–15
Reinforcement, p. 27

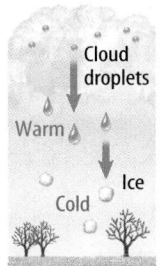  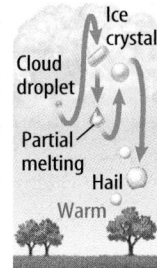 

C When the air near the ground is cold, sleet, which is made up of many small ice pellets, falls.

D Hailstones are pellets of ice that form inside a cloud.

Hail Hail is precipitation in the form of lumps of ice. Hail forms in cumulonimbus clouds of a thunderstorm when water freezes in layers around a small nucleus of ice. Hailstones grow larger as they're tossed up and down by rising and falling air. Most hailstones are smaller than 2.5 cm but can grow larger than a softball. Of all forms of precipitation, hail produces the most damage immediately, especially if winds blow during a hailstorm. Falling hailstones can break windows and destroy crops.

If you understand the role of water vapor in the atmosphere, you can begin to understand weather. The relative humidity of the air helps determine whether a location will have a dry day or experience some form of precipitation. The temperature of the atmosphere determines the form of precipitation. Studying clouds can add to your ability to forecast weather.

Section ① Assessment

1. When does water vapor in air condense?
2. What is the difference between humidity and relative humidity?
3. How do clouds form?
4. How does precipitation occur and what determines the type of precipitation that falls to Earth?
5. **Think Critically** Cumulonimbus clouds form when warm, moist air is suddenly lifted. How can the same cumulonimbus cloud produce rain and hail?

Skill Builder Activities

6. **Concept Mapping** Make a network-tree concept map that compares clouds and their descriptions. Use these terms: *cirrus, cumulus, stratus, feathery, fair weather, puffy, layered, precipitation, clouds, dark,* and *steady precipitation.* **For more help, refer to the** Science Skill Handbook.
7. **Making and Using Graphs** Use **Figure 4** to determine how much water vapor can be present in air when the temperature is 40°C. **For more help, refer to the** Science Skill Handbook.

Reteach

Collect a variety of cloud photographs. Identify each cloud type on the back of its picture. Have students work in pairs. Suggest that one student show the pictures, while the other identifies the clouds. Then have students switch roles. L2
COOP LEARN Ⓝ **Visual-Spatial**

Challenge

Have students observe and record the pattern of precipitation for several days. Have them also observe the cloud patterns that occur before and after precipitation. Challenge students to use this information to write a paragraph that describes how clouds can predict precipitation. L3

✓ *Assessment*

Content Have student pairs work together to write songs that explain how different types of precipitation form. Use **Performance Assessment in the Science Classroom,** p. 151.

SCIENCE *Online*
Internet Addresses

_____
_____

Explore the Glencoe Science Web site at **science.glencoe.com** to find out more about topics in this section.

Answers to Section Assessment

1. when it cools to the dew point
2. humidity: amount of water vapor in air; relative humidity: amount of water vapor present in air compared to the amount that is needed for saturation at a specific temperature
3. Moist, warm air is lifted and cools to its dew point; water vapor condenses

around dust particles and forms cloud drops.
4. Cloud droplets combine and grow large enough to fall to Earth; the temperature of the atmosphere.
5. Near the top of the cloud, water droplets freeze around small ice nuclei, forming ice crystals. Hailstones may grow as updrafts in the

cloud toss ice crystals up and down. Rain forms when falling ice crystals melt or when large water droplets fall from lower parts of the cloud.

6.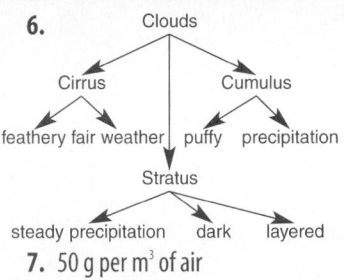

7. 50 g per m³ of air

Weather Patterns

1 Motivate

Bellringer Transparency

Display the Section Focus Transparency for Section 2. Use the accompanying Transparency Activity Master. L2

ELL

Tie to Prior Knowledge

Ask students if they have ever experienced a thunderstorm. Have students take turns describing what they saw, felt, and heard during such a storm. Tell students they will learn how thunderstorms form in the upcoming section.

As You Read

What You'll Learn

- **Describe** how weather is associated with fronts and high- and low-pressure areas.
- **Explain** how tornadoes develop from thunderstorms.
- **Discuss** the dangers of severe weather.

Vocabulary

air mass   hurricane
front   blizzard
tornado

Why It's Important

Air masses, pressure systems, and fronts cause weather to change.

Figure 9
Six major air masses affect weather in the United States. Each air mass has the same characteristics of temperature and moisture content as the area over which it formed.

Weather Changes

When you leave for school in the morning, the weather might be different from what it is when you head home in the afternoon. Because of the movement of air and moisture in the atmosphere, weather constantly changes.

Air Masses An **air mass** is a large body of air that has properties similar to the part of Earth's surface over which it develops. For example, an air mass that develops over land is dry compared with one that develops over water. An air mass that develops in the tropics is warmer than one that develops over northern regions. An air mass can cover thousands of square kilometers. When you observe a change in the weather from one day to the next, it is due to the movement of air masses. **Figure 9** shows air masses that affect the United States.

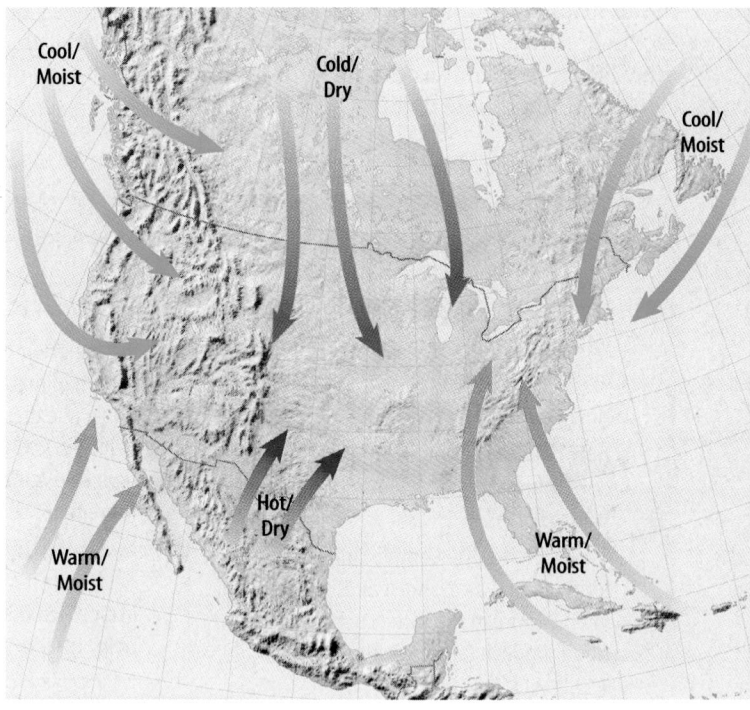

Cool/ Moist

Cold/ Dry

Cool/ Moist

Hot/ Dry

Warm/ Moist

Warm/ Moist

Section ✓*Assessment* Planner

PORTFOLIO
Use Science Words, p. 319
PERFORMANCE ASSESSMENT
Skill Builder Activities, p. 325
See page 336 for more options.

CONTENT ASSESSMENT
Section, p. 325
Challenge, p. 325
Chapter, pp. 336–337

Highs and Lows

Atmospheric pressure varies over Earth's surface. Anyone who has watched a weather report on television has heard about high- and low-pressure systems. Recall that winds blow from areas of high pressure to areas of low pressure. As winds blow into a low-pressure area in the northern hemisphere, Earth's rotation causes these winds to swirl in a counterclockwise direction. Large, swirling areas of low pressure are called cyclones and are associated with stormy weather.

 **Reading Check** *How do winds move in a cyclone?*

Winds blow away from a center of high pressure. Earth's rotation causes these winds to spiral clockwise in the northern hemisphere. High-pressure areas are associated with fair weather and are called anticyclones. Air pressure is measured using a barometer, like the one shown in **Figure 10.**

Variation in atmospheric pressure affects the weather. Low pressure systems at Earth's surface are regions of rising air. In Section 1, you learned that clouds form when air is lifted and cools. Areas of low pressure usually have cloudy weather. Sinking motion in high-pressure air masses makes it difficult for air to rise and clouds to form. That's why high pressure usually means good weather.

Fronts

A boundary between two air masses of different density, moisture, or temperature is called a **front.** If you've seen a weather map in the newspaper or on the evening news, you've seen fronts represented by various types of curving lines.

Cloudiness, precipitation, and storms sometimes occur at frontal boundaries. Four types of fronts include cold, warm, occluded, and stationary.

Cold and Warm Fronts A cold front, shown on a map as a blue line with triangles, occurs when colder air advances toward warm air. The cold air wedges under the warm air like a plow. As the warm air is lifted, it cools and water vapor condenses, forming clouds. When the temperature difference between the cold and warm air is large, thunderstorms and even tornadoes may form.

Warm fronts form when lighter, warmer air advances over heavier, colder air. A warm front is drawn on weather maps as a red line with red semicircles.

Figure 10
A barometer measures atmospheric pressure. The red pointer points to the current pressure. Watch how atmospheric pressure changes over time when you line up the white pointer to the one indicating the current pressure each day.

Data Update Visit the Glencoe Science Web site at **science.glencoe.com** to find the current atmospheric pressure, temperature, and wind direction in your town or nearest city. Look up these weather conditions for a city west of your town. Forecast the weather for your town based on your research.

---

2 Teach

Weather Changes

Discussion
Why don't pressure systems always remain in one place? Because global winds move them.

 Reading Check

Answer counterclockwise in the northern hemisphere

Use Science Words

Word Meaning In the 1920s, the term *front* was used to describe the boundary between two air masses because this boundary was similar to the front along which opposing armies fought during a war. Norwegian meteorologists first used the term. Have students write a brief paragraph comparing military fronts with weather fronts. In both cases, there is a line between two opposing forces. Eventually, one side advances, often pushing the other out of the way. L2 IS Linguistic P

Internet Addresses

Explore the Glencoe Science Web site at **science.glencoe.com** to find out more about topics in this section.

Resource Manager

Chapter Resources Booklet
Directed Reading for Content Mastery, p. 21
Transparency Activity, p. 45
Reading and Writing Skill Activities, p. 3

Inclusion Strategies

Visually Impaired Have students listen to daily weather reports on the radio or TV and identify how meteorologists use the terms mentioned in the text. Students can use cassette recorders to make audio reports on what they find and share their reports with the class. Students should include terms such as precipitation, front, high, low, temperature, and relative humidity.

Fronts

Visual Learning

Figure 11 Why is it unlikely that towering clouds will form at a warm front? The slope of the front is too gentle—it doesn't allow for air to be pushed up steeply to form towering clouds.

Teacher FYI

Atmospheric pressure drops before a front passes a region and rises after the front has passed. Also, as a front passes the wind changes direction. In the northern hemisphere, winds usually shift from southwest to northwest after a cold front has passed and from southeast to southwest after a warm front has passed.

Figure 11
Cold, warm, occluded, and stationary fronts occur at the boundaries of air masses. Cloudiness and precipitation occur at front boundaries.

Occluded and Stationary Fronts An occluded front involves three air masses of different temperatures—colder air, cool air, and warm air. An occluded front may form when a cold air mass moves toward cool air with warm air between the two. The colder air forces the warm air upward, closing off the warm air from the surface. Occluded fronts are shown on maps as purple lines with triangles and semicircles.

A stationary front occurs when a boundary between air masses stops advancing. Stationary fronts may remain in the same place for several days, producing light wind and precipitation. A stationary front is drawn on a weather map as an alternating red and blue line. Red semicircles point toward the cold air and blue triangles point toward the warm air. **Figure 11** summarizes the four types of fronts.

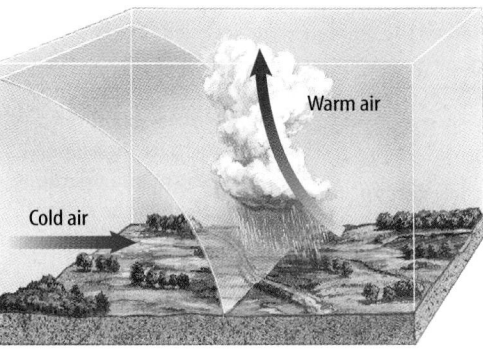

A A cold front can advance rapidly. Thunderstorms often form as warm air is suddenly lifted up over the cold air.

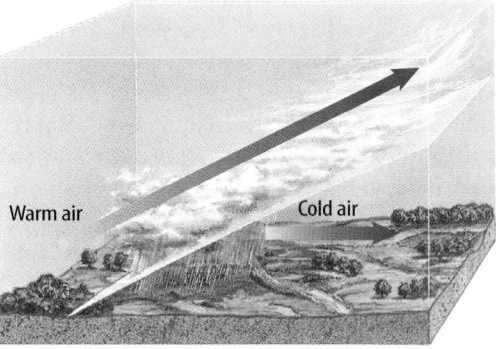

B Warm air slides over colder air along a warm front, forming a boundary with a gentle slope. This can lead to hours, if not days, of wet weather.

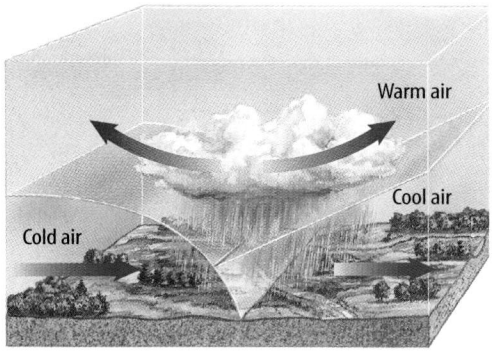

C The term *occlusion* means "closure." Colder air forces warm air upward, forming an occluded front that closes off the warm air from the surface.

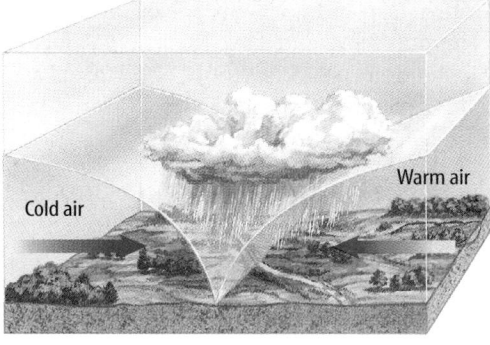

D A stationary front results when neither cold air nor warm air advances.

Inclusion Strategies

Learning Disabled Have students practice drawing symbols for fronts and describing the weather at each frontal boundary.

Curriculum Connection

Geography Obtain a simple weather map of the United States from a recent newspaper or access the Glencoe Science Web site. The map should show fronts. Display or copy the map for students. Have them use the fronts to describe the weather in at least two locations in the U.S. Several students can take turns using the map to present their weather forecasts to the class. [L2]
 [IS] **Visual-Spatial**

Severe Weather

Despite the weather, you usually can do your daily activities. If it's raining, you still go to school. You can still get there even if it snows a little. However, some weather conditions, such as those caused by thunderstorms, tornadoes, and blizzards, prevent you from going about your normal routine. Severe weather poses danger to people, structures, and animals.

Thunderstorms In a thunderstorm, heavy rain falls, lightning flashes, thunder roars, and hail might fall. What forces cause such extreme weather conditions? Thunderstorms occur in warm, moist air masses and along fronts. Warm, moist air can be forced upward where it cools and condensation occurs, forming cumulonimbus clouds that can reach heights of 18 km, like the one in **Figure 12.** When rising air cools, water vapor condenses into water droplets or ice crystals. Smaller droplets collide to form larger ones, and the droplets fall through the cloud toward Earth's surface. The falling droplets collide with still more droplets and grow larger. Raindrops cool the air around them. This cool, dense air then sinks and spreads over Earth's surface. Sinking, rain-cooled air and strong updrafts of warmer air cause the strong winds associated with thunderstorms. Hail also may form as ice crystals alternately fall to warmer layers and are lifted into colder layers by the strong updrafts inside cumulonimbus clouds.

Thunderstorm damage Sometimes thunderstorms can stall over a region, causing rain to fall heavily for a period of time. When streams cannot contain all the water running into them, flash flooding can occur. Flash floods can be dangerous because they occur with little warning.

Strong winds generated by thunderstorms also can cause damage. If a thunderstorm is accompanied by winds traveling faster than 89 km/h, it is classified as a severe thunderstorm. Hail from a thunderstorm can dent cars and the aluminum siding on houses. Although rain from thunderstorms helps crops grow, hail has been known to flatten and destroy entire crops in a matter of minutes.

Figure 12
Tall cumulonimbus clouds may form quickly as warm, moist air rapidly rises.

SECTION 2 Weather Patterns **321**

Severe Weather

Extension

Have students research how the average annual damage from severe thunderstorms affects your local economy.

Teacher FYI

A thunderstorm has a three-stage life cycle. The initial stage, or cumulus stage, of strong updrafts lasts for about 15 minutes. The mature stage is the most intense period and begins as rain falls from the base of the clouds. Lightning, turbulence, and hail can be most severe during this stage. The falling rain produces downdrafts that spread outward along the ground. The downdrafts finally cut off the updrafts of warm air. This signals the beginning of the final stage. With the supply of warm air cut off by cooler air on the ground, cloud growth and precipitation cease and the storm ends.

Fun Fact

The largest officially measured hailstone in the United States fell on September 3, 1970, in Coffeyville, Kansas. Having a mass of 0.76 kg and a circumference of 45 cm, it was about the size of a cantaloupe. Larger stones have been reported, but they were never officially measured.

Resource Manager

Science Inquiry Labs, p. 27

Science Journal

Weather Effects Have students write in their Science Journals about the direct and indirect ways weather affects their lives. One indirect effect is paying more for fruits and vegetables when an agricultural region experiences an unusually wet or dry growing season. L2 **IS Intrapersonal and Linguistic**

IDENTIFYING Misconceptions

Students may think that lightning travels only from clouds to the ground. In less than 1/10 second, a single lightning discharge goes back and forth many times between a cloud and the ground. Although these discharges usually begin in clouds, sometimes they begin at Earth's surface.

Discussion

Why don't you see lightning and hear the thunder it causes at the same time? Light travels 904,924.6 times faster than sound in air. Only when lightning strikes nearby are thunder and lightning sensed at nearly the same time.

✔ Reading Check

Answer A wind shear can form a rotating column of air parallel to the ground. A thunderstorm's updraft can tilt the rotating column, forming a funnel cloud.

SCIENCE Online
Internet Addresses

_____

_____

_____

_____

Explore the Glencoe Science Web site at **science.glencoe.com** to find out more about topics in this section.

Figure 13
This time-elapsed photo shows a thunderstorm over Arizona.

SCIENCE Online

Research Visit the Glencoe Science Web site at **science.glencoe.com** to research the number of lightning strikes in your state during the last year. Compare your findings with previous years. Communicate to your class what you learn.

Lightning and Thunder

What are lightning and thunder? Inside a storm cloud, warm air is lifted rapidly as cooler air sinks. This movement of air can cause different parts of a cloud to become oppositely charged. When current flows between regions of opposite electrical charge, lightning flashes. Lightning, as shown in **Figure 13,** can occur within a cloud, between clouds, or between a cloud and the ground.

Thunder results from the rapid heating of air around a bolt of lightning. Lightning can reach temperatures of about 30,000°C, which is more than five times the temperature of the surface of the Sun. This extreme heat causes air around the lightning to expand rapidly. Then it cools quickly and contracts. The rapid movement of the molecules forms sound waves heard as thunder.

Tornadoes Some of the most severe thunderstorms produce tornadoes. A **tornado** is a violent, whirling wind that moves in a narrow path over land. In severe thunderstorms, wind at different heights blows in different directions and at different speeds. This difference in wind speed and direction, called wind shear, creates a rotating column parallel to the ground. A thunderstorm's updraft can tilt the rotating column upward into the thunderstorm creating a funnel cloud. If the funnel comes into contact with Earth's surface, it is called a tornado.

✔ Reading Check   *What causes a tornado to form?*

A tornado's destructive winds can rip apart buildings and uproot trees. High winds can blow through broken windows. When winds blow inside a house, they can lift off the roof and blow out the walls, making it look as though the building exploded. The updraft in the center of a powerful tornado can lift animals, cars, and even houses into the air. Although tornadoes rarely exceed 200 m in diameter and usually last only a few minutes, they often are extremely destructive. In May 1999, multiple thunderstorms produced more than 70 tornadoes in Kansas, Oklahoma, and Texas. This severe tornado outbreak caused 40 deaths, 100 injuries, and more than $1.2 billion in property damage.

Curriculum Connection

History In 1752, Benjamin Franklin proved that lightning is an electrical discharge. Later, he invented a lightning rod. Have students research his experiments. In his best-known experiment, he attached a key to a kite string and flew the kite early in a storm, before lightning had come near him. A spark jumped from the key to his hand, thereby showing that electricity was present. L2 IS **Linguistic**

Tornado Chasing Inform students that some scientists chase tornadoes to study them. They look for places where conditions are right for tornadoes to form. Then they go to these areas and try to place instruments in a storm's path. Have students write a short essay on why they would or would not want to do this type of research. IS **Logical-Mathematical**

Figure 14

Tornadoes are extremely rapid, rotating winds that form at the base of cumulonimbus clouds. Smaller tornadoes may even form inside larger ones. Luckily, most tornadoes remain on the ground for just a few minutes. During that time, however, they can cause considerable—and sometimes strange—damage, such as driving a fork into a tree.

Tornadoes often form from a type of cumulonimbus cloud called a wall cloud. Strong, spiraling updrafts of warm, moist air may form in these clouds. As air spins upward, a low-pressure area forms, and the cloud descends to the ground in a funnel. The tornado sucks up debris as it moves along the ground, forming a dust envelope.

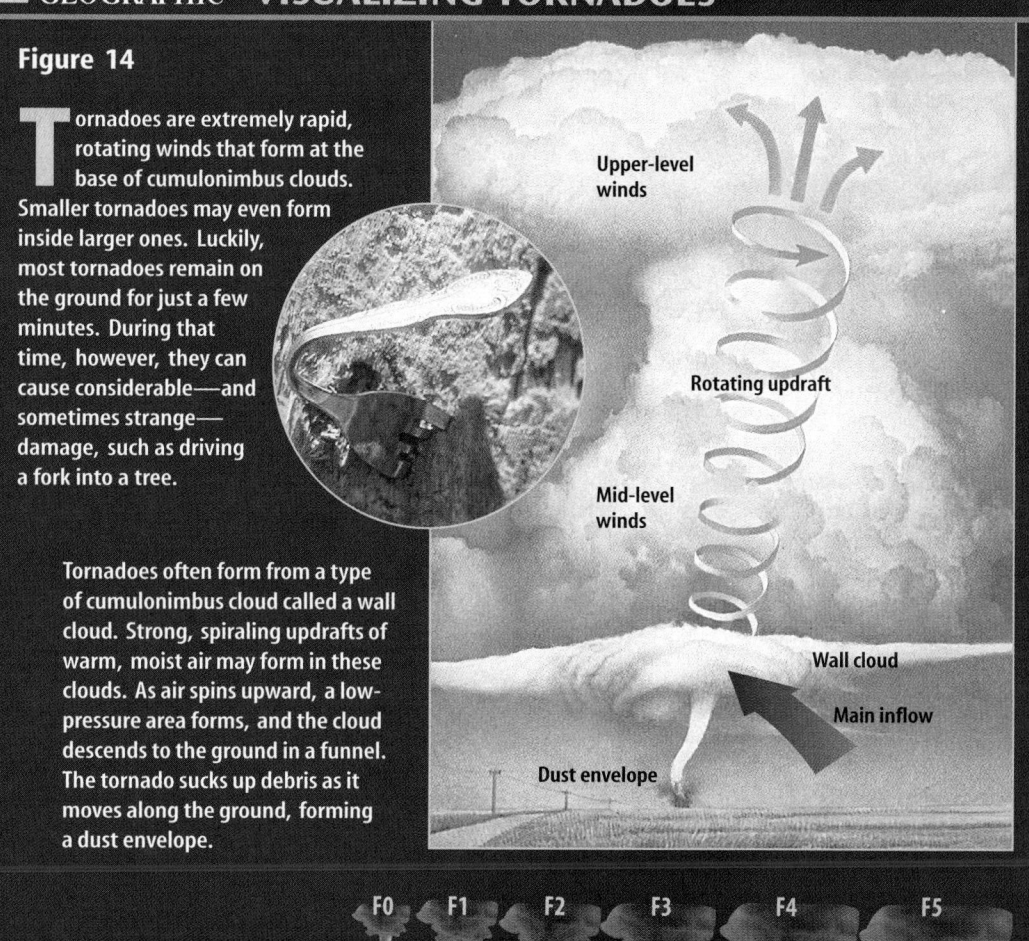

Upper-level winds

Rotating updraft

Mid-level winds

Wall cloud

Main inflow

Dust envelope

The Fujita Scale

F0 F1 F2 F3 F4 F5

	Wind speed (km/h)	Damage
F0	<116	Light: broken branches and chimneys
F1	116–180	Moderate: roofs damaged, mobile homes upturned
F2	181–253	Considerable: roofs torn off homes, large trees uprooted
F3	254–332	Severe: trains overturned, roofs and walls torn off
F4	333–419	Devastating: houses completely destroyed, cars picked up and carried elsewhere
F5	420–512	Incredible: total demolition

The Fujita scale, named after tornado expert Theodore Fujita, ranks tornadoes according to how much damage they cause. Fortunately, only one percent of tornadoes are classified as violent (F4 and F5).

323

Visualizing Tornadoes

Have students examine the pictures and read the captions. Then ask the following questions.

What do you think causes most injuries and deaths during a tornado? Why do you think this is? Most are caused by flying objects that are blown around by the very strong winds of a tornado.

If a tornado were heading toward you, why would a car not be a safe place to stay? Cars can be overturned or even picked up and carried away by tornado winds.

Activity

Have small groups of students research the average number of tornadoes that occur each year in each state. Ask them to prepare an outline map of the United States with the data for each state on it. Then ask them to identify the area known as "tornado alley" and write an explanation of why so many tornadoes occur in this region. L2 COOP LEARN
IS Linguistic and Visual-Spatial

Extension

Challenge students to find out how Doppler radar allows meteorologists to detect and track possible tornadoes. Have them prepare a labeled diagram of their findings. L2
IS Visual-Spatial

Resource Manager

Reading and Writing Skill Activities, p. 45

Severe Weather, continued

Activity

Have students work together to make mobiles showing different types of severe storms. L1

ELL | COOP LEARN | IS Visual-Spatial

Environmental Science
INTEGRATION

Hurricanes may become more common and more intense.

Teacher FYI

- A storm is classified as a tropical depression if its winds are less than 63 km/h, a tropical storm if winds are 63–119 km/h, and a hurricane if winds exceed 119 km/h.
- The strongest hurricane winds are within 80 km of the eye.
- During El Niño years, there are usually fewer hurricanes in the Atlantic. During the 1997 El Niño, there were 30% fewer tropical storms than normal. El Niño causes the tropical jet stream to curve eastward across the Atlantic Ocean, preventing tropical storms from moving west toward the Americas.
- The Saffir-Simpson Scale measures the intensity of hurricanes with numbers from 1 to 5. A Category 5 hurricane is the most intense, with sustained wind speed greater than 250 km/h. Category 1 hurricanes are the weakest, with sustained winds just past the hurricane threshold of 119 km/h.

Environmental Science
INTEGRATION

Some scientists hypothesize that Earth's ocean temperatures are increasing due to global warming. In your Science Journal, predict what might happen to the strength of hurricanes if Earth's oceans become warmer.

Figure 15
In this hurricane cross section, the small, red arrows indicate rising, warm, moist air. This air forms cumulus and cumulonimbus clouds in bands around the eye. The green arrows indicate cool, dry air sinking in the eye and between the cloud bands.

Hurricanes The most powerful storm is the hurricane. A **hurricane,** illustrated in **Figure 15,** is a large, swirling, low-pressure system that forms over the warm Atlantic Ocean. It is like a machine that turns heat energy from the ocean into wind. A storm must have winds of at least 119 km/h to be called a hurricane. Similar storms are called typhoons in the Pacific Ocean and cyclones in the Indian Ocean.

Hurricanes are similar to low-pressure systems on land, but they are much stronger. In the Atlantic and Pacific Oceans, low pressure sometimes develops near the equator. In the northern hemisphere, winds around this low pressure begin rotating counterclockwise. The strongest hurricanes affecting North America usually begin as a low-pressure system west of Africa. Steered by surface winds, these storms can travel west, gaining strength from the heat and moisture of warm ocean water.

When a hurricane strikes land, high winds, tornadoes, heavy rains, and high waves can cause a lot of damage. Floods from the heavy rains can cause additional damage. Hurricane weather can destroy crops, demolish buildings, and kill people and other animals. As long as a hurricane is over water, the warm, moist air rises and provides energy for the storm. When a hurricane reaches land, however, its supply of energy disappears and the storm loses power.

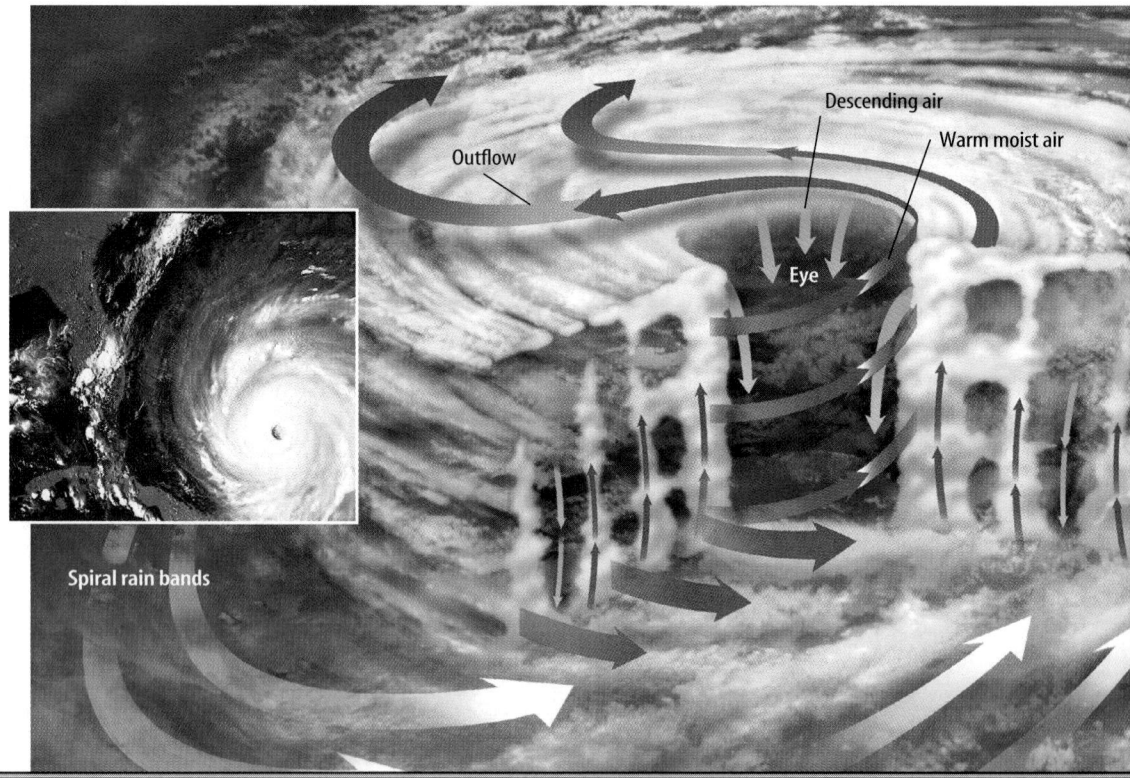

Descending air
Warm moist air
Outflow
Eye
Spiral rain bands

Curriculum Connection

Math The locations of the five deadliest hurricanes to strike the U.S. since 1900 are: (1) Galveston, TX, 1900, 8,000 deaths; (2) Florida, 1928, 1,836 deaths; (3) Southern TX, 1919, 600 deaths; (4) New England, 1938, 600 deaths; and (5) Florida Keys, 1935, 408 deaths. Have students make bar graphs of these data, with location on the *x*-axis and number of deaths on the *y*-axis. Students should determine a scale.

Resource Manager

Chapter Resources Booklet
  Reinforcement, p. 28
  Enrichment, p. 31

Blizzards Severe storms also can occur in winter. If you live in the northern United States, you may have awakened from a winter night's sleep to a cold, howling wind and blowing snow, like the storm in **Figure 16.** The National Weather Service classifies a winter storm as a **blizzard** if the winds are 56 km/h, the temperature is low, the visibility is less than 400 m in falling or blowing snow, and if these conditions persist for three hours or more.

Severe Weather Safety When severe weather threatens, the National Weather Service issues a watch or warning. Watches are issued when conditions are favorable for severe thunderstorms, tornadoes, floods, blizzards, and hurricanes. During a watch, stay tuned to a radio or television station reporting the weather. When a warning is issued, severe weather conditions already exist. You should take immediate action. During a severe thunderstorm or tornado warning, take shelter in the basement or a room in the middle of the house away from windows. When a hurricane or flood watch is issued, be prepared to leave your home and move farther inland.

Blizzards can be blinding and have dangerously low temperatures with high winds. During a blizzard, stay indoors. Spending too much time outside can result in severe frostbite.

Figure 16
Blizzards can be extremely dangerous because of their high winds, low temperatures, and poor visibility.

Section Assessment

1. Why is fair weather common during periods of high pressure?
2. How does a cold front form? What effect does a cold front have on weather?
3. What causes lightning and thunder in a thunderstorm?
4. What is the difference between a watch and a warning? How can you keep safe during a tornado warning?
5. **Think Critically** Explain why some fronts produce stronger storms than others.

Skill Builder Activities

6. **Recognizing Cause and Effect** Describe how an occluded front may form over your city and what effects it can have on the weather. **For more help, refer to the Science Skill Handbook.**
7. **Using an Electronic Spreadsheet** Make a spreadsheet comparing warm fronts, cold fronts, occluded fronts, and stationary fronts. Indicate what kind of clouds and weather systems form with each. **For more help, refer to the Technology Skill Handbook.**

Have students research specific hurricanes that have been especially destructive and present oral reports. Examples include Hurricanes Camille, Agnes, Gloria, Hugo, Andrew, Floyd, and Mitch.

3 Assess

Reteach

Have pairs of students make tables that compare and contrast tornadoes and hurricanes according to relative size, origin, type of pressure system, and damage. L2 COOP LEARN

Challenge

Have student pairs use the Internet to research severe weather safety. Encourage them to make posters that contain a list of safety tips with illustrations for hurricanes, tornadoes, thunderstorms, or blizzards. COOP LEARN

✔Assessment

Performance To assess students' abilities to describe the effects of weather systems, ask them to predict the resulting weather if a fast-moving cold air mass overtakes a slow-moving warm air mass over Texas in July. thunderstorms Use **Performance Assessment in the Science Classroom,** p. 89.

Answers to Section Assessment

1. Clouds can't form in the descending air of a high-pressure system.
2. Cold air moves into and pushes up warm air; thunderstorms are common.
3. Lightning is a current flow between areas of opposite electrical charge. Thunder results from rapid heating of air around the lightning bolt.
4. Watch: conditions are favorable for severe weather; warning: severe weather exists; take shelter in the basement or in a room away from windows.
5. The strongest storms form at the steepest frontal boundaries.
6. Possible answer: Cool air is over the city, with warmer air to the west.

Fast-moving cold air comes from the west and forces the warm air up. Rain and wind may result.
7. Possible answer: warm: layers of stratus clouds, light precipitation; cold: tall clouds, strong storms; stationary: light wind, precipitation; occluded: winds, heavy precipitation possible.

1 Motivate

Bellringer Transparency

Display the Section Focus Transparency for Section 3. Use the accompanying Transparency Activity Master. L2
ELL

Tie to Prior Knowledge

Based on weather forecasts they have seen or heard, have students recall how far ahead weather forecasters predict the weather, and if forecasts are usually accurate. about five days; accuracy varies Explain that they will learn how the weather is predicted in this section.

Text Question Answer

Weather concerns might include hurricanes, tornadoes, blizzards, ice storms, or hail.

3 Weather Forecasts

As You Read

What You'll Learn
- **Explain** how data are collected for weather maps and forecasts.
- **Identify** the symbols used in a weather station model.

Vocabulary
meteorologist	isotherm
station model	isobar

Why It's Important
Weather observations help you predict future weather events.

Figure 17
A meteorologist uses Doppler radar to track a tornado. Since the nineteenth century, technology has greatly improved weather forecasting.

Weather Observations

You can determine current weather conditions by checking the thermometer and looking to see whether clouds are in the sky. You know when it's raining. You have a general idea of the weather because you are familiar with the typical weather where you live. If you live in Florida, you don't expect snow in the forecast. If you live in Maine, you assume it will snow every winter. What weather concerns do you have in your region?

A **meteorologist** (meet ee uh RAH luh jist) is a person who studies the weather. Meteorologists take measurements of temperature, air pressure, winds, humidity, and precipitation. Computers, weather satellites, Doppler radar shown in **Figure 17,** and instruments attached to balloons are used to gather data. Such instruments improve meteorologists' ability to predict the weather. Meteorologists use the information provided by weather instruments to make weather maps. These maps are used to make weather forecasts.

Forecasting Weather Meteorologists gather information about current weather and use computers to make predictions about future weather patterns. Because storms can be dangerous, you do not want to be unprepared for threatening weather. However, meteorologists cannot always predict the weather exactly because conditions can change rapidly.

The National Weather Service depends on two sources for its information—data collected from the upper atmosphere and data collected on Earth's surface. Meteorologists of the National Weather Service collect information recorded by satellites, instruments attached to weather balloons, and from radar. This information is used to describe weather conditions in the atmosphere above Earth's surface.

326 CHAPTER 11 Weather

Section ✓Assessment Planner

PORTFOLIO
Challenge, p. 328
PERFORMANCE ASSESSMENT
Try at Home MiniLAB, p. 327
Skill Builder Activities, p. 328
See page 336 for more options.

CONTENT ASSESSMENT
Section, p. 328
Challenge, p. 328
Chapter, pp. 336–337

Station Models When meteorologists gather data from Earth's surface, it is recorded on a map using a combination of symbols, forming a **station model.** A station model, like the one in **Figure 18,** shows the weather conditions at a specific location on Earth's surface. Information provided by station models and instruments in the upper atmosphere is entered into computers and used to forecast weather.

Temperature and Pressure In addition to station models, weather maps have lines that connect locations of equal temperature or pressure. A line that connects points of equal temperature is called an **isotherm** (I suh thurm). *Iso* means "same" and *therm* means "temperature." You probably have seen isotherms on weather maps on TV or in the newspaper.

An **isobar** is a line drawn to connect points of equal atmospheric pressure. You can tell how fast wind is blowing in an area by noting how closely isobars are spaced. Isobars that are close together indicate a large pressure difference over a small area. A large pressure difference causes strong winds. Isobars that are spread apart indicate a smaller difference in pressure. Winds in this area are gentler. Isobars also indicate the locations of high- and low-pressure areas.

✔ **Reading Check**   *How do isobars indicate wind speed?*

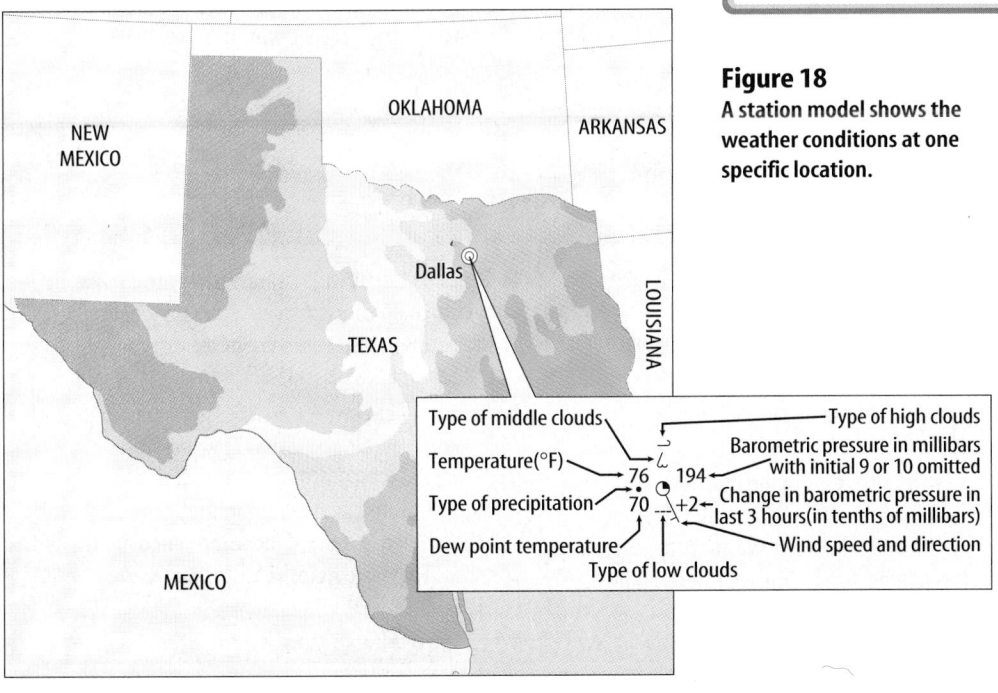

Figure 18
A station model shows the weather conditions at one specific location.

TRY AT HOME
Mini LAB

Measuring Rain
Procedure
1. You will need a **straight-sided container,** such as a soup or coffee can, **duct tape,** and a **ruler.**
2. Tape the ruler to the inner wall of your container.
3. Place the container on a level surface outdoors away from buildings or plants.
4. Measure the amount of water in your container after it rains. Continue to take measurements for a week.

Analysis
1. What was the average daily rainfall?
2. Why is it necessary to use containers with straight sides?

Weather Observations, continued

Extension

Invite a meteorologist to visit the class and talk about the tools that are used to forecast the weather.

3 Assess

Reteach

Have students examine daily weather maps and identify isotherms, the positions of high- and low-pressure areas, and fronts. L2 **LS Visual-Spatial**

Challenge

Have students research whether weather trends (climate) have changed over the years in your area. Direct them to write a report on what they find. Historical weather data are available from the National Weather Service, local meteorologists at universities or TV stations, or through searching local newspapers. If the trends have changed, encourage students to infer why they might have changed and to include this information in their reports. L3 **LS Linguistic P**

✔Assessment

Process Assess students' abilities to interpret scientific illustrations. Have students locate your area in **Figure 19**. Tell them to locate and identify the closest front and pressure system. Answers will vary with location. Use **Performance Assessment in the Science Classroom**, p. 99.

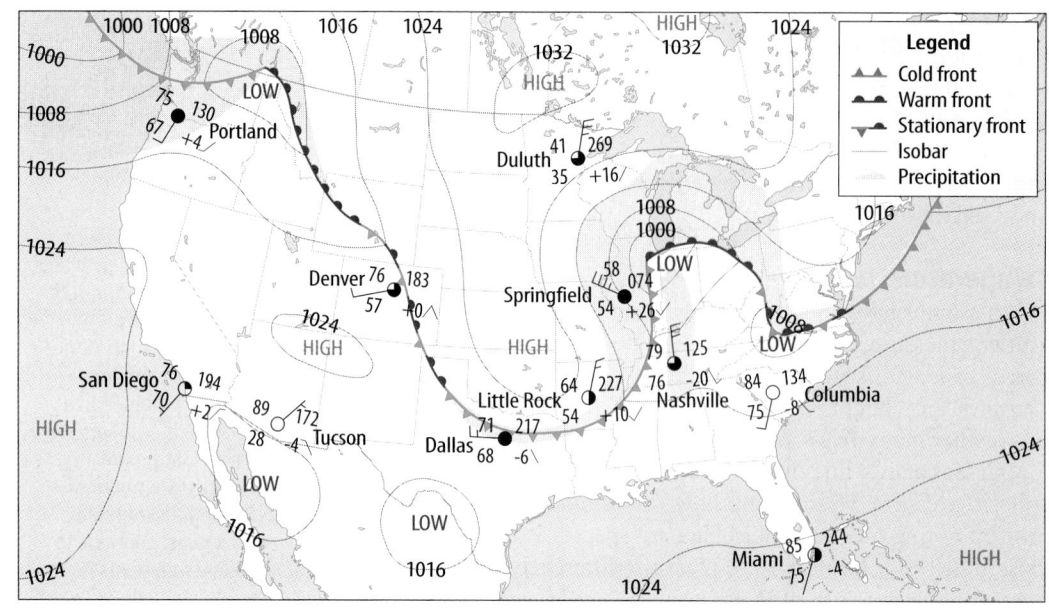

Figure 19
Highs, lows, isobars, and fronts on this weather map help meteorologists forecast the weather.

Weather Maps On a weather map like the one in **Figure 19**, pressure areas are drawn as circles with the word High or Low in the middle of the circle. Fronts are drawn as lines and symbols. When you watch weather forecasts on television, notice how weather fronts move from west to east. This is a pattern that meteorologists depend on to forecast weather.

Section 3 Assessment

1. What instruments do meteorologists use to collect weather data?
2. What is a station model?
3. How does the National Weather Service make weather maps?
4. What do closely spaced isobars on a weather map indicate?
5. **Think Critically** In the morning you hear a meteorologist forecast today's weather as sunny and warm. After school, it is raining. Why is the weather so hard to predict?

Skill Builder Activities

6. **Concept Mapping** Using a computer, make an events chain concept map for how a weather forecast is made. **For more help, refer to the Science Skill Handbook.**
7. **Communicating** Research what happened to American colonial troops at Valley Forge during the winter of 1777–1778. Imagine that you were a soldier during that winter. In your Science Journal, describe your experiences. **For more help, refer to the Science Skill Handbook.**

Answers to Section Assessment

1. Computers, weather satellites, Doppler radar, and instruments attached to balloons measure temperature, air pressure, wind, humidity, and precipitation.
2. symbols on a map that show weather conditions at one specific location
3. plotting weather data on a map,
then drawing isobars and fronts connecting the data
4. strong winds
5. Atmospheric conditions can rapidly change, making forecasting difficult.
6. Data from Earth's surface and upper atmosphere are collected by National Weather Service meteorologists. Computers are used to make weather
maps from data, meteorologists interpret maps, and forecasts are made.
7. Descriptions will vary. Strong winds, piercing cold, and snowfall took their toll on the many soldiers who were without proper clothing or shelter.

Activity

Reading a Weather Map

Meteorologists use a series of symbols to provide a picture of local and national weather conditions. With what you know, can you interpret weather information from weather map symbols?

What You'll Investigate
How do you read a weather map?

Materials
hand lens
Weather Map Symbols Appendix
Figure 19

Goals
■ **Learn** how to read a weather map.
■ **Use** information from a station model and a weather map to forecast weather.

Procedure
Use the information provided in the questions below and the Weather Map Symbols Appendix to learn how to read a weather map.

1. Find the station models on the map for Portland, Oregon, and Miami, Florida. Find the dew point, wind direction, barometric pressure, and temperature at each location.

2. Looking at the placement of the isobars, determine whether the wind would be stronger at Springfield, Illinois, or at San Diego, California. Record your answer. What is another way to determine the wind speed at these locations?

3. **Determine** the type of front near Dallas, Texas. Record your answer.

4. The triangles or half-circles are on the side of the line toward the direction the front is moving. In which direction is the cold front located over Washington state moving?

Conclude and Apply

1. Locate the pressure system over southeast Kansas. Predict what will happen to the weather of Nashville, Tennessee, if this pressure system moves there.

2. Prevailing westerlies are winds responsible for the movement of much of the weather across the United States. Based on this, would you expect Columbia, South Carolina, to continue to have clear skies? Explain.

3. The direction line on the station model indicates the direction from which the wind blows. The wind is named for that direction. Infer from this the name of the wind blowing at Little Rock, Arkansas.

*C*ommunicating
Your Data

Pretend you are a meteorologist for a local TV news station. Make a poster of your weather data and present a weather forecast to your class. **For more help, refer to the Science Skill Handbook.**

ACTIVITY 329

*C*ommunicating
Your Data

Students may wish to use a word-processing program to make labels for their posters. Encourage students to be informative and creative in their presentations.

Resource Manager

Chapter Resources Booklet
Transparency Activity, p. 47–48
Activity Worksheet, pp. 5–6
Reinforcement, p. 29

Activity

Purpose Students read and interpret a weather map. L2
IS Visual-Spatial
Process Skills recording, observing, interpreting scientific illustrations, using numbers, predicting
Time Required 45 minutes
Teaching Strategy If an opaque projector is available, project the weather map onto a screen.
Troubleshooting Some students will need to review the location of the states and major U.S. cities before this activity. Post a U.S. map in the classroom.

Answers to Procedure Steps
1. Portland: dew point—67°F, wind direction—SW, pressure—1013mb; Miami: dew point—75°F, wind direction—SW, pressure—1024.4mb, temperature—85°F
2. Springfield; look at the station models
3. cold front
4. south

Answers to Questions
1. Weather would be fair.
2. No; a cold front is approaching
3. north wind

✔ *Assessment*

Performance To assess students' abilities to interpret scientific illustrations, have them compare the weather shown on the map for Midland, Texas, and Birmingham, Alabama. Use **PASC**, p. 99.

Activity

Recognize the Problem

Purpose
Students will design and invent an instrument or system for measuring wind speed.

Process Skills
making models, observing, analyzing

Time Required
40 minutes/daily observations and measurements for one to two weeks

Thinking Critically

Discussion
Tell students to consider the effects of different speed winds on dead leaves, tree branches, and litter. Ask how they could create materials of different weights or shapes that would be influenced by different strength winds in observable patterns. What lightweight materials could they use that would travel small distances even in the slightest breeze? Have students evaluate their own designing skills to determine whether they should create an invention or a wind speed system. Provide Beaufort's scale of wind speeds as a reference source. Ask students to apply Beaufort's scale to determine the wind speed on different days so that they can see how a wind speed scale functions.

Possible Materials
Dried foods such as ground potato flakes or gelatin powder could be used instead of confetti or grass clippings. Students could also use paper of different weights, sizes or shapes. Pick up any litter after the activity.

Activity *Model and Invent*

Measuring Wind Speed

When you watch a gust of wind blow leaves down the street, do you wonder how fast the wind is moving? For centuries, people could only guess at wind speeds, but in 1805, Admiral Beaufort of the British navy invented a method for estimating wind speeds based on their effect on sails. Later, Beaufort's system was modified for use on land. Meteorologists use a simple instrument called an anemometer to measure wind speeds, and they still use Beaufort's system to estimate the speed of the wind. What type of instrument or system can you invent to measure wind speed?

Recognize the Problem

How could you use simple materials to invent an instrument or system for measuring wind speeds?

Thinking Critically

What observations do you use to estimate the speed of the wind?

Goals
- **Invent** an instrument or devise a system for measuring wind speeds using common materials.
- **Devise** a method for using your invention or system to compare different wind speeds.

Possible Materials
paper
scissors
confetti
grass clippings
meterstick
*measuring tape
*Alternate materials

Data Source
Refer to Section 1 for more information about anemometers and other wind speed instruments. Consult the data table for information about Beaufort's wind speed scale.

SCIENCE *Online*
Internet Addresses
_____
_____
_____

Explore the Glencoe Science Web site at **science.glencoe.com** to find out more about topics in this activity.

Resource Manager

Chapter Resources Booklet
   Activity Worksheet, pp. 7–8
Lab Management and Safety, p. 4

Planning the Model

1. Scan the list of possible materials and choose the materials you will need to devise your system.

2. **Devise** a system to measure different wind speeds. Be certain the materials you use are light enough to be moved by slight breezes.

Check the Model Plans

1. **Describe** your plan to your teacher. Provide a sketch of your instrument or system and ask your teacher how you might improve its design.

2. Present your idea for measuring wind speed to the class in the form of a diagram or poster. Ask your classmates to suggest improvements in your design that will make your system more accurate or easier to use.

Making the Model

1. Confetti or grass clippings that are all the same size can be used to measure wind speed by dropping them from a specific height. Measuring the distances they travel in different strength winds will provide data for devising a wind speed scale.

2. Different sizes and shapes of paper also could be dropped into the wind, and the strength of the wind would be determined by measuring the distances traveled by these different types of paper.

Beaufort's Wind Speed Scale	
Description	**Wind Speed (km/h)**
calm—smoke drifts up	less than 1
light air—smoke drifts with wind	1–5
light breeze—leaves rustle	6–11
gentle breeze—leaves move constantly	12–19
moderate breeze—branches move	20–29
fresh breeze—small trees sway	30–39
strong breeze—large branches move	40–50
moderate gale—whole trees move	51–61
fresh gale—twigs break	62–74
strong gale—slight damage to houses	75–87
whole gale—much damage to houses	88–101
storm—extensive damage	102–120
hurricane—extreme damage	more than 120

Analyzing and Applying Results

1. **Explain** why it is important for meteorologists to measure wind speeds.

2. **Compare** your results with Beaufort's wind speed scale.

3. **Develop** a scale for your method.

4. **Evaluate** how well your system worked in gentle breezes and strong winds.

5. **Analyze** what problems may exist in the design of your system and suggest steps you could take to improve your design.

Communicating
Your Data

Demonstrate your system for the class. **Compare** your results and measurements with the results of other classmates.

ACTIVITY 331

Communicating
Your Data

Use an electric fan and a large painting tarp to test student inventions and systems inside the classroom.

Planning the Model

Teaching Strategies

- Have the Beaufort scale of wind speeds posted in your room as a reference.
- Tell students to make a decision on creating an invention or a wind speed scale. Instruct them not to do both without first speaking to you.
- Ask students to make a checklist of items they will need to make their models.

Making the Model

Expected Outcome

Students should design and build an invention or create a system that accurately compares different wind speeds.

Analyzing and Applying Results

Answers

1. Aid in weather forecasts, warn of severe weather, warn air traffic of dangerous winds, and decide on locations for using wind power to generate electricity.
2. Answers will vary.
3. Answers will vary.
4. Answers will vary but students should discuss how their instruments or measuring systems would measure and compare increases in wind speed or wind gusts.
5. Answers will vary.

Assessment

Process Ask students to compare their methods for measuring wind speed with Beaufort's scale. Use **Performance Assessment in the Science Classroom,** p. 91.

Content Background

Before it can rain, water droplets in clouds have to grow large enough to reach the ground without evaporating.

Raindrops form by one of two processes, depending on the temperature of the clouds. In warm clouds, where temperatures are above freezing, small water droplets grow as they collide and merge with one another. Eventually, the drops are large enough to fall from the cloud as rain. Cold clouds, with temperatures at or below freezing, contain a mixture of ice crystals and supercooled water droplets. Supercooled water droplets are liquid water drops that exist below the freezing point. When a water droplet collides with an ice crystal, it freezes on impact, forming a larger ice crystal. When the crystal is large enough, it falls to the ground. Whether it falls as rain or snow depends on the air temperature below the cloud.

Cloud seeding attempts to promote rain by introducing condensation nuclei (particles intended to trigger condensation) into clouds. In warm clouds, large water drops are introduced. In cold clouds, cloud seeding attempts stimulate crystal growth by either chilling the air with dry ice or providing seed crystals. Silver iodide crystals are used as seeds because they form crystals similar to ice crystals.

TIME
SCIENCE AND
Society

SCIENCE ISSUES THAT AFFECT YOU!

Rain

You listen to a meteorologist give the long-term weather forecast. Another week with no rain in sight. As a farmer, you are concerned that your crops are withering in the fields. Home owners' lawns are turning brown. Wildfires are possible. Cattle are starving. And, if farmers' crops die, there could be a shortage of food and prices will go up for consumers.

332

Resources for Teachers and Students

The Atmosphere: An Introduction to Meteorology. Frederick K. Lutgens and Edward J. Tarbuck, Prentice Hall, 1998.

Meteorology: The Atmosphere and the Science of Weather. Joseph M. Moran and Michael D. Morgan, Prentice Hall, 1997.

Human Impacts on Weather and Climate. W.R. Cotton and R.A. Pielke, Cambridge Univ. Press, 1995.

Cloud seeding is an inexact science

makers

Flares contain chemicals which will seed clouds.

Meanwhile, several states away, another farmer is listening to the weather report calling for another week of rain. Her crops are getting so water soaked that they are beginning to rot.

Weather. Can't scientists find a way to better control it? The answer is...not exactly. Scientists have been experimenting with methods to control our weather since the 1940s. And nothing really works.

Cloud seeding is one such attempt. It uses technology to enhance the natural rainfall process. The idea has been used to create rain where it is needed or to reduce hail damage. Government officials also use cloud seeding or weather modification to try to reduce the force of a severe storm.

Some people seed a cloud by flying a plane above it and releasing highway-type flares with chemicals, such as silver iodide. Another method is to fly beneath the cloud and spray a chemical that can be carried into the cloud by air currents.

Flares are lodged under a plane. The pilot will drop them into potential rain clouds.

Cloud seeding doesn't work with clouds that have little water vapor or are not near the dew point. Seeding chemicals must be released into potential rain clouds. The chemicals provide nuclei for water molecules to cluster around. Water then falls to Earth as precipitation.

Cloud seeding does have its critics. If you seed clouds and cause rain for your area, aren't you preventing rain from falling in another area? Would that be considered "rain theft" by people who live in places where the cloudburst would naturally occur? What about those cloud-seeding agents? Could the cloud-seeding chemicals, such as silver iodide and acetone, affect the environment in a harmful way? Are humans meddling with nature and creating problems in ways that haven't been determined?

Currently, Montana, Pennsylvania, and New Mexico are states that don't allow cloud seeding within their state boundaries. But officials in Texas and California, the two states with the largest number of cloud-seeding programs, feel strongly that cloud seeding is an important technology when it comes to dealing with weather.

CONNECTIONS Debate Learn more about cloud seeding and other methods of changing weather. Then debate whether or not cloud seeding can be considered "rain theft."

Online

For more information, visit science.glencoe.com

CONNECTIONS Have students role-play a town meeting to debate the issue of "rain theft." Roles may include a chairman of the meeting (the town mayor) and citizen groups for and against cloud seeding. Both groups must have citizens representing each of the following: farmers, scientific experts, a chief executive of a cloud seeding company, and environmental activists.

Online

Internet Addresses

Explore the Glencoe Science Web site at **science.glencoe.com** to find out more about topics in this feature.

Discussion

Ask students to brainstorm other questions that might arise from cloud seeding. Possible questions: Does cloud seeding cause flooding or excessive snowfall? Who pays for damages caused by such flooding? Can cloud seeding reduce rainfall? Are the chemicals used harmful to the environment? Does cloud seeding "steal" rain from other areas?

Activity

Rainmaking attempts have an interesting history. Native Americans have contributed to this history with ceremonial rain dances. Use your library to investigate the myths and traditions of Native American rain dances. Have students prepare oral presentations to share their information with the class.

Investigate the Issue

Divide the class into two groups: those for and those against cloud seeding. For each group assign student roles for the mock town meeting (see Connections). Instruct students to develop their argument from the standpoint of the citizen group they represent. Farmers should consider agricultural concerns; scientific experts and environmental activists should look into current and past projects involving cloud seeding. The chief executives should investigate cloud seeding companies. Another area that may be explored is cost to local communities.

Chapter 11 Study Guide

Reviewing Main Ideas

Preview

Students can answer the questions in their Science Journals. Discuss the answers as you go through the chapter. **LS Linguistic**

Review

Students can write their answers, then compare them with those of other students. **LS Interpersonal**

Reteach

Students can look at the illustrations and describe details that support the main ideas of the chapter. **LS Visual-Spatial**

Answers to Chapter Review

SECTION 1

3. Hail forms in cumulonimbus clouds. Ice crystals acquire a thin layer of water at lower levels in the cloud. Updrafts then carry the ice crystals to higher levels of the cloud where the water freezes. This process repeats many times to produce hail.

SECTION 2

4. Its energy supply (warm, moist air over the ocean) is gone.

SECTION 3

2. 30°F

Reviewing Main Ideas

Section 1 What is weather?

1. Important factors that determine weather include air pressure, wind, temperature, and the amount of moisture in the air.

2. More water vapor can be present in warm air than in cold air. Water vapor condenses when the dew point is reached. Clouds are formed when warm, moist air rises and cools to its dew point.

3. Rain, hail, sleet, and snow are types of precipitation. *What causes hail to form during severe thunderstorms?*

Section 2 Weather Patterns

1. Fronts form when air masses with different characteristics, such as temperature, moisture, or density, meet. Types of fronts include cold fronts, warm fronts, occluded fronts, and stationary fronts.

2. High atmospheric pressure at Earth's surface usually means good weather. Cloudy and stormy weather occurs under low pressure.

3. Tornadoes are intense, whirling windstorms that can result from wind shears inside a thunderstorm.

4. Hurricanes and blizzards are large, severe storms with strong winds. *Why does a hurricane, shown below, lose strength as it moves over land?*

Section 3 Weather Forecasts

1. Meteorologists use information from radar, satellites, computers, and other weather instruments to make weather maps and forecasts.

2. Symbols on a station model indicate the weather at a particular location. *What is the dew point temperature on the station model shown here?*

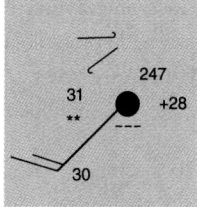

3. Weather maps include information about temperature and air pressure.

FOLDABLES Reading & Study Skills

After You Read

To help you review facts about weather, use the Foldable you made at the beginning of the chapter.

FOLDABLES Reading & Study Skills

After You Read

After students have read the chapter and completed the Foldable described in Before You Read, have them do the activity on the student page.

Dinah Zike

Visualizing Main Ideas

Complete the following concept map about air temperature, water vapor, and pressure.

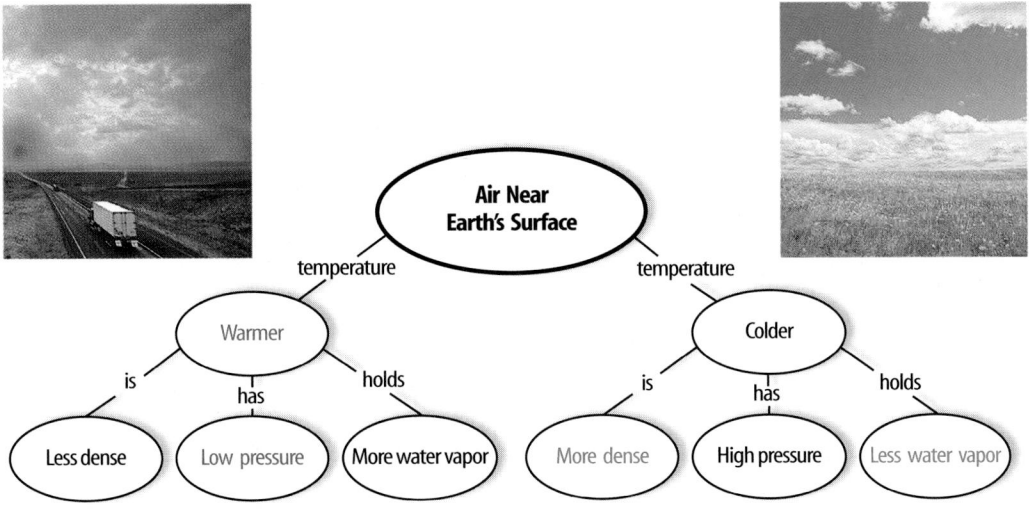

Vocabulary Review

Vocabulary Words

a. air mass
b. blizzard
c. dew point
d. fog
e. front
f. humidity
g. hurricane
h. isobar
i. isotherm
j. meteorologist
k. precipitation
l. relative humidity
m. station model
n. tornado
o. weather

THE PRINCETON REVIEW **Study Tip**

After each day's lesson, make a practice quiz for yourself. Later, when you're studying for the test, take the practice quizzes that you created.

Using Vocabulary

Explain the differences between the vocabulary words in each of the following sets.

1. air mass, front
2. humidity, relative humidity
3. relative humidity, dew point
4. dew point, precipitation
5. hurricane, tornado
6. blizzard, fog
7. meteorologist, station model
8. precipitation, fog
9. isobar, isotherm
10. isobar, front

CHAPTER STUDY GUIDE   335

Visualizing Main Ideas

See student page.

Vocabulary Review

Using Vocabulary

1. air mass: large body of air of uniform temperature and moisture; front: boundary between air masses
2. humidity: amount of water vapor in air; relative humidity: ratio of humidity in air to the amount of water vapor needed for saturation at a specific temperature
3. relative humidity: ratio of humidity in air to the amount of water vapor needed for saturation; dew point: temperature at which condensation occurs
4. dew point: temperature at which condensation occurs; precipitation: water falling from clouds
5. hurricane: large, swirling tropical low-pressure system; tornado: violent whirling wind produced by thunderstorms
6. blizzard: winter storm with high wind, freezing temperatures, and low visibility; fog: cloud that forms near the ground
7. meteorologist: scientist who studies weather; station model: symbols on a map that describe weather in one place
8. precipitation: water falling from clouds; fog: cloud that forms near the ground
9. isobar: line on map that connects points of equal air pressure; isotherm: line on map that connects points of equal temperature
10. isobar: line on map that connects points of equal air pressure; front: boundary between air masses

Chapter 11 Assessment

Checking Concepts

1. D
2. A
3. A
4. D
5. A
6. D
7. D
8. C
9. C
10. A

Thinking Critically

11. If humidity remains constant, relative humidity increases as temperature decreases.

12. Heat from the Sun causes water to evaporate, forming water vapor in the air. The water vapor rises and cools to form clouds, and then falls as precipitation.

13. The weather in Washington is influenced by air masses that form over water. The weather in west Texas is influenced by air masses that form over arid land.

14. The air has 79% of the water vapor that is needed for saturation at that temperature.

15. Hurricanes derive energy from warm waters. The water in polar regions is too cold

Checking Concepts

Choose the word or phrase that best answers the question.

1. Which type of air has a relative humidity of 100 percent?
   A) humid
   B) temperate
   C) dry
   D) saturated

2. What is a large body of air that has the same properties as the area over which it formed called?
   A) air mass
   B) station model
   C) front
   D) isotherm

3. At what temperature does water vapor in air condense?
   A) dew point
   B) station model
   C) front
   D) isobar

4. Which type of precipitation forms when water vapor changes directly into a solid?
   A) rain
   B) hail
   C) sleet
   D) snow

5. Which type of the following clouds are high feathery clouds made of ice crystals?
   A) cirrus
   B) nimbus
   C) cumulus
   D) stratus

6. Which type of front may form when cool air, cold air and warm air meet?
   A) warm
   B) cold
   C) stationary
   D) occluded

7. Which is issued when severe weather conditions exist and immediate action should be taken?
   A) front
   B) watch
   C) station model
   D) warning

8. Which term means the amount of water vapor in the air?
   A) dew point
   B) precipitation
   C) humidity
   D) relative humidity

9. What does an anemometer measure?
   A) air pressure
   B) relative humidity
   C) wind speed
   D) precipitation

10. What is a large, swirling storm that forms over warm, tropical water called?
    A) hurricane
    B) tornado
    C) blizzard
    D) hailstorm

Thinking Critically

11. Explain the relationship between temperature and relative humidity.

12. Describe how air, water, and the Sun interact to cause weather.

13. Explain why northwest Washington often has rainy weather and southwest Texas is dry.

14. What does it mean if the relative humidity is 79 percent?

15. Why don't hurricanes form in Earth's polar regions?

Developing Skills

16. **Comparing and Contrasting** Compare and contrast the weather at a cold front to that at a warm front.

17. **Observing and Inferring** You take a hot shower. The mirror in the bathroom fogs up, like the one below. Infer from this information what has happened.

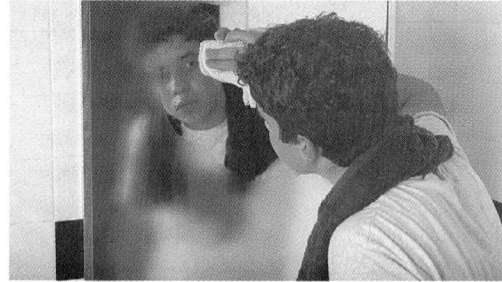

Chapter ✓Assessment Planner

Portfolio Encourage students to place in their portfolios one or two items of what they consider to be their best work. Examples include:
- Life Science Integration, p. 311
- Use Science Words, p. 319
- Challenge, p. 328

Performance Additional performance assessments, Performance Task Assessment Lists, and rubrics for evaluating these activities can be found in Glencoe's **Performance Assessment in the Science Classroom.**

18. Interpreting Scientific Illustrations Use the cloud descriptions in **Section 1** to describe the weather at your location today. Then try to predict tomorrow's weather.

19. Concept Mapping Complete the sequence map below showing how precipitation forms.

```
                  ┌──────────────┐
                  │ Water vapor  │
  ┌───────────┐   │ condenses into│
  │ Air cools.│──▶│   clouds.    │
  └───────────┘   └──────────────┘
        ▲                 │
        │                 ▼
  ┌──────────┐     ┌──────────────┐
  │Warm, moist│    │ Precipitation│
  │ air rises.│    │   occurs.    │
  └──────────┘     └──────────────┘
        ▲                 │
        │                 ▼
  ┌──────────────────────────────┐
  │        Earth's Surface        │
  └──────────────────────────────┘
```

20. Comparing and Contrasting Compare and contrast tornadoes and thunderstorms.

Performance Assessment

21. Board Game Make a board game using weather terms. You could make cards to advance or retreat a token.

22. Design your own weather station. Record temperature, precipitation, and wind speed for one week.

TECHNOLOGY

Go to the Glencoe Science Web site at **science.glencoe.com** or use the **Glencoe Science CD-ROM** for additional chapter assessment.

THE PRINCETON REVIEW   Test Practice

Hurricanes are rated on a scale based on their wind speed and barometric pressure. The table below lists the hurricane category by the wind speed and pressure of the storm.

Hurricane Rating Scale		
Category	**Wind Speed (km/h)**	**Barometric Pressure (millibars)**
1	119–154	>980
2	155–178	965–980
3	179–210	945–964
4	211–250	920–944
5	>250	<920

Study the table and answer the following questions.

1. In 1992, Hurricane Andrew, with winds of 233 km/hr and a pressure of 922 mb, struck southeast Florida. What category was Hurricane Andrew?

A) 1   **C)** 3
B) 2   **D)** 4

2. Which of the following best describes the pressure and wind when categorizing a hurricane?

F) Storm category increases as wind increases and pressure decreases.
G) Storm category increases as wind decreases and pressure increases.
H) Storm category increases as wind and pressure increase.
J) Storm category decreases as wind and pressure decrease.

THE PRINCETON REVIEW   Test Practice

The Test-Taking Tip was written by The Princeton Review, the nation's leader in test preparation.

1. D
2. F

Developing Skills

16. Both bring clouds and precipitation; cold front: possible thunderstorms and tornadoes; warm front: long period of steady, light precipitation.

17. The bathroom air is warm and full of water vapor. The air cooled to its dew point when it hit the surface of the cooler mirror, causing water vapor in the air to condense into liquid water on the glass.

18. Students should correctly identify and predict cloudiness, precipitation, or sunshine based on cloud observations.

19. See student page.

20. Both can produce strong, damaging winds. Thunderstorms produce heavy bursts of rainfall as well as lightning, thunder, and possibly hail. Severe thunderstorms can also produce tornadoes, which are swirling funnels of wind that move along the ground, destroying things in their path

Performance Assessment

21. Encourage students to be creative, include detailed instructions for playing the game, and use accurate information. Have students play each other's games. Use **PASC**, p. 117.

22. Check students' work. Use **PASC**, p. 117.

✓Assessment Resources

📁 Reproducible Masters

Chapter Resources Booklet
  Chapter Review, pp. 37–38
  Chapter Tests, pp. 39–42
  Assessment Transparency Activity, p. 49

Glencoe Science Web site
  Interactive Tutor
  Chapter Quizzes

Glencoe Technology
  🔧 Assessment Transparency
  💿 Interactive CD-ROM Chapter Quizzes
  💿 ExamView Pro Test Bank
  💿 Vocabulary PuzzleMaker Software
  📼 MindJogger Videoquiz

Section/Objectives	Standards		Activities/Features
Chapter Opener	**National**	**State/Local**	**Explore Activity:** Infer why oceans are salty, p. 339 **Before You Read,** p. 339
	See p. 7T for a Key to Standards.		
Section 1 Ocean Water 2 sessions 1 block 1. **State** the importance of Earth's oceans. 2. **Discuss** the origin of the oceans. 3. **Describe** the composition of seawater. 4. **Explain** how temperature and pressure vary with depth.	National Content Standards: UCP4, A1, B1, D1		**Science Online,** p. 343 **Activity:** Desalination, p. 345
Section 2 Ocean Currents and Climate 2 sessions 1 block 1. **State** how wind and the rotation of Earth influence surface currents. 2. **Discuss** how ocean currents affect weather and climate. 3. **Describe** the causes and effects of density currents. 4. **Explain** how upwelling occurs.	National Content Standards: UCP1, A1, B1, D1		**Science Online,** p. 347 **Chemistry Integration,** p. 348 **MiniLAB:** Modeling a Density Current, p. 349
Section 3 Waves 2 sessions 1 block 1. **Describe** how wind can form ocean waves. 2. **Explain** the movement of water particles in a wave. 3. **Describe** how the Moon and Sun cause Earth's tides. 4. **List** the forces that cause shoreline erosion.	National Content Standards: UCP1, A1, B1, D1		**MiniLAB:** Modeling Water Particle Movement, p. 352 **Science Online,** p. 353
Section 4 Life in the Oceans 4 sessions 2 blocks 1. **Describe** the characteristics of plankton, nekton, and bottom-dwelling organisms 2. **Distinguish** among producers, consumers, and decomposers. 3. **Discuss** how energy and nutrients are cycled in the oceans. 4. **Explain** how ocean organisms interact in food chains.	National Content Standards: UCP2, A1, C4, C5		**Life Science Integration,** p. 357 **Problem-Solving Activity:** Are fish that contain mercury safe to eat?, p. 358 **Visualizing Food Chains in a Food Web,** p. 359 **Activity:** Waves and Tides, p. 362 **Science Stats:** Ocean Facts, p. 364

NATIONAL GEOGRAPHIC

Teacher's Corner

PRODUCTS AVAILABLE FROM GLENCOE
To order call 1-800-334-7344:
CD-ROM
NGS PictureShow: Oceans

Curriculum Kit
GeoKit: Oceans
Transparency Set
NGS PicturePack: Oceans

PRODUCTS AVAILABLE FROM NATIONAL GEOGRAPHIC SOCIETY
To order call 1-800-368-2728:
Videos
Living Ocean; Oceans in Motion; Water: A Precious Resource

Activity Materials	Reproducible Resources	Section Assessment	Technology
Explore Activity: dry sand, salt, aluminum pie pan, bowl, water	**Chapter Resources Booklet** Foldables Worksheet, p. 17 Directed Reading Overview, p. 19 Note-taking Worksheets, pp. 35–37	*GLENCOE'S* **ASSESSMENT** *ADVANTAGE*	
Activity: large spoon, table salt, water, 2 250-mL beakers, large bowl, plastic wrap, tape, large marble	**Chapter Resources Booklet** Transparency Activity, p. 46 Enrichment, p. 31 Reinforcement, p. 27 Directed Reading, p. 20 Activity Worksheet, pp. 5–6 Lab Activity, pp. 9–12 **Cultural Diversity,** p. 27	Portfolio Curriculum Connection, p. 341 Performance Skill Builder Activities, p. 344 Content Section Assessment, p. 344	🔦 Section Focus Transparency 💿 Interactive CD-ROM 🎧 Guided Reading Audio Program
MiniLAB: paper cup, water, salt, food coloring, spoon, clear-plastic box, 2 thumbtacks, metric ruler *Need materials?* Contact Science Kit at 1-800-828-7777 or www.sciencekit.com on the Internet.	**Chapter Resources Booklet** Transparency Activity, p. 47 MiniLAB, p. 3 Enrichment, p. 32 Reinforcement, p. 28 Directed Reading, p. 20 **Earth Science Critical Thinking/ Problem Solving,** p. 16	Portfolio Cultural Diversity, p. 349 Performance MiniLAB, p. 349 Skill Builder Activities, p. 350 Content Section Assessment, p. 350	🔦 Section Focus Transparency 💿 Interactive CD-ROM 🎧 Guided Reading Audio Program
MiniLAB: large bowl, water, penny, toothpick, spoon	**Chapter Resources Booklet** Transparency Activity, p. 48 MiniLAB, p. 4 Enrichment, p. 33 Reinforcement, p. 29 Directed Reading, p. 21 Lab Activity, pp. 13–16	Portfolio Science Journal, p. 352 Performance MiniLAB, p. 352 Skill Builder Activities, p. 354 Content Section Assessment, p. 354	🔦 Section Focus Transparency 💿 Interactive CD-ROM 🎧 Guided Reading Audio Program
Activity: large basin; water; boards; sand, dirt, or gravel; chalk dust, salt, or sugar; bricks; rocks; plastic bottles; battery-operated fan	**Chapter Resources Booklet** Transparency Activity, p. 49 Enrichment, p. 34 Reinforcement, p. 30 Directed Reading, pp. 21, 22 Activity Worksheet, pp. 7–8 Transparency Activity, pp. 51–52 **Lab Management and Safety,** p. 73	Portfolio Extension, p. 357 Performance Problem-Solving Activity, p. 358 Skill Builder Activities, p. 361 Content Section Assessment, p. 361	🔦 Section Focus Transparency 🔦 Teaching Transparency 💿 Interactive CD-ROM 🎧 Guided Reading Audio Program

End of Chapter Assessment

GLENCOE'S **ASSESSMENT** *ADVANTAGE*

Blackline Masters	Technology	Professional Series
Chapter Resources Booklet Chapter Review, pp. 39–40 Chapter Tests, pp. 41–44 **Standardized Test Practice by The Princeton Review,** pp. 51–54	📼 MindJogger Videoquiz 💿 Interactive CD-ROM 💿 Vocabulary PuzzleMakers 💿 ExamView Pro Test Bank 💿 Interactive Lesson Planner 💿 Interactive Teacher Edition	Performance Assessment in the Science Classroom (PASC)

Transparencies

Section Focus

Section 1 Focus Transparency — Livin' Life Large

What's the biggest animal that ever lived? You might be surprised to learn that it's not a dinosaur, but the whale. The biggest blue whales are roughly 30 meters (100 feet) long and weigh about 136,000 kilograms (150 tons).

1. How does water help support the blue whale's massive size?
2. Name two ways animals in the ocean get oxygen.
3. In what ways do humans depend on the ocean?

L2

Section 2 Focus Transparency — Treacherous Current

Coursing around this peaceful island is the Maelstrøm, a swirling current caused by a combination of tide, wind, and configuration of sea floor. Running between two islands in the Norwegian Sea, the Maelstrøm poses a challenge to those who must navigate its waters.

1. What is a current?
2. How might a strong current make swimming dangerous?
3. Why do you think the Maelstrøm would be difficult to navigate?

L2

Section 3 Focus Transparency — Deadly Wave

Giant waves called tsunamis are created in the oceans by earthquakes or volcanoes. Tsunamis can be over 30 m (100 feet) high and are capable of traveling long distances. This photo shows a tsunami that struck Hilo, Hawaii, in 1946.

1. What happens when you drop a rock in water?
2. What do you think causes ocean waves?
3. Why are tsunamis more dangerous than regular waves?

L2

This is a representation of key blackline masters available in the Teacher Classroom Resources. See Resource Manager boxes within the chapter for additional information.

Assessment

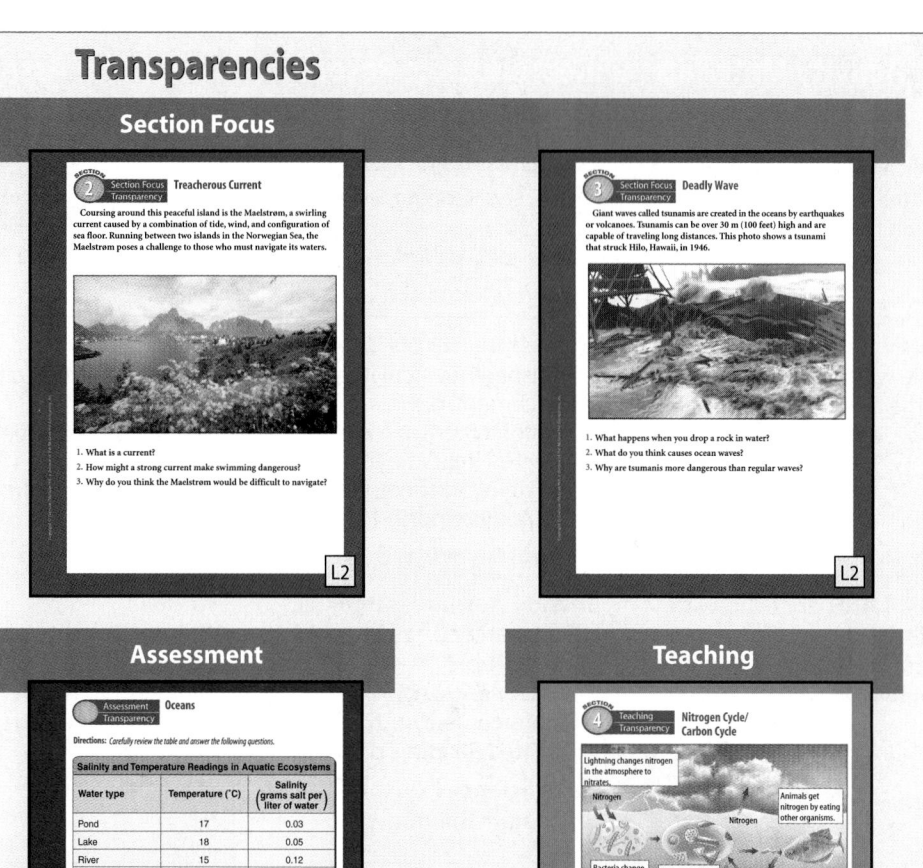

Assessment Transparency — Oceans

Directions: Carefully review the table and answer the following questions.

Salinity and Temperature Readings in Aquatic Ecosystems		
Water type	Temperature (°C)	Salinity (grams salt per liter of water)
Pond	17	0.03
Lake	18	0.05
River	15	0.12
Atlantic Ocean	12	34.5
Pacific Ocean	11	?

1. According to the table, which type of water has a temperature less than 13 degrees Celsius?
   A pond   C ocean
   B river   D lake
2. Using the data in the table as a guide, which of the following most closely describes the salinity of a stream?
   F 0.01   H 10.0
   G 0.10   J 100.0
3. These data were collected by testing water samples from different sources. When the salinity of the Pacific Ocean is tested, which of these is the value most likely to go in the table?
   A 34.5   C 0.03
   B 0.34   D 0.01

L2

Teaching

Section 4 Teaching Transparency — Nitrogen Cycle/Carbon Cycle

Lightning changes nitrogen in the atmosphere to nitrates.

Nitrogen

Animals get nitrogen by eating other organisms.

Nitrogen

Bacteria change nitrogen gas into nitrates.

Algae and plants use nitrates for growth.

Bacteria decompose dead organisms to produce nitrates and nitrogen gas.

Carbon dioxide

Carbon

Carbon dioxide

Algae and producers

Consumers

Carbon

Carbon dioxide

Carbon

Carbon

L2

Key to Teaching Strategies

The following designations will help you decide which activities are appropriate for your students.

L1 Level 1 activities should be appropriate for students with learning difficulties.

L2 Level 2 activities should be within the ability range of all students.

L3 Level 3 activities are designed for above-average students.

ELL ELL activities should be within the ability range of English Language Learners.

COOP LEARN Cooperative Learning activities are designed for small group work.

LS Multiple Learning Styles logos, as described on page 22T, are used throughout to indicate strategies that address different learning styles.

P These strategies represent student products that can be placed into a best-work portfolio.

Hands-on Activities

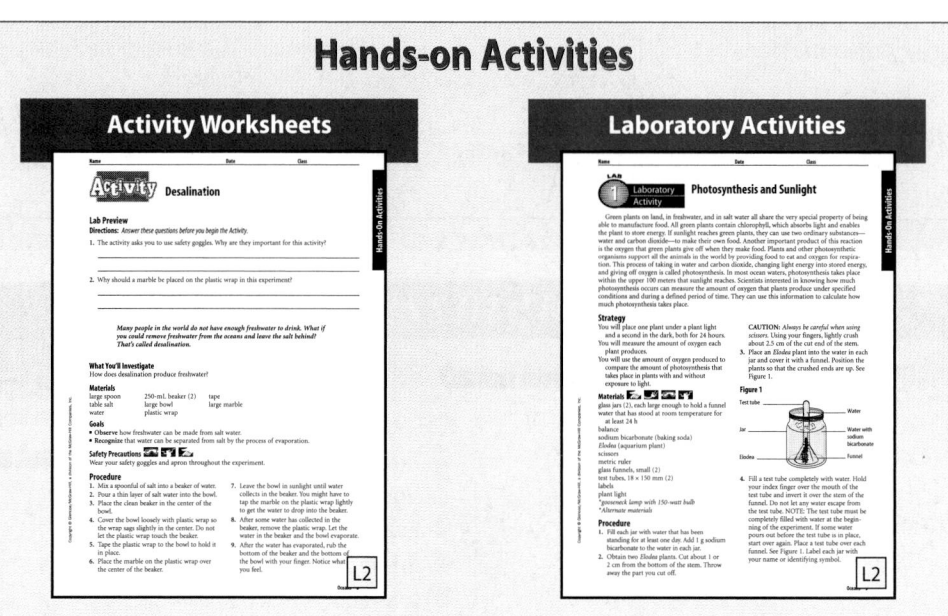

Activity Worksheets

Activity — Desalination

Lab Preview
Directions: Answer these questions before you begin the Activity.

1. The activity asks you to use safety goggles. Why are they important for this activity?

2. Why should a marble be placed on the plastic wrap in this experiment?

Many people in the world do not have enough freshwater to drink. What if you could remove freshwater from the oceans and leave the salt behind? That's called desalination.

What You'll Investigate
How does desalination produce freshwater?

Materials
large spoon   250-mL beaker (2)   tape
table salt   large bowl   large marble
water   plastic wrap

Goals
• Observe how freshwater can be made from salt water.
• Recognize that water can be separated from salt by the process of evaporation.

Safety Precautions
Wear your safety goggles and apron throughout the experiment.

Procedure
1. Mix a spoonful of salt into a beaker of water.
2. Pour a thin layer of salt water into the bowl.
3. Place the clean beaker in the center of the bowl.
4. Cover the bowl loosely with plastic wrap so the wrap sags slightly in the center. Do not let the plastic wrap touch the beaker.
5. Tape the plastic wrap to the bowl to hold it in place.
6. Place the marble on the plastic wrap over the center of the beaker.
7. Leave the bowl in sunlight until water collects in the beaker. You might have to tap the marble on the plastic wrap lightly to get the water to drop into the beaker.
8. After some water has collected in the beaker, remove the plastic wrap. Let the water in the beaker and the bowl evaporate.
9. After the water has evaporated, rub the bottom of the beaker and the bottom of the bowl with your finger. Notice what you feel.

L2

Laboratory Activities

Laboratory Activity — Photosynthesis and Sunlight

Green plants on land, in freshwater, and in salt water all share the very special property of being able to manufacture food. All green plants contain chlorophyll, which absorbs light and enables the plant to store energy. If sunlight reaches green plants, they can use two ordinary substances—water and carbon dioxide—to make their own food. Another important product of this reaction is the oxygen that green plants give off when they make food. Plants and other photosynthetic organisms support all the animals in the world by providing food to eat and oxygen for respiration. This process of taking in water and carbon dioxide, changing light energy into stored energy, and giving off oxygen is called photosynthesis. In most ocean waters, photosynthesis takes place within the upper 100 meters that sunlight reaches. Scientists interested in knowing how much photosynthesis occurs can measure the amount of oxygen that plants produce under specified conditions and during a defined period of time. They can use this information to calculate how much photosynthesis takes place.

Strategy
You will place one plant under a plant light and a second in the dark, both for 24 hours.
You will measure the amount of oxygen each plant produces.
You will use the amount of oxygen produced to compare the amount of photosynthesis that takes place in plants with and without exposure to light.

Materials
glass jars (2), each large enough to hold a funnel
water that has stood at room temperature for at least 24 h
sodium bicarbonate (baking soda)
Elodea (aquarium plant)
scissors
metric ruler
glass funnels, small (2)
test tubes, 18 × 150 mm (2)
labels
plant light
*generated lamp with 150-watt bulb
*Alternate materials

Procedure
1. Fill each jar with water that has been standing for at least one day. Add 1 g sodium bicarbonate to the water in each jar.
2. Choose two Elodea plants. Cut about 1 or 2 cm from the bottom of the stem. Throw away the part you cut off.

CAUTION: Always be careful when using scissors. Using your fingers, lightly crush about 2.5 cm of the cut end of the stem.
3. Place an Elodea plant into the water in each jar and cover it with a funnel. Position the plants so that the crushed ends are up. See Figure 1.

Figure 1

Test tube

Jar

Elodea

Water

Water with sodium bicarbonate

Funnel

4. Fill a test tube completely with water. Hold your index finger over the mouth of the test tube and invert it over the stem of the funnel. Do not let any water escape from the test tube. NOTE: The test tube must be completely filled with water at the beginning of the experiment. If some water pours out before the test tube is in place, start over again. Place a test tube over each funnel. See Figure 1. Label each jar with your name or identifying symbol.

L2

Meeting Different Ability Levels

Content Outline

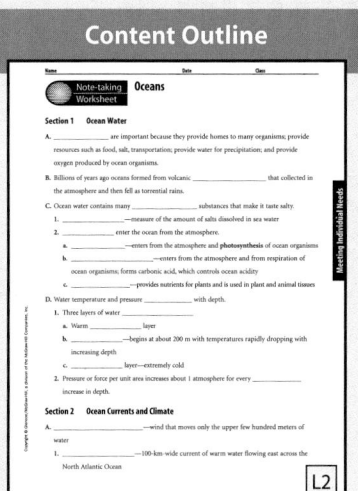

Reinforcement

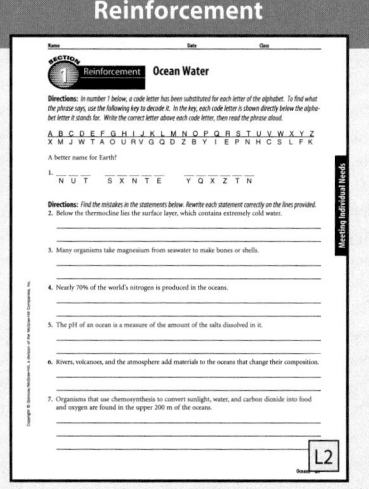

Directed Reading

Assessment

Chapter Tests

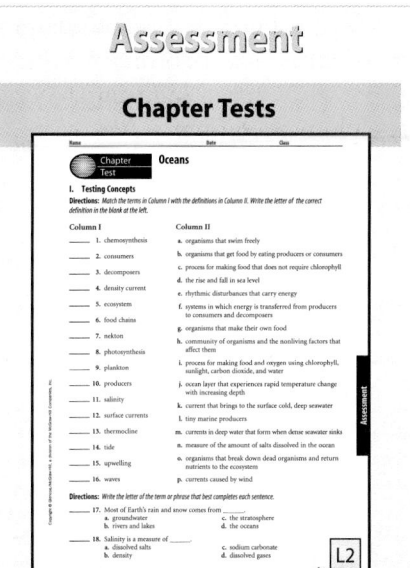

Enrichment

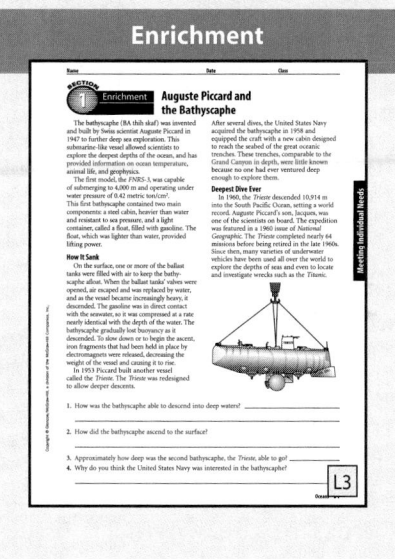

Spanish Directed Reading

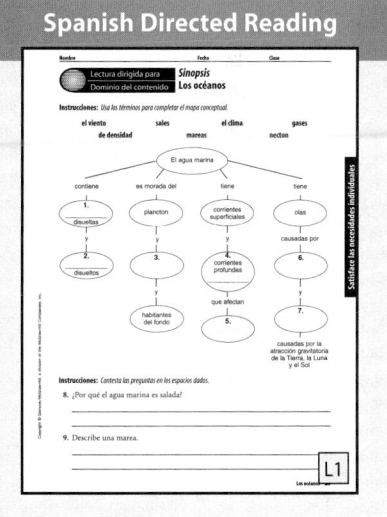

Test Practice Workbook

Chapter Review

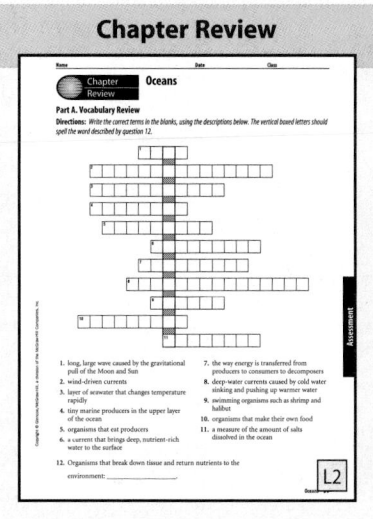

Science Content Background

SECTION 1
Ocean Water
Under the Sea
The water of the world's oceans covers a topography that is as rich and varied as that found on land. These features include mountains, valleys, and plains.

Student Misconception

The floor of the ocean is flat, with no topographic features.

Refer to the facing page for teaching strategies to address this misconception. Refer to pages 340–341 for content related to this topic.

SECTION 2
Ocean Currents and Climate
El Niño
El Niño events can cause severe weather disturbances on a localized level as well as globally. During the 1997–1998 El Niño, heavy rains in the eastern Pacific caused mudslides and flooding throughout Peru and Ecuador. Tornadoes swept across the southeastern United States in February of 1998. Drought struck other areas of the world, including Hawaii, southwestern Africa, and New Guinea, resulting in failed crops and starvation.

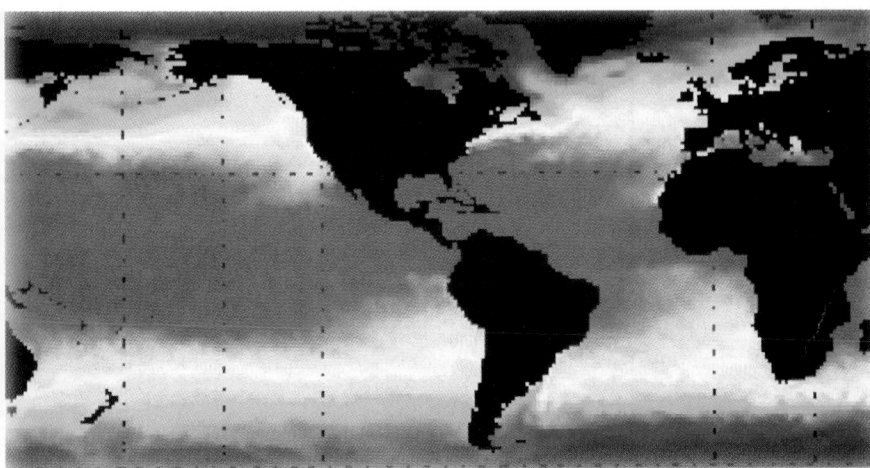

Warren Faidley/International Stock

SECTION 3
Waves
Wind Waves
When waves meet in the open ocean, they don't just pass over one another. Instead, they either add to or subtract from the crests and troughs of each other. This process is known as interference. In destructive interference, two waves meet and cancel each other out. This type of interaction is not dangerous, as the energy of each wave is dissipated. In constructive interference, waves meet and add to each other's height. Constructive interference can result in large, destructive waves. In some cases a rogue wave, which has a height of 30 m or more, is produced. The southeastern tip of Africa has a high incidence of rogue waves. When incoming waves reach the fast-moving current in this area, they can double in height and then break. Tankers have been broken in half by these rogue waves.

SECTION 4
Life in the Oceans
Coral Reefs
Reef-building corals have a mutualistic relationship with the dinoflagellate zooxanthellae, which grow in the tissues of the corals. The zooxanthellae receive a safe place to live and the carbon dioxide and nutrients given off by the corals during respiration. The corals receive oxygen and extra food in the form of carbohydrates from the zooxanthellae. It is this extra food that allows corals to build massive reef structures. Nonreef-building corals do not have zooxanthellae living in their tissues. These corals rely solely on filter feeding to capture food.

SCIENCE *Online*

For additional content background on this topic, go to the Glencoe Science Web site at science.glencoe.com.

Misconceptions

Find Out What Students Think

Students may think that . . .

- **The floor of the ocean is flat, with no topographic features.**

Students believe that, because they cannot see under the water, the floor of the ocean is flat like the surface of the water that covers it.

Demonstration

Provide students with maps of the ocean floor. Have them discuss the features that they observe. This will allow students to realize that the ocean floor has structures just like those on land.

Promote Understanding

Activity

Materials clay, cardboard shoe box with lid, straws, permanent marker, metric ruler, graph paper, scissors, glue

- Have each group of students use clay to make a model of the ocean floor in their shoe box. Encourage them to include features they noted when examining the map of the ocean floor.

- Have students glue the graph paper to the lids of their boxes. Using the scissors, have them poke straw-sized holes in the box lids at the intersection of every 10 graph-grid boxes. Have them label the grid on the long side of the box with numbers and the short side of the box with letters. The labeled graph paper thus forms a grid system for students to use when sampling. Then direct students to mark the straws in 1 cm increments. These will serve as depth gauges. Each group of students should then exchange models with another group so that they are sampling an "unknown"ocean floor.

- Each team should decide on a method of sampling and then carry it out. They should record their depth measurements on a clean sheet of graph paper, thus making a map showing the topography of the ocean floor.

- Encourage groups to share their results. Have the class discuss which sampling techniques were most useful. Then explain that scientists use sound in the same way that they used the straws to make pictures of the ocean floor.

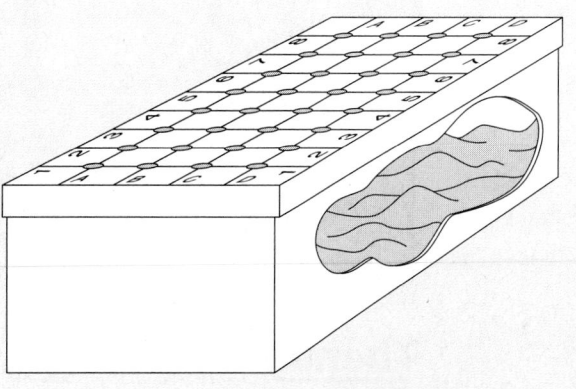

Assess

After completing the chapter, see *Identifying Misconceptions* in the Study Guide.

Oceans

Chapter Vocabulary

What do you think?

Science Journal The picture shows phytoplankton. Phytoplankton are an important food source for many ocean organisms. They also produce much of Earth's oxygen through the process of photosynthesis.

Oceans

Oceans seem so mysterious! Have you ever wondered why oceans taste salty or how oceans affect climates around the world? How do organisms find food and move around in the oceans? In this chapter, you'll learn the answers to these and other ocean mysteries. You'll learn about the composition of seawater. You also will discover what creates ocean waves, tides, and currents and how they affect the surrounding land. Finally, you'll find out about organisms in ocean ecosystems.

What do you think?

Science Journal Examine the photo below. Discuss what you think this might be or what is happening. Here's a hint: *Without these, the oceans would contain little life.* Write your answer or best guess in your Science Journal.

Theme Connection

Systems and Interactions This theme recurs throughout the chapter with explanations of how salts are formed when substances from volcanoes and rivers interact, how winds make waves, how the gravity of the Moon and Sun causes tides, how winds and the Coriolis force affect surface currents, how waves and currents cause shoreline erosion, and how organisms interact through food chains.

Ocean water tastes different from water in most lakes. Its salty taste comes from salts that are dissolved in the water. In the activity below, you will experiment to find out how some of those salts end up dissolved in ocean water.

Infer why oceans are salty

1. Mix five spoonfuls of dry sand with one spoonful of salt in a pie pan.

2. Bend a small section of the edge of the pie pan down so it is level with the bottom of the pan.

3. Hold the edge of the pie pan over a small bowl and sprinkle water on the salt and sand mixture. Don't wash the sand and salt out of the pie pan. Let the water filter through the mixture.

4. Allow the water to collect in the bowl. Place the bowl in sunlight or under a hot lamp and let the water evaporate. Observe what remains.

Observe

Describe in your Science Journal which material the water dissolved as it filtered through the salt and sand. Infer where some of the salt in the oceans comes from.

Before You Read

FOLDABLES
Reading & Study Skills

Making a Main Ideas Study Fold
Make the following Foldable to help you identify the major topics about oceans.

Waves
Life
Currents
Ocean Water

1. Stack two sheets of paper in front of you so the short side of both sheets is at the top.

2. Slide the top sheet up so that about four centimeters of the bottom sheet show.

3. Fold both sheets top to bottom to form four tabs and staple along the top fold. Turn the Foldable so the staples are at the bottom.

4. Label the flaps *Waves*, *Life*, *Currents*, and *Ocean Water*. Use scissors to cut or tear the top flap to look like waves, as shown.

5. As you read the chapter, write information on the tabs.

339

SECTION

1

Ocean Water

1 Motivate

Bellringer Transparency

Display the Section Focus Transparency for Section 1. Use the accompanying Transparency Activity Master. [L2]

[ELL]

Tie to Prior Knowledge

Have students who have visited the ocean describe their experiences with ocean water and how they may have discovered how it tastes. Explain that in this section, they will learn about the origin of the ocean's salts and more about the composition of seawater.

SECTION

1 Ocean Water

As You Read

What You'll Learn

- **State** the importance of Earth's oceans.
- **Discuss** the origin of the oceans.
- **Describe** the composition of seawater.
- **Explain** how temperature and pressure vary with depth.

Vocabulary
salinity
photosynthesis
thermocline

Why It's Important
Oceans affect all people's lives, even those who don't live near the ocean.

Importance of Oceans

Have you looked at a globe and noticed that oceans cover almost three fourths of the planet's surface? A better name for Earth might be "The Water Planet." You might live far away from an ocean, or maybe you've never seen the ocean. But oceans affect all living things—even those far from the shore.

Oceans provide a place for many organisms to live. Oceans transport seeds and animals and allow materials to be shipped across the world. Oceans also furnish people with resources including food, medicines, and salt. Some examples of resources from the ocean are shown in **Figure 1.** The water for most of Earth's rain and snow comes from the evaporation of ocean water. In addition, 70 percent of the oxygen on Earth is given off by ocean organisms.

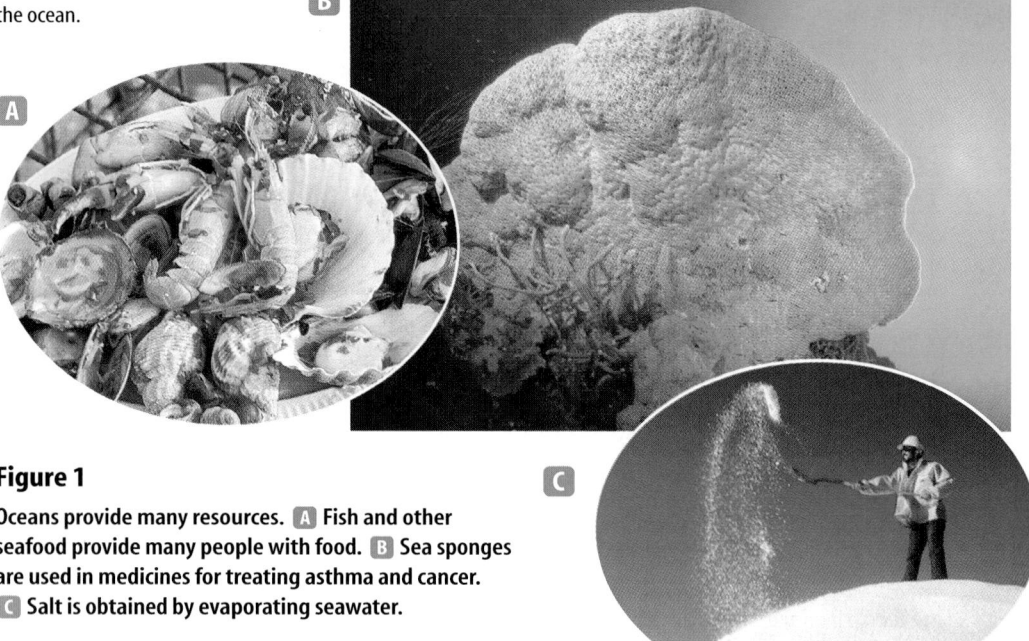

Figure 1

Oceans provide many resources. **A** Fish and other seafood provide many people with food. **B** Sea sponges are used in medicines for treating asthma and cancer. **C** Salt is obtained by evaporating seawater.

340 CHAPTER 12 Oceans

Section ✓*Assessment* Planner

PORTFOLIO
Curriculum Connection, p. 341
PERFORMANCE ASSESSMENT
Skill Builder Activities, p. 344
See page 368 for more options.

CONTENT ASSESSMENT
Section, p. 344
Challenge, p. 344
Chapter, pp. 368–369

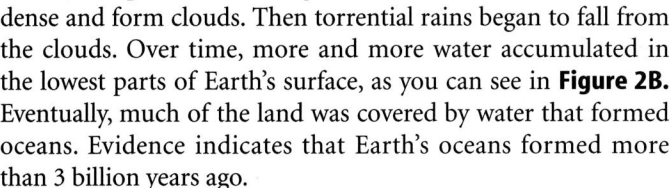

Figure 2
Ⓐ Oceans could have formed from water vapor that was released by volcanoes into Earth's atmosphere. Ⓑ When the water vapor cooled enough to form clouds and rain, water collected in low areas and formed oceans.

Ⓑ

Formation of Oceans

When Earth was still a young planet, many active volcanoes existed, as shown in **Figure 2A.** As they erupted, lava, ash, and gases were released from deep within Earth. The gases entered Earth's atmosphere. One of these gases was water vapor. Scientists hypothesize that about 4 billion years ago, water vapor began accumulating in the atmosphere. Over millions of years, the water vapor cooled enough to condense and form clouds. Then torrential rains began to fall from the clouds. Over time, more and more water accumulated in the lowest parts of Earth's surface, as you can see in **Figure 2B.** Eventually, much of the land was covered by water that formed oceans. Evidence indicates that Earth's oceans formed more than 3 billion years ago.

Composition of Ocean Water

If you taste seawater, you'll know immediately that it tastes different from water you normally drink. As a matter of fact, you really can't drink it. Dissolved substances cause the salty taste. Rivers and groundwater dissolve elements such as calcium, magnesium, and sodium from rocks and carry them to the ocean, as you saw in the Explore Activity. Erupting volcanoes add elements such as sulfur and chlorine to ocean water.

SECTION 1   Ocean Water   **341**

Curriculum Connection

Social Studies Today, oceans are not located in Michigan, Ohio, New York, Texas, Louisiana, or Kansas, but halite, salt from ancient oceans, is being mined in all of these states. Have students research uses for halite and have them write a paragraph about their findings. It is used to season and preserve food, to keep roadways free of winter ice, to soften water, and to manufacture textiles. L2
 **Linguistic** P

---

2 Teach

Formation of Oceans

Composition of Ocean Water

Quick Demo

To demonstrate how much salt seawater usually contains, measure 35 g of table salt with a triple-beam balance. Dissolve the salt in a beaker of 965 mL of water.

IDENTIFYING Misconceptions

Some students may think the ocean floor is flat, with no topographic features. Refer to page 338F for teaching strategies that address this misconception.

Composition of Ocean Water, continued

Discussion

Although the proportion and amount of dissolved salts in seawater remain in equilibrium, would you expect salinity to be constant throughout the oceans? Explain. No; salinity is a measure of the concentration of salt in the water. Evaporation, precipitation, and freezing and thawing of ice affect this concentration. For example, if 35 g of salt are dissolved in 965 mL of water, the concentration is 35 parts per 1,000 parts, or 3.5%. If 100 mL of fresh water are added, the concentration is then 35 parts per 1,100 parts, or 3.18%.

✔ Reading Check

Answer a measure of the amount of solids dissolved in seawater

Visual Learning

Figure 3 What percent of the dissolved solids in seawater are chloride? 55%

Salinity The two most abundant elements in the dissolved salts in seawater are sodium and chlorine. If seawater evaporates, the sodium and chloride ions combine to form a salt called halite. You use this salt to season food. Halite, as well as other salts and substances, give ocean water its unique taste.

Salinity (say LIHN ut ee) is a measure of the amount of solids, or salts, dissolved in seawater. It is measured in grams of dissolved solids per kilogram of water. One kilogram of ocean water usually contains about 35 g of dissolved solids, or 3.5 percent. **Figure 3** shows the most abundant salts in ocean water.

✔ Reading Check   *What is salinity?*

The proportions and amount of dissolved salts in seawater remain in equilibrium. This means that the composition of the oceans is in balance. Despite the fact that rivers, volcanoes, and the atmosphere constantly add substances to the ocean, its composition has remained nearly constant for hundreds of millions of years. Biological processes and chemical reactions remove many of the substances, such as calcium, from ocean water. For example, many organisms, such as oysters and clams, use calcium to make shells. Other marine animals use calcium to make bones. Calcium also can be removed from ocean water through chemical reactions, forming sediment on the ocean floor.

Figure 3
Every kilogram of ocean water contains about 35 g of dissolved solids. Sodium and chloride make up nearly 86 percent of this mass. This graph lists the most abundant dissolved solids.

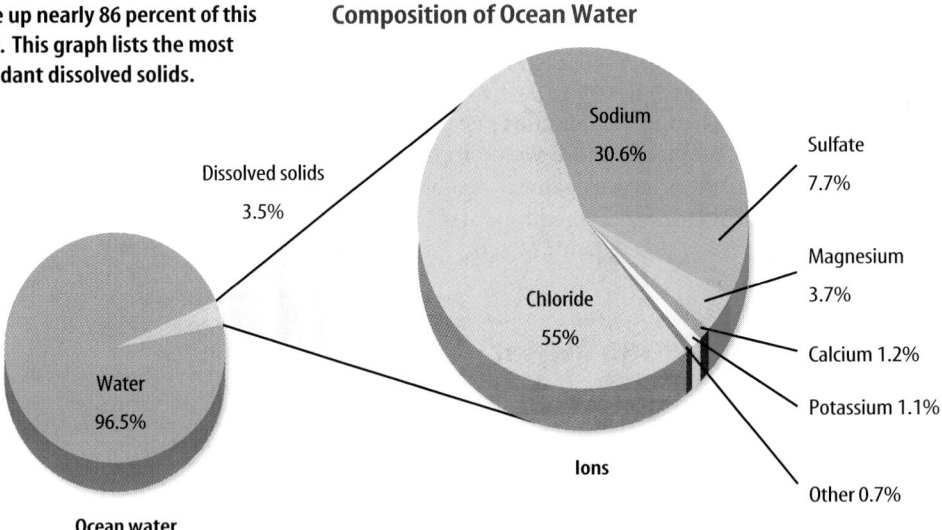

Composition of Ocean Water

Dissolved solids 3.5%

Water 96.5%

Ocean water

Sodium 30.6%

Sulfate 7.7%

Magnesium 3.7%

Chloride 55%

Calcium 1.2%

Potassium 1.1%

Other 0.7%

Ions

Curriculum Connection

Math Salinity is often reported in parts per thousand. The mathematical symbol for parts per thousand is ‰. Ask: **If you sampled water from the Atlantic Ocean and found that the percent of salt is 3.28%, what would the salinity be in parts per thousand?** 32.8‰ L2
IS **Logical-Mathematical**

Cultural Diversity

Middle East In most areas of the world, removing salts from seawater to obtain freshwater is too expensive. However, in arid countries such as Israel, Saudi Arabia, Kuwait, and the United Arab Emirates, the most cost-effective way to obtain freshwater is from seawater. Have students locate these countries on a map and determine the ocean(s) from which they get their water. L2 IS **Visual-Spatial**

Figure 4
Kelp growing in shallow water use sunlight to photosynthesize. During photosynthesis, oxygen is given off and dissolves in the water.

Carbon dioxide + Water $\xrightarrow{\text{Sunlight}}$ Food + Oxygen

Dissolved Gases Although all of the gases in Earth's atmosphere dissolve in seawater, three of the most important are oxygen, carbon dioxide, and nitrogen.

The greatest concentration of dissolved oxygen is near the surface of the ocean. There, oxygen enters seawater directly from the atmosphere. Also, organisms like the kelp in **Figure 4** produce oxygen by **photosynthesis**—a process in which organisms use sunlight, water, and carbon dioxide to make food and oxygen. Because sunlight is necessary for photosynthesis, organisms that carry on photosynthesis are found only in the upper 200 m of the ocean where sunlight reaches. Below 200 m, the level of dissolved oxygen drops rapidly. Here, many animals use oxygen for respiration and it is not replenished. However, more dissolved oxygen exists in very deep water than in water just below 200 m. This cold, deep water originates at the surface in polar regions and moves along the ocean floor.

 **Reading Check** *How does oxygen get into seawater?*

A large quantity of carbon dioxide is absorbed directly into seawater from the atmosphere. Carbon dioxide reacts with water molecules to form a weak acid called carbonic acid. Carbonic acid helps control the acidity of the oceans. In addition, during respiration, organisms use oxygen and give off carbon dioxide, adding more carbon dioxide to the oceans.

Nitrogen is the most abundant dissolved gas in the oceans. Some types of bacteria combine nitrogen with oxygen to form nitrates. These nitrates are important nutrients for plants. Nitrogen is also one of the important building blocks of plant and animal tissue.

SECTION 1 Ocean Water **343**

SCIENCE *Online*

Research Visit the Glencoe Science Web site at **science.glencoe.com** for more information about dissolved gases in the ocean. Make a poster illustrating what you learn.

SCIENCE *Online*
Internet Addresses

_____
_____
_____

Explore the Glencoe Science Web site at **science.glencoe.com** to find out more about topics in this section.

✔ **Reading Check**

Answer Oxygen enters from the atmosphere; it is also produced by organisms during photosynthesis.

Discussion

How do photosynthesis and respiration compare? These processes are opposites. In photosynthesis, producers use carbon dioxide and produce oxygen. In respiration, organisms use oxygen and produce carbon dioxide.

Resource Manager

Chapter Resources Booklet
   Enrichment, p. 31
   Lab Activity, pp. 9–12
Reading and Writing Skill Activities, p. 27

✔ **Active Reading**

Quickwrites This strategy, sometimes called freewrites, lets students use spontaneous writing to discover what they already know. Have students write a list of ideas about a topic, then share these ideas with the class. Next, have students write their ideas freely in a paragraph without worrying about punctuation, spelling, and grammar. Have students use a Quickwrite to share ideas during or after learning about oceans.

Water Temperature and Pressure

Activity

Invite an experienced scuba diver to talk to your class about the effects of high pressure on divers. Ask students to prepare questions for the speaker ahead of time. **IS** **Linguistic**

Caption Answer

Figure 5 It extends to 800 m (or a depth of 500 m).

3 Assess

Reteach

Play a review game. Organize the class into several teams. Have each student write three questions about the material in this section. Collect the questions. Then ask these questions of other teams, one at a time. Encourage members of each team to discuss the questions they are asked and have a team captain report their answers to the class. **L2** **ELL** **COOP LEARN** **IS** **Interpersonal**

Challenge

How does sunlight affect the amount of dissolved oxygen near the ocean's surface? It provides the energy needed for plants to photosynthesize and give off oxygen.

✔Assessment

Oral **What are two reasons for the rapid drop in dissolved oxygen below 200 m?** Light does not penetrate below 200 m, so there is no oxygen being added by photosynthetic organisms; animals living at these depths deplete the oxygen when they respire. **Use Performance Assessment in the Science Classroom, p. 91.**

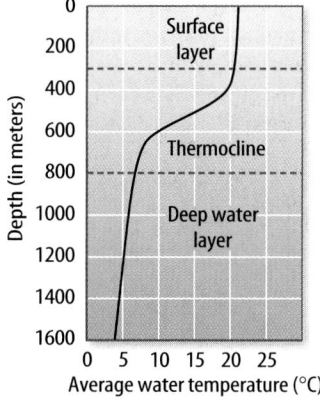

Water Temperature and Depth

Figure 5
The depth of the thermocline varies with location. In the location shown on this graph, the thermocline layer begins at 300 m. *How deep does the thermocline extend?*

Water Temperature and Pressure

Oceans have three temperature layers—the surface layer, the thermocline layer, and the deep-water layer, shown in **Figure 5.** The surface layer is warm because it receives solar energy. The warmest surface water is near the equator where the Sun's rays strike Earth at a direct angle. Water near the poles is cooler because the Sun's rays strike Earth at a lower angle.

The **thermocline** often begins at a depth of about 200 m, but this varies. In this layer, temperature drops quickly with increasing depth. This occurs because solar energy cannot penetrate this deep. Below the thermocline lies the deep-water layer, which contains extremely cold water.

 Physics INTEGRATION

Pressure, or force per unit area, also varies with depth. At sea level, the pressure of the atmosphere pushing down on the ocean surface is referred to as 1 atmosphere (atm) of pressure. An atmosphere is the pressure exerted on a surface at sea level by the column of air above it. As you go below the ocean's surface, the pressure increases because of the force of the water molecules pushing down. The pressure increases by about 1 atm for each 10-m increase in depth.

For example, at a depth of 20 m, a scuba diver would experience a pressure of 3 atm (1 atm of air + 2 atm of water). Divers must carry tanks that supply their lungs with air at the same pressure as the water around them. If they didn't, the water pressure would keep their lungs from inflating when they tried to inhale.

Section 1 Assessment

1. List at least four reasons the oceans are important to you.
2. According to scientific hypothesis, how were Earth's oceans formed?
3. Why does ocean water taste salty?
4. How and why do temperature and pressure vary with ocean depth?
5. **Think Critically** Explain why the compositions of river water and ocean water are not the same.

Skill Builder Activities

6. **Recognizing Cause and Effect** How does animal respiration affect the amount of dissolved oxygen in deeper water? **For more help, refer to the** Science Skill Handbook.

7. **Solving One-Step Equations** The pressure at sea level is 1 atmosphere. If pressure increases by 1 atmosphere for every 10 m in depth, what is the pressure at a depth of 200 m? **For more help, refer to the** Math Skill Handbook.

Answers to Section Assessment

1. Possible answers: for food, medicines, salt, oxygen, water cycle
2. Water vapor from volcanoes cooled and condensed; rains filled basins.
3. It contains dissolved substances.
4. Solar energy heats the upper 200 m. Below 200 m, temperature drops rapidly. Pressure increases with

depth because of the force of the water molecules pushing down.
5. Volcanoes and the atmosphere add additional chemicals to ocean water. Biological processes and chemical reactions in the oceans remove some substances like calcium that are abundant in river water.

6. Respiration removes oxygen.
7. 200 m ÷ 10 m = 20;
   20 × 1 atmosphere + 1 atmosphere = 21 atmospheres

Activity

Desalination

Many people in the world do not have enough freshwater to drink. What if you could remove freshwater from the oceans and leave the salt behind? That's called desalination.

What You'll Investigate
How does desalination produce freshwater?

Materials
large spoon	plastic wrap
table salt	tape
water	large marble
250 mL beaker (2)	
large bowl	

Goals
- **Observe** how freshwater can be made from salt water.
- **Recognize** that water can be separated from salt by the process of evaporation.

Safety Precautions

Wear your safety goggles and apron throughout the experiment.

Procedure
1. Mix a spoonful of salt into a beaker of water.
2. Pour a thin layer of salt water in the bowl.
3. Place the clean beaker in the center of the bowl.
4. Cover the bowl loosely with plastic wrap so the wrap sags slightly in the center. Do not let the plastic wrap touch the beaker.
5. Tape the plastic wrap to the bowl to hold it in place.
6. Place the marble on the plastic wrap over the center of the beaker.

7. Leave the bowl in sunlight until water collects in the beaker. You might have to tap the marble on the plastic wrap lightly to get the water to drop into the beaker.
8. After some water has collected in the beaker, remove the plastic wrap. Let the water in the beaker and the bowl evaporate.
9. After the water has evaporated, rub the bottom of the beaker and the bottom of the bowl with your finger. Notice what you feel.

Conclude and Apply
1. **Describe** what you found remaining in the bowl and in the beaker after all the water had evaporated.
2. What kind of water collected in the beaker—salt water or freshwater? Explain how you know.

*C*ommunicating
Your Data

Make a poster that illustrates how you would make water that you could drink if you were stranded on a deserted island in the middle of the ocean. **For more help, refer to the** Science Skill Handbook.

ACTIVITY 345

Purpose Students use desalination to produce freshwater. L2

ELL **IS** **Visual-Spatial**

Process Skills observing and inferring, drawing conclusions, communicating

Time Required 40 minutes

Safety Precautions Caution students to wear safety goggles throughout the experiment.

Teaching Strategy Use a light with a reflector to reduce the time it takes to evaporate the water.

Answers to Questions
1. The bowl contained salt, the beaker did not.
2. Freshwater; there was no salt left after the water was evaporated.

✔*Assessment*

Process Inform students that many precious metals are dissolved in seawater. **Is it practical to remove these metals using desalination?** It would require large volumes of seawater. The time and energy required to retrieve the metals would make this a very expensive process. Use **Performance Assessment in the Science Classroom**, p. 91.

Resource Manager

Chapter Resources Booklet
  Reinforcement, p. 27
  Activity Worksheet, pp. 5–6
Cultural Diversity, p. 27

*C*ommunicating
Your Data

Students should illustrate how seawater is collected, water is evaporated, and water vapor is collected and cooled.

Ocean Currents and Climate

SECTION

Ocean Currents and Climate

1 Motivate

Bellringer Transparency

Display the Section Focus Transparency for Section 2. Use the accompanying Transparency Activity Master. L2

ELL

As You Read

What You'll Learn

■ **State** how wind and the rotation of Earth influence surface currents.
■ **Discuss** how ocean currents affect weather and climate.
■ **Describe** the causes and effects of density currents.
■ **Explain** how upwelling occurs.

Vocabulary
surface current
density current
upwelling

Why It's Important
Ocean currents affect weather and climate.

Surface Currents

Ocean water never stands still. Currents move the water from place to place constantly. Ocean currents are like rivers that move within the ocean. They exist both at the ocean's surface and in deeper water. Major surface currents and winds are shown in **Figure 6.**

Causes of Surface Currents Powered by wind, **surface currents** usually move only the upper few hundred meters of seawater. When the global winds blow on the ocean's surface, they can set ocean water in motion. Because of Earth's rotation, the ocean currents that result do not move in straight lines. Earth's rotation causes surface ocean currents in the northern hemisphere to curve to the right and surface ocean currents in the southern hemisphere to curve to the left. You can see this in **Figure 6.** This turning of ocean currents is an example of the Coriolis effect.

Tie to Prior Knowledge

Have students recall what they learned about ocean salinity and temperature in the last section. In this section, they will learn how salinity and temperature affect deep ocean currents.

Caption Answer

Figure 6 clockwise

Figure 6
Earth's global winds create surface currents in the oceans.
Which way do currents rotate in the northern hemisphere?

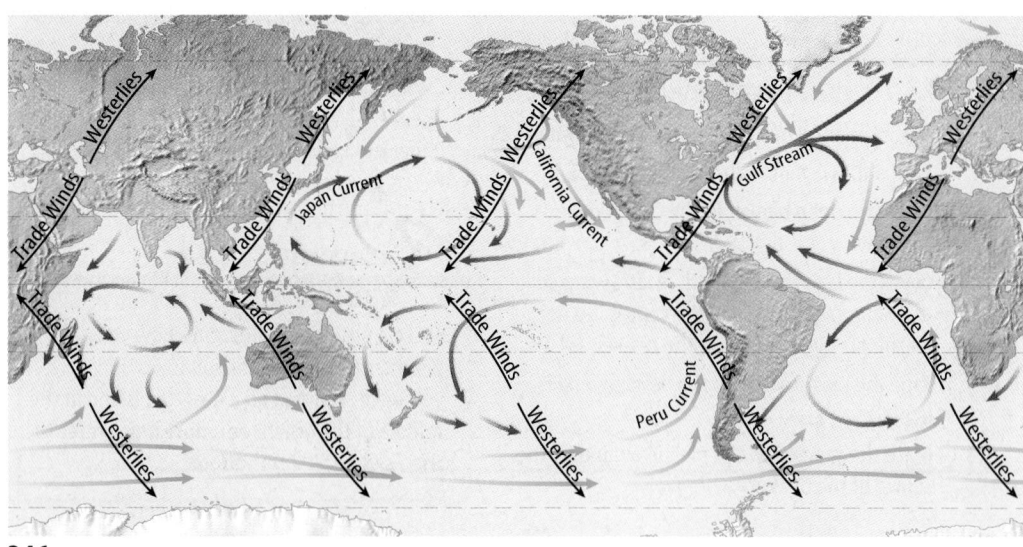

Section ✓ Assessment Planner

PORTFOLIO
Cultural Diversity, p. 349
PERFORMANCE ASSESSMENT
MiniLAB, p. 349
Skill Builder Activities, p. 350
See page 368 for more options.

CONTENT ASSESSMENT
Section, p. 350
Challenge, p. 350
Chapter, pp. 368–369

The Gulf Stream Much of what is known about surface currents comes from records kept by early sailors. Sailing ships depended on certain surface currents to carry them west and others to carry them east. One of the most important currents for sailing east across the North Atlantic Ocean is the Gulf Stream. This 100-km wide current was discovered in the 1500s by Ponce de Leon and his pilot Anton de Alaminos. In 1770, Benjamin Franklin published a map of the Gulf Stream drawn by Captain Timothy Folger, a Nantucket whaler.

The Gulf Stream, shown in **Figure 7,** flows from Florida northeastward toward North Carolina. There it curves toward the east and becomes slower and broader. Because the Gulf Stream originates near the equator, it is a warm current. Look back at **Figure 6.** Notice that currents on eastern coasts of continents, like the Gulf Stream, are usually warm, while currents on western coasts of continents are usually cold. Surface currents like the Gulf Stream distribute heat from equatorial regions to other areas. This can influence the climate of regions near these currents.

✓ **Reading Check** *What kind of current is the Gulf Stream?*

SCIENCE *Online*

Research Visit the Glencoe Science Web site at **science.glencoe.com** to learn more about the Gulf Stream and other surface currents. Communicate to your class what you learn.

Figure 7
In this satellite image, the warm water of the Gulf Stream appears red and orange.

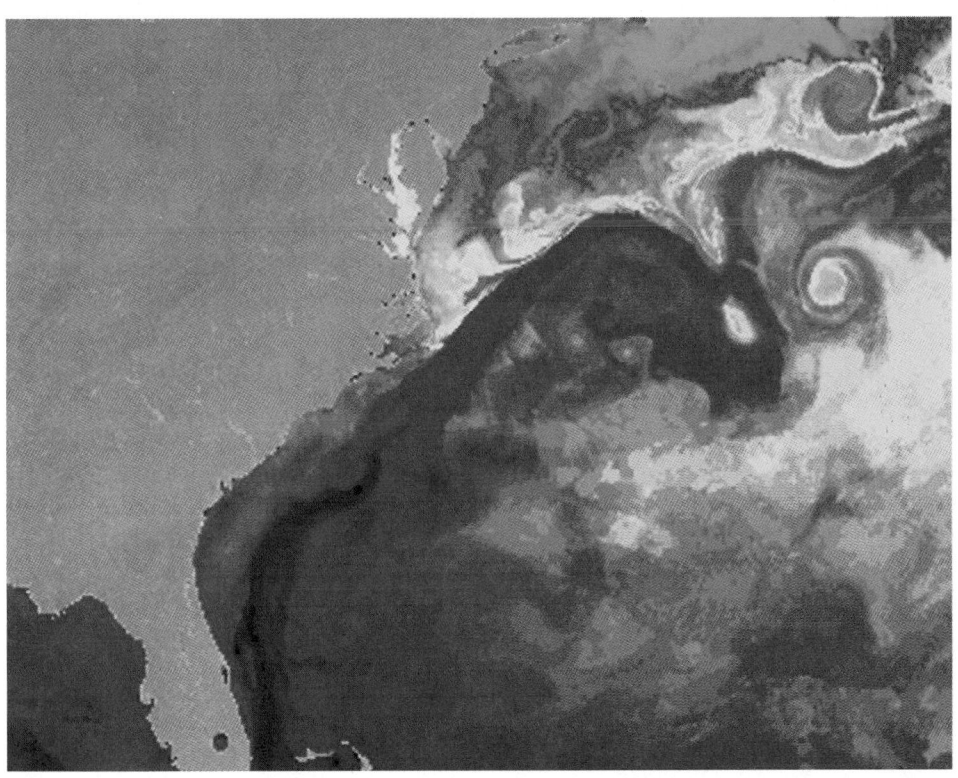

Surface Currents

Discussion

Why are currents along the eastern coasts of continents usually warm while those along the western coasts are cold? Currents along eastern coasts originate at the equator, where the amount of energy absorbed from the Sun is the greatest; currents along western coasts originate at high latitudes where water receives less solar energy.

✓ **Reading Check**

Answer warm surface current

Fun Fact

The Gulf Stream transports more than 50 times the combined volume of water that flows from all of Earth's rivers.

Visual Learning

Figure 7 Have students locate the Atlantic coast. Have them describe the temperature of the Gulf Stream along this coast. Possible answer: temperature of Gulf Stream is warmest at its origin and gets cooler as you go north. L2

LS Visual-Spatial

Resource Manager

Chapter Resources Booklet
Transparency Activity, p. 47
Directed Reading for Content Mastery, p. 20

Earth Science Critical Thinking/Problem Solving, p. 16

Teacher **FYI**

At lower latitudes, the Gulf Stream Current is narrow and fast moving. Along the southeastern shore of Florida, the current flows at an average velocity of 2 m per second. In this area, the width of the stream is about 80 km. Further north the Gulf Stream widens to over 450 km.

Density Currents

Chemistry
INTEGRATION

Increased salinity means an increase in the amount of dissolved solids. Therefore, when salinity increases, mass increases. When temperature increases, molecules move apart, and volume increases.

IDENTIFYING
Misconceptions

Most students know that ice floats on water. Students may think that this is true of many chemicals. Explain that the characteristic of the solid ice being less dense than the liquid water is unique to H_2O.

Teacher FYI
In September, the surface water temperature off Charleston, South Carolina is 27°C. Off San Diego, California, the surface water temperature is only 19°C. Both cities are at the same latitude.

Figure 8
A The warm water of the Gulf Stream helps moderate Iceland's climate. **B** The harbor at Reykjavik (RAY kyuh vihk), Iceland's capital, remains free of ice all year long.

Chemistry
INTEGRATION

The formula for determining density is mass/volume. When salinity increases, does it affect mass or volume? When temperature increases, does it affect mass or volume?

Climate As an example of how surface currents affect climate, locate Iceland on the map in **Figure 8A.** Based on its location and its name, you might expect it to have a cold climate. However, the Gulf Stream flows past Iceland. The current's warm water heats the surrounding air and keeps Iceland's climate mild and its harbors ice free year-round, as shown in **Figure 8B.**

Cold Surface Currents The currents on the western coasts of continents carry colder water back toward the equator. In **Figure 6,** find the California Current off the west coast of North America and the Peru Current along the west coast of South America. They are examples of cold surface currents. The California Current affects the climate of coastal cities. For example, San Francisco has cool summers and many foggy days because of the California Current.

Density Currents

In water at a depth of more than a few hundred meters, winds have no effect. Instead, currents develop because of differences in the density of the water. A **density current** forms when more dense seawater sinks beneath less dense seawater. Seawater becomes more dense when it gets colder or becomes more salty.

A density current exists in the Mediterranean Sea. In this sea, lots of water evaporates from the surface, leaving salts behind. Therefore, the remaining water is high in salinity. This more dense water sinks and moves out into the less dense water of the Atlantic Ocean. At the surface, less dense water from the Atlantic flows into the Mediterranean Sea.

LAB DEMONSTRATION

Purpose to observe the effects of temperature on water density

Materials 2 large beakers, 2 small beakers, hot plate, ice, water, food coloring, dropper

Preparation Use the large beakers to melt ice and heat water. Add a few drops of food coloring to the ice water.

Procedure Pour some of the warm water into a small beaker. Use a dropper to place some of the ice water on top of the warm water. Repeat the experiment, placing a few drops of warm water into a small beaker of ice water.

Expected Outcome The ice water sinks into the warm water.

✔Assessment

Infer why water sank in one beaker, but not in the other. Cold water is denser than warm water, and so it sank through the less dense warm water. The less dense warm water floated on the denser cold water.

Cold and Salty Water An important density current that affects many regions of Earth's oceans begins north of Iceland. In the winter months, the water at the surface starts to freeze. When water freezes, dissolved salts are left behind in the unfrozen water. Therefore, this unfrozen water is very dense because it is cold and salty. It sinks and slowly flows along the ocean floor toward the southern Atlantic Ocean, as shown in blue in **Figure 9.** There it spreads into the Indian and Pacific Oceans. As the water is sinking near Iceland, warm surface water of the Gulf Stream, shown in red, moves northward from the equator to replace it. The Gulf Stream water warms the continents that border the North Atlantic.

Density Currents and Climate Change Suppose density currents near Iceland stopped forming. Some scientists hypothesize that this has happened in Earth's past and could happen again. Increasing carbon dioxide concentrations in Earth's atmosphere could trap more of the Sun's heat, raising Earth's temperature. If Earth's temperature rose enough, ice couldn't easily form near the polar regions. Freshwater from melting glaciers on land also could reduce salinity of the ocean water. The density currents would weaken or stop. Scientists hypothesize that if dense water stopped flowing along the ocean bottom toward the southern Atlantic Ocean, warm water would no longer flow northward on the surface to replace the missing water. All of Earth could experience drastic climate shifts including changing rainfall patterns and temperatures.

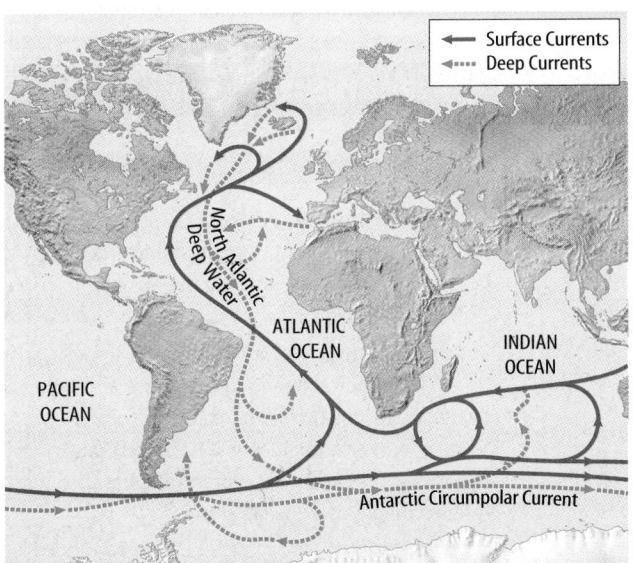

Surface Currents
Deep Currents

North Atlantic Deep Water

PACIFIC OCEAN

ATLANTIC OCEAN

INDIAN OCEAN

Antarctic Circumpolar Current

Figure 9
Like a giant conveyor belt, cold, salty water sinks in the northern Atlantic Ocean and flows southward, while warm surface water flows northward from the equator to replace it.

Modeling a Density Current

Procedure 🌊 🖐 🏊

1. Fill a **paper cup** three-fourths full of **water.**
2. Add two spoonfuls of **salt** and three drops of **food coloring** to the water. Stir with a **spoon** to dissolve the salt.
3. Push one **thumbtack** into the cup 1 cm from the bottom of the cup and another 3 cm from the bottom.
4. Carefully place the cup into a **clear-plastic box** and fill the box with water until the water level in the box is about 0.5 cm above the top tack.
5. Remove both tacks at the same time and record in your **Science Journal** what you observe.

Analysis

1. Infer what is happening at the two holes in the cup.
2. Make a sketch to describe the current's direction.
3. Explain what causes the density current to form.

Purpose Students model a density current. L2

🔲 **Visual-Spatial**

Materials paper cup, water, spoon, salt, food coloring, metric ruler, 2 thumbtacks, clear plastic box

Teaching Strategy Caution students to be careful when handling thumbtacks.

Analysis

1. At the top hole, freshwater enters the cup. At the bottom hole, salt water leaves the cup.
2. Sketches should show the MiniLAB setup. An arrow labeled "salt water" should point down and away from the bottom hole; an arrow labeled "freshwater" should point up to the top hole.
3. Salt water is denser than freshwater. As it sinks, it pushes the less dense freshwater up.

✔ Assessment

Oral Will a density current form where rivers enter an ocean? No, the less dense fresh water will remain as a layer on top of the denser salt water. Use **Performance Assessment in the Science Classroom,** p. 89.

Resource Manager

Chapter Resources Booklet
    MiniLAB, p. 3
    Enrichment, p. 32
    Reinforcement, p. 28

Cultural **Diversity**

Upwelling and Industry Off Peru's coast, phytoplankton live on nutrients brought to the surface by upwelling. The phytoplankton are eaten by anchovies. Many Peruvians work in factories that process fishmeal and fish oil from these anchovies. Have students infer and write a paragraph about what happens when the upwelling does not occur. Industry collapses; many people are out of work. P

Upwelling

Quick Demo

On the overhead, pour colored ice water into a rectangular, glass baking dish. Carefully place warm water on top of the cold water so that the warm water does not mix with the ice water. Use a spoon to gently pull the warm water away from the side of the dish. Students should see the colored water rise to the surface, representing an upwelling.

3 Assess

Reteach

Use **Figure 6** to review surface current directions.
L1 IS **Visual-Spatial**

Challenge

Ask students what they think the Gulf Stream would look like if the Isthmus of Panama were covered with water. Possible answer: Since surface currents are deflected by land masses, part of the Gulf Stream would be "lost" by flow between the now-separated continents of North and South America. The resulting current may not be as strong as the present Gulf Stream.

✔Assessment

Process Explain that currents that originate at the equator move faster than currents that originate at higher latitudes. Have students use **Figure 6** to identify fast-moving currents. Any current on the east coast of a continent is fast-moving. Use **PASC**, p. 89.

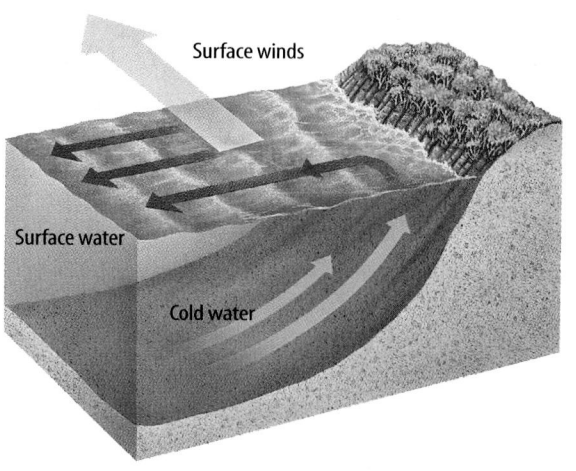

Figure 10
Winds push water away from shore along the South American coastline. This creates an upwelling of cold water.

Upwelling

An **upwelling** is a current in the ocean that brings deep, cold water to the ocean surface. This occurs along some coasts where winds cause surface water to move away from the land. Wind blowing parallel to the coast carries water away from the land because of the Coriolis effect. **Figure 10** shows upwelling as it occurs off the coast of Peru. Notice that when surface water is pushed away from the coast, deep water rises to the surface to take its place. This cold, deep water continually replaces the surface water that is pushed away from the coast.

The cold water contains high concentrations of nutrients produced when dead organisms decayed at depth. This concentration of nutrients causes tiny marine organisms to flourish and fish to be attracted to areas of upwelling. Upwelling also affects the climate of coastal areas. Upwelling contributes to San Francisco's cool summers and famous fogs.

El Niño During an El Niño (el NEEN yoh) event, the winds blowing water from the coast of Peru slacken, the eastern Pacific is warmed, and upwelling is reduced or stops. Without nutrients provided by upwelling, fish and other organisms cannot find food. Thus, the rich fishing grounds off of Peru are disrupted.

Section ② Assessment

1. How do winds create surface currents?
2. How does the rotation of Earth modify ocean currents in the northern hemisphere?
3. Why is surface water cooler near San Diego, California, than Charleston, South Carolina?
4. What causes the density current in the Mediterranean Sea?
5. **Think Critically** Explain why temperatures could decrease in some regions of Earth if global warming occurred.

Skill Builder Activities

6. **Comparing and Contrasting** Compare and contrast density currents and upwelling in the ocean. **For more help,** refer to the Science Skill Handbook.
7. **Communicating** Density currents are sometimes called thermohaline currents. Use a dictionary to look up *thermohaline.* In your Science Journal, explain why it is a good word to describe these currents. **For more help,** refer to the Science Skill Handbook.

Answers to Section Assessment

1. They push the water.
2. Surface currents curve to the right.
3. CA: currents originate in northern latitudes; SC: currents originate at the equator.
4. Surface evaporation produces salty, dense water. It sinks, and less dense Atlantic water flows in to replace it.

5. Density currents that form north of Iceland could become weak or stop. Warm water would no longer flow northward to warm the land.
6. Both involve vertical movement of water. A density current is caused by differences in salinity and temperature. An upwelling is caused when

wind causes surface water to move away from shore.
7. *Thermohaline* means "dependent on the effects of temperature and salinity." Density currents are affected by both temperature and salinity.

Waves

Waves Caused by Wind

Have you ever wanted to surf? By catching a high, curled wave, you can ride all the way to the beach. A **wave** in water is a rhythmic movement that carries energy through the water. Waves that surfers ride could have originated halfway around the world. Whenever wind blows across a body of water, friction pushes the water along with the wind. If the wind speed is great enough, the water begins piling up, forming a wave. Three things affect the height of a wave: the speed of the wind, the length of time the wind blows, and the distance over which the wind blows. A fast wind that blows over a long distance for a long time creates huge waves. Once a wave forms, it can travel a great distance. But when winds stop blowing, waves stop forming.

Parts of a Wave Each wave has a crest, its highest point, and a trough, its lowest point. Wave height is the vertical distance between the crest and trough. The wavelength is the horizontal distance between the crests or troughs of two successive waves. **Figure 11** shows the parts of a wave.

In the open ocean, most waves have heights of 2 m to 5 m. Ocean waves rarely reach heights of more than 15 m. However, storm winds can produce waves more than 30 m high—taller than a six-story building—that can capsize even large ships.

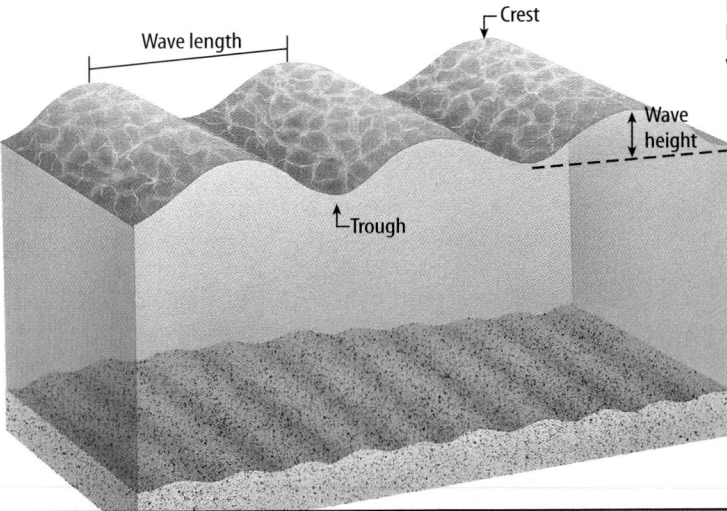

As You Read

What You'll Learn
- **Describe** how wind can form ocean waves.
- **Explain** the movement of water particles in a wave.
- **Describe** how the Moon and Sun cause Earth's tides.
- **List** the forces that cause shoreline erosion.

Vocabulary
wave
tide

Why It's Important
Wave erosion affects life in coastal regions.

Figure 11
Every wave has a crest, trough, wavelength, and wave height.

Section ✔*Assessment* Planner

PORTFOLIO
Science Journal, p. 352
PERFORMANCE ASSESSMENT
Try at Home MiniLAB, p. 352
Skill Builder Activities, p. 354
See page 368 for more options.

CONTENT ASSESSMENT
Section, p. 354
Challenge, p. 354
Chapter, pp. 368–369

SECTION

Waves

1 Motivate

Bellringer Transparency

Display the Section Focus Transparency for Section 3. Use the accompanying Transparency Activity Master. L2
ELL

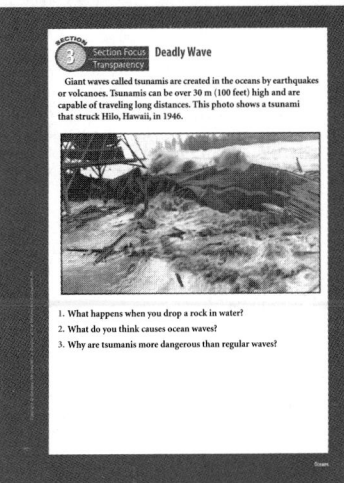

Tie to Prior Knowledge

Have students who have experience with ocean water describe how ocean waves look. Also, encourage students to describe the changing tides. Explain that in this section, students will learn what causes waves and tides.

Resource Manager

Chapter Resources Booklet
Transparency Activity, p. 48
Directed Reading for Content Mastery, p. 21
Lab Activity, pp. 13–16

② Teach

Waves Caused by Wind

Use an Analogy

When a rollerblader suddenly stops, friction stops the wheels, but the person's body keeps moving forward because of inertia. As a result, the person tumbles forward. In a breaking wave, friction with the ocean floor slows the bottom of the wave. The top of the wave keeps moving. In time, the wave breaks over on itself.

TRY AT HOME Mini LAB

Purpose Students model water particle movement in a wave.
L2 ELL IS Kinesthetic
Materials large bowl, water, penny, toothpick, spoon
Teaching Strategy Remind students to make gentle waves.
Analysis
1. The waves moved to the other end of the bowl. The toothpick stayed in position over the penny.
2. Both stay in about the same place as a wave passes.

✔Assessment

Oral Why was the penny used in the MiniLAB? It gave the observer a point of reference for keeping track of the toothpick's movement. Use **Performance Assessment in the Science Classroom**, p. 91.

✔ Reading Check

Answer The top of a wave is not slowed by friction, but the bottom is. When the top overtakes the bottom, the wave collapses and a breaker forms.

Figure 12
As a wave moves by, individual particles of water move around in circles. As a wave approaches shore, wavelength decreases and wave height increases. Eventually the bottom of the wave cannot support the top, and the wave falls over on itself, creating a breaker.

TRY AT HOME Mini LAB

Modeling Water Particle Movement

Procedure
1. Fill a large **bowl** with **water** and place a **penny** on the bottom in the center of the bowl.
2. Float a small piece of **toothpick** in the bowl directly above the penny.
3. Gently dip a **spoon** into the water to make small waves.

Analysis
1. Compare and contrast the movement of the waves and the toothpick.
2. Compare the movement of the toothpick with the movement of water particles in a wave.

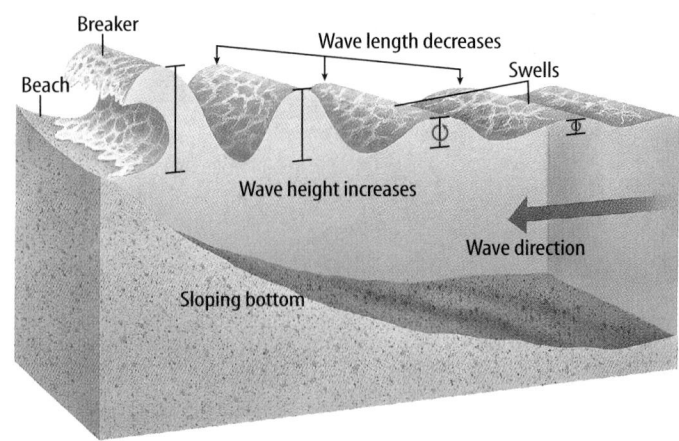

Wave Motion When you observe an ocean wave, it looks as though the water is moving forward. But unless the wave is breaking onto shore, the water does not move forward. Each molecule of water stays in about the same place in a passing wave. If you want to demonstrate how particles move in a wave, tie a ribbon to the middle of a rope. Then hold one end of the rope and have someone else hold the other end. Wiggle the rope until a wave starts moving toward the other person. Notice that the wave travels through the rope to the other person, but the ribbon moves only in small circles, not forward.

Breakers As a wave approaches a shore, it changes shape. Friction with the ocean floor slows the water at the bottom of the wave. Notice in **Figure 12** that as the bottom of the wave slows, the crest and trough come closer together and the wave height increases. Because the top of the wave is not slowed by friction, it moves faster than the bottom. Eventually, the wave top overtakes the bottom, and the wave collapses. Water tumbles over on itself. This collapsing wave is called a breaker. Breakers make the best waves for surfers to ride. After a wave breaks onto shore, gravity pulls the water back into the sea.

✔ **Reading Check** *What causes breakers to form?*

Along smooth, gently sloping coasts, waves deposit eroded sediments on shore, forming beaches. Beaches extend inland as far as the tides and waves are able to deposit sediments.

Waves usually approach a shore at slight angles. This creates a longshore current of water, which runs parallel to the shore. As a result, beach sediments are moved sideways. Longshore currents carry many metric tons of loose sediment from one beach to another.

Teacher FYI

A wave becomes a breaker when the depth of the water equals one-half the wavelength. When this occurs, friction begins to slow the bottom of the wave.

Science Journal

Sand Journey Have each student imagine that he or she is a grain of sand on a beach. Have them write stories in which they describe how tides, wind-driven waves, and longshore currents affect their movements along the beach. Encourage students to be creative. Suggest that they make sketches to accompany their stories. L2 ELL IS **Linguistic and Visual-Spatial** P

Tides

Throughout a day, the water level at the ocean's edge changes. This rise and fall in sea level is called a **tide.** A tide is a giant wave that can be thousands of kilometers long but only 1 m to 2 m high in the open ocean. As the crest of this wave reaches shore, sea level rises to form high tide. Later in the day, the trough of the wave reaches shore and sea level drops. This is low tide. The difference between sea level at high tide and low tide is the tidal range. The tidal range in some coastal areas can be as much as 20 m.

Causes of Tides Tides are not created by wind. They are created by the gravitational attraction of Earth and the Moon and Earth and the Sun. The Moon and Earth are relatively close together in space, so the Moon's gravity exerts a strong pull on Earth. This gravity pulls harder on particles closer to the Moon than on particles farther from the Moon, causing two bulges of water to form. One bulge forms directly under the Moon and one on the opposite side of Earth. As Earth rotates, these bulges move to follow the Moon on its daily passage. The crests of these bulges are high tides. Between these bulges are troughs that create low tides.

The Sun's gravity also affects the tides. When the Moon, Earth, and Sun line up together, the high tides are higher and the low tides are lower than normal, creating spring tides. When the Sun, Earth, and Moon form a right angle, high tides are lower and low tides are higher than normal, creating neap tides. **Figure 13** illustrates this effect.

SCIENCE Online

Collect Data Visit the Glencoe Science Web site at **science.glencoe.com** for data on tidal ranges around the world. Communicate to your class what you learn.

Figure 13
As the Moon and Earth revolve around a common center of mass, a bulge of water forms on the side of Earth closest to the Moon and on the side opposite the Moon.

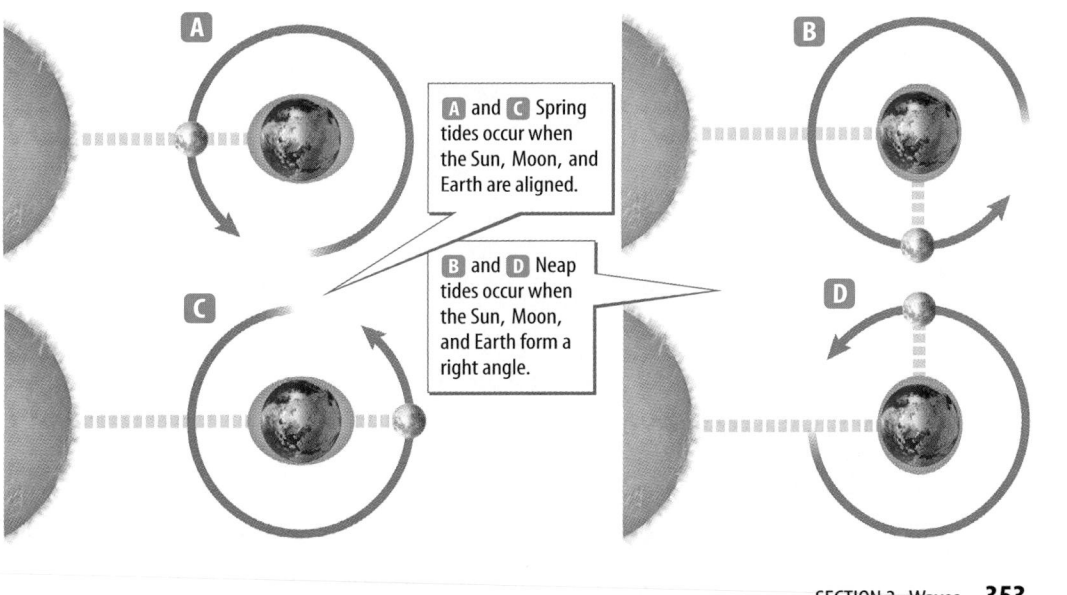

A and C Spring tides occur when the Sun, Moon, and Earth are aligned.

B and D Neap tides occur when the Sun, Moon, and Earth form a right angle.

SECTION 3 Waves **353**

Wave Erosion

Extension

Have students research the effectiveness of using groins to reduce beach erosion. Have them make diagrams to show how groins work. L2 ELL

LS **Kinesthetic**

Reteach

In order to demonstrate the movement of water particles in a wave, use the analogy of spectators in a stadium. Have five or more students line up their chairs side-by-side. Have them stand up and sit down in a precise order that imitates wave motion. Lead students to realize that as the wave motion moves down the row, the people do not move horizontally. COOP LEARN

LS **Kinesthetic and Interpersonal**

Challenge

Inform students that the waves north of Antarctica are extremely large. Challenge them to examine a world map and infer what may lead to these large waves. There are no landmasses to block the wind. The long distance over which the wind blows results in the formation of giant waves.

Assessment

Process Compare and contrast tides and most other surface waves. Tides, like all waves, have crests, troughs, and wavelengths. Tides are caused by the gravitational attraction of Earth and the Moon and Earth and the Sun. Most other surface waves are formed by wind. Use **PASC**, p. 99.

Figure 14
In a single day about 14,000 waves will crash onto this rocky shore.

Wave Erosion

Waves can erode many meters of land in a single season. They wear away rock at the base of rocky shorelines, as shown in **Figure 14.** Then overhanging rocks fall into the water, leaving a steep cliff. Houses built on ocean cliffs can be damaged or destroyed by the erosion below. At Tillamook Rock, Oregon, storm waves hurled a 61-kg rock high into the air. The rock crashed through the roof of a building 30 m above the water.

Beach Erosion Sandy shorelines also can be eroded by waves. Large storms and hurricanes can produce waves that move much of the sand from the beach and can destroy large parts of some nearshore islands. Longshore currents also can erode beaches. This happens most often when people build structures called groins that extend out into the water. Although groins may protect beaches in some places, they often cause erosion elsewhere.

Section Assessment

1. How does wind create waves? What factors determine the size of waves?
2. How does a water particle move in a wave? What causes a wave to break?
3. What causes tides? How do spring tides and neap tides differ?
4. How can waves erode shorelines?
5. **Think Critically** If a storm arrives at a beach during high tide, why is erosion especially damaging?

Skill Builder Activities

6. **Recognizing Cause and Effect** The city of Snyderville keeps pumping sand onto its beach, but the sand keeps disappearing. Explain where it is going. **For more help, refer to the** Science Skill Handbook.

7. **Using a Word Processor** Use a word processing program to write a creative poem about wave motion. **For more help, refer to the** Technology Skill Handbook.

Answers to Section Assessment

1. Friction from the wind pushes the water along. Factors affecting size include speed of the wind, length of time the wind blows, and distance over which the wind blows.
2. Water particles move in a circle. A wave breaks when its top overtakes its bottom.

3. gravitational attraction of Earth and the Moon and Earth and the Sun; spring tides: large tidal range; neap tides: small tidal range
4. The force of breaking waves removes sediments.
5. The combination of strong storm waves and high tide exposes more beach area to erosion.

6. Some sand is carried down the beach by the longshore current. Some is carried by waves and deposited offshore.
7. Poems should be both creatively written and accurate in their descriptions.

Life in the Oceans

Types of Ocean Life

Different types of organisms live in different parts of the ocean. Where an organism lives determines whether it is classified as plankton, nekton, or a bottom dweller.

Plankton Tiny marine organisms that float in the upper layers of oceans are called **plankton.** Most plankton are one-celled organisms, such as the diatoms (DI uh tahmz) pictured in **Figure 15B.** Some plankton can swim, but most drift with currents. You would need a microscope to see most of these organisms. Examples of animal plankton include eggs of ocean animals, very young fish, larvae jellyfish and crabs, and tiny adults of some organisms. **Figure 15A** shows a tiny jellyfish about 2 cm in diameter, and **Figure 15C** shows the eggs of corals being released into the water where they will float.

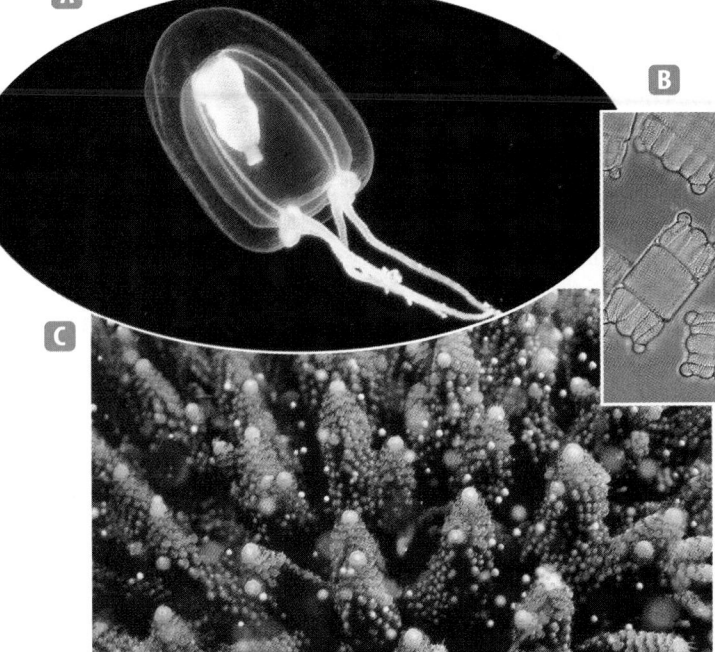

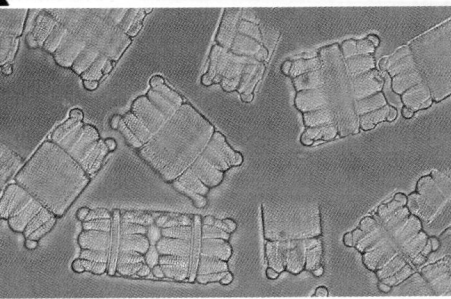

A

B

C

As You Read

What You'll Learn

- **Describe** the characteristics of plankton, nekton, and bottom-dwelling organisms.
- **Distinguish** among producers, consumers, and decomposers.
- **Discuss** how energy and nutrients are cycled in the oceans.
- **Explain** how organisms in the oceans interact in food chains.

Vocabulary

plankton	chemosynthesis
nekton	consumer
ecosystem	decomposer
producer	food chain

Why It's Important

Marine organisms provide people with much of the food they need to survive.

Figure 15
Plankton, such as tiny jellyfish **A** and diatoms **B**, are found in the surface waters of every ocean. **C** The eggs of corals are found only in warm ocean waters around reefs.

SECTION 4 Life in the Oceans **355**

SECTION

4

Life in the Oceans

1 Motivate

Bellringer Transparency

 Display the Section Focus Transparency for Section 4. Use the accompanying Transparency Activity Master. L2
ELL

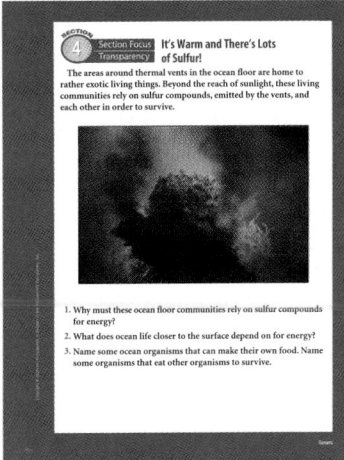

Tie to Prior Knowledge

Have students describe marine organisms they have seen at the beach or on nature programs on television. Explain that in this section, they will learn how these organisms are classified and how they interact.

Resource Manager

Chapter Resources Booklet
Transparency Activity, p. 49
Directed Reading for Content Mastery, pp. 21, 22
Physical Science Critical Thinking/Problem Solving, p. 23

Section ✔*Assessment* Planner

PORTFOLIO
Extension, p. 357
PERFORMANCE ASSESSMENT
Problem-Solving Activity, p. 358
Skill Builder Activities, p. 361
See page 368 for more options.

CONTENT ASSESSMENT
Section, p. 361
Challenge, p. 361
Chapter, pp. 368–369

Section 4 Life in the Oceans **355**

Types of Ocean Life

Use Science Words

Word Meaning Have students find out why jellyfish larvae and very young fish are called *zoo-plankton*, while diatoms and some other protists are called *phytoplankton*. *Zoo-* means animal; jellyfish larvae and young fish are animals. *Phyto-* means plant; like plants, diatoms and some other protists make their own food. *Plankton* means to wander or drift. Jellyfish larvae, very young fish, and diatoms drift in the surface currents. L2 IS **Linguistic**

Extension

Have students write biographies of important ocean explorers and researchers. Some people they might wish to study are Eugenie Clark, Sylvia Earl, Robert Ballard, Jacques-Yves Cousteau, William Beebe, Otis Barton, and Auguste Piccard. L2 IS **Linguistic**

Make a Model

Have students use chenille stems, aluminum foil, and duct tape to make models of marine organisms. After models are completed, have each student share whether his or her organism is plankton, nekton, or a bottom-dweller. Have students demonstrate how their organisms move and acquire food. L2 ELL COOP LEARN IS **Kinesthetic and Interpersonal**

Figure 16
Swimming animals, such as this anglerfish (left), are nekton.

Nekton Animals that can actively swim, rather than drift in the currents, are called **nekton.** Fish, whales, shrimp, turtles, and squid are nekton. Swimming allows these animals to search more areas for food. Some nekton, such as herring, come to the surface to feed on plankton, but others remain in deeper water.

Some of the nekton that live in the dark abyss of the deepest parts of the ocean have organs that produce light, which attracts live food. Shown in **Figure 16,** an anglerfish dangles a luminous lure over its head. When small animals like these shrimp bite at the lure, the anglerfish swallows them whole.

Bottom Dwellers Some organisms live on the ocean bottom. They can burrow in sediments, walk or swim on the bottom, or can be attached to the seafloor.

Bottom-dwelling animals include anemones, crabs, corals, snails, starfish, and some fish. Many of these animals, such as sea cucumbers, eat the partially decomposed matter that sinks to the ocean floor. Some, such as the sea star in **Figure 17A,** prey on other bottom dwellers. Others that are attached to the bottom, such as sponges, filter food particles from the water. Still others, such as anemones, corals, and the sea fans shown in **Figure 17B,** are found in coral reefs. They capture organisms that swim by.

Figure 17
Bottom dwellers vary greatly.
🅐 Many sea stars feed on other bottom dwellers such as clams.
🅑 Sea fans live attached to the bottom and cannot move from place to place.

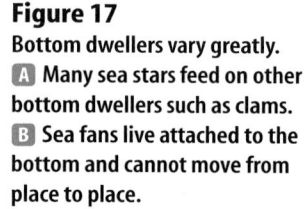

Inclusion Strategies

Learning Disabled Have students collect pictures of marine organisms from magazines. They should classify the organisms as plankton, nekton, or bottom-dwellers and mount the pictures on poster board for display in the classroom. L1 IS **Visual-Spatial**

Curriculum Connection

Literature Many authors have written about the oceans. Examples include Jules Verne's *Twenty Thousand Leagues Under the Sea*, Ernest Hemingway's *The Old Man and the Sea*, Yukio Mishima's "The Sound of Waves," Rachel Carson's *The Sea Around Us*, and Herman Melville's *Moby Dick*. Have students choose one of these to read. Have them share excerpts with their classmates. L2 ELL IS **Linguistic**

Ocean Ecosystems

The oceans are home to many different kinds of organisms. No matter where organisms live, they are part of an ecosystem. An **ecosystem** is a community of organisms and the nonliving factors that affect them, such as sunlight, water, nutrients, sediment, and gases. Every ecosystem has producer, consumer, and decomposer organisms.

Producers Producer organisms, such as those shown in **Figure 18,** form the base of all ecosystems. **Producers** are organisms that can make their own food. Producers near the ocean's surface contain chlorophyll. This allows them to make food and oxygen during photosynthesis.

In deep water, where sunlight does not penetrate, producers that use chlorophyll can't survive. In this part of the ocean, producers make food by a process called **chemosynthesis.** *Chemo* means "chemical." This process often takes place along mid-ocean ridges where hot water circulates through the crust. Bacteria produce food using dissolved sulfur compounds that escape from hot rock. The bacteria then are eaten by organisms such as crabs and tube worms.

Consumers and Decomposers Consumer and decomposer organisms depend upon producers for survival. Organisms that eat, or consume, producers are called **consumers.** Consumers get their energy from the food stored in the producers' cells. Some also eat other consumers to get energy. When producers and consumers die, decomposers digest them. **Decomposers,** such as bacteria, break down tissue and release nutrients and carbon dioxide back into the ecosystem.

> ✔ **Reading Check** *What is a consumer?*

Life Science INTEGRATION

Most fish have an organ called a swim bladder that regulates their buoyancy. By inflating or deflating the bladder, fish move up or down in the water column. If a swim bladder inflates, will the fish rise or sink? Why does a scuba diver wear a buoyancy vest?

Figure 18
Ⓐ Producers can be large like this sea grass. Ⓑ Sometimes they are as small as this microscopic algae. *What do all producers have in common?*

Magnification: 100×

Ocean Ecosystems

Activity

Show a video that features ocean organisms in their natural habitats. During the movie, have students list the producers and consumers they see. At the conclusion of the movie, have students share and discuss their lists. L2 ELL COOP LEARN
IS **Visual-Spatial and Interpersonal**

Extension

In 1977, Robert Ballard discovered organisms living in vents along the Mid-Atlantic Ridge. Have students research Ballard's trip and make poster displays of his discoveries. L2
IS **Linguistic and Visual-Spatial** P

Life Science INTEGRATION

The fish will rise. A scuba diver can regulate his or her buoyancy by inflating the vest to rise in the water column or by deflating it to sink.

> ✔ **Reading Check**

Answer an organism that gets energy from food stored in producers' and other consumers' cells

Caption Answer

Figure 18 All producers make their own food.

Resource Manager

Chapter Resources Booklet
　Enrichment, p. 34

Home and Community Involvement, p. 38

Life Science Critical Thinking/Problem Solving, p. 10

Curriculum Connection

Art Have student groups select a marine ecosystem to study in depth. Suggested ecosystems include sandy coastal region, coral reef, kelp forest, mid-ocean ridge, open water, and deep-ocean sea floor. After researching the ecosystem, have each group make a diorama of the ecosystem. L2 ELL IS **Kinesthetic**

Ocean Ecosystems,
continued

Discussion

As a result of rising temperatures in some oceans, some types of plankton are dying. **What effect will this have on the food webs in these areas?** Consumers that normally eat these plankton will have to depend on other food sources. If other food is not available, some consumers will die. Consumers that eat these consumers may also be affected. With additional organisms dying, decomposers will thrive.

Food Chains Throughout the oceans, energy is transferred from producers to consumers and decomposers through **food chains.** In **Figure 19,** notice that algae (producers) are eaten by krill that are, in turn, eaten by Adélie penguins. Leopard seals eat the penguins, and killer whales eat the leopard seals. At each stage in the food chain, energy obtained from one organism is used by other organisms to move, grow, repair cells, reproduce, and eliminate wastes. Energy not used in these life processes is transferred along the food chain.

All ecosystems have many complex feeding relationships. Most organisms depend on more than one species for food. Notice in **Figure 19** that krill eat more than algae and in turn are eaten by animals other than Adélie penguins. In the Antarctic Ocean, as in all ecosystems, food chains are interconnected to form highly complex systems called food webs.

Problem-Solving Activity

Are fish that contain mercury safe to eat?

When mercury, once used in pesticides, is added to oceans or bodies of fresh-water, bacteria change it to methyl mercury, which is a more toxic form of mercury. Fish then absorb the methyl mercury from the water as it flows over their gills or as they feed on aquatic organisms. Larger fish feed on the smaller fish, and humans often eat larger fish. The following table lists the methyl mercury ranges for a variety of fish.

Identifying the Problem

The average methyl mercury present in each fish is given in the chart in parts per million (ppm). The detection limit is 0.10 ppm. Any values less than 0.10 ppm are shown as ND (not detected). The FDA's (Food and Drug Administration) safe limit for human consumption is 1 ppm. Which species of fish could put you in danger of mercury poisoning if you eat them?

Solving the Problem

1. Which of the fish listed do not contain any methyl mercury? Explain.

Methyl Mercury Content in Domestic Fish		
Species	**Range (ppm)**	**Average (ppm)**
Catfish	ND–0.16	ND
Cod	ND–0.17	0.13
Crab	ND–0.27	0.13
Flounder	ND	ND
Halibut	0.12–0.63	0.24
Salmon	ND	ND
Tuna (canned)	ND–0.34	0.20
Tuna (fresh)	ND–0.76	0.38
Swordfish	0.36–1.68	0.88
Shark	0.30–3.52	0.84

2. The FDA limit of 1 ppm is ten times lower than levels found in fish that have caused illness. The FDA recommends eating shark or swordfish no more than once a week. Does this appear consistent with the information given in the data table? Explain. Which fish could you safely eat as often as you wanted?

Inclusion Strategies

Gifted Have students find out the meaning of the word *biodiversity* and make a collage of an ocean ecosystem. They should show and label many different life-forms, including micro as well as macro. Have them explain why biodiversity is important in ocean food webs. Biodiversity refers to the many different types of life that exist in an ecosystem. Complex food webs depend on biodiversity. If certain species become extinct, branches of the food web collapse. Remaining species will become more dependent on fewer sources of food. L3 **Linguistic**

Figure 19

A food web represents a network of interconnected food chains. It shows how energy moves through an ecosystem—from producers to consumers and eventually to decomposers. This diagram shows a food web in the Antarctic Ocean. Arrows indicate the direction in which energy is transferred from one organism to another.

B Some consumers get energy from one primary source. For example, crabeater seals, despite their name, dine almost exclusively on krill.

C Other consumers, such as the killer whale and the leopard seal, eat several different types of organisms to gain the energy they need.

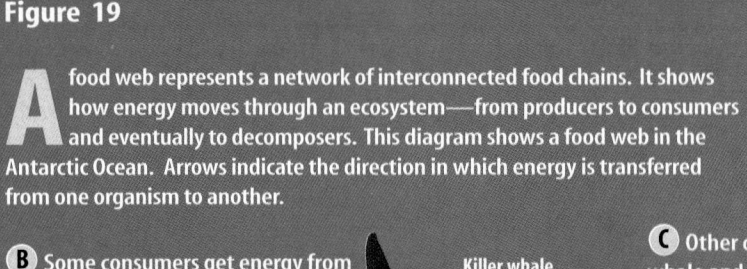
Killer whale

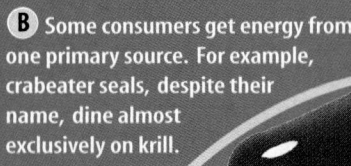
Crabeater seal

Leopard seal

Weddell seal

Adelie penguin

Cod

Squid

Small animals and other organisms

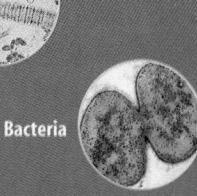
Krill   Algae

A All food chains begin with a producer—in this case, photosynthetic algae that drift through polar seas.

D Decomposers feed on wastes and dead organisms and return nutrients to the ecosystem in the process. In this way, decomposers are a vital link in the food web.

Bacteria

359

Visualizing Food Chains in a Food Web

Have students examine the pictures and read the captions. Then ask the following questions.

What might happen to the food web if overfishing greatly reduced the number of krill in the Antarctic Ocean? Possible answer: Other organisms that feed on krill would not have enough food. Many of these organisms might die of starvation and organisms that feed on them would then not have enough food.

What would happen if there were no decomposers in a food web? Wastes and the remains of dead organisms would accumulate in the ecosystem, and nutrients would not be returned to the ecosystem.

Activity

Have small groups of students select one organism within the food web to represent. Each student should make a sign indicating which organism he or she represents. Students should then stand in the proper order as each one describes what he or she represents and does in the food chain. For example, one student might say, "I am algae and I produce food by using the Sun's energy."

Extension

Challenge students to research the effects of overharvesting marine organisms on food webs in different areas of the ocean. Have students present oral reports on their findings.

Resource Manager

Chapter Resources Booklet
   Transparency Activity, pp. 51–52
Mathematics Skill Activities, p. 33
Cultural Diversity, p. 3

Ocean Nutrients

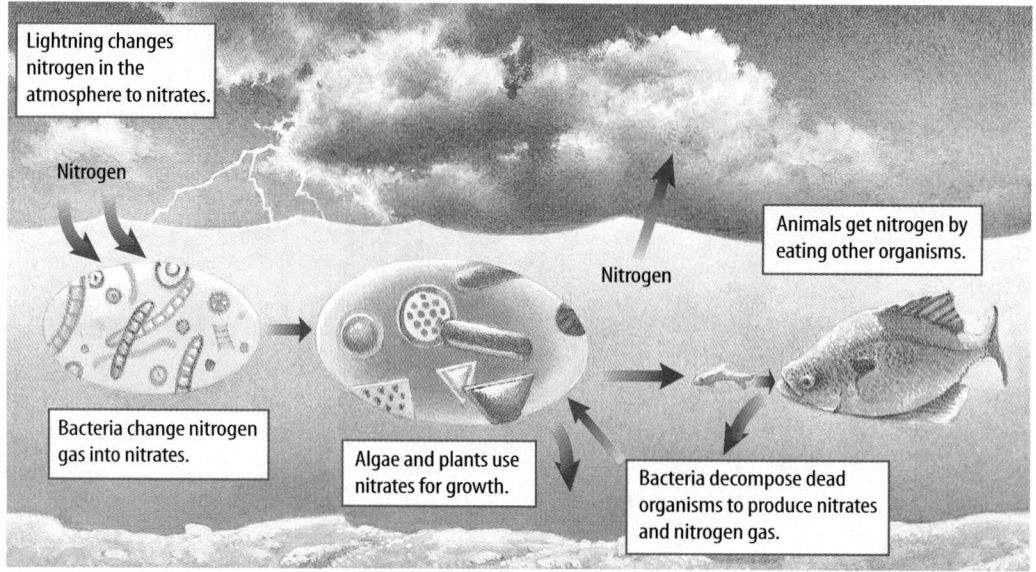

Lightning changes nitrogen in the atmosphere to nitrates.

Nitrogen

Animals get nitrogen by eating other organisms.

Nitrogen

Bacteria change nitrogen gas into nitrates.

Algae and plants use nitrates for growth.

Bacteria decompose dead organisms to produce nitrates and nitrogen gas.

Figure 20
Nitrogen cycles from nitrogen gas in the atmosphere to nitrogen compounds and back again.

Figure 21
Carbon cycles through the ocean and between the ocean and the atmosphere.

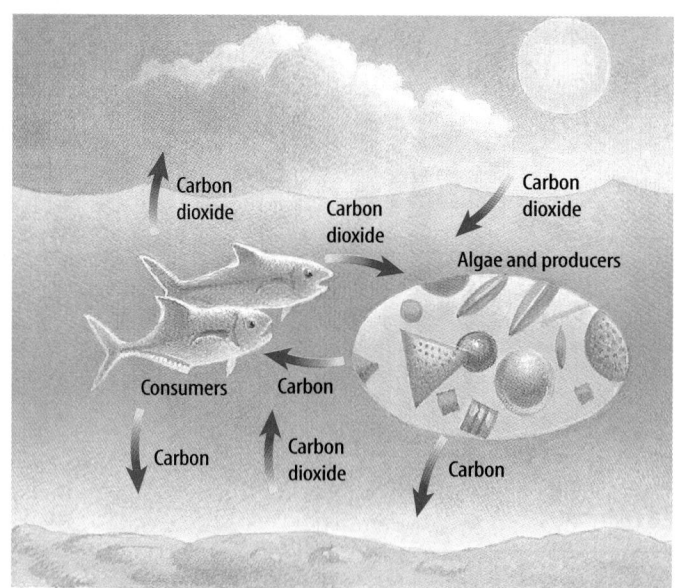

Carbon dioxide

Carbon dioxide

Carbon dioxide

Algae and producers

Consumers

Carbon

Carbon

Carbon dioxide

Carbon

Carbon dioxide

Ocean Nutrients

Nearly everything in an ecosystem is recycled. When organisms respire, carbon dioxide is released back into the ecosystem. When organisms excrete wastes or die and decompose, nutrients are recycled. All organisms need certain kinds of nutrients in order to survive. For example, plants need nitrogen and phosphorus. **Figure 20** shows how nitrogen cycles through the ocean.

Carbon also is recycled. You learned earlier in this chapter that oceans absorb carbon dioxide from the atmosphere. You also learned that producers use carbon dioxide to make food and to build their tissues. Carbon then can be transferred to consumers when producers are eaten. When organisms die and sink to the bottom, some carbon is incorporated into marine sediment. Over time, carbon is exchanged slowly between rocks, oceans, the atmosphere, and organisms, as seen in **Figure 21.**

Figure 22
Parrot fish are efficient recycling organisms. They turn coral into fine sand as they graze on the algae in the coral.

Extension
Have students write reports on the possible causes and results of coral bleaching. L2
IS **Linguistic**

3 Assess

Reteach
Display photographs of marine organisms. Have students classify each organism as plankton, nekton, or bottom-dweller; producer, consumer, or decomposer. L1 IS **Visual-Spatial**

Challenge
What are some ways that terrestrial ecosystems and marine ecosystems interact?
Possible answer: Sea birds and certain kinds of fish belong to food webs in both ecosystems; pollution on land is carried to the oceans by water and air; oxygen, carbon dioxide, and nitrogen cycle through both ecosystems.

Coral Reefs and Nutrient Recycling Coral reefs are ecosystems that need clear, warm, sunlit water. Each coral animal builds a hard calcium carbonate capsule around itself. Inside the animals' cells, live algae that provide the animals with nutrients and give them color. As corals build one on top of another, a reef develops. Other bottom-dwelling organisms and nekton begin living on and around the reef. Nearly 25 percent of all marine species and 20 percent of all known marine fish live on coral reefs. Coral reefs generally form in tropical regions in water no deeper than 30 m.

A healthy reef maintains a delicate balance of producers, consumers, and decomposers. Energy, nutrients, and gases are cycled among organisms in complex food webs in a coral reef. Look at **Figure 22** to see one example of how materials are cycled through a coral reef.

✔ Assessment

Process Ask students to infer an advantage nekton have over animal plankton when it comes to finding food. Because nekton actively swim, they are able to search more areas for food than can animal plankton, which rely on drifting in currents. Use **Performance Assessment in the Science Classroom,** p. 89.

Section 4 Assessment

1. List the characteristics of producers, consumers, and decomposers.
2. How is carbon cycled through the oceans? How is nitrogen cycled?
3. List the characteristics of plankton, nekton, and bottom-dwelling organisms.
4. Explain why every ecosystem must include producers as well as other organisms.
5. **Think Critically** Why are some organisms considered to be plankton in one stage of their life but nekton in another stage of their life?

Skill Builder Activities

6. **Forming Hypotheses** Write a hypothesis about how an increase in the amounts of ocean nutrients might affect plankton. **For more help, refer to the** Science Skill Handbook.

7. **Communicating** Invent a new sea creature. In your Science Journal, explain how it gets its energy and where it lives. Classify it as a producer, consumer, or decomposer and as plankton, nekton, or bottom dweller. Sketch your creature and draw its food chain. **For more help, refer to the** Science Skill Handbook.

Answers to Section Assessment

1. Producers: make own food; consumers: eat other organisms; decomposers: break down tissue, release nutrients and CO_2
2. Carbon: producers use CO_2 to make food; carbon is transferred to consumers when producers are eaten; animals and plants respire CO_2.

Carbon is deposited in organic sediments. Nitrogen: cycles from plant tissue to animal tissue to bacteria; bacteria produce nitrogen gas and nitrates; plants use nitrates.
3. Plankton: float in currents; nekton: actively swim; bottom-dwellers: live on bottom, some attached, some walk or swim.

4. Producers make food and oxygen that other organisms need to survive.
5. In the egg and larval stage, they drift in currents; as adults, they swim.
6. With more nutrients, plankton will increase in number and mass.
7. Creatures will vary.

Activity

Recognize the Problem

Purpose

Students will model waves and tides and infer how erosion might occur in the model.

Process Skills

designing and making a model, predicting, comparing, analyzing data

Time Required

45 minutes

Thinking Critically

Discussion

Ask students to describe what they see if they throw a pebble into a pond. Waves move outward from the place where the pebble contacted the water. Then ask them to think about other ways they have made waves in a bathtub or a swimming pool.

Possible Materials

Battery-operated fans reduce the risk of shock and are available at camping supply and hardware stores.

Alternate Materials

If fans that must be plugged into an electrical outlet are used, be sure to caution students not to let the fan or the cord get wet and not to touch the fan and the water at the same time.

Safety Precautions

Remind students to immediately wipe up any water that spills on the floor.

Activity *Model and Invent*

Waves and Tides

The water in coastal regions is subject to the same forces as water in the open ocean. Daily high and low tides affect the water level, and waves are involved in shoreline erosion. How can you simulate ocean waves and represent tidal changes in water level? How will the tides affect the amount of erosion in various areas?

Recognize the Problem

How can you model ocean waves and tides in the classroom?

Thinking Critically

Can you simulate waves and tides along the edge of an ocean using a basin of water in the classroom?

Goals

- ■ **Construct** a model of the edge of the ocean.
- ■ **Demonstrate** how you can simulate waves and tides in your model.
- ■ **Predict** how erosion might occur in your model.

Possible Materials

large basin
water
boards
sand
*gravel
bricks
rocks
plastic bottles
fan (battery-operated)
*Alternate materials

Safety Precautions

362 CHAPTER 12 Oceans

SCIENCE Online

Internet Addresses

_____

_____

_____

Explore the Glencoe Science Web site at **science.glencoe.com** to find out more about topics in this activity.

Cultural **Diversity**

Bore Rafting In Nova Scotia's Bay of Fundy rising tide water forms tidal bores in some rivers. A tidal bore is a large wave that flows upstream and reverses the river's flow. In these rivers, bore rafting is a popular sport. It combines the thrill of white-water rafting with bird watching, as eagles, ospreys, and seabirds fish the incoming tidal waters.

Planning the Model

1. **Determine** how you are going to create a model of the edge of the ocean. Draw a picture of what your model will look like.

2. Decide how you will create waves and tides in your model. What can you use to move the water? How can you simulate tides by changing how high the water level is?

3. **Predict** where in your model erosion may occur and where it may not. How might you be able to see where erosion will occur?

Check the Model Plans

1. **Compare** your model plans with those of other students in the class. Discuss why each of you chose the design you did.

2. Make sure that your teacher approves your model plans before you construct your model.

Making the Model

1. **Construct** your model based on your design plans.

2. Create waves in your model and observe what happens.

Record your observations in your Science Journal.

3. Change the tide by changing the water level and repeat step 2.

Analyzing and Applying Results

1. **Describe** what you observed when you created waves and tides in your ocean model.

2. Were you able to see any evidence of erosion in your model? If so, in what areas of your model was erosion present and where was it absent? If not, where would you expect to see erosion over a longer period of time? Explain.

3. Did the waves you created always look the same or did they seem to vary in wave height or wavelength? Explain. Did you see anything that

looked like breakers as the waves hit the shore?

4. In what ways was your model similar to and different from the edge of a real ocean? What features were you able to simulate and what features were missing from your model?

Communicating Your Data

Discuss with your family or students in other classes how ocean waves and tides affect erosion along the edge of oceans.

Planning the Model

Teaching Strategies Remind students not to make waves so large that they splash water out of the basin.

Troubleshooting Students may not observe any erosion if they don't generate waves consistently for a period of time.

Making the Model

Expected Outcome

Most results will show that beach erosion occurs as a result of wave action, and that erosion increases at high tide.

Analyzing and Applying Results

1. Waves push sand up onto some parts of the beach and carry it away in other parts. The process occurs higher up the beach when the tide is high.

2. Answers will depend on the model of shoreline created. All models should be expected to show erosion over a period of time.

3. Answers will depend on the method used to generate waves and the structure of the shoreline model.

4. Answers will depend on the model created, but students might not be able to model sea cliffs.

✔ Assessment

Process Show students photographs of large storm waves striking a shoreline and ask them what effect these waves would have on a shoreline. Use **Performance Assessment in the Science Classroom,** p. 89.

Communicating Your Data

Students could use a word processing program to outline the major points they want to make in their discussion.

Science Stats

Ocean Facts

Did You Know...

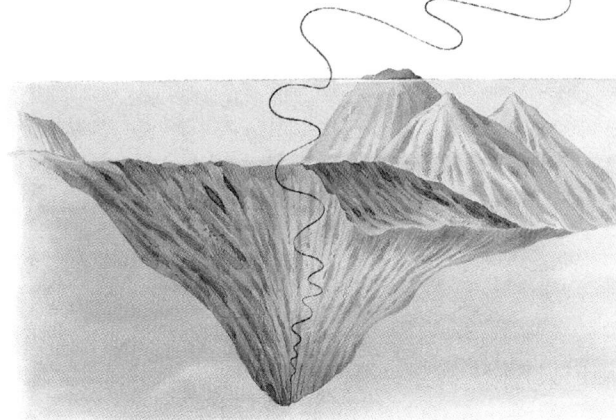

Content Background

In many ways the world under the oceans is similar to the landscape on dry ground. Mountains, valleys, and volcanoes give the ocean floor a varied topography. Stretching from the edges of continents are continental shelves, with an average width of 70 km and depth of about 145 m. From the continental shelf the sea floor drops off to the abyssal plain, which lies at a depth of about 4,000 m. Seamounts are underwater volcanoes that rise over 1,000 m from the ocean floor. Trenches form where the oceanic lithosphere sinks into Earth's mantle. In 1960, the bathyscaphe *Trieste* made the deepest dive ever—10,911 m—into the Marianas Trench.

Discussion

Why do you think scientists' knowledge of the ocean has grown so much in the last 60 years? Possible answer: It was very difficult to explore the deep parts of the ocean because of the cold temperatures and tremendous pressures until the development of technologies such as scuba gear, submersibles, and robots.

Activity

Have small groups of students research the history of undersea exploration and make illustrated timelines of some important discoveries and the technologies that allowed those discoveries to be made.

. . . The deepest place in the ocean is the Marianas Trench, located east of the Philippines. The deepest part of the Marianas Trench is the Challenger Deep, which extends 11,035 m down. That's deep enough to hold Mount Everest and the world's five tallest buildings stacked on top of one another.

. . . The oceans contain enough salt to cover Earth with a layer 15 stories high. The average salt content of the world's major oceans and seas is about 3.5 percent. Some isolated bays and lagoons can contain as much as 10 percent salt during certain seasons.

364 CHAPTER 12 Oceans

SCIENCE
Online
Internet Addresses

_____

_____

_____

Explore the Glencoe Science Web site at **science.glencoe.com** to find out more about topics in this feature.

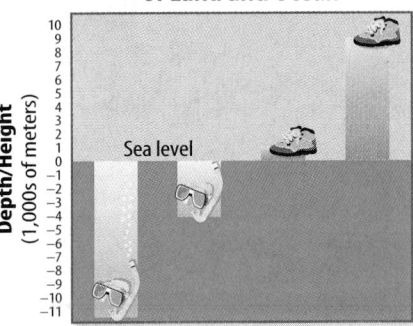

. . . The area of the Pacific Ocean, 165 million km², is greater than all the land on Earth combined—146 million km².

. . . Although the Arctic Ocean is the smallest ocean, it is larger than the area of the United States, which is about 9 million km².

Comparison of Land and Ocean

Depth/Height (1,000s of meters)

Sea level

Marianas Trench | Average ocean depth | Average land height | Mount Everest

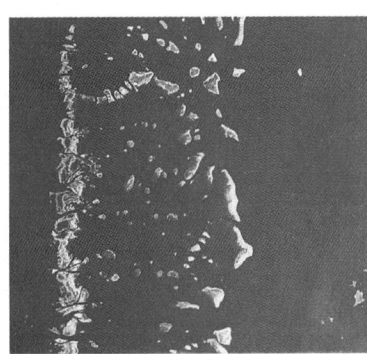

Great Barrier Reef

. . . At more than 2,000 km long, the Great Barrier Reef in the Coral Sea is the largest organic structure on Earth and can be seen clearly from space.

Do the Math

1. The average depth of the ocean is 3,730 m. About how many times deeper than this average depth is the Marianas Trench?
2. Use the graph to find out about how much deeper the Marianas Trench is than Mount Everest is high.
3. The Indian Ocean's total area is 73.6 million km², and the Arctic Ocean's total area is 14.1 million km². How many times larger is the Indian Ocean than the Arctic Ocean?

Go Further

Go to **science.glencoe.com** to find the surface area of the three largest oceans. Make a graph showing the relative sizes of these oceans.

Teaching Strategies

- Remind students to read the question carefully in order to choose the correct operation. They should choose division to calculate the answer for the first question in Do the Math.
- Remind students that estimating before doing any computation will help them know if their answer is reasonable. Tell students to first round both numbers and estimate the answer before doing the subtraction in the second question in Do the Math.
- Remind students that they can drop the *millions* in the numbers before doing the division in the third question in Do the Math.

Answers

1. almost 3 times as deep; $11,035 \div 3,730 = 2.96$
2. about 2,000 m; 11,035 m — 8,800 m = 2,235 m
3. a little more than 5 times as large; $73.6 \div 14.1 = 5.22$

Go Further

Discuss with students which type of graph would be best for presenting this type of information—a bar graph, a circle graph, or a line graph.

Visual Learning

Height and Depth Comparison of Land and Ocean Ask students how many meters each number on the side of the graph represents. 1,000 meters Then ask them to compare the average ocean depth with average land height. The average ocean depth is about 4,000 m, while the average land height is about 1,000 m, so the average ocean depth is about 4 times as great as the average land height. **How would this change if sea levels rose?** Answer: The average ocean depth would increase, while the average land height would decrease.

Reviewing Main Ideas

Preview

Students can answer the questions in their Science Journals. Discuss the answers as you go through the chapter. **Linguistic**

Review

Students can write their answers, then compare them with those of other students. **Interpersonal**

Reteach

Students can look at the illustrations and describe details that support the main ideas of the chapter. **Visual-Spatial**

Answers to Chapter Review

SECTION 1

4. 30 m ÷ 10 m = 3;
3 × 1 atmosphere + 1 atmosphere = 4 atmospheres

SECTION 3

3. Waves have worn away the rocks, creating a rugged coastline.

SECTION 4

1. nekton

Chapter 12 Study Guide

Reviewing Main Ideas

Section 1 Ocean Water

1. Oceans provide much of the oxygen and food for Earth's organisms. Oceans interact with the atmosphere to create weather and climate.

2. Scientists think early oceans formed when basins filled with water that condensed from the water vapor of erupting volcanoes.

3. Seawater is a combination of water, dissolved solids, and dissolved gases.

4. Ocean temperatures vary with latitude and depth. Water pressure is created by gravity pulling down water molecules. *What pressure would the scuba diver, shown here, experience at 30 m?*

Section 2 Ocean Currents and Climate

1. Winds blowing across oceans produce surface currents. Earth's rotation deflects surface currents.

2. Ocean surface currents can be warm or cold. The Gulf Stream is a warm surface current. The California Current and the Peru Current are cold surface currents. Ocean currents affect the climates of coastal regions.

3. Density currents develop because water masses have different temperatures and salinity. Upwelling occurs when winds push surface water away from a coast and cold, deep water rises to take its place. During an El Niño event, upwelling is reduced or stops.

Section 3 Waves

1. Winds cause water to pile up, forming waves.

2. Tides are created by the gravitational attraction of Earth and the Moon and Earth and the Sun.

3. Waves constantly erode shorelines. *How have waves affected the shoreline shown here?*

Section 4 Life in the Oceans

1. Plankton drift in ocean currents, and nekton actively swim. Some organisms live on the seafloor. *Which type of organism is the shark shown here?*

2. In an ecosystem, producers, consumers, and decomposers interact with each other and their surroundings.

3. Nutrients like nitrogen, phosphorus, and carbon are cycled in the oceans.

FOLDABLES Reading & Study Skills

After You Read

To help you review the major topics about oceans, use the Foldable you made at the beginning of the chapter.

FOLDABLES Reading & Study Skills

After You Read

After students have read the chapter and completed the Foldable described in Before You Read, have them do the activity on the student page.

Visualizing Main Ideas

Complete the following concept map about types of ocean organisms.

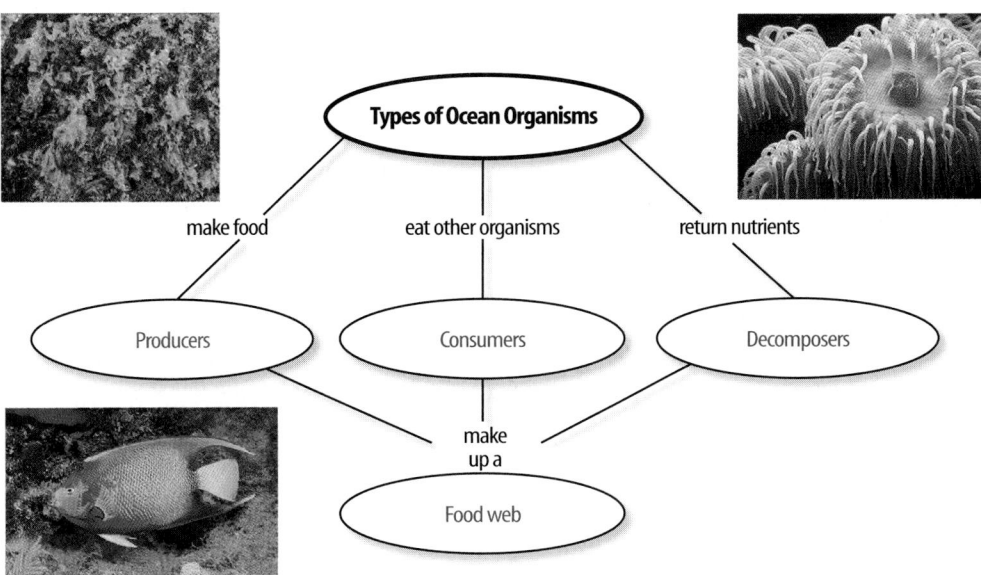

Types of Ocean Organisms

make food — eat other organisms — return nutrients

Producers — Consumers — Decomposers

make up a

Food web

Visualizing Main Ideas

See student page.

Vocabulary Review

Using Vocabulary

1. Plankton float in the upper layers of oceans.
2. Organisms that get their energy from eating other organisms are consumers.
3. Waves are caused by wind blowing across oceans.
4. Density currents are caused by differences in the ocean water's salinity.
5. The layer of ocean water where the temperature drops quickly with depth is the thermocline.

Vocabulary Review

Vocabulary Words

a. chemosynthesis
b. consumer
c. decomposer
d. density current
e. ecosystem
f. food chain
g. nekton
h. photosynthesis
i. plankton
j. producer
k. salinity
l. surface current
m. thermocline
n. tide
o. upwelling
p. wave

THE PRINCETON REVIEW **Study Tip**

Copy your own notes from class. As you do, explain each concept in more detail to make sure that you understand it completely.

Using Vocabulary

The sentences below include terms that have been used incorrectly. Change the incorrect terms so that the sentence reads correctly. Underline your change.

1. Nekton float in the upper layers of oceans.

2. Organisms that get their energy from eating other organisms are producers.

3. Tides are caused by wind blowing across oceans.

4. Surface currents are caused by differences in the ocean water's salinity.

5. The layer of ocean water where the temperature drops quickly with depth is the upwelling.

IDENTIFYING ▶ Misconceptions

Assess

Use the assessment as follow-up to page 340F after students have completed the chapter.

Procedure Have students use clay to construct a 3-D model of their unseen ocean floor and compare their constructed model to the actual model inside the shoebox.

Expected Outcome The students will be able to see how well sampling can be used to discover what features are on the ocean floor. This will reinforce the concept that the ocean floor is not flat.

Reinforcement Have students describe their sampling plans. Have students name the features that they found while sampling their ocean floor.

Checking Concepts

1. D
2. A
3. B
4. B
5. C
6. C
7. D
8. A
9. B
10. D

Thinking Critically

11. As waves pass by, the motion of the boat is similar to the motion of water particles in a wave.

12. The current off California originates near Alaska. The current near South Carolina originates near the equator.

13. Organisms that depend on plankton for food will need to rely on other food sources or they will die. With fewer plankton, there will be less dissolved oxygen in the water. As a result, some organisms will die.

14. Runoff from the land carries many nutrients to the ocean. Also, sunlight penetrates shallow water. With nutrients and sunlight, producers thrive. With a large amount of plankton to eat, there are many consumers in shallow water near shore.

15. Temperature differences result because different latitudes receive different amounts of solar energy. Currents that originate at high latitudes are cold. Currents that originate at low latitudes are warm.

Checking Concepts

Choose the word or phrase that best answers the question.

1. Which of the following is a measure of dissolved solids in seawater?
   A) density
   C) thermocline
   B) nekton
   D) salinity

2. Which of these organisms is an example of a bottom dweller?
   A) sea star
   C) shark
   B) seal
   D) diatom

3. Which substance is found in the most common ocean salt?
   A) calcium
   C) carbon
   B) chlorine
   D) cobalt

4. Which of the following terms is the high point of a wave?
   A) wavelength
   C) trough
   B) crest
   D) wave height

5. Which of the following terms is the low point of a wave?
   A) wavelength
   C) trough
   B) crest
   D) wave height

6. Which of these tides forms because the Sun, Moon, and Earth are aligned?
   A) high tide
   C) spring tide
   B) low tide
   D) neap tide

7. Which of these organisms is a producer?
   A) sea star
   C) seal
   B) coral
   D) algae

8. Which of these gases is produced during photosynthesis?
   A) oxygen
   C) nitrogen
   B) carbon dioxide
   D) water vapor

9. Which of these terms describes the daily rhythmic rise and fall of sea level?
   A) surface current
   C) density current
   B) tide
   D) upwelling

10. What is the process that occurs when bacteria near ocean vents make food from sulfur compounds?
    A) respiration
    C) photosynthesis
    B) decomposition
    D) chemosynthesis

Thinking Critically

11. Explain why a boat tied to a dock bobs up and down in the water.

12. Why is the water at a beach in southern California much colder than the water at a beach in South Carolina?

13. How would other ocean life in an area be affected if an oil spill killed much of the plankton in that area?

14. Discuss reasons why more marine creatures live in shallow water near shore than in any other region of the oceans.

15. Why aren't all ocean surface currents the same temperature?

Developing Skills

16. **Interpreting Scientific Illustrations** Use **Figure 20** to describe how nitrogen is cycled from the atmosphere to marine organisms.

17. **Classifying** A tiny crab larva, shown below, hatches from an egg, drifts with the surface currents, and eats microscopic organisms. Classify this organism.

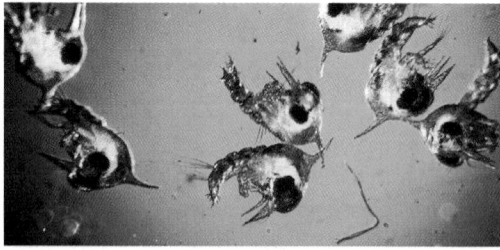

Chapter ✓Assessment Planner

Portfolio Encourage students to place in their portfolios one or two items of what they consider to be their best work. Examples include:
- Curriculum Connection, p. 341
- Cultural Diversity, p. 349
- Science Journal, p. 352
- Extension, p. 357

Performance Additional performance assessments, Performance Task Assessment Lists, and rubrics for evaluating these activities can be found in Glencoe's **Performance Assessment in the Science Classroom.**

18. Comparing and Contrasting Compare and contrast the way that consumers and decomposers get their energy.

19. Interpreting Scientific Illustrations Use the food web to infer what will happen to sea urchins and kelp if sea otters decline in number.

[Food web diagram showing: White sharks, People, Sheep head, Spiny lobsters, Sea otters, Sea stars, Abalone, Sea urchins, Kelp with arrows connecting them]

20. Drawing Conclusions Place the organisms in the proper sequence in a food chain: krill, killer whale, algae, cod, leopard seal.

Performance Assessment

21. Letter Write to the National Wildlife Federation about coral bleaching. Ask what is being done to protect coral reefs.

22. Pamphlet Research beach nourishment, jetties, and other ways that people have tried to reduce beach erosion. Create a pamphlet of your findings and pass it out to your classmates.

TECHNOLOGY

Go to the Glencoe Science Web site at **science.glencoe.com** or use the **Glencoe Science CD-ROM** for additional chapter assessment.

THE PRINCETON REVIEW — Test Practice

Ms. Mangan's class is studying different organisms. Here is a table of some of the organisms they have been studying.

Marine Organisms	
Producers	**Consumers**
Seaweed	Krill
Kelp	Squid
Algae	Seal

1. The producers are different from the consumers because only producers are able to _____ .
  A) swim in deep water
  B) make their own food
  C) contribute to the marine food web
  D) digest the nutrients in other organisms

2. What would happen to consumers if all producers perished?
  F) Consumers also would die.
  G) Consumers would begin making their own food.
  H) Consumers would decompose organic matter.
  J) Consumers would move to a new environment.

THE PRINCETON REVIEW — Test Practice

The Test-Taking Tip was written by The Princeton Review, the nation's leader in test preparation.
1. B
2. F

Developing Skills

16. Nitrogen-fixing bacteria change atmospheric nitrogen into nitrates. Marine producers use the nitrates and incorporate the nitrogen into their tissues. When consumers eat producers, nitrogen is cycled throughout the food web.

17. It is plankton and a consumer.

18. Both depend on producers for energy. Consumers get energy when they eat food stored in producers' and other consumers' tissues. Decomposers break down tissues of producers and consumers to get energy.

19. Sea urchins will increase in number with fewer sea otters to eat them. Kelp will decrease in number because there will be more sea urchins and abalone to eat them.

20. algae, krill, cod, leopard seal, killer whale

Performance Assessment

21. Letters should contain accurate information and be written in correct business style. Use **PASC**, p. 139.

22. Suggest that students use their word processing and graphic design skills to make their pamphlets. Pamphlets should contain accurate information. Use **PASC**, p. 129.

✔Assessment Resources

 Reproducible Masters

Chapter Resources Booklet
  Chapter Review, pp. 39–40
  Chapter Tests, pp. 41–44
  Assessment Transparency Activity, p. 53

Glencoe Science Web site
  Interactive Tutor
  Chapter Quizzes

Glencoe Technology
  🖌 Assessment Transparency
  💿 Interactive CD-ROM Chapter Quizzes
  💿 ExamView Pro Test Bank
  💿 Vocabulary PuzzleMaker Software
  📼 MindJogger Videoquiz

Question 1: B

Students must refer back to the reading passage in order to recall the chronology of events.

- **Choice A** No; this occurred second in the passage.
- **Choice B** Yes; this occurred first in the passage.
- **Choice C** No; this occurred last in the passage.
- **Choice D** No; this occurred third in the passage.

Question 2: H

Students must refer to the information in the reading passage to identify the correct answer, choice H, *119 km/h.*

Question 3: B

Students can use key words in the question such as *energy source* in order to find the important information, which is located in the second and in the last paragraph of the passage. Only answer choice B, *warm ocean water*, is supported by this information.

THE PRINCETON REVIEW

All questions written and validated by The Princeton Review.

Read the passage. Then read each question that follows the passage. Decide which is the best answer to each question.

Hurricanes: An Exchange Between Ocean and Atmosphere

Hurricanes are among the most feared of all weather storms in the Atlantic region. In the western Pacific they are known as typhoons, and in Australia and the Indian Ocean they are called cyclones. Hurricane season in the United States and Caribbean occurs each year between June and November.

Hurricanes over the Atlantic Ocean begin as low-pressure systems, usually in the tropical seas west of Africa. The trade winds blow these storms westward. Heat from the warm ocean water gives the system energy. Once the water temperature rises to 27°C, a hurricane can form.

To be classified as a hurricane, the wind speed of the storm must exceed 119 km/h. Hurricanes can last for several days and can reach heights up to 16 km above the water.

The Atlantic has about ten tropical storms each year. Of these, six of them might develop into full-blown hurricanes.

Hurricanes can cause severe damage to anything near them on the water. After a hurricane reaches land, it loses its source of energy—warm ocean water—and begins to weaken. Even though the strength of these storms fade as they reach shore, hurricanes frequently are responsible for billions of dollars of damage and loss of lives.

Test-Taking Tip   Take your time and read the passage carefully.

1. Which of the following was described first in the passage?
   - **A)** Hurricanes can reach heights up to 16 km above the surface of the water.
   - **B)** Hurricane season in the Atlantic region occurs between June and November.
   - **C)** Hurricanes start to lose energy upon reaching land.
   - **D)** Hurricanes can cause severe damage to anything near them on the water.

2. To classify as a hurricane, the wind speed of the storm must be more than _____.
   - **F)** 27 km/h
   - **G)** 16 km/h
   - **H)** 119 km/h
   - **J)** 140 km/h

3. What is the energy source of hurricanes?
   - **A)** high winds
   - **B)** warm ocean water
   - **C)** trade winds
   - **D)** cold air from land

Reasoning and Skills

Read each question and choose the best answer.

1. During El Niño years, upwelling of ocean water off the coast of Peru is greatly reduced, the water warms, and the number of fish decreases. Which of the following best explains why this occurs?
   A) The Coriolis effect shifts currents toward land.
   B) High concentrations of nutrients in the surface water increase its density.
   C) Winds blowing water from the coast slacken.
   D) The Eastern Pacific warms, thus changing the direction of currents off Peru.

Test-Taking Tip Think about what causes upwelling, then choose the answer that offers the most reasonable explanation for why it might stop.

Earth's Atmosphere	
Layer	**Characteristic**
Troposphere	Most water vapor and gases
Stratosphere	Contains ozone layer
Mesosphere	Falling temperatures
Thermosphere	Very high temperatures

2. According to the information in the table, rain would most likely originate in the _____.
   F) troposphere
   G) stratosphere
   H) mesosphere
   J) thermosphere

Test-Taking Tip Examine the table carefully. Find the words you would most closely associate with rain and follow the row back to the correct answer.

Tornado Damage	
Type of Tornado	**Damage**
F0	Light: Broken branches and chimneys
F1	Moderate: Roof damage
F2	Considerable: Roofs torn off, trees uprooted
F3	Severe: Heavy roofs and walls torn off
F4	Devastating: Houses leveled
F5	Incredible: Houses picked up
F6	Total demolition

3. What type of tornado occurred near this home?
   A) light
   B) moderate
   C) considerable
   D) severe

Test-Taking Tip Obtain a copy of the photograph above and circle all of the things damaged in the picture. Compare what you found to the information given in the table.

Standardized Test Practice

Reasoning and Skills

QUESTION 1: C
Students must understand that upwelling is caused by winds.

QUESTION 2: F
Students must use the information in the chart and make the connection between rain and water vapor in order to identify choice F, *troposphere*, as the layer of Earth's atmosphere in which rain originates.

QUESTION 3: C
Students must relate the damage shown in the picture to the information given in the table.

Teaching Tip

When questions ask about a table or chart, students should read the chart carefully to identify the relationships between columns.

UNIT 5

Unit Contents

✔ Pre-Reading Activity

Have students search through the chapters and identify any minerals, rocks, and landforms with which they are familiar.

UNIT 5 Earth and Space

How Are Rocks & Fluorescent Lights Connected?

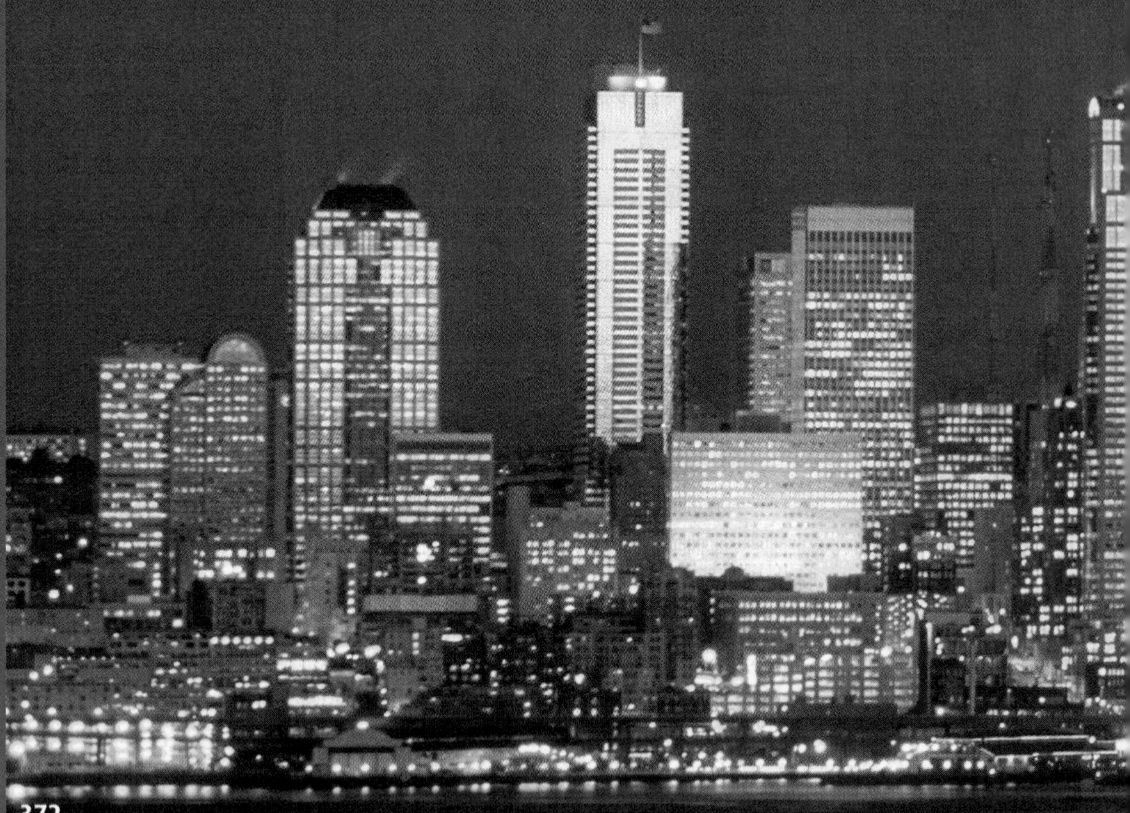

Teacher to Teacher

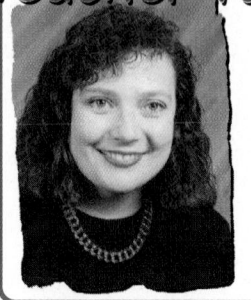

"To illustrate plate movement, I have students use graham crackers as plates and frosting as magma. Using the information they learned about convergent and divergent boundaries, have students recreate these movements using their materials. Remind students not to eat anything made or used in a laboratory."

Deborah Peters Huffine, Teacher
Noblesville Intermediate School
Noblesville, IN

Introducing the Unit

How Are Rocks & Fluorescent Lights Connected?

The emission of light by matter (luminescence) has always been known to exist. Lightning, the aurora borealis, and light emission by bacteria or in decaying matter are common natural phenomena.

There are many types of luminescence. Bioluminescence is luminescence produced by living organisms, such as glow-worms, fireflies, microscopic organisms living in the sea, and various fungi and bacteria found on rotting wood or decomposing flesh. Chemiluminescence is produced by certain chemical reactions. Electroluminescence is produced by electric discharges, which may appear when silk or fur is stroked or when adhesive surfaces are separated. Fluorescence, or luminescence emitted from a substance under stimulation by light, had been observed in rocks and certain other substances for hundreds of years.

Scientific investigation of luminescence didn't begin until 1603, when Vincenzo Casariolo, a Bolognian shoemaker and alchemist, accidentally prepared an artificial phosphor that glowed on its own after exposure to light. For the next three centuries scientists studied phosphorescence, and in 1911 the first fluorescent lighting was developed.

A round 1600, an Italian cobbler found a rock that contained a mineral that could be made to glow in the dark. The discovery led other people to seek materials with similar properties. Eventually, scientists identified many fluorescent and phosphorescent (fahs fuh RE sunt) substances—substances that react to certain forms of energy by giving off their own light. As seen above, a fluorescent mineral may look one way in ordinary light (front), but may give off a strange glow (back) when exposed to ultraviolet light. In the 1850s, a scientist wondered whether the fluorescent properties of a substance could be harnessed to create a new type of lighting. The scientist put a fluorescent material inside a glass tube and sent an electric charge through the tube, creating the first fluorescent lamp. Today, fluorescent light bulbs are widely used in office buildings, schools, and factories.

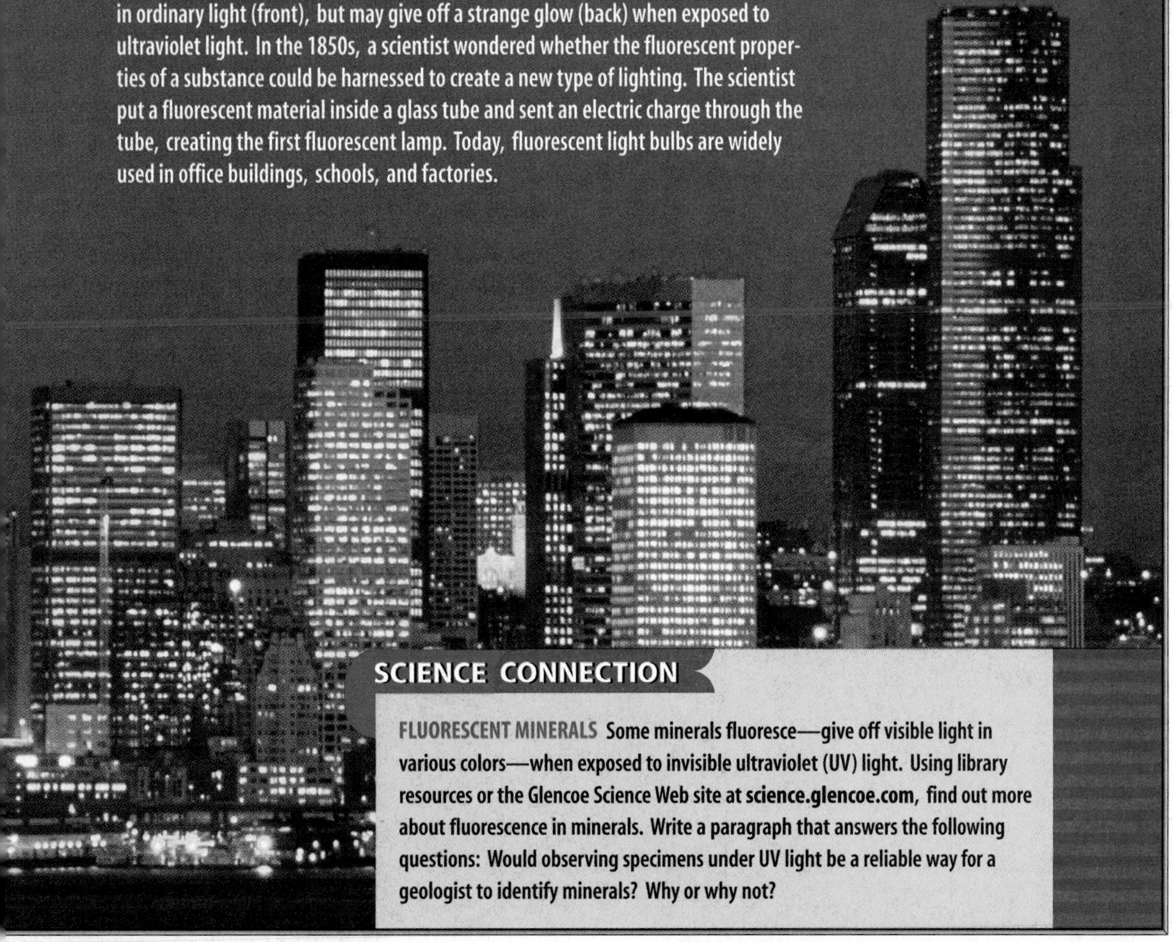

SCIENCE CONNECTION

FLUORESCENT MINERALS Some minerals fluoresce—give off visible light in various colors—when exposed to invisible ultraviolet (UV) light. Using library resources or the Glencoe Science Web site at science.glencoe.com, find out more about fluorescence in minerals. Write a paragraph that answers the following questions: Would observing specimens under UV light be a reliable way for a geologist to identify minerals? Why or why not?

SCIENCE *Online*
Internet Addresses
_____
_____
_____
_____

Explore the Glencoe Science Web site at **science.glencoe.com** to find out more about topics in this unit.

SCIENCE CONNECTION

Activity

When ultraviolet light strikes certain materials, it causes them to fluoresce. Because the spectrum of fluorescent light is characteristic of a material's composition, it can be used for screening minerals.

Section/Objectives	Standards		Activities/Features
Chapter Opener	**National**	**State/Local**	**Explore Activity:** Observe a rock, p. 375
	See p. 6T for a Key to Standards.		**Before You Read,** p. 375
Section 1 Minerals—Earth's Jewels 🕐 2 sessions 📦 1 block 1. **Identify** the difference between a mineral and a rock. 2. **Describe** the properties that are used to identify minerals.	National Content Standards: UCP3, A1, B1, D1		**Life Science Integration,** p. 377 **MiniLAB:** Classifying Minerals, p. 381 **Problem-Solving Activity:** How hard are these minerals?, p. 381 **Science Online,** p. 382
Section 2 Igneous and Sedimentary Rocks 🕐 2 sessions 📦 1 block 1. **Explain** how extrusive and intrusive igneous rocks are different. 2. **Describe** how different types of sedimentary rocks form.	National Content Standards: UCP1, A1, D1		**Physics Integration,** p. 387 **Visualizing Igneous Rock Features,** p. 388 **MiniLAB:** Modeling How Fossils Form Rocks, p. 390
Section 3 Metamorphic Rocks and the Rock Cycle 🕐 3 sessions 📦 1.5 blocks 1. **Describe** the conditions needed for metamorphic rocks to form. 2. **Explain** how all rocks are linked by the rock cycle.	National Content Standards: UCP2, UCP3, UCP4, A1, D1, G1, G2	.	**Science Online,** p. 394 **Activity:** Gneiss Rice, p. 397 **Activity:** Classifying Minerals, p. 398 **Oops! Accidents in Science:** Going for the Gold, p. 400

NATIONAL GEOGRAPHIC

Teacher's Corner

PRODUCTS AVAILABLE FROM GLENCOE
To order call 1-800-334-7433:
CD-ROM
NGS Picture Show: Geology
Posters
GeoKit: Rocks and Minerals
NGS Picture Show: Rocks and Minerals

INDEX TO NATIONAL GEOGRAPHIC SOCIETY
The following articles may be used for research relating to this chapter:
"Black Pearls of French Polynesia," by David Doubilet, June 1997.
"Rubies and Sapphires," by Fred Ward, October 1991.

"Emeralds," by Fred Ward, July 1990.
"Jade: Stone of Heaven," by Fred Ward, September 1987.
"The Pearl," by Fred Ward, August 1985.

Activity Materials	Reproducible Resources	Section Assessment	Technology
Explore Activity: sparkling rock, hand lens	**Chapter Resources Booklet** Foldables Worksheet, p. 17 Directed Reading Overview, p. 19 Note-taking Worksheets, pp. 33–35	GLENCOE'S ASSESSMENT ADVANTAGE	
MiniLAB: magnet; samples of quartz, calcite, hornblende, magnetite; beaker; vinegar; water *Need materials?* Contact Science Kit at 1-800-828-7777 or www.sciencekit.com on the Internet.	**Chapter Resources Booklet** Transparency Activity, p. 44 MiniLAB, p. 3 Enrichment, p. 30 Reinforcement, p. 27 Directed Reading, p. 20 Lab Activities, pp. 9–11 **Mathematics Skill Activities,** p. 1 **Cultural Diversity,** p. 35 **Science Inquiry Labs,** p. 23	Portfolio Life Science Integration, p. 377 Performance MiniLAB, p. 381 Problem-Solving Activity, p. 381 Skill Builder Activities, p. 384 Content Section Assessment, p. 384	♪ Section Focus Transparency ◉ Interactive CD-ROM ∩ Guided Reading Audio Program
MiniLAB: small aluminum pie pan, dry macaroni, white glue, water, mixing bowl or beaker, sample of fossiliferous limestone	**Chapter Resources Booklet** Transparency Activity, p. 45 MiniLAB, p. 4 Enrichment, p. 31 Reinforcement, p. 28 Directed Reading, p. 21 Lab Activities, pp. 13–16 **Reading and Writing Skill Activities,** p. 21 **Earth Science Critical Thinking/Problem Solving,** p. 10	Portfolio Science Journal, p. 387 Performance MiniLAB, p. 390 Skill Builder Activities, p. 391 Content Section Assessment, p. 391	♪ Section Focus Transparency ◉ Interactive CD-ROM ∩ Guided Reading Audio Program
Activity: rolling pin, lump of modeling clay, uncooked rice (wild rice, if available), granite sample, gneiss sample **Activity:** set of minerals, hand lens, putty knife, streak plate, Mohs scale, minerals field guide	**Chapter Resources Booklet** Transparency Activity, p. 46 Activity Worksheet, pp. 5–8 Enrichment, p. 32 Reinforcement, p. 29 Directed Reading, pp. 21, 22 Transparency Activity, pp. 47–48 **Earth Science Critical Thinking/Problem Solving,** p. 4 **Home and Community Involvement,** p. 43 **Lab Management and Safety,** p. 55	Portfolio Science Journal, p. 393 Performance Skill Builder Activities, p. 396 Content Section Assessment, p. 396	♪ Section Focus Transparency ♪ Teaching Transparency ◉ Interactive CD-ROM ∩ Guided Reading Audio Program

End of Chapter Assessment

GLENCOE'S ASSESSMENT ADVANTAGE

Blackline Masters	Technology	Professional Series
Chapter Resources Booklet Chapter Review, pp. 37–38 Chapter Tests, pp. 39–42 **Standardized Test Practice by The Princeton Review,** pp. 55–58	▭ MindJogger Videoquiz ◉ Interactive CD-ROM ◉ Vocabulary PuzzleMakers ◉ ExamView Pro Test Bank ◉ Interactive Lesson Planner ◉ Interactive Teacher Edition	Performance Assessment in the Science Classroom (PASC)

Transparencies

Section Focus

Section Focus Transparency 1: Phosphate Was Everywhere!

Nauru is a tiny island in the Pacific Ocean near Papua New Guinea. Despite its small size, Nauru is one of the richest developing nations. Its wealth, however, comes from phosphate deposits that are expected to run out early in the twenty-first century.

1. Judging from the picture, how is phosphate mined on Nauru?
2. Do you think the phosphate is ready for use as fertilizer straight from the mine? Why or why not?
3. Name some other valuable materials that are mined from Earth.

L2

Section Focus Transparency 2: Beautiful Blue

Crater Lake, in western Oregon, was formed over 6,000 years ago by volcanic processes. Subsequent eruptions and lava flows formed Wizard Island, shown below. In 1902, the region including Crater Lake (a total of 647 km²) became a national park.

1. Given Crater Lake's origin, how do you think many of the area's rocks were formed?
2. Name some other formations resulting from volcanic activity.

L2

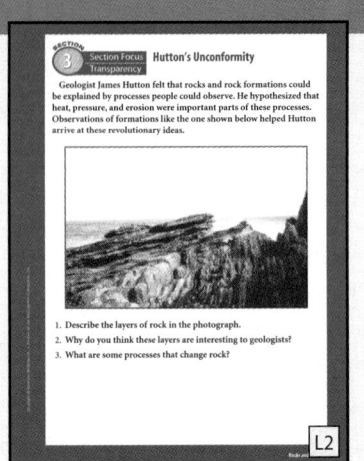

Section Focus Transparency 3: Hutton's Unconformity

Geologist James Hutton felt that rocks and rock formations could be explained by processes people could observe. He hypothesized that heat, pressure, and erosion were important parts of these processes. Observations of formations like the one shown below helped Hutton arrive at these revolutionary ideas.

1. Describe the layers of rock in the photograph.
2. Why do you think these layers are interesting to geologists?
3. What are some processes that change rock?

L2

This is a representation of key blackline masters available in the Teacher Classroom Resources. See Resource Manager boxes within the chapter for additional information.

Assessment

Assessment Transparency: Rocks and Minerals

Directions: Carefully review the diagram and answer the following questions.

Folded Rock Layers

1. Which sequence shows the rock layers in correct order from youngest to oldest?
   A R, S, T, Q   C Q, S, T, R
   B S, Q, R, T   D T, Q, R, S
2. Which of the following would be the correct order for a core sample from the oil well?
   F T, R, Q, S   H S, R, Q, T
   G Q, S, T, R   J R, S, T, Q
3. The rock layers in the diagram are folded because they have been subject to extreme pressure and heat. What kind of rock is formed by high temperatures and pressures?
   A sedimentary rock
   B metamorphic rock
   C igneous rock
   D detrital rock

L2

Teaching

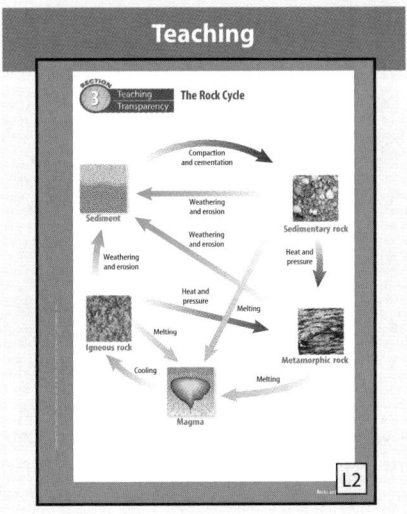

Teaching Transparency: The Rock Cycle

L2

Key to Teaching Strategies

The following designations will help you decide which activities are appropriate for your students.

L1 Level 1 activities should be appropriate for students with learning difficulties.

L2 Level 2 activities should be within the ability range of all students.

L3 Level 3 activities are designed for above-average students.

ELL ELL activities should be within the ability range of English Language Learners.

COOP LEARN Cooperative Learning activities are designed for small group work.

LS Multiple Learning Styles logos, as described on page 22T, are used throughout to indicate strategies that address different learning styles.

P These strategies represent student products that can be placed into a best-work portfolio.

Hands-on Activities

Activity Worksheets

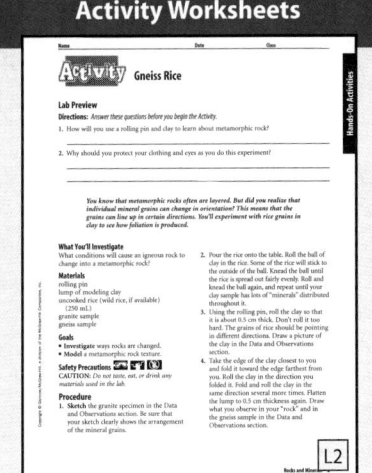

Activity: Gneiss Rice

Lab Preview

Directions: Answer these questions before you begin the Activity.

1. How will you use a rolling pin and clay to learn about metamorphic rock?

2. Why should you protect your clothing and eyes as you do this experiment?

You know that metamorphic rocks often are layered. But did you realize that individual mineral grains can change in orientation? This means that the grains can line up in certain directions. You'll experiment with rice grains in clay to see how foliation is produced.

What You'll Investigate
What conditions will cause an igneous rock to change into a metamorphic rock?

Materials
rolling pin
lump of modeling clay
uncooked rice (wild rice, if available) (250 mL)
granite sample
gneiss sample

Goals
• Investigate ways rocks are changed.
• Model a metamorphic rock texture.

Safety Precautions
CAUTION: Do not taste, eat, or drink any materials used in the lab.

Procedure
1. Sketch the granite specimen in the Data and Observations section. Be sure that your sketch clearly shows the arrangement of the mineral grains.

2. Pour the rice onto the table. Roll the ball of clay in the rice. Some of the rice will stick to the outside of the ball. Knead the ball until the rice is spread out fairly evenly. Roll and knead the ball again, and repeat until your clay sample has lots of "minerals" distributed throughout it.
3. Using the rolling pin, roll the clay so that it is about 0.5 cm thick. Don't roll it too hard. The grains of rice should be pointing in different directions. Draw a picture of the clay in the Data and Observations section.
4. Take the edge of the clay closest to you and fold it toward the edge farthest from you. Roll the clay in the direction you folded it. Fold and roll the clay in the same direction several more times. Flatten the lump to 0.5 cm thickness again. Draw what you observe in your "rock" and in the gneiss sample in the Data and Observations section.

L2

Laboratory Activities

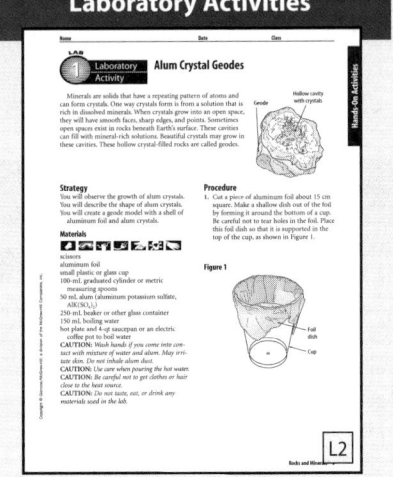

Laboratory Activity: Alum Crystal Geodes

Minerals are solids that have a repeating pattern of atoms and can form crystals. One way crystals form is from a solution that is rich in dissolved minerals. When crystals grow into an open space, they will have smooth faces, sharp edges, and points. Sometimes open spaces exist in rocks beneath Earth's surface. These cavities can fill with mineral-rich solutions. Beautiful crystals may grow in these cavities. These hollow crystal-filled rocks are called geodes.

Strategy
You will observe the growth of alum crystals.
You will describe the shape of alum crystals.
You will create a geode model with a shell of aluminum foil and alum crystals.

Materials
scissors
aluminum foil
small plastic or glass cup
100-mL graduated cylinder or metric measuring spoons
50 mL alum (aluminum potassium sulfate, AlK(SO₄)₂)
250-mL beaker or other glass container
250 mL boiling water
hot plate and 4-qt saucepan or an electric coffee pot to boil water
CAUTION: Wash hands if you come into contact with mixture of water and alum. May irritate skin. Do not inhale alum dust.
CAUTION: Use care when pouring the hot water.
CAUTION: Be careful not to get clothes or hair close to the heat source.
CAUTION: Do not taste, eat, or drink any materials used in the lab.

Procedure
1. Cut a piece of aluminum foil about 15 cm square. Make a shallow dish out of the foil by forming it around the bottom of a cup. Be careful not to form any holes in the foil. Place this foil dish so that it is supported in the top of the cup, as shown in Figure 1.

Figure 1

L2

Meeting Different Ability Levels

Content Outline

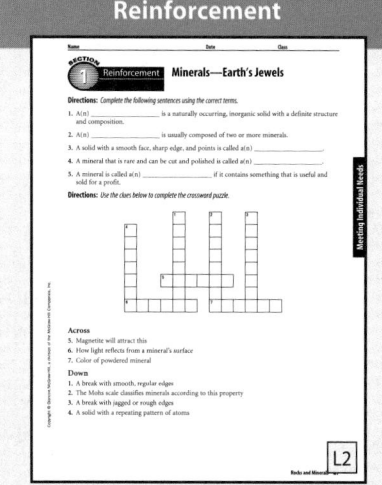

Reinforcement

Directed Reading

Assessment

Chapter Tests

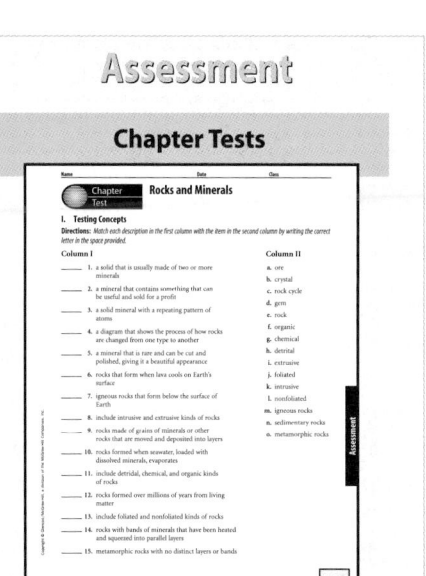

Enrichment

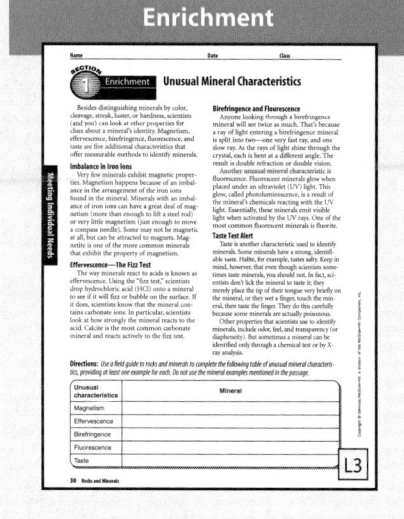

Spanish Directed Reading

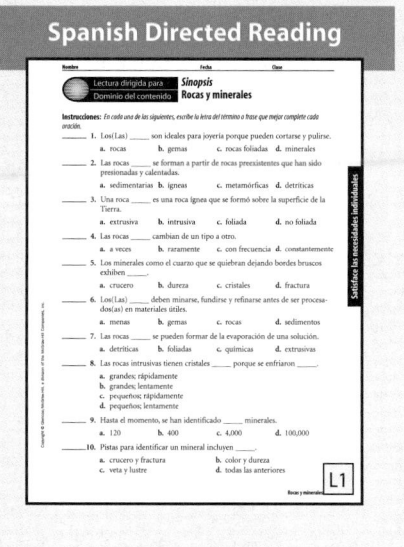

Test Practice Workbook

Chapter Review

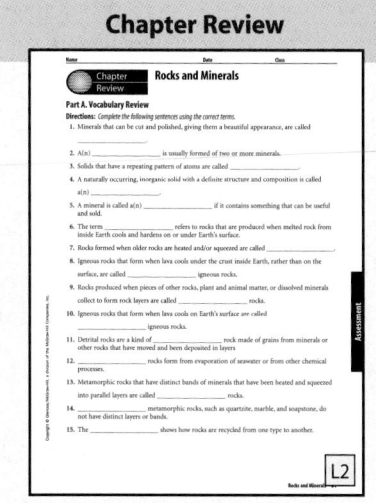

Science Content Background

Runk/Schoenberger/Grant Heilman Photography, Inc.

SECTION 1

Minerals—Earth's Jewels
What is a mineral?

A mineral can be defined as a naturally occurring, inorganic solid with an ordered atomic structure and definite but not fixed chemical makeup. This definition excludes some solids, such as organic solids. It also excludes some naturally occurring inorganic solids, such as opal, that look like minerals but do not have an ordered atomic structure. These solids are called mineraloids.

Rocks are commonly described as aggregates of minerals, but several rocks don't actually fit this definition. Examples are coal and obsidian, which are composed mainly of solids that are not minerals. For this reason, geologists use a more inclusive definition. A rock is a mixture of minerals, mineraloids, organic material, or glass.

Crystals

Crystals start to grow when minute "seed" crystal forms, and ions and molecules migrate to their surfaces. Some substances form lots of seed crystals and smaller crystals, but others form fewer seed crystals and larger crystals. The rate of cooling also influences crystal size; slower cooling leads to larger crystals.

Cleavage and Fracture

Minerals may cleave in one or many directions. Micas, like muscovite, have one cleavage. Feldspars break along two directions of cleavage to form prism-shaped fragments. Calcite has three directions of cleavage that together outline rhombohedron-shaped pieces of the mineral. Fluorite has four directions of cleavage, and the mineral sphalerite has six.

Fracture may be either conchoidal or uneven. A mineral displaying conchoidal fracture breaks along smooth, curved surfaces. This type of fracture is well displayed by obsidian, an igneous rock. The mineral quartz also has conchoidal fracture. Other minerals break in a more random fashion. These minerals have uneven fracture.

Hardness

A mineral's hardness depends on the strength of its atomic bonds and can be measured by determining the mineral's resistance to scratching. Most minerals have uniform hardness, but some minerals, like calcite, are harder on certain surfaces than on others.

Fun Fact

Atoms of carbon can crystallize in one atomic structure to form graphite and in another to form diamonds.

Specific Gravity

A mineral's specific gravity (also known as heft) is the ratio of the mineral's weight to the weight of an equal volume of water. If a cubic centimeter of a mineral weighs four times more than a cubic centimeter of water, its specific gravity is four.

SECTION 2

Igneous and Sedimentary Rocks
Rocks from Lava

Pumice has a glassy texture with holes or spaces in the structure caused by the rapid expansion of gases upon reaching Earth's surface. Occasionally, lava that contains large mineral crystals that grew at depth may erupt at Earth's surface. When this lava cools, a rock with large crystals surrounded by small crystals will form.

Rocks from Magma

Intrusive igneous rocks form when magma, which is less dense than surrounding rock, rises, cools, and solidifies before reaching Earth's surface.

Sedimentary Rocks

Sedimentary rocks tend to display visible layering, or bedding. Most sedimentary rocks form when sediments are deposited and then compacted or cemented together, or both. Cementation occurs as mineral cements such as silica (quartz), calcite, clay minerals, and iron oxides precipitate in the pore spaces of the sediment.

Many sedimentary rocks form when broken pieces of preexisting rock, also known as detritus, are deposited and lithified (turn to solid rock). Because they are made of detritus, these rocks are called detrital sedimentary rocks.

SECTION 3 — Metamorphic Rocks and the Rock Cycle

New Rock from Old Rock

Rocks change in response to changes in heat, pressure, and fluid activity. New minerals often form, and preexisting minerals may be recrystallized. Minerals also may acquire a preferred orientation.

The heat, pressure, and chemical reactions that cause rocks to change are generated in different ways. Contact metamorphism occurs when hot magma comes into contact with surrounding rocks. Regional metamorphism occurs when large areas of Earth are subjected to increased pressure and temperature, such as during mountain building.

Fun Fact

Erosion-resistant intrusive rock formations can be found at Gettysburg, Pennsylvania, where ridges provided protection for Union and Confederate troops during the American Civil War.

The Rock Cycle

Matter has been cycling through Earth throughout history. Melting, weathering and erosion, and metamorphism continue the process today.

SCIENCE Online

For additional content background on this topic, go to the Glencoe Science Web site at science.glencoe.com.

Darrell Gulin/DRK Photo

Chapter Vocabulary

What do you think?

Science Journal The photo shows columnar basalt. This igneous rock formed as lava flowed across Earth's surface. The columns formed as the basalt cooled and contracted, forming hexagonal arrays of fractures.

Rocks and Minerals

Spectacular natural scenes like this one at Pikes Peak in Colorado are often shaped by rock formations. How did rocks form? What are they made of? In this chapter you will learn the answers. In addition you will find out where gemstones and valuable metals such as gold and copper come from. Rocks and minerals are the basic materials of Earth's surface. Read on to discover how they are classified and how they are related.

What do you think?

Science Journal Look at the picture below with a classmate. Discuss what you think this might be or what is happening. Here's a hint: *It is far cooler now than it used to be.* Write your answer or best guess in your Science Journal.

374

Theme Connection

Scale and Structure and **Stability and Change** The theme of scale and structure is presented as the properties of minerals are related to the arrangement of their atoms. The theme of stability and change is emphasized through the study of the rock cycle.

The view is spectacular! You and a friend have successfully scaled Pikes Peak. Now that you have reached the top, you also have a chance to look more closely at the rock you've been climbing. First, you notice that it sparkles in the Sun because of the silvery specks that are stuck in the rock. Looking closer, you also see clear, glassy pieces and pink, irregular chunks. What is the rock made of? How did it get here?

Observe a rock

1. Obtain a sparkling rock from your teacher. You also will need a hand lens.
2. Observe the rock with the hand lens. Your job is to observe and record as many of the features of the rock as you can.
3. Return the rock to your teacher.
4. Describe your rock so other students could identify it from a variety of rocks.

Observe

How do the parts of the rock fit together to form the whole thing? Describe this in your Science Journal and make a drawing. Be sure to label the colors and shapes in your drawing.

Before You Read

FOLDABLES
Reading & Study Skills

Making a Venn Diagram Study Fold **Make the following Foldable to compare and contrast the characteristics of rocks and minerals.**

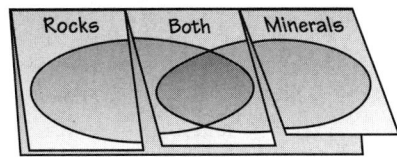

1. Place a sheet of paper in front of you so the long side is at the top. Fold the paper in half from top to bottom.
2. Fold both sides in. Unfold the paper so three sections show.
3. Through the top thickness of paper, cut along each of the fold lines to the top fold, forming three tabs. Label each tab *Rocks, Both,* and *Minerals* and draw ovals across the front of the paper as shown.
4. As you read the chapter, write what you learn about rocks and minerals under the left and right tabs.

375

1 Motivate

Bellringer Transparency

Display the Section Focus Transparency for Section 1. Use the accompanying Transparency Activity Master. L2 ELL

Tie to Prior Knowledge

Have students recall that matter is composed of atoms and that atoms combine to form compounds. In this section, students will learn that the structures and properties of minerals are determined by their internal arrangement of atoms.

SECTION

1 Minerals—Earth's Jewels

As You Read

***What* You'll Learn**
- **Identify** the difference between a mineral and a rock.
- **Describe** the properties that are used to identify minerals.

Vocabulary

mineral	gem
rock	ore
crystal	

***Why* It's Important**
Minerals are the basic substances of nature that humans use for a variety of purposes.

Figure 1
You use minerals every day without realizing it. Minerals are used to make many common objects.

What is a mineral?

Suppose you were planning an expedition to find minerals (MIHN uh ruhlz). Where would you look? Do you think you'll have to crawl into a cave or brave the depths of a mine? Well, put away your flashlight. You can find minerals in your own home—in the salt shaker and in your pencil. Metal pots, glassware, and ceramic dishes are products made from minerals. Minerals and products from them, shown in **Figure 1,** surround you.

Minerals Defined **Minerals** are inorganic, solid materials found in nature. Inorganic means they usually are not formed by plants or animals. You could go outside and find minerals that occur as gleaming crystals—or as small grains in ordinary rocks. X-ray patterns of a mineral show an orderly arrangement of atoms that looks something like a garden trellis. Evidence of this orderly arrangement is the beautiful crystal shape often seen in minerals. The particular chemical makeup and arrangement of the atoms in the crystal is unique to each mineral. **Rocks,** such as the one used in the Explore Activity, usually are made of two or more minerals. Each mineral has unique characteristics you can use to identify it. So far, more than 4,000 minerals have been identified.

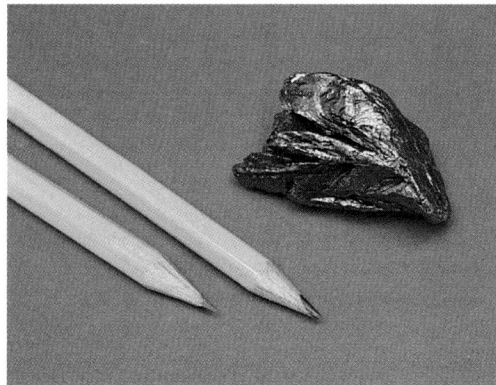

A The "lead" in a pencil is not lead. It is the mineral graphite.

B The mineral quartz is used to make the glass that you use every day.

376 **CHAPTER 13** Rocks and Minerals

Section ✓*Assessment* Planner

PORTFOLIO
Life Science Integration, p. 377
PERFORMANCE ASSESSMENT
Problem-Solving Activity, p. 381
MiniLAB, p. 381
Skill Builder Activities, p. 384
See page 404 for more options.

CONTENT ASSESSMENT
Section, p. 384
Challenge, p. 384
Chapter, pp. 404–405

How do minerals form? Minerals form in several ways. One way is from melted rock inside Earth called magma. As magma cools, atoms combine in orderly patterns to form minerals. Minerals also form from melted rock that reaches Earth's surface. Melted rock at Earth's surface is called lava.

Evaporation can form minerals. Just as salt crystals appear when seawater evaporates, other dissolved minerals, such as gypsum, can crystallize. A process called precipitation (prih sih puh TAY shun) can form minerals, too. Water can hold only so much dissolved material. Any extra separates and falls out as a solid. Large areas of the ocean floor are covered with manganese nodules that formed in this way. These metallic spheres average 25 cm in diameter. They crystallized directly from seawater containing metal atoms.

Formation Clues Sometimes, you can tell how a mineral formed by how it looks. Large mineral grains that fit together like a puzzle seem to show up in rocks formed from slow-cooling magma. If you see large, perfectly formed crystals, it means the mineral had plenty of space in which to grow. This is a sign they may have formed in open pockets within the rock.

The crystals you see in **Figure 2** grew this way from a solution that was rich in dissolved minerals. To figure out how a mineral was formed, you have to look at the size of the mineral crystal and how the crystals fit together.

Properties of Minerals

The cheers are deafening. The crowd is jumping and screaming. From your seat high in the bleachers, you see someone who is wearing a yellow shirt and has long, dark hair in braids, just like a friend you saw this morning. You're only sure it's your friend when she turns and you recognize her smile. You've identified your friend by physical properties that set her apart from other people—her clothing, hair color and style, and facial features. Each mineral, too, has a set of physical properties that can be used to identify it. Most common minerals can be identified with items you have around the house and can carry in your pocket, such as a penny or a steel file. With a little practice you soon can recognize mineral shapes, too. Next you will learn about properties that will help you identify minerals.

Figure 2
This cluster of fluorite crystals formed from a solution rich in dissolved minerals.

Life Science
INTEGRATION

Bones, such as those found in humans and horses, contain tiny crystals of the mineral apatite. Research apatite and report your findings to your class.

Properties of Minerals, continued

✔ **Reading Check**

Answer orderly internal atomic arrangement

Caption Answers

Figure 3 Pyrite has a gold color and metallic luster that makes it look like gold.

Figure 4B The three directions of cleavage at right angles produce a cubic external shape.

Visual Learning

Figures 3 and 4B Share with the class samples of several crystals, such as halite (cubic), corundum (hexagonal), and pyrite (cubic). Draw the internal atomic arrangement of a cubic crystal (halite) on the board and have students compare it with the salt shown in **Figure 4B**.

IDENTIFYING Misconceptions

Have students describe what comes to mind when they think of the word *crystal*. Students may think that a mineral has a crystalline structure only if the sample shows the crystal shape, such as cubic salt crystals. Emphasize that a mineral's crystalline structure refers to the internal arrangement of atoms. Even if a mineral shows no crystal shape, it still has an internal crystalline structure.

Figure 3
The mineral pyrite often forms crystals with six faces. *Why do you think pyrite also is called "fool's gold"?*

Crystals All minerals have an orderly pattern of atoms. The atoms making up the mineral are arranged in a repeating pattern. Solid materials that have such a pattern of atoms are called **crystals.** Sometimes crystals have smooth surfaces called crystal faces. The mineral pyrite commonly forms crystals with six crystal faces, as shown in **Figure 3.**

✔ **Reading Check** *What distinguishes crystals from other types of solid matter?*

Cleavage and Fracture Another clue to a mineral's identity is the way it breaks. Minerals that split into pieces with smooth, regular planes that reflect light are said to have cleavage (KLEE vihj). The mineral mica in **Figure 4A** shows cleavage by splitting into thin sheets. Splitting one of these minerals along a cleavage surface is something like peeling off a piece of presliced cheese. Cleavage is caused by weaknesses within the arrangement of atoms that make up the mineral.

Not all minerals have cleavage. Some break into pieces with jagged or rough edges. Instead of neat slices, these pieces are shaped more like hunks of cheese torn from an unsliced block. Materials that break this way, such as quartz, have what is called fracture (FRAK chur). **Figure 4C** shows the fracture of flint.

Figure 4
Some minerals have one or more directions of cleavage. If minerals do not break along flat surfaces, they have fracture.

A Mica has one direction of cleavage and can be peeled off in sheets.

B The mineral halite, also called rock salt, has three directions of cleavage at right angles to each other. *Why might grains of rock salt look like little cubes?*

C Fracture can be jagged and irregular or smooth and curvy like in flint.

Teacher FYI

Minerals that have the same chemical composition but different internal structures are called *polymorphs.* An excellent example of polymorphs is diamond and graphite. Both minerals are composed only of carbon. In diamond, each carbon atom is bonded tightly with four other carbon atoms. Because of this, diamond is the hardest known mineral. In graphite, each carbon atom is bonded tightly to other carbon atoms within a layer. The layers are held together weakly. This structure makes graphite one of the softest known minerals. Graphite is used in pencil lead because it is soft enough to leave a mark on paper. It also is used as a lubricant because of its softness.

Figure 5
The mineral calcite can form in a wide variety of colors. The colors are caused by slight impurities.

Color The reddish-gold color of a new penny shows you that it contains copper. The bright yellow color of sulfur is a valuable clue to its identity. Sometimes a mineral's color can help you figure out what it is. But color also can fool you. The common mineral pyrite (PI rite) has a shiny, gold color similar to real gold—close enough to disappoint many prospectors during the California Gold Rush in the 1800s. Because of this, pyrite also is called fool's gold. While different minerals can look similar in color, the same mineral can occur in a variety of colors. The mineral calcite, for example, can be many different colors, as shown in **Figure 5.**

Streak and Luster Scraping a mineral sample across an unglazed, white tile, called a streak plate, produces a streak of color, as shown in **Figure 6.** Oddly enough, the streak is not necessarily the same color as the mineral itself. This streak of powdered mineral is more useful for identification than the mineral's color. Gold prospectors could have saved themselves a lot of heartache if they had known about the streak test. Pyrite makes a greenish-black or brownish-black streak, but real gold makes a yellow streak.

Is the mineral shiny? Dull? Pearly? Words like these describe another property of minerals called luster. Luster describes how light reflects from a mineral's surface. If it shines like a metal, the mineral has metallic (muh TA lihk) luster. Nonmetallic minerals can be described as having pearly, glassy, dull, or earthy luster. You can use color, streak, and luster to help identify minerals.

Figure 6
Streak is the color of the powdered mineral. The mineral hematite has a characteristic reddish-brown streak. *How do you obtain a mineral's streak?*

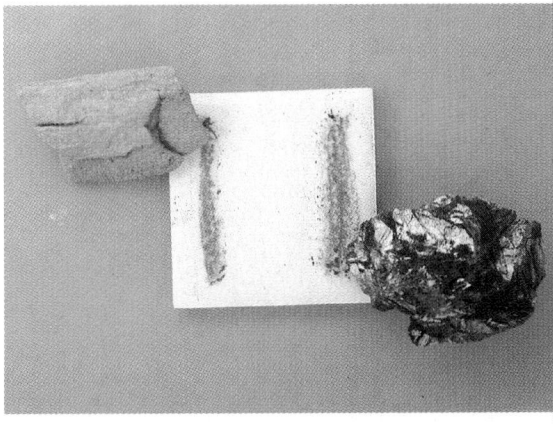

Use an Analogy

To help students understand why some minerals cleave, relate the weaknesses in the arrangement of the mineral's atoms to the weakness of icing between layers of cake. Cleavage occurs along planes of weak bonds just as the cake can easily be separated between iced layers. When no distinct plane of weakness exists between atoms, it is like a piece of cake without icing. The breakage can occur in any direction.

Activity

Obtain samples of specular hematite, earthy hematite, and oolitic hematite. Ask students to make a table in their Science Journals to compare and contrast the appearance of each sample and to describe the streaks of each sample. Samples of hematite can look very different. Some are red, some are steel gray, and some are a shiny metallic color. But no matter what color the sample is, hematite's streak color is dark red-brown. L1 **Visual-Spatial and Linguistic**

Fun Fact

Minerals with metallic luster generally have dark streaks.

Caption Answer

Figure 6 by scraping a mineral sample across an unglazed, white porcelain tile (streak plate)

Resource Manager

Chapter Resources Booklet
    Enrichment, p. 30
Mathematics Skill Activities, p. 1

✔ Active Reading

Buddy Interviews Have students interview one another to find out what helps them to understand what they are reading, how they find answers, and how they assimilate new vocabulary terms. Have students use Buddy Interviews to help them master the concepts related to Properties of Minerals in this section.

Properties of Minerals, continued

Extension

Have students collect rocks and minerals from near their homes and bring them to class. Invite a geologist to come to class and discuss his or her career. After the discussion, ask the geologist to identify the students' samples. Then, have the students organize the samples into labeled sets. L1 ELL
IS Visual-Spatial

Discussion

Why do some carbonate minerals react more readily with hydrochloric acid than others? The fizzing reaction is the release of CO_2 from the mineral. The more easily the CO_2 is released, the more the mineral will fizz.

Teacher FYI

When dilute HCl acid is placed on a sample of calcite or any rock that has calcite in it, water is produced and carbon dioxide gas is released in the following reaction:
$$CaCO_3 + 2HCl \rightarrow H_2O + CO_2 + CaCl_2$$

Table 1 Mohs Scale

Mineral	Hardness	Hardness of Common Objects
Talc	1 (softest)	
Gypsum	2	fingernail (2.5)
Calcite	3	copper penny (3.5)
Fluorite	4	iron nail (4.5)
Apatite	5	glass (5.5)
Feldspar	6	steel file (6.5)
Quartz	7	streak plate (7)
Topaz	8	
Corundum	9	
Diamond	10 (hardest)	

Figure 7
Calcite has the unique property of double refraction.

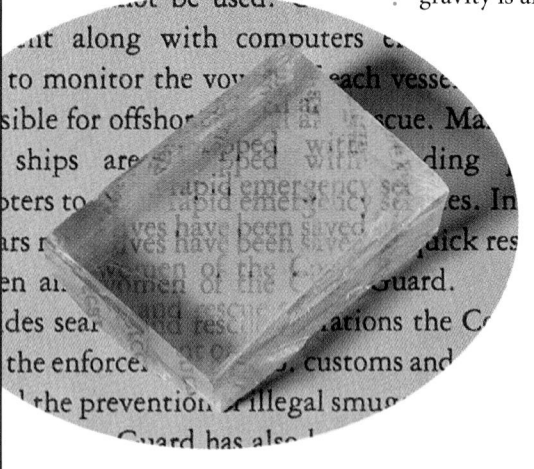

Hardness As you investigate different minerals, you'll find that some are harder than others. Some minerals, like talc, are so soft that they can be scratched with a fingernail. Others, like diamond, are so hard that they can be used to cut almost anything else.

In 1822, an Austrian geologist named Friedrich Mohs also noticed this property. He developed a way to classify minerals by their hardness. The Mohs scale, shown in **Table 1**, classifies minerals from 1 (softest) to 10 (hardest). You can determine hardness by trying to scratch one mineral with another to see which is harder. For example, fluorite (4 on the Mohs scale) will scratch calcite (3 on the scale), but fluorite cannot scratch apatite (5 on the scale). You also can use a homemade mineral identification kit—a penny, a nail, and a small glass plate with smooth edges. Simply find out what scratches what. Is the mineral hard enough to scratch a penny? Will it scratch glass?

Specific Gravity Some minerals are heavier for their size than others. Specific gravity compares the weight of a mineral with the weight of an equal volume of water. Pyrite—or fool's gold—is about five times heavier than water. Real gold is more than 15 times heavier than water. You easily could sense this difference by holding each one in your hand. Measuring specific gravity is another way you can identify minerals.

Other Properties Some minerals have other unusual properties that can help identify them. The mineral magnetite will attract a magnet. The mineral calcite has two unusual properties. It will fizz when it comes into contact with an acid like vinegar. Also, if you look through a clear calcite crystal, you will see a double image, as shown in **Figure 7**. Scientists taste some minerals to identify them, but you should not try this yourself. Halite, also called rock salt, has a salty taste.

Together, all of the properties you have read about are used to identify minerals. Learn to use them and you can be a mineral detective.

380   CHAPTER 13 Rocks and Minerals

Curriculum Connection

Geography Invite a jeweler from your community to visit the class and explain how tests are used to determine the value of gems brought in by customers. As an example, ask the speaker to explain how it is determined whether a diamond ring contains actual diamonds. Have the speaker tell where diamonds are found, and have students pinpoint these places on a map. L2

Resource Manager

Chapter Resources Booklet
MiniLAB, p. 3
Science Inquiry Labs, p. 23

Common Minerals

In the Chapter Opener, the rocks making up Pikes Peak were made of minerals. But only a small number of the more than 4,000 minerals make up most rocks. These minerals often are called the rock-forming minerals. If you can recognize these minerals, you will be able to identify most rocks. Other minerals are much rarer. However, some of these rare minerals also are important because they are used as gems or are ore minerals, which are sources of valuable metals.

Most of the rock-forming minerals are silicates, which contain the elements silicon and oxygen. The mineral quartz is pure silica (SiO_2). More than half of the minerals in Earth's crust are forms of a silicate mineral called feldspar. Other important rock-forming minerals are carbonates—or compounds containing carbon and oxygen. The carbonate mineral calcite makes up the common rock limestone.

✔ **Reading Check** *Why is the silicate mineral feldspar important?*

Other common minerals can be found in rocks that formed at the bottom of ancient, evaporating seas. Rock comprised of the mineral gypsum is abundant in many places, and rock salt, made of the mineral halite, underlies large parts of the Midwest.

Mini LAB

Classifying Minerals

Procedure 🥽 👕 🚰
1. Touch a **magnet** to samples of **quartz, calcite, hornblende,** and **magnetite.** Record which mineral attracts the magnet.
2. Place each sample in a small **beaker** that is half full of **vinegar.** Record what happens.
3. Rinse samples with **water.**

Analysis
1. Describe how each mineral reacted to the tests in steps 1 and 2.
2. Describe in a data table the other physical properties of the four minerals.

Problem-Solving Activity

How hard are these minerals?

Some minerals, like diamonds, are hard. Others, like talc, are soft. How can you determine the hardness of a mineral?

Identifying the Problem

The table at the right shows the results of a hardness test done using some common items as tools (a fingernail, penny, nail, and steel file) to scratch certain minerals (halite, turquoise, an emerald, a ruby, and graphite). The testing tools are listed at the top from softest (fingernail) to hardest (steel file). The table shows which minerals were scratched by which tools. Examine the table to determine the relative hardness of each mineral.

Hardness Test

Mineral	Fingernail	Penny	Nail	Steel File
Turquoise	N	N	Y	Y
Halite	N	Y	Y	Y
Ruby	N	N	N	N
Graphite	Y	Y	Y	Y
Emerald	N	N	N	N

Solving the problem

1. Is it possible to rank the five minerals from softest to hardest using the data in the table above? Why or why not?
2. What method could you use to determine whether the ruby or the emerald is harder?

Inclusion Strategies

Learning Disabled Assist students in accomplishing the MiniLAB by providing them with specific instructions on how the magnet helps identify magnetic properties and how to prepare the beaker of vinegar. Help students prepare their data tables, using an example on the board or pairing students with others who understand how the data table should be organized. L1 ELL
IS **Interpersonal**

✔ Assessment

Oral Which two tests would distinguish quartz from calcite? hardness and reaction to vinegar Use **Performance Assessment in the Science Classroom,** p. 89.

Common Minerals

Mini LAB

Purpose to investigate how properties can be used to identify minerals L2 ELL
IS **Kinesthetic**
Materials quartz, calcite, hornblende, magnetite, small beaker, vinegar, magnet, water
Teaching Strategy Caution students to wear goggles and aprons.
Analysis
1. Magnetite is attracted to a magnet. Calcite fizzes when placed in vinegar.
2. Possible answers: Quartz is harder than glass and has a glassy luster; hornblende is black and has two directions of cleavage; calcite can be scratched by copper and has three directions of cleavage; magnetite is black with a black streak.

✔ Reading Check

Answer Varieties of feldspar make up more than half of the minerals in Earth's crust.

Problem-Solving Activity

National Math Standards
Correlation to Mathematics Objectives
2, 5–10

Answers
1. No; it is possible to determine that graphite is the softest, followed by halite and turquoise. But it is not possible to tell whether emerald or ruby is harder, as they show the same data.
2. Scratch the ruby with the emerald and the emerald with the ruby. Whichever scratches the other is the harder mineral (ruby).

Discussion

Mining gems and ores often requires more than just digging. Gold, for example, may be present in rocks in tiny specks. Have students research how ores are mined. Then have them discuss the problems that might be caused by mining for gems or precious metals. One way to get gold out of ore is to crush the rock and mix it with chemicals such as cyanide and zinc. The major problem with these mining operations is that they can produce large amounts of toxic waste.

SCIENCE *Online*

Internet Addresses

_____

_____

_____

_____

Explore the Glencoe Science Web site at **science.glencoe.com** to find out more about topics in this section.

Figure 8

A This garnet crystal is encrusted with other minerals but still shines a deep red. **B** Cut garnet is a prized gemstone.

SCIENCE *Online*

Research Visit the Glencoe Science Web site at **science.glencoe.com** for more information about gems. Communicate to your class what you learn.

Figure 9
Diamonds sometimes are found in kimberlite deposits.

Gems Which would you rather win, a diamond ring or a quartz ring? A diamond ring would be more valuable. Why? The diamond in a ring is a kind of mineral called a gem. **Gems** are minerals that are rare and can be cut and polished, giving them a beautiful appearance, as shown in **Figure 8.** This makes them ideal for jewelry. To be gem quality, most minerals must be clear with no blemishes or cracks. A gem also must have a beautiful luster or color. Few minerals meet these standards. That's why the ones that do are rare and valuable.

The Making of a Gem One reason why gems are so rare is that they are produced under special conditions. Diamond, for instance, is a form of the element carbon. Scientists can make artificial diamonds in laboratories, but they must use extremely high pressures. These pressures are greater than any found within Earth's crust. Therefore, scientists suggest that diamond forms deep in Earth's mantle. It takes a special kind of volcanic eruption to bring a diamond close to Earth's surface, where miners can find it. This type of eruption forces magma from the mantle toward the surface of Earth at high speeds, bringing diamond right along with it. This type of magma is called kimberlite magma. **Figure 9** shows a rock from a kimberlite deposit in South Africa that is mined for diamond. Kimberlite deposits are found in the necks of ancient volcanoes.

Science Journal

Gems and Gemstones Minerals are used as gems or gemstones because of certain favorable properties. Ask students to write a paragraph explaining how gems and gemstones differ from other minerals. Ask them to write a paragraph in which they name and describe a new gemstone that they have discovered. Gems are generally hard and can be cut into shapes that reflect light. L2 IS **Linguistic**

Curriculum Connection

History French chemist Marc Gaudin produced the first synthetic ruby in 1873. He melted compounds that decomposed to form aluminum oxide, the material rubies are made of. He then added chromium to the aluminum oxide for color, producing synthetic rubies. Have students find out how synthetic rubies compare with real gems. Synthetic rubies often contain microscopic bubbles and striations. L2

Figure 10
To be profitable, ores must be found in large deposits or rich veins. Mining is expensive. Copper ore is obtained from this mine in Arizona.

Ores A mineral is called an **ore** if it contains enough of a useful substance that it can be sold for a profit. Many of the metals that humans use come from ores. For example, the iron used to make steel comes from the mineral hematite, lead for batteries is produced from galena, and the magnesium used in vitamins comes from dolomite. Ores of these useful metals must be extracted from Earth in a process called mining. A copper mine is shown in **Figure 10.**

Ore Processing After an ore has been mined, it must be processed to extract the desired mineral or element. **Figure 11** shows a copper smelting plant that melts the ore and then separates and removes most of the unwanted materials. After this smelting process, copper can be refined, which means that it is purified. Then it is processed into many materials that you use every day. Examples of useful copper products include sheet metal products, electrical wiring in cars and homes, and just about anything electronic. Some examples of copper products are shown in **Figure 12.**

Early settlers in Jamestown, Virginia, produced iron by baking moisture out of ore they found in salt marshes. Today much of the iron produced in the United States is highly processed from ore found near Lake Superior.

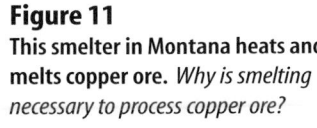

Figure 11
This smelter in Montana heats and melts copper ore. *Why is smelting necessary to process copper ore?*

Visual Learning

Figure 10 Copper-bearing minerals occur in coarse-grained igneous rocks in this mine. These ores often are referred to as porphyry copper deposits. Have students determine what is meant by the term *porphyry*. The term *porphyry* means that at least two distinct crystal sizes are present in a rock. ⬛ **Linguistic**

Extension

Have students research ways to safely dispose of wastes from mining operations. Students can present their findings on posters or on a class bulletin board. Waste is placed on top of clay or artificial liners. Fluids derived from the waste are collected and contained to prevent them from contaminating potable water sources. The piles of waste are covered with dirt and plants are grown on them. Scientists monitor the waste piles and local water supplies to ensure that no leakage occurs. L3 ⬛ **Linguistic**

Caption Answer

Figure 11 to extract and purify the copper

Resource Manager

Chapter Resources Booklet
  Reinforcement, p. 27
  Lab Activity, pp. 9–11
Cultural Diversity, p. 35

3 Assess

Reteach

Have student pairs review the photographs of minerals in this section and discuss how each could be described using the properties they have learned about. L1 COOP LEARN

LS Interpersonal

Challenge

Display four different minerals that can be recognized easily by one or two characteristics, and have students identify the minerals. Some minerals that may be used are quartz (hardness of 7), sulfur (yellow color), calcite (three directions of cleavage or reaction to hydrochloric acid), and hematite (red-brown streak). L2 **LS Visual-Spatial**

✔ Assessment

Content Have students work in groups of two or three to write a song with lyrics in their Science Journals about the definition of a mineral. Use **Performance Assessment in the Science Classroom,** p. 151.

Figure 12
Many metal objects you use every day are made with copper. *What other metals are used to produce everyday objects?*

Minerals Around You Now you have a better understanding of minerals and their uses. Can you name five things in your classroom that come from minerals? Can you go outside and find a mineral right now? You will find that minerals are all around you and that you use minerals every day. Next, you will look at rocks, which are Earth materials made up of combinations of minerals.

Section 1 Assessment

1. Explain the difference between a mineral and a rock. Name five common rock-forming minerals.

2. List five properties that are used most commonly to identify minerals.

3. Where in Earth is diamond formed? Describe an event that must occur in order for diamond to reach Earth's surface.

4. When is a mineral considered to be an ore? Describe the steps of mining, smelting, and refining that are used to extract minerals or elements from ores.

5. **Think Critically** Would you want to live close to a working gold mine? Explain.

Skill Builder Activities

6. **Comparing and Contrasting** Gems and ores are some of Earth's rarer minerals. Compare and contrast gems and ores. Why are they so valuable? Explain the importance of both in society today. **For more help, refer to the** Science Skill Handbook.

7. **Using Percentages** In 1996, the United States produced approximately 2,340,000 metric tons of refined copper. In 1997, about 2,440,000 metric tons of refined copper were produced. Compared to the 1996 amount, copper production increased by what percentage in 1997? **For more help, refer to the** Math Skill Handbook.

384 CHAPTER 13 Rocks and Minerals

Answers to Section Assessment

1. Mineral: naturally occurring, inorganic solid with a definite composition and orderly internal atomic arrangement; rock: usually comprised of two or more minerals; rock forming minerals include quartz, feldspar, calcite, gypsum, and halite; among others

2. Possible answers: color, luster, streak, hardness, cleavage, magnetism

3. Diamonds form in Earth's mantle under conditions of high pressure. Diamonds erupt to the surface via volcanic eruptions.

4. When it can be mined for profit; Ores are removed from the crust and melted to remove unwanted material. Then the remaining material is refined, or purified, and processed.

5. Answers will vary. Some students may feel that it would be an advantage to live close to a gold mine, as jobs might be available at the mine. Others might be wary of environmental problems caused by the mine.

6. Both deal with minerals. Gems are rare and can be cut and polished. Ores contain enough of a mineral that it

can be mined at a profit. Both are valuable because of the uses they have in today's society. Ores are probably more important to society because they have a wider use for most people.

7. $2,440,000t - 2,340,000t = 100,000t$; $100,000t/2,340,000t \times 100 = 4.3\%$

Igneous and Sedimentary Rocks

Igneous Rock

A rocky cliff, a jagged mountain peak, and a huge boulder probably all look solid and permanent to you. Rocks seem as if they've always been here and always will be. But little by little, things change constantly on Earth. New rocks form, and old rocks wear away. Such processes produce three main kinds of rocks—igneous, sedimentary, and metamorphic.

The deeper you go into the interior of Earth, the higher the temperature is and the greater the pressure is. Deep inside Earth, it is hot enough to melt rock. **Igneous** (IHG nee us) **rocks** form when melted rock from inside Earth cools. The cooling and hardening that result in igneous rock can occur on Earth, as seen in **Figure 13,** or underneath Earth's surface. When melted rock cools on Earth's surface, it makes an **extrusive** (ehk STREW sihv) igneous rock. Melted rock that cools below Earth's surface forms **intrusive** (ihn trew sihv) igneous rock.

Chemical Composition The chemicals in the melted rock determine the color of the resulting rock. If it contains a high percentage of silica and little iron, magnesium, or calcium, the rock will be light in color. Light-colored igneous rocks are called granitic (gra NIH tihk) rocks. If the silica content is far less, but it contains more iron, magnesium, or calcium, a dark-colored or basaltic (buh SAWL tihk) rock will result. Intrusive igneous rocks often are granitic, and extrusive igneous rocks often are basaltic. These two categories are important in classifying igneous rocks.

Figure 13
Sakurajima is a volcano in Japan. During the 1995 eruption, molten rock and solid rock were thrown into the air.

Section 2

Igneous and Sedimentary Rocks

①Motivate

Bellringer Transparency
Display the Section Focus Transparency for Section 2. Use the accompanying Transparency Activity Master. L2
ELL

Tie to Prior Knowledge
Help students recall that rocks can be made of more than just minerals. Both coal (made of organic material) and obsidian (made of volcanic glass) are rocks.

Section ✔*Assessment* Planner

PORTFOLIO
Science Journal, p. 387
PERFORMANCE ASSESSMENT
Try at Home MiniLAB, p. 390
Skill Builder Activities, p. 391
See page 404 for more options.

CONTENT ASSESSMENT
Section, p. 391
Challenge, p. 391
Chapter, pp. 404–405

Section 2 Igneous and Sedimentary Rocks   **385**

Igneous Rock

Discussion

Describe a rock that formed from magma that began to cool slowly underground and then erupted onto Earth's surface. These events result in a rock that has large crystals contained within a mass of smaller crystals. Large crystals begin to form when the magma is underground. When the lava erupts, it cools rapidly and forms tiny crystals or glass. This type of rock is said to have a porphyritic texture.

✔ Reading Check

Answer a large crack in Earth's crust from which lava erupts

Activity

Remind students that minerals containing higher concentrations of silicon and oxygen are light in color, and minerals containing less silicon and oxygen and more iron and magnesium are dark in color. Show students samples of granite, rhyolite, gabbro, and basalt. Ask them to work in small groups to determine which minerals are contained in each sample. L2
COOP LEARN **Interpersonal**

Rocks from Lava Extrusive igneous rocks form when melted rock cools on Earth's surface. Liquid rock that reaches Earth's surface is called lava. Lava cools quickly before large mineral crystals have time to form. That's why extrusive igneous rocks usually have a smooth, sometimes glassy appearance.

Extrusive igneous rocks can form in two ways. In one way, volcanoes erupt and shoot out lava and ash. Also, large cracks in Earth's crust, called fissures (FIH shurz), can open up. When they do, the lava oozes out onto the ground or into water. Oozing lava from a fissure or a volcano is called a lava flow. In Hawaii, lava flows are so common that you can observe one almost every day. Lava flows quickly expose melted rock to air or water. The fastest cooling lava forms no grains at all. This is how obsidian, a type of volcanic glass, forms. Lava trapping large amounts of gas can cool to form igneous rocks containing many holes.

✔ Reading Check   *What is a fissure?*

Figure 14
Extrusive igneous rocks form at Earth's surface. Intrusive igneous rocks form inside Earth. Wind and water can erode rocks to expose features such as dikes, sills, and volcanic necks.

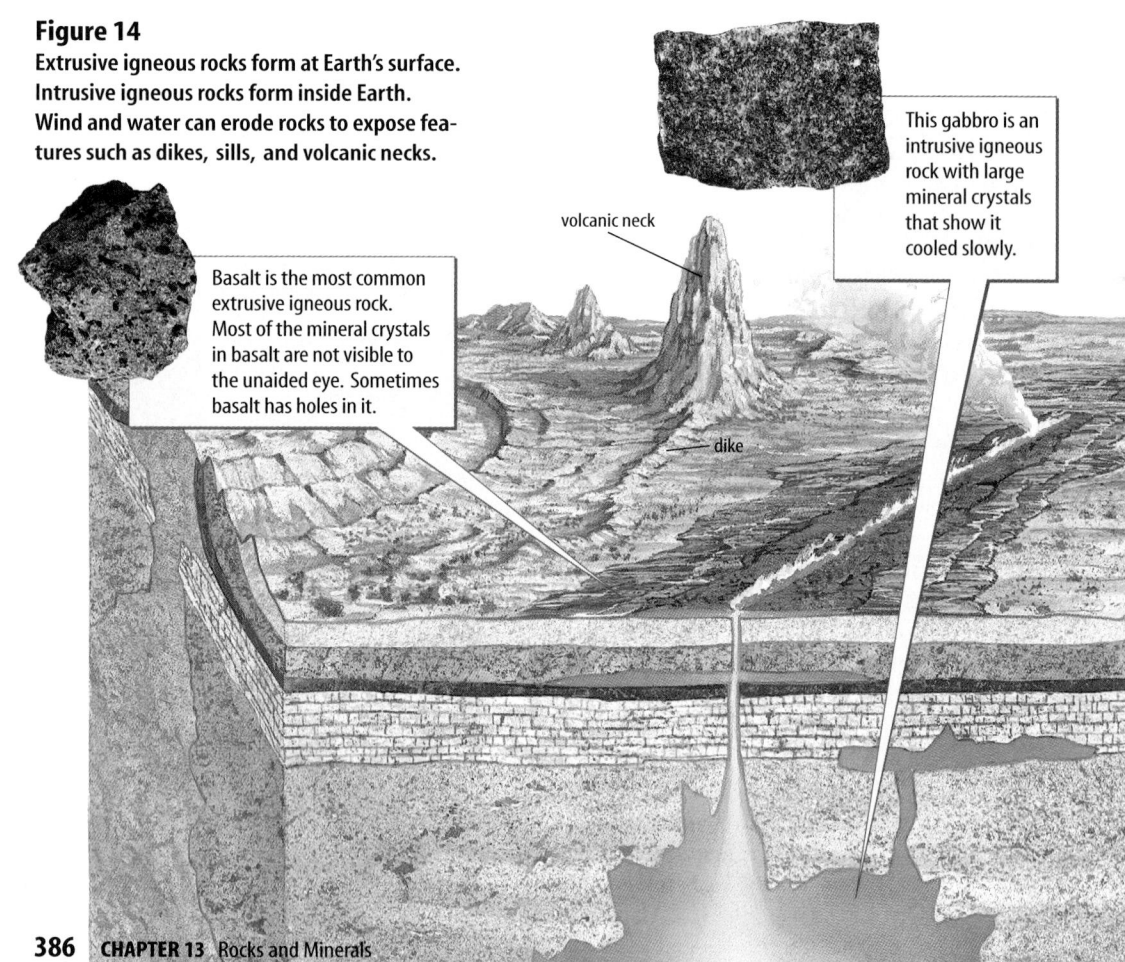

This gabbro is an intrusive igneous rock with large mineral crystals that show it cooled slowly.

volcanic neck

Basalt is the most common extrusive igneous rock. Most of the mineral crystals in basalt are not visible to the unaided eye. Sometimes basalt has holes in it.

dike

386   CHAPTER 13 Rocks and Minerals

🔬 LAB DEMONSTRATION

Purpose to show that igneous rocks can be identified by density and color
Materials 2 beakers (500 mL), pumice, scoria, water
Preparation Samples of pumice and scoria must be thoroughly dry.

Procedure Float pumice in one beaker of water and scoria in the other.
Expected Outcome Students observe that light-colored pumice floats, but that dark-colored scoria sinks. They should realize that scoria is denser than pumice. Sample colors indicate that scoria contains more iron and magnesium than does pumice.

✔ *Assessment*

Explain why pumice floats but scoria doesn't. Pumice is richer in silica and thus is not as dense as scoria. This, along with air bubbles that are trapped in the rock, allows it to float in water.

Rocks from Magma Some melted rock never reaches the surface. Such underground melted rock is called magma. Intrusive igneous rocks are produced when magma cools below the surface of Earth, as shown in **Figure 14.**

Intrusive igneous rocks form when a huge glob of magma from inside Earth rises toward the surface but never reaches it. It's similar to when a helium balloon rises and gets stopped by the ceiling. This hot mass of rock sits under the surface and cools slowly over millions of years until it is solid. The cooling is so slow that the minerals in the magma have time to form large crystals. The size of the mineral crystals is the main difference between intrusive and extrusive igneous rocks. Intrusive igneous rocks have large crystals that are easy to see. Extrusive igneous rocks do not have large crystals that you can see easily. **Figure 15** shows some igneous rock features.

✔ **Reading Check** *How do intrusive and extrusive rocks appear different?*

Physics INTEGRATION

The extreme heat found inside Earth has several sources. Some is left over from Earth's formation, and some comes from radioactive isotopes that constantly emit heat while they decay deep in Earth's interior. Research to find detailed explanations of these heat sources. Use your own words to explain them in your Science Journal.

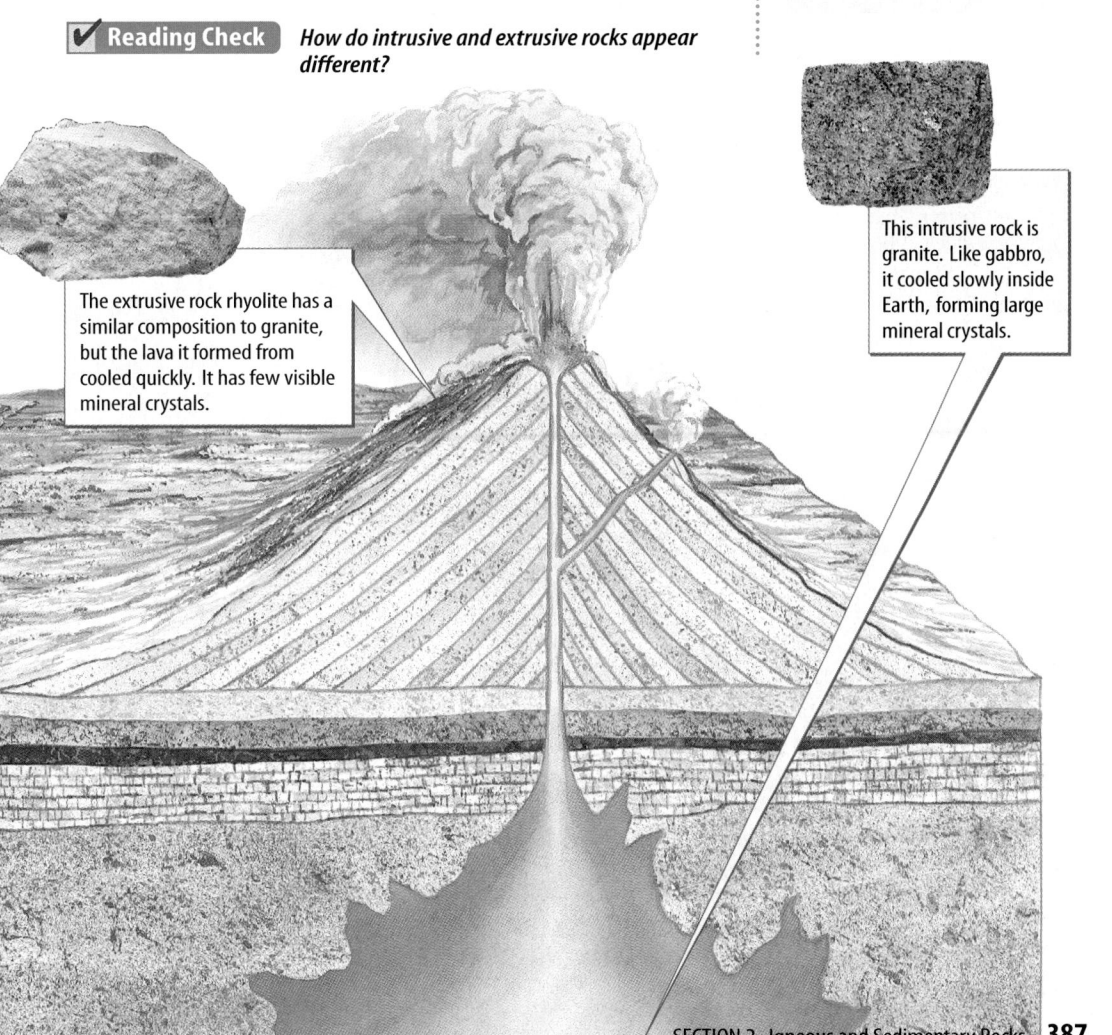

The extrusive rock rhyolite has a similar composition to granite, but the lava it formed from cooled quickly. It has few visible mineral crystals.

This intrusive rock is granite. Like gabbro, it cooled slowly inside Earth, forming large mineral crystals.

Use Science Words

Word Origin The roots of the words *intrusive* and *extrusive* are *in-*, in; *ex-*, out; and *trudere*, to push. Have students find other words with these roots and explain their meanings. intrude, to push in; interior, within; extrude, to push out; exterior, on the outside [L2] **Linguistic**

Physics INTEGRATION

Radioactive isotopes such as ^{40}K, ^{235}U, ^{238}U, ^{40}Ca, and many others are contained in minerals and other Earth materials. The decay processes that such isotopes undergo release energy in the form of heat.

✔ **Reading Check**

Answer Intrusive rocks have large crystals that can be easily seen; extrusive igneous rocks do not have large crystals that can be easily seen.

Activity

To help students understand why crystal size in igneous rocks is affected by how much time passes during the cooling process, give each student a strip of paper and tape. Tell students that when you say "go," they are to form loops from their paper and attach them to other students' loops. They are to continue until you say "stop" or until all loops are connected. At first, give students very little time in order to model crystals forming quickly. They should note that a high number of small groups of loops have formed. Now have students return to their original position. Give students more time to model crystals forming slowly. Students should note that fewer locations of larger groups of loops have formed. [L2] **Kinesthetic**

Science Journal

Igneous Rock Formation Have students research and write a creative short story in their Science Journals about what happens to a mineral crystal in magma or lava as an igneous rock forms. Their stories should include where cooling occurs, how long it takes, and what size the crystals are when the rock has solidified. [L2] **Linguistic** [P]

Resource Manager

Chapter Resources Booklet
  Directed Reading for Content Mastery, p. 21
Reading and Writing Skill Activities, p. 21

Visualizing Igneous Rock Features

Have students examine the pictures and read the captions. Then ask the following questions.

- **How do sills and dikes differ?** Sills are features that run parallel to the rock layers, while dikes cut across the rock layers.

- **Which is older, the sill or the rock surrounding it? Explain.** The rock surrounding the sill is older. It was in place before the sill formed as magma was forced between existing rock layers.

Activity

Have small groups of students research an area where intrusive igneous rock features can be visited, such as Yosemite National Park, California; Shiprock, New Mexico; Big Bend National Park, Texas; Devils Tower National Monument, Wyoming; or Navajo Volcanic Field, Arizona. Ask each group to prepare a travel brochure for the area that includes information on the intrusive features. [L2] COOP LEARN [IS] **Linguistic**

Extension

Have students research and write brief reports on the relationship between volcanic pipes, such as those near Kimberly, South Africa and in northern Canada, and diamonds. Students should find that the pipes formed from the magma that carried the diamonds toward Earth's surface from the mantle.

Figure 15

Intrusive igneous rocks are formed when a mass of liquid rock, or magma, rises toward Earth's surface and then cools before emerging. The magma cools in a variety of ways. Eventually the rocks may be uplifted and erosion may expose them at Earth's surface. A selection of these formations is shown here.

▶ This dike in Israel's Negev Desert formed when magma squeezed into cracks that cut across rock layers.

▶ A batholith is a very large igneous rock body that forms when rising magma cools below the ground. Towering El Capitan, right, is just one part of a huge batholith. It looms over the entrance to the Yosemite Valley.

▲ Sills such as this one in Death Valley, California, form when magma is forced into spaces that run parallel to rock layers.

▶ Volcanic necks like Shiprock, New Mexico, form when magma hardens inside the vent of a volcano. Because the volcanic rock in the neck is harder than the volcanic rock in the volcano's cone, only the volcanic neck remains after erosion wears the cone away.

388 CHAPTER 13 Rocks and Minerals

Resource Manager

Chapter Resources Booklet
Lab Activity, pp. 13–16

Earth Science Critical Thinking/Problem Solving, p. 10

Sedimentary Rocks

Pieces of broken rock, shells, mineral grains, and other materials make up what is called sediment (SE duh munt). The sand you squeeze through your toes at the beach is one type of sediment. As shown in **Figure 16,** sediment can collect in layers to form rocks. These are called **sedimentary** (sed uh MEN tuh ree) **rocks.** Rivers, ocean waves, mud slides, and glaciers can carry sediment. Sediment also can be carried by the wind. When sediment is dropped, or deposited, by wind, ice, gravity, or water, it collects in layers. After sediment is deposited, it begins the long process of becoming rock. Most sedimentary rocks take thousands to millions of years to form. The changes that form sedimentary rocks occur continuously. As with igneous rock, there are several kinds of sedimentary rocks. They fall into three main categories.

✔ **Reading Check** *How is sediment transported?*

Detrital Rocks When you mention sedimentary rocks, most people think about rocks like sandstone, which is a detrital (dih TRI tuhl) rock. Detrital rocks, shown in **Figure 17,** are made of grains of minerals or other rocks that have moved and been deposited in layers by water, ice, gravity, or wind. Other minerals dissolved in water act to cement these particles together. The weight of sediment above them also squeezes or compacts the layers into rock.

Figure 16
The layers in these rocks are the different types of sedimentary rocks that have been exposed at Sedona, in Arizona. *What causes the layers seen in sedimentary rocks?*

Figure 17
Four types of detrital sedimentary rocks include shale, siltstone, sandstone, and conglomerate.

Siltstone

Conglomerate

Sandstone

Shale

Sedimentary Rocks

Caption Answer
Figure 16 Sediment normally is deposited in horizontal layers parallel to Earth's surface.

✔ Reading Check

Answer Possible answers: rivers, ocean waves, wind, mudslides, and glaciers

Make a Model

Have students make a model that shows how detrital rocks form from broken pieces of other rocks. Provide teams of students with small chips of wood for a model of rock fragments and a bottle of wood glue or white glue. Have students mix the wood chips into the glue and then place the mixture between two sheets of waxed paper. Tell them to apply pressure to the mixture and then set it aside to dry. When it is dry, students will have a model of a detrital rock. [L2] ELL COOP LEARN [N] **Kinesthetic**

Visual Learning

Figure 17 The sizes of grains in a detrital rock are related to the energy of transport. For example, it takes fast-flowing water to move large particles. Have students rank the rocks shown in order of increasing energy of transport. shale, siltstone, sandstone, conglomerate [L2]

Curriculum Connection

Geography Have students pinpoint the location of the Bonneville Salt Flats and find out what processes occurred to form the salt flats. The Bonneville Salt Flats cover about 260 km² (100 mi²) in northwestern Utah. The flats, part of the Great Salt Lake Desert, are a remnant of the bed of an ancient lake formed about 30,000 years ago. As the water evaporated, the flats were formed from accumulating salts. [L3]

TRY AT HOME
Mini LAB

Purpose Students make models of an organic sedimentary rock with a clastic texture. L1

ELL COOP LEARN IS **Kinesthetic**

Materials small, disposable aluminum pie pan; broken macaroni (about 2 cups); white glue; water; fossiliferous limestone; mixing bowl

Teaching Strategies Suggest that students use macaroni of different shapes and sizes.

Analysis

1. The glue solution was the cement that held the "rock" together. It represents the calcite that holds limestone together.

2. Suggest that students use shape and texture to match the macaroni in their rocks to intact macaroni fossils.

✔ Assessment

Portfolio Have students make labeled posters of their artificial fossil drawings and of actual fossil drawings from true fossil rock samples. Ask students to share their posters with the class. Encourage them to include their posters in their portfolios. Use **PASC**, p. 145.

Fun Fact

Because organic sedimentary rocks form as a result of biochemical reactions, they can also be classified as biochemical rocks.

TRY AT HOME
Mini LAB

Modeling How Fossils Form Rocks

Procedure 🖐 🥽

1. Fill a small **aluminum pie pan** with pieces of broken **macaroni**. These represent various fossils.

2. Mix 50 mL of **white glue** into 250 mL of **water.** Pour this solution over the macaroni and set it aside to dry.

3. When your fossil rock sample has set, remove it from the pan and compare it with an actual **fossil limestone** sample.

Analysis

1. Explain why you used the glue solution and what this represents in nature.

2. Using whole macaroni samples as a guide, match the macaroni "fossils" in your "rock" to the intact macaroni. Draw and label them in your **Science Journal.**

Figure 18
The minerals left behind after a geyser erupts form layers of chemical rock.

Identifying Detrital Rocks To identify a detrital sedimentary rock, you use the size of the grains that make up the rock. The smallest, clay-sized grains feel slippery when wet and make up a rock called shale. Silt-sized grains are slightly larger than clay. These make up the rougher-feeling siltstone. Sandstone is made of yet larger, sand-sized grains. Pebbles are larger still. Pebbles mixed and cemented together with other sediment make up rocks called conglomerates (kun GLAHM ruts).

Chemical Rocks Some sedimentary rocks form when seawater, loaded with dissolved minerals, evaporates. Chemical sedimentary rock also forms when mineral-rich water from geysers, hot springs, or salty lakes evaporates, as shown in **Figure 18.** As the water evaporates, layers of the minerals are left behind. If you've ever sat in the Sun after swimming in the ocean, you probably noticed salt crystals on your skin. The seawater on your skin evaporated, leaving behind deposits of halite. The halite was dissolved in the water. Chemical rocks form this way from evaporation or other chemical processes.

Organic Rocks Would it surprise you to know that the chalk your teacher is using on the chalkboard might also be a sedimentary rock? Not only that, but coal, which is used as a fuel to produce electricity, is also a sedimentary rock.

Chalk and coal are examples of the group of sedimentary rocks called organic rocks. Organic rocks form over millions of years. Living matter dies, piles up, and then is compressed into rock. If the rock is produced from layers of plants piled on top of one another, it is called coal. Organic sedimentary rocks also form in the ocean and usually are classified as limestone.

Resource Manager 📖

Chapter Resources Booklet
  Reinforcement, p. 28
  MiniLAB, p. 4

Teacher FYI

Detrital sedimentary rocks, as well as any rock made of broken pieces of other rocks or fossils, are said to have clastic textures. For this reason, detrital sedimentary rocks are often called clastic rocks. Rocks composed of broken pieces of seashells also have a clastic texture, although they are organic rocks.

Figure 19
There are a variety of organic sedimentary rocks.

A The pyramids in Egypt are made from fossiliferous limestone.

B A thin slice through the limestone shows that it contains many small fossils.

Fossils Chalk and other types of fossiliferous limestone are made from the fossils of millions of tiny organisms, as shown in **Figure 19.** A fossil is the remains or trace of a once-living plant or animal. A dinosaur bone and footprint are both fossils.

Section 2 Assessment

1. Contrast the ways in which extrusive and intrusive igneous rocks are formed.

2. Infer why igneous rocks that solidify underground cool so slowly.

3. Diagram how each of the three kinds of sedimentary rocks forms. List one example of each kind of rock: detrital, chemical, and organic.

4. List in order from smallest to largest the grain sizes used to identify detrital rocks.

5. **Think Critically** If someone handed you a sample of an igneous rock and asked you whether it is extrusive or intrusive, what would you look for first? Explain.

Skill Builder Activities

6. **Concept Mapping** Coal is an organic sedimentary rock that can be used as fuel. Research to find out how coal forms. On a computer, develop an events-chain concept map showing the steps in its formation. **For more help, refer to the** Science Skill Handbook.

7. **Communicating** Research a national park or monument where volcanic activity has taken place. Read about the park and the features that you'd like to see. Then describe the features in your Science Journal. Be sure to explain how each feature formed. **For more help, refer to the** Science Skill Handbook.

Section 2 Igneous and Sedimentary Rocks **391**

---

③ Assess

Reteach

How is salt that forms on your skin after swimming in the ocean similar to the formation of chemical sedimentary rock? In both cases, deposits of salt form as water containing salt in solution evaporates. L1 **IS Logical-Mathematical**

Challenge

Conglomerate and breccia are both detrital rocks that form from gravel-sized sediment. Conglomerate contains rounded gravel; breccia contains angular gravel. Have students infer which rock is formed from sediment that is deposited near its source. Abrasion has not smoothed the angular sediment in breccia; therefore, it must have formed close to its sediment source. L3
IS Logical-Mathematical

✔Assessment

Oral Why are rocks such as sandstone and shale called sedimentary rocks? They form from sediment. **How can you distinguish extrusive from intrusive igneous rocks?** Intrusive rocks contain crystals that can be seen with the unaided eye. Use **Performance Assessment in the Science Classroom,** p. 89.

Answers to Section Assessment

1. Extrusive igneous rocks cool quickly from lava, producing no or small crystals. Intrusive igneous rocks cool slowly from magma, producing large crystals.

2. The surrounding rock insulates the cooling magma.

3. detrital rocks—pieces of other rocks, sandstone; chemical rocks— precipitation of minerals from solution, rock salt; organic rocks— from fossils, coal

4. clay, silt, sand, and gravel

5. The crystals; if they are visible to the unaided eye, the rock is intrusive.

6. Possible answer: plant material dies → becomes buried → is compressed into rock

7. Students might research and describe Hawaii Volcanoes National Park, Sunset Crater Volcano National Park, Capulin Volcano National Monument, Mount Rainier National Park, Sunset Crater Volcano National Monument, Lava Beds National Monument, Lassen Volcanic National Park, or Big Bend National Park, among others.

SECTION

3

Metamorphic Rocks and the Rock Cycle

1 Motivate

Bellringer Transparency

Display the Section Focus Transparency for Section 1. Use the accompanying Transparency Activity Master. L2
ELL

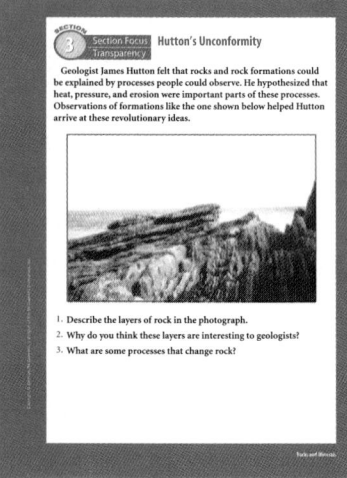

As You Read

What You'll Learn
- **Describe** the conditions needed for metamorphic rocks to form.
- **Explain** how all rocks are linked by the rock cycle.

Vocabulary
metamorphic rock   nonfoliated
foliated   rock cycle

Why It's Important
Metamorphic rocks and the rock cycle show that Earth is a constantly changing planet.

New Rock from Old Rock

The land around you changed last night—perhaps not measurably, but it changed. Even if you can't detect it, Earth is changing constantly. Wind relocates soil particles. Layers of sediment are piling up on lake bottoms where streams carrying sediment flow into them. Wind and rain are gradually wearing away cliffs. Landmasses are moving at a rate of a few centimeters per year. Rocks are disappearing slowly below Earth's surface. Some of these changes can cause existing rocks to be heated and squeezed, as shown in **Figure 20.** In the process, new rocks form.

It can take millions of years for rocks to change. That's the amount of time that often is necessary for extreme pressure to build while rocks are buried deeply or continents collide. Sometimes existing rocks are cooked when magma moves upward into Earth's crust, changing their mineral crystals. All these events can make new rocks out of old rocks.

✔ Reading Check   *What events can change rocks?*

Tie to Prior Knowledge

Remind students of the characteristics of granite. Then show them gneiss, a metamorphic rock. Have them compare and contrast granite and gneiss.

✔ Reading Check

Answer change in pressure or temperature conditions

Figure 20
The rocks of the Labrador Peninsula in Canada were squeezed into spectacular folds. This photo was taken during the space shuttle *Challenger* mission *STS-41G* in 1984.

392   CHAPTER 13 Rocks and Minerals

Section ✔ *Assessment* Planner

PORTFOLIO
Science Journal, p. 393
PERFORMANCE ASSESSMENT
Skill Builder Activities, p. 396
See page 404 for more options.

CONTENT ASSESSMENT
Section, p. 396
Challenge, p. 396
Chapter, pp. 404–405

Figure 21
High pressure and temperature can cause existing rocks to change into new metamorphic rocks. **A** Granite can change to gniess. **B** The sedimentary rock sandstone can become quartzite, and **C** limestone can change to marble.

Metamorphic Rocks Do you recycle your plastic milk jugs? After the jugs are collected, sorted, and cleaned, they are heated and squeezed into pellets. The pellets later can be made into useful new products. It takes millions of years, but rocks get recycled, too. This process usually occurs thousands of meters below Earth's surface where temperatures and pressures are high. New rocks that form when existing rocks are heated or squeezed are called **metamorphic** (me tuh MOR fihk) **rocks.** The word *metamorphic* means "change of form." This describes well how some rocks take on a whole new look when they are under great temperatures and pressures.

✔ **Reading Check** *What does the word metamorphic mean?*

Figure 21 shows three kinds of rocks and what they change into when they are subjected to the forces involved in metamorphism. Not only do the resulting rocks look different, they have recrystallized and might be chemically changed, too. The minerals often align in a distinctive way.

New Rock from Old Rock

Discussion

The pressure, as well as the heat and chemical reactions, that causes rocks to change can be generated in several different ways. **What Earth processes could generate the pressure needed for metamorphic changes?** mountain building, movement along a fault, burial beneath other rock layers

Activity

Provide students with samples of marble and quartzite and a glass plate. Explain that quartz in sandstone has a hardness of 7; calcite in limestone has a hardness of 3. Have them use this information and the glass plate to determine which rock forms from sandstone and which rock forms from limestone. Quartzite will scratch glass, marble will not. Thus quartzite forms from sandstone, and marble forms from limestone. Students should be careful when using the glass plates. They can break if too much pressure is applied. L2 **Kinesthetic**

✔ **Reading Check**

Answer change of form

Science Journal

Rock Uses Have students go on a scavenger hunt in your community for examples of uses for metamorphic rocks. Examples might include slate roofs, marble buildings and statues, and graphite in pencils and lubricants. Have students write paragraphs in their Science Journals explaining why each metamorphic rock is used for the purpose observed. L2 P

Resource Manager

Chapter Resources Booklet
Activity Worksheets, pp. 5–8
Enrichment, p. 32
Directed Reading for Content Mastery, pp. 21, 22

New Rock from Old Rock, continued

Fun Fact

Slate is used as flooring and as a roofing material because of the way it separates when broken. Slate breaks along smooth, flat surfaces called rock cleavage.

Quick Demo

Present samples of metamorphic rocks and the parent rocks from which they form. Some examples to use are slate–shale, quartzite–sandstone, marble–limestone, and gneiss–granite. Explain that the type of metamorphic rock that forms has to do with the intensity of metamorphism. Demonstrate with samples of shale, which changes to slate, then phyllite, then schist, then gneiss as metamorphic intensity increases. Explain that, in this case, crystal size increases with increasing intensity of metamorphism.

LS Visual-Spatial

Extension

Remind students that calcite reacts with acid. Metamorphic rocks formed from limestone, such as marble, also contain calcite and should also react with acid. Have students test some metamorphic rocks to determine whether any calcite is present. Caution students to wear safety goggles and aprons when testing rocks. L2 ELL LS **Kinesthetic**

Figure 22
There are many different types of metamorphic rocks.

A This statue is made from marble, a nonfoliated metamorphic rock.

B The roof of this house is made of slate, a foliated metamorphic rock.

SCIENCE Online

Collect Data Visit the Glencoe Science Web site at **science.glencoe.com** for data about the rock cycle. Make your own diagram of the rock cycle.

Types of Changed Rocks New metamorphic rocks can form from any existing type of rock—igneous, sedimentary, or metamorphic. A physical characteristic helpful for classifying all rocks is the texture of the rocks. This term refers to the general appearance of the rock. Texture differences in metamorphic rocks divide them into two main groups—foliated (FOH lee ay tud) and nonfoliated, as shown in **Figure 22.**

Foliated rocks have visible layers or elongated grains of minerals. The term *foliated* comes from the Latin *foliatus,* which means "leafy." These minerals have been heated and squeezed into parallel layers, or leaves. Many foliated rocks have bands of different-colored minerals. Slate, gneiss (NISE), phyllite (FIHL ite), and schist (SHIHST) are all examples of foliated rocks.

Nonfoliated rocks do not have distinct layers or bands. These rocks, such as quartzite, marble, and soapstone, often are more even in color than foliated rocks. If the mineral grains are visible at all, they do not seem to line up in any particular direction. Quartzite forms when the quartz sand grains in sandstone fuse after they are squeezed and heated. You can fuse ice crystals in a similar way if you squeeze a snowball. The presssure from your hands creates grains of ice inside.

SCIENCE Online

Internet Addresses

_____

_____

_____

Explore the Glencoe Science Web site at **science.glencoe.com** to find out more about topics in this section.

Resource Manager

Chapter Resources Booklet
Transparency Activity, p. 46

Earth Science Critical Thinking/Problem Solving, p. 4

Home and Community Involvement, p. 43

The Rock Cycle

Rocks are changing constantly from one type to another. If you wanted to describe these processes to someone, how would you do it? Would you use words or pictures? Scientists have created a model in diagram form called the **rock cycle** to show how different kinds of rock are related to one another and how rocks change from one type to another. Each rock is on a continuing journey through the rock cycle, as shown in **Figure 23.** A trip through the rock cycle takes millions of years.

Figure 23
This diagram of the rock cycle shows how rocks are recycled constantly from one kind of rock to another.

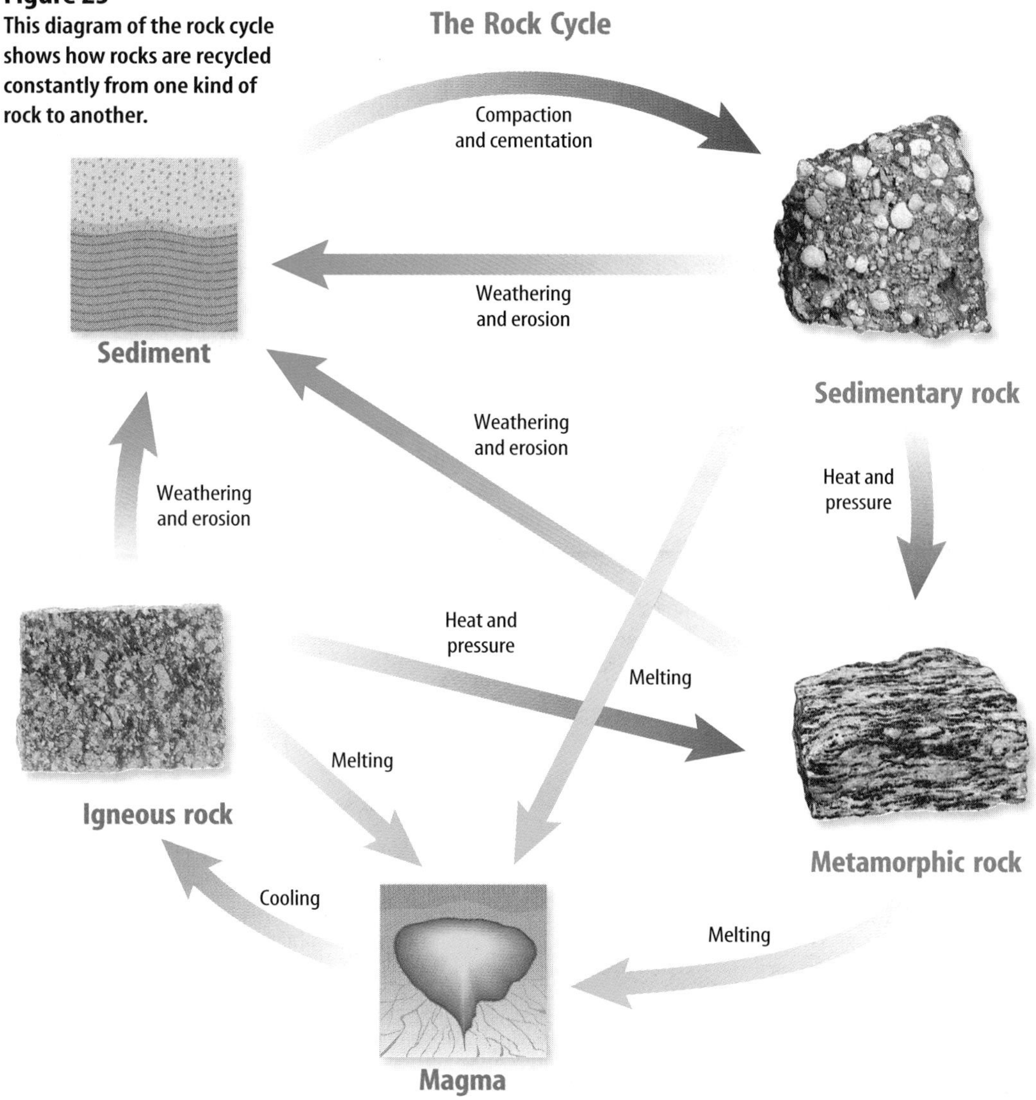

The Rock Cycle

- Compaction and cementation
- Weathering and erosion
- Sediment
- Weathering and erosion
- Weathering and erosion
- Sedimentary rock
- Heat and pressure
- Heat and pressure
- Melting
- Igneous rock
- Melting
- Metamorphic rock
- Cooling
- Melting
- Magma

Teacher FYI

Certain minerals produced by specific conditions of metamorphism can be used to indicate what degree of metamorphism has occurred. If these minerals are found in a rock, the conditions of metamorphism, such as pressure or temperature, that the rock underwent can be estimated. Minerals of this type are referred to as *index minerals*. Some examples are chlorite, garnet, staurolite, and sillimanite.

Use Science Words

Word Meaning Have students find out why nonfoliated rocks are also classified as recrystallized metamorphic rocks. When the parent rocks of nonfoliated rocks go through metamorphism, their mineral grains normally are not rearranged into flat layers. Instead, the mineral grains grow bigger, as they recrystallize into new, larger, interlocking crystals. L2
Linguistic

The Rock Cycle

Visual Learning

Figure 23 Emphasize that each arrow represents a process that changes rock from one form to another. Have students write a separate sentence that describes each arrow in the rock cycle diagram. L2 **Linguistic**

Cultural Diversity

Archaeology Rocks and minerals have been important resources for a wide variety of cultures for a long time.

- The oldest stone tool from Kenya dates from about 2.6 million years ago.
- Obsidian, or volcanic glass, provided extremely sharp cutting edges and could be fashioned into beautiful artwork. Obsidian

trade routes ran throughout the Americas by 200 B.C. and throughout Asia as early as 9000 B.C.

- The earliest paintings, preserved in caves throughout the world, are masterpieces created with charcoal, chalk, and various shades of ochre.

The Rock Cycle, continued

Answer If metamorphic rock is heated enough to melt, magma forms. Once the magma cools and crystallizes, igneous rock forms.

③ Assess

Reteach

Have students sketch foliated and nonfoliated metamorphic rocks. Ask individual students to describe what their sketches show. L2 ELL IS **Visual-Spatial**

Challenge

Slate, schist, and gneiss all are foliated metamorphic rocks formed by different intensities of metamorphism. Individual foliated mineral grains are easily visible in gneiss and to a lesser degree in schist. They are not visible in slate. Based on the size of the mineral grains, have students hypothesize the order in which the three rocks normally form. slate, schist, gneiss

✔Assessment

Portfolio Have students write a letter in which they describe a rock. The letter must describe the rock well enough without naming it that another student can identify it. Use **Performance Assessment in the Science Classroom,** p. 139.

Figure 24
This lava in Hawaii is flowing into the ocean and cooling rapidly.

The Journey of a Rock Pick any point on the diagram of the rock cycle in **Figure 23,** and you will see how a rock in that part of the cycle could become any other kind of rock. Start with a blob of lava that oozes to the surface and cools, as shown in **Figure 24.** It forms an igneous rock. Wind, rain, and ice wear away at the rock, breaking off small pieces. These pieces are now called sediment. Streams and rivers carry the sediment to the ocean where it piles up over time. The weight of sediment above compresses the pieces below. Mineral-rich water seeps through the sediment and glues, or cements, it together. It becomes a sedimentary rock. If this sedimentary rock is buried deeply, pressure and heat inside Earth can change it into a metamorphic rock. Metamorphic rock deep inside Earth can melt and begin the cycle again. In this way, all rocks on Earth are changed over millions and millions of years. This process is taking place right now.

Reading Check *Describe how a metamorphic rock might change into an igneous rock.*

Section ③ Assessment

1. Identify two factors that can produce metamorphic rocks.
2. List examples of foliated and nonfoliated rocks. Explain the difference between the two types of metamorphic rocks.
3. Igneous rocks and metamorphic rocks can form at high temperatures and pressures. Explain the difference between these two rock types.
4. Scientists have diagrammed the rock cycle. Explain what this diagram shows.
5. **Think Critically** Trace the journey of a piece of granite through the rock cycle. Explain how this rock could be changed from an igneous rock to a sedimentary rock and then to a metamorphic rock.

Skill Builder Activities

6. **Drawing Conclusions** Describe an event that is a part of the rock cycle you can observe occurring around you or that you see on television news. Explain the steps leading up to this part of the rock cycle, and the steps that could follow to continue the cycle. **For more help, refer to the** Science Skill Handbook.
7. **Using an Electronic Spreadsheet** Using a spreadsheet program, create a data table to list the properties of different rocks and minerals that you have studied in this chapter. After you've made your table, cut and paste the different rows so as to group like rocks and minerals together. **For more help, refer to the** Technology Skill Handbook.

Answers to Section Assessment

1. two of the following: heat, pressure, chemical reactions
2. Foliated: gneiss, slate, phyllite, schist (mineral layering); nonfoliated: marble, quartzite, soapstone (no layering)
3. Igneous rocks form from completely melted rock (magma or lava).

Metamorphic rocks can form as a result of increases in temperature and pressure without melting.
4. It shows how one rock type is changed to another in a never-ending cycle.
5. Igneous rock (granite) is weathered into sediment. Sediment is deposited where it is compacted and cemented

to form sedimentary rocks. Sedimentary rocks are squeezed, heated, and changed chemically to form metamorphic rocks.
6. Students might describe erosion and deposition caused by floods or landslides or deposition of volcanic rock during a volcanic eruption.

7. Characteristics students might include in their tables are: minerals: hardness, color, streak, luster, cleavage; igneous rocks: intrusive and extrusive; sedimentary rocks: detrital, chemical, and organic; metamorphic rocks: foliated and nonfoliated

Gneiss Rice

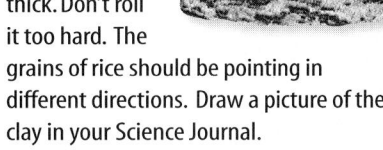

You know that metamorphic rocks often are layered. But did you realize that individual mineral grains can change in orientation? This means that the grains can line up in certain directions. You'll experiment with rice grains in clay to see how foliation is produced.

What You'll Investigate
What conditions will cause an igneous rock to change into a metamorphic rock?

Materials
rolling pin
lump of modeling clay
uncooked rice (wild rice, if available) (200 g)
granite sample
gneiss sample

Goals
■ **Investigate** ways rocks are changed.
■ **Model** a metamorphic rock texture.

Safety Precautions

WARNING: *Do not taste, eat, or drink any materials used in the lab.*

Procedure
1. **Sketch** the granite specimen in your Science Journal. Be sure that your sketch clearly shows the arrangement of the mineral grains.
2. Pour the rice onto the table. Roll the ball of clay in the rice. Some of the rice will stick to the outside of the ball. Knead the ball until the rice is spread out fairly evenly. Roll and knead the ball again, and repeat until your clay sample has lots of "minerals" distributed throughout it.

3. Using the rolling pin, roll the clay so it is about 0.5 cm thick. Don't roll it too hard. The grains of rice should be pointing in different directions. Draw a picture of the clay in your Science Journal.
4. Take the edge of the clay closest to you and fold it toward the edge farthest from you. Roll the clay in the direction you folded it. Fold and roll the clay in the same direction several more times. Flatten the lump to 0.5 cm in thickness again. Draw what you observe in your "rock" and in the gneiss sample in your Science Journal.

Conclude and Apply
1. What features did the granite and the first lump of clay have in common?
2. What force caused the positions of rice grains in the lump of clay to change? How is this process similar to and different from what happens in nature?

*C*ommunicating
Your Data

Refer to your Science Journal diagrams and the rock samples provided for you in this activity and make a poster relating this activity to processes in the rock cycle. Be sure to include diagrams of what you did, as well as information on how similar events occur in nature. **For more help, refer to the** Science Skill Handbook.

ACTIVITY 397

Purpose Students demonstrate how pressure causes a realignment of mineral grains, forming a metamorphic rock. L2 ELL COOP LEARN Kinesthetic

Process Skills observing, inferring, recognizing cause and effect, interpreting scientific illustrations, making models

Time Required 30 minutes

Teaching Strategy Have students roll small amounts of clay into the rice. Then put smaller pieces together and knead the clay until the rice is thoroughly mixed in.

Answers to Questions
1. The granite has many mineral crystals arranged randomly throughout. The clay has many rice grains distributed randomly.
2. Compression forced rice grains to change orientation. In nature, compression forces mineral grains to realign. Heat and chemical changes caused by fluids also can cause metamorphism.

✓*Assessment*

Process Provide students with three different metamorphic rocks and the rocks from which they formed. Have students determine which rock changed to form a foliated metamorphic rock, similar to the layered clay rock in the activity. Rocks to use are sandstone-quartzite, granite-gneiss, and shale-slate. Use **PASC**, p. 97.

Resource Manager

Chapter Resources Booklet
Activity Worksheet, pp. 5–6
Reinforcement, p. 29
Transparency Activity, pp. 47–48

*C*ommunicating
Your Data

Encourage students to include images of granite and photos of their first lump of clay to show what they have in common. Images of gneiss could be included along with a photo of the clay after it has been flattened to represent metamorphism.

Activity

BENCH TESTED

What You'll Investigate

Purpose

Students will test a variety of mineral samples and use a field guide to identify each sample.

Process Skills

testing, observing, collecting and interpreting data, inferring, identifying

Time Required

one class period

Materials

It is not necessary that each group have the same set of mineral samples to classify. Try to have samples for each group that vary enough in their properties so students will be able to easily identify them.

Alternate Materials

If specimens do not have numbers tagged or painted on them, you might put them in numbered containers. Students should replace each sample in its correct container.

You also might want to have students test samples for attraction to a magnet.

Safety Precautions

Remind students to keep goggles on at all times. Have students wash their hands after they are finished handling samples.

Activity

Classifying Minerals

You are hiking along a trail and encounter what looks like an interesting rock. You notice that it is uniform in color and shows distinct crystal faces. You think it must be a mineral and you want to identify it so you open a guidebook to rocks and minerals. What observations must you make in order to identify it? What tests can you make in the field?

What You'll Investigate

How to classify a set of minerals.

Materials

set of minerals	streak plate
hand lens	Mohs scale
putty knife	minerals field guide

Safety Precautions

WARNING: *Be careful when using a knife. Never taste any materials used in a lab.*

Goals

- **Test** and observe important mineral characteristics.

Resource Manager

Chapter Resources Booklet
Activity Worksheet, pp.7–8
Lab Management and Safety, p. 55

Procedure

1. Copy the data table below into your Science Journal. Based on your observations and streak and hardness tests, fill in columns 2 to 6. In the sixth column— "Scratches which samples?"—list the number of each mineral sample that this sample was able to scratch. Use this information to rank each sample from softest to hardest. Compare these ranks to Mohs scale to help identify the mineral. Consult the rocks and minerals field guide to fill in the last column after compiling all the characteristics.

2. Obtain a classroom set of minerals.

3. **Observe** each sample and conduct appropriate tests to complete as much of your data table as possible.

Mineral Characteristics							
Sample Number	Crystal Shape	Cleavage/ Fracture	Color	Streak and Luster	Scratches which samples?	Hardness Rank	Mineral Name
1							
2							
…			Answers will vary				
No. of samples							

Conclude and Apply

1. Based on the information in your data table, identify each mineral.

2. Did you need all of the information in the table to identify each mineral? Explain why or why not.

3. Which characteristics were easy to determine? Which were somewhat more difficult? Explain.

4. Were some characteristics more useful as indicators than others?

5. Would you be able to identify minerals in the field after doing this activity? Which characteristics would be easy to determine on the spot? Which would be difficult?

6. **Describe** how your actions in this activity are similar to those of a scientist. What additional work might a scientist have done to identify these unknown minerals?

Communicating
Your Data

Create a visually appealing poster showing the minerals in this activity and the characteristics that were useful for identifying each one. Be sure to include informative labels on your poster.

Assessment

Oral Ask students to explain why more than one characteristic must be observed before identifying a mineral sample. Use **Performance Assessment in the Science Classroom,** p. 89.

Communicating
Your Data

Each group can present their poster to the class. Discuss any differing opinions as to the characteristics that were useful for identifying each mineral.

Procedure

Teaching Strategies
Students should gather data on one mineral sample at a time to avoid confusion.

Tie to Prior Knowledge
Most students have used a rock, stone, or chalk to draw on a sidewalk, so they know that a softer mineral can leave a streak on a harder substance, and that a harder substance will not leave a streak but will scratch a softer substance.

Expected Outcome
Most results will indicate that students are able to use the characteristics of minerals to identify samples.

Conclude and Apply

1. Answers will depend on the samples students observed.

2. Answers will vary depending on samples, but some minerals, such as sulfur, may be easy to identify based only on color.

3. Color and streak are easy to determine. Crystal shape and cleavage/fracture may be more difficult for students to determine.

4. Hardness and streak are probably more useful than some other characteristics.

5. Color and possibly crystal shape (if crystals were large) would be easy to spot in the field. Hardness and streak would be more difficult to test in the field.

6. Possible answers: actions involved use of science process skills; actions followed procedures. Additional tests might include testing for magnetism, testing with acid, and analyzing chemistry.

Error Analysis
Have each group compare their results with your key to the minerals. If the identifications of the samples do not agree, have students list possible reasons for the discrepancies.

Content Background

In nature, gold is usually found as a pure metal, often in the form of nuggets or flakes. It is fairly widely distributed throughout the world and is often found associated with quartz and pyrite ("fool's gold"). In its pure state, gold is one of the most beautiful minerals. Its chemical symbol, Au, comes from the Latin word *aurum*, which means "shining dawn."

The gold rushes of California and Alaska have become an important part of the early history of the American West. Much of the gold in California was recovered from placer deposits by panning. When miners swirled gold-bearing sand around in shallow pans, the sand and gravel washed over the rim, leaving the heavier gold flakes or nuggets behind.

Discussion

Why did so many people rush to California to prospect for gold? Gold is very valuable and they wanted to become wealthy.

Why is gold such a valuable mineral? Possible answers: It is not a common mineral, so that makes it more valuable. It doesn't tarnish or corrode like most other metals.

Fun Fact

The largest gold nugget ever found had a mass of about 70 kg. It was found in Victoria, Australia, in 1869.

Oops! Accidents in SCIENCE

SOMETIES GREAT DISCOVERIES HAPPEN BY ACCIDENT!

Going for the

A time line history of the accidental discovery of gold in California

CALIFORNIA REPUBLIC

1840

California is a quiet place. Only a few hundred people live in the small town of San Francisco.

1848

On January 24, Marshall notices something glinting in the water. Is it a nugget of gold? Aware that all that glitters is not gold, Marshall hits it with a rock. Marshall knows that "fool's gold" shatters when hit. But this shiny metal bends. More nuggets are found. Marshall shows the gold nugget to Sutter. After some more tests, they decide it is gold! Sutter and Marshall try to keep the discovery a secret, but word leaks out.

1850

California becomes the thirty-first state.

Sutter's Mill

1847

John Sutter hires James Marshall to build a sawmill on his ranch. Marshall and local Native Americans work quickly to harness the water power of the American River. They dig a channel from the river to run the sawmill. The water is used to make the waterwheel work.

Miners hope to strike it rich.

1849

The Gold Rush hits! A flood of people from around the world descends on northern California. They're dubbed "forty-niners" because they leave home in 1849 to seek their fortunes. San Francisco's population grows to 25,000. Many people become wealthy—but not Marshall or Sutter. Since Sutter doesn't have a legal claim to the land, the U.S. government claims it.

400

Resources for Teachers and Students

The Gold Rush, by Liza Ketchum, Little, Brown, 1996.

The California Gold Rush in American History, by Linda Jacobs Altman, Enslow Publishers, 1997.

The Diary of David R. Leeper: Rushing for Gold, edited by Connie and Peter Roop, Benchmark Books, 2001.

The California Gold Rush, by Jean F. Blashfield, Compass Point Books, 2001.

Gold Rush: Hands-On Projects About Mining the Riches of California, by Jennifer Quasha, Powerkids Press, 2001.

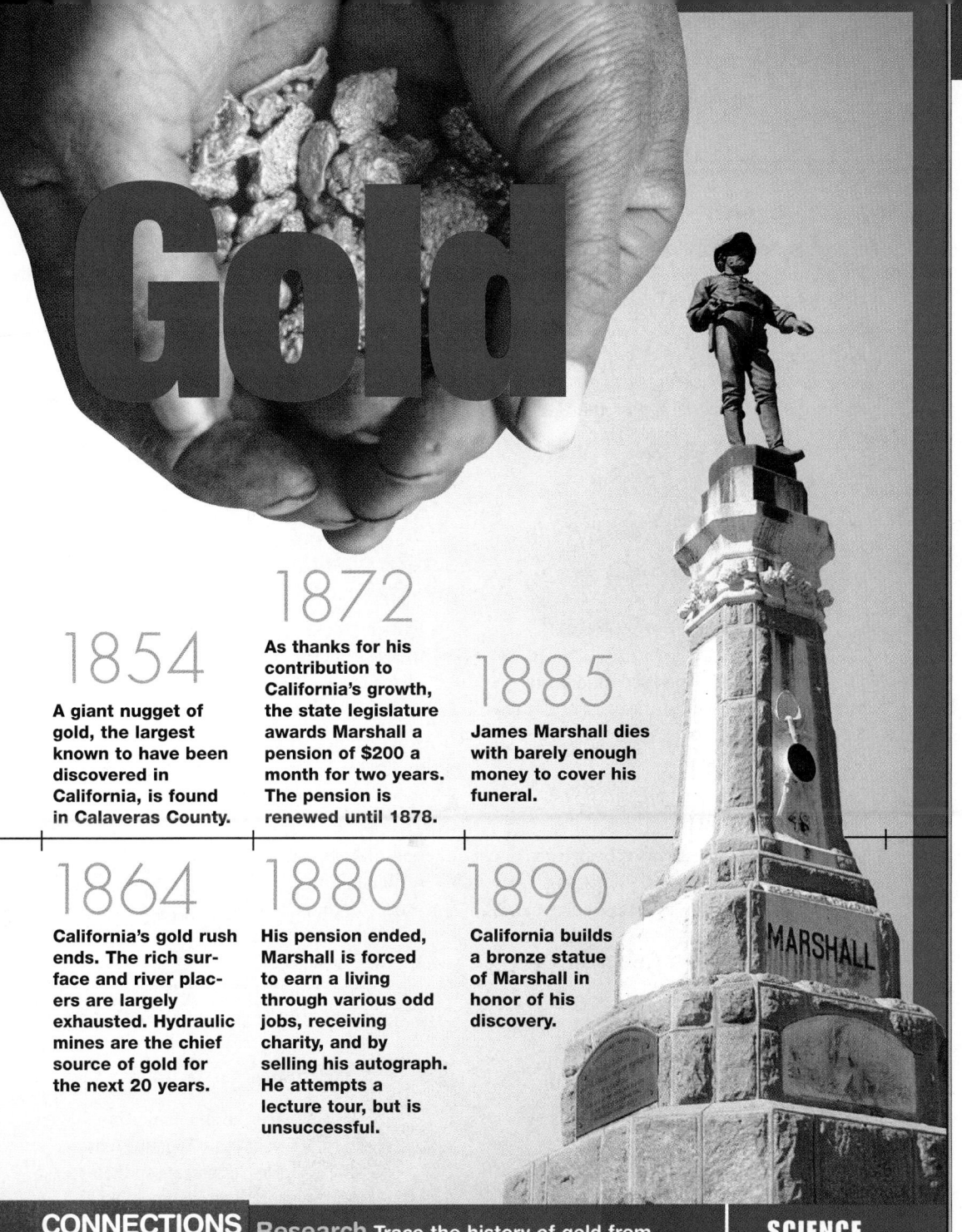

Gold

1854

A giant nugget of gold, the largest known to have been discovered in California, is found in Calaveras County.

1872

As thanks for his contribution to California's growth, the state legislature awards Marshall a pension of $200 a month for two years. The pension is renewed until 1878.

1885

James Marshall dies with barely enough money to cover his funeral.

1864

California's gold rush ends. The rich surface and river placers are largely exhausted. Hydraulic mines are the chief source of gold for the next 20 years.

1880

His pension ended, Marshall is forced to earn a living through various odd jobs, receiving charity, and by selling his autograph. He attempts a lecture tour, but is unsuccessful.

1890

California builds a bronze statue of Marshall in honor of his discovery.

MARSHALL

Activity

Allow students to simulate the method used by miners during the California Gold Rush. In a shallow aluminum pie pan, have them mix a handful each of sand and fine gravel. Then have them mix in a few pieces of lead shot to simulate gold. Point out to students that lead, like gold, is more dense than the other materials. Finally have them stir in about 100 mL of water. Have students gently shake the pie pan back and forth over a large dishpan, so that the water and lighter materials slosh out. The lead shot will remain in the bottom of the pan when it is nearly empty.

Analyze the Event

- **What might have happened if James Marshall had not known that "fool's gold" shatters when hit?** Possible answer: He might not have realized that he had found gold and the gold rush might never have happened.

- **Why do you think Sutter and Marshall tried to keep the discovery a secret?** Possible answer: If other people hadn't found out about the gold, they would have been able to retrieve more gold for themselves and would have become very rich.

CONNECTIONS
Research Trace the history of gold from ancient civilizations to the present. How was gold used in the past? How is it used in the present? What new uses for gold have been discovered? Report to the class.

SCIENCE *Online*
For more information, visit science.glencoe.com

CONNECTIONS
Gold was made into simple ornaments as early as 3000 B.C. in Egypt. Excavations in Sumeria (present-day Iraq) have yielded sophisticated goldwork dating to about 2500 B.C. By 2000 B.C. the techniques of filigree work were known to Minoan goldsmiths in Crete. In the past, gold has been widely used for decorative purposes. However, its current uses include as a coating for space vehicles, coating large windows to prevent the greenhouse effect in buildings, and coating electronic switches and connectors.

SCIENCE *Online*

Internet Addresses

_____

_____

Explore the Glencoe Science Web site at **science.glencoe.com** to find out more about topics in this feature.

Reviewing Main Ideas

Preview

Students can answer the questions in their Science Journals. Discuss the answers as you go through the chapter. IS **Linguistic**

Review

Students can write their answers, then compare them with those of other students. IS **Interpersonal**

Reteach

Students can look at the illustrations and describe details that support the main ideas of the chapter. IS **Visual-Spatial**

Answers to Chapter Review

SECTION 1

1. The shape of this amethyst's crystals is an indication of its internal atomic arrangement.

SECTION 2

4. compaction and cementation

SECTION 3

3. extrusive igneous rocks

Reviewing Main Ideas

Section 1 Minerals—Earth's Jewels

1. Minerals are inorganic solid materials found in nature. They generally have the same chemical makeup, and the atoms always are arranged in an orderly pattern. Rocks are combinations of two or more minerals. *In what way does this amethyst reflect the orderly pattern of its atoms?*

2. These properties can be used to identify minerals—crystal shape, cleavage and fracture, color, streak, luster, hardness, and specific gravity.

3. Gems are minerals that are rare. When cut and polished they are beautiful.

4. Ores of useful minerals must be extracted from Earth in a process called mining. Ores usually must be processed to produce metals.

Section 2 Igneous and Sedimentary Rocks

1. Igneous rocks form when melted rock from inside Earth cools and hardens.

2. Extrusive igneous rocks are formed on Earth's surface and have small or no crystals. Intrusive igneous rocks harden underneath Earth's surface and have large crystals.

3. Sedimentary rocks are made from pieces of other rocks, minerals, or plant and animal matter that collect in layers.

4. There are three groups of sedimentary rocks. Rocks formed from grains of minerals or other rocks are called detrital rocks. *What two processes occurred to change sand into this sandstone?*

5. Rocks formed from a chemical process such as evaporation of mineral-rich water are called chemical rocks. Rocks formed from fossils or plant remains are organic rocks.

Section 3 Metamorphic Rocks and the Rock Cycle

1. Existing rocks change into metamorphic rocks after becoming heated or squeezed inside Earth. The result is a rock with an entirely different appearance.

2. Foliated metamorphic rocks are easy to spot due to the layers of minerals. Nonfoliated metamorphic rocks lack distinct layers.

3. The rock cycle shows how all rocks are related and the processes that change them from one type to another. *What rock type would result from this volcanic eruption?*

FOLDABLES
Reading & Study Skills

After You Read

Use the information in your Venn Diagram Study Fold to compare and contrast rocks and minerals. Write common characteristics under the *Both* tab.

FOLDABLES
Reading & Study Skills

After You Read

After students have read the chapter and completed the Foldable described in Before You Read, have them do the activity on the student page.

Dinah Zike

Visualizing Main Ideas

Complete the concept map using the following terms and phrases: extrusive, organic, foliated, intrusive, chemical, nonfoliated, detrital, metamorphic, *and* sedimentary.

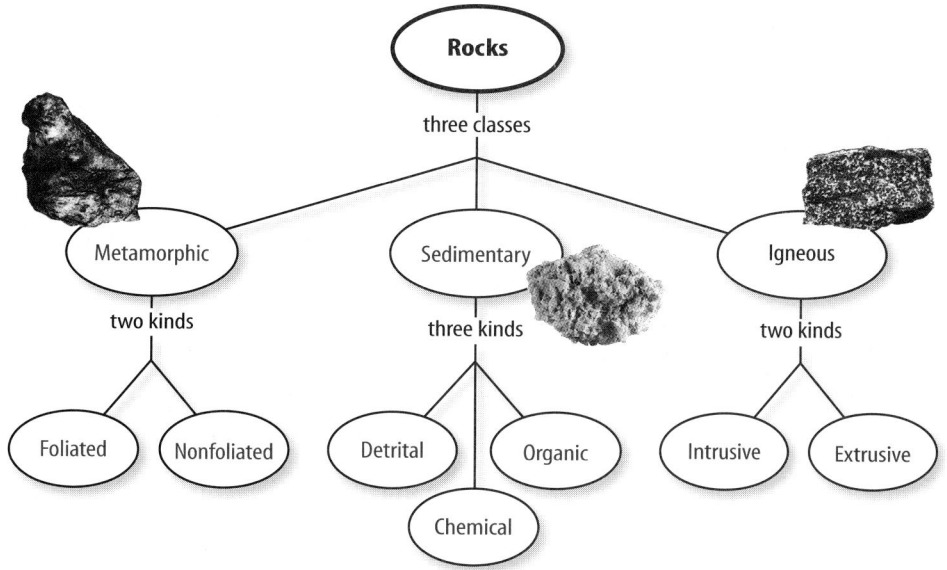

Rocks — three classes

- Metamorphic — two kinds: Foliated, Nonfoliated
- Sedimentary — three kinds: Detrital, Organic, Chemical
- Igneous — two kinds: Intrusive, Extrusive

Vocabulary Review

Vocabulary Words

a. crystal
b. extrusive
c. foliated
d. gem
e. igneous rock
f. intrusive
g. metamorphic rock
h. mineral
i. nonfoliated
j. ore
k. rock
l. rock cycle
m. sedimentary rock

 **THE PRINCETON REVIEW** **Study Tip**

Make sure to read over your class notes after each lesson. Reading them will help you better understand what you've learned, as well as prepare you for the next day's lesson.

Using Vocabulary

Explain the difference between each pair of vocabulary words.

1. mineral, rock
2. crystal, gem
3. cleavage, fracture
4. hardness, streak
5. rock, rock cycle
6. intrusive, extrusive
7. igneous rock, metamorphic rock
8. foliated, nonfoliated
9. rock, ore
10. metamorphic rock, sedimentary rock

Visualizing Main Ideas

See student page.

Vocabulary Review

Using Vocabulary

1. Minerals are composed of orderly arrangements of atoms. Most rocks are composed of minerals.
2. Crystals are solid materials that have an orderly arrangement of atoms. Gems are rare and beautiful minerals that often are cut from crystals.
3. Cleavage is the breaking of a mineral along smooth, flat planes. Fracture is breakage with an uneven or curved surface.
4. Hardness is a measure of how easily a mineral can be scratched. Streak is the color of the powdered mineral.
5. Most rocks are aggregates of minerals. The rock cycle is a model showing how rocks change.
6. Intrusive rocks form inside Earth. Extrusive rocks form at or near Earth's surface.
7. Igneous rock forms from magma or lava. Metamorphic rock forms when preexisting rocks are altered by heat, pressure, or fluids.
8. Foliated rocks have layers of mineral grains. Nonfoliated rocks have mostly no layers.
9. A rock is an aggregate of minerals. An ore is a rock that can be mined at a profit.
10. Metamorphic rocks form from changes in temperature, pressure, or chemical conditions. Sedimentary rocks form from sediment or by precipitation from solution.

Chapter 13 Assessment

Checking Concepts

1. B
2. D
3. B
4. D
5. D
6. B
7. A
8. B
9. A
10. A

Thinking Critically

11. No; sugar comes from plants. Minerals are inorganic.

12. Possible answers: The deposits are too small or the expense of mining in remote areas is too high.

13. If gneiss, granite, and basalt were all exposed to erosion, pieces of all three could be moved and deposited together to form a conglomerate.

14. No; the heat, pressure, and chemical changes that form metamorphic rocks would likely destroy the dinosaur bone.

15. Quartz forms in igneous rocks as magma cools. If such a rock is weathered, eroded, and deposited as sediment, the quartz can be cemented and compacted into sedimentary rock.

Checking Concepts

Choose the word or phrase that best answers the question.

1. Which of the following describes what rocks usually are composed of?
   A) pieces
   B) minerals
   C) fossil fuels
   D) foliations

2. When do metamorphic rocks form?
   A) when layers of sediment are deposited
   B) when lava solidifies in seawater
   C) when particles of rock break off at Earth's surface
   D) when heat and pressure change rocks

3. How can sedimentary rocks be classified?
   A) foliated or nonfoliated
   B) organic, chemical, or detrital
   C) extrusive or intrusive
   D) gems or ores

4. What kind of rocks are produced by volcanic eruptions?
   A) detrital
   B) foliated
   C) organic
   D) extrusive

5. Which of the following must be true for a substance to be considered a mineral?
   A) It must be organic.
   B) It must be glassy.
   C) It must be a gem.
   D) It must be naturally occurring.

6. Which of the following describes grains in igneous rocks that form slowly from magma below Earth's surface?
   A) no grains
   B) visible grains
   C) sedimentary grains
   D) foliated grains

7. How do sedimentary rocks form?
   A) They are deposited on Earth's surface.
   B) They form from magma.
   C) They are squeezed into foliated layers.
   D) They form deep in Earth's crust.

8. Which of these is NOT a physical property of a mineral?
   A) cleavage
   B) organic
   C) fracture
   D) hardness

9. Which is true of all minerals?
   A) They are inorganic solids.
   B) They have a glassy luster.
   C) They have a conchoidal fracture.
   D) They are harder than a penny.

10. Which is true about how all detrital rocks form?
    A) form from grains of preexisting rocks
    B) form from lava
    C) form by evaporation
    D) form from plant remains

Thinking Critically

11. Is a sugar crystal a mineral? Explain.

12. Metal deposits in Antarctica are not considered to be ores. List some reasons for this.

13. How is it possible to find pieces of gneiss, granite, and basalt in a single conglomerate?

14. Would you expect to find a well-preserved dinosaur bone in a metamorphic rock like schist? Explain.

15. Explain how the mineral quartz could be in an igneous rock and in a sedimentary rock.

Developing Skills

16. **Communicating** You are hiking in the mountains and as you cross a shallow stream, you see an unusual rock. You notice that it is full of fossil shells. Your friend asks you what it is. What do you say and why?

Chapter ✔Assessment Planner

Portfolio Encourage students to place in their portfolios one or two items of what they consider to be their best work. Examples include:
- Life Science Integration, p. 377
- Science Journal, p. 387
- Science Journal, p. 393

Performance Additional performance assessments, Performance Task Assessment Lists, and rubrics for evaluating these activities can be found in Glencoe's **Performance Assessment in the Science Classroom.**

17. **Classifying** Your teacher gives you two clear minerals. What quick test could you do in order to determine which is halite and which is calcite?

18. **Concept Mapping** Complete this concept map about minerals.

Minerals

Identifying properties include

- Hardness
- Streak and luster
- Cleavage and fracture
- Specific gravity
- Color

19. **Testing a Hypothesis** Your teacher gives you a glass plate, a nail, a penny, and a bar magnet. On a computer, describe how you would use these items to determine the hardness and special property of the mineral magnetite. Refer to **Table 1** for help.

Performance Assessment

20. **Making models** Determine what materials and processes you would need to use to set up a working model of the rock cycle. Describe the ways in which your model is accurate and the ways in which it falls short. Present your model to the class.

TECHNOLOGY

Go to the Glencoe Science Web site at **science.glencoe.com** or use the **Glencoe Science CD-ROM** for additional chapter assessment.

THE PRINCETON REVIEW — Test Practice

A student was studying for an Earth science test and made the following table to keep track of information.

Type of Rocks	
Type of Rock	**Characteristics**
Igneous	Form from lava or magma
Sedimentary	Layers of sediment or organic remains
Metamorphic	Result of high temperature or pressure

Examine the table and answer the questions

1. According to the chart, igneous rocks form from _____ .
   A) sediment
   B) lava or magma
   C) plant/animal matter
   D) high pressures

2. A rock made up of fossil shells would be a _____ .
   F) sedimentary rock
   G) igneous rock
   H) metamorphic rock
   J) fissure.

3. Rocks that form from high heat and pressure are _____ .
   A) sedimentary rocks
   B) chemical rocks
   C) metamorphic rocks
   D) organic rocks

The Test-Taking Tip was written by The Princeton Review, the nation's leader in test preparation.

1. B
2. F
3. C

Developing Skills

16. The rock is an organic sedimentary rock. It is a fossil-rich limestone.

17. Two tests could be used. HCl acid will react with the calcite and not the halite. The calcite will produce a double image if looked through, but the halite will not.

18. See student page.

19. Try to scratch each item with the magnetite. If the magnetite scratches the item, the magnetite is harder than that item. Magnetite scratches the penny, the iron nail, and the glass plate. Its hardness is greater than 5.5, the hardness of the glass plate. Use the bar magnet to determine that magnetite is attracted to a magnet.

Performance Assessment

20. Use **Performance Assessment in the Science Classroom**, p. 123 to evaluate students' models.

✓Assessment Resources

📁 Reproducible Masters

Chapter Resources Booklet
Chapter Review, pp. 37–38
Chapter Tests, pp. 39–42
Assessment Transparency Activity, p. 49

Glencoe Science Web site
Interactive Tutor
Chapter Quizzes

Glencoe Technology

- Assessment Transparency
- Interactive CD-ROM Chapter Quizzes
- ExamView Pro Test Bank
- Vocabulary PuzzleMaker Software
- MindJogger Videoquiz

Section/Objectives	Standards		Activities/Features
Chapter Opener	**National**	**State/Local**	**Explore Activity:** Model stress buildup along faults, p. 407 **Before You Read,** p. 407
	See p. 5T for a Key to Standards.		
Section 1 Forces Inside Earth ⏱ 2 sessions ▢ 1 block 1. **Explain** how earthquakes result from the buildup of energy in rocks. 2. **Describe** how compression, tension, and shear forces make rocks move along faults. 3. **Distinguish** among normal, reverse, and strike-slip faults.	National Content Standards: UCP2, B2, B3, D1		
Section 2 Features of Earthquakes ⏱ 2 sessions ▢ 1 block 1. **Explain** how earthquake energy travels in seismic waves. 2. **Distinguish** among primary, secondary, and surface waves. 3. **Describe** the structure of Earth's interior.	National Content Standards: UCP2, A1, B2, B3, D1		**Physics Integration,** p. 413 **Visualizing Seismic Waves,** p. 414 **Science Online,** p. 415 **MiniLAB:** Interpreting Seismic Wave Data, p. 417 **Activity:** Epicenter Location, p. 420
Section 3 People and Earthquakes ⏱ 3 sessions ▢ 1.5 blocks 1. **Explain** where most earthquakes in the United States occur. 2. **Describe** how scientists measure earthquakes. 3. **List** ways to make your classroom and home more earthquake-safe.	National Content Standards: UCP2, A1, B2, B3, D1, F1, F3, F5, G2		**Physics Integration,** p. 423 **Science Online,** p. 424 **Math Skills Activity:** Using Multiplication to Compare Earthquake Energy, p. 425 **MiniLAB:** Modeling Seismic-Safe Structures, p. 426 **Activity:** Earthquake Depths, pp. 428–429 **Science Stats:** Moving Earth!, pp. 430–431

Activity Materials	Reproducible Resources	Section Assessment	Technology
Explore Activity: medium-grain sandpaper (2 sheets); tape; textbook; large, thick rubber bands (2)	**Chapter Resources Booklet** Foldables Worksheet, p. 19 Directed Reading Overview, p. 21 Note-taking Worksheets, pp. 35–37	GLENCOE'S ASSESSMENT ADVANTAGE	
Need materials? Contact Science Kit at 1-800-828-7777 or www.sciencekit.com on the Internet.	**Chapter Resources Booklet** Transparency Activity, p. 46 Enrichment, p. 32 Reinforcement, p. 29 Directed Reading, p. 22 Transparency Activity, pp. 49–50	Portfolio Activity, p. 410 Performance Skill Builder Activities, p. 411 Content Section Assessment, p. 411	Section Focus Transparency Teaching Transparency Interactive CD-ROM Guided Reading Audio Program
MiniLAB: Figure 11 graph **Activity:** string, metric ruler, globe, chalk	**Chapter Resources Booklet** Transparency Activity, p. 47 MiniLAB, p. 3 Lab Activity, pp. 9–13 Enrichment, p. 33 Reinforcement, p. 30 Directed Reading, p. 23 Activity Worksheet, pp. 5–6 **Home and Community Involvement,** p. 40	Portfolio Science Journal, p. 415 Performance MiniLAB, p. 417 Skill Builder Activities, p. 419 Content Section Assessment, p. 419	Section Focus Transparency Interactive CD-ROM Guided Reading Audio Program
MiniLAB: building blocks, rubber bands (medium and large sizes) **Activity:** graph paper, pencil	**Chapter Resources Booklet** Transparency Activity, p. 48 MiniLAB, p. 4 Lab Activity, pp. 15–18 Enrichment, p. 34 Reinforcement, p. 31 Directed Reading, pp. 23, 24 Activity Worksheet, pp. 7–8 **Lab Management and Safety,** p. 65	Portfolio Extension, p. 422 Performance Math Skills Activity, p. 425 MiniLAB, p. 426 Skill Builder Activities, p. 427 Content Section Assessment, p. 427	Section Focus Transparency Interactive CD-ROM Guided Reading Audio Program

GLENCOE'S ASSESSMENT ADVANTAGE	End of Chapter Assessment		
Blackline Masters		**Technology**	**Professional Series**
Chapter Resources Booklet Chapter Review, pp. 39–40 Chapter Tests, pp. 41–44 **Standardized Test Practice by The Princeton Review,** pp. 51–54		MindJogger Videoquiz Interactive CD-ROM Vocabulary PuzzleMakers ExamView Pro Test Bank Interactive Lesson Planner Interactive Teacher Edition	Performance Assessment in the Science Classroom (PASC)

Transparencies

Section Focus

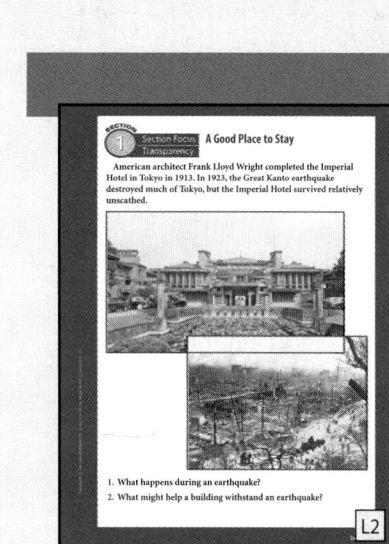

Section 1 Section Focus Transparency — A Good Place to Stay

American architect Frank Lloyd Wright completed the Imperial Hotel in Tokyo in 1913. In 1923, the Great Kanto earthquake destroyed much of Tokyo, but the Imperial Hotel survived relatively unscathed.

1. What happens during an earthquake?
2. What might help a building withstand an earthquake?

L2

Section 2 Section Focus Transparency — A Beautiful Detector

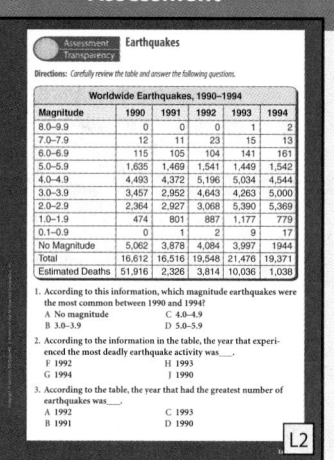

Seismographs are instruments that scientists use to gather information about earthquakes. They are very sensitive to motion, and they record tremors that people can't feel. The first instrument to detect earthquakes was invented in 132 A.D. by Chang Heng, a Chinese scientist and mathematician.

1. What do you think the blue lines on the drum represent?
2. As you get further from the location of an earthquake, what happens to your perception of the earthquake?
3. Do you think China experiences a lot of earthquakes? Why or why not?

L2

Section 3 Section Focus Transparency — The World of Earthquakes

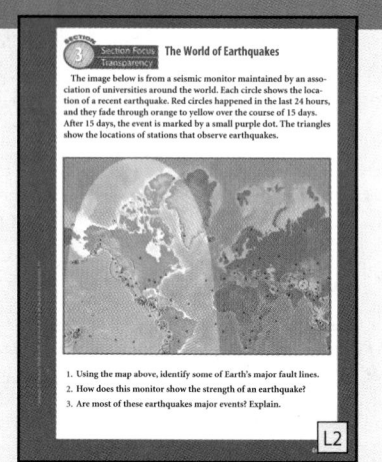

The image below is from a seismic monitor maintained by an association of universities around the world. Each circle shows the location of a recent earthquake. Red circles happened in the last 24 hours, and they fade through orange to yellow over the course of 15 days. After 15 days, the event is marked by a small purple dot. The triangles show the locations of stations that observe earthquakes.

1. Using the map above, identify some of Earth's major fault lines.
2. How does this monitor show the strength of an earthquake?
3. Are most of these earthquakes major events? Explain.

L2

This is a representation of key blackline masters available in the Teacher Classroom Resources. See Resource Manager boxes within the chapter for additional information.

Assessment

Assessment Transparency — Earthquakes

Directions: Carefully review the table and answer the following questions.

Worldwide Earthquakes, 1990–1994					
Magnitude	**1990**	**1991**	**1992**	**1993**	**1994**
8.0–9.9	0	0	0	1	2
7.0–7.9	12	11	23	15	13
6.0–6.9	115	105	104	141	161
5.0–5.9	1,635	1,469	1,541	1,449	1,542
4.0–4.9	4,493	4,372	5,196	5,034	4,544
3.0–3.9	3,457	2,952	4,643	4,263	5,000
2.0–2.9	2,364	2,927	3,068	5,390	5,369
1.0–1.9	474	801	887	1,177	779
0.1–0.9	0	1	2	9	17
No Magnitude	5,062	3,878	4,084	3,997	1944
Total	16,612	16,516	19,548	21,476	19,371
Estimated Deaths	51,916	2,326	3,814	10,036	1,038

1. According to this information, which magnitude earthquakes were the most common between 1990 and 1994?
   A No magnitude   C 4.0–4.9
   B 3.0–3.9   D 5.0–5.9
2. According to the information in the table, the year that experienced the most deadly earthquake activity was___.
   F 1992   H 1993
   G 1994   J 1990
3. According to the table, the year that had the greatest number of earthquakes was___.
   A 1992   C 1993
   B 1991   D 1990

L2

Teaching

Section 1 Teaching Transparency — Faults

L2

Key to Teaching Strategies

The following designations will help you decide which activities are appropriate for your students.

L1 Level 1 activities should be appropriate for students with learning difficulties.

L2 Level 2 activities should be within the ability range of all students.

L3 Level 3 activities are designed for above-average students.

ELL ELL activities should be within the ability range of English Language Learners.

COOP LEARN Cooperative Learning activities are designed for small group work.

LS Multiple Learning Styles logos, as described on page 22T, are used throughout to indicate strategies that address different learning styles.

P These strategies represent student products that can be placed into a best-work portfolio.

Hands-on Activities

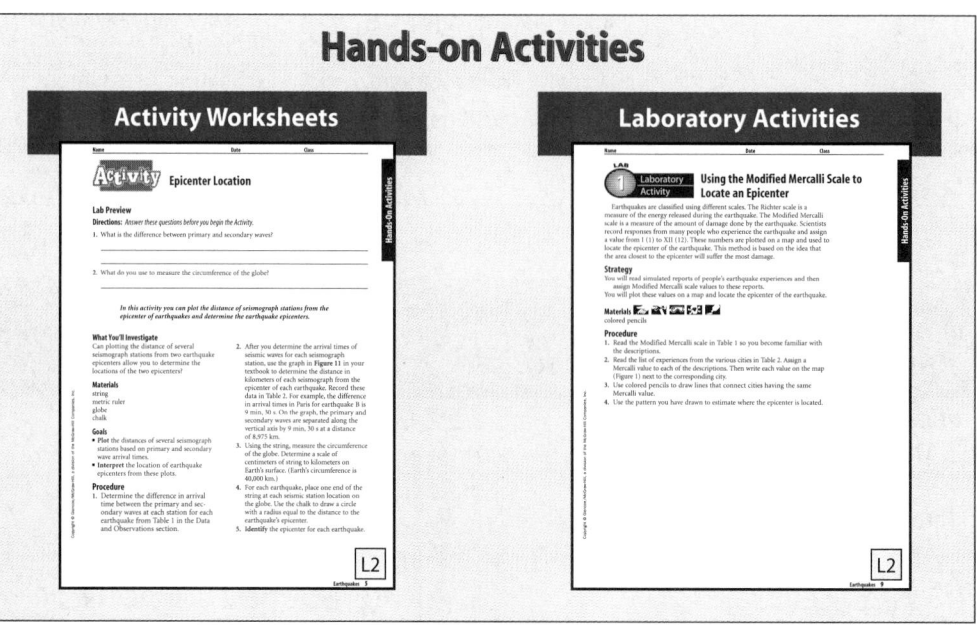

Activity Worksheets

Activity — Epicenter Location

Lab Preview
Directions: Answer these questions before you begin the Activity.

1. What is the difference between primary and secondary waves?

2. What do you use to measure the circumference of the globe?

In this activity you can plot the distance of seismograph stations from the epicenter of earthquakes and determine the earthquake epicenters.

What You'll Investigate
Can plotting the distance of several seismograph stations from two earthquake epicenters allow you to determine the locations of the two epicenters?

Materials
string
metric ruler
globe
chalk

Goals
• **Plot** the distances of several seismograph stations based on primary and secondary wave arrival times.
• **Interpret** the location of earthquake epicenters from these plots.

Procedure
1. Determine the difference in arrival time between the primary and secondary waves at each station for each earthquake from Table 1 in the Data and Observations section.

2. After you determine the arrival times of seismic waves for each seismograph station, use the graph in **Figure 11** in your textbook to determine the distance in kilometers of each seismograph from the epicenter of each earthquake. Record these data in Table 2. For example, the difference in arrival times in Paris for earthquake B is 9 min, 30 s. On the graph, the primary and secondary waves are separated along the vertical axis by 9 min, 30 s at a distance of 8,975 km.
3. Using the string, measure the circumference of the globe. Determine a scale of centimeters of string to kilometers on Earth's surface. (Earth's circumference is 40,000 km.)
4. For each earthquake, place one end of the string at each seismic station location on the globe. Use the chalk to draw a circle with a radius equal to the distance to the earthquake's epicenter.
5. **Identify** the epicenter for each earthquake.

L2

Laboratory Activities

Laboratory Activity — Using the Modified Mercalli Scale to Locate an Epicenter

Earthquakes are classified using different scales. The Richter scale is a measure of the energy released during the earthquake. The Modified Mercalli scale is a measure of the amount of damage done by the earthquake. Scientists record responses from many people who experience the earthquake and assign a value from I (1) to XII (12). These numbers are plotted on a map and used to locate the epicenter of the earthquake. This method is based on the idea that the area closest to the epicenter will suffer the most damage.

Strategy
You will read simulated reports of people's earthquake experiences and then assign Modified Mercalli scale values to these reports.
You will plot these values on a map and locate the epicenter of the earthquake.

Materials
colored pencils

Procedure
1. Read the Modified Mercalli scale in Table 1 so you become familiar with the descriptions.
2. Read the list of experiences from the various cities in Table 2. Assign a Mercalli value to each of the descriptions. Then write each value on the map (Figure 1) next to the corresponding city.
3. Use colored pencils to draw lines that connect cities having the same Mercalli value.
4. Use the pattern you have drawn to estimate where the epicenter is located.

L2

Meeting Different Ability Levels

Content Outline

Reinforcement

Directed Reading

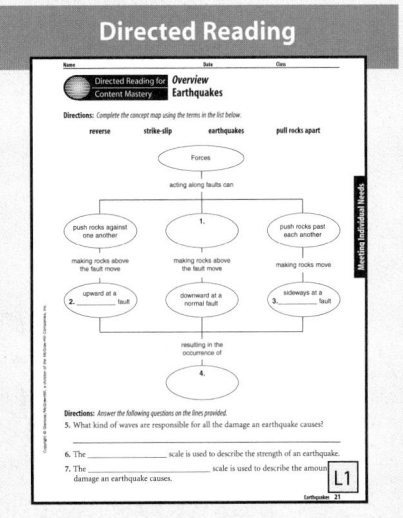

Assessment

Chapter Tests

Enrichment

Spanish Directed Reading

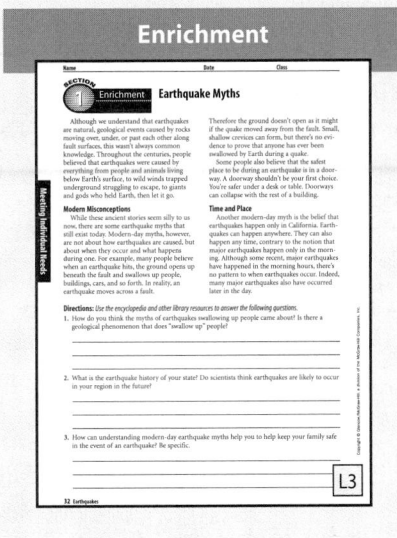

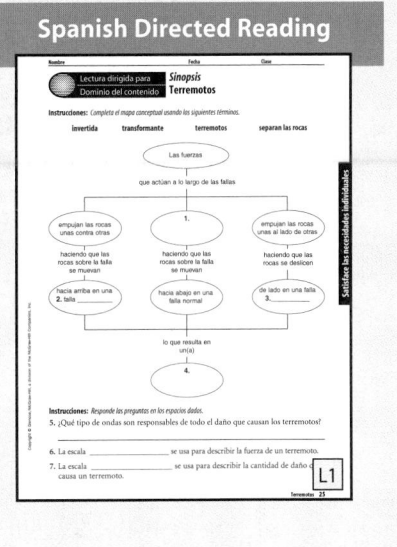

Test Practice Workbook

Chapter Review

Science Content Background

Forces Inside Earth
Types of Earthquakes

Shallow-focus earthquakes occur in three places: where two of Earth's plates are moving apart, near the edges of plates that are converging, and where two plates are moving past each other. Intermediate and deep-focus earthquakes occur where one plate subducts under another. Subduction zone quakes account for almost one-half of the destructive quakes.

Student Misconception

Earthquakes occur only in California.
Refer to the facing page for teaching strategies to address this misconception. Refer to pages 408–409 for content related to this topic.

Features of Earthquakes
Predicting Earthquakes

One method that is used in predicting earthquakes is the study of seismic gaps. Seismic gaps are areas of a fault zone that have not produced a major earthquake during a specific time interval. When a seismic gap area is located, researchers estimate how long it has been since the fault zone in question has experienced an earthquake. Using this information and knowledge of the average earthquake recurrence interval along the fault segment, scientists predict a time range over which the area could expect to experience a major earthquake.

Although much information is used in an attempt to predict earthquakes, success has been limited. Stress begins to build up in an area as soon as an earthquake has occurred. Without knowing how much stress can accumulate before rocks must shift, it is difficult to predict an earthquake with any amount of accuracy.

People and Earthquakes
Earthquake Magnitude

The extent of the damage caused by an earthquake depends on the distance to the epicenter, the type of bedrock in the area, the local soil or sediment types, and the number and type of structures subjected to the quake, among other factors.

Seismic-Safe Structures

Most loss of life in an earthquake occurs when people are trapped in and on crumbling structures, such as buildings, bridges, and highways. Making structures seismic-safe can reduce the loss of life in an earthquake. Seismic-safe structures are resistant to vibrations that occur during an earthquake.

The two main strategies for building seismic-safe structures are shock absorption and reinforcement. The goals of these building techniques are to prevent structures from collapsing and to minimize falling debris.

Gerald French/FPG International

SCIENCE *Online*

For additional content background on this topic, go to the Glencoe Science Web site at **science.glencoe.com**.

IDENTIFYING Misconceptions

Find Out What Students Think

Students may think that . . .

• **Earthquakes occur only in California.**

Much of the publicity found in the media features California earthquakes. As a result, many students think that the major location for earthquakes in the world is in California. Actually, earthquakes occur throughout the world, including many areas of the United States. Thus, it is important to feature earthquakes from a variety of areas of the world as students learn about this topic.

Activity

Use the Internet to find information on recent earthquakes. Useful links for earthquake information can be accessed through the Glencoe Science website at **science.glencoe.com**. Have students plot on a world map earthquakes that have occurred over the last 30 days to begin to develop the idea that earthquakes occur worldwide.

Promote Understanding

Activity

After students understand that earthquakes are a world-wide phenomenon, reinforce the importance of having an "earthquake survival kit," especially if you live in an earthquake-prone area. Tell students that they have been hired to design the ideal kit. Explain that the kit must meet several minimum requirements:

• It should provide supplies for a family of four.

• It should provide enough supplies for three days.

• It should be able to be stored for long periods of time without spoiling.

Have students work in small groups to discuss what they would put in their kits. Have each group prepare a list of items they would include, giving both the item name and a quantity. Remind students that after a major earthquake many of the things we take for granted would not be available.

When students have made their lists, have groups compare their ideas. Are all items the same? What were some of the issues that different families might face? Prompt students to think of families with small children or infants. Discuss the types of foods that might be stored safely for long periods of time. Remind students that obtaining safe drinking water can be a major problem after an earthquake.

After students finish designing their kits, suggest they compare their ideas to those of the Red Cross or other disaster-management groups. What have they overlooked? What might your students recommend to these groups?

Assess

After completing the chapter, see *Identifying Misconceptions* in the Study Guide.

Earthquakes

Chapter Vocabulary

What do you think?

Science Journal This is a record of vibrations produced by an earthquake. The record is a seismogram, produced by a seismograph.

Earthquakes

More than 20,000 deaths and at least 166,000 injuries resulted from a powerful earthquake in India on January 26, 2001. Collapse of structures, such as this building in Ahmedabad, India, is among the greatest dangers associated with earthquakes. What causes earthquakes? Why do some areas experience repeated earthquakes while other areas rarely do? In this chapter you'll learn the answers to these and other questions. You'll also learn how earthquake damage can be reduced.

What do you think?

Science Journal Look at the picture below with a classmate. Discuss what you think this might be. Here's a hint: *Something must have been shaking to make these waves.* Write your answer or best guess in your Science Journal.

406

Theme Connection

Energy The energy theme is highlighted as students learn how earthquakes unleash tremendous amounts of energy inside Earth's crust. That energy can change Earth's surface and affect both people and structures.

EXPLORE ACTIVITY

Why do earthquakes occur? The bedrock beneath the soil can break and form cracks known as faults. When blocks of rock move past each other along a fault, they cause the ground to shake. Why don't rocks move all the time, causing constant earthquakes? You'll find out during this activity.

Model stress buildup along faults

1. Tape a sheet of medium-grain sandpaper to the tabletop.

2. Tape a second sheet of sandpaper to the book cover on a textbook.

3. Place the book on the table so that both sheets of sandpaper meet.

4. Tie two large, thick rubber bands together and loop one of the rubber bands around the edge of the book so that it is not touching the sandpaper.

5. Pull on the free rubber band until the book moves and observe this movement.

Observe

Write a paragraph in your Science Journal describing how the book moved and explaining how this activity modeled the buildup of stress along a fault.

Before You Read

FOLDABLES
Reading & Study Skills

Making a Cause and Effect Study Fold Make the following Foldable to help you understand the cause and effect relationship of earthquakes and Earth's crust.

1. Place a sheet of paper in front of you so the long side is at the top. Fold the paper in half from the left side to the right side and then unfold.

2. Label the left side of the paper *Cause* and the right side *Effect*. Refold the paper.

3. Before you read the chapter, draw a cross section of Earth's crust showing what you think happens during an earthquake on the outside of your Foldable.

4. As you read the chapter, change your drawing and list causes of earthquakes on the inside of your Foldable.

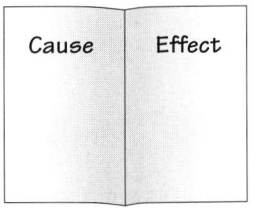

Cause	Effect

EXPLORE ACTIVITY

Purpose Students explore the cause of earthquake activity at faults. **IS** **Kinesthetic**

Preparation Sandpaper can be bought at a hardware store.

Materials two sheets medium-grain sandpaper, textbook, two large rubber bands, tape

Teaching Strategy Have students work in pairs.

Safety Precautions Caution students to avoid scrapes or cuts when handling sandpaper.

Observe

The book moves with a quick jerk once the pulling force overcomes the friction between the two pieces of sandpaper. Rocks along fault lines build up stress in a similar manner until they rapidly slip past each other, causing an earthquake.

✔ Assessment

Process Have students create a labeled diagram that illustrates what happened in the activity. Use **Performance Assessment in the Science Classroom**, p. 163.

FOLDABLES
Reading & Study Skills

Dinah Zike Study Fold

Purpose Have students make and use a Foldable to diagram and explain what they think happens when an earthquake is taking place. As they read the chapter, have students collect information on the causes and effects of earthquakes and amend their initial diagram if necessary.

For additional help, see Foldables Worksheet, p. 19 in **Chapter Resources Booklet,** or go to the Glencoe Science Web site at **science.glencoe.com.** See After You Read in the Study Guide at the end of this chapter.

Before You Read

Forces Inside Earth

Forces Inside Earth

1 Motivate

Bellringer Transparency

Display the Section Focus Transparency for Section 1. Use the accompanying Transparency Activity Master. L2

ELL

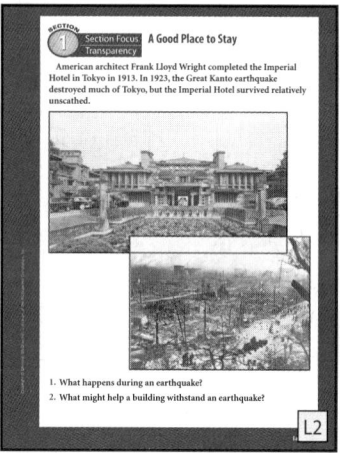

Tie to Prior Knowledge

Ask students to recall any recent earthquakes they have heard about or experienced. Discuss with students where the earthquakes occurred and what happened as a result of them. Then tell students they will find out why earthquakes occur in this section.

As You Read

What You'll Learn

- **Explain** how earthquakes result from the buildup of energy in rocks.
- **Describe** how compression, tension, and shear forces make rocks move along faults.
- **Distinguish** among normal, reverse, and strike-slip faults.

Vocabulary

fault
earthquake
normal fault
reverse fault
strike-slip fault

Why It's Important

Earthquakes are among the most dramatic of all natural disasters on Earth.

Earthquake Causes

Recall the last time you used a rubber band. Rubber bands stretch when you pull them. Because they are elastic, they return to their original shape once the force is released. However, if you stretch a rubber band too far, it will break. A wooden craft stick behaves in a similar way. When a force is first applied to the stick, it will bend and change shape, as shown in **Figure 1A.** The energy needed to bend the stick is stored inside the stick as potential energy. If the force keeping the stick bent is removed, the stick will return to its original shape, and the stored energy will be released as energy of motion.

Fault Formation There is a limit to how far a wooden craft stick can bend. This is called its elastic limit. Once its elastic limit is passed, the stick breaks, as shown in **Figure 1B.** Rocks behave in a similar way. Up to a point, applied forces cause rocks to bend and stretch, undergoing what is called elastic deformation. Once the elastic limit is passed, the rocks may break. When rocks break, they move along surfaces called **faults.** A tremendous amount of force is required to overcome the strength of rocks and to cause movement along a fault. Rock along one side of a fault can move up, down, or sideways in relation to rock along the other side of the fault.

Figure 1
The **A** bending and **B** breaking of wooden craft sticks are similar to how rocks bend and break.

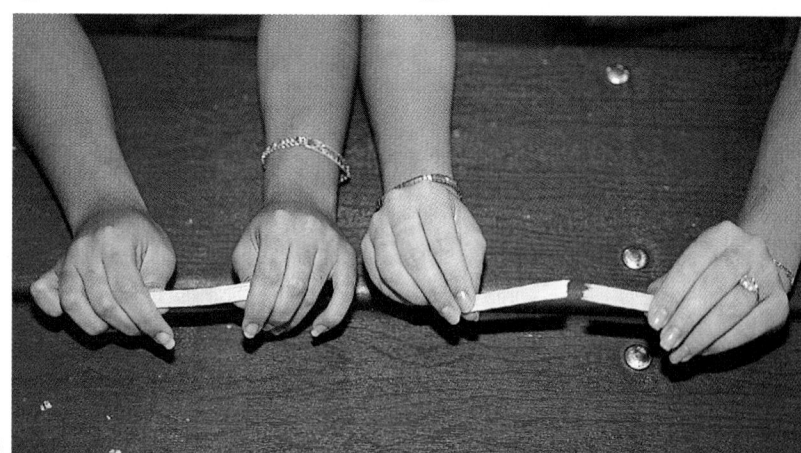

408 CHAPTER 14 Earthquakes

Section ✓*Assessment* Planner

PORTFOLIO
Activity, p. 410
PERFORMANCE ASSESSMENT
Skill Builder Activities, p. 411
See page 434 for more options.

CONTENT ASSESSMENT
Section, p. 411
Challenge, p. 411
Chapter, pp. 434–435

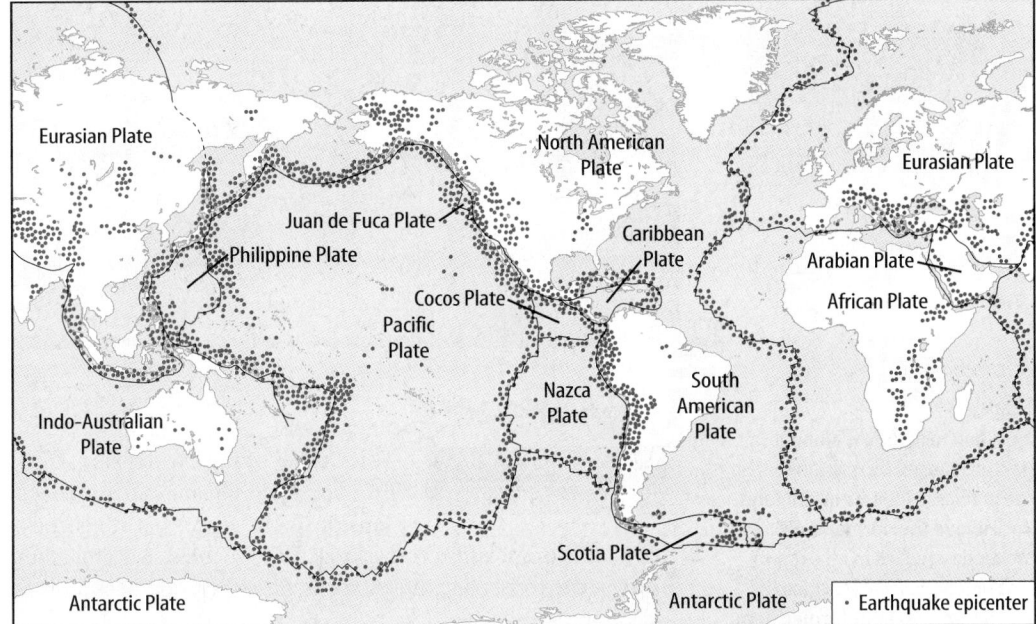

Figure 2
The dots represent the epicenters of major earthquakes over a ten-year period. Note that most earthquakes occur near plate boundaries. *Why do earthquakes rarely occur in the middle of plates?*

What causes faults? What produces the forces that cause rocks to break and faults to form? The surface of Earth is in constant motion because of forces inside the planet. These forces cause sections of Earth's surface, called plates, to move. This movement puts stress on the rocks near the plate edges. To relieve this stress, the rocks tend to bend, compress, or stretch. If the force is great enough, the rocks will break. An **earthquake** is the vibrations produced by the breaking of rock. **Figure 2** shows how the locations of earthquakes outline the plates that make up Earth's surface.

✔ **Reading Check** *Why do most earthquakes occur near plate boundaries?*

How Earthquakes Occur As rocks move past each other along a fault, their rough surfaces catch, temporarily halting movement along the fault. However, forces keep driving the rocks to move. This action builds up stress at the points where the rocks are stuck. The stress causes the rocks to bend and change shape. When the rocks are stressed beyond their elastic limit, they break, move along the fault, and return to their original shapes. An earthquake results. Earthquakes range from unnoticeable vibrations to devastating waves of energy. Regardless of their intensity, most earthquakes result from rocks moving over, under, or past each other along fault surfaces.

---

② Teach

Earthquake Causes

Caption Answer
Figure 2 Because most of the stress on plates is at their edges, rock is more likely to break and cause quakes there than in central areas.

Activity
Different materials have different elastic limits. Have students bend the following materials to see what happens once the elastic limit is reached: a piece of cardboard; a plastic drinking straw; a wooden tongue depressor; a thin, steel wire; some silicon putty; a thin sheet of slate or shale. Have students wear goggles during this activity. L2 ELL IS **Kinesthetic**

✔ **Reading Check**

Answer Most stress is at boundaries where plates meet.

Fun Fact
There is no spot on Earth that cannot experience an earthquake, but earthquakes are less likely to occur in Antarctica than in any other place.

IDENTIFYING
Misconceptions
Some students think that earthquakes occur only in California. Refer to page 406F for teaching strategies that address this misconception.

✔ **Active Reading**

Buddy Interviews This strategy helps students understand and clarify the reading. Have students interview one another to find out what helps them to understand what they are reading, how they find answers, and how they assimilate new vocabulary terms. Have students use Buddy Interviews to help them master the concept of what causes earthquakes.

Resource Manager

Chapter Resources Booklet
Transparency Activity, p. 46
Directed Reading for Content Mastery, pp. 21, 22
Enrichment, p. 32

Types of Faults

Discussion

Would it be possible to stand at a fault and not know it was there? Explain. Yes; the fault could be the site of hills or mountains, and the actual fault could have been covered by soil and rock as the result of erosion.

Activity

Have pairs of students apply compression, tension, and shear forces to bars of taffy. Tell students to make drawings that show what happens to the taffy in each instance. Have students write a paragraph relating this to what happens to rocks when forces are applied. Depending on the amount of force applied, students should see the taffy bend or break, which is what happens when force is applied to rock.

L2 COOP LEARN **LS** **Interpersonal**
P

Quick Demo

Contrast the three types of faults by preparing a large, triple-decker peanut butter and jelly sandwich. Cut off the crusts so the individual layers can be seen. Construct a fault at about a 30° angle by cutting through the sandwich. Move the separate halves of the sandwich to demonstrate normal, reverse, and strike-slip faults.
LS **Visual-Spatial**

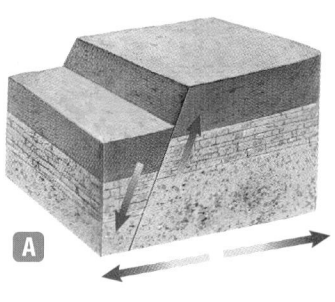
A

B

Figure 3
A When rock moves along a fracture caused by tension forces, the break is called a normal fault. Rock above the normal fault moves downward in relation to rock below the fault surface.
B This normal fault formed near Kanab, Utah.

Figure 4
A Compression forces in rocks form reverse faults. The rock above the reverse fault surface moves upward in relation to the rock below the fault surface.
B Rock layers have been offset along this reverse fault.

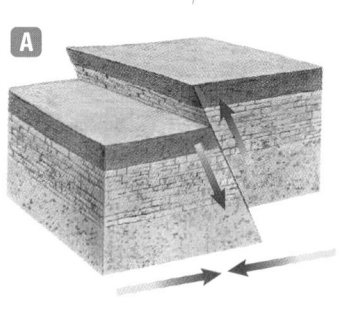
A

Types of Faults

Physics
INTEGRATION

Three types of forces—tension, compression, and shear—act on rocks. Tension is the force that pulls rocks apart, and compression is the force that squeezes rocks together. Shear is the force that causes rocks on either side of a fault to slide past each other.

Normal Faults Tensional forces inside Earth cause rocks to be pulled apart. When rocks are stretched by these forces, a normal fault can form. Along a **normal fault,** rock above the fault surface moves downward in relation to rock below the fault surface. The motion along a normal fault is shown in **Figure 3A.** Notice the normal fault shown in the photograph in **Figure 3B.**

Reverse Faults Reverse faults result from compression forces that squeeze rock. **Figure 4A** shows the motion along a reverse fault. If rock breaks from forces pushing from opposite directions, rock above a **reverse fault** surface is forced up and over the rock below the fault surface. **Figure 4B** shows a large reverse fault in California.

B

410 **CHAPTER 14** Earthquakes

Visual Learning

Figure 3 The arrows at the bottom of the figure illustrate how the tension forces are being applied. The arrows beside the fault line illustrate the relationship between the two blocks of rock. **Do the two pairs of arrows illustrate whether one block moved up or down?** No, the movement is relative. Either or both blocks could have moved.

Resource Manager

Chapter Resources Booklet
Reinforcement, p. 29
Transparency Activity, pp. 49–50

Earth Science Critical Thinking/Problem Solving, pp. 1, 8, 10

Figure 5

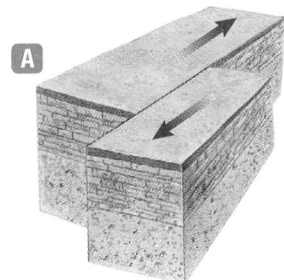

A Shear forces push on rock in opposite—but not directly opposite—horizontal directions. When they are strong enough, these forces split rock and create strike-slip faults. Little vertical movement occurs along a strike-slip fault. **B** The North American Plate and the Pacific Plate slide past each other along the San Andreas Fault, a strike-slip fault, in California.

Strike-Slip Faults At a **strike-slip fault,** shown in **Figure 5A,** rocks on either side of the fault are moving past each other without much upward or downward movement. **Figure 5B** shows the largest fault in California—the San Andreas Fault—which stretches more than 1,100 km through the state. The San Andreas Fault is the boundary between two of Earth's plates that are moving sideways past each other.

 Reading Check *What is a strike-slip fault?*

Section 1 Assessment

1. What is an earthquake?

2. The Himalaya in Tibet formed when two of Earth's plates collided. What type of faults would you expect to find in these mountains? Why?

3. In what direction do rocks above a normal fault surface move?

4. Why is California's San Andreas Fault a strike-slip fault?

5. **Think Critically** Why is it easier to predict where an earthquake will occur than it is to predict when it will occur?

Skill Builder Activities

6. **Forming Hypotheses** Hypothesize why the chances of an earthquake occurring along a fault increase rather than decrease as time since the last earthquake passes. **For more help, refer to the** Science Skill Handbook.

7. **Using Graphics Software** Use a graphics program to make models of the three types of faults—normal, reverse, and strike-slip. Add arrows to show the directions of movement along both sides of each type. **For more help, refer to the** Technology Skill Handbook.

Answers to Section Assessment

1. An earthquake is a vibration produced by the breaking of rock.
2. Reverse faults; they are the result of compression forces.
3. downward in relation to rocks below the fault
4. Rocks on either side of the fault move past each other.
5. Scientists know that most earthquakes occur near plate boundaries, but they cannot predict when rocks in the crust will break in response to the forces acting on them.
6. The longer the time between earthquakes, the more stress that builds up, and the more likely the chances of an earthquake.
7. Students' models should show appropriate crustal movement for each of the three fault types.

Types of Faults,
continued

Discussion
Why is folding more likely with compression than with tension forces? Compression causes bending and therefore folding, while tension causes thinning and cracking.

✔ Reading Check

Answer a fault where rocks on either side are moving past each other in a horizontal direction

③ Assess

Reteach
Have students use their hands to demonstrate the movement that occurs along each of the three kinds of faults.

Challenge
Challenge students to do research on the Internet to find out what coastal California will look like in several million years because of the movement of plates along the San Andreas Fault. Instruct them to include diagrams to illustrate their answers. Because the Pacific Plate is moving northwest in relation to the North American Plate, a piece of crust containing Los Angeles will one day be adjacent to San Francisco. L2 **Visual-Spatial**

✔ Assessment

Content Have students write a brief paragraph to explain why streambeds are offset at the San Andreas Fault. Rocks on either side of the fault move past each other, causing the streambeds to be offset. Use **Performance Assessment in the Science Classroom,** p. 159.

SECTION

2

1 Motivate

Bellringer Transparency

Display the Section Focus Transparency for Section 2. Use the accompanying Transparency Activity Master. L2

ELL

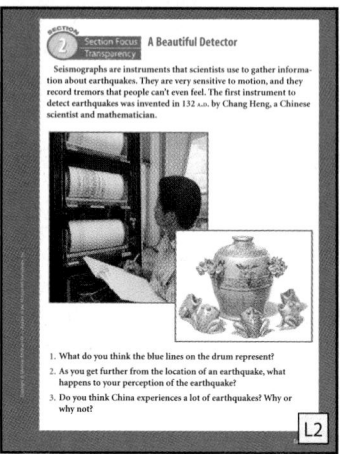

Tie to Prior Knowledge

Tell students that the energy of earthquakes travels in waves. Ask students to recall other types of energy that travel in waves. *Possible answers: sound, electromagnetic radiation such as visible light, energy in ocean waves* Tell students that in this section they will find out how earthquakes that happen inside Earth's crust can affect people and things on the surface.

Features of Earthquakes

What You'll Learn
- **Explain** how earthquake energy travels in seismic waves.
- **Distinguish** among primary, secondary, and surface waves.
- **Describe** the structure of Earth's interior.

Vocabulary
seismic wave   surface wave
focus   epicenter
primary wave   seismograph
secondary wave

Why It's Important
Seismic waves are responsible for most damage caused by earthquakes.

Seismic Waves

When two people hold opposite ends of a rope and shake one end, as shown in **Figure 6,** they send energy through the rope in the form of waves. Like the waves that travel through the rope, **seismic** (SIZE mihk) **waves** generated by an earthquake travel through Earth. During a strong earthquake, the ground moves forward and backward, heaves up and down, and shifts from side to side. The surface of the ground can ripple like waves do in water. Imagine trying to stand on ground that had waves traveling through it. This is what you might experience during a strong earthquake.

Origin of Seismic Waves You learned earlier that rocks move past each other along faults, creating stress at points where the rocks' irregular surfaces catch each other. The stress continues to build up until the elastic limit is exceeded and energy is released in the form of seismic waves. The point where this energy release first occurs is the **focus** (plural, *foci*) of the earthquake. The foci of most earthquakes are within 65 km of Earth's surface. A few have been recorded as deep as 700 km. Seismic waves are produced and travel outward from the earthquake focus.

Figure 6
Some seismic waves are similar to the wave that is traveling through the rope. Note that the rope moves perpendicular to the wave direction.

Section ✔*Assessment* Planner

PORTFOLIO
Science Journal, p. 415
PERFORMANCE ASSESSMENT
MiniLAB, p. 417
Skill Builder Activities, p. 419
See page 434 for more options.

CONTENT ASSESSMENT
Section, p. 419
Challenge, p. 419
Chapter, pp. 434–435

Primary Waves When earthquakes occur, three different types of seismic waves are produced. All of the waves are generated at the same time, but each behaves differently within Earth. **Primary waves** (P-waves) cause particles in rocks to move back and forth in the same direction that the wave is traveling. If you squeeze one end of a coiled spring and then release it, you cause it to compress and then stretch as the wave travels through the spring, as shown in **Figure 7**. Particles in rocks also compress and then stretch apart, transmitting primary waves through the rock.

Secondary and Surface Waves **Secondary waves** (S-waves) move through Earth by causing particles in rocks to move at right angles to the direction of wave travel. The wave traveling through the rope shown in **Figure 6** is an example of a secondary wave.

Surface waves cause most of the destruction resulting from earthquakes. **Surface waves** move rock particles in a backward, rolling motion and a side-to-side, swaying motion, as shown in **Figure 8**. Many buildings are unable to withstand intense shaking because they are made with stiff materials. The buildings fall apart when surface waves cause different parts of the building to move in different directions.

 **Reading Check** *Why do surface waves damage buildings?*

Surface waves are produced when earthquake energy reaches the surface of Earth. Surface waves travel outward from the epicenter. The earthquake **epicenter** (EH pi sen tur) is the point on Earth's surface directly above the earthquake focus. Find the focus and epicenter in **Figure 9**.

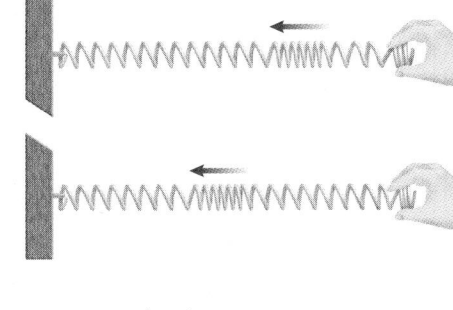

Figure 7
Primary waves move through Earth the same way that a wave travels through a coiled spring.

 Physics
INTEGRATION

When sound is produced, waves move through air or some other material. Research sound waves to find out which type of seismic wave they are similar to.

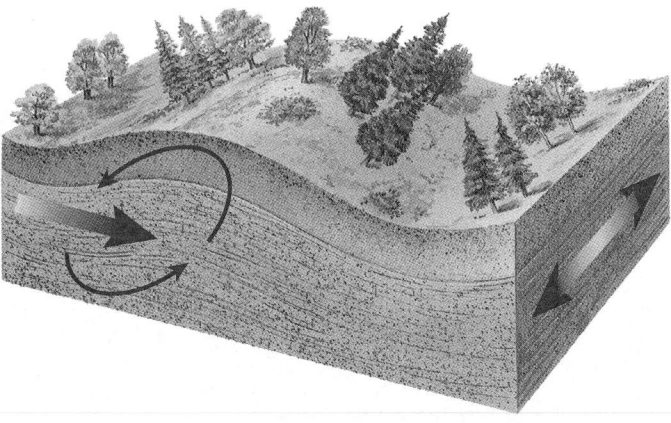

Figure 8
Surface waves move rock particles in a backward, rolling motion and a side-to-side, swaying motion. *How does this movement differ from rock movement caused by secondary waves?*

SECTION 2 Features of Earthquakes **413**

Teacher FYI

If the energy of an earthquake is strong enough to shake a house, light fixtures can fall, refrigerators and other large items can move, bookcases and TVs can topple over, and cabinet doors can fly open causing the contents to spill out.

Visualizing Seismic Waves

Have students examine the pictures and read the captions. Then ask the following questions.

Which type of wave would a seismograph first record after an earthquake? A seismograph would first record a primary wave, then a secondary wave. Surface waves would be recorded last.

Why do some earthquakes cause more damage than others? Possible answers: Damage can be greater if the magnitude is higher or the focus is near Earth's surface. More damage also can occur if the epicenter is near populated areas or if buildings are not constructed to withstand earthquakes.

Activity

Have students demonstrate seismic waves using a coiled spring toy, stretched 1-2 meters on a table. Have a student hold one end of the spring firmly. Have another student demonstrate P-waves by quickly pushing the other end of the spring toward the first student. S-waves can be demonstrated by moving the spring up and down. Gently moving one end of the spring side to side while at the same time moving it in a rolling motion will demonstrates surface waves. Caution: Students should wear goggles when performing this activity.

Extension

Challenge your students to research the different types of surface waves and illustrate their movement.

Figure 9

A s the plates that form Earth's lithosphere move, great stress is placed on rocks. They bend, stretch, and compress. Occasionally, rocks break, producing earthquakes that generate seismic waves. As shown here, different kinds of seismic waves—each with distinctive characteristics—move outward from the focus of the earthquake.

C The point on Earth's surface directly above an earthquake's focus is known as the epicenter. Surface waves spread out from the epicenter like ripples in a pond.

D The amplitudes, or heights, of surface waves are greater than those of primary and secondary waves. Surface waves cause the most damage during an earthquake.

B Primary waves and secondary waves originate at the focus and travel outward in all directions. Primary waves travel about twice as fast as secondary waves.

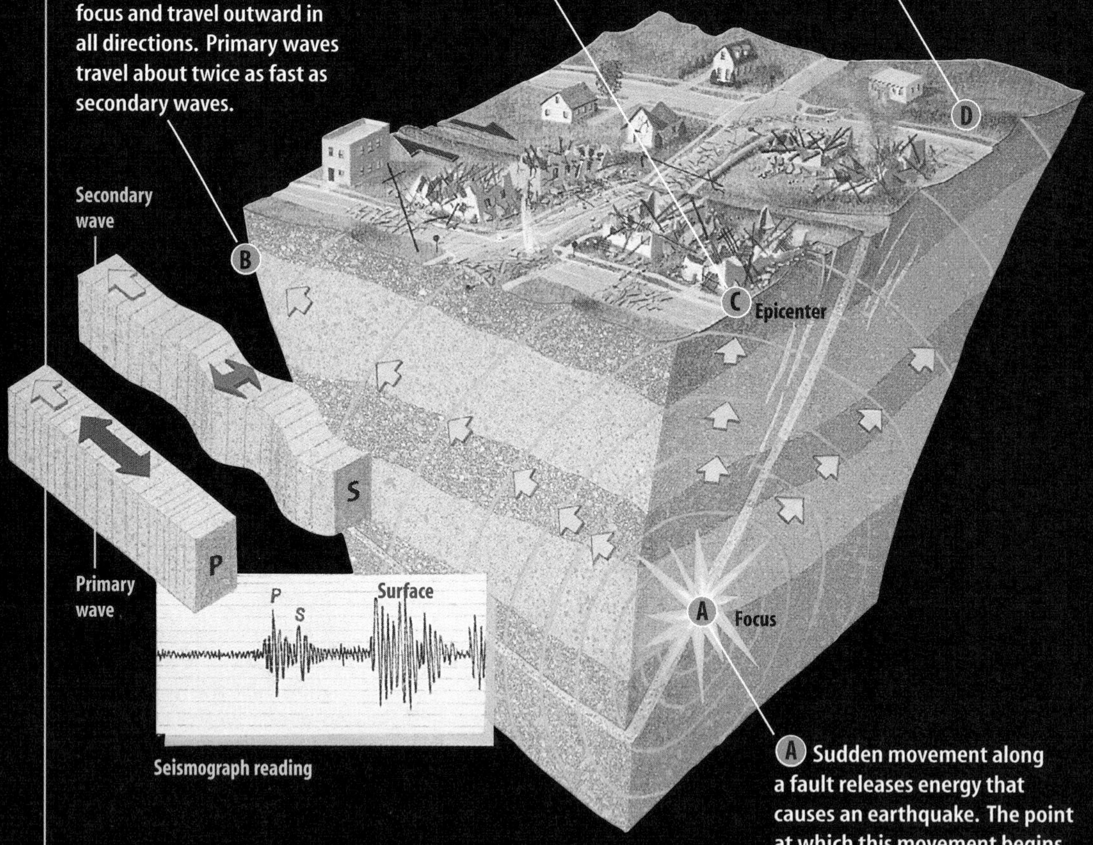

Secondary wave

Primary wave

P   S   Surface

Seismograph reading

Epicenter

Focus

A Sudden movement along a fault releases energy that causes an earthquake. The point at which this movement begins is called the earthquake's focus.

Resource Manager

Chapter Resources Booklet
Enrichment, p. 33
Lab Activity, pp. 9–13

Locating an Epicenter

Different seismic waves travel through Earth at different speeds. Primary waves are the fastest, secondary waves are slower, and surface waves are the slowest. Can you think of a way this information could be used to determine how far away an earthquake epicenter is? Think of the last time you saw two people running in a race. You probably noticed that the faster person got further ahead as the race continued. Like runners in a race, seismic waves travel at different speeds.

Scientists have learned how to use the different speeds of seismic waves to determine the distance to an earthquake epicenter. When an epicenter is far from a location, the primary wave has more time to put distance between it and the secondary and surface waves, just like the fastest runner in a race.

Measuring Seismic Waves Seismic waves from earthquakes are measured with an instrument known as a **seismograph.** Seismographs register the waves and record the time that each arrived. Seismographs consist of a rotating drum of paper and a pendulum with an attached pen. When seismic waves reach the seismograph, the drum vibrates but the pendulum remains at rest. The stationary pen traces a record of the vibrations on the moving drum of paper. The paper record of the seismic event is called a seismogram. **Figure 10** shows two types of seismographs that measure either vertical or horizontal ground movement, depending on the orientation of the drum.

SCIENCE Online

Research Visit the Glencoe Science Web site at **science.glencoe.com** to learn about the National Earthquake Information Center and the World Data Center for Seismology. Share what you learn with your class.

Figure 10
Seismographs differ according to whether they are intended to measure horizontal or vertical seismic motions. *Why can't one seismograph measure both horizontal and vertical motions?*

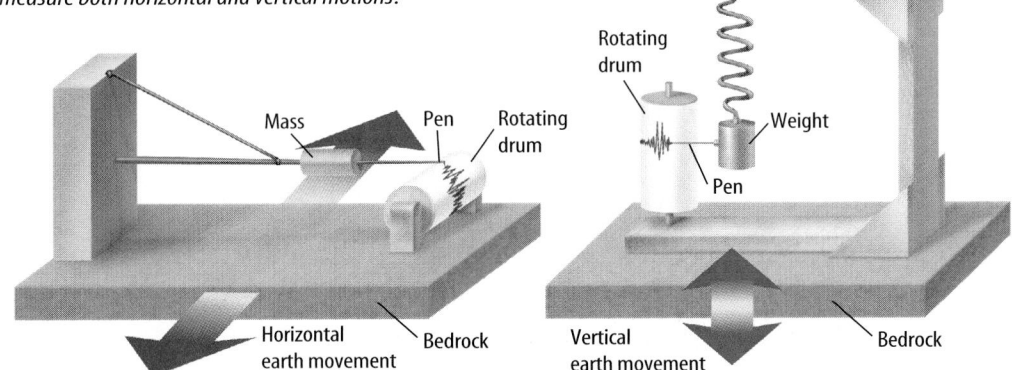

Mass — Pen — Rotating drum
Horizontal earth movement — Bedrock

Rotating drum — Weight — Pen
Vertical earth movement — Bedrock

Locating an Epicenter

SCIENCE Online
Internet Addresses

Explore the Glencoe Science Web site at **science.glencoe.com** to find out more about topics in this section.

Fun Fact

Primary waves travel at about 6.0 km/s, secondary waves at about 3.5 km/s, and surface waves at about 3.0 km/s through granite crust.

IDENTIFYING Misconceptions

Students may think that scientists can predict earthquakes. However, they can figure only the probability that an earthquake will happen in a certain place in the future based on scientific data. For example, geologists can't say for certain when the next major earthquake in San Francisco will happen. But they can estimate that the probability of a major earthquake there in the next 30 years is 70 percent.

Caption Answer
Figure 10 The drum on the seismograph can be oriented to measure either horizontal or vertical motion, but not both.

Science Journal

Landers Quake Have students write a summary in their Science Journals after researching the 1992 earthquake in Landers, California. Have them explain why this event is so important to the study of faults and earthquakes. Data obtained from the Landers quake may indicate that a new fault is being formed in that area of the desert. P

Teacher FYI

Primary waves generated at the focus of an earthquake travel outward through Earth's interior. Sometimes these waves enter Earth's atmosphere and cause the loud noises associated with earthquakes.

Locating an Epicenter, continued

Discussion

Would buildings on Earth's surface start to sway as soon as primary waves move out from the focus of a quake? Explain. Probably not much; primary waves move more quickly than the surface waves that cause most of the damage during quakes.

Quick Demo

Place a large, flat pan of water in front of the class. Drop a small rock into the water. Have students observe the waves that are generated and write a paragraph in their Science Journals that explains how the wave movement in water is similar to the movement of certain types of earthquake waves at Earth's surface. L2 **IS** Linguistic

Caption Answer

Figure 11B One station will only indicate the distance to the epicenter, not its exact location. The three stations are needed in order to pinpoint the exact location.

Figure 11
Primary waves arrive at a seismograph station before secondary waves do.

A This graph shows the distance that primary and secondary waves travel over time. By measuring the difference in arrival times, a seismologist can determine the distance to the epicenter.

Seismograph Stations Each type of seismic wave reaches a seismograph station at a different time based on its speed. Primary waves arrive first at seismograph stations, and secondary waves, which travel slower, arrive second, as shown in the graph in **Figure 11A.** Because surface waves travel slowest, they arrive at seismograph stations last.

If seismic waves reach three or more seismograph stations, the location of the epicenter can be determined. To locate an epicenter, scientists draw circles around each station on a map. The radius of each circle equals that station's distance from the earthquake epicenter. The point where all three circles intersect, shown in **Figure 11B,** is the location of the earthquake epicenter.

Seismologists usually describe earthquakes based on their distances from the seismograph. Local events occur less than 100 km away. Regional events occur 100 km to 1,400 km away. Teleseismic events are those that occur at distances greater than 1,400 km.

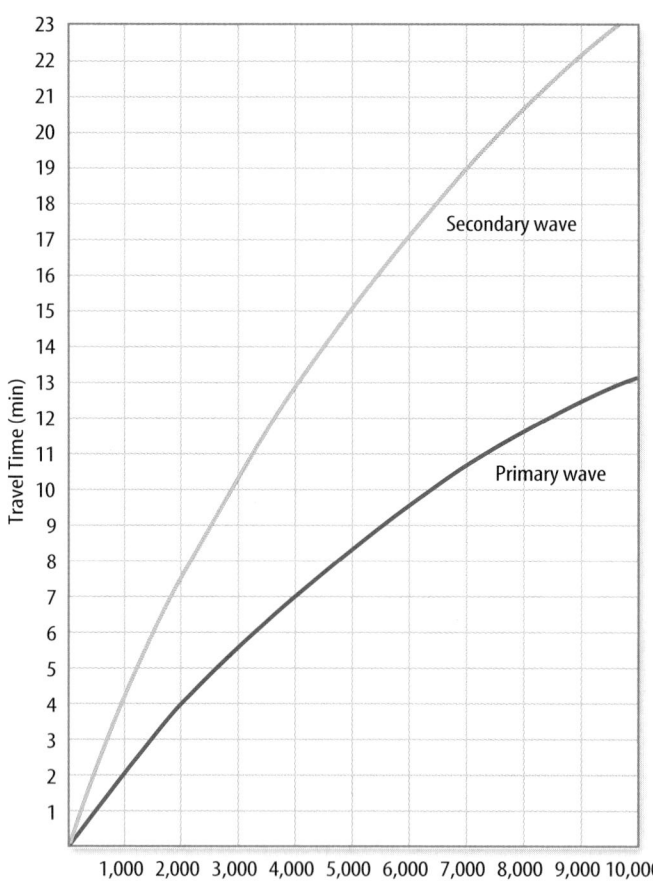

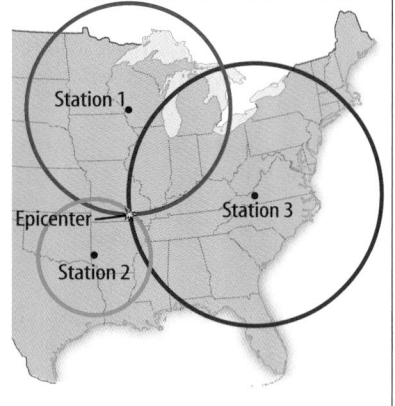

B The radius of each circle is equal to the distance from the epicenter to each seismograph station. The intersection of the three circles is the location of the epicenter. *Why is one seismograph station not enough?*

LAB DEMONSTRATION

Purpose to demonstrate each of the three types of seismic waves

Materials a coiled-spring toy

Preparation Tie pieces of string on the spring at five evenly spaced intervals.

Procedure Demonstrate primary waves by compressing about 20 coils together and

releasing them, secondary waves by moving the spring from side to side, and a surface wave by moving the spring in an elliptical path while also moving it from side to side.

Expected Outcome Students will see that each wave causes a different type of movement in the material through which it is moving.

Assessment

Ask students which type of wave would cause the most damage. Surface waves would cause the most damage because of the large amount of motion associated with them.

Basic Structure of Earth

Figure 12 shows Earth's internal structure. At the very center of Earth is a solid, dense inner core made mostly of iron with smaller amounts of nickel, oxygen, silicon, and sulfur. Pressure from the layers above causes the inner core to be solid. Above the solid inner core lies the liquid outer core, which also is made mainly of iron.

> ✔ **Reading Check**   *How do the inner and outer cores differ?*

Earth's mantle is the largest layer, lying directly above the outer core. It is made mostly of silicon, oxygen, magnesium, and iron. The mantle often is divided into an upper part and a lower part based on changing seismic wave speeds. A portion of the upper mantle, called the asthenosphere (as THE nuh sfihr), consists of weak rock that can flow slowly.

Earth's Crust   The outermost layer of Earth is the crust. Together, the crust and a part of the mantle just beneath it make up Earth's lithosphere (LIH thuh sfihr). The lithosphere is broken into a number of plates that move over the asthenosphere beneath it.

The thickness of Earth's crust varies. It is more than 60 km thick in some mountainous regions and less than 5 km thick under some parts of the oceans. Compared to the mantle, the crust contains more silicon and aluminum and less magnesium and iron. Earth's crust generally is less dense than the mantle beneath it.

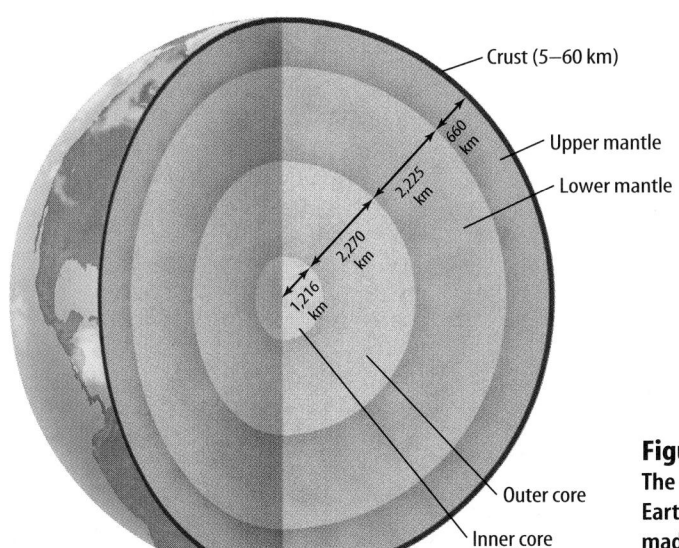

Crust (5–60 km)
660 km
2,225 km
2,270 km
1,216 km
Upper mantle
Lower mantle
Outer core
Inner core

Figure 12
The internal structure of Earth shows that it is made of different layers.

Mini LAB

Interpreting Seismic Wave Data

Procedure
1. Use the **graph** in **Figure 11** to determine the difference in arrival times for primary and secondary waves at the distances listed in the data table below. Two examples are provided for you.

Wave Data	
Distance (km)	**Difference in Arrival Time**
1,500	2 min, 50 s
2,250	
2,750	
3,000	
4,000	5 min, 55 s
7,000	
9,000	

2. Use the graph to determine the differences in arrival times for the other distances in the table.

Analysis
1. What happens to the difference in arrival times as the distance from the earthquake increases?
2. If the difference in arrival times at a seismograph station is 6 min, 30 s, how far away is the epicenter?

Basic Structure of Earth

Mini LAB

Purpose Students will use seismic wave data to determine the distance to an earthquake epicenter. L2
LS Logical-Mathematical P
Materials **Figure 11** graph
Teaching Strategy Make sure students understand the graph before beginning.
Analysis
1. The difference in arrival times is a direct but not constant relationship. The difference in times increases with distance to the earthquake epicenter.
2. about 4,750 km

✔ *Assessment*

Performance Have students determine distances to earthquakes whose primary and secondary wave arrival times are separated by 5 minutes and 7 minutes. 5 min—3,250 km; 7 min—5,400 km Use **PASC**, p. 89.

> ✔ **Reading Check**

Answer The inner core is solid while the outer core is liquid.

Visual Learning

Figure 12 Which is the thinnest of Earth's layers? the crust

Curriculum Connection

Literature Have students do a library search to find science fiction books that have been written about journeys to Earth's center. Have students choose such a book and write a brief scientific critique comparing what the author imagined with the reality of Earth's interior. Have students read their reports in class as part of a class discussion.

Resource Manager

Chapter Resources Booklet
   MiniLAB, p. 3
Home and Community Involvement, p. 40

Basic Structure of Earth, continued

Make a Model

Have students make a model of Earth's interior using clay, cut paper, plaster of paris, or any other readily available materials. Have students share their models in a class presentation. L2

 **Kinesthetic**

Using an Analogy

Explain to students that the internal structure of a peach is analogous to Earth's internal structure. The peach pit is like Earth's core. The meat of the peach, which is its thickest part, can be compared with the thickest part of Earth's interior, the mantle. The thin peach skin corresponds to Earth's crust, which is extremely thin compared with the planet's other layers.

✔ Reading Check

Answer They change speed as the density of rock inside Earth changes.

Mapping Earth's Internal Structure As shown in **Figure 13,** the speeds and paths of seismic waves change as they travel through materials with different densities. By studying seismic waves that have traveled through Earth, scientists have identified different layers with different densities. In general, the densities increase with depth as pressures increase. Studying seismic waves has allowed scientists to map Earth's internal structure without being there.

Early in the twentieth century, scientists discovered that large areas of Earth don't receive seismic waves from an earthquake. In the area on Earth between 105° and 140° from the earthquake focus, no waves are detected. This area, called the shadow zone, is shown in **Figure 13.** Secondary waves are not transmitted through a liquid, so they stop when they hit the liquid outer core. Primary waves are slowed and bent but not stopped by the liquid outer core. Because of this, scientists concluded that the outer core and mantle are made of different materials. Primary waves speed up again as they travel through the solid inner core. The bending of primary waves and the stopping of secondary waves create the shadow zone.

✔ Reading Check
Why do seismic waves change speed as they travel through Earth?

Figure 13
Seismic waves bend and change speed as the density of rock changes. Primary waves bend when they contact the outer core, and secondary waves are stopped completely. This creates a shadow zone where no seismic waves are received.

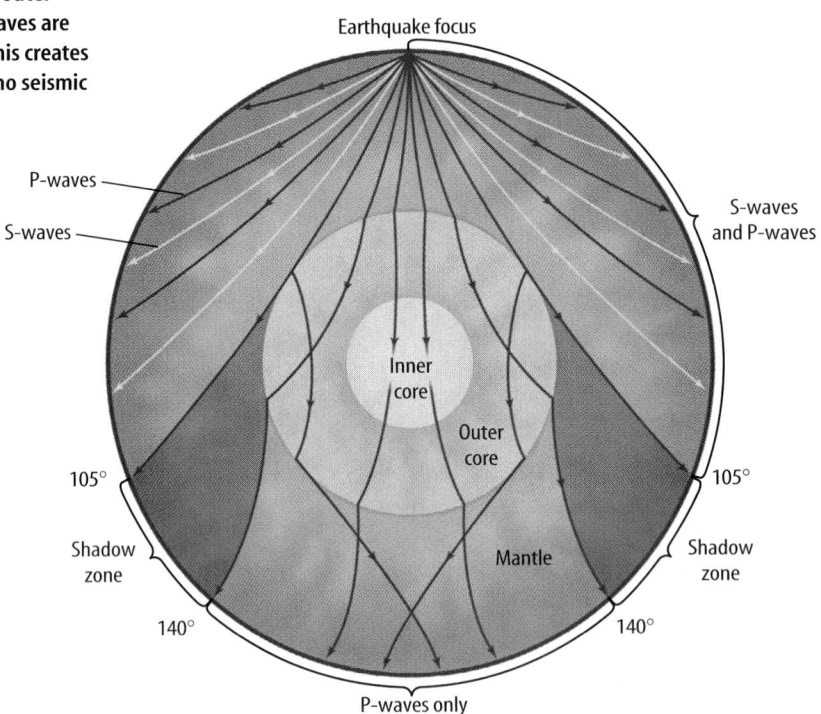

Resource Manager

Chapter Resources Booklet
Reinforcement, p. 30
Activity Worksheet, pp. 5–6

Inclusion Strategies

Learning Disabled To help these students, build a model of Earth's interior layers from modeling clay. First, make a ball of clay with a radius of 24 mm. Cut this ball in half and mold a 45-mm layer of different-colored clay around it. Around this second layer, mold a 58-mm-thick layer of a third color of clay. Mold a very thin layer of a fourth color around this third layer.

Layer Boundaries Figure 14 shows how seismic waves change speed as they pass through layers of Earth. Seismic waves speed up when they pass through the bottom of the crust and enter the upper mantle, shown on the far left of the graph. This boundary between the crust and upper mantle is called the Mohorovicic discontinuity (moh huh ROH vee chihch • dis kahn tuh NEW uh tee), or Moho.

The mantle is divided into layers based on changes in seismic wave speeds. For example, primary and secondary waves slow down again when they reach the asthenosphere. Then, they generally speed up as they move through a more solid region of the mantle below the asthenosphere.

The core is divided into two layers based on how seismic waves travel through it. Secondary waves do not travel through the liquid outer core, as you can see in the graph. Primary waves slow down when they reach the outer core, but they speed up again upon reaching the solid inner core.

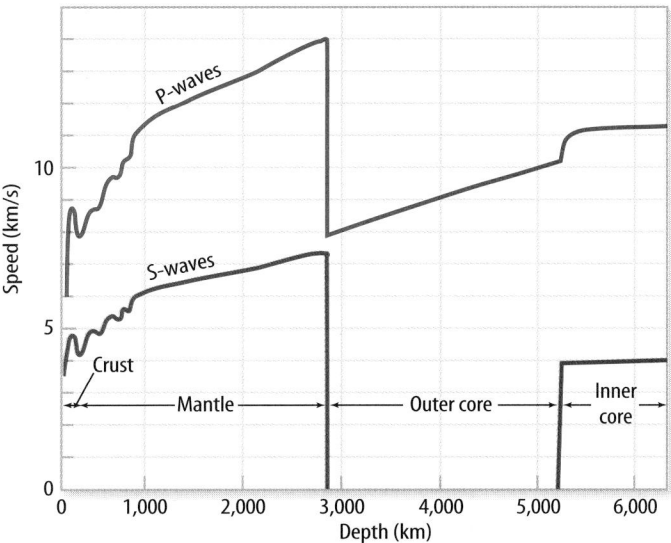
Seismic Wave Speeds

Figure 14
Changes in the speeds of seismic waves allowed scientists to detect boundaries between Earth's layers. S waves in the inner core form when P waves strike its surface.

Section 2 Assessment

1. How many seismograph stations are needed to determine the location of an epicenter? Explain.

2. Name the layers of Earth's interior.

3. What makes up most of Earth's inner core?

4. What are the three types of seismic waves? Which one does the most damage to property?

5. **Think Critically** Why do some seismograph stations receive both primary and secondary waves from an earthquake but other stations don't?

Skill Builder Activities

6. **Predicting** What will happen to the distance between two opposite walls of a room as primary waves move through the room? **For more help, refer to the** Science Skill Handbook.

7. **Solving One-Step Equations** Primary waves travel about 6 km/s through Earth's crust. The distance from Los Angeles, California, to Phoenix, Arizona, is about 600 km. How long would it take primary waves to travel between the two cities? **For more help, refer to the** Math Skill Handbook.

Reteach
Work with students to devise a large chart on the bulletin board or chalkboard that lists the properties and effects of the different types of seismic waves covered in this section.

Challenge
Challenge students to write reports on the work of seismologists and other scientists who study earthquakes. Reports should include the types of places they work, what they do, and how their work is helpful to society. Encourage interested students to interview such a scientist about what he or she does. Have students share what they find in class. L2
LS Linguistic

✓Assessment

Performance Assess students' abilities to make and use graphs. Ask students to use **Figure 11** and determine travel times for primary waves at a distance of 3,000 km, 4,000 km, and 6,000 km. 5 minutes, 40 s; 7 minutes, 10 s; 9 minutes, 40 s Use **Performance Assessment in the Science Classroom,** p. 89.

Answers to Section Assessment

1. Three; circles are drawn around each seismograph station representing the distance of the station from the earthquake epicenter. The point at which the circles around the three stations meet is the epicenter.

2. crust, mantle, outer core, inner core

3. iron

4. primary waves, secondary waves, surface waves; surface waves

5. Secondary waves do not pass through liquids; therefore, they are stopped by Earth's outer core. Seismograph stations within the outer core's secondary wave shadow zone, but beyond its primary wave shadow zone, will record only primary waves. Other stations might lie within both shadow zones.

6. Earth's surface in the region would alternately compress and then expand. This would cause the walls to move toward and then away from each other.

7. 100 seconds; 1 minute and 40 seconds

Activity

Purpose Students will interpret data on an earthquake wave distance-time graph to determine the locations of earthquake epicenters. L2 ELL COOP LEARN
LS **Logical-Mathematical** P

Process Skills using numbers, interpreting data, making and using tables, making and using graphs, comparing and contrasting

Time Required 45 minutes

Teaching Strategy Be sure students understand how to use **Figure 11** before beginning this activity.

Answers to Questions

1. The difference in arrival time between P- and S-waves increases as the distance of the seismograph station from the earthquake increases. This time interval can be used to calculate the distance between the seismograph and the earthquake.

2. A: Mexico City, Mexico; B: San Francisco, California

3. a minimum of three

4. Those seismograph stations were probably within the outer core's shadow zone.

Activity

Epicenter Location

In this activity you can plot the distance of seismograph stations from the epicenters of earthquakes and determine the earthquake epicenters.

What You'll Investigate
Can plotting the distance of several seismograph stations from two earthquake epicenters allow you to determine the locations of the two epicenters?

Materials
string   globe
metric ruler   chalk

Goals
- **Plot** the distances from several seismograph stations based on primary and secondary wave arrival times.
- **Interpret** the location of earthquake epicenters from these plots.

Earthquake Data			
Location of Seismograph	Wave	Wave Arrival Times	
		Earthquake A	Earthquake B
New York, New York	P	2:24:05 P.M.	1:19:42 P.M.
	S	2:29:15 P.M.	1:25:27 P.M.
Seattle, Washington	P	2:24:40 P.M.	1:14:37 P.M.
	S	2:30:10 P.M.	1:16:57 P.M.
Rio de Janeiro, Brazil	P	2:29:10 P.M.	—
	S	2:37:50 P.M.	—
Paris, France	P	2:30:30 P.M.	1:24:57 P.M.
	S	2:40:10 P.M.	1:34:27 P.M.
Tokyo, Japan	P	—	1:24:27 P.M.
	S	—	1:33:27 P.M.

Procedure

1. Determine the difference in arrival time between the primary and secondary waves at each station for each earthquake listed in the table.

2. After you determine the arrival time differences for each seismograph station, use the graph in **Figure 11** to determine the distance in kilometers of each seismograph from the epicenter of each earthquake. Record these data in a data table. For example, the difference in arrival times in Paris for earthquake B is 9 min, 30 s. On the graph, the primary and secondary waves are separated along the vertical axis by 9 min, 30 s at a distance of 8,975 km.

3. Using the string, measure the circumference of the globe. Determine a scale of centimeters of string to kilometers on Earth's surface. (Earth's circumference is 40,000 km.)

4. For each earthquake, place one end of the string at each seismic station location on the globe. Use the chalk to draw a circle with a radius equal to the distance to the earthquake's epicenter.

5. **Identify** the epicenter for each earthquake.

Conclude and Apply

1. How is the distance of a seismograph from the earthquake related to the arrival times of the waves?

2. What is the location of the epicenter for each earthquake?

3. How many stations were needed to locate each epicenter accurately?

4. **Explain** why some seismographs didn't receive secondary waves from some quakes.

Assessment

Performance Ask students to explain why data from two seismograph stations are not enough to locate an earthquake epicenter. Use **Performance Assessment in the Science Classroom**, p. 91.

Inclusion Strategies

Physically Challenged Help these students by assigning each one a partner who will provide support as he or she measures distances on the globe. Encourage helpers to provide each physically challenged student with just enough assistance to accomplish the task.

People and Earthquakes

Earthquake Activity

Imagine awakening in the middle of the night with your bed shaking, windows shattering, and furniture crashing together. That's what many people in Northridge, California, experienced at 4:30 A.M. on January 17, 1994. The ground beneath Northridge shook violently—it was an earthquake.

Although the earthquake lasted only 15 s, it killed 51 people, injured more than 9,000 people, and caused $44 billion in damage. More than 22,000 people were left homeless. **Figure 15A** shows some of the damage caused by the Northridge earthquake. **Figure 15B** shows the record of the Northridge earthquake on a seismogram.

Earthquakes are natural geological events that provide information about Earth. Unfortunately, they also cause billions of dollars in property damage and kill an average of 10,000 people every year. With so many lives lost and such destruction, it is important for scientists to learn as much as possible about earthquakes to try to reduce their impact on society.

As You Read

What You'll Learn
- **Explain** where most earthquakes in the United States occur.
- **Describe** how scientists measure earthquakes.
- **List** ways to make your classroom and home more earthquake-safe.

Vocabulary
magnitude
liquefaction
tsunami

Why It's Important
Earthquake preparation can save lives and reduce damage.

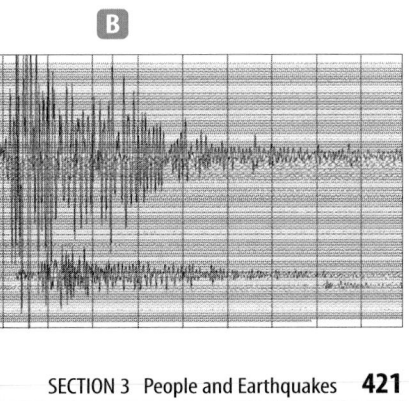

A

Figure 15
The 1994 Northridge, California, earthquake was a costly disaster. **A** Several major highways were damaged. **B** A seismograph made this record, called a seismogram, of the earthquake.

B

SECTION
3

People and Earthquakes

1 Motivate

Bellringer Transparency
Display the Section Focus Transparency for Section 3. Use the accompanying Transparency Activity Master. L2 ELL

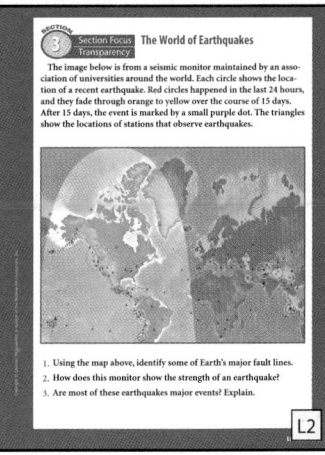

Tie to Prior Knowledge
Help students recall photographs of the destruction caused by earthquakes they may have seen in newspapers, in magazines, or on television.

Resource Manager

Chapter Resources Booklet
Transparency Activity, p. 48
Directed Reading for Content Mastery, pp. 23, 24

Section ✓*Assessment* Planner

PORTFOLIO
Extension, p. 422

PERFORMANCE ASSESSMENT
Math Skills Activity, p. 425
MiniLAB, p. 426
Skill Builder Activities, p. 427
See page 434 for more options.

CONTENT ASSESSMENT
Section, p. 427
Challenge, p. 427
Chapter, pp. 434–435

2 Teach

Earthquake Activity

Make a Model

Tape a stiff sheet of paper to the side of a closed shoe box. Have a volunteer slowly draw a straight line from the top of the sheet to the bottom. Then, have the volunteer attempt the same feat as another student bounces a small rubber ball on the top of the box. Use this model to explain how a seismograph works. **Visual-Spatial**

Extension

Have students write two or three paragraphs in their Science Journals about what it might be like at the epicenter of an earthquake. Encourage them to relate what might happen to buildings, bridges, and other structures. Have them address whether they would be able to feel any of the seismic waves they have learned about. L2 **Linguistic** P

Discussion

Instruct students to look at **Table 1. Why did some strong earthquakes cause so much loss of life while others caused little?** Possible answers: Some areas were more populous than others; the buildings in some areas were more able to withstand earthquake vibrations.

Visual Learning

Table 1 Ask students to identify the most powerful earthquake listed in the table. the 1960 earthquake in Chile Which earthquake resulted in the most deaths? the 1556 earthquake in China

Figure 16
The 1999 earthquake in Turkey released about 32 times more energy than the 1994 Northridge earthquake did.

Table 1 Large-Magnitude Earthquakes			
Year	Location	Magnitude	Deaths
1556	Shensi, China	?	830,000
1755	Lisbon, Portugal	8.8 (est.)	70,000
1811–12	New Madrid, MO	8.3 (est.)	few
1886	Charleston, SC	?	60
1906	San Francisco, CA	8.3	700 to 800
1923	Tokyo, Japan	9.2	143,000
1960	Chile	9.5	490 to 2,290
1964	Prince William Sound, AK	8.5	131
1976	Tangshan, China	8.2	242,000
1990	Iran	7.7	50,000
1995	Kobe, Japan	6.9	5,378
2000	Indonesia	7.9	90
2001	India	7.7	>20,000

422 CHAPTER 14 Earthquakes

Studying Earthquakes Scientists who study earthquakes and seismic waves are seismologists. As you learned earlier, the instrument that is used to record primary, secondary, and surface waves from earthquakes all over the world is called a seismograph. Seismologists can use records from seismographs, called seismograms, to learn more than just where the epicenter of an earthquake is located.

Measuring Earthquake Magnitude The height of the lines traced on the paper record of a seismograph is a measure of the energy that is released, or the **magnitude,** of the earthquake. The Richter magnitude scale is used to describe the strength of an earthquake and is based on the height of the lines on the seismogram. The Richter scale has no upper limit. However, scientists think that a value of about 9.5 would be the maximum strength an earthquake could register. For each increase of 1.0 on the Richter scale, the height of the line on a seismogram is ten times greater. However, about 32 times as much energy is released for every increase of 1.0 on the scale. For example, an earthquake with a magnitude of 8.5 releases about 32 times more energy than an earthquake with a magnitude of 7.5. **Figure 16** shows damage from the 7.8-magnitude earthquake in Turkey in 1999. **Table 1** is a list of some large-magnitude earthquakes that have occurred around the world and the damage they have caused.

Most of the earthquakes you hear about are large ones that cause great damage. However, of all the earthquakes detected throughout the world each year, most have magnitudes too low to be felt by humans. Scientists record thousands of earthquakes every day with magnitudes of less than 3.0. Each year, about 55,000 earthquakes are felt but cause little or no damage. These minor earthquakes have magnitudes that range from approximately 3.0 to 4.9 on the Richter scale.

Resource Manager

Chapter Resources Booklet
  Lab Activity, pp. 15–18

Earth Science Critical Thinking/Problem Solving, p. 9

Inclusion Strategies

Learning Disabled Have students use the information in **Table 1** to design and draw a time line of major earthquakes. Encourage students to illustrate the time line. Also encourage students to research other major earthquakes and add them to their timelines.

Describing Earthquake Intensity Earthquakes also can be described by the amount of damage they cause. The modified Mercalli intensity scale describes the intensity of an earthquake using the amount of structural and geologic damage in a specific location. The amount of damage done depends on the strength of the earthquake, the nature of surface material, the design of structures, and the distance from the epicenter. Under ideal conditions, only a few people would feel an intensity-I earthquake, and it would cause no damage. An intensity-IV earthquake would be felt by everyone indoors during the day but would be felt by only a few people outdoors. Pictures might fall off walls and books might fall from shelves. However, an intensity-IX earthquake would cause considerable damage to buildings and would cause cracks in the ground. An intensity-XII earthquake would cause total destruction of buildings, and objects such as cars would be thrown upward into the air. The 1994 6.8-magnitude earthquake in Northridge, California, was listed at an intensity of IX because of the damage it caused.

Liquefaction Have you ever tried to drink a thick milkshake from a cup? Sometimes the milkshake is so thick that it won't flow. How do you make the milkshake flow? You shake it. Something similar can happen to very wet soil during an earthquake. Wet soil can be strong most of the time, but the shaking from an earthquake can cause it to act more like a liquid. This is called **liquefaction.** When liquefaction occurs in soil under buildings, the buildings can sink into the soil and collapse, as shown in **Figure 17.** People living in earthquake regions should avoid building on loose soils.

Physics INTEGRATION

In 1975, Chinese scientists successfully predicted an earthquake by measuring a slow tilt of Earth's surface and small changes in Earth's magnetism. Many lives were saved as a result of this prediction. Do research to find out why most earthquakes have not been predicted.

Physics INTEGRATION

Many earthquakes occur with no prior warning. Seismologists can determine areas where earthquakes are likely to occur, but they can't determine exactly when.

Discussion

Why would the buildings in San Francisco's Marina district have been more susceptible to damage, having been built on a landfilled marsh? The soils of the filled-in marsh were probably not very compact and could be infiltrated with water, causing them to be susceptible to liquefaction.

Figure 17
San Francisco's Marina district suffered extensive damage from liquefaction in a 1989 earthquake because it is built on a landfilled marsh.

Teacher FYI

Moment Magnitude Moment magnitude, which is more precise than the Richter scale, is derived by multiplying the rigidity of the rock by the area of the fault rupture and then again by the amount of rock movement. This provides the seismic moment of the earthquake. Seismic moment is based on the concept of torque. The interaction of different segments of Earth on opposing sides of a fault set up internal torques that cause earthquakes. The magnitude usually first reported is Richter scale magnitude modified for modern equipment. After further study, the moment magnitude can be determined and is applied to the earthquake.

Earthquake Activity,
continued

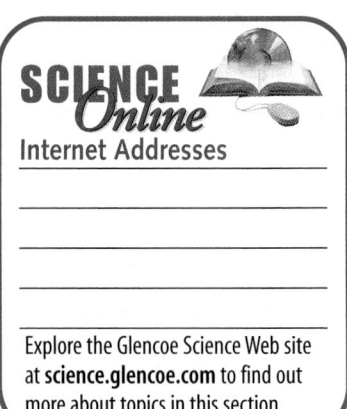

SCIENCE *Online*
Internet Addresses

_____

_____

_____

Explore the Glencoe Science Web site at science.glencoe.com to find out more about topics in this section.

Extension

Have students research and report to the class on the Tsunami Warning System developed by the United States. The Tsunami Warning System was developed in 1948 after a tsunami hit the Aleutian and Hawaiian Islands two years earlier. After a 1964 Alaskan wave took 103 lives, an improved Regional TWS was developed. Now data from GOES (Geostationary Operational Environmental Satellite) satellites are able to help scientists issue tsunami warnings in as little as two minutes in some cases.

Caption Answer

Figure 18 Flooding could occur as the huge wave comes ashore. Buildings might be destroyed, boats and other objects on shore could be swept out to sea, and people could be killed.

SCIENCE *Online*

Research Visit the Glencoe Science Web site at **science.glencoe.com** for more information about tsunamis. Make a poster to illustrate what you learn.

Figure 18
A tsunami begins over the earthquake focus. *What might happen to towns located near the shore?*

Tsunamis Most earthquake damage occurs when surface waves cause buildings, bridges, and roads to collapse. People living near the seashore, however, have another problem. An earthquake under the ocean causes a sudden movement of the ocean floor. The movement pushes against the water, causing a powerful wave that can travel thousands of kilometers in all directions. Far from shore, a wave caused by an earthquake is so long that a large ship might ride over it without anyone noticing. But when one of these waves breaks on a shore, as shown in **Figure 18,** it forms a towering crest that can reach 30 m in height.

Ocean waves caused by earthquakes are called seismic sea waves, or **tsunamis** (soo NAH meez). Just before a tsunami crashes onto shore, the water along a shoreline might move rapidly toward the sea, exposing a large portion of land that normally is underwater. This should be taken as a warning sign that a tsunami could strike soon, and you should head for higher ground immediately.

Because of the number of earthquakes that occur around the Pacific Ocean, the threat of tsunamis is constant. To protect lives and property, a warning system has been set up in coastal areas and for the Pacific islands to alert people if a tsunami is likely to occur. The Pacific Tsunami Warning Center, located near Hilo, Hawaii, provides warning information including predicted tsunami arrival times at coastal areas.

However, even tsunami warnings can't prevent all loss of life. In the 1960 tsunami that struck Hawaii, 61 people died when they ignored the warning to move away from coastal areas.

Cultural **Diversity**

Tsunami! Tsunamis occur in many areas around the world and have been reported since ancient times. One of the earliest recorded tsunamis struck Syria around 2,000 B.C. Thera, one of the Cyclades Islands in the Mediterranean, may be the remnant of a volcano that erupted—causing tsunamis that ended the Minoan civilization on Crete. Tsunami is a Japanese word for "harbor wave." Many have struck the Japanese shore. Because Japan is an island nation, the threat of tsunamis is a national safety concern. Today, by using expected tsunami characteristics, the Japan Meteorological Agency can forecast tsunami heights for the Japanese coastline. This provides residents with the knowledge necessary to move a safe distance away from the shore.

Earthquake Safety

You have learned that earthquakes can be destructive, but the damage and loss of life can be minimized. Although earthquakes cannot be predicted reliably, **Figure 19** shows where earthquakes are most likely to occur in the United States.

Knowing where large earthquakes are likely to occur helps in long-term planning. Cities in such regions can take action to prevent damage to buildings and loss of life. Many buildings withstood the 1989 San Francisco earthquake because they were built with the expectation that such an earthquake would occur someday.

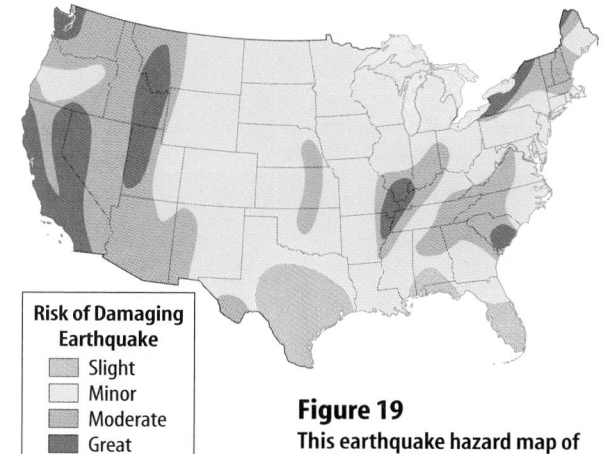

Risk of Damaging Earthquake
- Slight
- Minor
- Moderate
- Great

Figure 19
This earthquake hazard map of the United States shows where earthquakes are most likely to cause severe damage.

Math Skills Activity

Using Multiplication to Compare Earthquake Energy

Example Problem

The Richter scale is used to measure the magnitude of earthquakes. For each number increase on the Richter scale, 32 times more energy is released. How much more energy is released by a magnitude 6 earthquake than by a magnitude 3 earthquake?

Solution

1 *This is what you know:*   magnitude 6 earthquake, magnitude 3 earthquake, energy increases 32 times per magnitude number

2 *This is what you need to find out:*   amount of additional energy released

3 *This is the procedure you need to use:*   Find the difference in magnitude numbers, then use that number of <u>multiples</u> of 32 to find the amount of additional energy released.

4 *Solve the equation:*   difference in magnitude = 6 − 3 = 3
multiply 32 times itself 3 times: $32 \times 32 \times 32 = 32{,}768$
32,768 times more energy is released

Practice Problem

Calculate the difference in the amount of energy released between a magnitude 7 earthquake and a magnitude 2 earthquake.

For more help, refer to the Math Skill Handbook.

Tsunami at Papua New Guinea Have students search newspaper articles online to write brief descriptions in their Science Journals of the damage done when a tsunami hit the northern coast of Papua New Guinea, on July 17, 1998. Trees and houses were swept away by the tsunami and at least 2,000 people died.

Resource Manager

Chapter Resources Booklet
   Enrichment, p. 34
Mathematics Skill Activities, p. 9
Cultural Diversity, p. 47

Earthquake Safety

Visual Learning

Figure 19 Have students determine whether your community has a high probability of having an earthquake. Answers will vary depending on your location.

Discussion

Of what use is a map that shows earthquake probability? It can alert people who live in certain areas of the country that there is a good chance they will experience an earthquake and that they should be prepared for one.

Math Skills Activity

National Math Standards
Correlation to Mathematics Objectives
1, 2, 6, 8, 9

Teaching Strategy
Follow the steps in the example problem. The difference in magnitude numbers is 5. Multiply 32 times itself 5 times.

Answer to Practice Problem
33,554,432 times more energy is released.

Earthquake Safety,
continued

Text Question Answer

Buildings can be designed to withstand the shaking of earthquakes.

 **Reading Check**

Answer those built to resist damage from the shaking of earthquakes

Caption Answer

Figure 20 The rubber acts like a cushion to absorb earthquake waves.

 **Mini LAB**

Purpose Students will model seismic-safe methods of construction. [L2] ELL COOP LEARN
[IS] **Interpersonal**

Materials blocks, rubber bands of two sizes

Teaching Strategy Review Earthquake-Resistant Structures with students before having them complete the activity.

Analysis
1. Structures with rubber bands around them are more likely to withstand the "earthquake."
2. Concrete cement pillars could be wrapped with steel supports. The supports would decrease the chances of the pillars' breaking during an earthquake.

 **Assessment**

Performance Have students build a model seismic-safe highway. Use **Performance Assessment in the Science Classroom**, p. 123.

Mini LAB

Modeling Seismic-Safe Structures

Procedure
1. On a **tabletop,** build a structure out of **building blocks** by simply placing one block on top of another.
2. Build a second structure by wrapping sections of three blocks together with **rubber bands.** Then, wrap larger rubber bands around the entire completed structure.
3. Set the second structure on the tabletop next to the first one and pound on the side of the table with a slow, steady rhythm.

Analysis
1. Which of your two structures was better able to withstand the "earthquake" caused by pounding on the table?
2. How might the idea of wrapping the blocks with rubber bands be used in construction of supports for elevated highways?

Quake-Resistant Structures During earthquakes, buildings, bridges, and highways can be damaged or destroyed. Most loss of life during an earthquake occurs when people are trapped in or on these crumbling structures. What can be done to reduce loss of life?

Seismic-safe structures stand up to vibrations that occur during an earthquake. **Figure 20** shows how buildings can be built to resist earthquake damage. Today in California, some new buildings are supported by flexible, circular moorings placed under the buildings. The moorings are made of steel plates filled with alternating layers of rubber and steel. The rubber acts like a cushion to absorb earthquake waves. Tests have shown that buildings supported in this way should be able to withstand an earthquake measuring up to 8.3 on the Richter scale without major damage.

In older buildings, workers often install steel rods to reinforce building walls. Such measures protect buildings in areas that are likely to experience earthquakes.

✔ **Reading Check** *What are seismic-safe structures?*

Figure 20
The rubber portions of this building's moorings absorb most of the wave motion of an earthquake. The building itself only sways gently. *What purpose does the rubber serve?*

Curriculum Connection

Art Have students research what to do to keep safe during an earthquake. Then have them take one aspect of what they find and create a poster with one important "Earthquake Safety Tip." Hang the posters in class and use them as a foundation for a class discussion on earthquake safety.
[IS] **Visual-Spatial**

Resource Manager

Chapter Resources Booklet
MiniLAB, p. 4
Reinforcement, p. 31

Performance Assessment in the Science Classroom, p. 42

Before an Earthquake To make your home as earthquake-safe as possible, certain steps can be taken. To reduce the danger of injuries from falling objects, move heavy objects from high shelves and place them on lower shelves. Learn how to turn off the gas, water, and electricity in your home. To reduce the chance of fire from broken gas lines, make sure that hot-water heaters and other gas appliances are held securely in place, as shown in **Figure 21**. A newer method that is being used to minimize the danger of fire involves placing sensors on gas lines. The sensors automatically shut off the gas when earthquake vibrations are detected.

During an Earthquake If you're indoors, move away from windows and any objects that could fall on you. Seek shelter in a doorway or under a sturdy table or desk. If you're outdoors, stay in the open—away from power lines or anything that might fall. Stay away from buildings—chimneys or other parts of buildings could fall on you.

After an Earthquake Check water and gas lines for damage. If any are damaged, shut off the valves. If you smell gas, leave the building immediately and call authorities from a phone away from the leak area. Stay out of and away from damaged buildings. Be careful around broken glass and rubble that could contain sharp edges and wear boots or sturdy shoes to keep from cutting your feet. Finally, stay away from beaches. Tsunamis sometimes hit after the ground has stopped shaking.

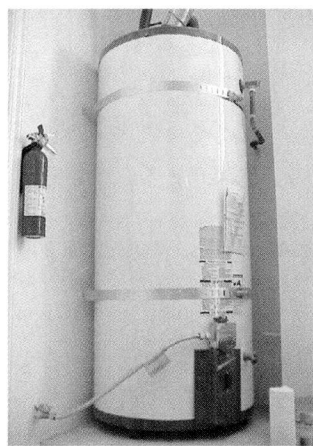

Figure 21
Securing gas water heaters to walls with sturdy straps helps reduce the danger of fires from broken gas lines.

Section Assessment

1. How can you determine whether or not you live in an area where an earthquake is likely to occur?
2. What can you do to make your home more safe during an earthquake?
3. How is earthquake magnitude measured?
4. Name three ways that an earthquake can cause damage.
5. **Think Critically** How are shock absorbers on a car similar to the circular moorings used in modern earthquake-safe buildings? How do they absorb shock?

Skill Builder Activities

6. **Forming Hypotheses** Hypothesize why some earthquakes with smaller magnitudes result in more deaths than earthquakes with larger magnitudes. **For more help, refer to the** Science Skill Handbook.

7. **Solving One-Step Equations** What is the difference in energy released between an earthquake of Richter magnitude 8.5 and one of magnitude 4.5? Between one of magnitude 3.5 and one of magnitude 5.5? **For more help, refer to the** Math Skill Handbook.

Reteach
Use the Internet to gather a number of magazine and newspaper articles about recent earthquakes and tsunamis and the damage they caused. Allow each student to choose an article to read, summarize, and report on to the class. Use the reports as a basis for class discussion about quakes and their effects.

Challenge
Challenge students to use their imaginations and information in this section to come up with designs that might make homes, office buildings, bridges, or other structures earthquake resistant. Students should work in groups of two or three to make sketches or models. Set aside class time for students to present their designs. COOP LEARN

✔ Assessment

Performance Have students make concept maps that show what people should do before, during, and after earthquakes to keep safe. Allow students to make large drawings on construction paper. Use **Performance Assessment in the Science Classroom,** p. 161.

Answers to Section Assessment

1. Check maps or written sources to find out whether the area has had earthquakes in the past.
2. Move heavy objects to low shelves. Make sure hot-water heaters and gas appliances are held securely in place. Place sensors on gas lines.
3. As the drum of a seismograph vibrates under a stationary pen in response to the seismic waves of an earthquake, a record is made.
4. Possible answers: shaking that damages or destroys buildings, fires, liquefaction, tsunamis
5. The rubber portion of the moorings absorbs shock similar to the way fluid in a car's shock absorber absorbs shock.
6. The buildings in the areas with less-powerful quakes may not be as able to withstand the movement caused by the quake; some small quakes might occur in more heavily populated areas.
7. about 1,048,576 times more energy; about 1,024 times more energy

Activity

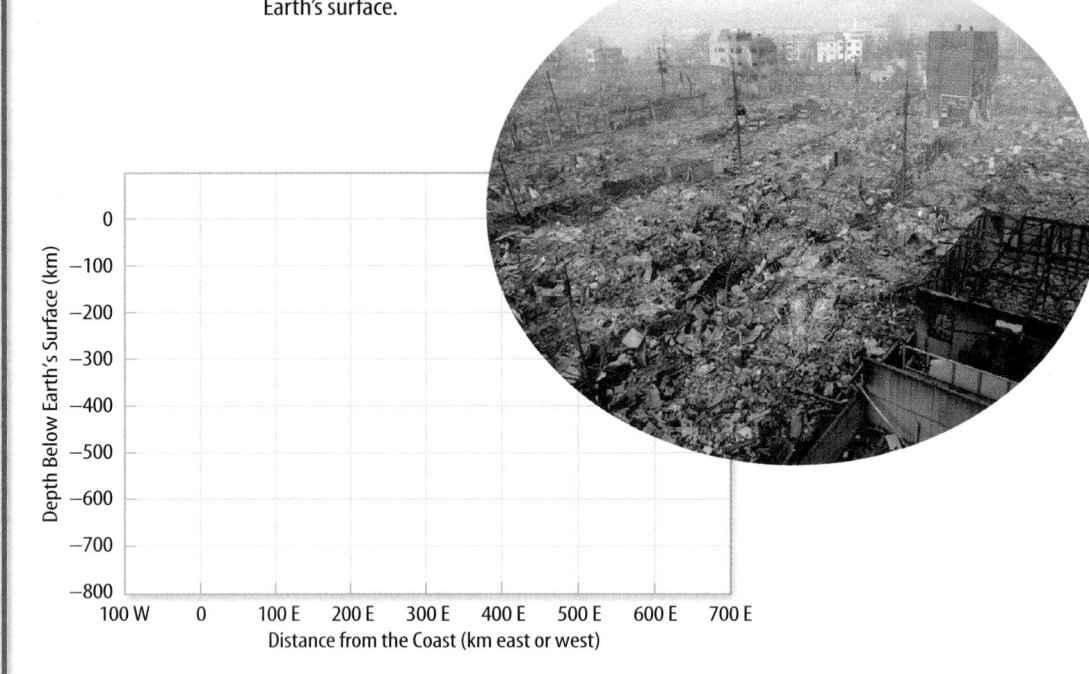

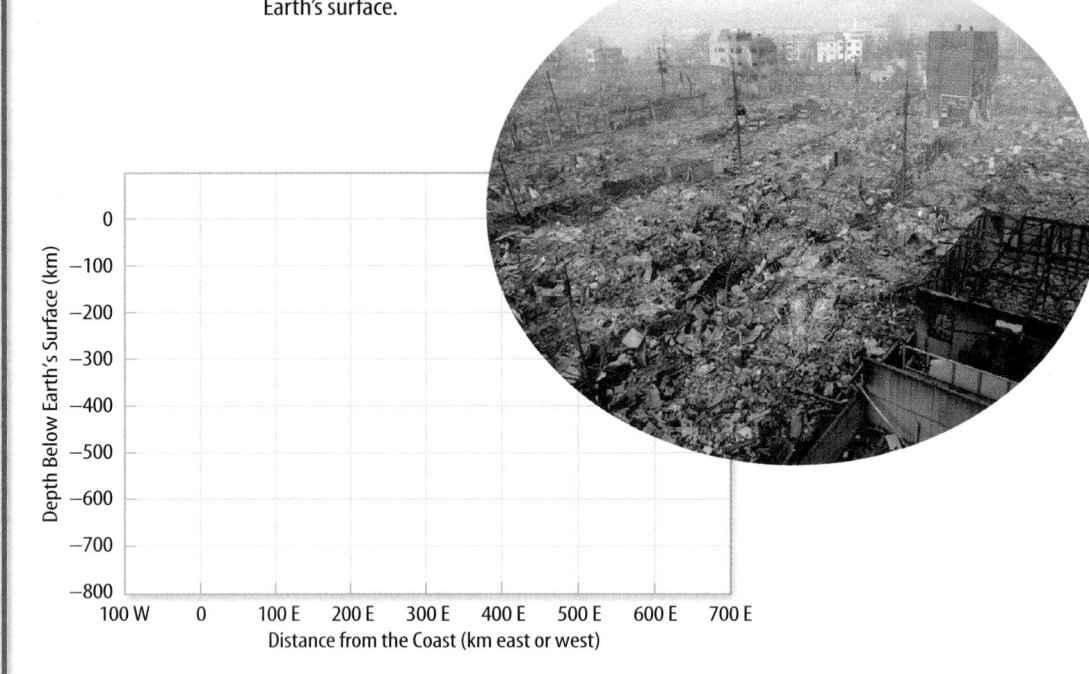

BENCH TESTED

What You'll Investigate

Purpose

Students investigate whether there is a relationship between the depth of earthquake foci and epicenter locations and the movements of plates. [L2]

COOP LEARN

IS Logical-Mathematical [P]

Process Skills

observing and inferring, communicating, using numbers, interpreting data, hypothesizing, using tables, making and using graphs, comparing and contrasting, separating and controlling variables

Time Required

45 minutes

Procedure

Teaching Strategies

• Review the definitions of focus and epicenter before starting the activity.

• Draw a blank version of the focus depth versus distance graph. Indicate the location of the coast on the graph. Help students begin by plotting the first two locations.

Expected Outcome

Students should find that earthquake foci occur deeper the farther they are from the shore.

Activity

Earthquake Depths

You learned earlier in this chapter that Earth's crust is broken into sections called plates. Stresses caused by movement of these plates generate energy within rocks that must be released. When this release of energy is sudden and rocks break, an earthquake occurs.

What You'll Investigate

Can a study of the foci of earthquakes tell you anything about plate movement in a particular region?

Goals

■ **Observe** any connection between earthquake-focus depth and epicenter location using the data provided on the next page.

■ **Describe** any observed relationship between earthquake-focus depth and the movement of plates at Earth's surface.

Materials

graph paper
pencil

428 **CHAPTER 14** Earthquakes

Curriculum Connection

Geography Have students research where on Earth the distribution of earthquake foci might be similar to that in this activity. Possible answer: the west coast of South America

Inclusion Strategies

Visually Impaired Ask some of your students to prepare copies of the maps and charts being used in this activity in a manner useful to those who are visually impaired. Outline the locations under study with thick lines, and identify earthquake foci by raised bumps on the maps. Students who are able could produce maps and charts using Braille.

Procedure

1. Use graph paper and the data table on the right to make a graph plotting the depths of earthquake foci and the distances from the coast of a continent for each earthquake epicenter.

2. Use the graph on the previous page as a reference to draw your own graph. Place *Distance from the Coast* on the horizontal axis. Begin labeling at the far left with 100 km west. To the right of it should be 0 km, then 100 km east, 200 km east, 300 km east, and so on through 700 km east. What point on your graph represents the coast?

3. Label the vertical axis *Depth Below Earth's Surface*. Label the top of the graph 0 km to represent Earth's surface. Label the bottom of the vertical axis −800 km.

4. **Plot** the focus depths against the distance and direction from the coast for each earthquake in the table to the right.

Conclude and Apply

1. **Describe** any observed relationship between the location of earthquake epicenters and the depth of earthquake foci.

2. Based on the graph you have completed, hypothesize what is happening to the plates at Earth's surface in the vicinity of the plotted earthquake foci.

3. **Infer** what process is causing the earthquakes you plotted on your graph paper.

4. Hypothesize why none of the plotted earthquakes occurred below 700 km.

5. Based on what you have plotted, infer what continent these data could apply to. Explain what you based your answer on.

Focus and Epicenter Data

Earthquake	Focus Depth (km)	Distance of Epicenter from Coast (km)
A	−55	0
B	−295	100 east
C	−390	455 east
D	−60	75 east
E	−130	255 east
F	−195	65 east
G	−695	400 east
H	−20	40 west
I	−505	695 east
J	−520	390 east
K	−385	335 east
L	−45	95 east
M	−305	495 east
N	−480	285 east
O	−665	545 east
P	−85	90 west
Q	−525	205 east
R	−85	25 west
S	−445	595 east
T	−635	665 east
U	−55	95 west
V	−70	100 west

ommunicating

Your Data

Compare your graph with those of other members of your class. **For more help, refer to the** Science Skill Handbook.

Conclude and Apply

Answers to Questions

1. The earthquakes near the coast are shallow-focus earthquakes. Moving inland, the earthquake foci become progressively deeper.

2. Two plates are colliding, with one possibly being subducted beneath the other.

3. It's possible that an ocean plate is sliding beneath a land plate. As one plate slides under the other, earthquakes occur at increasing depth.

4. Generally, earthquakes occur because of the fracturing of solids. Because of the heat and pressure at a depth of 700 km, the consistency of the slab is like plastic, and stress is absorbed without fracturing.

5. South America, part of North America

Error Analysis

Students who do not get the correct outcome should check whether they have transferred data correctly from the table to the graph. Incorrect plotting of the graph itself also could introduce errors.

Process Ask students to draw the plate boundary described by the data in this activity. Students should draw a convergent boundary where a sea plate meets a land plate and the sea plate is subducted. Use **Performance Assessment in the Science Classroom,** p. 127.

Resource Manager

Chapter Resources Booklet
  Activity Worksheet, pp. 7–8
Lab Management and Safety, p. 65

ommunicating

Your Data

Use a spreadsheet computer program to make a line graph to display the focus and epicenter data.

Content Background

Students might have heard tsunamis referred to as tidal waves. This term is incorrect, as tsunamis have nothing to do with tides. The word *tsunami* actually means "harbor wave" in Japanese, and has become the accepted term for waves generated by seismic activity. Sometimes a drop in sea level precedes the arrival of a tsunami. People have been killed after moving out to inspect exposed sea life, and then suddenly being faced with a fast-moving wall of water.

Discussion

- **What preparations for a tsunami could the people of Hawaii make if given several hours notice?** They could move ships out of harbors to the open sea and evacuate low-lying areas.

- **How might the duration of an earthquake contribute to its severity?** The longer the shaking, the more opportunity for damage. The psychological toll exacted by an earthquake on residents is greater the longer the shaking continues.

Activity

Have the class act out the nearly five minute duration of the Alaskan earthquake, imagining the panic and dangers involved. Use a stopwatch to give them accurate start and end times. Have them record their impressions in their science journals.

LS Kinesthetic and Linguistic

Science Stats

Moving Earth!

Did you know...

... The most powerful earthquake to hit the United States in recorded history shook Alaska in 1964. At 8.5 on the Richter scale, the quake shook all of Alaska for nearly 5 min, which is a long time for an earthquake. Nearly 320 km of roads near Anchorage suffered damage, and almost half of the 204 bridges had to be rebuilt.

... Snakes can sense the vibrations made by a small rodent up to 23 m away. Does this mean that they can detect vibrations prior to major earthquakes? Unusual animal behavior was observed just before a 1969 earthquake in China—an event that was successfully predicted.

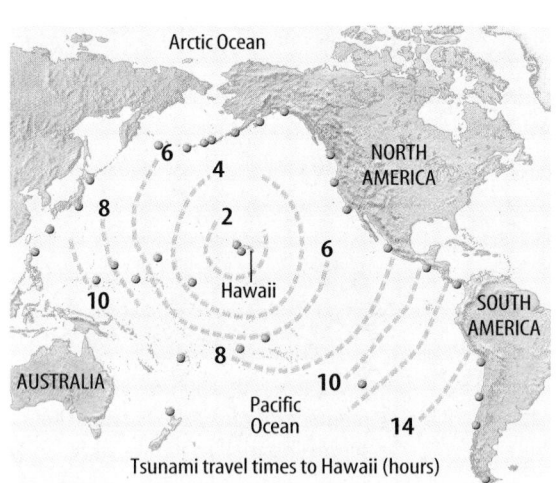

Tsunami travel times to Hawaii (hours)

... Earthquakes beneath the ocean floor can cause seismic sea waves, or tsunamis. Traveling at speeds of up to 950 km/h—as fast as a commercial jet—a tsunami can strike with little warning. Since 1945, more people have been killed by tsunamis than by the ground shaking from earthquakes.

430 CHAPTER 14 Earthquakes

SCIENCE *Online*
Internet Addresses

_____

_____

_____

Explore the Glencoe Science Web site at **science.glencoe.com** to find out more about topics in this section.

... Tsunamis can reach heights of 30 m. A wave that tall would knock over this lighthouse.

... On December 16, 1811, a strong earthquake occurred near New Madrid, Missouri. This earthquake was so strong that it changed the course of the Mississippi River. The earthquake also was reported to have rung the bell of St. Phillip's Steeple in Charleston, South Carolina.

Do the Math

1. On the Richter scale, a whole number increase means that the height of the largest recorded seismic wave increases by ten. How much higher is the largest wave from an 8.5 earthquake than the largest wave from a 3.5 earthquake?
2. Look at the tsunami warning system map on the previous page. About how long would a tsunami triggered near the Aleutian Islands take to reach Hawaii?

Go Further

Visit the Glencoe Science Web site at **science.glencoe.com.** Research the history and effects of earthquakes in the United States. Describe how the San Francisco earthquake of 1906 stimulated earthquake research.

SCIENCE STATS 431

Do the Math

Teaching Strategies

- Help students to identify what fact(s) they have been given and what they are asked to solve in the first Do the Math problem. Then have students determine which operation or operations they can use to solve the problem.
- To help students complete the second question in Do the Math, have them inspect the diagram showing tsunami travel times. Discuss what the dotted lines show.

Answers

1. 50 times higher
2. 6 hours

Go Further

Have students make charts to organize what they learn about various U.S. earthquakes. They can include columns to show the date, location, magnitude and effects of each earthquake.

Visual Learning

Earthquakes Beneath the Ocean Floor What is presumed to be occurring on each of the dotted lines shown in the diagram? earthquakes Use the times shown in the diagram to extrapolate: Predict how much time it would take a tsunami to reach Hawaii from an earthquake occurring near the southern tip of South America. About 16 hours **Approximately how distant is the epicenter of an earthquake if it takes 15 hours for the tsunami to reach Hawaii?** 15 hours times 950 km/h equals 14,250 km.

Reviewing Main Ideas

Preview

Students can answer the questions in their Science Journals. Discuss the answers as you go through the chapter. **Linguistic**

Review

Students can write their answers, then compare them with those of other students. **Interpersonal**

Reteach

Students can look at the illustrations and describe details that support the main ideas of the chapter. **Visual-Spatial**

Answers to Chapter Review

SECTION 1

3. a normal fault

SECTION 2

1. surface waves
2. San Francisco

SECTION 3

1. a seismogram

Reviewing Main Ideas

Section 1 Forces Inside Earth

1. Plate movements put stress on rocks. To a certain point, the rocks bend and stretch. If the force is beyond the elastic limit, the rocks might break.

2. Earthquakes are vibrations that are created when rocks break along a fault.

3. Normal faults form when rocks undergo tension. Compression produces reverse faults. Strike-slip faults result from shearing forces. *What type of fault is shown here?*

Section 2 Features of Earthquakes

1. Primary waves compress and stretch rock particles as the waves move. Secondary waves move by causing particles in rocks to move at right angles to the direction of the waves. Surface waves move in a backward rolling motion and a side-to-side swaying motion. *Which kind of earthquake wave caused the damage shown here?*

2. Scientists can locate earthquake epicenters by recording seismic waves. *Where is the epicenter of the earthquake shown here?*

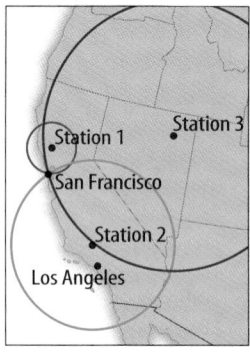

3. By observing the speeds and paths of seismic waves, scientists are able to determine the boundaries between Earth's internal layers.

Section 3 People and Earthquakes

1. A seismograph is the instrument used to measure earthquake magnitude. *What is this record of an earthquake produced by a seismograph called?*

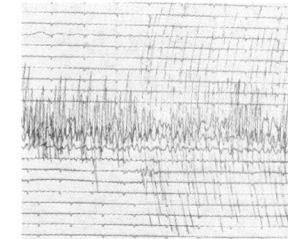

2. The magnitude of an earthquake is a measure of the energy released by the quake. The Richter scale describes how much energy an earthquake releases. The scale has no upper limit.

3. Earthquakes can cause liquefaction of wet soil and tsunamis, both of which increase the amount of structural damage produced by an earthquake.

FOLDABLES
Reading & Study Skills

After You Read

Using what you learned in this chapter, list and explain the effects of earthquakes on the inside of your Foldable.

FOLDABLES
Reading & Study Skills

After You Read

After students have read the chapter and completed the Foldable described in Before You Read, have them do the activity on the student page.

Dinah Zike

Visualizing Main Ideas

Complete the following concept map on earthquake damage.

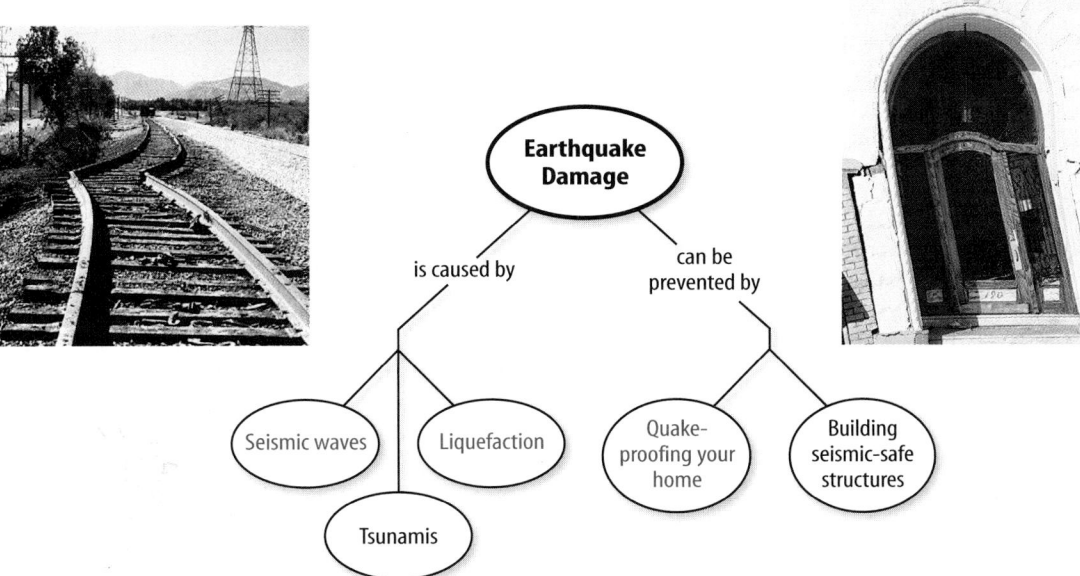

Earthquake Damage

is caused by

can be prevented by

Seismic waves

Liquefaction

Tsunamis

Quake-proofing your home

Building seismic-safe structures

Visualizing Main Ideas

See student page.

Vocabulary Review

Using Vocabulary

1. surface waves
2. strike-slip fault
3. epicenter
4. magnitude
5. tsunami

Vocabulary Review

Vocabulary Words

a. earthquake
b. epicenter
c. fault
d. focus
e. liquefaction
f. magnitude
g. normal fault
h. primary wave

i. reverse fault
j. secondary wave
k. seismic wave
l. seismograph
m. strike-slip fault
n. surface wave
o. tsunami

THE PRINCETON REVIEW **Study Tip**

Be a teacher! Gather a group of friends and assign each one a section of the chapter to teach. Teaching helps you remember and understand information.

Using Vocabulary

Replace the underlined words with the correct vocabulary words.

1. Most earthquake damage results from <u>primary waves</u>.

2. At a <u>normal fault</u>, rocks move past each other without much upward or downward movement.

3. The point on Earth's surface directly above the earthquake focus is the <u>fault</u>.

4. The measure of the energy released during an earthquake is its <u>seismograph</u>.

5. An earthquake under the ocean can cause a <u>surface wave</u> that travels thousands of kilometers.

CHAPTER STUDY GUIDE **433**

IDENTIFYING **Misconceptions**

Assess

Use the assessment as follow-up to page 406F after students have completed the chapter.

Activity Have students bring in newspaper articles describing earthquakes around the world. Have the class work together to make a bulletin board display showing the location of different earthquakes, and describing their intensity and the damage done. Have students compare their findings with the map in **Figure 2**. Have students explain why earthquakes are found where they are, and why everyone should know how to respond to an earthquake.

Chapter 14 Assessment

Checking Concepts

1. C
2. A
3. B
4. B
5. A
6. B
7. B
8. D
9. A
10. C

Thinking Critically

11. The earthquake generated tsunamis that caused the damage.
12. It is unlikely that anything will fall on him or her.
13. If the pendulum remains still, any movement recorded by the attached pen will be the result of seismic waves.
14. Tsunamis are caused by earthquakes on the ocean floor and have nothing to do with tides.
15. The single-story wood-frame house; the wood would probably give more with vibrations than would bricks, which are more likely to crumble and fall apart.

Checking Concepts

Choose the word or phrase that best answers the question.

1. Earthquakes can occur when which of the following is passed?
   A) tension limit
   B) seismic unit
   C) elastic limit
   D) shear limit

2. When the rock above the fault surface moves down relative to the rock below the fault surface, what kind of fault forms?
   A) normal   C) reverse
   B) strike-slip D) shearing

3. From which of the following do primary and secondary waves move outward?
   A) epicenter   C) Moho
   B) focus   D) tsunami

4. What kind of earthquake waves stretch and compress rocks?
   A) surface   C) secondary
   B) primary   D) shear

5. What are the slowest seismic waves?
   A) surface   C) secondary
   B) primary   D) pressure

6. What is the fewest number of seismograph stations that are needed to locate the epicenter of an earthquake?
   A) two   C) four
   B) three   D) five

7. What happens to primary waves when they pass from liquids into solids?
   A) slow down   C) stay the same
   B) speed up   D) stop

8. What part of a seismograph does not move during an earthquake?
   A) sheet of paper C) drum
   B) fixed frame   D) pendulum

9. How much more energy does an earthquake of magnitude 7.5 release than an earthquake of magnitude 6.5?
   A) 32 times more   C) twice as much
   B) 32 times less   D) about half as much

10. What are the recorded lines from an earthquake called?
    A) seismograph   C) seismogram
    B) Mercalli scale D) Richter scale

Thinking Critically

11. The 1960 earthquake in the Pacific Ocean off the coast of Chile caused damage and loss of life in Chile and also in Hawaii, Japan, and other areas along the Pacific Ocean border. How could this earthquake do so much damage to areas thousands of kilometers from its epicenter?

12. Why is a person who is standing outside in an open field relatively safe during a strong earthquake?

13. Explain why the pendulum of a seismograph remains at rest.

14. Tsunamis often are called tidal waves. Explain why this is incorrect.

15. Which probably would be more stable during an earthquake—a single-story wood-frame house or a brick building? Explain.

Developing Skills

16. **Communicating** Imagine you are a science reporter assigned to interview the mayor about the earthquake safety of buildings in your city. What buildings would you be most concerned about? Make a list of questions about earthquake safety that you would ask the mayor.

Chapter ✓Assessment Planner

Portfolio Encourage students to place in their portfolios one or two items of what they consider to be their best work. Examples include:
- Activity, p. 410
- Science Journal, p. 415
- Extension, p. 422

Performance Additional performance assessments, Performance Task Assessment Lists, and rubrics for evaluating these activities can be found in Glencoe's **Performance Assessment in the Science Classroom.**

17. Measuring in SI Use an atlas and a metric ruler to answer the following question. Primary waves travel at about 6 km/s in continental crust. How long would it take a primary wave to travel from San Francisco, California, to Reno, Nevada?

18. Interpreting Data Use the data table below and a map of the United States to determine the location of the earthquake epicenter.

Seismograph Station Data

Station	Latitude	Longitude	Distance from Earthquake
1	45° N	120° W	1,300 km
2	35° N	105° W	1,200 km
3	40° N	115° W	790 km

19. Forming Hypotheses Hypothesize how seismologists could assign magnitudes to earthquakes that occurred before modern seismographs and the Richter scale were developed.

Performance Assessment

20. Model Use layers of different colors of clay to illustrate the three different kinds of faults. Label each model, explaining the forces involved and the rock movement.

21. Display Make a display showing why data from two seismograph stations are not enough to determine the location of an earthquake epicenter.

TECHNOLOGY

Go to the Glencoe Science Web site at **science.glencoe.com** or use the **Glencoe Science CD-ROM** for additional chapter assessment.

THE PRINCETON REVIEW Test Practice

Seismologists used the modified Mercalli intensity scale to determine the intensity of the same earthquake from four different cities. They recorded their data in the following table.

Earthquake Intensity

City	Intensity
A	VII 7
B	X 10
C	V 5
D	IX 9

Study the table and answer the following questions.

1. According to the table, which city probably was the closest to the epicenter of the earthquake?
A) city A
B) city B
C) city C
D) city D

2. Which of the following would be an accurate conclusion based on the intensity in city B?
F) The earthquake was not felt by very many people.
G) The earthquake destroyed well-built wooden and stone structures.
H) Destruction was minimal. Dishes rattled in cabinets, and pictures fell off of walls.
J) The earthquake was only felt indoors.

CHAPTER ASSESSMENT 435

THE PRINCETON REVIEW Test Practice

The Test-Taking Tip was written by The Princeton Review, the nation's leader in test preparation.
1. B
2. G

Developing Skills

16. Most concern: hospital, police and fire stations; Do you have an emergency plan in place in case of major earthquake damage? Have you educated the public about what to do? Are buildings earthquake resistant? Accept all reasonable answers.
17. about 50 seconds (d = 300 km)
18. The epicenter is near (just south of) Los Angeles, California.
19. It could be done by comparing the amount of damage done by early earthquakes to damage done by earthquakes today when the magnitude is known.

Performance Assessment

20. Models should show the relative movement of rock layers and the direction of forces acting at the fault. Use **Performance Assessment in the Science Classroom**, p. 123.
21. Answers will vary but students should conclude that the third location is needed to pinpoint the location of the epicenter.

✔Assessment Resources

📂 **Reproducible Masters**

Chapter Resources Booklet
  Chapter Review, pp. 39–40
  Chapter Tests, pp. 41–44
  Assessment Transparency Activity, p. 51

Glencoe Science Web site
  Interactive Tutor
  Chapter Quizzes

Glencoe Technology
  🖌 Assessment Transparency
  💿 Interactive CD-ROM Chapter Quizzes
  💿 ExamView Pro Test Bank
  💿 Vocabulary PuzzleMaker Software
  📼 MindJogger Videoquiz

Section/Objectives	Standards		Activities/Features
Chapter Opener	**National**	**State/Local**	**Explore Activity:** Describe landforms, p. 437 **Before You Read,** p. 437
	See p. 5T for a Key to Standards.		
Section 1 Landforms 🕐 2 sessions 📦 1 block 1. **Discuss** differences between plains and plateaus. 2. **Describe** folded, upwarped, fault-blocked and volcanic mountains.	National Content Standards: UCP5, A1, D1		**MiniLAB:** Profiling the United States, p. 440 **Science Online,** p. 441
Section 2 Viewpoints 🕐 2 sessions 📦 1 block 1. **Define** latitude and longitude. 2. **Explain** how latitude and longitude are used to identify locations on Earth. 3. **Determine** the time and date in different time zones.	National Content Standards: UCP3, A1, D1, F5		**MiniLAB:** Interpreting Latitude and Longitude, p. 445 **Life Science Integration,** p. 446
Section 3 Maps 🕐 3 sessions 📦 1.5 blocks 1. **Explain** the differences among Mercator, Robinson, and conic projections. 2. **Describe** features of topographic maps, geologic maps, and satellite maps.	National Content Standards: UCP2, A1, D1, E2, F5, G3		**Physics Integration,** p. 450 **Visualizing Topographic Maps,** p. 451 **Science Online,** p. 452 **Problem-Solving Activity:** How can you create a cross section from a geologic map?, p. 453 **Activity:** Making a Topographic Map, p. 455 **Activity:** Constructing Landforms, pp. 456–457 **Science and History:** Location, Location, pp. 458–459

NATIONAL GEOGRAPHIC

Teacher's Corner

PRODUCTS AVAILABLE FROM NATIONAL GEOGRAPHIC SOCIETY
To order call 1-800-368-2728:
Books
Exploring Your World: the Adventure of Geography
National Geographic Satellite Atlas for

Young Explorers
National Geographic World Atlas for Young Explorers
Maps and Globe
Explorer Globe; Physical Earth
World Satellite
World Physical/Ocean Floor

Videos
Latitude and Longitude
Mapping Your World
Physical Geography of the Continent Series (6 videos)
When We Learn About Earth from Space

Activity Materials	Reproducible Resources	Section Assessment	Technology
Explore Activity: globe, atlas, or world map	**Chapter Resources Booklet** Foldables Worksheet, p. 15 Directed Reading Overview, p. 17 Note-taking Worksheets, pp. 31–32	GLENCOE'S **ASSESSMENT** ADVANTAGE	
MiniLAB: piece of paper, pencil, map of the United States	**Chapter Resources Booklet** Transparency Activity, p. 42 MiniLAB, p. 3 Enrichment, p. 28 Reinforcement, p. 25 Directed Reading, p. 18 Transparency Activity, pp. 45–46 **Cultural Diversity,** p. 33	Portfolio Cultural diversity, p. 440 Performance MiniLAB, p. 440 Skill Builder Activities, p. 443 Content Section Assessment, p. 443	Section Focus Transparency Teaching Transparency Interactive CD-ROM Guided Reading Audio Program
MiniLAB: world map *Need materials?* Contact Science Kit at 1-800-828-7777 or www.sciencekit.com on the Internet.	**Chapter Resources Booklet** Transparency Activity, p. 43 MiniLAB, p. 4 Lab Activities, pp. 9–11, 13–14 Enrichment, p. 29 Reinforcement, p. 26 Directed Reading, p. 19	Portfolio Challenge, p. 447 Performance MiniLAB, p. 445 Skill Builder Activities, p. 447 Content Section Assessment, p. 447	Section Focus Transparency Interactive CD-ROM Guided Reading Audio Program
Activity: plastic model of a landform, water tinted with food coloring, transparency, transparency marker, clear plastic storage box with lid, beaker, metric ruler, tape **Activity:** U.S. Geological Survey 7.5 minute quadrangle maps, sandbox sand, rolls of brown paper towels, spray bottle filled with water, ruler	**Chapter Resources Booklet** Transparency Activity, p. 44 Enrichment, p. 30 Reinforcement, p. 27 Directed Reading, pp. 19, 20 Activity Worksheets, pp. 5–6, 7–8 **Earth Science Critical Thinking/ Problem Solving,** p. 5 **Cultural Diversity,** pp. 27, 49 **Reading and Writing Skill Activities,** p. 21 **Lab Management and Safety,** p. 66	Portfolio Extension, p. 451 Performance Problem-Solving Activity, p. 453 Skill Builder Activities, p. 454 Content Section Assessment, p. 454	Section Focus Transparency Interactive CD-ROM Guided Reading Audio Program

GLENCOE'S **ASSESSMENT** ADVANTAGE

End of Chapter Assessment

Blackline Masters	Technology	Professional Series
Chapter Resources Booklet Chapter Review, pp. 35–36 Chapter Tests, pp. 37–40 **Standardized Test Practice by The Princeton Review,** pp. 31–34	MindJogger Videoquiz Interactive CD-ROM Vocabulary PuzzleMakers ExamView Pro Test Bank Interactive Lesson Planner Interactive Teacher Edition	Performance Assessment in the Science Classroom (PASC)

Transparencies

Section Focus

Section Focus Transparency 1 — Sacred Heights

Mount Fuji, or Fujiyama, is Japan's highest mountain at 3,776 m (12,388 feet) high. Below is a photo of the mountain along with a topographical image made by a satellite. Mount Fuji is considered a sacred mountain, and its name means "everlasting life."

1. What might Mount Fuji's shape and surrounding terrain tell you about the way in which it was formed?
2. How might wind and water change the shape of a mountain?

L2

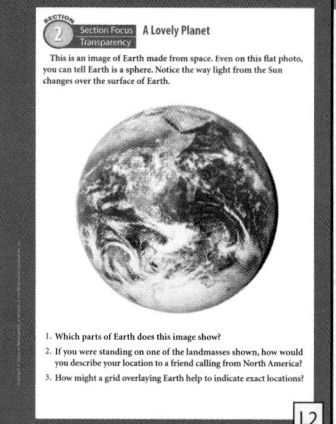

Section Focus Transparency 2 — A Lovely Planet

This is an image of Earth made from space. Even on this flat photo, you can tell Earth is a sphere. Notice the way light from the Sun changes over the surface of Earth.

1. Which parts of Earth does this image show?
2. If you were standing on one of the landmasses shown, how would you describe your location to a friend calling from North America?
3. How might a grid overlaying Earth help to indicate exact locations?

L2

Section Focus Transparency 3 — A Map of the Times

This is a map of the world that was made in Europe around 1617. Map making dates to prehistoric times when maps were used to show hunting and fishing grounds. Today, map makers can use images from satellites to help them make better maps.

1. Judging from this map, what parts of the world did Europeans know well in 1617? What parts of the world are mapped inaccurately?
2. How do you think explorers affected map making?
3. Think about different maps of your state that you have seen. Do all maps provide the same information? How many different kinds of maps can you name?

L2

Assessment

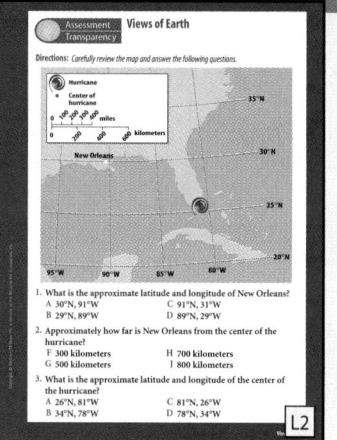

Assessment Transparency — Views of Earth

Directions: Carefully review the map and answer the following questions.

1. What is the approximate latitude and longitude of New Orleans?
   A 30°N, 91°W   C 91°N, 31°W
   B 29°N, 89°W   D 89°N, 29°W
2. Approximately how far is New Orleans from the center of the hurricane?
   F 300 kilometers   H 700 kilometers
   G 500 kilometers   J 800 kilometers
3. What is the approximate latitude and longitude of the center of the hurricane?
   A 26°N, 81°W   C 81°N, 26°W
   B 34°N, 78°W   D 78°N, 34°W

L2

Teaching

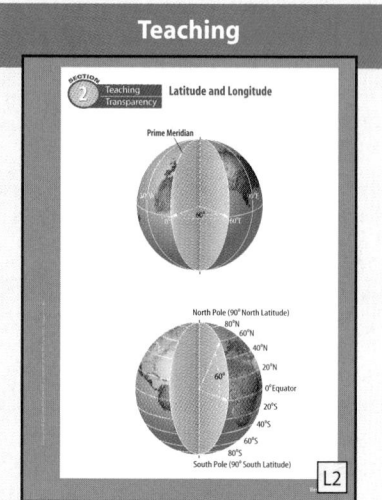

Teaching Transparency 2 — Latitude and Longitude

L2

This is a representation of key blackline masters available in the Teacher Classroom Resources. See Resource Manager boxes within the chapter for additional information.

Key to Teaching Strategies

The following designations will help you decide which activities are appropriate for your students.

L1 Level 1 activities should be appropriate for students with learning difficulties.

L2 Level 2 activities should be within the ability range of all students.

L3 Level 3 activities are designed for above-average students.

ELL ELL activities should be within the ability range of English Language Learners.

COOP LEARN Cooperative Learning activities are designed for small group work.

LS Multiple Learning Styles logos, as described on page 22T, are used throughout to indicate strategies that address different learning styles.

P These strategies represent student products that can be placed into a best-work portfolio.

Hands-on Activities

Activity Worksheets

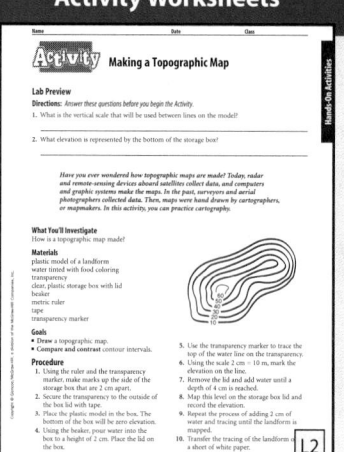

Activity — Making a Topographic Map

Lab Preview

Directions: Answer these questions before you begin the Activity.

1. What is the vertical scale that will be used between lines on the model?

2. What elevation is represented by the bottom of the storage box?

Have you ever wondered how topographic maps are made? Today, radar and remote-sensing devices aboard satellites collect data, and computers and graphic imaging make the maps. In the past, surveyors and aerial photographers collected data. Then, maps were hand drawn by cartographers, or mapmakers. In this activity, you can practice cartography.

What You'll Investigate
How is a topographic map made?

Materials
plastic model of a landform
water tinted with food coloring
transparency
clear, plastic storage box with lid
beaker
metric ruler
tape
transparency marker

Goals
• Draw a topographic map.
• Compare and contrast contour intervals.

Procedure
1. Using the ruler and the transparency marker, make marks up the side of the storage box that are 2 cm apart.
2. Secure the transparency to the outside of the box lid with tape.
3. Place the plastic model in the box. The bottom of the box will be zero elevation.
4. Using the beaker, pour water into the box to a height of 2 cm. Place the lid on the box.
5. Use the transparency marker to trace the top of the water line on the transparency.
6. Using the scale 2 cm = 10 m, mark the elevation on the line.
7. Remove the lid and add water until a depth of 4 cm is reached.
8. Map this level on the storage box lid and record the elevation.
9. Repeat the process of adding 2 cm of water and tracing until the landform is mapped.
10. Transfer the tracing of the landform to a sheet of white paper.

L2

Views of Earth 5

Laboratory Activities

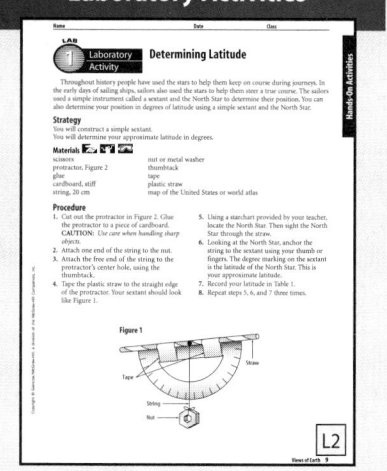

Laboratory Activity 1 — Determining Latitude

Throughout history people have used the stars to help them keep on course during journeys. In the early days of sailing ships, sailors also used the stars to help them steer a true course. The sailors used a simple instrument called a sextant and the North Star to determine their position. You can also determine your position in degrees of latitude using a simple sextant and the North Star.

Strategy
You will construct a simple sextant.
You will determine your approximate latitude in degrees.

Materials
scissors
protractor, Figure 2
glue
cardboard, stiff
string, 20 cm
nut or metal washer
thumbtack
tape
plastic straw
map of the United States or world atlas

Procedure
1. Cut out the protractor in Figure 2. Glue the protractor to a piece of cardboard. CAUTION: Use care when handling sharp objects.
2. Attach one end of the string to the nut.
3. Attach the free end of the string to the protractor's center hole, using the thumbtack.
4. Tape the plastic straw to the straight edge of the protractor. Your sextant should look like Figure 1.
5. Using a starchart provided by your teacher, locate the North Star. Then sight the North Star through the straw.
6. Looking at the North Star, anchor the string to the sextant using your thumb or fingers. The degree marking on the sextant is the latitude of the North Star. This is your approximate latitude.
7. Record your latitude in Table 1.
8. Repeat steps 5, 6, and 7 three times.

Figure 1

L2

Views of Earth 9

Meeting Different Ability Levels

Content Outline

Note-taking Worksheet — **Views of Earth**

Section 1   Landforms

A. _____—large, flat areas which often have thick, fertile soils and grassy meadows
1. _____ plains stretch along coastal areas and are often called lowlands.
2. _____ plains in the central part of a continent.
B. _____—flat, raised areas of land made up of nearly horizontal rocks; their edges rise steeply from the area around them.
C. _____ tower above the surrounding land.
1. _____ mountains form when rock layers are squeezed from opposite sides, causing the rock layers to fold like a rug pushed up against the wall.
2. Forces inside Earth push the crust up to form _____.
3. _____ mountains form when tilted blocks of rock are separated by faults from the surrounding rock.
4. Layers of molten material pile up forming cone-shaped _____ mountains.

Section 2   Viewpoints

A. Latitude and longitude lines identify exact locations on Earth by means of an imaginary _____ system; when stating a location latitude always comes before longitude.
1. _____—lines running parallel to the **equator**
2. Running from the North Pole through Greenwich Observatory near London, England, the _____ is the reference point for lines of **longitude**, distances in degrees east or west.
3. East lines of longitude meet west lines of longitude at the _____, which is opposite the prime meridian.
B. Earth is divided into 24 _____ zones, each about fifteen degrees of longitude wide and exactly one hour different from the zones on either side of it.
C. Calendar dates begin and end at midnight; the _____ is located at the 180° meridian.

L2   Views of Earth 31

Reinforcement

SECTION 1 Reinforcement — **Landforms**

Directions: *Complete the paragraphs using the words listed below. Some words may be used more than once.*

plateaus   river   plains   Colorado Plateau
uplifted   landforms   Grand Canyon   Great Plains
Great Plains   mountains   Gulf   coastal
lowlands   Atlantic   interior

Features that make up the shape of the land at Earth's surface are called
1. _____. There are three basic types of landforms, 2. _____,
3. _____, and 4. _____. Plains are large, relatively
5. _____ areas. In the United States, plains cover about one-half of all the land areas. 6. _____ plains are broad areas along coastlines. These plains are called
7. _____ because of their low elevation. The coastal plain along the East Coast of the United States is called the 8. _____ Coastal Plain. The plain that surrounds the Gulf of Mexico is the 9. _____ Coastal Plain.
10. _____ plains extend across the center of the United States. The
11. _____ make up a large portion of the interior plains.
Relatively flat areas of land that rise steeply from the land around them are called
12. _____. They are areas of nearly horizontal rocks that have been
13. _____ by forces within Earth. An example of a plateau in the United States is the 14. _____, which lies just west of the Rocky Mountains. Here the Colorado 15. _____ has cut deep into the rock layers, forming the
16. _____.

Directions: *Name the four kinds of mountains and give one example of each.*
17. _____
18. _____
19. _____
20. _____

L2   Views of Earth 23

Directed Reading

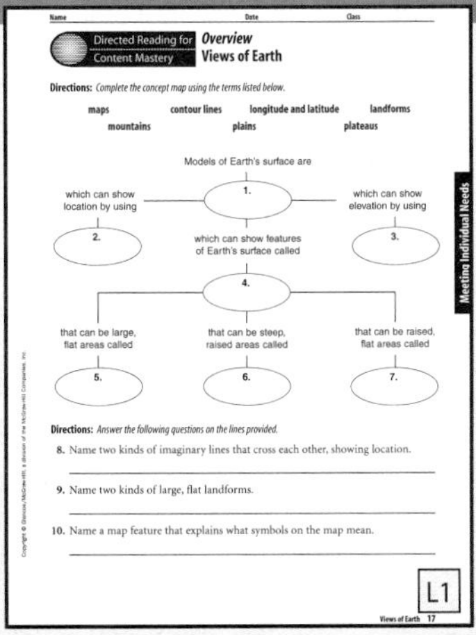

Directed Reading for Content Mastery — *Overview* **Views of Earth**

Directions: *Complete the concept map using the terms listed below.*

maps   contour lines   longitude and latitude   landforms
mountains   plains   plateaus

Models of Earth's surface are

1. _____

which can show location by using   2. _____

which can show features of Earth's surface called   4. _____

which can show elevation by using   3. _____

that can be large, flat areas called   5. _____
that can be steep, raised areas called   6. _____
that can be raised, flat areas called   7. _____

Directions: *Answer the following questions on the lines provided.*

8. Name two kinds of imaginary lines that cross each other, showing location.
_____

9. Name two kinds of large, flat landforms.
_____

10. Name a map feature that explains what symbols on the map mean.
_____

L1   Views of Earth 17

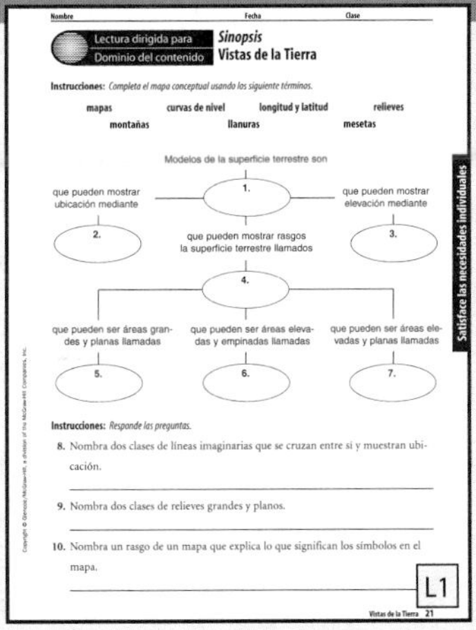

Assessment

Chapter Tests

Chapter Test — **Views of Earth**

I.   Testing Concepts

Directions: *Match the description in Column I with the term in Column II. Write the letter of the correct term in the blank at the left.*

Column I
1. distances in degrees east or west of the prime meridian
2. large, flat landforms
3. a way of collecting information about Earth from a distance
4. landforms formed when horizontal rock layers are squeezed together and buckle
5. map projection that shows correct shapes of continents but distorts their areas
6. landforms made of layers of molten rock
7. shows the changes in elevation of Earth's surface
8. explains what the symbols used on the map mean
9. landforms formed by forces pushing up Earth's crust
10. flat, raised areas of land
11. imaginary line that represents 0° longitude
12. map projection showing fairly accurate shapes and land areas of continents
13. the distance in degrees either north or south of the equator
14. the transition line for calendar days
15. projection useful for producing maps of small areas
16. the difference in elevation between two side-by-side contour lines
17. the relationship between the distances on the map and actual distances on Earth
18. imaginary line that circles Earth exactly halfway between the north and south poles
19. line on a map that connects points of equal elevation
20. landforms made of huge, tilted blocks of rocks that are separated from surrounding rocks by faults

Column II
a. plains
b. plateaus
c. folded mountains
d. upwarped mountains
e. fault-block mountains
f. volcanic mountains
g. latitude
h. prime meridian
i. longitude
j. International Date Line
k. Mercator projection
l. Robinson projection
m. conic projection
n. topographic map
o. contour line
p. contour interval
q. map scale
r. remote sensing
s. map legend
t. equator

L2   Views of Earth 37

Test Practice Workbook

Standardized Test Practice — Teacher Edition

The Princeton Review

Glencoe **Science**

LEVEL RED

L2

Enrichment

SECTION 1 Enrichment — **Building New Landforms**

People have always changed the land to create more space. San Francisco, New York City, and Boston are examples of places where people have filled in bays with soil to extend their land area. Japan and Hong Kong have built airports in their bays.
One of the best-known examples of extending a coastal plain is in the Netherlands. Over the centuries, the Dutch have built polders, tracts of lowland reclaimed from the sea, lakes, or marshes. First, dikes of sand and rock are built. Then the polder area is pumped dry. In years past, the windmills that dot the Netherlands provided the power needed to pump the sea water out. Now, electrical pumps do the work.

A Need for Land
The Netherlands occupies a small area of land, with more than 6 million people. The population density is high, 421 people per square kilometer. (The United States population density is 29 people per square kilometer.) The Dutch use every bit of land they have. They even use median strips of highways for crops. In the Netherlands, the largest cities and richest farmland are found on the polders.

IJsselmeer (Lake IJssel), a lake created by the IJsselmeer Dam when the first polder was created, gets its water from the Rhine. It is used to store water for the northern Netherlands. This water is used for drinking, industrial purposes, and irrigation. Any excess water is pumped into the Wadden Sea.

Environmental Change
Unfortunately, this system of water control that protects the polders depends heavily on maintaining things as they are. Due to global warming, which causes increased temperatures, the Dutch must re-evaluate their water management system. Rising temperatures will cause polar ice caps to melt, which will cause water levels to rise. Higher temperatures will also cause more water to evaporate and become rain in other areas, leaving less water available to the Dutch during the summer. The Netherlands might have too much water in the winter and too little in the summer.
The Dutch realize now that new dams and dike reinforcements will be necessary, but they are interested in working with the natural flow of water. The Dutch face a huge task, but they have worked for centuries to protect their land. They are confident they will continue to succeed.

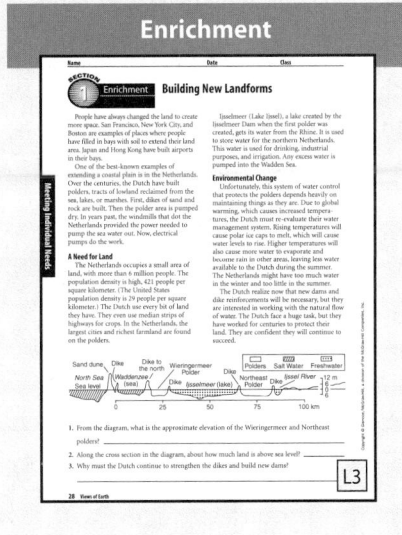

1. From the diagram, what is the approximate elevation of the Wieringermeer and Northeast polders? _____
2. Along the cross section in the diagram, about how much land is above sea level? _____
3. Why must the Dutch continue to strengthen the dikes and build new dams? _____

L3   28   Views of Earth

Spanish Directed Reading

Lectura dirigida para Dominio del contenido — *Sinopsis* **Vistas de la Tierra**

Instrucciones: *Completa el mapa conceptual usando los siguiente términos.*

mapas   curvas de nivel   longitud y latitud   relieves
montañas   llanuras   mesetas

Modelos de la superficie terrestre son

1. _____

que pueden mostrar ubicación mediante   2. _____

que pueden mostrar rasgos la superficie terrestre llamados   4. _____

que pueden mostrar elevación mediante   3. _____

que pueden ser áreas grandes y planas llamadas   5. _____
que pueden ser áreas elevadas y empinadas llamadas   6. _____
que pueden ser áreas elevadas y planas llamadas   7. _____

Instrucciones: *Responde las preguntas.*

8. Nombra dos clases de líneas imaginarias que se cruzan entre sí y muestran ubicación. _____

9. Nombra dos clases de relieves grandes y planos. _____

10. Nombra un rasgo de un mapa que explica lo que significan los símbolos en el mapa. _____

L1   Vistas de la Tierra 21

Chapter Review

Chapter Review — **Views of Earth**

Part A. Vocabulary Review

Directions: *Circle the term or phrase in parentheses that best completes each statement.*

1. Imaginary lines used to determine distances north and south are called (meridians, latitude lines, longitude lines).
2. On a (Robinson, Mercator, conic) projection, lines of latitude are parallel and lines of longitude are curved, resulting in less distortion.
3. About one-half of the land area in the United States is made up of (plateaus, plains, mountains).
4. On a topographic map, (contour lines, distance scales, contour intervals) are used to connect points of equal elevation.
5. On a road map, a (Robinson, Mercator, conic) projection would be used.
6. Maps show distance using (contour lines, map scales, map legends).
7. (Upwarped, Folded, Volcanic) mountains were formed when crust was pushed up by forces inside Earth.
8. Lines of longitude can be used to determine the exact (north/south, east/west, north/east) location of a place.
9. The 180° meridian is the (equator, prime meridian, International Date Line).
10. Relatively flat, raised areas of land are called (plateaus, plains, mountains).
11. Mountains that begin when molten material reaches Earth's surface through a weak area of crust are (upwarped, fault-blocked, volcanic) mountains.
12. A contour interval shows the difference in (projection, elevation, scale) between two side-by-side contour lines.
13. A map projection showing correct shapes of continents with distorted areas is a (Robinson, Mercator, conic) projection.
14. The exact location of a place on a map can be found using (latitude lines, longitude lines, latitude and longitude lines).
15. Zero longitude is designated by the (equator, prime meridian, International Date Line).
16. The Appalachians, the older North American mountains, are an example of (volcanic, folded, upwarped) mountains.
17. Sharp, jagged peaks are characteristic of (fault-blocked, folded, upwarped) mountains.

L2   Views of Earth 35

Science Content Background

SECTION 1

Landforms
Plains and Mountains

Plains form in a variety of ways. Some are formed by the erosion of plateaus and mountains. Others are formed by the deposition of sediments into depressions. Mountains are classified according to their most dominant characteristics. These characteristics are caused by the processes involved in mountain building, such as folding, faulting, upwarping, and igneous activities.

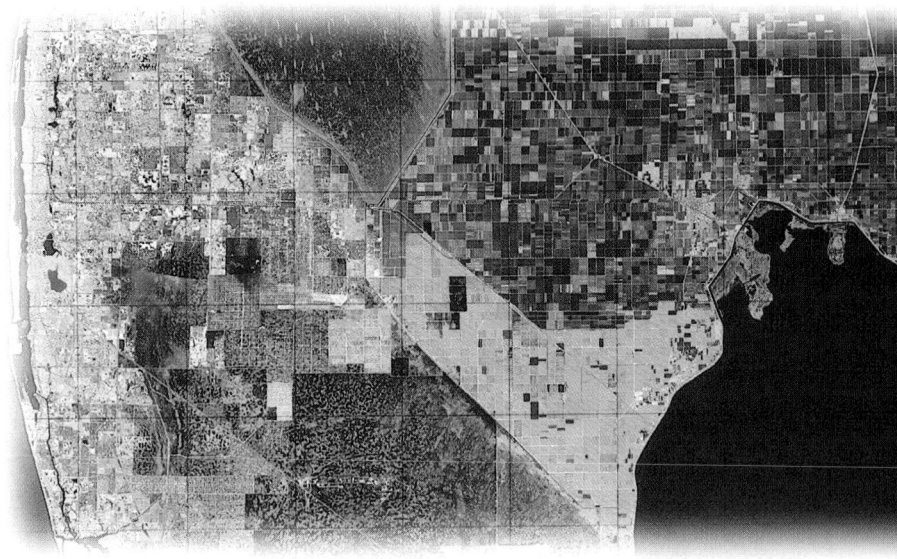

Earth Satellite Corporation/Science Photo Library/Photo Researchers, Inc.

SECTION 2

Viewpoints
Latitude and Longitude

Latitude is defined as the angle formed between the point in the sky directly above an observer (zenith) and the plane of Earth's equator. Each degree of latitude represents a distance of about 111 km over Earth's surface. Lines of latitude form imaginary circles around Earth that are parallel to the equator. The diameter of these circles decrease with distance from the equator. At the poles, the circles are mere points.

Student Misconception

Earth is not a sphere, but is flat.

Refer to the facing page for teaching strategies to address this misconception. Refer to pages 444–447 for content related to this topic.

Lines of longitude, or meridians, are not parallel. They converge toward Earth's poles. The distance between lines of longitude varies with distance from the equator. At the poles, the distance shrinks to zero.

SECTION 3

Maps
Map Projections

A map projection is made by transferring data about Earth onto paper. Because Earth is round and paper is flat, some distortion is always present in map projections. The larger the area covered by the map, the greater the distortion. Gerhardus Mercator developed the projection named for him in 1569. In a Mercator projection, the size of Greenland is exaggerated 1,500 percent. When Arthur Robinson created his projection in 1963, he visualized how each country should look on a map, then used mathematics and computers to draw their shapes. The Robinson projection has a 60 percent exaggeration of the size of Greenland.

SCIENCE *Online*

For additional content background on this topic, go to the Glencoe Science Web site at **science.glencoe.com**.

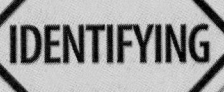

Misconceptions

Find Out What Students Think

Students may think that . . .

• Earth is not a sphere, but is flat.
This misconception is a result of students' common experience—from the ground, Earth's surface looks flat. In addition, many students have yet to grasp the idea of gravity pulling all parts of Earth, and the people and other objects on its surface, toward its center. Thus students think that if Earth were a sphere, people on the bottom would "fall off."

Demonstration
Evidence, both direct and indirect, needs to be provided to students to help them understand that Earth is spherical and that it rotates. Evidence could include

• satellite photos of Earth.

S. Nielsen/DRK Photo

• photographs showing Earth's curved shadow on the Moon during a lunar eclipse.

Promote Understanding

Activity
Provide each pair of students with construction paper, scissors, tape, and a basketball or other sports ball.

• Have students make a small representation of a sail boat using the construction paper and tape. Instruct them to tape the boat onto the basketball.

• Have students stand about 3 m from their partners. Direct the partner to hold the basketball in front of his or her body, with the boat toward the partner's body. Then have him or her rotate the ball so the boat appears to move up and over the top of the ball.

• As the ship appears, have the watching partner closely observe which parts of the boat appear first. Then have students switch roles.

Discussion
After all students have observed the approach of the boat, bring the class together and discuss their observations. Bring out the idea that as a ship disappears over the horizon the last part that one observes is the mast. As it approaches, the first thing one sees is the mast. If Earth were flat, one would see the entire boat either appear or disappear.

Assess
After completing the chapter, see *Identifying Misconceptions* in the Study Guide.

Chapter Vocabulary

What do you think?

Science Journal A hand-held receiver for a global positioning system (GPS) is shown. The GPS is a system of 24 satellites in orbit around Earth. A person holding a GPS receiver can pinpoint his or her exact location on Earth's surface by receiving signals from those satellites. This is especially useful for hiking in the woods, boating in the ocean, driving in an unfamiliar city, or flying a small airplane over unfamiliar terrain.

Views of Earth

Viewing Earth from satellites, often called remote sensing, is a powerful way to learn about Earth's landforms, weather, and vegetation. This colorful image shows the metropolitan area of New York City and surrounding regions. Vegetation shows up as green, uncovered land is red, water is blue, and human-made structures appear gray. In this chapter, you will learn about studying Earth from space. You'll learn about Earth's major landforms, and you'll learn how to locate places on Earth's surface.

What do you think?

Science Journal Look at the picture below with a classmate. Discuss what you think this might be. Here's a hint: *It can keep you from getting lost on land or at sea.* Write your answer or best guess in your Science Journal.

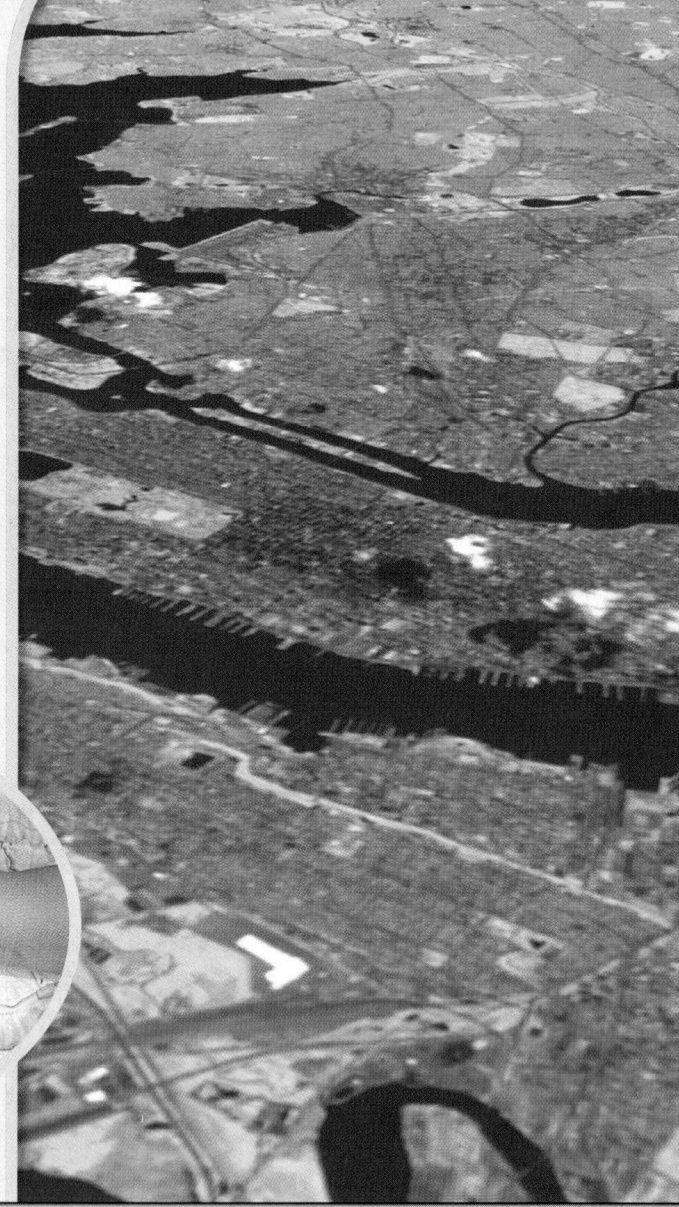

436

Theme Connection

Scale and Structure The structural differences among major landforms are examined. Students also focus on understanding the scale and structure of maps.

Pictures of Earth from space are acquired by instruments attached to satellites. Scientists use these images to make maps because they show features of Earth's surface, such as mountains and rivers. In the activity below, use a map or a globe to explore Earth's surface.

Describe landforms
Using a globe, atlas, or a world map, locate the following features and describe their positions on Earth relative to other major features. Provide any other details that would help someone else find them.

1. Andes mountains
2. Amazon, Ganges, and Mississippi Rivers
3. Indian Ocean, the Sea of Japan, and the Baltic Sea
4. Australia, South America, and North America

Observe
Choose one country on the globe or map and describe its major physical features in your Science Journal.

Purpose Students reinforce map skills by using a world map or globe to observe and record the relative positions of Earth's land-forms. L2 ELL IS **Visual-Spatial**

Preparation Be sure the maps and globes you use have the listed features clearly labeled.

Materials globe or world map for every three students

Teaching Strategy Have students practice describing landform locations before they begin the activity. For example, have them describe the location of the Rocky Mountains. north-south mountain range in western North America

Observe
Answers will vary depending on the country chosen.

✓Assessment

Performance Ask students to describe in writing how mountains and rivers are indicated on the globe or world map they used. Use **Performance Assessment in the Science Classroom,** p. 159.

Before You Read

FOLDABLES
Reading & Study Skills

Making a Main Ideas Study Fold Make the following Foldable to help you identify the major topics about landforms.

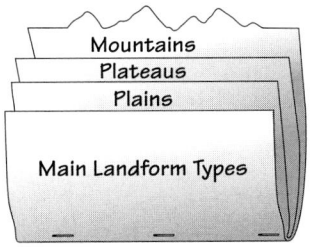
Mountains
Plateaus
Plains
Main Landform Types

1. Stack two sheets of paper in front of you so the short side of both sheets is at the top.
2. Slide the top sheet up so about 4 cm of the bottom sheet show.
3. Fold both sheets top to bottom to form four tabs and staple along the fold. Turn the Foldable so the staples are at the bottom. Cut mountain shapes on the top tab.
4. Label the tabs *Main Landform Types, Plains, Plateaus,* and *Mountains.* Before you read the chapter, write what you know about each landform under the tabs.
5. As you read the chapter, add to and correct what you have written.

437

FOLDABLES
Reading & Study Skills

Before You Read

Dinah Zike Study Fold
Purpose Determine what students know about the three main landform types before reading the chapter. Provide a Foldable for recording and organizing notes on plains, plateaus, and mountains as they read.

For additional help, see Foldables Worksheet, p. 15 in **Chapter Resources Booklet,** or go to the Glencoe Science Web site at **science.glencoe.com.** See After You Read in the Study Guide at the end of this chapter.

SECTION

1

Landforms

1 Motivate

Bellringer Transparency

Display the Section Focus Transparency for Section 1. Use the accompanying Transparency Activity Master. L2

ELL

Tie to Prior Knowledge

Have students brainstorm the names of prominent landforms in or near your community. List them on the board. Tell students they will learn about several types of landforms in this section.

SECTION

1 Landforms

As You Read

What You'll Learn

- **Discuss** differences between plains and plateaus.
- **Describe** folded, upwarped, fault-block, and volcanic mountains.

Vocabulary

plain
plateau
folded mountain
upwarped mountain
fault-block mountain
volcanic mountain

Why It's Important

Landforms influence how people can use land.

Figure 1
Three basic types of landforms are plains, plateaus, and mountains.

Plains

Earth offers abundant variety—from tropics to tundras, deserts to rain forests, and freshwater mountain streams to saltwater tidal marshes. Some of Earth's most stunning features are its landforms, which can provide beautiful vistas, such as vast, flat, fertile plains; deep gorges that cut through steep walls of rock; and towering, snowcapped peaks. **Figure 1** shows the three basic types of landforms—plains, plateaus, and mountains.

Even if you haven't ever visited mountains, you might have seen hundreds of pictures of them in your lifetime. Plains are more common than mountains, but they are more difficult to visualize. **Plains** are large, flat areas, often found in the interior regions of continents. The flat land of plains is ideal for agriculture. Plains often have thick, fertile soils and abundant, grassy meadows suitable for grazing animals. Plains also are home to a variety of wildlife, including foxes, ground squirrels, and snakes. When plains are found near the ocean, they're called coastal plains. Together, interior plains and coastal plains make up half of all the land in the United States.

Mountains

Plateau

Plain

Section ✔ Assessment Planner

PORTFOLIO
Cultural Diversity, p. 440
PERFORMANCE ASSESSMENT
Try at Home MiniLAB, p. 440
Skill Builder Activities, p. 443
See page 462 for more options.

CONTENT ASSESSMENT
Section, p. 443
Challenge, p. 443
Chapter, pp. 462–463

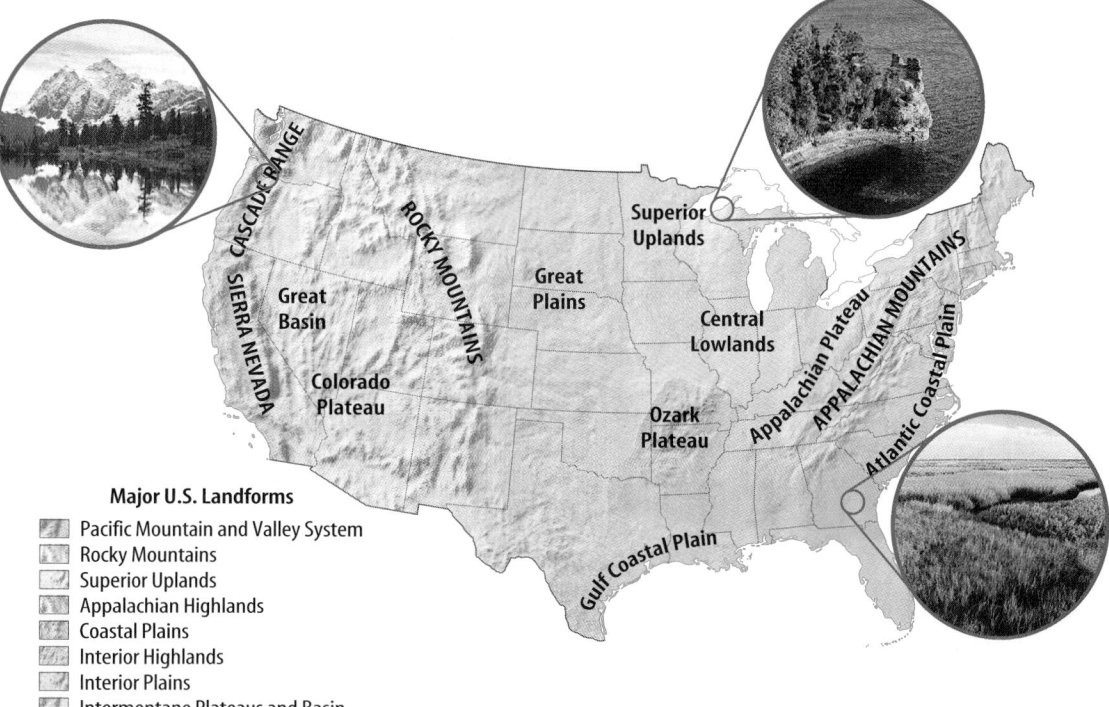

Major U.S. Landforms
- ▨ Pacific Mountain and Valley System
- ▨ Rocky Mountains
- ▨ Superior Uplands
- ▨ Appalachian Highlands
- ▨ Coastal Plains
- ▨ Interior Highlands
- ▨ Interior Plains
- ▨ Intermontane Plateaus and Basin

Coastal Plains A coastal plain often is called a lowland because it is lower in elevation, or distance above sea level, than the land around it. You can think of the coastal plains as being the exposed portion of a continental shelf. The continental shelf is the part of a continent that extends into the ocean. The Atlantic Coastal Plain is a good example of this type of landform. It stretches along the east coast of the United States from New Jersey to Florida. This area has low rolling hills, swamps, and marshes. A marsh is a grassy wetland that usually is flooded with water.

The Atlantic Coastal Plain, shown in **Figure 2,** began forming about 70 million years ago as sediment began accumulating on the ocean floor. Sea level eventually dropped, and the seafloor was exposed. As a result, the coastal plain was born. The size of the coastal plain varies over time. That's because sea level rises and falls. During the last ice age, the coastal plain was larger than it is now because so much of Earth's water was contained in glaciers.

The Gulf Coastal Plain includes the lowlands in the southern United States that surround the Gulf of Mexico. Much of this plain was formed from sediment deposited in deltas by the many rivers that enter the Gulf of Mexico.

✔ **Reading Check** *How are coastal plains formed?*

Figure 2
The United States has eight major landform regions, which include plains, mountains, and plateaus. **After looking at this map, describe the region that you live in.**

Curriculum Connection

Social Studies More than half the world's population lives on plains. Have students research possible explanations for this fact. Students should discover that plains are often fertile farmlands. L2
▨ **Logical-Mathematical**

Resource Manager

Chapter Resources Booklet
Transparency Activity, p. 42
Directed Reading for Content Mastery, pp. 17, 18
Note-taking Worksheets, pp. 31–32

---

② Teach

Plains

Activity
Display a relief map of North America. Have students compare and contrast the different landforms. L2 ▨ **Visual-Spatial**

IDENTIFYING Misconceptions
Students may think that because plains are flat, they are always found at much lower elevations than mountains. Explain that plains can be found at any elevation. For example, Denver, Colorado, is at the western edge of the Great Plains at an elevation of 1609 m. In comparison, the average elevation of the Appalachian Mountains is less than 2,000 m above sea level.

Extension
Encourage several students to interview a city or county engineer to find out why he or she needs to know about local landforms when planning new roads and other projects. Have students share this information with their classmates. L2 ▨ **Interpersonal**

✔ **Reading Check**

Answer Coastal plains form when sea level drops and the seafloor is exposed or from sediment deposited in deltas by rivers.

TRY AT HOME
Mini LAB

Purpose Students make a profile that shows the major landforms of the United States. L2

IS Visual-Spatial

Materials **Figure 2**, metric ruler, pencil, physical map of the United States.

Teaching Strategy If possible, project a transparency of **Figure 2**. With a clear transparency as an overlay, use a marking pen to show students how to make the profile.

Analysis

1. Profiles progress from mountains near the west coast, to a high elevation basin, and then to a wide set of steep mountains representing the Rockies. A wide plain should stretch from these mountains through much of the central area of the country. A range of lower mountains lies between the central plain and the coastal plain.

2. Many landforms run north-south in the United States, thus these profiles would not show as much change in elevation.

✔ Assessment

Performance Have students write a travelogue describing the landforms they would see along the route shown in their profiles. Use **PASC,** p. 159.

TRY AT HOME
Mini LAB

Profiling the United States

Procedure

1. Place the bottom edge of a piece of **paper** across the middle of **Figure 2,** extending from the west coast to the east coast.
2. Mark where different landforms are located along this edge.
3. Use a **map of the United States** and the **descriptions of the landforms in Section 1** to help you draw a profile, or side view, of the United States. Use steep, jagged lines to represent mountains. Low, flat lines can represent plains.

Analysis

1. Describe how your profile changed shape as you moved from west to east.
2. Describe how the shape of your profile would be different if you oriented your paper north to south.

Figure 3
Plains and plateaus are fairly flat, but plateaus have higher elevation. **A** This short-grass prairie in Kansas is part of an interior plain. **B** The Colorado River has carved the Grand Canyon into the Colorado Plateau.

Interior Plains The central portion of the United States is comprised largely of interior plains. Shown in **Figure 3,** you'll find them between the Rocky Mountains, the Appalachian Mountains, and the Gulf Coastal Plain. They include the Central Lowlands around the Missouri and Mississippi Rivers and the rolling hills of the Great Lakes area.

A large part of the interior plains is known as the Great Plains. This area lies between the Mississippi River and the Rocky Mountains. It is a flat, grassy, dry area with few trees. The Great Plains also are referred to as the high plains because of their elevation, which ranges from 350 m above sea level at the eastern border to 1,500 m in the west. The Great Plains consist of nearly horizontal layers of sedimentary rocks.

Plateaus

At somewhat higher elevations, you will find plateaus (pla TOHZ). **Plateaus** are flat, raised areas of land made up of nearly horizontal rocks that have been uplifted by forces within Earth. They are different from plains in that their edges rise steeply from the land around them. Because of this uplifting, it is common for plateaus, such as the Colorado Plateau, to be cut through by deep river valleys and canyons. The Colorado River, as shown in **Figure 3,** has cut deeply into the rock layers of the plateau, forming the Grand Canyon. Because the Colorado Plateau is located mostly in what is now a dry region, only a few rivers have developed on its surface. If you hiked around on this plateau, you would encounter a high, rugged environment.

Cultural Diversity

Landforms and Ancient Builders Among the mountains and canyons of northwestern New Mexico is Pueblo Bonito, a three-acre stone and mortar structure built by many generations of Anasazi Indian masons. The builders used the sandstone to fashion rectangular blocks for the walls of the structure. Mud and water mortar knits the blocks together. Pueblo Bonito contains more than 600 rooms. Like many Anasazi structures, it was abandoned about 900 years ago when a prolonged drought made living in this dry area difficult. Many of the structures are still partially standing. Have students use the Internet to research the ruins of Chaco Canyon, including Pueblo Bonito. Have them write short reports on what they find. L2 **IS** **Linguistic** P

Mountains

Mountains with snowcapped peaks often are shrouded in clouds and tower high above the surrounding land. If you climb them, the views are spectacular. The world's highest mountain peak is Mount Everest in the Himalaya—more than 8,800 m above sea level. By contrast, the highest mountain peaks in the United States reach just over 6,000 m. Mountains also vary in how they are formed. The four main types of mountains are folded, upwarped, fault-block, and volcanic.

✔ Reading Check *What is the highest mountain peak on Earth?*

Folded Mountains The Appalachian Mountains and the Rocky Mountains in Canada, shown in **Figure 4,** are comprised of folded rock layers. In **folded mountains,** the rock layers are folded like a rug that has been pushed up against a wall.

To form folded mountains, tremendous forces inside Earth squeeze horizontal rock layers, causing them to fold. The Appalachian Mountains formed between 480 million and 250 million years ago and are among the oldest and longest mountain ranges in North America. The Appalachians once were higher than the Rocky Mountains, but weathering and erosion have worn them down. They now are less than 2,000 m above sea level. The Ouachita (WAH shuh tah) Mountains of Arkansas are extensions of the same mountain range.

Research Visit the Glencoe Science Web site at **science.glencoe.com** to learn how landforms can affect economic development.

Figure 4
Folded mountains form when rock layers are squeezed from opposite sides. These mountains in Banff National Park, Canada, consist of folded rock layers.

Mountains

✔ Reading Check

Answer Mount Everest

Use Science Words

Word Usage Obtain photographs of the three basic kinds of landforms: plains, plateaus, and mountains. Have students write a sentence using each term. L2
IS Linguistic

Fun Fact

The Colorado Plateau has been rising approximately 0.3 cm every year for the last 10 million years. It is presently 2 km higher than the area that surrounds it.

Quick Demo

Demonstrate the formation of folded mountains by laying a sheet of paper on a flat surface. Have a student place a hand on one end. Have another student place a hand on the other end. Tell the students to slide the ends of the paper toward the center. Have the class note the high folded loop that forms. L1 ELL
COOP LEARN **IS Visual-Spatial**

Internet Addresses

_____
_____
_____

Explore the Glencoe Science Web site at **science.glencoe.com** to find out more about topics in this section.

Teacher FYI

The highest mountain peak in the United States is Mount McKinley, which rises 6,194 m in the Alaska Range. The mountain was named for President William McKinley. The Athabaskan Indians of the area called the peak Denali, which means "The Great One." The preserve surrounding the mountain now bears the Indian name, as Denali National Park.

Resource Manager

Chapter Resources Booklet
  MiniLAB, p. 3
  Enrichment, p. 28
Reading and Writing Skill Activities, p. 3

Mountains, continued

Make a Model

Have students use clay to make models of the different kinds of mountains discussed in this section. L1 ELL
LS Kinesthetic

Discussion

Tell students that the Ridge and Valley area of Pennsylvania is composed of parallel lines of rounded ridges with lowlands between them. **Is this area more likely to be composed of folded or fault-block mountains?** Folded mountains; resistant rock layers in the folds stand up as ridges; weak rock forms valleys. Some students may recognize that the mountains of Pennsylvania are part of the Appalachians, which are identified as folded mountains in the text.

Caption Answer

Figure 6 Fault-block mountains form as a result of movement along a fault. Upwarped mountains form because of broad uplift of rock.

Activity

Have students use a world map to locate major volcanic mountain chains. Have them write a statement in their Science Journals about where most of these mountains occur. L2
LS Visual-Spatial and Linguistic

Figure 5
The southern Rocky Mountains are upwarped mountains that formed when crust was pushed up by forces inside Earth.

Upwarped Mountains The Adirondack Mountains in New York, the southern Rocky Mountains in Colorado and New Mexico, and the Black Hills in South Dakota are upwarped mountains. **Figure 5** shows a mountain range in Colorado. Notice the high peaks and sharp ridges that are common to this type of mountain. **Upwarped mountains** form when blocks of Earth's crust are pushed up by forces inside Earth. Over time, the soil and sedimentary rocks at the top of Earth's crust erode, exposing the hard, crystalline rock underneath. As these rocks erode, they form the peaks and ridges.

Fault-Block Mountains **Fault-block mountains** are made of huge, tilted blocks of rock that are separated from surrounding rock by faults. These faults are large fractures in rock along which mostly vertical movement has occurred. The Grand Tetons of Wyoming, shown in **Figure 6,** and the Sierra Nevada in California, are examples of fault-block mountains. As **Figure 6** shows, when these mountains formed, one block was pushed up, while the adjacent block dropped down. This mountain-building process produces majestic peaks and steep slopes.

Figure 6
Fault-block mountains such as the Grand Tetons are formed when faults occur. Some rock blocks move up, and others move down. *How are fault-block mountains different from upwarped mountains?*

Resource Manager

Chapter Resources Booklet
   Reinforcement, p. 25
   Transparency Activity, pp. 45–46
Cultural Diversity, p. 33

Science Journal

Young Mountains Tell students that the Himalayas are still growing. Have students locate these mountains on a map and describe in their Science Journals why these mountains are still growing. Students should discover that the Himalayas are being pushed up as the Indian plate converges with the Asian plate. L2

Figure 7
Mount Shasta is a volcanic mountain made up of layers of lava flows and ash.

Volcanic Mountains **Volcanic mountains,** like the one shown in **Figure 7,** begin to form when molten material reaches the surface through a weak area of the crust. The deposited materials pile up, layer upon layer, until a cone-shaped structure forms. Two volcanic mountains in the United States are Mount St. Helens in Washington and Mount Shasta in California. The Hawaiian Islands are the peaks of huge volcanoes that sit on the ocean floor. Measured from the base, Mauna Loa in Hawaii would be higher than Mount Everest.

Plains, plateaus, and mountains offer different kinds of landforms to explore. They range from low, coastal plains and high, desert plateaus to mountain ranges thousands of meters high.

Section Assessment

1. Describe the eight major landform regions in the United States that are mentioned in this chapter.
2. How do plains and plateaus differ?
3. Why are some mountains folded and others upwarped?
4. How are volcanic mountains different from other mountains?
5. **Think Critically** If you wanted to know whether a particular mountain was formed by movement along a fault, what would you look for?

Skill Builder Activities

6. **Concept Mapping** Make an events-chain concept map to explain how upwarped mountains form. **For more help, refer to the** Science Skill Handbook.
7. **Using an Electronic Spreadsheet** Design a spreadsheet that compares the origin and features of the following: *folded, upwarped, fault-block,* and *volcanic mountains.* Then, explain an advantage of using a spreadsheet to compare different types of mountains. **For more help, refer to the** Technology Skill Handbook.

Mountains, continued

Visual Learning

Figure 7 **What visual clue tells you that Mount Shasta is a volcanic mountain?** Mount Shasta has a cone shape.

③ Assess

Reteach
Use wooden blocks or rectangular sponges cut at various angles to demonstrate the formation of fault-block mountains. L1 ELL IS **Visual-Spatial**

Challenge
Challenge partners to do research to compare and contrast the processes that formed the Appalachian Mountains with those that formed the Black Hills. Encourage students to use labeled diagrams to illustrate the processes. Students should find that lateral forces formed the Appalachians and vertical forces formed the Black Hills. L3 IS **Interpersonal**

✓ Assessment

Process Have students make a concept map that shows how volcanic mountains form. Use **PASC,** p. 161.

Answers to Section Assessment

1. Pacific Mountain and Valley System: system of ranges and valleys; Rocky Mountains: high mountain range; Superior Uplands: rugged highlands; Appalachian Highlands: old mountain range; Coastal plains: low-elevation, flat areas near the ocean; Interior highlands: mature hills;

Interior plains: expansive region of flat land; Intermontane plateaus and basins: mountains and valleys of the Great Basin
2. Plateau edges rise steeply from the land around them; the edges of plains do not.

3. folded: rock layers were squeezed; upwarped: forces within Earth caused upward arching of rock layers
4. Other mountains form when crust is squeezed or pushed upward. Volcanoes form when molten material is deposited on Earth's surface.

5. nearby faults and blocky-looking mountains
6. crust blocks pushed up → soil erodes → hard rocks exposed forming sharp peaks
7. Check students' work. Spreadsheets organize material in a way that makes comparisons easy to see.

SECTION

2 Viewpoints

Viewpoints

1 Motivate

Bellringer Transparency

Display the Section Focus Transparency for Section 2. Use the accompanying Transparency Activity Master. **L2**

ELL

Tie to Prior Knowledge

Have students recall the appearance of maps and globes, and the lines that form a grid on them. Explain that in this section, they will learn how these lines help pinpoint locations on Earth's surface.

IDENTIFYING Misconceptions

Some students may think that Earth is not a sphere, but flat. See page 436F for strategies that address this misconception.

As You Read

What You'll Learn
- **Define** latitude and longitude.
- **Explain** how latitude and longitude are used to identify locations on Earth.
- **Determine** the time and date in different time zones.

Vocabulary

equator   prime meridian
latitude   longitude

Why It's Important
Latitude and longitude allow you to locate places on Earth.

Figure 8
Latitude and longitude are measurements that are used to indicate locations on Earth's surface.

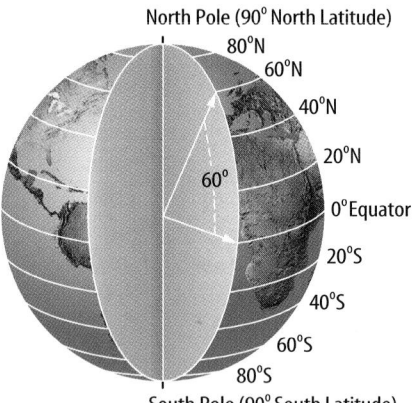

A Latitude is the measurement of the imaginary angle created by the equator, the center of Earth, and a location on Earth.

B Longitude is the measurement of the angle along the equator, between the prime meridian, the center of Earth, and a meridian on Earth.

444 CHAPTER 15 Views of Earth

Latitude and Longitude

During hurricane season, meteorologists track storms as they form in the Atlantic Ocean. To identify the exact location of a storm, latitude and longitude lines are used. These lines form an imaginary grid system that allows people to locate any place on Earth accurately.

Latitude Look at **Figure 8.** The **equator** is an imaginary line around Earth exactly halfway between the north and south poles. It separates Earth into two equal halves called the northern hemisphere and the southern hemisphere. Lines running parallel to the equator are called lines of **latitude,** or parallels. Latitude is the distance, measured in degrees, either north or south of the equator. Because they are parallel, lines of latitude do not intersect, or cross, one another.

The equator is at 0° latitude, and the poles are each at 90° latitude. Locations north and south of the equator are referred to by degrees north latitude and degrees south latitude, respectively. Each degree is further divided into segments called minutes and seconds. There are 60 minutes in one degree and 60 seconds in one minute.

Section ✔ Assessment Planner

PORTFOLIO
Challenge, p. 447

PERFORMANCE ASSESSMENT
MiniLAB, p. 445
Skill Builder Activities, p. 447
See page 462 for more options.

CONTENT ASSESSMENT
Section, p. 447
Challenge, p. 447
Chapter, pp. 462–463

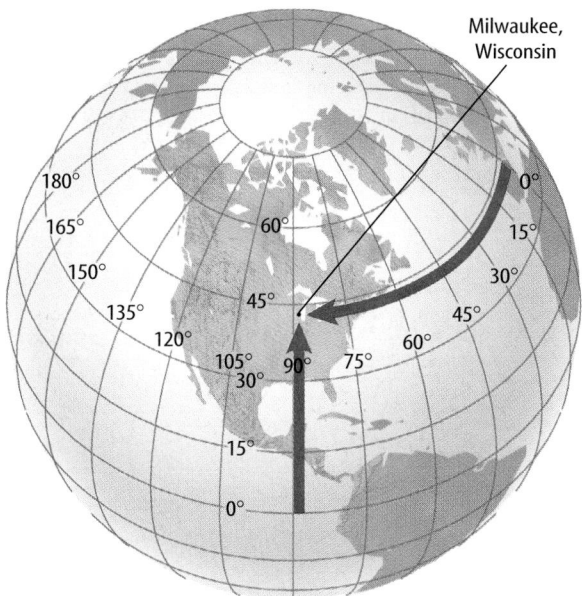

Milwaukee,
Wisconsin

Figure 9
The city of Milwaukee, Wisconsin is
located at about 43°N, 88°W. *How
is latitude different from longitude?*

Longitude The vertical lines, seen in **Figure 8B,** have two names—meridians and lines of longitude. Longitude lines are different from latitude lines in many important ways. Just as the equator is used as a reference point for lines of latitude, there's a reference point for lines of longitude—the **prime meridian.** This imaginary line represents 0° longitude. In 1884, astronomers decided the prime meridian should go through the Greenwich (GREN ihtch) Observatory near London, England. The prime meridian had to be agreed upon, because no natural point of reference exists.

Longitude refers to distances in degrees east or west of the prime meridian. Points west of the prime meridian have west longitude measured from 0° to 180°, and points east of the prime meridian have east longitude, measured similarly.

Prime Meridian The prime meridian does not circle Earth as the equator does. Rather, it runs from the north pole through Greenwich, England, to the south pole. The line of longitude on the opposite side of Earth from the prime meridian is the 180° meridian. East lines of longitude meet west lines of longitude at the 180° meridian. You can locate places accurately using latitude and longitude as shown in **Figure 9.** Note that latitude position always comes first when a location is given.

 **Reading Check** *What line of longitude is found opposite the prime meridian?*

SECTION 2 Viewpoints **445**

Caption Answer
Figure 9 Both are part of a grid system for locating places on Earth; latitude refers to distances north and south of the equator; longitude refers to distances east and west of the prime meridian.

Resource Manager

Chapter Resources Booklet
Transparency Activity, p. 43
Directed Reading for Content Mastery, p. 19
MiniLAB, p. 4

Time Zones

Visual Learning

Figure 10 What time is it where we live when it is 7:00 a.m. in Denver? Answers will vary depending on your location.

Caption Answer

Figure 10B 6:00 P.M.

Quick Demo

Demonstrate the concept of Earth time using a bright light to represent the Sun and a rotating globe. Point out that noon, midnight, 6 P.M., and 6 A.M. remain stationary with regard to the Sun, while positions on Earth's surface rotate toward or away from a specific time.

Discussion

Why do you think each time zone is about 15° of longitude wide? If students need a hint, remind them that Earth's circumference equals 360°. 360° divided by 24 hours is 15° per hour.

Life Science
INTEGRATION

Have students discuss what it felt like, how long it took to recover, and whether they took any special action to get over jet lag, such as drinking fruit juices, eating special foods, or taking vitamins.

✔ Reading Check

Answer Each day has 24 hours.

Figure 10
The United States has six time zones.

B But students in Seattle, Washington, which lies in the Pacific time zone, are eating dinner. *What time would it be in Seattle when the students in Washington, D.C., are sleeping at 9:00 P.M.?*

Life Science
INTEGRATION

If you travel east or west across three or more time zones, you could suffer from jet lag. Jet lag occurs when your internal time clock does not match the new time zone. Jet lag can disrupt the daily rhythms of sleeping and eating. Have you or any of your classmates ever suffered from jet lag?

A Washington, D.C., lies in the eastern time zone. Students there would be going to sleep at 9:00 P.M.

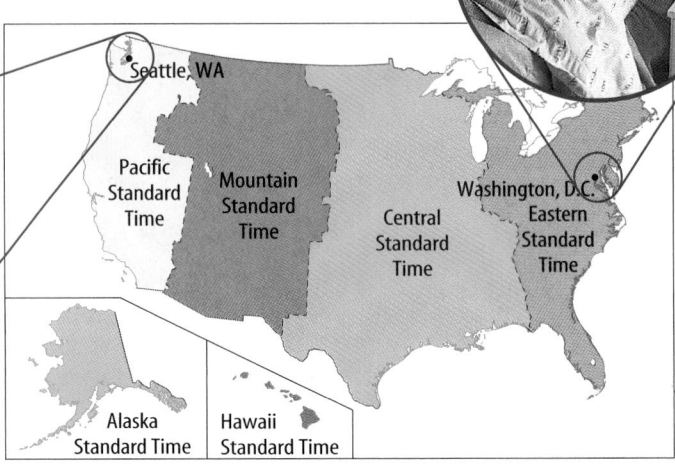

Time Zones

What time it is depends on where you are on Earth. Time is measured by tracking Earth's movement in relation to the Sun. Each day has 24 h, so Earth is divided into 24 time zones. Each time zone is about 15° of longitude wide and is 1 h different from the zones on each side of it. The United States has six different time zones. As you can see in **Figure 10,** people in different parts of the country don't experience dusk simultaneously. Because Earth rotates, the eastern states end a day while the western states are still in sunlight.

✔ Reading Check
What is the basis for dividing Earth into 24 time zones?

Time zones do not follow lines of longitude strictly. Time zone boundaries are adjusted in local areas. For example, if a city were split by a time zone boundary, the results would be confusing. In such a situation, the time zone boundary is moved outside of the city.

Calendar Dates

In each time zone, one day ends and the next day begins at midnight. If it is 11:59 P.M. Tuesday, then 2 min later it will be 12:01 A.M. Wednesday in that particular time zone.

Resource Manager

Chapter Resources Booklet
Lab Activity, pp. 9–11, 13–14
Enrichment, p. 29
Reinforcement, p. 26

Teacher FYI

In 1884, an international committee agreed upon our current system of 24 time zones, 15° apart, starting with the Prime Meridian through Greenwich, England. Daylight saving time was instituted during World War I to conserve fuel for the war effort by extending evening daylight hours.

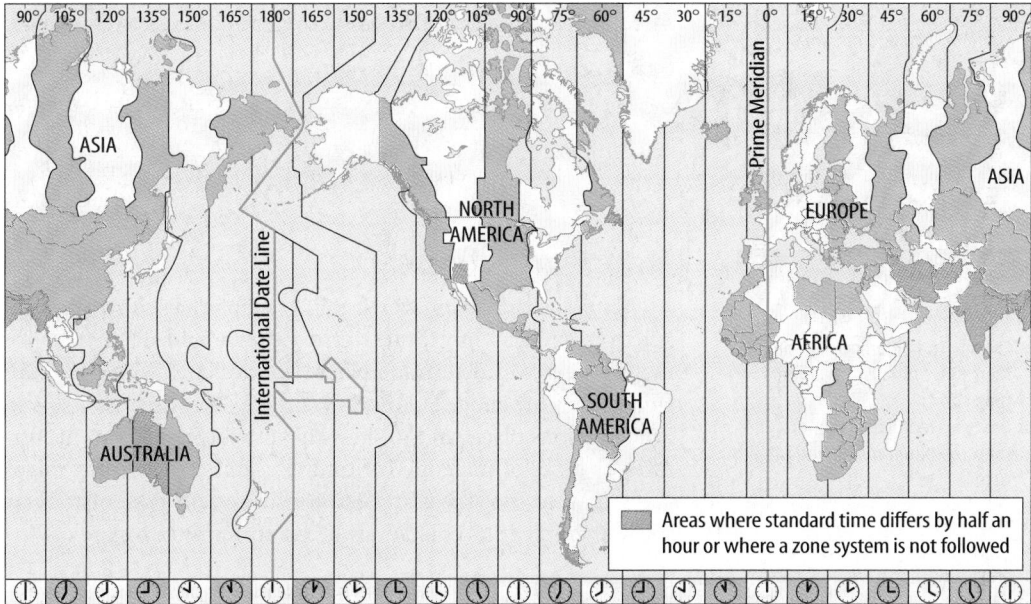

Areas where standard time differs by half an hour or where a zone system is not followed

International Date Line You gain or lose time when you enter a new time zone. If you travel far enough, you can gain or lose a whole day. The International Date Line, shown on **Figure 11,** is the transition line for calendar days. If you were traveling west across the International Date Line, located near the 180° meridian, you would move your calendar forward one day. If you were traveling east when you crossed it, you would move your calendar back one day.

Figure 11
Lines of longitude roughly determine the locations of time zone boundaries. These boundaries are adjusted locally to avoid splitting cities and other political subdivisions, such as counties, into different time zones.

Section 2 Assessment

1. What are latitude and longitude?

2. How do lines of latitude and longitude help people find locations on Earth?

3. What are the latitude and longitude of New Orleans, Louisiana?

4. If it were 7:00 P.M. in New York City, what time would it be in Los Angeles?

5. **Think Critically** How could you leave home on Monday to go sailing on the ocean, sail for 1 h on Sunday, and return home on Monday?

Skill Builder Activities

6. **Interpreting Scientific Illustrations** Use a world map to find the latitude and longitude of the following locations: Sri Lanka; Tokyo, Japan; and the Falkland Islands. **For more help, refer to the** Science Skill Handbook.

7. **Using Fractions** If you started at the prime meridian and traveled east one fourth of the way around Earth, what line of longitude would you reach? **For more help, refer to the** Math Skill Handbook.

SECTION 2 Viewpoints **447**

1 Motivate

Bellringer Transparency

Display the Section Focus Transparency for Section 3. Use the accompanying Transparency Activity Master. L2 ELL

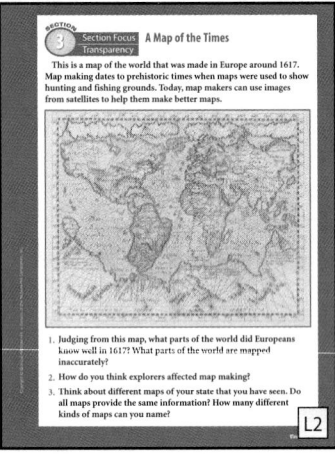

Tie to Prior Knowledge

Ask students if they've ever noticed that maps of the same place on Earth often look very different. To illustrate, show students two maps of the United States made with two different map projections. Have students observe how the maps differ.

Resource Manager

Chapter Resources Booklet
Transparency Activity, p. 44
Directed Reading for Content Mastery, pp. 19, 20

As You Read

What You'll Learn

■ **Explain** the differences among Mercator, Robinson, and conic projections.
■ **Describe** features of topographic maps, geologic maps, and satellite maps.

Vocabulary

conic projection   map scale
topographic map   map legend
contour line

Why It's Important

Maps help people navigate and understand Earth.

Figure 12
Lines of longitude are drawn parallel to one another in Mercator projections. *What happens near the poles in Mercator projections?*

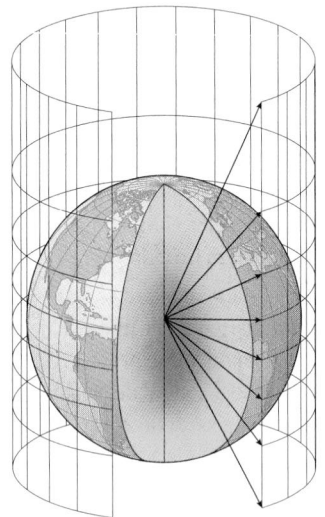

Map Projections

Maps—road maps, world maps, maps that show physical features such as mountains and valleys, and even treasure maps—help you determine where you are and where you are going. They are models of Earth's surface. Scientists use maps to locate various places and to show the distribution of various features or types of material. For example, an Earth scientist might use a map to plot the distribution of a certain type of rock or soil. Other scientists could draw ocean currents on a map.

✔ **Reading Check** *What are possible uses a scientist would have for maps?*

Many maps are made as projections. A map projection is made when points and lines on a globe's surface are transferred onto paper, as shown in **Figure 12.** Map projections can be made in several different ways, but all types of projections distort the shapes of landmasses or their areas. Antarctica, for instance, might look smaller or larger than it is as a result of the projection that is used for a particular map.

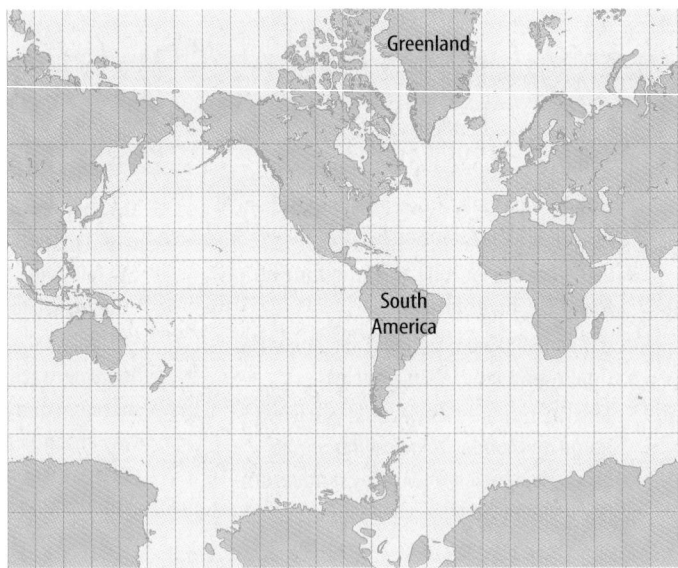

Section ✓ *Assessment* Planner

PORTFOLIO
Extension, p. 451
PERFORMANCE ASSESSMENT
Problem-Solving Activity, p. 453
Skill Builder Activities, p. 454
See page 462 for more options.

CONTENT ASSESSMENT
Section, p. 454
Challenge, p. 454
Chapter, pp. 462–463

Figure 13
Robinson projections show little distortion in continent shapes and sizes.

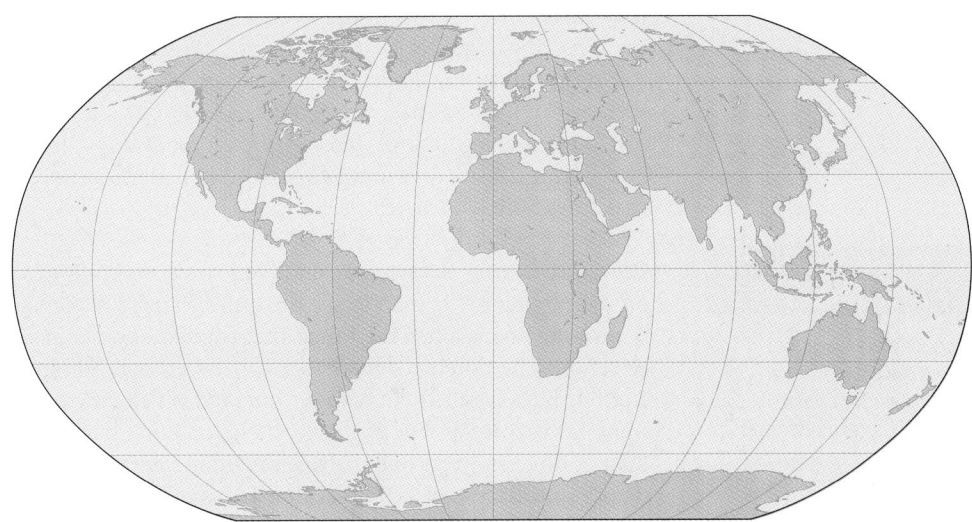

Mercator Projection
Mercator (mer KAY ter) projections are used mainly on ships. They project correct shapes of continents, but the areas are distorted. Lines of longitude are projected onto the map parallel to each other. As you learned earlier, only latitude lines are parallel. Longitude lines meet at the poles. When longitude lines are projected as parallel, areas near the poles appear bigger than they are. Greenland, in the Mercator projection in **Figure 12,** appears to be larger than South America, but Greenland is actually smaller.

Robinson Projection
A Robinson projection shows accurate continent shapes and more accurate land areas. As shown in **Figure 13,** lines of latitude remain parallel, and lines of longitude are curved as they are on a globe. This results in less distortion near the poles.

Conic Projection
When you look at a road map or a weather map, you are using a conic (KAH nihk) projection. Conic projections, like the one shown in **Figure 14,** often are used to produce maps of small areas. These maps are well suited for middle latitude regions but are not as useful for mapping polar or equatorial regions. **Conic projections** are made by projecting points and lines from a globe onto a cone.

✔ **Reading Check** *How are conic projections made?*

Figure 14
Small areas are mapped accurately using conic projections.

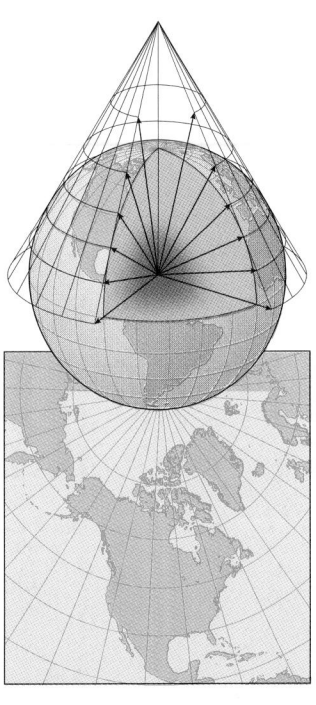

Map Projections

✔ **Reading Check**

Answer to locate various places and to show the distribution of various features or types of material

Caption Answer
Figure 12 Size is exaggerated.

Quick Demo
Illustrate a different map projection by drawing a rough world map on a grapefruit. Then slice the grapefruit into eight identical wedges. Remove the fruit and press the wedges down side by side on a flat surface as they were on the fruit. Have students observe the way this "projection" shows the world. Discuss the pros and cons of such a projection. Pros: It doesn't distort the size of land areas. Cons: The features are interrupted, making the map hard to use.
IS **Visual-Spatial**

✔ **Reading Check**

Answer by projecting points and lines from a globe onto a cone

---

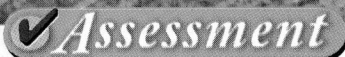

LAB DEMONSTRATION

Purpose to make a Mercator projection grid
Materials globe, large sheet of tracing paper, marking pen, meterstick
Procedure Form a paper cylinder around the globe as shown in **Figure 12.** Trace latitude lines by bending the paper so that it is touching the globe. Mark where longitude lines intersect the equator. Remove the paper from the globe and use a meterstick to draw the longitude lines perpendicular to the equator.
Expected Outcome A Mercator projection grid is created.

✔ *Assessment*

Where is the greatest distortion on the projection? near the poles **Which area has the least distortion?** areas near the equator

Topographic Maps

Text Question Answer

It avoids having contour lines too close together or too far apart. If a small interval were used for a mountainous area, the closely-spaced contours would be impossible to read. If a large contour interval were used for a flat area, the lines would be so widely spaced that it would be difficult to interpret elevation.

Activity

Obtain two topographic maps of your area, one up-to-date and the other as old as possible. Have students compare and contrast the two maps. Students may find that one map contains features such as buildings or roads not found on the other map. Have students use their observations of these maps to explain why maps should be regularly updated. L2

ELL  **Visual-Spatial**

Physics
INTEGRATION

The data collected by these probes provides scientists information on elevation at various points on the surface. Contour maps of the planets' surfaces can be made using these data.

Physics
INTEGRATION

Topographic maps of Venus and Mars have been made by space probes. The probes send a radar beam or laser pulses to the surface and measure how long it takes for the beam or pulses to return to the probe.

Topographic Maps

For nature hiking, a conic map projection can be helpful by directing you to the location where you will start your hike. On your hike, however, you would need a detailed map identifying the hills and valleys of that specific area. A **topographic map,** shown in **Figure 15,** models the changes in elevation of Earth's surface. With such a map, you can determine your location relative to identifiable natural features. Topographic maps also indicate cultural features such as roads, cities, dams, and other structures built by people.

Contour Lines Before your hike, you study the contour lines on your topographic map to see the trail's changes in elevation. A **contour line** is a line on a map that connects points of equal elevation. The difference in elevation between two side-by-side contour lines is called the contour interval, which remains constant for each map. For example, if the contour interval on a map is 10 m and you walk between two lines anywhere on that map, you will have walked up or down 10 m.

In mountainous areas, the contour lines are close together. This situation models a steep slope. However, if the change in elevation is slight, the contour lines will be far apart. Often large contour intervals are used for mountainous terrain, and small contour intervals are used for fairly flat areas. Why? **Table 1** gives additional tips for examining contour lines.

Index Contours Some contour lines, called index contours, are marked with their elevation. If the contour interval is 5 m, you can determine the elevation of other lines around the index contour by adding or subtracting 5 m from the elevation shown on the index contour.

Table 1 Contour Rules

1. **Contour lines close around hills and basins.** To decide whether you're looking at a hill or basin, you can read the elevation numbers or look for hachures (ha SHOORZ). These are short lines drawn at right angles to the contour line. They show depressions by pointing toward lower elevations.

2. **Contour lines never cross.** If they did, it would mean that the spot where they cross would have two different elevations.

3. **Contour lines form Vs that point upstream when they cross streams.** This is because streams flow in depressions that are beneath the elevation of the surrounding land surface. When the contour lines cross the depression, they appear as Vs pointing upstream on the map.

Inclusion Strategies

Gifted Have students interview a cartographer, and then write a report detailing the steps involved in the map-making process, from obtaining raw data to making the actual map. Encourage students to illustrate each step. L3

Interpersonal

✔ Active Reading

Buddy Interviews This strategy helps students understand and clarify the reading. Have students interview one another to find out what helps them understand what they are reading, how they find answers, and how they assimilate new vocabulary terms. Have students use Buddy Interviews to help them master the concept of topographic maps.

Figure 15

Planning a hike? A topographic map will show you changes in elevation. With such a map, you can see at a glance how steep a mountain trail is, as well as its location relative to rivers, lakes, roads, and cities nearby. The steps in creating a topographic map are shown here.

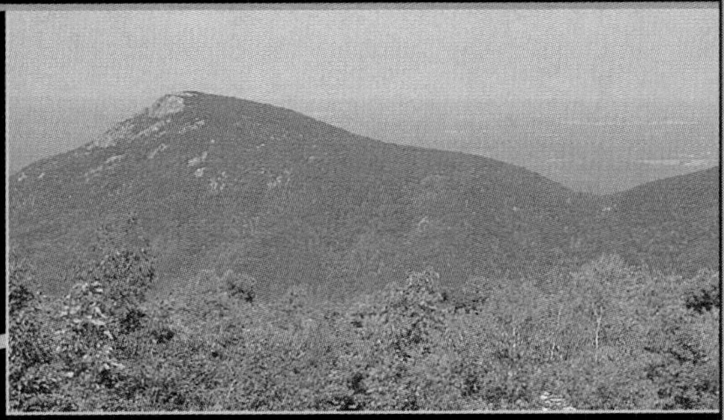

A To create a topographic map of Old Rag Mountain in Shenandoah National Park, Virginia, mapmakers first measure the elevation of the mountain at various points.

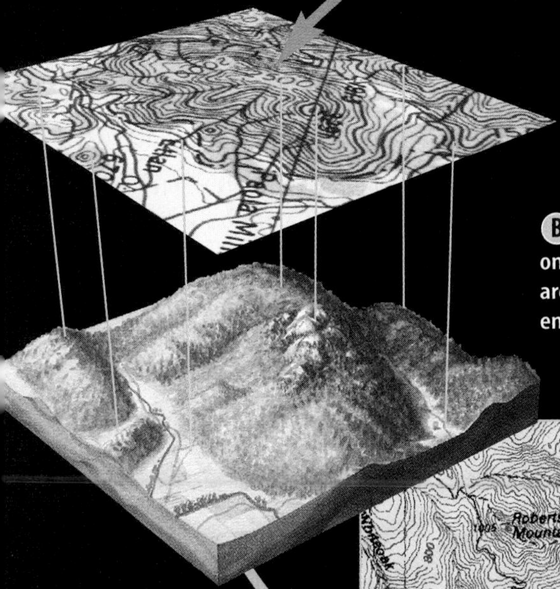

B These points are then projected onto paper. Points at the same elevation are connected, forming contour lines that encircle the mountain.

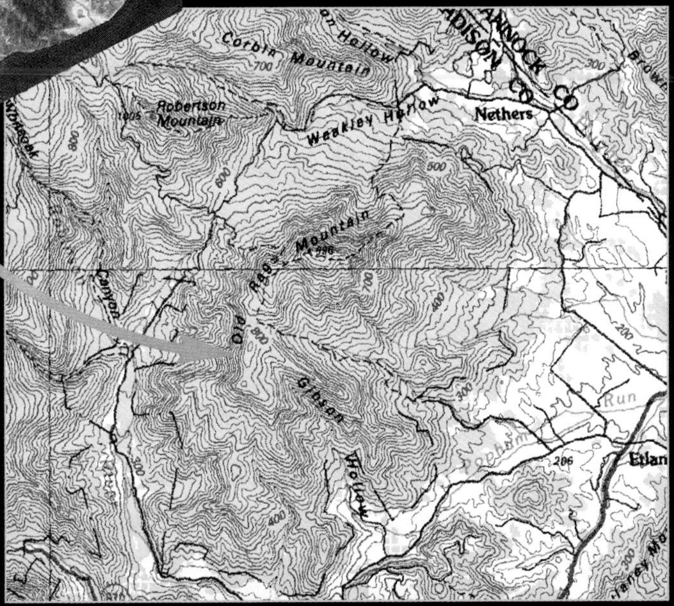

C Where contour lines on a topographic map are close together, elevation is changing rapidly—and the trail is very steep!

Visualizing Topographic Maps

Have students examine the pictures and read the captions. Then ask the following questions.

Besides hiking, what are some other reasons people would use a topographic map? Possible answers: For planning highways, bridges, and tunnels

How would a topographic map help someone planning to build a house? These maps could be used to show the differences in elevation, the steepness of slopes, the location of streams, and the proximity to roads.

Activity

Take students to an area near school where they can observe a prominent landscape feature. Take along a topographic map and have students explain how the feature compares to its representation on the map.

Extension

Have students prepare brief written reports on the sport of orienteering. L2 LS **Linguistic** P

Resource Manager

Earth Science Critical Thinking/Problem Solving, p. 5

Cultural Diversity, p. 27

Reading and Writing Skill Activities, p. 21

Topographic Maps, continued

Discussion

What is the contour interval of a map if two side-by-side contour lines represent elevations of 200 m and 300 m? 100 m Suppose a student draws a map using the scale 1 cm: 100 miles. **Is this a proper scale? Explain.** No; units of measurement on each side of the ratio must be the same.

Geologic Maps

Extension

Tell students to find a geologic map of the area in which you live. Have them write a paragraph that describes the geology of the area as portrayed by the map. L2 ELL COOP LEARN
 Visual-Spatial

Text Question Answer

Drill into rock or soil to get core samples or other evidence.

Figure 16
Geologists use block diagrams to understand Earth's subsurface. The different colors represent different rock layers.

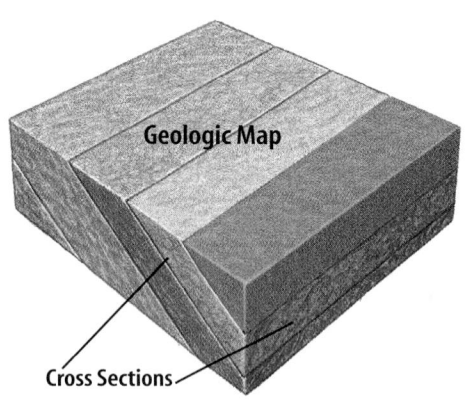

Geologic Map

Cross Sections

Map Scale When planning your hike, you'll want to determine the distance to your destination before you leave. Because maps are small models of Earth's surface, distances and sizes of things shown on a map are proportional to the real thing on Earth. Therefore, real distances can be found by using a scale.

The **map scale** is the relationship between the distances on the map and distances on Earth's surface. Scale often is represented as a ratio. For example, a topographic map of the Grand Canyon might have a scale that reads 1:80,000. This means that one unit on the map represents 80,000 units on land. If the unit you wanted to use was a centimeter, then 1 cm on the map would equal 80,000 cm on land. The unit of distance could be feet or millimeters or any other measure of distance. However, the units of measure on each side of the ratio must always be the same. A map scale also can be shown in the form of a small bar that is divided into sections and scaled down to match real distances on Earth.

Map Legend Topographic maps and most other maps have a legend. A **map legend** explains what the symbols used on the map mean. Some frequently used symbols for topographic maps are shown in the appendix at the back of the book.

Map Series Topographic maps are made to cover different amounts of Earth's surface. A map series includes maps that have the same dimensions of latitude and longitude. For example, one map series includes maps that are 7.5 minutes of latitude by 7.5 minutes of longitude. Other map series include maps covering larger areas of Earth's surface.

Geologic Maps

One of the more important tools to Earth scientists is the geologic map. Geologic maps show the arrangement and types of rocks at Earth's surface. Using geologic maps and data collected from rock exposures, a geologist can infer how rock layers might look below Earth's surface. The block diagram in **Figure 16** is a 3-D model that illustrates a solid section of Earth. The top surface of the block is the geologic map. Side views of the block are called cross sections, which are derived from the surface map. Developing geologic maps and cross sections is extremely important for the exploration and extraction of natural resources. What can a scientist do to determine whether a cross section accurately represents the underground features?

Inclusion Strategies

Learning Disabled Draw a contour map with five concentric contours, each 2 cm apart. Draw a straight reference line from the center of the map to any point along the outermost contour. Give students a copy of the map. Have them cut along the outermost contour line, then trace the circular pattern on a piece of cardboard. Have them place an X where the reference line meets the cardboard. Direct students to cut out the cardboard along the traced line. Have them repeat this process with each of the other four contours, moving inward. Be sure students place an X where the reference line meets the cardboard for each cut. When all the contours have been cut out, have students paste the cardboard cutouts together, one on top of the other, lining up the X's. The stair-step result is a model of a hill. **Kinesthetic**

Three-Dimensional Maps Topographic maps and geologic maps are two-dimensional models that are used to study features of Earth's surface. To visualize Earth three dimensionally, scientists often rely on computers. Using computers, information is digitized to create a three-dimensional view of features such as rock layers or river systems. Digitizing is a process by which points are plotted on a coordinate grid.

Map Uses As you have learned, Earth can be viewed in many different ways. Maps are chosen depending upon the situation. If you wanted to determine New Zealand's location relative to Canada and you didn't have a globe, you probably would examine a Mercator projection. In your search, you would use lines of latitude and longitude, and a map scale. If you wanted to travel across the country, you would rely on a road map, or conic projection. You also would use a map legend to help locate features along the way. To climb the highest peak in your region, you would take along a topographic map.

Problem-Solving Activity

How can you create a cross section from a geologic map?

Earth scientists are interested in knowing the types of rocks and their configurations underground. To help them visualize this, they use geologic maps. Geologic maps offer a two-dimensional view of the three-dimensional situation found under Earth's surface. You don't have to be a professional geologist to understand a geologic map. Use your ability to create graphs to interpret this geologic map.

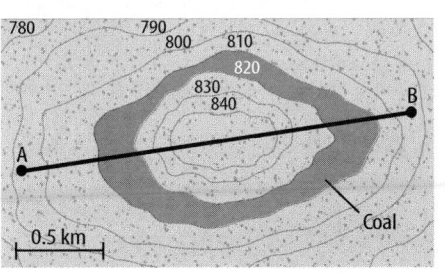

Identifying the Problem

Above is a simple geologic map showing where a coal seam is found on Earth's surface. Place a straight edge of paper along the line marked A–B and mark the points where it meets a contour. Make a different color mark where it meets the exposure of coal. Make a graph on which the various elevations (in meters) are marked on the *y*-axis. Lay your marked edge of paper along the *x*-axis and transfer the points directly above onto the proper elevation line. Now connect the dots to draw in the land's surface and connect the marks you made for the coal seam separately.

Solving the Problem

1. What type of topography does the map represent?
2. At what elevation is the coal seam?
3. Does this seam tilt, or is it horizontal? Explain how you know.

Geologic Maps,
continued

Use Science Words

Word Origin Have students use dictionaries to find the meaning and origin of the word *cartography*. Students will discover that cartography is the science of making maps. The word has two roots: *carte* comes from the French word meaning "card" or "map"; *-ography* comes from the Latin *-graphia*, meaning "writing." Ask students the technical name for a mapmaker. cartographer

Problem-Solving Activity

National Math Standards

Correlation to Mathematics Objectives

2, 6, 8–10

Answers

1. a hill
2. 810 to 820 m
3. Horizontal; the lines representing the top and bottom of the coal seam are horizontal.

Teacher FYI

Two common types of maps are thematic maps and inventory maps. A thematic map shows the distribution of a particular feature over a certain area, for example, the difference in population density or amount of rainfall over a state or country. An inventory map shows the location of a certain type of item over an area, for example, the location of nuclear power plants in a state.

Resource Manager

Chapter Resources Booklet
  Enrichment, p. 30
  Reinforcement, p. 27
Cultural Diversity, p. 49

3 Assess

Reteach

Have pairs of students prepare one type of map that gives the reader information about your community. The map can be a topographic map of a neighborhood, a road map, an inventory map showing the location of schools, or some other type. Have students present their maps to the class and explain how they were made. L2 COOP LEARN
IS Interpersonal

Challenge

Challenge students to find out how Landsat images can be obtained. (These images can be obtained on the Internet.) Have students obtain imagery for your area, and write a short paragraph that explains how the images are interpreted. Discuss in class what the image shows.
IS Visual-Spatial

✓Assessment

Process Have students prepare charts that compare and contrast topographic and geologic maps. Use **Performance Assessment in the Science Classroom,** p. 109.

Figure 17
Sensors on *Landsat 7* detect light reflected off landforms on Earth.

Remote Sensing

Scientists use remote-sensing techniques to collect much of the data used for making maps. Remote sensing is a way of collecting information about Earth from a distance, often using satellites.

Landsat One way that Earth's surface has been studied is with data collected from Landsat satellites, as shown in **Figure 17.** These satellites take pictures of Earth's surface using different wavelengths of light. The images can be used to make maps of snow cover over the United States or to evaluate the impact of forest fires, such as those that occurred in the western United States during the summer of 2000. The newest Landsat satellite is *Landsat 7,* which was launched in April of 1999. It can acquire the most detailed Landsat images yet.

Global Positioning System The Global Positioning System, or GPS, is a satellite-based, radio-navigation system that allows users to determine their exact position anywhere on Earth. Twenty-four satellites orbit 20,200 km above the planet. Each satellite sends a position signal and a time signal. The satellites are arranged in their orbits so that signals from at least six can be picked up at any given moment by someone using a GPS receiver. By processing the signals, the receiver calculates the user's exact location. GPS technology is used to navigate, to create detailed maps, and to track wildlife.

Section 3 Assessment

1. How do Mercator, Robinson, and conic projections differ?
2. Why does Greenland appear to be larger on a Mercator projection than it does on a Robinson projection?
3. Why can't contour lines ever cross?
4. What is a geologic map?
5. **Think Critically** Would a map that covers a large area have the same map scale as a map that covers a small region? How would the scales differ?

Skill Builder Activities

6. **Making Models** Architects make detailed maps called scale drawings to help them plan their work. Make a scale drawing of your classroom. **For more help, refer to the** Science Skill Handbook.
7. **Communicating** Draw a map in your Science Journal that your friends could use to get from school to your home. Include a map legend and a map scale. **For more help, refer to the** Science Skill Handbook.

Answers to Section Assessment

1. Areas of distortion differ, so they are best for different purposes. Mercator has great distortion in polar areas. Robinson has less distortion at the poles. Conic projections are accurate for relatively small areas of Earth's surface.

2. Lines of longitude are parallel on a Mercator, stretching any landmasses in polar areas. There is less distortion in polar areas on a Robinson projection, so Greenland isn't as stretched out.

3. One location cannot have two different elevations.
4. a map that shows the arrangement of rocks at Earth's surface
5. No; the ratio for the scale would be much smaller on a map that shows a larger area.

6. Encourage students to start by making a grid system for the class and determining a scale, such as 1:100.
7. Maps should show a route with streets and symbols for landmarks.

Activity

Making a Topographic Map

Have you ever wondered how topographic maps are made? Today, radar and remote-sensing devices aboard satellites collect data, and computers and graphic systems make the maps. In the past, surveyors and aerial photographers collected data. Then, maps were hand drawn by cartographers, or mapmakers. In this activity, you can practice cartography.

Materials

plastic model of a landform
water tinted with food coloring
transparency
clear, plastic storage box with lid
beaker
metric ruler
tape
transparency marker

What You'll Investigate

How is a topographic map made?

Goals

■ **Draw** a topographic map.
■ **Compare and contrast** contour intervals.

Procedure

1. Using the ruler and the transparency marker, make marks up the side of the storage box that are 2 cm apart.
2. Secure the transparency to the outside of the box lid with tape.
3. Place the plastic model in the box. The bottom of the box will be zero elevation.
4. Using the beaker, pour water into the box to a height of 2 cm. Place the lid on the box.
5. Use the transparency marker to trace the top of the water line on the transparency.

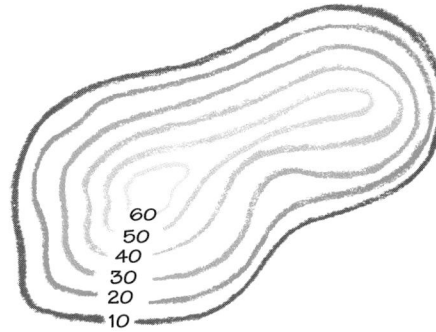

6. Using the scale 2 cm = 10 m, mark the elevation on the line.
7. Remove the lid and add water until a depth of 4 cm is reached.
8. Map this level on the storage box lid and record the elevation.
9. Repeat the process of adding 2 cm of water and tracing until the landform is mapped.
10. Transfer the tracing of the landform onto a sheet of white paper.

Conclude and Apply

1. What is the contour interval of this topographic map?
2. How does the distance between contour lines on the map show the steepness of the slope on the landform model?
3. **Determine** the total elevation of the landform you have selected.
4. How was elevation represented on your map?
5. How are elevations shown on topographic maps?
6. Must all topographic maps have a contour line that represents 0 m of elevation? Explain.

ACTIVITY 455

Communicating
Your Data

Have students compare the topographic maps produced by other groups with their own.

Purpose Students make a topographic map from a landform model. **L2** **ELL** **COOP LEARN** **LS** **Kinesthetic**

Process Skills measuring in SI, making models, interpreting data, comparing and contrasting

Time Required 45–50 minutes

Teaching Strategy Suggest that students stand directly over the model with one eye closed to make each tracing, so that each will be done from the same position.

Troubleshooting Some students may need extra help in understanding the scale to be used.

Answers to Questions

1. 10 m
2. The closer the contour lines, the steeper the slope.
3. Answers will vary, but they should equal the height of the model in centimeters multiplied by 500. (2 cm = 10 m; therefore 1 cm = 5 m or 500 cm)
4. lines drawn on the transparency
5. contour lines
6. No, the 0-m contour line is only on maps with elevations at sea level.

✔Assessment

Performance To further assess students' understanding of making topographic maps from landform models, have them repeat the activity using a second landform model. Have them compare and contrast their two completed topographic maps. Use **Performance Assessment in the Science Classroom,** p. 123.

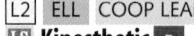

Recognize the Problem

Purpose

Students will show the relationship between topographic maps and landforms by making a 3-D model from a topographic map.

L2 ELL COOP LEARN

Kinesthetic P

Process Skills

interpreting scientific illustrations, making models, using numbers, observing and inferring

Time Required

45 minutes

Thinking Critically

Discussion

Ask students to discuss how they would walk across a sloping field while keeping their eyes level. Students will walk on a line of equal elevation, similar to a contour line on a topographic map. Mention to students that steep slopes are shown on a topographic map as areas where contour lines are very close.

Possible Materials

Obtain 7.5 minute quadrangle maps from the U.S. Geological Survey and the book, *100 Topographic Maps*, by Richard Debruin, available from Hubbard. Obtain sandbox sand from a local hardware store. Ask maintenance for rolls of brown paper towels and empty spray bottles.

Activity *Model and Invent*

Constructing Landforms

Most maps perform well in helping you get from place to place. A road map, for example, will allow you to choose the shortest route from one place to another. If you are hiking, though, distance might not be so important. You might want to choose a route that avoids steep terrain. In this case you need a map that shows the highs and lows of Earth's surface, called relief. Topographic maps use contour lines to show the landscape in three dimensions. Among their many uses, such maps allow hikers to choose routes that maximize the scenery and minimize the physical exertion.

Recognize the Problem

What does a landscape depicted on a two-dimensional topographic map look like in three dimensions?

Thinking Critically

How can you model a landscape?

Goals

- **Research** how contour lines show relief on a topographic map.
- **Determine** what scale you can best use to model a landscape of your choice.

- Working cooperatively with your classmates, model a landscape in three dimensions from the information given on a topographic map.

Possible Materials

U.S. Geological Survey 7.5 minute quadrangle maps
sandbox sand
rolls of brown paper towels
spray bottle filled with water
ruler

Data Source

SCIENCE *Online* Go to the Glencoe Science Web site at **science.glencoe.com** for more information about topographic maps.

Inclusion Strategies

Physically Challenged Place your physically challenged students with other students who will help them make their models. Provide a large flat board on which lab groups can work on their models. This will enable them to move the project from place to place, making it easier for physically challenged students to participate.

SCIENCE *Online*
Internet Addresses

_____

_____

_____

Explore the Glencoe Science Web site at **science.glencoe.com** to find out more about topics in this section.

Planning the Model

1. **Choose** a topographic map showing a landscape easily modeled using sand. Check to see what contour interval is used on the map. Use the index contours to find the difference between the lowest and the highest elevations shown on the landscape. Check the distance scale to determine how much area the landscape covers.

2. **Determine** the scale you will use to convert the elevations shown on your map to heights on your model. Make sure the scale is proportional to the distances on your map.

3. **Plan** a model of the landscape in sand by sketching the main features and their scaled heights onto paper. Note the degree of steepness found on all sides of the features.

Check the Model Plans

1. **Prepare** a document that shows the scale you plan to use for your model and the calculations you used to derive that scale. Remember to use the same scale for distance as you use for height. If your landscape is fairly flat, you can exaggerate the vertical scale by a factor of two or three. Be sure your paper is neat, is easy to follow, and includes all units. Present the document to your teacher for approval.

2. **Research** how the U.S. Geological Survey creates topographic maps and find out how it decides upon a contour interval for each map. This information can be obtained from the Glencoe Science Web site.

Making the Model

1. Using the sand, spray bottle, and ruler, create a scale model of your landscape on the brown paper towels.

2. **Check** your topographic map to be sure your model includes the landscape features at their proper heights and proper degrees of steepness.

Analyzing and Applying Results

1. Did your model accurately represent the landscape depicted on your topographic map? Discuss the strengths and weaknesses of your model.

2. Why was it important to use the same scale for height and distance? If you exaggerated the height, why was it important to indicate the exaggeration on your model?

3. Why did the mapmakers choose the contour interval used on your topographic map?

4. **Predict** the contour intervals mapmakers might choose for topographic maps of the world's tallest mountains—the Himalaya—and for topographic maps of Kansas, which is fairly flat.

ACTIVITY 457

Planning the Model

Teaching Strategies

- Have students use a topographic map that has a feature on which at least four contour lines have been drawn.

- Some students will need help in making their sand models of the topographic map. They should begin with the highest and lowest elevations and shape the sand in between to the proper contours.

Making the Model

Expected Outcome

The model will look like a hill, a slope, or a valley as presented on the topographic map. The model should show a gradual increase in elevation from one contour line to the next.

Analyzing and Applying Results

1. Students should note that their models approximate the shape of landforms on their maps. One strength is the fact that the sand models actual land features. One weakness is that it is difficult to keep the sand from shifting.

2. If the same scale is not used, the shape of the landform will be distorted. Indicating how the model was exaggerated will help explain distortions in the model.

3. The contour interval is based on how great the change in elevation is on the map.

4. 100 meters; 5 meters

✓Assessment

Performance To further assess students' understanding of making a 3-D landform model from a topographic map, have them make a model using the topographic map they made in the activity. Have them compare their completed model with the plastic model used in that activity. Use **Performance Assessment in the Science Classroom**, p. 123.

Communicating
Your Data

Students can prepare an oral report that is given to the class. In their reports, students should explain how their models are similar to the actual landforms and the method used to make the model. Students should also explain any exaggerations used in the making of the model.

TIME
SCIENCE AND HISTORY
SCIENCE CAN CHANGE THE COURSE OF HISTORY!

Content Background

Cultural geography is the study of the relationship between people and their environment. A major focus of cultural geographers is how culture and the surrounding environment fit together.

The environment includes landforms, climate, and natural resources such as water, soil, and vegetation. Culture is a way of life developed by a population for getting along with each other and their environment. It consists of beliefs, philosophies, knowledge, arts, science, technologies, and economies.

When studying the interactions between these people and their environment, geographers try to answer certain questions. How did the people living in an area get there? What aspects of the environment enticed people to settle in the area? How has the environment influenced the people's livelihood? How have the people influenced their environment? If culture or the environment changes, will the people be able to keep up with the changes?

The general consensus among geographers is that the environment does not solely determine culture nor does culture control the environment. Rather they interact and influence each other, thus shaping the lives of the people living in an area.

LOCATION,

New York Harbor in 1849   Rich Midwest farmland   Georgia peaches

Why is New York City at the mouth of the Hudson River and not 300 km inland? Why are there more farms in Iowa than in Alaska? What's the reason for growing lots of peaches in Georgia but not in California's Death Valley? It's all about location. The landforms, climate, soil, and resources in an area determine where cities and farms grow and what people connected with them do.

Landforms Are Key

When many American cities were founded hundreds of years ago, waterways were the best means of transportation. Old cities such as New York City and Boston are located on deep harbors where ships could land with people and goods. Rivers also were major highways centuries ago. They still are. A city such as New Orleans, located at the mouth of the Mississippi River, receives goods from the entire river valley.

It then ships the goods from its port to places far away.

Topography and soil also play a role in where activities such as farming take root. States such as Iowa and Illinois have many farms because they have lots of flat land and fertile soil. Growing crops is more difficult in mountainous areas or where soil is stony and poor.

Climate and Soil

Climate limits the locations of cities and farms, as well. The fertile soil and warm, moist climate of Georgia make it a perfect place to grow peaches. California's Death Valley can't support such crops because it's a hot desert. Deserts are too dry to grow much of anything without irrigation. Deserts also don't have large population centers unless water is brought in from far away. Los Angeles and Las Vegas are both desert cities that are huge only because they pipe in water from hundreds of miles away.

458

Resources for Teachers and Students

Cultural Geography: A Critical Introduction, by Don Mitchell. Blackwell Publishers, Malden, MA, 2000.

People, Land and Time, by Peter Atkins, Ian Simmons, and Brian Roberts. John Wiley & Sons, New York, 1998.

Explorations in the Understanding of Landscape: A Cultural Geography, by William Norton. Greenwood Press, New York, 1989.

Resources Rule

The location of an important natural resource can change the rules. A gold deposit or an oil field can cause a town to grow in a place where the topography, soil, and climate are not favorable. For example, thousands of people now live in parts of Alaska only because of the great supply of oil there. People settled in rugged areas of the Rocky Mountains to mine gold and silver. Maine has a harsh climate and poor soil. But people settled along its coast because they could catch lobsters and fish in the nearby North Atlantic.

LOCATION

Alaska pipeline

Maine fishing and lobster industry

The rules that govern where towns grow and where people live are a bit different now than they used to be. Often information, not goods, moves from place to place on computers that can be anywhere. But as long as people farm, use minerals, and transport goods from place to place, the natural environment and natural resources will always help determine where people are and what they do.

Cities, farms, and industries grow in logical places

CONNECTIONS Research Why was your community built where it is? Research its history. What types of economic activity were important when it was founded? Did topography, climate, or resources determine its location? Are they important today? Report to the class.

SCIENCE Online
For more information, visit
science.glencoe.com

SCIENCE Online
Internet Addresses _____
_____
_____
_____

Explore the Glencoe Science Web site at **science.glencoe.com** to find out more about topics in this feature.

Discussion

Facilitate a brainstorming session in which students list the factors that might affect where people settle. Have students discuss how each factor might affect the establishment and success of a community. Possible answers might include landforms, climate, soil conditions, and resources of various types. Landforms such as mountains might make transportation and settlement difficult, but might provide needed resources such as minerals and water. Desert settlements have to address the need for water and good soil. Settling near waterways presents numerous advantages including rich soil for agriculture, transportation, and commerce.

Historical Significance

Throughout history civilizations have established themselves in areas that supported their daily needs. Early hunters and gatherers gave way to village life, as agriculture became the main source of food. Trade routes opened villages to resources that were unavailable locally. In general, populations flourished in areas of mild climate where the terrain was level and the soil was fertile. Additionally, settlements were established where other natural resources, fresh water, and minerals also were abundant.

These conditions were found along waterways and coastal areas. Over time, populations began expanding into the interior regions. These inland areas tend to be drier and lacking in natural resources. As a result, new challenges had to be met in order for populations to succeed.

Reviewing Main Ideas

Preview

Students can answer the questions in their Science Journals. Discuss the answers as you go through the chapter. **IS Linguistic**

Review

Students can write their answers, then compare them with those of other students. **IS Interpersonal**

Reteach

Students can look at the illustrations and describe details that support the main ideas of the chapter. **IS Visual-Spatial**

Answers to Chapter Review

SECTION 1

2. mountains

SECTION 2

4. six (Eastern, Central, Mountain, Pacific, Alaska, Hawaii-Aleutian)

SECTION 3

2. a topographic map

Reviewing Main Ideas

Section 1 Landforms

1. The three main types of landforms are plains, plateaus, and mountains.

2. Plains are large, flat areas. Plateaus are relatively flat, raised areas of land made up of nearly horizontal rocks that have been uplifted. Mountains rise high above the surrounding land. *Which type of landform is shown in the photograph below?*

Section 2 Viewpoints

1. Latitude and longitude form an imaginary grid system that enables points on Earth to be located exactly.

2. Latitude is the distance in degrees north or south of the equator. Longitude is the distance in degrees east or west of the prime meridian.

3. Reference lines have been established for measuring latitude and longitude. Latitude is measured from Earth's equator, an imaginary line halfway between Earth's poles. Longitude is measured from the prime meridian. The prime meridian runs from pole to pole through Greenwich, England.

4. Earth is divided into 24 time zones. Each time zone represents a 1-h difference. The International Date Line separates different calendar days. *How many time zones are in the United States?*

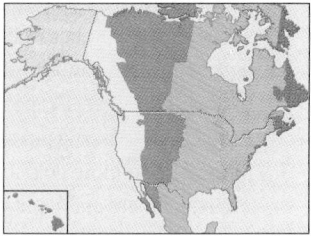

Section 3 Maps

1. Mercator, Robinson, and conic projections are made by transferring points and lines on a globe's surface onto paper.

2. Topographic maps show the elevation of Earth's surface. Geologic maps show the types of rocks that make up Earth's surface. *What type of map is shown here?*

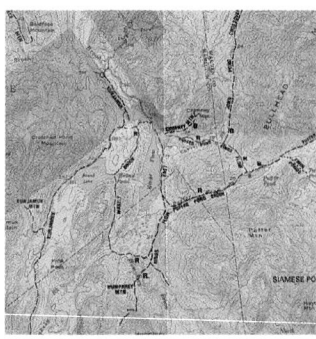

3. Remote sensing is a way of collecting information about Earth from a distance. Satellites are important remote-sensing devices.

FOLDABLES
Reading & Study Skills

After You Read

To help you review the three main landform types, use the Foldable you made at the beginning of this chapter.

FOLDABLES
Reading & Study Skills

After You Read

After students have read the chapter and completed the Foldable described in Before You Read, have them do the activity on the student page.

Dinah Zike

Visualizing Main Ideas

Complete the following concept map on landforms.

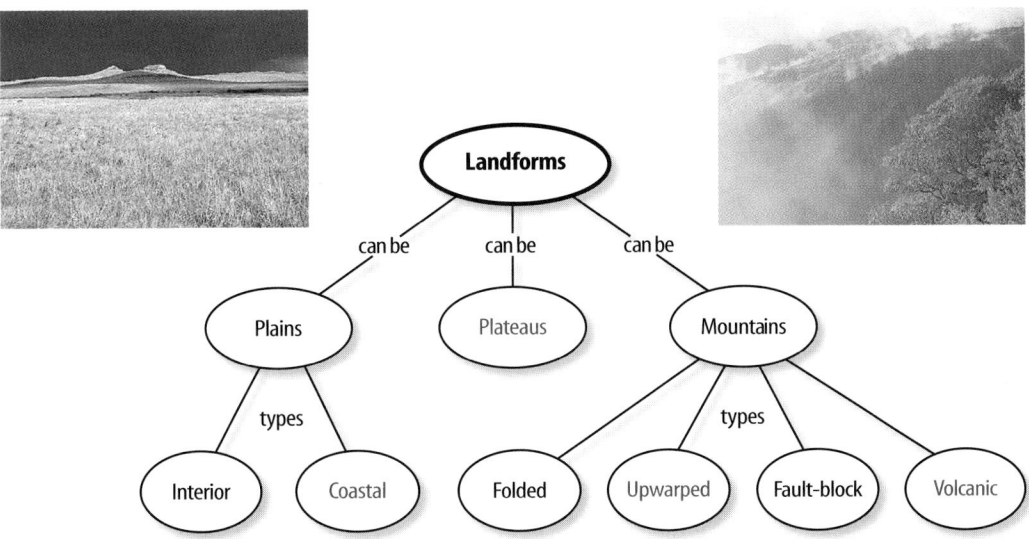

```
                    Landforms
            can be    can be    can be
        Plains      Plateaus      Mountains
        types                     types
   Interior  Coastal    Folded  Upwarped  Fault-block  Volcanic
```

Vocabulary Review

Vocabulary Words

a. conic projection
b. contour line
c. equator
d. fault-block mountain
e. folded mountain
f. latitude
g. longitude
h. map legend

i. map scale
j. plain
k. plateau
l. prime meridian
m. topographic map
n. upwarped mountain
o. volcanic mountain

THE PRINCETON REVIEW   Study Tip

Make a plan! Before you start your homework, write a checklist of what you need to do for each subject. As you finish each item, check it off.

Using Vocabulary

For each set of terms below, choose the one term that does not belong and explain why it does not belong.

1. upwarped mountain, equator, volcanic mountain

2. plain, plateau, prime meridian

3. topographic map, contour line, volcanic mountain

4. prime meridian, equator, folded mountain

5. fault-block mountain, upwarped mountain, plateau

6. prime meridian, map scale, contour line

CHAPTER STUDY GUIDE   461

Visualizing Main Ideas

See student page.

Vocabulary Review

Using Vocabulary

1. The equator is not a type of mountain.
2. The prime meridian is not a landform.
3. A volcanic mountain is not part of a topographic map.
4. A folded mountain is not a reference point on a map grid.
5. A plateau is not a type of mountain.
6. The prime meridian would not be found on most topographic maps.

IDENTIFYING Misconceptions

Assess

Use the assessment as follow-up to page 436F after students have completed the chapter.

Activity Organize the class into small groups. Challenge each group to devise a skit that they can perform for the class. The skit should illustrate what might happen if Earth were flat. For example, they might act out a ship sailing off the edge of the world or Earth's shadow on the Moon as having a straight edge. After each group acts out its skit, have the class explain what actually happens on Earth, since it is a sphere.

Expected Outcome Students should understand by this point that Earth is a sphere, not flat.

Checking Concepts

1. B
2. D
3. B
4. A
5. C
6. D
7. B
8. B
9. C
10. B

Thinking Critically

11. The map of the Atlantic Coastal Plain would show little change in elevation, and the contour interval would be small. The map of the Rockies would show many closed contours indicating mountain peaks, and the contour interval would be large.
12. Tuesday
13. 160°
14. Anchorage, San Francisco, Denver, Houston, Bangor
15. The map with a scale of 1:50,000 would show less detail than the map with a scale of 1:24,000.

Checking Concepts

Choose the word or phrase that best answers the question.

1. What makes up about 50 percent of all land areas in the United States?
   A) plateaus
   C) mountains
   B) plains
   D) volcanoes

2. Where is the north pole located?
   A) 0°N
   C) 50°N
   B) 180°N
   D) 90°N

3. What kind of mountains are the Hawaiian Islands?
   A) fault-block
   C) upwarped
   B) volcanic
   D) folded

4. What are lines that are parallel to the equator called?
   A) lines of latitude
   C) lines of longitude
   B) prime meridians
   D) contour lines

5. How many degrees apart are the 24 time zones?
   A) 10
   C) 15
   B) 34
   D) 25

6. Which type of map is most distorted at the poles?
   A) conic
   C) Robinson
   B) topographic
   D) Mercator

7. Which type of map shows changes in elevation at Earth's surface?
   A) conic
   C) Robinson
   B) topographic
   D) Mercator

8. What is measured with respect to sea level?
   A) contour interval
   C) conic projection
   B) elevation
   D) sonar

9. What kind of map shows rock types making up Earth's surface?
   A) topographic
   C) geologic
   B) Robinson
   D) Mercator

10. Which major U.S. landform includes the Grand Canyon?
    A) Great Plains
    B) Colorado Plateau
    C) Gulf Coastal Plain
    D) Appalachian Mountains

Thinking Critically

11. How would a topographic map of the Atlantic Coastal Plain differ from a topographic map of the Rocky Mountains?

12. If you left Korea early Wednesday morning and flew to Hawaii, on what day of the week would you arrive?

13. If you were flying directly south from the north pole and reached 70° north latitude, how many more degrees of latitude would you pass over before reaching the south pole?

14. Using the map below, arrange these cities in order from the city with the earliest time to the one with the latest time on a given day: Anchorage, Alaska; San Francisco, California; Bangor, Maine; Denver, Colorado; Houston, Texas.

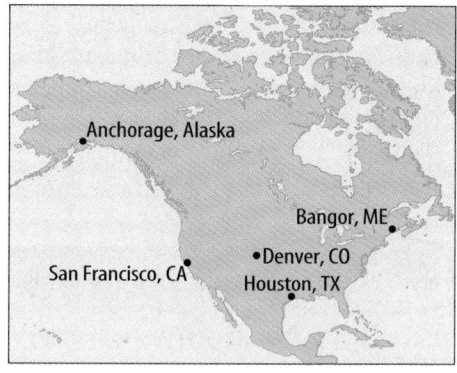

15. How is a map with a scale of 1:50,000 different from a map with a scale of 1:24,000?

Chapter ✓Assessment Planner

Portfolio Encourage students to place in their portfolios one or two items of what they consider to be their best work. Examples include:
- Cultural Diversity, p. 440
- Challenge, p. 447
- Extension, p. 451

Performance Additional performance assessments, Performance Task Assessment Lists, and rubrics for evaluating these activities can be found in Glencoe's **Performance Assessment in the Science Classroom.**

Developing Skills

16. Comparing and Contrasting Compare and contrast Mercator, Robinson, and conic map projections.

17. Forming Hypotheses You are visiting a mountain in the northwest part of the United States. The mountain has steep sides and is not part of a mountain range. A crater can be seen at the top of the mountain. Hypothesize about what type of mountain you are visiting.

18. Concept Mapping Complete the following concept map about parts of a topographic map.

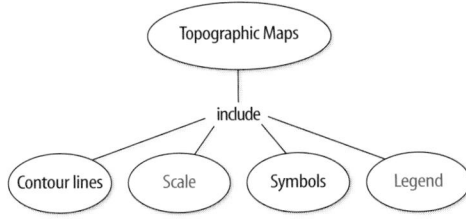

Performance Assessment

19. Poem Create a poem about the different types of landforms. Include characteristics of each landform in your poem. Display your poem with those of your classmates.

20. Poster Create a poster showing how satellites can be used for remote sensing.

TECHNOLOGY

Go to the Glencoe Science Web site at **science.glencoe.com** or use the **Glencoe Science CD-ROM** for additional chapter assessment.

THE PRINCETON REVIEW — Test Practice

Alicia was looking at a map of the United States because her science teacher suggested that she learn about the land-form regions in the United States.

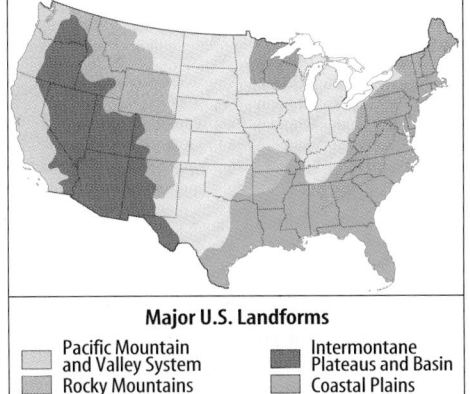

Major U.S. Landforms

- Pacific Mountain and Valley System
- Rocky Mountains
- Superior Uplands
- Appalachian Highlands
- Intermontane Plateaus and Basin
- Coastal Plains
- Interior Highlands
- Interior Plains

Study the diagram and answer the following questions.

1. Which technological development would have had the greatest impact on the accuracy of Alicia's map?
 A) radio communications
 B) measurement with lasers
 C) computer-assisted design
 D) satellite imaging

2. Which of the following landform regions would contain high, rugged mountains?
 F) Coastal Plains
 G) Interior Plains
 H) Appalachian Highlands
 J) Rocky Mountains

THE PRINCETON REVIEW — Test Practice

The Test-Taking Tip was written by The Princeton Review, the nation's leader in test preparation.
1. D
2. J

Developing Skills

16. Each depicts a round Earth on a flat surface. Mercator projections exaggerate the areas near the poles and are used mainly for navigation. Robinson projections are good for depicting accurate continent shapes and have less distortion near the poles. Conic projections are good for mapping small areas and are used for road maps.
17. volcanic mountain
18. See student page.

Performance Assessment

19. Poems may be simple as long they describe different types of landforms. Encourage students to be creative. Use **PASC**, p. 151.
20. Posters should correctly show how satellites can be used for remote sensing. Use **PASC**, p. 145.

✓ Assessment Resources

📁 Reproducible Masters

Chapter Resources Booklet
 Chapter Review, pp. 35–36
 Chapter Tests, pp. 37–40
 Assessment Transparency Activity, p. 47

Glencoe Science Web site
 Interactive Tutor
 Chapter Quizzes

Glencoe Technology

- Assessment Transparency
- Interactive CD-ROM Chapter Quizzes
- ExamView Pro Test Bank
- Vocabulary PuzzleMaker Software
- MindJogger Videoquiz

Section/Objectives	Standards		Activities/Features
Chapter Opener	**National**	**State/Local**	**Explore Activity:** Model water erosion, p. 465 **Before You Read,** p. 465
	See p. 7T for a Key to Standards.		
Section 1 Weathering and Soil Formation 🕐 3 sessions 📦 1.5 blocks 1. **Identify** processes that break rock apart. 2. **Describe** processes that chemically change rock. 3. **Explain** how soil evolves.	National Content Standards: UCP3, A1, B1, D1, F2		**MiniLAB:** Rock Dissolving Acids, p. 469 **MiniLAB:** Analyzing Soils, p. 470 **Activity:** Classifying Soils, p. 472
Section 2 Erosion of Earth's Surface 🕐 4 sessions 📦 2 blocks 1. **Identify** agents of erosion. 2. **Describe** the effects of erosion.	National Content Standards: UCP3, A1, B1, D1, F2, G1, G3		**Visualizing Mass Movements,** p. 474 **Physics Integration,** p. 475 **Science Online,** p. 476 **Problem-Solving Activity:** Can evidence of sheet erosion be seen in a farm field?, p. 479 **Science Online,** p. 480 **Activity:** Measuring Soil Erosion, p. 482 **Science and History:** Crumbling Monuments, p. 484

Teacher's Corner

PRODUCTS AVAILABLE FROM GLENCOE
To order call 1-800-334-7344:
CD-ROM
NGS PictureShow: Dynamic Earth
NGS PictureShow: Geology
Curriculum Kit
GeoKit: Dynamic Earth

Transparency Sets
NGS PicturePack: Dynamic Earth
NGS PicturePack: Geology
PRODUCTS AVAILABLE FROM NATIONAL GEOGRAPHIC SOCIETY
To order call 1-800-368-2728:

Video
Our Dynamic Earth

INDEX TO NATIONAL GEOGRAPHIC SOCIETY
The following article may be used for research relating to this chapter: "Acid Rain: How Great a Menace?" Anne La Bastille, November 1981.

Activity Materials	Reproducible Resources	Section Assessment	Technology
Explore Activity: bread pan, sand, plastic washtub, brick or wood block, access to a faucet, clock	**Chapter Resources Booklet** Foldables Worksheet, p. 17 Directed Reading Overview, p. 19 Note-taking Worksheets, pp. 31–32	GLENCOE'S **ASSESSMENT** ADVANTAGE	
MiniLAB: dropper, vinegar, pieces of chalk and limestone, hand lens, 5 percent hydrochloric acid **MiniLAB:** soil sample, sheet of newspaper **Activity:** soil sample, stereomicroscope	**Chapter Resources Booklet** Transparency Activity, p. 42 Activity Worksheet, pp. 5–6 Enrichment, p. 29 Reinforcement, p. 27 Directed Reading, p. 20 Lab Activity, pp. 9–12 MiniLAB, pp. 3, 4 Transparency Activity, pp. 45–46 **Cultural Diversity,** p. 33 **Science Inquiry Labs,** p. 35	Performance MiniLAB, p. 469 MiniLAB, p. 470 Skill Builder Activities, p. 471 Content Section Assessment, p. 471	🔦 Section Focus Transparency 🔦 Teaching Transparency 💿 Interactive CD-ROM 🎧 Guided Reading Audio Program
Activity: blocks of wood, 2 paint trays, soil, grass sod, water, 2 pails, 1,000-mL beaker, triple-beam balance, calculator, watch *Need materials?* Contact Science Kit at 1-800-828-7777 or www.sciencekit.com on the Internet.	**Chapter Resources Booklet** Transparency Activity, p. 43 Activity Worksheet, pp. 7–8 Enrichment, p. 30 Reinforcement, p. 28 Directed Reading, pp. 21, 22 Lab Activity, pp. 13–16 **Lab Management and Safety,** p. 58 **Mathematics Skill Activities,** p. 9 **Reading and Writing Skill Activities,** p. 27 **Home and Community Involvement,** p. 37	Portfolio Activity, p. 474 Science Journal, p. 476 Performance Problem-Solving Activity, p. 479 Skill Builder Activities, p. 481 Content Section Assessment, p. 481	🔦 Section Focus Transparency 💿 Interactive CD-ROM 🎧 Guided Reading Audio Program

End of Chapter Assessment

GLENCOE'S **ASSESSMENT** ADVANTAGE

Blackline Masters	Technology	Professional Series
Chapter Resources Booklet Chapter Review, pp. 35–36 Chapter Tests, pp. 37–40 **Standardized Test Practice by The Princeton Review,** pp. 67–70	📼 MindJogger Videoquiz 💿 Interactive CD-ROM 💿 Vocabulary PuzzleMakers 💿 ExamView Pro Test Bank 💿 Interactive Lesson Planner 💿 Interactive Teacher Edition	Performance Assessment in the Science Classroom (PASC)

Transparencies

Section Focus

This is a representation of key blackline masters available in the Teacher Classroom Resources. See Resource Manager boxes within the chapter for additional information.

Assessment

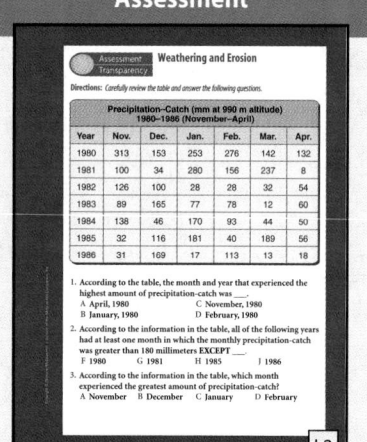

Teaching

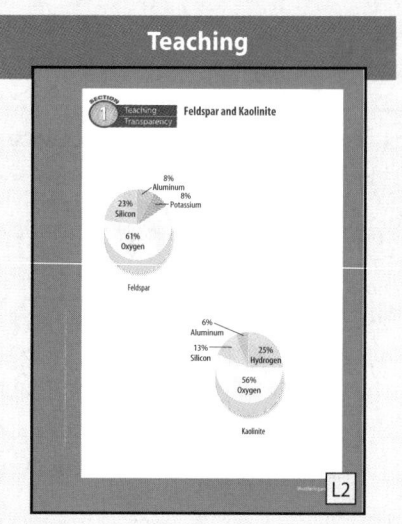

Key to Teaching Strategies

The following designations will help you decide which activities are appropriate for your students.

L1 Level 1 activities should be appropriate for students with learning difficulties.

L2 Level 2 activities should be within the ability range of all students.

L3 Level 3 activities are designed for above-average students.

ELL ELL activities should be within the ability range of English Language Learners.

COOP LEARN Cooperative Learning activities are designed for small group work.

LS Multiple Learning Styles logos, as described on page 22T, are used throughout to indicate strategies that address different learning styles.

P These strategies represent student products that can be placed into a best-work portfolio.

Hands-on Activities

Activity Worksheets

Laboratory Activities

Meeting Different Ability Levels

Content Outline

Note-taking Worksheet — **Weathering and Erosion**

Section 1   Weathering and Soil Formation

A. Natural process that causes rocks to break down is called _____.

B. _____—breaks rocks into smaller pieces without changing them chemically

  1. _____ is the freezing and thawing cycle that breaks rocks apart.
  2. Plant _____ and burrowing _____ exert pressure on rocks.

C. When the chemical composition of rock changes, _____ has occurred.

  1. _____, from water and carbon dioxide, reacts chemically with many rocks.
  2. _____, formed from a plant's release of tannin, dissolves some rock minerals.
  3. Oxygen can cause rocks containing iron to rust in the process of _____.

D. _____—mixture of weathered rock, organic matter, water, and air that supports the growth of plant life

  1. The _____ affects what kind of soil develops.
  2. _____ influences soil development.
  3. The _____ in tropical regions increases the rate of weathering forming soil more quickly than in deserts.
  4. Rocks take _____, perhaps thousands of years, to weather into soil.
  5. _____ affect soil development.

L2

Reinforcement

Reinforcement — **Weathering and Soil Formation**

Directions: *Answer the following questions on the lines provided.*

1. What is weathering?

2. What is the principal difference between mechanical weathering and chemical weathering?

Directions: *Complete the following sentences using the correct terms.*

3. Two causes of mechanical weathering are ice wedging and _____.
4. Chemical weathering takes place fastest in a _____ and _____ climate.
5. _____ takes place when the composition of the rock changes.
6. When minerals in rocks combine with _____ in the air, chemical weathering takes place.
7. _____ is a mixture of weathered rock, organic matter, water, and air.
8. The lack of thick soils on steep hills is an example of how _____ influences soil development.

Directions: *Circle the term in parentheses that correctly completes the sentence.*

9. Ice wedging occurs because a given amount of ice has a volume (greater than, less than, the same as) an equal amount of water.
10. A growing plant can cause (mechanical, chemical, both mechanical and chemical) weathering.
11. (Carbon dioxide, Oxygen, Nitrogen) in air reacts with water to dissolve rocks such as marble and limestone.
12. Deep soils develop quickly where rock weathers (slowly, rapidly, either slowly or quickly).
13. In a tropical climate, (sandy soil, clayey soil, humus) develops.
14. Many plants produce (carbonic acid, tannic acid, rust), which causes weathering in rocks.

L2

Directed Reading

Directed Reading for Content Mastery — *Overview* **Weathering and Erosion**

Directions: *Use the terms in the list below to complete the concept maps.*

gravity   water   rock slides   mudflows
creep   mechanical   ice

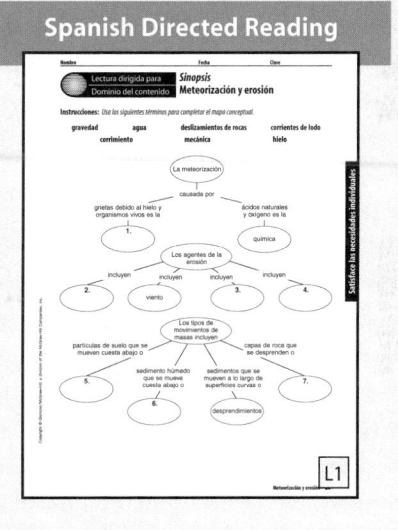

L1

Assessment

Chapter Tests

Chapter Test — **Weathering and Erosion**

I. Testing Concepts

Directions: *On the lines provided, write a complete sentence using each term.*

1. weathering
2. mechanical weathering
3. chemical weathering
4. soil
5. erosion
6. mass movement
7. deflation
8. abrasion
9. runoff
10. glacier
11. streams
12. slump
13. creep

L2

Enrichment

Enrichment — **Rain Forest Soils**

Tropical rain forests are very hot and steamy places. The average annual temperature is about 25°C. Rainfall is usually between 150 cm and 350 cm per year, with the greatest rainfalls reaching 900 cm per year or more. Many different living things flourish in these warm, moist conditions, but there is a difficult side to these conditions, too. While the plentiful rain and warm temperatures nurture a wide variety of plants and animals, they also make it particularly difficult for tropical rain forests to recover from deforestation.

The problem is that plants and animals cannot use all the water that falls as rain, and the Sun cannot evaporate the excess water. Therefore, excess water runs off the soil, taking nutrients and organic material with it. As a result, the layer of soil that contains nutrients is very thin.

Effects of Rapid Decomposition

Leaves falling from trees are one of the many factors that influence soil nutrients. In tropical rain forests, different trees shed their leaves at different times. This means there is only a thin layer of leaf litter on the ground at any time. Decomposers, such as bacteria and fungi, thrive in hot, wet conditions. The result is that leaf litter and other sources of nutrients break down quickly. Decomposers often can break down dead animals and plants within 24 hours.

Other plants take up the nutrients almost as soon as they are released. Rain forest trees have shallow root systems that allow them to absorb nutrients from the forest floor. They do this so rapidly that nutrients don't have time to be stored in the soil. Therefore, unlike soil in temperate forests, the humus layer of rain forest soil is very thin.

Effects of Deforestation

As long as trees and plants growing in forest soil can quickly absorb the nutrients, many living things can thrive in these conditions. When rain forests are cleared for farming or cattle grazing, however, the soil can support crops or grasses for only a few years. By then, most of the remaining nutrients have been removed. The land is then abandoned. The soil is bare and exposed to the effects of rain, heat, and wind. Erosion quickly washes away the top soil and any remaining nutrients, leaving behind a subsurface layer called laterite. This soil is colored red by aluminum and iron oxides. Exposed to the hot Sun, this layer can become as hard as concrete. It is nearly impossible for rain forests to regrow under these conditions.

Meanwhile loggers, farmers, and cattle ranchers move to new areas of rain forest and destruction begins again. In some areas, about 2,000 trees per minute are cut down in the rain forests. Scientists estimate that an area of tropical rain forest about the size of the state of Wisconsin is being destroyed every year.

1. Why would it be difficult to replant trees in an area of tropical rainforest that has been cleared? What do you think would have to be done before this could be attempted?

2. How would the soil in a tropical rainforest be different from the soil in a tropical forest that has a wet season and a dry season?

L3

Spanish Directed Reading

Lectura dirigida para Dominio del contenido — *Sinopsis* **Meteorización y erosión**

Instrucciones: *Usa los siguientes términos para completar el mapa conceptual.*

gravedad   agua   deslizamientos de rocas   corrientes de lodo
corrimiento   mecánica   hielo

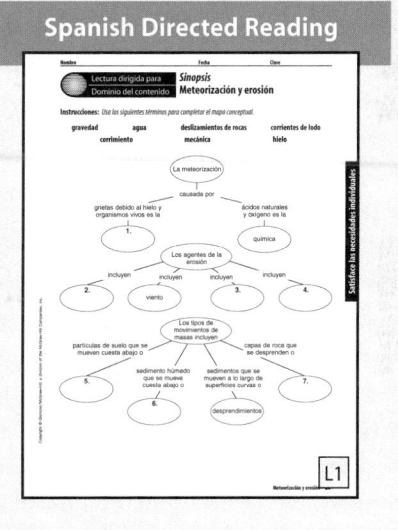

L1

Test Practice Workbook

Standardized Test Practice
Teacher Edition

Glencoe **Science**

LEVEL RED

L2

Chapter Review

Chapter Review — **Weathering and Erosion**

Part A. Vocabulary Review

Directions: *Use the clues below to complete the crossword puzzle.*

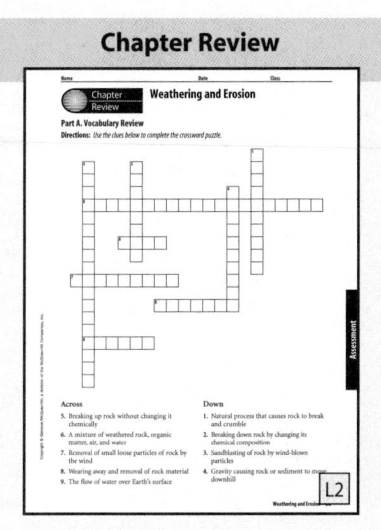

Across

5. Breaking up rock without changing it chemically
6. A mixture of weathered rock, organic matter, air, and water
7. Removal of small loose particles of rock by the wind
8. Wearing away and removal of rock material
9. The flow of water over Earth's surface

Down

1. Natural process that causes rock to break and crumble
2. Breaking down rock by changing its chemical composition
3. Sandblasting of rock by wind-blown particles
4. Gravity causing rock or sediment to move downhill

L2

Science Content Background

Weathering and Soil Formation

Mechanical Weathering

In hot, dry areas, a force that can contribute to the mechanical weathering of rock is the growth of salt crystals. Under certain conditions salt crystals can form from solution in rocks. Cracks and crevices can widen under the force applied as salt crystals grow. Salt crystal growth has the greatest effect on porous rocks, such as sandstone and limestone. Most often found in desertlike conditions, salt crystal growth also can occur in caves in coastal regions where the salt is derived from seawater.

Chemical Weathering

The pH of normal rainwater is slightly acidic at 5.6. The growing problem of acid rain, which has a pH of less than 5.0; acid snow; and acid fog, which has a pH as low as 1.7 in highly industrialized areas, is leading to increased chemical weathering of rocks such as limestone, marble, and sandstone. Acid rain also has left its mark on buildings, monuments, and tombstones. Acid rain results from several sources. The release of excess carbon dioxide from the burning of fossil fuels leads to increased amounts of carbonic acid in the atmosphere. Nitric acid is formed from the release of nitrogen oxide by

Corbis

Student Misconception

Soil is only one color, such as black, red, or yellow.

Refer to the facing page for teaching strategies to address this misconception. Refer to pages 469–471 for content related to this topic.

internal combustion engines. The largest source of acid rain results from the release of sulfur dioxide into the atmosphere from burning coal that contains sulfur. Sulfur dioxide combines with oxygen to form sulfuric acid.

Soil Formation

Soil is a mixture of weathered rock, organic matter, water, and air. A major factor affecting soil color is the type of rock that has been weathered.

Erosion of Earth's Surface

Wind

During the 1930s the Great Plains of the United States experienced repeated, severe dust storms, which resulted in the entire area being referred to as the Dust Bowl. A severe drought, in combination with the earlier replacement of deep-rooted grasses with shallow-rooted grains, allowed the strong winds that swept across the plains during this time to strip away large amounts of topsoil. During several extreme storms, great quantities of topsoil were carried away from the plains to places as far away as New York and New England.

SCIENCE Online

For additional content background on this topic, go to the Glencoe Science Web site at science.glencoe.com.

IDENTIFYING ▷ Misconceptions

Find Out What Students Think

Students may think that . . .

- **Soil is only one color, such as black, red, or yellow.**

Students think that soil is only one color; that is, the color of the soil where they live is the color of all soil.

Activity

Display small pieces of different-colored rocks. Samples might include limestone, sandstone, and shale. While wearing goggles, wrap each sample in a towel and crush with a rock hammer. Have students examine each crushed sample. Discuss how the color of each parent rock would affect the color of a soil that developed from it.

Promote Understanding

Activity

Organize the class into small groups. Provide each group with a variety of soils of different colors. Also provide each group with the parent rocks that could have altered to form each soil type.

- Have students work with group members to match each soil sample to the correct type of parent rock.

- Then have students discuss how they matched the samples. Discuss how soils develop from the alteration of parent rocks. The parent rock often lends its color to the soil formed from it.

- Discuss other factors that can add color to soils. Explain that the presence of humus,

Charles O'Rear/Corbis

or organic materials, can make soils appear darker. Iron oxides can also add colors such as yellow or red to soils.

Assess

After completing the chapter, see *Identifying Misconceptions* in the Study Guide.

Weathering and Erosion

Chapter Vocabulary

What do you think?

Science Journal These rocks have striations cut into them by the glacier that passed over them. Two sets of striations identify two different flow directions.

Weathering and Erosion

Erosion can be a devastating problem in many places in the world, especially in hilly or mountainous regions. Rock and sediment tend to move downhill under the influence of gravity. This mudflow in California threatened lives and destroyed a house. In this chapter, you will learn how weathering and erosion affect rocks. You also will learn how soil develops from weathered rock.

What do you think?

Science Journal Look at the picture below with a classmate. Discuss what this might be. Here's a hint: *Glaciers don't always flow in the same direction.* Write your answer or best guess in your Science Journal.

464

Theme Connection

Stability and Change Landforms may appear to be unchanging. But actually, they are constantly changing as a result of the effects of weathering and erosion.

The Grand Canyon is 440 km long, up to 24 km wide, and up to 1,800 m deep. The water of the Colorado River carved the canyon out of rock by wearing away particles and carrying them away for millions of years. The process of wearing away rock is called erosion. Over time, erosion has shaped and reshaped Earth's surface many times. In this activity, you will explore how running water formed the Grand Canyon.

Model water erosion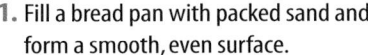

1. Fill a bread pan with packed sand and form a smooth, even surface.

2. Place the bread pan in a plastic wash tub. Position one end of the wash tub in a sink under the faucet.

3. Place a brick or wood block under the end of the bread pan beneath the faucet.

4. Turn on the water to form a steady trickle of water falling into the pan and observe for 10 min. The wash tub should catch the eroded sand.

Observe

In your Science Journal, draw a top view picture of the erosion pattern formed in the sand by the running water. Write a paragraph describing what the sand would look like if you had left the water running overnight.

Before You Read

FOLDABLES
Reading & Study Skills

Making a Compare and Contrast Study Fold **Make the following Foldable to help you see how weathering and erosion are similar and different.**

1. Place a sheet of paper in front of you so the short side is at the top. Fold the paper in half from top to bottom and then unfold.

2. Fold in to the centerfold line to divide the paper into fourths.

3. Label the flaps *Weathering* and *Erosion*. Label the middle portion inside your Foldable *Both*. Before you read the chapter, write the definition of each on the front of the flaps.

4. As you read the chapter, write information you learn on the back of the two flaps.

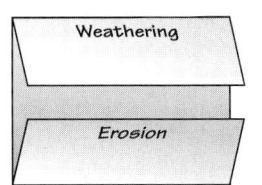

465

EXPLORE ACTIVITY

Purpose Students will model the soil erosion caused by running water.

Preparation Purchase a bread pan and washtub for each student group and assign each group a sink.

Materials bread pan, sand, plastic washtub, wood block, clock and access to a faucet for each student group

Teaching Strategy Have students layer the bread pan with several different colors of sand so that they can more clearly see the erosion process. As the trickle of water cuts a deeper groove into the sand, new colors will be exposed by erosion.

Observe

A deep "gorge" was eroded into the sand.

✓Assessment

Performance Ask students to leave the faucets running at a slow trickle the entire day and then draw the pattern of the colored layers exposed by the erosion. Use **Performance Assessment in the Science Classroom,** p. 127.

Before You Read

FOLDABLES
Reading & Study Skills

Dinah Zike Study Fold

Purpose Students make and use a Foldable to define and collect examples of weathering and erosion, and then use what they learn to explain what weathering and erosion have in common.

📁 For additional help, see Foldables Worksheet, p. 17 in **Chapter Resources Booklet,** or go to the Glencoe Science Web site at **science.glencoe.com.** See After You Read in the Study Guide at the end of this chapter.

Weathering and Soil Formation

1 Motivate

Bellringer Transparency

Display the Section Focus Transparency for Section 1. Use the accompanying Transparency Activity Master. L2

ELL

Tie to Prior Knowledge

Have students discuss what they know about the formation and use of soil. Explain that in this section they will learn how soil forms through the weathering of rock.

Caption Answer

Figure 1 The granite was broken into smaller pieces without changing chemically.

Weathering and Soil Formation

As You Read

***What* You'll Learn**
- **Identify** processes that break rock apart.
- **Describe** processes that chemically change rock.
- **Explain** how soil evolves.

Vocabulary
weathering
mechanical weathering
chemical weathering
soil
topography

***Why* It's Important**
Soil forms when rocks break apart and change chemically. Soil is home to many organisms and most plants need soil in order to grow.

Weathering

Have you noticed potholes in roadways and broken concrete in sidewalks and curbs? When a car rolls over a pothole in the road in late winter or when you step over a broken sidewalk, you know things aren't as solid or permanent as they look. Holes in roads and broken sidewalks show that solid materials can be changed by nature. **Weathering** is a natural process that causes rocks to change, breaks them down, and causes them to crumble. Freezing and thawing, oxygen in the air, and even plants and animals can affect the stability of rock. These are some of the things that cause rocks on Earth's surface to weather, and in some cases, to become soils.

Mechanical Weathering

When a sidewalk breaks apart, a large slab of concrete is broken into many small pieces. The concrete looks the same. It's just broken apart. This is similar to mechanical weathering. **Mechanical weathering** breaks rocks into smaller pieces without changing them chemically. The small pieces are identical in composition to the original rock, as shown in **Figure 1.** Two of the many causes of mechanical weathering are ice wedging and living organisms.

Figure 1
The forces of mechanical weathering break apart rocks. *How do you know that the smaller pieces of granite were produced by mechanical weathering?*

466

Section ✓*Assessment* Planner

PERFORMANCE ASSESSMENT	CONTENT ASSESSMENT
MiniLAB, p. 469	Section, p. 471
Try at Home MiniLAB, p. 470	Challenge, p. 471
Skill Builder Activities, p. 471	Chapter, pp. 488–489
See page 488 for more options.	

Figure 2
Over time, freezing water can break apart rock.

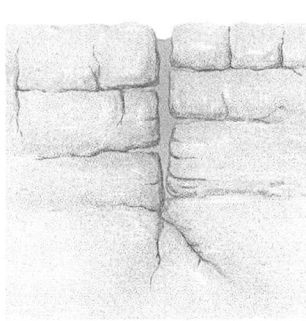

A Water seeps into cracks. The deeper the cracks are, the deeper water can seep in.

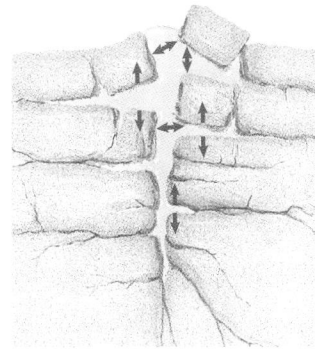

B The water freezes and expands forcing the cracks to open further.

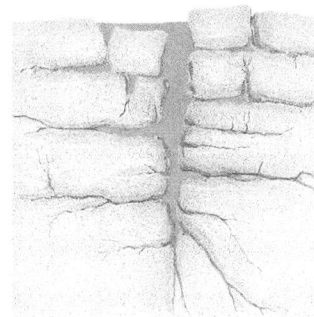

C The ice melts. If the temperature falls below freezing again, the process will repeat itself.

Ice Wedging In some areas of the world, air temperature drops low enough to freeze water. Then, when the temperature rises, the ice thaws. This freezing and thawing cycle breaks up rocks. How can this happen? When it rains or snow melts, water seeps into cracks in rocks. If the temperature drops below freezing, ice crystals form. As the crystals grow, they take up more space than the water did because ice is less dense than water. This expansion exerts pressure on the rocks. With enough force, the rocks will crack further and eventually break apart, as shown in **Figure 2.** Ice wedging also causes potholes to form in roadways.

✔ Reading Check *Explain how ice wedging can break rock apart.*

Plants and Animals Plants and animals also cause mechanical weathering. As shown in **Figure 3,** plants can grow in what seem to be the most inconvenient places. Their roots grow deep into cracks in rock where water collects. As they grow, roots become thicker and longer, slowly exerting pressure and wedging rock apart.

Gophers and prairie dogs also weather rock—as do other animals that burrow in the ground. As they burrow through sediment or soft sedimentary rock, animals break rock apart. They also push some rock and sediment to the surface where another kind of weathering, called chemical weathering, takes place more rapidly.

Figure 3
Tree roots can break rock apart.

Mechanical Weathering

Activity

Have students half-fill hard plastic jars with water and use grease pencils to mark the height of the water on the sides of the jars. Then have them put the jars in a freezer. The next day, have students examine the jars. They should observe that ice occupies more space in the jar than the water did. L1 ELL **IS** **Visual-Spatial**

✔ Reading Check

Answer As ice crystals form, they take up more space than liquid water and thus wedge the rock apart.

Use an Analogy

The process that occurs when ice wedging splits rocks into pieces is similar to the process of using a wedge to split wood. A triangular metal wedge is placed into a crack in a log. When hit with a mallet, the thicker part of the wedge is driven into the crack, and the wood splits apart. In ice wedging, water freezes in cracks, takes up more space, and splits the rock apart.

Resource Manager

Chapter Resources Booklet

Transparency Activity, p. 42

Directed Reading for Content Mastery, pp. 19, 20

Note-taking Worksheets, pp. 31–32

✔ Active Reading

Synthesis Journal In this strategy, students reflect on a project, a paper, or a performance in light of their own experiences and plan for personal application. Have each student divide a piece of paper into three sections. Have them record "What I did," "What I learned," and "How I can use it." Have students write a Synthesis Journal entry about the activity on this page.

Chemical Weathering

Caption Answer

Figure 4 It contains hydrogen and no potassium.

✔ Reading Check

Answer The tropics are more likely to be moist and warm, which accelerates chemical weathering.

Visual Learning

Table 1 Have students analyze the data in the table and determine the rate of chemical weathering occurring in your area. Answers will depend on location.

Discussion

Chemical weathering occurs on the surface of rocks. **What happens to the rate of chemical weathering if a rock is broken into smaller pieces?** Because the rock's surface area has increased, the rate of chemical weathering also increases.

Figure 4
Chemical weathering changes the chemical composition of minerals and rocks. *How is kaolinite different from feldspar?*

Elements in Feldspar

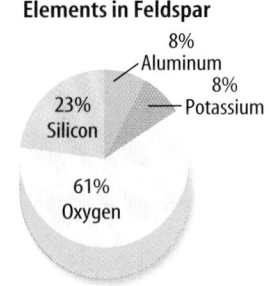

8% Aluminum
8% Potassium
23% Silicon
61% Oxygen

Elements in Kaolinite

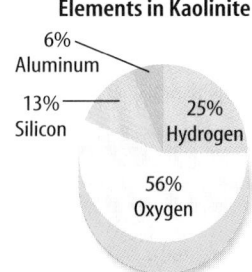

6% Aluminum
13% Silicon
25% Hydrogen
56% Oxygen

A Feldspar crystals react with carbonic acid.

B The mineral kaolinite is formed.

Chemical Weathering

Chemical weathering occurs when the chemical composition of rock changes. This kind of weathering is rapid in tropical regions where it's moist and warm most of the time. Because desert areas have little rainfall and polar regions have low temperatures, chemical weathering occurs slowly in these areas. **Table 1** summarizes the rates of chemical weathering for different climates. Two important causes of chemical weathering are natural acids and oxygen.

✔ Reading Check

Why is chemical weathering rapid in the tropics?

Table 1 Rates of Weathering

Climate	Chemical Weathering
Hot and dry	Slow
Hot and wet	Fast
Cold and dry	Slow
Cold and wet	Slow

Natural Acids Some rocks react chemically with natural acids in the environment. When water mixes with carbon dioxide in air or soil, for example, carbonic acid forms. Carbonic acid can change the chemical composition of minerals in rocks, as shown in **Figure 4.**

Although carbonic acid is weak, it reacts chemically with many rocks. Vinegar reacts with the calcium carbonate in chalk, dissolving it. In a similar way, when carbonic acid comes in contact with rocks like limestone, dolomite, and marble, they dissolve. Other rocks also weather when exposed to carbonic acid.

LAB DEMONSTRATION

Purpose to make an acid

Materials small beaker, phenol red or phenolphthalein, drinking straw

Preparation Explain that phenol red is an indicator that changes color when exposed to acids.

Procedure Fill a small beaker with phenol red. Exhale into the beaker through the straw. *Caution: Do not suck liquid in through the straw.* Have students observe what happens to the color of the phenol red.

Expected Outcome The phenol red turns yellow.

✔ Assessment

What gas was exhaled into the beaker? carbon dioxide **What natural acid was produced?** carbonic acid **How do you know?** The color change in the phenol red indicated the presence of an acid.

Plant Acids Plant roots also produce acid that reacts with rocks. Many plants produce a substance called tannin. In solution, tannin forms tannic acid. This acid dissolves some minerals in rocks. When minerals dissolve, the remaining rock is weakened, and it can break into smaller pieces. The next time you see moss or other plants growing on rock, as shown in **Figure 5**, peel back the plant. You'll likely see discoloration of the rock where plant acids are reacting chemically with some of the minerals in the rock.

Figure 5
Moss growing on rocks can cause chemical weathering.

Effect of Oxygen When you see rusty cars, reddish soil, or reddish stains on rock, you witness oxidation, the effects of chemical changes caused by oxygen. When iron-containing materials such as steel are oxidized a chemical reaction causes the material to rust. Rocks chemically weather in a similar way. When some iron-containing minerals are exposed to oxygen, they can weather to minerals that are like rust. This leaves the rock weakened, and it can break apart. As shown in **Figure 6**, some rocks also can be colored red or orange when iron-bearing minerals in them react with oxygen.

Figure 6
Oxidation occurs in rocks and cars.

A Even a tiny amount of iron in rock can combine with oxygen and form a reddish iron oxide.

B The iron contained in metal objects such as this truck also can combine with oxygen and form a reddish iron oxide called rust.

Table 2 Factors that Affect Soil Formation

Parent Rock	Slope of Land	Climate	Time	Organisms

Soil

Make a Model

Have students make a compost pile to model the formation of the organic component of soil. Get permission to use an area of the school yard as a compost pile. Encourage students to add grass clippings, straw, and non-meat or dairy food wastes to the pile. Turn the pile frequently to provide aeration. Adding worms will speed the process. Have students periodically examine the compost with a hand lens. Finished compost is dark, smells "earthy," and has few recognizable components.
L2 ELL Kinesthetic

TRY AT HOME
Mini LAB

Purpose Student will examine a soil sample.

Materials soil sample, sheet of newspaper

Teaching Strategy Be sure students wash their hands thoroughly after handling the soil.

Analysis

1. Answers will be subjective and based on the students' soil samples. Students may mention water and air which, although present, will not be observable.

2. Answers will vary, depending on the soil sample.

✔Assessment

Performance Have students separate soil components into different piles: rock fragments, sand, clay, topsoils, humus, and organisms. Use **PASC**, p. 89

TRY AT HOME
Mini LAB

Analyzing Soils

Procedure 🖐 🚫

1. Obtain a sample of **soil** from near your home.
2. Spread the soil out over a piece of **newspaper.**
3. Carefully sort through the soil. Separate out organic matter from weathered rock.
4. Wash hands thoroughly after working with soils.

Analysis

1. Besides the organic materials and the remains of weathered rock, what else is present in the soil?
2. Is some of the soil too fine-grained to tell if it is organic or weathered rock?

470 CHAPTER 16 Weathering and Erosion

Soil

Is soil merely dirt under your feet, or is it something more important? **Soil** is a mixture of weathered rock, organic matter, water, and air that supports the growth of plant life. Organic matter includes decomposed leaves, twigs, roots, and other material. Many factors affect soil formation.

Parent Rock As listed in **Table 2,** one factor affecting soil formation is the kind of parent rock that is being weathered. For example, where limestone is chemically weathered, clayey soil is common because clay is left behind when the limestone dissolves. In areas where sandstone is weathered, sandy soil forms.

The Slope of the Land The **topography,** or surface features of an area also influence the types of soils that develop. You've probably noticed that on steep hillsides, soil has little chance of developing. This is because rock fragments move downhill constantly. However, in lowlands where the land is flat, wind and water deposit fine sediments that help form thick soils.

Climate Climate affects soil evolution, too. If rock weathers quickly, deep soils can develop rapidly. This is more likely to happen in tropical regions where the climate is warm and moist. Climate also affects the amount of organic material in soil. Soils in desert climates contain little organic material. However, in mild, humid climates, vegetation is lush and much organic material is present. When plants and animals die, decomposition by fungi and bacteria begins. The result is the formation of a dark-colored material called humus, as shown in the soil profile in **Figure 7.** Most of the organic matter in soil is humus. Humus helps soil hold water and provides nutrients that plants need to grow.

Visual Learning

Figure 7 Why are soil layers different colors?
Soil layers can get their color from organic matter, mineral precipitates, and the rock and mineral grains in the soil. Organic matter often colors surface horizons. Subsurface horizons are colored by mineral precipitates or parent material.

Resource Manager

Chapter Resources Booklet
MiniLAB, p. 4
Lab Activity, pp. 9–12

Earth Science Critical Thinking/Problem Solving, p. 6

Time It takes time for rocks to weather. It can take thousands of years for some soils to form. As soils develop, they become less like the rock from which they formed. In young soils, the parent rock determines the soil characteristics. As weathering continues, however, the soil resembles the parent rock less and less. Thicker, well-developed soils often are found in areas where weathering has gone on undisturbed for a long period of time. For this to happen, soil materials must not be eroded away and new sediment must not be deposited over the land's surface too quickly.

Organisms Organisms influence soil development. Lichens are small organisms that consist of an alga and a fungus that live together for mutual benefit. You may have seen lichens in the form of multicolored patches growing on tree branches or cliff faces. Interestingly, lichens can grow directly on rock. As they grow, they take nutrients from the rock that they are starting to break down, forming a thin soil. After a soil has formed, many types of plants such as grasses and trees can grow.

The roots of these plants further break down the parent rock. Dead plant material such as leaves accumulates and adds organic matter to the soil. Some plants contribute more organic matter to soil than others. For example, soil under grassy areas often is richer in organic matter than soil developing under forests. This is why some of the best farmland in the midwestern United States is where grasslands used to be.

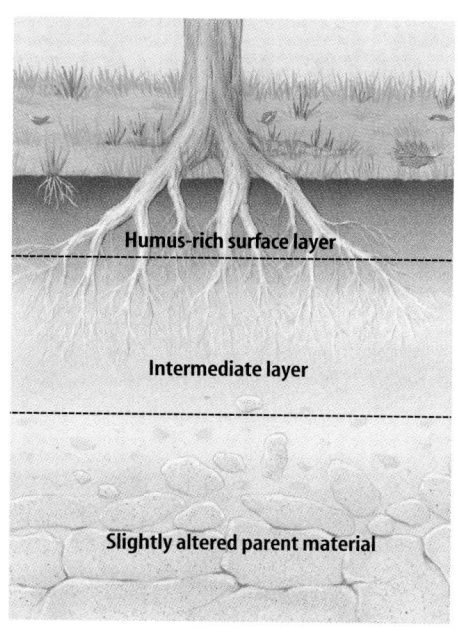

Humus-rich surface layer

Intermediate layer

Slightly altered parent material

Figure 7
Soils contain layers that are created by weathering, the flow of water and chemicals, and the activities of organisms. *What part do microorganisms play in soil development?*

Section 1 Assessment

1. What are two ways that rocks are mechanically weathered?
2. Name two agents of chemical weathering.
3. How does carbonic acid weather rocks?
4. How does soil form? What factors are important?
5. **Think Critically** How could climate affect rates of mechanical weathering? What about chemical weathering? How are the two kinds of weathering related?

Skill Builder Activities

6. **Comparing and Contrasting** Compare and contrast mechanical weathering caused by ice wedging with mechanical weathering caused by growing roots. **For more help, refer to the Science Skill Handbook.**

7. **Communicating** Write a descriptive poem in your Science Journal that explains different ways rocks are weathered. **For more help, refer to the Science Skill Handbook.**

Answers to Section Assessment

1. by plant roots and ice wedging
2. natural acids and oxygen
3. It dissolves some minerals in rocks.
4. when organic matter, water, and air are combined with weathered rock particles; parent material, shape of the land, climate, time, and organisms
5. In warm, moist climates, the rate of mechanical weathering is fast

because plant roots wedge rocks apart. The rate is rapid in temperate climates because water freezes and thaws, causing ice wedging. The rate is slow in warm, dry regions, and cold, dry regions where there are few plants and no ice wedging. Table 1 lists rates of chemical weathering in various climates.

6. Both wedge rocks apart. Mechanical weathering by plant roots occurs as plants grow and require more space; ice wedging occurs as water freezes and expands in fractured rock.
7. Poems should include accurate information about weathering.

Quick Demo

Fill a flowerpot with peat moss and another pot of equal size with the same amount of sand. Slowly pour water into each pot and determine the quantity of water that can be held by each material before water leaks from the bottom of the pot. Expected outcome: Humus (peat moss) will hold much more water than sand.

Caption Answer

Figure 7 They decompose organic matter.

3 Assess

Reteach

Make a drawing of a soil profile on the overhead projector. Have students describe each layer as you point to it. Characteristics mentioned should include amount of humus and rock particles in each layer. L1
Visual-Spatial

Challenge

Have students examine a partially decomposed log. Have them list the organisms they see and relate how each type of organism contributes to the formation of humus. L3
Visual-Spatial

Assessment

Process Have students design a spider concept map of factors that affect weathering. Use **Performance Assessment in the Science Classroom,** p. 161.

Activity

BENCH TESTED

Purpose Students use a classification key to determine the texture of a soil sample. L2

IS **Kinesthetic and Visual-Spatial**

Process Skills observing and inferring, classifying, drawing conclusions, communicating

Time Required 40 minutes

Alternate Materials hand lens

Safety Precautions Caution students to wash their hands after handling the soil.

Teaching Strategy Cover work surfaces with newspaper to help decrease clean-up time.

Answers to Questions

1. Answers will vary depending on local soils.
2. Loamy soil is smooth and holds water well.
3. Sandy loamy soil is gritty and will make a firm ball when squeezed.
4. Answers may include rock particles, decomposing leaf material, and insects.

Assessment

Oral Have students explain the relationship between worms and soil fertility. Worms move organic matter throughout the soil, add nitrates to the soil, and dig tunnels that allow air to go deep into the soil. Use **Performance Assessment in the Science Classroom,** p. 89.

Activity
Classifying Soils

Not all soils are the same. Geologists and soil scientists classify soils based on the amounts and kinds of particles they contain.

What You'll Investigate
How is soil texture determined?

Materials
soil sample
stereomicroscope
*hand lens
*Alternate materials

Safety Precautions
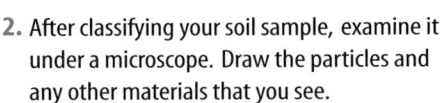

Goals
- **Classify** a soil using an identification key.
- **Observe** soil with a stereomicroscope.

Procedure

1. Place a small sample of moistened soil between your fingers. Then follow the directions in the classification key below.
   a. Slide your fingers back and forth past each other. If your sample feels gritty, go to **b**. If it doesn't feel gritty, go to **c**.
   b. If you can mold the soil into a firm ball, it's sandy loam soil. If you cannot mold it into a firm ball, it's sandy soil.
   c. If your sample is sticky, go to **d**. If your sample isn't sticky, go to **e**.
   d. If your sample can be molded into a long, thin ribbon, it's clay soil. If your soil can't be molded into a long, thin ribbon it's clay loam soil.
   e. If your sample is smooth, it's silty loam soil. If it isn't smooth, it's loam soil.

2. After classifying your soil sample, examine it under a microscope. Draw the particles and any other materials that you see.
3. Wash your hands thoroughly after you are finished working with soils.

Conclude and Apply

1. **Determine** the texture of your soil sample.
2. **Describe** two characteristics of loam soil.
3. **Describe** two features of sandy loam soil.
4. Based on your observations with the stereomicroscope, what types of particles and other materials did you see? Did you observe any evidence of the activities of organisms?

Communicating Your Data

Compare your conclusions with those of other students in your class. **For more help, refer to the** Science Skill Handbook.

Communicating Your Data

Suggest students make a table in which they can organize their observations. Students should discuss why their conclusions did or did not agree.

Resource Manager

Chapter Resources Booklet
  Reinforcement, p. 27
Performance Assessment in the Science Classroom, p. 44
Science Inquiry Labs, p. 35

Erosion of Earth's Surface

Agents of Erosion

Imagine looking over the rim of the Grand Canyon at the winding Colorado River below or watching the sunset over Utah's famous arches. Features such as these are spectacular examples of Earth's natural beauty, but how can canyons and arches form in solid rock? These features and many other natural landforms are a result of erosion of Earth's surface. **Erosion** is the wearing away and removal of rock or sediment. Erosion occurs because gravity, ice, wind, and water sculpt Earth's surface.

Gravity

Gravity is a force that pulls every object toward every other object. Gravity pulls everything on Earth toward its center. As a result, water flows downhill and rocks tumble down slopes. When gravity alone causes rock or sediment to move down a slope, the erosion is called **mass movement.** Mass movements can occur anywhere there are hills or mountains. One place where they often occur is near volcanoes, as shown in **Figure 8.** Creep, slump, rock slides, and mudflows are four types of mass movements, as seen in **Figure 9.**

As You Read

What You'll Learn
- **Identify** agents of erosion.
- **Describe** the effects of erosion.

Vocabulary
erosion
mass movement
creep
slump
deflation
abrasion
runoff

Why It's Important
Erosion shapes Earth's surface.

Figure 8
The town of Weed, California, was built on top of a landslide that moved down the volcano known as Mount Shasta.

473

Erosion of Earth's Surface

1 Motivate

Bellringer Transparency

Display the Section Focus Transparency for Section 2. Use the accompanying Transparency Activity Master. L2
ELL

Tie to Prior Knowledge

Remind students that in Section 1, they learned how rocks are weathered. Have students list ways in which they think those weathered particles are moved from place to place. Then explain that in this section, they will learn how erosional agents transport weathered sediments.

Section ✓Assessment Planner

PORTFOLIO
Activity, p. 474
Science Journal, p. 476

PERFORMANCE ASSESSMENT
Problem-Solving Activity, p. 479
Skill Builder Activities, p. 481
See page 488 for more options.

CONTENT ASSESSMENT
Section, p. 481
Challenge, p. 481
Chapter, pp. 488–489

NATIONAL GEOGRAPHIC

Visualizing Mass Movements

Have students examine the pictures and read the captions. Then ask the following questions.

What role does the degree of slope play in mass movement? Because the force of gravity is behind all mass movement, the steeper the slope, the greater the likelihood of mass movement.

How does water contribute to the types of mass movement shown here? In the case of creep and slump, moisture weakens the soil's resistance to movement down a slope. A sudden influx of water can initiate a mudflow. Rock slides can occur when rainwater seeps into weak layers underlying slabs of rock.

Activity

Have students go online to research a major rock slide or mudflow that has made the news. Have them make posters showing the landscape before and after these events, as well as detailing the consequences. L2 **LS Visual-Spatial** P

Extension

Challenge students to design an investigation to test the roles played by slope and water in mass movement events. Have them make a hypothesis and design an experiment identifying the independent and dependent variables. Ask them to list factors that would remain constants in their investigations.

NATIONAL GEOGRAPHIC **VISUALIZING MASS MOVEMENTS**

Figure 9

When the relentless tug of gravity causes a large chunk of soil or rock to move downhill—either gradually or with sudden speed—the result is what geologists call a mass movement. Weathering and water often contribute to mass movements. Several kinds are shown here.

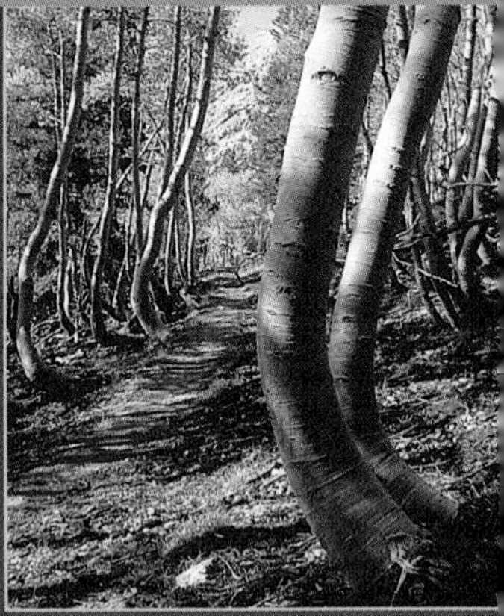

A CREEP When soil on a slope moves very slowly downhill, a mass movement called creep occurs. Some of the trees at right have been gradually bent because of creep's pressure on their trunks.

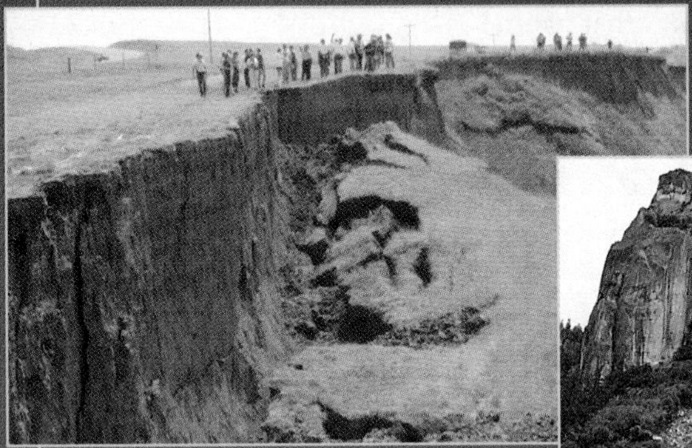

B SLUMP This cliff in North Dakota shows the effects of the mass movement known as slump. Slumping often occurs after earthquakes or heavy and prolonged rains.

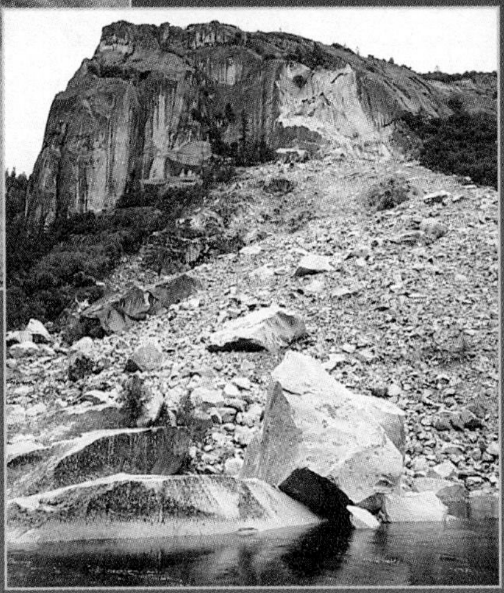

C ROCK SLIDES When rocks break free from the side of a cliff or a mountain, they crash down in what is called a rock slide. Rock slides, like the one at the left in Yosemite National Park, can occur with little warning.

D MUDFLOWS A Japanese town shows the devastation that a fourth type of mass movement—a mudflow—can bring. When heavy moisture saturates sediments, mudflows can develop, sending a pasty mix of water and sediment downhill over the ground's surface.

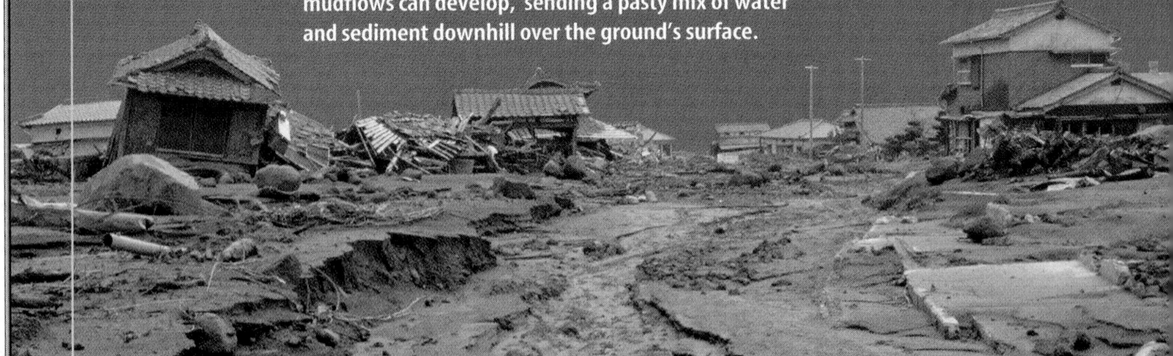

474 CHAPTER 16 Weathering and Erosion

Resource Manager

Chapter Resources Booklet

Transparency Activity, p. 43

Directed Reading for Content Mastery, pp. 21, 22

Mathematics Skill Activities, p. 9

Creep **Creep** is the name for a process in which sediments move slowly downhill, as shown in **Figure 9A.** Creep is common where freezing and thawing occur. As ice expands in soil, it pushes sediments up. Then as soil thaws, the sediments move farther downslope. **Figure 10** shows how small particles of sediment can creep downslope. Over time, creep can move large amounts of sediment, possibly causing damage to some structures. Do you live in an area where you can see the results of creep?

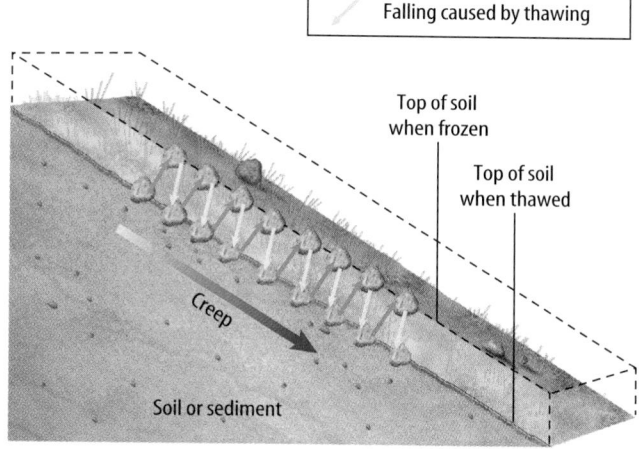

↗ Expansion caused by freezing

↙ Falling caused by thawing

Top of soil when frozen

Top of soil when thawed

Creep

Soil or sediment

Slump A **slump** occurs when a mass of rock or sediment moves downhill along a curved surface, as shown in **Figure 9B.** Slumps are most common in thick layers of loose sediment, but they also form in sedimentary rock. Slumps frequently occur on slopes that have been undercut by erosion, such as those above the bases of cliffs that have been eroded by waves. Slumping of this kind is common along the coast of Southern California where it threatens to destroy houses and other buildings.

Rock Slides Can you imagine millions of cubic meters of rock roaring down a mountain at speeds greater than 100 km/h? This can happen when a rock slide occurs. During a rock slide layers of rock break loose from slopes and slide to the bottom. The rock layers often bounce and break apart during movement. This produces a huge, jumbled pile of rocks at the bottom of the slope, as you can see in **Figure 9C.** Rock slides can be destructive, sometimes destroying entire villages or causing hazards on roads in mountainous areas.

Mudflows Where heavy rains or melting snow and ice saturate sediments, mudflows, as shown in **Figure 9D,** can develop. A mudflow is a mass of wet sediment that flows downhill over the ground surface. Some mudflows can be thick and flow slowly downhill at rates of a few meters per day. Other mudflows can be much more fluid and move down slope at speeds approaching 70 km/h. This type of mudflow is common on some volcanoes.

✔ Reading Check *What is the slowest of the four kinds of mass movement?*

Figure 10
When soil freezes, particles are lifted. When it thaws, the particles are pulled downhill by gravity. Eventually, large amounts of sediment are moved by this process.

Physics
INTEGRATION

Slumps and rock slides often occur when sediment becomes saturated by rain. Water between sediment grains helps lift up overlying rock and sediment. This makes it easier for the sediment to overcome the forces holding it in place. Can you think of a way some slopes might be protected from slumps and rock slides? Explain.

Section 2 Erosion of Earth's Surface **475**

Ice

Use Science Words

Word Origin The term *glacier* comes from the French word *glace*. Have students find the meaning of glace. It means ice.

Activity

The following data show ice flow speeds across a small alpine glacier. Have students identify patterns in the data using average, frequency, and range. Students should graph these data to observe the pattern of ice speeds.

Distance Across Glacier (m)	Speed (m/yr)
0	20
50	40
100	80
200	100
300	80
350	40
400	20

Average = 54 m/yr; range = 100 m/yr – 20m/yr; frequency: 20 m/yr = 2, 40 m/yr = 2, 80 m/yr = 2, 100 m/yr = 1. Graph should be a symmetric curve.

Fun Fact

The names for the countries Greenland and Iceland are misleading. Greenland is covered by a continental glacier. Iceland is not.

SCIENCE *Online*
Internet Addresses

_____

_____

_____

_____

Explore the Glencoe Science Web site at **science.glencoe.com** to find out more about topics in this section.

Figure 11
Glaciers form in cold regions.

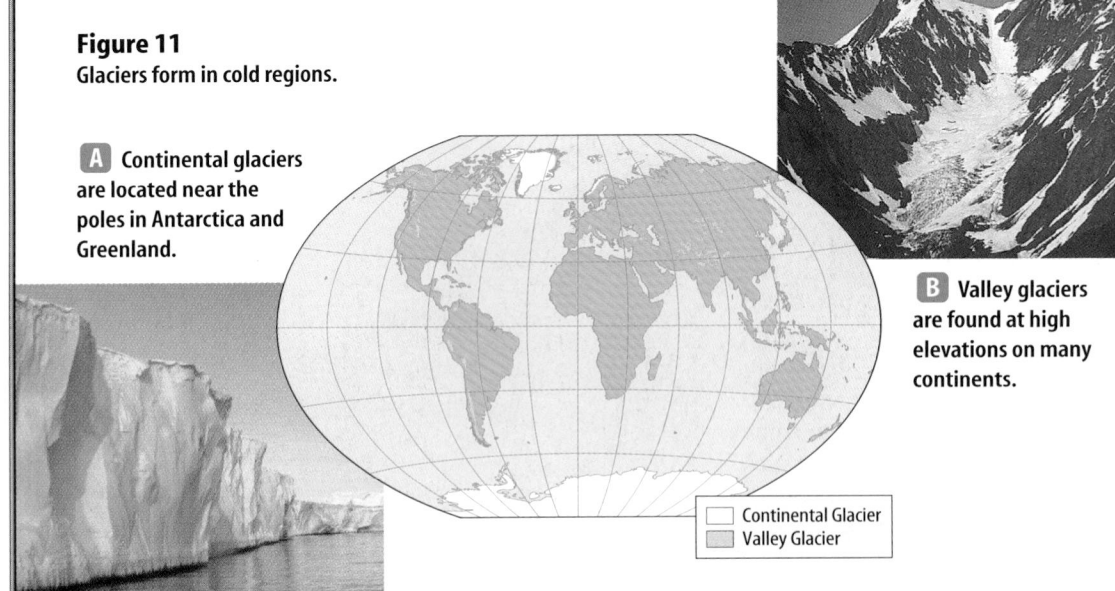

A Continental glaciers are located near the poles in Antarctica and Greenland.

B Valley glaciers are found at high elevations on many continents.

Continental Glacier
Valley Glacier

SCIENCE *Online*

Research Visit the Glencoe Science Web site at **science.glencoe.com** for more information about glacial erosion and deposition. Communicate to your class what you learned.

Ice

In some parts of the world, ice is an agent of erosion. In cold regions, more snow might fall than melts. Over many years, the snow can accumulate to form large, deep masses of ice called glaciers. When the ice in a glacier becomes thick enough, its own weight causes it to flow downhill under the influence of gravity. As glaciers move over Earth's surface, they erode materials from some areas and deposit sediment in other areas. **Figure 11** shows the two kinds of glaciers—continental glaciers and valley glaciers.

Today, continental glaciers in polar regions cover about ten percent of Earth. These glaciers are so large and thick that they can bury mountain ranges. Valley glaciers are much smaller and are located in high mountains where the average temperature isn't warm enough to melt the ice sheets. Continental and valley glaciers move and cause erosion.

Glacial Erosion Glaciers can erode rock in two different ways. If the rock that the glacier is sliding over has cracks in it, the ice can pull out pieces of rock. This causes the rock to erode slowly. The loose pieces of rock freeze into the bottom of the glacier and are dragged along as the glacier moves. As these different-sized fragments of rock are dragged over Earth's surface, they scratch the rock below like giant sheets of sandpaper. This scratching is the second way that glaciers can erode rock. Scratching produces large grooves or smaller striations in the rock underneath. The scratching also can wear rock into a fine powder called rock flour.

476 CHAPTER 16 Weathering and Erosion

Cultural Diversity

Sherpas Sherpas live on the high southern slopes of the Himalaya, thus glaciers are a very important part of their lives. Many Sherpas are guides for mountain climbing expeditions to Mount Everest. Have students research the role Sherpas have had in Mount Everest expeditions and the dangers they face. L2 IS **Linguistic**

Science Journal

Tour Guide After researching Glacier National Park, have students write travel brochures that describe the glacial structures that can be seen at the park. L2 IS **Linguistic** P

Figure 12
Many high-altitude areas owe their distinctive appearance to glacial erosion.

A Mountain glaciers can carve bowl-shaped depressions called cirques.

B Glaciers can widen valleys giving them a U-shaped profile.

Effects of Glacial Erosion Glacial erosion of rock can be a powerful force shaping Earth's surface. In mountains, valley glaciers can remove rock from the mountaintops to form large bowls, called cirques (SURKS), and steep peaks. When a glacier moves into a stream valley, it erodes rock along the valley sides, producing a wider, U-shaped valley. These features are shown in **Figure 12.** Continental glaciers also shape Earth's surface. These glaciers can scour large lakes and completely remove rock layers from the land's surface.

Glacial Deposition Glaciers also can deposit sediments. When stagnant glacier ice melts or when ice melts at the bottom of a flowing glacier or along its edges, the sediment the ice was carrying gets left behind on Earth's surface. This sediment, deposited directly from glacier ice, is called till. Till is a mixture of different-sized particles, ranging from clay to large boulders.

As you can imagine, a lot of melting occurs around glaciers, especially during summer. So much water can be produced that rivers often flow away from the glacier. These rivers carry and deposit sediment. Sand and gravel deposits laid down by these rivers, shown in **Figure 13,** are called outwash. Unlike till, outwash usually consists of particles that are all about the same size.

Figure 13
This valley in New Zealand has been filled with outwash. *How could you distinguish outwash from till?*

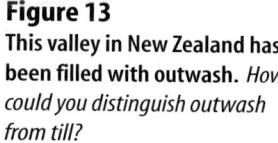 SECTION 2 Erosion of Earth's Surface **477**

Curriculum Connection

Geography The Matterhorn, called Mont Cervin by the French and Monte Cervino by the Italians, formed during the Pleistocene Epoch. Have students locate it on a map. It is in the Alps between Switzerland and Italy. L2  **Visual-Spatial**

Make a Model

Use the following procedures to demonstrate glacial erosion. Place gravel of different sizes into the compartments of an ice tray. Fill the tray with water. Freeze the tray overnight. Fill a large flat box or tray with sand. Have students use the ice cube "glaciers" to demonstrate how glaciers scratch grooves and striations into rock. L2 **Kinesthetic**

Extension

Have students research the origin of the Great Lakes. Have them make maps that show the evolution of the Great Lakes during the Pleistocene Epoch of geologic time. L2 **Visual-Spatial**

Discussion

You find a large rock in the middle of a flat field. Could this be a glacial deposit? Explain. Yes, a glacier might have deposited till, including the rock, as it melted.

Caption Answer

Figure 13 Till is a mixture of different-sized particles of sediment. Outwash is sorted by size.

Wind

✔ Reading Check

Answer Sediment particles carried by wind strike rocks, making pits and smooth, polished surfaces.

Discussion

Why do you think farmers often plant rows of trees along their fields? When wind hits the trees, it slows down, thus reducing erosion of the soil in the fields. The reduction in speed also causes sediment carried by the wind to be deposited.

Teacher FYI

- Strong winds that deflated glacial outwash during and following the ice ages deposited large amounts of loess near the Mississippi River. These buff-colored deposits have evolved into fertile soils.

- Loess deposits that originated from silts deflated from the Gobi and Ordos deserts give China's Yellow River (Huang He) its color.

Visual Learning

Figure 15 How can you tell the direction a sand dune is migrating? A dune migrates in the direction the wind is blowing. The wind rolls sand particles up the gentle side and over the top of the dune. Thus, the gentle side of the dune points away from the direction of migration.

Figure 14
In a desert, where small particles have been carried away by wind, larger sediments called desert pavement remain behind.

Figure 15
Wind transportation of sand creates sand dunes.

A Sand dunes do not remain in one location—they migrate.

Wind

If you've had sand blow into your eyes, you've experienced wind as an agent of erosion. When wind blows across loose sediments like silt and sand, it lifts and carries it. As shown in **Figure 14,** wind often leaves behind particles too heavy to move. This erosion of the land by wind is called **deflation.** Deflation can lower the land's surface by several meters.

Wind that is carrying sediment can wear down, or abrade, other rocks just as a sandblasting machine would do. **Abrasion** is a form of erosion that can make pits in rocks and produce smooth, polished surfaces. Abrasion is common in some deserts and in some cold regions with strong winds.

✔ Reading Check *How does abrasion occur?*

When wind blows around some irregular feature on Earth's surface, such as a rock or clump of vegetation, it slows down. This causes sand carried by the wind to be deposited. If this sand deposit continues to grow, a sand dune like that shown in **Figure 15A** might form. Sand dunes move when wind carries sand up one side of the dune and it avalanches down the other, as shown in **Figure 15B.**

Sometimes, wind carries only fine sediment called silt. When this sediment is deposited, an accumulation of silt called loess (LOOS) can blanket Earth's surface. Loess is as fine as talcum powder. Loess often is deposited downwind of some large deserts and near glacial streams.

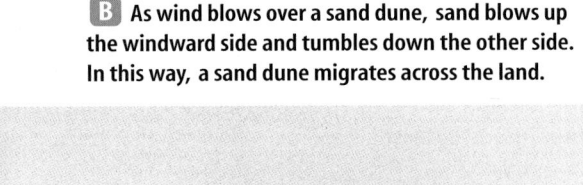

B As wind blows over a sand dune, sand blows up the windward side and tumbles down the other side. In this way, a sand dune migrates across the land.

Dune movement

478 CHAPTER 16 Weathering and Erosion

Inclusion Strategies

Gifted Have pairs of students work together to design experiments to study the effects of different variables on deflation. Variables to be tested might include soil moisture, wind velocity, and plant cover. Have students make posters explaining their results. L3 COOP LEARN

Ⓚ Kinesthetic

Cultural Diversity

Sacred Rock The largest sandstone monolith in the world is in Australia's Northern Territory. Shaped by wind-blown sands, Ayers Rock is the remains of a sandstone that formed about 500 million years ago. To the Aboriginal people, Ayers Rock, called Uluru, is a sacred site. Have students discuss why they think the Aboriginal people might consider Uluru sacred.

Water

You probably have seen muddy water streaming down a street after a heavy rain. You might even have taken off your shoes and waded through the water. Water that flows over Earth's surface is called **runoff.** Runoff is an important agent of erosion. This is especially true if the water is moving fast. The more speed water has, the more material it can carry with it. Water can flow over Earth's surface in several different ways, as you will soon discover.

Sheet Flow As raindrops fall to Earth, they break up clumps of soil and loosen small grains of sediment. If these raindrops are falling on a sloped land surface, a thin sheet of water might begin to move downhill. You have observed something similar if you've ever washed a car and seen sheets of water flowing over the hood, as shown in **Figure 16.** When water flows downhill as a thin sheet, it is called sheet flow. This thin sheet of water can carry loose sediment grains with it, and cause erosion of the land. This erosion is called sheet erosion.

Figure 16
Water flows over the hood of a car as a thin sheet. *How is this similar to sheet flow on Earth's surface?*

Problem-Solving Activity

Can evidence of sheet erosion be seen in a farm field?

If you've ever traveled through parts of your state where there are farms, you might have seen bare, recently cultivated fields. Perhaps the soil was prepared for planting a crop of corn, oats, or soybeans. Do you think sheet erosion can visibly affect the soil in farm fields?

Identifying the Problem

The top layer of most soils is much darker than layers beneath it because it contains more organic matter. This layer is the first to be removed from a slope by sheet flow. How does the photo show evidence of sheet erosion?

Solving the Problem
1. Observe the photo and write a description of it in your Science Journal.

2. Infer why some areas of the field are darker colored than others are. Where do you think the highest point(s) are in this field?
3. Make a generalization about the darker areas of the field.

Resource Manager

Chapter Resources Booklet
Lab Activity, pp. 13–16

Science Inquiry Labs, p. 5

Life Science Critical Thinking/Problem Solving, p. 23

Science Journal

Runoff Have students take pictures of runoff or write paragraphs in their Science Journals about their observations of runoff. Challenge them to identify the source of the runoff (rainfall, snowmelt, sprinkler, or garden hose). L2 IS **Linguistic and Visual-Spatial**

Water

Make a Model

Spread a layer of soil onto one end of a cookie sheet or rectangular tray. Form a slight downward slope by placing a book under the end of the tray containing the soil. Have students observe the effects of dripping different sized drops of water from different heights onto the soil. Students should observe the "raindrops" break up clumps of soil and loosen small grains of sediment. As they continue adding water, a sheet flow will develop and eroded materials will collect along the bottom of the tray. L2 ELL IS **Kinesthetic and Visual-Spatial**

Caption Answer

Figure 16 Water flows down a slope as a thin sheet over Earth's surface when sheet flow occurs.

Problem-Solving Activity

National Math Standards

Correlation to Mathematics Objectives
6,7

Answers

1. Students' descriptions should be of a recently cultivated field and should include color and slope of the ground.
2. Sheet wash has moved organic-rich topsoil to low areas of the field. The high points are lighter colored.
3. They have soil with a higher humus content.

Activity

Have students draw a series of pictures that show how a rill can evolve into a gully. L2 ELL IS **Visual-Spatial**

Water, continued

Visual Learning

Figure 17 Why do gullies often form on vegetation-free slopes? Soil is easily eroded without plant roots to help hold it in place.

Use an Analogy

Just as paths form near the school building where students walk over the same area of grass day after day, rills form where water flows over the same area after every rain. After continuous use by students, paths are eroded deeper into the sediments. After recurring rains, rills develop into gullies.

SCIENCE Online
Internet Addresses
_____
_____
_____
_____

Explore the Glencoe Science Web site at science.glencoe.com to find out more about topics in this section.

Teacher FYI

- As water erodes the sides and bottom of a channel, its profile becomes V-shaped.
- The winding parts where streams snake back and forth are called meanders.

Figure 17
Gullies often form on vegetation-free slopes.

SCIENCE Online

Research Visit the Glencoe Science Web site at **science.glencoe.com** for more information about how running water shapes Earth's surface. Communicate to your class what you learn.

Figure 18
Streams that flow down steep slopes such as this one in Yosemite National Park often have whitewater rapids and waterfalls.

480

Rills and Gullies Where a sheet of water flows around obstacles and becomes deeper, rills can form. Rills are small channels cut into the sediment at Earth's surface. These channels carry more sediment than can be moved by sheet flow. In some cases, a network of rills can form on a slope after just one heavy rain. Large amounts of sediment can be picked up and carried away by rills.

As runoff continues to flow through the rills, more sediment erodes and the channel widens and deepens. When the channels get to be about 0.5 m across, they are called gullies, as shown in **Figure 17.**

Streams Gullies often connect to stream channels. Streams can be so small that you could jump to the other side or large enough for huge river barges to transport products along their course. Most streams have water flowing through them continually, but some have water only during part of the year.

In mountainous and hilly regions, as in **Figure 18,** streams flow down steep slopes. These streams have a lot of energy and often cut into the rock beneath their valleys. This type of stream typically has white-water rapids and may have waterfalls. As streams move out of the mountains and onto flatter land, they begin to flow more smoothly. The streams might snake back and forth across their valley, eroding and depositing sediments along their sides. All streams eventually must flow into the ocean or a large lake. The level of water in the ocean or lake determines how deeply a river can erode.

Curriculum Connection

Social Studies Dams are built to prevent flooding, provide reservoirs for drinking water, and allow the harnessing of the energy of moving water. Dams also trap sediments and reduce the flow of water downstream. Hoover Dam is located on the Nevada-Arizona border along the Colorado River. Have students research how people downstream are affected by this dam. L2 IS **Linguistic**

Resource Manager

Chapter Resources Booklet
    Reinforcement, p. 28
Earth Science Critical Thinking/Problem Solving, p. 7

Shaping Earth's Surface If you did the Explore activity at the beginning of the chapter, you saw a small model of erosion by a stream. You might not think about them much, but streams are the most important agent of erosion on Earth. They shape more of Earth's surface than ice, wind, or gravity. Over long periods of time, water moving in a stream can have enough power to cut large canyons into solid rock. Many streams together can sculpt the land over a wide region, forming valleys and leaving some rock as hills. Streams also shape the land by depositing sediment. Rivers can deposit sand bars along their course, and can build up sheets of sand across their valleys. When rivers enter oceans or lakes, the water slows and sediment is deposited. This can form large accumulations of sediment called deltas, as in **Figure 19.** The city of New Orleans is built on the delta formed by the Mississippi River.

Figure 19
A triangular area of sediment near the mouth of a river is called a delta. Ancient deltas that are now dry land are often excellent places to grow crops.

Effects of Erosion

As you've learned, all agents of erosion change Earth's surface. Rock and sediment are removed from some areas only to be deposited somewhere else. Where material is removed, canyons, valleys, and mountain bowls can form. Where sediment accumulates, deltas, sand bars, sand dunes, and other features make up the land.

Section ② Assessment

1. List four agents of erosion. Which of these is the fastest agent of erosion? The slowest? Explain your answers.

2. How does deflation differ from abrasion?

3. How does a cirque form?

4. When do streams deposit sediments? When do they erode them?

5. **Think Critically** Why might a river that was eroding and depositing sediment along its sides start to cut into Earth to form a canyon?

Skill Builder Activities

6. **Recognizing Cause and Effect** Why might a river start filling its valley with sediment? **For more help, refer to the** Science Skill Handbook.

7. **Solving One-Step Equations** If wind is eroding an area at a rate of 2 mm per year and depositing it in a smaller area at a rate of 7 mm per year, how much lower will the first area be in meters after 2 thousand years? How much higher will the second area be? **For more help, refer to the** Math Skill Handbook.

Fun Fact

A placer is a deposit formed by the sorting action of moving water. Denser and often valuable minerals may be concentrated in this way in streams, lakes, or oceans. South African diamond and Alaskan gold placers are mined.

③ Assess

Reteach
Have students place a small pile of a sand and gravel mixture in one end of a large plastic or metal tray. Have them move the pile to the other end of the tray by modeling agents of erosion. L2 ELL IS **Kinesthetic**

Challenge
Explain how rocks can be abraded by a variety of erosional agents. Flowing water and blowing wind carry sediments that abrade rock. Ice and the sediments it contains also abrade rocks.

✓Assessment

Process Have students predict what will happen to a stream if its bed is uplifted. A stream will respond to the uplift by cutting downward toward lower elevations. This results in increased erosion of the stream channel. Use **PASC,** p. 89.

Answers to Section Assessment

1. Gravity, ice, wind, water; gravity is fastest, ice is often slowest.
2. Deflation: wind blows away tiny sediments; abrasion: fine sediments scratch and pit rocks they hit.
3. Ice wedging plucks out rock; valley glacier removes rock, leaving bowl.

4. deposit: when energy isn't great enough to suspend sediments, for example, in stream bed where current is not strong and at mouth of stream where it enters lake or ocean; erode: when fast-moving water suspends sediments and carries them away

5. If the land is uplifted, there is increased erosion of the stream bed.
6. If more sediment is supplied to a river than can be transported, the river valley will fill.

7. 2 mm/yr × 2,000 yr = 4,000 mm, 4,000 mm ÷ 1,000 mm/m = 4 m; 7 mm/yr × 2,000 yr = 14,000 mm, 14,000 mm ÷ 1,000 mm/m = 14 m

Activity

Recognize the Problem

Purpose

Students measure to what extent vegetation reduces soil erosion.

L2 COOP LEARN **Visual-Spatial**

Process Skills

forming a hypothesis, designing an experiment to test a hypothesis, identifying and manipulating variables, measuring in SI, using numbers, drawing conclusions

Time Required

45 minutes to plan the activity, and 45 minutes to carry out and analyze the activity

Safety Precautions

Caution students to wear goggles and use hot pads when boiling water.

Form a Hypothesis

Possible Hypothesis

Students will likely predict that the tray with sod will have much less erosion.

Test Your Hypothesis

Possible Procedures

Cover the bottoms of trays with soil. Cover soil in one tray with sod. Place identical blocks of wood under one end of each tray. Determine the mass of the empty beakers. Fill each pail with 1,000 mL of water. Pour the water into the trays at the same rate. Wait several minutes, and pour the muddy water from each tray into a beaker. Evaporate the water in the beakers. Measure the masses of the beakers. Compute the mass of eroded soil. Calculate percentage of soil loss.

Activity *Design Your Own Experiment*

Measuring Soil Erosion

During urban highway construction, surface mining, forest harvesting, or agricultural cultivation, surface vegetation can be removed from soil. These practices expose soil to water and wind. Does vegetation significantly reduce soil erosion?

Recognize the Problem

How much does vegetation reduce soil erosion?

Form a Hypothesis

Based on what you've read and observed, hypothesize about how much less soil will be eroded from a sodded field than from bare soil.

Safety Precautions

Wash your hands thoroughly when you are through working with soils.

Possible Materials

blocks of wood   pails (2)
books   1,000 mL beaker
paint trays (2)   triple-beam balance
soil   calculator
grass sod   watch
water
Alternate materials

Goals

- **Design** an experiment to measure soil loss from grass-covered soil and from soil without grass cover.
- **Calculate** the percent of soil loss with and without grass cover.

Curriculum Connection

History In the 1930s, drought plus poor farming practices led to severe wind erosion in the Great Plains of the United States. This area became known as the Dust Bowl. Have students research farming practices used today to prevent soil erosion. L2 **Linguistic**

Resource Manager

Chapter Resources Booklet
    Activity Worksheet, pp. 7–8
Lab Management and Safety, p. 58

Test Your Hypothesis

Plan

1. As a group, agree upon the hypothesis and decide how you will test it. Identify which results will falsify or confirm the hypothesis.

2. **List** the steps you will need to take to test your hypothesis. Describe exactly what you will do in each step.

3. **Prepare** a data table in your Science Journal to record your observations.

4. Read over the entire experiment to make sure all steps are in logical order, and that you have all necessary materials.

5. **Identify** all constants and variables and the control of the experiment. A control is a standard for comparing the results of an experiment. One possible control for this experiment

would be the results of the treatment for the uncovered soil sample.

Do

1. Make sure your teacher approves your plan before you start.

2. Carry out the experiment step by step as planned.

3. While doing the experiment, record your observations and complete the data table in your Science Journal.

Vegetation and Erosion			
	(A) Mass of Soil at Start	(B) Mass of Eroded Soil	% of Soil Loss (B/A) × 100
Covered Soil Sample		Answers	
Uncovered Soil Sample		will vary.	

Analyze Your Data

1. **Compare** the percent of soil loss from each soil sample.

2. **Compare** your results with those of other groups.

3. What was your control in this experiment? Why?

4. Which were the variables you kept constant? Which did you vary?

Draw Conclusions

1. Did the results support your hypothesis? Explain.

2. **Infer** what effect other types of plants would have in reducing soil erosion. Do you think that grass is better or worse than most other plants at reducing erosion?

Communicating Your Data

Write a letter to the editor of a newspaper. In your letter, **summarize** what you learned in your experiment about the effect of plant cover on soil erosion.

ACTIVITY 483

Communicating Your Data

Have students use a word processing program on the computer to write their business letters to editors.

Content Background

Acid rain is not a new occurrence. It was first recognized and named in 1872 by Robert Angus Smith in Scotland. Rain is naturally acidic, forming a mild solution of carbonic acid from its contact with CO_2 in the atmosphere. Neutral solutions have a pH of 7. A lower number indicates a solution is acidic, and a higher number indicates it is alkaline. Rain is normally in the pH range of 5 to 6, but some acid rains are as low as 3.

When water mixes with sulfur or nitrogen oxides in the air, it forms acids of various kinds, largely sulfuric and nitric acid. The effects of acidity on building materials such as granite are less because granite is crystalline and less reactive. Softer stones such as marble and sandstone contain high proportions of alkaline substances. These substances react with the acid to form other compounds and cause the deterioration of the stone. Most large stone structures have been built with these softer stones and are at some risk from acid rain.

The acid rain caused by pollution usually falls away from its source, often crossing political borders. In other words, acid rain that falls in one country may have its origins in another country. The result is a problem of international proportions.

TIME SCIENCE AND HISTORY

SCIENCE CAN CHANGE THE COURSE OF HISTORY!

Acid rain is destroying some of the world's most famous monuments

CRUMBLING

The Taj Mahal in India, the Acropolis in Greece, and the Colosseum in Italy, have stood for centuries. They've survived wars, souvenir-hunters, and natural weathering from wind and rain. But now, something far worse threatens their existence— acid rain. Over the last few decades, this form of pollution has eaten away at some of history's greatest monuments.

Acid rain leads to health and environmental risks. It also harms human-made structures.

Most of these structures are made of sandstone, limestone, and marble. Acid rain causes the calcium in these stones to form calcium sulfate, or gypsum. Gypsum's powdery little blotches are sometimes called "marble cancer." When it rains, the gypsum washes away, along with some of the surface of the monument. In many cases, acidic soot falls into the cracks of monuments. When rainwater seeps into the cracks, acidic water is formed, which further damages the structure.

484

Acid rain has not been kind to this Mayan figure.

Parts of India's Taj Mahal are turning yellow from pollutants.

Resources for Teachers and Students

US EPA Clean Air Markets Division
1200 Pennsylvania Avenue, NW
Mail Code 6204N, Washington, DC 20460

National Park Service Air Resources Division
1849 C Street NW
Washington, DC 20240
Phone: (202) 208-6843

U.S. Department of the Interior
U.S. Geological Survey
12201 Sunrise Valley Drive,
Reston, VA 20192

An Introduction to Global Environmental Issues (2nd Ed.) by K. T. Pickering & L. A. Owen.
London&NY. Routledge (1997)

Greece's Parthenon is slowly being eaten away by acid rain.

MONUMENTS

In Agra, India, the smooth, white marble mausoleum called the Taj Mahal has stood since the seventeenth century. But acid rain is making the surface of the building yellow and flaky. The pollution is caused by hundreds of factories surrounding Agra that emit damaging chemicals.

What moisture, molds, and the roots of vegetation couldn't do in 1,500 years, acid rain is doing in decades. It is destroying the Mayan ruins of Mexico. Pollution is causing statues to crumble and paintings on walls to flake off. The culprits are oil burning refineries and exhaust from tour buses.

Acid rain is a huge problem affecting national monuments and treasures in just about every urban location in the world.

These include the Capitol building in Washington, D.C., churches in Germany, and stained-glass windows in Sweden. Because of pollution, many corroding statues displayed outdoors have been brought inside museums. In London, acid rain has forced workers to repair and replace so much of Westminster Abbey that the structure is becoming a mere copy of the original.

Throughout the world, acid rain has weathered many structures more in the last 20 years than in the 2,000 years before. This is one reason some steps have been taken in Europe and the United States to reduce emissions from the burning of fossil fuels. If these laws don't work, many irreplaceable art treasures may be gone forever.

CONNECTIONS Identify Which monuments and buildings represent the United States? Brainstorm a list with your class. Then choose a monument and, using your school's media center or the Glencoe Science Web site, learn more about it. Is acid rain affecting it in any way?

Online
For more information, visit science.glencoe.com

CONNECTIONS Pick a reasonable number of monuments in different communities throughout the United States. Assign each group a different monument to investigate how it might be affected by acid rain. Suggest that students also try to obtain information from sources in those communities regarding the actual state of those structures and how the community is dealing with the problem, if at all.

Online
Internet Addresses

_____

_____

_____

Explore the Glencoe Science Web site at **science.glencoe.com** to find out more about topics in this feature.

Discussion

Do we need historical monuments in order to learn about the past they represent? Explain. Possible answers: Some students may suggest that pictures in textbooks might be sufficient for learning about a particular monument or the culture and events it represents. Others may suggest that without the monument, there will be less factual data to help us understand the past.

Historical Significance

As old or ancient structures deteriorate and disappear, the past tends to disappear with them. Students should understand that ancient buildings like the Parthenon and the Coliseum are tangible links to history that lead people to consider the events that occurred in and around them. The carvings on old temples and the images in ancient statues are indicators of the world view of their creators that are much more immediate and lively than textbook descriptions of them. The more these images deteriorate, the more information is lost. Also, explain to students that archaeologists, anthropologists, and other scientists analyze inanimate objects, including historic structures, in order to gain factual knowledge about them and the cultures that built them.

Chapter 16 Study Guide

Reviewing Main Ideas

Preview

Students can answer the questions in their Science Journals. Discuss the answers as you go through the chapter. **LS Linguistic**

Review

Students can write their answers, then compare them with those of other students. **LS Interpersonal**

Reteach

Students can look at the illustrations and describe details that support the main ideas of the chapter. **LS Visual-Spatial**

Answers to Chapter Review

SECTION 1

3. oxidation of iron-bearing minerals
4. No, gravity would cause rock particles and any soil that forms to erode.

SECTION 2

1. The rocks have striations made by glaciers.
2. wind

Reviewing Main Ideas

Section 1 Weathering and Soil Formation

1. Weathering includes processes that break down rock.

2. During mechanical weathering, physical processes break rock into smaller pieces.

3. During chemical weathering, the chemical composition of rocks is changed. *What causes the reddish color of these rocks?*

4. Soil evolves over time from weathered rock. Parent rock, topography, climate, and organisms affect soil formation. *Do you think a thick soil layer could form on this surface? Why or why not?*

Section 2 Erosion of Earth's Surface

1. Erosion is the wearing away and removal of rock. *In the photo below, what evidence do you see that erosion has occurred?*

2. Agents of erosion include gravity, ice, wind, and water. *Which agent of erosion is responsible for this unusual structure?*

3. All agents of erosion move rock and sediment. When energy of motion decreases, sediment is deposited.

4. Erosion and deposition determine the shape of the land.

FOLDABLES
Reading & Study Skills

After You Read

Identify common characteristics of weathering and erosion and write them on the middle section of your Foldable.

FOLDABLES
Reading & Study Skills

After You Read

After students have read the chapter and completed the Foldable described in Before You Read, have them do the activity on the student page.

Dinah Zike

Visualizing Main Ideas

Fill in the following table, which compares erosion and deposition by different agents.

Erosion and Deposition		
Erosional Agent	**Evidence of Erosion**	**Evidence of Deposition**
Gravity	curved slump scars, leaning fence posts, steep cliffs	material piled at bottom of slopes
Ice	cirques, striations, U-shaped valleys	till, outwash
Wind	desert pavement pitted rocks	sand dunes, loess
Surface Water	rills, gullies, stream valleys	bars, deltas

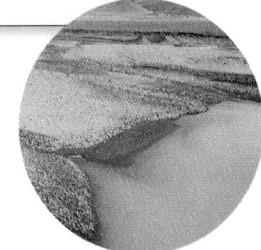

Vocabulary Review

Vocabulary Words

a. abrasion
b. chemical weathering
c. creep
d. deflation
e. erosion
f. mass movement
g. mechanical weathering
h. runoff
i. slump
j. soil
k. topography
l. weathering

Study Tip

Read the chapters before you go over them in class. Being familiar with the material before your teacher explains it gives you a better understanding and provides you with a good opportunity to ask questions.

Using Vocabulary

Use each of the following pairs of terms in a sentence.

1. chemical weathering, mechanical weathering
2. erosion, weathering
3. deflation, runoff
4. mass movement, weathering
5. soil, abrasion
6. soil, erosion
7. mass movement, mechanical weathering
8. weathering, chemical weathering
9. creep, slump
10. topography, runoff

Visualizing Main Ideas

See student page.

Vocabulary Review

Using Vocabulary

1. Chemical weathering changes the chemical composition of a rock; mechanical weathering breaks rocks into small pieces without changing them chemically.
2. Weathering is the process that breaks rocks into small pieces; erosion is the moving of those pieces from one place to another.
3. Deflation is erosion by wind; runoff is the flowing of water across the surface.
4. Weathering is the process that breaks rocks into small pieces; mass movement is the movement of those pieces down a slope because of gravity.
5. Soil is a mixture of weathered rock, organic matter, water, and air; abrasion occurs as soil and sediment carried by the wind wears away rock.
6. Possible answer: Plants can slow the erosion of soil.
7. Possible answer: The particles produced by mechanical weathering are moved down a slope by mass movement.
8. Weathering alters rock mechanically or chemically; chemical weathering breaks down rock by changing its composition.
9. Creep is the slow movement of sediments downhill; slump is the downhill movement of a large mass of sediments or rock.
10. Possible answer: the type of runoff depends partly on the topography of the surrounding land.

IDENTIFYING ▷ **Misconceptions**

Assess

Use the assessment as follow-up to page 464F after students have completed the chapter.

Materials parent rock samples, soil samples of various colors that are related to the parent rocks

Procedure Have students develop a concept map showing how a particular color of soil could be related to a particular parent rock, such as: red sandy soil → red sandstone.

Expected Outcome Students will realize that soil color is partly related to the parent rock color.

Reinforcement Show students color photographs of rock outcrops from a variety of areas from around the world. Have the students infer the soil color that they might expect to see on a visit to that location.

Checking Concepts (Teacher Answers)

1. C
2. D
3. B
4. A
5. A
6. B
7. C
8. A
9. D
10. A

Thinking Critically (Teacher Answers)

11. Water makes sediments heavier. It also lifts up overlying rock and sediment. This makes it easier for sediments to overcome the forces that hold the slope in place.
12. Soil evolution is faster in warm, moist climates where materials break down quickly.
13. by not over steepening slopes or by planting vegetation on slopes
14. No; the climate is cold and dry and thus not conducive to chemical weathering.
15. Some kinds of rocks dissolve when exposed to natural acids. Others do not.

Checking Concepts

Choose the word or phrase that best answers the question.

1. Which of the following agents of erosion forms U-shaped valleys?
   A) gravity
   C) ice
   B) surface water
   D) wind

2. In which of these places is chemical weathering most rapid?
   A) deserts
   C) polar regions
   B) mountains
   D) tropical regions

3. Which of the following forms when carbon dioxide combines with water?
   A) calcium carbonate
   C) tannic acid
   B) carbonic acid
   D) dripstone

4. Which process causes rocks to weather to a reddish color?
   A) oxidation
   C) carbon dioxide
   B) deflation
   D) frost action

5. Which type of mass movement occurs when sediments slowly move downhill because of freezing and thawing?
   A) creep
   C) slump
   B) rock slide
   D) mudflow

6. Which of the following helps form cirques and U-shaped valleys?
   A) rill erosion
   C) deflation
   B) ice wedging
   D) till

7. What is windblown, fine sediment called?
   A) till
   C) loess
   B) outwash
   D) delta

8. Which of the following refers to water that flows over Earth's surface?
   A) runoff
   B) slump
   C) chemical weathering
   D) till

9. Which of the following is an example of chemical weathering?
   A) Plant roots grow in cracks in rock and break the rock apart.
   B) Freezing and thawing of water widens cracks in rocks.
   C) Wind blows sand into rock, scratching the rock.
   D) Oxygen causes iron-bearing minerals in rock to break down.

10. Which one of the following erosional agents creates desert pavement?
    A) wind
    C) water
    B) gravity
    D) ice

Thinking Critically

11. Explain why mass movement is more common after a heavy rainfall.

12. How does climate affect the development of soils?

13. How could some mass movement be prevented?

14. Would chemical weathering be rapid in Antarctica?

15. Why do caves form only in certain types of rock?

Developing Skills

16. **Recognizing Cause and Effect** Explain how water creates stream valleys.

17. **Forming Hypotheses** Form hypotheses about how deeply water could erode and about how deeply glaciers could erode.

Chapter ✔Assessment Planner

Portfolio Encourage students to place in their portfolios one or two items of what they consider to be their best work. Examples include:
- Activity, p. 474
- Science Journal, p. 476

Performance Additional performance assessments, Performance Task Assessment Lists, and rubrics for evaluating these activities can be found in Glencoe's **Performance Assessment in the Science Classroom.**

18. Recognizing Cause and Effect Explain how valley glaciers create U-shaped valleys.

19. Classifying Classify the following by the agent that deposits each: sand dune, delta, till, and loess.

20. Concept Mapping Complete the concept map showing the different types of mass movements.

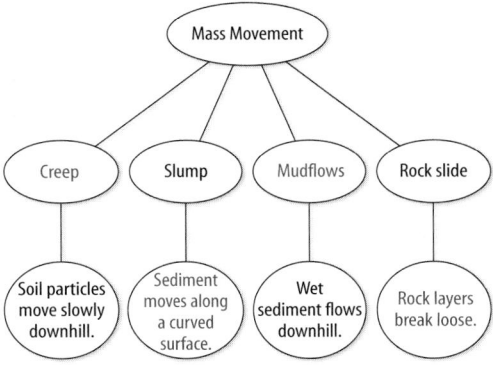

Performance Assessment

21. Poster Use photographs from old magazines to make a poster that illustrates different kinds of weathering and erosion. Display your poster in your classroom.

22. Model Use polystyrene, cardboard and clay to make a model of a glacier. Include a river of meltwater leading away from the glacier. Use markers to label the areas of erosion and deposition. Show and label areas where till and outwash sediments could be found. Display your model in your classroom.

TECHNOLOGY

Go to the Glencoe Science Web site at **science.glencoe.com** or use the **Glencoe Science CD-ROM** for additional chapter assessment.

THE PRINCETON REVIEW — Test Practice

Geologists measured the amount of cumulative precipitation and the amount of land movement along highway 50 in California to see if there was a relationship between them.

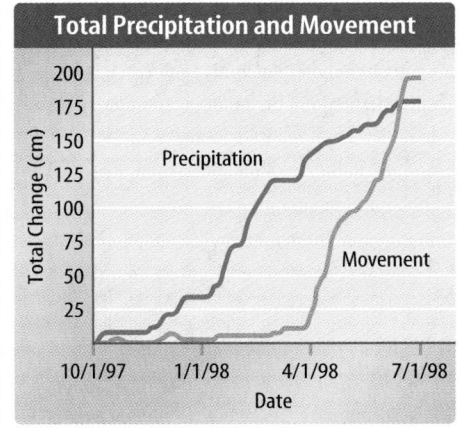

Study the graph and answer the following questions.

1. According to this information, at which precipitation level did soil movement begin?

A) about 125 cm   **C)** about 75 cm
B) about 50 cm   **D)** about 100 cm

2. Based on this information, which of the following is a reasonable conclusion to make about the relationship between precipitation and movement?

F) As precipitation decreases, movement increases.
G) As movement decreases, precipitation increases.
H) There is almost no movement until precipitation reaches a certain level.
J) There is no relationship.

THE PRINCETON REVIEW — Test Practice

The Test-Taking Tip was written by The Princeton Review, the nation's leader in test preparation.

1. A
2. H

Developing Skills

16. Water erodes the sides and bottom of its channel.
17. Water can erode to sea level. Glaciers can erode deeper.
18. Along the sides of the glacier, ice plucking breaks rocks. When the glacier moves, it erodes these particles, leaving steep cliffs. The bottom of the valley is abraded by the glacier. These actions combine to form a U-shaped valley.
19. sand dune—wind; delta—water; till—glacier; loess—wind
20. See student page.

Performance Assessment

21. Students should label the agent(s) of weathering or erosion for every photograph they include on their posters. Use **Performance Assessment in the Science Classroom**, p. 145.
22. Check students' work. Use **Performance Assessment in the Science Classroom**, p. 123.

Assessment Resources

 Reproducible Masters

Chapter Resources Booklet
  Chapter Review, pp. 35–36
  Chapter Tests, pp. 37–40
  Assessment Transparency Activity, p. 47

Glencoe Science Web site
  Interactive Tutor
  Chapter Quizzes

Glencoe Technology
  Assessment Transparency
  Interactive CD-ROM Chapter Quizzes
  ExamView Pro Test Bank
  Vocabulary PuzzleMaker Software
  MindJogger Videoquiz

Section/Objectives	Standards		Activities/Features
Chapter Opener	**National**	**State/Local**	**Explore Activity:** Estimate grains of rice, p. 491 **Before You Read,** p. 491
	See p. 7T for a Key to Standards.		
Section 1 Earth's Place in Space 🕐 2 sessions 📦 1 block 1. **Explain** why Earth has seasons. 2. **Describe** the motions that cause Moon phases.	National Content Standards: UCP2, A1, B2, D3		**Science Online,** p. 493 **MiniLAB:** Observing Distance and Size, p. 495 **Activity:** Moon Phases, p. 497
Section 2 The Solar System 🕐 2 sessions 📦 1 block 1. **Explain** how to measure distance in the solar system. 2. **List** the various objects in the solar system. 3. **Describe** important characteristics of each planet.	National Content Standards: UCP1, D3		**Science Online,** p. 499 **Life Science Integration,** p. 500 **Problem-Solving Activity:** How can you model distances in the solar system?, p. 503
Section 3 Stars and Galaxies 🕐 3 sessions 📦 1.5 blocks 1. **Explain** how a star is born. 2. **Describe** the galaxies that make up the universe. 3. **Explain** how to measure distances in space beyond Earth's solar system.	National Content Standards: UCP4, A1, D3, E1, G1		**MiniLAB:** Modeling Constellations, p. 507 **Science Online,** p. 508 **Visualizing Galaxies,** p. 510 **Physics Integration,** p. 512 **Activity:** Space Colony, pp. 514–515 **Science and Language Arts:** The Sun and the Moon, pp. 516–517

Teacher's Corner

PRODUCTS AVAILABLE FROM GLENCOE
To order call 1-800-334-7344:
CD-ROMs: *NGS PictureShow: Solar System; NGS PictureShow: Stars and Galaxies*
Transparency Set: *NGS PicturePack: Solar System*

Videodiscs: *STV: Earth, Moon, and Stars; STV: Solar System*
PRODUCTS AVAILABLE FROM NATIONAL GEOGRAPHIC SOCIETY
To order call 1-800-368-2728:

Books: *Discover Mars; Mars: Uncovering the Secrets of the Red Planet; National Geographic Satellite Atlas of the World*
Poster: *Solar System/Celestial Family*
Video: *Asteroids: Deadly Impact*

Activity Materials	Reproducible Resources	Section Assessment	Technology
Explore Activity: white crayon or chalk, metric ruler, black construction paper, uncooked rice	**Chapter Resources Booklet** Foldables Worksheet, p. 17 Directed Reading Overview, p. 19 Note-taking Worksheets, pp. 33–35	GLENCOE'S ASSESSMENT ADVANTAGE	
MiniLAB: basketball, table, penny **Activity:** drawing paper, softball, flashlight, scissors	**Chapter Resources Booklet** Transparency Activity, p. 44 MiniLAB, p. 3 Enrichment, p. 30 Reinforcement, p. 27 Directed Reading, p. 20 Activity Worksheet, pp. 5–6 Lab Activity, pp. 9–11 Transparency Activity, pp. 47–48 **Science Inquiry Labs,** p. 41	Portfolio Activity, p. 494 Performance MiniLAB, p. 495 Skill Builder Activities, p. 496 Content Section Assessment, p. 496	Section Focus Transparency Teaching Transparency Interactive CD-ROM Guided Reading Audio Program
Need materials? Contact Science Kit at 1-800-828-7777 or www.sciencekit.com on the Internet.	**Chapter Resources Booklet** Transparency Activity, p. 45 Enrichment, p. 31 Reinforcement, p. 28 Directed Reading, p. 21 Lab Activity, pp. 13–16 **Science Inquiry Labs,** p. 39 **Mathematics Skill Activities,** p. 39 **Reading and Writing Skill Activities,** p. 11	Portfolio Life Science Integration, p. 500 Performance Problem-Solving Activity, p. 503 Skill Builder Activities, p. 505 Content Section Assessment, p. 505	Section Focus Transparency Interactive CD-ROM Guided Reading Audio Program
MiniLAB: black construction paper, scissors, cardboard cylinder (oatmeal box), tape, pencil, flashlight **Activity:** drawing paper, markers, books about the planets	**Chapter Resources Booklet** Transparency Activity, p. 46 MiniLAB, p. 4 Enrichment, p. 32 Reinforcement, p. 29 Directed Reading, pp. 21, 22 Activity Worksheet, pp. 7–8 **Home and Community Involvement,** p. 31 **Lab Management and Safety,** p. 73	Portfolio Physics Integration, p. 512 Performance MiniLAB, p. 507 Skill Builder Activities, p. 513 Content Section Assessment, p. 513	Section Focus Transparency Interactive CD-ROM Guided Reading Audio Program

End of Chapter Assessment

GLENCOE'S ASSESSMENT ADVANTAGE

Blackline Masters	Technology	Professional Series
Chapter Resources Booklet Chapter Review, pp. 37–38 Chapter Tests, pp. 39–42 **Standardized Test Practice by The Princeton Review,** pp. 71–74	MindJogger Videoquiz Interactive CD-ROM Vocabulary PuzzleMakers ExamView Pro Test Bank Interactive Lesson Planner Interactive Teacher Edition	Performance Assessment in the Science Classroom (PASC)

Transparencies

Section Focus

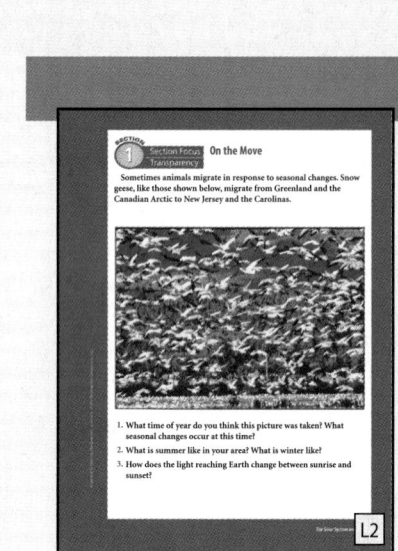

On the Move

Sometimes animals migrate in response to seasonal changes. Snow geese, like those shown below, migrate from Greenland and the Canadian Arctic to New Jersey and the Carolinas.

1. What time of year do you think this picture was taken? What seasonal changes occur at this time?
2. What is summer like in your area? What is winter like?
3. How does the light reaching Earth change between sunrise and sunset?

L2

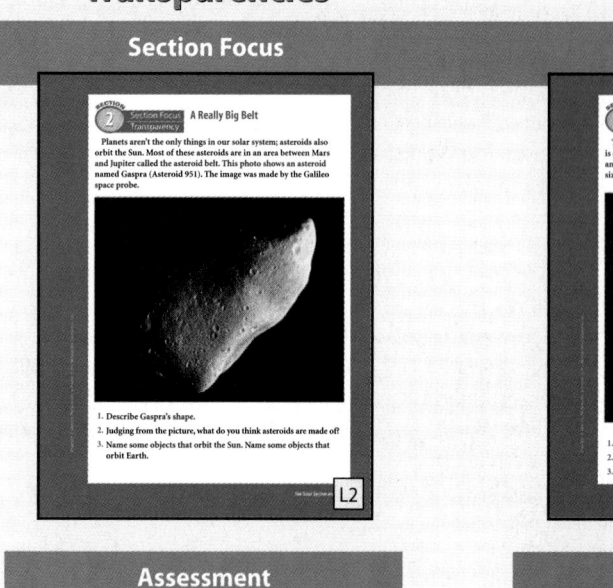

A Really Big Belt

Planets aren't the only things in our solar system; asteroids also orbit the Sun. Most of these asteroids are in an area between Mars and Jupiter called the asteroid belt. This photo shows an asteroid named Gaspra (Asteroid 951). The image was made by the Galileo space probe.

1. Describe Gaspra's shape.
2. Judging from the picture, what do you think asteroids are made of?
3. Name some objects that orbit the Sun. Name some objects that orbit Earth.

L2

Fiery Sun

The star nearest Earth is our very own Sun. Scientists think the Sun is about 4.6 billion years old and that it will continue to shine for another five billion years or so. As far as stars go, the Sun is medium-sized.

1. What would our Sun look like from a distant galaxy?
2. How do people group stars in the night sky?
3. Why do some stars appear brighter than others?

L2

This is a representation of key blackline masters available in the Teacher Classroom Resources. See Resource Manager boxes within the chapter for additional information.

Key to Teaching Strategies

The following designations will help you decide which activities are appropriate for your students.

L1 Level 1 activities should be appropriate for students with learning difficulties.

L2 Level 2 activities should be within the ability range of all students.

L3 Level 3 activities are designed for above-average students.

ELL ELL activities should be within the ability range of English Language Learners.

COOP LEARN Cooperative Learning activities are designed for small group work.

LS Multiple Learning Styles logos, as described on page 22T, are used throughout to indicate strategies that address different learning styles.

P These strategies represent student products that can be placed into a best-work portfolio.

Assessment

The Solar System and Beyond

Directions: Carefully review the table and answer the following question.

Inner Planets

Planet	Diameter (km)	Distance from Sun (AU)	Temperature (°C)
Mercury	4,875	0.39	−170–450
Venus	12,104	0.72	470
Earth	12,756	1.00	−50–55
Mars	6,794	1.52	−170–27

1. According to the table, the inner planet with the largest diameter is ___.
   A Mercury
   B Venus
   C Earth
   D Mars
2. According to this information, which planet is closest to the Sun?
   F Mercury
   G Venus
   H Earth
   J Mars
3. According to the table, a space probe sitting on an inner planet with a temperature of 470°C is probably on ___.
   A Mercury
   B Venus
   C Earth
   D Mars

L2

Teaching

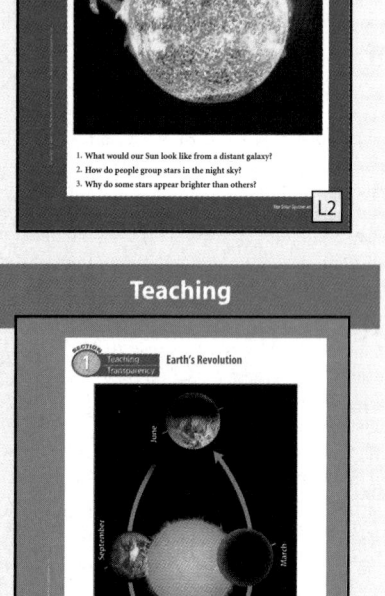

Earth's Revolution

L2

Hands-on Activities

Activity Worksheets

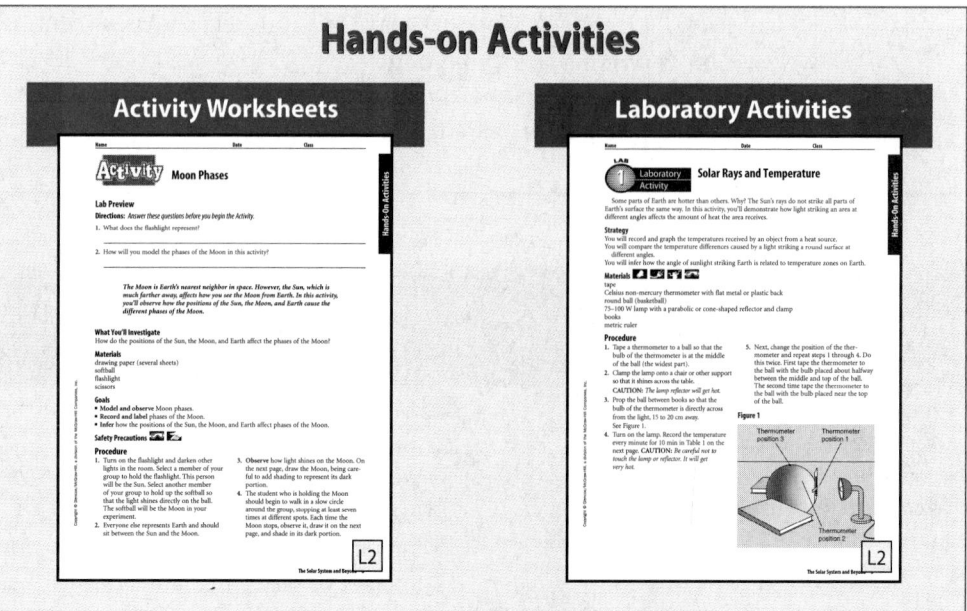

Activity Moon Phases

Lab Preview

Directions: Answer these questions before you begin the Activity.

1. What does the flashlight represent?

2. How will you model the phases of the Moon in this activity?

The Moon is Earth's nearest neighbor in space. However, the Sun, which is much farther away, affects how you see the Moon from Earth. In this activity, you'll observe how the positions of the Sun, the Moon, and Earth cause the different phases of the Moon.

What You'll Investigate
How do the positions of the Sun, the Moon, and Earth affect the phases of the Moon?

Materials
drawing paper (several sheets)
softball
flashlight
scissors

Goals
• **Model and observe** Moon phases.
• **Record and label** phases of the Moon.
• **Infer** how the positions of the Sun, the Moon, and Earth affect phases of the Moon.

Safety Precautions

Procedure
1. Turn on the flashlight and darken other lights in the room. Select a number of your group to hold the flashlight. This person will be the Sun. Select another member of your group to hold up the softball so that the light shines directly on the ball. The softball will be the Moon in your experiment.
2. Everyone else represents Earth and should sit between the Sun and the Moon.
3. Observe how light shines on the Moon. On the next page, draw the Moon, being careful to add shading to represent its dark portion.
4. The student who is holding the Moon should begin to walk in a slow circle around the group, stopping at least seven times at different spots. Each time the Moon stops, observe it, draw it on the next page, and record its dark portion.

L2

Laboratory Activities

Laboratory Activity Solar Rays and Temperature

Some parts of Earth are hotter than others. Why? The Sun's rays do not strike all parts of Earth's surface the same way. In this activity, you'll demonstrate how light striking an area at different angles affects the amount of heat the area receives.

Strategy
You will record and graph the temperatures received by an object from a heat source.
You will compare the temperature differences caused by a light striking a round surface at different angles.
You will infer how the angle of sunlight striking Earth is related to temperature zones on Earth.

Materials
tape
Celsius non-mercury thermometer with flat metal or plastic back
round ball (basketball)
75–100 W lamp with a parabolic or cone-shaped reflector and clamp
books
metric ruler

Procedure
1. Tape a thermometer to a ball so that the bulb of the thermometer is at the middle of the ball (the widest part).
2. Clamp the lamp onto a chair or other support so that it shines across the table.
3. Prop the ball between books so that the bulb of the thermometer is directly across from the light, 15 to 20 cm away. See Figure 1.
4. Turn on the lamp. Record the temperature every minute for 10 min in Table 1 on the next page. CAUTION: Be careful not to touch the lamp or reflector. It will get very hot.
5. Next, change the position of the thermometer and repeat steps 1 through 4. Do this twice. First tape the thermometer to the ball with the bulb placed about halfway between the middle and top of the ball. The second time tape the thermometer to the ball with the bulb placed near the top of the ball.

Figure 1

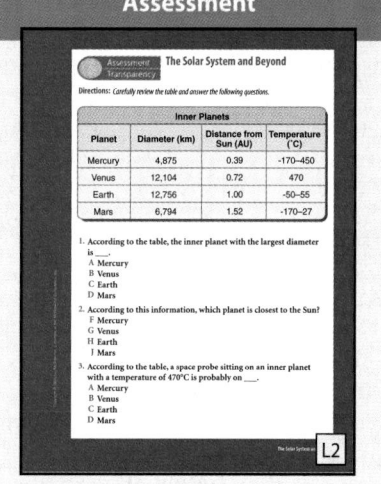

L2

RESOURCE MANAGER

Meeting Different Ability Levels

Content Outline
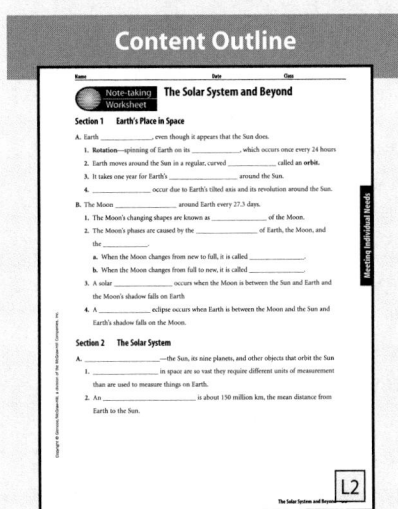

Reinforcement
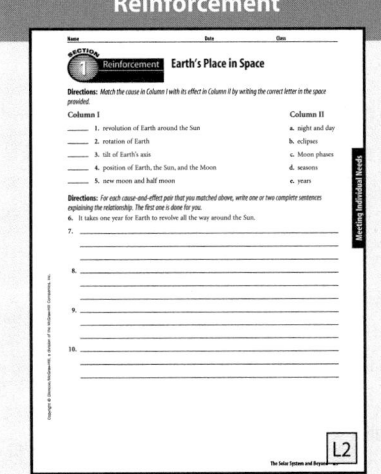

Directed Reading

Assessment

Chapter Tests
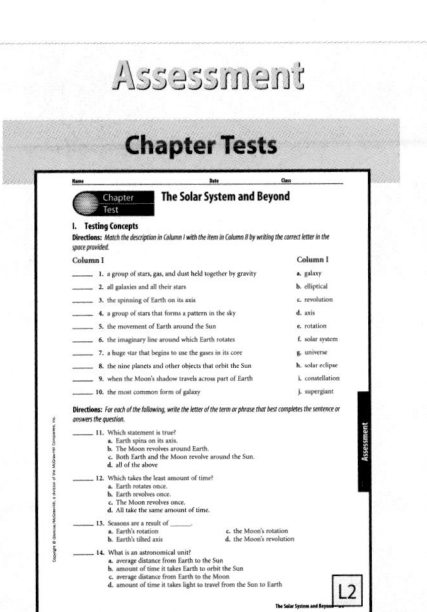

Enrichment
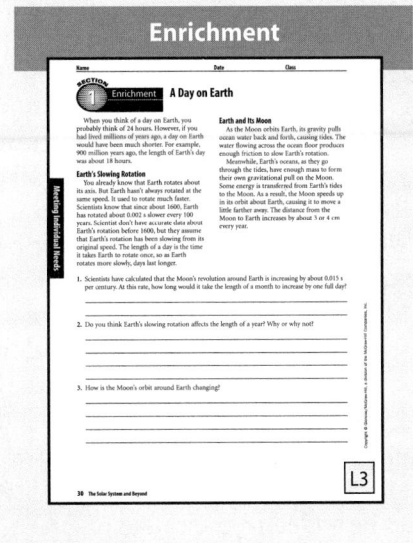

Spanish Directed Reading
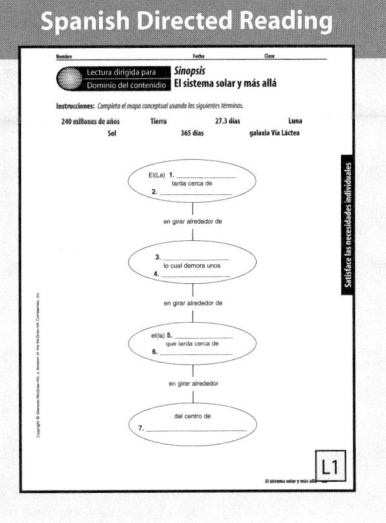

Test Practice Workbook

Chapter Review

Science Content Background

SECTION 1 — Earth's Place in Space

Earth's Rotation and Revolution

Like most of the planets in our solar system, Earth rotates from west to east about an imaginary axis that runs through the geographic north and south poles. This rotation results in the apparent daily motion of the Sun, the stars, and the Moon across the sky. One complete rotation, measured with respect to the position of the Sun, occurs every 24 hours.

> ## Student Misconception
>
> Planets and stars are about the same distance away from Earth.
>
> **Refer to the facing page for teaching strategies to address this misconception. Refer to pages 498–505 for content related to this topic.**

Earth's Revolution

Earth revolves around the Sun once in approximately 365.26 days. Because the calendar year cannot contain a fraction of a day, an extra day—February 29th—must be added to the calendar every fourth year (leap year). Earth's orbit around the Sun is elliptical. This also is true for all the other planets in our solar system. Earth moves faster in its orbit when it is close to the Sun and slower in its orbit when it is farther away from the Sun.

SECTION 2 — The Solar System

Inner Planets

The inner planets—Mercury, Venus, Earth, and Mars—are small and rocky with relatively high average densities. Venus has a thick atmosphere shrouded in clouds of sulfuric acid. Mars is a cold, dry planet with a thin atmosphere consisting mostly of carbon dioxide. The surface of Mars has many fascinating features, including ancient water-cut channels and the largest volcanoes in our solar system. Mars is probably lifeless now, but it may have supported bacteria billions of years ago.

The Outer Planets

The Jovian planets—Jupiter, Saturn, Uranus, and Neptune—are the largest planets. They have thick, gaseous atmospheres consisting mostly of hydrogen with small amounts of helium, methane, ammonia, and water. Clouds composed of ice crystals of ammonia, methane, or other compounds are blown over the planets' surfaces by strong winds. The cores of Jupiter and Saturn are surrounded by a thick layer of liquid hydrogen.

NASA/Tom Stack & Associates

SECTION 3 — Stars and Galaxies

The Lives of Stars

Most stars do not form alone, but as parts of groups of stars known as clusters. Often as these clusters break up, two or more stars will orbit a common center of mass. In these binary stars, when one star expands as it evolves into a giant or supergiant, its companion star can pull off mass from the giant star, thus changing the life cycles of both stars.

SCIENCE Online

For additional content background on this topic, go to the Glencoe Science Web site at **science.glencoe.com.**

IDENTIFYING Misconceptions

Find Out What Students Think

Students may think that . . .

- **Planets and stars are about the same distance away from Earth.**

Students often think that, since planets and stars are both objects in the sky, they are about the same distance from Earth. This idea is "confirmed" when they observe the bright objects in the night sky.

Discussion

Ask the class to brainstorm a list of objects they have observed in the night sky. Lists might include stars, the Moon, planets, airplanes, falling "stars," and satellites.

- Discuss how students can determine which of the objects they observe are manufactured, and which are natural objects. Manufactured objects (airplanes and satellites) are lighted objects that move with some speed across the sky. Falling "stars" glow brightly, but only for a moment or two. They do not follow an extended path across the sky. Other objects appear to move slowly across the sky throughout the night.

- Then ask students how they can tell planets from stars as they observe the night sky. Because planets are so much closer to Earth than the stars, they often don't "twinkle" as stars do.

Promote Understanding

Activity

Remind students that, even though the planets are very far away, they are much closer than any of the stars we see in the night sky. Use this activity to reinforce the distances to the planets in the solar system and to the nearest stars, other than our Sun.

- Give each group of students a large roll of toilet paper or adding machine tape, a meterstick, and a marker.

- Direct the class to the data shown in the table. Have students make a model of the solar system on their paper rolls, using these distances to the planets from the Sun.

- When students have completed their models, provide them with this data. Explain that these distances use the same scale as students used to build their solar system. Alpha Centauri: 145.1 km; Sirius: 293.6 km; Deneb: 47,645.6 km

- Discuss with students where these stars would be on the solar system model. Underscore that these, the closest stars other than our Sun, are far outside the solar system. Thus, even though they look to be the same distance from Earth when viewed in the night sky, they are actually very far apart.

Planet	Distance	Planet	Distance
Mercury	0.208 m	Saturn	5.126 m
Venus	0.388 m	Uranus	10.31 m
Earth	0.537 m	Neptune	16.164 m
Mars	0.818 m	Pluto	21.24 m
Jupiter	2.795 m		

Assess

After completing the chapter, see *Identifying Misconceptions* in the Study Guide.

The Solar System and Beyond

Chapter Vocabulary

What do you think?

Science Journal This is a time exposure photograph of the circumpolar stars, that is, the stars in the part of the sky around Polaris, the north star. You can see by the photograph that as Earth spins on its axis, the stars appear to move in a circle around Polaris.

The Solar System and Beyond

It doesn't feel as if Earth is moving. Does Earth move through space? Does the Moon? What's out there besides Earth, the Moon, the Sun, and stars? In this chapter you will find the answers to these questions. In addition, you will learn why the Moon changes its appearance, how comets appear, and where meteorites come from. You also will read about constellations, galaxies, and the life cycles of stars.

What do you think?

Science Journal Look at the picture below with a classmate. Discuss what you think this might be or what is happening. Here's a hint: *It's a time exposure.* Write your answer or best guess in your Science Journal.

490

Theme Connection

Scale and Structure The immensity, composition, and relatedness of objects in the solar system support this ongoing theme.

EXPLORE ACTIVITY

When you gaze at the night sky, what do you see? On a clear night, the sky is full of sparkling points of light. With the unaided eye, you can see dozens—no, hundreds—of these sparkles. How many stars are there?

Estimate grains of rice

1. Using white crayon or chalk and a ruler, draw grid lines on a sheet of black construction paper, dividing it into 5-cm squares.

2. Spill 4 g of rice grains onto the black paper.

3. Count the number of grains of rice in one square. Repeat this step with a different square. Add the number of grains of rice in the two squares, then divide this number by two to calculate the average number of grains of rice in the two squares.

4. Multiply this number by the number of squares on the paper. This will give you an estimate of the number of grains of rice on the paper.

Observe

How could scientists use this same method to estimate the number of stars in the sky? In your Science Journal, describe the process scientists might use.

Before You Read

FOLDABLES Reading & Study Skills

Making an Organizational Study Fold **Make the following Foldable to help you organize your thoughts into clear categories about the solar system and beyond.**

1. Stack six sheets of paper in front of you so the short sides are at the top.

2. Slide the top sheet up so that about four centimeters of the next sheet show. Move each sheet up so about four centimeters of the next sheet show.

3. Fold the sheets top to bottom to form 12 tabs. Staple along the top fold.

4. Label the tabs *Sun, Mercury, Venus, Earth, Mars, Jupiter, Saturn, Uranus, Neptune, Pluto, Beyond the Solar System: Stars,* and *Beyond the Solar System: Galaxies.*

5. Before you read the chapter, write what you know about each under the tabs. As you read the chapter, correct and add to what you've written.

| Sun |
| Mercury |
| Venus |
| Earth |
| Mars |
| Jupiter |
| Saturn |
| Uranus |
| Neptune |
| Pluto |
| Beyond the Solar System: Stars |
| Beyond the Solar System: Galaxies |

491

Purpose Use the Explore Activity to introduce students to the concepts of random sampling and estimation. L2 ELL COOP LEARN **KS** Kinesthetic

Preparation Review how averages are calculated.

Materials black construction paper; ruler; white crayon or chalk; dry, uncooked rice

Teaching Strategies
- Have students test the accuracy of their estimate by counting the rice grains and comparing their estimate to the actual number.
- Discuss other areas where estimation is important. population size, monthly costs for a family, the weight of people in an elevator

Observe

Scientists could divide the night sky into sections and use the method described here to estimate the total number of visible stars.

Assessment

Oral Have students use a parallel procedure to estimate the number of students in their school (count the number of children in two classrooms, find average, then multiply by the number of classrooms in the school). Have them compare the accuracy of their estimates to the actual student population. Use **Performance Assessment in the Science Classroom,** p. 97.

Before You Read

FOLDABLES Reading & Study Skills

Dinah Zike Study Fold

Purpose Students will make and use a Foldable to organize information about the solar system and beyond. Writing down what they already know before reading the chapter will uncover misconceptions about space. Organizing the information as they read will help them understand the content.

📁 For additional help, see Foldables Worksheet, p. 17 in **Chapter Resources Booklet,** or go to the Glencoe Science Web site at **science.glencoe.com.**

See After You Read in the Study Guide at the end of this chapter.

SECTION

Earth's Place in Space

1 Motivate

Bellringer Transparency

Display the Section Focus Transparency for Section 1. Use the accompanying Transparency Activity Master. L2

ELL

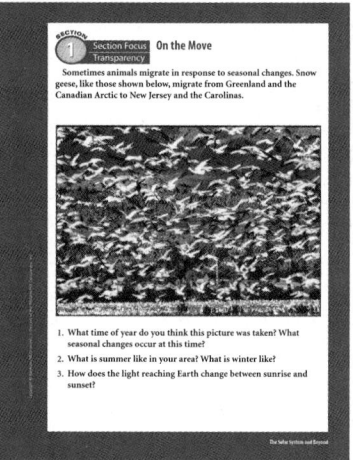

Section Focus Transparency — On the Move

Sometimes animals migrate in response to seasonal changes. Snow geese, like those shown below, migrate from Greenland and the Canadian Arctic to New Jersey and the Carolinas.

1. What time of year do you think this picture was taken? What seasonal changes occur at this time?
2. What is summer like in your area? What is winter like?
3. How does the light reaching Earth change between sunrise and sunset?

The Solar System and Beyond

Tie to Prior Knowledge

Have students brainstorm and recall facts they know about the relationships between the Sun, Earth, and the Moon. Encourage them to include information about the movements of Earth and the Moon. Have students list everyday events that result from movements of Earth or the Moon.

As You Read

What You'll Learn
- **Explain** why Earth has seasons.
- **Describe** the motions that cause Moon phases.

Vocabulary
rotation   revolution
orbit   eclipse

Why It's Important
When you understand Earth's movements you'll understand night and day as well as the seasons.

Figure 1
The rotation of Earth on its axis causes night and day.

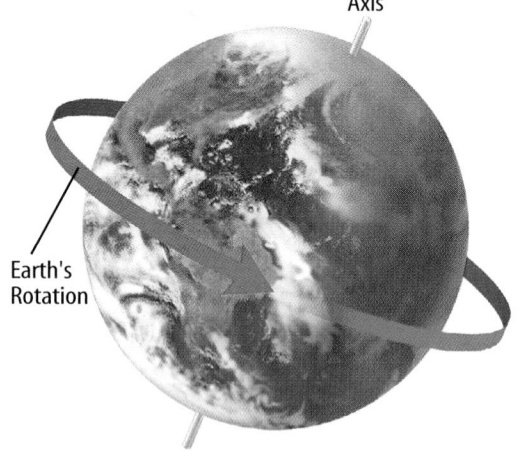

Axis

Earth's
Rotation

Earth Moves

You wake up, stretch and yawn, then glance out your window to see the first rays of dawn. By lunchtime, the Sun is high in the sky. As you sit down to dinner in the evening, the Sun appears to sink below the horizon. Although it seems like the Sun moves across the sky, it is Earth that is moving.

Earth's Rotation Earth spins in space like a twirling figure skater. Your planet spins around an imaginary line running through its center called an axis. **Figure 1** shows how Earth spins on its axis.

The spinning of Earth on its axis is called Earth's **rotation** (roh TAY shun). Earth rotates once every 24 h. The Sun appears each morning due to Earth's rotation. Throughout the day, Earth continues to rotate and the Sun appears to move across the sky. In the evening, the Sun seems to go down because the place where you are on Earth is rotating away from the Sun.

You can see how this works by standing and facing a lamp. Pretend you are Earth and the lamp is the Sun. Now, without pivoting your head, turn around slowly in a counterclockwise direction. The lamp seems to move across your vision, then disappear. You rotate until you finally see the lamp again. The lamp didn't move—you did. When you rotated, you were like Earth rotating in space, causing different parts of the planet to face the Sun at different times. The rotation of Earth—not movement of the Sun—causes night and day.

✔ **Reading Check** *Why does the Sun appear to move across the sky?*

Because the Sun only appears to move across the sky, this movement is called apparent motion. Can you think of any other objects you encounter that might display apparent motion?

Section ✔*Assessment* Planner

PORTFOLIO
Activity, p. 494

PERFORMANCE ASSESSMENT
Skill Builder Activities, p. 496
MiniLAB, p. 495
See page 520 for more options.

CONTENT ASSESSMENT
Section, p. 496
Challenge, p. 496
Chapter, pp. 520–521

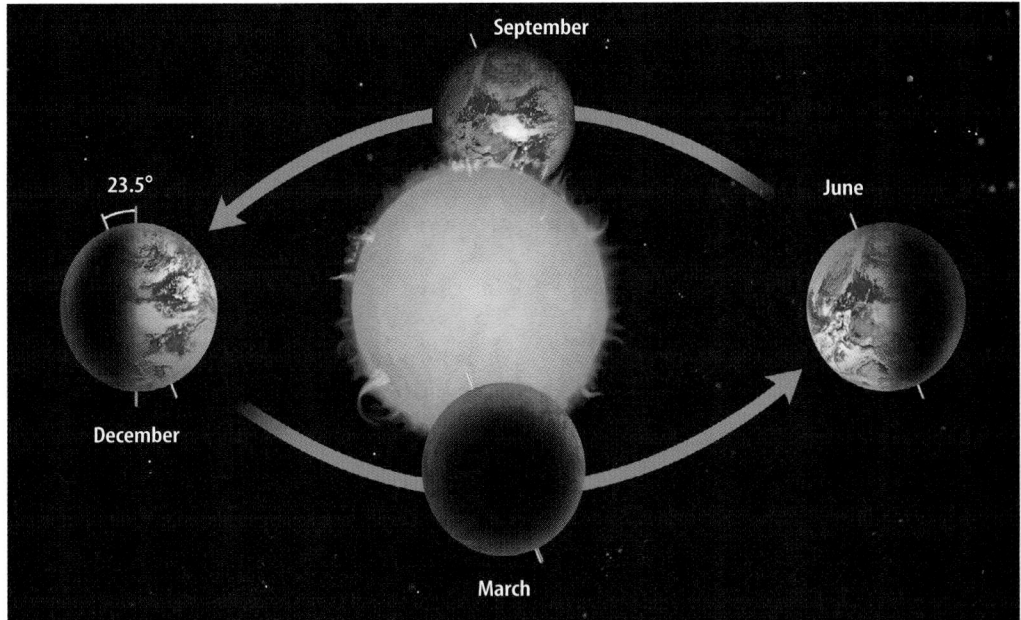

September

23.5°

December

June

March

Earth's Revolution Earth rotates in space, but it also moves in other ways. Like an athlete running around a track, Earth moves around the Sun in a regular, curved path called an **orbit**. The movement of Earth around the Sun is known as Earth's **revolution** (reh vuh LEW shun). A year on Earth is the time it takes for Earth to complete one revolution, as seen in **Figure 2**.

Seasons Who doesn't love summer? The long, warm days are great for swimming, biking, and relaxing. Why can't summer last all year? Blame it on Earth's axis and revolution around the Sun. The axis is not straight up and down like a skyscraper—it is slightly tilted. It's due to this tilt and Earth's revolution that you experience seasons.

Look at **Figure 2**. Summer occurs when your part of Earth is tilted toward the Sun. Then it receives more direct sunlight and thus more energy from the Sun than the part of Earth that is tilted away from the Sun. The Sun appears high in the sky. The days are long and the nights are short. Six months later, when the part of Earth that you live on is tilted away from the Sun, you have winter. During this time, the slanted rays of the Sun are weak. The Sun appears low in the sky. The days are short and the nights are long. Autumn and spring occur when Earth is not tilted toward or away from the Sun.

 **Reading Check** *What causes seasons?*

Figure 2
Earth takes one year to revolve around the Sun. The Sun's rays strike more directly in the summer, so they are more powerful than the weak, spread-out rays that strike in winter.

SCIENCE Online

Collect Data Visit the Glencoe Science Web site at **science.glencoe.com** for data on Earth's distance from the Sun at various times of the year. Why does the distance change? Communicate to your class what you learn.

---

2 Teach

Earth Moves

 **Reading Check**

Answer Because Earth rotates.

IDENTIFYING
Misconceptions

Many people think that Earth is closest to the Sun in summer. Actually, for those in the northern hemisphere, the opposite is true. Earth is closest to the Sun in January. The tilt of Earth's axis, not Earth's distance from the Sun, determines the season.

Reading Check

Answer Earth's tilt and its revolution around the Sun

Teacher FYI

The tilt of a planet's axis is determined by the intersection of the line around which it rotates with a line perpendicular to its ecliptic (path around the Sun). Earth's axis is tilted at an angle of 23.5°.

SCIENCE Online
Internet Addresses

_____

_____

_____

Explore the Glencoe Science Web site at **science.glencoe.com** to find out more about topics in this section.

Curriculum Connection

Geography The Sun is directly over the tropic of Cancer (23.5°N) at the northern hemisphere summer solstice. At the northern hemisphere winter solstice, the Sun is directly over the tropic of Capricorn (23.5°S). Have students locate these latitudes on a map or globe. [L2]
LS Visual-Spatial

Resource Manager

Chapter Resources Booklet
Transparency Activity, p. 44
Note-taking Worksheets, pp. 33–35
Enrichment, p. 30
Directed Reading for Content Mastery, pp. 19, 20

Movements of the Moon

Caption Answer
Figure 3 bottom of column 1

Use an Analogy

Scientists estimate the Sun's diameter to be 1,391,994 km. Earth, at 12,756 km in diameter, is about 109 times smaller than the Sun. The Moon's diameter of 3,476 km is a little more than 1/4 the size of Earth's. To help students grasp these relative sizes, tell them that if the Sun, Earth, and the Moon were placed on a football field, the Moon would be about the size of a football, Earth would take up one yard, and the Sun would stretch from goalpost to goalpost.

✔ **Reading Check**

Answer During a lunar cycle you see different portions of the daylight side of the Moon.

Use Science Words

Word Origin *Gibbous* is a description of the Moon phase between first quarter and full Moon or between full Moon and third quarter. Have students find the origin of this word and explain why it is used to describe these phases of the Moon. *Gibbous* comes from a Latin word meaning "humped" like a camel. The Moon appears to have a hump on its side during these phases. [L2] [IS] **Linguistic**

Activity

Have students observe and record the shape of the Moon for one month. Their drawings can be arranged on a sheet of paper or in a flip book. Before students begin, explain that there will be times when the Moon is not visible because of cloud cover or the position of the Moon in its orbit. Remind students that for some time during the month, the Moon will be visible only during the day or in the early morning. [L2] [IS] **Visual-Spatial** [P]

Figure 3
The phase of the Moon is determined by the relative positions of the Sun, Earth, and the Moon. *Which photo below shows a full moon?*

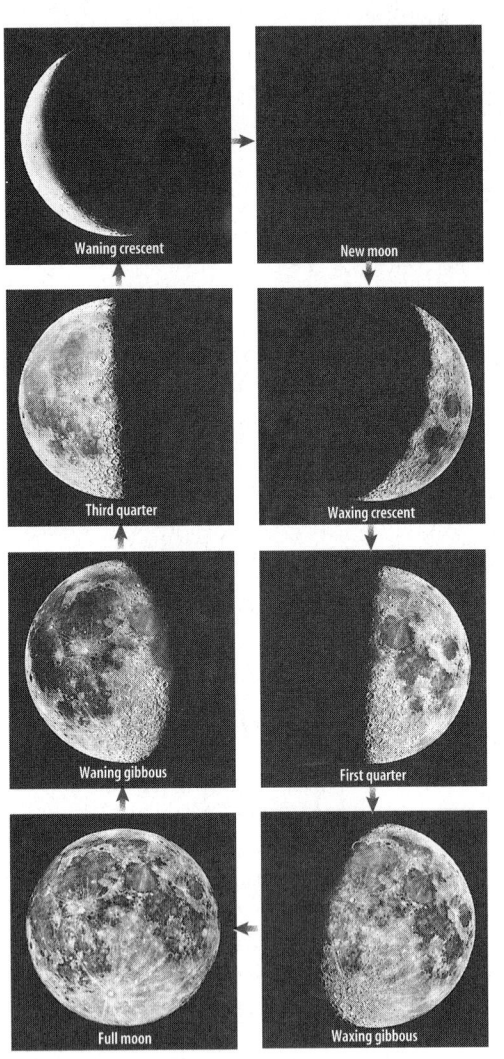

Movements of the Moon

Imagine a fly buzzing around the head of a jogger on a track. That's how the Moon moves around Earth. Just like that relentless fly around the jogger's head, the Moon constantly circles Earth as Earth revolves around the Sun. The Moon revolves around Earth once every 27.3 days. As you probably have noticed, the Moon does not always look the same from Earth. Sometimes it looks like a big, glowing disk. Other times, it appears to be a thin sliver.

Moon Phases How many different Moon shapes have you seen? Have you seen the Moon look round or maybe like a half circle? Although the Moon looks different at different times of the month, it doesn't change. What does change is the way the Moon appears from Earth. These changes are called phases of the Moon. **Figure 3** shows the various phases of the Moon.

Light from the Sun The phase of the Moon that you see on any given night depends on the positions of the Moon, the Sun, and Earth in space. The Sun lights up the Moon, just as it lights up Earth. Also, just as half of Earth experiences day while the other half experiences night, one half of the Moon is lit by the Sun while the other half is dark. It takes the Moon about one month to go through its phases. During that time, also called a lunar cycle, you see different portions of the daylight side of the Moon. Once each cycle, when the Moon and Sun are on opposite sides of Earth, you can see all of the lit portion of the Moon. This is called a full moon. Nearly two weeks later, the Moon is on the same side as the Sun and it is a new moon. Half the Moon is still lit by the Sun, but none of that half is visible to you. The Moon appears in a slightly different shape each night throughout the lunar cycle as it circles Earth and goes from full to new to full again. The Moon is waning during that portion of the month when it changes from full to new. A waxing moon grows bigger each night on the way from new to full.

✔ **Reading Check** *Describe the lunar cycle.*

Resource Manager

Chapter Resources Booklet
MiniLAB, p. 3
Lab Activity, pp. 9–11
Science Inquiry Labs, p. 41

Visual Learning

Figure 3 The phase of the Moon is determined by the relative positions of the Sun, the Moon, and Earth. **How might Earth appear to an observer on the Moon?** Earth would appear to go through phases, just as the Moon does.

Figure 4
During a solar eclipse, the Moon moves between the Sun and Earth. The Sun's corona is visible during a total solar eclipse. *What phase must the Moon be in for a solar eclipse to occur?*

Sun

Area of partial eclipse

Moon

Area of total eclipse

Earth

Solar Eclipse Have you ever tried to watch TV with someone standing between you and the screen? You can't see a thing. The picture from the screen can't reach your eyes because someone is blocking it. Sometimes the Moon is like that person standing in front of the TV. It moves between the Sun and Earth in a position that blocks sunlight from reaching Earth. The Moon's shadow travels across parts of Earth. This event, shown in **Figure 4,** is an example of an **eclipse** (ih KLIHPS). Because it is an eclipse of the Sun, it is known as a solar eclipse. The Moon is much smaller than the Sun, so it casts a tiny shadow on Earth. Sunlight is blocked completely only in the small area of Earth where the Moon's darker shadow falls. In that area, the eclipse is said to be a total solar eclipse.

✔ **Reading Check** *What causes solar eclipses?*

Due to the small size of the shadow—about 269 km wide—only a lucky few get to experience each solar eclipse. For the few minutes the total eclipse lasts, the sky darkens, flowers close, and some planets and brighter stars appear. The Sun's spectacular corona, its pearly white, outermost layer, appears. Far more people will be in the lighter part of the Moon's shadow and will experience a partial solar eclipse.

Mini LAB

Observing Distance and Size

Procedure

1. Place a **basketball** on a **table** at the front of the classroom. Then stand at the back of the room.
2. Holding a **penny,** extend your arm, close one eye, and try to block the ball from sight with the penny.
3. Slowly move the penny closer to you until it completely blocks your view of the basketball.

Analysis

1. In your **Science Journal,** describe what you observed. When did the penny block your view of the basketball?
2. A small object can sometimes block a larger object from view. Explain how this relates to a solar eclipse.

SECTION 1 Earth's Place in Space **495**

Mini LAB

Purpose Students observe the relationship between the distance and size of an object relative to another object. [L2]
IS Interpersonal
Materials basketball, penny
Teaching Strategy Before beginning the activity, ask students if they think that something small could hide something large; for example, "Could a peanut hide an elephant?"
Analysis
1. The penny will probably cover the ball when the student's arm is about halfway toward his or her body. Answers will vary depending on classroom size.
2. Students should realize that even though the Moon is much smaller than the Sun, it can block out the Sun's light because the Moon is much closer to Earth than the Sun is.

✔ Assessment

Performance Have each student draw a diagram of the relationship between his or her eye, the penny, and the ball. The lines should radiate straight from the eye past the penny toward the basketball. Use **PASC,** p. 127.

✔ **Reading Check**

Answer A solar eclipse occurs when the Moon passes directly between Earth and the Sun.

Cultural Diversity

Lunar Calendar Some Middle Eastern and Far Eastern cultures use the lunar calendar. Obtain a calendar from one such culture for students to examine. Using the calendar, have students correlate the beginnings of the months to the new Moon. Students will find that the beginnings of lunar months occur within two or three days of the new Moon. They do not necessarily coincide with the months used in the United States. Students will also find that each month contains either 29 or 30 days. Since the lunar month is based on the time from new Moon to new Moon, or 29.5 days, the lunar year is 11 days shorter than the solar year. Adding seven months to the lunar calendar every 19 years compensates for this difference. Also, because of this 11-day difference, some years will have 12 full lunar cycles and part of a thirteenth. [L2]

③ Assess

Reteach

Have students sketch and label the positions of the Sun and Earth during summer and winter solstice (June 21 or 22 and December 21 or 22) in the northern hemisphere. L2 ELL
Visual-Spatial

Challenge

Have students research and report on the conditions that are necessary for an annular solar eclipse to occur. Possible answer: The Moon is too far from Earth to cover the Sun completely. The Moon is too small to cover the entire Sun.

Assessment

Process Have students research and write a short paragraph explaining why the same side of the Moon always faces Earth. The Moon rotates once and also revolves once every 27.3 days. Thus, the same side of the Moon always faces Earth. Use **Performance Assessment in the Science Classroom,** p. 159.

Figure 5
During a lunar eclipse, Earth moves between the Sun and the Moon. The Moon often appears red during a lunar eclipse. *Why is a lunar eclipse more common than a solar eclipse?*

Moon

Earth

Sun

Lunar Eclipse Sometimes Earth gets between the Sun and the Moon, blocking sunlight from reaching the Moon. When Earth's shadow falls on the Moon, an eclipse of the Moon occurs, which is called a lunar eclipse. Earth's shadow is big compared to the Moon, so everyone on the nighttime side of Earth, weather permitting, gets to see a lunar eclipse. When eclipsed, the full moon grows faint and sometimes turns deep red, as shown in **Figure 5.**

Section Assessment

1. Explain the difference between Earth's revolution and rotation.

2. Describe how Earth's revolution and the tilt of its axis contribute to the seasons.

3. Explain why Earth's shadow often covers the entire Moon during a lunar eclipse, but only a small part of Earth is covered by the Moon's shadow during a solar eclipse.

4. Which phase of the Moon would occur during a lunar eclipse?

5. **Think Critically** The tilt of Earth's axis contributes to the seasons. What would seasons be like if Earth's axis were not tilted?

Skill Builder Activities

6. **Concept Mapping** Draw a Venn diagram in your Science Journal. In one circle, write what you know about solar eclipses. In the second circle, write what you know about lunar eclipses. Where the circles overlap, write the facts that apply to lunar and solar eclipses. **For more help, refer to the** Science Skill Handbook.

7. **Solving One-Step Equations** Light travels 300,000 km/s. There are 60 s in 1 min. If it takes 8 min for the Sun's light to reach Earth, how far is the Sun from Earth? **For more help, refer to the** Math Skill Handbook.

Answers to Section Assessment

1. revolution—movement of Earth around the Sun; rotation—spinning of Earth on its axis
2. Earth's revolution and tilt cause the northern and southern hemispheres to receive different amounts of radiation at different times of the year.

3. Earth's larger shadow covers the Moon. The Moon's smaller shadow only covers a small section of Earth's surface.

4. full moon
5. There would be no seasons.
6. solar eclipse side—Moon between Earth and Sun, new Moon; lunar

eclipse side—Earth between Sun and Moon, full Moon; center area—Sun, Moon, and Earth in line, shadow of one object falls on another
7. 60 s/minute × 8 minutes = 480 s; 480 s × 300,000 km/s = 144,000,000 km

Activity

Moon Phases

The Moon is Earth's nearest neighbor in space. However, the Sun, which is much farther away, affects how you see the Moon from Earth. In this activity, you'll observe how the positions of the Sun, the Moon, and Earth cause the different phases of the Moon.

What You'll Investigate
How do the positions of the Sun, the Moon, and Earth affect the phases of the Moon?

Materials
drawing paper (several sheets)
softball
flashlight
scissors

Goals
- ■ **Model and observe** Moon phases.
- ■ **Record and label** phases of the Moon.
- ■ **Infer** how the positions of the Sun, the Moon, and Earth affect phases of the Moon.

Safety Precautions 🥽 ✂

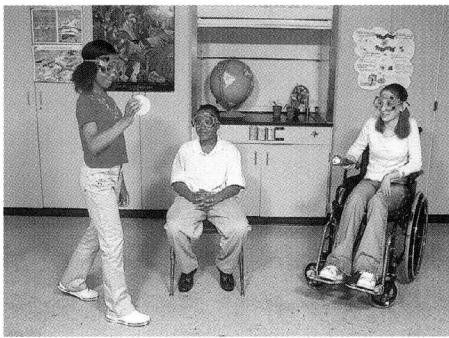

Procedure
1. Turn on the flashlight and darken other lights in the room. Select a member of your group to hold the flashlight. This person will be the Sun. Select another member of your group to hold up the softball so that the light shines directly on the ball. The softball will be the Moon in your experiment.

2. Everyone else represents Earth and should sit between the Sun and the Moon.

3. **Observe** how light shines on the Moon. Draw the Moon, being careful to add shading to represent its dark portion.

4. The student who is holding the Moon should begin to walk in a slow circle around the group, stopping at least seven times at different spots. Each time the Moon stops, observe it, draw it, and shade in its dark portion.

Conclude and Apply
1. **Compare and contrast** your drawings with those of other students. Discuss similarities and differences in the drawings.

2. In your own words, explain how the positions of the Sun, the Moon, and Earth affect the phase of the Moon that is visible from Earth.

3. **Compare** your drawings with **Figure 3**. Which phase is the Moon in for each drawing? Label each drawing with the correct Moon phase.

𝒞ommunicating Your Data
Use your drawings to make a poster explaining phases of the moon. **For more help, refer to the** Science Skill Handbook.

Activity

BENCH TESTED

Purpose Students observe phases of the Moon. [L2] [ELL] [COOP LEARN] [IS] **Visual-Spatial** [P]

Process Skills observing, comparing and contrasting, inferring, analyzing, modeling

Time Required 40 minutes

Safety Precautions Caution students to handle scissors with care.

Teaching Strategies
- The terminator—the line that separates the Moon's light and dark sides—should be drawn first. The darkened part of the sphere should be shaded.
- The student holding the softball should move in a counterclockwise direction in order to get the phases in correct order.

Answers to Questions
1. Students should compare and contrast the location of the terminator and correct shape of the shaded portion of the Moon at each phase.
2. As the Moon moves more nearly opposite the Sun, more of its lighted side is visible from Earth.
3. Student drawings should correspond to Figure 3.

✔Assessment
Portfolio Many cultures have myths and legends about the phases of the Moon. Have students research one myth, then write short stories or poems about the Moon based on their research. They can use their Moon sketches to illustrate their stories. Use **Performance Assessment in the Science Classroom,** p. 159.

𝒞ommunicating Your Data
Students should discuss how their drawings compared or contrasted with the drawings of other students. Students could draw on the board to show where they placed the terminator and the portion of the Moon they shaded as they drew specific phases.

The Solar System

1 Motivate

Bellringer Transparency

Display the Section Focus Transparency for Section 2. Use the accompanying Transparency Activity Master. L2

ELL

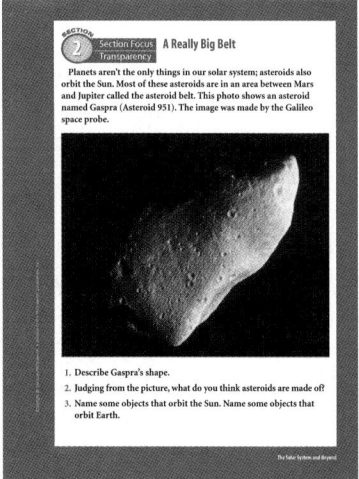

Tie to Prior Knowledge

Have students recall recent discoveries about the planets that have been in the news, such as the possibility of water flowing on Mars or the possibility of seas existing under the crust of Europa, one of Jupiter's moons.

As You Read

What You'll Learn

- **Explain** how to measure distance in the solar system.
- **List** the various objects in the solar system.
- **Describe** important characteristics of each planet.

Vocabulary

solar system   comet
astronomical unit   meteorite

Why It's Important

Much can be learned about Earth by studying the other planets.

Distances in Space

Imagine that you are an astronaut living in the future, doing research on a space station in orbit around Earth. You've been working hard for a long time and need a vacation. Where will you go? How about a tour of the solar system? The **solar system,** shown in **Figure 6,** is made up of the nine planets and numerous other objects that orbit the Sun, all held in place by the Sun's immense gravity. How long will your tour take?

✔ **Reading Check**   *What holds the solar system together?*

The *Voyagers 1* and *2* spacecraft left Earth in 1977 to explore the solar system. It took *Voyager 2* two years to reach the planet Jupiter, four years to pass Saturn, and more than eight years to reach Uranus. *Voyager 2* passed Neptune, the farthest planet on its itinerary, 12 years after it left the launchpad on Earth.

Figure 6
The Sun is the center of the solar system, which is made up of the nine planets and other objects that orbit the Sun.

498   CHAPTER 17   The Solar System and Beyond

Section ✔*Assessment* Planner

PORTFOLIO
Life Science Integration, p. 500
PERFORMANCE ASSESSMENT
Problem-Solving Activity, p. 503
Skill Builder Activities, p. 505
See page 520 for more options.

CONTENT ASSESSMENT
Section, p. 505
Challenge, p. 505
Chapter, pp. 520–521

Measuring Space Distances in space are hard to imagine because space is so vast. Suppose you had to measure your pencil, the hallway outside your classroom, and the distance from your home to school. Would you use the same units for each measurement? No. You probably would measure your pencil in centimeters. You would use something bigger to measure the length of the hallway, such as meters. You might measure the trip from your home to school in kilometers. Larger units are used to measure longer distances. Imagine trying to measure the trip from your home to school in centimeters. If you didn't lose count, you'd end up with a huge number.

Astronomical Unit Kilometers are fine for measuring long distances on Earth, such as the distance from New York to Chicago (about 1,200 km). Even bigger units are needed to measure vast distances in space. One such measure is the **astronomical** (as truh NAHM ih kul) **unit.** An astronomical unit equals 150 million km, which is the mean distance from Earth to the Sun. Astronomical unit is abbreviated *AU*. If something is 3 *AU* away from the Sun, then the object is three times farther from the Sun than Earth is. The *AU* is a convenient unit for measuring distances in the solar system.

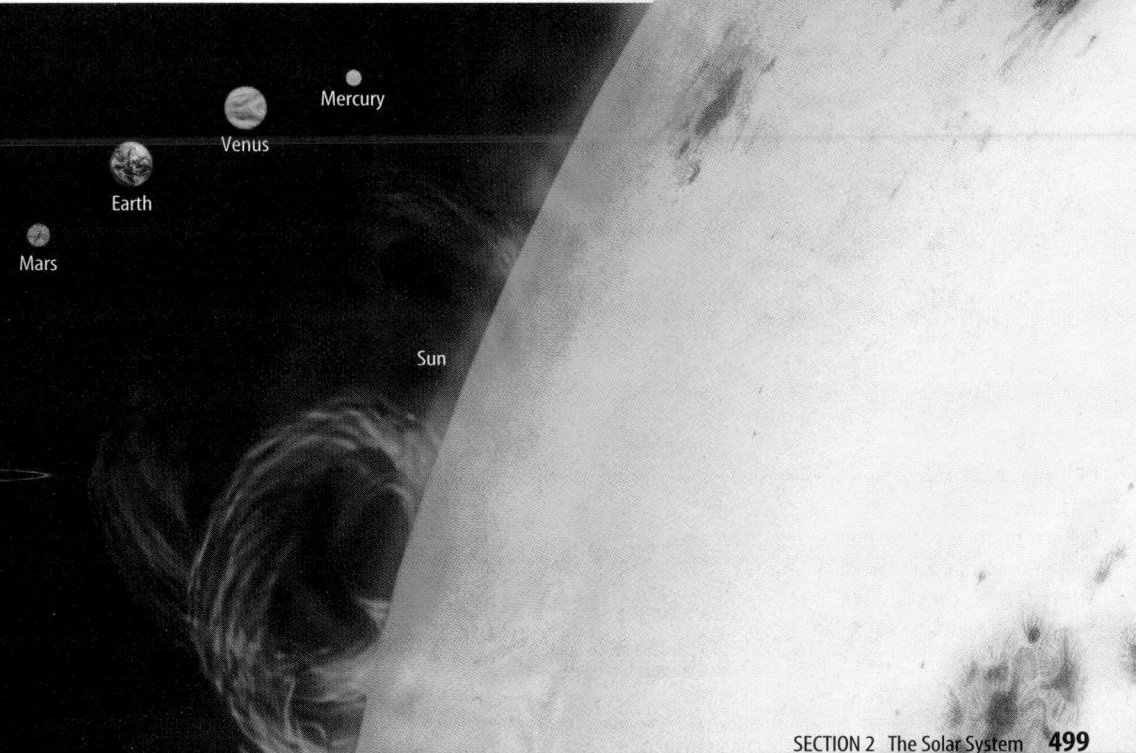

Mercury
Venus
Earth
Mars
Sun

SECTION 2 The Solar System **499**

Touring the Solar System

Activity

As students learn about each of the planets in the solar system, have them make a chart on the bulletin board or chalkboard that compares and contrasts each planet to Earth. Remind students that Earth is the only planet where water exists as a gas, a liquid, and a solid. Encourage students to come up with additional ways that Earth differs from other planets. L2

Inner Planets

Life Science
INTEGRATION

Some weaknesses for the hypothesis could be that the surface environment could be very hostile, and Mars has low temperatures and little atmosphere. Strengths of the hypothesis could be that volcanic activity on Mars could make temperatures more appropriate for life on Mars; another strength could be that on Earth bacteria can live at great depths in groundwater, and that might also be possible on Mars. L2

Life Science
INTEGRATION

Recent discoveries indicating that water might occasionally seep from the surface of Mars have caused some people to hypothesize that microscopic life might exist on Mars. Research this hypothesis and critique its strengths and weaknesses using current scientific evidence and information.

Touring the Solar System

Now you know a little more about how to measure distances in the solar system. Next, you can travel outward from the Sun and take a look at the objects in the solar system. Maybe you can find a nice destination for your next vacation. Strap yourself into your spacecraft and get ready to travel. It's time to begin your journey. What will you see first?

Inner Planets

The first group of planets you pass are the inner planets. These planets are mostly solid, with minerals similar to those on Earth. As with all the planets, much of what is known comes from spacecraft that send data back to Earth. Various spacecraft took the photographs shown in **Figure 7** and the rest of this section. Some were taken while in orbit and others upon landing.

Mercury The first planet that you will visit is the one that is closest to the Sun. Mercury, shown in **Figure 7A,** is the second-smallest planet. Its surface has many craters. Craters form when meteorites, which are chunks of rock or metal that fall from the sky, strike a planet's surface. You will read about meteorites later in this section. Because of Mercury's small size and low gravity, most gases that could form an atmosphere escape into space. The nearly absent atmosphere and the closeness of this planet to the Sun cause great extremes in temperature on Mercury. Its surface temperature can reach 430°C during the day and drop to −180°C at night, making the planet unfit for life.

A

✔ Reading Check   *Why does Mercury have almost no atmosphere?*

Venus You won't be able to see much at your next stop, shown in **Figure 7B.** Venus, the second-closest planet to the Sun, is hard to see because its surface is surrounded by thick clouds. These clouds trap the solar energy that reaches the surface of Venus. That energy causes surface temperatures to hover around 470°C—hot enough to bake a clay pot.

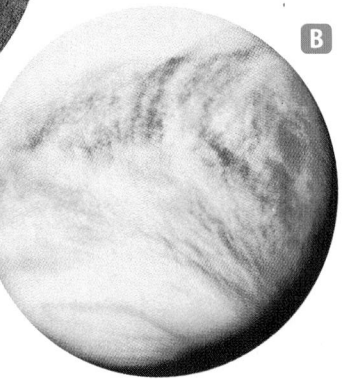
B

Figure 7
A Mercury is the closest planet to the Sun. Like the Moon, its surface is scarred by craters. **B** Earth's closest neighbor, Venus, is covered in clouds.

🗂 LAB DEMONSTRATION   ✔ *Assessment*

Purpose to observe the shape of an elliptical orbit

Materials pushpins (2), piece of string, large, flat piece of cardboard, marker

Preparation Cover the cardboard with paper and insert two pushpins about 8 cm apart.

Procedure Tie the ends of the string to make a loop. Drop the loop of string over the pins and use the string to guide a felt-tipped marker, thereby drawing an ellipse.

Expected Outcome Students observe the shape of an ellipse.

Explain that the ellipse is a model of a planet's orbit with the Sun located at one of the pins. **What would happen to the shape of the ellipse if the pins were placed closer together?** The ellipse would be less flattened and more circular.

Earth Home sweet home. You've reached Earth, the third planet from the Sun. You didn't realize how unusual your home planet was until you saw other planets. Earth's surface temperatures allow water to exist as a solid, a liquid, and a gas. Also, ozone in Earth's atmosphere works like a screen to limit the number of ultraviolet (ul truh VI uh lut) rays that reach the planet's surface. Ultraviolet rays are harmful rays from the Sun. Because of Earth's atmosphere, life can thrive on the planet. You would like to linger on Earth, shown in **Figure 8,** but you have six more planets to explore.

Mars Has someone else been here? You see signs of earlier visits to Mars, the fourth of the inner planets. Tiny robotic explorers have been left behind. However, it wasn't a person who left them here. Spacecraft that were sent from Earth to explore Mars's surface left the robots. If you stay long enough and look around, you might notice that Mars, shown in **Figure 9,** has seasons and polar ice caps. Signs indicate that the planet once had liquid water. Water might even be shaping the surface of Mars today. You'll also notice that the planet looks red. That's because the rocks on its surface contain iron oxide, which is rust. Two small moons, Phobos and Deimos, orbit Mars.

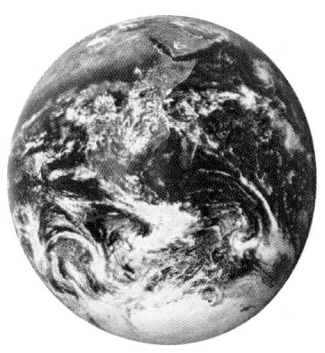

Figure 8
As far as scientists know, Earth is the only planet that supports life. It is one of the four inner planets.

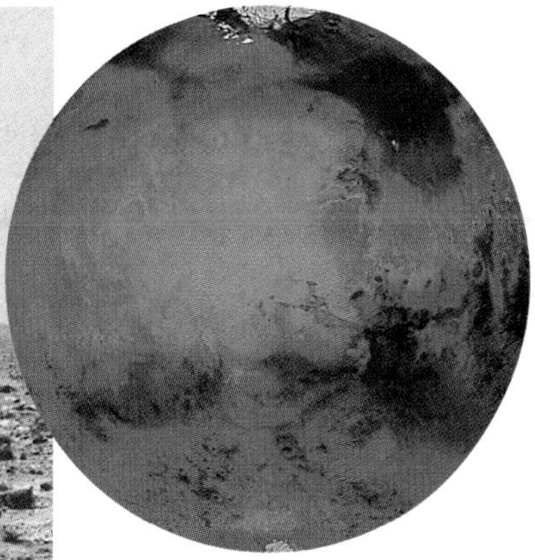

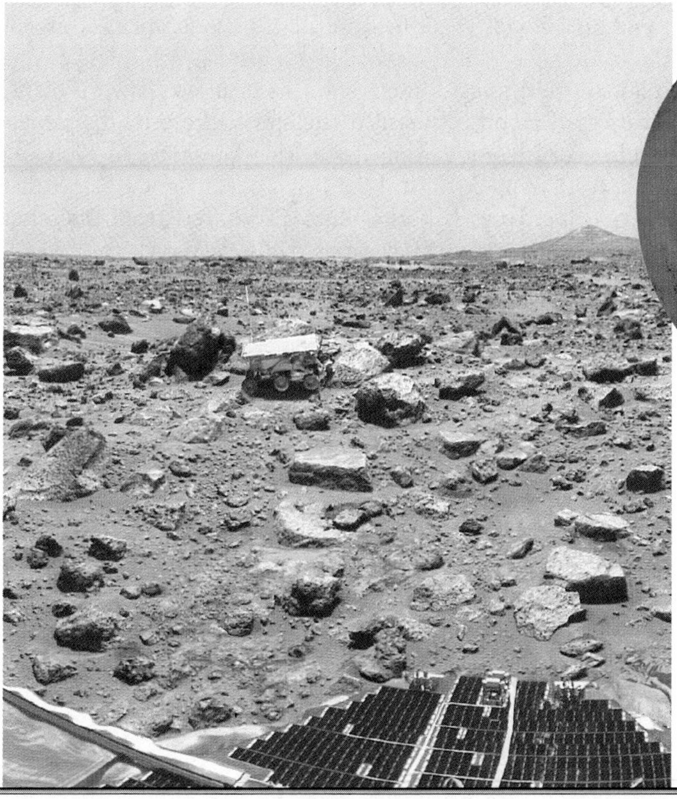

Figure 9
Mars often is called the Red Planet. ***What causes Mars's surface to appear red?***

Quick Demo

Many planets, including Venus, Mars, Jupiter, and Saturn, can be seen with the unaided eye, small binoculars, or a small telescope. Show students how to use binoculars or a telescope to observe planets. Consider conducting a night observation and demonstrating how to find and observe these and other planets.

Fun Fact

The misconception that Mars has canals was actually the result of a linguistic error. The Italian astronomer Schiaparelli wrote of seeing *canali* on Mars, which means "channels." This was mistakenly translated to "canals." The movement of any liquid can make channels naturally. Canals, on the other hand, imply construction by intelligent beings.

Visual Learning

Figure 9 The small roving vehicle, *Sojourner,* enabled the *Pathfinder* mission to study a large area of the Martian surface. **Contrast the surfaces of Mars and Earth.** Mars is barren and dry. Its surface looks red due to iron oxide in its rocks. Much of Earth is green and covered with vegetation. Water flows freely over Earth's surface.

Caption Answer

Figure 9 iron oxide in the rocks

Active Reading

Write-Draw-Discuss This strategy encourages students to actively participate in reading and lectures, assimilating content creatively. Have students write about an idea, clarify it, then make an illustration or drawing. Ask students to share responses with the class and display several examples. Have students Write-Draw-Discuss about the aspect of the solar system that interests them the most.

Resource Manager

Mathematics Skill Activities, p. 39

Cultural Diversity, p. 25

Science Inquiry Labs, p. 39

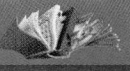

Inner Planets,
continued

Make a Model

Have students make a model of a mining operation in the asteroid belt. Student models should indicate how asteroids would be collected and processed. Robotic asteroid collectors could collect the smaller asteroids. These could be returned to a large processing plant on one of the larger asteroids. [L2] [IS] **Kinesthetic and Logical-Mathematical**

Outer Planets

Extension

Have students research the four Galilean satellites of Jupiter—Io, Europa, Ganymede, and Callisto. Then have them compare and contrast these four large moons. Possible answer: All four orbit Jupiter. Io is volcanically active. Europa may have water beneath its thin crust. Ganymede has its own magnetic field. Callisto also may have an ocean inside. [L2] [IS] **Linguistic**

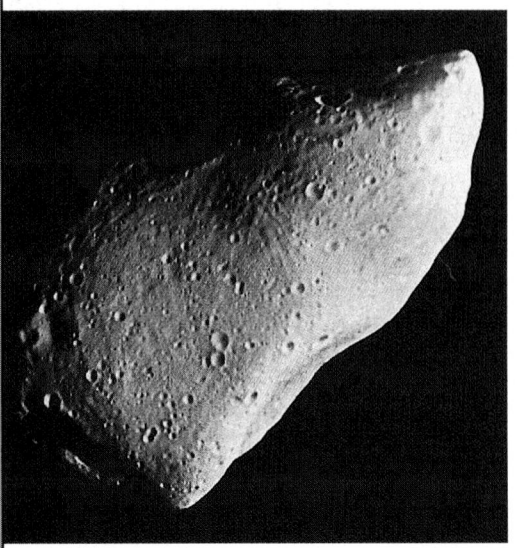

Figure 10
This close-up of the asteroid Gaspra was taken by the *Galileo* spacecraft in 1991.

Figure 11
Jupiter is the largest planet in the solar system. This gas giant has 28 moons.

Asteroid Belt Look out for asteroids. On the next part of your trip, you must make your way through the asteroid belt that lies between Mars and the next planet, Jupiter. As you can see in **Figure 10,** asteroids are pieces of rock made of minerals similar to those that formed the rocky planets and moons. In fact, these asteroids might have become a planet if it weren't for the giant planet, Jupiter. Jupiter's huge gravitational force might have prevented a small planet from forming in the area of the asteroid belt. The asteroids also might be the remains of larger bodies that broke up in collisions. The asteroid belt separates the solar system's planets into two groups—the inner planets, which you've already visited, and the outer planets, which are coming next.

✔ **Reading Check** *What are asteroids?*

Outer Planets

Moving past the asteroids, you come to the outer planets. The outer planets are Jupiter, Saturn, Uranus, Neptune, and Pluto. Let's hope you aren't looking for places to stop and rest. Trying to stand on most of these planets would be like trying to stand on a cloud. That's because all of the outer planets, except Pluto, are huge balls of gas called gas giants. Each might have a solid core, but none of them has a solid surface. The gas giants have lots of moons, also called satellites, which orbit the planets just like Earth's Moon orbits Earth. They have rings surrounding them that are made of dust and ice. The only outer planet that doesn't have rings is Pluto. Pluto also differs from the other outer planets because it is composed of ice and rock.

Jupiter If you're looking for excitement, you'll find it on Jupiter, which is the largest planet in the solar system and the fifth from the Sun. It also has the shortest day—less than 10 h long—which means this giant planet is spinning faster than any other planet. Watch out for a huge, red whirlpool near the middle of the planet. That's the Great Red Spot, a giant storm on Jupiter's surface. Jupiter, shown in **Figure 11,** almost looks like a miniature solar system. It has 28 moons. One called Ganymede (GA nih meed) is larger than the planet Mercury. Ganymede, along with two other moons, Europa and Callisto, might have liquid water under their icy crust. Another of Jupiter's moons, Io, has more active volcanoes than any other object in the solar system.

Inclusion Strategies

Gifted Galileo first saw the four largest moons of Jupiter (Io, Europa, Ganymede, and Callisto) from Earth through a telescope. If possible, bring a telescope to class and let students examine its structure. Have students research and write a report about the astronomical accomplishments of Galileo. Galileo observed the phases of Venus and craters and maria on the Moon. [L2] [IS] **Linguistic**

Science Journal

Galileo **and** *Cassini* **Spacecraft** Have students research the discoveries of the *Galileo* spacecraft to Jupiter and the goals of the *Cassini* mission expected to arrive at Saturn in 2004. Have them write a report in their Science Journals. *Galileo*—information about Jupiter and its moons; *Cassini*—atmosphere of Titan and Saturn's atmosphere, rings, and other moons [L2] [IS] **Linguistic**

Saturn You might have thought that Jupiter was unusual. Wait until you see Saturn, the sixth planet from the Sun. You'll be dazzled by its rings, shown in **Figure 12.** Saturn's several broad rings are made up of hundreds of smaller rings, which are made up of pieces of ice and rock. Some of these pieces are like specks of dust. Others are many meters across. Saturn is orbited by at least 30 moons, the largest of which is Titan. Titan has an atmosphere that resembles the atmosphere on Earth in primitive times. Some scientists hypothesize that Titan's atmosphere might provide clues about how life formed on Earth.

Uranus After Saturn, you come to Uranus, the seventh planet from the Sun. Uranus warrants a careful look because of the interesting way it spins on its axis. The axis of most planets is tilted just a little, somewhat like the handle of a broom that is leaning against a wall. Uranus, also shown in **Figure 12,** is nearly lying on its side. Its axis is tilted almost even with the plane of its orbit like a broomstick lying on the floor. Uranus's atmosphere is made mostly of hydrogen with smaller amounts of helium and methane. The methane gives Uranus its distinctive bluish-green color. Uranus has rings and is thought to have at least 21 moons.

Figure 12
Saturn and Uranus are two of the four gas giant planets.

IDENTIFYING
Misconceptions

Many students may think that the planets are lined up in a straight line outward from the Sun. Stress to them that the planets orbit in different planes and at different speeds. Illustrating the planets in a line and learning about the planets "in order" is simply a convenient way to study the solar system.

Problem-Solving Activity

How can you model distances in the solar system?

The distances between the planets and the Sun are unimaginably large but definitely measurable. Astronomers have developed a system of measurement to describe these distances in space. Could you represent these vast distances in a simple classroom model? Use your knowledge of SI and your ability to read a data table to find out.

Identifying the Problem

The table to the right shows the distances in astronomical units between the planets and the Sun. Notice that the inner planets are fairly close together, and the outer planets are far apart. Study the distances carefully, then answer the questions.

Solving the Problem

1. Based on the distances shown in the table, how would you make a scale model of the solar system that would fit in your classroom? What unit would you use to show the distances between the planets?

2. Show the conversion between astronomical units and the SI unit you would use for your model.

Solar System Data	
Planet	**Distance from the Sun (AU)**
Mercury	0.39
Venus	0.72
Earth	1.00
Mars	1.52
Jupiter	5.20
Saturn	9.54
Uranus	19.19
Neptune	30.07
Pluto	39.48

SECTION 2 The Solar System **503**

Problem-Solving Activity

National Math Standards

Correlation to Mathematics Objectives

1, 2, 4, 5, 6–10

Answers

1. Possible answer: The easiest way to make a model of the solar system would be to convert to centimeters, using a meterstick. Given the vast distances from the Sun to the outer planets, students may realize that the distance to some planets, such as Mercury, would be measured in centimeters, while the distances to others, such as Pluto, would be measured in meters.

2. Possible answer: 1 AU = 10 cm

Use Science Words

Word Origin Have students research and write in their Science Journals about the mythological roots of the names Pluto and Charon. In Greek mythology, Charon was the boatman who ferried dead souls across the river Styx to Hades. In Roman mythology, Pluto was the god of the underworld. L2 [IS] **Linguistic**

Inclusion Strategies

Learning Disabled Help students achieve success on the Problem-Solving Activity by providing a simple scale of 1 AU = 1 cm to use in constructing their models of the solar system. This scale will allow students to construct a model with an overall size of less than a meter. It also avoids using a mathematical multiplier since the units are one-to-one. L1

Resource Manager

Chapter Resources Booklet
Enrichment, p. 31

Physical Science Critical Thinking/Problem Solving, p. 4

Earth Science Critical Thinking/Problem Solving, p. 8

IDENTIFYING
Misconceptions

Students may think that planets and stars are about the same distance from Earth. Refer to page 490F for teaching strategies that address this misconception.

Discussion

Should Pluto be considered a planet like others in the solar system? Possible answer: Some students may say that Pluto is so small, it should be considered a moon. In fact, Pluto is much smaller than the other planets, and its moon is very large in relation to Pluto. Based on their sizes and other data, some scientists hypothesize that Pluto and Charon could be large members of the Kuiper belt of comets, located just beyond Pluto's orbit.

Caption Answer

Figure 14 Comets glow for two reasons. Sunlight reflects from dust particles in the comet's tail, and gases produced when a comet's ice is vaporized fluoresce.

Teacher **FYI**

The closer a comet gets to the Sun, the longer its tail becomes. Often two tails are visible, one made of dust and one made of ions.

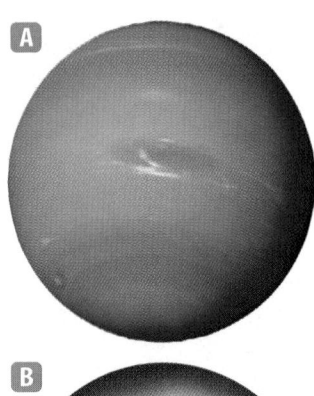

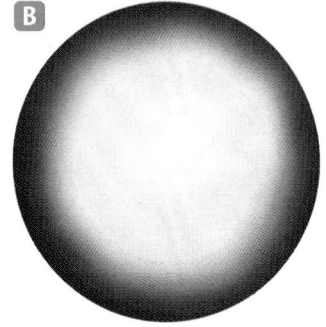

Figure 13
The outermost planets are A Neptune and B Pluto. This is the best image available of Pluto, which was not visited by *Voyager* spacecraft.

Figure 14
The tails of comets point away from the Sun, pushed by solar wind. Solar wind is a stream of charged particles heading outward from the Sun. *Why do comets appear to glow?*

504

Neptune Neptune is the next stop in your space travel. Neptune, shown in **Figure 13A,** is the eighth planet from the Sun. Between 1979 and 1999, Pluto was closer to the Sun than Neptune was because their orbits overlap. However, even then Neptune was considered the eighth planet. Neptune's atmosphere is composed of hydrogen, helium, and methane. Methane and helium give the planet a blue color. Neptune is the last of the big, gas planets with rings around it. It also has eight moons. Triton, the largest of these, has geysers that shoot gaseous nitrogen into space. The low number of craters on Triton indicates that lava still flows onto its surface.

Pluto The last planet that you come to on your tour is Pluto, a small, rocky planet with a frozen crust. Pluto was discovered in 1930 and is farthest from the Sun. It is the smallest planet in the solar system—smaller even than Earth's Moon—and the one scientists know the least about. It is the only planet in the solar system that has never been visited by a spacecraft. Pluto, shown in **Figure 13B,** has one moon, Charon, which is nearly half the size of the planet itself.

Comets

A **comet** is a large body of ice and rock that travels around the Sun in an elliptical orbit. These objects are like dirty snowballs that measure a few kilometers across. Comets might originate in a cloud of objects far beyond the orbit of Pluto known as the Oort Cloud. This belt is 50,000 AU from the Sun. Some comets also originate in the Kuiper Belt, which lies just beyond the orbit of Pluto. As a comet approaches the Sun, radiation vaporizes some of the material. Solar winds blow vaporized gas and dust away from the comet, forming what appears from Earth as a bright, glowing tail, shown in **Figure 14**.

✔ **Reading Check** *Where do comets come from?*

Reading Check

Answer Comets might come from the Oort Cloud beyond the orbit of Pluto. Some comets may come from the Kuiper Belt.

Resource Manager

Chapter Resources Booklet
 Reinforcement, p. 28
 Lab Activity, pp. 13–16

Life Science Critical Thinking/Problem Solving, p. 14

Teacher **FYI**

The existence of an eighth planet in our solar system was predicted in the 1840s by analyzing observed anomalies in Uranus's orbit. Neptune was later discovered amazingly close to its theoretically predicted position. Two scientists worked separately on the discovery of Neptune and both are credited with its discovery. Their names are John Couch Adams and Urbain Leverrier.

Meteorites Occasionally, chunks of extraterrestrial rock and metal fall to Earth. **Meteorites** are any fragments from space that survive their plunge through the atmosphere and land on Earth's surface. Small ones are no bigger than pebbles. The one in **Figure 15** has a mass of 14.5 metric tons. Hundreds of meteorites fall to Earth each year. Luckily, strikes on buildings or other human-made objects are rare. In fact, only a tiny fraction of the meteorites that fall are ever found. Scientists are extremely interested in those that are, as they yield important clues from space. For example, many seem to be about 4.5 billion years old, which provides a rough estimate of the age of the solar system. Several thousand meteorites have been collected in Antarctica, where moving ice sheets concentrate them in certain areas. Any rock seen on an ice sheet in Antarctica is probably a meteorite, because few other rocks are exposed. Meteorites can be one of three types—irons, stones, and stoney-irons. Irons are almost all iron, with some nickel mixed in. Stones are rocky. The rarest, stoney irons, are a mixture of metal and rock.

Figure 15
This meteorite on display at the American Museum of Natural History in New York has a mass of 14.5 metric tons. *Why are meteorites rare?*

3 Assess

Reteach
Have students make a Book of Planets listing various characteristics of each planet, such as size, number of moons, and speed of rotation. L1 IS **Linguistic**

Challenge
Have students research which spacecraft is responsible for mapping almost the entire surface of Venus. Ask them to explain how Venus's cloud-covered surface could be mapped. Between 1990 and 1994, the *Magellan* space probe used radar to map Venus's surface. L2

✔Assessment

Process The United States is hoping to launch a crewed mission to Mars early in the twenty-first century. Have students research and write about the goals of the mission, as well as the obstacles NASA faces. Use **Performance Assessment in the Science Classroom,** p. 159.

Section 2 Assessment

1. Explain how the astronomical unit is useful for measuring distances in space.

2. In general, how are the outer planets different from the inner planets? How are they alike?

3. Describe the objects other than planets that are located within Earth's solar system.

4. How is Saturn's largest satellite different from satellites of other planets?

5. **Think Critically** Larger units of measure are used to express increasingly larger distances. How do scientists express tiny distances, such as the distances between molecules or atoms?

Skill Builder Activities

6. **Developing Multimedia Presentations** Use your knowledge of the solar system to develop a multimedia presentation. You might begin by drawing a labeled poster that includes the Sun, the planets with their moons, the asteroid belt, and comets. **For more help, refer to the** Technology Skill Handbook.

7. **Using an Electronic Spreadsheet** Using the table in the Problem Solving Activity, make a spreadsheet showing the distances of the planets from the Sun. Add columns for additional data such as day and year lengths and the diameters of each planet. **For more help, refer to the** Technology Skill Handbook.

Answers to Section Assessment

1. Distances in space are very large. Large units, such as the AU, are needed to make distances more understandable.

2. Outer: gas giants with rings and multiple moons (except Pluto); Inner: solid and rocky. All planets rotate and revolve.

3. moons—rocky masses in orbit around planets; asteroids—small rocky bodies; comets—masses of rock and ice orbiting the Sun

4. It has an atmosphere that resembles Earth's early atmosphere.

5. Small units of measurement such as Angstroms are used to measure distances between atoms.

6. Student presentations should reflect the unique characteristics of each object included in their displays.

7. Students' spreadsheets should look like the table in the activity, with additional columns added. Each column should be labeled as to the information it contains.

SECTION

3

Stars and Galaxies

1 Motivate

Bellringer Transparency

Display the Section Focus Transparency for Section 3. Use the accompanying Transparency Activity Master. L2

ELL

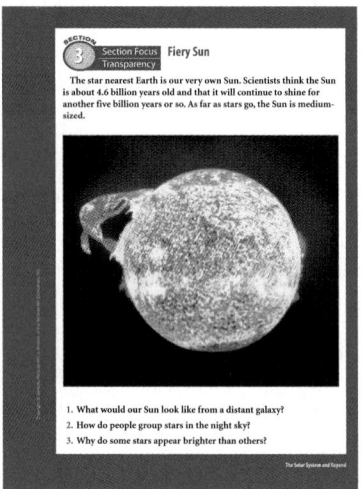

Section Focus Transparency — Fiery Sun

The star nearest Earth is our very own Sun. Scientists think the Sun is about 4.6 billion years old and that it will continue to shine for another five billion years or so. As far as stars go, the Sun is medium-sized.

1. What would our Sun look like from a distant galaxy?
2. How do people group stars in the night sky?
3. Why do some stars appear brighter than others?

The Solar System and Beyond

Tie to Prior Knowledge

Have students recall walking outside on a clear, dark night and seeing many stars. Ask them if they have ever identified patterns or shapes formed by groups of stars. Remind them of the Big Dipper, part of the constellation Ursa Major.

As You Read

What You'll Learn
- **Explain** how a star is born.
- **Describe** the galaxies that make up the universe.
- **Explain** how to measure distances in space beyond Earth's solar system.

Vocabulary
constellation   galaxy
supernova   light-year

Why It's Important
Understanding the vastness of the universe will help you appreciate Earth's place in space.

Figure 16
Find the Big Dipper in the constellation Ursa Major. *Why do you think people call it the Big Dipper?*

Stars

Every night, a whole new world opens to you as the stars come out. The fact is, stars are always in the sky. You can't see them during the day because the Sun's light makes Earth's atmosphere so bright that it hides them. The Sun is a star, too. In fact, it is the closest star to Earth. You can't see the Sun at night because as Earth rotates, your part of Earth is facing away from it.

Constellations Ursa Major, Orion, Taurus—do these names sound familiar? They are **constellations** (kahn stuh LAY shunz), or groups of stars that form patterns in the sky. **Figure 16** shows some constellations.

Constellations are named after animals, objects, and people—real or imaginary. Many of the names that early Greek astronomers gave to the constellations are still in use. However, throughout history, different groups of people have seen different things in the constellations. In early England, people thought the Big Dipper, found in the constellation Ursa Major, looked like a plow. Native Americans saw a horse and rider. To the Chinese, it looked like a governmental official and his helpers moving on a cloud. What image does the Big Dipper bring to your mind?

Ursa Minor

Polaris

Cepheus

Ursa Major

Cassiopeia

506

Section ✔*Assessment* Planner

PORTFOLIO
Physics Integration, p. 512
PERFORMANCE ASSESSMENT
Try at Home MiniLAB, p. 507
Skill Builder Activities, p. 513
See page 520 for more options.

CONTENT ASSESSMENT
Section, p. 513
Challenge, p. 513
Chapter, pp. 520–521

Starry Colors When you glance at the sky on a clear night, the stars look like tiny pinpoints of light. From a distance, they look alike, but stars are different sizes and colors.

Most stars in the universe are cool and small. However, some smaller and medium-sized stars can be hot, and many larger stars are fairly cool. How is a star's temperature measured? The color of a star is a clue. Just as the red flames in a campfire are cooler, red stars are the coolest visible stars. Yellow stars are of medium temperature. Bluish-white stars, like the blue flames on a gas stove, are the hottest. The Sun is a yellow, medium-sized star. The giant, red star called Betelgeuse (BEE tul jews) is much bigger than the Sun. If this huge star were in the same place as Earth's Sun, it would swallow Mercury, Venus, Earth, and Mars.

✔ Reading Check *How is star color related to temperature?*

Apparent Magnitude Look at the sky on a clear night and you can easily notice that some stars are brighter than others. A system called apparent magnitude is used for classifying how bright a star appears from Earth. The dimmest stars that are visible to the unaided eye measure 6 on the apparent magnitude scale. A star with an apparent magnitude of 5 is 2.5 times brighter. The smaller the number is, the brighter the star is. The brightest star in the sky, Sirius, has an apparent magnitude of −1.5, and the Sun's apparent magnitude is −26.7.

Compared to other stars, the Sun is medium in size and temperature. It looks so bright because it is so close to Earth. Apparent magnitude is a measure of how bright a star looks from Earth but not a measure of its actual brightness, known as absolute magnitude. As **Figure 17** shows, a small, close star would look brighter than a giant star that is far away.

Figure 17
This flashlight looks brighter than the car headlights because it is closer. In a similar way, a small but close star will appear brighter than a more distant, giant star.

TRY AT HOME

Mini LAB

Modeling Constellations

Procedure

1. Draw a dot pattern of a constellation on a piece of **black construction paper.** Choose a known constellation or make up your own.
2. With an adult's help, cut off the end of a **cardboard cylinder** such as an oatmeal box. You now have a cylinder with both ends open.
3. Place the cylinder over the constellation. Trace around the rim. Cut the paper along the traced line.
4. **Tape** the paper to the end of the cylinder. Using a **pencil,** carefully poke holes through the dots on the paper.
5. Place a **flashlight** inside the open end of the cylinder. Darken the room and observe your constellation on the ceiling.

Analysis

1. Turn on the overhead light and view your constellation again. Can you still see it? Why or why not?
2. The stars are always in the sky, even during the day. How is the overhead light similar to the Sun? Explain.

---

② Teach

Stars

Caption Answer

Figure 16 It looks like a large dipper with a handle.

✔ Reading Check

Answer Surface temperatures of stars decrease as colors go from the violet end of the spectrum toward the red end of the spectrum.

TRY AT HOME

Mini LAB

Purpose Students investigate light diffusion. **Kinesthetic**

Materials black construction paper; round, empty cornmeal or oats box; scissors; flashlight; pencil; tape

Teaching Strategies Cut off the ends of the boxes for students.

Safety Precautions Caution students to handle scissors with care.

Analysis

1. No, the diffused overhead light on the ceiling is brighter than the flashlight forming the stars.
2. In the same way that the diffused overhead light is brighter than the stars formed by the flashlight, our Sun's light diffused by Earth's atmosphere is brighter than starlight.

✔Assessment

Content Constellations are named after animals, objects, and people—real and imaginary. Have students make a cartoon illustrating what their constellation represents. Use **PASC,** p. 133.

Inclusion Strategies

Learning Disabled Show students the constellation Orion. Explain that this constellation gets its name from a mythological Greek hunter. Have them draw the figure of a hunter over the constellation. Tell them to color the star to the upper left red and the one to the lower right blue. These are Betelgeuse and Rigel, respectively. Help them find these stars in a star atlas. L1 **Visual-Spatial**

Resource Manager

Chapter Resources Booklet
Transparency Activity, p. 46
MiniLAB, p. 4
Home and Community Involvement, p. 31

Caption Answer

Figure 18 A supernova occurs.

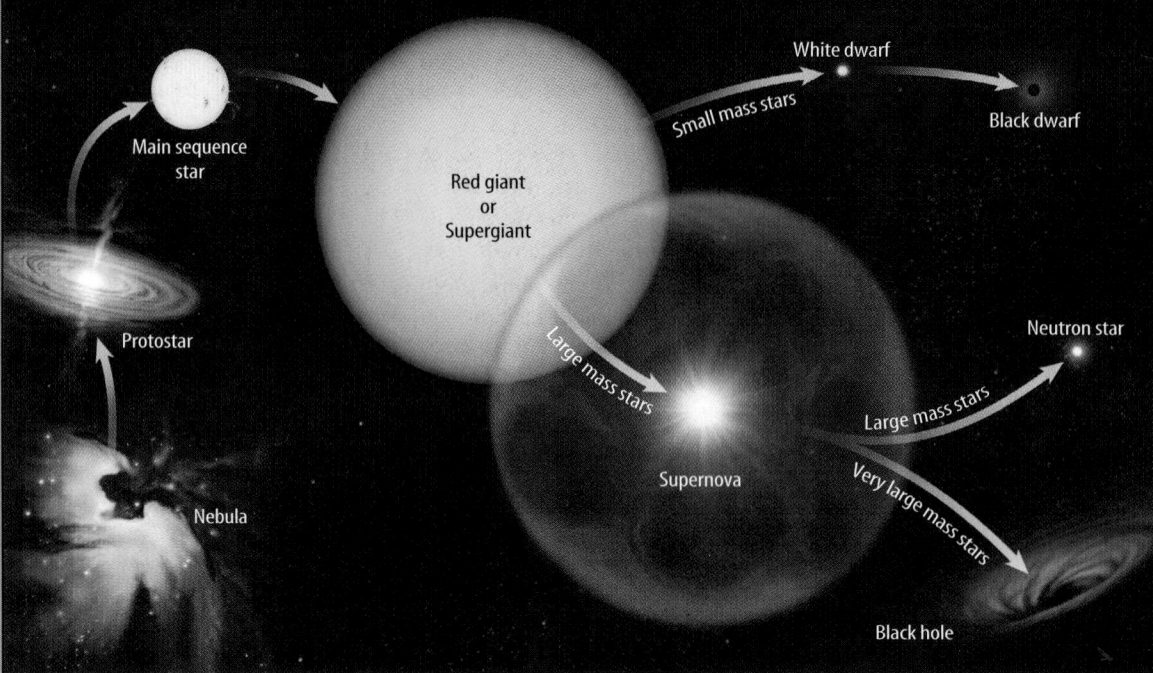

Teacher **FYI**

The way in which a star evolves throughout its life cycle is determined by its original mass. Stars with a mass similar to the Sun's do not become supernovas. They end as a black dwarf, a burned out white dwarf. Stars many times more massive than the Sun can evolve through the supergiant stage, eventually ending up as a neutron star. If the neutron star is massive enough, it can become a black hole.

✔ Reading Check

Answer Small and medium mass stars: star, giant star, white dwarf, black dwarf; large mass stars: star, giant star, super nova, neutron star or black hole.

Extension

Have students research what happens inside a star that causes a supernova to occur. Have them illustrate their findings on a poster or bulletin board. When a massive star uses much of the hydrogen fuel at its core, the core partially collapses under gravity. Heat released by the collapsing core initiates fusion reactions in the outer layers, forming heavier and heavier elements. Finally iron forms in the core. Iron does not fuel further fusion and the core collapses again. The core becomes compressed, stops, and then rebounds with a tremendous outward force. A huge shock wave moves outward through the star, blasting the outer layers into space. L2
LS **Linguistic and Visual-Spatial**

Figure 18
The events in the lifetime of a star depend greatly on the star's mass. *What happens to supergiants when their cores collapse?*

SCIENCE *Online*

Collect Data Visit the Glencoe Science Web site at **science.glencoe.com** for data on supernovas that astronomers have observed in distant galaxies over the past year. How many were found? How far away did these events occur? Communicate to your class what you learn.

The Lives of Stars

You've grown up and changed a lot since you were born. You've gone through several stages in your life, and you'll go through many more. Stars go through stages in their lives, too.

The stages a star goes through in its life depend on the star's size. When a medium-sized star like the Sun uses up some of the gases in its center, it expands to become a giant star. The Sun will become a giant in about 5 billion years. At that time it will expand to cover the orbits of Mercury, Venus, and possibly Earth. It will remain that way for about a billion years. The Sun then will lose its outer shell and shrink to a hot white dwarf. Eventually, it will cool and become a black dwarf. Stars more massive than the Sun complete their life cycles in shorter periods of time. The smallest stars shine the longest. **Figure 18** illustrates how the course of a star's life is determined by its mass.

✔ Reading Check *What stages does a star go through in its life?*

Scientists hypothesize that stars begin their lives as huge clouds of gas and dust. The force of gravity, which causes attraction between objects, causes the dust and gases to move closer together. When this happens, temperatures within the cloud begin to rise. A star is formed when this cloud gets so dense and hot that the atoms within it merge. This process is known as fusion, and it changes matter to the energy that powers the star.

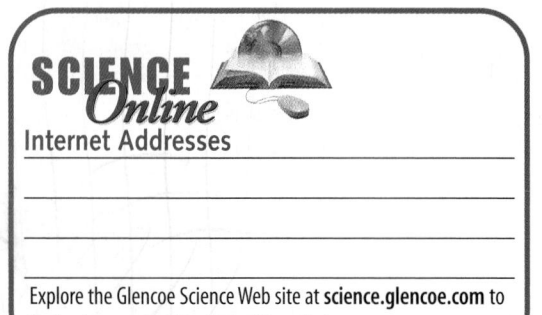

SCIENCE *Online*
Internet Addresses _____
_____
_____
_____
Explore the Glencoe Science Web site at **science.glencoe.com** to find out more about topics in this section.

Science **Journal**
_____
Stellar Evolution Have students research all stages in the life cycle of a star like the Sun. Ask them to make an illustration of the stages involved in their Science Journals. nebula—proto-star—main sequence—giant—white dwarf—black dwarf L2 **ELL** **LS** **Kinesthetic and Visual-Spatial**

Supergiants When a large star begins to use up the fuel in its core, it becomes a supergiant. Over time, the core of a supergiant collapses. Then a **supernova** occurs, in which the outer part of the star explodes and becomes bright. For a few brief days, the supernova might shine more brightly than a whole galaxy. The dust and gases released by this explosion, shown in **Figure 19,** eventually might form other stars.

Meanwhile, the core of the supergiant is still around. It now is called a neutron star. If the neutron star is massive enough, it could become a black hole rapidly. Black holes, shown in **Figure 20,** are so dense that even light cannot escape their gravity. Light shone into them disappears, and no light can escape from them.

Galaxies

What do you see when you look at the night sky? If you live in a city, you might not see much. The glare from city lights makes it hard to see the stars. If you go to a dark place, far from the lights of towns and cities, you can see much more. In a dark area, you might be able to use a powerful telescope to see dim clumps of stars grouped together. These groups of stars are galaxies (GA luk seez). A **galaxy** is a group of stars, gas, and dust held together by gravity.

Types of Galaxies You now know how planets and stars differ from one another. Galaxies come in different shapes and sizes, too. The three major types of galaxies are elliptical, spiral, and irregular. Elliptical galaxies are very common. They're shaped like huge footballs or spheres. Spiral galaxies have arms radiating outward from the center, somewhat like a giant pinwheel. As shown in **Figure 21,** some spiral galaxies have bar-shaped centers. Irregular galaxies are just that—irregular. They come in all sorts of different shapes and can't be classified easily. Irregular galaxies are usually smaller than other galaxies. They are also common.

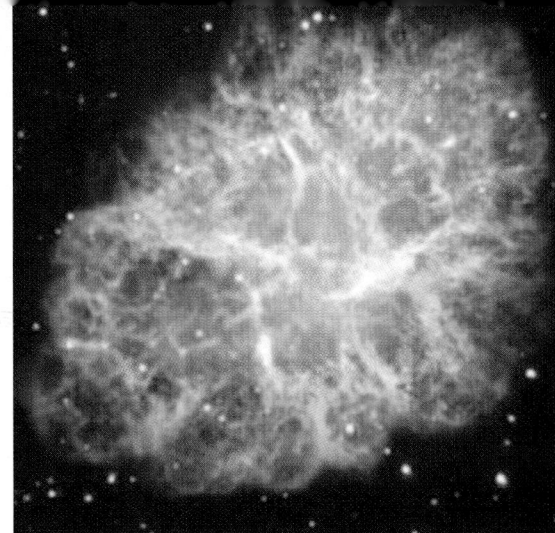

Figure 19
This photo shows the remains of a supernova located trillions of kilometers from Earth.

Figure 20
A black hole has so much gravity that not even light can escape. This drawing shows a black hole stripping gas from a nearby star. *How do black holes form?*

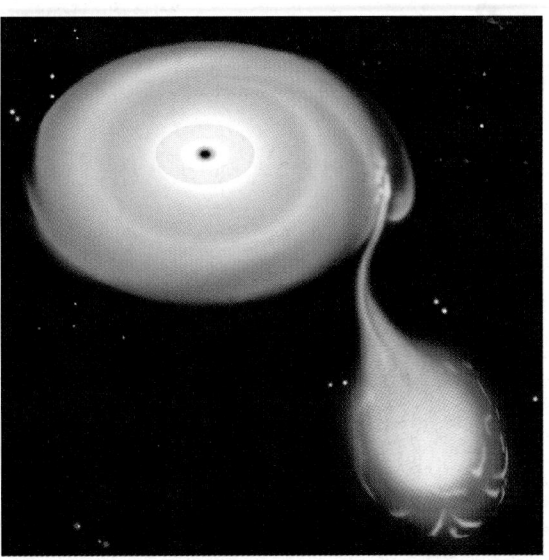

SECTION 3 Stars and Galaxies **509**

Visualizing Galaxies

Figure 21

Have students examine the pictures and read the captions. Then ask the following questions.

If the members of the class were to arrange themselves in the shape of a spiral galaxy, how would they arrange themselves and where would most of them stand? Most would stand in the center of the group, with some extending out in pinwheel fashion.

How would you rearrange yourselves to represent an irregular galaxy? An elliptical galaxy? To represent an irregular galaxy, students could just arrange themselves randomly in the room; to represent an elliptical galaxy, they would cluster together to form an oval shape.

Activity

Have small groups of students use black construction paper, white glue, and sand and salt to make models of the four shapes of galaxies. Ask students what each grain of salt or sand represents in their models. a star

Extension

Ask students to research the relative frequency of the different categories of galaxies and identify which galaxies of each type are closest to the Milky Way. Have students write a brief report on their findings.

Figure 21

Most stars visible in the night sky are part of the Milky Way Galaxy. Other galaxies, near and far, vary greatly in size and mass. The smallest galaxies are just a few thousand light-years in diameter and a million times more massive than the Sun. Large galaxies—which might be more than 100,000 light-years across—have a mass several trillion times greater than the Sun. Astronomers group galaxies into four general categories, as shown here.

▶ **SPIRAL GALAXIES** Spiral galaxies consist of a large, flat disk of interstellar gas and dust with star clusters extending from the disk in a spiral pattern. The Andromeda Galaxy, one of the Milky Way Galaxy's closest neighbors, is a spiral galaxy.

▲ **ELLIPTICAL GALAXIES** They are nearly spherical to oval in shape and consist of a tightly packed group of relatively old stars.

▲ **IRREGULAR GALAXIES** A few galaxies are neither spiral nor elliptical. Their shape seems to follow no set pattern, so astronomers have given them the general classification of irregular.

◀ **BARRED SPIRAL GALAXIES** Sometimes the flat disk that forms the center of a spiral galaxy is elongated into a bar shape. Two arms containing clusters of stars swirl out from either end of the bar, forming what is known as a barred spiral galaxy.

510 **CHAPTER 17** The Solar System and Beyond

Resource Manager

Chapter Resources Booklet
Enrichment, p. 32

Teacher FYI

The Milky Way is a large spiral galaxy with a diameter of about 100,000 light-years. Spiral arms consisting of younger stars surround old stars near the center of the galaxy. Our Sun is located about halfway along one of these spiral arms. Some astronomers think a super-massive black hole exists at the center of the Milky Way and in other galaxies as well.

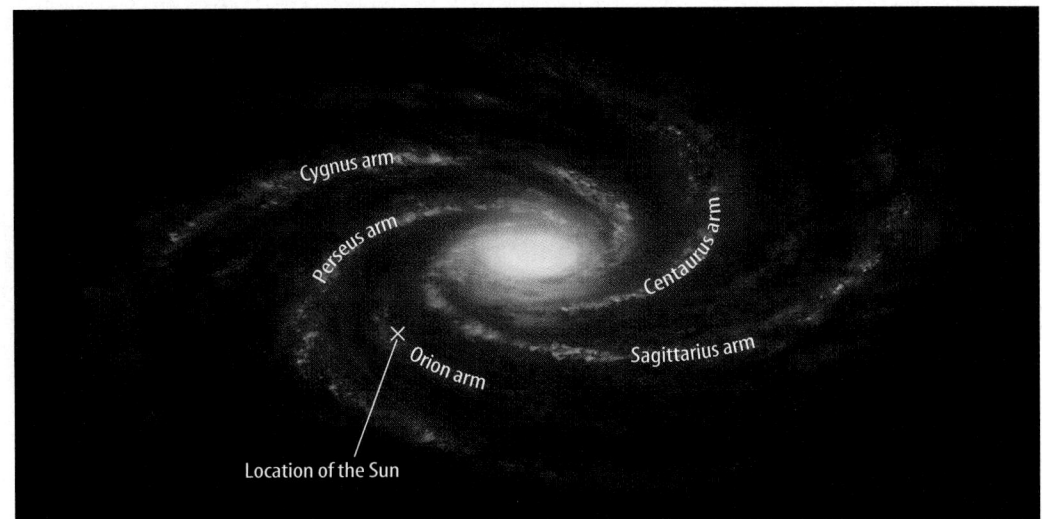

Cygnus arm
Perseus arm
Centaurus arm
Orion arm
Sagittarius arm
Location of the Sun

The Milky Way Galaxy Which type of galaxy do you live in? Look at **Figure 22.** You live in the Milky Way, which is a giant spiral galaxy. Hundreds of billions of stars are in the Milky Way, including the Sun. Just as Earth revolves around the Sun, stars revolve around the centers of galaxies. The Sun revolves around the center of the Milky Way about once every 240 million years.

A View from Within You can see part of the Milky Way as a band of light across the night sky. However, you can't see the whole Milky Way. To understand why, think about boarding a Ferris wheel and looking straight up. Can you really tell what the ride looks like? Because you are at the bottom looking up, you get a limited view. Your view of the Milky Way from Earth is like the view of the Ferris wheel from the bottom. As you can see in **Figure 23,** you can view only parts of this galaxy because you are within it.

✔ **Reading Check** *Why can't you see the entire Milky Way from Earth?*

The faint band of light across the sky that gives the Milky Way its name is the combined glow of stars in the galaxy's disk. In 1609, when the Italian astronomer Galileo looked at the Milky Way with a telescope, he showed that the band was actually made of countless individual stars. The galaxy is vast—bigger and brighter than most of the galaxies in the universe. Every star you see in the sky with your naked eye is a member of the Milky Way Galaxy.

Figure 22
The Sun, one of billions of stars in the galaxy, is located toward the edge of the Milky Way.

Figure 23
This is the view of the Milky Way from inside the galaxy. *Why is it called the Milky Way?*

SECTION 3 Stars and Galaxies **511**

Caption Answer

Figure 23 The many stars in the galaxy form a diffuse band of white across the sky that looks like a road, or "way." Because it is white, it is called the Milky Way.

Galaxies, continued

The universe is very large and is expanding. Edwin Hubble discovered that the light from most galaxies is shifted toward the red end of the spectrum because, as these galaxies are moving away from Earth, their light waves become "stretched out." This stretching is called the Doppler effect. Have students write reports on what they discover about Edwin Hubble, red and blue shifts, and the Doppler effect. [L3]
IS **Linguistic** **P**

Teacher FYI

The Cartwheel Galaxy, located about 500 million light-years from Earth, is thought to have formed when a smaller galaxy collided head-on with a larger one. A similar process may be occurring on the other side of the Milky Way. A dwarf elliptical galaxy has been discovered just 50,000 light-years from the Milky Way's nucleus. It lies on the other side of the Milky Way from Earth, and it appears that our galaxy is tearing it apart. Researchers think that within another billion years, the stars from this small galaxy will be incorporated into our own Milky Way.

✔ Reading Check

Answer Distances between galaxies are vast, much larger than the distances within the solar system, so a larger unit of measurement is needed.

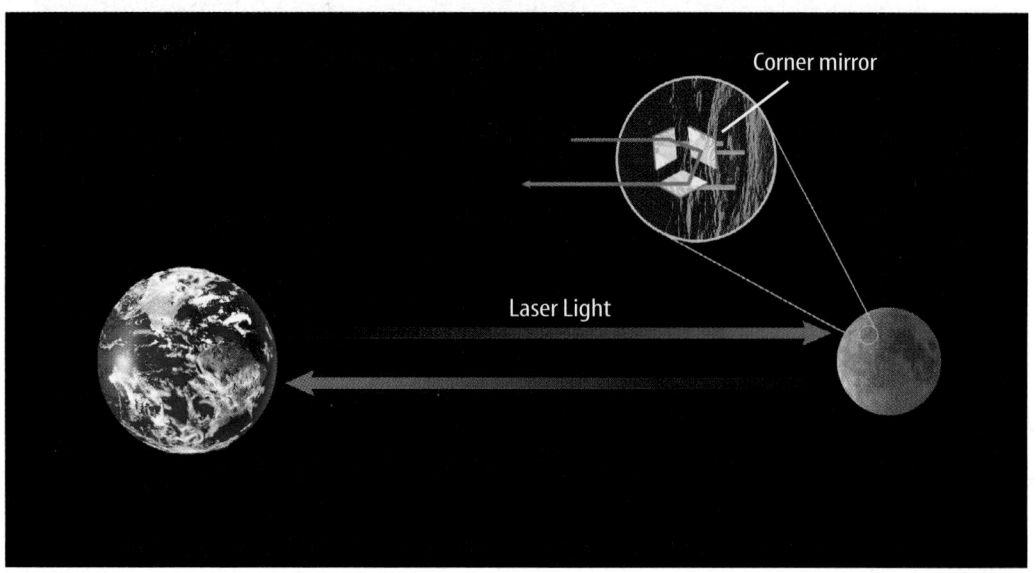

Figure 24
The constant speed of light through space helps astronomers in many ways. For example, the distance to the Moon has been determined by bouncing a laser beam off mirrors left by *Apollo 11* astronauts.

Physics
INTEGRATION

The Milky Way belongs to a cluster of galaxies called the Local Group. Scientists have determined that galaxies outside of the Local Group are moving away from Earth. Based on this, what can you infer about the size of the universe? Research the phenomenon known as red shift and describe to the class how it has helped astronomers learn about the universe.

Speed of Light The speed of light is unique. Light travels through space at about 300,000 km/s—so fast it could go around Earth seven times in 1 s. You can skim across ocean waves quickly on a speedboat, but no matter how fast you go, you can't gain on light waves. It's impossible to go faster than light. Most galaxies are moving away from the Milky Way and a few are moving closer, but the light from all galaxies travels toward Earth at the same speed. The constant speed of light is useful to astronomers, as shown in **Figure 24.**

Light-Years Earlier you learned that distances between the planets are measured in astronomical units. However, distances between galaxies are vast. Measuring them requires an even bigger unit of measure. Scientists often use light-years to measure distances between galaxies. A **light-year** is the distance light travels in one year—about 9.5 trillion km.

✔ **Reading Check** *Why is a light-year better than an astronomical unit for measuring distances between galaxies?*

Would you like to travel back in time? In a way, that's what you're doing when you look at a galaxy. The galaxy might be millions of light-years away. The light that you see started on its journey long ago. You are seeing the galaxy as it was millions of years ago. On the other hand, if you could look at Earth from this distant galaxy, you would see events that happened here millions of years ago. That's how long it takes the light to travel the vast distances through space.

Resource Manager

Chapter Resources Booklet
Reinforcement, p. 29
Directed Reading for Content Mastery, pp. 21, 22

Science Journal

Distances in the Universe Have students research the distances to Betelgeuse, Deneb, and the Large Magellanic Cloud. Instruct them to select a scale that will enable them to illustrate their distances from Earth. Have them place their illustrations in their Science Journals. Betelgeuse, 490 ly; Deneb, 1,400 ly; Large Magellanic Cloud, 169,000 ly
[L3] **IS** **Logical-Mathematical and Kinesthetic**

The Universe

Each galaxy contains billions of stars. Some might have as many stars as the Milky Way, and a few might have more. As many as 100 billion galaxies might exist. All these galaxies with all of their countless stars make up the universe.

Look at **Figure 25.** The *Hubble Space Telescope* spent ten days in 1995 photographing a tiny sector of the sky to produce this image. More than 1,500 galaxies were discovered. Astronomers think a similar picture would appear if they photographed any other sector of the sky. In this great vastness of exploding stars, black holes, star-filled galaxies, and empty space is one small planet called Earth. If you reduced the Sun to the size of a period on this page, the next-closest star would be more than 16 km away. Earth looks even lonelier when you consider that the universe also seems to be expanding. Most other galaxies are moving away at speeds as fast as 20,000 km/s. In relation to the immensity of the universe, Earth is an insignificant speck of dust. Could it be the only place where life exists?

Figure 25
The Hubble Deep Field Image shows hundreds of galaxies in one tiny sector of the sky. *What does this image tell you about the sky?*

 **Reading Check** *How do other galaxies move relative to Earth?*

Section Assessment

1. What are the three major types of galaxies? What type of galaxy is the Milky Way?

2. Describe how a star forms.

3. Describe the size and temperature of most stars that exist in the universe.

4. How long has light from a star that is 50 light-years away been traveling when it reaches Earth?

5. **Think Critically** Some stars might no longer be in existence, but you still see them in the night sky. Why?

Skill Builder Activities

6. **Making Models** The Milky Way is 100,000 light-years in diameter. Outline a plan for how you would build a model of the Milky Way. **For more help, refer to the** Science Skill Handbook.

7. **Communicating** Observe the stars in the night sky. In your Science Journal, draw the stars you observed. Now draw your own constellation based on those stars. Give your constellation a name. Why did you choose that name? **For more help, refer to the** Science Skill Handbook.

Answers to Section Assessment

1. Elliptical, spiral, irregular; the Milky Way is a spiral galaxy.
2. Scientists hypothesize that stars begin as huge clouds of gas and dust which eventually come together because of gravity.
3. small and cool

4. 50 years
5. Some stars are so far away that it takes a long time for their light to reach Earth. It is possible for us to see the light from a faraway star that long ago stopped emitting light.

6. Possible answer: Use a scale of 1 cm = 1,000 light years. With this scale, the galaxy would be 100 cm or 1 m in diameter.
7. Students should explain why they selected a particular name for their constellation.

Visual Learning

Figure 25 What advantages might there be for placing instruments such as the Hubble Space Telescope in orbit? In orbit, the instrument is not affected by clouds, light, or distortions caused by the atmosphere.

3 Assess

Reteach

Have pairs of students make flash cards of the three types of galaxies. Have them draw the galaxy on one side and write its type on the other. Student pairs can then test each other using the flash cards. [L1] COOP LEARN [IS] **Interpersonal**

Challenge

Have small groups of students take turns stating one fact about stars. When the groups have covered what was learned in this section, have each group propose one characteristic of stars that they would like to resear and report on to the class. [L COOP LEARN [IS] **Interpersonal**

✔ Assessment

Performance Have students write and perform a skit explaining the relationships among stars, solar systems, galaxies, and the universe. Use **PASC,** p. 147.

Caption Answer

Figure 25 There are a large number of galaxies in the entire sky.

✔ Reading Check

Answer Most other galaxies are moving away from Earth.

Activity

Activity
Design Your Own Experiment

Recognize the Problem

Purpose

Students will hypothesize how conditions on a planet affect the type of space colony that could be built there. L2 COOP LEARN

IS Logical-Mathematical

Process Skills

designing an experiment, forming a hypothesis, inferring, classifying, communicating, comparing and contrasting

Time Required

one class period

Materials

Reference books for students include: *The Planets in Our Solar System* by Franklyn M. Branley, HarperCollins, 1998; *The Planets* by David McNab and James Younger, Yale University Press, 1999; *The Incredible Journey to the Planets*, by Nicholas Harris, Peter Bedrick Books, 1999; and *Across the Solar System*, by Rod Theodorou, Heinemann Library, 2000.

Form a Hypothesis

Possible Hypothesis

Regardless of the planet chosen, most student hypotheses will reflect the need for oxygen, water, protection/shelter from extreme heat and/or cold, and food sources.

Space Colony

Many fictional movies and books describe astronauts from Earth living in space colonies on other planets. Some of these make-believe societies seem far-fetched. So far, humans haven't built a space colony on another planet. However, if it happens, what would it look like?

Recognize the Problem

How would conditions on a planet affect the type of space colony that might be built there?

Form a Hypothesis

Research a planet. Review conditions on the surface of the planet. Make a hypothesis about the things that would have to be included in a space colony to allow humans to survive on the planet.

Possible Materials
drawing paper
markers
books about the planets

Goals
■ **Infer** what a space colony might look like on another planet.
■ **Classify** planetary surface conditions.
■ **Draw** a space colony for a planet.

514

Test Your Hypothesis

Possible Procedures

List all the planet's surface features and conditions. Identify ways to protect humans from features and conditions that would not allow them to survive. Design structures and equipment that would allow humans to survive on the planet. Draw exterior and interior views of the space colony. Include labels and explanations on the drawings.

Resource Manager

Chapter Resources Booklet
   Activity Worksheet, pp. 7–8
Lab Management and Safety, p. 73

Test Your Hypothesis

Plan

1. Select a planet and study the conditions on its surface.
2. **Classify** the surface conditions in the following ways.
   a. solid, liquid, or gas
   b. hot, cold, or a range of temperatures
   c. heavy atmosphere, thin atmosphere, or no atmosphere
   d. bright or dim sunlight
   e. unique conditions
3. **List** the things that humans need to survive. For example, humans need air to breathe. Does your planet have air that humans can breathe, or would your space colony have to provide the air?
4. Make a table for the planet showing its surface conditions and the features the space colony would have to have so that humans could survive on the planet.
5. **Discuss** your decisions as a group to make sure they make sense.

Do

1. Make sure your teacher approves your plan before you start.
2. **Draw** a picture of the space colony. Draw another picture showing the inside of the space colony. Label the parts of the space colony and explain how they aid in the survival of its human inhabitants.

Analyze Your Data

1. **Compare and contrast** your space colony with those of other students who researched the same planet you did. How are they alike? How are they different?
2. Would you change your space colony after seeing other groups' drawings? If so, what changes would you make? Explain your reasoning.

Draw Conclusions

1. What was the most interesting thing you learned about the planet you studied?
2. Was your planet a good choice for a space colony? Explain.
3. Would humans want to live on your planet? Why or why not?
4. Could your space colony be built using present technology? Explain.

𝒞ommunicating
Your Data

Present your drawing and your table to the class. Make a case for why your planet would make a good home for a space colony. **For more help, refer to the** Science Skill **Handbook.**

✔Assessment

Content Have students work in groups of two or three to write a letter home to relatives on Earth describing what it's like to live in their space colony. Use **Performance Assessment in the Science Classroom,** p. 139.

𝒞ommunicating
Your Data

Students could use a word-processing program to prepare their table and the information they want to present for why their planet would be a good place for a space colony.

Teaching Strategies

You might want to have students read about the problems faced by researchers in the Biosphere 2 project for additional information on problems that might be faced by a space colony.

Expected Outcome

Most drawings should show that students have planned ways to produce their own oxygen, obtain water, recycle their wastes, provide for protection from extremes in temperature, and produce food.

Analyze Your Data

1. Comparisons will depend on the planets chosen for the space colonies. All space colonies should be alike in that they provide for the basic needs for human survival. They will probably differ in how those needs are met.
2. Students may decide to make changes after seeing a better way to provide for a particular need of space colonists.

Error Analysis

Have students examine their drawings to evaluate if there was any survival need that they did not consider or account for.

Draw Conclusions

1. Answers will depend on the planet chosen. If Mars was chosen, students might mention the possibility that water exists on the planet.
2. Some planets are better choices than others—those with solid surfaces and less extreme conditions are better.
3. Accept any answers that students can reasonably justify.
4. Probably not, since more detailed information would be needed and most planets present extremely hostile environments for humans.

The Sun and the Moon
A Korean Folktale

✔ Pre-Reading Activity

Lead a class discussion in which students brainstorm about the definition of a cause-and-effect relationship. Encourage responses without giving away what they will learn in the feature. After reading the feature you can go back and address how close they were with their definitions.

Respond to the Reading

Active Reading Strategies

Question Have students check that they understand what they have read. Have them reread sentences if their meaning is unclear.

Question Tell students to ask themselves while they read this passage, is this story set in the present day or at a time in the past?

Review Have students review what they have read. Explain that by looking back over several paragraphs, they can see how the information fits together. Ask students what they have learned about the existence of the Sun and the Moon.

Answers to Questions

1. The folktale was created to try to make sense of the people's observations of the Sun and Moon.

2. We know that the girl is modest because she shone brightly so that people could not look at her. We know that she is not willing to try new things—she asks to be the sun because she is "not familiar with the night." It could also be said that the girl is determined or bold because she makes a request of the Heavenly King. The king is fair. He made everyone work equally. He also listened to the girl's request and gave her a more fitting duty.

Respond to the Reading

1. What is the purpose of this folktale?

2. Describe the personalities of the girl and the king. What clues does the folktale give us about each of their personalities?

The two children lived peacefully in the Heavenly Kingdom, until one day the Heavenly King said to them, "We can not allow anyone to sit here and idle away the time. So I have decided on duties for you. The boy shall be the Sun, to light the world of men, and the girl shall be the Moon, to shine by night." Then the girl answered, "Oh King, I am not familiar with the night. It would be better for me not to be the Moon." So the King made her the Sun instead, and made her brother the Moon.

It is said that when she became the Sun, the people used to gaze up at her in the sky. But she was modest, and greatly embarrassed by this. So she shone brighter and brighter, so that it was impossible to look at her directly. And that is why the Sun is so bright, that her modesty might be forever respected.

516 CHAPTER 17 The Solar System and Beyond

Reading Further

Other sources on this topic include:

Inquiry Into the Relation of Cause and Effect, by Thomas Brown, Scholars Facsimilies & Reprint, 1999.

Older Brother, Younger Brother: A Korean Folk Tale, illustrated by Wengi Ma, Viking Penguin, 1997.

Understanding Literature

Cause and Effect In the folktale you just read, a story was created to explain why the Sun and the Moon exist, as well as why you should never look directly at the Sun. When one event brings about a second event, you are dealing with cause and effect. In this folktale, the Heavenly King says that no one is allowed to be idle in the Heavenly Kingdom. This is a cause. The effect is that the girl and boy are given the duties of being the Sun and the Moon. Many cultures create their own explanations, like this folktale, of why things happen or exist?

Science Connection In this chapter, you learned that a cause-and-effect relationship between Earth and the Sun is responsible for the changing seasons. According to the scientific explanation, the tilt of Earth's axis and Earth's revolution around the Sun cause the seasons to change. When the part of Earth you live on is tilted towards the Sun, you experience summer. When your part of Earth is tilted away from the Sun, you experience winter. Autumn and spring occur when Earth is not tilted toward or away from the Sun.

Linking Science and Writing

Create a Folktale Many early cultures used stories called folktales or myths to explain things that they didn't understand scientifically. Think of something that happens in nature that you don't understand scientifically. Write a one-page folktale that explains why it happens. You might explain what causes thunder, why the sky is blue, or how a spider knows how to spin its web.

Career Connection

Astronaut and physician

Dr. Mae Jemison finds ways to use space to help humans on Earth. She was a Science Mission Specialist on the space shuttle *Endeavor.* In space, she studied bone cells and biofeedback. On Earth, she directs the Jemison Institute. This institute brings new technology to countries that need it. It is working on a satellite system called Alafiya— which is Yoruba for "good health." Alafiya helps countries share information about health care. Using the satellite in space, people can learn about health education, disease prevention, and health resources.

SCIENCE *Online* To learn more about a career as an astronaut, visit the Glencoe Science Web site at **science.glencoe.com**.

Understanding Literature

Science Connection

Also related to cause and effect with regard to the seasons is the changing colors of leaves in autumn. In certain places on Earth, days shorten and temperatures become colder so the green of summer foliage is transformed into an autumn palette of golds, reds, and browns. During the growing season the chlorophyll is continually produced and broken down, so leaves appear green. As nights grow longer in autumn, chlorophyll production slows down and then stops. Eventually all the chlorophyll is destroyed. The carotenoids and anthocyanins that are present in the leaf are then unmasked and show their colors.

Linking Science and Writing

Teaching Strategies

Lead students in a brainstorming activity in which they think of a number of phenomena in nature they do not fully grasp. This will give them ideas to start their writing activity. Remind the students what they have learned about cause and effect.

Career Connection

Astronauts like Mae Jemison come from a wide variety of academic backgrounds. They often begin by pursuing a Bachelor of Science degree in science, engineering, or aeronautics. Then many go on to complete advanced degrees or, like Dr. Jemison, attend medical school. After leaving the space program, astronauts often work to benefit society in other ways.

SCIENCE *Online*
Internet Addresses

_____

_____

_____

Explore the Glencoe Science Web site at **science.glencoe.com** to find out more about topics in this feature.

Reviewing Main Ideas

Preview

Students can answer the questions in their Science Journals. Discuss the answers as you go through the chapter. **Linguistic**

Review

Students can write their answers, then compare them with those of other students. **Interpersonal**

Reteach

Students can look at the illustrations and describe details that support the main ideas of the chapter. **Visual-Spatial**

Answers to Chapter Review

SECTION 1

3. A lunar eclipse occurs when Earth moves between the Sun and the Moon. A solar eclipse occurs when the Moon moves between the Sun and Earth.

SECTION 2

3. Pluto is a small, rocky planet, not a gaseous giant.

SECTION 3

1. The hottest visible stars are blue; the coolest are red.

3. Scientists use special units of measurements because distances in space are so vast.

Chapter 17 Study Guide

Reviewing Main Ideas

Section 1 Earth's Place in Space

1. Earth spinning on its axis is called rotation. This movement causes night and day.

2. Earth orbits the Sun in a regular, curved path. This movement is known as Earth's revolution. Earth's revolution and the tilt of its axis are responsible for seasons.

3. The Moon moves, too, as it orbits Earth. The different positions of Earth, the Sun, and the Moon in space cause Moon phases and eclipses. *Explain the difference between a lunar eclipse and the solar eclipse shown here.*

Section 2 The Solar System

1. The solar system is made up of the nine planets and numerous other objects that orbit the Sun. Planets are classified as inner planets or outer planets.

2. The inner planets—Mercury, Venus, Earth, and Mars—are closest to the Sun.

3. The outer planets—Jupiter, Saturn, Uranus, Neptune, and Pluto—are much farther away. Most of the outer planets are large, gas giants with rings and moons. *How is Pluto different from the other outer planets?*

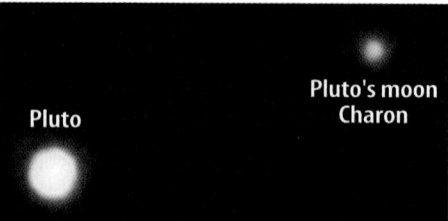

Pluto

Pluto's moon Charon

Section 3 Stars and Galaxies

1. Constellations are groups of stars that form patterns in the sky. Although stars might look the same from Earth, they differ greatly in temperature, size, and color. The Sun, for instance, is a medium-sized, yellow star. *What color are the hottest stars? The coolest?*

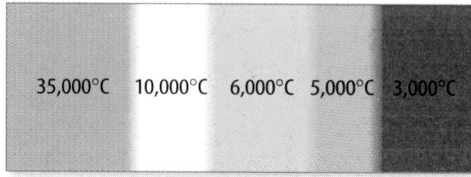

| 35,000°C | 10,000°C | 6,000°C | 5,000°C | 3,000°C |

2. Stars begin as gas and dust that are pulled together by gravity. Eventually, a star begins to produce light as hydrogen atoms fuse. The course of the life cycle for each star is determined by its size. Supernovas and black holes are the results of huge stars that have completed their life cycles.

3. Galaxies are groups of stars, gas, and dust held together by gravity. The three main types of galaxies are elliptical, spiral, and irregular. You live in the Milky Way, a spiral galaxy. Distances between galaxies are measured in light-years. A light-year is the distance light travels in one year—about 9.5 trillion km. *Why are special units needed for studying distances in space?*

FOLDABLES
Reading & Study Skills

After You Read

To help you review characteristics of the solar system, stars, and galaxies, use the Foldable you made at the beginning of the chapter.

FOLDABLES
Reading & Study Skills

After You Read

After students have read the chapter and completed the Foldable described in Before You Read, have them do the activity on the student page.

Dinah Zike

Visualizing Main Ideas

Use the following terms to fill in the concept map below: asteroid belt, galaxy, universe, inner planets, comets and meteorites, *and* outer planets.

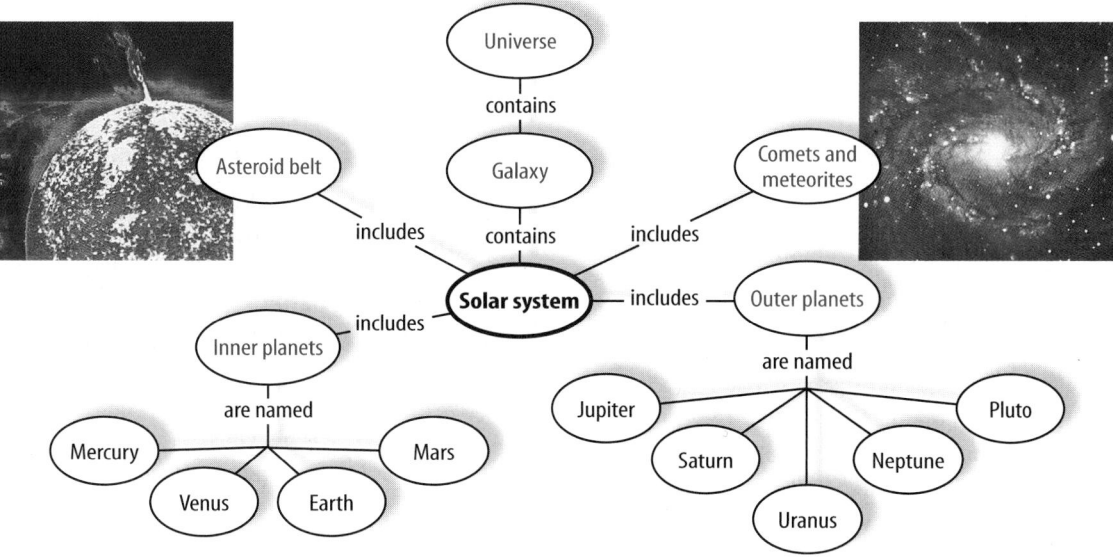

Universe — contains — Galaxy — contains — **Solar system**

Asteroid belt — includes

Comets and meteorites — includes

Solar system — includes — Outer planets

Inner planets — includes

Inner planets — are named — Mercury, Venus, Earth, Mars

Outer planets — are named — Jupiter, Saturn, Uranus, Neptune, Pluto

Visualizing Main Ideas

See student page.

Vocabulary Review

Using Vocabulary

1. eclipse
2. rotation
3. galaxy
4. constellation
5. revolution

Vocabulary Review

Vocabulary Words

a. astronomical unit
b. comet
c. constellation
d. eclipse
e. galaxy
f. light-year
g. meteorite
h. orbit
i. revolution
j. rotation
k. solar system
l. supernova

 **THE PRINCETON REVIEW** **Study Tip**

Design experiments that you could perform to test some of the principles discussed in this chapter.

Using Vocabulary

Each question below asks about a vocabulary word from the list. Write the word that best answers each question.

1. What event occurs when Earth's shadow falls on the Moon or when the Moon's shadow falls on Earth?

2. Which motion of Earth produces day and night and causes the planets and stars to rise and set?

3. What is a large group of stars, gas, and dust held together by gravity called?

4. What is a group of stars that forms a pattern in the sky called?

5. Which movement of Earth causes it to travel around the Sun?

CHAPTER STUDY GUIDE   519

IDENTIFYING Misconceptions

Assess

Use the assessment as follow-up to page 490F after students have completed the chapter.

Procedure Visit the Glencoe Science Web site to find information about the movement of the planets around the Sun and the apparent movement of planets and stars in the sky. Have each student select a planet and a star and graph and analyze the data about the objects chosen.

Expected Outcome Students will recognize that planets are much closer to Earth than stars are. They will also recognize that we can determine whether or not an object in the sky is a planet or star, based partly on its motion.

Chapter 17 Assessment

Checking Concepts

1. D
2. B
3. B
4. C
5. D
6. A
7. C
8. D
9. A
10. B

Thinking Critically

11. Earth's surface temperatures allow water to exist as a solid, a liquid, and a gas. Also, Earth's atmosphere keeps most ultraviolet rays from reaching the planet's surface.

12. Answers will vary. Students may say that Mars is most like Earth because of its temperature and atmosphere. Jupiter may be students' choice as most different. It is a gas giant, has no firm surface, and has multiple moons.

13. Eclipses are possible only when the Moon is crossing Earth's orbital plane. By plotting the orbits of Earth and the Moon, scientists can predict the day and time of a solar eclipse.

14. The changing position of the Moon from night to night is a real motion because the Moon is orbiting Earth. The movement of the Moon westward across the sky is an apparent motion caused by Earth's rotation.

Checking Concepts

Choose the word or phrase that best answers the question.

1. What is caused by the tilt of Earth's axis and Earth's revolution?
   A) eclipses
   C) day and night
   B) phases
   D) seasons

2. What is occurring when the Moon's phases are waning?
   A) Phases are growing larger.
   B) Phases are growing smaller.
   C) a full moon
   D) a new moon

3. An astronomical unit equals the distance from Earth to which of the following?
   A) the Moon
   C) Mercury
   B) the Sun
   D) Pluto

4. Earth is which planet from the Sun?
   A) first
   C) third
   B) second
   D) fourth

5. How many galaxies could be in the universe?
   A) 1 billion
   C) 50 billion
   B) 10 billion
   D) 100 billion

6. Which results from Earth's rotation?
   A) night and day
   C) Moon phases
   B) summer and winter
   D) solar eclipses

7. What unit often is used to measure large distances in space, such as between stars or galaxies?
   A) kilometer
   C) light-year
   B) astronomical unit
   D) centimeter

8. How many planets are in the solar system?
   A) six
   C) eight
   B) seven
   D) nine

9. Which object's shadow travels across part of Earth during a solar eclipse?
   A) the Moon
   C) Mars
   B) the Sun
   D) a comet

10. If a star is massive enough, what can result after it produces a supernova?
    A) a galaxy
    C) a black dwarf
    B) a black hole
    D) a superstar

Thinking Critically

11. What conditions on Earth allow life to thrive?

12. Which of the planets in the solar system seems most like Earth? Which seems most different? Explain your answers using facts about the planets.

13. How might a scientist predict the day and time of a solar eclipse?

14. Which of the Moon's motions are real? Which are apparent? Explain why each occurs.

Developing Skills

15. **Making and Using Tables** Research the size, period of rotation, and period of revolution for each planet. Show this information in a table. How do tables help you better understand information?

16. **Comparing and Contrasting** Compare and contrast the inner planets and the outer planets.

17. **Making a Model** Based on what you have learned about the Sun, the Moon, and Earth, model a lunar or a solar eclipse using simple classroom materials.

Chapter ✓Assessment Planner

Portfolio Encourage students to place in their portfolios one or two items of what they consider to be their best work. Examples include:
- Activity, p. 494
- Life Science Integration, p. 500
- Physics Integration, p. 512

Performance Additional performance assessments, Performance Task Assessment Lists, and rubrics for evaluating these activities can be found in Glencoe's **Performance Assessment in the Science Classroom.**

18. Concept Mapping Complete the following concept map using these terms: *full, red surface, corona, solar,* and *few.*

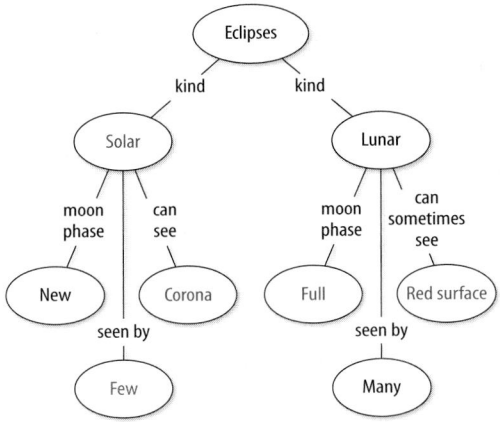

19. Comparing and Contrasting Compare and contrast Earth and other bodies in the solar system in terms of their ability to support life.

Performance Assessment

20. Model Make a three-dimensional model including a light source for the Sun that shows how Earth's tilted axis and its orbit around the Sun combine to cause changes in the lengths of day and night throughout the year.

21. Poster Research the moons of Jupiter, Saturn, Uranus, or Neptune. Make a poster showing the special characteristics of these moons. Display your poster for your class.

TECHNOLOGY

Go to the Glencoe Science Web site at **science.glencoe.com** or use the **Glencoe Science CD-ROM** for additional chapter assessment.

THE PRINCETON REVIEW — Test Practice

The way that Earth moves in space creates night and day and different seasons. The picture below shows Earth and the Sun in space.

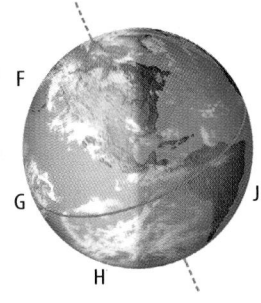

Study the picture and answer the following questions.

1. Which of the following processes contributes to the fact that it is summertime at location F?
  A) The rotation of Earth
  B) The core of Earth
  C) The tilt of Earth on its axis
  D) The phases of the Moon

2. In the picture of Earth, it is nighttime at location _____.
  F) F   **H)** H
  G) G   **J)** J

3. Why would location G not experience very much seasonal temperature change?
  A) It is facing the Sun.
  B) It is near Earth's equator.
  C) It is in the southern hemisphere.
  D) It is in the northern hemisphere.

THE PRINCETON REVIEW — Test Practice

The Test-Taking Tip was written by The Princeton Review, the nation's leader in test preparation.
1. C
2. J
3. B

Developing Skills

15. Tables allow you to compare a lot of information at a glance.

Solar System Information			
Planet	Diameter (km)	Period of rotation	Period of revolution
Mercury	4,878	59 d	87.97 d
Venus	12,104	243 d	224.70 d
Earth	12,756	24 h	365.26 d
Mars	6,794	24.6 h	686.98 d
Jupiter	142,796	10 h	11.86 y
Saturn	120,660	10.6 h	29.46 y
Uranus	51,118	17.2 h	84.04 y
Neptune	49,528	16 h	164.79 y
Pluto	2,290	6 d	248.53 y

16. All planets orbit the Sun. The inner planets are small and rocky; the outer (except for Pluto) are gas giants.
17. Check student's work.
18. See student page.
19. Earth's unique position with respect to the Sun and its atmosphere allow liquid water and life to exist. Features on Mars suggest liquid water has in the past, and may still, be present there. An ocean of water is thought to exist beneath the surface of Europa, one of Jupiter's moons.

Performance Assessment

20. Use **PASC,** p. 123.
21. Use **PASC,** p. 145.

✓Assessment Resources

📁 Reproducible Masters

Chapter Resources Booklet
  Chapter Review, pp. 37–38
  Chapter Tests, pp. 39–42
  Assessment Transparency Activity, p. 49

Glencoe Science Web site
  Interactive Tutor
  Chapter Quizzes

Glencoe Technology
  🖱 Assessment Transparency
  💿 Interactive CD-ROM Chapter Quizzes
  💿 ExamView Pro Test Bank
  💿 Vocabulary PuzzleMaker Software
  📼 MindJogger Videoquiz

QUESTION 1: B

Students must use clues from the passage such as *rocks will melt. This molten rock*, to identify that the best meaning of the word *molten* is choice B, *melted.*

QUESTION 2: F

Students must refer to the first paragraph in order to identify the correct answer.

QUESTION 3: B

Students must reread the passage carefully to decide which choice is supported by the reading passage.

- **Choice A** No; rapid cooling produces small crystals or glass.
- **Choice B** Yes; this is supported by the passage.
- **Choice C** No; this is not mentioned in the passage.
- **Choice D** No; heat and pressure over time form metamorphic rocks.

THE PRINCETON REVIEW — All questions written and validated by The Princeton Review.

Read the passage. Then read each question that follows the passage. Decide which is the best answer to each question.

Obsidian Uses

From the top of the highest mountain to the bottom of the deepest ocean, Earth is made mostly of rock. Geologists classify rocks according to three different categories, depending upon how the rocks were formed. These are igneous, sedimentary, and metamorphic.

Igneous rocks are formed from rock that melted and later cooled and solidified. When temperature and pressure conditions are just right, deep within Earth, rocks will melt. This molten rock, called magma, moves up toward the surface of Earth over time and might reach the surface in a volcanic eruption. When magma erupts at Earth's surface, it is called lava. When lava cools, mineral crystals will form. If it cools very quickly, volcanic glass can form.

Obsidian is a type of volcanic rock. It also is volcanic glass because few or no crystals are present within it. It was a prized material among prehistoric cultures because it fractures with sharp edges and can be used as a weapon or tool. Knives, arrowheads, and spear points were made from obsidian. Prehistoric people also used obsidian as mirrors. In modern times, obsidian has been used for surgical scalpel blades.

The beauty and mystery of igneous rocks have inspired many artists. Some artists carefully sculpt volcanic rock into beautiful, one-of-a-kind pieces of art.

> **Test-Taking Tip** As you read the passage, write a one-sentence summary for each paragraph.

This is obsidian, a type of volcanic glass.

1. In this passage, the word <u>molten</u> means
   - **A)** deep
   - **B)** melted
   - **C)** igneous
   - **D)** cooled

2. According to the passage, the three categories, or groups, of rocks are _____.
   - **F)** igneous, metamorphic, and sedimentary
   - **G)** volcanic, glassy, and irregular
   - **H)** chemical, organic, and detrital
   - **J)** residual, original, and primitive

3. Which conclusion is best supported by information given in the passage?
   - **A)** When magma cools rapidly, it produces rocks with many large crystals.
   - **B)** Igneous rocks can be made into tools and pieces of art.
   - **C)** Obsidian was used by prehistoric cultures to build stone houses.
   - **D)** Igneous rock forms when rocks are exposed to heat and pressure over time.

Standardized Test Practice

Reasoning and Skills

Read each question and choose the best answer.

Igneous Rocks

Formed	Light-colored	Dark-colored
Below Earth's Surface	granite	gabbro
At Earth's Surface	rhyolite	basalt

1. According to the chart, lava that flows onto the surface from a volcano should cool to form the dark-colored rock _____.

  A) granite   **C)** rhyolite
  B) gabbro   **D)** basalt

Test-Taking Tip   Reread the question and think about the color of the rock and where the rock was formed.

2. Earth's crust is estimated to be composed of about 46% oxygen, 28% silicon, 8% aluminum, and 18% other elements. Which area of the graph represents aluminum?

  F) Q
  G) R
  H) S
  J) T

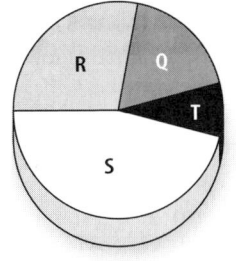

Test-Taking Tip   Think about the quantity of the element the question refers to compared to the sizes of each portion of the graph.

3. The chart shows the average distance of each planet from the Sun. Which planet is almost 8 times as far from the Sun as Jupiter?

  A) Mercury
  B) Saturn
  C) Neptune
  D) Pluto

Solar System Data

Planet	Distance from the Sun (AU)
Mercury	0.39
Venus	0.72
Earth	1
Mars	1.52
Jupiter	5.20
Saturn	9.54
Uranus	19.19
Neptune	30.07
Pluto	39.48

Test-Taking Tip   Multiply the distance to Jupiter by 8, and find the distance closest to the answer. Then follow the chart across to find which planet it is.

4. The erosion pictured is most likely caused by the force of _____.

  F) water   **H)** wind
  G) gravity   **J)** glacier movement

Test-Taking Tip   Think about the forces that help cause erosion.

Reasoning and Skills

QUESTION 1: D

Students must read the question carefully and then refer to the table. Key words in the question are *onto the surface* and *dark-colored rock*. Only choice D, *basalt*, forms at the surface and is dark-colored.

QUESTION 2: J

Students must compare information from the question with the graph in order to identify the correct answer. Aluminum is the smallest percentage given in the question, and choice J, *T*, is the smallest slice of the pie chart.

Teaching Tip

Tell students to think about the size of the portion of the graph the question asks for compared with the size of the other portions.

QUESTION 3: D

Students must multiply the distance of Jupiter from the Sun by eight and then find in the chart the planet that is approximately equal to that distance.

QUESTION 4: F

Students must understand the forces that cause erosion and use the information in the pictures to identify choice F, *water*, as the correct answer.

Unit Contents

✔ Pre-Reading Activity

Have students choose a chapter in this unit and write five things they want to know about the topic. Then have them skim the text for key words to help them locate passages where they think their questions may be answered.

UNIT **6** Matter, Forces, and Energy

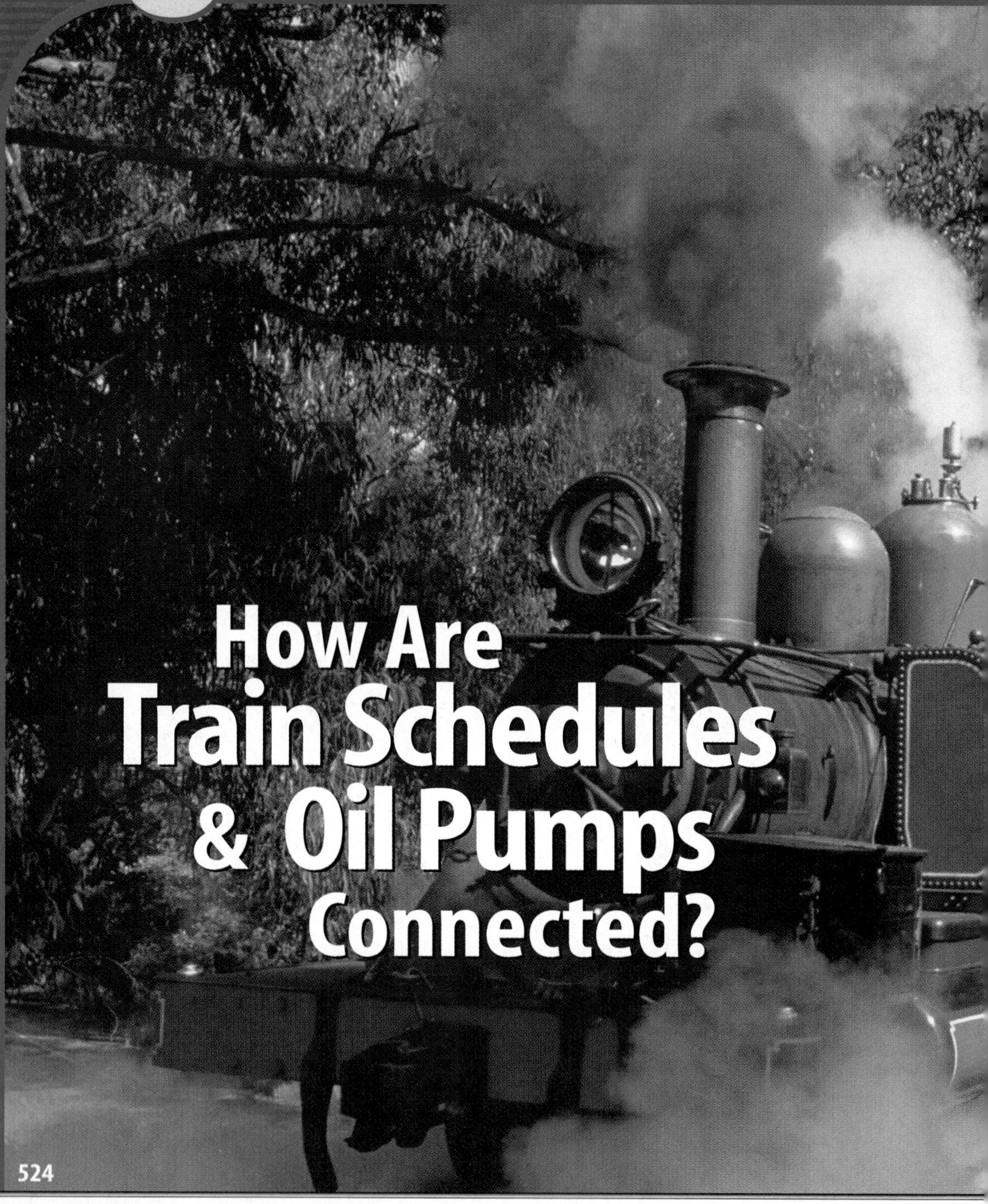

How Are Train Schedules & Oil Pumps Connected?

524

Teacher to Teacher

"Introduce students to the concept of chemical change by having them heat sugar in an aluminum foil scoop over a candle. This decomposition reaction illustrates that in chemical changes, a substance's chemical properties change and new products are formed."

John E. Burns, Teacher
Ramona Junior High School
Chino, CA

In the 1800s, trains had to make frequent stops so that their moving parts could be lubricated. Without lubrication, the parts would have worn out due to friction. When the train stopped, a worker had to get out and oil the parts by hand. The process was very time-consuming and made it hard for trains to stay on schedule. Around 1870, an engineer named Elijah McCoy developed the first automatic lubricating device, which oiled the engine while the train was running. (A later version of his automatic lubricator is seen at lower right.) Since then, many kinds of automatic lubricating devices have been developed. Today, automobiles have oil pumps that automatically circulate oil to the moving parts of the engine. When you go for a ride in a car, you can thank Elijah McCoy that you don't have to stop every few miles to oil the engine by hand!

Introducing the Unit

How Are Train Schedules & Oil Pumps Connected?

All matter is composed of atoms. Atoms of various kinds are attracted to other atoms. The moving parts of train engines contact one another. The attraction between atoms in these parts produces resistance to motion; this resistance is what we call friction. As the parts move against one another the attractions between atoms are broken. Gradually the matter of the contacting parts is worn away. As the bonds between atoms break, the energy holding them together (potential energy) is released as heat (a form of kinetic energy). The use of lubricants reduces the force of friction between objects by forming a thin layer of frictionless molecules between moving parts. This reduces the damage to the parts and the heat generated by motion. The result is longer-lasting parts and a more efficient use of fuels to produce motion.

SCIENCE CONNECTION

FRICTION AND LUBRICANTS A lubricant is a substance that reduces friction between surfaces that touch one another. Some of the world's first lubricants were animal and plant products such as lard and vegetable oils. Conduct research to identify a variety of modern-day lubricants. Select one lubricant you learned about and create a poster that shows its source, how it is made or processed, its special properties, and how it is used to reduce friction.

SCIENCE Online
Internet Addresses
_____
_____
_____
_____

Explore the Glencoe Science Web site at **science.glencoe.com** to find out more about topics in this unit.

SCIENCE CONNECTION

Activity

Demonstrate that the energy attracting atoms to one another is released as kinetic energy, or heat, when those bonds are broken. Give each student a rubber band. Instruct them to hold it against their upper lip and to note how warm or cool the material feels. Have the students stretch the rubber band while the bands are in contact with their skin. The rubber band will feel quite warm. As the band resumes its original shape they will feel the material cool down. Explain that stretching the rubber broke some of the forces of attraction between atoms. This energy was released as heat.

Section/Objectives	Standards		Activities/Features
	National	**State/Local**	
Chapter Opener	See p. 7T for a Key to Standards.		**Explore Activity:** Classify Coins, p. 527 **Before You Read,** p. 527
Section 1 Physical Properties and Changes ⏱ 4 sessions ▥ 2 blocks 1. **Identify** physical properties of matter. 2. **Describe** the states of matter. 3. **Classify** matter using physical properties.	National Content Standards: UCP2, A1, B1		**Science Online,** p. 529 **Science Online,** p. 530 **MiniLAB:** Changing Density, p. 531 **Earth Science Integration,** p. 533 **Visualizing Dichotomous Keys,** p. 536
Section 2 Chemical Properties and Changes ⏱ 5 sessions ▥ 2.5 blocks 1. **Recognize** chemical properties. 2. **Identify** chemical changes. 3. **Classify** matter according to chemical properties. 4. **Describe** the law of conservation of mass.	National Content Standards: UCP2, A1, B1, G2, G3		**Health Integration,** p. 541 **MiniLAB:** Observing Yeast, p. 544 **Problem-Solving Activity:** Do light sticks conserve mass?, p. 545 **Activity:** Liquid Layers, p. 547 **Activity:** Fruit Salad Favorites, p. 548

NATIONAL GEOGRAPHIC

Teacher's Corner

INDEX TO NATIONAL GEOGRAPHIC SOCIETY
The following articles may be used for research relating to this chapter: "Worlds Within the Atom," by John Boslough, May 1985.

"Unlocking the Climate Puzzle," by Curt Supple, May 1998.

Activity Materials	Reproducible Resources	Section Assessment	Technology
Explore Activity: collection of pennies	**Chapter Resources Booklet** Foldables Worksheet, p. 17 Directed Reading Overview, p. 19 Note-taking Worksheets, pp. 31–32	GLENCOE'S ASSESSMENT ADVANTAGE	

MiniLAB: tablespoon of baking soda, warm water, vinegar, 2 clear glasses, 3 raisins, plastic knife
 	
Need materials?
Contact Science Kit at 1-800-828-7777 or www.sciencekit.com on the Internet.
	Chapter Resources Booklet
	Transparency Activity, p. 42
	MiniLAB, p. 3
	Enrichment, p. 29
	Reinforcement, p. 27
	Directed Reading, p. 20
	Lab Activity, pp. 9–11
	Transparency Activity, pp. 45–46
	Science Inquiry Labs, pp. 25,
	    43, 45
	**Reading and Writing Skill
	    Activities,** p. 17
		Portfolio
		Curriculum Connection, p. 532
		Performance
		MiniLAB, p. 531
		Skill Builder Activities, p. 539
		Content
		Section Assessment, p. 539
			Section Focus Transparency
			Teaching Transparency
			Interactive CD-ROM
			Guided Reading Audio
			    Program

MiniLAB: paper plate or lab tray, clear cup or beaker, dry yeast, hand lens, warm water, sugar
Activity: 250-mL beaker, graduated cylinder, corn syrup, glycerin, water, corn oil, rubbing alcohol, penny, wood sphere, rubber ball
Activity: bananas, apples, pears, 2 mixing bowls, lemon-water solution, paring knife
	Chapter Resources Booklet
	Transparency Activity, p. 43
	MiniLAB, p. 4
	Enrichment, p. 30
	Reinforcement, p. 28
	Directed Reading, pp. 21, 22
	Activity Worksheet, pp. 5–6, 7–8
	Lab Activity, pp. 13–15
	Mathematics Skill Activities,
	    p. 9
	**Reading and Writing Skill
	    Activities,** p. 1
	**Life Science Critical Thinking/
	    Problem Solving,** p. 8
	Lab Management and Safety,
	    p. 38
		Portfolio
		Science Journal, p. 543
		Curriculum Connection, p. 544
		Performance
		MiniLAB, p. 544
		Problem-Solving Activity, p. 545
		Skill Builder Activities, p. 546
		Content
		Section Assessment, p. 546
			Section Focus Transparency
			Interactive CD-ROM
			Guided Reading Audio
			    Program

GLENCOE'S ASSESSMENT ADVANTAGE	End of Chapter Assessment		
	Blackline Masters	**Technology**	**Professional Series**
	Chapter Resources Booklet Chapter Review, pp. 35–36 Chapter Tests, pp. 37–40 **Standardized Test Practice by The Princeton Review,** pp. 75–78	MindJogger Videoquiz Interactive CD-ROM Vocabulary PuzzleMakers ExamView Pro Test Bank Interactive Lesson Planner Interactive Teacher Edition	Performance Assessment in the Science Classroom (PASC)

Transparencies

Section Focus

Section Focus Transparency **Water, Water Everywhere**

How much water can you find here? Actually, water is almost everywhere.

1. Where do you see water as a solid? A liquid?
2. What happens to snow on a sunny, warm day? What happens to water in a kettle if you light a burner underneath? How are these events similar?

L2

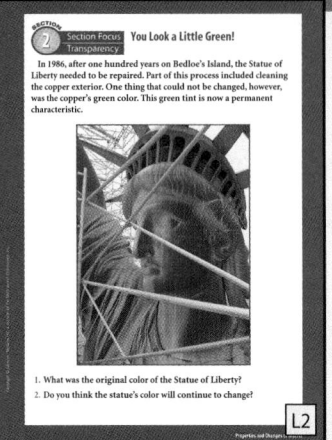

Section Focus Transparency **You Look a Little Green!**

In 1986, after one hundred years on Bedloe's Island, the Statue of Liberty needed to be repaired. Part of this process included cleaning the copper exterior. One thing that could not be changed, however, was the copper's green color. This green tint is now a permanent characteristic.

1. What was the original color of the Statue of Liberty?
2. Do you think the statue's color will continue to change?

L2

This is a representation of key blackline masters available in the Teacher Classroom Resources. See Resource Manager boxes within the chapter for additional information.

Assessment

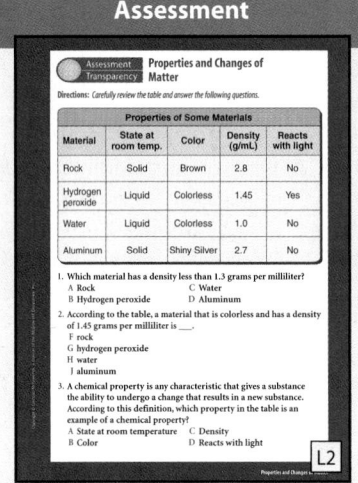

Assessment Transparency **Properties and Changes of Matter**

Directions: Carefully review the table and answer the following questions.

Properties of Some Materials

Material	State at room temp.	Color	Density (g/mL)	Reacts with light
Rock	Solid	Brown	2.8	No
Hydrogen peroxide	Liquid	Colorless	1.45	Yes
Water	Liquid	Colorless	1.0	No
Aluminum	Solid	Shiny Silver	2.7	No

1. Which material has a density less than 1.3 grams per milliliter?
   A Rock   C Water
   B Hydrogen peroxide   D Aluminum
2. According to the table, a material that is colorless and has a density of 1.45 grams per milliliter is ___.
   F rock
   G hydrogen peroxide
   H water
   J aluminum
3. A chemical property is any characteristic that gives a substance the ability to undergo a change that results in a new substance. According to this definition, which property in the table is an example of a chemical property?
   A State at room temperature   C Density
   B Color   D Reacts with light

L2

Teaching

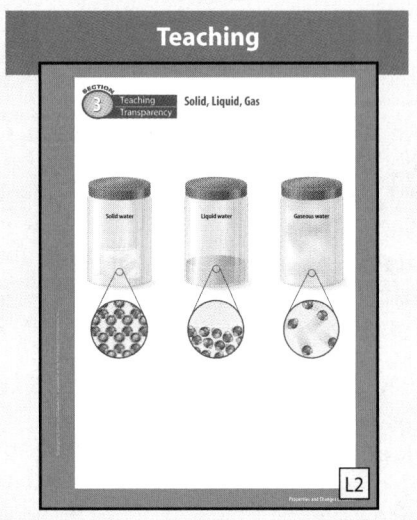

Teaching Transparency **Solid, Liquid, Gas**

Solid water   Liquid water   Gaseous water

L2

Key to Teaching Strategies

The following designations will help you decide which activities are appropriate for your students.

L1 Level 1 activities should be appropriate for students with learning difficulties.

L2 Level 2 activities should be within the ability range of all students.

L3 Level 3 activities are designed for above-average students.

ELL ELL activities should be within the ability range of English Language Learners.

COOP LEARN Cooperative Learning activities are designed for small group work.

LS Multiple Learning Styles logos, as described on page 22T, are used throughout to indicate strategies that address different learning styles.

P These strategies represent student products that can be placed into a best-work portfolio.

Hands-on Activities

Activity Worksheets

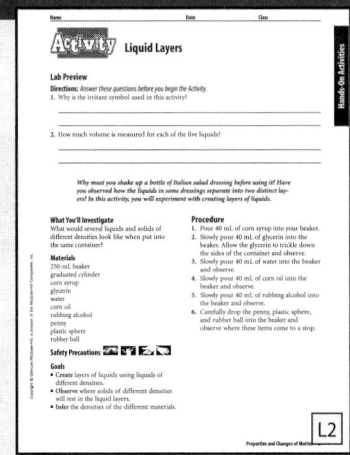

Name _____ Date _____ Class _____

Activity **Liquid Layers**

Lab Preview

Directions: Answer these questions before you begin the Activity.
1. Why is the irritant symbol used in this activity?

2. How much volume is measured for each of the five liquids?

Why must you shake up a bottle of Italian salad dressing before using it? Have you observed how the liquids in some dressings separate into two distinct layers? In this activity, you will experiment with creating layers of liquids.

What You'll Investigate
What would several liquids and solids of different densities look like when put into the same container?

Materials
250-mL beaker
graduated cylinder
corn syrup
glycerin
water
corn oil
rubbing alcohol
penny
plastic sphere
rubber ball

Safety Precautions

Goals
• Create layers of liquids using liquids of different densities.
• Observe where solids of different densities will rest in the liquid layers.
• Infer the densities of the different materials.

Procedure
1. Pour 40 mL of corn syrup into your beaker.
2. Slowly pour 40 mL of glycerin into the beaker. Allow the glycerin to trickle down the sides of the container and observe.
3. Slowly pour 40 mL of water into the beaker and observe.
4. Slowly pour 40 mL of corn oil into the beaker and observe.
5. Slowly pour 40 mL of rubbing alcohol into the beaker and observe.
6. Carefully drop the penny, plastic sphere, and rubber ball into the beaker and observe where these items come to a stop.

L2

Laboratory Activities

Name _____ Date _____ Class _____

Laboratory Activity **Density of Solids**

Suppose you cut a piece of copper rod into sections of equal volume. If each section of rod had a volume of 1 cm³, you would find that all the pieces would have the same mass when massed on a balance. That is, for a unit volume of material is the same for all samples of a substance, but usually differs for different substances. The mass of a unit volume, or density, is therefore a characteristic physical property of a substance. How can you determine whether samples that share other similar physical properties are made of the same substance? One way is to determine the densities of the samples.

Strategy
You will measure the mass and volume of several samples of solids.
You will calculate the density of each solid.
You will determine if any of the samples are made of the same substance.
You will identify samples based on their densities.

Materials
sheets of paper (2)
metal blocks (3)
balance
metric ruler
small rocks (2)
50-mL graduated cylinder
water

Procedure
1. Place the three blocks on a sheet of paper. On the paper, make a circle around each block. Label one circle A, label another circle B, and a third circle C, as shown in Figure 1. Take only one block off the paper at a time. Keep the other blocks in their circles so you don't get them mixed up.

Figure 1

2. Use a balance to measure the mass of each block to the nearest 0.1 gram. Record the masses in Table 1.
3. Measure the dimensions of each of the three blocks as accurately as you can. Record the dimensions in the table.
4. Calculate the volume of each block by multiplying length, width, and height. Record the volume in the table.
5. Calculate the density of each block by dividing the mass by the volume. Record the density of each block in the table.
6. Place the two rocks on another sheet of paper. On the paper, make a circle around each rock. Label one circle A and label the other circle B. Take only one rock off the paper at a time. Keep the other rock in its circle so you don't get them mixed up.
7. Use the balance to measure the masses of each rock sample. Record the masses in Table 2.

L2

Meeting Different Ability Levels

Content Outline

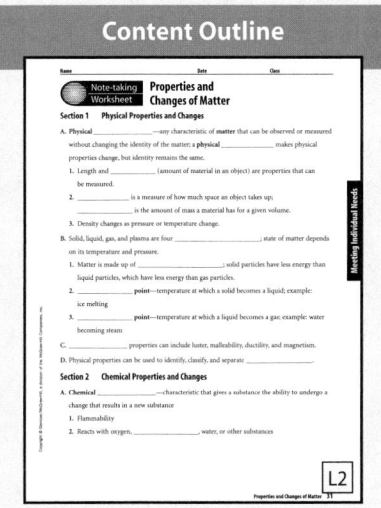

Reinforcement

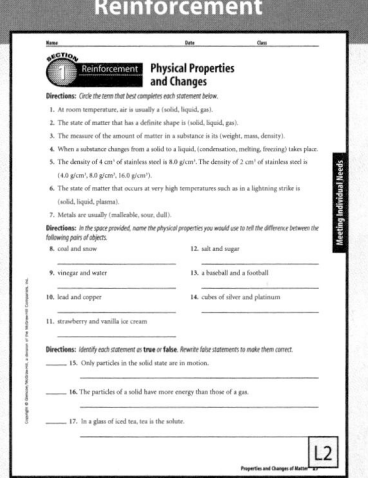

Directed Reading

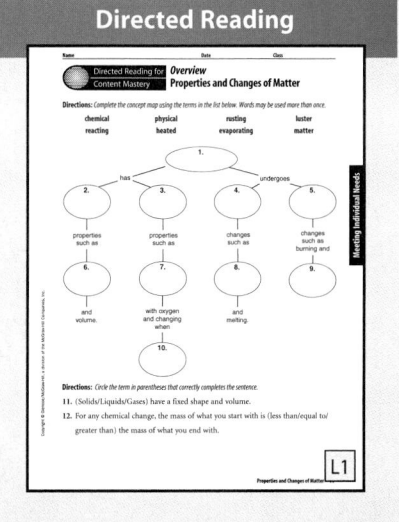

Assessment

Chapter Tests

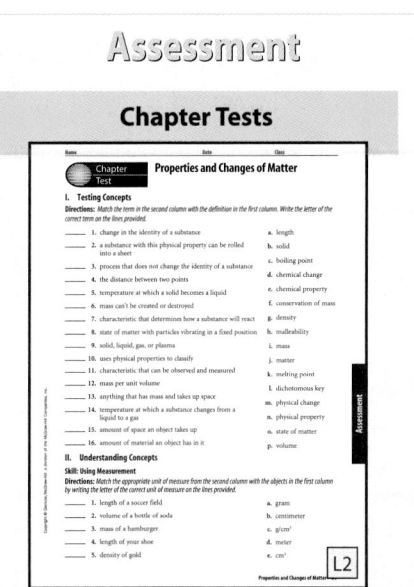

Enrichment

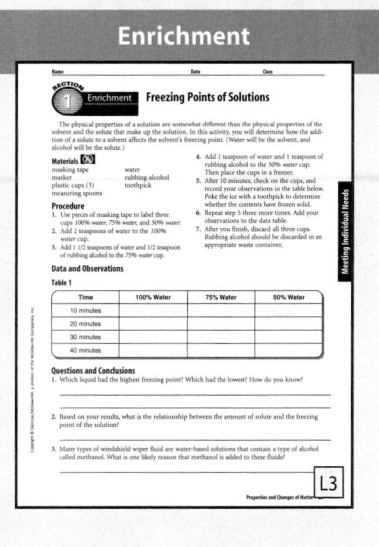

Spanish Directed Reading

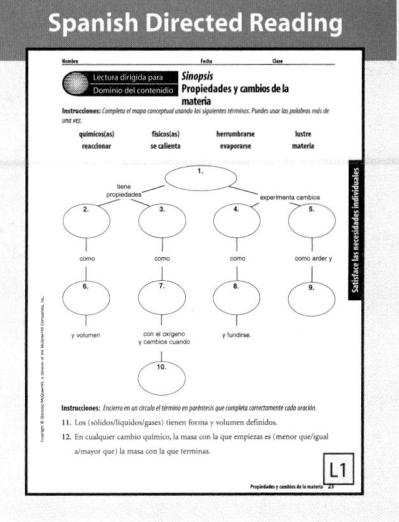

Test Practice Workbook

Chapter Review

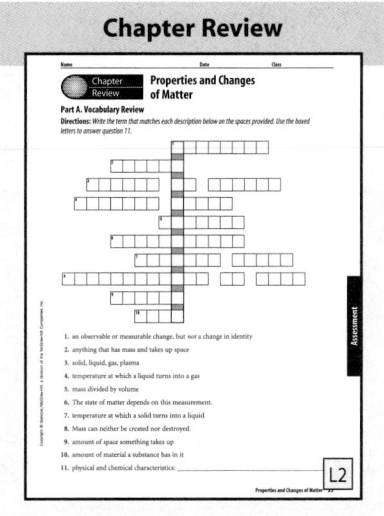

Science Content Background

SECTION
1

Physical Properties and Changes

Physical Properties

Care must be taken in describing some physical properties, particularly properties such as solubility. Describing solubility can involve a reaction and, for that reason, may not be a true physical property. For example, if you say that sodium is soluble in water, that would imply that the sodium simply dissolves in water. Instead, sodium reacts with water to form hydrogen gas and an aqueous sodium hydroxide solution.

Physical Changes

Knowledge of physical changes and the circumstances under which they occur can be used to separate mixtures. Distillation is a change-of-state operation that is used to separate substances with different boiling points. Distillation is used to separate drinking water from seawater and hydrocarbons, such as gasoline and kerosene, from petroleum.

Fun Fact

Salt has been purified for thousands of years by using a physical change process—evaporation.

Intensive and Extensive Properties

Properties can also be classified as either intensive or extensive, depending on whether the value changes with the size of the sample. Intensive properties, such as melting point and temperature, have values that do not depend on the amount of the sample. Extensive properties, such as mass, length, and volume, have values that do depend on the sample size. Density is an intensive physical property that relates the mass of an object to its volume. Density is temperature dependent because most substances change in volume when heated or cooled.

Fun Fact

Icebergs float because solid ice is less dense than liquid water. Hydrogen is used to inflate weather balloons because it is much less dense than air.

Anna E. Zuckerman/PhotoEdit

Chemical Properties and Changes
Chemical Properties

A substance's chemical properties describe its ability to react with other substances or to decompose. For example, one chemical property of limestone, calcium carbonate, is its ability to react with hydrochloric acid, producing carbon dioxide, water, and calcium chloride. Another chemical property of calcium carbonate is the ability to decompose, forming calcium oxide and carbon dioxide when heated.

The ability to corrode many metals is a chemical property of some acids. For example, when sulfuric acid corrodes aluminum, the aluminum atoms are oxidized (lose electrons) to form positively charged aluminum ions, while the hydrogen ions in the sulfuric acid are reduced (gain electrons) to form hydrogen atoms.

Chemical Changes

Chemical reaction is another term for chemical change. In a chemical change, atoms are rearranged and may lose or gain electrons. A rule of thumb states that if a precipitate, gas, color change, or energy change occurs, a chemical change has taken place. Almost all chemical changes involve either the taking in (endothermic) or giving off (exothermic) energy. Cold packs used by athletic trainers take advantage of endothermic changes.

SCIENCE
Online

For additional content background on this topic, go to the Glencoe Science Web site at science.glencoe.com.

Charles D. Winters/Photo Researchers, Inc.

Properties and Changes of Matter

Chapter Vocabulary

physical property, p. 528
matter, p. 529
physical change, p. 529
density, p. 530
state of matter, p. 531
melting point, p. 533
boiling point, p. 533
chemical property, p. 540
chemical change, p. 541
conservation of mass, p. 545

What do you think?

Science Journal The colored band is a thermometer that records the temperature of the water in the fish tank.

Properties and Changes of Matter

Wendy Craig Duncan carried the Olympic flame underwater on the way to the 2000 Summer Olympics in Sydney, Australia. How many different states of matter can you find in this picture? What chemical and physical changes are taking place? In this chapter, you will learn about the four states of matter, the physical and chemical properties of matter, and how those properties can change.

What do you think?

Science Journal What is the colored band on this fish tank? Why would it change colors? Here's a hint: *Would you want your fish to be chilly?* Write your thoughts and ideas in your Science Journal.

526

Theme Connection

Stability and Change Matter can be described by its physical and chemical properties. Matter is capable of undergoing physical and chemical changes based upon these properties.

Your teacher has given you a collection of pennies. It is your task to separate these pennies into groups while using words to describe each set. In this chapter, you will learn how to identify things based on their physical and chemical properties. With an understanding of these principles of matter, you will discover how things are classified or put into groups.

Classify coins

1. Observe the collection of pennies.

2. Choose a characteristic that will allow you to separate the pennies into groups.

3. Classify and sort each penny based on the chosen feature. Tally your data in a frequency table.

4. Explain how you classified the pennies. Compare your system of classification with those of others in the classroom.

Observe

Think about how your group classified its pennies. Describe the system your group used in your Science Journal.

FOLDABLES
Reading & Study Skills

Before You Read

Making an Organizational Study Fold **Make the following Foldable to help you organize your thoughts into clear categories about properties of matter.**

1. Place a sheet of paper in front of you so the long side is at the top. Fold the paper in half from the left side to the right side. Unfold.

2. Fold each side in to the center fold line to divide the paper into fourths. Fold the paper in half from top to bottom. Unfold.

3. Through the top thickness of paper, cut along both of the middle fold lines to form four tabs. Label the tabs *Physical Properties*, *Physical Changes*, *Chemical Properties*, and *Chemical Changes*.

4. Before you read the chapter, define each term on the front of the tabs. As you read the chapter, correct your definitions and write about each under the tabs.

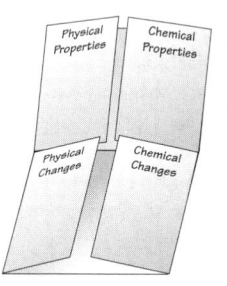

527

Purpose Use the Explore Activity to help students understand that observable properties are used to identify and classify matter. L1 ELL COOP LEARN

IS Interpersonal

Preparation Collect coins for each group of students.

Materials one set of approximately 20 pennies for each group

Teaching Strategy Ask students to share possible categories they could use to classify the pennies. Possible answers: date, amount of wear, shininess, place minted

Observe

Descriptions should be clear and should include any difficulties experienced in classifying specific pennies.

✓**Assessment**

Oral **What can you learn about a penny from how you classify it?** Categories such as amount of wear and shininess reflect amount of use and how that use has affected the substance from which pennies are made; date and place minted reflect the original manufacture. **How could descriptions of groups of pennies assist a person in identifying a particular coin?** The person could use the information to match it with a group thus narrowing the possible choices for the penny's identity. Use **Performance Assessment in the Science Classroom,** p. 89.

FOLDABLES
Reading & Study Skills

Before You Read

Dinah Zike Study Fold

Purpose Use this activity to determine what students know about matter's physical and chemical properties and changes before reading the chapter. Have them use the Foldable to record and organize notes as they read.

📁 For additional help, see Foldables Worksheet, p. 17 in **Chapter Resources Booklet,** or go to the Glencoe Science Web site at **science.glencoe.com.** See After You Read in the Study Guide at the end of this chapter.

SECTION

Physical Properties and Changes

1 Motivate

1 Motivate

Bellringer Transparency

Display the Section Focus Transparency for Section 1. Use the accompanying Transparency Activity Master. L2

ELL

Section Focus Transparency — Water, Water Everywhere

How much water can you find here? Actually, water is almost everywhere.

1. Where do you see water as a solid? A liquid?
2. What happens to snow on a sunny, warm day? What happens to water in a kettle if you light a burner underneath? How are these events similar?

Tie to Prior Knowledge

Have students recall past experiences of being asked to sort things into groups. They may have sorted laundry into piles of white, dark, and other, or they may have gone through their own clothing to separate items that fit from items that were too small. In this section, students will learn how matter can be described according to properties and how changes in these properties occur.

As You Read

What You'll Learn

- **Identify** physical properties of matter.
- **Describe** the states of matter.
- **Classify** matter using physical properties.

Vocabulary

physical property
matter
physical change
density
state of matter
melting point
boiling point

Why It's Important

Observing physical properties will help you interpret the world around you.

Using Your Senses

As you look in your empty wallet and realize that your allowance isn't coming anytime soon, you decide to get an after-school job. You've been hired at the new grocery store that will open next month. They are getting everything ready for the grand opening, and you will be helping make decisions about where things will go and how they will be arranged.

When you come into a new situation or have to make any kind of decision, what do you usually do first? Most people would make some observations. Observing involves seeing, hearing, tasting, touching, and smelling.

Whether in a new job or in the laboratory, you use your senses to observe materials. Any characteristic of a material that can be observed or measured without changing the identity of the material is a **physical property.** However, it is important to never taste, touch, or smell any of the materials being used in the lab without guidance, as noted in **Figure 1.** For safety reasons you will rely mostly on other observations.

Figure 1
For safety reasons, in the laboratory you usually use only two of your senses—sight and hearing. Many chemicals can be dangerous to touch, taste, and smell.

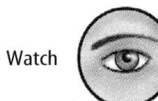 Watch

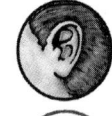 Listen

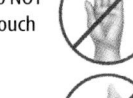 Do NOT touch

 Do NOT smell

 Do NOT taste

528

Section ✓Assessment Planner

PORTFOLIO
Curriculum Connection, p. 532

PERFORMANCE ASSESSMENT
Try at Home MiniLAB, p. 531
Skill Builder Activities, p. 539
See page 552 for more options.

CONTENT ASSESSMENT
Section, p. 539
Challenge, p. 539
Chapter, pp. 552–553

Physical Properties

On the first day of your new job, the boss gives you an inventory list and a drawing of the store layout. She explains that every employee is going to give his or her input as to how the merchandise should be arranged. Where will you begin?

You decide that the first thing you'll do is make some observations about the items on the list. One of the key senses used in observing physical properties is sight, so you go shopping to look at what you will be arranging.

Color and Shape Everything that you can see, touch, smell, or taste is matter. **Matter** is anything that has mass and takes up space. What things do you observe about the matter on your inventory list? The list already is organized by similarity of products, so you go to an aisle and look.

Color is the first thing you notice. The laundry detergent bottles you are looking at come in every color. Maybe you will organize them in the colors of the rainbow. You make a note and look more closely. Each bottle or box has a different shape. Some are square, some rectangular, and some are a free-form shape. You could arrange the packages by their shape.

When the plastic used to make the packaging is molded, it changes shape. However, the material is still plastic. This type of change is called a physical change. It is important to realize that in a **physical change,** the physical properties of a substance change, but the identity of the substance does not change. Notice **Figure 2.** The detergent bottles are made of high-density polyethylene regardless of the differences in the physical properties of color or shape.

✔ Reading Check *What is matter?*

SCIENCE Online

Research Visit the Glencoe Science Web site at **science.glencoe.com** for more information about classifying matter by its physical properties. Communicate to your class what you learn.

---

2 Teach

Using Your Senses

Safety Precautions

Use caution when handling acids. Wear *goggles, gloves,* and an *apron.*

Quick Demo

Bring to class a beaker of 6 M hydrochloric acid and a beaker of water. Without identifying their contents, set them side by side for students to look at. Explain that although the liquids in both beakers look like water, only one of them is water. Put a piece of denim fabric into each liquid. The water will not react with the denim, but the acid will. Explain to students that in a lab, dangerous substances can look like safe substances. Therefore, they should never taste, touch, or smell lab materials. [L2] [IS] **Visual-Spatial**

Physical Properties

Quick Demo

Show students a sheet of notebook paper, and have them describe its size and shape. Crumple the paper into a wad, and have students again describe its size and shape. Explain that while the description of the paper has changed, the paper remains paper. Crumpling paper is therefore an example of a physical change. [L2] [ELL] [IS] **Visual-Spatial**

✔ Reading Check

Answer anything that has mass and takes up space

SCIENCE Online
Internet Addresses
_____
_____
_____

Explore the Glencoe Science Web site at **science.glencoe.com** to find out more about topics in this section.

Physical Properties,
continued

Use Science Words

Word Usage Have students use the term *physical property* as they describe an object in their backpacks or desks. Possible answer: My ruler has the physical properties of being shaped long, narrow, and thin. [L2] ELL

IS Linguistic

IDENTIFYING
Misconceptions

Students may think that mass and weight are the same. Mass is a measure of the amount of matter in a substance, while weight is the measure of the force of gravity on it. Ask students what would happen to the mass and weight of a desk if it were transported to the moon. Its mass would stay the same, but its weight would decrease to one-sixth of its weight on Earth.

SCIENCE Online
Internet Addresses
_____
_____
_____
_____

Explore the Glencoe Science Web site at **science.glencoe.com** to find out more about topics in this section.

SCIENCE Online

Collect Data Visit the Glencoe Science Web site at **science.glencoe.com** for information about density. Communicate to your class what you learn.

Figure 3
The length of any object can be measured with the appropriate tool.

Length and Mass Some properties of matter can be identified by using your senses, and other properties can be measured. How much is there? How much space does it take up?

One useful and measurable physical property is length. Length is measured using a ruler, meterstick, or tape measure, as shown in **Figure 3.** Objects can be classified by their length. For example, you could choose to organize the French bread in the bakery section of your store by the length of the loaf. But, even though the dough has been shaped in different lengths, it is still French bread.

Back in the laundry aisle, you notice a child struggling to lift one of the boxes of detergent. That raises a question. How much detergent is in each box? Mass is a physical property that describes the amount of material in an object. Some of the boxes are heavy, but, the formula of the detergent hasn't changed from the small box to the large box. Organizing the boxes by mass is another option.

Volume and Density Mass isn't the only physical property that describes how much of something you have. Another measurement is volume. Volume measures the amount of space an object takes up. Liquids usually are measured by volume. The juice bottles on your list could be organized by volume.

Another measurable physical property related to mass and volume is **density**—the amount of mass a material has for a given volume. You notice this property when you try to lift two things of equal volume that have different masses. Density is found by dividing the mass of an object by its volume.

$$\text{density} = \text{mass/volume, or } D = m/V$$

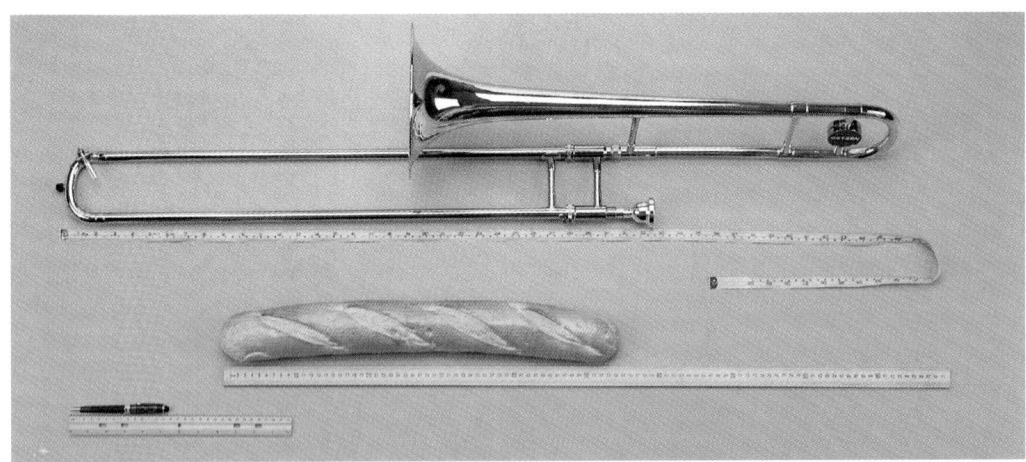
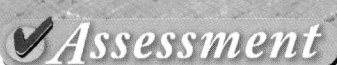

LAB DEMONSTRATION

✔ Assessment

Purpose to demonstrate volume and density as properties of matter

Materials water, 100-mL graduated cylinder, 10 g clay, string

Preparation Pour water into the graduated cylinder to the 50-mL mark. Shape the clay to fit into the graduated cylinder.

Procedure Cut a piece of string, and attach it to the clay. Use the string to lower the clay into the graduated cylinder. Be careful not to splash out any water.

Expected Outcome The volume and density of the clay will vary.

What is the volume of the clay? (the volume of the clay + water) − 50 mL **What is the density of the clay?** 10 g/volume of clay **How would the density change if you used a larger piece of clay?** It would not change.

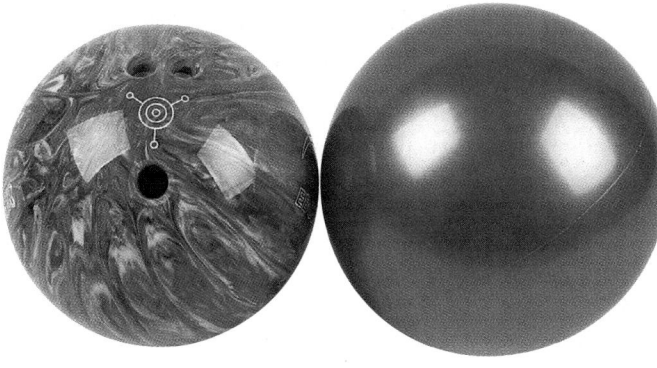

Bowling ball   **Kickball**

Figure 4
These balls take up about the same space, but the bowling ball on the left has more mass than the kickball on the right. Therefore, the bowling ball is more dense.

Same Volume, Different Mass **Figure 4** shows two balls that are the same size but not the same mass. The bowling ball is more dense than the kickball. The customers of your grocery store will notice the density of their bags of groceries if the baggers load all of the canned goods in one bag and put all of the cereal and napkins in the other.

The density of a material stays the same as long as pressure and temperature stay the same. Water at room temperature has a density of 1.00 g/cm³. However, when you do change the temperature or pressure, the density of a material can change. Water kept in the freezer at 0°C is in the form of ice. The density of that ice is 0.9168 g/cm³. Has the identity of water changed? No, but something has changed.

> ✔ **Reading Check**   *What two measurements are related in the measurement of density?*

States of Matter

What changes when water goes from 20°C to 0°C? It changes from a liquid to a solid. The four **states of matter** are solid, liquid, gas, and plasma (PLAZ muh). The state of matter of a substance depends on its temperature and pressure. Three of these states of matter are things you talk about or experience every day, but the term *plasma* might be unfamiliar. The plasma state occurs at very high temperatures and is found in fluorescent (floo RE sunt) lightbulbs, the atmosphere, and in lightning strikes.

As you look at the products to shelve in your grocery store, you might make choices of classification based on the state of matter. The state of matter of a material is another physical property. The liquid juices all will be in one place, and the solid, frozen juice concentrates will be in another.

TRY AT HOME
Mini LAB

Changing Density

Procedure
1. Stir three tablespoons of **baking soda** in 3/4 cup of **warm water.** Set aside.
2. Pour **vinegar** into a **clear glass** until it is half full.
3. Slowly pour the baking soda and warm water mixture into the glass of vinegar.
4. After most of the fizzing has stopped, place three halves of **raisins** in the glass.
5. Record your observations in your Science Journal or on a computer.

Analysis
1. How did the bubbles affect the raisins?
2. Infer what changed the density of the raisins.

TRY AT HOME
Mini LAB

Purpose to observe change in density L2 IS **Kinesthetic**

Materials tablespoon, baking soda, warm water, two clear glasses, vinegar, three raisins

Teaching Strategy Cut the raisins in half ahead of time.

Analysis
1. The bubbles pushed the raisins around.
2. The gas in the bubbles adhered to the outside of the raisins, making the density of the raisins and bubbles combined less than the density of just the raisins.

✔Assessment

Process Have students put three halves of raisins in a glass of water and observe how they move. Ask students to write paragraphs in their Science Journals comparing and contrasting the behavior of the raisins in the two situations. Use **Performance Assessment in the Science Classroom,** p. 89.

> ✔ **Reading Check**

Answer mass and volume

Teacher FYI
Plasma can be found in the part of the atmosphere called the ionosphere.

Resource Manager

Chapter Resources Booklet
  MiniLAB, p. 3
  Note-taking Worksheets, pp. 31–32
Science Inquiry Labs, p. 25

Visual Learning

Figure 4 What physical properties do the two balls in Figure 4 share? shape, size, volume, state **What physical properties are different for these two items?** mass, density, color L2
IS **Visual-Spatial**

Visual Learning

Figure 5 Point out to students the illustrations showing the motion of particles in solids, liquids, and gases. Ask a volunteer to explain how the motion of particles in a gas is different from the motion of particles in a liquid. The particles in a gas move faster than the particles in a liquid and move independently of one another. Also point out to students that the amount of gaseous water in the third jar is much less than the amount in the first two jars because gaseous water takes up much more volume than solid or liquid water. L2 𝕀𝕊 **Visual-Spatial**

Make a Model

Have students use gumdrops and toothpicks to make models that show how particles in solids, liquids, and gases are arranged and how they can move. For a solid, students should connect the gumdrops with the toothpicks to form a rigid structure. For a liquid, gumdrops should be connected to form layers. The gumdrops in each layer should be connected, but the layers should not be connected to each other. For a gas, the gumdrops should not be connected at all. L2 𝕀𝕊 **Kinesthetic**

Moving Particles Matter is made up of moving particles. The state of matter is determined by how much energy the particles have. The particles of a solid vibrate in a fixed position. They remain close together and give the solid a definite shape and volume. The particles of a liquid are moving much faster and have enough energy to slide past one another. This allows a liquid to take the shape of its container. The particles of a gas are moving so quickly that they have enough energy to move freely away from other particles. The particles of a gas take up as much space as possible and will spread out to fill any container. **Figure 5** illustrates the differences in the states of water.

✔ **Reading Check** *Which state of matter doesn't conform to the shape of the container?*

Changes of State You witness a change of state when you put ice cubes in water and they melt. You still have water but in another form. The opposite physical change happens when you put liquid water in ice-cube trays and pop them in your freezer. The water doesn't change identity—only the state it is in.

For your job, you will need to make some decisions based on the ability of materials to change state. You don't want all those frozen items thawing out and becoming slushy liquid. You also don't want some of the liquids to get so cold that they freeze.

Figure 5
Water can be in three different states: solid, liquid, and gas. The molecules in a solid are tightly packed and vibrate in place, but in a liquid they can slip past each other because they have more energy to move. In a gas, they move freely all around the container with even more energy.

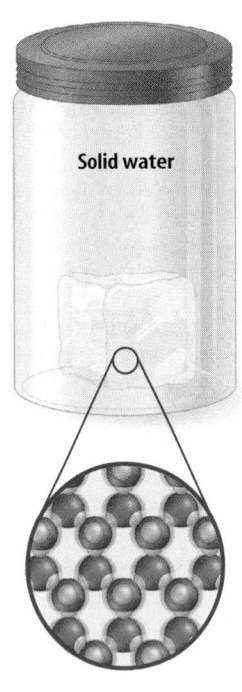
Solid water

Liquid water

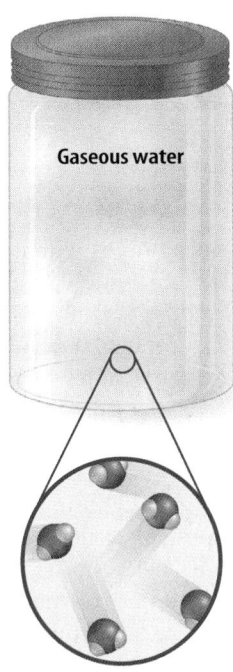
Gaseous water

532 CHAPTER 18 Properties and Changes of Matter

Curriculum Connection

Art Glass is a solid that has been used to make artistic and practical objects since before 2000 B.C. To make these objects, glass must be heated until it changes state and becomes a liquid. In the liquid state, it can be blown or molded into almost any form, which it keeps when it cools down and again becomes a solid. Have students bring in pictures of works of art made from glass. L2 𝕀𝕊 **Visual-Spatial** P

Melting and Boiling Points At what temperature will water in the form of ice change into a liquid? The temperature at which a solid becomes a liquid is its **melting point.** The melting point of a pure substance does not change with the amount of the substance. This means that a small sliver of ice and a block of ice the size of a house both will melt at 0°C. Lead always melts at 327.5°C. When a substance melts, it changes from a solid to a liquid. This is a physical change and the melting point is a physical property.

At what temperature will liquid water change to a gas? The **boiling point** is the temperature at which a substance in the liquid state becomes a gas. Each pure substance has a unique boiling point at atmospheric pressure. The boiling point of water is 100°C at atmospheric pressure. The boiling point of nitrogen is −195.8°C, so it changes to a gas when it warms after being spilled into the open air, as shown in **Figure 6.** The boiling point, like the melting point, does not depend on the amount of the substance.

 **Reading Check** *What physical change takes place at the boiling point?*

However, the boiling point and melting point can help to identify a substance. If you observe a clear liquid that boils at 56.1°C at atmospheric pressure, it is not water. Water boils at 100°C. If you know the boiling points and melting points of substances, you can classify substances based on those points.

Metallic Properties

Other physical properties allow you to classify substances as metals. You already have seen how you can classify things as solids, liquids, or gases or according to color, shape, length, mass, volume, or density. What properties do metals have?

How do metals look and act? Often the first thing you notice about something that is a metal is its shiny appearance. This is due to the way light is reflected from the surface of the metal. This shine is called luster. New handlebars on a bike have a metallic luster. Words that describe the appearance of nonmetallic objects are *pearly, milky,* or *dull.*

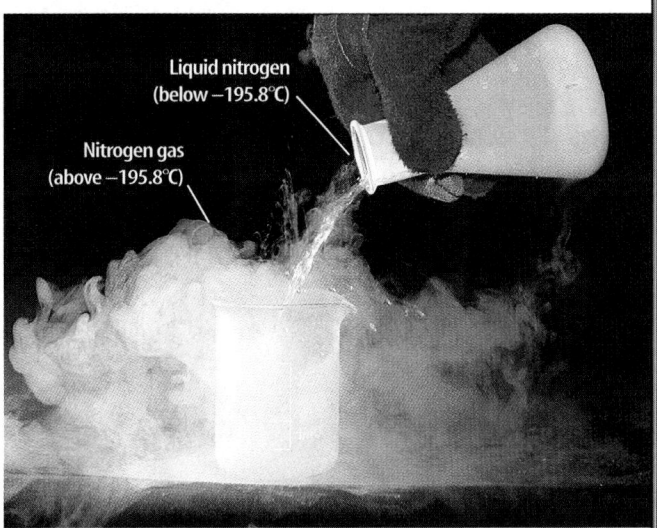

Liquid nitrogen (below −195.8°C)

Nitrogen gas (above −195.8°C)

Figure 6
When liquid nitrogen is poured from a flask, you see an instant change to gas because nitrogen's boiling point is −195.8°C, which is much lower than room temperature.

 Earth Science
INTEGRATION

When geologists describe rocks, they use specific terms that have meaning to all other scientists who read their descriptions. To describe the appearance of a rock or mineral, they use the following terms: *metallic, adamantine, vitreous, resinous, pearly, silky,* and *greasy.* Research these terms and write a definition and example of each in your Science Journal.

Section 1 Physical Properties and Changes **533**

Resource Manager

Chapter Resources Booklet
Enrichment, p. 29

Science Inquiry Labs, p. 43

 **Cultural Diversity**

Bronze Age As early as 4000 B.C., people in what is now the Middle East discovered they could melt together copper and tin to make bronze. Bronze is strong, hard, and resistant to corrosion and has a low melting point. Ancient metal workers shaped and pounded it into jewelry, weapons, coins, tools, and art works. Women of ancient Egypt, Greece, and Rome used mirrors of shiny polished bronze.

Quick Demo

Place 200 mL of crushed ice into a beaker. Place a thermometer into the beaker and note the temperature. Heat the beaker using a Bunsen burner and tongs. Note the temperature every 30 seconds as the ice melts. Explain that as the ice melts, the temperature remains constant at the melting point of ice. If heat is added after all the ice has melted, the temperature of the water will start to rise again. L2
Visual-Spatial

 **Reading Check**

Answer change of state from liquid to gas

Metallic Properties

 **Earth Science**
INTEGRATION

metallic: shines like a metal—pyrite, galena; adamantine: shines like a diamond—cassiterite; vitreous: glassy—fluorite, calcite, quartz; resinous: less brilliant than greasy—sphalerite; pearly: shining, silvery—muscovite mica; silky: finely fibrous with many parallel needles—gypsum; greasy: a little less brilliant than diamond—halite

Discussion

Have students identify items in the classroom that have a metallic luster. Possible answers: chrome legs on classroom chairs, frame around the board, parts of wristwatch Have students think of other shiny metal objects not found in the classroom. Possible answers: car, faucet, refrigerator door handle, aluminum foil L2 ELL
Visual-Spatial

Metallic Properties,
continued

Visual Learning ─○

Figure 7 Name other objects that use the properties of ductility or malleability in their construction. Possible answers: bridges, playground equipment, power lines, appliance cords, brass musical instruments

Use Science Words

Word Usage *Malleable* means "capable of being shaped by hammering, rolling, or pressing." Use the word *malleable* in a sentence describing a metal object found in the classroom. Sample answer: The file cabinet is made from malleable metal sheets. L2

IS **Linguistic**

Discussion

Ask students to think of everyday instances when they either observed bent metal or personally bent a metal object. Possible answers: dent in car or filing cabinet, paper clip, staple, bent spoon, coat hanger, electric cord, steel wool

Figure 7
This artist has taken advantage of the ductility of metal by choosing wire as the medium for her sculpture.

Figure 8
This junkyard magnet pulls scrap metal that can be salvaged from the rest of the debris. It is sorting by a physical property.

Uses of Metals Metals can be used in unique ways because of some of the physical properties they have. For example, many metals can be hammered, pressed, or rolled into thin sheets. This property of metals is called malleability (mal lee uh BIH luh tee). The malleability of copper makes it an ideal choice for artwork such as the Statue of Liberty. Many metals can be drawn into wires as shown in **Figure 7.** This property is called ductility (duk TIH luh tee). The wires in buildings and most electrical equipment and household appliances are made from copper. Silver and platinum are also ductile.

You probably observe another physical property of some metals every day when you go to the refrigerator to get milk or juice for breakfast. Your refrigerator door is made of metal. Some metals respond to magnets. Most people make use of that property and put reminder notes, artwork, and photos on their refrigerators. Some metals have groups of atoms that can be affected by the force of a magnet, and they are attracted to the magnet because of that force. The magnet in **Figure 8** is being used to select metallic objects.

At the grocery store, your employer might think about these properties of metals as she looks at grocery carts and thinks about shelving. Malleable carts can be dented. How could the shelf's attraction of magnets be used to post advertisements or weekly specials? Perhaps the prices could be fixed to the shelves with magnetic numbers. After you observe the physical properties of an object, you can make use of those properties.

534   CHAPTER 18 Properties and Changes of Matter

Inclusion Strategies

Gifted Ask groups of students to make sculptures using wire or aluminum foil. They should identify the physical properties of their projects, including color, luster, shape, length, mass, volume, state, and whether they show malleability, ductility, and/or attraction to magnets. L3

COOP LEARN IS **Kinesthetic**

Using Physical Properties

In the previous pages, many physical properties were discussed. These physical properties—such as appearance, state, shape, length, mass, volume, ability to attract a magnet, density, melting point, boiling point, malleability, and ductility— can be used to help you identify, separate, and classify substances.

For example, salt can be described as a white solid. Each salt crystal, if you look at it under a microscope, could be described as having a three-dimensional cubic structure. You can measure the mass, volume, and density of a sample of salt or find out if it would attract a magnet. These are examples of how physical properties can be used to identify a substance.

Figure 9
Coins can be sorted by their physical properties. Sorting by size is used here.

Sorting and Separating When you do laundry, you sort according to physical properties. Perhaps you sort by color. When you select a heat setting on an iron, you classify the clothes by the type of fabric. When miners during the Gold Rush panned for gold, they separated the dirt and rocks by density of particles. **Figure 9** shows a coin sorter that separates the coins based on their size. Iron filings can be separated from sand by using a magnet.

Life Science
INTEGRATION

Scientists who work with animals use physical properties or characteristics to determine the identity of a specimen. They do this by using a tool called a dichotomous (di KAH tuh mus) key. The term *dichotomous* refers to two parts or divisions. Part of a dichotomous key for identifying hard-shelled crabs is shown in **Figure 10.** To begin the identification of your unknown animal, you are given two choices. Your animal will match only one of the choices. In the key in **Figure 10,** you are to determine whether or not your crab lives in a borrowed shell. Based on your answer, you are either directed to another set of choices or given the name of the crab you are identifying.

SECTION 1 Physical Properties and Changes **535**

Using Physical Properties

Activity

Provide groups of students with a tile streak plate, a magnet, and unidentified, numbered samples of graphite (1), magnetite (2), talc (3), and fluorite (4). Explain that they will identify the samples using physical properties. First, have students rub each sample on the streak plate and record the color of each mineral's streak. Then have students try to scratch each sample with a fingernail. Finally, have students determine which is attracted to the magnet. When students have completed the activity, reveal the identity of each sample. Graphite: gray/black streak, can be scratched, is not attracted by magnet; magnetite: black streak, cannot be scratched, attracted by magnet; talc: white streak, scratched by a fingernail, not attracted by a magnet; fluorite: white streak, cannot be scratched, not attracted by magnet. L2 COOP LEARN
IS Kinesthetic

Life Science
INTEGRATION

Have students work in groups to develop dichotomous keys that lead to the identification of a specific animal. Possible questions include: Does this animal have hair or scales? Does this animal make a barking sound or a meowing sound? Does this animal have paws or hooves? L2 COOP LEARN
IS Logical-Mathematical

Resource Manager

Chapter Resources Booklet
Lab Activity, pp. 9–11

Physical Science Critical Thinking/Problem Solving, p. 10

Inclusion Strategies

Visually Impaired Ask these students to describe physical properties that can be identified by nonvisual means. Possible answers: solid—shape, size, texture, density, smell; liquid—thickness, slipperiness, smell; gas—smell L2 IS **Kinesthetic**

Visualizing Dichotomous Keys

Have students examine the pictures and read the captions, and then ask the following questions.

Have students identify each crab pictured. **What physical property did you use to identify each one?** The crab in the lower right has a borrowed shell; the crab in the upper right has a shell that overlaps its walking leg; the crab on the left has walking legs that are exposed.

What are some other items that could be identified using a dichotomous key? Possible answers: trees; flowers; rocks; minerals

Activity

Divide the class into small groups. Give each group five or six different objects, such as a pen, a pencil, a piece of chalk, a paint brush, a ruler, and an eraser. Ask each group to develop a dichotomous key that could be used to identify the objects, based on their physical properties. Have each group present its key to the class and have other groups critique the key. L2 COOP LEARN
IS Visual-Spatial and Interpersonal

Extension

Have students research the physical properties of the elements gold, silver, copper, mercury, iodine, and sulfur. Challenge them to make a dichotomous key that other students could use to identify these elements. L3
IS Logical-Mathematical

Figure 10

Whether in the laboratory or in the field, scientists often encounter substances or organisms that they cannot immediately identify. One approach to tracking down the identity of such "unknowns" is to use a dichotomous key, such as the one shown. The key is designed so a user can compare physical properties or characteristics of the unknown substance or organism—in this case, a crab—with characteristics of known organisms in a stepwise manner. With each step, a choice must be made. Each choice leads to subsequent steps that guide the user through the key until a positive identification is made.

Dichotomous Key	
1. A. Lives in a "borrowed" shell (usually some type of snail shell)	Hermit Crab
B. Does not live in a "borrowed" shell	go to #2
2. A. Shell completely overlaps the walking legs	Box Crab
B. Walking legs are exposed	Kelp Crab

Can you identify the three crabs shown here by following this dichotomous key?

Resource Manager

Chapter Resources Booklet
   Reinforcement, p. 27
   Transparency Activity, pp. 45–46
Science Inquiry Labs, p. 45

Everyday Examples Identification by physical properties is a subject in science that is easy to observe in the real world. Suppose you volunteer to help your friend choose a family pet. While visiting the local animal shelter, you spot a cute dog. The dog looks like the one in **Figure 11.** You look at the sign on the cage. It says that the dog is male, one to two years old, and its breed is unknown. You and your friend wonder what breed of dog he is. What kind of information do you and your friend need to figure out the dog's breed? First, you need a thorough description of the physical properties of the dog. What does the dog look like? Second, you need to know the descriptions of various breeds of dogs. Then you can match up the description of the dog with the correct breed. The dog you found is a white, medium-sized dog with large black spots on his back. He also has black ears and a black mask around his eyes. The manager of the shelter tells you that the dog is close to full-grown. What breed is the dog?

Narrowing the Options To find out, you may need to research the various breeds of dogs and their descriptions. Often, determining the identity of something that is unknown is easiest by using the process of elimination. You figure out all of the breeds the dog can't be. Then your list of possible breeds is smaller. Upon looking at the descriptions of various breeds, you eliminate small dog and large dog breeds. You also eliminate breeds that do not contain white dogs. With the remaining breeds, you might look at photos to see which ones most resemble your dog. Scientists use similar methods to determine the identities of living and nonliving things.

Substances

Matter—everything that has mass and takes up space—can be classified by its physical properties. One way to classify matter is based on its chemical composition. Matter that has the same composition and properties throughout is called a substance. There are two types of substances—elements and compounds.

Elements Substances that are made up of only one type of atom are called elements. **Figure 12** shows examples of elements. Oxygen is a substance made up of only oxygen atoms. A bar of gold is a substance made up of only gold atoms. Aluminum foil is made up of only aluminum atoms. Elements cannot be broken down into simpler substances by physical or chemical means. However, different elements can combine to form new substances—called compounds.

Figure 11
Physical descriptions are used to determine the identities of unknown things. *What physical properties are used to describe this dog?*

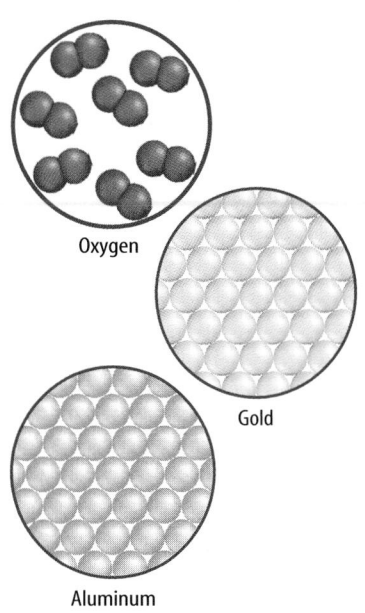

Oxygen

Gold

Aluminum

Figure 12
Elements such as oxygen, gold, and aluminum are made up of only one type of atom.

SECTION 1 Physical Properties and Changes **537**

Cultural Diversity

Ocher Ocher, a naturally occurring iron oxide (Fe_2O) is formed by the weathering of rocks. Historically, ocher has been used to produce rock paintings and continues to be used for artwork today. It comes in a variety of colors, depending on the percentage of iron oxide present. Hematite ore, one source of ocher that can be ground to produce a bright red color, appears to have been mined in Swaziland, Africa, as early as 44,000 years ago. Ocher has also been found in burial plots in Rome, Mayan caves, the great pyramids in Egypt, and with the Aborigines in Australia. Have students find out the other colors produced by iron oxide ores. Other colors produced include black (magnetite), yellow (limonite), and brown (siderite and pyrite).

Discussion

What is the difference between an element and a compound? Elements are made of only one type of atom. Compounds are made of more than one type of element.

Make a Model

While discussing the law of difinite proportions, have students make models of simple compounds using gumdrops and toothpicks. Examples of compounds are: H_2O, NaCl, KBr, and CO_2. Have them share their models with the class.

Mixtures

Discussion

What are the two types of mixtures? homogeneous and heterogeneous

What is the difference between the two types of mixtures? Homogeneous mixtures are the same throughout and heterogeneous mixtures have sections that are different throughout.

Use Science Words

Word Usage Ask students to classify these mixtures as heterogeneous or homogeneous: sand heterogeneous water homogeneous Italian-style salad dressing heterogeneous

Discussion

Remind students that a compound is a pure substance whose smallest unit is made up of atoms of more than one element. **What compounds do you use in your daily activities?** Examples include table salt, water, and sugar.

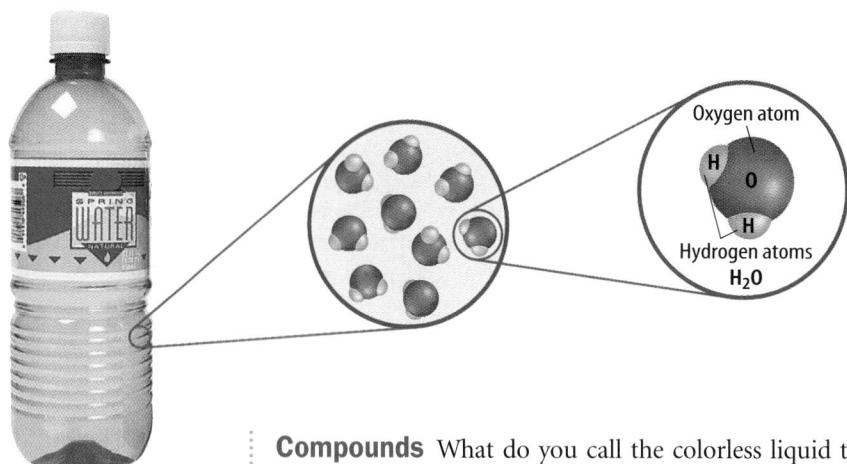

Figure 13
Compounds contain more than one type of atom bonded together. Water contains a ratio of two hydrogen atoms bonded to one oxygen atom.

Compounds What do you call the colorless liquid that flows from the kitchen faucet? You probably call it water, but maybe you've seen it written as H_2O. The elements hydrogen and oxygen exist separately as colorless gases. However, these two elements can combine to form the compound water, shown in **Figure 13,** with properties that are different from the individual gases that make it up. A compound is a substance that is made up of atoms of more than one element chemically bonded together. The smallest unit of water is made up of two hydrogen atoms and one oxygen atom bonded together.

Compounds have a fixed ratio—or proportion of atoms throughout. For example, every drop of water contains a ratio of two hydrogen atoms to one oxygen atom. Every sample of carbon dioxide contains a ratio of one carbon atom to two oxygen atoms.

Compounds can be broken down only by chemical means into the elements that combined to make them. For example, boiling, freezing, stirring or filtering will not separate the hydrogen atoms from the oxygen atom. However, if electricity is added to water, it can be broken down into hydrogen gas and oxygen gas.

Mixtures

When two or more substances come together but don't chemically combine or bond to make a new substance, a mixture results. Unlike compounds, the proportions of the substances in a mixture can be changed without changing the identity of the mixture. For example, if you put some sand into a bucket of water, the sand doesn't chemically combine with the water. If you add more sand or more water, it's still a mixture of sand and water. Physical properties can be used to separate mixtures into simpler substances. For example, solid sand can be filtered from liquid water using a sieve.

538   CHAPTER 18 Properties and Changes of Matter

Curriculum Connection

Art Have students make collages that demonstrate elements, compounds, and mixtures. Students should identify which are homogeneous and heterogeneous mixtures. Have them search through magazines to collect illustrations for their collages. L2 **Kinesthetic**

Homogeneous Mixtures Mixtures can be classified as homogeneous or heterogeneous based on their physical properties. *Homogeneous* means "the same throughout." Homogeneous mixtures contain more than one substance evenly mixed but not chemically bonded together. You can't see the different parts in a homogeneous mixture no matter how closely you look. In fact, it is difficult to see the difference between a homogeneous mixture and a substance because they both look uniform, or even, throughout.

Homogeneous mixtures can be solid, liquid or gas. The brass in a trumpet is a solid mixture of zinc and copper—two elements. Sugar water is a homogeneous liquid mixture of sugar and water—both compounds. Air is a homogeneous mixture of elements—nitrogen, oxygen, argon, neon and helium—and two compounds—carbon dioxide and water. Another name for a homogeneous mixture is a solution.

Heterogeneous Mixtures A heterogeneous mixture is one of two or more substances that are not mixed evenly. You can see the different parts of a heterogeneous mixture, such as a mixture of sand and water. A pizza is a tasty kind of heterogeneous mixture. Other examples of this kind of mixture include salad, a bookshelf full of books, or a toolbox full of nuts and bolts. **Figure 14** shows examples of heterogeneous and homogeneous mixtures.

Figure 14
The salad and the pizza are heterogeneous mixtures. The fruit drink is a homogeneous mixture.

Section 1 Assessment

1. What property of matter is used to measure the amount of space an object takes?

2. What are the four states of matter? Describe each and give an example.

3. How might a substance such as water have two different densities?

4. Compare and contrast heterogeneous and homogeneous mixtures.

5. **Think Critically** Explain why the boiling point is the same for 1 L and 3 L of water. Will it take the same amount of time for each volume of water to begin to boil?

Skill Builder Activities

6. **Concept Mapping** Using a computer, draw a cycle concept map with the steps for changing an ice cube into steam. Use the terms *melting point* and *boiling point* in your answer. **For more help, refer to the Science Skill Handbook.**

7. **Solving One-Step Equations** Calculate the volume of an object that has a length of 10 cm, a width of 10 cm, and a height of 10 cm. Use the formula for volume: $V = lwh$. Express your answer using cubic centimeters (cm^3). **For more help, refer to the Math Skill Handbook.**

Answers to Section Assessment

1. volume
2. The four states of matter are solid, which has a definite shape and volume, such as ice; liquid, which has a definite volume but takes the shape of its container, such as water; gas, which fills the shape and volume of its container, such as air; and plasma, which occurs at very high temperatures and is found in fluorescent lightbulbs.
3. by changing the temperature or pressure
4. Both heterogenous and homogenous mixtures contain two or more substances that are not chemically combined. Homogenous mixtures contain evenly mixed substances. Heterogenous mixtures contain unevenly mixed substances.
5. Boiling point at a particular pressure is a physical property that does not change with the amount of a substance. A larger volume of water will take longer to boil because there are more particles to which energy must be added.
6. Check student work.
7. 1,000 cm^3

1 Motivate

Bellringer Transparency

Display the Section Focus Transparency for Section 2. Use the accompanying Transparency Activity Master. L2

ELL

Tie to Prior Knowledge

Review the concepts of physical properties and changes. Ask students to give examples of each. Explain that substances also have chemical properties and undergo chemical changes that result in new substances.

Chemical Properties and Changes

As You Read

What You'll Learn
- **Recognize** chemical properties.
- **Identify** chemical changes.
- **Classify** matter according to chemical properties.
- **Describe** the law of conservation of mass.

Vocabulary
chemical property
chemical change
conservation of mass

Why It's Important
Knowing the chemical properties will allow you to distinguish differences in matter.

Figure 12
These are four examples of chemical properties.

Ability to Change

It is time to celebrate. You and your coworkers have cooperated in classifying all of the products and setting up the shelves in the new grocery store. The store manager agrees to a celebration party and campfire at the nearby park. Several large pieces of firewood and some small pieces of kindling are needed to start the campfire. After the campfire, all that remains of the wood is a small pile of ash. Where did the wood go? What property of the wood is responsible for this change?

All of the properties that you observed and used for classification in the first section were physical properties that you could observe easily. In addition, even when those properties changed, the identity of the object remained the same. Something different seems to have happened in the bonfire example.

Some properties do indicate a change of identity for the substances involved. A **chemical property** is any characteristic that gives a substance the ability to undergo a change that results in a new substance. **Figure 12** shows some properties of substances that can be observed only as they undergo a chemical change.

Reading Check *What does a chemical property give a substance the ability to do?*

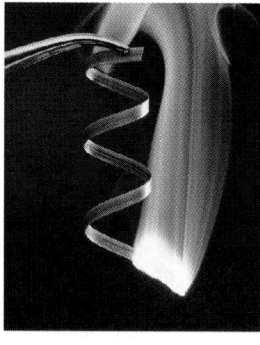
Flammability

Reacts with oxygen

Reacts with light

Reacts with water

540 CHAPTER 18 Properties and Changes of Matter

Section ✔ *Assessment* Planner

PORTFOLIO
Science Journal, p. 543
Curriculum Connection, p. 544

PERFORMANCE ASSESSMENT
MiniLAB, p. 544
Skill Builder Activities, p. 546
See page 552 for more options.

CONTENT ASSESSMENT
Section, p. 546
Challenge, p. 546
Chapter, pp. 552–553

A

B

C

Common Chemical Properties

You don't have to be in a laboratory to see changes that take place because of chemical properties. These are called chemical changes. A **chemical change** is a change in the identity of a substance due to the chemical properties of that substance. A new substance or substances are formed in such a change.

The campfire you enjoyed to celebrate the opening of the grocery store resulted in chemical changes. The oxygen in the air reacted with the wood to form a new substance called ash. Wood can burn. This chemical property is called flammability. Some products have warnings on their labels about keeping them away from heat and flame because of the flammability of the materials. Sometimes after a campfire you see stones that didn't burn around the edge of the ashes. These stones have the chemical property of inflammability.

Common Reactions An unpainted iron gate, such as the one shown in **Figure 13A**, will rust in time. The rust is a result of oxygen in the air reacting with the iron and causing corrosion. The corrosion produces a new substance called iron oxide. Other chemical reactions occur when metals interact with other elements. **Figure 13B** shows tarnish, the grayish-brown film that develops on silver when it reacts with sulfur in the air. The ability to react with oxygen or sulfur is a chemical property. **Figure 13C** shows another example of this chemical property.

Have you ever sliced an apple or banana and left it sitting on the table? The brownish coloring that you notice is a chemical change that occurs between the fruit and the oxygen in the air. Those who work in the produce department at the grocery store must be careful with any fruit they slice to use as samples. Although nothing is wrong with brown apples, they don't look appetizing.

Figure 13
Many kinds of interactions with oxygen can occur.
A An untreated iron gate will rust. **B** Silver dishes develop tarnish. **C** Copper sculptures develop a green patina, which is a mixture of copper compounds.

 **Health**
INTEGRATION

Researchers have discovered an enzyme in fruit that is involved in the browning process. They are doing experiments to try to grow grapevines in which the level of this enzyme, polyphenol oxidase (PPO), is reduced. This could result in grapes that do not brown as quickly. Write a paragraph in your Science Journal about why this would be helpful to fruit growers, store owners, and customers.

SECTION 2 Chemical Properties and Changes **541**

② Teach

Ability to Change

✔ **Reading Check**

Answer undergo a change that results in a new substance

Common Chemical Properties

IDENTIFYING
Misconceptions

When students see a substance such as water change state, they may think there has been a chemical change, resulting in a different substance. Point out that ice, water, and steam (water vapor) all have the same chemical makeup and formula, H_2O.

 Health
INTEGRATION

Cells of fruit damaged by cutting or rubbing release polyphenol oxidase. This enzyme catalyzes the conversion of monophenols to quinones, which oxidize to form brown polyphenolic pigments. In the grapevines, the gene for polyphenol oxidase has been switched off by genetic modification. Students may suggest that these grapes may be more attractive to consumers, and that growers and store owners would suffer less loss from fruit damage.

Resource Manager

Chapter Resources Booklet
Transparency Activity, p. 43
Directed Reading for Content Mastery, pp. 21, 22
Life Science Critical Thinking/Problem Solving, p. 8

Teacher FYI

One way to prevent iron from rusting is to coat it with another material that will corrode first. *Galvanizing* with zinc works because the zinc coating reacts with the oxygen in the air to form a thin protective layer of zinc oxide.

Something New

Use an Analogy

During a chemical change, atoms are regrouped into new, different substances. As an analogy, imagine taking a car apart and reshaping and regrouping its components to make a lawn mower, two sofas, and a shed. What had been a car is now several entirely different things.

Quick Demo

To demonstrate chemical change and physical change, bring to class two pennies, a rough surface, a glass beaker, a small amount of diluted hydrochloric acid, a torch, and heat-resistant tongs. **CAUTION:** *Wear a laboratory apron and safety goggles.* Use the rough surface to scratch the edge of the penny, exposing the zinc center. Place the penny in a small amount of dilute hydrochloric acid in a beaker. Students will observe a chemical reaction between the zinc and the acid, while the outer layer of the penny will remain intact. Now scratch the other penny on a rough surface to expose the zinc center. Using tongs, grip the penny and place it near the flame. The zinc will melt, which is a physical change that causes a separation between the zinc and the outside covering of the penny. **CAUTION:** *The inside of the penny will melt and fall out. It will be extremely hot.* L2 ELL
IS Visual-Spatial

Visual Learning

Figure 14 Many chemical reactions, such as this one, are potentially dangerous. A photograph can be used to observe the reaction safely. Teachers are not to demonstrate this experiment in a middle school classroom, nor should students attempt this at school or at home. L2
IS Visual-Spatial

Figure 14
When sugar and sulfuric acid combine, a chemical change occurs and a new substance forms. During this reaction, the mixture foams and a toxic gas is released, leaving only water and air-filled carbon behind. (Because a toxic gas is released, students should never perform this as an activity.)

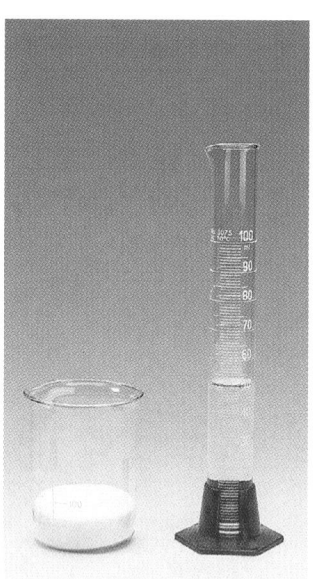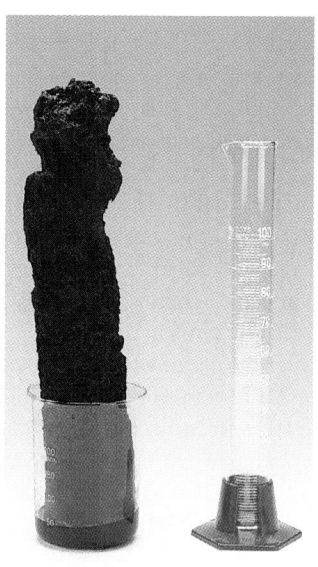

Heat and Light Vitamins often are dispensed in dark-brown bottles. Do you know why? Many vitamins have the ability to change when exposed to light. This is a chemical property. They are protected in those colored bottles from undergoing a chemical change with light.

Some substances are sensitive to heat and will undergo a chemical change only when heated or cooled. One example is limestone. Limestone is generally thought of as unreactive. Some limestone formations have been around for centuries without changing. However, if limestone is heated, it goes through a chemical change and produces carbon dioxide and lime, a chemical used in many industrial processes. The chemical property in this case is the ability to change when heated.

Another chemical property is the ability to change with electrical contact. Electricity can cause a change in some substances and decompose some compounds. Water is one of those compounds that can be broken down with electricity.

Something New

The important difference in a chemical change is that a new substance is formed. Because of chemical changes, you can enjoy many things in life that you would not have experienced without them. What about that perfect, browned marshmallow you roasted at the bonfire? A chemical change occurred as a result of the fire to make the taste and the appearance different.

Sugar is normally a white, crystalline substance, but after you heat it over a flame, it turns to a dark-brown caramel. A new substance has been formed. Sugar also can undergo a chemical change when sulfuric acid is added to it. The new substance is obviously different from the original, as shown in **Figure 14.**

You could not enjoy a birthday cake if the eggs, sugar, flour, baking powder, and other ingredients didn't change chemically. You would have what you see when you pour the gooey batter into the pan.

✔ Active Reading

Double Entry Journal In this strategy, the student takes notes and adds his or her own reflections while reading the student text. Students are encouraged to explore ideas, make responses, and take risks in giving opinions about the reading. Have them divide the paper in half. On the left, identify a particular passage or quotation of significance in the reading. The reader records anything luminous, enigmatic, stimulating, or disturbing. On the right, the reader responds, questions, elaborates, makes personal connections, evaluates, reflects, analyzes, or interprets. Have students make a Double Entry Journal for the discussion of chemical properties and chemical changes in this section.

Signs of Change

Signs of Change How do you know that you have a new substance? Is it just because it looks different? You could put a salad in a blender and it would look different, but a chemical change would not have occurred. You still would have lettuce, carrots, and any other vegetables that were there to begin with.

You can look for signs when evaluating whether you have a new substance as a result of a chemical change. Look at the piece of birthday cake in **Figure 15.** When a cake bakes, gas bubbles form and grow within the ingredients. Bubbles are a sign that a chemical change has taken place. When you look closely at a piece of cake, you can see the airholes left from the bubbles.

Other signs of change include the production of heat, light, smoke, change in color, and sound. Which of these signs of change would you have seen or heard during the campfire?

Is it reversible? One other way to determine whether a physical change or a chemical change has occurred is to decide whether or not you can reverse the change by simple physical means. Physical changes usually can be reversed easily. For example, melted butter can become solid again if it is placed in the refrigerator. A figure made of modeling clay, like the one in **Figure 16,** can be smashed to fit back into a container. However, chemical changes can't be reversed using physical means. For example, the ashes in a fireplace cannot be put back together to make the logs that you had to start with. Can you find the egg in a cake? Where is the white flour?

✔ **Reading Check** *What kind of change can be reversed easily?*

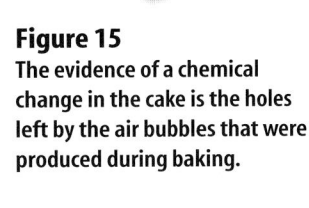

Figure 15
The evidence of a chemical change in the cake is the holes left by the air bubbles that were produced during baking.

Figure 16
A change such as molding clay or changing shape can be undone easily.

Pizza is produced by a combination of chemical and physical changes. For example, the yeast in the dough reacts chemically with the sugar and other substances, causing the dough to rise while it bakes. The melting of the cheese is a physical change.

Activity

Have student groups make posters for the classroom about chemical change. Each poster should include a colorful illustration demonstrating one or more signs that a chemical change is occurring or has occurred. L1
ELL COOP LEARN **Visual-Spatial**

Text Question Answer

You'd have heard crackling sounds, seen light, felt heat, seen smoke, and seen a color change in the wood as it burned.

Extension

Tell students that a water molecule contains two hydrogen atoms and one oxygen atom. Explain that two water molecules can decompose to form two molecules of hydrogen gas and one molecule of oxygen gas. A molecule of hydrogen gas contains two hydrogen atoms, and a molecule of oxygen gas contains two oxygen atoms. Have students use gumdrops and toothpicks to make models of several water molecules and then use the models to simulate the decomposition of water. L3
ELL COOP LEARN **Visual-Spatial**

Resource Manager

Chapter Resources Booklet
  Enrichment, p. 30
Reading and Writing Skill Activities, p. 1
Earth Science Critical Thinking/Problem Solving, p. 17

Science Journal

Chemistry Notes Ask students to record their observations of chemical changes they encounter at home. They should write down the initial substances, the resulting substances, and the signs that the change was chemical rather than physical. L2 **Intrapersonal** P

✔ **Reading Check**

Answer a physical change

Something New, continued

Mini LAB

Purpose Students observe gas formation during a chemical reaction. L2 ELL COOP LEARN

IS Kinesthetic

Materials paper plate or lab tray, dry yeast, hand lens, warm water, sugar, clear cup or beaker

Teaching Strategy Have students place a small amount of dry yeast on the paper plate or lab tray to make their initial observation.

Analysis

1. The bubbles that form show that a new substance, a gas, is formed when the sugar, water, and yeast are combined.
2. This is a chemical change because gas is produced.

✔ Assessment

Oral Ask students to explain the results of their investigation. Have them use information given in the text under the heading *Signs of Change* to support their answer. Use **Performance Assessment in the Science Classroom**, p. 143.

Mini LAB

Observing Yeast

Procedure 👓 👕 🚫

1. Observe a **tablespoon** of **dry yeast** with a **hand lens.** Draw and describe what you observe.
2. Put the yeast in 50 mL of warm, not hot, **water.**
3. Compare your observations of the dry yeast with those of the wet yeast.
4. Put a pinch of **sugar** in the water and observe for 15 minutes.
5. Record your observations.

Analysis

1. Are new substances formed when sugar is added to the water and yeast? Explain.
2. Do you think this is a chemical change or a physical change? Explain.

Table 1 Comparing Properties	
Physical Properties	color, shape, length, mass, volume, density, state, ability to attract a magnet, melting point, boiling point, malleability, ductility
Chemical Properties	flammability; ability to react with: oxygen, electricity, light, water, heat, vinegar, bleach, etc.

Classifying According to Chemical Properties Classifying according to physical properties is often easier than classifying according to chemical properties. **Table 1** summarizes the two kinds of properties. The physical properties of a substance are easily observed, but the chemical properties can't be observed without changing the substance. However, once you know the chemical properties, you can classify and identify matter based on those properties. For example, if you try to burn what looks like a piece of wood but find that it won't burn, you can rule out the possibility that it is untreated wood.

In a grocery store, the products sometimes are separated according to their flammability or sensitivity to light or heat. You don't often see the produce section in front of big windows where heat and light come in. The fruit and vegetables would undergo a chemical change and ripen too quickly. You also won't find the lighter fluid and rubbing alcohol near the bakery or other places where heat and flame could be present.

Architects and product designers have to take into account the chemical properties of materials when they design buildings and merchandise. For example, children's sleepwear and bedding can't be made of a flammable fabric. Also, some of the architects designing the most modern buildings are choosing materials like titanium because it does not react with oxygen like many other metals do.

Conservation of Mass

It was so convenient to turn the firewood into the small pile of ash left after the campfire. You began with many kilograms of flammable substances but ended up with just a few kilograms of ash. Could this be a solution to the problems with landfills and garbage dumps? Why not burn all the trash? If you could make such a reduction without creating undesirable materials, this would be a great solution.

Curriculum Connection

Language Arts Have students write a diamond poem about physical and chemical properties. Form: Line 1, first topic; Line 2, two adjectives describing Line 1; Line 3, three participles related to Line 1; Line 4, four nouns—the first two related to Line 1 and the next two to Line 7; Line 5, three participles related to Line 7; Line 6, two adjectives describing Line 7; Line 7, second topic. P

Example:

physical
color, texture
smelling, feeling, seeing
rock, pillow, fire, bubble
burning, baking, rusting
flammable, reactive
chemical

Mass Is Not Destroyed Before you celebrate your discovery, think this through. Did mass really disappear during the fire? It appears that way when you compare the mass of the pile of ashes to the mass of the firewood you started with. The law of **conservation of mass** states that the mass of what you end with is always the same as the mass of what you start with.

This law was first investigated about 200 years ago, and many investigations since then have proven it to be true. One experiment done by French scientist Antoine Lavoisier was a small version of a campfire. He determined that a fire does not make mass disappear or truly get rid of anything. The question, however, remains. Where did the mass go? The ashes aren't heavy enough to account for the mass of all of the pieces of firewood.

Where did the mass go? If you look at the campfire example more closely, you see that the law of conservation of mass is true. When flammable materials burn, they combine with oxygen. Ash, smoke, and gases are produced. The smoke and gases escape into the air. If you could measure the mass of the oxygen and all of the original flammable materials that were burned and compare it to the remaining mass of the ash, smoke, and gas, they would be equal.

Problem-Solving Activity

Do light sticks conserve mass?

Light sticks often are used on Halloween to light the way for trick-or-treaters. They make children visible to drivers. They also are used as toys, for camping, marking trails, emergency traffic problems, by the military, and they work well underwater. A light stick contains two chemicals in separate tubes. When you break the inner tube, the two chemicals react producing a greenish light. The chemicals are not toxic, and they will not catch fire.

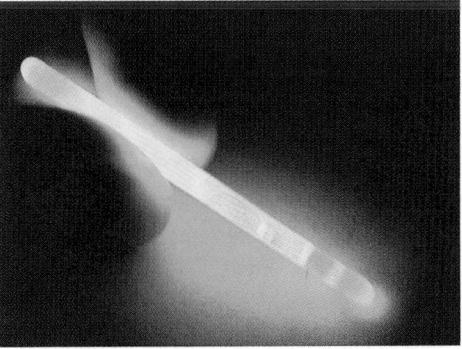

Identifying the Problem
In all reactions that occur in the world, mass is never lost or gained. This is the law of conservation of mass. An example of this phenomenon is the light stick. How can you prove this?

Solving the Problem
Describe how you could show that a light stick does not gain or lose mass when you allow the reaction to take place. Is this reaction a chemical or physical change? What is your evidence?

SECTION 2 Chemical Properties and Changes **545**

Have students work in groups to name signs that indicate that a chemical change has occurred. Ask each group then to identify one situation in which one of these signs is present but in which no chemical change has occurred. Signs include the production of heat, light, smoke, color change, gas bubbles, sound, and the ease with which the change can be reversed. Gas bubbles are produced when water boils, but this is a physical change, not a chemical change.

L2 IS **Logical-Mathematical**

Challenge

Fire is one chemical reaction that we sometimes want to stop quickly. Have students work in small groups to think of as many ways as they can to put out a fire. Ask each group to choose one and explain why it works.

L2 COOP LEARN IS **Interpersonal**

✔Assessment

Oral Have students think of chemical changes in which the product appears larger than the original substances and in which the product appears smaller. bread rising; wood burning Have them explain how mass is conserved in these chemical changes. The expansion of bread is caused by the formation of a gas, which pushes on the bread and makes it rise. Combustion produces a large amount of gas, which in this case is able to move freely away from the fire, leaving only a small amount of solid products behind. Use **PASC,** p. 89.

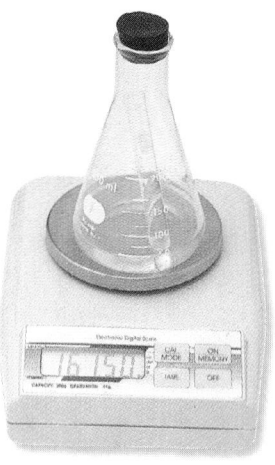
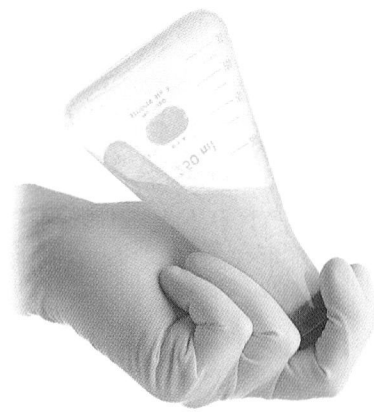
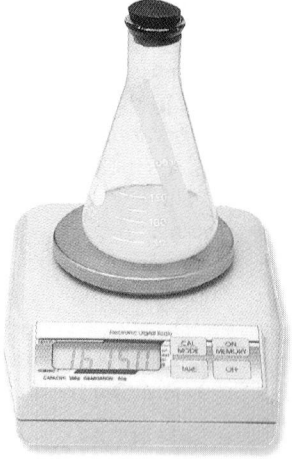

Figure 17
This reaction demonstrates the conservation of mass. Although a chemical change has occurred and new substances were made, the mass remained constant.

Before and After Mass is not destroyed or created during any chemical change. The conservation of mass is demonstrated in **Figure 17.** In the first photo, you see one substance in the flask and a different substance contained in a test tube inside the flask. The total mass is 16.150 g. In the second photo, the flask is turned upside down. This allows the two substances to mix and react. Because the flask is sealed, nothing is allowed to escape. In the third photo, the flask is placed on the balance again and the total mass is determined to be 16.150 g. If no mass is lost or gained, what happens in a reaction? Instead of disappearing or appearing, the particles in the substances rearrange into different combinations with different properties.

Section **Assessment**

1. What is a chemical property?
2. List four chemical properties.
3. What are some of the signs that a chemical change has occurred?
4. Describe the law of conservation of mass. Give an example.
5. **Think Critically** You see a bright flash and then flames as your teacher performs a demonstration for the class. Is this an example of a physical change or a chemical change? Explain.

Skill Builder Activities

6. **Comparing and Contrasting** Compare and contrast physical change and chemical change. **For more help, refer to the** Science Skill Handbook.
7. **Solving One-Step Equations** A student heats 4.00 g of a blue compound to produce 2.56 g of a white compound and an unknown amount of colorless gas. What is the mass of this gas? **For more help, refer to the** Math Skill Handbook.

546 **CHAPTER 18** Properties and Changes of Matter

Answers to Section Assessment

1. any characteristic that gives a substance the ability to undergo a change that results in a new substance
2. Possible answers: ability to burn, to react with O_2, to react to heat or light, to break down with electricity
3. Possible answers: production of heat, light, smoke, color change, gas bubbles, sound

4. The law of conservation of mass states that the mass of the products of a chemical change is always the same as the mass of the original substances. The mass of wood and oxygen before the wood burns is the same as the mass of the products formed.
5. Production of heat and light are signs of a chemical change.

6. In a physical change, the properties of a substance change but the substance itself remains the same. In a chemical change, a new substance is formed.
7. The mass of the gas produced is 1.44g.

Activity

Liquid Layers

Why must you shake up a bottle of Italian salad dressing before using it? Have you observed how the liquids in some dressings separate into two distinct layers? In this activity, you will experiment with creating layers of liquids.

What You'll Investigate
What would several liquids and solids of different densities look like when put into the same container?

Goals
- ■ **Create** layers of liquids using liquids of different densities.
- ■ **Observe** where solids of different densities will rest in the liquid layers.
- ■ **Infer** the densities of the different materials.

Materials
250-mL beaker	corn oil
graduated cylinder	rubbing alcohol
corn syrup	penny
glycerin	hollow plastic sphere
water	rubber ball

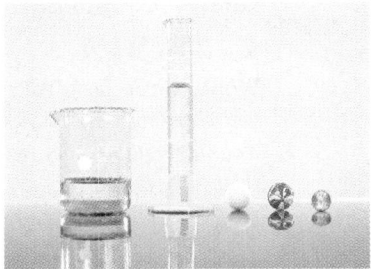

Safety Precautions 🧤 👓 🔬 ✋

Procedure
1. Pour 40 mL of corn syrup into your beaker.
2. Slowly pour 40 mL of glycerin into the beaker.

Allow the glycerin to trickle down the sides of the container and observe.
3. Slowly pour 40 mL of water into the beaker and observe.
4. Slowly pour 40 mL of corn oil into the beaker and observe.
5. Slowly pour 40 mL of rubbing alcohol into the beaker and observe.
6. Carefully drop the penny, hollow plastic sphere, and rubber ball into the beaker and observe where these items come to a stop.

Conclude and Apply
1. In your Science Journal, draw a picture of the liquids and solids in your flask. Label your diagram.
2. **Describe** what happened to the five liquids when you poured them into the beaker.
3. **Infer** why the liquids behaved this way.
4. **Describe** what happened to the three solids you placed into the beaker.
5. **List** the substances you used in your activity in order from those with the highest density to those with the lowest density.
6. If water has a density of 1 g/cm^3, what can you infer about the densities of the solids and other liquids?

𝒞ommunicating
Your Data

Draw a labeled poster of the substances you placed in your beaker. Research the densities of each substance and include these densities on your poster. **For more help, refer to the Science Skill Handbook.**

𝒞ommunicating
Your Data

Densities: corn syrup, 1.360 g/cm^3; glycerin, 1.260 g/cm^3; water, 1.0 g/cm^3; corn oil, 0.91 g/cm^3; rubbing alcohol, 0.791 g/cm^3; penny (copper and zinc), about 8.0 g/cm^3. The densities of the plastic sphere and the rubber ball will vary.

Activity

Purpose Students observe the behavior of liquids and solids of different densities. [L2] [ELL]
[KS] **Kinesthetic**

Process Skills observing, sequencing, inferring, communicating, recognizing cause and effect

Time Required 20 minutes

Safety Precautions Remind students not to taste any of the materials used for this activity.

Teaching Strategy Pouring the liquids in such a way that the layers remain intact can be tricky. Before having students do this activity, practice pouring the liquids yourself so you can show them how to do it.

Troubleshooting Make sure the beaker is clean and dry at the beginning of this activity.

Answers to Questions
1. Check students' work.
2. The liquids formed separate layers, one on top of the other.
3. They have different densities.
4. The penny sank to the bottom, the rubber ball floated on top, and the plastic sphere was suspended between the penny and the ball.
5. penny, corn syrup, glycerin, water, corn oil, rubbing alcohol, plastic sphere, rubber ball
6. The densities of the penny, corn syrup, and glycerin are greater than 1 g/cm^3, and the densities of the corn oil, rubbing alcohol, plastic sphere, and rubber ball are less than 1 g/cm^3.

✔ Assessment

Performance Have students test their inferences. Ask them to clean the beaker and then pour into it 40 mL of corn oil followed by 40 mL of water. Use **Performance Assessment in the Science Classroom,** p. 97.

Activity

BENCH TESTED

Recognize the Problem

Purpose
Students observe and partici-pate in controlling a chemical change. [L2] ELL COOP LEARN
IS Interpersonal

Process Skills
designing an experiment, form-ing a hypothesis, observing and inferring, communicating, recognizing cause and effect, separating and controlling vari-ables, interpreting data

Time Required
two 45-minute periods

Materials
bananas, apples, pears, plastic or glass mixing bowls, 500 mL lemon/water solution, paring knife

Alternate Materials
other fruit that browns; possible containers: plastic shoe box or disposable container

Safety Precautions
Be careful when handling the paring knife. If students will use the knife, show them the safe way to cut fruit, to hand over the knife, and to position the knife when it's not in use. Num-ber the knives and collect them before the class ends.

Form a Hypothesis

Possible Hypotheses
Most students' hypotheses will reflect that a chemical change can be controlled.

Activity Design Your Own Experiment

Fruit Salad Favorites

When you are looking forward to enjoying a tasty, sweet fruit salad at a picnic, the last thing you want to see is brown fruit in the bowl. What can you do about this problem? Your teacher has given you a few different kinds of fruit. It is your task to per-form a test in which you will observe a physical change and a chemical change.

Recognize the Problem
Can a chemical change be controlled?

Form a Hypothesis
Based on your reading and observations, state a hypothesis about whether you can control a chemical change.

Goals
■ **Design** an experiment that identi-fies physical changes and chemical changes in fruit.
■ **Observe** whether chemical changes can be controlled.

Possible Materials
bananas
apples
pears
plastic or glass mixing bowls (2)
lemon/water solution (500 mL)
paring knife

Safety Precautions

WARNING: *Be careful when working with sharp objects. Always keep hands away from sharp blades. Never eat any-thing in the laboratory.*

Test Your Hypothesis

Possible Procedures
Slice fruit and place an even amount in each of two containers. In one container place 500 mL lemon/water solution. Make observations of each container every 5 minutes.

Resource Manager

Chapter Resources Booklet
    Activity Worksheet, pp. 7–8
Lab Management and Safety, p. 38

Test Your Hypothesis

Plan

1. As a group, agree upon the hypothesis and decide how you will test it. Identify what results will confirm the hypothesis.

2. **List** each of the steps you will need in order to test your hypothesis. Be specific. Describe exactly what you will do in each step. List all of your materials.

3. Prepare a data table in your Science Journal or on a computer for your observations.

4. Read the entire investigation to make sure all steps are in logical order.

5. **Identify** all constants, variables, and controls of the investigation.

Do

1. Ask your teacher to approve your plan and choice of constants, variables and controls before you start.

2. Perform the investigation as planned.

3. While doing the investigation, record your observations and complete the data table you prepared in your Science Journal.

Analyze Your Data

1. **Compare and contrast** the changes you observe in the control and the test fruit.

2. **Compare** your results with those of other groups.

3. What was your control in this investigation?

4. What are your variables?

5. Did you encounter any problems carrying out the investigation?

6. Do you have any suggestions for changes in a future investigation?

Draw Conclusions

1. Did the results support your hypothesis? Explain.

2. **Describe** what effect refrigerating the two salads would have on the fruit.

3. What will you do with the fruit from this experiment? Could it be eaten?

*C*ommunicating
Your Data

Write a page for an illustrated cookbook explaining the benefits you found in this experiment. Include drawings and a step-by-step procedure. **For more help, refer to the Science Skill Handbook.**

ACTIVITY 549

Oral Have students explain what chemical reaction is inhibited in this experiment. Freshly cut fruit reacts with oxygen in the air to turn brown. Use **Performance Assessment in the Science Classroom,** p. 89.

*C*ommunicating
Your Data

Students may base their directions on the procedure used in their experiments. Have them review an illustrated cookbook for ideas on how to communicate what they have learned. L2 IN **Linguistic**

Teaching Strategies

Tie to Prior Knowledge Most students know that fresh fruit, when cut, will begin to brown in a short period of time.

Troubleshooting Fruit may be cut by the teacher prior to the investigation. If so, cut fruit while students are creating and recording their plan, keeping in mind that it will soon begin to brown. Distribute fruit once a group's procedure is approved.

Expected Outcome

Fresh fruit, when cut, will react quickly with the oxygen in the air, resulting in a brown tint on the freshly cut surface of the fruit. A lemon/water solution will retard the oxidation process and leave the fruit looking fresh and crisp.

Analyze Your Data

1. The fruit with the lemon/water solution did not brown; the fruit without the solution turned brown.
2. Results should be similar.
3. the freshly cut fruit that was not in the lemon/water solution
4. the presence of lemon/water, different types of fruit
5. Answers will vary.
6. Answers will vary.

Draw Conclusions

1. Answers will vary.
2. Refrigerating the two salads would cause the fruit without the lemon/water solution to brown more slowly.
3. Encourage students to think of practical and safe disposal methods, possibly including feeding classroom animals (if appropriate), composting, etc. It is most important that they articulate that no students should eat anything in a lab situation.

Reviewing Main Ideas

Preview

Students can answer the questions in their Science Journals. Discuss the answers as you go through the chapter. **Linguistic**

Review

Students can write their answers, then compare them with those of other students. **Interpersonal**

Reteach

Students can look at the illustrations and describe details that support the main ideas of the chapter. **Visual-Spatial**

Answers to Chapter Review

SECTION 1

1. color, shape, length, mass, volume, state of different body components
5. color, shape

SECTION 2

1. flammability
3. physical

Reviewing Main Ideas

Section 1 Physical Properties and Changes

1. Any characteristic of a material that can be observed or measured is a physical property. *What can you observe or measure about the baby in the photo?*

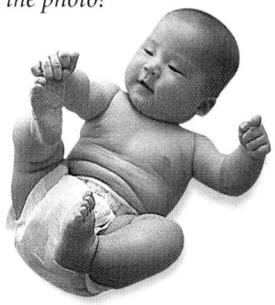

2. The four states of matter are solid, liquid, gas, and plasma. The state of matter is a physical property that is dependent on temperature and pressure.

3. State, color, shape, length, mass, volume, attraction by a magnet, density, melting point, boiling point, luster, malleability, and ductility are common physical properties.

4. In a physical change the properties of a substance change but the identity of the substance always stays the same.

5. You can classify materials according to their physical properties. *What different physical properties could you use to classify the objects in the photo?*

Section 2 Chemical Properties and Changes

1. Chemical properties give a substance the ability to undergo a chemical change. *What chemical property is being displayed in the photo?*

2. Common chemical properties include: ability to burn, reacts with oxygen, reacts with heat or light, and breaks down with electricity.

3. In a chemical change substances combine to form a new material. *Is the balloon about to undergo a chemical or physical change?*

4. The mass of the products of a chemical change is always the same as the mass of what you started with.

5. A chemical change results in a substance with a new identity, but matter is not created or destroyed.

FOLDABLES Reading & Study Skills

After You Read

Use the information in your Foldable to compare and contrast physical and chemical properties of matter. Write about each on the back of the tabs.

FOLDABLES Reading & Study Skills

After You Read

After students have read the chapter and completed the Foldable described in Before You Read, have them do the activity on the student page.

Dinah Zike

Visualizing Main Ideas

Complete the following table comparing properties of different objects.

Properties of Matter		
Type of Matter	**Physical Properties**	**Chemical Properties**
log	brown, round, might have length, solid	flammability
pillow	soft, might describe color, size, solid	flammability
bowl of cookie dough	color, gooey, chunks in it, solid	reacts with heat
book	might describe size, rectangle, color, solid	flammability
glass of orange juice	might describe volume, liquid, color	reacts with bleach

Vocabulary Review

Vocabulary Words

a. boiling point
b. chemical change
c. chemical property
d. conservation of mass
e. density
f. matter
g. melting point
h. physical change
i. physical property
j. states of matter

Study Tip

Make a study schedule for yourself. If you have a planner, write down exactly which hours you plan to spend studying and stick to it.

Using Vocabulary

The sentences below include terms that have been used incorrectly. Change the incorrect terms so the sentence reads correctly.

1. The <u>boiling point</u> is the temperature at which matter in a solid state changes to a liquid.

2. <u>Matter</u> is a measure of the mass of an object in a given volume.

3. A <u>chemical change</u> is easily observed or measured without changing the object.

4. <u>Physical changes</u> result in a new substance and cannot be reversed by physical means.

5. The four states of matter are solid, <u>volume</u>, liquid, and <u>melting point</u>.

Visualizing Main Ideas

See student page.

Vocabulary Review

Using Vocabulary

1. The <u>melting point</u> is the temperature at which matter in a solid state changes to a liquid.

2. <u>Density</u> is a measure of the mass of an object in a given volume.

3. A <u>physical property</u> is easily observed or measured without changing the object.

4. <u>Chemical changes</u> result in a new substance and cannot be reversed by physical means.

5. The four states of matter are solid, <u>gas</u>, liquid, and <u>plasma</u>.

Chapter 18 Assessment

Checking Concepts

1. C
2. D
3. C
4. A
5. B
6. D
7. C
8. B
9. A
10. D

Thinking Critically

11. All of the atoms of the reacting substances become part of the new substances formed.
12. A solid has a definite shape and volume, a liquid has definite volume but takes the shape of its container, a gas has the shape and volume of its container, and plasma occurs at very high temperatures.
13. The globe is spherical. Without changing its state, one could determine its mass, diameter, volume, density, color, and ability to attract a magnet.
14. volume and mass

Checking Concepts

Choose the word or phrase that best answers the question.

1. What statement describes the physical property of density?
   A) the distance between two points
   B) how light is reflected from an object's surface
   C) the amount of mass for a given volume
   D) the amount of space an object takes up

2. Which of the following is an example of a physical change?
   A) tarnishing   C) burning
   B) rusting   D) melting

3. Which of the choices below describes a boiling point?
   A) a chemical property
   B) a chemical change
   C) a physical property
   D) a color change

4. Which of the following is a sign that a chemical change has occurred?
   A) smoke   C) change in shape
   B) broken pieces   D) change in state

5. Which describes what volume is?
   A) the area of a square
   B) the amount of space an object takes up
   C) the distance between two points
   D) the temperature at which boiling begins

6. What property is described by the ability of metals to be hammered into sheets?
   A) mass   C) volume
   B) density   D) malleability

7. Which of these is a chemical property?
   A) size
   B) density
   C) flammability
   D) volume

8. When iron reacts with oxygen, what substance is produced?
   A) tarnish
   B) rust
   C) patina
   D) ashes

9. What kind of change results in a new substance being produced?
   A) chemical   C) physical
   B) mass   D) change of state

10. What is conserved during any change?
    A) color   C) identity
    B) volume   D) mass

Thinking Critically

11. Use the law of conservation of matter to explain what happens to atoms when they combine to form a new substance.

12. Describe the four states of matter. How are they different?

13. A globe is placed on your desk and you are asked to identify its physical properties. How would you describe the globe?

14. What information do you need to know about a material to find its density?

Developing Skills

15. **Classifying** Classify the following as a chemical or physical change: an egg breaks, a newspaper burns in the fireplace, a dish of ice cream is left out and melts, and a loaf of bread is baked.

Chapter ✔Assessment Planner

Portfolio Encourage students to place in their portfolios one or two items of what they consider to be their best work. Examples include:
- Curriculum Connection, p. 532
- Science Journal, p. 543
- Curriculum Connection, p. 544

Performance Additional performance assessments, Performance Task Assessment Lists, and rubrics for evaluating these activities can be found in Glencoe's **Performance Assessment in the Science Classroom.**

16. Measuring in SI Find the density of the piece of lead that has a mass of 49.01 g and a volume of 4.5 mL.

17. Concept Mapping Use the spider-mapping skill to organize and define physical properties of matter. Include the concepts of color, shape, length, density, mass, states of matter, volume, density, melting point, and boiling point.

18. Making and Using Tables Complete the table by supplying the missing information.

States of Matter

Type	Definition	Examples
solid	Particles vibrate in a fixed position.	books, desk, chair, ice cubes
liquid	Particles do not stay in one position. They move past each other.	water, juice, tea, soft drink, etc.
gas	Particles move freely with energy. They move all around.	oxygen, helium, vapor

19. Drawing Conclusions List the physical and chemical properties and changes that describe the process of scrambling eggs.

Performance Assessment

20. Comic Strip Create a comic strip demonstrating a chemical change in a substance. Include captions and drawings that demonstrate your understanding of conservation of matter.

TECHNOLOGY

Go to the Glencoe Science Web site at **science.glencoe.com** or use the **Glencoe Science CD-ROM** for additional chapter assessment.

Test Practice

Unknown matter can be identified by taking a sample of it and comparing its physical properties to those of already identified substances.

Physical Properties

Substance	Density (g/ml)	Color
Gasoline	0.703	Clear
Aluminum	2.700	Silver
Methane	0.466	Colorless
Water	1.000	Clear

Study the table and answer the following questions.

1. A scientist has a sample of a substance with a density greater than 1 g/mL. According to the table, which of these substances has a density greater than 1 g/mL?
A) gasoline
B) water
C) aluminum
D) methane

2. A physical change occurs when the form or appearance of a substance is changed. All of the following are examples of physical changes EXCEPT _____.
F) the vaporization of gasoline
G) corrosion of aluminum
H) methane diluted by air
J) water freezing into ice

CHAPTER ASSESSMENT 553

Test Practice

The Test-Taking Tip was written by The Princeton Review, the nation's leader in test preparation.
1. C
2. G

Developing Skills

15. chemical changes: a newspaper burns in the fireplace, a loaf of bread is baked; physical changes: an egg breaks, a dish of ice cream is left out and melts
16. 49.01 g/4.5 mL = 10.89 g/mL
17. Check students' work.
18. See student page.
19. The yolk and white of the eggs are mixed (physical change), the eggs are heated and cooked (chemical change to form bonds that harden the eggs).

Performance Assessment

20. Comic strips will vary but should identify the substances both before and after the chemical change and should indicate that matter has been conserved. Use **PASC**, p. 133.

✔Assessment Resources

📁 Reproducible Masters

Chapter Resources Booklet
 Chapter Review, pp. 35–36
 Chapter Tests, pp. 37–40
 Assessment Transparency Activity, p. 47

Glencoe Science Web site
 Interactive Tutor
 Chapter Quizzes

Glencoe Technology

 🖌 Assessment Transparency
 Interactive CD-ROM Chapter Quizzes
 ExamView Pro Test Bank
 Vocabulary PuzzleMaker Software
 MindJogger Videoquiz

Section/Objectives	Standards		Activities/Features
	National	State/Local	
Chapter Opener	See p. 6T for a Key to Standards.		**Explore Activity:** Model skateboard motion, p. 555 **Before You Read,** p. 555
Section 1 Motion 🕐 2 sessions 📦 1 block 1. **Define** speed and acceleration. 2. **Relate** acceleration to change in speed. 3. **Calculate** distance, speed, and acceleration.	National Content Standards: UCP3, B2		**Math Skills Activity:** Calculating Average Speed, p. 557 **Earth Science Integration,** Calculating Distance, p. 558 **Math Skills Activity:** Calculating Distance, p. 558 **Math Skills Activity:** Calculating Acceleration, p. 560
Section 2 Newton's Laws of Motion 🕐 4 sessions 📦 2 blocks 1. **Describe** how forces affect motion. 2. **Calculate** acceleration using Newton's second law of motion. 3. **Explain** Newton's third law of motion.	National Content Standards: UCP3, A1, B2		**Life Science Integration,** p. 563 **MiniLAB:** Determining Weights in Newtons, p. 564 **Science Online,** p. 566 **Math Skills Activity:** Newton's Second Law—Calculating Acceleration, p. 566 **Visualizing Newton's Laws and Space Travel,** p. 568
Section 3 Work and Simple Machines 🕐 4 sessions 📦 2 blocks 1. **Define** work. 2. **Distinguish** the different types of simple machines. 3. **Explain** how machines make work easier.	National Content Standards: UCP3, A1, B2, E1, E2, F5, G1		**Life Science Integration,** p. 571 **Math Skills Activity:** Calculating Work, p. 571 **Science Online,** p. 572 **MiniLAB:** Observing Mechanical Advantage—Pulleys, p. 573 **Activity:** Motion, p. 577 **Activity:** Methods of Travel, p. 578 **Science Stats,** Fastest Facts, p. 580

Teacher's Corner

INDEX TO NATIONAL GEOGRAPHIC SOCIETY
The following articles may be used for research relating to this chapter: "What's Got Pull? Gravity," by Allen Fallow, November 1995.

"Searching for the Secrets of Gravity," by John Boslough, May 1989.

Activity Materials	Reproducible Resources	Section Assessment	Technology
Explore Activity: 2–4 books, heavy paper or cardboard, marble	**Chapter Resources Booklet** Foldables Worksheet, p. 15 Directed Reading Overview, p. 17 Note-taking Worksheets, pp. 31–33	*GLENCOE'S* **ASSESSMENT** *ADVANTAGE*	
Need materials? Contact Science Kit at 1-800-828-7777 or www.sciencekit.com on the Internet.	**Chapter Resources Booklet** Transparency Activity, p. 42 Enrichment, p. 28 Reinforcement, p. 25 Directed Reading, p. 18 Lab Activity, pp. 9–11 **Mathematics Skill Activities,** p. 9 **Reading and Writing Skill Activities,** p. 35	Portfolio Earth Science Integration, p. 558 Performance Math Skills Activity, p. 557 Math Skills Activity, p. 558 Math Skills Activity, p. 560 Skill Builder Activities, p. 561 Content Section Assessment, p. 561	Section Focus Transparency Interactive CD-ROM Guided Reading Audio Program
MiniLAB: bathroom scale, large book, chair, heavy coat, another heavy object, calculator	**Chapter Resources Booklet** Transparency Activity, p. 43 MiniLAB, p. 3 Enrichment, p. 29 Reinforcement, p. 26 Directed Reading, p. 18 Lab Activity, pp. 13–14 Transparency Activity, pp. 45–46 **Physical Science Critical Thinking/Problem Solving,** p. 3 **Cultural Diversity,** p. 63	Portfolio Extension, p. 564 Performance MiniLAB, p. 564 Skill Builder Activities, p. 569 Content Section Assessment, p. 569	Section Focus Transparency Teaching Transparency Interactive CD-ROM Guided Reading Audio Program
MiniLAB: 2 broomsticks or 2 dowels, rope (3-m long) **Activity:** small ball or marble, meterstick or tape measure, stopwatch, or clock with second hand, graph paper **Activity:** no materials needed	**Chapter Resources Booklet** Transparency Activity, p. 44 MiniLAB, p. 4 Enrichment, p. 30 Reinforcement, p. 27 Directed Reading, pp. 19, 20 Activity Worksheet, pp. 5–6, 7–8 **Lab Management and Safety,** p. 71	Portfolio Cultural Diversity, p. 571 Performance Math Skills Activity, p. 571 MiniLAB, p. 573 Skill Builder Activities, p. 576 Content Section Assessment, p. 576	Section Focus Transparency Interactive CD-ROM Guided Reading Audio Program

End of Chapter Assessment

GLENCOE'S **ASSESSMENT** *ADVANTAGE*

Blackline Masters	Technology	Professional Series
Chapter Resources Booklet Chapter Review, pp. 35–36 Chapter Tests, pp. 37–40 **Standardized Test Practice by The Princeton Review,** pp. 79–82	MindJogger Videoquiz Interactive CD-ROM Vocabulary PuzzleMakers ExamView Pro Test Bank Interactive Lesson Planner Interactive Teacher Edition	Performance Assessment in the Science Classroom (PASC)

Transparencies

Section Focus

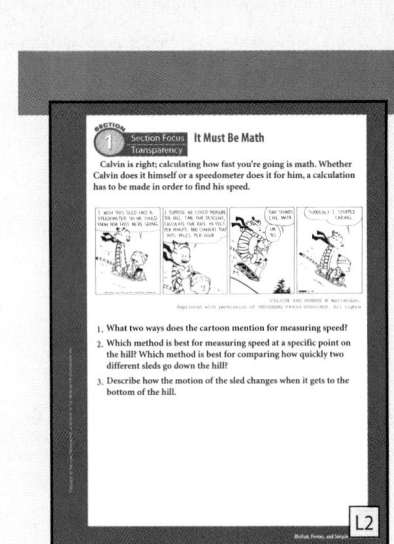

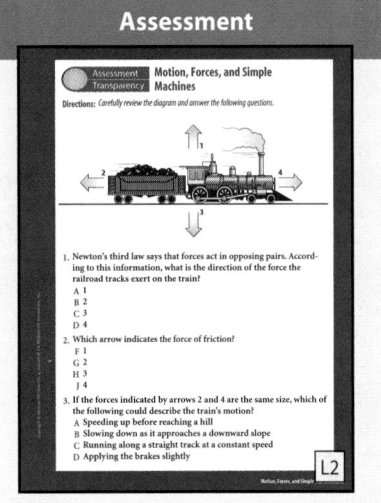

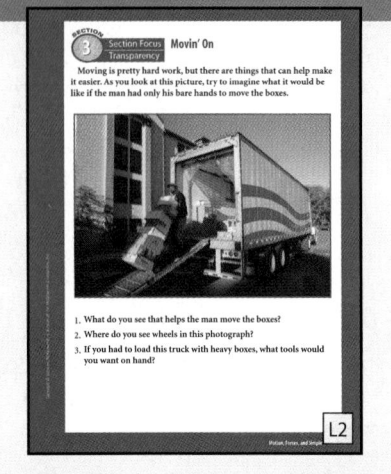

This is a representation of key blackline masters available in the Teacher Classroom Resources. See Resource Manager boxes within the chapter for additional information.

Assessment

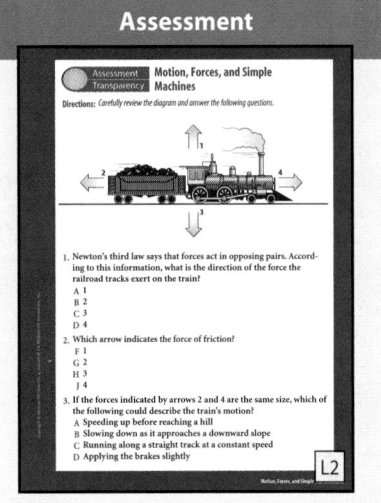

Teaching

Key to Teaching Strategies

The following designations will help you decide which activities are appropriate for your students.

L1 Level 1 activities should be appropriate for students with learning difficulties.

L2 Level 2 activities should be within the ability range of all students.

L3 Level 3 activities are designed for above-average students.

ELL ELL activities should be within the ability range of English Language Learners.

COOP LEARN Cooperative Learning activities are designed for small group work.

LS Multiple Learning Styles logos, as described on page 22T, are used throughout to indicate strategies that address different learning styles.

P These strategies represent student products that can be placed into a best-work portfolio.

Hands-on Activities

Activity Worksheets

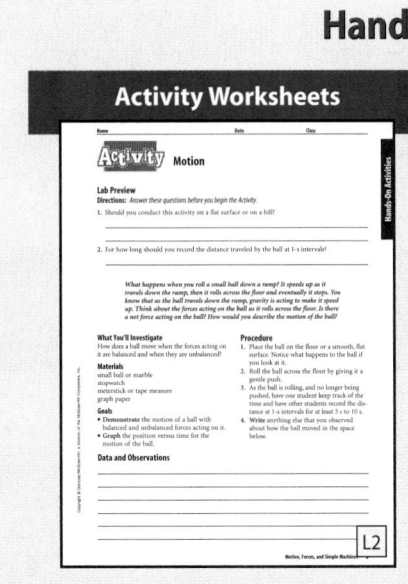

Laboratory Activities

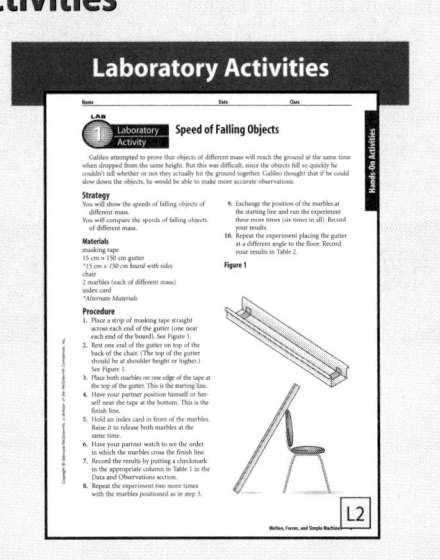

Meeting Different Ability Levels

Content Outline

Note-taking Worksheet — Motion, Forces, and Simple Machines

Section 1 Motion

A. _____ involves distance and time.
1. _____ speed—calculated as total distance traveled divided by travel time
2. _____ speed—an object's speed at a particular moment
3. When instantaneous speed does not change, an object is moving at _____ speed; average speed and instantaneous speed are the _____ in this situation.
4. Distance can be calculated if an object is moving at constant speed over a particular time period; total distance traveled equals _____ times time.
5. Speed and direction of motion is _____.
C. _____ is the change in velocity divided by the time needed for the change to occur.
1. Acceleration can be calculated using a formula: acceleration equals change in _____ divided by time.
2. Acceleration can be shown on a speed-time graph.

Section 2 Newton's Laws of Motion

A. _____—a push or a pull
1. When a force acts on an object, it _____ the object's acceleration.
2. Two or more forces that cancel each other out are _____ forces.
3. Two or more forces that do not cancel each other out are _____ forces.
4. The combination of all forces acting on an object is the _____ force.
B. Newton's _____—explain how forces cause motion
1. Newton's first law—a moving object moves in a straight line with _____ speed unless a force acts on it.
a. _____—a force that resists movement between two surfaces in contact
b. An object's tendency to resist a change in motion is _____; the more mass an object has, the greater its inertia.

Motion, Forces, and Simple Machines **L2**

Reinforcement

Section 1 Reinforcement — Motion

Directions: *Identify what each of the following formulas is used to find.*
1. (change in speed)/time
2. acceleration × time
3. (total distance traveled)/time
4. 1/2 (acceleration)(time)²

Directions: *The graph shows the various speeds that a worm travels over a 10-minute interval. Use the graph to answer the questions that follow.*
5. What is the greatest speed the worm reaches?
6. What is the worm's acceleration during the first 2 minutes?
7. How fast is the worm traveling as it goes from A to B?
8. How far does the worm travel from A to B?
9. What is the worm's acceleration from A to B?
10. How does the worm's motion change from B to C?
11. What is the worm's acceleration during the last 2 minutes?
12. How would you describe the worm's motion during the last 2 minutes?
13. How far does the worm travel during the last 2 minutes?

Motion, Forces, and Simple Machines **L2**

Directed Reading

Directed Reading for Content Mastery — Overview — Motion, Forces, and Simple Machines

Directions: *Use the formula* $v = d/t$ *to answer the following question.*
1. Julio rides his bike 12 km in 1.5 h. Determine the average speed at which Julio rode.

Directions: *The figure below illustrates Newton's third law of motion. Use it to answer the questions below.*

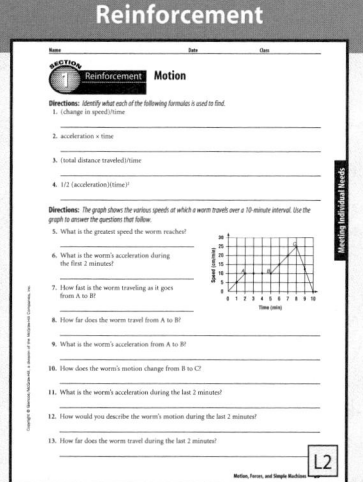

2. Draw arrows on the figure above to show the direction in which the oars must move to send the boat forward.
3. Do the arrows you drew in the figure represent an action force or a reaction force?

Directions: *Answer the following question about weight.*
4. If your weight is 490 N and you stand on a box that exerts a normal force of 440 N, what will happen?

Directions: *Answer the following question on the lines provided.*
5. A third-class lever has a mechanical advantage of less than one. Why are third-class levers used if this is the case?

Motion, Forces, and Simple Machines **L1**

Enrichment

Section 1 Enrichment — The Art of Motion

Think back to the last time you read a comic book or saw a cartoon in the newspaper. Chances are that somewhere in that comic strip, the cartoonist showed a character in motion. Do you remember how it was done? Perhaps the cartoonist inserted horizontal lines to show motion. Maybe the cartoonist altered the actual shape of an object. List three techniques for showing motion in cartoons.
1. _____
2. _____
3. _____

Directions: *Using simple figures, motion lines, or other techniques, draw three cartoon panels of two automobiles on a highway. One is moving at a constant speed and one is accelerating.*

4. What formulas did your cartoon illustrate?

Motion, Forces, and Simple Machines **L3**

Spanish Directed Reading

Lectura dirigida para Dominio del contenido — Sinopsis — Movimiento, fuerzas y máquinas simples

Instrucciones: *Usa la fórmula* $v = d/t$ *para contestar la siguiente pregunta.*
1. Julio anda en bicicleta 12 km en 1.5 h. Determina la rapidez promedio de Julio en esta travesía.

Instrucciones: *La figura ilustra la tercera ley del movimiento de Newton. Úsala para contestar las preguntas.*

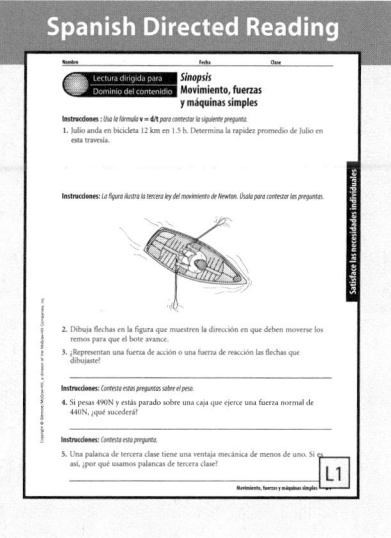

2. Dibuja flechas en la figura que muestren la dirección en que deben moverse los remos para que el bote avance.
3. ¿Representan una fuerza de acción o una fuerza de reacción las flechas que dibujaste?

Instrucciones: *Contesta estas preguntas sobre el peso.*
4. Si pesas 490N y estás parado sobre una caja que ejerce una fuerza normal de 440N, ¿qué sucederá?

Instrucciones: *Contesta esta pregunta.*
5. Una palanca de tercera clase tiene una ventaja mecánica de menos de uno. Si es así, ¿por qué usamos palancas de tercera clase?

Movimiento, fuerzas y máquinas simples **L1**

Assessment

Chapter Tests

Chapter Test — Motion, Forces, and Simple Machines

I. Testing Concepts

Directions: *In the blank at the left, write the letter of the term that best completes each statement.*

____ 1. It would probably be easiest to ride a bicycle across _____.
a. a sidewalk   b. the grass   c. sand   d. gravel
____ 2. The force that always acts opposite to the direction of the motion of an object is called _____.
a. gravity   b. inertia   c. friction   d. none of these
____ 3. According to Newton's third law, forces always occur in _____ pairs.
a. equal but opposite   c. unequal but complementary
b. unequal but opposite   d. equal but complementary
____ 4. Newton first described gravity while watching _____.
a. smoke rise   b. a car accelerate   c. someone walking   d. an apple falling
____ 5. You would NOT use _____ to find the acceleration of an object.
a. time   b. initial speed   c. final speed   d. weight
____ 6. Newton's _____ law of motion explains why you may lean sideways in a car if the driver turns a corner too quickly.
a. primary   b. first   c. second   d. third
____ 7. _____ is the speed of an object and its direction of motion.
a. Friction   b. Mass   c. Gravity   d. Velocity
____ 8. To calculate an average speed, you would use _____.
a. weight and time   c. acceleration
b. weight and distance   d. distance and time
____ 9. _____ is used to describe an object slowing down because of decreasing speed.
a. Acceleration   c. Negative acceleration
b. Average speed   d. Inertia
____ 10. A bottle opener is a(n) _____.
a. first-class lever   b. second-class lever   c. third-class lever   d. inclined plane
____ 11. An object that has a _____ will accelerate in the direction of the force.
a. normal force   b. net force   c. frictional force   d. speed
____ 12. _____ is the rate at which an object covers a given distance.
a. Acceleration   b. Speed   c. Force   d. Motion
____ 13. _____ is NOT a force.
a. Gravity   b. Mass   c. Friction   d. all of these
____ 14. A 1-cm screw with a 4-cm thread would have a mechanical advantage of _____.
a. one   b. two   c. three   d. four
____ 15. Stepping from a wagon and watching the wagon move away from you is an example of Newton's _____ law.
a. first   b. second   c. third   d. gravitational

Motion, Forces, and Simple Machines **L2**

Test Practice Workbook

Standardized Test Practice — Teacher Edition

Glencoe **Science**

- Correlated to the National Science Standards
- Prepares students for ITBS, SAT-9, and TerraNova
- Two pages of questions for each chapter
- Written by The Princeton Review

LEVEL RED

L2

Chapter Review

Chapter Review — Motion, Forces, and Simple Machines

Part A. Vocabulary Review

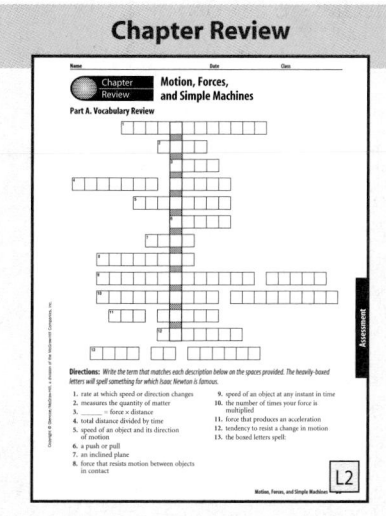

Directions: *Write the term that matches each description below on the spaces provided. The heavily-boxed letters will spell something for which Isaac Newton is famous.*

1. rate at which speed or direction changes
2. measures the quantity of matter
3. _____ = force × distance
4. total distance divided by time
5. speed of an object and its direction of motion
6. a push or pull
7. an inclined plane
8. force that resists motion between objects in contact
9. speed of an object at any instant in time
10. the number of times your force is multiplied
11. force that produces an acceleration
12. tendency to resist a change in motion
13. the boxed letters spell:

Motion, Forces, and Simple Machines **L2**

Science Content Background

SECTION 1

Motion
Acceleration

When an object's motion changes the object is accelerating. Acceleration is the rate of change with time of an object's velocity. Acceleration always has units of speed divided by time, or meter/second divided by seconds. Because the velocity of an object has direction, an object is accelerating when it changes its direction of motion, as well as when it speeds up or slows down.

SECTION 2

Newton's Laws of Motion
Newton's First Law

Constant, straight-line motion is just as natural as rest. This can approximately be demonstrated in a variety of ways using balanced forces, but it is impossible to produce a completely friction free environment. An air-hockey puck skimming a cushion of air works as an example of an approximate continuous straight-line motion.

Student Misconception

If an object is moving, there is a force acting on it in the direction of the motion.

Refer to the facing page for teaching strategies to address this misconception. Refer to pages 564–566 for content related to this topic.

When a ball is thrown upward, an upward force is exerted on the ball that is greater than the downward force of gravity. This upward force is exerted on the ball only while the ball is in contact with the thrower's hand.

Newton's Second Law

When an unbalanced force acts upon an object, the object will accelerate in the direction of this force according to $F_{net} = ma$. When an object falls and air resistance is negligible, the net force is just the weight of the object. On the surface of the Earth, weight can be calculated using $w = mg$. When this is substituted as F_{net} in Newton's second law, the masses cancel on both sides of the equation. This is a very profound result that bothered Newton. Are inertia (an object's tendency to resist a change in motion) and gravitational mass the same quantity? Einstein later resolved the issue when he stated his principle for equivalence, which says that an object falling in a gravitational field is identical to an object being accelerated by another means. Therefore, inertia and gravitational masses are the same.

SECTION 3

Work and Simple Machines
Work

Simple machines often enable less effort to be used to do a job, such as moving a heavy object. However, machines do not reduce the amount of work needed to do a job. Even though less effort may be needed, this effort must be exerted over a longer distance.

What is a machine?

In all machines friction converts some of the input work into heat that warms the machine and its surroundings. As a result, the output work is always less than the input work and no machine is 100 percent efficient.

SCIENCE Online

For additional content background on this topic, go to the Glencoe Science Web site at science.glencoe.com.

IDENTIFYING Misconceptions

Find Out What Students Think

Students may think that . . .

- **If an object is moving, there is a force acting on it in the direction of the motion.**

Friction makes it seem that an object will move only while a force is being applied. If a box on the floor is given a push, it slides in the direction of the push and then stops. If the box were placed on an icy surface and pushed, it would slide much farther. Without friction, the box would continue moving with constant velocity, even though no force was being exerted on it.

Activity

Give each group of students a marble. Ask students to practice rolling the marble on a flat surface until they can get it to roll about one meter and then stop. When they are able to do this, ask why the marble stops after they have started it rolling. Have students in each group discuss this question, and then ask groups to explain their answers. Some students will explain that the marble stopped because it ran out of force.

Promote Understanding

Activity

Give each student a piece of clear plastic tubing and a marble that can roll easily inside the tubing.

- Demonstrate for students how to curl the tubing so that it forms part of a circle. Lift up one end of the tubing a little so gravity helps the marble roll down the circle.

- Ask students each to draw a diagram showing how the ball will roll after it leaves the tubing.

- Have students hold the tubing so that it forms part of a circle and then roll the marble through it. Tell students to repeat the process until they are confident of their results.

- Students should see that the marble continues in a straight line after it leaves the tubing. Ask students why the marble doesn't curve after it leaves the tubing.

- Make sure they realize that the marble moved in a curve inside the tubing because the walls

of the tubing exerted forces on the marble that pushed in the curve.

- Once the marble was free of the tubing, those forces were no longer acting on it, so it continued in straight-line motion. The tubing could exert forces on the marble only while the marble and tubing were in contact.

Mark M. Lawrence/The Stock Market

Assess

After completing the chapter, see *Identifying Misconceptions* in the Study Guide.

Motion, Forces, and Simple Machines

What do you think?

Science Journal This photo shows a very small electric motor.

Motion, Forces, and Simple Machines

This rollerblader pauses in the air as he changes direction and begins his descent. But he can't stay airborne long. How does his motion change as he reaches the bottom of the half-pipe and starts up the other side? What happens when he reaches the top? In this chapter, you will learn how forces affect motion, speed, acceleration, and direction.

What Do You Think?

Science Journal Look at the picture below with a classmate. Discuss what this might be or what is happening. Here's a hint: *You could use this in a hair dryer, if you were a hundred times smaller.* Write your answer or your best guess in your Science Journal.

554

Theme Connection

Systems and Interactions The study of the motion of macroscopic objects involves applying Newton's laws to a system of objects. The interactions between objects in this system can be described by Newton's second and third laws. If the objects are not interacting, Newton's first law applies.

Skateboarders who can ride half-pipes make it look easy. They race down one side and up the other. They rise above the ledge and appear to float as they spin and return. They practice these tricks many times until they get them right. In this chapter, you'll learn how this complicated motion can be explained by forces such as gravity. With an understanding of forces and how they make things move, you will begin to unravel the secrets of these tricks.

Model skateboard motion

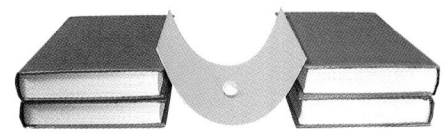

1. Use heavy paper or cardboard to make a model of a half-pipe like the one in the picture. A marble will model the skateboard.

2. Release the marble from a point near the bottom of the curve. Observe the motion. How high does it go? When is its speed greatest?

3. Release the marble from a point near the top of the curve. Observe the motion. Compare this to the marble's motion in step 2.

Science Journal

In your Science Journal, describe your experiment and what you discovered. How did the different starting points affect how high the marble rolled up the other side?

Before You Read

FOLDABLES
Reading & Study Skills

Making a Know-Want-Learn Study Fold **Make the following Foldable to help identify what you already know and what you want to know about motion and forces.**

1. Place a sheet of paper in front of you so the long side is at the top. Fold the paper in half from top to bottom.

2. Fold both sides in to form three equal sections. Unfold the paper so three sections show.

3. Through the top thickness of paper, cut along each of the fold lines to the topfold, forming three tabs. Label the tabs *Know, Want,* and *Learned.*

4. Before you read the chapter, write what you know and what you want to know under the tabs. As you read the chapter, correct what you have written and add more questions.

| Know | Want | Learned |

555

EXPLORE ACTIVITY

Purpose Students model the motion of an object rolling down and up a ramp. They will observe and manipulate the variables affected by gravity. [L1]
[ELL] [IS] **Kinesthetic**

Preparation Have different sizes of heavy paper on hand.

Materials various sizes of heavy paper or thin cardboard, marble, tape, marking pen, books

Teaching Strategies

• Suggest that students mark a scale on the paper to help measure the height the marble rises up the side of the half-pipe.

Observe

The marble travels fastest at the bottom of the ramp, and the farther up the ramp it is released, the higher it rises on the other side. The height to which the marble rises is nearly the same as the height from which it was released.

✔ *Assessment*

Performance Have students use their results to predict where they must release the marble to reach a height that you choose on the other side. Use **Performance Assessment in the Science Classroom,** p. 89.

FOLDABLES
Reading & Study Skills

Before You Read

Dinah Zike Study Fold

Purpose This activity will provide students with an opportunity to review what they know and think about what they would like to know about motion and forces. The resulting Foldable can be used as an assessment tool at the end of the chapter to determine what students have learned.

📁 For additional help, see Foldables Worksheet, p. 15 in **Chapter Resources Booklet,** or go to the Glencoe Science Web site at **science.glencoe.com.** See After You Read in the Study Guide at the end of this chapter.

SECTION

1

Motion

1 Motivate

Bellringer Transparency

Display the Section Focus Transparency for Section 1. Use the accompanying Transparency Activity Master. L2

ELL

Section Focus Transparency

1 It Must Be Math

Calvin is right; calculating how fast you're going is math. Whether Calvin does it himself or a speedometer does it for him, a calculation has to be made in order to find his speed.

1. What two ways does the cartoon mention for measuring speed?
2. Which method is best for measuring speed at a specific point on the hill? Which method is best for comparing how quickly two different sleds go down the hill?
3. Describe how the motion of the sled changes when it gets to the bottom of the hill.

Tie to Prior Knowledge

Ask students what they think their fastest speed is on their bike or skateboard. A typical bike speed is about 4 m/s, and a typical skateboard speed is about 3 m/s. Tell them that in this section they will learn different ways of describing speed.

Caption Answer

Figure 1 It would increase.

SECTION

1

Motion

As You Read

***What* You'll Learn**

■ **Define** speed and acceleration.
■ **Relate** acceleration to change in speed.
■ **Calculate** distance, speed, and acceleration.

Vocabulary

average speed   velocity
instantaneous speed   acceleration

***Why* It's Important**

Motion can be described using distance, time, speed, and acceleration.

Speed

Think of skateboarding down the side of a half-pipe for the first time. Your heart pounds as you move faster. As you reach the bottom, you are going fast, and you feel excitement and maybe even fear. You flow through the change in direction as you start up the other side. Your speed decreases as you move higher up the wall. When you reach the top, you are at a near standstill. If you think fast, you can grab hold of the ledge and take a break. Otherwise, back down you go—with or without the skateboard.

To understand how to describe motion, think about the movement of the bicycle in **Figure 1.** To describe how fast the bicycle is traveling, you have to know two things about its motion. One is the distance it has traveled, or how far it has gone. The other is how much time it took to travel that distance.

Average Speed A bike rider can speed up and slow down several times in a certain time period. One way to describe the bike rider's motion over this time period is to give the average speed. To calculate **average speed,** divide the distance traveled by the time it takes to travel that distance.

$$\text{average speed} = \frac{\text{total distance traveled}}{\text{travel time}}$$

If you let s stand for the average speed, d stand for distance, and t stand for time, you can write this equation as follows.

$$s = \frac{d}{t}$$

Figure 1
To find the biker's average speed, divide the distance down the hill by the time taken to cover that distance. *What would happen to the average speed if the hill were steeper?*

Because average speed is calculated by dividing distance by time, its units always will be a distance unit divided by a time unit. For example, the average speed of a car can have units of kilometers per hour rather than meters per second.

556   CHAPTER 19 Motion, Forces, and Simple Machines

Section ✓*Assessment* Planner

PORTFOLIO
Earth Science Integration, p. 558

PERFORMANCE ASSESSMENT
Math Skills Activities, pp. 557, 558, 560
Skill Builder Activities, p. 561
See page 584 for more options.

CONTENT ASSESSMENT
Section, p. 561
Challenge, p. 561
Chapter, pp. 584–585

Math Skills Activity

Calculating Average Speed

Example Problem

Riding your bike, it takes you 30 min to get to your friend's house, which is 9 km away. What is your average speed?

Solution

1 *This is what you know:*   distance: $d = 9$ km
time: $t = 30$ min $= 0.5$ h

2 *This is what you need to know:*   speed: s

3 *This is the equation you need to use:* $s = d/t$

4 *Substitute the known values:* $s = 9$ km/0.5 h $= 18$ km/h

Check your answer by multiplying it by the time. Do you calculate the same distance that was given?

Practice Problem

If an airplane travels 1,350 km in 3 h, what is its average speed?

For more help, refer to the Math Skill Handbook.

Instantaneous Speed Average speed is useful if you don't care about the details of the motion. For example, suppose you went on a long road trip and traveled 640 km in 8 h. Your average speed was 80 km/h, even though you might have stopped for red lights, got stuck in a traffic jam, or enjoyed a long stretch of high speed on a highway.

When your motion is speeding up and slowing down, it might be useful to know how fast you are going at a certain time. For example, suppose the speed limit over a 100-km section of freeway is 100 km/h. Even though a car might travel this distance with an average speed of 90 km/h, it can be moving faster than the speed limit at different times.

To keep from exceeding the speed limit, the driver would need to know the **instantaneous speed**—the speed of an object at any instant of time. When you ride in a car, the instantaneous speed is given by the speedometer, as shown in **Figure 2.** How does your instantaneous speed change as you skateboard down the side of the half-pipe?

Figure 2
The odometer in a car measures the distance traveled. The speedometer measures instantaneous speed. *How could you use this speedometer to measure average speed?*

✔ **Reading Check**   *How is instantaneous speed different from average speed?*

Resource Manager

Chapter Resources Booklet
Transparency Activity, p. 42
Note-taking Worksheets, pp. 31–33
Mathematics Skill Activities, p. 9

Curriculum Connection

Music The pattern of speed is one of the things that changes individual notes into music. Have students investigate speed in music and demonstrate what they learn to the class. The tempo (rate of speed) of a song is usually described by Italian words such as *adagio* (leisurely) or *vivace* (lively). Rhythm describes the pattern of the beat. L3 **IS** **Auditory-Musical**

---

2 Teach

Speed

Math Skills Activity

National Math Standards
Correlation to Mathematics Objectives
1, 2, 4, 6, 8, 9

Answer to Practice Problem

- This is what you know: distance: $d = 1350$ km; time: $t = 3$ h
- This is what you need to know: speed: s
- This is the equation you need to use: $s = d/t$
- Substitute the known values: $s = 1,350$ km/3 $h = 450$ km/h
- Avg. Speed $= 450$ km/h

Extension

Position and speed are always measured relative to a reference point. Have students find out the average speed of a student sitting in a chair when the reference point is the Sun. Earth travels through the solar system around the Sun, a distance of about 940,100,000 km, in one year, which is equal to about 365 days, or about 8,766 hours. Earth's average speed, and therefore the average speed of the student sitting at the desk, is about 107,200 km/h. L3

IS **Logical-Mathematical**

Caption Answer

Figure 2 Measure the distance traveled using the odometer, and divide that distance by the time needed to travel the distance.

✔ **Reading Check**

Answer Instantaneous speed is speed at any instant; average speed is speed over a time interval.

Speed, continued

Earth Science
INTEGRATION

The rate of plate motion varies widely. The slowest movement is along the Arctic Ridge, which moves less than 2.5 cm/yr. The fastest movement is at the East Pacific Rise, west of South America. Here the Pacific Plate and the Nazca Plate move about 15 cm/yr relative to one another. Occasionally a plate will have a sudden movement much faster than its normal rate. For example, the Pacific Plate normally moves northwest relative to the North American Plate at a rate of about 5 cm per year. In 1906, however, the Pacific Plate suddenly moved about 6 m, resulting in the famous San Francisco earthquake.

Math Skills Activity

National Math Standards

Correlation to Mathematics Objectives

1, 2, 4, 6, 8, 9

Answer to Practice Problem

- This is what you know: speed: $s = 5$ km/h; time: $t = $ h
- This is what you need to know: distance: d
- This is the equation you need to use: $d = st$

  Substitute the known values:
  $d = (5 \text{ km/h}) \times (6 \text{ h}) = 30 \text{ km}$

Earth Science
INTEGRATION

The outer part of Earth is the crust. Earth's crust is broken into huge pieces called plates that move slowly. Research how fast plates can move. In your Science Journal, make a table showing the speeds of some plates.

Constant Speed Sometimes an object is moving such that its instantaneous speed doesn't change. You may have noticed that the speedometer needle will hardly move when the driver is using cruise control. When the instantaneous speed doesn't change, an object is moving with constant speed. Then the average speed and the instantaneous speed are the same.

Calculating Distance If an object is moving with constant speed, then the distance it travels over any period of time can be calculated using the equation for average speed. When both sides of this equation are multiplied by the time, you have the following new equation.

$$\text{total distance traveled} = \text{average speed} \times \text{time}$$
$$d = s \times t$$

For example, if a marathon runner can maintain a constant speed of 16 km/h, how far can she run in 24 min or 0.4 h? The distance covered by the runner is as follows.

$$d = s \times t = (16 \text{ km/h}) \times (0.4 \text{ h}) = 6.4 \text{ km}$$

Notice that units of time in the speed, s, and in the time, t, have to be the same. Otherwise, these units of time won't cancel.

Math Skills Activity

Calculating Distance

Example Problem

It takes your family 2 h to drive to an amusement park at an average speed of 73 km/h. How far away is the amusement park?

1. *This is what you know:*   speed: $s = 73$ km/h
         time: $t = 2$ h
2. *This is what you need to know:*   distance: d
3. *This is the equation you need to use:* $d = s \times t$
4. *Substitute the known values:* $d = 73 \text{ km/h} \times 2 \text{ h} = 146 \text{ km}$

Check your answer by dividing it by the time. Do you calculate the same speed that was given?

Practice Problem

You and your friends walk at an average speed of 5 km/h on a nature hike. After 6 h, you reach the ranger station. How far did you hike?

For more help, refer to the Math Skill Handbook.

Science Journal

Speeds Have students measure the speed of their movements several times in a day. Ask them to write in their Science Journals at least one example each of a constant speed, an instantaneous speed, and an average speed at which they moved that day. [L2] [IN] **Naturalist**

✔ Active Reading

Reflective Journal Have students divide sheets of paper into several columns and record their thoughts under headings such as "What I did," "What I learned," "What questions I have," "What surprises I experienced," and "Overall response." Have students write a Reflective Journal for the Math Skills Activities in this section.

Velocity

Suppose you are walking with a constant speed on a street, headed north. You turn when you reach an intersection and start walking with the same speed, but you now are headed east, as shown in **Figure 3.** Your motion has changed, even though your speed has remained constant. To completely describe your movement you would have to tell not only how fast you were moving, but also your direction. The **velocity** of an object is the speed of an object and its direction of motion.

Velocity changes when the speed changes, the direction of motion changes, or both change. When you turned the corner at the intersection, your direction of motion changed, even though your speed remained constant. Therefore, your velocity changed.

 **Reading Check** *What are two ways that you can change your velocity?*

Acceleration

At the top of a skateboard half-pipe, you are at rest. Your speed is zero. When you start down, you smoothly speed up, going faster and faster. If the angle of the half-pipe were steeper, you would speed up at an even greater rate.

How could you describe how your speed is changing? If you changed direction, how could you describe how your velocity was changing? Just as speed describes how the distance traveled changes with time, acceleration describes how the velocity changes with time. **Acceleration** is the change in velocity divided by the time needed for the change to occur. **Figure 4** shows some examples of acceleration.

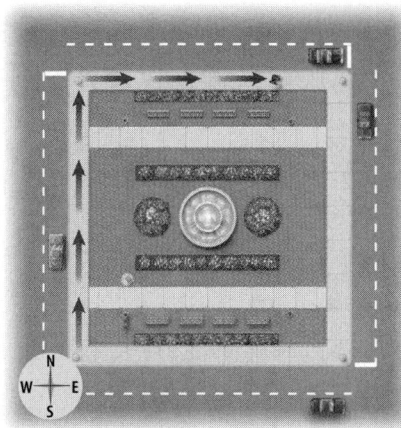

Figure 3
If you are walking north at a constant speed and then turn east, continuing at the same speed, you have changed your velocity. *What is another way to change your velocity?*

Figure 4
If the velocity of an object is changing, the object has acceleration. The direction of the acceleration depends on whether the object is speeding up or slowing down.

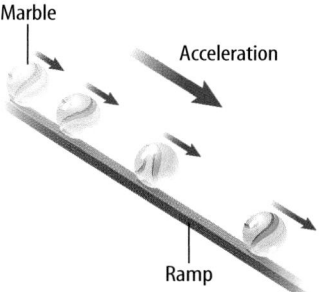

A A marble rolling down a hill speeds up. Its motion and acceleration are in the same direction.

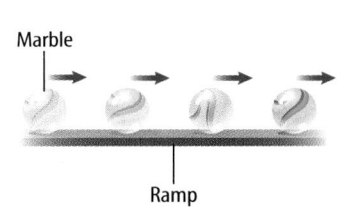

B This marble is rolling on a level surface with constant velocity. Its acceleration is zero.

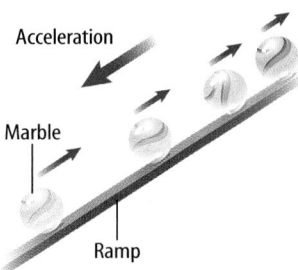

C A marble rolling up a hill slows down. Its motion and acceleration are in opposite directions.

SECTION 1 Motion **559**

Activity
Give students the following scenario. At 5:00 a.m. a newspaper truck leaves the printer's with two loads of newspapers to deliver. It travels on a highway at 80 km/h for 30 minutes. Then it travels on side roads for 20 minutes at 15 km/h, reaching its first delivery at 5:50 a.m. It takes the driver 10 minutes to deliver the first load of papers. Then the truck travels 15 minutes at 20 km/h to reach its second delivery. There it takes the driver 15 minutes to unload the papers. At 6:30 a.m. the empty truck heads back to the printer. **What was its instantaneous speed at 5:10 a.m.?** 80 km/h **How far did the truck travel to deliver its two loads?** 80 km/h for 0.5 hr = 40 km + 15 km/h for 0.33 hr = 5 km + 0 km/h for 0.17 h = 0 km + 20 km/h for 0.25 h = 4 km + 0 km/h for 0.25 h = 0 km = 49 km **What was the truck's average speed?** 49 km/1.5 h = 32.67 km/h

Velocity

Caption Answer
Figure 3 increase or decrease your speed

Acceleration

 Reading Check

Answer Change your speed or change your direction.

Acceleration, continued

Fun Fact

Negative acceleration is frequently called deceleration.

Math Skills Activity

National Math Standards

Correlation to Mathematics Objectives

1,2,4,6,8,9

Answer to Practice Problem

- This is what you know: time: $t = 5$ s; initial speed $= 8$ m/s; final speed $= 18$ m/s
- This is what you need to know: acceleration: a
- This is the equation you need to use: $a = $ (final speed $-$ initial speed)/t
- Substitute the known values: $a = (18\,\text{m/s} - 8\,\text{m/s})/5\text{s} = 2\,\text{m/s}^2$

Teacher FYI

Acceleration describes how speed changes with time, just as speed describes how distance changes with time. The slope of a speed-time graph gives instantaneous acceleration, just as the slope of a distance-time graph gives instantaneous speed.

Extension

Tell students that gravity causes a constant acceleration on all objects falling near Earth's surface. Have students research what that constant acceleration is. $9.8\,\text{m/s}^2$ **After falling for 10s, how fast would an object be moving?** $9.8\,\text{m/s}^2 \times 10\text{s} = 98$ m/s
L3 IS **Logical-Mathematical** P

Calculating Acceleration If the direction of motion isn't changing, the motion is along a straight line. Then the acceleration can be calculated from the following formula.

$$\text{acceleration} = \text{change in speed/time}$$
$$a = (\text{final speed} - \text{initial speed})/t$$

The initial speed is the speed at the beginning of the time period, and the final speed is the speed at the end of the time period. The initial speed of an object that starts from rest is 0 m/s. If an object at rest accelerates to a final speed of 10 m/s in 2 s, the acceleration is found as follows.

$$a = \frac{(10\,\text{m/s} - 0\,\text{m/s})}{2\,\text{s}} = 5\,\text{m/s}^2$$

An object that is slowing down also is accelerating. Suppose an object has a speed of 10 m/s and then comes to a stop in 2 s. Then the initial speed is 10 m/s and the final speed is 0 m/s. The acceleration is $-5\,\text{m/s}^2$.

Math Skills Activity

Calculating Acceleration

Example Problem

You are sliding on a snow-covered hill at a speed of 8 m/s. There is a drop that increases your speed to 18 m/s in 5 s. Find your acceleration.

1. *This is what you know:*   initial speed $= 8$ m/s
    final speed $= 18$ m/s
    time: $t = 5$ s

2. *This is what you need to know:*   acceleration: a

3. *This is the equation you need to use:* $a = (\text{final speed} - \text{initial speed})/t$

4. *Substitute the known values:* $a = (18\,\text{m/s} - 8\,\text{m/s})/5$ s
    $a = 10\,\text{m/s}/5\,\text{s} = 2\,\text{m/s}^2$

Check your answer by multiplying it by the time. Subtract the initial speed. Do you calculate the same final speed that was given?

Practice Problem

The roller coaster you are on is moving at 10 m/s. 5 s later it does a loop-the-loop and is moving at 25 m/s. What is the roller coaster's acceleration over this time?

For more help, refer to the Math Skill Handbook.

Resource Manager

Chapter Resources Booklet

Reinforcement, p. 25

Directed Reading for Content Mastery, pp. 17, 18

Performance Assessment in the Science Classroom, p. 35

Science Journal

Sports Science Have students write descriptions in their Science Journals of how speed, velocity, and acceleration are important in several sports. Descriptions might include the velocity (speed and direction) with which a bowling ball hits the pins or how a skier accelerates while traveling down a snowy slope.
L2 IS **Linguistic**

Graphing Speed Picture yourself skating down the side of a hill, across a level valley, then up another hill on the opposite side. If you were to graph your speed over time, it would look similar to the graph in **Figure 5.**

As you start down the hill, your speed will increase with time, as shown in segment A. The line on the graph rises when acceleration is in the direction of motion. When you travel across the level pavement, you move at a constant speed. Because your speed doesn't change, the line on the graph will be horizontal as shown in segment B. A horizontal line shows that the acceleration is zero. On the opposite side, when you are moving up the hill, your speed will decrease, as shown in segment C. Anytime you slow down, acceleration is opposite the direction of motion and the line on a speed-time graph will slant downward.

Figure 5
The acceleration of an object can be shown on a speed-time graph.

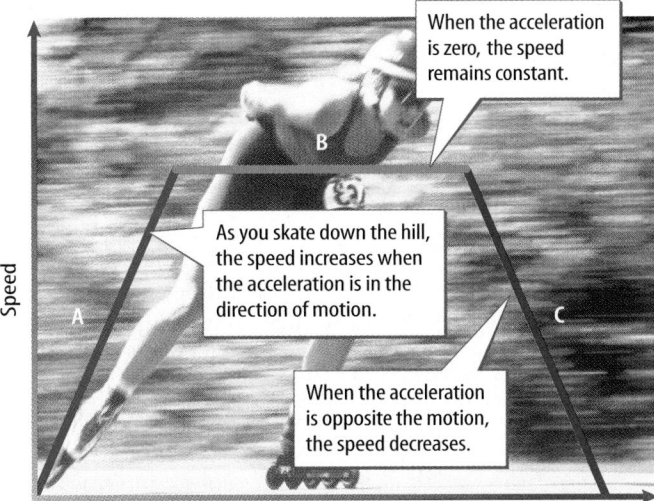

When the acceleration is zero, the speed remains constant.

As you skate down the hill, the speed increases when the acceleration is in the direction of motion.

When the acceleration is opposite the motion, the speed decreases.

Speed

Time

Section 1 Assessment

1. During rush-hour traffic in a big city, it can take 1.5 h to travel 45 km. What is the average speed in km/h for this trip?

2. A car traveling 20 m/s brakes and takes 3 s to stop. What is the acceleration in m/s²?

3. A runner accelerates from 0 m/s to 3 m/s in 12 s. What is the acceleration?

4. If an airplane is flying at a constant speed of 500 km/h, can it be accelerating? Explain.

5. **Think Critically** Describe the motion of a skateboard as it accelerates down one side of a half-pipe and up the other side. What would happen if the up side of the pipe were not as steep as the down side?

Skill Builder Activities

6. **Making and Using Graphs** Make a speed-time graph of a roller-coaster ride. Begin at the top of the first hill and graph the motion through two smaller hills. Compare the speed at the bottom and top of each hill. **For more help, refer to the Science Skill Handbook.**

7. **Solving One-Step Equations** The space shuttle takes 8 min between blastoff and reaching its orbit. During this time, it accelerates at 16 m/s². Express 8 min in seconds. How fast, in kilometers per second, is the shuttle going when it reaches its orbit? **For more help, refer to the Math Skill Handbook.**

Answers to Section Assessment

1. 30 km/h
2. about − 12 m/s²
3. (3 m/s)/12 s = 0.25 m/s²
4. Yes; it could be changing direction.
5. The skateboard speeds up as it goes down the ramp and slows down as it rises up the other side. If the two sides are symmetrical, the skateboard will speed up and slow down with about the same acceleration. If the up side were not as steep, the skateboard would slow down at a slower rate and travel a greater distance.
6. Check students' work.
7. Eight minutes is 480 s. The shuttle is moving at (16 m/s²)(480 s) = 7,680 m/s = 7.7 km/s.

Newton's Laws of Motion

1 Motivate

Bellringer Transparency

Display the Section Focus Transparency for Section 2. Use the accompanying Transparency Activity Master. L2

ELL

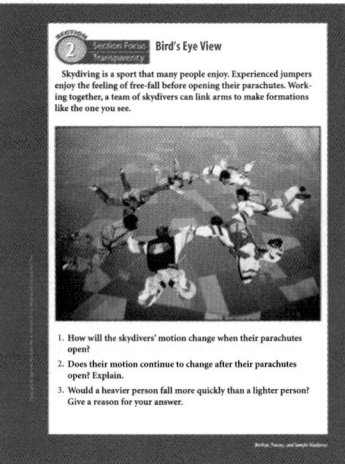

Section Focus
Transparency 2   **Bird's Eye View**

Skydiving is a sport that many people enjoy. Experienced jumpers enjoy the feeling of free-fall before opening their parachutes. Working together, a team of skydivers can link arms to make formations like the one you see.

1. How will the skydivers' motion change when their parachutes open?

2. Does their motion continue to change after their parachutes open? Explain.

3. Would a heavier person fall more quickly than a lighter person? Give a reason for your answer.

Tie to Prior Knowledge

When two people push on opposite sides of a swinging door, the door swings away from the person who pushes harder and stays still if they push with the same force. In this section students will learn how force affects motion.

As You Read

What You'll Learn

- **Describe** how forces affect motion.
- **Calculate** acceleration using Newton's second law of motion.
- **Explain** Newton's third law of motion.

Vocabulary

force
friction
inertia

Why It's Important

Newton's laws explain motions as simple as walking and as complicated as a rocket's launch.

Figure 6
After a golf ball is thrown, it follows a curved path toward the ground. *How does this curved path show that the ball is accelerating?*

Force

What causes objects to move? In the lunchroom you pull a chair away from a table before you sit down and push it back under the table when you leave. You exert a force on the chair and cause it to move. A **force** is a push or a pull. In SI units, force is measured in newtons. One newton is about the amount of force it takes to lift a quarter-pound hamburger.

Force and Acceleration Exerting a force on an object causes its motion to change. So, a force causes an object to accelerate. For example, when you throw a ball your hand exerts a force on the ball, causing it to speed up. The ball has acceleration because the speed of the ball has increased.

A force also can change the direction of an object's motion. After the ball leaves your hand, if no one catches it, its path curves downward and it hits the ground. Gravity pulls the ball downward and causes it to change direction, as shown in **Figure 6.** Recall that an object has acceleration when its direction of motion changes. The force of gravity has caused the ball to accelerate. Anytime a force acts on something, its speed changes or its direction of motion changes, or both.

Section ✔Assessment Planner

PORTFOLIO

Extension, p. 564

PERFORMANCE ASSESSMENT

Try at Home MiniLAB, p. 564
Math Skills Activity, p. 566
Skill Builder Activities, p. 569
See page 585 for more options.

CONTENT ASSESSMENT

Section, p. 569
Challenge, p. 569
Chapter, pp. 584–585

Applied forces **Force 1** **Force 2**   Net forces **Net force**

A When two forces act in the same direction on an object, like a box, the net force is equal to the sum of the two forces.

Force 1 **Force 2**   Net force = 0

B If two forces of equal strength act on the box in opposite directions, the forces will cancel, resulting in a net force of zero.

Force 1 **Force 2**   Net force

C When two unequal forces act in opposite directions on the box, the net force is the difference of the two forces.

Figure 7
When more than one force acts on an object, the forces combine to form a net force.

Balanced and Unbalanced Forces More than one force can act on an object without causing its motion to change. If both you and your friend push on a door with the same force in opposite directions, the door doesn't move. Two or more forces are balanced forces if their effects cancel each other and they do not cause a change in an object's motion. If the effects of the forces don't cancel each other, the forces are unbalanced forces.

Combining Forces Suppose you push on a door to open it. At the same time, someone on the other side of the door also is pushing. What is the motion of the door? When more than one force acts on an object, the forces combine. The combination of all the forces acting on an object is the net force.

How do forces combine to form the net force? If the forces are in the same direction, they add together to form the net force. If two forces are in opposite directions, the net force is the difference between the two forces and is in the direction of the larger force. **Figure 7** shows some examples of how forces combine to form the net force. If you push on the door with a larger force than the person on the other side pushes, the door moves in the direction of your push. If you push with the same force as the other person, the two forces will cancel and the net force is zero.

Life Science
INTEGRATION

For a fragile seedling to grow, it must exert enough force to push through the soil above it. The force exerted by the seedling as it pushes its way through the soil is due to the water pressure created inside its cells. New cells form as the seedling begins to grow underground. These cells take up water and expand, exerting a pressure that can be 20 times greater than atmospheric pressure. Research some of the factors that can affect how seedlings germinate. Write a paragraph in your Science Journal summarizing what you learned.

---

2 Teach

Force

Caption Answer
Figure 6 by a change in direction

Quick Demo
Have a volunteer work with you to move a box, as shown in **Figure 7**. Have students describe the motion that results in each scenario. First, both of you push in the same direction. Then, both of you push on the box from opposite sides using equal strength. Finally, have the volunteer push on his or her side of the box harder than you push on your side of the box. Have the volunteer describe how the application of force felt in each instance.

Activity
Have students choose several activities and describe all forces that cause the motion. Activities might include swinging, ice skating, or swimming. For horizontal motion, be sure students remember to include gravity and normal force, even though they cancel each other. L2
IS Linguistic

Life Science
INTEGRATION

Students may describe the effects of absorption of water, passage of time, chilling, warming, oxygen availability, or light exposure.

TRY AT HOME
Mini LAB

Purpose Students measure weights in pounds and convert them to newtons. [L2] [ELL]
[COOP LEARN] [IS] **Kinesthetic**

Materials bathroom scale, large book, chair, heavy coat

Teaching Strategy
Have students place the scale on a hard floor instead of carpet.

Analysis
1. Answers will vary.
2. Answers will vary.
3. Answers will vary.

✓Assessment

Process Show students a picture of a student next to an animal. Ask students to estimate the weight of the animal in newtons. Answers will vary depending on the size of the animal in the picture. Use **PASC,** p. 89.

Newton's First Law

Extension

During earthquakes, buildings tend to remain at rest as the ground underneath them moves, which can cause them to collapse. In many large cities, buildings are now constructed to better withstand earthquakes. Have students research ways this is done. Have them write a report on their findings. Some buildings are built on rubber pads, some are designed to sway during an earthquake, and some are made stronger so they won't be destroyed by an earthquake. [L3]
[IS] **Linguistic** [P]

TRY AT HOME
Mini LAB

Determining Weights in Newtons

Procedure:
1. Stand on a **bathroom scale** and measure your weight.
2. Hold a **large book,** stand on the scale, and measure the combined weight of you and the book.
3. Repeat step #2 using a **chair, heavy coat,** and a **fourth object** of your choice.

Analysis
1. Subtract your weight from each of the combined weights to calculate the weight of each object in pounds.
2. Multiply the weight of each object in pounds by 4.4 to calculate its weight in newtons.
3. Calculate your own weight in newtons.

Figure 8
After the ball has been hit, it will move along the ground in a straight line, until it is acted on by another force.

564 CHAPTER 19

Resource Manager

Chapter Resources Booklet
 MiniLAB, p. 3
Cultural Diversity, p. 63

Gravity

One force you are familiar with is gravity. If you hold a basketball and then let it go, it falls to the ground. The force pulling the ball down to the ground is gravity. Gravity is the pull that all objects exert on each other. When you dropped the basketball, Earth pulled it downward.

Objects like Earth and the basketball don't have to be touching to exert a gravitational pull on each other. However, the force of gravity between two objects becomes weaker as the objects get farther apart. Also, the gravitational force is weaker between objects of less mass, such as you and this book, compared to objects of greater mass, such as you and Earth.

Newton's First Law

When you give a book on a table a push, it slides and comes to a stop. After you throw or hit a baseball and it hits the ground, it soon rolls to a stop. In fact, it seems that anytime you set something in motion, it stops moving after awhile. You might conclude that to keep an object moving, a net force must be exerted on the object at all times.

The British scientist Isaac Newton and a few others before him realized that an object could be moving even if no net force was acting on it. According to Newton's first law of motion, an object will not change its motion unless a force acts on it. Therefore, an object that is not moving, like a book sitting on a table, remains at rest until something pushes or pulls it.

What if an object is already moving, like a football you've just thrown to someone? Newton's first law says the motion of the football won't change unless a force is exerted on it. This means that after the ball is in motion, a force has to be applied to make it speed up, slow down, or change direction. In other words, a moving object, like the ball in **Figure 8,** moves in a straight line with constant speed unless a force acts on it.

Curriculum Connection

History Newton published the results of his scientific studies in one of the most famous books of all time. Have students find the name of the book and the year it was published. *Philosophiae naturalis principia mathematica* (The Mathematical Principles of Natural Philosophy) published in 1687. [L3]
[IS] **Linguistic**

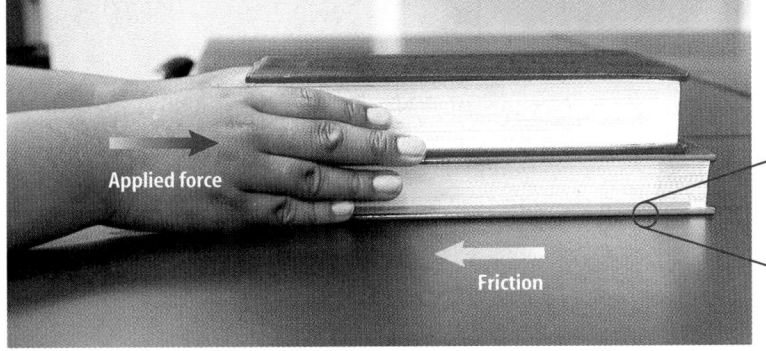
Applied force
Friction

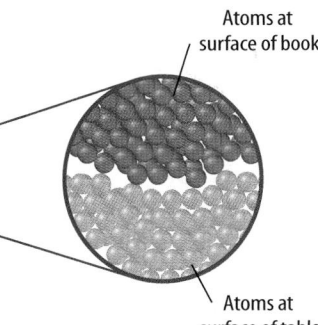
Atoms at surface of book

Atoms at surface of table

Friction Newton's first law states that a moving object should never slow down or change direction until a force is exerted on it. Can you think of any moving objects that never slow down or change direction? A book slid across a table, slowed down, and came to a stop. Because its motion changed, a force must have acted on it and caused it to stop. This force is called friction. **Friction** is a force that resists motion between two surfaces that are in contact. It always acts opposite to the direction of motion, as shown in **Figure 9.** To keep an object moving when friction is acting on it, you have to keep pushing or pulling on the object to overcome the frictional force.

✔ **Reading Check** *In what direction is the force of friction exerted?*

The size of the friction force depends on the two surfaces involved. In general, the rougher the surfaces are, the greater the friction will be. For example, if you push a hockey puck on an ice rink, it will go a great distance before it stops. If you try to push it with the same force on a smooth floor, it won't slide as far. If you push the puck on a rough carpet, it will barely move.

Inertia and Mass You might have noticed how hard it is to move a heavy object, such as a refrigerator, even when it has wheels. If you try pushing someone who is much bigger than you are—even someone who is wearing skates or standing on a skateboard—the person won't budge easily. It's easier to push someone who is smaller. You also might have noticed that it is hard to stop someone who is much bigger than you are after that person is moving. In each case, including the one shown in **Figure 10,** the object resists having its motion changed. This tendency to resist a change in motion is called **inertia**.

You know from experience that heavy objects are harder to move and harder to stop than light objects are. The more matter an object has, the harder it will be to move or stop. Mass measures the quantity of matter. The more mass an object has, the greater its inertia is.

Figure 9
Friction is caused by the roughness of the surfaces in contact. The enlargement shows how the table and book surfaces might look if you could see their atoms.

Figure 10
The cart has inertia and resists moving when you push it.

Newton's Second Law

Discussion

If you double the net force on an object, how is its acceleration affected? The equation $F = m \times a$ shows that force is directly proportional to acceleration, so doubling the force will also double the acceleration.

Activity

Have students do a unit analysis to calculate why, if force is expressed in newtons, and mass is given in kilograms, acceleration will be in m/s^2. $a = F/m$; $a = $ newtons/kilograms; $a = kg \times m/s^2 \div kg = m/s^2$. L2 **LS** **Logical-Mathematical**

SCIENCE *Online*

Data Update Visit the Glencoe Science Web site at **science.glencoe.com** for information about the contributions made to science and mathematics by Sir Isaac Newton. Make a time line to show what you learn.

IDENTIFYING Misconceptions

Students may think that if an object is moving, there is a force acting on it in the direction of the motion. See page 554F for teaching strategies that address this misconception.

Math Skills Activity

National Math Standards

Correlation to Mathematics Objectives

1, 2, 4, 6, 8, 9

Answer to Practice Problem

- What you know: mass: $m = 20$ kg; force: $F = 40$N
- What you need to know: acceleration: a
- This is equation you need to use: $a = F_{net}/m$
- Substitute the known values:
  $a = 40$N/20 kg
  $a = 2$ m/s^2

Newton's Second Law

According to Newton's first law, a change in motion occurs only if a net force is exerted on an object. Newton's second law tells how a net force acting on an object changes the motion of the object. According to Newton's second law, a net force changes the velocity of the object, and causes it to accelerate.

Newton's second law states two things. One is that if an object is acted upon by a net force, the change in velocity will be in the direction of the net force. The other is that the acceleration can be calculated from the following formula:

$$\text{acceleration} = \frac{\text{net force}}{\text{mass}}$$

If a stands for the acceleration, F_{net} for the net force, and m for the mass, this formula can be written as follows:

$$a = \frac{F_{net}}{m}$$

In this formula the force is in newtons, the mass is in kilograms, and the acceleration is in meters per second squared.

Math Skills Activity

Newton's Second Law—Calculating Acceleration

Example Problem

You throw a 0.5-kg basketball with a force of 10 N. What is the ball's acceleration?

1. *This is what you know:*   mass: $m = 0.5$ kg
   force: $F = 10$ N

2. *This is what you need to know:*   acceleration: a

3. *This is the equation you need to use:* $a = F_{net}/m$

4. *Substitute in known values:*   10 N/0.5 kg = 20 m/s^2

   Check your answer by multiplying it by the mass of the ball. Do you calculate the same force that was given?

Practice Problem

You push a 20-kg crate with a force of 40 N. What is the crate's acceleration?

For more help, refer to the Math Skill Handbook.

566   **CHAPTER 19**   Motion, Forces, and Simple Machines

Resource Manager

Chapter Resources Booklet
Enrichment, p. 29
Lab Activity, pp. 13–14

Performance Assessment in the Science Classroom, p. 36

SCIENCE *Online*
Internet Addresses
_____
_____
_____
_____

Explore the Glencoe Science Web site at **science.glencoe.com** to find out more about topics in this section.

Mass and Acceleration When a net force acts on an object, its acceleration depends on its mass. The more mass an object has or the more inertia it has, the harder it is to accelerate. Imagine using the same force to push an empty grocery cart that you would use to push a refrigerator, as shown in **Figure 11.** The refrigerator has more mass. With the same force acting on the two objects, the refrigerator will have a smaller acceleration compared to the empty cart. More mass means less acceleration if the force acting on the objects is the same.

Newton's Third Law

Suppose you push on a wall. It might surprise you to know that the wall pushes back on you. According to Newton's third law, when one object exerts a force on a second object, the second object exerts an equal force in the opposite direction on the first object. For example, when you walk, you push back on the sidewalk and the sidewalk pushes forward on you with an equal force.

The force exerted by the first object is the action force. The force exerted by the second object is the reaction force. In **Figure 12,** the action force is the swimmer's push on the pool wall. The reaction force is the push of the pool wall on the swimmer. The action and reaction forces are equal, but in opposite directions.

Figure 13 on the next page shows how Newton's laws affect astronauts in space and the motion of the space shuttle.

Figure 11
A When pushing a refrigerator, a large force is required to achieve a small acceleration.
B If you were to push an empty grocery cart with the same force, its acceleration would be larger.

Figure 12
When the swimmer pushes against the pool wall, the wall pushes back with an equal and opposite force.

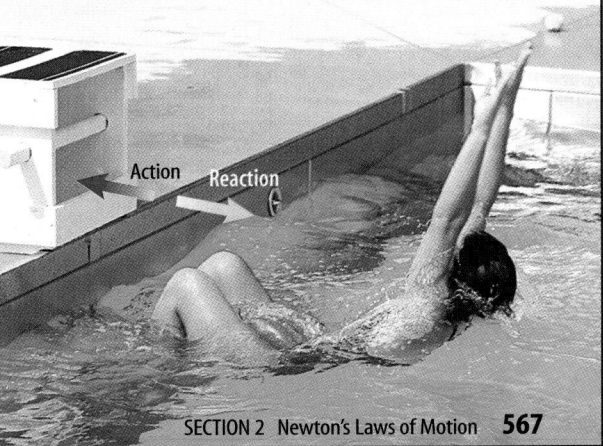

Newton's Third Law

Discussion
Ask students to explain what happens when they jump forward off a skateboard. The skateboard moves back, as explained by Newton's third law of motion.

IDENTIFYING
Misconceptions
Students may think that the shuttle is launched into space by the exploding gases pushing against the ground. Explain that if this were true, the shuttle wouldn't be able to move in space with no ground to push against. According to Newton's third law, the gases exploding downward, out the bottom of the shuttle, push the vehicle upward.

LAB DEMONSTRATION

Purpose to demonstrate Newton's laws of motion
Materials 2-g mass, 50-g mass, cart, book (about 0.5 kg), string, 2 spring scales
Preparation Attach the string to the book, and record the mass of the book.
Procedure First, place the masses in the cart. Roll it sharply against a barrier and

ask students to observe what happens to the masses. Next, have students calculate the force needed to hold up the book and verify this using the spring scale. Finally, use spring scales to pull opposite sides of the book.

Expected Outcome Have students explain the results, using Newton's laws.

If you used a spring scale to pull a book across the table at a constant speed, what force would you measure on the scale? friction How would the force recorded on the scale differ if the mass of the book were doubled? It would double.

Visualizing Newton's Laws and Space Travel

Have students examine the pictures and read the captions. Then ask the following questions.

- **How is a blown-up balloon that you release like a space shuttle taking off?** As the balloon contracts, it pushes air toward the back. As the air leaves, it pushes on the balloon, moving it forward. This is similar to the forces acting on the shuttle.

- **If an astronaut with a tool belt accidentally pushed off from the shuttle, how could the tools in the belt be used to return to the shuttle?** If the astronaut threw the tools, one at a time, away from the shuttle, an equal and opposite reaction would move the astronaut back toward the shuttle. If the astronaut had enough tools to throw, the shuttle could be reached.

Activity

Have small groups of students work together to write and illustrate a story about how they would use a rocket belt that is propelled by gases that shoot out of moveable nozzles. Allow groups to exchange and read one another's stories. L2 COOP LEARN
LS Linguistic and Interpersonal

Extension

Have students research and write brief reports that explain the motion of satellites in terms of Newton's laws of motion. Ask students to present their reports to the class. **LS Linguistic and Logical-Mathematical**

Figure 13

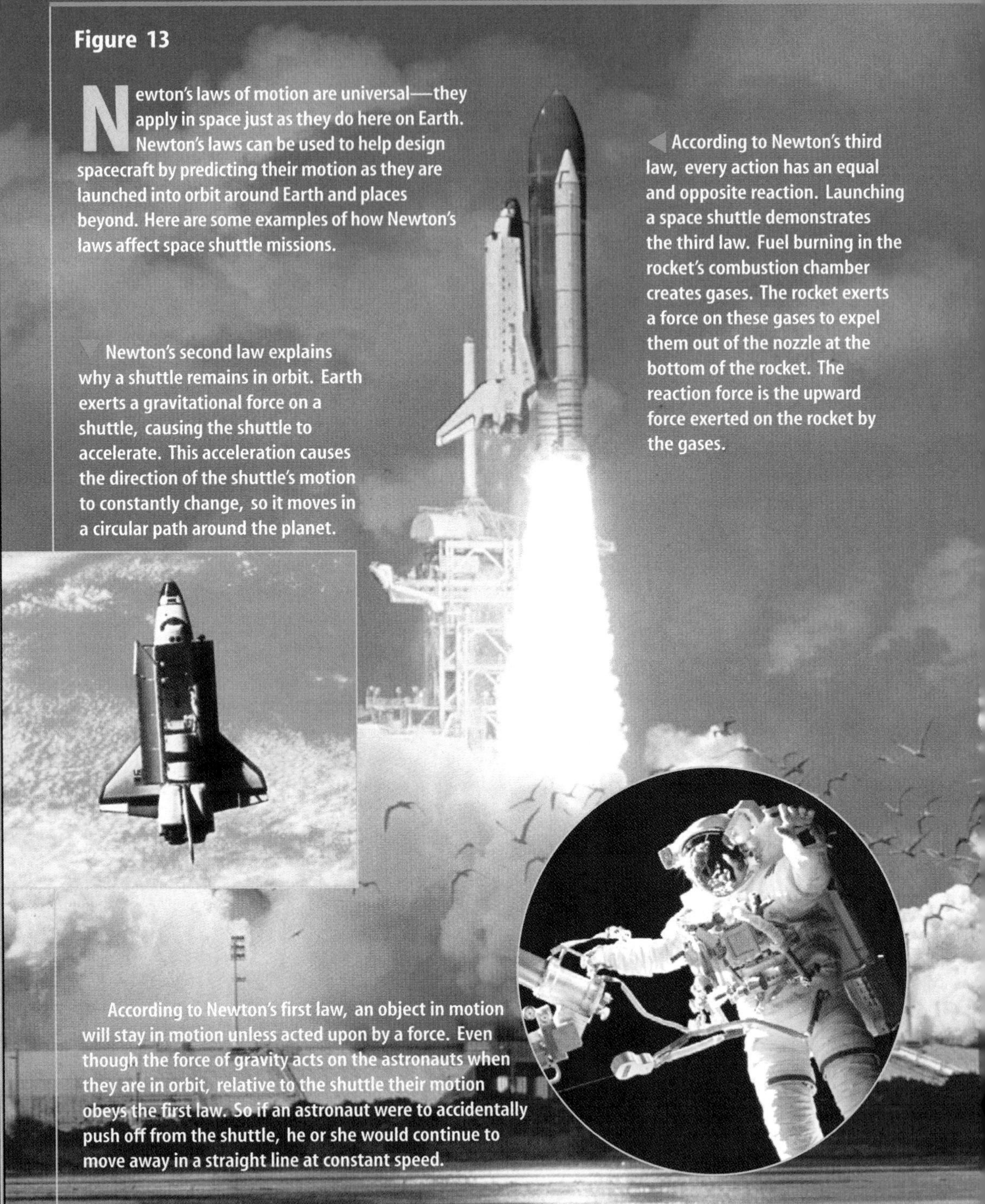

Newton's laws of motion are universal—they apply in space just as they do here on Earth. Newton's laws can be used to help design spacecraft by predicting their motion as they are launched into orbit around Earth and places beyond. Here are some examples of how Newton's laws affect space shuttle missions.

Newton's second law explains why a shuttle remains in orbit. Earth exerts a gravitational force on a shuttle, causing the shuttle to accelerate. This acceleration causes the direction of the shuttle's motion to constantly change, so it moves in a circular path around the planet.

According to Newton's third law, every action has an equal and opposite reaction. Launching a space shuttle demonstrates the third law. Fuel burning in the rocket's combustion chamber creates gases. The rocket exerts a force on these gases to expel them out of the nozzle at the bottom of the rocket. The reaction force is the upward force exerted on the rocket by the gases.

According to Newton's first law, an object in motion will stay in motion unless acted upon by a force. Even though the force of gravity acts on the astronauts when they are in orbit, relative to the shuttle their motion obeys the first law. So if an astronaut were to accidentally push off from the shuttle, he or she would continue to move away in a straight line at constant speed.

568 CHAPTER 19 Motion, Forces, and Simple Machines

Resource Manager

Chapter Resources Booklet
  Reinforcement, p. 26
  Transparency Activity, pp. 45–46

Force Pairs Act on Different Objects If forces always occur in equal but opposite pairs, how can anything ever move? Won't the forces acting on an object always cancel each other? If you push on a book and the book pushes back on you with an equal but opposite force, won't the forces cancel? Recall that in Newton's third law, the equal and opposite forces act on different objects. When you push on the book, a force is acting on the book. When the book pushes back on you, a force is acting on you. One force of the force pair acts on the book, and the other force acts on you. Because the forces act on different objects, they don't cancel.

 Reading Check *How is net force different from action-reaction forces?*

Examples of Newton's Third Law Think about what happens when you jump from a boat, as shown in **Figure 14.** If you jump off a small boat, the boat moves back. You are pushing the boat back with your feet with the same force with which it is pushing you forward. Because you have more mass than the boat, it will accelerate more and move farther than you do. This situation is reversed when you jump off a big boat. Because the mass of the boat is so large, the force you exert on the boat gives it only a tiny acceleration. You don't notice the large boat moving at all, but the force it exerts on you easily propels your smaller mass to the dock.

Force from boat   Force from person

Figure 14
When you jump off a boat, your feet exert a force on the boat, which pushes it backward. The boat also exerts a force on your feet, which pushes you forward.

Section ② Assessment

1. Using a computer, make a table listing Newton's laws of motion. For each law, include the definition and give at least one example from your everyday life. Do not use examples already listed in the chapter.

2. Does a force act on a car if it moves at a constant speed while turning? Explain.

3. You throw a ball to your friend. If the ball has a mass of 0.15 kg and it accelerates at 20 m/s², what force did you exert on the ball?

4. **Think Critically** Give at least two examples of using inertia to your advantage.

Skill Builder Activities

5. **Recognizing Cause and Effect** Newton's third law is a good example of cause and effect. Explain why, using a ball bouncing off a wall as an example. **For more help, refer to the Science Skill Handbook.**

6. **Using an Electronic Spreadsheet** Enter the formula $a = F_{net}/m$ in a spreadsheet. Find the acceleration given to various masses by a force of 100 N. Use masses 10 kg, 20 kg, ... 100 kg. Also use your own mass, the mass of a car, and other familiar examples. **For more help, refer to the Technology Skill Handbook.**

 Reading Check

Answer Net force is the sum of forces on one object. Action-reaction forces are equal and opposite, but they act on two different objects.

③ Assess

Reteach

Display pictures showing examples of how Newton's laws of motion affect everyday life. Have students discuss the pictures and tell which of Newton's laws are demonstrated. [L2]
Visual-Spatial

Challenge

Using Newton's laws of motion, explain how a car's headrest protects you from neck injury. By Newton's first law, if the car is struck from behind, your head will tend to fly back relative to the car, and this motion can injure your neck. The headrest acts according to Newton's third law, pushing against your head and keeping your neck from being injured. [L3]
Logical-Mathematical

✔ Assessment

Performance Have students work in small groups to prepare a demonstration in which they act out and explain each of Newton's laws. The groups can present their demonstrations to the class. Use **Performance Assessment in the Science Classroom,** p. 147.

Answers to Section Assessment

1. Possible examples: First law, a car slides on an icy road; second law, a soccer ball travels in the direction it is kicked; third law, the ground pushes against you with the same force as your weight.

2. Negative acceleration; it always acts in the direction opposite the motion of an object.

3. F = m × a = 3 N

4. Possible answer: It takes a large force to stop a heavy running football player.

5. The ball pushes on the wall, causing the wall to push back.

6. Check students' work.

Work and Simple Machines

Work and Simple Machines

1 Motivate

Bellringer Transparency

Display the Section Focus Transparency for Section 3. Use the accompanying Transparency Activity Master. L2 ELL

Tie to Prior Knowledge

Ask students to name the simple machines. They may think all machines are big and complex. In this chapter they will learn that many machines are very simple, and many large machines are combinations of simple machines.

Resource Manager

Chapter Resources Booklet
Transparency Activity, p. 44
Directed Reading for Content Mastery, pp. 19, 20

As You Read

What You'll Learn
- **Define** work.
- **Distinguish** the different types of simple machines.
- **Explain** how machines make work easier.

Vocabulary
work
simple machine
compound machine
mechanical advantage
pulley
lever
inclined plane

Why It's Important
Machines make doing work easier.

Work

Newton's laws explain how forces change the motion of an object. If you apply a force upward on the box in **Figure 15A,** it will move upward. Have you done any work on the box? When you think of work, you might think of doing household chores—a job at an office, factory, or farm; or even the homework you do every night. In science, the definition of work is more specific—**work** is done when a force causes an object to move in the same direction that the force is applied.

Effort Doesn't Always Equal Work If you push against a wall, do you do work? For work to be done, two things must occur. First, you must apply a force to an object. Second, the object must move in the same direction as the force you apply. If the wall didn't move, no work was done.

Picture yourself lifting the box in **Figure 15A.** You can feel your arms exerting a force upward as you lift the box. The box moves upward in the direction of your force, therefore you have done work. If you carry the box forward, as in **Figure 15B,** you still can feel your arms applying an upward force on the box, but the box is moving forward. Because the direction of motion is not in the same direction as the force applied by your arms, no work is done by your arms.

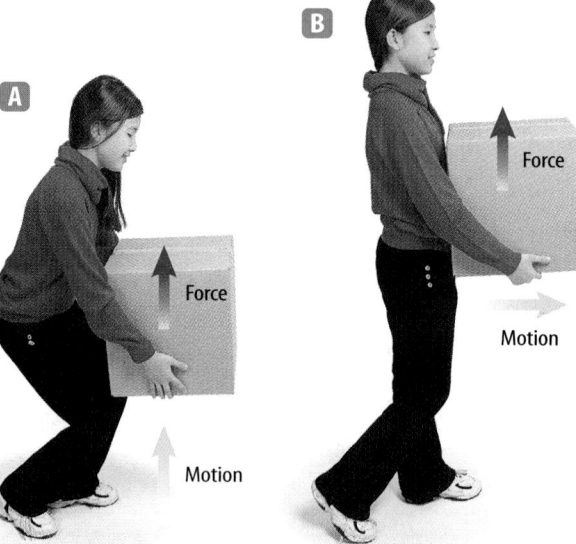

Figure 15
Work is done only when an object moves in the direction of the applied force.
A You do work when you lift a box upward, because the box moves upward.
B Even though the box moves forward, your arms are exerting an upward force and do no work.

570 CHAPTER 19 Motion, Forces, and Simple Machines

Section ✓ Assessment Planner

PORTFOLIO
Cultural Diversity, p. 571
PERFORMANCE ASSESSMENT
Math Skills Activity, p. 571
Skill Builder Activities, p. 576
See page 584 for more options.

CONTENT ASSESSMENT
Section, p. 576
Challenge, p. 576
Chapter, pp. 584–585

Calculating Work

To do work a force must be applied and an object must move. The greater the force that is applied that makes an object move, the more work that is done. Which of these tasks would involve more work—lifting a shoe from the floor to your waist or lifting a pile of books the same distance? Even though the shoe and the books move the same distance, more work is done in lifting the books because it takes more force to lift the books. The work done can be calculated from the equation below.

$$\text{work} = \text{force} \times \text{distance}$$

If W represents the work done, F stands for the force applied, and d stands for distance, this equation can be written as follows:

$$W = F \times d$$

The force is measured in newtons (N), and the distance is measured in meters (m). Work, like energy, is measured in joules (J). The joule is named for James Prescott Joule, a nineteenth-century British physicist who showed that work and energy are related. To lift a baseball from the ground to your waist requires about 1 J of work.

Life Science
INTEGRATION

Even though the wall doesn't move, you may find yourself feeling tired when you push against a wall. Muscles in your body contract when you push. This contraction is caused by chemical reactions in your muscles that cause molecules to move past each other. As a result work is done by your body when you push. Research how a muscle contracts and describe what you learned in your Science Journal.

Math Skills Activity

Calculating Work

Example Problem

A weight lifter lifts a 500-N weight a distance of 2 m from the floor to a position over his head. How much work does he do?

1. *This is what you know:*   force: $F = 500$ N
                distance: $d = 2$ m

2. *This is what you need to know:*   work: W

3. *This is the equation you need to use:* $W = F \times d$

4. *Substitute the known values:* $W = 500 \text{ N} \times 2 \text{ m} = 1{,}000$ J

Check your answer by dividing your answer by the distance. Do you calculate the same force that was given?

Practice Problem

Using a force of 50 N, you push a computer cart 10 m across a classroom floor. How much work did you do?

For more help, refer to the Math Skill Handbook.

---

2 Teach

Calculating Work

Life Science
INTEGRATION

Muscle tissue is made up of fibers, which in turn are made up of myofibrils. Each myofibril is made up of thick and thin protein filaments. During contraction, the thin filaments slide toward one another, shortening the myofibril. When the muscle relaxes, the filaments return to their original position.

Math Skills Activity

National Math Standards

Correlation to Mathematics Objectives

1, 2, 4, 6, 8, 9

Answer to Practice Problem

- What you know: force: $F = 50$N; distance: $d = 10$m
- What you need to know: work: W
- Equation you need to use: $W = F \times d$
- Substitute known values: $W = 50$N $\times$ 10m
$W = 500$J

Cultural Diversity

Early Machines Around the first century A.D., the Greek mathematician Hero of Alexandria wrote a series of books entitled *Mechanics*. The second book in this series described simple machines and how they could be applied to everyday tasks. Hero explained how using a lever, pulley, wedge, or screw made lifting and transporting objects easier. Have students research and write a report about how simple machines made life easier for people before the invention of modern, powered machinery. Possible answers: lifting a heavy rock with a lever, raising a bucket from a well using a pulley, hunting with a sharp spear tip or arrowhead (wedge). L2
Logical-Mathematical P

What is a machine?

Discussion

The six simple machines can be classified into two groups, the inclined plane group and the lever group. Discuss with students these two groups and the characteristics of the simple machines. **Which simple machines belong to the inclined plane group?** the wedge, inclined plane, and screw **Which belong to the lever group?** the lever, wheel and axle, and pulley L2  **Logical-Mathematical**

✔ Reading Check

Answer by changing the size of the force you apply or by changing the direction of the force

Discussion

Have students discuss why a machine that changes the direction of input force but doesn't multiply force might be useful. Possible answer: Changing direction so you are pulling down rather than pushing up makes the work easier if you are located below the object.

Figure 16
The can opener changes the small force of your hand on the handles to a large force on the blade that cuts into the can.

Research Visit the Glencoe Science Web site at **science.glencoe.com** for information about early tools. Communicate to your class what you learn.

What is a machine?

How many machines have you used today? Why did you use them? A machine is a device that makes work easier. The can opener like the one in **Figure 16** is a machine that changes a small force applied by your hand into a larger force that makes it easier to open the can.

A **simple machine** is a machine that uses only one movement. A screwdriver is an example of a simple machine. It only requires one motion—turning it. Simple machines include the inclined plane, wedge, screw, lever, wheel and axle, and pulley. A **compound machine** is a combination of simple machines. The can opener is a compound machine that combines several simple machines. Machines can make work easier in two ways. They can change the size of the force you apply. They also can change the direction of the force.

✔ Reading Check   *How do machines make work easier?*

Mechanical Advantage Some machines are useful because they increase the force you apply. The number of times the applied force is increased by a machine is called the **mechanical advantage** (MA) of the machine.

When you push on the handles of the can opener, the force you apply is called the input force (F_i). The can opener changes your input force to the force that is exerted by the metal cutting blade on the can. The force exerted by a machine is called the output force (F_o). The mechanical advantage is the ratio of the output force to the input force.

$$\text{mechanical advantage} = \text{output force/input force}$$
$$MA = F_o/F_i$$

Work In and Work Out In a simple machine the input force and the output force do work. For example, when you push on the handles of a can opener and the handles move, the input force does work. The output force at the blade of the can opener does work as the blade moves down and punctures the can.

An ideal machine is a machine in which there is no friction. Then the work done by the input force is equal to the work done by the output force. In other words, for an ideal machine the work you do on the machine—work in—would be equal to the work done by the machine—work out.

$$\text{work in} = \text{work out}$$

Increasing Force A simple machine can change a small input force into a larger output force. Recall that work equals force times distance. So, if the work in is equal to the work out, a smaller input force must be applied over a larger distance than the larger output force. Think again about the can opener. The can opener increases the force you apply at the handle. So the distance you move the handle is large compared to the distance the blade of the can opener moves as it pierces the can.

In all real machines, friction always occurs as one part moves past another. Friction causes some of the input work to be changed into heat, which can't be used to do work. So for a real machine, work out always will be less than work in.

The Pulley

To raise a window blind, you pull down on a cord. The blind uses a pulley to change the direction of the force. A **pulley** is an object with a groove, like a wheel, with a rope or chain running through the groove. A pulley changes the direction of the input force. A rope thrown over a railing can be used as a pulley. A simple pulley such as the one shown in **Figure 17A,** changes only the direction of the force, so its mechanical advantage is 1.

It is possible to have a large mechanical advantage if more than one pulley is used. A double-pulley system like the one in **Figure 17B** has a mechanical advantage of 2. Each supporting rope holds half of the weight, so you need to supply only half the input force to lift it.

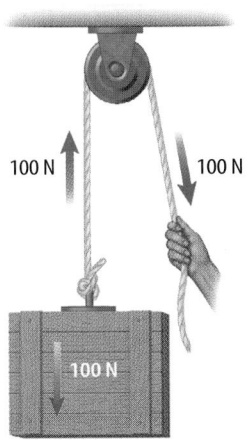

100 N   100 N

100 N

A A single pulley changes the direction of the input force.

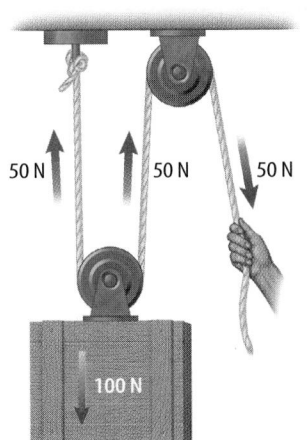

50 N   50 N   50 N

100 N

B A combination of pulleys decreases the input force, so the mechanical advantage is greater than one.

Figure 17
A pulley changes the direction of the input force and can decrease the input force.

SECTION 3 Work and Simple Machines **573**

The Lever

Activity

Have students use a spring scale to find the mechanical advantage of first-, second-, and third-class levers by fastening the scale at the point where the effort force is applied. Levers can be easily constructed using objects such as rulers and blocks of wood. L2 ELL COOP LEARN
Kinesthetic

Visual Learning

Figure 18 The classification of a lever is determined by whether the fulcrum, input force, or output force is in the middle. However, the distance between the fulcrum and the input and output forces determines how much effort is required to lift the load. For example, in **Figure 18A,** if the fulcrum is moved closer to the output force, the mechanical advantage increases. Have students experiment with various levers to see this effect. L2 ELL
Kinesthetic

Figure 18
A lever is classified according to the location of the input force, output force, and fulcrum.

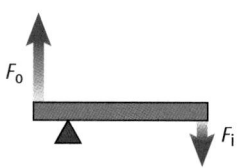 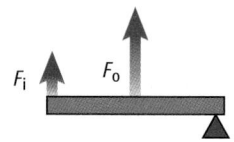 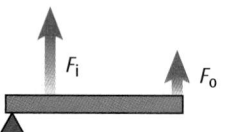

A Sometimes a screwdriver is used as a first-class lever. The fulcrum is between the input and output forces.

B A wheelbarrow is a second-class lever. The fulcrum is the wheel, and the input force is applied on the handles. The load is between the input force and the fulcrum.

C A hockey stick is a third-class lever. The fulcrum is your upper hand, and the input force is applied by your lower hand.

The Lever

Probably the first simple machine invented by humans was the lever. A **lever** is a rod or plank that pivots about a fixed point. The pivot point is called the fulcrum. Levers can increase force or increase the distance over which a force is applied. There are three types, or classes, of levers. The three classes depend on the position of the input force, output force, and the fulcrum.

In a first-class lever, the fulcrum is located between the input force and output force. Usually a first-class lever is used to increase force, like the screwdriver in **Figure 18A.**

If the output force is between the input force and the fulcrum, like the wheelbarrow in **Figure 18B,** the lever is a second-class lever. The output force always is greater than the input force for this type of lever.

A hockey stick, like the one in **Figure 18C,** is a third-class lever. In a third-class lever, the input force is located between the output force and the fulcrum. The mechanical advantage of a third-class lever always is less than one. A third-class lever increases the distance over which the input force is applied.

Resource Manager

Chapter Resources Booklet
  Enrichment, p. 30

Physical Science Critical Thinking/Problem Solving, p. 7

Teacher FYI

Students might benefit from a mnemonic to help remember the different classifications of levers. Tell them to remember the word FREE. For a first-class lever, the fulcrum (F) is in the middle. For a second-class lever, the resistance (R) is in the middle. For a third-class lever, the effort (E) is in the middle.

The Wheel and Axle Try turning a doorknob by holding the narrow base of the knob. It's much easier to turn the larger knob. A doorknob is an example of a wheel and axle. Look at **Figure 19.** A wheel and axle is made of two round objects that are attached and rotate together about the same axis. Usually, the larger object is called the wheel and the smaller object is the axle. The mechanical advantage of a wheel and axle can be calculated by dividing the radius of the wheel by the radius of the axle.

The Inclined Plane

An **inclined plane** is a sloped surface, sometimes called a ramp. It allows you to lift a heavy load by using less force over a greater distance. Imagine having to lift a couch 1 m off the ground onto a truck. If you used an inclined plane or ramp, as shown in **Figure 20,** you would have to move the couch farther than if you lifted it straight up. Either way, the amount of work needed to move the couch would be the same. Because the couch moves a longer distance up the ramp, doing the same amount of work takes less force.

The mechanical advantage of an inclined plane is the length of the inclined plane divided by its height. The longer the ramp is, the less force it takes to move the object. Ramps might have enabled the ancient Egyptians to build their pyramids. To move limestone blocks having a mass of more than 1,000 kg each, archaeologists hypothesize that the Egyptians built enormous ramps.

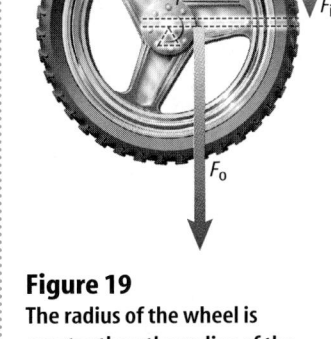

Figure 19
The radius of the wheel is greater than the radius of the axle. The mechanical advantage of the wheel and axle is greater than one.

Figure 20
It is much easier to load this couch into a truck using a ramp. Even though they push it a greater distance, it requires less force.

The Inclined Plane

Activity

Demonstrate the advantage of using an inclined plane by having students use a spring scale to compare the force needed to pull a load up a ramp. Lean two boards against books. One should be at about a 30° angle to the floor and the other at about a 45° angle to the floor. Attach the scale to a load and observe the difference in force required to pull it up the ramps.
L1 ELL **Kinesthetic**

Extension

Work can be done against friction, inertia, or gravity. Have students make posters showing examples of work done against each of these. Advise them that some work is against more than one force. Possible answers: Pushing a heavy box across a floor is work against friction because the box rubs against the floor, and it is work against inertia because the box has a tendency to stay still. Lifting the box is work against gravity. L2
Visual-Spatial

Quick Demo

Demonstrate how a wheel and axle is essentially the same as a lever by drawing a wheel and axle on the board as shown:

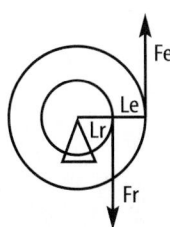

Point out the corresponding components. For example, the axis of rotation corresponds to the fulcrum, and the radius of the wheel corresponds to the lever arm.

Reteach

Bring in objects that are either simple or compound machines. Have students describe the simple machines involved in each of them. [L2]  **Visual-Spatial**

Challenge

According to legend, Archimedes, a mathematician in ancient Greece, once said about levers, "Give me a place to stand and I will move the Earth." **Explain what this means.** A first-class lever multiplies force by increasing the input force distance. If Archimedes had a large enough lever and input force distance, he could produce enough force to move Earth. [L3] **Logical-Mathematical**

Assessment

Oral Ask students why third-class levers are not useful for lifting heavy objects. They increase the distance the load moves but don't multiply the force. Use **Performance Assessment in the Science Classroom,** p. 143.

Figure 21
Plant-eaters and meat-eaters have different teeth.

A These wedge-shaped teeth enable a meat-eater to tear meat.

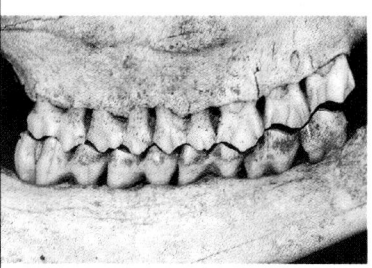

B The teeth of a plant-eater are flatter and used for grinding.

Life Science INTEGRATION

The Wedge When you take a bite out of an apple, you are using wedges. A wedge is a moving inclined plane with one or two sloping sides. Your front teeth are wedges. A wedge changes the direction of the input force. As you push your front teeth into the apple, the downward input force is changed by your teeth into a sideways force that pushes the skin of the apple apart. Knives and axes also are wedges that are used for cutting.

Figure 21 shows that the teeth of meat-eaters, or carnivores, are more wedge-shaped than the teeth of plant-eaters, or herbivores. The teeth of carnivores are used to cut and rip meat, while herbivores' teeth are used for grinding plant material. Scientists can determine what a fossilized animal ate when it was living by examining its teeth.

The Screw Roads going up a mountain usually wrap around the mountain. The mountain road is less steep than a road straight up the side of the mountain, so it's easier to climb. However, you travel a greater distance to climb the mountain on the mountain road. The mountain road is similar to a screw. A screw is an inclined plane wrapped around a post. The inclined plane forms the screw threads. Just like a wedge, a screw also changes the direction of the force you apply. When you turn a screw, the input force is changed by the threads to an output force that pulls the screw into the material. Friction between the threads and the material holds the screw tightly in place.

Section Assessment

1. How much work would it take to lift a 1,000-kg limestone block 146 m to the top of the Great Pyramid?

2. Explain how you can tell if work is being done on an object.

3. Using a pulley system with a mechanical advantage of 10, how large an input force would be needed to lift a stone slab weighing 2,500 N?

4. Compare a wheel and axle to a lever.

5. **Think Critically** Identify two levers in your body. What class of lever is each?

Skill Builder Activities

6. **Making and Using Tables** Make a table to represent the six simple machines. For each machine, list the following: its name, how to find its mechanical advantage, and at least three examples of each. **For more help, refer to the** Science Skill Handbook.

7. **Communicating** Write a paragraph in your Science Journal that explains how the lever, wedge, and wheel and axle are used in a can opener. **For more help, refer to the** Science Skill Handbook.

Answers to Section Assessment

1. $W = (m \times g) \times d = 1{,}000\,\text{N} \times 9.8\,\text{m/s}^2 \times 146\,\text{m} = 1{,}430{,}800\,\text{J}$
2. A force must be applied, and the object must move.
3. $F_i = F_o/MA = 250\,\text{N}$
4. The center of the axle is similar to the fulcrum. The radius of the axle is similar to the distance from the fulcrum to the output force. The radius of the wheel is similar to the distance from the fulcrum to the input force.
5. Your upper arm, forearm, and hand are third-class levers with your shoulder, elbow, and wrist as fulcrums. When you hold an object at arm's length, you don't use your forearm as a lever.
6. Check students' work.
7. Paragraphs might describe the can opener's handle as a lever and the cutter as a wedge. The cutter is held on by a wheel and axle.

Activity

Motion

What happens when you roll a small ball down a ramp? It speeds up as it travels down the ramp, then it rolls across the floor and eventually it stops. You know that as the ball travels down the ramp, gravity is acting to make it speed up. Think about the forces that are acting on the ball as it rolls across the floor. Is there a net force acting on the ball? How would you describe the motion of the ball?

What You'll Investigate
How does a ball move when the forces acting on it are balanced and when they are unbalanced?

Materials
small ball or marble   stopwatch
meter stick or tape measure   graph paper

Goals
- ■ **Demonstrate** the motion of a ball with unbalanced and balanced forces acting on it.
- ■ **Graph** the position versus time for the motion of the ball.

Procedure

1. Place the ball on the floor or a smooth, flat surface.

2. Roll the ball across the floor by giving it a gentle push.

3. As the ball is rolling, and no longer being pushed, have one student announce the time every second and have other students record the distance at 1-s intervals for at least 5 s to 10 s.

4. **Write** anything else that you observed about how the ball moved.

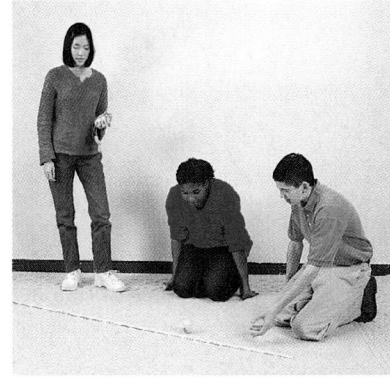

Conclude and Apply

1. Describe the motion of the ball when you placed it on the floor.

2. **Graph** the position of the ball versus time. Does the slope of the graph change in the different time intervals?

3. **Calculate** the speed of the ball in three of the time intervals. How does the speed change in those intervals?

4. What forces were acting on the ball when you placed it on the floor? Were the forces acting on the ball balanced or unbalanced? Explain.

5. What forces were acting on the ball when it was rolling across the floor? Was there an unbalanced force? Explain.

6. **Compare and contrast** the situations you described in questions 4 and 5.

*C*ommunicating

Compare your graphs and results with those of other students in your class. **For more help, refer to the** Science Skill Handbook.

Resource Manager

Chapter Resources Booklet
Reinforcement, p. 27
Activity Worksheet, pp. 5–6

*C*ommunicating
Your Data

Encourage students to create their graphs and data tables electronically.

Purpose Students will observe the motion of balls when balanced and unbalanced forces act upon them. L2 🤚 **Kinesthetic**

Process Skills observing, graphing, calculating, comparing and contrasting

Time Required 25 minutes

Alternate Materials Basketballs or tennis balls can replace the small balls or marbles.

Safety Precautions Caution students to never throw a ball during class.

Teaching Strategies
- Instruct the student keeping track of time to count aloud in 1-second intervals so group members can mark off distances.
- Clear away floor space for student groups to work.

Answers to Questions
1. It remains stationary.
2. The slope changes with time because the ball travels less distance during each subsequent time interval.
3. Answers will vary, but the slowest speed will occur during the last time interval.
4. Gravity and friction; because the ball's motion did not change, the forces were balanced.
5. Friction; friction was the unbalanced force that caused the motion of the ball to change.
6. Accept all reasonable answers.

✔*Assessment*

Process Ask students to infer what conditions would be necessary for a ball to continue to roll indefinitely. **Could these conditions ever exist?** An infinitely smooth surface and the absence of friction. No, in everyday phenomena some friction is always present. Use **PASC**, p. 89.

Activity

Recognize the Problem

Internet Students will use Internet sites that can be accessed through the Glencoe Science Web site at **science.glencoe.com.** They will investigate methods of travel between locations to determine the fastest way to get from one place to the other.

Non-Internet Sources Ask travel agencies for maps and travel guides.

Time Required

about two days

Preparation

Internet Access the Glencoe Science Web site at **science.glencoe.com** to run through the steps that the students will follow.

Non-Internet Sources Collect maps and travel brochures that provide distance and travel information.

Form a Hypothesis

Possible Hypotheses

Students will investigate travel distances and methods between two locations. They will hypothesize which travel method will get them between locations in the shortest amount of time. For example, the fastest way to get from Chicago, Illinois, to Indianapolis, Indiana is by car.

Activity *Use the Internet*

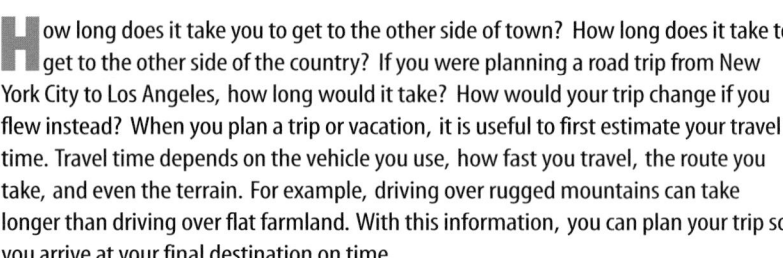

Methods of Travel

How long does it take you to get to the other side of town? How long does it take to get to the other side of the country? If you were planning a road trip from New York City to Los Angeles, how long would it take? How would your trip change if you flew instead? When you plan a trip or vacation, it is useful to first estimate your travel time. Travel time depends on the vehicle you use, how fast you travel, the route you take, and even the terrain. For example, driving over rugged mountains can take longer than driving over flat farmland. With this information, you can plan your trip so you arrive at your final destination on time.

Recognize the Problem

What's the fastest way to travel between two specific locations?

Form a Hypothesis

What's the fastest way to get from one place to another? Is flying always better than driving? What would you encounter along the way that could change your travel time? Form a hypothesis about what is the fastest form of travel.

Goals

- ■ **Research** travel times.
- ■ **Compare** travel times for different methods of travel.
- ■ **Evaluate** the fastest way to travel between two locations.
- ■ **Design** a table to display your findings and communicate them to other students.

Data Source

SCIENCE *Online* Go to the Glencoe Science Web site at **science.glencoe.com** for more information on travel times, methods of travel, distances between locations, and data from other students.

578 CHAPTER 19 Motion, Forces, and Simple Machines

Resource Manager

Chapter Resources Booklet
  Activity Worksheet, pp. 7–8
Lab Management and Safety, p. 71

SCIENCE *Online*
Internet Addresses

_____

_____

_____

_____

Explore the Glencoe Science Web site at **science.glencoe.com** to find out more about topics in this activity.

Test Your Hypothesis

Plan

1. **Choose** a starting point and a final destination.

2. **Identify** the routes commonly used between these two locations.

3. **Study** the common forms of travel between these two locations.

4. **Research** how to estimate travel time. What factors can make your trip take more or less time?

Do

1. Make sure your teacher approves your plan before you start.

2. Visit the Glencoe Science Web site for links to sites that estimate travel times and distances.

3. **Calculate** the travel time and distance between your two locations for different methods of travel.

4. **Record** your data in your Science Journal.

Analyze Your Data

1. **Analyze** the data recorded in your Science Journal to determine the fastest method of travel. Was it better to drive or fly? Did you investigate another method of travel?

2. **Calculate** the average speed of the methods of travel you investigated. Which method had the fastest speed? Which method had the slowest?

3. Use a computer (home, library, or computer lab) to create a chart that compares the travel time, average speed, and distances for different methods of travel. Use your chart to determine the fastest method of travel. What factors add to travel time?

4. **Share** your data by posting it on the Glencoe Science Web site.

Draw Conclusions

1. **Compare** your findings to those of your classmates and data posted on the Glencoe Science Web site. What is the farthest distance investigated? The shortest?

2. What factors can affect travel time for the different methods? How would your travel time be different if you didn't have a direct flight?

3. **Infer** how the average speed of an airplane flight would change if you included your trips to and from the airport and waiting time in your total travel time.

Communicating
Your Data

Find this *Use the Internet* activity on the Glencoe Science Web site at **science.glencoe.com.** Post your data in the table provided. Combine your data with that of other students and make a class travel booklet that estimates travel times for various locations around the world.

ACTIVITY 579

Test Your Hypothesis

Teaching Strategies

As students analyze methods of travel, remind them that airline travel may not always be the fastest way of getting from one place to another. One of their destinations may not be located near an airport.

Analyze Your Data

1. Answers will be subjective and based on the students' individual research.

2. Remind students that speed is calculated by dividing distance traveled by amount of time for the trip.

3. Students may conclude that the fastest method may not always be the most convenient. Factors such as flight schedules may influence their decisions.

4. Have students evaluate the posted data to find other methods of travel between their two destinations.

Draw Conclusions

1. Answers will vary based on the students' individual research.

2. Weather conditions may affect travel times. Layovers can significantly add to travel time.

3. Average speed would decrease, as the time spent traveling to and from airports as well as waiting time can be significant.

✔*Assessment*

Portfolio Have students make travel brochures for the trip between the two locations. Suggest they include the travel distance, identify the travel methods investigated, and provide data to support the travel time between locations. They should also describe the factors that would influence choosing the fastest means of travel. Use **PASC,** p. 129.

Communicating
Your Data

Suggest students use a spreadsheet to collect travel data and describe factors that would influence choosing each travel method.

Science Stats

Content Background

The peregrine falcon is a bird of prey that has become rare throughout most of its range. It has become rare because of the widespread use of chlorinated hydrocarbons used in insecticides, primarily DDT.

DDT found its way into the food chain via runoff into waterways. The chemicals become concentrated in the tissues of the falcon because the prey that the falcons eat contains DDT.

DDT interrupts the reproduction cycle when it causes the eggshells of the falcons to be unusually thin, which causes the developing embryo to die. This has caused a drastic decline in the number of peregrine falcons and other birds of prey such as the American bald eagle. The American peregrine falcon is on the endangered species list. It is hoped that the peregrine falcon's numbers will increase since the use of DDT has been restricted since 1972.

Activity

Have the students choose one of the items in the feature and write a song about it. Ask for student volunteers to share their song with the class.

Science Stats

Fastest Facts

Did you know...

...Nature's fastest creature is the peregrine falcon. It swoops down on its prey, traveling at speeds of more than 300 km/h. That tremendous speed enables the peregrine falcon to catch and kill other birds, which are its main prey.

...The fastest serve in women's tennis history was hit by Venus Williams in 1998. Williams's serve clocked in at 201 km/h—faster than the top speed of most trains in the United States.

...The fastest animal on land is the cheetah. This large cat can sprint at speeds of over 100 km/h. That is about as fast as a car traveling at freeway speeds, though the cheetah can only maintain top speed for a few hundred meters.

580   CHAPTER 19   Motion, Forces, and Simple Machines

SCIENCE Online
Internet Addresses

_____

_____

_____

_____

Explore the Glencoe Science Web site at **science.glencoe.com** to find out more about topics in this feature.

Human World Speed Records

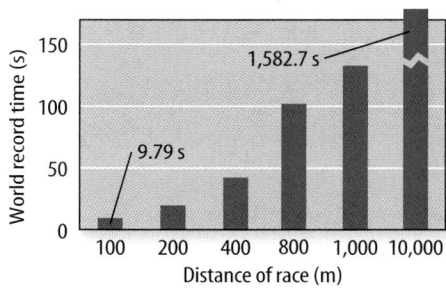

Do the Math

Teaching Strategies
- Review with the students how to calculate time using the formula d = vt.
- Provide graph paper to help students complete the second question in Do the Math.

Answers
1. 18.7 h
2. Students should draw a bar graph showing the Maglev train as the fastest, the tennis serve as the next fastest, and the cheetah as the slowest.
3. 16 min 19 s

Go Further
Answers will vary.

...The Supersonic Transport (SST), the world's fastest passenger jet, cruises at twice the speed of sound. Traveling at 2,150 km/h, the SST can travel from New York to London—a distance of about 5,600 km—in 2 h, 55 min 45 s.

...The world's fastest train is in Japan. Called the Maglev because it's magnetically levitated, or lifted up, it has reached a speed of 552 km/h. It reaches such high speeds partly because friction with the tracks is eliminated.

Do the Math

1. How long would it take a peregrine falcon moving at top speed to fly from New York to London?
2. Make a bar graph that compares the speeds of the fastest serve, the cheetah, and the Maglev train.
3. Look at the Human World Speed Record graph. If a runner could maintain the 100-m world record speed, how long would it take the athlete to run 10,000 m?

Go Further
Do library research to find the top speeds of four or five land animals. Create a bar graph that compares the speeds.

SCIENCE STATS 581

Visual Learning

Human World Speed Records Using information from the graph, what was the average speed during the 800 m race. 8 m/s What was the average speed during the 10,000 m race? 6.3 m/s What is the difference in these two speeds? 1.7 m/s

Chapter 19 Study Guide

Reviewing Main Ideas

Preview

Students can answer the questions in their Science Journals. Discuss the answers as you go through the chapter. **Linguistic**

Review

Students can write their answers, then compare them with those of other students. **Interpersonal**

Reteach

Students can look at the illustrations and describe details that support the main ideas of the chapter. **Visual-Spatial**

Answers to Chapter Review

SECTION 1

3. Yes; it slows down as it rises and speeds up as it falls.

SECTION 2

3. Gravity pulls the shuttle downward. The gases exploding out the bottom of the shuttle exert an upward force on the shuttle. A net upward force enables the shuttle to launch.

SECTION 3

2. It decreases the force necessary to lift something by increasing distance and changing the direction of applied force.

Reviewing Main Ideas

Section 1 Motion

1. Speed, velocity, and acceleration are ways to describe motion.

2. Average speed is the distance traveled divided by the time.

3. Acceleration describes how velocity changes with time. An object is accelerating when either its speed or direction of motion changes. *Is the ball in this photo accelerating? Explain.*

4. Acceleration can be calculated by dividing the change in speed by the time.

Section 2 Newton's Laws of Motion

1. Inertia is a measurement of how difficult it is to change an object's motion.

2. Newton's first law states that an object will remain at rest or move at constant speed if no net force is acting on it.

3. Newton's second law describes how unbalanced or net forces act on an object. The object will accelerate according to the formula $a = F_{net}/m$. *What forces act on the space shuttle when it launches? In what direction is the net force?*

4. Newton's third law states that forces occur in equal but opposite pairs.

Section 3 Work and Simple Machines

1. Work is done when an applied force causes an object to move in the direction of the force. Work equals the force applied times the distance over which the force is applied.

2. A machine is a device that makes work easier. A simple machine does work with one movement. A machine can increase force, increase distance, or change the direction of an applied force. *How does this crowbar make work easier?*

3. The mechanical advantage is the output force divided by the input force. For an ideal machine, the work in is equal to the work out.

4. The six types of simple machines are inclined plane, wedge, screw, lever, wheel and axle, and pulley. A compound machine is made up of simple machines.

FOLDABLES
Reading & Study
Skills

After You Read

Write what you learned under the *Learned* tab of your Foldable. Explain the relationship between motion and force.

FOLDABLES
Reading & Study
Skills

After You Read

After students have read the chapter and completed the Foldable described in Before You Read, have them do the activity on the student page.

Visualizing Main Ideas

Complete the following concept map on simple machines.

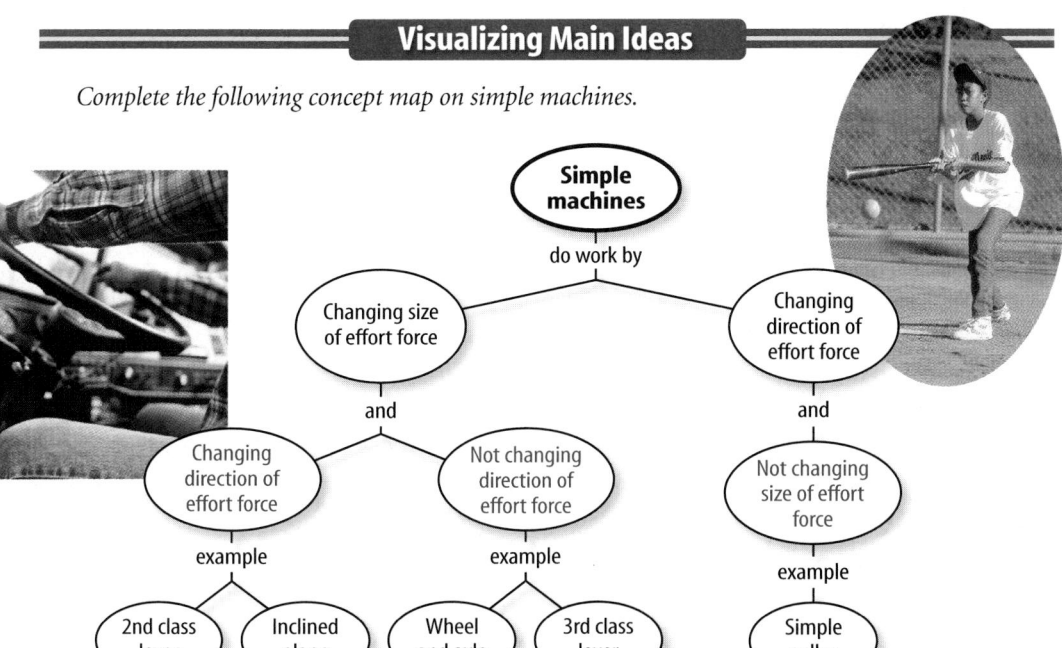

Simple machines

do work by

Changing size of effort force

Changing direction of effort force

and

and

Changing direction of effort force

Not changing direction of effort force

Not changing size of effort force

example

example

example

2nd class lever

Inclined plane

Wheel and axle

3rd class lever

Simple pulley

Vocabulary Review

Vocabulary Words

a. acceleration
b. average speed
c. compound machine
d. force
e. friction
f. inclined plane
g. inertia
h. instantaneous speed
i. lever
j. mechanical advantage
k. pulley
l. simple machine
m. velocity
n. work

THE PRINCETON REVIEW **Study Tip**

After each day's lesson, make a practice quiz for yourself. Later, when you're studying for the test, take the practice quizzes you created.

Using Vocabulary

For each set of vocabulary words below, explain the relationship that exists.

1. inertia, force

2. acceleration, velocity

3. lever, pulley

4. force, work

5. work, simple machine

6. average speed, velocity

7. friction, force

8. force, mechanical advantage

9. average speed, instantaneous speed

10. simple machine, compound machine

CHAPTER STUDY GUIDE   583

Visualizing Main Ideas

See student page.

Vocabulary Review

Using Vocabulary

1. The more mass an object has, the greater its inertia and the greater amount of force needed to move it.
2. Acceleration is how velocity changes with time.
3. A lever can increase force or increase the distance over which a force is applied. A pulley changes the direction of an input force and can decrease an input force.
4. Work is done when a force causes an object to move in the same direction the force is applied.
5. A simple machine is a device that uses only one movement and makes work easier by changing the size and/or direction of the force applied.
6. An object's average speed over a period of time is the total distance traveled divided by the total time elapsed. Its velocity during that time depends on direction traveled.
7. Friction is a force that resists motion between two surfaces that are in contact.
8. Mechanical advantage is a machine's output force divided by its input force.
9. If an object travels at a constant speed, its instantaneous speed equals its average speed.
10. A simple machine is a machine that uses only one movement whereas a compound machine is a combination of simple machines.

IDENTIFYING ▷ Misconceptions

Assess

Use the assessment as follow-up to page 554F after students have completed the chapter.

Procedure Tell students that when a tennis player hits a ball with a tennis racket, he or she only gives the ball a force when it is touching the strings of the racket. Divide the class into groups and have them discuss why following through hitting the ball gives a tennis player more power.

Expected Outcome Students should begin to realize that a force is only imparted when the ball is in contact with the strings of the racket. Following through increases the amount of time the ball and strings are in contact so more force is applied to the ball.

Checking Concepts

1. B
2. A
3. A
4. A
5. B
6. A
7. A
8. C
9. D
10. D

Thinking Critically

11. It increases because you ran the second distance faster.
12. slowing down
13. $MA = 4$
14. Its large mass gives it so much inertia that it is difficult to stop.
15. $F = m \times a = 60{,}000{,}000$ N

Chapter ⑲ Assessment

Checking Concepts

Choose the word or phrase that best answers the question.

1. What decreases friction?
   A) rough surfaces
   B) smooth surfaces
   C) more speed
   D) more surface area

2. What will an object acted upon by a net force do?
   A) accelerate
   B) remain at rest
   C) gain mass
   D) become balanced

3. What is an example of a simple machine?
   A) baseball bat
   B) scissors
   C) can opener
   D) car

4. What simple machines make up an ax?
   A) a lever and a wedge
   B) two levers
   C) a wedge and a pulley
   D) a lever and a screw

5. A car is driving at constant velocity. Which of the following is NOT true?
   A) All the forces acting are balanced.
   B) A net force keeps it moving.
   C) The car is moving in a straight line with constant speed.
   D) The car is not accelerating.

6. A large truck bumps a small car. Which of the following is true?
   A) The force of the truck on the car is greater.
   B) The force of the car on the truck is greater.
   C) The forces are the same.
   D) No force is involved.

7. What is the unit for acceleration?
   A) m/s^2
   B) $kg\ m/s^2$
   C) m/s
   D) N

8. What is inertia related to?
   A) speed
   B) gravity
   C) mass
   D) Newton's first law

9. A force of 30 N exerted over a distance of 3 m does how much work?
   A) 3 J
   B) 10 J
   C) 30 J
   D) 90 J

10. Which of the following is a force?
    A) inertia
    B) acceleration
    C) speed
    D) friction

Thinking Critically

11. You run 100 m in 25 s. If you then run the same distance in less time, does your average speed increase or decrease? Explain.

12. A sprinter's speed over a 100-m dash is shown in the graph below. Was the sprinter speeding up, slowing down, or running at a constant speed?

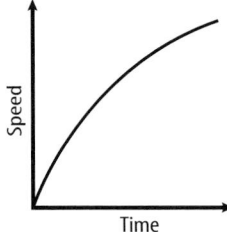

13. What is the mechanical advantage of a ramp 8 m long that extends from the sidewalk to a 2-m high porch?

14. Explain why a fast-moving freight train might take a few kilometers to stop after the brakes have been applied.

15. What is the force exerted by the rocket engines on a space shuttle that has a mass of 2 million kg if it accelerates at 30 m/s^2?

Chapter ✔ *Assessment* Planner

Portfolio Encourage students to place in their portfolios one or two items of what they consider to be their best work. Examples include:
- Earth Science Integration, p. 558
- Extension, p. 564
- Cultural Diversity, p. 571

Performance Additional performance assessments, Performance Task Assessment Lists, and rubrics for evaluating these activities can be found in Glencoe's **Performance Assessment in the Science Classroom.**

Developing Skills

16. Making and Using Graphs The graph below is a distance-time graph of Marion's bicycle ride. What is Marion's average speed? How long did it take her to travel 25 km?

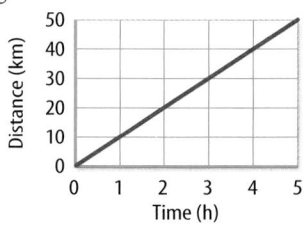

17. Measuring in SI Which of the following speeds is the fastest: 20 m/s, 200 cm/s, or 0.2 km/s? Here's a hint: *Express all the speeds in meters per second and compare.*

18. Drawing Conclusions You are rolling backward down a hill on your bike and use your brakes to stop. In what direction was the acceleration?

19. Solving One-Step Equations At the 1976 Olympics, Vasili Aleseev shattered the world record for weight lifting when he lifted 2,500 N from the floor to over his head, a point 2 m above the ground. How much work did he do?

Performance Assessment

20. Oral Presentation Prepare a presentation, with props, to explain one of Newton's laws of motion to a third-grade class.

TECHNOLOGY

Go to the Glencoe Science Web site at **science.glencoe.com** or use the **Glencoe Science CD-ROM** for additional chapter assessment.

THE PRINCETON REVIEW **Test Practice**

A scientist is beginning an experiment on force and acceleration using three blocks held in the air with ropes. The blocks are all the same distance from the ground.

Block	Mass	Force	Time to Reach Ground
M	100 kg	980 N	
N	10 kg	98 N	
O	1 kg	9.8 N	

Study the table and answer the following questions.

1. A scientist prepared the above table to record data from an experiment. Which of the following is most likely the scientist's hypothesis?
A) Gravity pulls blocks in different directions.
B) The three blocks protect each other from gravity's pull.
C) To produce force, the blocks need time.
D) The three blocks take the same amount of time to fall.

2. After collecting the data shown, the scientist also decides to study one more block with a mass of 1,000 kg. What is the force on the 1,000-kg block?
F) 98 N   **H)** 9,800 N
G) 980 N   **J)** 98,000 N

THE PRINCETON REVIEW **Test Practice**

The Test-Taking Tip was written by The Princeton Review, the nation's leader in test preparation.
1. D
2. H

Developing Skills

16. Marion traveled 50 km in 5 h, so her average speed was 10 km/h. The graph is a diagonal line starting at (0,0) and passing through (1,10). The time to travel 25 km is 2.5 h.
17. 0.2 km/s
18. toward the top of the hill
19. 5,000 J

Performance Assessment

20. Use **Performance Assessment in the Science Classroom**, p. 143.

✓Assessment Resources

 Reproducible Masters

Chapter Resources Booklet
Chapter Review, pp. 35–36
Chapter Tests, pp. 37–40
Assessment Transparency Activity, p. 47

Glencoe Science Web site
Interactive Tutor
Chapter Quizzes

Glencoe Technology
🖋 Assessment Transparency
💿 Interactive CD-ROM Chapter Quizzes
💿 ExamView Pro Test Bank
💿 Vocabulary PuzzleMaker Software
📼 MindJogger Videoquiz

Section/Objectives	Standards		Activities/Features
Chapter Opener	National	State/Local	**Explore Activity:** Observe energy conversions, p. 587 **Before You Read,** p. 587
	See p. 6T for a Key to Standards.		
Section 1 Energy Changes 🕐 3 sessions 📦 1.5 blocks 1. **Explain** what energy is. 2. **Describe** the forms energy takes. 3. **Compare and contrast** potential energy and kinetic energy.	National Content Standards: UCP3, A1, B3		**Life Science Integration,** p. 590 **Visualizing Kinetic Energy,** p. 591 **MiniLAB:** Comparing Kinetic Energy, p. 593 **Science Online,** p. 594
Section 2 Temperature 🕐 2 sessions 📦 1 block 1. **Distinguish** between temperature and heat. 2. **Identify** important uses of heat. 3. **Explain** how heat moves.	National Content Standards: UCP4, A1, B3		**Problem-Solving Activity:** Can you be fooled by temperature?, p. 597 **Life Science Integration,** p. 600 **MiniLAB:** Comparing Energy Content, p. 602
Section 3 Chemical Energy 🕐 4 sessions 📦 2 blocks 1. **Determine** how chemical energy is produced. 2. **Explain** how reaction rates are changed.	National Content Standards: UCP3, A1, B3, E1, F4, G1		**Science Online,** p. 607 **Activity:** Converting Potential and Kinetic Energy, p. 609 **Activity:** Comparing Temperature Changes, pp. 610–611 **Science and Language Arts:** Hiroshima, pp. 612–613

Activity Materials	Reproducible Resources	Section Assessment	Technology
Explore Activity: beaker, hot plate, flashlight, pencil, baseball, clay	**Chapter Resources Booklet** Foldables Worksheet, p. 15 Directed Reading Overview, p. 17 Note-taking Worksheets, pp. 31–32	*GLENCOE'S* **ASSESSMENT** *ADVANTAGE*	
MiniLAB: clay, piece of cardboard, baseball, golf ball, or orange, meter stick *Need materials?* Contact Science Kit at 1-800-828-7777 or www.sciencekit.com on the Internet.	**Chapter Resources Booklet** Transparency Activity, p. 42 MiniLAB, p. 3 Enrichment, p. 28 Reinforcement, p. 25 Directed Reading, p. 18 Transparency Activity, pp. 45–46 **Reading and Writing Skill Activity,** p. 35 **Home and Community Involvement,** p. 38	Portfolio Assessment, p. 595 Performance MiniLAB, p. 593 Skill Builder Activities, p. 595 Content Section Assessment, p. 595	Section Focus Transparency Teaching Transparency Interactive CD-ROM Guided Reading Audio Program
MiniLAB: 3 transparent containers hot, cold, and room-temperature water dropper food coloring	**Chapter Resources Booklet** Transparency Activity, p. 43 MiniLAB, p. 4 Enrichment, p. 29 Reinforcement, p. 26 Directed Reading, p. 19 Lab Activity, pp. 9–11 **Mathematics Skill Activities,** p. 37 **Reading and Writing Skill Activities,** p. 33	Portfolio Assessment, p. 603 Performance Problem-Solving Activity, p. 597 MiniLAB, p. 602 Skill Builder Activities, p. 603 Content Section Assessment, p. 603	Section Focus Transparency Interactive CD-ROM Guided Reading Audio Program
Activity: piece of cardboard, triple-beam balance, table-tennis ball, tennis ball, baseball, stopwatch, meterstick **Activity:** 4 thermometers, 2 self-sealing freezer bags, 100 mL water, 2–3 ice cubes, 100 mL pancake syrup, 4 400 to 600-mL beakers, spoon or stirring rod	**Chapter Resources Booklet** Transparency Activity, p. 44 Enrichment, p. 30 Reinforcement, p. 27 Directed Reading, pp. 19, 20 Activity Worksheets, pp. 5–6, 7–8 Lab Activity, pp. 13–14 **Life Science Critical Thinking/ Problem Solving,** p. 8 **Physical Science Critical Thinking/ Problem Solving,** p. 10 **Lab Management and Safety,** p. 37	Portfolio Visual Learning, p. 596 Performance Skill Builder Activities, p. 608 Content Section Assessment, p. 608	Section Focus Transparency Interactive CD-ROM Guided Reading Audio Program

GLENCOE'S ASSESSMENT ADVANTAGE	End of Chapter Assessment	
Blackline Masters	**Technology**	**Professional Series**
Chapter Resources Booklet Chapter Review, pp. 35–36 Chapter Tests, pp. 37–40 **Standardized Test Practice by The Princeton Review,** pp. 83–86	MindJogger Videoquiz Interactive CD-ROM Vocabulary PuzzleMakers ExamView Pro Test Bank Interactive Lesson Planner Interactive Teacher Edition	Performance Assessment in the Science Classroom (PASC)

Transparencies

Section Focus

Section Focus Transparency 1 High Energy

A body needs a lot of energy to participate in physical activities like basketball. Energy also refers to the position and motion of objects.

1. How is energy being used in the photo?
2. Where do you get energy for exercise?

L2

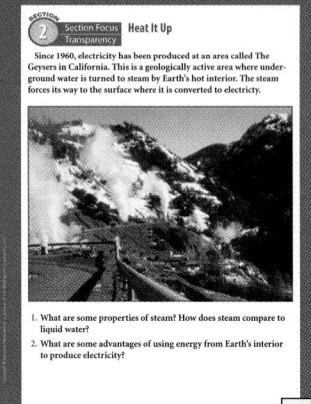

Section Focus Transparency 2 Heat It Up

Since 1960, electricity has been produced at an area called The Geysers in California. This is a geologically active area where underground water is turned to steam by Earth's hot interior. The steam forces its way to the surface where it is converted to electricity.

1. What are some properties of steam? How does steam compare to liquid water?
2. What are some advantages of using energy from Earth's interior to produce electricity?

L2

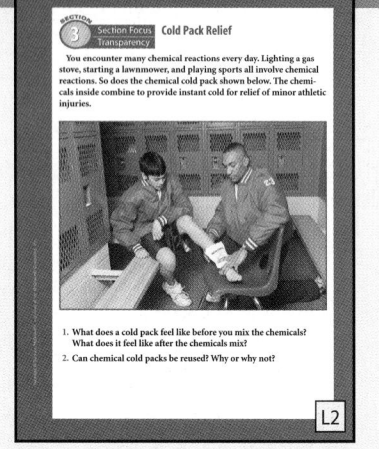

Section Focus Transparency 3 Cold Pack Relief

You encounter many chemical reactions every day. Lighting a gas stove, starting a lawnmower, and playing sports all involve chemical reactions. So does the chemical cold pack shown below. The chemicals inside combine to provide instant cold for relief of minor athletic injuries.

1. What does a cold pack feel like before you mix the chemicals? What does it feel like after the chemicals mix?
2. Can chemical cold packs be reused? Why or why not?

L2

This is a representation of key blackline masters available in the Teacher Classroom Resources. See Resource Manager boxes within the chapter for additional information.

Assessment

Assessment Transparency Energy

Directions: Carefully review the diagram and answer the following question.

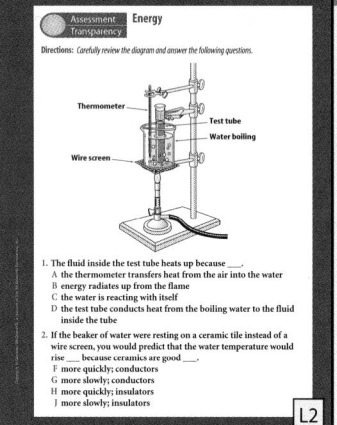

Thermometer
Test tube
Water boiling
Wire screen

1. The fluid inside the test tube heats up because ___.
   A the thermometer transfers heat from the air into the water
   B energy radiates up from the flame
   C the water is reacting with itself
   D the test tube conducts heat from the boiling water to the fluid inside the tube
2. If the beaker of water were resting on a ceramic tile instead of a wire screen, you would predict that the water temperature would rise ___ because ceramics are good ___.
   F more quickly; conductors
   G more slowly; conductors
   H more quickly; insulators
   J more slowly; insulators

L2

Teaching

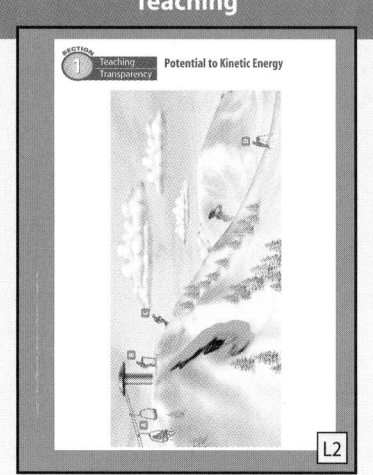

Teaching Transparency 1 Potential to Kinetic Energy

L2

Key to Teaching Strategies

The following designations will help you decide which activities are appropriate for your students.

L1 Level 1 activities should be appropriate for students with learning difficulties.

L2 Level 2 activities should be within the ability range of all students.

L3 Level 3 activities are designed for above-average students.

ELL ELL activities should be within the ability range of English Language Learners.

COOP LEARN Cooperative Learning activities are designed for small group work.

LS Multiple Learning Styles logos, as described on page 22T, are used throughout to indicate strategies that address different learning styles.

P These strategies represent student products that can be placed into a best-work portfolio.

Hands-on Activities

Activity Worksheets

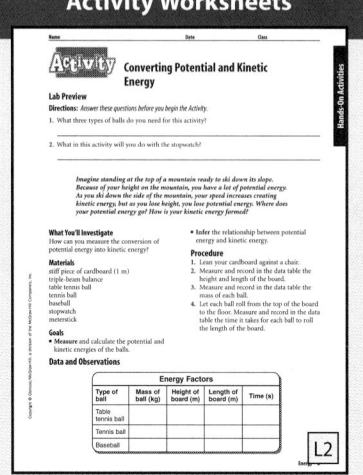

Activity Converting Potential and Kinetic Energy

Lab Preview
Directions: Answer these questions before you begin the Activity.

1. What three types of balls do you need for this activity?

2. What in this activity will you do with the stopwatch?

Imagine standing at the top of a mountain ready to ski down its slope. Because of your height on the mountain, you have a lot of potential energy. As you ski down the side of the mountain, your speed increases creating kinetic energy, but as you lose height, you lose potential energy. Where does your potential energy go? How is your kinetic energy formed?

What You'll Investigate
How can you measure the conversion of potential energy into kinetic energy?

Materials
stiff piece of cardboard (1 m)
triple-beam balance
table tennis ball
tennis ball
baseball
stopwatch
meterstick

Goals
• **Measure** and calculate the potential and kinetic energies of the balls.

• **Infer** the relationship between potential energy and kinetic energy.

Procedure
1. Lean your cardboard against a chair.
2. Measure and record in the data table the height and length of the board.
3. Measure and record in the data table the mass of each ball.
4. Let each ball roll from the top of the board to the floor. Measure and record in the data table the time it takes for each ball to roll the length of the board.

Data and Observations

Energy Factors				
Type of ball	Mass of ball (kg)	Height of board (m)	Length of board (m)	Time (s)
Table tennis ball				
Tennis ball				
Baseball				

L2

Laboratory Activities

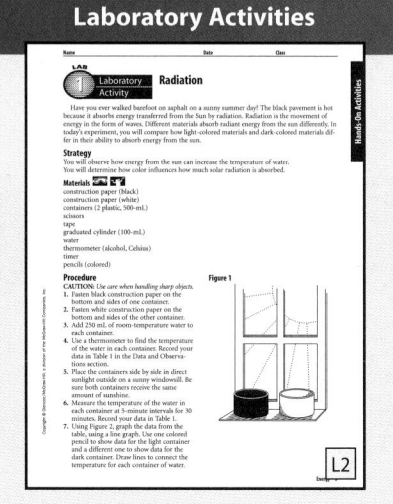

Laboratory Activity Radiation

Have you ever walked barefoot on asphalt on a sunny summer day? The black pavement is hot because it absorbs energy transferred from the Sun by radiation. Radiation is the movement of energy in the form of waves. Different materials absorb radiant energy from the sun differently. In today's experiment, you will compare how light-colored materials and dark-colored materials differ in their ability to absorb energy from the sun.

Strategy
You will observe how energy from the sun can increase the temperature of water. You will determine how color influences how much solar radiation is absorbed.

Materials
construction paper (black)
construction paper (white)
containers (2 plastic, 500-mL)
scissors
tape
graduated cylinder (100-mL)
water
thermometer (alcohol, Celsius)
timer
pencils (colored)

Procedure
CAUTION: Use care when handling sharp objects.
1. Fasten black construction paper on the bottom and sides of one container.
2. Fasten white construction paper on the bottom and sides of the other container.
3. Add 250 mL of room-temperature water to each container.
4. Use a thermometer to find the temperature of the water in each container. Record your data in Table 1 in the Data and Observations section.
5. Place the containers side by side in direct sunlight outside on a sunny windowsill. Be sure both containers receive the same amount of sunshine.
6. Measure the temperature of the water in each container at 5-minute intervals for 30 minutes. Record your data in Table 1.
7. Using Figure 2, graph the data from the table, using a line graph. Use one colored pencil to show data for the light container and a different one to show data for the dark container. Draw lines to connect the temperature for each container of water.

Figure 1

L2

Meeting Different Ability Levels

Content Outline

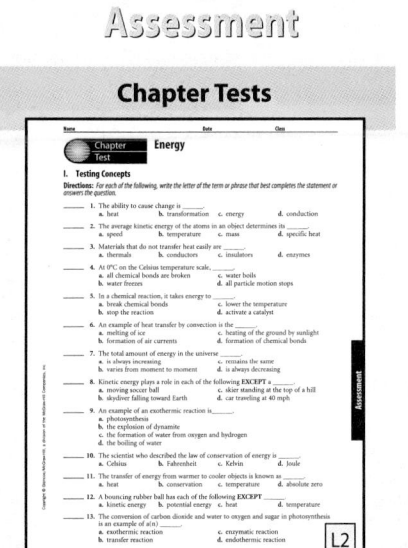

Reinforcement

Directed Reading

Assessment

Chapter Tests

Enrichment

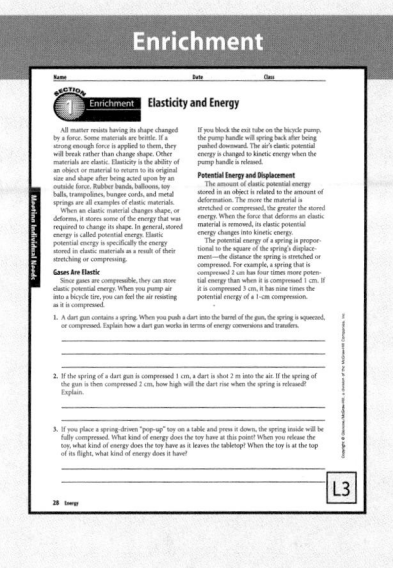

Spanish Directed Reading

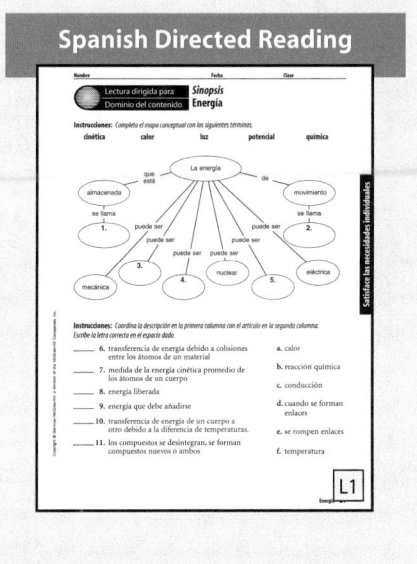

Test Practice Workbook

Chapter Review

Science Content Background

SECTION 1

Energy Changes
What is Energy?

A moving baseball has energy; you can see and feel the change that occurs as you catch it in your hand. Light is a form of energy; it can cause change in pigments in photographic film and in the retina of the eye. It can also cause a sunburn. The concept of energy can be divided into two categories: forms of stored energy and forms of energy involved in transfer and/or transformation.

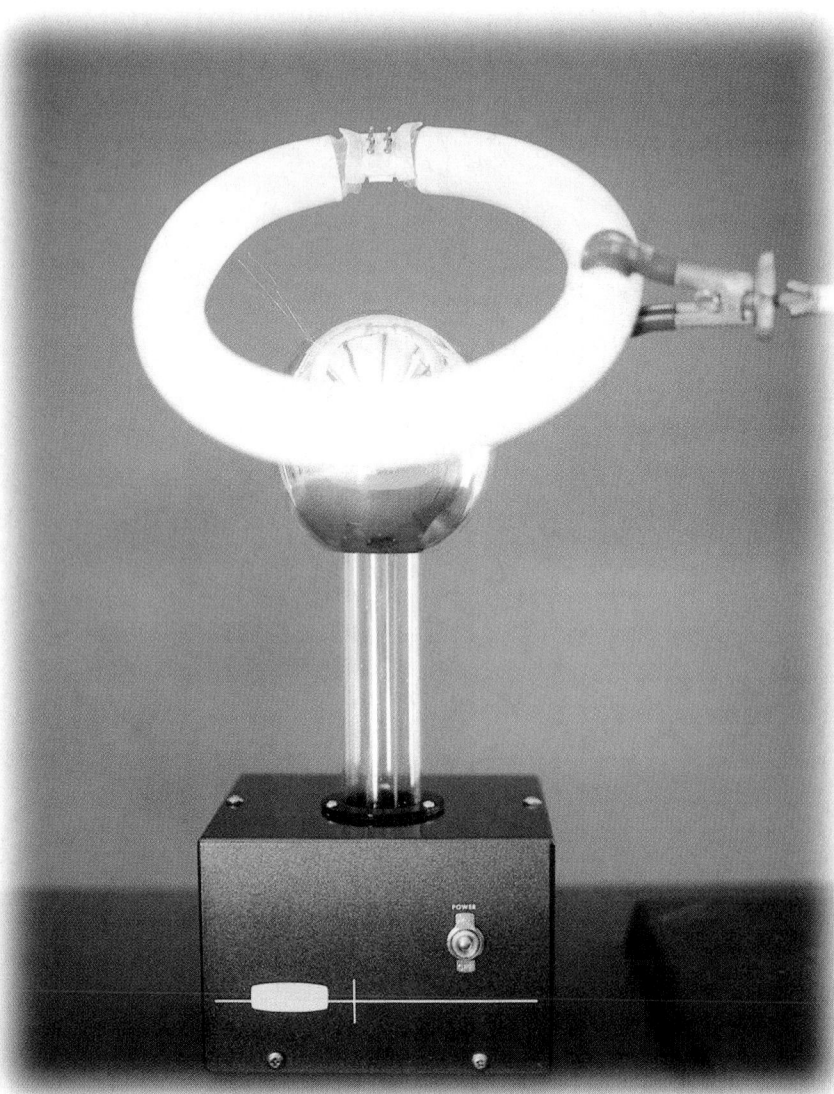

Runk/Schoenberger/Grant Heilman Photography, Inc.

Energy Transfers and Transformations

There are many examples of transfer or transformations of energy. Perhaps the most familiar is work. Work is the transfer of mechanical energy. The transfer of energy resulting from the collision between molecules is heat. Sound and light are two examples of waves that can transfer energy. Other examples of energy transformations are chemical and nuclear reactions, which commonly transform potential energy into other types of energy.

Potential Energy

Potential energy is associated with the fundamental forces in nature. Each force—gravitational, electromagnetic, and nuclear forces—can be thought of in terms of a field. Energy stored because of position in one of these fields is potential energy. Consequently, there are three basic types of potential energy: gravitational, electromagnetic, and nuclear. Two other types of potential energy are commonly discussed: elastic potential energy and chemical potential energy. Both of these types fundamentally are the result of electromagnetic interactions between atoms and molecules.

> ## Fun Fact
>
> Gravity can do work on an object to increase or decrease its kinetic energy. When a ball is thrown into the air, gravity does work to slow it down. Once the ball has reached the highest point in its flight, gravity does work to speed it up.

SECTION 2

Temperature
Temperature and Kinetic Energy

In a gas, temperature is proportional to the average kinetic energy of the molecules. By comparing the temperatures of two samples of material, you are also comparing the average kinetic energy of their particles.

Kinetic energy is directly related to speed. Under normal conditions, the average speed of nitrogen molecules in air is about 450 m/s. These nitrogen molecules are continually colliding and exchanging energy with other molecules. The nitrogen molecules have a range of speeds. A few nitrogen molecules will move slowly, less than 100 m/s, and a few will be going quite fast, greater than 1,000 m/s.

Measuring Temperature

In the kinetic theory, the temperature of a substance is proportional to the average kinetic energy of its molecules. This seems to imply that the temperature of the material would be zero if the average kinetic energy were zero. In other words, molecules would stop moving at 0 K, or absolute zero. However, at very low temperatures, effects due to the internal structure of atoms and molecules become important. As a result, all motion does not cease at absolute zero. Instead molecules still have some kinetic energy, called the zero-point energy.

Heat will be transferred from an object at a higher temperature to an object at a lower temperature if they are in contact. If no thermal energy is transferred between two objects in contact, they are at the same temperature.

Heat and Temperature

Temperature and thermal energy are related, but they have distinct properties. Temperature is a measure of the average kinetic energy of particles in any object, whereas thermal energy is the total energy of the particles. A cup of 90°C tea is much hotter than a bathtub full of 42°C water, but there is more thermal energy in the bathtub of water because the amount of water in the bathtub is much greater. After standing for half an hour, the tea is near room temperature, and the bathtub water's temperature has barely gone down. One reason the tea loses thermal energy more quickly is that it has far less energy to lose.

SECTION 3 — Chemical Energy
Chemical Reactions and Energy

To break bonds means to pull atoms apart, which requires energy input to overcome the electrostatic force of attraction between the atoms. Likewise, when bonding atoms accelerate toward each other to form a chemical bond, energy is released.

An exothermic reaction can sustain itself as long as there are reactants. However, for an endothermic reaction to continue, there must be not only reactants but also an energy supply from the environment.

Changing the Rate of Reaction

Enzymes can increase the reaction rate billions of times faster than it would occur if the enzyme weren't present. For example, in aerobic respiration, toxic hydrogen peroxide is produced. The enzyme catalase can convert 40 million molecules of hydrogen peroxide into harmless water and oxygen every second. This is the same reaction that you see when you pour hydrogen peroxide on a wound. Catalase from injured cells rapidly breaks down the hydrogen peroxide, producing oxygen gas and water.

Fun Fact

Temperature is one factor controlling the rate of a chemical reaction. Sometimes the same reactants will produce different products if the reaction occurs at different temperatures.

SCIENCE Online

For additional content background on this topic, go to the Glencoe Science Web site at science.glencoe.com.

CHAPTER 20

Energy

Chapter Vocabulary

energy, p. 588
kinetic energy, p. 590
potential energy, p. 592
law of conservation of energy, p. 594
temperature, p. 597
heat, p. 599
conduction, p. 600
convection, p. 602
radiation, p. 603
endothermic reaction, p. 606
exothermic reaction, p. 607
catalyst, p. 608

What do you think?

Science Journal This photograph shows steam coming out of a tea kettle.

CHAPTER 20

Energy

A powerful wave pounds the entrance to a lighthouse on Les Sables D'Olonne harbor in France. Hours earlier, this angry ocean was a gentle body of water, and waves calmly lapped the shore. Have you ever wondered what could change a calm, friendly ocean into a ferocious body of movement? In this chapter you'll learn how changes are caused by the transfer of energy. You'll also learn how temperature and heat are related, and how energy is involved in chemical reactions.

What do you think?

Science Journal Look at the picture below with a classmate. Discuss what you think this might be or what is happening. Here's a hint: *Though it looks harmless, touching it can cause severe burns.* Write your answer or your best guess in your Science Journal.

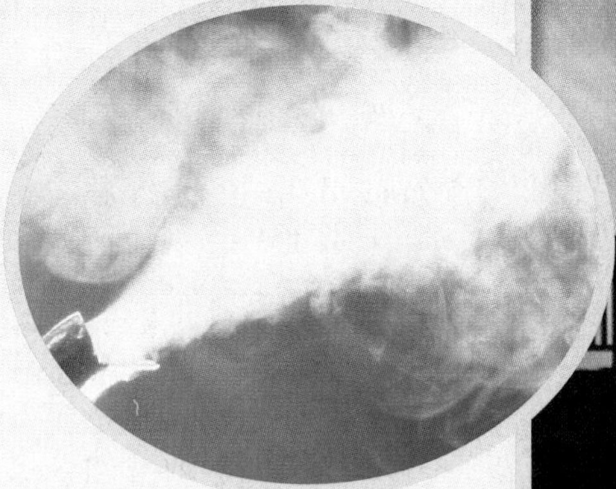

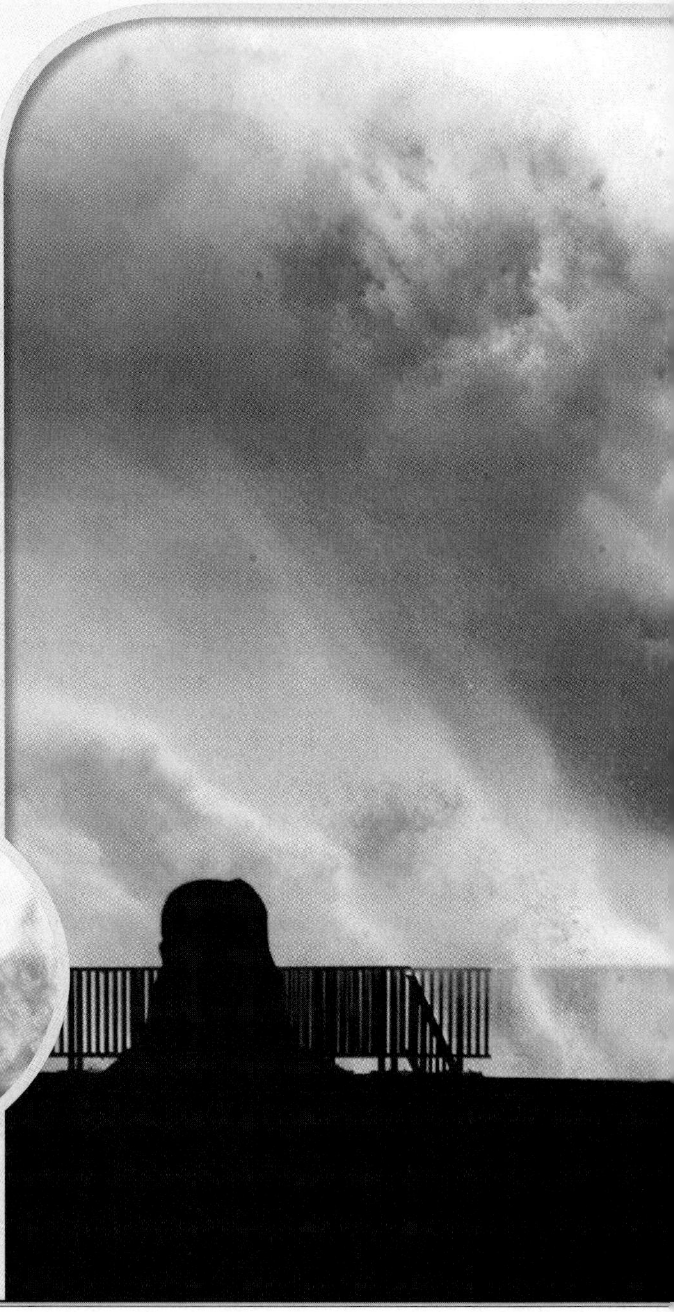

586

Theme Connection

Energy This chapter discusses energy and how it can be transformed, transferred, released, and absorbed in systems.

Think of all the things you do every day such as walking to class, riding to school, switching on a light, cooking food, playing music, or stopping your bike. All of the actions of your daily life involve energy and changing energy from one form to another. What forms can energy take? In what ways can energy change from one form to another? Find out during this activity.

Observe energy conversions

1. Place a beaker filled with water on a hotplate and bring the water to a boil.

2. Switch on a flashlight.

3. Rub a pencil back and forth between your palms as fast as you can.

4. Drop a baseball from a height of 2 m into a layer of clay.

Observe

During each step of this activity, you converted one form of energy into another form. Write a paragraph in your Science Journal describing the changes that occurred in each step of this activity.

Before You Read

FOLDABLES
Reading & Study
Skills

Making a Cause and Effect Study Fold Make the following Foldable to help you understand the different ways energy can be transformed.

1. Place a sheet of paper in front of you so the long side is at the top. Fold the paper in half from top to bottom. Fold the top down and the bottom up. Unfold all the folds.

2. Using the fold lines as a guide, refold the paper into a fan. Unfold all the folds again.

3. Title the top fold *Form of Energy* and *Changed to* as shown. List under Form of Energy *Electrical to, Chemical to, Heat to, Kinetic to,* and *Potential to.*

4. As you read the chapter, write answers to what each form of energy can be changed to under *Changed to* on your Foldable.

Form of Energy	Changed to
Electrical to	
Chemical to	
Heat to	
Kinetic to	
Potential to	

587

Purpose Use this Explore Activity to introduce students to some of the ways energy changes from one form to another. L2 ELL **N** **Kinesthetic**

Preparation Set up a hotplate for each group and collect flashlights and baseballs.

Materials beaker of water, hotplate, flashlight, pencil, baseball, clay

Teaching Strategy Assign four students to each group and have each group member decide which task he or she will demonstrate. Suggest students perform the other three tasks while waiting for the water to boil.

Observe

In the first step electricity was converted to heat. In step 2 chemical energy was converted to electrical energy, which was converted to light. In the third step kinetic energy was converted to heat. In step 4 the potential energy of the baseball was converted to kinetic energy.

✓ *Assessment*

Process Provide students with a diagram of the power plant that supplies electrical energy to your school and ask students to identify the energy conversion used by the plant. Possible energy sources include fossil fuels (chemical energy), nuclear reactions (nuclear energy), solar collectors (solar energy), windmills (wind power), and hydroelectric power. Use **PASC,** p. 89.

Before You Read

FOLDABLES
Reading & Study
Skills

Dinah Zike Study Fold
Purpose Students make and use a Foldable to record examples of energy changes. Students use the data collected to explain the causes of these changes and their effects.

📁 For additional help, see Foldables Worksheet, p. 15 in **Chapter Resources Booklet,** or go to the Glencoe Science Web site at **science.glencoe.com.** See After You Read in the Study Guide at the end of this chapter.

SECTION

1

Energy Changes

Bellringer Transparency

Display the Section Focus Transparency for Section 1. Use the accompanying Transparency Activity Master. L2

ELL

Tie to Prior Knowledge

Have students recall changes they have noticed in matter or the environment. Tell them that whenever anything changes in nature, the change is due to energy.

Text Question Answer

Possible answers: electric or magnetic energy, solar energy, energy of athlete in motion

---

SECTION

1 Energy Changes

As You Read

What You'll Learn

- **Explain** what energy is.
- **Describe** the forms energy takes.
- **Compare and contrast** potential energy and kinetic energy.

Vocabulary

energy
kinetic energy
potential energy
law of conservation of energy

Why It's Important

Energy causes all the changes that take place around you.

Figure 1
Lightning causes dramatic change as it lights up the sky.

Energy

Energy is a term you probably use every day. You might say that eating a plate of spaghetti gives you energy, or that a gymnast has a lot of energy. Do you realize that a burning fire, a bouncing ball, and a tank of gasoline also have energy?

What is energy? The word *energy* comes from the ancient Greek word *energos,* which means "active." You probably have used the word *energy* in the same way. When you say you have a lot of energy, what does this mean? **Energy** is the ability to cause change. For example, energy can change the temperature of a pot of water, or it can change the direction and speed of a baseball. The energy in a thunderstorm, like the one shown in **Figure 1,** produces lightning that lights up the sky and thunder that can rattle windows. Energy can change the arrangement of atoms in molecules and cause chemical reactions to occur. You use energy when you change the speed of a bicycle by pedaling faster or when you put on the brakes.

✔ **Reading Check** *What are some things energy can change?*

Forms of Energy

If you ask your friends what comes to mind when they think of energy, you probably will get many different answers. Some might mention candy bars or food. Others might think of the energy needed to run a car. Energy does come in different forms from a variety of sources. Food provides energy in the form of chemical energy. Your body converts chemical energy in the food you eat into the energy it needs to move, think, and grow. Nuclear power plants use nuclear energy contained in the center or nucleus of the atom to produce electricity. What other forms of energy can you think of?

588 CHAPTER 20

Section ✔*Assessment* Planner

PORTFOLIO
Assessment, p. 595
PERFORMANCE ASSESSMENT
Try at Home MiniLAB, p. 593
Skill Builder Activities, p. 595
See page 616 for more options.

CONTENT ASSESSMENT
Section, p. 595
Challenge, p. 595
Chapter, pp. 616–617

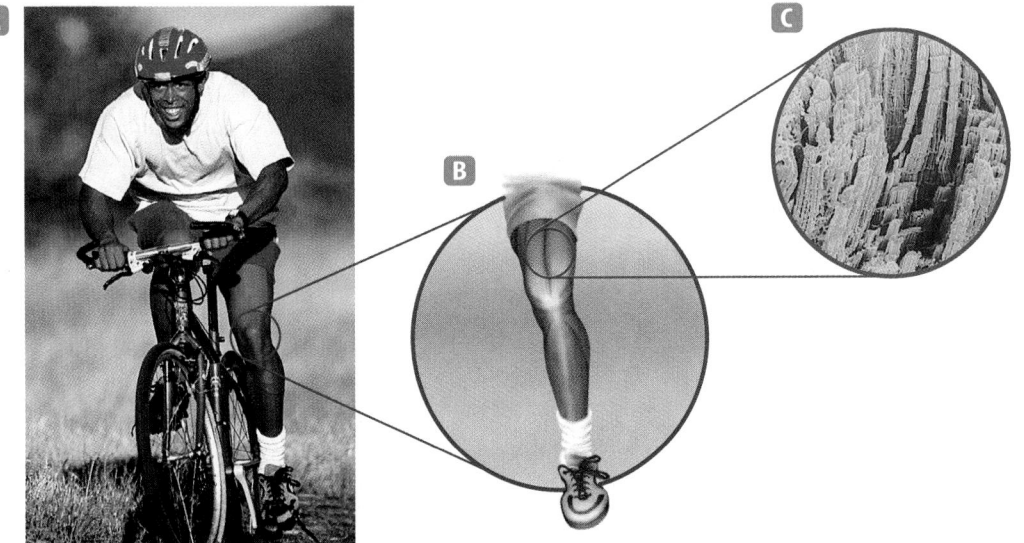

Energy Transformations Energy is stored in the chemical compounds in your muscles. When you push down on a bicycle pedal, chemical energy is used to make your legs move.

An energy transformation occurs if energy changes from one form to another. Energy transformations go on all around you and inside of you all the time. The chemical energy stored in your muscles changes to energy of motion, as you can see in **Figure 2.** When a car sits in the Sun all day, the energy in sunlight changes to heat energy that warms the inside of the car. The energy you use to stretch and move a rubber band also changes into heat energy that raises the temperature of the rubber band.

During these and other types of energy transformations, the total amount of energy stays the same. Energy is never lost or gained—it only changes form.

Using Energy Transformations Since the earliest times, humans have used different forms of energy. When humans first learned to make fires, they used the chemical energy in wood and other fuels to cook, stay warm, and light their way in the dark. Today, a gas stove, like the one in **Figure 3,** transforms the chemical energy in natural gas to heat energy that boils water and cooks food. An electric current that flows in a wire carries electrical energy that can be used in many ways. A hair dryer converts electrical energy into heat energy. A lightbulb converts electrical energy into heat and light energy when you flip on a switch.

Figure 2
🅐 You pedal a bicycle with your legs. 🅑 Muscles cause your leg to move by contracting.
🅒 Your muscles are made of these microscopic fibers. They cause your muscles to contract by becoming shorter when certain chemical reactions release chemical energy.

Figure 3
As natural gas burns in a gas stove, it gives off energy that heats the water.

Teacher FYI

When a force does work on an object, energy is transferred to the object. The work on an object is defined as the force exerted on the object multiplied by the distance the object moved in the direction of the force. The change in energy of the system (the object and its surroundings) is equal to the amount of work done.

IDENTIFYING Misconceptions

Students often think of energy as a substance rather than a property. Saying that energy flows or moves can lead to confusion; particles and waves flow or move, carrying energy with them. Energy is transferred or transformed.

Resource Manager

Chapter Resources Booklet
  Note-taking Worksheets, pp. 31–32
  Transparency Activity, p. 42
Reading and Writing Skill Activity, p. 35

Science Journal

Transfer and Transformation Students need to distinguish clearly between a transfer of energy and the transformation of energy. Have students describe the difference between these two processes and write in their Science Journals a sentence using each. L2 ELL 🄻🄢 **Linguistic**

Kinetic Energy

Use Science Words

Word Meaning Have students use a dictionary to find the meaning of *kinetic*. relating to or caused by motion L2 ELL **Linguistic**

Extension

Introduce advanced students to the formula for kinetic energy, $KE = 1/2mv^2$. Do several examples with different numbers. **How fast would a 50-kg person have to be going to have the kinetic energy of a 1,000-kg car moving 1 m/s or 3.6 km/h?** The car has kinetic energy $KE = 1/2 \times 1,000$ kg $(1 \text{ m/s})^2 = 500$ J. To find the speed of a person with that much kinetic energy, solve $KE = 1/2mv^2$ for v: $500 \text{ J} = 1/2 \times 50 \text{ kg} \times v^2; 20 = v^2; v = 4.47$ m/s, about 16 km/h. L3

Logical-Mathematical

Activity

Bring in balls of several different masses. Have students roll the balls at different speeds and see how hard they are to stop. **When does each ball have the most kinetic energy?** when it is moving the fastest The more kinetic energy a ball has, the harder it will be to stop. Point out that catching a fast-moving baseball takes more force than stopping a slowly rolling bowling ball. However, if the balls move at the same speed, the bowling ball will be harder to stop. It has more kinetic energy because it is more massive. L2

ELL **Kinesthetic**

Figure 4
Any moving object has energy because it can cause change.

Kinetic Energy

One soccer ball is sitting on the ground and another is rolling toward the net. How does the energy of the moving ball compare to the one at rest? A moving ball certainly has the ability to cause change. For example, a moving bowling ball shown in **Figure 4** causes the bowling pins to fall. A moving ball has energy due to its motion. The energy an object has due to its motion is called **kinetic** (kih NET ihk) **energy.** A football thrown by a quarterback has kinetic energy. A sky diver or a leaf falling toward Earth also has kinetic energy.

Mass, Speed, and Kinetic Energy Although moving objects have kinetic energy, not all moving objects have the same amount of kinetic energy. What determines the amount of kinetic energy in a moving object? The amount of kinetic energy an object has depends on the mass and speed of the object, as shown in **Figure 5.** Imagine a small rock and a large boulder rolling down a hillside at the same speed. Which would have more kinetic energy? Think about the damage the rock and the boulder could do if they hit something at the bottom of the hill. The large boulder could cause more damage, so it has more kinetic energy. Even though the rock and the boulder were moving at the same speed, the boulder had more kinetic energy than the rock because it had more mass.

Kinetic energy also depends on speed. The faster a bowling ball moves, the more pins it can knock down. When more pins are knocked down, a greater change has occured. So the faster the bowling ball moves, the more kinetic energy it has. Kinetic energy increases as speed increases.

Curriculum Connection

Art Kinetic art is a form of art designed to be set in motion. Ask students to describe kinetic art works they have seen or heard of. Examples: sculptures in which balls roll and drop down along different paths, fountains, mobiles, some gardens. You might want to ask local museums if they include any kinetic art in their collections. L3 ELL **Visual-Spatial**

Visual Learning

Figure 4 Which has more kinetic energy: a bowling ball, or a pin moving at the same speed as the bowling ball? the bowling ball, because it has more mass L2 **Logical-Mathematical**

Figure 5

The amount of kinetic energy of a moving object depends on the mass and the speed of the object. For example, the fastest measured speed a baseball has been thrown is about 45 m/s. The kinetic energy of a baseball traveling at that speed is about 150 J.

▲ There is evidence that a meteorite 10 km in diameter collided with Earth about 65 million years ago and might have caused the extinction of dinosaurs. The meteorite may have been moving 400 times faster than the baseball and would have a tremendous amount of kinetic energy due to its enormous mass and high speed—about a trillion trillion joules.

▼ A 600-kg race car, traveling at about 50 m/s, has about 5,000 times the kinetic energy of the baseball.

▼ Earth's atmosphere is continually bombarded by particles called cosmic rays, which are mainly high-speed protons. The mass of a proton is about a 100 trillion trillion times smaller than the mass of a baseball. Yet, some of these particles travel so fast, they have nearly the same kinetic energy as the baseball.

 A sprinter with a mass of about 55 kg and running at 9 m/s has kinetic energy about 15 times greater than the baseball.

591

Visualizing Kinetic Energy

Have students examine the pictures and read the captions. Then ask the following questions.

The baseball in the feature is traveling at 45 m/s and the race car is traveling at 9 m/s. **Why does the car have 1,600 times the kinetic energy of the baseball?** because the race car has significantly more mass

What is the kinetic energy of the sprinter in the feature? KE of sprinter $= 15 \times$ KE of baseball $= 15 \times 150$ J $= 2,250$ J

Activity

Have students research some of the possible effects due to the collision of a meteorite with Earth 65 million years ago. Answers could include tsunamis and earthquakes caused by the shock wave, firestorms caused by release of methane gas from the ocean floor, acid rain formed by the combustion products of the firestorms, and global cooling due to the effects of the dust ejected from the impact and the smog formed by the firestorms.

Extension

When the space shuttle reenters Earth's atmosphere, it has a tremendous amount of kinetic energy. Have students research how the kinetic energy of the shuttle is reduced so that astronauts can land safely.

Resource Manager

Chapter Resources Booklet
   Transparency Activity, pp. 45–46

Life Science Critical Thinking/Problem Solving, p. 15

Physical Science Critical Thinking/Problem Solving, p. 6

Kinetic Energy,
continued

Discussion

When you kick a ball, how do the kinetic energy of your foot and the kinetic energy of the ball change? Your foot slows down, so its kinetic energy decreases. The ball speeds up, so its kinetic energy increases. L2

IS **Logical-Mathematical**

Quick Demo

Place marbles equally spaced along a level track made from two metersticks taped one marble-width apart or from the groove in a ruler. Roll a marble from one end. Notice how the kinetic energy is transferred in each collision. (Note that friction with the track will cause all the marbles to come to a stop fairly quickly as the kinetic energy is transformed to thermal energy. With no such loss, the collisions could go on indefinitely.) L2 ELL IS **Visual-Spatial**

Potential Energy

Visual Learning ——

Figure 7 Notice that energy is needed to increase the skier's potential energy. Where does it come from? chemical energy from fuel running the ski lift, or chemical energy used in the skier's muscles if she skis up L3 IS **Logical-Mathematical**

Figure 6
Kinetic energy is transferred from domino to domino by tapping the first one in line.

Figure 7
Potential and kinetic energy change as the skier moves up and down the slope. **A** The skier's potential energy increases as the ski lift carries her up the hill. **B** Her potential energy is largest at the top of the hill. **C** As she skis down, potential energy transforms into kinetic energy. **D** Here her kinetic energy is greatest and her potential energy is smallest.

Transferring Kinetic Energy Kinetic energy can be transferred from one object to another when they collide. Think about the transfer of energy during bowling. Even if the bowling ball does not touch all of the pins, it still can knock them all down with one roll. The bowling ball transfers kinetic energy to a few pins. These pins move and bump into other pins, transferring the kinetic energy to the remaining pins and knocking them down.

A transfer of kinetic energy also takes place when dominoes fall. You need to give only the first domino in the row a bit of kinetic energy by lightly tapping it to make it fall against the next domino. As the first domino falls into the next one, its kinetic energy is transferred to the second domino, as shown in **Figure 6.** This transfer of kinetic energy continues from domino to domino until the last one falls and hits the table. Then, the last domino's kinetic energy is transferred to the table.

Potential Energy

Suppose the ski lift in **Figure 7** takes a skier to the top of a hill. The skier has no kinetic energy when she is standing at the top of the hill. But as she skis down and moves faster, her kinetic energy increases. Where does this kinetic energy come from? Gravity pulls the skier down the hill. If the skier were standing at the bottom of the hill, gravity would not start her moving, as it does when she is at the top of the hill. When the skier's position is at the top of the hill, she has a form of energy called potential energy. **Potential energy** is energy that is stored because of an object's position. By using the ski lift to take her to the top of the hill, the skier increased her potential energy by changing her position.

592

Cultural Diversity

Chain Drives The chain drive, familiar to students from bicycles, was invented in China by Chang Ssu-Hsun to power a mechanical clock in 976 A.D. Chain drives did not appear in Europe until 1770. Show students an illustration of a chain drive and ask how the chain drive on a bicycle transfers energy. The kinetic energy of a foot on the pedals is transferred by the chain to the wheels. L2 IS **Visual-Spatial**

Teacher FYI

There are three basic types of potential energy: gravitational potential energy, electrical/magnetic potential energy, and nuclear potential energy. Chemical potential energy is a type of electrical potential energy stored in the bonds of molecules. Elastic potential energy (the force stored in a stretched rubber band) is also related to electromagnetic force.

Increasing Potential Energy When you raise an object above its original position, it has the potential to fall. If it does fall, it has kinetic energy. To raise an object, you have to transfer energy to the object. The ski lift uses energy when it takes a skier up a hill and transfers some of that energy to the skier. This energy becomes stored as potential energy in the skier. As the skier goes down the hill, the potential energy she had at the top of the hill is converted to kinetic energy.

If the skier were lifted higher, her potential energy would increase. The higher an object is lifted above Earth, the greater its potential energy.

Converting Potential and Kinetic Energy

When a skier skis down a hill, potential energy is transformed to kinetic energy. Kinetic energy also can be transformed into potential energy. Suppose you throw a ball straight up into the air. The muscles in your body cause the ball to move upward when it leaves your hand. Because it is moving, the ball has kinetic energy. Look at **Figure 8.** As the ball gets higher and higher, its potential energy is increasing. At the same time, the ball is slowing down and its kinetic energy is decreasing.

What happens when the ball reaches its highest point? The ball comes to a stop for an instant before it starts to fall downward again. At its highest point, the ball has no more kinetic energy. All the kinetic energy the ball had when it left your hand has been converted to potential energy, and the ball will go no higher. As the ball falls downward, its potential energy is converted back into kinetic energy. If you catch the ball at the same height above the ground as when you threw it upward, its kinetic energy will be the same as when it left your hand.

TRY AT HOME
Mini LAB

Comparing Kinetic Energy and Height

Procedure:
1. Lay a 3-cm-thick layer of smooth modeling **clay** on a piece of **cardboard.** Place the cardboard on the floor.
2. Drop an object such as a **baseball, golf ball,** or **orange** into the clay from a height of 10 cm. Measure and record the depth of the hole made by the object.
3. Repeat step 2 from a height of 50 cm and 1 m.

Analysis
1. How does the depth of the hole depend on the height of the ball?
2. How does the kinetic energy of the falling ball depend on the distance it fell?

Figure 8
Energy is transformed as a ball rises and falls.

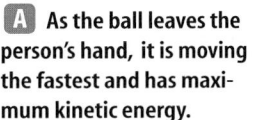
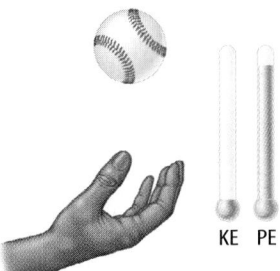
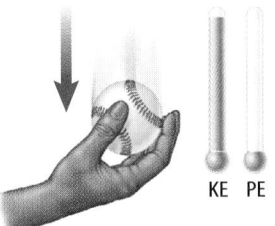

KE PE   KE PE   KE PE

A As the ball leaves the person's hand, it is moving the fastest and has maximum kinetic energy.

B As the ball moves upward, it slows down as its kinetic energy is transformed into potential energy.

C As the ball moves downward, it speeds up as its potential energy is transformed into kinetic energy.

SECTION 1 Energy Changes **593**

Converting Potential and Kinetic Energy

TRY AT HOME
Mini LAB

Purpose Students will observe and compare the effects of potential and kinetic energy.
[L2] [IS] **Kinesthetic**

Materials clay, cardboard, baseball, golf ball, orange, meter stick

Teaching Strategy Make sure students drop the objects the same way each time.

Analysis
1. The greater the distance the ball fell, the greater the depth of the hole.
2. The kinetic energy of the ball just before it hits the clay is greater if the ball is dropped from a greater height.

✔Assessment

Process Have each student write a newspaper article describing this MiniLAB and the results. Have students write headlines for the articles and remind them they can use tables and illustrations in the articles. Use **Performance Assessment in the Science Classroom,** p. 141.

Discussion

What are some positions other than height above Earth that give an object potential energy? a stretched rubber band, a pulled spring [L3]
[IS] **Logical-Mathematical**

Resource Manager

Chapter Resources Booklet
MiniLAB, p. 3
Enrichment, p. 28
Home and Community Involvement, p. 38

Teacher **FYI**

Kinetic energy is regularly transformed to thermal energy by friction. When doing classroom demonstrations, keep friction in mind. Tell students that thermal energy is another form of energy, so energy is still conserved—kinetic energy is lost, but an equal amount of thermal energy is gained.

Converting Potential and Kinetic Energy, continued

 **Reading Check**

Answer kinetic energy

Conserving Energy

Quick Demo

Split a 1-m length of plastic tubing that is about 1 cm in diameter. Clamp each end of the tubing to a ring stand so that it forms a shallow, U-shaped track. Hold a marble slightly above one end of the track and ask students to predict the height that the marble will reach on the opposite side. Release the marble and have students observe the height it reaches. Rearrange the tubing to form variously shaped ramps and discuss the motion of the marble, stressing the conservation of energy. L1
ELL **Visual-Spatial**

Figure 9
The potential energy of water can be transformed into electrical energy. **A** The potential energy of water behind the dam is converted to kinetic energy as the water falls through pipes. **B** The kinetic energy of the moving water spins generators like these that produce electricity.

Energy Changes in Falling Water You might have stood close to a large waterfall and heard the roar of the water. Just like a ball falling to the ground, the potential energy that the water has at the top of the falls is transformed into kinetic energy as the water falls downward.

The kinetic energy of falling water can be used to generate electricity. As shown in **Figure 9,** water backs up behind a dam on a river, forming a lake or reservoir. The water near the top of the dam then falls downward. The kinetic energy of the moving water spins generators, which produce electricity. The potential energy of the water behind the dam is transformed into electrical energy.

 Reading Check *The potential energy of falling water is transformed into what form of energy?*

Conserving Energy

Following the trail of energy as it is transformed can be a challenge. Sometimes it might seem that energy disappears or is lost. But that's not the case. In 1840, James Joule demonstrated the law of conservation of energy. According to the **law of conservation of energy,** energy cannot be created or destroyed. It only can be transformed from one form into another, so the total amount of energy in the universe never changes. The only change is in the form that energy appears in.

Kinetic energy can be converted into heat energy when two objects rub against each other. As a book slides across a table, it will slow down and eventually stop. The book's kinetic energy isn't lost. It is converted into heat energy as the book rubs against the surface of the table.

A

B

 **Resource Manager**

Chapter Resources Booklet
Reinforcement, p. 25
Directed Reading for Content Mastery, pp. 17, 18

Inclusion Strategies

Learning Disabled Reinforce the idea of conservation of energy. Collect a number of small blocks, marbles, or other identical units. Label 4 containers chemical energy, kinetic energy, potential energy, and thermal energy. Show how a given amount of energy (e.g., 20 units) can be distributed among the containers. The total amount of energy stays the same, but it can be in different forms. L1 ELL **Kinesthetic**

Figure 10
Energy can take different forms, but it can never be created or destroyed.

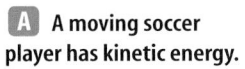

A A moving soccer player has kinetic energy.

B Kinetic energy from the player's moving leg is transferred to the ball.

C When the ball rolls, its kinetic energy is transformed by friction into heat as the ball rubs against the grass.

Following the Energy Trail The flow of energy as a soccer ball is kicked is shown in **Figure 10.** Chemical energy in the soccer player's leg muscles is converted into kinetic energy when she swings her leg. When the ball is kicked, this kinetic energy is transferred to the ball. After the ball rolls for a while, it comes to a stop. The kinetic energy of the ball seems to have disappeared, but it hasn't. As the ball rolled, its kinetic energy was transformed into heat energy as the ball rubbed against the grass.

Section Assessment

1. Imagine a roller coaster as it climbs to the top of the steepest hill on its track. When does the first car have the greatest potential energy?

2. If you are riding in a roller coaster, how is your kinetic energy related to your speed?

3. State the law of conservation of energy.

4. What is energy? Can it change an object?

5. **Think Critically** The following happens: You get up in the morning, get dressed, eat breakfast, walk to the bus stop, and ride to school. List three different energy transformations that have taken place.

Skill Builder Activities

6. **Making and Using Graphs** A pendulum swings seven times per minute. If the string were half as long, the pendulum would swing ten times per minute. If it were twice as long, it would swing five times per minute. Make a bar graph that shows these data. Draw a conclusion from the results. **For more help, refer to the** Science Skill Handbook.

7. **Communicating** In your Science Journal, list energy transformations that take place when you roast marshmallows over a fire. **For more help, refer to the** Science Skill Handbook.

Answers to Section Assessment

1. at the top of the track
2. As speed increases, so does kinetic energy. If speed decreases, kinetic energy decreases.
3. Energy cannot be created or destroyed, only transformed.
4. Energy is the ability to cause change; yes, all changes to an object involve energy.

5. Possible answer: When you get up, you transform chemical energy to kinetic energy to potential energy. When you eat breakfast, you use kinetic energy to get chemical energy. When you ride the bus, chemical energy in the fuel is transformed to kinetic energy.

6. As the length of the string increases, the number of swings per minute decreases.
7. Possible answer: chemical to kinetic as you put marshmallow on stick and place over fire; thermal energy transforms the marshmallow's chemistry, browning the outside.

---

3 Assess

Reteach
Energy is conserved within a closed system. Point out to students that when a system gains energy (for example, a plant getting energy from the Sun) another system must be losing energy (the Sun is sending out the energy). Together, these two systems make a larger system in which energy has been conserved.
L2 IS **Logical-Mathematical**

Challenge
Give students the formula for gravitational potential energy, GPE = mgh, with g = 10 m/s^2, and ask them to find the kinetic, potential, and total energy of a 0.3-kg ball dropped from a height of 8 m at the top, midpoint, and bottom of the fall. The total energy at the top is PE = mgh = 0.3 kg × 10 m/s^2 × 8 m = 24 J; KE = 0. At the midpoint, PE = 12 J; KE = 24 J − 12 J = 12 J. At the bottom, PE = 0; KE = 24 J.
L3 IS **Logical-Mathematical**

✓Assessment

Process Show students a pendulum and ask them to draw diagrams and write descriptions that explain the energy conversions that take place as the pendulum swings. Ask why a pendulum will not rise higher than the point at which it was dropped. It would have more potential energy, so energy would not be conserved. Use **Performance Assessment in the Science Classroom,** p. 127. P

SECTION

2

Temperature

1 Motivate

Bellringer Transparency

Display the Section Focus Transparency for Section 2. Use the accompanying Transparency Activity Master. L2

ELL

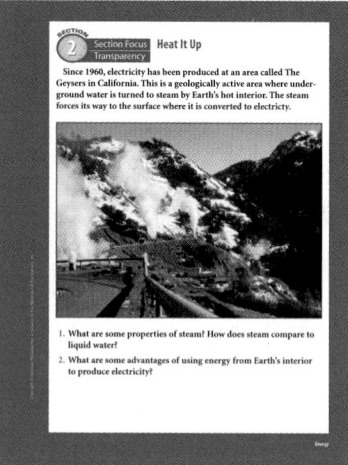

Tie to Prior Knowledge

Discuss with students where the heat we feel comes from—the Sun, transformation of chemical energy inside our bodies, and geothermal energy from inside Earth.

SECTION

2

Temperature

As You Read

What You'll Learn

- **Distinguish** between temperature and heat.
- **Identify** important uses of heat.
- **Explain** how heat moves.

Vocabulary

temperature   convection
heat   radiation
conduction

Why It's Important

The flow of heat warms Earth, produces weather, cooks your food, and warms and cools your home.

Figure 11
In gases, atoms are free to move in all directions.

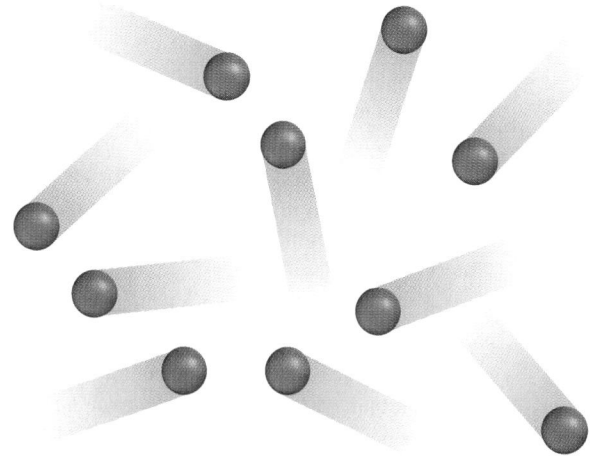

Temperature

What's today's temperature? If you looked at a thermometer, listened to a weather report on the radio, or saw a weather map on television, you probably used the air temperature to help you decide what to wear. Some days are so hot you don't need a jacket. Others are so cold you want to bundle up.

Hot and *cold* are words used in everyday language to describe temperature. However, they are not scientific words because they mean different things to different people. A summer day that seems hot to one person might seem just right to another. If you grew up in Texas but moved to Minnesota, you might find the winters unbearably cold. Have you ever complained that a classroom was too cold when other students insisted that it was too warm?

Temperature and Kinetic Energy What is temperature? Remember that any material or object is made up of atoms. The atoms in objects are moving constantly, even if the object appears to be perfectly still. Every object you can think of—your hand, the pencil on your desk, or even the desktop—contains atoms that are in constant motion. In solids, liquids, and gases the atoms do not move in a single direction. Instead, they move in all directions. In a gas, atoms are far apart and can move as shown in **Figure 11.** In liquids, atoms are closer together and can't move as far as in a gas. In solids, atoms are bound more tightly together and can move only short distances. Instead of moving freely as shown in **Figure 11,** atoms in a solid vibrate back and forth. The motion of atoms in all directions in solids, liquids, and gases is called random motion. Because the atoms are moving, they have kinetic energy. The faster the atoms are moving, the more kinetic energy they have.

596   CHAPTER 20 Energy

Section ✓Assessment Planner

PORTFOLIO
Assessment, p. 603
PERFORMANCE ASSESSMENT
MiniLAB, p. 602
Skill Builder Activities, p. 603
See page 616 for more options.

CONTENT ASSESSMENT
Section, p. 603
Challenge, p. 603
Chapter, pp. 616–617

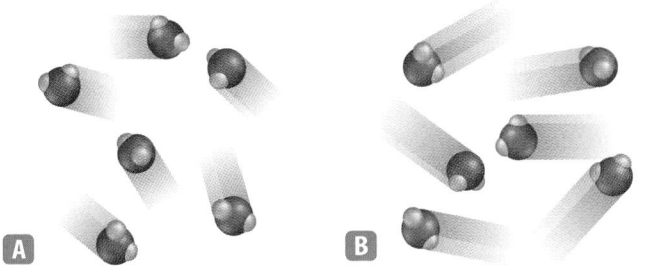

Temperature is a measure of the average kinetic energy of the atoms in an object. When an object's temperature is higher, its atoms have more kinetic energy. **Figure 12** shows gas molecules in the air at 0°C (A) and at 30°C (B). At the higher temperature, the molecules are moving faster and have more kinetic energy.

Problem-Solving Activity

Can you be fooled by temperature?

On a cold, wintry morning, you may have heard a local meteorologist caution you to "Bundle up, because the wind chill index is minus 20 degrees." While wind cannot lower the temperature of the outside air, it can make your body lose heat faster, and make you feel as if the temperature were lower.

Identifying the Problem

A wind chill index of –29°C presents little danger to you if you are properly dressed. Below this temperature, however, your skin can become frostbitten within minutes. Use the table to find wind chill values for conditions that present the greatest dangers.

Wind Chill Index

Temperature (°C)	Wind Speed (km/h)							
	10	20	30	40	50	60	70	80
20	18°C	16°C	14°C	13°C	13°C	12°C	12°C	12°C
12	9°C	5°C	3°C	1°C	0°C	0°C	−1°C	−1°C
0	−4°C	−10°C	−14°C	−17°C	−18°C	−19°C	−20°C	−21°C
−20	−26°C	−36°C	−43°C	−47°C	−49°C	−51°C	−52°C	−53°C
−36	−44°C	−57°C	−65°C	−71°C	−74°C	−77°C	−78°C	−79°C

Solving the Problem

1. Assuming you live in an area where wind speeds in the winter rarely reach 50 km/h, at which air temperature should you be certain to take extra precautions?
2. What happens to the wind chill index as wind speeds get higher and temperatures get lower?

Teacher FYI

Temperature measures the *average* kinetic energy of the molecules in a substance. There is no way to measure the individual kinetic energy of each molecule. In a large group of molecules, the energies of the molecules follow a distribution curve. For a large group of atoms, the energy distribution can be very accurately predicted.

Resource Manager

Chapter Resources Booklet
Transparency Activity, p. 43
Mathematics Skill Activities, p. 37

2 Teach

Temperature

Caption Answer

Figure 12 The particles in B are moving faster than those in A.

Quick Demo

Pour sand into a plastic container until it is one-fourth full. Measure the temperature of the sand. Place a lid on the container and shake it vigorously for several minutes (you may want to have student volunteers take turns at this). Stop shaking and immediately measure the temperature of the sand. Discuss how the sand got its extra thermal energy. from the kinetic energy of the sand during the shaking [L1]
ELL **IS** **Visual-Spatial**

Discussion

Ask students to describe the motion of atoms in a solid, a liquid, and a gas. In a solid the atoms are held close together and vibrate back and forth. In a liquid the atoms are held less tightly than in a solid, and can move past one another. In a gas, the atoms are not held together, and they move in straight lines. [L1]
IS **Linguistic**

Problem-Solving Activity

National Math Standards

Correlation to Mathematics Objectives
1, 2, 4, 5, 6, 7–10

Teaching Strategy

Because the exact temperature at which the wind chill index reaches –29°C when the wind speed is 50 km/h is not given in the table, students' answers will be approximate.

Answers

1. somewhere between 0 and −10°C
2. It decreases.

Discussion

Ask students to give examples of times when their perception of hot and cold depended on the temperature they were used to. Possible answers include getting into a swimming pool—at first the water feels cold, then you get used to it and it feels warmer. L2 🔢 **Logical-Mathematical**

Extension

Have students find out about how other types of thermometers, such as electronic fever thermometers and liquid crystal thermometers, work. Have them make displays illustrating their findings. Electronic fever thermometers use a thermistor to measure temperature. A thermistor is a semiconductor device whose ability to conduct electricity increases with temperature. In liquid crystal thermometers, the configuration of the liquid crystals changes with temperature, and the different configurations reflect different colors of light. Each number on the thermometer has a slightly different liquid crystal behind it so each number becomes colored at a different temperature. L3 🔢 **Linguistic**

✔ Reading Check

Answer because atoms are so small and objects contain so many of them

Measuring Temperature

Some people might say that the water in a swimming pool feels warm, although others might say it feels cool. Because the temperature of the water feels different to different people, you cannot describe or measure temperature accurately by how it feels. Remember that temperature is related to the kinetic energy of all the atoms in an object. You might think that to measure temperature, you must measure the kinetic energy of the atoms. But atoms are so small that even a tiny piece of material consists of trillions and trillions of atoms. Because they are so small and objects contain so many of them, it is impossible to measure the kinetic energy of all the individual atoms. However, a practical way to measure temperature is to use a thermometer, as shown in **Figure 13.**

✔ Reading Check
Why can't the kinetic energy of all the atoms in an object be measured?

The Fahrenheit Scale One temperature scale you might be familiar with is the Fahrenheit (FAYR un hite) scale. On the Fahrenheit scale, the freezing point of water is given the temperature 32°F, and the boiling point is 212°F. The space between the boiling point and the freezing point is divided into 180 equal degrees. The Fahrenheit scale today is used mainly in the United States.

Figure 13
How do thermometers work?
Many materials expand as their temperature increases. For example, the height of a liquid such as alcohol in a hollow tube increases as the temperature of the liquid increases. To make a Celsius thermometer, follow the steps below.

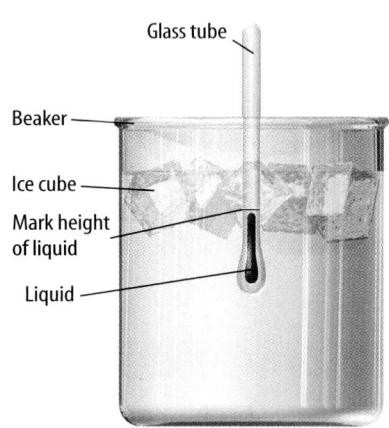

Glass tube
Beaker
Ice cube
Mark height of liquid
Liquid

A Place a glass tube containing the liquid in freezing water and mark the height of the liquid.

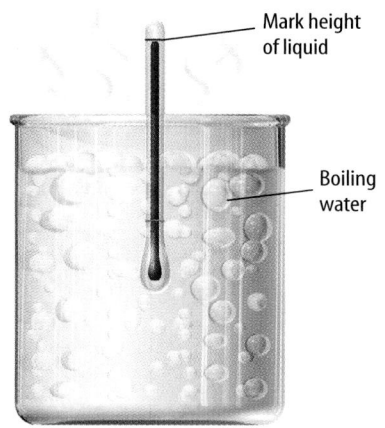

Mark height of liquid
Boiling water

B Place the tube in boiling water and mark the height of the liquid.

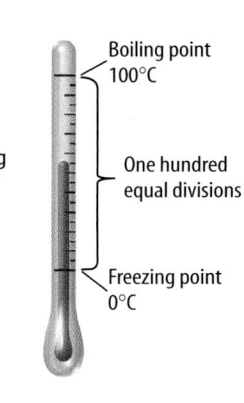

Boiling point 100°C
One hundred equal divisions
Freezing point 0°C

C To make a temperature scale, divide the distance between the marks into equal degrees.

✔ Active Reading

Bubble Map Using a bubble map helps students start ideas flowing about a given topic. Words are clustered to describe a topic or idea that is studied. Students can use a bubble map for prewriting, to generate ideas before writing in their Journals, or to review for a test. Have students design a bubble map to organize the ideas about heat and temperature discussed in this chapter.

The Celsius Scale Another temperature scale that is used more widely throughout the world is the Celsius (SEL see us) scale. On the Celsius temperature scale, the freezing point of water is given the temperature 0°C and the boiling point is given the temperature 100°C. Because there are only 100 Celsius degrees between the boiling and freezing points of water, a temperature change of one Celsius degree is bigger than a change of one Fahrenheit degree.

Heat

On a warm, sunny day when you tilt your head back, you can feel the warmth of the Sun on your face. On a chilly day, putting your cold hands near an open fire warms them up. In both cases, you could feel heat from the Sun and from the fire making you warmer. What is heat?

Look at **Figure 14.** Suppose you pick up a tall glass of iced tea. If you hold the glass for a while, the drink warms up. Your hand is at a higher temperature than the tea, so the atoms and molecules in your hand have a higher kinetic energy than the ones in the iced tea. Kinetic energy from the moving atoms and molecules in your hand is transferred by collisions to the atoms and molecules in the tea.

A transfer of energy from one object to another due to a difference in temperature is called **heat.** Heat flows from warmer objects to cooler ones. In the example just given, heat flows out of your hand and into the glass of iced tea. As you hold the glass, the temperature of the tea increases and the temperature of your skin touching the glass decreases. Heat will stop flowing from your hand to the glass of tea when the temperatures of your hand and the glass are the same.

Heat and Temperature

How much does the temperature of something increase when heat is transferred to it? It depends on two things. One is the amount of material in the object. The other is the kinds of atoms the material is made of. For example, compared to other materials, water is an unusual substance in that it must absorb a large amount of heat before its temperature rises by one degree. Water often is used as a coolant. The purpose of the water in a car's radiator is to carry a large amount of heat away from the engine and keep the engine from being damaged by overheating, as shown in **Figure 15.**

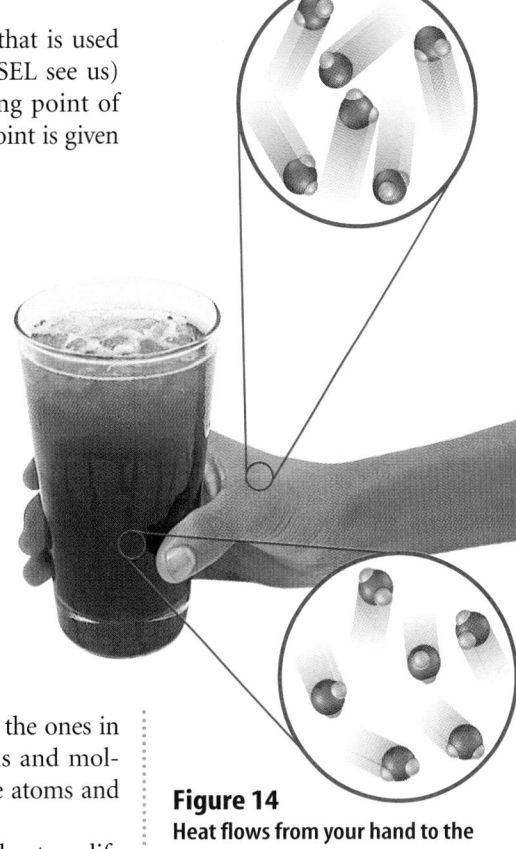

Figure 14
Heat flows from your hand to the glass of iced tea, making your hand feel cold. *Why do people wear gloves in cold weather?*

Figure 15
This car's engine overheated because its cooling system didn't carry enough heat from the engine.

SECTION 2 Temperature **599**

Fun Fact

The Kelvin scale is another temperature scale. One kelvin is equal to one degree Celsius, but the zero of the Kelvin scale is at −273°C. Zero kelvin corresponds to the temperature at which molecules have the least amount of thermal energy. This temperature is called absolute zero.

Heat

Caption Answer

Figure 14 to slow down the rate at which heat flows from their hands to the surroundings

Heat and Temperature

Visual Learning

Figure 15 When a car is overheating, it helps to turn on the heat. How does this help? This helps heat flow away from the engine as it moves into the passenger compartment.

Discussion

Explain that slides on most playgrounds used to be made of metal. Now many are made of plastic. Ask students to compare the way metal and plastic slides react to the Sun's heat. Metal slides become hot in the Sun. Plastic slides can absorb an equal amount of heat without becoming as hot.

Resource Manager

Chapter Resources Booklet
Enrichment, p. 29

Reading and Writing Skill Activities, p. 33

Curriculum Connection

History Steam engines convert thermal energy to mechanical energy. Have students find out about the development of the steam engine and how it affected scientists' understanding of heat and energy. James Watt patented the first practical steam engine in 1769. Thermodynamics and an understanding of energy conservation developed in conjunction with the invention of the steam engine.  L1 **IS** **Linguistic**

Heat and Temperature, *continued*

Discussion

Which would you expect to have a more steady temperature, a pool of water or the dry ground next to it? the pool of water L2 IS **Logical-Mathematical**

Heat on the Move

Use Science Words

Word Usage Have students use the word *conduct* in both its scientific and everyday meanings. Possible answer: Metals conduct heat well. The guide conducted a tour through the museum. Note that in science, conductors and insulators can be used in reference to electricity or heat. L1 ELL IS **Linguistic**

Life Science
INTEGRATION

Have students research the preferred temperature for plants in their area. The U.S. plant zones in a seed catalog or gardening book can be helpful. The zones contain microclimates, even within a large yard, of warmer or cooler areas. Ask students what sort of local plants couldn't grow well if the temperature increased or decreased. L3 IS **Naturalist**

A   Winter   Summer   **B**

Figure 16
Water can absorb and lose a great deal of heat without changing temperature much.
A During the winter, the lake is warmer than the surrounding land. **B** During the summer, the lake is cooler than the surrounding land.

Life Science
INTEGRATION

Heat can be a form of pollution. Sometimes hot water released from power plants can upset river and lake ecosystems, killing fish and other organisms. Research sources of heat pollution in your area.

Lakes and Air Temperature How does the temperature of water in a lake compare to the temperature of the surrounding air on a hot summer day? How do these temperatures compare at night when the air has cooled off? You might have noticed that the water is cooler than the air during the day and warmer than the air at night. This is because it takes longer for a large body of water to warm up or cool down than it does for the surrounding air and land to change temperature. Even from season to season, a large body of water can change temperature less than the surrounding land, as shown in **Figure 16.**

Heat on the Move

A transfer of energy occurs if there is a temperature difference between two areas in contact. Heat is transferred from warm places to cooler ones. This transfer can take place in three ways—radiation, conduction, and convection. Conduction transfers heat mainly through solids and liquids. Convection transfers heat through liquids and gases. Radiation can transfer energy through space.

Conduction Have you ever picked up a metal spoon that was in a pot of boiling water and dropped it right away because the spoon had become hot? The spoon handle became hot because of conduction. **Conduction** (kun DUK shun) is the transfer of energy by collisions between the atoms in a material.

As the part of the spoon in the boiling water became warmer, its atoms and molecules moved faster. These particles then collided with slower-moving particles in the spoon. In these collisions, kinetic energy was transferred from the faster-moving to the slower-moving particles farther up the spoon's handle.

600   CHAPTER 20 Energy

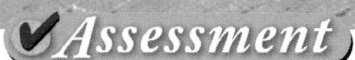
LAB DEMONSTRATION

Purpose to model thermodynamic collisions
Materials 10 marbles (same size), glass pie pan, overhead projector
Procedure Place 5 marbles in the pan on an overhead projector. Shake the pan slightly to imitate a cold substance and rapidly to simulate a hot substance. Then "mix" the substances by adding 5 fast-moving

marbles to a pan of stationary or slowly moving marbles.
Expected Outcome As marbles collide, the faster marbles transfer kinetic energy to the slower ones. The "hot" atoms slow down as the "cold" atoms speed up, until all are moving at the same average speed.

✔️ *Assessment*

What would happen if you added a few stationary marbles to a plate of rapidly moving marbles? The moving marbles would transfer kinetic energy to the stationary ones, so that the marbles originally moving quickly would slow down and those that were stationary would speed up.

Bumping Along Even though conduction is a transfer of kinetic energy from particle to particle, in a solid the particles involved don't travel from one place to another. As shown in **Figure 17,** they simply move back and forth in place, bumping into each other and transferring energy from faster-moving particles to slower-moving ones. Conduction usually occurs in solids.

✔ **Reading Check** *How is energy transferred by conduction?*

Conductors It's dinnertime and the hamburgers are frozen solid. This is one time when you want to transfer heat rapidly. You could put a frozen hamburger on a metal tray to speed up the thawing process. Materials through which it is easy to transfer energy are thermal conductors. Most metals are good conductors of heat. Metals such as gold, silver, and copper are the best thermal conductors. Copper is widely available and less expensive than gold or silver. Some cooking pans are made of steel but have copper bottoms. A copper bottom conducts heat more evenly. It helps spread heat across the bottom surface of the pan to prevent hot spots from forming. This allows food to cook evenly.

Insulators Some materials are poor conductors of heat. These materials can be used as thermal insulators. When you are cold, for example, you can put on a sweater or a jacket or add another blanket to your bed. You are keeping yourself warm by adding insulation. The clothes and the blanket are poor conductors of heat. In fact, they make it more difficult for heat to escape from your body. By trapping your body heat around you, you feel warmer.

Blankets and clothes help keep you warm because they are made of materials that contain many air spaces, as shown in **Figure 18.** Air is a good insulator, so materials that contain air are also good insulators. For example, building insulation is made from materials that contain air spaces. Materials made of plastics also are often good insulators. If you put a plastic spoon in boiling water, it takes a long time for it to get hot. Many cooking pans have plastic handles that won't melt instead of metal ones. These handles remain at a comfortable temperature while the pans are used for cooking. Other examples of insulators include wood, rubber, and ceramic materials such as tiles.

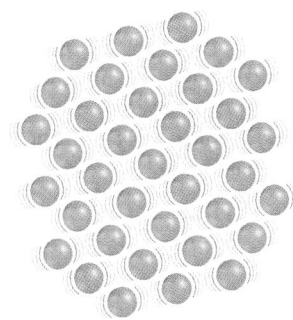

Figure 17
In a solid, atoms collide with each other as they vibrate back and forth.

Figure 18
Under high magnification, this insulating material is seen to contain many air spaces.

SECTION 2 Temperature **601**

Purpose Students see the relationship between temperature and kinetic energy. L1 ELL

LS **Visual-Spatial**

Materials three transparent plastic cups, supply of hot, room-temperature and cold water, dropper, food coloring

Teaching Strategy Ask students whether it is important to use the same number of drops in each container. yes; to control variables

Safety Precaution Make sure the water is not hot enough to burn students.

Analysis

1. Hot water was fastest, cold water slowest. The higher the temperature, the faster the particles moved.
2. The greater the water temperature, the more motion the water molecules had, and the more they pushed the food coloring particles.
3. the hot-water cup

✓Assessment

Performance Ask the students to design a similar experiment to compare the energy of hot and cold gases. **What could be used to measure the rate of dispersion?** smoke or smells Use **Performance Assessment in the Science Classroom**, p. 105.

Figure 19
The furnace's fan helps circulate hot air through your home. Warmer air particles move upward while cooler air particles move downward.

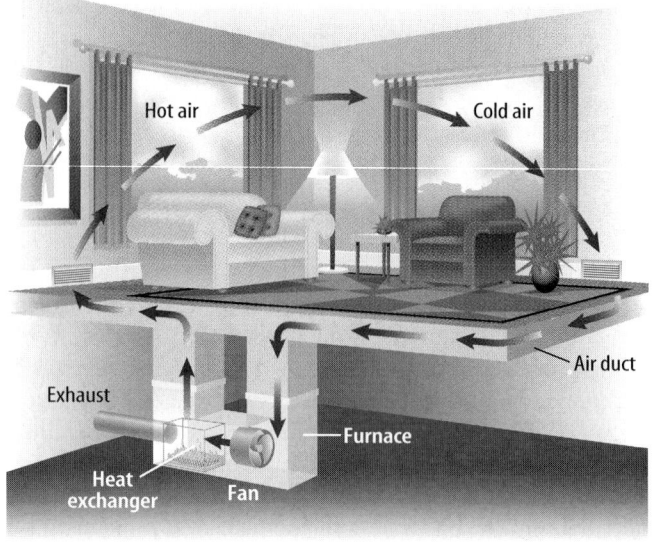

Hot air　Cold air

Air duct

Exhaust

Heat exchanger　Fan　Furnace

Mini LAB

Comparing Energy Content

Procedure

1. Pour equal amounts of **hot, cold, and room-temperature water** into each of **three transparent, labeled containers.**
2. Measure and record the temperature of the water in each container.
3. Use a **dropper** to gently put a drop of **food coloring** in the center of each container.
4. After 2 min, observe each container.

Analysis

1. Based on the speed at which the food coloring spreads through the water, rank the containers from fastest to slowest.
2. Infer how water temperature affected the movement of the food coloring.
3. In which container do the water particles have the most kinetic energy?

Feeling the Heat Think about getting into a car that has been closed up on a sunny day. Do you prefer a car that has fabric-covered or vinyl-covered seats? Even though the masses of the seats are similar and the temperatures of the surroundings are the same, the vinyl material feels hotter on your skin than the fabric does. How hot something feels also is affected by how fast heat flows, as well as the actual temperature. Vinyl is a better conductor than fabric, so heat flows to your skin more rapidly from the vinyl than from the fabric. As a result, the vinyl feels hotter than the fabric does.

Convection Heat also can be transferred by particles that do not stay in one place but rather move from one place to another. **Convection** (kun VEK shun) transfers heat when particles move between objects or areas that differ in temperature. This type of transfer is most common in gases and liquids. As temperature increases, particles move around more quickly, and the distance between particles increases. This causes density to decrease as temperature increases. Cooler, denser material then forces the warmer, less dense material to move upward.

Some homes are heated by convection. Look at **Figure 19.** Air is warmed in the furnace. The warm, less dense air is then forced up through the air duct by the furnace fan. The warm air gets pushed up through the room by the cooler air around it. As the warm air cools, it becomes more dense. Cool, dense air sinks and is then pulled into the return air duct by the furnace fan to be warmed again and recirculated.

Resource Manager

Chapter Resources Booklet
MiniLAB, p. 4
Reinforcement, p. 26
Directed Reading for Content Mastery, p. 19

Cultural Diversity

Igloos The Inuit demonstrated an understanding of convection in the design of igloos. The entrance is a tunnel lower than the inside of the igloo. Cold air sinks into the tunnel, but warm air stays in the igloo.

Examples of Convection Eagles and hawks float effortlessly high in the air. Sometimes a bird can stay in the air without flapping its wings because it is held up by a thermal.

As shown in **Figure 20,** a thermal is a column of warm air that is forced up as cold air around it sinks. It is a convection current in the air.

Convection also occurs in liquids. In a pot of boiling water, the warmer, less dense water is forced up as the cooler, denser water sinks. Convection currents on a larger scale are formed in oceans by cold water flowing from the poles and warm water flowing from tropical regions.

Radiation Radiation (ray dee AY shun) transfers energy by waves. These waves can be visible light waves or types of waves that you cannot see. When these waves strike an object, their energy can be absorbed and the object's temperature rises. Radiation can travel through air and even through a vacuum.

The Sun transfers energy to Earth through radiation. You take advantage of radiation when you warm yourself by a fire. Heat is transferred by radiation from the fire and you become warmer. You also can use radiation to cook food. A microwave oven cooks food by using microwave radiation to transfer energy to the food.

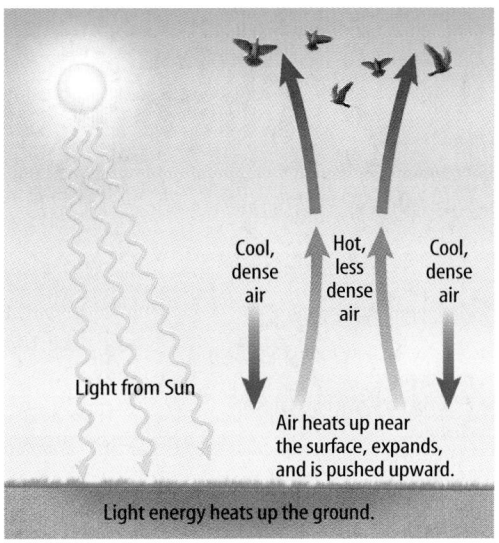

Cool, dense air
Hot, less dense air
Cool, dense air

Light from Sun

Air heats up near the surface, expands, and is pushed upward.

Light energy heats up the ground.

Figure 20
Thermals form when hot, thin air rises up through cooler, denser air.

Section 2 Assessment

1. List three ways that heat is transferred and give an example for each.

2. How are temperature and heat different?

3. What condition must exist for transfer of heat to occur?

4. Which type of energy transfer can take place with little or no matter present? Explain.

5. **Think Critically** Popcorn can be cooked in a hot-air popper, in a microwave oven, or in a pan on the stove. Identify how energy is transferred in each method.

Skill Builder Activities

6. **Classifying** Classify the following events into energy transfer by conduction, convection, or radiation: *sunlight heats water, pot handle gets hot, smoke rises, hot metal glows,* and *ice feels cold.* **For more help, refer to the** Science Skill Handbook.

7. **Solving One-Step Equations** To change a temperature from Fahrenheit to Celsius, subtract 32 from the Fahrenheit temperature then multiply by 5/9. If the temperature is 77°F, what is the Celsius temperature? **For more help, refer to the** Math Skill Handbook.

SECTION 2 Temperature **603**

Assess

Reteach

Illustrate the three types of heat transfer by reminding students of sitting by a fire. The warm smoke rises upward through the cooler air, transferring heat by convection. The heat from the fire radiates in waves. If one end of a metal tool is put into the fire, it will conduct heat to the other end, burning your hand. L2 ELL **Linguistic**

Challenge

Define pressure for students as force per unit area. The more numerous or forceful the collisions of a gas with the walls of a container, the greater the pressure. Ask them to explain why raising the temperature of a fixed volume of gas would raise the pressure of the gas. When the temperature is raised, the molecules in the gas move faster. They collide more frequently and at higher speeds with the sides of the container, increasing the pressure. L3 **Logical-Mathematical**

✓Assessment

Process Tell students to draw an illustration of a pot of water heating on the stove. On the drawing, indicate the source of energy, what kind of energy it is, how it is transferred to the pot and then to the water, and what happens to the water as it heats. Use **Performance Assessment in the Science Classroom,** p. 127. P

SECTION

Chemical Energy

Bellringer Transparency

Display the Section Focus Transparency for Section 3. Use the accompanying Transparency Activity Master. L2

ELL

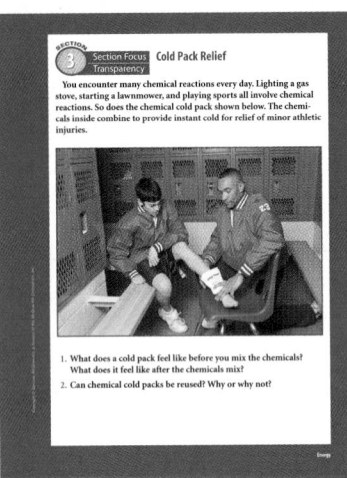

Tie to Prior Knowledge

Discuss with students what they have learned about ways energy can be stored. Remind them that energy can be stored gravitationally by lifting an object and that chemical energy is stored in food and muscles.

As You Read

What You'll Learn

■ **Determine** how chemical energy is produced.
■ **Explain** how reaction rates are changed.

Vocabulary
endothermic reaction
exothermic reaction
catalyst

Why It's Important
Chemical energy makes it possible for your body to move, grow, and stay warm.

Figure 21
Chemical reactions can produce light energy.
A Each point of greenish light in this picture is a firefly.
B A chemical reaction inside a firefly's body produces light.

Chemical Reactions and Energy

On a hot summer night, you might have seen fireflies glowing, like those in **Figure 21.** Did you ever wonder how they make their eerie, blinking light? If you have seen light sticks, which glow for a short period of time, you have observed the same process that causes the fireflies' glow. Energy in the form of light is released when a chemical reaction takes place inside the light stick. A burner on a gas stove releases heat and light energy because of a chemical reaction taking place. You might not realize it, but every day you make use of the energy released by many chemical reactions.

What is a chemical reaction? In a chemical reaction, compounds are broken down or new compounds are formed. Sometimes both processes occur. Some chemical reactions occur when atoms or molecules come together. New compounds are formed when atoms and molecules combine and bonds form between them. A compound is broken down when the bonds between the atoms that make up the compound are broken. These atoms are then available to recombine to form new compounds.

When a fire burns, a chemical reaction occurs. Bonds between the atoms in some of the compounds that make up the wood are broken. These atoms then combine with atoms in the air and form new compounds. As these new compounds are formed, heat and light are given off.

Section ✔Assessment Planner

PORTFOLIO
Visual Learning, p. 605
PERFORMANCE ASSESSMENT
Skill Builder Activities, p. 608
See page 616 for more options.

CONTENT ASSESSMENT
Section, p. 608
Challenge, p. 608
Chapter, pp. 616–617

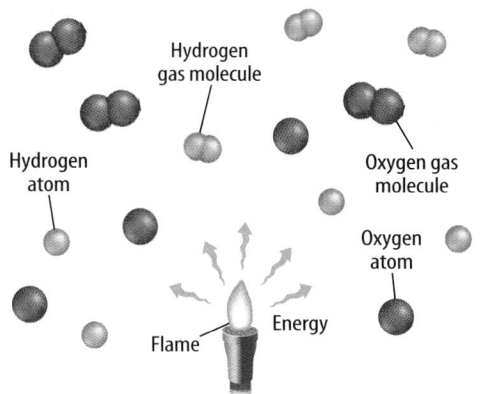

A The added energy from the flame causes the bonds to break in the oxygen gas and hydrogen gas.

B When the new bonds form between hydrogen and oxygen to produce water particles, energy is released.

Chemical Bonds Energy is stored in the bonds between the atoms in a compound. The stored energy in the chemical bonds is a form of potential energy called chemical energy.

The chemical energy stored in oil, gas, and coal is an important source of energy that is used every day. The chemical energy stored in food provides a source of energy for your body. The muscles in your body transform some of this chemical energy into kinetic energy and heat when they move. List some of the other sources of chemical energy you used today.

Energy in Reactions

In every chemical reaction, transformations in energy occur. To break bonds, energy must be added. The reverse is also true. When bonds form, energy is released. Often energy must be added before the reaction can begin. For example, energy is needed to start the reaction between hydrogen and oxygen to form water. Look at **Figure 22.** When a lighted match is placed in a mixture of hydrogen gas and oxygen gas, the mixture will explode and water will form. The energy to begin the reaction comes from the heat supplied by the flame. As the reaction occurs, bonds form between hydrogen and oxygen atoms, and water molecules form. The energy released as the bonds form results in the explosion.

After the hydrogen and oxygen atoms are bound together to form a water molecule, it is difficult to split them apart. Energy—usually supplied by electricity, heat, or light—is required to break the chemical bonds.

✔ **Reading Check** *What is required to break chemical bonds?*

Figure 22
Oxygen and hydrogen gas will not react unless energy is added.

Visual Learning

Figure 22 Review with students the synthesis of water shown in Figures 22A and B. Have students follow the process with their fingers as you read the description from the text. Make sure students understand that energy is needed to initiate the process, but once started, the process gives off more than enough energy to keep itself going. L1 ELL **IS Visual-Spatial**

Chemical Reactions and Energy

Quick Demo

The energy stored in chemical bonds can be transformed to light energy when you crush certain crystals. Use a glass to crush wintergreen candies in a completely dark room, and students will see sparks. L1 ELL
IS Visual-Spatial

Energy in Reactions

Make a Model

Have students use two magnetic balls to make an analogy to making and breaking chemical bonds. When you pull the magnets apart, you put energy into the reaction to break the bond. When the magnets are allowed to pull together, energy is released; the potential energy of their position is transformed into the kinetic energy of motion. L2 **IS Kinesthetic**

Teacher **FYI**

An explosion occurs when a substance expands very quickly. In the synthesis of water, the energy released by the reaction gives the newly formed water molecules a large amount of kinetic energy, which makes them move very quickly. This causes the gaseous water to expand and explode.

✔ **Reading Check**

Answer energy

Extension

Have students identify some endothermic processes and determine the kind of energy that is used to make them happen. The dissolution of Epsom salt in water is an endothermic process. The molecules of Epsom salt take thermal energy from the water, so as they dissolve, the temperature of the water decreases. L3 IS **Linguistic**

Teacher FYI

The dissolving of a substance is a physical change, not a chemical change. Therefore, when a substance uses energy to dissolve, the process cannot be called an endothermic chemical reaction. It is, nonetheless, an endothermic process.

Visual Learning ——○

Figure 23 Have students make a concept map sequencing the events shown in this figure. P

IDENTIFYING
Misconceptions

Students may think that because energy is needed to start a particular reaction, the reaction is endothermic. In fact, many reactions that require energy to start are exothermic. This is because as the chemicals react, they release more energy than they absorb.

Energy-Absorbing Reactions Some chemical reactions need a constant supply of energy to keep them going. These reactions absorb energy. A chemical reaction that absorbs heat energy is called an **endothermic** (en duh THUR mihk) **reaction.** Endothermic chemical reactions often take place in the preparation of food. Thermal energy is absorbed by the food as it cooks. For example, an endothermic reaction takes place in baking some kinds of cookies. The baking soda absorbs energy and produces a gas that puffs up the cookies.

Chemical reactions occur when sunlight strikes the leaves of green plants. These chemical reactions convert the energy in sunlight into chemical energy contained in a type of sugar. Oxygen also is produced by these chemical reactions. This process, shown in **Figure 23,** is called photosynthesis. When the plant is deprived of sunlight, the reactions stop. Photosynthesis is probably the most important endothermic process on Earth. Plants provide you, and almost all other living things, with food and oxygen through photosynthesis.

Figure 23
In photosynthesis, plants absorb light energy and make oxygen and sugar from water and carbon dioxide.

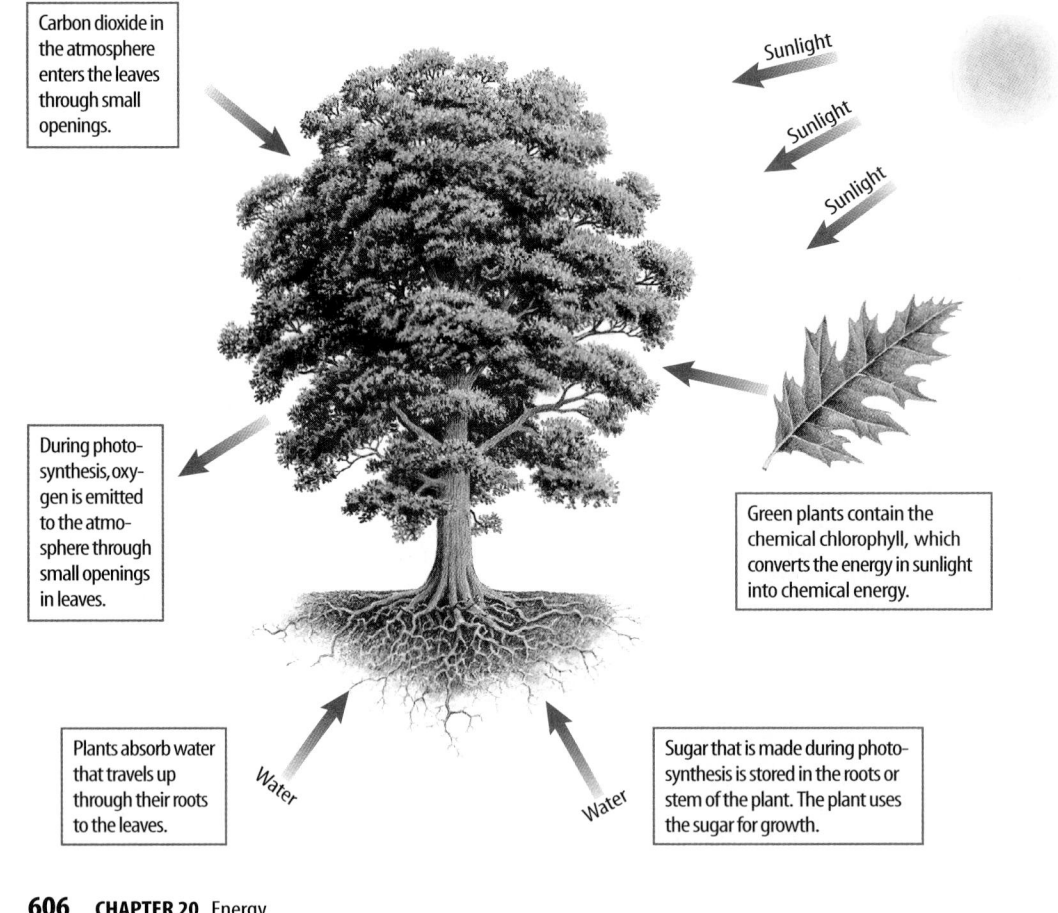

Carbon dioxide in the atmosphere enters the leaves through small openings.

During photosynthesis, oxygen is emitted to the atmosphere through small openings in leaves.

Sunlight

Sunlight

Sunlight

Green plants contain the chemical chlorophyll, which converts the energy in sunlight into chemical energy.

Plants absorb water that travels up through their roots to the leaves.

Water

Water

Sugar that is made during photosynthesis is stored in the roots or stem of the plant. The plant uses the sugar for growth.

Inclusion Strategies

Learning Disabled The following endothermic process produces a difference in temperature that can be felt with bare skin. Dissolve a large amount of table salt in one of two plastic cups of room-temperature water. Hold both cups to your cheeks and compare the temperature. Energy was absorbed to break the chemical bonds between sodium and chlorine ions. L1
ELL IS **Kinesthetic**

Curriculum Connection

Health Portable cold packs taken camping and hiking and used to treat athletic injuries use endothermic processes. Have students find out how these packs work. To start the reaction, a pack is kneaded. This breaks a barrier and mixes two substances together. The resulting endothermic reaction makes the pack cold. L3 IS **Linguistic**

Energy-Releasing Reactions Endothermic chemical reactions are usually important because of the compounds the reactions produce. Other reactions are important because they release energy. **Exothermic** (ek soh THUR mihk) **reactions** are chemical reactions that release heat energy. A chemical hand warmer releases heat when an exothermic reaction takes place inside the hand warmer. When a substance burns, atoms in the substance combine with oxygen atoms in the air. An exothermic reaction occurs, and energy in the form of heat and light is released. The exothermic reaction that occurs when a material burns by combining with oxygen is called combustion. Burning oil, coal, and gas produces much of the energy needed to heat homes and schools. What are some other exothermic reactions?

 **Reading Check** *What are chemical reactions that give off energy called?*

Rate of Reaction Chemical reactions can occur at different rates. They occur very fast when fireworks explode. However, if you leave tools or a skateboard outside for a long time, you might notice the metal parts slowly becoming rusty, as shown in **Figure 24.** Rusting is a chemical reaction that occurs when a metal combines with oxygen. It occurs much more slowly than a fireworks explosion. Likewise, when silver is exposed to air, it tarnishes. This chemical reaction, however, occurs much more slowly than the burning of a candle's wick.

In your body an enormous number of chemical reactions are occurring every second. The rates of these reactions are carefully controlled by your body to enable it to function properly.

SCIENCE Online

Research Visit the Glencoe Science Web site at **science.glencoe.com** for information about the heat released at deep-sea vents. Make a poster describing what you learn.

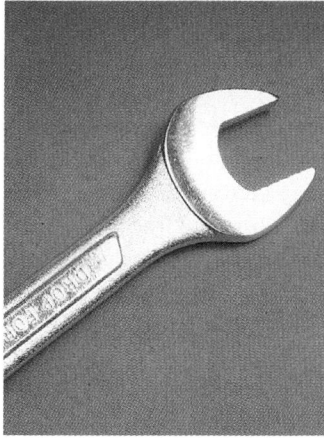

Figure 24
Rust is a chemical combination of iron and oxygen.

 **A** This photo shows a wrench before it rusts.

B This photo shows a wrench after it rusts.

Use Science Words

Word Meaning To help students keep exothermic reactions and endothermic reactions straight, have them find out what the prefixes *ex-* and *endo-* can mean. Then ask them to list other words with these prefixes. The prefix *ex-* means "outside" or "away from." Words include *extrude, exceed, extraterrestrial,* and *exercise.* The prefix *endo-* means "within." Words include *endocrine gland,* a gland that secretes hormones directly into the bloodstream. L2 ELL [N] **Linguistic**

Quick Demo

Light a match as an example of an exothermic reaction. Point out that you have to use energy to start the reaction. L2
[N] **Visual-Spatial**

 **Reading Check**

Answer exothermic reactions

Discussion

Why are foods stored at cold temperatures to prevent spoilage? At cold temperatures, the chemical reactions that spoil food occur much more slowly. Milk, for example, will keep for a week in the refrigerator but less than a day on the countertop.

Resource Manager

Chapter Resources Booklet
　Enrichment, p. 30
　Reinforcement, p. 27
Physical Science Critical Thinking/Problem Solving, p. 10

SCIENCE Online
Internet Addresses
_____
_____
_____
Explore the Glencoe Science Web site at **science.glencoe.com** to find out more about topics in this section.

Reteach

Tell students that when iron oxide is heated, it reacts with carbon to form iron and carbon dioxide. **Is this an exothermic or an endothermic reaction?** endothermic L2

IS Logical-Mathematical

Challenge

You want to develop a soda can that will chill the soda when it is opened. How would you do this? Find a rapid endothermic reaction that absorbs a large amount of thermal energy. Figure out a way to have the opening of the can start the reaction. The thermal energy absorbed from the soda by the reaction will cool the soda. Make sure the reaction does not take place in the soda. The reactants must be safe to use with food, even if they are separated from it. L3

IS Logical-Mathematical

✔ Assessment

Oral What effect would chilling a chemical reaction have on its reaction rate? Why? It would slow the reaction rate, because with less kinetic energy the reactants could not mix to break and form bonds as quickly. Use **PASC**, p. 89.

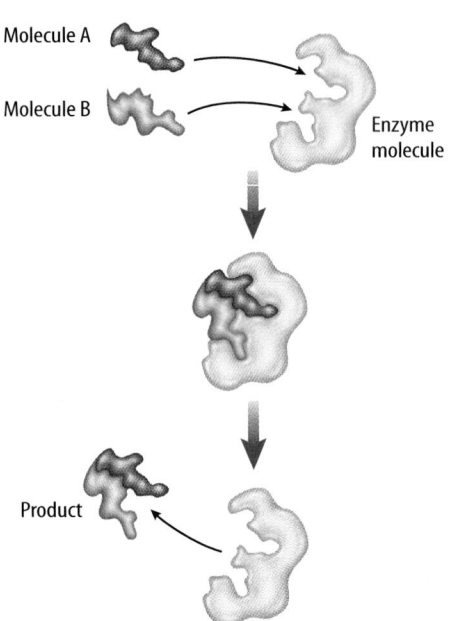

Molecule A

Molecule B

Enzyme molecule

Product

Figure 25
An enzyme makes a chemical reaction go faster by bringing certain molecules together. Only the molecules that have the right shape to fit on the surface of the enzyme will react.

Changing the Rate of Reaction

Two ways to change the rate of a chemical reaction are changing the temperature and adding a type of compound called a catalyst. For example, if you pour cake batter into a pan and leave it on a table for several hours, nothing seems to happen. However, if you put the pan in a hot oven, the cake batter becomes a cake. Raising the temperature of the cake batter in the hot oven causes substances in the batter to react more quickly.

A **catalyst** (KAT ul ust) is a substance that changes the rate of a chemical reaction without any permanent change to its own structure. Many cell processes in your body are controlled by the presence of catalysts, called enzymes, as shown in **Figure 25.** Enzymes are found throughout your body and are important for growth, respiration, and digestion. When you chew a piece of bread, glands in your mouth produce saliva that contains an enzyme. The enzyme in saliva acts as a catalyst to help break down starches in food into smaller molecules.

Many other chemical reactions depend on catalysts to help them go faster. The production of vegetable shortening, synthetic rubber, and high-octane gasoline are all chemical processes that occur with the help of catalysts.

Section 3 Assessment

1. How is chemical energy produced?
2. What happens to bonds when new products are made?
3. Name two ways to speed up a reaction.
4. Describe how radiant light energy from the Sun is transformed into chemical energy by the process of photosynthesis.
5. **Think Critically** Gasoline can react explosively with oxygen in air. Why doesn't the gasoline in a car's gas tank explode when the gas cap is removed?

Skill Builder Activities

6. **Drawing Conclusions** Identify three processes that take place in your classroom that involve chemical reactions. Which of these reactions are endothermic? Exothermic? **For more help, refer to the** Science Skill Handbook.
7. **Using a Word Processor** On a word processor, write one sentence per paragraph to summarize the main idea of each paragraph in this section. **For more help, refer to the** Technology Skill Handbook.

608 CHAPTER 20 Energy

Answers to Section Assessment

1. It is produced in chemical reactions in which bonds are formed as energy is added.
2. They are formed or broken.
3. raise the temperature, stir, add a catalyst
4. Light energy from the Sun is absorbed by chlorophyll in plant leaves. A chemical reaction occurs that converts CO_2 and H_2O into a sugar. Chemical energy is stored in the chemical bonds of the sugar molecule.
5. Energy needs to be added.
6. Check students' work. Reactions that produce energy, such as those in a burner, are exothermic. Reactions that absorb energy, such as those in a plant growing on the windowsill, are endothermic.
7. Check students' sentences.

Activity

Converting Potential and Kinetic Energy

Imagine standing at the top of a mountain ready to ski down its slope. Because of your height on the mountain, you have potential energy. As you ski down the side of the mountain, your speed and kinetic energy increase, but as you lose height, your potential energy decreases. Where does your potential energy go? Where does your kinetic energy come from?

What You'll Investigate
How can you measure the conversion of potential energy into kinetic energy?

Materials
stiff piece of card-
board (1 m)
triple-beam balance
table tennis ball
tennis ball

baseball
stopwatch
meterstick

Goals
- ■ **Measure** and calculate the potential and kinetic energies of the balls.
- ■ **Observe** the conversion between potential energy and kinetic energy.

Procedure

1. Copy the data table into your Science Journal.
2. Lean your cardboard against a chair.
3. **Measure** and record the height and length of the board.
4. **Measure** and record the mass of each ball.
5. Let each ball roll from the top of the board to the floor. Measure and record the time it takes for each ball to roll the length of the board.

Conclude and Apply

1. **Calculate** the potential energy of each ball at the top of the board by multiplying the mass times the height times 9.8.
2. **Calculate** the average velocity of each ball as it reaches the floor by dividing the length of the board by the time.

Energy Factors				
Type of Ball	Mass of Ball (kg)	Height of Board (m)	Length of Board (m)	Time (s)
Table tennis ball	(0.02)	(0.7)	(1)	(2.54)
Tennis ball	(0.06)	(0.7)	(1)	(2.13)
Baseball	(0.15)	(0.7)	(1)	(1.45)

3. **Calculate** the average kinetic energy of each ball as it rolled down the board by multiplying the mass times the velocity squared, and dividing by 2.
4. Which ball had the greatest kinetic energy? Infer why this ball had more kinetic energy.
5. **Infer** how the table tennis ball could have more potential energy than the baseball.
6. **Infer** the relationship between each ball's potential energy at the top of the slope and its average kinetic energy.

Communicating Your Data

Compare your data with the data collected by your classmates. **For more help, refer to the** Science Skill Handbook.

Resource Manager

Chapter Resources Booklet
Lab Activity, pp. 13–14
Activity Worksheet, pp. 5–6

Communicating Your Data

Students should discuss why their conclusions did or did not agree. They can cite their references to support their arguments.

Activity

BENCH TESTED

Purpose Students will observe potential energy converting to kinetic energy. [L2] **IS** **Kinesthetic**

Process Skills collecting data, measuring, making and using tables, recording data, interpreting data

Time Required 40 minutes

Safety Precautions Students should wear safety goggles during all lab activities.

Teaching Strategy A student should catch the balls at the end of the board to keep the balls from disturbing other groups.

Answers to Questions
1. Answers will vary. Students should use the equation $PE = mgh$.
2. Answers will vary.
3. Answers will vary. Students should use the equation $KE = mv^2/2$.
4. The baseball; it had the greatest mass.
5. If the table-tennis ball were high enough, its increased height could make up for its lower mass.
6. They should be nearly equal. There are some differences in the calculations due to friction and experimental error.

✓ *Assessment*

Oral What law does this lab illustrate? The law of conservation of energy. Use **Performance assessment in the Science Classroom,** p. 89.

Activity

What You'll Investigate

Purpose

Students will compare how two different substances absorb thermal energy. L2 ELL COOP LEARN
IS Visual-Spatial

Process Skills

comparing and contrasting, identifying and controlling variables, making and using tables, interpreting data, forming operational definitions

Time Required

50 minutes

Safety Precautions

For safety, you may want to dispense the hot water to students. Do not use water hot enough to cause burns.

Procedure

Teaching Strategy

Explain to students that when the temperature of the water no longer changes, the water is at the same temperature as the material inside the bag.

Tie to Prior Knowledge

Ask students about any prior experience heating substances in the kitchen. **What substances heat quickly or slowly in a microwave?** bread quickly, water slowly **Does it take as long to boil a large pot of water as a small pot?** A pot with more water, over the same heat source, will take longer to come to a boil than a pot with less water.

Activity

Comparing Temperature Changes

How does the temperature of a substance change as heat is added to it? The temperatures of equal amounts of different substances change differently as they are heated. In this lab you will determine how the temperatures of two different materials change as they absorb and release heat.

What You'll Investigate

Which material increases in temperature the least as it absorbs heat?

Goals

- **Measure** temperature.
- **Calculate** temperature change.
- **Infer** a material's ability to absorb heat.

Materials

−10°C to 110°C range thermometers (4)
*computer probe
self-sealing freezer bags (2)
water (100 mL)
ice cubes (2 to 3)
pancake syrup (100 mL)
*corn syrup
400 to 600 mL beakers (4)
*heat-safe glass containers
spoon or stirring rod
*Alternate materials

Safety Precautions 🥽 🧤 🧼 💧

Use care when handling the heated bags and hot water. Do not taste, eat, or drink any materials used in the lab. Take care when handling glass thermometers.

Inclusion Strategies

Learning Impaired Students should heat two bags with equal amounts of water and syrup in two beakers of hot water. After a set amount of time, the bag containing syrup should be warmer to the touch than the bag containing water.

Procedure

1. **Design** two data tables to record your temperature measurements of the hot- and cold-water beakers. Use the sample table to help you.

2. Pour 200 mL of hot tap water (about 90°C) into each of two large beakers.

3. Pour 200 mL of cool tap water into each of two large beakers. Add two or three ice cubes and stir until the ice melts.

4. Pour 100 mL of room-temperature water into one bag and 100 mL of syrup into the other bag. Tightly seal both bags.

5. **Record** the starting water temperature of each hot-water beaker. Place each bag into its own beaker of hot water.

6. **Record** the water temperature in each of the hot-water beakers every 2 minutes until the temperature does not change.

7. **Record** the starting water temperature of each cold-water beaker. If any ice cubes remain, remove them from the cold water.

8. Carefully remove the bags from the hot water and put each into its own beaker of cold water.

9. **Record** the water temperature in each of the cold-water beakers every 2 minutes until no change in temperature occurs.

Water Temperatures—Hot Beaker			
Water Bag		Syrup Bag	
Time (min)	Temp. (°C)	Time (min)	Temp. (°C)
0		0	
2	Answers	2	Answers
4	will	4	will
6	vary.	6	vary.
8		8	

Conclude and Apply

1. Look at your data. Which beaker of hot water reached a lower temperature—the beaker with the water-filled or syrup-filled bag?

2. In which beaker of cold water did you observe the greater temperature change after adding the bags?

3. Which material absorbed more heat? Which released more heat?

4. **Infer** from your results whether 100 mL of water or 100 mL of syrup at the same temperature contains more energy. Explain.

ommunicating Your Data

Compare your results with the results of other students in your classroom. Explain any differences in your data or your conclusions. **For more help, refer to the** Science Skill Handbook.

Expected Outcome

Results will vary depending on the type of syrup. Students will observe that the beaker with the water-filled bag will warm up more slowly than the beaker with the syrup-filled bag. Likewise, the beaker with the water-filled bag will cool more slowly than the beaker with the syrup-filled bag.

Conclude and Apply

1. the beaker with the syrup-filled bag
2. the cold-water beaker containing the syrup-filled bag
3. The syrup absorbed more heat. The syrup also released more heat.
4. Because the syrup caused a larger temperature change, it contains more thermal energy.

Error Analysis

There could be loss or gain of heat to the environment. Unless they are dried off between experiments, bags of water and syrup could carry hot water into the cold beakers.

✔Assessment

Oral Have students verbally describe the reasoning they used to answer the questions. Encourage them to think of examples to help them describe the effects of thermal energy transfer between different types and amounts of materials. Use **Performance Assessment in the Science Classroom,** p. 143.

ommunicating Your Data

Graphs of the data would make it easy for students to compare their results. Refer to Making Graphs in the Skill Handbook.

Resource Manager

Chapter Resources Booklet
    Activity Worksheet, pp. 7–8
Lab Management and Safety, p. 37

Science and Language Arts

Hiroshima

by Lawrence Yep

On August 6, 1945, an American B-29 bomber dropped a new weapon called the atom bomb on the Japanese city of Hiroshima. The bomb destroyed 60 percent of the city, killing between 90,000 and 140,000 people.

Everything is made up of tiny particles called atoms. They are so small they are invisible to the eye. Energy holds these parts together like glue. When the atom breaks up into its parts, the energy goes free and there is a big explosion.

Inside the bomb, one uranium atom collides with another. Those atoms both break up. Their parts smash into more atoms and split them in turn.[1]

This is called a chain reaction. There are millions and millions of atoms inside the bomb. When they all break up, it is believed that the atom bomb will be equal to 20,000 tons of dynamite. In 1945, it is the most powerful weapon ever made....

Up until then, no single bomb has ever caused so much damage or so many deaths.

The wind mixes their dust with the dirt and debris. Then it sends everything boiling upward in a tall purple-gray column. When the top of the dust cloud spreads out, it looks like a strange, giant mushroom.

The bomb goes off 580 meters above the ground. The temperature reaches several million degrees Celsius immediately.

One mile away, the fierce heat starts fires.

Even two miles away, people are burned by the heat.

[1] A chain reaction occurs when the nuclei of unstable uranium atoms emit particles called neutrons. These neutrons strike other uranium nuclei, causing them to split and emit more neutrons, and so on.

Pre-Reading Activity

Students should take turns reading aloud Toshi Maruki's non-fiction storybook, *Hiroshima No Pika (The Flash of Hiroshima)*, which recalls her own experiences as a child when Hiroshima was bombed. They should then do a reading reaction quick-write, putting themselves in Maruki's shoes.

Respond to the Reading

Active Reading Strategies

Visualize Suggest to students that they keep the image of a city in their mind's eye as they read this selection. They can form pictures in their minds of how the force of the bomb might change the appearance of a city. Tell them to pay attention to the details the writer gives that might help them visualize the destruction. Ask them how they picture Hiroshima after the bombing.

Respond Have students think about their reactions as they read about the power of the atom bomb and the heat it produced. After they finish reading the selection, have them imagine the effects the bomb had on the human and animal populations as well as the environment.

Answers to Questions

1. The bombing of Hiroshima was one of the most significant events of the twentieth century.
2. It uses a chain reaction to release energy.
3. It resulted in more damage and more deaths than any other single bomb.

Reading Further

Other sources on this topic include:

National Japanese American Historical Society, 1855 Folsom Street #161, San Francisco, CA 94103

Our World Class of '44 Project, compiled by Diane Honda, funded by the Civil Liberties Public Education Fund/printed by Herff Jones Yearbook Company, 1998

Inferno: The Firebombing of Japan, March 9–August 15, 1945, by Edwin P. Hoyt, Madison Books, 2000

Desert Exile: The Uprooting of a Japanese American Family, by Yoshiko Uchida, University of Washington Press, 1982

Understanding Literature

Summarize When you summarize something, you mention only the main ideas and necessary supporting details. Much of the information of the original text will not be mentioned in the summary, but the main ideas should be obvious.

Instead of providing a complete account, the author of *Hiroshima* has chosen to summarize the events. He briefly explains the science behind the atom bomb. He also gives some details about the destruction after the bomb was dropped on Hiroshima, Japan. The author has not completely explained how the bomb worked. He also has omitted specifics about the damage to Hiroshima. He is trying to give only a general idea of what happened.

Science Connection In this chapter you learned that energy can be released by exothermic chemical reactions when the bonds between atoms are broken. In this excerpt from *Hiroshima*, Lawrence Yep describes the effects of the energy released in a different process—the energy released when the nuclei of atoms are split. This reaction released an enormous amount of energy that destroyed a city.

Linking Science and Writing

Write a Summary You are summarizing when you tell a friend about a movie or sporting event that you watched. Scientists summarize when they report their findings from experiments. Reread one of the sections in this chapter and identify the main ideas and important, supporting details. Imagine that you have one minute to explain the information in the section to a new student. Write a one- or two-paragraph summary of the section.

Career Connection

Nuclear Physicist

Dr. Shirley Ann Jackson was chairperson of the U.S. Nuclear Regulatory Commission from 1995–1999. Her job was to use her scientific background to ensure that American nuclear power plants were run safely. An authority on semiconductor systems, Dr. Jackson has worked on research teams across the United States and in Europe. She also has been a professor and a consultant to private companies, and is now president of a technical institute. Jackson holds degrees in physics, as well as five honorary doctoral degrees.

SCIENCE *Online* To learn more about careers in nuclear physics, visit the Glencoe Science Web site at **science.glencoe.com.**

Understanding Literature

Science Connection

An atomic bomb contains a hollow sphere of uranium or plutonium. To detonate the bomb, a source of neutrons is shot by a detonator into the center of the sphere, which is crushed by explosives. The neutrons cannot escape. A chain reaction results and fission flashes through the uranium or plutonium in a fraction of a second. With power equal to tens of thousands of tons of TNT, the bomb explodes. Extreme radiation also is produced, and fallout from a nuclear explosion spreads through the atmosphere carrying lethal amounts of radiation.

Linking Science and Writing

Teaching Strategies

In preparation for the writing activity, review with students the main ideas and supporting details in the excerpt they just read. Write an outline form on the blackboard and have students help fill in the blanks. Start with the main idea under Roman numeral I and list supporting details as A., B., etc. Suggest that students create a similar outline of whatever section they choose to reread in the chapter for the writing activity.

Career Connection

Students interested in nuclear physics need to study science, mathematics and computer technology. A Ph.D. is usually required for a career in this field. Most nuclear physicists work in research and development, devising theories that describe the fundamental forces and laws of nature. Many physicists teach in colleges and universities; some work in private industry.

Internet Addresses

_____

_____

_____

Explore the Glencoe Science Web site at **science.glencoe.com** to find out more about topics in this feature.

Chapter 20 Study Guide

Reviewing Main Ideas

Preview

Students can answer the questions in their Science Journals. Discuss the answers as you go through the chapter. **Linguistic**

Review

Students can write their answers, then compare them with those of other students. **Interpersonal**

Reteach

Students can look at the illustrations and describe details that support the main ideas of the chapter. **Visual-Spatial**

Answers to Chapter Review

SECTION 1
2. electrical to light and heat

SECTION 2
3. radiation

SECTION 3
2. exothermic

Reviewing Main Ideas

Section 1   Energy Changes

1. Energy is the ability to cause change. It can change the temperature, shape, speed, or direction of an object.

2. Energy can change from one form to another. Some common forms of energy are kinetic, chemical, heat, light, and electrical. *What energy transformations are shown here?*

3. Moving objects have kinetic energy. The kinetic energy of an object increases if either its speed or its mass increases. The higher an object is above Earth's surface, the larger its potential energy is. Potential energy is stored energy.

4. Kinetic energy, as well as other forms of energy, can be transferred from one object to another. When energy is transferred or changes form, the total amount of energy stays the same. Energy cannot be created or destroyed.

Section 2   Temperature

1. Temperature is a measure of the average kinetic energy of the particles in a material. The temperature increases as the kinetic energy increases.

2. The movement of energy from a warmer object to a cooler one is called heat.

3. Heat can be transferred by conduction, convection, and radiation. *What type of heat transfer is shown here?*

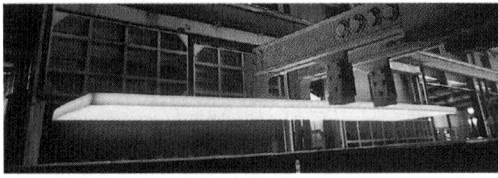

Section 3   Chemical Energy

1. The energy stored in chemical bonds is chemical energy. The energy stored in food and oil is an important source of chemical energy.

2. Chemical reactions can release or absorb energy. Exothermic reactions are chemical reactions that release energy. Endothermic reactions absorb energy. *What type of chemical reaction is shown here?*

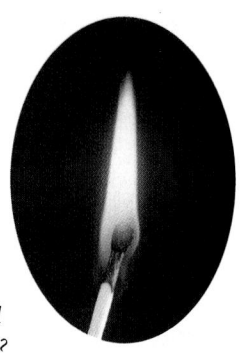

3. Changing the temperature and adding catalysts can change the rate of chemical reactions.

FOLDABLES
Reading & Study Skills

After You Read

On the back of your Foldable describe what caused each form of energy to change and explain the effects of the change.

FOLDABLES
Reading & Study Skills

After You Read

After students have read the chapter and completed the Foldable described in Before You Read, have them do the activity on the student page.

Dinah Zike

Visualizing Main Ideas

Complete the following concept map on energy.

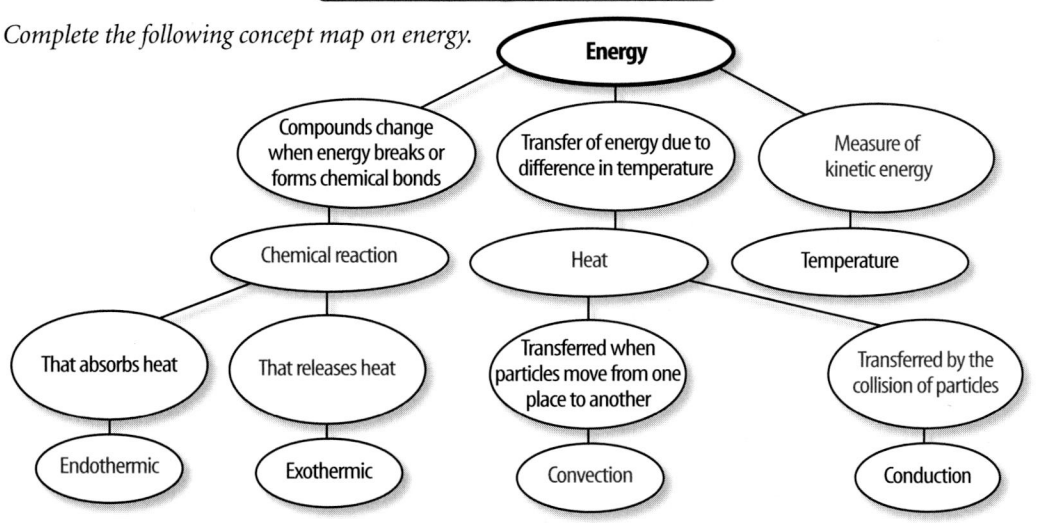

Visualizing Main Ideas

See student page.

Vocabulary Review

Using Vocabulary

1. conduction
2. kinetic energy
3. heat
4. temperature
5. potential energy
6. conduction
7. radiation
8. endothermic reaction
9. catalyst

Vocabulary Review

Vocabulary Words

a. catalyst
b. conduction
c. convection
d. endothermic reaction
e. energy
f. exothermic reaction
g. heat
h. kinetic energy
i. law of conservation of energy
j. potential energy
k. radiation
l. temperature

 **Study Tip**

Keep all your homework assignments and read them over from time to time. Make sure you understand any questions you answered incorrectly.

Using Vocabulary

Make each sentence true by replacing the underlined word or words with a vocabulary word.

1. Energy transfer by contact is <u>radiation</u>.

2. Energy of motion is <u>potential energy</u>.

3. The movement of energy from warm to cool objects is <u>temperature</u>.

4. A measure of the kinetic energy of the atoms in a substance is called <u>heat</u>.

5. <u>Kinetic energy</u> is energy that is stored.

6. <u>Convection</u> is the transfer of energy by collisions between the particles in a material.

7. Energy transferred by waves is called <u>kinetic energy</u>.

8. A reaction that absorbs energy is an <u>exothermic reaction</u>.

9. A <u>conductor</u> is a substance that changes the rate of a chemical reaction.

Chapter 20 Assessment

Checking Concepts

1. D
2. C
3. A
4. C
5. C
6. B
7. B
8. D
9. A
10. C

Thinking Critically

11. People and other heat-producing objects are closer together in cities, as are structures that can retain heat.
12. Heat flows out of the hot liquid into the air. Heat flows out of the air into the cold liquid.
13. They transformed chemical energy in their bodies to kinetic energy. As they climbed the hill, they gained potential energy. When each fell, potential energy was transformed to kinetic energy.
14. The fiberglass insulation would help keep thermal energy from being conducted out of the house into the air.
15. −40°F

Checking Concepts

Choose the word or phrase that best answers the question.

1. Which of the following correctly describes energy?
   A) can be created
   B) can be destroyed
   C) cannot change form
   D) can cause change

2. What is an object's temperature related to?
   A) heat
   B) total energy of its atoms
   C) kinetic energy of its atoms
   D) total chemical energy

3. What happens if two objects at different temperatures are touching?
   A) Heat moves from the warmer object.
   B) Heat moves from the cooler object.
   C) Heat moves to the warmer object.
   D) No heat transfer takes place.

4. During an energy transfer, what happens to the total amount of energy?
   A) It increases.
   B) It decreases.
   C) It stays the same.
   D) It depends on the energy form being transferred.

5. How is energy from the Sun transferred to Earth?
   A) conduction
   B) convection
   C) radiation
   D) insulation

6. When would you have the most potential energy?
   A) walking up the hill
   B) sitting at the top of the hill
   C) running up the hill
   D) sitting at the bottom of the hill

7. Which of the following kinds of chemical reactions absorb energy?
   A) exothermic
   B) endothermic
   C) catalysts
   D) thermals

8. What kind of material transfers heat easily?
   A) plastic
   B) insulator
   C) glass
   D) conductor

9. What increases as the speed of an object increases?
   A) kinetic energy
   B) mass
   C) nuclear energy
   D) potential energy

10. Thermals are produced by what type of energy transfer?
    A) radiation
    B) conduction
    C) convection
    D) atmospheric

Thinking Critically

11. Cities are usually warmer in the winter than the surrounding countryside. What do you think causes this?

12. If heat flows in only one direction, how can hot and cold liquids reach room temperature as they sit on a table?

13. Think about what happens to Jack and Jill in the nursery rhyme. What kinds of energy are used? How was each energy form used?

14. Use what you know about the movement of heat to explain why you would fill the walls of a house you were building with fiberglass insulation.

15. Graph the data in the table with the Celsius temperature on the *x*-axis and the Fahrenheit temperature on the *y*-axis. From your graph, what is the Fahrenheit temperature when the Celsius temperature is –40°C?

°C	°F
100	212
50	122
0	32
−50	−58

Chapter ✓Assessment Planner

Portfolio Encourage students to place in their portfolios one or two items of what they consider to be their best work. Examples include:
- Assessment, p. 595
- Assessment, p. 603
- Visual Learning, p. 606

Performance Additional performance assessments, Performance Task Assessment Lists, and rubrics for evaluating these activities can be found in Glencoe's **Performance Assessment in the Science Classroom.**

Developing Skills

16. Concept Mapping Below is a concept map of the energy changes of a gymnast bouncing on a trampoline. Complete the map by indicating the type of energy—kinetic, potential, or both—the gymnast has at each of the following stages: halfway up, the highest point, halfway down, and just before hitting the trampoline.

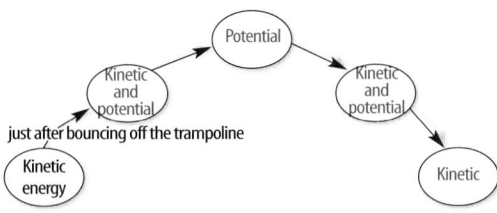

17. Comparing and Contrasting Compare and contrast convection, radiation, and conduction.

18. Making and Using Tables Make a table of your activities today and the types of energy changes that occurred while you did them.

19. Communicating Write a short paragraph about the main ideas of this chapter. Include a short example in your own words about one kind of energy change.

Performance Assessment

20. Poster Research some of the forms of energy you use each day. Make a poster that shows how you use each.

TECHNOLOGY

Go to the Glencoe Science Web site at **science.glencoe.com** or use the **Glencoe Science CD-ROM** for additional chapter assessment.

 **Test Practice**

A chemist is studying a chemical reaction where substance X is changed to substance Y under different conditions.

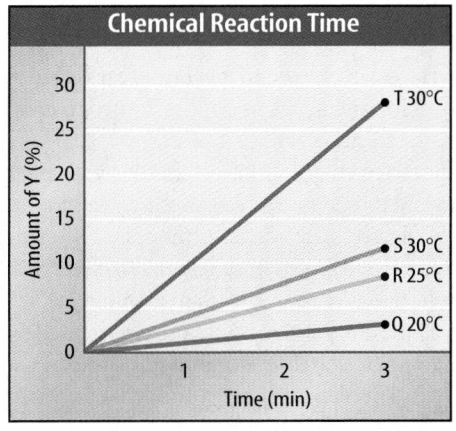

Chemical Reaction Time

1. According to this chart, at which temperature is the rate of reaction the greatest?
   - **A)** 0°C
   - **B)** 20°C
   - **C)** 25°C
   - **D)** 30°C

2. A catalyst is any substance that can accelerate a chemical reaction without getting changed itself. According to that definition, which of the lines above demonstrates the effects of using a catalyst?
   - **F)** Q
   - **G)** R
   - **H)** S
   - **J)** T

 **Test Practice**

The Test-Taking Tip was written by The Princeton Review, the nation's leader in test preparation.
1. D
2. J

Developing Skills

16. See student page.
17. All three are ways of transferring heat. Conduction transfers energy between touching atoms. Convection transfers energy when hot atoms move to a place where the temperature is different. Radiation transfers energy in waves.
18. Check students' work. Tables should include transfers between chemical energy (digestion), kinetic to potential and back (going up or down), and chemical to kinetic (movement).
19. Energy is the ability to cause change. Types of energy are potential energy, kinetic energy, electric energy, chemical energy, light energy, and heat energy. Energy can be transferred and transformed, but not created or destroyed.

Performance Assessment

20. Evaluate students' posters. Several types of energy transfer should be included. Use **PASC**, p. 145.

✓Assessment Resources

 Reproducible Masters

Chapter Resources Booklet
Chapter Review, pp. 35–36
Chapter Tests, pp. 37–40
Assessment Transparency Activity, p. 47

Glencoe Science Web site
Interactive Tutor
Chapter Quizzes

Glencoe Technology
- Assessment Transparency
- Interactive CD-ROM Chapter Quizzes
- ExamView Pro Test Bank
- Vocabulary PuzzleMaker Software
- MindJogger Videoquiz

Reading Comprehension

Reading Comprehension

Read the passage. Then read each question that follows the passage. Decide which is the best answer to each question.

Electric Cars: The Cars of the Future?

Have you ever wondered how a car is able to move? In car engines gasoline is burned to convert chemical energy into thermal energy. The engine then changes some of this thermal energy into kinetic energy that causes the wheels to turn. However, some car manufacturers are also exploring whether cars can be developed that will run on electrical energy rather than gasoline.

These electric cars would use electrical energy to power an electric motor that turns the car's wheels. The electrical energy would be provided by a battery. In a battery chemical reactions occur that convert chemical energy into electrical energy. Eventually, the chemicals in the battery are used up and the battery can no longer produce electrical energy. When rechargeable batteries are recharged, the chemical reactions in the battery are reversed. Then the chemicals in the battery that produce electrical energy are restored.

While electric cars would produce no pollution from the car, there are potential environmental problems. The rechargeable batteries used by electric cars are heavy, expensive, and contain hazardous materials such as lead. As a result, the manufacture and disposal of these batteries can create environmental problems. Also, the electricity used to charge these batteries usually is generated by power plants which can produce air pollution and other wastes.

Other types of electric cars are being developed that use a hydrogen fuel cell instead of batteries. In this fuel cell hydrogen gas reacts with oxygen to produce electricity. The hydro-

gen gas can be obtained from water. Although the fuel cell produces almost no pollution, electricity from power plants still is needed to generate the hydrogen gas the fuel cells uses. Research is being done to find other ways to produce hydrogen gas that would result in less pollution.

Recently several carmakers have developed hybrid cars that combine an internal combustion engine, a battery, and an electric motor. The electric motor assists the internal combustion engine in providing power. During braking, about half of the engine's kinetic energy is recovered and is stored in the battery.

Test-Taking Tip Read the passage slowly to make sure you don't miss any important details.

1. From the story, you can infer that <u>rechargeable</u> means _____.
   A) brand new
   B) reusable
   C) paid by credit card
   D) disposable

2. The hydrogen gas used in a hydrogen fuel cell can be obtained from _____.
   F) water
   G) electric cars
   H) power plants
   J) hybrid cars

Reasoning and Skills

Read each question and choose the best answer.

| Water | Soda | Apple Juice | Milk |

1. The picture shows an experiment that tests which liquid will boil first. Which of the following would make it a better-designed experiment?

A) Put a thermometer in one container.
B) Use a different amount of liquid in each container.
C) Use the same size container for each liquid.
D) Use solids instead of liquids.

Test-Taking Tip Experiments should test one factor at a time.

2. What most likely is being measured in the picture?

F) the volume of the rock
G) the mass of the rock
H) the length of the rock
J) the texture of the rock

Test-Taking Tip Think about which characteristic a scale measures.

3. Less friction acts on objects moving across slippery surfaces than on objects moving across rough surfaces. On which surface could you slide the farthest?

A) rug
B) cement
C) dirt
D) ice

Test-Taking Tip Which surface would have the least amount of friction for you to slide on?

4. A marshmallow was held over a fire too long and it burned. Which of the following was observed?

F) physical property
G) size-dependent property
H) physical change
J) chemical change

Consider this question carefully before writing your answer on a separate sheet of paper.

5. Usually, more than one force is acting on an object. These forces can be balanced or unbalanced. Describe a situation where the forces acting on an object are balanced. Be sure to explain what the forces are.

Test-Taking Tip When the forces acting on an object are balanced, that object won't move.

Reasoning and Skills

QUESTION 1: C

Students should understand that a controlled experiment can have only one independent variable.

Teaching Tip

When presented with a diagram of an experiment, students should check to see that it conforms to the definition of a controlled experiment.

QUESTION 2: G

Students should use their experiences with laboratory apparatus to identify that a laboratory scale is used to measure mass.

QUESTION 3: D

Students should understand that of the four choices, choice D, *ice*, has the least amount of friction and is therefore the most slippery.

QUESTION 4: J

Students should understand that burning is always a chemical change.

QUESTION 5: Answers will vary.

Students should mention that where the forces acting on an object are balanced, the object's motion (or lack thereof) does not change.

UNIT 7

Unit Contents

✔ Pre-Reading Activity

Have students list electrical appliances and devices and tell their major function, such as heating, cooling, lighting, motion, and so forth. They can conduct a scavenger hunt and try to find pictures of these items in this unit.

UNIT 7

Electricity and Magnetism

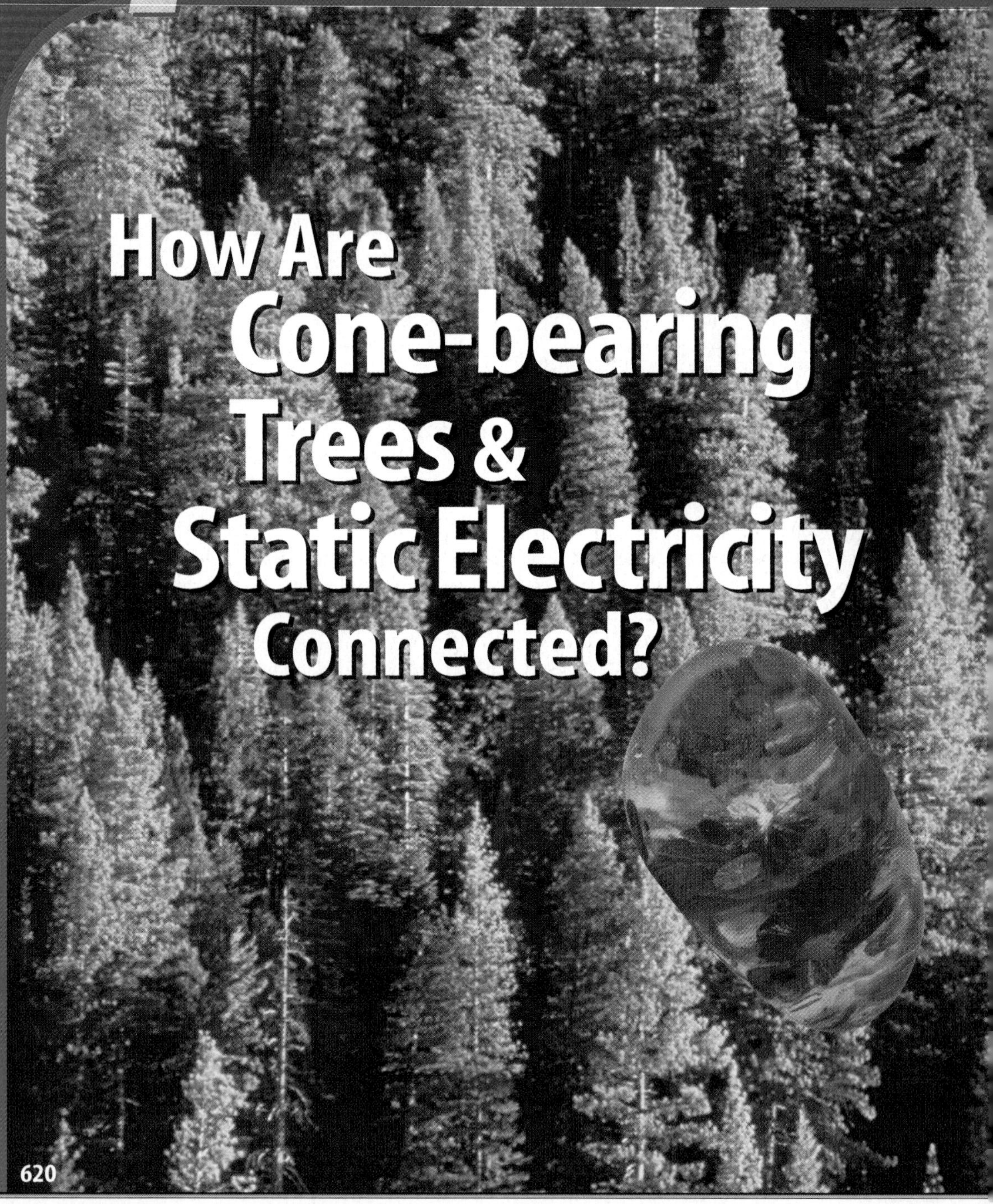

How Are Cone-bearing Trees & Static Electricity Connected?

620

Teacher to Teacher

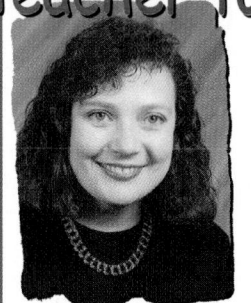

"I have groups of six to eight students create a human circuit by hooking themselves up. The class identifies the circuit as a series or parallel and predicts whether it will work. Using a set of electrical equipment, have another group create the demonstrated circuit."

Deborah Peters Huffine, Teacher
Noblesville Intermediate School
Noblesville, IN

When the bark of a cone-bearing tree is broken it secretes resin, which hardens and seals the tree's wound. The resin of some ancient trees fossilized over time, forming a golden, gemlike substance called amber. The ancient Greeks prized amber highly, not only for its beauty, but also because they believed it had magical qualities. They had noticed that when amber was rubbed with wool or fur, small bits of straw or ash would stick to it. Because of amber's color and its unusual properties, some believed that amber was solidified sunshine. The Greek name for amber was *elektron* which means "substance of the Sun."

By the seventeenth century, the behavior of amber had sparked the curiosity of a number of scientists, and an explanation of amber's behavior finally emerged. When amber is rubbed by wool or fur, static electricity is produced. Today, a device called a Van de Graaff generator, like the one shown below, can produce static electricity involving millions of volts, and has been used to explore the nature of matter in atom-smashing experiments.

SCIENCE CONNECTION

STATIC ELECTRICITY When you dry clothes in a gas or electric dryer, the fabrics often stick together. This "clinging" is due to static electricity. Using the Glencoe Science Web site at **science.glencoe.com** or library resources, find out how clothing becomes charged in a dryer, and how anti-static products work. Write a paragraph in your Science Journal about what you find.

SCIENCE CONNECTION

Activity

When two materials are in contact, electrons can be transferred from one material to the other. For example, rubbing a balloon on wool causes electrons to be transferred from the wool to the balloon. The balloon then has a negative charge and is attracted to the positively-charged wool. Have students try this with different materials and discuss the results. Suggest that advanced students try to construct a static generator. **ⓁⓈ Kinesthetic**

Introducing the Unit

How Are Cone-Bearing Trees & Static Electricity Connected?

The properties of amber, which eventually became known as its electrical properties, were known to the Greeks. The philosopher Thales of Miletus thought that amber's ability to attract feathers and other light objects when the amber was rubbed, was evidence of a soul.

Post-Renaissance investigation of the electrical properties of amber helped lead to an understanding of electricity. In 1600, William Gilbert invented the term *Electrica*, from the Latin name for amber, *electrum*, for any material that could be made to act like amber and hold a static charge. Metals like steel and copper were called *non-electrics* because they conducted the charge away.

In 1660 Otto Von Guericke built the first stactic generator from a glass sphere turned by a handle against woolen cloth. By placing a little mercury in the sphere and evacuating the air, Francis Hauksbee in 1705 was able to make the sphere glow brightly enough to read by.

SCIENCE *Online*

Internet Addresses

_____

_____

_____

_____

Explore the Glencoe Science Web site at **science.glencoe.com** to find out more about topics in this unit.

Section/Objectives	Standards		Activities/Features
Chapter Opener	National	State/Local	**Explore Activity:** Investigate electric forces, p. 623 **Before You Read,** p. 623
	See p. 7T for a Key to Standards.		
Section 1 Electric Charge 🕐 2 sessions 📦 1 block 1. **Describe** how objects can become electrically charged. 2. **Explain** how electric charges affect other electric charges. 3. **Distinguish** between insulators and conductors. 4. **Describe** how electric discharges such as lightning occur.	National Content Standards: UCP2, B3, C1, D1, F3		**Visualizing Nerve Impulses,** p. 626 **Science Online,** p. 628
Section 2 Electric Current 🕐 2 sessions 📦 1 block 1. **Relate** voltage to the electrical energy carried by an electric current. 2. **Describe** a battery and how it produces an electric current. 3. **Explain** electrical resistance.	National Content Standards: UCP2, A1, B3, E2		**MiniLAB:** Investigating the Electric Force, p. 632 **Chemistry Integration,** p. 633
Section 3 Electric Circuits 🕐 4 sessions 📦 2 blocks 1. **Explain** how voltage, current, and resistance are related in an electric circuit. 2. **Investigate** the difference between series and parallel circuits. 3. **Determine** the electrical power used in a circuit. 4. **Describe** how to avoid dangerous electric shock.	National Content Standards: UCP2, A1, B3, E2, F1, F5, G2		**Math Skills Activity:** Calculating the Current Used by Lightbulbs, p. 637 **MiniLAB:** Identifying Simple Circuits, p. 638 **Math Skills Activity:** Calculating the Wattage of Lightbulbs, p. 640 **Science Online,** p. 641 **Life Science Integration,** p. 642 **Activity:** Current in a Parallel Circuit, p. 643 **Activity:** A Model for Voltage and Current, p. 644 **Science and Society:** Fire in the Forest, p. 646

◻ NATIONAL GEOGRAPHIC

Teacher's Corner

PRODUCTS AVAILABLE FROM GLENCOE
To order call 1-800-334-7344:
Videodisc
STV: Electricity and Simple Machines

PRODUCTS AVAILABLE FROM NATIONAL GEOGRAPHIC SOCIETY
To order call 1-800-368-2728:
Videos
Introduction to Circuits

INDEX TO NATIONAL GEOGRAPHIC SOCIETY
The following articles may be used for research relating to this chapter:
"A Comeback for Nuclear Power? Our Electric Future" by Peter Miller, August 1991;
"Conservation: Can We Live Better on Less?" by Rick Gore, February 1981.

Activity Materials	Reproducible Resources	Section Assessment	Technology
Explore Activity: 2 rubber balloons, small bits of paper, piece of wool	**Chapter Resources Booklet** Foldables Worksheet, p. 17 Directed Reading Overview, p. 19 Note-taking Worksheets, pp. 33–35	GLENCOE'S **ASSESSMENT** ADVANTAGE	
Need materials? Contact Science Kit at 1-800-828-7777 or www.sciencekit.com on the Internet.	**Chapter Resources Booklet** Transparency Activity, p. 44 Enrichment, p. 30 Reinforcement, p. 27 Directed Reading, p. 20 Lab Activity, pp. 9–12 **Life Science Critical Thinking/ Problem Solving,** p. 2	Portfolio Assessment, p. 630 Performance Skill Builder Activities, p. 630 Content Section Assessment, p. 630	Section Focus Transparency Interactive CD-ROM Guided Reading Audio Program
MiniLAB: salt, plate, pepper, rubber or plastic comb, wool cloth	**Chapter Resources Booklet** Transparency Activity, p. 45 MiniLAB, p. 3 Enrichment, p. 31 Reinforcement, p. 28 Directed Reading, p. 21 Transparency Activity, pp. 47–48 Lab Activity, pp. 13–15 **Science Inquiry Labs,** p. 9	Portfolio Assessment, p. 635 Performance MiniLAB, p. 632 Skill Builder Activities, p. 635 Content Section Assessment, p. 635	Section Focus Transparency Teaching Transparency Interactive CD-ROM Guided Reading Audio Program
MiniLAB: flashlight bulb, wire, battery **Activity:** 1.5-V lightbulbs (4), 1.5-V batteries (2), 10-cm-long pieces of insulated wire (8), 2 battery holders, 4 mini-bulb sockets **Activity:** plastic funnel, 1-m lengths of rubber or plastic tubing of different diameters, meterstick, ring stand with ring, stopwatch, hose clamp, 500-mL beakers (2)	**Chapter Resources Booklet** Transparency Activity, p. 46 MiniLAB, p. 4 Enrichment, p. 32 Reinforcement, p. 29 Directed Reading, pp. 21, 22 Activity Worksheets, pp. 5–6, 7–8 **Mathematics Skill Activities,** p. 11 **Physical Science Critical Thinking/Problem Solving,** p. 8 **Lab Management and Safety,** p. 71	Portfolio Visual Learning, p. 638 Performance Math Skills Activity, p. 637 MiniLAB, p. 638 Math Skill Activity, p. 640 Skill Builder Activities, p. 642 Content Section Assessment, p. 642	Section Focus Transparency Interactive CD-ROM Guided Reading Audio Program

End of Chapter Assessment

GLENCOE'S **ASSESSMENT** ADVANTAGE

Blackline Masters	Technology	Professional Series
Chapter Resources Booklet Chapter Review, pp. 37–38 Chapter Tests, pp. 39–42 **Standardized Test Practice by The Princeton Review,** pp. 87–90	MindJogger Videoquiz Interactive CD-ROM Vocabulary PuzzleMakers ExamView Pro Test Bank Interactive Lesson Planner Interactive Teacher Edition	Performance Assessment in the Science Classroom (PASC)

Transparencies

Section Focus

A Spritely Vision

The lightning that we usually see is below the clouds, but there is activity high above the clouds, too. These events have some pretty fanciful names, like sprites, elves, and blue jets. This photo shows the red flash of a sprite, which sometimes occurs during thunderstorms.

1. When do you usually see lightning?
2. How does this sprite appear similar to lightning? Different?
3. How is a flash of lightning different from a glowing lightbulb?

L2

Go with the Flow!

Highways in heavily used areas are designed with many lanes to keep traffic moving, but sometimes it doesn't work.

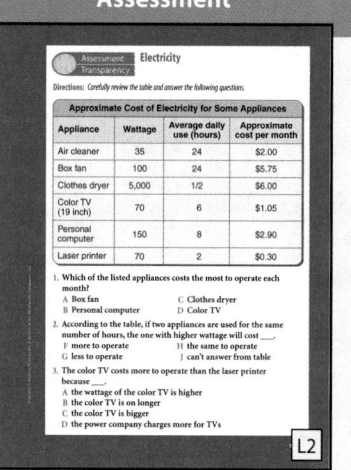

1. Describe what is happening in the picture. What would traffic be like if there were the same number of cars but fewer lanes? What would traffic be like if there were the same number of cars but twice as many lanes?
2. How might the flow of traffic on a road be like the flow of electricity in a wire?

L2

In the Chips

A few decades ago, a single computer was the size of a classroom. Today's laptops, however, are smaller, faster, and have more memory. Much of this change is due to the development of microcircuits like the silicon chip in this photo.

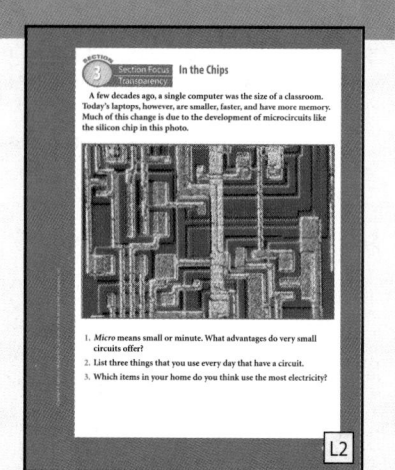

1. *Micro* means small or minute. What advantages do very small circuits offer?
2. List three things that you use every day that have a circuit.
3. Which items in your home do you think use the most electricity?

L2

This is a representation of key blackline masters available in the Teacher Classroom Resources. See Resource Manager boxes within the chapter for additional information.

Assessment

Electricity

Directions: *Carefully review the table and answer the following questions.*

Approximate Cost of Electricity for Some Appliances			
Appliance	Wattage	Average daily use (hours)	Approximate cost per month
Air cleaner	35	24	$2.00
Box fan	100	24	$5.75
Clothes dryer	5,000	1/2	$6.00
Color TV (19 inch)	70	6	$1.05
Personal computer	150	8	$2.90
Laser printer	70	2	$0.30

1. Which of the listed appliances costs the most to operate each month?
 A Box fan C Clothes dryer
 B Personal computer D Color TV
2. According to the table, if two appliances are used for the same number of hours, the one with higher wattage will cost ___.
 F more to operate H the same to operate
 G less to operate J can't answer from table
3. The color TV costs more to operate than the laser printer because ___.
 A the wattage of the color TV is higher
 B the color TV is on longer
 C the color TV is bigger
 D the power company charges more for TVs

L2

Teaching

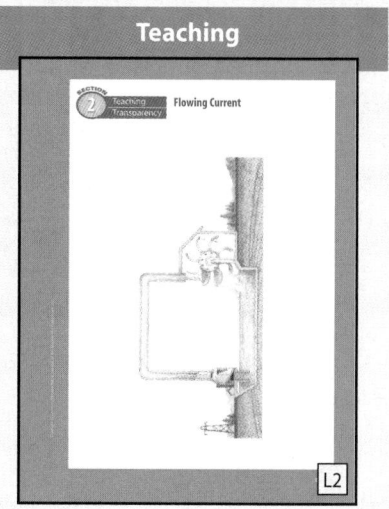

Flowing Current

L2

Key to Teaching Strategies

The following designations will help you decide which activities are appropriate for your students.

L1 Level 1 activities should be appropriate for students with learning difficulties.

L2 Level 2 activities should be within the ability range of all students.

L3 Level 3 activities are designed for above-average students.

ELL ELL activities should be within the ability range of English Language Learners.

COOP LEARN Cooperative Learning activities are designed for small group work.

LS Multiple Learning Styles logos, as described on page 22T, are used throughout to indicate strategies that address different learning styles.

P These strategies represent student products that can be placed into a best-work portfolio.

Hands-on Activities

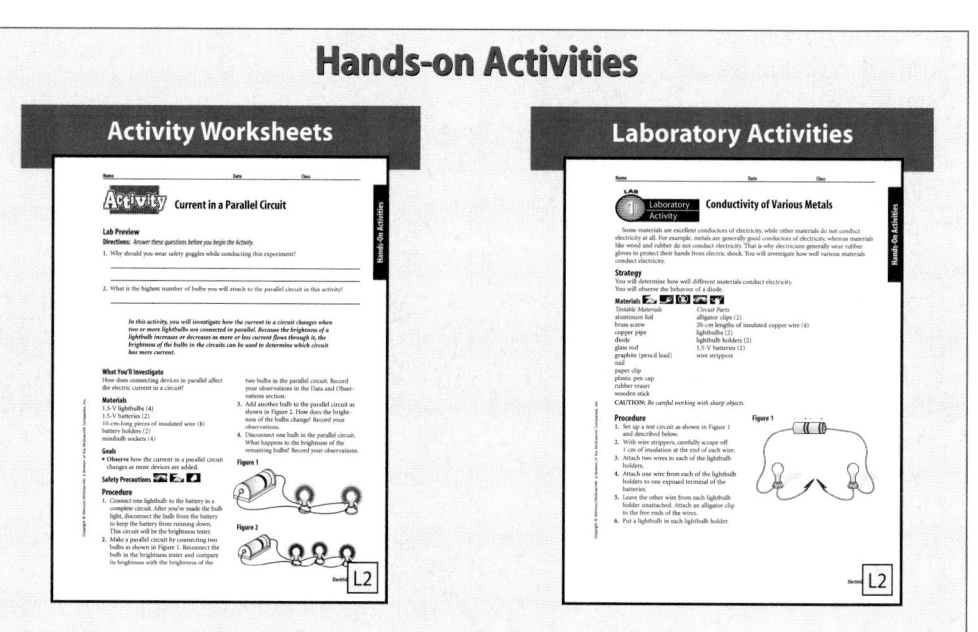

Activity Worksheets

Current in a Parallel Circuit

Lab Preview
Directions: *Answer these questions before you begin the Activity.*

1. Why should you wear safety goggles while conducting this experiment?

2. What is the highest number of bulbs you will attach to the parallel circuit in this activity?

In this activity, you will investigate how the current in a circuit changes when two or more lightbulbs are connected in parallel. Because the brightness of a lightbulb increases or decreases as more or less current flows through it, the brightness of the bulbs in the circuits can be used to determine which circuit has more current.

What You'll Investigate
How does connecting devices in parallel affect the electric current in a circuit?

Materials
1.5-V lightbulbs (4)
1.5-V batteries (2)
10-cm-long pieces of insulated wire (8)
battery holders (2)
minibulb sockets (4)

Goals
• Observe how the current in a parallel circuit changes as more devices are added.

Safety Precautions

Procedure
1. Connect one lightbulb to the battery in a complete circuit. After you've made the bulb light, disconnect the bulb from the battery to keep the battery from running down. This circuit will be the brightness tester.
2. Make a parallel circuit by connecting two bulbs as shown in Figure 1. Reconnect the bulb in the brightness tester and compare its brightness with the brightness of the

Figure 1

Figure 2

two bulbs in the parallel circuit. Record your observations in the Data and Observations section.
3. Add another bulb to the parallel circuit as shown in Figure 2. How does the brightness of the bulbs change? Record your observations.
4. Disconnect one bulb in the parallel circuit. What happens to the brightness of the remaining bulbs? Record your observations.

L2

Laboratory Activities

Conductivity of Various Metals

Some materials are excellent conductors of electricity, while other materials do not conduct electricity at all. For example, metals are generally good conductors of electricity, whereas materials like wood and rubber do not conduct electricity. That is why electricians generally wear rubber gloves to protect their hands from electric shock. You will investigate how well various materials conduct electricity.

Strategy
You will determine how well different materials conduct electricity. You will observe the behavior of a diode.

Materials

Testable Materials
aluminum foil
brass screw
copper pipe
diode
glass rod
graphite (pencil lead)
nail
paper clip
plastic pen cap
rubber eraser
wooden stick

Circuit Parts
alligator clips (2)
20-cm lengths of insulated copper wire (4)
lightbulbs (2)
lightbulb holders (2)
1.5-V batteries (2)
wire strippers

CAUTION: *Be careful working with sharp objects.*

Procedure
1. Set up a test circuit as shown in Figure 1 and described below.
2. With wire strippers, carefully scrape off 1 cm of insulation at the end of each wire.
3. Attach two wires to each of the lightbulb holders.
4. Attach one wire from each of the lightbulb holders to one exposed terminal of the batteries.
5. Leave the other wire from each lightbulb holder unattached. Attach an alligator clip to the free ends of the wires.
6. Put a lightbulb in each lightbulb holder.

Figure 1

L2

Meeting Different Ability Levels

Content Outline
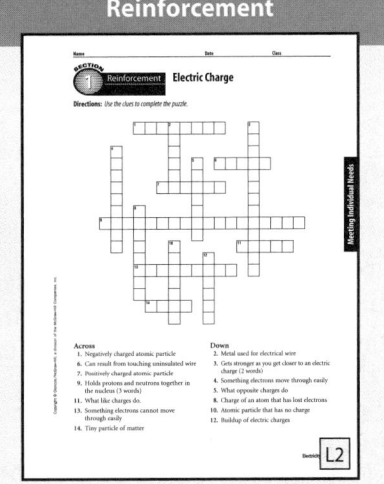

Reinforcement

Directed Reading
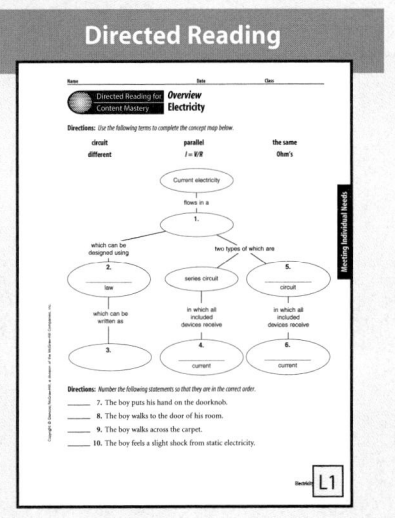

Assessment

Chapter Tests
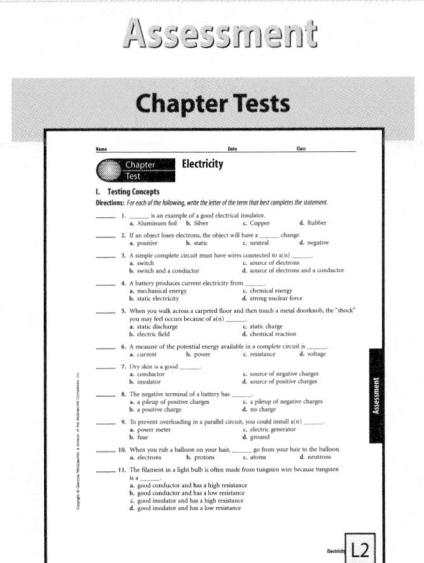

Enrichment
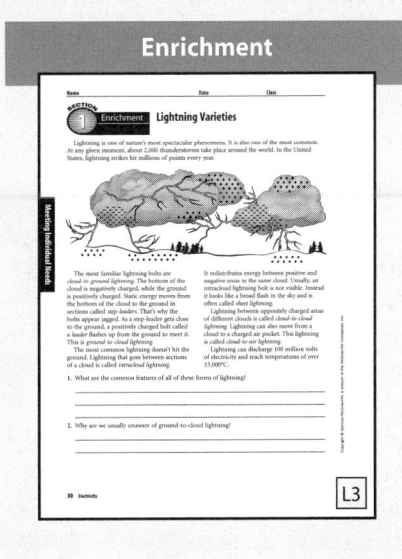

Spanish Directed Reading
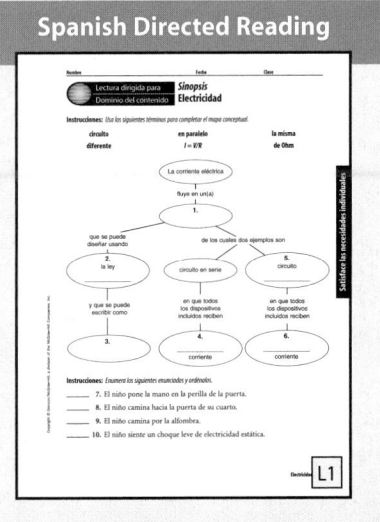

Test Practice Workbook

Chapter Review
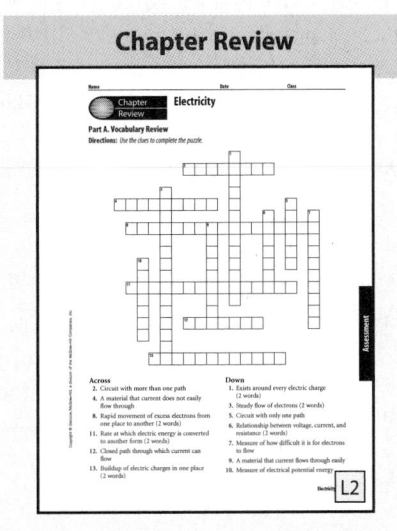

Science Content Background

SECTION 1

Electric Charge
Electricity

Charge is an abstract idea and is not a substance. Charge is the name given to a property acquired by objects, a property that seems to leak away, can be restored by rubbing, can move between objects, is highly mobile on metals, and so on. From observing the interactions between objects, we can infer the existence of a property called charge, but we cannot observe the charge itself, only the interactions it produces. In all of science, the appropriate starting point is not the model but the observation. The concept of charge was invented to provide a plausible explanation for scientists' observations.

SECTION 2

Electric Current
Flow of Charge

Pekka Parviainen/
Photo Researchers, Inc.

Benjamin Franklin's charge model of positive and negative, with conventional current going from positive to negative, is still used today. Electrons were discovered almost one hundred and fifty years later and exhibit the characteristics of negative charge. Franklin defined objects repelled by rubber rods stroked with rabbit fur as negative. They could easily have been defined as positive. Because rubber rods that have been stroked with rabbit fur repel electrons, we consider electrons to be negative. When a wire is used as the conductor, the electrons in the metal carry negative charge through the wire. In a fluid conductor, such as the electrolyte inside a battery, positive and negative charges (ions) are free to move.

Student Misconception

Electricity travels from a battery to a light-bulb and stops there.

Refer to the facing page for teaching strategies to address this misconception. Refer to pages 631–634 for content related to this topic.

Students may wonder about the names of batteries. There are AA, AAA, C, and D; why are there no A or B batteries? In the 1920s, there were A and B batteries, which were used to power crank telephones and early radios. They are no longer produced today.

SECTION 3

Electric Circuits
Electrical Safety

In electrical shock, the amount and duration of electrical current moving through the body determines the extent of the damage it does. Low voltage does not imply low hazard. A wall voltage of 120 V is not a particularly high voltage, yet it can be lethal because of the large current that can flow out of the wall socket. An example of the importance of current is to consider the balloon experiment in the opening Explore Activity. Rubbing a balloon on your hair can charge the balloon to several thousand volts. Even if you touch such a balloon, you will feel no shock because the amount of current is so small.

SCIENCE Online

For additional content background on this topic, go to the Glencoe Science Web site at science.glencoe.com.

Misconceptions

Students may think that . . .

- **Electricity travels from a battery to a light bulb and stops there.**

Most students have little experience with simple electric circuits. It might seem to students that electricity flows into appliances connected to an electric outlet just as gasoline flows into a car connected by a hose to a gas pump. In fact, an electric current will flow only if there is a closed path for the charges to follow.

Demonstration

Hold up a flashlight and turn it on. Ask students to write down their predictions about what would happen if you left the flashlight on for a couple of days. Ask them to write down why they think their predictions would happen. Hold up one D battery, one flashlight bulb, and one wire with the insulation stripped off both ends. Ask students to draw one way they could make the bulb light using only these materials.

Promote Understanding

Activity

Give each pair of students one wire, one flashlight bulb, and one D battery and ask them to do the following:

- Connect the items as shown in your drawings and see if the bulb lights.

- Try other ways to get the bulb to light.

- Draw all the arrangements you attempt—both those that don't work and those that do work.

   After 25 minutes some pairs probably will have determined how to complete the circuit to get the bulb to light. Possible ways to make the bulb light include touching the bulb to one side of the battery, while touching one end of the wire to the other side of the bulb, and touching the other end of the wire to the other side of the battery.

On one side of the board, have students draw ways that the materials were connected so that the bulbs did not light up. On the other side of the board, have students draw ways the materials were connected to produce a lit bulb.

   Ask how the drawings on one side of the board are different from the drawings on the other side.

   Based on the drawings, what is necessary to get a bulb to light? Establish that a complete circuit gives electrons a closed path through which to travel, while an energy source, such as the battery, gives electrons the energy needed to move through the circuit.

Assess

After completing the chapter, see *Identifying Misconceptions* in the Study Guide.

Electricity

Chapter Vocabulary

What do you think?

Science Journal The photo shows electric discharges from high-voltage transmission wires. The electric field surrounding the wires causes ions in the air to accelerate and collide with other molecules. These collisions produce many additional ions. Light is emitted when electrons recombine with positive ions.

Electricity

This spark generator uses voltages of millions of volts to produce these electric discharges that resemble lightning. Other electric discharges, like those that occur when you walk across a carpeted floor, are not as visible. In your home, electric currents flow through wires, and also power lights, televisions, and other appliances. In this chapter, you will learn about electric charges and the forces they exert on each other. You also will learn how electric charges moving in a circuit can do useful work.

What do you think?

Science Journal Look at the picture below with a classmate. Discuss what this might be. Here's a hint: *Think power—lots of power.* Write your answer or best guess in your Science Journal.

622

Theme Connection

Systems and Interactions Electric charges interact in observable ways with their environment. Electric circuits are systems of moving electric charges. The movement of electric charges in a circuit is controlled by interactions between parts of the circuit.

N o computers? No CD players? No video games? Can you imagine life without electricity? You depend on it every day, and not just to make life more fun. Electricity heats and cools homes and provides light. It provides energy that can be used to do work. This energy comes from the forces that electric charges exert on each other. What is the nature of these electric forces?

Investigate electric forces

1. Inflate a rubber balloon.
2. Put some small bits of paper on your desktop and bring the balloon close to the bits of paper. Observe what happens.
3. Charge the balloon by holding it by the knot and rubbing the balloon on your hair or on a piece of wool.
4. Bring the balloon close to the bits of paper and observe what happens.
5. Charge two balloons using the procedure in step 3 and bring them close to each other, holding them by their knots.
6. Repeat step 3, then touch the balloon with your hand. Now what happens when you bring the balloon close to the bits of paper?

Observe

Record your observations of electric forces in your Science Journal.

Before You Read

Making a Vocabulary Study Fold **Make the following Foldable to help you better understand the terms *charge*, *current*, and *circuit*.**

1. Stack two sheets of paper in front of you so the short side of both sheets is at the top.
2. Slide the top sheet up so that about 4 cm of the bottom sheet show.
3. Fold both sheets top to bottom to form four tabs and staple along the fold.
4. Label the tabs *Electricity*, *Charge*, *Current*, and *Circuit*.
5. Before you read the chapter, write your definition of charge, current, and circuit under the tabs. As you read the chapter, correct your definition and write more information about each.

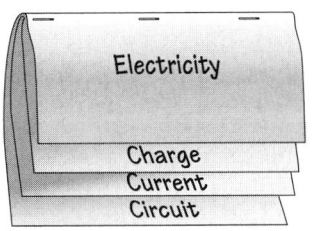

623

Before You Read

Dinah Zike Study Fold

Purpose To determine what students know about electricity before reading the chapter, and to provide a Foldable for recording and organizing notes on charges, currents, and circuits as students read

📁 For additional help, see Foldables Worksheet, p. 17 in **Chapter Resources Booklet,** or go to the Glencoe Science Web site at **science.glencoe.com.** See After You Read in the Study Guide at the end of this chapter.

Purpose Use the Explore Activity to introduce the concept of electric charge. The moving paper in this activity is evidence that a force is being applied and that work is being done. L2 ELL
IS **Visual Spatial**

Preparation To save time, inflate balloons before class.

Materials balloons, tissue paper, wool cloth

Teaching Strategies After students charge the balloon using their hair, ask whether their hair acts differently or feels odd. Have students describe the connection between charging the balloon and the behavior of their hair.

Observe

In Step 2 the balloon has no effect on the paper. In Step 4 the balloon attracts the pieces of paper. In Step 5 the balloons repel each other. In Step 6 the balloon no longer affects the pieces of paper.

✔ *Assessment*

Performance Have students develop lists of questions about their observations. Questions should focus on the science concepts being explored; for example, why might the balloon and paper attract and why might they repel? Use **Performance Assessment in the Science Classroom,** p. 91.

Teacher FYI

Activities involving the production of static electricity work better when the humidity in the room is low. Humid air is a better electrical conductor than dry air. As a result, an object will lose excess electric charge more rapidly in humid air than in dry air.

Electric Charge

SECTION

Electric Charge

① Motivate

Bellringer Transparency

Display the Section Focus Transparency for Section 1. Use the accompanying Transparency Activity Master. [L2] ELL

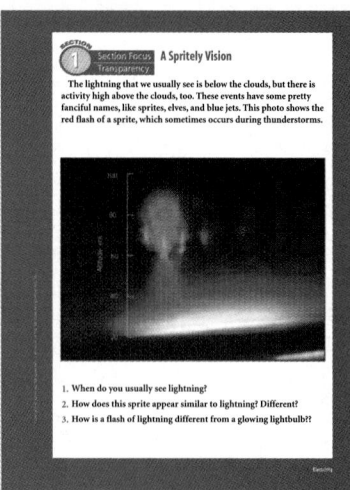

Tie to Prior Knowledge

Ask students to describe experiences they have had with static electricity. They may mention that socks and sweaters cling together when first taken out of a dryer and make a snapping sound when pulled apart. They may also mention getting a shock when touching a doorknob after walking across a room. Tell students that this section explains how the accumulation of excess electric charges causes these things to happen.

Caption Answer

Figure 1 the nucleus

As You Read

What You'll Learn

- **Describe** how objects can become electrically charged.
- **Explain** how electric charges affect other electric charges.
- **Distinguish** between insulators and conductors.
- **Describe** how electric discharges such as lightning occur.

Vocabulary

ion	insulator
static charge	conductor
electric force	electric discharge
electric field	

Why It's Important

All electrical phenomena result from the behavior of electric charges.

Figure 1
An atom is made of positively charged protons (orange), negatively charged electrons (red), and neutrons (blue) with no electric charge. *Where are the protons and neutrons located in an atom?*

Electricity

You can't see, smell, or taste electricity, so it might seem mysterious. However, electricity is not so hard to understand when you start by thinking small—very small. All solids, liquids, and gases are made of tiny particles called atoms. Atoms, as shown in **Figure 1,** are made of even smaller particles called protons, neutrons, and electrons. Protons and neutrons are held together tightly in the nucleus at the center of an atom, but electrons swarm around the nucleus in all directions. Protons and electrons possess electric charge, but neutrons have no electric charge.

Positive and Negative Charge Two types of electric charge exist—positive and negative. Protons carry a positive charge, and electrons carry a negative charge. The amount of negative charge on an electron is exactly equal to the amount of positive charge on a proton. Because atoms have equal numbers of protons and electrons, the amount of positive charge on all the protons in the nucleus of an atom is exactly balanced by the negative charge on all the electrons moving around the nucleus. Therefore, atoms are electrically neutral, which means they have no overall electric charge.

Some atoms can become negatively charged if they gain extra electrons. Other atoms can easily lose electrons thereby becoming positively charged. A positively or negatively charged atom is called an **ion** (I ahn).

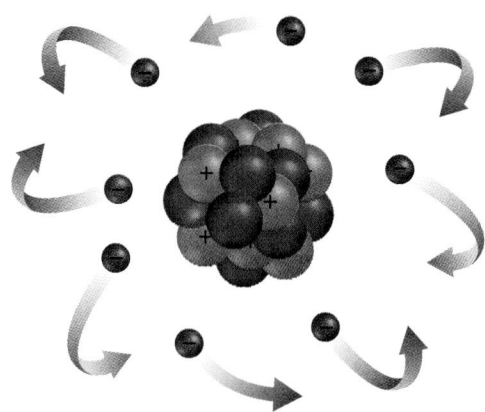

Section ✔*Assessment* Planner

PORTFOLIO
Assessment, p. 630
PERFORMANCE ASSESSMENT
Skill Builder Activities, p. 630
See page 650 for more options.

CONTENT ASSESSMENT
Section, p. 630
Challenge, p. 630
Chapter, pp. 650–651

Figure 2
Rubbing can move electrons from one object to another. Because hair holds electrons more loosely than the balloon holds them, electrons are pulled off the hair when the two make contact. *Which object has become positively charged and which has become negatively charged?*

Electrons Move in Solids Electrons can move from atom to atom and from object to object. Rubbing is one way that electrons can be transferred. If you ever have taken clinging clothes from a clothes dryer, you have seen what happens when electrons are transferred from one object to another.

Suppose you rub a balloon on your hair. The atoms in your hair hold their electrons more loosely than the atoms on the balloon hold theirs. As a result, electrons are transferred from the atoms in your hair to the atoms on the surface of the balloon, as shown in **Figure 2.** Because your hair loses electrons, it becomes positively charged. The balloon gains electrons and becomes negatively charged. Your hair and the balloon become attracted to one another and make your hair stand on end. This imbalance of electric charge on an object is called a **static charge.** In solids, static charge is due to the transfer of electrons between objects. Protons cannot be removed easily from the nucleus of an atom and usually do not move from one object to another.

✔ **Reading Check** *How does an object become electrically charged?*

Ions Move in Solutions Sometimes, a flow of charge can be caused by the movement of ions instead of the movement of electrons. Table salt—sodium chloride—is made of sodium ions and chloride ions that are fixed in place and cannot move through the solid. However, when salt is dissolved in water, the sodium and chloride ions break apart and spread out evenly in the water forming a solution, as shown in **Figure 3.** Now the positive and negative ions are free to move. Solutions containing ions play an important role in enabling different parts of your body to communicate with each other. **Figure 4** shows how a nerve cell uses ions to transmit signals. These signals moving throughout your body enable you to sense, move, and even think.

Figure 3
When table salt (NaCl) dissolves in water, the sodium ions and chloride ions break apart. These ions now are able to carry electric energy.

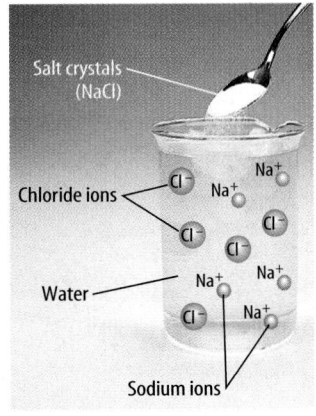

Salt crystals (NaCl)

Chloride ions

Water

Sodium ions

Cultural **Diversity**
Electric Amber The word *electricity* comes from the Greek word for amber, *elektron.* Ancient Greeks found that when amber was rubbed with fur, the amber attracted small pieces of straw.

Resource Manager

Chapter Resources Booklet
Transparency Activity, p. 44
Directed Reading for Content Mastery, pp. 19, 20
Note-taking Worksheets, pp. 33–35

Visualizing Nerve Impulses

Have students examine the pictures and read the captions. Then ask the following questions.

How are the outside and inside of a nerve cell membrane charged when the cell is not transmitting an impulse? The outside of the membrane is positively charged and the inside is negatively charged.

What happens to the charge on the inside of the cell membrane as the nerve impulse moves along the cell? The inside of the membrane becomes positively charged as sodium ions move from the outside to the inside of the membrane.

Once the impulse reaches the end of one nerve cell, how is the message continued on to the next nerve cell? A neurotransmitter is released that causes the next nerve cell to begin the process.

Activity

Have students write and perform a skit that illustrates the nerve impulse process. L2
IS Kinesthetic

Extension

Challenge students to research and find out how various diseases interrupt the process by which nerve cells transmit impulses. Have students present their finding to the class using visual aids.
L3 **IS Linguistic**

Figure 4

The control and coordination of all your bodily functions involves signals traveling from one part of your body to another through nerve cells. Nerve cells use ions to transmit signals from one nerve cell to another.

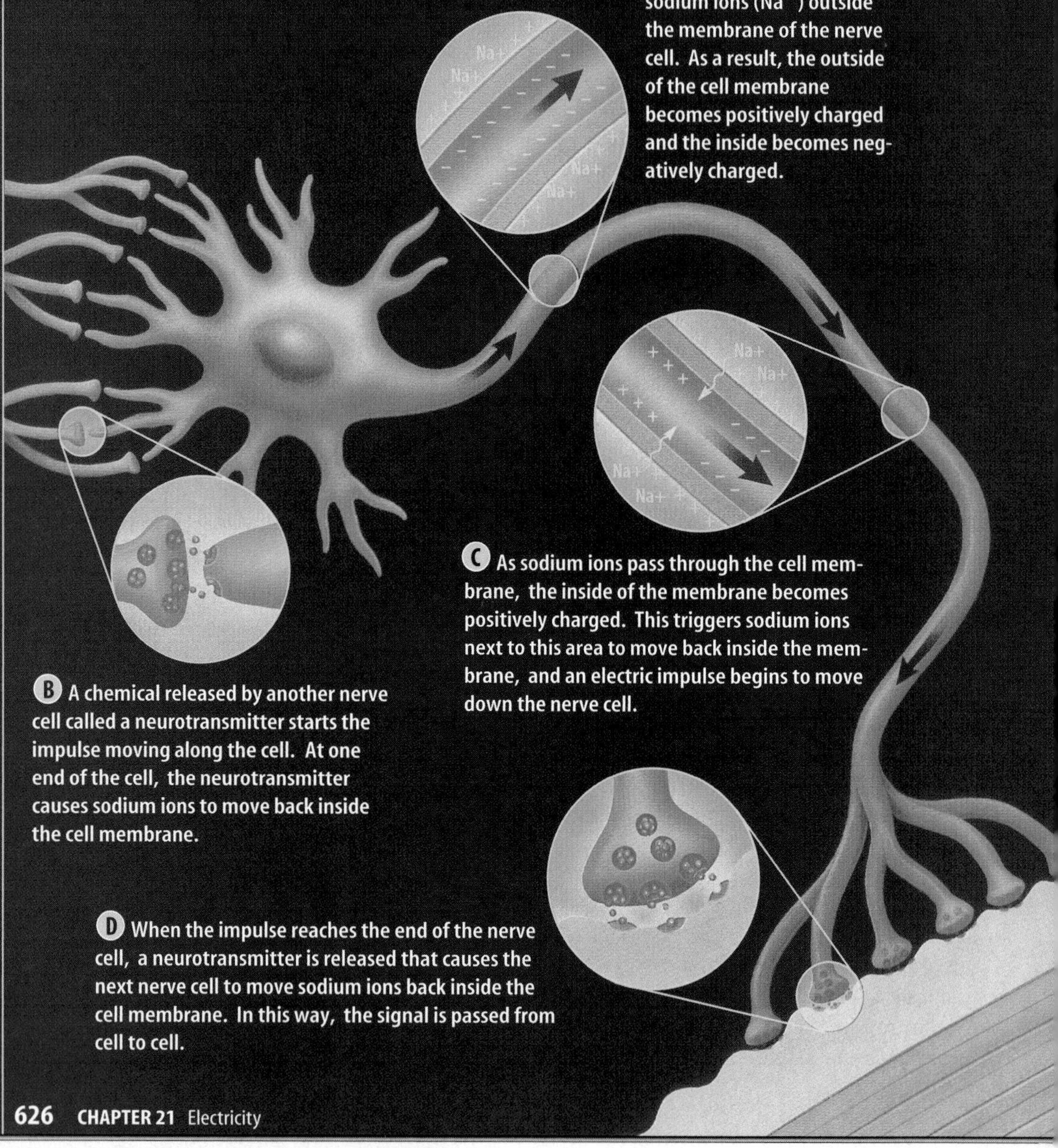

A When a nerve cell is not transmitting a signal, it moves positively charged sodium ions (Na$^+$) outside the membrane of the nerve cell. As a result, the outside of the cell membrane becomes positively charged and the inside becomes negatively charged.

C As sodium ions pass through the cell membrane, the inside of the membrane becomes positively charged. This triggers sodium ions next to this area to move back inside the membrane, and an electric impulse begins to move down the nerve cell.

B A chemical released by another nerve cell called a neurotransmitter starts the impulse moving along the cell. At one end of the cell, the neurotransmitter causes sodium ions to move back inside the cell membrane.

D When the impulse reaches the end of the nerve cell, a neurotransmitter is released that causes the next nerve cell to move sodium ions back inside the cell membrane. In this way, the signal is passed from cell to cell.

626 CHAPTER 21 Electricity

Resource Manager

Chapter Resources Booklet
Enrichment, p. 30
Lab Activity, pp. 9–12

Unlike charges attract.

Like charges repel.   Like charges repel.

Electric Forces

The electrons in an atom swarm around the nucleus. What keeps these electrons close to the nucleus? The positively charged protons in the nucleus exert an attractive electric force on the negatively charged electrons. All charged objects exert an **electric force** on each other. The electric force between two charges can be attractive or repulsive, as shown in **Figure 5**. Objects with the same type of charge repel one another and objects with opposite charges attract one another. This rule is often stated as "like charges repel, and unlike charges attract."

The electric force between two electric charges gets stronger as the distance between them decreases. A positive and a negative charge are attracted to each other more strongly if they are closer together. Two like charges are pushed away more strongly from each other the closer they are. The electric force on two objects that are charged, such as two balloons that have been rubbed on wool, also increases if the amount of charge on the objects increases.

Electric Fields You might have noticed examples of how charged objects don't have to be touching to exert an electric force on each other. For instance, two charged balloons push each other apart even though they are not touching. Also, bits of paper and a charged balloon don't have to be touching for the balloon to attract the paper. How are charged objects able to exert forces on each other without touching?

Electric charges exert a force on each other at a distance through an **electric field** that exists around every electric charge. **Figure 6** shows the electric field around a positive and a negative charge. An electric field gets stronger as you get closer to a charge, just as the electric force between two charges becomes greater as the charges get closer together.

Figure 6
The lines with arrowheads represent the electric field around charges. The direction of each arrow is the direction a positive charge would move if it were placed in the field.

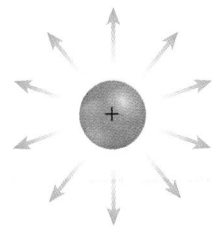

A The electric field arrows point away from a positive charge.

B The electric field arrows point toward a negative charge. *Why are these arrows in the opposite direction of the arrows around the positive charge?*

✔ Active Reading

Metacognition Journal In this strategy, each student analyzes his or her own thought processes. Have students divide the paper in half down the center. On the left, have them record what they have learned about electric charges. On the right, have them record the reason they learned it.

Electric Forces

Fun Fact

The process of charging things by rubbing is not completely understood. This branch of science is called triboelectricity.

IDENTIFYING Misconceptions

Students may think that static charge is caused by friction or that electrons are literally rubbed off one surface and onto another. Explain that static charge results from contact between two surfaces. Rubbing only increases the amount of contact area of the two bodies.

Quick Demo

To show how an electric charge can build up on a balloon, rub a balloon vigorously with a foam cup or a piece of plastic foam. In a dark room, quickly bring the charged balloon near a fluorescent light bulb. A small spark will jump, making the lightbulb flash. This works best on a cold, dry day.
L2 **IS Visual-Spatial**

Extension

Have students find out why the strong force is strong enough to hold protons and neutrons together but doesn't act on the electrons in an atom. The strong force acts only at extremely short distances—distances that are too short to affect the electrons moving around the nucleus of the atom. L3
IS Linguistic

Caption Answer

Figure 6B The arrows point in the direction a positive charge would move. A positive charge would move toward a negative charge and away from a positive charge.

Use Science Words

Word Origins Have students look up the word *conductor* and explain where it comes from. The word *conductor* comes from the Latin word *conducere,* which means "to lead or bring together." Conductors bring together opposite electric charges. L2

K Linguistic

Activity

Have groups of students brainstorm a list of objects and predict whether the objects are conductors or insulators. Then have each group use a battery, two wires, and a flashlight bulb to make a simple circuit tester and test the objects. Ask each group to make a table to summarize results. L3 ELL
COOP LEARN **K** Kinesthetic

Visual Learning

Figure 7 Point out to students that the different ways excess charges spread out on conductors and insulators is similar to the different ways water behaves on various surfaces. For example, water that falls on the freshly waxed surface of a car beads up and stays in one place. However, water that falls on a piece of wood spreads out because the wood is porous. L2

K Visual-Spatial

Figure 7
Electric charges move more easily through conductors than through insulators.

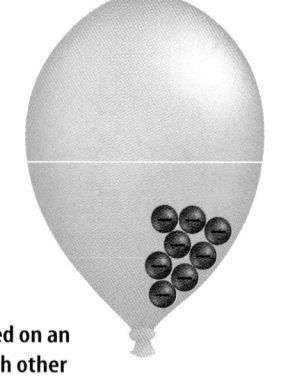 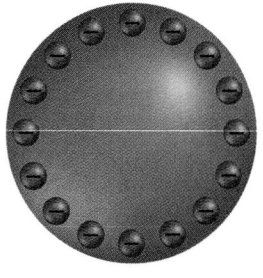

A Charges placed on an insulator repel each other but cannot move easily on the surface of the insulator. As a result, the charges remain in one place.

B Charges placed on a conductor repel each other but can move easily on the conductor's surface. Thus, they spread out as far apart as possible.

SCIENCE Online

Research Visit the Glencoe Science Web site at **science.glencoe.com** for news on recent breakthroughs in superconductor research. Communicate to your class what you learn.

Insulators and Conductors

Rubbing a balloon on your hair transfers electrons from your hair to the balloon. However, only the part of the balloon that was rubbed on your hair becomes charged because electrons cannot move easily through rubber. As a result, the electrons that were rubbed onto the balloon stay in one place, as shown in **Figure 7A.** A material in which electrons cannot move easily from place to place is called an **insulator.** Examples of insulators are plastic, wood, glass, and rubber.

Materials that are **conductors** contain electrons that can move more easily through the material. Look at **Figure 7B.** Excess electrons on the surface of a conductor spread out over the entire surface.

Metals as Conductors The best conductors are metals such as copper, gold, and aluminum. In metal atoms, a few electrons are not attracted as strongly to the nucleus as the other electrons and are loosely held by the atom. When metal atoms form a solid, the metal atoms can move only short distances. However, the electrons that are loosely held by the atoms can move easily through the solid piece of metal. In an insulator, the electrons are held tightly in the atoms that make up the insulator and therefore cannot move easily.

An electric wire is made from a conductor coated with an insulator such as plastic. Electrons move easily through the copper but do not move easily through the plastic insulation. This prevents electrons from moving through the insulation and causing an electric shock if someone touches the wire.

628 CHAPTER 21 Electricity

SCIENCE Online
Internet Addresses

_____

_____

_____

Explore the Glencoe Science Web site at **science.glencoe.com** to find out more about topics in this section.

Induced Charge

Has this ever happened to you? You walk across a carpet and as you reach for a metal doorknob, you feel an electric shock. Maybe you even see a spark jump between your fingertip and the doorknob. To find out what happened, look at **Figure 8.**

As you walk, electrons are rubbed off the rug by your shoes. The electrons then spread over the surface of your skin. As you bring your hand close to the doorknob, the electric field around the excess electrons on your hand repel the electrons in the doorknob. Because the doorknob is a good conductor, its electrons move easily. The part of the doorknob closest to your hand then becomes positively charged. This separation of positive and negative charges due to an electric field is called an **induced charge.**

If the electric field in the space between your hand and the knob is strong enough, charge can be pulled across that space, as shown in **Figure 8C.** This rapid movement of excess charge from one place to another is an **electric discharge.** Lightning is also an electric discharge. In a storm cloud, air currents cause the bottom of the cloud to become negatively charged. This negative charge induces a positive charge in the ground below the cloud. Lightning occurs when electric charge moves between the cloud and the ground.

Lightning can occur in ways other than from a cloud to the ground. To find out more about lightning, see the **Lightning Field Guide** at the back of the book.

Figure 8
A spark that jumps between your fingers and a metal doorknob starts at your feet.

A As you walk across the floor, you rub electrons from the carpet onto the bottom of your shoes. These electrons then spread out over your skin, including your hands.

B As you bring your hand close to the metal doorknob, electrons on the doorknob move as far away from your hand as possible. The part of the doorknob closest to your hand is left with a positive charge.

C The attractive electric force between the electrons on your hand and the induced positive charge on the doorknob might be strong enough to pull electrons from your hand to the doorknob. You might see this as a spark and feel a mild electric shock.

SECTION 1 Electric Charge **629**

③ Assess

Reteach

Ask students to look up the word *static* and tell one reason this word is appropriate for the term *static electricity* and one reason the word is misleading. The word *static* means "not moving." It is true that static electricity is not in continual motion like current electricity. However, a static discharge is far from motionless; it is a very rapid, though noncontinuous, transfer of charge. L2
I.S Linguistic

Challenge

Electrons and protons are electrically attracted to each other. However, all particles with mass are gravitationally attracted to one another. **Why do we ignore gravitational effects when we discuss the attraction of electrons and protons?** The masses of the particles are so small that the gravitational attraction is insignificant compared to the electrical attraction. L3
I.S Logical-Mathematical

 Assessment

Portfolio Have students draw pictures representing the charging of a balloon and the subsequent attraction of bits of paper. Encourage students to use symbols to represent positive and negative charge. Use **PASC,** p. 127. P

Figure 9
A lightning rod can protect a building from being damaged by a lightning strike. *Should a lightning rod be an insulator or a conductor?*

Grounding

Lightning is an electric discharge that can cause damage and injury because a lightning bolt releases an extremely large amount of electric energy. Even electric discharges that release small amounts of energy can damage delicate circuitry in devices such as computers. One way to avoid the damage caused by electric discharges is to make the excess charges flow harmlessly into Earth's surface. Earth can be a conductor, and because it is so large, it can absorb an enormous quantity of excess charge.

The process of providing a pathway to drain excess charge into Earth is called grounding. The pathway is usually a conductor such as a wire or a pipe. You might have noticed lightning rods at the top of buildings and towers, as shown in **Figure 9.** These rods are made of metal and are connected to metal cables that conduct electric charge into the ground if the rod is struck by lightning.

 **Reading Check** *How can tall structures be protected against lightning strikes?*

Section ① Assessment

1. What is the difference between an object that is negatively charged and one that is positively charged?
2. Two electrically charged objects repel each other. What can you say about the type of charge on each object?
3. Contrast insulators and conductors. List three materials that are good insulators and three that are good conductors.
4. Why does an electric discharge occur?
5. **Think Critically** Excess charge placed on the surface of a conductor tends to spread over the entire surface, but excess charge placed on an insulator tends to stay where it was placed originally. Explain.

Skill Builder Activities

6. **Recognizing Cause and Effect** Clothes that are dried on a clothesline outdoors don't stick to each other when they are taken out of the laundry basket. Clothes that are dried in a clothes dryer do tend to stick to each other. What is the reason for this difference? **For more help, refer to the Science Skill Handbook.**
7. **Communicating** You are sitting in a car. You slide out of the car seat, and as you start to touch the metal car door, a spark jumps from your hand to the door. In your Science Journal, describe how the spark was formed. Use at least four vocabulary words in your explanation. **For more help, refer to the Science Skill Handbook.**

630 CHAPTER 21 Electricity

Answers to Section Assessment

1. Negatively charged objects have an excess of electrons while positively charged objects have a deficit of electrons.
2. The two objects have the same type of charge.
3. In conductors electrons move easily and in insulators they do not. Accept all reasonable examples.

4. Because an electric field is strong enough to pull excess charge through air, which is normally an insulator.
5. Charge can move easily on conductors but not on insulators.
6. In a dryer, clothes continually rub against each other while on a clothesline they do not.

7. Your clothes rubbed electrons off the car seat. These then built up a static charge on your skin. When you brought your hand close to the car door, a conductor, the part of the door nearest to it became positively charged. The electric field was great enough to cause an electric discharge across the space.

Electric Current

Flow of Charge

An electric discharge, such as a lightning bolt, can release a huge amount of energy in an instant. However, electric lights, refrigerators, TVs, and stereos need a steady source of electric energy that can be controlled. This source of electric energy comes from an **electric current,** which is the flow of electric charge. In solids, the flowing charges are electrons. In liquids, the flowing charges are ions, which can be positively or negatively charged. Electric current is measured in units of amperes (A). A model for electric current is flowing water. Water flows downhill because a gravitational force acts on it. Similarly, electrons flow because an electric force acts on them.

A Model for a Simple Circuit How does a flow of water provide energy? If the water is separated from Earth by using a pump, the higher water now has gravitational potential energy, as shown in **Figure 10.** As the water falls and does work on the waterwheel, the water loses potential energy and the waterwheel gains kinetic energy. For the water to flow continuously, it must flow through a closed loop. Electric charges will flow continuously only through a closed conducting loop called a **circuit.**

As You Read

What You'll Learn

- **Relate** voltage to the electric energy carried by an electric current.
- **Describe** a battery and how it produces an electric current.
- **Explain** electrical resistance.

Vocabulary

electric current   voltage
circuit   resistance

Why It's Important

The electric appliances you use rely on electric current.

Figure 10
The potential energy of water is increased when a pump raises the water above Earth. The greater the height is, the more energy the water has. *How can this energy be used?*

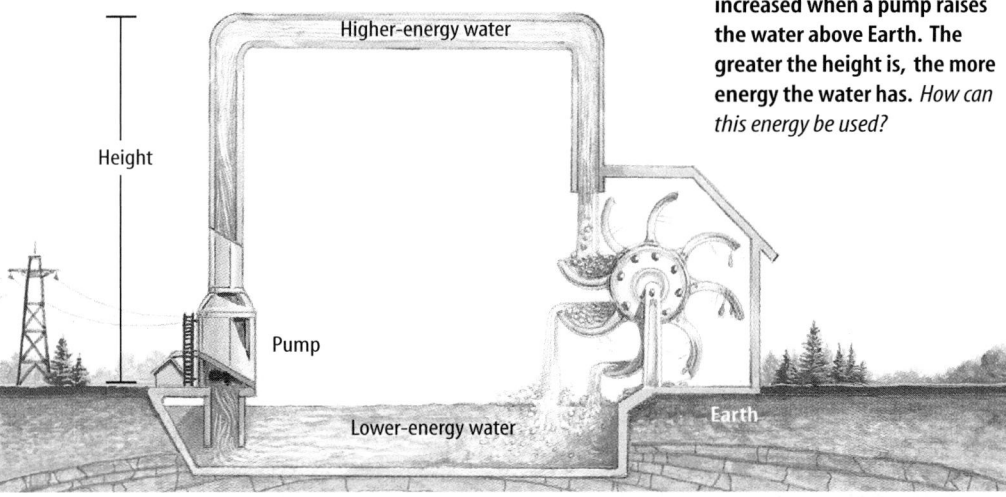

Higher-energy water

Height

Pump

Lower-energy water

Earth

SECTION 2 Electric Current **631**

Section ✓*Assessment* Planner

PORTFOLIO
Assessment, p. 635
PERFORMANCE ASSESSMENT
Try At Home MiniLAB, p. 632
Skill Builder Activities, p. 635
See page 650 for more options.

CONTENT ASSESSMENT
Section, p. 635
Challenge, p. 635
Chapter, pp. 650–651

1 Motivate

Bellringer Transparency

Display the Section Focus Transparency for Section 2. Use the accompanying Transparency Activity Master. L2
ELL

Tie to Prior Knowledge

Ask students what happens to devices like tape players when the batteries get old. They either run more slowly or stop working. Explain that this occurs because the batteries no longer produce adequate electric current.

Caption Answer

Figure 10 to do work

Resource Manager

Chapter Resources Booklet
Transparency Activity, p. 45
Directed Reading for Content Mastery, p. 21

Section 2 Electric Current **631**

Purpose Students observe static electricity with a comb. L2

ELL IS **Kinesthetic**

Materials plate, salt, pepper, plastic comb, wool clothing

Teaching Strategy Instruct students to rub the comb on the wool vigorously for several seconds and then comb through the particles immediately.

Analysis
1. The comb attracted the pepper flakes and some small crystals of salt.
2. Salt crystals are larger and heavier than pepper flakes, and the electric force is only strong enough to lift the smaller crystals.

Performance Ask students to perform this activity for their family or friends as a "magic" trick. Have them explain how the trick works using static electricity. Use **PASC**, p. 97.

TRY AT HOME
Mini LAB

Investigating the Electric Force

Procedure
1. Pour a layer of **salt** on a **plate.**
2. Sparingly sprinkle grains of **pepper** on top of the salt. Do not use too much pepper.
3. Rub a **rubber** or **plastic comb** on an article of **wool clothing.**
4. Slowly drag the comb through the salt and observe.

Analysis
1. How did the salt and pepper react to the comb?
2. Explain why the pepper reacted differently than the salt.

Figure 11
As long as there is a closed path for electrons to follow, electrons flow in a circuit from the negative battery terminal to the positive terminal.

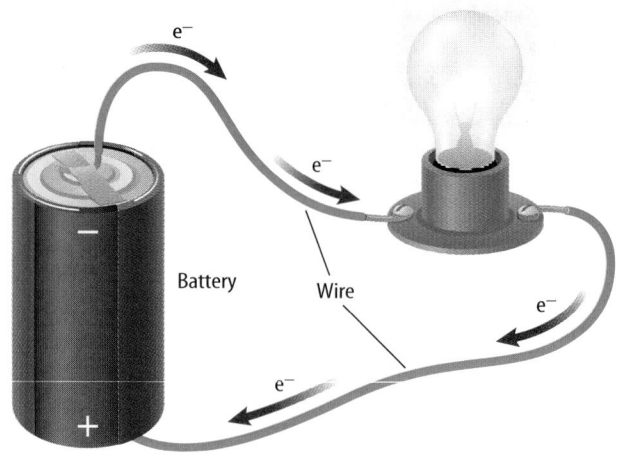

Electric Circuits The simplest electric circuit contains a source of electrical energy, such as a battery, and an electric conductor, such as a wire, connected to the battery. For the simple circuit shown in **Figure 11,** a closed path is formed by wires connected to a lightbulb and to a battery. Electric current flows in the circuit as long as none of the wires, including the glowing filament wire in the lightbulb, is disconnected or broken.

Voltage In a water circuit, a pump increases the gravitaional potential energy of the water by raising the water from a lower level to a higher level. In an electric circuit, a battery increases the electric potential energy of electrons. This electric potential energy can be transformed into other forms of energy. The **voltage** of a battery is a measure of how much electric potential energy each electron can gain. As voltage increases, more electric potential energy is available to be transformed into other forms of energy. Voltage is measured in volts (V).

How a Current Flows You may think that when an electric current flows in a circuit, electrons travel completely around the circuit. Actually, individual electrons move slowly through a wire in an electric circuit. When the ends of the wire are connected to a battery, electrons in the wire begin to move toward the positive battery terminal. As an electron moves it collides with other electric charges in the wire, and is deflected in a different direction. After each collision, the electron again starts moving toward the positive terminal. A single electron may undergo more than ten trillion collisions each second. As a result, it may take several minutes for an electron in the wire to travel one centimeter.

Cultural **Diversity**

Lewis Latimer Thomas Edison's first successful electric lamp had treated paper filaments that burned out quickly. In 1881, African American inventor Lewis Latimer patented an improved carbon-based filament that lasted much longer. Latimer also improved the lightbulb's socket. As part of Edison's team, Latimer helped supervise the installation of electric lights in New York, Philadelphia, Montreal, and London.

Resource Manager

Chapter Resources Booklet
MiniLAB, p. 3
Lab Activity, pp. 13–15
Transparency Activity, pp. 47–48

Batteries A battery supplies energy to an electric circuit. When the positive and negative terminals in a battery are connected in a circuit, the electric potential energy of the electrons in the circuit is increased. As these electrons move toward the positive battery terminal, this electric potential energy is transformed into other forms of energy, just as gravitational potential energy is converted into kinetic energy as water falls.

A battery supplies energy to an electric circuit by converting chemical energy to electric potential energy. For the alkaline battery shown in **Figure 12,** the two terminals are separated by a moist paste. Chemical reactions in the moist paste cause electrons to be transferred to the negative terminal, and from the atoms in the positive terminal. As a result, the negative terminal becomes negatively charged and the positive terminal becomes positively charged. This causes electrons in the circuit to be pushed away from the negative terminal and to be attracted to the positive terminal.

Battery Life Batteries don't supply energy forever. Maybe you know someone whose car wouldn't start after the lights had been left on overnight? Why do batteries run down? Batteries contain only a limited amount of the chemicals that react to produce chemical energy. These reactions go on as the battery is used and the chemicals are changed into other compounds. Once the original chemicals are used up, the chemical reactions stop and the battery is "dead."

Chemistry
INTEGRATION

Many chemicals are used to make an alkaline battery. Zinc is a source of electrons and positive ions, manganese dioxide is used to collect the electrons at the positive terminal, and water is used to carry ions through the battery. Visit the Glencoe Science Web site at **science.glencoe.com** for information about the chemistry of batteries.

Chemistry
INTEGRATION

In an acidic dry cell, the ammonium chloride (NH_4Cl) is reduced: $2NH_4^+ + 2MnO_2 + 2e^- \rightarrow Mn_2O_3 + 2NH_3 + H_2O$. A thin zinc cylinder serves as the anode and it undergoes oxidation: $Zn\ (s) \rightarrow Zn^{2+} + 2e^-$. This dry cell produces about 1.5 volts. In the alkaline version, the ammonium chloride is replaced by KOH or NaOH and the half-cell reactions are: $Zn + 2OH^- \rightarrow ZnO + H_2O + 2e^-$ and $2MnO_2 + 2e^- + H_2O \rightarrow Mn_2O_3 + 2OH^-$. The alkaline dry cell lasts much longer as the zinc anode corrodes less rapidly under basic conditions than under acidic conditions.

IDENTIFYING
Misconceptions

The net speed of charges in a wire carrying current is only about 1mm/s. Why does a light turn on immediately even though the lamp cord is long? The circuit that is completed when the switch is turned on sets up an electric field along the entire wire almost instantaneously. The charges already in the wire respond to the electric field, and the current starts throughout the wire all at once.

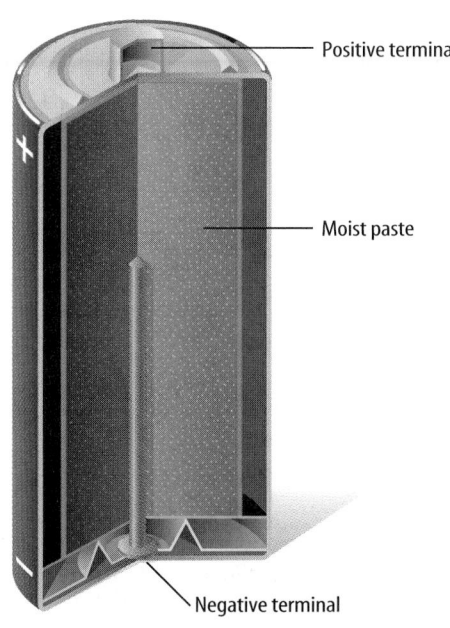

Positive terminal

Moist paste

Negative terminal

Figure 12
When this alkaline battery is connected in an electric circuit, chemical reactions occur in the moist paste of this alkaline battery that move electrons from the positive terminal to the negative terminal.

LAB DEMONSTRATION

Purpose to show how a battery works

Materials 10 pennies, 10 nickels, salt, water, paper towel, voltmeter

Alternate materials 10 pieces of aluminum foil, 10 dimes

Procedure Add as much salt to a cup of water as will dissolve. Soak a paper towel in the salt water. Make a stack by alternating pennies and nickels with pieces of the wet paper towel between them. Connect the voltmeter to each end of the stack and measure the voltage.

Expected Outcome Students should see the voltmeter jump slightly when the wires are connected.

✔Assessment

What is happening in the stack of pennies and nickels? Chemical reactions are sending electrons to one end of the stack, making it negative and the other end positive. **How might this battery wear out?** The towel might dry out.

Resistance

Use an Analogy

Electrons encounter atoms and other electrons as they make their way through a wire in a way that is similar to the way you constantly bump against other people and objects as you move through a crowded hallway. You can't move as fast as you'd like because you must zigzag to avoid other people and objects. As you move, you lose some of your energy to the people you bump into.

✔ Reading Check

Answer Yes; it can provide heat and light.

Caption Answer

Figure 13 to heat in the wire

Resistance

Electrons can move much more easily through conductors than through insulators, but even conductors interfere somewhat with the flow of electrons. The measure of how difficult it is for electrons to flow through a material is called **resistance.** The unit of resistance is the ohm (Ω). Insulators generally have much higher resistance than conductors.

As electrons flow through a circuit, they collide with the atoms and other electric charges in the materials that make up the circuit. Look at **Figure 13.** These collisions cause some of the electrons' electric energy to be converted into thermal energy—heat—and sometimes into light. The amount of electric energy that is converted into heat and light depends on the resistance of the materials in the circuit.

Wires and Filaments The amount of electric energy that is converted into thermal energy increases as the resistance of the wire increases. Copper, which is one of the best electric conductors, has low resistance. Copper is used in household wiring because little electric energy is lost as electrons flow through copper wires. As a result, not much heat is produced. Because copper wires don't heat up much, the wires don't become hot enough to melt through their insulation, which makes fires less likely to occur. On the other hand, tungsten wire has a higher resistance. As electrons flow through tungsten wire, it becomes extremely hot—so hot, in fact, that it glows with a bright light. The high temperature makes tungsten a poor choice for household wiring, but the light it gives off makes it an excellent choice for the filaments of lightbulbs.

✔ Reading Check
Is having resistance in electrical wires ever beneficial?

Figure 13
As electrons flow through a wire, they travel in a zigzag path as they collide with atoms and other electrons. These collisions cause the electrons to lose some electric energy. *Where does this electric energy go?*

Resource Manager

Chapter Resources Booklet
Enrichment, p. 31
Reinforcement, p. 28

Teacher FYI

Some substances lose all resistance and become superconductors when they are cooled to temperatures approaching absolute zero (0 K). Scientists theorize that at these low temperatures electrons travel in connected groups of pairs. This enables them to move through the material without being scattered by collisions.

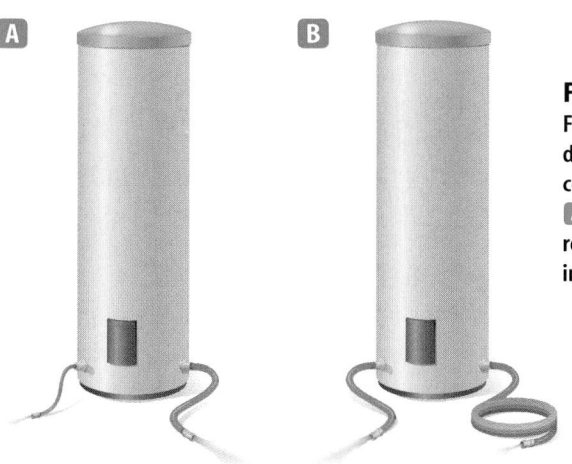

Figure 14
For water and electrons, the diameter and length of the conductor influence resistance. **A** A narrow hose increases the resistance. **B** A long hose also increases the resistance.

Slowing the Flow The electric resistance of a wire also depends on the length and thickness of the wire. Imagine water flowing through a hose, as shown in **Figure 14.** As the hose becomes more narrow or longer, the water flow decreases. In a similar way, the length and diameter of a wire affects electron flow. The electric resistance increases as the wire becomes longer or as it becomes narrower.

Section Assessment

1. How does increasing the voltage in a circuit affect the energy of the electrons flowing in the circuit?

2. How does a battery cause electrons to move in an electric circuit?

3. For the same length, which has more resistance—a garden hose or a fire hose? Which has more resistance—a thin wire or a thick wire?

4. Why is copper often used in household wiring?

5. **Think Critically** Some electrical devices require two batteries, usually placed end to end. How does the voltage of the combination compare with the voltage of a single battery? Try it.

Skill Builder Activities

6. **Drawing Conclusions** Observe the size of various batteries, such as a watch battery, a camera battery, a flashlight battery, and an automobile battery. Conclude whether the voltage produced by a battery is related to its physical size. **For more help, refer to the Science Skill Handbook.**

7. **Communicating** The terms *circuit, current,* and *resistance* are often used in everyday language. In your Science Journal, record several different ways of using the words *circuit, current,* and *resistance.* Compare and contrast the everyday use of the words with their scientific definitions. **For more help, refer to the Science Skill Handbook.**

3 Assess

Reteach
Ask students to relate current and voltage in a wire to the flow of water in a pipe. Water will flow through a pipe if the pressure at one end of the pipe is different from the pressure at the other end. Likewise, current flows through a wire if the voltage at one end of the wire is different from the voltage at the other end. L2 LS **Linguistic**

Challenge
Ask students to explain why rechargeable batteries recharge when a current passes through them. The current makes the chemical reaction run the opposite way. Once the battery is recharged, the original chemicals are again present. L3 LS **Logical-Mathematical**

✔Assessment

Portfolio Have students make detailed posters of a particular type of battery. Labels should indicate the chemical reactions taking place and which way the charges will flow. Use **Performance Assessment in the Science Classroom,** p. 145. P

Answers to Section Assessment

1. It gives the electrons in the circuit more energy.
2. chemical reactions in the battery
3. the garden hose; a thin wire
4. It is a good conductor and does not heat up much.
5. The combination has twice the voltage. The voltages of the batteries add together to produce the total voltage.
6. The voltage of a battery is not related to size. A car battery is 12 V. A D-cell battery is 1.5 V. A smaller camera battery is 6 V.
7. The word *circuit* refers to a path that is in the form of a closed loop. In electricity, a circuit is a closed path through which electrons flow. In everyday use, the word *current* refers to flow, as in currents of water in the ocean. In electricity, current describes the flow of electrons. When used in discussions of electricity, resistance means opposition to the flow of electrons. In everyday use, the word *resistance* also describes opposition.

Section 2 Electric Current **635**

SECTION

3

Electric Circuits

1 Motivate

Bellringer Transparency

Display the Section Focus Transparency for Section 3. Use the accompanying Transparency Activity Master. L2

ELL

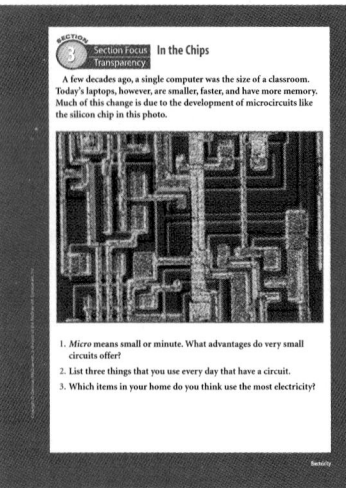

SECTION

3 Section Focus Transparency   In the Chips

A few decades ago, a single computer was the size of a classroom. Today's laptops, however, are smaller, faster, and have more memory. Much of this change is due to the development of microcircuits like the silicon chip in this photo.

1. *Micro* means small or minute. What advantages do very small circuits offer?
2. List three things that you use every day that have a circuit.
3. Which items in your home do you think use the most electricity?

Electricity

Tie to Prior Knowledge

What happens to the water flowing from a hose that has been perforated with holes? Water flows out of all the holes, making the flow at the end of the hose weaker. Tell students that in this section they will learn how voltage and current can be modified as electric charge flows through a wire.

SECTION

3 **Electric Circuits**

As You Read

What You'll Learn

■ **Explain** how voltage, current, and resistance are related in an electric circuit.
■ **Investigate** the difference between series and parallel circuits.
■ **Determine** the electric power used in a circuit.
■ **Describe** how to avoid dangerous electric shock.

Vocabulary
Ohm's law
series circuit
parallel circuit
electric power

Why It's Important
Understanding how circuits work will help you better use electricity.

Controlling the Current

When you connect a conductor, such as a wire or a lightbulb, between the positive and negative terminals of a battery, electrons flow in the circuit. The amount of current is determined by the voltage supplied by the battery and the resistance of the conductor. To help understand this relationship, imagine a bucket with a hose at the bottom, as shown in **Figure 15.** If the bucket is raised, water will flow out of the hose faster than before. Increasing the height will increase the current.

Voltage and Resistance Think back to the pump and waterwheel in **Figure 10.** Recall that the raised water has energy that is lost when the water falls. Increasing the height from which the water falls increases the energy of the water. Increasing the height of the water is similar to increasing the voltage of the battery. Just as the water current increases when the height of the water increases, the electric current in a circuit increases as voltage increases.

If the diameter of the tube in **Figure 15** is decreased, resistance is greater and the flow of the water decreases. In the same way, as the resistance in an electric circuit increases, the current in the circuit decreases.

Figure 15
Raising the bucket higher increases the potential energy of the water in the bucket. This causes the water to flow out of the hose faster.

Section ✔*Assessment* Planner

PORTFOLIO	Skill Builder Activities, p. 642
Visual Learning, p. 638	See page 650 for more options.
PERFORMANCE ASSESSMENT	CONTENT ASSESSMENT
Math Skills Activity, p. 637	Section, p. 642
MiniLAB, p. 638	Challenge, p. 642
Math Skills Activity, p. 640	Chapter, pp. 650–651

Ohm's Law A nineteenth-century German physicist, Georg Simon Ohm, carried out experiments that measured how changing the voltage and resistance in a circuit affected the current. The relationship he found among voltage, current and resistance is now known as **Ohm's law.** In equation form, Ohm's law is written as follows.

$$\text{current} = \frac{\text{voltage}}{\text{resistance}}$$

$$I\,(\text{A}) = \frac{V\,(\text{V})}{R\,(\Omega)}$$

According to Ohm's law, when the voltage in a circuit increases the current increases, just as water flows faster from a bucket that is raised higher. However, when the resistance is increased, the current in the circuit decreases.

Math Skills Activity

Calculating the Current Used by Lightbulbs

Example Problem
In homes, the standard electric outlet provides 110 V. What is the current through a lightbulb with a resistance of 220 Ω?

Solution

1 *This is what you know:*   voltage: $V = 110$ V
                                     resistance: $R = 220$ Ω

2 *This is what you need to find:*   current: I

3 *This is the equation you need to use:* $I = V/R$

4 *Substitute the known values:* $I = (110\text{ V})/(220\ \Omega)$
                                           $= 0.5$ A

Check your answer by multiplying it by the resistance of 220 Ω. Do you calculate the given voltage of 110 V?

Practice Problems

1. What is the resistance of a lightbulb connected to a 110-V outlet that requires a current of 0.2 A?
2. Which draws more current at the same voltage, a lightbulb with higher resistance or a lightbulb with lower resistance? Use a mathematical example to answer this question.

For more help, refer to the Math Skill Handbook.

Curriculum Connection

History Ask students to find out more about Georg Simon Ohm. Georg Simon Ohm lived from 1789 to 1854. Ohm found that the resistance of a wire was independent of the current flowing through it. He theorized that electricity moved from particle to particle in a wire and formulated the law named for him. [L2] **IS** **Linguistic**

Resource Manager

Chapter Resources Booklet
    Transparency Activity, p. 46
    Directed Reading for Content Mastery, pp. 21, 22

---

② Teach

Controlling the Current

Discussion

The text states that narrowing a tube will increase the resistance to the flow of water through the tube. This is similar to using a thinner wire to conduct charge. In what other ways could you increase resistance to the flow of water in a tube, and what would be similar ways to increase resistance to electric current in a conductor? Making the tube longer would be similar to making the current path in a circuit longer. Adding material in the tube to reduce the flow at various places would be similar to putting resistors in a circuit. [L2] **IS**
Logical-Mathematical

Make a Model

Have interested students make a mechanical model of an electric circuit. Students might rig a small motor to lift marbles to a height. These marbles would be dropped into a tube filled with marbles, pushing some marbles out the other end, and then returning them to the lift mechanism. Have students present their models to the class, describing how each segment represents one aspect of an electric circuit. [L3]
IS **Kinesthetic**

Math Skills Activity

National Math Standards
Correlation to Mathematics Objectives
1, 2, 4, 6, 8, 9

Answers to Practice Problems

1. 500Ω
2. A lightbulb with a lower resistance draws more current. Accept all reasonable examples.

Series and Parallel Circuits

Mini LAB

Identifying Simple Circuits

Procedure

1. The filament in a lightbulb is a piece of wire. For the bulb to light, an electric current must flow through the filament in a complete circuit. Examine the base of a **flashlight bulb** carefully. Where are the ends of the filament connected to the base?
2. Connect one piece of **wire,** a **battery,** and a flashlight bulb to make the bulb light. (There are four possible ways to do this.)

Analysis

Draw and label a diagram showing the path that is followed by the electrons in your circuit. Explain your diagram.

Figure 16
This circuit is an example of a series circuit. A series circuit has only one path for electric current to follow. *What happens to the current in this circuit if any of the connecting wires are removed?*

Series and Parallel Circuits

Circuits control the movement of electric current by providing a path for electrons to follow. For current to flow, the circuit must provide an unbroken path for current to follow. Have you ever been putting up holiday lights and had a string that would not light because a single bulb was missing or had burned out and you couldn't figure out which one it was? Maybe you've noticed that some strings of lights don't go out no matter how many bulbs burn out or are removed. These two strings of holiday lights are examples of the two kinds of basic circuits—series and parallel.

Wired in a Line A **series circuit** is a circuit that has only one path for the electric current to follow, as shown in **Figure 16.** If this path is broken, then the current no longer will flow and all the devices in the circuit stop working. If the entire string of lights went out when only one bulb burned out, then the lights in the string were wired as a series circuit. When the bulb burned out, the filament in the bulb broke and the current path through the entire string was broken.

✔ **Reading Check** *How many different paths can electric current follow in a series circuit?*

In a series circuit, electrical devices are connected along the same current path. As a result, the current is the same through every device. However, each new device that is added to the circuit decreases the current throughout the circuit. This is because each device has electrical resistance, and in a series circuit, the total resistance to the flow of electrons increases as each additional device is added to the circuit. By Ohm's law, as the resistance increases, the current decreases.

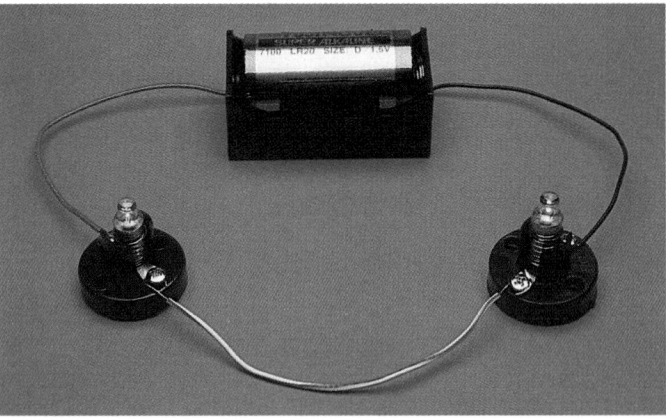

Branched Wiring What if you wanted to watch TV and had to turn on all the lights, a hair dryer, and every other electrical appliance in the house to do so? That's what it would be like if all the electrical appliances in your house were connected in a series circuit.

Instead, houses, schools, and other buildings are wired using parallel circuits. A **parallel circuit** is a circuit that has more than one path for the electric current to follow, as shown in **Figure 17.** The current branches so that electrons flow through each of the paths. If one path is broken, electrons continue to flow through the other paths. Adding or removing additional devices in one branch does not break the current path in the other branches, so the devices on those branches continue to work normally.

In a parallel circuit, the resistance in each branch can be different, depending on the devices in the branch. The lower the resistance is in a branch, the more current flows in the branch. So the current in each branch of a parallel circuit can be different.

Figure 17
This circuit is an example of a parallel circuit. A parallel circuit has more than one path for electric current to follow. *What happens to the current in the circuit if either of the wires connecting the two lightbulbs is removed?*

Protecting Electric Circuits

In a parallel circuit, the current that flows out of the battery or electric outlet increases as more devices are added to the circuit. As the current through the circuit increases, the wires heat up.

To keep the wire from becoming hot enough to cause a fire, the circuits in houses and other buildings have fuses or circuit breakers like those shown in **Figure 18** that limit the amount of current in the wiring. When the current becomes larger than 15 A or 20 A, a piece of metal in the fuse melts or a switch in the circuit breaker opens, stopping the current. The cause of the overload can then be removed, and the circuit can be used again by replacing the fuse or resetting the circuit breaker.

Figure 18
You might have fuses in your home that prevent electric wires from overheating.

 **In some buildings, each circuit is connected to a fuse. The fuses are usually located in a fuse box.**

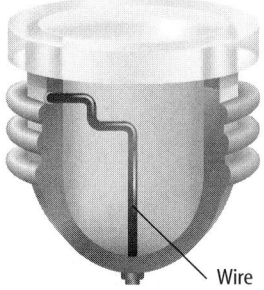
Wire

B **A fuse contains a piece of wire that melts and breaks when the current flowing through the fuse becomes too large.**

SECTION 3 Electric Circuits **639**

Quick Demo
Connect one flashlight bulb to a battery and have students note the brightness. Then connect another bulb in series and have students identify what happens. The brightness of the two bulbs is less than the brightness of the single bulb. Next connect the bulbs in parallel and have students note the difference. Both should glow more brightly than the single bulb did.

IDENTIFYING Misconceptions

Emphasize to students that current is not used up when passing through an electric circuit. The electrons that move in a circuit when a battery is connected are in the conductors that make up the circuit. A battery produces an electric field that causes these electrons to drift slowly toward the positive battery terminal. Electrons continue to move as long as the battery is connected.

Protecting Electric Circuits

Fun Fact

Today, many electrical devices have various types of circuit breakers of their own. The large plugs on many hairdryers and the buttons on the sides of power strips are circuit breakers that prevent these devices from drawing too much current or overheating.

Resource Manager

Chapter Resources Booklet
MiniLAB, p. 4
Enrichment, p. 32

Electric Power

Visual Learning

Table 1 Have students identify the appliances in most homes that use the most power. toaster, hairdryer **Why do these use the most power?** They produce heat. They have circuits that have low resistance and so draw a large current. L2

Logical-Mathematical

Make a Model

Explain to students that a circuit diagram is a model of an electric circuit. It shows the source of electric power, the arrangement of the wiring, and all of the devices that use electric power. Have students draw circuit diagrams of the wiring in one or two rooms in a house. Ask them to include in their diagrams at least three devices that use electricity. Students may use standard electrical symbols, or they may make up their own. Make sure they include a key to the symbols they use. L2 **Visual-Spatial**

Math Skills Activity

National Math Standards

Correlation to Mathematics Objectives

1, 2, 6, 8, 9

Answer to Practice Problem

0.23A

Table 1	Power Ratings of Common Appliances
Appliance	**Power (W)**
Computer	150
Color TV	140
Stereo	60
Refrigerator	350
Toaster	1,100
Microwave	800
Hair dryer	1,200

Electric Power

Electric energy is used in many ways to do useful jobs. Toasters and electric ovens convert electric energy to heat, stereos convert electric energy to sound, and a fan blade rotates as electric energy is converted to mechanical energy. The rate at which an appliance converts electric energy to another form of energy is the **electric power** used by the appliance.

Calculating Power The rate at which energy is used in the circuit is related to the amount of energy carried by the electrons, which increases as the voltage increases. The power that is used also is related to the rate at which electrons flow into the circuit. As a result, the power that is used in a circuit can be determined by multiplying the current by the voltage.

$$\text{Power} = \text{current} \times \text{voltage}$$
$$P\,(\text{W}) = I\,(\text{A}) \times V\,(\text{V})$$

Table 1 lists the power required by several common appliances. The unit of power is the watt, W.

Math Skills Activity

Calculating the Wattage of Lightbulbs

Example Problem

How much power does a lightbulb use if the current is 0.55 A and the voltage is 110 V?

Solution

1 This is what you know: voltage: $V = 110$ V
    current: $I = 0.55$ A

2 This is what you need to find: power: P

3 This is the equation you need to use: $P = I \times V$

4 Substitute the known values: $P = 0.55\,\text{A} \times 110\,\text{V}$
    $= 60$ W

Check your answer by dividing it by the current of 0.55 A. Did you calculate the given voltage of 110 V?

Practice Problem

How much current does a 25-W bulb require in a 110-V circuit?

For more help, refer to the Math Skill Handbook.

640   CHAPTER 21 Electricity

Power in the Home Have students collect the power information from some of the appliances in their homes. Have them calculate how much power each device uses in a month and write their findings in their Science Journals. L2 **Logical-Mathematical**

Resource Manager

Chapter Resources Booklet
Reinforcement, p. 29

Cost of Electric Energy Power is the rate at which energy is used, or the amount of energy that is used per second. When you use a hair dryer, the amount of electric energy that is used depends on the power of the hair dryer and the amount of time you use it. If you used it for 5 min yesterday and 10 min today, you used twice as much energy today as yesterday.

Using electric energy costs money. Electric companies generate electric energy and sell it in units of kilowatt-hours to homes, schools, and businesses. One kilowatt-hour, kWh, is an amount of electric energy equal to using 1 kW of power continuously for 1 h. This would be the amount of energy needed to light ten 100-W lightbulbs for 1 h, or one 100-W lightbulb for 10 h.

 **Reading Check** *What does kWh stand for and what does it measure?*

An electric company usually charges its customers for the number of kilowatt-hours they use every month. The number of kilowatt-hours used in a building such as a house or a school is measured by an electric meter, which usually is attached to the outside of the building, as shown in **Figure 19.**

Electrical Safety

Health **INTEGRATION**

Have you ever had a mild electric shock? You probably felt only a mild tingling sensation, but electricity can have much more dangerous effects. In 1997, electric shocks killed an estimated 490 people in the United States. **Table 2** lists a few safety tips to help prevent electrical accidents.

Table 2 Situations to Avoid
Never use appliances with frayed or damaged electric cords.
Unplug appliances before working on them, such as when prying toast out of a jammed toaster.
Avoid all water when using plugged-in appliances.
Never touch power lines with anything, including kite string and ladders.
Always respect warning signs and labels.

Figure 19
Electric meters measure the amount of electric energy used in kilowatt-hours. *Find the electric meter that records the electric energy used in your house.*

SCIENCE Online

Data Update Visit the Glencoe Science Web site at **science.glencoe.com** to find the cost of electric energy in various parts of the world. Communicate to your class what you learn.

✔ **Reading Check**

Answer kWh stands for kilowatt-hours. A kWh is the amount of electrical energy equal to using 1 kW of power continuously for an hour.

Electrical Safety

Teacher **FYI**

Current following a left-hand-to-either-foot path through the body poses the greatest threat of causing cardiac arrest. The damage done by electric shock depends on the amount of electric current and the length of time of the shock. For the average adult experiencing a 200 mA left-hand-to-either-foot current, the threshold for muscular contractions causing breathing difficulties is approximately 50 ms, while the threshold for ventricular fibrillation is about 400 ms.

IDENTIFYING
Misconceptions

Students may think that a higher voltage is always more dangerous than a lower voltage. Remind them that a higher voltage can be less dangerous than a lower voltage if the lower voltage produces more current. For example, a balloon can be charged to thousands of volts. Yet touching the balloon does not cause a dangerous shock because only a small current flows from the balloon. However, a 110-volt electric outlet can cause a dangerous shock because the current flowing into the body can be large.

Curriculum Connection

Math Have students read the electric meters for their homes at the beginning of the week and at the end of the week. If they can find the price per kilowatt-hour, have them calculate the cost of the week's electric usage. L2 **Logical-Mathematical**

SCIENCE Online
Internet Addresses _____

_____

_____

_____

Explore the Glencoe Science Web site at **science.glencoe.com** to find out more about topics in this section.

Electrical Safety, continued

Life Science
INTEGRATION

Have students investigate the first-aid procedures for treating electric shock. What first-aid procedures should you be aware of? Possible answer: CPR to restart the heart and treatment for shock [L2]
[IS] **Kinesthetic**

3 Assess

Reteach

Bring to class an energy-rating label from a new appliance. Have students use the energy specifications of the appliance to determine the energy it will use and its power. Have them estimate the cost to run the appliance for one year. [L2]
[IS] **Logical-Mathematical**

Challenge

With students, do an electrical safety check of the classroom. Identify electrical hazards, such as frayed cords and too many appliances running from a single outlet. Also check the placement of appliances and consider whether any might be in a dangerous spot. [L2] [IS] **Visual-Spatial**

✔Assessment

Process Provide students with basic circuit diagrams. Have them describe which devices are in series and which devices are in parallel. Have them predict the changes that occur when one device is turned off or removed. Use **Performance Assessment in the Science Classroom,** p. 89.

Life Science
INTEGRATION

The scale below shows how the effect of electric current on the human body depends on the amount of current that flows into the body.

0.0005 A	Tingle
0.001 A	Pain threshold
0.01 A	Inability to let go
0.025 A	
0.05 A	Difficulty breathing
0.10 A	
0.25 A	
0.50 A	Heart failure
1.00 A	

Electric Shock You experience an electric shock when an electric current enters your body. In some ways your body is like a piece of insulated wire. The fluids inside your body are good conductors of current. The electrical resistance of dry skin is much higher. Skin insulates the body like the plastic insulation around a copper wire. Your skin helps keep electric current from entering your body.

A current can enter your body when you accidentally become part of an electric circuit. Whether you receive a deadly shock depends on the amount of current that flows into your body. The current that flows through the wires connected to a 60 W light-bulb is 0.5 A. This amount of current entering your body could be deadly. Even a current as small as 0.001 A can be painful.

Lightning Safety On average, more people are killed every year by lightning in the United States than by hurricanes or tornadoes. Most lightning deaths and injuries occur outdoors. If you are outside and can see lightning or hear thunder, you should take shelter in a large, enclosed building if possible. A metal vehicle such as a car, bus, or van can provide protection if you avoid contact with metal surfaces.

You should avoid high places and open fields, and stay away from isolated high objects such as trees, flagpoles, or light towers. Avoid picnic shelters, baseball dugouts, bleachers, metal fences, and bodies of water. If you are caught outdoors, get in the lightning-safety position—squat low to the ground on the balls of your feet with your hands on your knees.

Section 3 Assessment

1. As the resistance in a simple circuit increases, what happens to the current?
2. What are the differences between a series circuit and a parallel circuit?
3. You have the stereo on while you're working on the computer. Which appliance is using more power?
4. How is your body like a piece of insulated wire?
5. **Think Critically** What determines whether a 100-W lightbulb costs more to use than a 1,200-W hair dryer does?

Skill Builder Activities

6. **Making and Using Graphs** Using 1,000 W for 1 h costs around $0.20. Calculate the cost of using each of the appliances in **Table 1** for 24 h. Present your results in a table. **For more help, refer to the** Science Skill Handbook.
7. **Using Proportions** A typical household uses 1,000 kWh of electrical energy every month. If a power company supplies electrical energy to 10,000 households, how much electrical energy must it supply every year? **For more help, refer to the** Math Skill Handbook.

642 CHAPTER 21 Electricity

Answers to Section Assessment

1. It decreases.
2. Series circuits have only one path for current to follow. Parallel circuits have multiple paths.
3. the computer
4. Your dry skin is a much better insulator than the solutions in the tissues inside your body.

5. The length of time that each is used determines the energy consumed and so the cost of using each.
6. Using the formula P/1000 × 0.2 × 24, to run 24 hours, the computer would cost $0.72, color TV would cost $0.67, stereo would cost $0.29, refrigerator would cost $1.68,

toaster would cost $5.28, microwave would cost $3.84, hair dryer would cost $5.76.
7. 1,000 kWh/month × 12 months = 12,000 kWh; 12,000 kWh/household × 10,000 households = 120,000,000 kWh

Activity

Current in a Parallel Circuit

In this activity, you will investigate how the current in a circuit changes when two or more lightbulbs are connected in parallel. Because the brightness of a lightbulb increases or decreases as more or less current flows through it, the brightness of the bulbs in the circuits can be used to determine which circuit has more current.

Materials
1.5-V lightbulbs (4)
1.5-V batteries (2)
10-cm-long pieces of insulated wire (8)
battery holders (2)
minibulb sockets (4)

What You'll Investigate
How does connecting devices in parallel affect the electric current in a circuit?

Goal
■ **Observe** how the current in a parallel circuit changes as more devices are added.

Safety Precautions

Procedure
1. Connect one lightbulb to the battery in a complete circuit. After you've made the bulb light, disconnect the bulb from the battery to keep the battery from running down. This circuit will be the brightness tester.

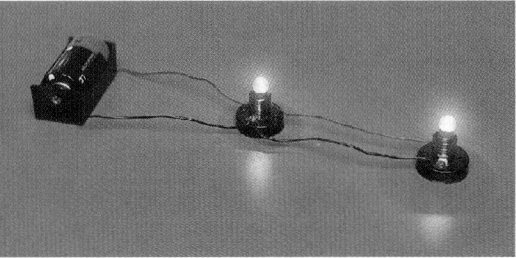

2. Make a parallel circuit by connecting two bulbs as shown in the diagram. Reconnect the bulb in the brightness tester and compare its brightness with the brightness of the two bulbs in the parallel circuit. Record your observations.

3. Add another bulb to the parallel circuit as shown in the figure. How does the brightness of the bulbs change?

4. Disconnect one bulb in the parallel circuit. What happens to the brightness of the remaining bulbs?

Conclude and Apply
1. Compared to the brightness tester, is the current in the parallel circuit more or less?
2. How does adding additional devices affect the current in a parallel circuit?
3. Are the electric circuits in your house wired in series or parallel? How do you know?

*C*ommunicating
Your Data

Compare your conclusions with those of other students in your class. **For more help, refer to the** Science Skill Handbook.

*C*ommunicating
Your Data

Have students use a computer drawing program to draw the circuits they made in this activity. Encourage them to devise symbols for the different elements in the circuits (i.e., batteries and bulbs).

Resource Manager

Chapter Resources Booklet
  Activity Worksheet, pp. 5–6

Purpose Students determine how adding and removing devices affects parallel circuits.
L2 IS **Kinesthetic**

Process Skills observing, comparing and contrasting, classifying, forming operational definitions, experimenting

Time Required 30 minutes

Safety Precautions The wires can become hot, especially if the wires short-circuit the battery. Rechargeable batteries are particularly susceptible to becoming hot when short-circuited. Bulbs can break. Be sure students are aware of classroom safety procedures for taking care of broken glass.

Troubleshooting If repeated trials fail to light the bulb, replace each element of the circuit with a component known to be in working order so as to isolate the defective circuit element.

Answers to Questions
1. The current is greater in the parallel circuit.
2. It causes the current to increase.
3. The electric circuits in a house are wired in parallel. When one device is turned off, the other devices do not stop working.

✓*Assessment*

Performance Have each student design and make a circuit. Have students place construction paper over their circuits and cut holes where the bulbs are. By only unscrewing and rescrewing lightbulbs, have other students try to determine the hidden wiring pattern. Use **PASC**, p. 97.

Activity

What You'll Investigate

Purpose

Students investigate how the height of a water source and width of a tube affect the flow of water and relate the results to current, voltage, and resistance in electric circuits. [L2] ELL [LS]
Kinesthetic

Process Skills

measuring, experimenting, making a model, making and using a table, recognizing cause and effect

Time Required

50 minutes

Procedure

Teaching Strategies

- Discuss with students how to measure the diameter of tubing.
- Students may need help calculating rate. Present a simple calculation of rate on the board. Rate = volume ÷ time

Tie to Prior Knowledge Before the experiment, have students discuss potential energy. **What does gravitational potential energy depend upon?** mass, gravity, and height **What variable is manipulated in the experiment?** height

Troubleshooting Demonstrate the proper way to connect tubing of different diameters to the funnels.

Expected Outcome

The flow rate is lower with the smaller diameter tubing and when the funnel is lower.

Activity

A Model for Voltage and Current

The flow of electrons in an electric circuit is something like the flow of water. By raising or lowering the height of a water tank, you can increase or decrease the potential energy of the water. In this activity, you will use a water system to investigate how the flow of water in a tube depends on the height of the water and the diameter of the tube.

What You'll Investigate

How is the flow of water through a tube affected by changing the height of a container of water and the diameter of the tube?

Materials

plastic funnel
rubber or plastic tubing of different
    diameters (1 m each)
meterstick
ring stand with ring
stopwatch
*clock displaying seconds
hose clamp
*binder clip
500-mL beakers (2)
*Alternate Materials

Goal

■ **Model** the flow of current in a simple circuit.

Safety Precautions 🥽 ✋

Flow Rate Data

Trial	Height (cm)	Diameter (mm)	Time (s)	Flow Rate (mL/s)
1	40	0.5	4	25
2	40	0.25	15	6.7
3	30	0.5	5	20
4	20	0.5	6	17

644   CHAPTER 21 Electricity

Inclusion Strategies

Behaviorally Disordered The day before students do the activity, provide them with a step-by-step description of the procedure. Explain that the objective of the activity is to observe how the rate of the flow of water changes as the diameter of the tubing changes. Give them time to read the description, and answer any questions they have. Tell them when the activity will occur and how long they will have to complete it.

Procedure

1. **Design** a data table in which to record your data. It should be similar to the table on the previous page.

2. Connect the tubing to the bottom of the funnel and place the funnel in the ring of the ring stand.

3. **Measure** the inside diameter of the rubber tubing. Record your data.

4. Place a 500-mL beaker at the bottom of the ring stand and lower the ring so the open end of the tubing is in the beaker.

5. Use the meterstick to measure the height from the top of the funnel to the bottom of the ring stand.

6. Working with a classmate, pour water into the funnel fast enough to keep the funnel full but not overflowing. Measure and record the time needed for 100 mL of water to flow into the beaker. Use the hose clamp to start and stop the flow of water.

7. Connect tubing with a different diameter to the funnel and repeat steps 2 through 6.

8. Reconnect the original piece of tubing and repeat steps 4 through 6 for several lower positions of the funnel, lowering the height by 10 cm each time.

9. **Calculate** the rate of flow for each trial by dividing 100 mL by the measured time.

Conclude and Apply

1. Make a graph that shows how the rate of flow depends on the funnel height. How does the rate of flow depend on the height of the funnel?

2. How does the rate of flow depend on the diameter of the tubing? Is this what you expected to happen? Explain.

3. Which of the variables that you changed in your trials corresponds to the voltage in a circuit? The resistance?

4. Based on your results, how would the current in a circuit depend on the voltage? How would the current depend on the resistance?

Communicating Your Data

Share your graph with other students in your class. Did other students draw the same conclusions as you? **For more help, refer to the** Science Skill Handbook.

Conclude and Apply

1. Student graphs should indicate that flow rate increases as height increases.

2. As the diameter of the tube decreases, the rate of flow of the water decreases.

3. The height of the funnel corresponds to voltage. The diameter of the tube corresponds to resistance.

4. As voltage increases, the current increases. As resistance increases, the current decreases.

Error Analysis

Ask students whether their answers make intuitive sense. Have them explain why they did or didn't expect their results. Have students work with their lab partners to brainstorm possible errors that might have occurred in the experiment, including using different pouring techniques and errors in measuring tube diameter, funnel height, and time.

Oral This activity uses an analogy between voltage and gravitational potential energy. Ask students to explain the real difference between these two quantities. Use **Performance Assessment in the Science Classroom**, p. 89.

Resource Manager

Chapter Resources Booklet
   Activity Worksheet, pp. 7–8
Lab Management and Safety, p. 71

Communicating Your Data

Suggest that students use pencil and paper or computer drawing software to design other systems of tubing for water to flow through. Have them identify the areas of their designs that offer the greatest resistance to the flow of water.

Content Background

Fuel, oxygen, and heat must be present for a fire to continue burning. Therefore, modern fire-fighting tactics concentrate on removing one or more of these elements to suppress or contain forest fires.

Typically, the initial attack effort involves making a fuel break. To do this, hand crews and bulldozers remove unburned fuel from the path of a fire. The fire-fighters use specialized tools to form a fire line, in which all vegetation is removed down to the mineral soil. These tools include shovels, chain saws, and combination tools like the Pulaski. The Pulaski has a hatchet blade that is used for chopping and a hoe-type blade that is used for digging. Backfires are another, riskier technique used to remove unburned fuel. Backfires are fires that are purposely set between a fuel break and the front of a forest fire.

Helicopters and airplanes are also used to fight fires. Helicopters shuttle firefighting crews and supplies and also may be used to transport and drop water on a fire. Airplanes are used to transport smoke jumpers, specialized firefighters who parachute to the fire, and to drop water or fire retardant chemicals on the fire.

After a fire has been contained, the mop up activity begins. Mopping up involves putting out hot spots still burning within the fire perimeter.

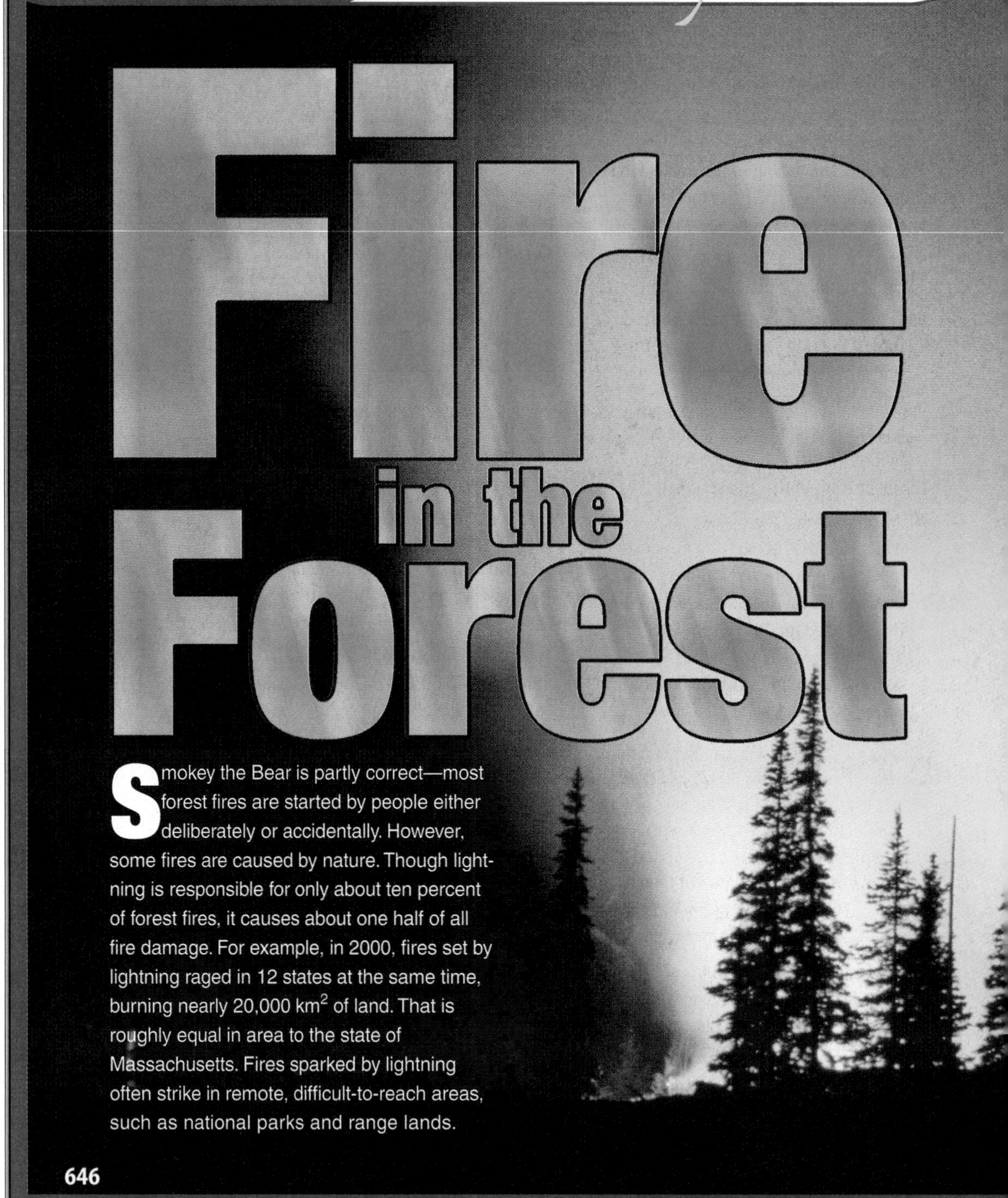

Fire in the Forest

Smokey the Bear is partly correct—most forest fires are started by people either deliberately or accidentally. However, some fires are caused by nature. Though lightning is responsible for only about ten percent of forest fires, it causes about one half of all fire damage. For example, in 2000, fires set by lightning raged in 12 states at the same time, burning nearly 20,000 km² of land. That is roughly equal in area to the state of Massachusetts. Fires sparked by lightning often strike in remote, difficult-to-reach areas, such as national parks and range lands.

646

Resources for Teachers and Students

Fire: Friend or Foe, Dorothy Hinshaw Patent, Clarion Books, 1998.

Forests On Fire: The Fight to Save Our Trees, Gregory Vogt, An Impact Book, Franklin Watts, 1990.

Smoke Jumper, Keith Elliot Greenberg, Blackbirch Press, Inc., 1995.

Young Men and Fire, Norman Maclean, University of Chicago Press, 1992.

Burning undetected for days, these fires can spread out of control and are hard to extinguish. Sometimes, firefighters must jump into the heart of these blazing areas to put the fires out. In addition to threatening lives, the fires can destroy millions of dollars worth of homes and property. Air pollution caused by smoke from forest fires also can have harmful effects on people. When wood products and fossil fuels are burned, they release particulate matter into the atmosphere. This can damage the human respiratory system, especially for those with preexisting conditions, such as asthma.

People aren't the only victims of forest fires. The fires kill animals, as well. Those who survive the blaze often perish because their habitats have been destroyed. Monster blazes also cause damage to the environment. They spew carbon dioxide and other gases into the atmosphere. Some of these gases may contribute to the greenhouse effect that warms the planet. In addition, fires give off carbon monoxide, which can cause ozone to form. In the lower atmosphere, ozone can damage vegetation, kill trees, and irritate lung tissue. Moreover, massive forest fires harm the logging industry, cause soil erosion in the ruined land, and are responsible for the loss of water reserves that normally collect in a healthy forest.

Plant life returns after a forest fire in Yellowstone National Park.

But fires caused by lightning also have some positive effects. In old, thick forests, trees often become diseased and insect-ridden. By removing these unhealthy trees, fires allow healthy trees greater access to water and nutrients. Fires also clean away a forest's dead trees, underbrush, and needles. This not only clears out space for new vegetation, it provides new food for them, as well. Dead organic matter returns its nutrients to the ground as it decays, but it can take a century for dead logs to rot completely.

Fires ignited by lightning might not be all bad

A fire completes the decay process almost instantly, allowing nutrients to be recycled a lot faster. The removal of these combustible materials prevents more widespread fires from occurring. It also lets new grasses and trees grow on the burned ground. The new types of vegetation attract new types of animals. This, in turn, creates a healthier and more diverse forest.

CONNECTIONS Research Find out more about the job of putting out forest fires. What training is needed? What gear do firefighters wear? Why would people risk their lives to save a forest? Use the media center to learn more about forest firefighters and their careers. Report to the class.

Online
For more information, visit science.glencoe.com

CONNECTIONS Large fires require a number of support personnel to perform a variety of tasks, including setting up and maintaining communications, supplying provisions and fuel, coordinating crews and equipment, monitoring the weather, and catering food. Ask each student to find information on a task provided by a member of a fire support team and prepare a report for the class.

Online

Internet Addresses

_____

_____

_____

Explore the Glencoe Science Web site at **science.glencoe.com** to find out more about topics in this feature.

Discussion

Scientists have determined that some fires may be beneficial to forests. **What are some positive effects caused by forest fires?** Possible responses: Clearing away diseased trees gives healthy trees greater access to the remaining water and nutrients; removing dead trees and underbrush creates space for new vegetation; regular removal of fuels helps prevent large, uncontrollable fires; burned vegetation returns some nutrients to the soil quicker than rotting vegetation; heat is needed for some seeds to germinate. L2
LS Logical-Mathematical

Activity

Have students search the newspaper or the Glencoe Science Web site for articles related to controlling forest fires. Suggest each student summarize the article in three sentences and then copy these sentences onto a sheet of construction paper. Arrange the papers on the bulletin board. L2 **LS Logical-Mathematical**

Investigate the Issue

Oxygen, fuel, and heat must be present for a fire to burn. Ask students to speculate how firefighters remove oxygen, fuel, and heat from a fire. Explain that water is used to remove oxygen and to cool flames and that fire lines and backfires are used to remove fuels. Mention that chemicals may be added to water to form a foam that will adhere to materials and smother flames more effectively.

Chapter 21 Study Guide

Reviewing Main Ideas

Preview

Students can answer the questions in their Science Journals. Discuss the answers as you go through the chapter. **Linguistic**

Review

Students can write their answers, then compare them with those of other students. **Interpersonal**

Reteach

Students can look at the illustrations and describe details that support the main ideas of the chapter. **Visual-Spatial**

Answers to Chapter Review

SECTION 1
4. The electric charge is directed to the ground by a lightning rod.

SECTION 2
4. because the path has been broken

SECTION 3
4. The button is part of a circuit breaker that stops the flow of current in the hairdryer if it becomes too great. The reset mechanism works by reconnecting the circuit inside the hairdryer.

Reviewing Main Ideas

Section 1 Electric Charge

1. The two types of electric charge are positive and negative. Like charges repel and unlike charges attract.

2. An object becomes negatively charged if it gains electrons and positively charged if it loses electrons.

3. Electrically charged objects have an electric field surrounding them and exert electric forces on one another.

4. Electrons can move easily in conductors, but not so easily in insulators. *Why isn't the building shown below harmed when lightning strikes it?*

Section 2 Electric Current

1. Electric current is the flow of charges—usually either electrons or ions.

2. The energy carried by the current in a circuit increases as the voltage in the circuit increases.

3. In a battery, chemical reactions provide the energy that causes electrons to flow in a circuit.

4. As electrons flow in a circuit, some of their electrical energy is lost due to resistance in the circuit. *In a simple circuit, why do electrons stop flowing if the circuit is broken?*

Section 3 Electric Circuits

1. In an electric circuit, the voltage, current, and resistance are related by Ohm's law, expressed as $I = V / R$.

2. The two basic kinds of electric circuits are parallel circuits and series circuits. A series circuit has only one path for the current to follow, but a parallel circuit has more than one path.

3. The rate at which electric devices use electrical energy is the electric power used by the device. Electric companies charge customers for using electrical energy in units of kilowatt-hours.

4. The amount of current flowing through the body determines how much damage occurs. The current from wall outlets can be dangerous. *Hair dryers often come with a reset button. What is the purpose of the button, and how might the reset mechanism work?*

FOLDABLES
Reading & Study Skills

After You Read

Using the information on your Foldable, under the *Electricity* tab, explain the differences between the two types of charges and between the two types of circuits.

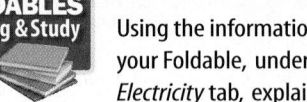

FOLDABLES
Reading & Study Skills

After You Read

After students have read the chapter and completed the Foldable described in Before You Read, have them do the activity on the student page.

Visualizing Main Ideas

Correctly order the following concept map, which illustrates how electric current moves through a simple circuit.

- Negative electrons recombine with positive ions. — 5
- Electrons are released at the negative battery terminal. — 2
- Opposite charges attract, forcing electrons to move in the circuit. — 4
- Chemical reactions separate electrons from atoms. — 1
- Positive ions produced are at the positive battery terminal. — 3

Vocabulary Review

Vocabulary Words

a. circuit
b. conductor
c. electric current
d. electric discharge
e. electric field
f. electric force
g. electric power
h. insulator
i. ion
j. Ohm's law
k. parallel circuit
l. resistance
m. series circuit
n. static charge
o. voltage

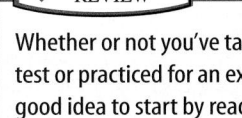

Study Tip

Whether or not you've taken a particular type of test or practiced for an exam many times, it's a good idea to start by reading the instructions provided at the beginning of each section. It only takes a moment.

Using Vocabulary

Answer the following questions using complete sentences.

1. What is the term for the flow of charge?

2. What is the relationship among voltage, current, and resistance in a circuit?

3. In which material do electrons move easily?

4. What is the name for the unbroken path that current follows?

5. What is the term for an excess of electric charge in one place?

6. What is an atom that has lost or gained electrons called?

7. Which circuits have more than one path for electrons to follow?

8. What is the rate at which electrical energy is converted to other forms of energy?

CHAPTER STUDY GUIDE   649

Chapter 21 Study Guide

Visualizing Main Ideas

See student page.

Vocabulary Review

Using Vocabulary

1. Electric current is the flow of charge.
2. Ohm's law states that current equals voltage divided by resistance.
3. Electrons move most easily in conductors.
4. The unbroken path through which a charge flows is a circuit.
5. A buildup of charge in one place is a static charge.
6. An atom that has gained or lost electrons is called an ion.
7. Parallel circuits have more than one path for electrons.
8. The rate at which electric energy is converted into another form of energy is electric power.

IDENTIFYING Misconceptions

Assess

Use the assessment as follow-up to page 622F after students have completed the chapter.

Materials 2 ammeters, circuit with battery and bulb, **Figure 1**

Procedure Show students **Figure 1**. Ask if the number of electrons passing through point A is the same as the number of electrons passing through point B. Place ammeters in the circuit at points A and B.

Expected Outcome The two points have the same current and therefore the same number of electrons passing through them.

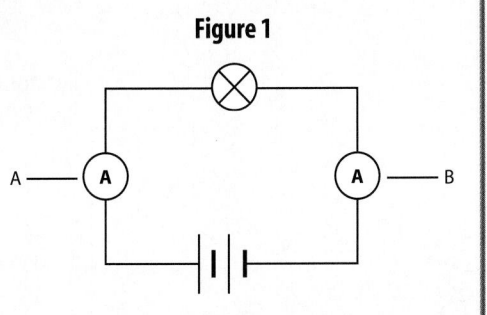

Figure 1

Checking Concepts

1. B
2. D
3. D
4. A
5. C
6. D
7. B
8. D
9. D
10. A

Thinking Critically

11. Electrons collide with the atoms and other electrons in the material. This causes the electrons to lose energy and slow down.
12. The charge on the balloon induces an opposite charge on the wall. The charges in the balloon and the charges in the wall attract each other.
13. No. Think of two tanks of water connected by a hose at the bottom. One tank also has a nozzle at the bottom from which water can flow out. If you were to open that nozzle, water could only flow as quickly as the water pressure in that tank was pushing it out. If the tanks had been placed in series, however (one on top of the other), the water pressure would have been greater and so would have pushed more water out.
14. Bring the two objects together. If they move toward each other, they are of opposite charge. If they move away from each other, they have the same charge.
15. Plastic is an insulator and prevents the electric current inside the appliance from flowing into your body when you handle the appliance.

Checking Concepts

Choose the word or phrase that best answers the question.

1. An object that is positively charged _____ .
   A) has more neutrons than protons
   B) has more protons than electrons
   C) has more electrons than protons
   D) has more electrons than neutrons

2. What is the force between two electrons?
   A) unbalanced   C) attractive
   B) neutral   D) repulsive

3. How much power does the average hair dryer use?
   A) 20 W   C) 750 W
   B) 75 W   D) 1,200 W

4. What property of a wire increases when it is made thinner?
   A) resistance   C) current
   B) voltage   D) charge

5. What property does Earth have that causes grounding to drain static charges?
   A) It is a planet.
   B) It has a high resistance.
   C) It is a conductor.
   D) It is like a battery.

6. Why is a severe electric shock dangerous?
   A) It can stop the heart from beating.
   B) It can cause burns.
   C) It can interfere with breathing.
   D) All of the above are true.

7. Because an air conditioner uses more electric power than a lightbulb in a given amount of time, what also must be true?
   A) It must have a higher resistance.
   B) It must use more energy every second.
   C) It must have its own batteries.
   D) It must be wired in series.

8. What unit of electrical energy is sold by electric companies?
   A) ampere   C) volt
   B) ohm   D) kilowatt-hour

9. What surrounds electric charges that causes them to affect each other even though they are not touching?
   A) an induced charge C) a conductor
   B) a static discharge D) an electric field

10. As more devices are added to a series circuit, what happens to the current?
   A) decreases   C) stays the same
   B) increases   D) stops

Thinking Critically

11. Why do materials have electrical resistance?

12. Explain why a balloon that has a static charge will stick to a wall.

13. If you connect two batteries in parallel, will the lightbulb glow brighter than if just one battery is used? Explain, using water as an analogy.

14. If you have two charged objects, how can you tell whether the type of charge on them is the same or different?

15. Explain why the outside cases of electric appliances usually are made of plastic.

Developing Skills

16. **Classifying** Look at several objects around your home. Classify these objects as insulators or conductors.

Chapter ✓Assessment Planner

Portfolio Encourage students to place in their portfolios one or two items of what they consider to be their best work. Examples include:
- Assessment, p. 630
- Assessment, p. 635
- Visual Learning, p. 638

Performance Additional performance assessments, Performance Task Assessment Lists, and rubrics for evaluating these activities can be found in Glencoe's **Performance Assessment in the Science Classroom.**

17. Making and Using Graphs The following data show the current and voltage in a circuit containing a portable CD player and in a circuit containing a portable radio.

a. Make a graph with the horizontal axis as current and the vertical axis as voltage. Plot the data for both appliances.

b. Which line is more horizontal—the plot of the radio data or the CD player data?

c. Use Ohm's law to determine the electrical resistance of each device.

d. For which device is the line more horizontal—the device with the higher or lower resistance?

Portable Radio		Portable CD Player	
Voltage (V)	Current (A)	Voltage (V)	Current (A)
2.0	1.0	2.0	0.5
4.0	2.0	4.0	1.0
6.0	3.0	6.0	1.5

18. Collecting Data Determine the total cost of keeping all the lights turned on in your living room for 24 h if the cost of electricity is $0.08 per kilowatt-hour.

Performance Assessment

19. Design a Board Game Design a board game about a series or parallel circuit. The rules of the game could be based on opening or closing the circuit, adding fuses, and/or resetting a circuit breaker.

TECHNOLOGY

Go to the Glencoe Science Web site at **science.glencoe.com** or use the **Glencoe Science CD-ROM** for additional chapter assessment.

THE PRINCETON REVIEW **Test Practice**

A student is interested in setting up and comparing four different circuits. The table below lists her results.

Type of Electric Circuit			
Circuit	Number of Resistors	Circuit Type	Battery Voltage
A	2	Series	6 V
B	3	Parallel	12 V
C	4	Series	4 V
D	5	Parallel	8 V

Study the chart above and answer the following questions.

1. The voltage across a resistor in a parallel circuit equals the battery voltage. In a series circuit, the voltage across a resistor is less than the battery voltage. In which circuit is the voltage across an individual resistor the greatest?

A) Circuit A
B) Circuit B
C) Circuit C
D) Circuit D

2. An electric motor requires at least 5 volts to run. According to the table, the battery in which circuit could NOT be used to run the motor?

F) Circuit A
G) Circuit B
H) Circuit C
J) Circuit D

THE PRINCETON REVIEW **Test Practice**

The Test-Taking Tip was written by The Princeton Review, the nation's leader in test preparation.

1. B
2. H

Developing Skills

16. Accept all reasonable answers.
17. a. Both graphs are straight lines. The line for the CD player has a steeper slope
   b. radio
   c. $R = V/I$; for the radio $R = (2\,V)/(1\,A) = 2\,\Omega$; for the CD player $R = (2\,V)/(0.5\,A) = 4\,\Omega$
   d. the device with the lower resistance
18. Answers will depend on the number and type of lights.

Performance Assessment

19. Check student's games. Use **PASC**, p. 117.

✓*Assessment* **Resources**

Reproducible Masters

Chapter Resources Booklet
  Chapter Review, pp. 37–88
  Chapter Tests, pp. 39–42
  Assessment Transparency Activity, p. 49

Glencoe Science Web site
  Interactive Tutor
  Chapter Quizzes

Glencoe Technology
  Assessment Transparency
  Interactive CD-ROM Chapter Quizzes
  ExamView Pro Test Bank
  Vocabulary PuzzleMaker Software
  MindJogger Videoquiz

Section/Objectives	Standards		Activities/Features
Chapter Opener	National	State/Local	**Explore Activity:** Observe and measure force between magnets, p. 653 **Before You Read,** p. 653
	See p. 7T for a Key to Standards.		
Section 1 What is magnetism? ⏱ 3 sessions 📦 1.5 blocks 1. **Describe** the behavior of magnets. 2. **Relate** the behavior of magnets to magnetic fields. 3. **Explain** the source of all magnetic fields.	National Content Standards: UCP2, A1, B1, B2, E2		**Problem-Solving Activity:** Finding the Magnetic Declination, p. 657 **MiniLAB:** Observing Magnetic Fields, p. 658 **Activity:** Make a Compass, p. 660
Section 2 Electricity and Magnetism ⏱ 4 sessions 📦 2 blocks 1. **Describe** the relationship between electricity and magnetism. 2. **Explain** how electricity can produce motion. 3. **Explain** how motion can produce electricity.	National Content Standards: UCP2, A1, B1, B2, B3, D2, F5, G1		**MiniLAB:** Assembling an Electromagnet, p. 662 **Visualizing Maglev Trains,** p. 663 **Science Online,** p. 667 **Activity:** How does an electric motor work?, p. 670 **Science and Language Arts:** Aagjuuk and Sivulliit, p. 672

NATIONAL GEOGRAPHIC   Teacher's Corner

PRODUCTS AVAILABLE FROM NATIONAL GEOGRAPHIC SOCIETY
To order call 1-800-368-2728:
Book
Waves: The Electromagnetic Universe

Video
Introduction to Magnetism

Activity Materials	Reproducible Resources	Section Assessment	Technology
Explore Activity: 2 bar magnets, sheet of paper	**Chapter Resources Booklet** Foldables Worksheet, p. 13 Directed Reading Overview, p. 15 Note-taking Worksheets, pp. 27–28	*GLENCOE'S* **ASSESSMENT** *ADVANTAGE*	
MiniLAB: iron filings, plastic petri dish, tape, several magnets **Activity:** petri dish, water, sewing needle, magnet, tape, marker, paper, plastic spoon	**Chapter Resources Booklet** Transparency Activity, p. 38 MiniLAB, p. 3 Enrichment, p. 25 Reinforcement, p. 23 Directed Reading, p. 16 Lab Activity, pp. 9–10 Activity Worksheet, pp. 5–6 **Earth Science Critical Thinking/ Problem Solving,** p. 8	Portfolio Assessment, p. 658 Performance Problem Solving Activity, p. 657 MiniLAB, p. 658 Skill Builder Activities, p. 659 Content Section Assessment, p. 659	🔋 Section Focus Transparency 💿 Interactive CD-ROM 🎧 Guided Reading Audio Program
MiniLAB: wire, 16-penny steel nail, D-cell battery, battery holder, paper clips **Activity:** 22-gauge enameled wire (4 m), steel knitting needle, 4 nails, hammer, 2 ceramic magnets, 18-gauge insulated wire (60 cm), masking tape, fine sandpaper, 15-cm wooden board, 2 wooden blocks, 6-V battery, wire cutters *Need materials? Contact Science Kit at 1-800-828-7777 or www.sciencekit.com on the Internet.*	**Chapter Resources Booklet** Transparency Activity, p. 39 MiniLAB, p. 4 Enrichment, p. 26 Reinforcement, p. 24 Directed Reading, pp. 17, 18 Lab Activity, pp. 11–12 Transparency Activity, pp. 41–42 Activity Worksheet, pp. 7–8 **Lab Management and Safety,** p. 64 **Science Inquiry Labs,** pp. 9, 55 **Physical Science Critical Thinking/ Problem Solving,** p. 20	Portfolio Cultural Diversity, p. 665 Performance MiniLAB, p. 662 Skill Builder Activities, p. 669 Content Section Assessment, p. 669	🔋 Section Focus Transparency 🔋 Teaching Transparency 💿 Interactive CD-ROM 🎧 Guided Reading Audio Program

End of Chapter Assessment

GLENCOE'S **ASSESSMENT** *ADVANTAGE*

Blackline Masters	Technology	Professional Series
Chapter Resources Booklet Chapter Review, pp. 31–32 Chapter Tests, pp. 33–36 **Standardized Test Practice by The Princeton Review,** pp. 91–94	📼 MindJogger Videoquiz 💿 Interactive CD-ROM 💿 Vocabulary PuzzleMakers 💿 ExamView Pro Test Bank 💿 Interactive Lesson Planner 💿 Interactive Teacher Edition	Performance Assessment in the Science Classroom (PASC)

Transparencies

Section Focus

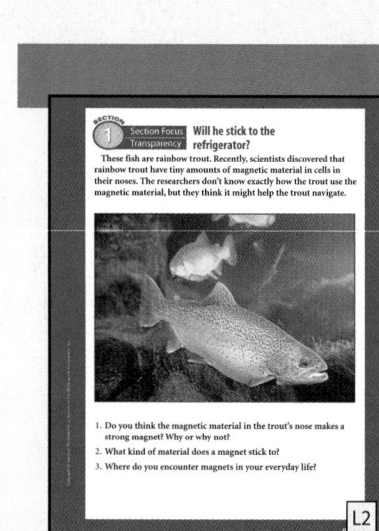

Section Focus Transparency 1 — Will he stick to the refrigerator?

These fish are rainbow trout. Recently, scientists discovered that rainbow trout have tiny amounts of magnetic material in cells in their noses. The researchers don't know exactly how the trout use the magnetic material, but they think it might help the trout navigate.

1. Do you think the magnetic material in the trout's nose makes a strong magnet? Why or why not?
2. What kind of material does a magnet stick to?
3. Where do you encounter magnets in your everyday life?

L2

Section Focus Transparency 2 — Heavy Duty

In a salvage yard it is necessary to move large amounts of scrap material. One way to do this is with a powerful magnet such as the magnet shown in the picture.

1. What does all the scrap material that the magnet can pick up have in common?
2. Would the magnet also be able to pick up old car seats or wind-shield glass? Explain.
3. How do you think the crane operator releases the scrap material from the large magnet?

L2

This is a representation of key blackline masters available in the Teacher Classroom Resources. See Resource Manager boxes within the chapter for additional information.

Key to Teaching Strategies

The following designations will help you decide which activities are appropriate for your students.

L1 Level 1 activities should be appropriate for students with learning difficulties.

L2 Level 2 activities should be within the ability range of all students.

L3 Level 3 activities are designed for above-average students.

ELL ELL activities should be within the ability range of English Language Learners.

COOP LEARN Cooperative Learning activities are designed for small group work.

LS Multiple Learning Styles logos, as described on page 22T, are used throughout to indicate strategies that address different learning styles.

P These strategies represent student products that can be placed into a best-work portfolio.

Assessment

Assessment Transparency — Magnetism

Directions: Carefully review the graph and answer the following questions.

Sunspot Activity

1. According to the graph, what year had the greatest number of sunspots?
   A 1948   C 1965
   B 1958   D 1980
2. Which year experienced the fewest sunspots?
   F 1954   H 1976
   G 1964   J 1983
3. What is the approximate length of time between points of low sunspot activity?
   A 1 year   C 11 years
   B 5 years   D 20 years

L2

Teaching

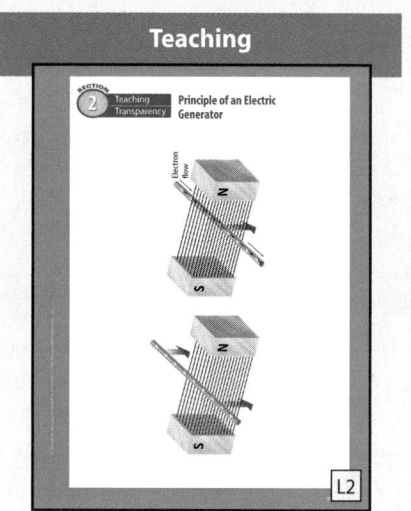

Teaching Transparency 2 — Principle of an Electric Generator

L2

Hands-on Activities

Activity Worksheets

Activity — Make a Compass

Lab Preview
Directions: Answer the following questions before you begin the Activity.

1. How do you use the needle in this activity?

2. Is the magnetic field stronger or weaker as you go farther from the poles?

A valuable tool for any nature enthusiast is a compass. More than 1,000 years ago, Chinese inventors found a way to magnetize pieces of iron. They used this method to manufacture compasses. You can use the same procedure to make a compass.

What You'll Investigate
How do you construct a compass?

Materials
petri dish
*clear bowl
water
sewing needle
magnet
tape
marker
paper
plastic spoon
*Alternate materials

Goals
• Observe induced magnetism.
• Build a compass.

Safety Precautions

Procedure
1. Reproduce the circular protractor shown. Tape it under the bottom of your dish, so it can be seen but not get wet. Add water until the dish is half full.

2. Mark one end of the needle with a marker. Magnetize the needle by placing it on the magnet aligned north and south for 1 min.

L2

Laboratory Activities

Laboratory Activity 1 — Earth's Magnetism

Earth is surrounded by a magnetic field that is similar to the magnetic field around a bar magnet. Magnets have a north magnetic pole and a south magnetic pole. Earth's south magnetic pole is near the north geographic pole, and its north magnetic pole is near the south geographic pole.

You usually do not notice Earth's magnetic field because it is weak. In your classroom, wires carrying electric current also produce magnetic fields that add to Earth's magnetic field and can change its direction. A compass can show the direction of the magnetic field. A compass needle is a small bar magnet that aligns itself along the magnetic field lines around the compass. You can use a compass to map the magnetic field in your classroom.

Strategy
You will use a compass.
You will map the magnetic field in your classroom.

Materials
compass
graph paper

Procedure
1. Draw a floor plan of the classroom on the graph paper. (The floor plan does not have to be to scale.) Indicate north, south, east, and west on the floor plan.
2. Mark the desk locations on the floor plan with a small circle and a number.
3. Take a compass reading at each numbered location. Note the compass needle's direction. See Figure 1. Draw it neatly on the floor plan. Record each angle in Table 1.

Data and Observations
Table 1

Location	Angle
1	
2	
3	
4	
5	
6	
7	

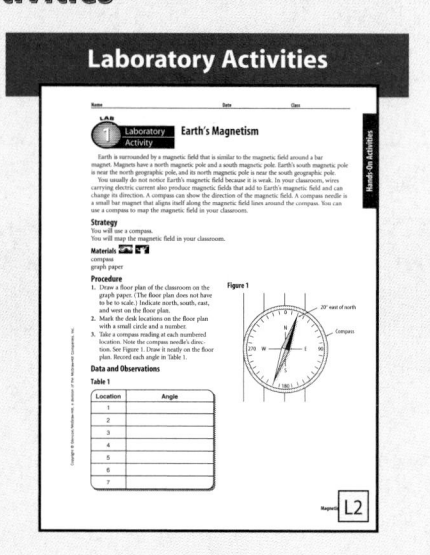

Figure 1

L2

Meeting Different Ability Levels

Content Outline

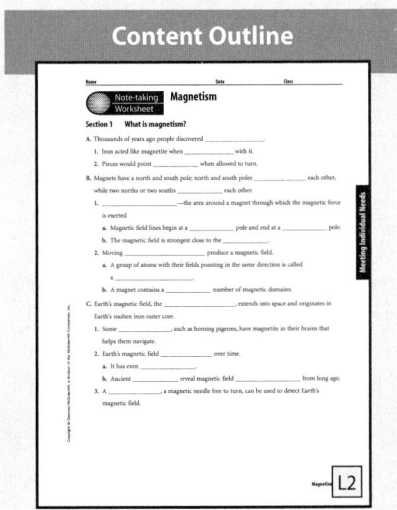

Reinforcement

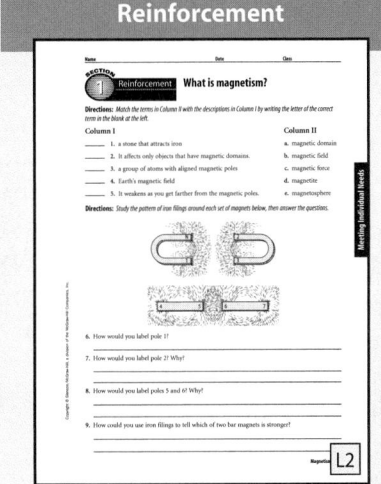

Directed Reading

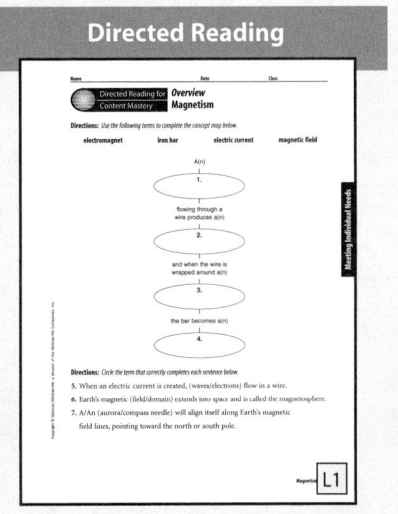

Assessment

Chapter Tests

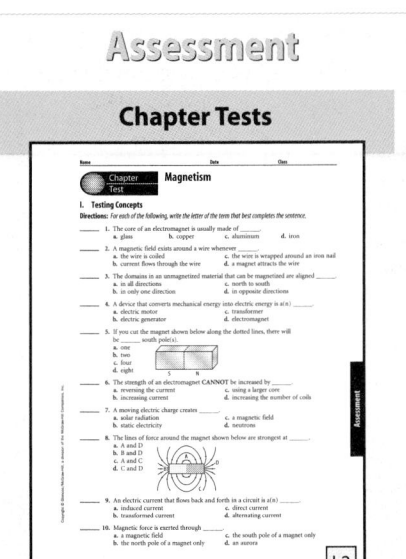

Enrichment

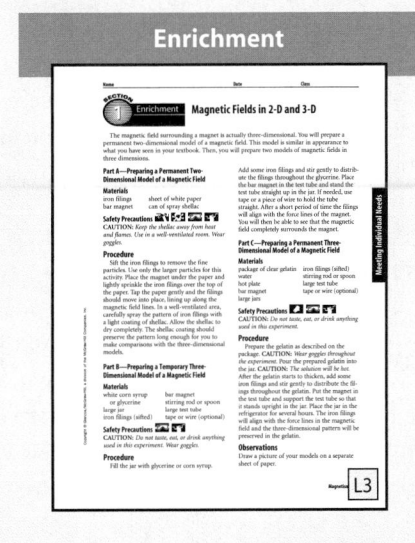

Spanish Directed Reading

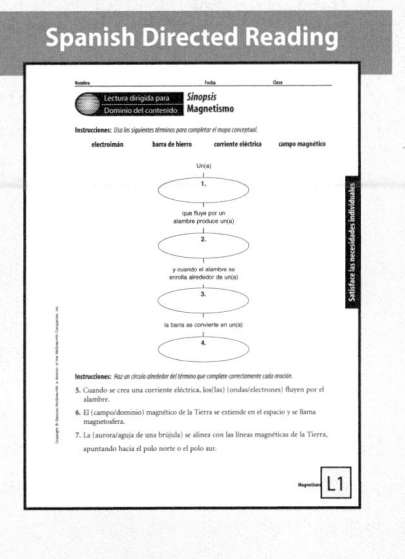

Test Practice Workbook

Chapter Review

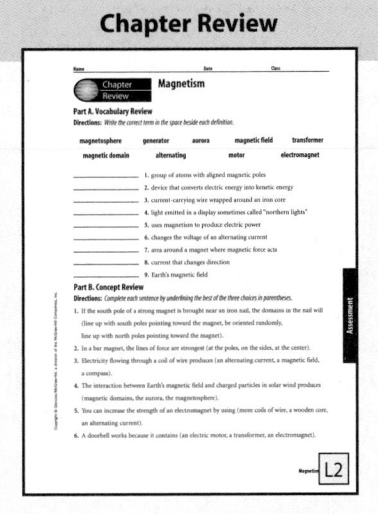

Science Content Background

SECTION 1

What is magnetism?
Magnets

Electrons spin as they move around the nucleus of an atom. Because the electron has charge, its motion around the nucleus and its spin both produce magnetic fields. In most elements these magnetic fields cancel. But in a few elements, such as iron, cobalt, and nickel, the magnetic fields produced by the electron spins add together. These elements can be made into permanent magnets.

The lines that represent magnetic fields are called magnetic field lines. By convention, the lines are shown going from north poles to south poles. These lines can be used to describe any magnetic fields: the field around a magnet, the field between two or more magnets, the field around celestial objects such as Earth, or the field produced by a changing electric field.

Student Misconception

Students may think that Earth's geographic North Pole is a magnetic north pole and Earth's geographic South Pole is a magnetic south pole.

Refer to the facing page for teaching strategies to address this misconception. Refer to pages 657–659 for content related to this topic.

Earth's Magnetic Field

The naming of a magnet's poles can cause some confusion. By convention we call one pole of a magnet north and the other part south. The part of a freely turning magnet that faces geographic north is called the north pole of the magnet. Like poles repel and unlike poles attract. Thus, Earth's north pole is really a south magnetic pole because it attracts the north end of magnets. If you picture Earth's magnetic field as being produced by a large bar magnet, the magnet's south pole would be at Earth's north pole, attracting the north poles of compass needles. This is confusing for many people.

Another way of explaining this is to say that magnetic field lines go into south poles and come out of north poles. Compasses show the direction of the magnetic field lines. Thus if the north end of a compass points at something it must be a magnetic south pole.

SECTION 2

Electricity and Magnetism
Moving Charge Forms a Magnet

In 1820, Hans Christian Oersted discovered that an electric current could deflect a magnetic compass needle. Michael Faraday's experimental work and James Clerk Maxwell's mathematical development of Faraday's ideas established electricity and magnetism as two aspects of one force, electromagnetism. Electromagnetism is one of the four fundamental forces known. Gravity, the strong nuclear force, and the weak nuclear force are the other three. These fundamental forces all act at a distance through a field. They are fundamental because they explain other forces. Familiar contact forces, such as friction between a book and a table, the normal force of the table holding up the book, or your ability to push a book with your hand, are due to the electromagnetic force of the atoms in the books, your hand, and the tabletop.

SCIENCE *Online*

For additional content background on this topic, go to the Glencoe Science Web site at science.glencoe.com.

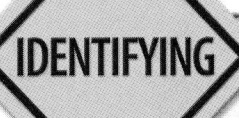

IDENTIFYING Misconceptions

Find Out What Students Think

Students may think that . . .

- **Earth's north and south geographic poles are corresponding north and south magnetic poles.**

Most people assume that we call the north pole "north" because it is close to a magnetic north pole. This is logical reasoning. However, opposite magnetic poles attract, so Earth's geographic north pole is actually close to its magnetic south pole because it attracts the north end of a magnet. The convention for naming north and south came about in a logical way. The part of a magnet that pointed to the north was called the north magnetic pole. Later, people realized that the north pointing part of a magnet is actually attracted to a south magnetic pole. Since the convention naming north and south on Earth was already established it has been kept, even though it causes confusion.

Demonstration

Give each group sheets of paper, a strip of masking tape, and a bar magnet that is labeled N (north) and S (south). Ask them to use the bar magnet as the center of Earth and to draw around the magnet to make a model of Earth. Direct students to label the equator, the northern hemisphere, and the southern hemisphere. Then have them decide whether the N or the S end of the magnet should be in the Northern Hemisphere.

Promote Understanding

Activity

- Give each group of students a compass.

- Review with students that the north end of the compass needle points to the northern part of our planet.

- Ask students to check their models using the compass to make sure the north end of the compass needle points toward the Northern Hemisphere of their models.

- If the compass needle points the wrong way, have students rearrange their models to make the compass needle point to the Northern Hemisphere.

    Many students will have made models of Earth with the north pole of the magnet in the Northern Hemisphere. They will see that the north end of the compass needle points away from this rather than towards it. In their models, the south pole of the magnet should be in the Northern Hemisphere.

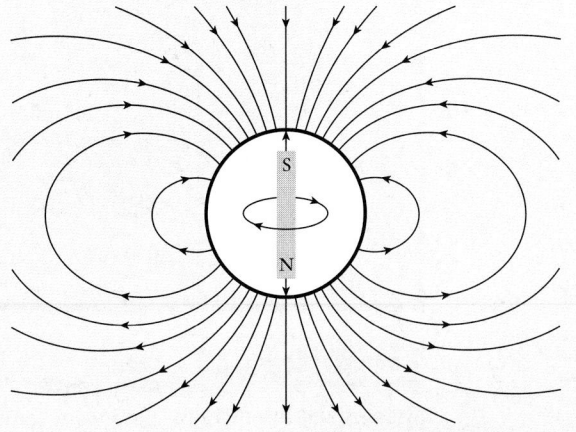

Assess

After completing the chapter, see *Identifying Misconceptions* in the Study Guide.

Magnetism

Chapter Vocabulary

magnetic field, p. 652
magnetic domain, p. 656
magnetosphere, p. 657
electromagnet, p. 661
motor, p. 653
aurora, p. 665
generator, p. 666
alternating current, p. 666
transformer, p. 668

What do you think?

Science Journal The photo shows two neodymium magnets. These magnets are strong enough to attract each other even when separated by a distance equal to the thickness of a hand.

Magnetism

This maglev train is designed to travel at speeds up to 500 km/h. However, you won't see any steam or exhaust coming out of its engine. In fact this train is not even touching the track. That's because it is suspended by magnetic forces and propelled by a traveling magnetic field. In this chapter, you will learn why magnets attract certain materials. You will also learn how electricity and magnetism are connected, and how an electric current can create a magnetic field.

What do you think?

Science Journal Look at the picture below with a classmate. Discuss what is happening. Here's a hint: *No glue or tape is involved.* Write your answer or best guess in your Science Journal.

652

Theme Connection

Systems and Interactions Changing electric and magnetic fields form a system in which one of the fields produces the other.

EXPLORE ACTIVITY

Perhaps you've driven bumper cars with your friends, and remember the jolt you felt when you crashed into another car. Quite a force can be generated from that small car powered by an electric motor. How does the motor produce a force that gets the tires moving? The answer involves magnetism. The following activity will demonstrate how a magnet is able to exert forces.

Observe and measure force between magnets 👓

1. Place two bar magnets on opposite ends of a sheet of paper.

2. Slowly slide one magnet toward the other until it moves. Measure the distance between the magnets.

3. Turn one magnet around 180°. Repeat the activity. Then turn the other magnet and repeat again.

4. Repeat the activity with one magnet perpendicular to the other, in a T shape.

Observe

In your Science Journal, record your results. In each case, how close did the magnets have to be to affect each other? Did the magnets move together or apart? How did the forces exerted by the magnets change as the magnets were moved closer together? Explain.

Before You Read

Making a Compare and Contrast Study Fold   Make the following Foldable to help you see how magnetic forces and magnetic fields are similar and different.

1. Place a sheet of paper in front of you so the long side is at the top. Fold the paper in half from the left side to the right side. Unfold.

2. Fold each side in to the fold line to divide the paper into fourths.

3. Label the flaps *Magnetic Force* and *Magnetic Field*.

4. As you read the chapter, write information about each topic on the inside of each flap.

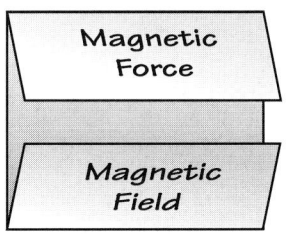

Magnetic Force

Magnetic Field

Purpose Use the Explore Activity to introduce students to the forces between two magnets. [L2]
ELL [IS] **Kinesthetic**

Materials paper, metric ruler, two bar magnets

Teaching Strategy Graph paper can be substituted for the paper and ruler. If it is, review with students how to use graph paper to measure distance.

Observe

The magnets move together when unlike poles face each other and move apart when like poles face each other. If the magnets were big enough, they could be used to move large things such as a train.

Assessment

Process Have students sketch each arrangement of the magnets and draw arrows to indicate the direction of movement. Use **Performance Assessment in the Science Classroom,** p. 127.

Before You Read

Dinah Zike Study Fold

Purpose Students use this Foldable to differentiate between "magnetic force" and "magnetic field." They then use what they have learned to explain what they have in common.

📁 For additional help, see Foldables Worksheet p. 13 in **Chapter Resources Booklet** or go to the Glencoe Science Web site at **science.glencoe.com.** See After You Read in the Study Guide at the end of this chapter.

SECTION

What is magnetism?

1 Motivate

Bellringer Transparency

Display the Section Focus Transparency for Section 1. Use the accompanying Transparency Activity Master. L2

ELL

Tie to Prior Knowledge

Ask students to think of examples of the effects of magnetism that they have experienced. List these on the chalkboard. Refrigerator magnets, cabinet locks, and audiotapes or videotapes are possibilities.

What is magnetism?

As You Read

What You'll Learn
- **Describe** the behavior of magnets.
- **Relate** the behavior of magnets to magnetic fields.
- **Explain** why some materials are magnetic.

Vocabulary
magnetic field
magnetic domain
magnetosphere

Why It's Important
Magnetism is one of the basic forces of nature.

Figure 1
Two north poles or two south poles repel each other. North and south magnetic poles are attracted to each other.

Early Uses

Do you use magnets to attach papers to a metal surface such as a refrigerator? Have you ever wondered why magnets and some metals attract? Thousands of years ago, people noticed that a mineral called magnetite attracted other pieces of magnetite and bits of iron. They discovered that when they rubbed small pieces of iron with magnetite, the iron began to act like magnetite. When these pieces were free to turn, one end pointed north. These might have been the first compasses. The compass was an important development for navigation and exploration, especially at sea. Before compasses, sailors had to depend on the Sun or the stars to know in which direction they were going.

Magnets

A piece of magnetite is a magnet. Magnets attract objects made of iron or steel, such as nails and paper clips. Magnets also can attract or repel other magnets. Every magnet has two ends, or poles. One end is called the north pole and the other is the south pole. As shown in **Figure 1,** a north magnetic pole always repels other north poles and always attracts south poles. Likewise, a south pole always repels other south poles and attracts north poles.

Two north poles repel   Two south poles repel

Opposite poles attract

Section ✔Assessment Planner

PORTFOLIO
MiniLAB Assessment, p. 658
PERFORMANCE ASSESSMENT
Problem-Solving Activity, p. 657
MiniLAB, p. 658
Skill Builder Activities, p. 659
See page 676 for more options.

CONTENT ASSESSMENT
Section, p. 659
Challenge, p. 659
Chapter, pp. 676–677

The Magnetic Field You have to handle a pair of magnets for only a short time before you can feel that magnets attract or repel without touching each other. How can a magnet cause an object to move without touching it? Recall that a force is a push or a pull that can cause an object to move. Just like gravitational and electric forces, a magnetic force can be exerted even when objects are not touching. And like these forces, the magnetic force becomes weaker as the magnets get farther apart. This magnetic force is exerted through a **magnetic field.** Magnetic fields surround all magnets. If you sprinkle iron filings near a magnet, the iron filings will outline the magnetic field around the magnet. Take a look at **Figure 2A.** The iron filings form a pattern of curved lines that start on one pole and end on the other. These curved lines are called magnetic field lines. Magnetic field lines help show the direction of the magnetic field.

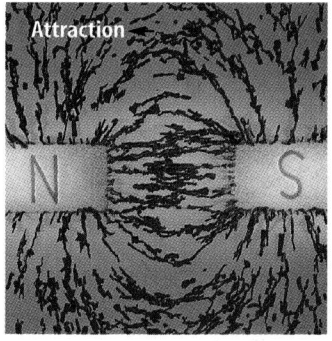

A Iron filings show the magnetic field lines around a bar magnet.

B Magnetic field lines start at the north pole of the magnet and end on the south pole.

✔ **Reading Check** *What is the evidence that a magnetic field exists?*

Magnetic field lines begin at a magnet's north pole and end on the south pole, as shown in **Figure 2B.** The field lines are close together where the field is strong and get farther apart as the field gets weaker. As you can see in the figures, the magnetic field is strongest close to the magnetic poles and grows weaker farther from the poles.

Field lines that curve toward each other show attraction. Field lines that curve away from each other show repulsion. **Figure 3** illustrates the magnetic field lines between a north and a south pole and the field lines between two north poles.

Figure 2
A magnetic field surrounds a magnet. Where the magnetic field lines are close together, the field is strong. *For this magnet, where is the field strongest?*

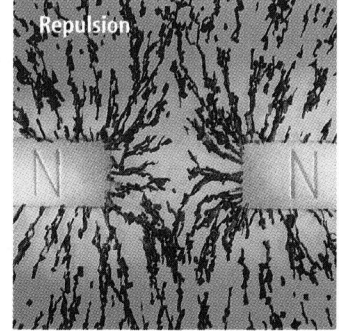
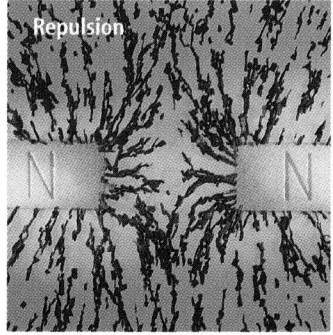

Figure 3
Magnetic field lines show attraction and repulsion. *What would the field between two south poles look like?*

SECTION 1 What is magnetism? **655**

Caption Answer

Figure 4 Motion through space and spinning, just as Earth spins as it revolves around the Sun.

Use an Analogy

Magnetizing an object is analogous to giving an object a static charge. When you rub a balloon against a piece of wool, you cause the electrons to move in a way that induces a temporary static charge in the wool and in the balloon. When you rub a magnet against a steel nail, you can cause the electrons in the nail to line up in a way that induces a temporary magnetic field around the nail.

IDENTIFYING Misconceptions

Students may think that all magnets are made of iron. Explain that magnets also can be made from nickel and cobalt. Some magnets are made from ceramics. These ceramics are made from compounds that contain iron, nickel, or cobalt atoms.

Activity

Have students practice inducing magnetism in different objects by rubbing the objects in the same direction about 20 times with a magnet. Then ask students to determine the strength of any magnetic field induced. For example, they can test to see how many paper clips a magnetized paper clip will attract. L2 ELL IS Kinesthetic

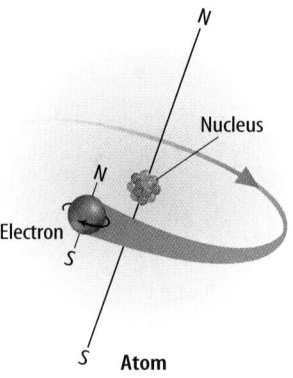

Figure 4
Movement of electrons produces magnetic fields. *What are the two types of motion shown in the illustration?*

Figure 5
Some materials can become temporary magnets.

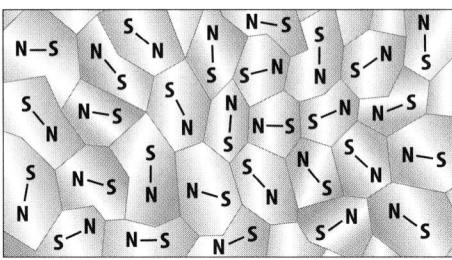

A Microscopic sections of iron and steel act as tiny magnets. Normally, these domains are oriented randomly and their magnetic fields cancel each other.

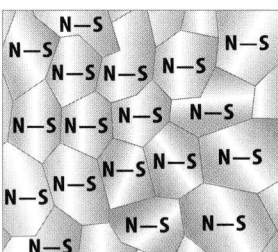

B When a strong magnet is brought near the material, the domains line up, and their magnetic fields add together.

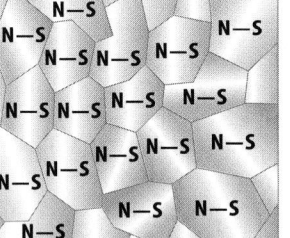

C The bar magnet magnetizes the paper clips. The top of each paper clip is now a north pole, and the bottom is a south pole.

Making Magnetic Fields A magnet is surrounded by a magnetic field that enables the magnet to exert a magnetic force. How are magnetic fields made? A moving electric charge creates a magnetic field.

Inside every magnet are moving charges. All atoms contain negatively charged particles called electrons. Not only do these electrons swarm around the nucleus of an atom, they also spin, as shown in **Figure 4**. Because of its movement, each electron produces a magnetic field. The atoms that make up magnets have their electrons arranged so that each atom is like a small magnet. In a material such as iron, a large number of atoms will have their magnetic fields pointing the same direction. This group of atoms, with their fields pointing in the same direction, is called a **magnetic domain**.

A material that can become magnetized, such as iron or steel, contains many magnetic domains. When the material is not magnetized, these domains are oriented in different directions, as shown in **Figure 5A**. The magnetic fields created by the domains cancel, so the material does not act like a magnet.

A magnet contains a large number of magnetic domains that are lined up and pointing in the same direction. Suppose a strong magnet is held close to a material such as iron or steel. The magnet causes the magnetic field in many magnetic domains to line up with the magnet's field, as shown in **Figure 5B**. As you can see in **Figure 5C** this method magnetizes paper clips.

Teacher FYI

Ancient writings suggest that 2,000 years ago in Egypt, magnets were used to make statues appear as if they were floating in midair. The statues were made of iron, and naturally-occurring magnets called lodestones were arranged on the floors or walls to overcome the effect of gravity on the statues.

Inclusion Strategies

Visually Impaired Pair these students with sighted students. Provide each pair with two magnets, one large and one small, and have them map the magnetic field of the large magnet by moving the small magnet around it. Have the sighted student use raised lines (of glue, for example) to make tactile models of the magnetic field. The visually impaired student can then feel the field lines with his or her hands.

Earth's Magnetic Field

Magnetism isn't limited to bar magnets. Earth has a magnetic field, as shown in **Figure 6.** The region of space affected by Earth's magnetic field is called the **magnetosphere** (mag NEE tuh sfihr). The origin of Earth's magnetic field is thought to be deep within Earth in the outer core layer. One theory is that movement of molten iron in the outer core is responsible for generating Earth's magnetic field. The shape of Earth's magnetic field is similar to that of a huge bar magnet tilted about 11° from Earth's geographic north and south poles.

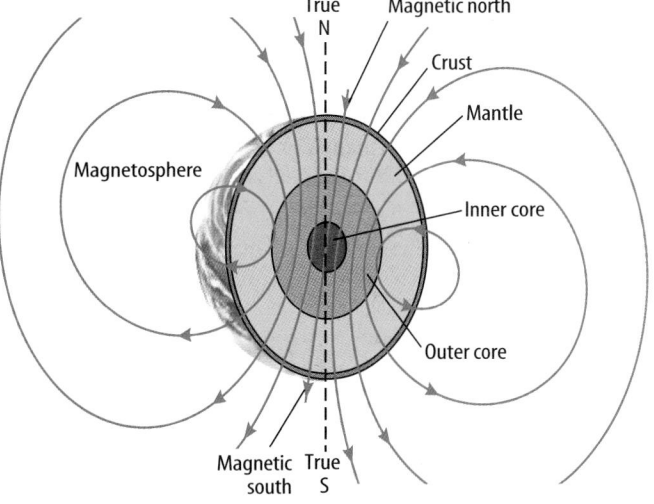

Figure 6
Earth has a magnetic field similar to the field of a bar magnet.

Problem-Solving Activity

Finding the Magnetic Declination

The north pole of a compass points toward the magnetic pole, rather than true north. Imagine drawing a line between your location and the north pole, and a line between your location and the magnetic pole. The angle between these two lines is called the magnetic declination. Sometimes knowing the magnetic declination can be important if you need to know the direction to true north, rather than to the magnetic pole. However, the magnetic declination changes depending on your position.

Identifying the Problem

Suppose your location is at 50° N and 110° W. You wish to head true north. The location of the north pole is at 90° N and 110° W, and the location of the magnetic pole is at about 80° N and

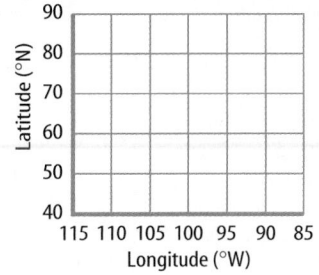

105° W. What is the magnetic declination angle at your location?

Solving the Problem
1. Label a graph like the one shown above.
2. On the graph, plot your location, the location of the magnetic pole, and the location of the north pole.
3. Draw a line from your location to the north pole, and a line from your location to the magnetic pole.
4. Using a protractor measure the angle between the two lines.

✔ Active Reading

Quickwrite Have students write a list of ideas about magnetism and then share these ideas with the class. Next, have students write their ideas about magnetism freely in a paragraph without worrying about punctuation, spelling, and grammar. Have students then share their paragraphs.

Resource Manager

Chapter Resources Booklet
  Enrichment, p. 25

Physical Science Critical Thinking/Problem Solving, p. 18

Earth's Magnetic Field

Quick Demo

Put a clear plate or petri dish over a piece of a natural magnet and use iron filings to show the shape of the magnetic field. Discuss why the shape of the field around the natural magnet is irregular. Ask students whether Earth's magnetic field is completely uniform. Possible answer: No, it is strongest near the poles. L3
IS Logical-Mathematical

Discussion

How are gravity, electricity, and magnetism alike? How are they different? All have fields and act at a distance. Gravity always attracts, but electricity and magnetism can attract or repel. Gravity exists between all objects, while only certain objects are affected by electric and magnetic fields. L2
IS Logical-Mathematical

IDENTIFYING
Misconceptions

Some students think that Earth's north and south geographic poles are corresponding north and south magnetic poles. See page 652F for teaching strategies that address this misconception.

Problem-Solving Activity

National Math Standards
Correlation to Mathematics Objectives
2, 3, 4, 6, 8, 9, 10

Answer to Practice Problem
The Magnetic declination is about 20°.

Caption Answer

Figure 7 farther north

Mini LAB

Purpose Students use iron filings to observe magnetic fields. L2 **Kinesthetic**

Materials iron filings, plastic petri dish, tape, magnets

Safety Precaution Make sure to use iron *filings* only. DO NOT use iron *powder*, as it may contain ultrafine particles that present a serious risk of fire and explosion.

Troubleshooting

Seal the petri dish with tape or glue to keep the filings off the magnets. Filings can be hard to remove.

Teaching Strategies

Field lines around magnets can be illustrated with an overhead projector, using a clear petri dish containing iron filings and magnets of different shapes and strengths.

Analysis

1. Filings are densest at the poles. They are less dense farther away from the poles.
2. The stronger the magnet, the denser the filings.

Performance Have students use iron filings to design an experiment to show whether flexible magnetic strips are a single magnet or a series of magnets, each with a north and south pole. Use **Performance Assessment in the Science Classroom**, p. 95. P

Mini LAB

Observing Magnetic Fields

Procedure
1. Place **iron filings** in a **plastic petri dish.** Cover the dish and **tape** it closed.
2. Collect **several magnets.** Place the magnets on the table and hold the dish over each one. Draw a diagram of what happens to the filings in each case.
3. Arrange two or more magnets under the dish. Observe the pattern of the filings.

Analysis
1. What happens to the filings close to the poles? Far from the poles?
2. Compare the fields of the individual magnets. How can you tell which magnet is strongest? Weakest?

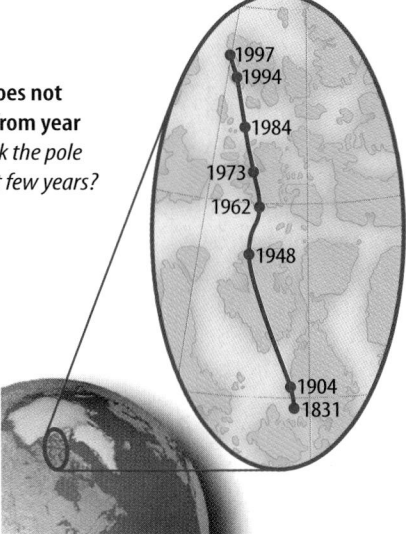

Figure 7
Earth's magnetic pole does not remain in one location from year to year. *How do you think the pole might move over the next few years?*

Nature's Magnets Honeybees, rainbow trout, and homing pigeons have something in common with sailors and hikers. They take advantage of magnetism to find their way. Instead of using compasses, these animals and others have tiny pieces of magnetite in their bodies. These pieces can be so small that they may contain a single magnetic domain. Scientists have shown that some animals use these natural magnets to detect Earth's magnetic field. They appear to use Earth's magnetic field, along with other clues like the position of the Sun or stars, to help them navigate.

Earth's Changing Magnetic Field Earth's magnetic poles do not stay in one place. The magnetic pole in the north today, as shown in **Figure 7,** is in a different place from where it was 20 years ago. In fact, not only does the position of the magnetic poles move, but Earth's magnetic field sometimes reverses direction. For example, 700 thousand years ago, a compass needle that now points north would point south. During the past 20 million years, Earth's magnetic field has reversed direction more than 70 times. The magnetism of ancient rocks contains a record of these magnetic field changes. When some types of molten rock cool, magnetic domains of iron in the rock line up with Earth's magnetic field. After the rock cools, the orientation of these domains is frozen into position. Consequently, these old rocks preserve the orientation of Earth's magnetic field as it was long ago.

Resource Manager

Chapter Resources Booklet
  MiniLAB, p. 3
  Lab Activity, pp. 9–10

Performance Assessment in the Science Classroom, p. 35

Visual Learning

Figure 7 The illustration shows that Earth's magnetic field is changing. **What does this suggest is going on inside Earth?** If the magnetic field arises from Earth's molten-iron core, it suggests that the process in the core are changing, also. L3

Logical-Mathematical

Figure 8
The compass needles align with the magnetic field lines around the magnet. *What happens to the compass needles when the bar magnet is removed?*

The Compass How can humans detect and measure Earth's magnetic field? The compass is a useful tool for finding and mapping magnetic fields. A compass has a needle that is free to turn. The needle itself is a small magnet with a north and a south magnetic pole. A magnet placed close to a compass causes the needle to rotate until it is aligned with the magnetic field line that passes through the compass, as shown in **Figure 8.**

Earth's magnetic field also causes a compass needle to rotate. The north pole of the compass needle points toward Earth's magnetic pole that is near the geographic north pole. Unlike poles attract, so this magnetic pole is actually a magnetic south pole. Earth's magnetic field is like that of a bar magnet with the magnet's south pole near Earth's north pole.

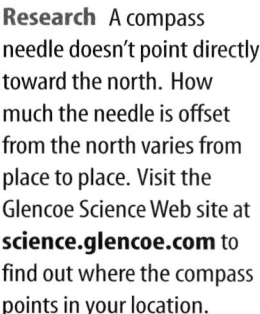

SCIENCE *Online*

Research A compass needle doesn't point directly toward the north. How much the needle is offset from the north varies from place to place. Visit the Glencoe Science Web site at **science.glencoe.com** to find out where the compass points in your location.

Section 1 Assessment

1. Why do atoms behave like magnets?
2. Explain why magnets attract iron but do not attract paper.
3. How is the behavior of electric charges similar to that of magnetic poles?
4. Around a magnet, where is the field the strongest? Where is it the weakest?
5. **Think Critically** A horseshoe magnet is a bar magnet bent into the shape of the letter U. When would two horseshoe magnets attract each other? Repel? Have little effect?

Skill Builder Activities

6. **Comparing and Contrasting** Compare and contrast the three phenomena of *gravity, electricity,* and *magnetism.* Use the terms *force* and *field* in your comparison. **For more help, refer to the** Science Skill Handbook.
7. **Communicating** Imagine you are an early explorer. In your Science Journal, explain how a compass would change your work. Describe the difficulties of working without a compass. **For more help, refer to the** Science Skill Handbook.

Answers to Section Assessment

1. They contain moving electrons.
2. Some metals have magnetic domains in which atoms are oriented in the same direction. Paper does not.
3. Yes, the material around you would not block Earth's magnetic field.
4. The field is strongest near the magnet's poles and weakest far from the poles.
5. If like poles face each other, the magnets will repel each other. If opposite poles face each other, the magnets will attract each other. If the rounded parts of the magnets face each other, the magnets will have little effect on each other.
6. All act at a distance through fields whose force decreases with distance. In electricity and magnetism, like repels like and opposites attract. Gravity has no charges or poles.
7. It would tell you the direction in which you were traveling, even if you could not see the Sun or stars.

Caption Answer
Figure 8 They align with Earth's magnetic field.

SCIENCE *Online*
Internet Addresses

Explore the Glencoe Science Web site at **science.glencoe.com** to find out more about topics in this section.

3 Assess

Reteach
Use iron filings to display the magnetic fields surrounding a variety of magnets. Have students identify where the fields are strongest and weakest.
Visual-Spatial

Challenge
Some metal alloys made of combinations of iron, cobalt, nickel and other elements can be strong magnets. Have students research the properties of the alloys alnico and permalloy, and how they are used. What elements do these two alloys contain? Alnico is a mixture of aluminum, nickel, iron, and cobalt. Permalloy is a mixture of iron and nickel.

 **Assessment**

Performance Have students use a paper clip, a magnet, and materials such as paper or aluminum foil to determine whether materials can shield magnetic forces. Use **Performance Assessment in the Science Classroom,** p. 97.

Activity

Purpose Students discover how magnetism can be used to find direction on Earth. L2 ELL

IS Kinesthetic

Process Skills observing, inferring, comparing and contrasting, interpreting data

Time Required 45 minutes

Safety Precautions Caution students about responsible and careful handling of the needles. Collect and count needles before the end of class.

Teaching Strategies Needles can be difficult to handle; help students place them on the water.

Troubleshooting Caution students about disturbing the water and needle as little as possible when moving the dish.

Answers to Questions

1. The needle always aligns itself north-south.
2. The compass needle moved to align itself with the magnet's field.
3. The north pole of the needle will be attracted to the south pole of the magnet, and the needle's south pole will be attracted to the magnet's north pole.

Assessment

Performance Have students find out what orienteering is. Have them learn how to find places using only a compass and directions. Ask them to write about what they find. Use **PASC**, p. 159.

Activity

Make a Compass

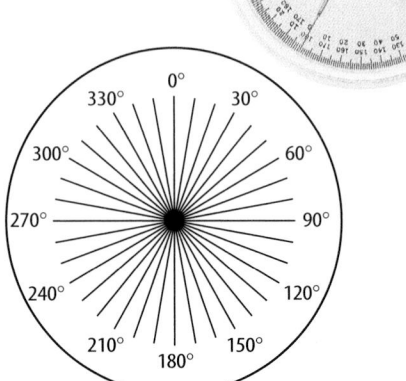

A valuable tool for hikers and campers is a compass. Almost 1,000 years ago, Chinese inventors found a way to magnetize pieces of iron. They used this method to manufacture compasses. You can use the same procedure to make a compass.

What You'll Investigate
How do you construct a compass?

Materials

petri dish	tape
*clear bowl	marker
water	paper
sewing needle	plastic spoon
magnet	*Alternate material

Goals
■ **Observe** induced magnetism.
■ **Build** a compass.

Safety 🔍 👓 🧤

Procedure

1. Reproduce the circular protractor shown. Tape it under the bottom of your dish so it can be seen but not get wet. Add water until the dish is half full.

2. Mark one end of the needle with a marker. Magnetize a needle by placing it on the magnet aligned north and south for 1 min.

3. Float the needle carefully in the dish. Use a plastic spoon to lower the needle onto the water. Turn the dish so the marked part of the needle is above the 0° mark. This is your compass.

4. Bring the magnet near your compass. Observe how the needle reacts. Measure the angle the needle turns.

Conclude and Apply

1. **Explain** why the marked end of the needle always pointed the same way in step 3, even though you rotated the dish.

2. **Describe** the behavior of the compass when the magnet was brought close.

3. Does the marked end of your needle point to the north or south pole of the bar magnet? Infer whether the marked end of your needle is a north or a south pole. How do you know?

Communicating Your Data

Make a half-page insert that will go into a wilderness survival guide to describe the procedure for making a compass. Share your half-page insert with your classmates. **For more help, refer to the** Science Skill Handbook.

Communicating Your Data

Students can use a word processing program and a scanner to help them produce their directions for making a compass. Scanned photos could show how to magnetize a needle and how to mount it.

Resource Manager

Chapter Resources Booklet
Activity Worksheet, pp. 5–6

Electricity and Magnetism

Electromagnets

Magnetic fields are produced by moving electric charges. Electrons moving around the nuclei of atoms produce magnetic fields. The motion of these electrons causes some materials, such as iron, to be magnetic. You cause electric charges to move when you flip a light switch or turn on a portable CD player. When electric current flows in a wire, electric charges move in the wire. As a result, a wire that contains an electric current also is surrounded by a magnetic field. **Figure 9A** shows the magnetic field produced around a wire that carries an electric current.

Look at the magnetic field lines around the coils of wire in **Figure 9B.** The magnetic fields around each coil of wire add together to form a stronger magnetic field inside the coil. When the coils are wrapped around an iron core, the magnetic field of the coils magnetizes the iron. The iron then becomes a magnet, which adds to the strength of the magnetic field inside the coil. A current-carrying wire wrapped around an iron core is called an **electromagnet,** as shown in **Figure 9C.**

As You Read

What You'll Learn
- **Describe** the relationship between electricity and magnetism.
- **Explain** how electricity can produce motion.
- **Explain** how motion can produce electricity.

Vocabulary

electromagnet	generator
motor	alternating current
aurora	transformer

Why It's Important
The electric current that comes from your wall socket is available because of magnetism.

Figure 9
A current-carrying wire produces a magnetic field.

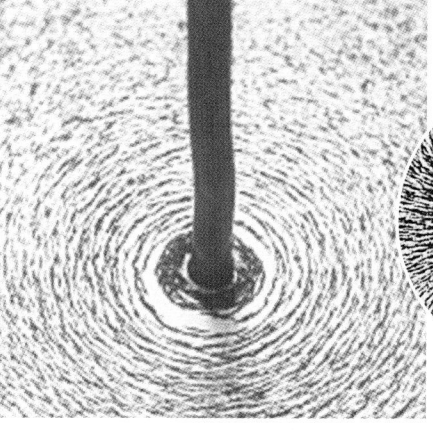

A Iron particles show the magnetic field lines around a current-carrying wire.

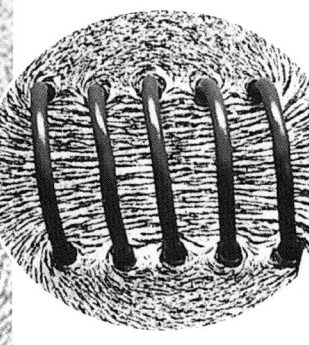

B When a wire is wrapped in a coil, the field inside the coil is made stronger.

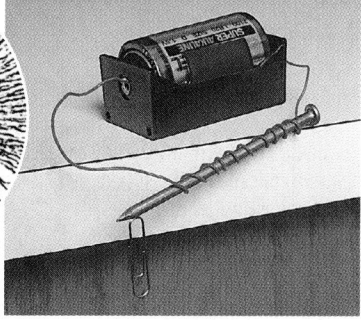

C An iron core inside the coils increases the magnetic field because the core becomes magnetized.

SECTION 2 Electricity and Magnetism **661**

SECTION

Electricity and Magnetism

1 Motivate

Bellringer Transparency
Display the Section Focus Transparency for Section 2. Use the accompanying Transparency Activity Master. L2 ELL

Tie to Prior Knowledge
Ask students in what context, other than when discussing magnetism, they've heard that like repels like and opposites attract. electricity Explain that in this section they will learn more about how electricity and magnetism are related.

Section ✔Assessment Planner

PORTFOLIO
Cultural Diversity, p. 665
PERFORMANCE ASSESSMENT
Try At Home MiniLAB, p. 662
Skill Builder Activities, p. 669
See page 676 for more options.

CONTENT ASSESSMENT
Section, p. 669
Challenge, p. 669
Chapter, pp. 676–677

2 Teach

Moving Charge Creates a Magnet

Caption Answer
Figure 10 by opening the circuit

TRY AT HOME
Mini LAB

Purpose Students build an electromagnet. L2

IS Kinesthetic

Materials insulated wire, 16-penny steel nail, D-cell battery, paper clips

Teaching Strategy Provide sealed iron filings or compasses so students can investigate the fields produced by their electromagnets.

Safety Precautions Make sure students do not leave the electromagnets connected to the battery for long periods of time.

Troubleshooting Make sure students use insulated wire and do not short the batteries by wiring directly across the terminals.

Analysis
1. The more coils on the electromagnet, the more paper clips it picked up.
2. The five-coil electromagnet should pick up about half as many paper clips as the ten-coil electromagnet.

✔Assessment

Oral Have students summarize the relationship between the number of coils and the number of paper clips an electromagnet can pick up. The more coils, the greater the number of paper clips that can be picked up. Use **PASC**, p. 89.

Figure 10
An electric doorbell uses an electromagnet. Each time the electromagnet is turned on, the hammer strikes the bell. *How is the electromagnet turned off?*

TRY AT HOME
Mini LAB

Assembling an Electromagnet

Procedure
1. Wrap a **wire** around a **16-penny steel nail** ten times. Connect one end of the wire to a **D-cell battery,** as shown in **Figure 9C.** Leave the other end loose until you use the electromagnet. **WARNING:** *When current is flowing in the wire, it can become hot over time.*
2. Connect the wire. Observe how many **paper clips** you can pick up with the magnet.
3. Disconnect the wire and rewrap the nail with 20 coils. Connect the wire and observe how many paper clips you can pick up. Disconnect the wire again.

Analysis
1. How many paper clips did you pick up each time? Did more coils make the electromagnet stronger or weaker?
2. Graph the number of coils versus number of paper clips attracted. Predict how many paper clips would be picked up with five coils of wire. Check your prediction.

Bell

D When the hammer strikes the bell, the circuit is open, and the electromagnet is turned off.

C The electromagnet attracts the hammer that strikes the bell.

E A spring pulls the hammer back, closing the circuit and starting the cycle over.

B When the circuit is closed, an electromagnet is turned on.

Power source

A Pressing the button closes the circuit.

Using Electromagnets The magnetic field of an electromagnet is turned on or off when the electric current is turned on or off. By changing the current, the strength and direction of the magnetic field of an electromagnet can be changed. This has led to a number of practical uses for electromagnets. A doorbell, as shown in **Figure 10,** is a familiar use of an electromagnet. When you press the button by the door, you close a switch in a circuit that includes an electromagnet. The magnet attracts an iron bar attached to a hammer. The hammer strikes the bell. When the hammer strikes the bell, the hammer has moved far enough to open the circuit again. The electromagnet loses its magnetic field, and a spring pulls the iron bar and hammer back into place. This movement closes the circuit, and the cycle is repeated as long as the button is pushed.

One use of electromagnets is in high-speed trains. A new generation of trains uses powerful electromagnets for lift and propulsion, as shown in **Figure 11.** These trains, know as maglev (magnetic levitation) trains, can reach speeds of more than 500 km/h.

Inclusion Strategies

Physically Challenged An electromagnet can be made with larger equipment that will make the manipulation easier. A tall metal cylinder can be used in place of the nail and a spray-painted metal spring toy can be used in place of the wire. **IS** Kinesthetic

Visual Learning

Figure 10 Have students use the illustration and text description to make a flowchart that traces the sequence of events that results in a doorbell ringing. Possible answer: Pushing the button creates an electric current, which activates the electromagnet and causes an iron bar to move a hammer that strikes a bell. The bell rings, and the hammer movement opens the circuit again, shutting off the current. L2 **IS** Visual-Spatial

Figure 11

Imagine speeding along in a train at more than 500 kph and never actually touching the ground. Someday you may experience that in a maglev or "magnetic levitation" train. A maglev train uses magnets to lift, guide, and move the train over a special track. Several countries, including Japan and Germany, are experimenting with maglev technology.

A maglev train runs suspended, or levitated, one to ten centimeters above a track, or guideway, that contains wire coils and electromagnets. The train never touches the guideway, eliminating friction. Because energy isn't being converted into heat by friction, a maglev train can reach higher speeds using less energy.

In the design shown here the train is lifted by the attraction between the track magnet and the train magnet, while the guidance magnets keep the train centered in the guideway. A varying electric current running through electromagnets in the guideway creates magnetic forces that move the train forward.

- Guidance magnet
- Track magnet
- Train magnet
- Track

SECTION 2 Electricity and Magnetism **663**

Visualizing Maglev Trains

Have students examine the pictures and read the captions. Then ask the following questions. **What are some advantages to maglev trains not mentioned here?** Possible answers: quieter than regular trains; carries no combustible fuel in case of accidents; no friction means no wearing out of parts; faster travel times for people and products **Do you think there are any disadvantages to maglev trains?** Possible answer: safety concerns with higher speeds

Activity

Give each group of students a paper clip, a 30-cm piece of sewing thread, a 20-cm piece of string, a piece of masking tape, a bar magnet, and a ring stand with a ring attached. Ask them to determine a way to use these materials to magnetically levitate the paper clip above the surface of a table. Use the string to hang the magnet from the ring. Tie the paper clip to the thread. Attach the thread to the table with tape below the magnet. Adjust the length of the thread so the paper clip will be attracted to the magnet, but not touch it. L2 IS **Kinesthetic**

Extension

Have students research the difference in designs for maglev trains. Encourage them to prepare a written report with diagrams explaining what they learn. IS **Linguistic**

Resource Manager

Chapter Resources Booklet
   Transparency Activity, p. 39
   MiniLAB, p. 4
Home and Community Involvement, p. 49

Magnets Push Currents

Quick Demo

Show students how electricity and magnetism are related by setting up a DC circuit and showing how the needle of a compass is deflected in opposite directions when the compass is held over and under the wire. If possible, set this up on an overhead projector so students can see it better. Ask students to describe a way to move the wire that will keep the compass spinning. L3 **IS** **Logical-Mathematical**

Visual Learning

Figure 13 The illustration shows that the current loop spins because of the force exerted on it by the magnetic field. Help students see that to keep the loop spinning, some mechanism must be in place that changes the direction of the current each half-turn. This is done by two split rings connected to the ends of the loop. These establish connections with the battery terminals. When the loop spins, the rings also spin and come in contact with the opposite terminals. This changes the direction of the current and keeps the motor operating. L2 **IS** **Visual-Spatial**

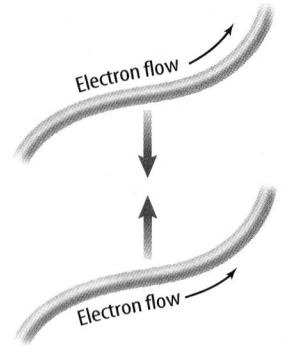

Figure 12
Two wires carrying current in the same direction attract each other, just as unlike magnetic poles do.

Figure 13
In an electric motor, the force a magnet exerts on a current-carrying wire transforms electric energy into kinetic energy.

Magnets Push and Pull Currents

Look around for electric appliances that produce motion, such as a fan. How does the electric energy entering the fan become transformed into the kinetic energy of the moving fan blades? Recall that current-carrying wires produce a magnetic field. This magnetic field behaves the same way as the magnetic field that a magnet produces. Two current-carrying wires can attract each other as if they were two magnets, as shown in **Figure 12.**

Electric Motor Just as two magnets exert a force on each other, a magnet and a current-carrying wire exert forces on each other. The magnetic field around a current-carrying wire will cause it to be pushed or pulled by a magnet, depending on the direction the current is flowing in the wire. As a result, some of the electric energy carried by the current is converted into kinetic energy of the moving wire, as shown in **Figure 13A.** Any device that converts electric energy into kinetic energy is a **motor.** To keep a motor running, the current-carrying wire is formed into a loop so the magnetic field can force the wire to spin continually, as shown in **Figure 13B.**

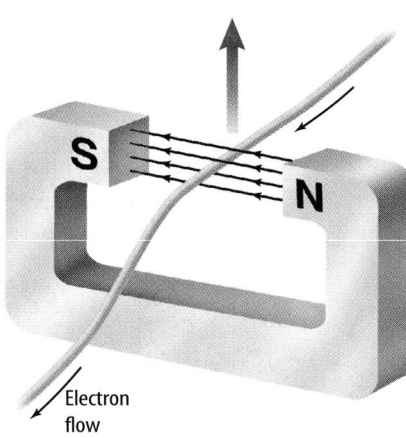

A A magnetic field like the one shown will push a current-carrying wire upward.

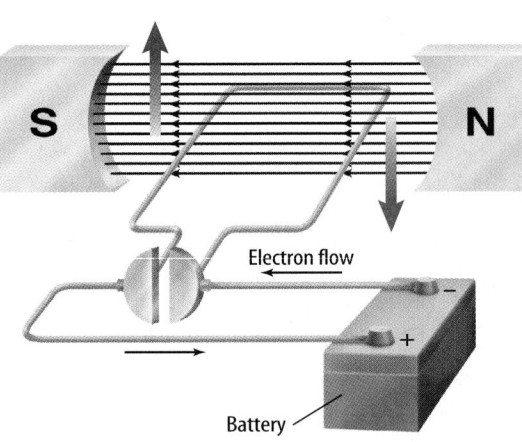

B The magnetic field exerts a force on the wire loop, causing it to spin as long as current flows in the loop.

Teacher FYI

Electromagnetic interactions are important in the operation of television sets. Magnets control the beam of electrons that forms the television picture. Many laboratory balances also work by balancing a weight with an electromagnetic force.

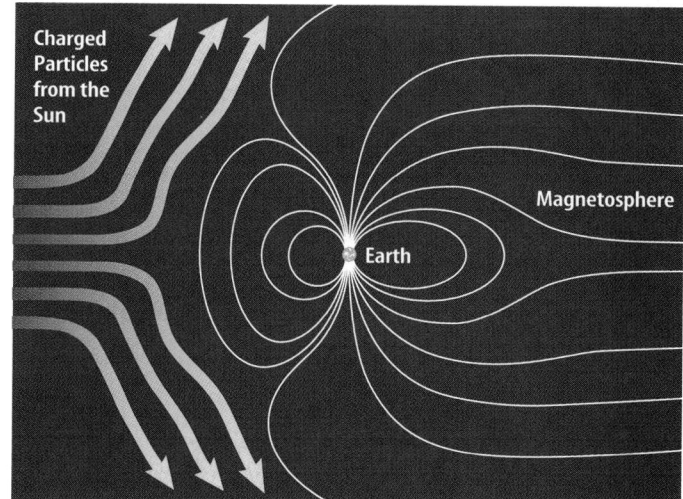

Charged Particles from the Sun

Magnetosphere

Earth

Pushing on Currents in Space The Sun emits charged particles that stream through the solar system like an enormous electric current. Just like a current-carrying wire is pushed or pulled by a magnetic field, Earth's magnetic field pushes and pulls on the electric current generated by the Sun. This causes most of the charged particles in this current to be deflected so they never strike Earth, as shown in **Figure 14.** As a result, living things on Earth are protected from damage that might be caused by these charged particles. At the same time, the solar current pushes on Earth's magnetosphere so it is stretched away from the Sun.

The Aurora Sometimes the Sun ejects a large number of charged particles all at once. Most of these charged particles are deflected by Earth's magnetosphere. However, some of the ejected particles from the Sun produce other charged particles in Earth's outer atmosphere. These charged particles spiral along Earth's magnetic field lines toward Earth's magnetic poles. There they collide with atoms in the atmosphere. These collisions cause the atoms to emit light. The light emitted causes a display known as the aurora (uh ROR uh), as shown in **Figure 15.** In northern latitudes, the aurora sometimes is called the northern lights.

Figure 15
An aurora is a natural light show that occurs in the southern and northern skies.

SECTION 2 Electricity and Magnetism **665**

A Magnet Pushes on Moving Charge

Fun Fact

The frequency of alternating current in Europe is 50 cycles per second.

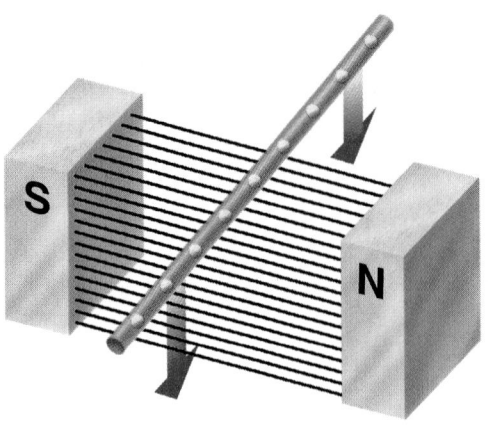

A If a wire is pulled downward through a magnetic field, the electrons in the wire also move downward through the field.

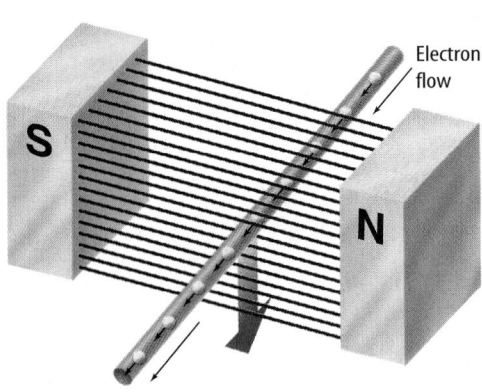

Electron flow

B The magnetic field then exerts a force on the moving electrons, causing them to move along the wire.

Figure 16
When a wire is made to move through a magnetic field, an electric current can be produced in the wire.

Figure 17
In a generator, a power source spins a wire loop in a magnetic field. Every half turn, the current will reverse direction. This type of generator supplies alternating current to the lightbulb.

A Magnet Pushes on Moving Charge

In an electric motor, a magnetic field turns electricity into motion. A device called a **generator** uses a magnetic field to turn motion into electricity. Electric motors and electric generators both involve conversions between electric energy and kinetic energy. In a motor, electric energy is changed into kinetic energy. In a generator, kinetic energy is changed into electric energy. **Figure 16** shows how a current can be produced in a wire that moves in a magnetic field. As the wire moves, the electrons in the wire also move in the same direction, as shown in **Figure 16A.** The magnetic field exerts a force on the moving electrons that pushes them along the wire, as shown in **Figure 16B,** creating an electric current.

Generating Electricity To produce electric current, the wire is fashioned into a loop, as in **Figure 17.** A power source provides the kinetic energy to spin the wire loop. With each half turn, the current in the loop changes direction. This causes the current to alternate from positive to negative. Such a current is called an **alternating current** (AC). In the United States, electric currents change from positive to negative to positive 60 times each second.

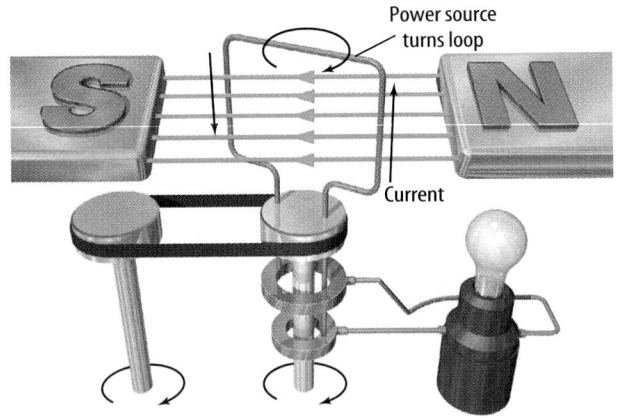

Power source turns loop

Current

LAB DEMONSTRATION

Purpose to build an electric generator
Materials four small bar magnets; 70 m #30 wire; holiday lightbulb; small cardboard box; 1 long nail, tape
Procedure Poke holes in the long sides of the box. Insert the nail so that it spans the box opening and spins freely. Tape the magnets to the nail, 2 on each side, so that

the north poles point in the same direction. Wrap wire around the sides of the box. Use tape to keep the wire away from the nail holes. Attach each wire end to one wire of the bulb. Hand spin the nail vigorously.

Expected Outcome The bulb glows dimly. To increase brightness, clamp the nail into the chuck of a hand drill.

Assessment

Why does the bulb light only dimly? Not much current is produced. **Why is the bulb brighter when the nail is turned faster?** The faster the magnets rotate, the more current is generated.

Types of Current A battery produces direct current instead of alternating current. In a direct current (DC) electrons flow in one direction. In an alternating current, electrons change their direction of movement many times each second. Some generators are built to produce direct current instead of alternating current.

✓ Reading Check *What type of currents can be produced by a generator?*

Power Plants Electric generators produce almost all of the electric energy used all over the world. Small generators can produce energy for one household, and large generators in electric power plants can provide electric energy for thousands of homes. Different energy sources such as gas, coal, and water are used to provide the kinetic energy to rotate coils of wire in a magnetic field. Coal-burning power plants, like the one pictured in **Figure 18,** are the most common. More than half of the electric energy generated by power plants in the United States comes from burning coal.

Voltage The electric energy produced at a power plant is carried to your home in wires. Recall that voltage is a measure of how much energy that electric charges in a current are carrying. The electric transmission lines from electric power plants transmit electric energy at a high voltage of about 700,000 V. Transmitting electric energy at a low voltage is less efficient because more electric energy is converted into heat in the wires. However, high voltage is not safe for use in homes and businesses. A device is needed to reduce the voltage.

SCIENCE *Online*

Research Visit the Glencoe Science Web site at **science.glencoe.com** for more information about the different types of power plants used in your region of the country. Communicate to your class what you learn.

SCIENCE *Online*
Internet Addresses

Explore the Glencoe Science Web site at **science.glencoe.com** to find out more about topics in this section.

✓ Reading Check

Answer direct current and alternating current

Quick Demo

To illustrate the difference between alternating and direct current, make a circuit with an AC power source, a lightbulb, and an ammeter. Have students note how the needle fluctuates between positive and negative values. Next, connect the ammeter to a DC power source, and have students note the constant positive value. L2
LS Visual-Spatial

Figure 18
Coal-burning power plants supply much of the electric energy for the world.

Science Journal

Providing Power Have students research in more detail how power gets from the power plant to their homes. Ask them to outline the steps in their Science Journals, paying particular attention to those steps that in some way involve magnetism. L2 **LS Linguistic**

Resource Manager

Chapter Resources Booklet
    Enrichment, p. 26
    Lab Activity, pp. 11–12
Science Inquiry Labs, pp. 9, 55

Changing Voltage

Activity

Collect several discarded transformers from used or broken appliances and break open their outer, plastic casings. Organize the class into groups and give each a transformer and its casing. Describe the power-converting specifications of each transformer. If possible, tell students what device each transformer was used to operate. Have students identify the input coil, output coil, and iron core. Have them try to determine from the windings to what voltage the transformer converts the 120 V from an outlet and whether their findings match the rating stated on the case. L3

✔ Reading Check

Answer It can increase or decrease voltage of an alternating current.

IDENTIFYING Misconceptions

Make sure students understand that transformers work only with alternating current and not with direct current. This is because the constant electrical field of direct current produces a constant magnetic field that cannot induce an electrical field in the secondary winding.

Caption Answer
Figure 20 180V

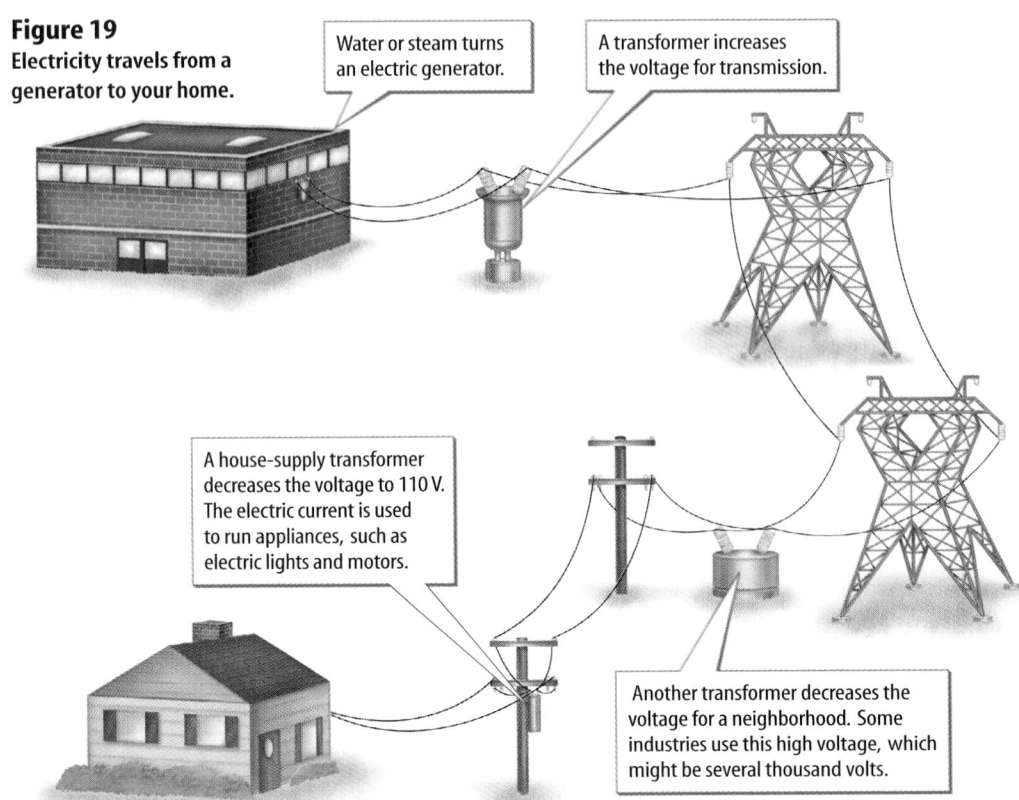

Figure 19
Electricity travels from a generator to your home.

Water or steam turns an electric generator.

A transformer increases the voltage for transmission.

A house-supply transformer decreases the voltage to 110 V. The electric current is used to run appliances, such as electric lights and motors.

Another transformer decreases the voltage for a neighborhood. Some industries use this high voltage, which might be several thousand volts.

Figure 20
A transformer can increase or decrease voltage. The ratio of input coils to output coils equals the ratio of input voltage to output voltage. *If the input voltage here is 60 V, what is the output voltage?*

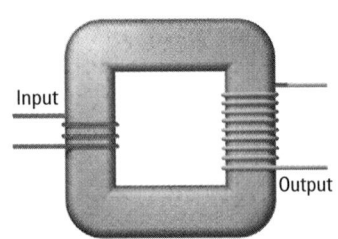
Input
Output

Changing Voltage

A **transformer** is a device that changes the voltage of an alternating current with little loss of energy. Transformers are used to increase the voltage before transmitting an electric current through the power lines. Other transformers are used to decrease the voltage to the level needed for home or industrial use. Such a power system is shown in **Figure 19.** Transformers also play a role in power adaptors. For battery-operated devices, a power adaptor must change the 110 V from the wall outlet to a voltage that matches the device's batteries.

✔ Reading Check *Why is a transformer important?*

A transformer usually has two coils of wire wrapped around an iron core, as shown in **Figure 20.** One coil is connected to an alternating current source. The current creates a magnetic field in the iron core, just like in an electromagnet. Because the current is alternating, the magnetic field it produces also switches direction. This alternating magnetic field in the core then causes an alternating current in the other wire coil.

Science Journal

AC versus DC When Thomas Edison first installed his electric lamps, he powered them with direct current. Have students find out and write in their Science Journals why alternating current became the preferred electrical current. Alternating current could be transmitted at a high voltage that could be stepped down by transformers for household use. L2  **Linguistic**

Resource Manager

Chapter Resources Booklet
    Reinforcement, p. 24
    Transparency Activity, pp. 41–42

The Transformer Ratio How a transformer increases or decreases the voltages depends on the number of coils on each side. The ratio of coils on the input side to coils on the output side is the same as the ratio of the input voltage to the output voltage. For example, the transformer in **Figure 20** has a ratio of input coils to output coils of 3 to 9. If the input voltage is 10 V, the output voltage will be 30 V. By varying the ratio of coils, the voltage can be increased or decreased.

Connecting Electricity and Magnetism

Electricity and magnetism have many similarities. Both forces depend on charges such as electrons. Both forces can repel or attract. In both cases, like forces repel and unlike forces attract. Moving charges produce magnetic fields, and magnetic fields can generate electric currents. People use this connection in many ways, including the electric guitar shown in **Figure 21.**

In an electric guitar, small magnets produce a magnetic field around the strings. This field causes the magnetic domains in the strings to line up, producing a magnetic field of their own. When you strum the guitar, the strings vibrate producing a change in the surrounding magnetic field. Charges in the coil start to vibrate in response to the changing magnetic field. The motion of these charges is an electric current that eventually is amplified and sent to a speaker to create sound.

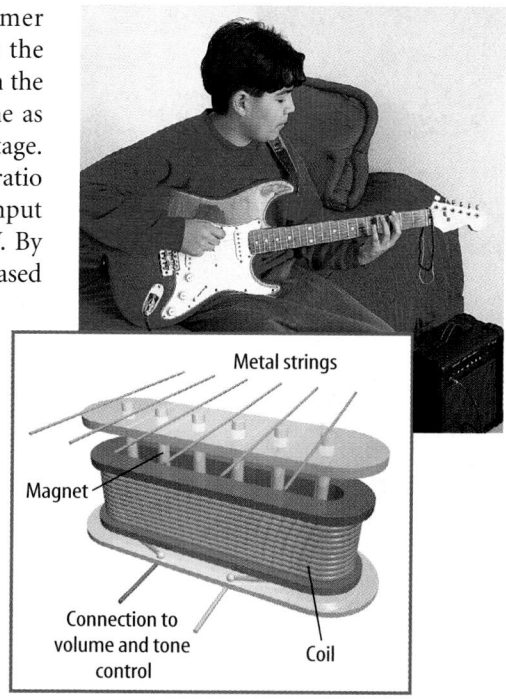

Figure 21
Electric guitars illustrate the connection between electricity and magnetism.

Section 2 Assessment

1. What is an electromagnet? How can you make one in the classroom?

2. How does a transformer work?

3. How does a magnetic field affect a current-carrying wire?

4. How does a generator turn motion into electrical energy?

5. **Think Critically** How is an electric motor similar to an aurora? Use the terms current, field, and kinetic energy in your answer.

Skill Builder Activities

6. **Researching Information** Research how electricity is generated in your state. Make a poster showing the fuels that are used. **For more help, refer to the** Science Skill Handbook.

7. **Calculating Ratios** A transformer has ten turns of wire on the input side and 50 turns of wire on the output side. If the input voltage is 120 V, what will the output voltage be? **For more help, refer to the** Math Skill Handbook.

Answers to Section Assessment

1. A device that uses electricity to generate magnetism; wind wire around an iron nail and attach the wire to a battery.

2. An alternating current in the input coil induces a magnetic field in the core. This induces an alternating current in the output coil.

3. It exerts a force on the wire.

4. A power source spins a wire loop surrounded by a magnet. The movement of the wire relative to the magnetic field induces current in the wire.

5. In an electric motor, a magnetic field exerts a force on an electric current, converting electric energy into kinetic energy. In an aurora, charged particles transfer kinetic energy to atmospheric atoms, which re-emit the energy as light.

6. Check students' posters.

7. (50 turns ÷ 10 turns) × 120 V = 600 V

Make a Model

Have students roll cardboard into a tube and wind different colors of string around it to make a model of a transformer. Give them several different voltage conversions to model, such as 60 V to 120 V, 120 V to 3 V, and 120 V to 220 V. L2
LS Kinesthetic

3 Assess

Reteach

Ask students to predict how various electromagnets with different numbers of windings compare. Then give students sample transformer ratios and ask them whether each will increase or decrease voltage. L2
LS Logical-Mathematical

Challenge

Stereo speakers rely on interactions between magnets and electricity to produce sound. Have students find out how the magnets in stereo speakers work. A stereo speaker has a permanent magnet and an electromagnet. The electromagnet can move and is attached to a cone of paper. The varying electrical signal carrying the information about the sound flows through the electromagnet, causing a varying magnetic field around it. This magnetic field interacts with the constant magnetic field of the permanent magnet, causing the electromagnet, and the paper cone to which it is attached, to move. This motion of the paper cone creates the sounds heard from the speaker. L3
LS Logical-Mathematical

✓ Assessment

Performance Have students take an inventory of their homes and list all the items that make use of an electric motor. Have them summarize their findings in a spreadsheet or table. Use **Performance Assessment in the Science Classroom,** p. 109.

Activity

BENCH TESTED

What You'll Investigate

Purpose

Students build an electric motor.

[L2] ELL IK **Kinesthetic**

Process Skills

observing and inferring, recognizing cause and effect, interpreting scientific illustrations, formulating models

Time Required

1 class period

Materials

You can obtain wood blocks from your school's wood shop or from a lumber yard's scraps.

Safety Precautions

Caution students to hold only the insulated part of each wire when wires are attached to the battery.

Procedure

Teaching Strategy

Show students how to use sandpaper to strip the insulation off the wire without cutting the wire itself. Make certain all batteries are charged.

Tie to Prior Knowledge

Ask students whether they have ever seen a tiny, electric motor in a toy or model. Did they notice that there were magnets in it?

Troubleshooting

Be sure students attach the wire securely to the battery terminals and to the knitting needles.

Activity

How does an electric motor work?

Electric motors are used in many appliances. For example, a computer contains a cooling fan and motors to spin the hard drive. A CD player contains electric motors to spin the CD. Some cars contain electric motors that move windows up and down, change the position of the seats, and blow warm or cold air into the car's interior. All these electric motors consist of an electromagnet and a permanent magnet. In this activity you will build a simple electric motor that will work for you.

What You'll Investigate

How can you change electric energy into motion?

Goals

- **Assemble** a small electric motor.
- **Observe** how the motor works.

670

Safety Precautions

Hold only the insulated part of each wire when they are attached to the battery. Use care when hammering the nails. After cutting the wire, the ends will be sharp.

Materials

22-gauge enameled wire (4 m)
steel knitting needle
*steel rod
nails (4)
hammer
ceramic magnets (2)
18-gauge insulated wire (60 cm)
masking tape
fine sandpaper
approximately 15-cm wooden board
wooden blocks (2)
6-V battery
*1.5-V batteries connected in a series (4)
wire cutters
*scissors
*Alternate materials

Inclusion Strategies

Physically Challenged Pair these students with others who work well in the lab. Have the physically challenged student read the instructions aloud as the other student builds the model. Have both students evaluate the setup to make sure the needle is as close to the magnets as possible.

✔ Active Reading

Synthesis Journal In this strategy, students reflect on a project, a paper, or a performance in light of their own experiences and plan for personal application. Have each student divide a piece of paper into three sections. Have them record "What I did," "What I learned," and "How I can use it." Have students write a Synthesis Journal entry related to this activity.

Procedure

1. Use sandpaper to strip the enamel from about 4 cm of each end of the 22-gauge wire.

2. Leaving the stripped ends free, make this wire into a tight coil of at least 30 turns. A D-cell battery or a film canister will help in forming the coil. Tape the coil so it doesn't unravel.

3. Insert the knitting needle through the coil. Center the coil on the needle. Pull the wire's two ends to one end of the needle.

4. Near the ends of the wire, wrap masking tape around the needle to act as insulation. Then tape one bare wire to each side of the needle at the spot where the masking tape is.

5. Tape a ceramic magnet to each block so that a north pole extends from one and a south pole from the other.

6. Make the motor. Tap the nails into the wood block as shown in the figure. Try to cross the nails at the same height as the magnets so the coil will be suspended between them.

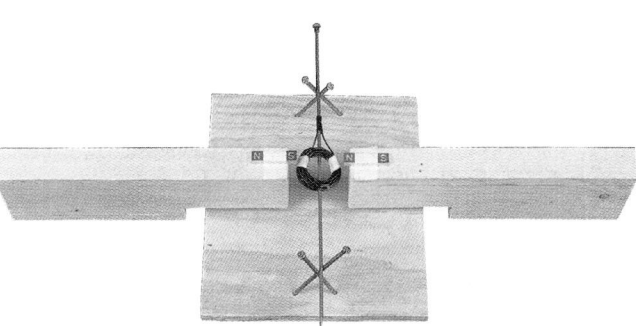

7. Place the needle on the nails. Use bits of wood or folded paper to adjust the positions of the magnets until the coil is directly between the magnets. The magnets should be as close to the coil as possible without touching it.

8. Cut two 30-cm lengths of 18-gauge wire. Use sandpaper to strip the ends of both wires. Attach one wire to each terminal of the battery. Holding only the insulated part of each wire, place one wire against each of the bare wires taped to the needle to close the circuit. Observe what happens.

Conclude and Apply

1. **Describe** what happens when you close the circuit by connecting the wires. Were the results expected?

2. **Describe** what happens when you open the circuit.

3. **Predict** what would happen if you used twice as many coils of wire.

*C*ommunicating
Your Data

Compare your conclusions with other students in your class. **For more help, refer to the** Science Skill Handbook.

Expected Outcome

The wire coil will spin when the current is turned on and stop when the current stops.

Conclude and Apply

1. The coil starts to spin.
2. The coil stops spinning.
3. A larger magnetic field would be induced by the coil, so the coil would spin faster.

Error Analysis

If the motor doesn't turn, have students move the magnet closer to the coil. Also, have students make sure the knitting needle is centered between the magnets.

 **✔ *Assessment***

Performance Have students design machines that could use this motor. They should consider how much force this motor can apply. Possibilities include using the motor as a fan, to spin an artistic design, or to lift a small object. Use **Performance Assessment in the Science Classroom,** p. 117.

Resource Manager

Chapter Resources Booklet
Activity Worksheet, pp. 7–8
Lab Management and Safety, p. 64

*C*ommunicating
Your Data

Have students make diagrams of their motors including explanations of how the parts worked, what worked well, and what didn't work.

Science and Language Arts

"Aagjuuk[1] and Sivulliit[2]"
from Intellectual Culture of the Copper Eskimos
by Knud Rasmussen, told by Tatilgak

Respond to the Reading

Active Reading Strategies

Listen Ask volunteers to read the passage aloud. Point out to students that these words are meant to be passed on to other people by word of mouth.

Question Discuss with students what might happen if the next generation did not learn this chant from the elders.

Connect Have students find the constellations Aquila and Bootes on a star map. Suggest students find out when these constellations are visible in the sky in your area and look for them in the night sky.

Evaluate The translation of this passage into English makes it somewhat awkward. Work with students to identify the passages that are particularly awkward and reword them to make them clearer.

Answers to Questions
1. The verse mentions the names of two constellations.
2. In winter it is dark in the morning in the arctic region where the Inuit live.

Respond to the Reading

1. How can you tell the importance of constellations to the Inuit for telling direction?
2. How is it possible that the Inuit could see the constellations in the morning sky?

The following are "magic words" that are spoken before the Inuit (IH noo wut) people go seal hunting. Inuit are native people that live in the arctic region. Because the Inuit live in relative darkness for much of the winter, they have learned to find their way by looking at the stars to guide them.

The verse below was collected by an ethnographer. An ethnographer studies the practices and beliefs of people in different cultures. The poem is about two constellations that are important to the Inuit people because their appearance marks the end of winter when the Sun begins to appear in the sky again.

By which way, I wonder the mornings—
You dear morning, get up!
See I am up!
By which way, I wonder,
the constellation *Aagjuuk* rises up in the sky?
By this way—perhaps—by the morning
It rises up!

Morning, you dear morning, get up!
See I am up!
By which way, I wonder,
the constellation *Sivulliit*
Has risen to the sky?
By this way—perhaps—by the morning.
It rises up!

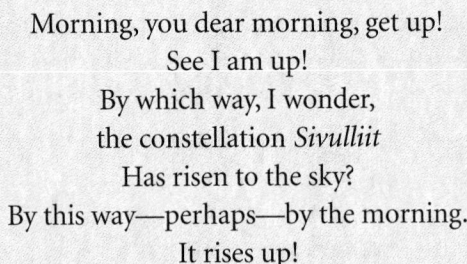

[1] Inuit name for the constellation of stars called Aquila (A kwuh luh)
[2] Inuit name for the constellation of stars called Bootes (boh OH teez)

672   CHAPTER 22 Magnetism

Reading Further

Other sources on this topic include:

A Walk Through the Heavens: A Guide to Stars and Constellations and Their Legends by Milton D. Heifetz and Wil Tirion, Cambridge University Press (March 1998).

The Starlore Handbook : An Essential Guide to the Night Sky by Geoffrey Cornelius, Chronicle Books (April 1997).

Exploring the Night Sky: The Equinox Astronomy Guide for Beginners by Terrence Dickinson and John Bianchi (Illustrator), Firefly Books (March 1988).

Understanding Literature

Ethnography Ethnography is a description of a culture. To write an ethnography, an ethnographer collects cultural stories, poems, or other oral tales from the culture that he or she is studying. Ethnographies of the Inuit are full of stories about the stars and constellations, but other forms of navigation are also important to the Inuit. It is important for the Inuit to be skilled in navigation because they must travel over vast areas of frozen ground that has few landmarks. The Inuit use other clues to navigate such as wind direction, sea currents, snowdrifts, and clouds.

Science Connection In this chapter you learned that Earth has a magnetic field. Earth's magnetic field causes the north pole of a compass needle to point in a northerly direction. Using a compass helps a person to navigate and find their way. However, at the far northern latitudes where the Inuit live, a compass becomes more difficult to use. Some Inuit live north of Earth's northern magnetic pole. In these locations a compass needle points in a southerly direction. As a result, the Inuit developed other ways to navigate.

Linking Science and Writing

Expository Writing Pretend your family is traveling from St. Louis, Missouri, to Madison, Wisconsin, on a summer evening. Use the library or the Internet to research the constellations in the summer sky in North America. Then write a paragraph describing the constellations that will help you and your family navigate north toward Wisconsin.

Career Connection

Astrophysicist

France Anne Cordova is familiar with the properties of gravity and magnetism in her innovative work with telescopes. Cordova was born in Paris, France to a Mexican American diplomat and grew up in California taking care of her 11 brothers and sisters. As a college student she became inspired by the first *Apollo* space mission and went on to earn a Ph.D. in physics from the California Institute of Technology. She was one of only two women in her graduating class. Cordova now serves as the vice chancellor for research at the University of California at Santa Barbara.

SCIENCE*Online* To learn more about careers in astrophysics, visit the Glencoe Science Web site at **science.glencoe.com**.

Understanding Literature

Science Connection

At high northern latitudes, a compass needle still points toward Earth's magnetic north pole. However, because the compass is close to the magnetic pole, the direction the compass needle point changes as the position of the compass changes. As a result, a compass needle at high northern latitudes doesn't point in a single direction. Instead the direction depends on the location. This makes a compass more difficult to use for determining direction. In 1993, the magnetic pole was located in northern Canada, at about 78°27' N, 104°24'W.

Linking Science and Writing

Teaching Strategies

After students conduct their research on the constellations in the summer sky, help them draw a map of the sky that illustrates all the northern hemisphere constellations. Have students work in groups to draw maps on large pieces of paper.

When students are finished, ask them which stars they would use to navigate their return trip from St. Louis to Wisconsin.

Career Connection

Students wishing to pursue a career in astronomy or astrophysics should get an early start by taking advanced math and science in high school. Precalculus as well as chemistry and physics courses are also strongly recommended in high school to prepare for college. Many astronomy students entering college have taken advanced placement calculus and/or physics.

SCIENCE *Online*

Internet Addresses

_____

_____

_____

Explore the Glencoe Science Web site at **science.glencoe.com** to find out more about topics in this feature.

Chapter 22 Study Guide

Reviewing Main Ideas

Preview

Students can answer the questions in their Science Journals. Discuss the answers as you go through the chapter. **LS** **Linguistic**

Review

Students can write their answers, then compare them with those of other students. **LS** **Interpersonal**

Reteach

Students can look at the illustrations and describe details that support the main ideas of the chapter. **LS** **Visual-Spatial**

Answers to Chapter Review

Section 1

2. Magnets stick to materials that can be magnetized. These materials are magnetized when a magnetic field causes the magnetic fields produced by individual atoms in the material to line up and add together.

4. charged particles from the Sun hitting Earth's magnetosphere

Section 2

1. An electric current flowing through a wire coil produces a magnetic field. This magentic field can be made larger by wrapping the coil around an iron core.

4. the input coil

Reviewing Main Ideas

Section 1 What is magnetism?

1. All magnets have two poles—north and south. Like poles repel each other and unlike poles attract.

2. Electrons act like tiny magnets. Groups of atoms can align to form magnetic domains. If domains align, then a magnet is formed. *Why do magnets stick to some objects, such as refrigerators, but not others?*

3. A magnetic force acts through a magnetic field. Magnetic fields extend through space and point from a north pole to a south pole.

4. Earth has a magnetic field that can be detected using a compass. *What might be the cause for these green and red lights above Earth in the photo taken from the space shuttle in orbit?*

Section 2 Electricity and Magnetism

1. Electric current creates a magnetic field. Electromagnets are made from a coil of wire that carries a current, wrapped around an iron core. *How is this crane able to lift the scrap iron particles?*

2. A magnetic field exerts a force on a moving charge or a current-carrying wire.

3. Motors transform electric energy into kinetic energy. Generators transform kinetic energy into electric energy.

4. Transformers are used to increase and decrease voltage in AC circuits. *In this step-down transformer, which has more turns, the input coil or the output coil?*

FOLDABLES
Reading & Study Skills

After You Read

Using the information on your Foldable, compare and contrast the terms *magnetic force* and *magnetic field*. Write your observations under the flaps in your Foldable.

FOLDABLES
Reading & Study Skills

After You Read

After students have read the chapter and completed the Foldable described in Before You Read, have them do the activity on the student page.

Dinah Zike

Visualizing Main Ideas

Complete the following concept map.

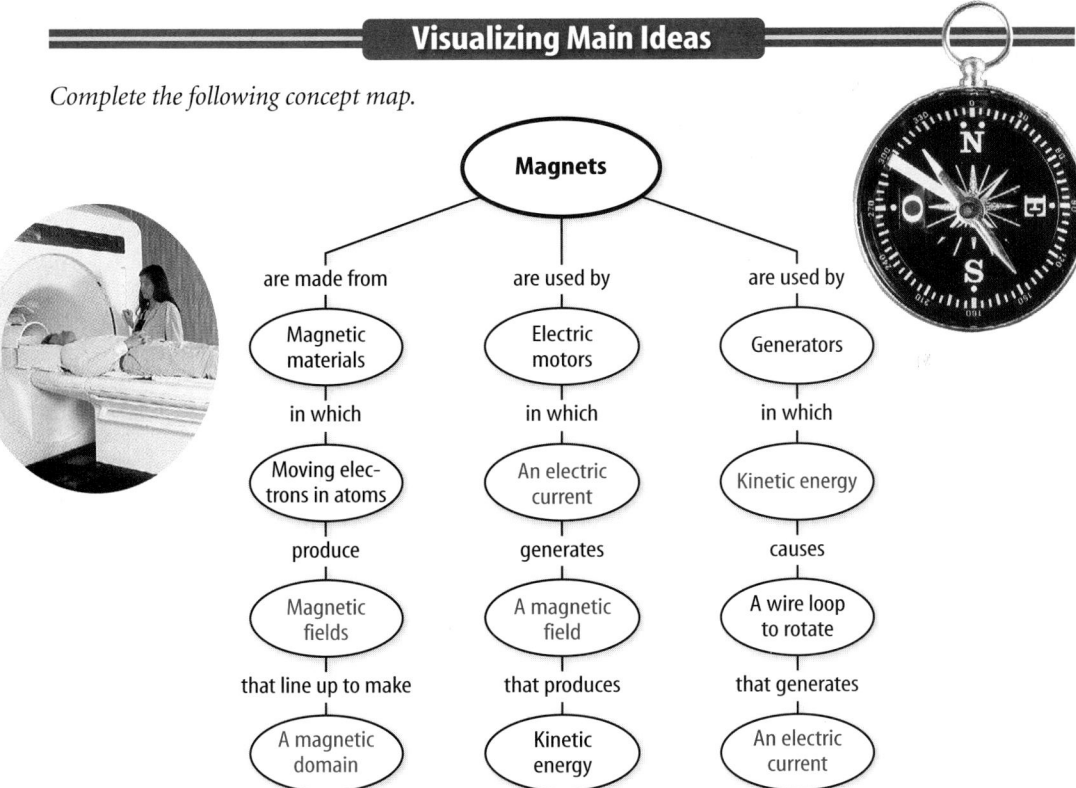

Magnets

are made from → **Magnetic materials** → in which → **Moving electrons in atoms** → produce → **Magnetic fields** → that line up to make → **A magnetic domain**

are used by → **Electric motors** → in which → **An electric current** → generates → **A magnetic field** → that produces → **Kinetic energy**

are used by → **Generators** → in which → **Kinetic energy** → causes → **A wire loop to rotate** → that generates → **An electric current**

Vocabulary Review

Vocabulary Words

a. alternating current
b. aurora
c. electromagnet
d. generator
e. magnetic domain
f. magnetic field
g. magnetosphere
h. motor
i. transformer

THE PRINCETON REVIEW | **Study Tip**

Look for examples in your home of what you are studying in science class. For instance, where can you find electric motors in your home?

Using Vocabulary

Explain the relationship that exists between each set of vocabulary words below.

1. generator, transformer
2. magnetic force, magnetic field
3. alternating current, direct current
4. current, electromagnet
5. motor, generator
6. electron, magnetism
7. magnetosphere, aurora
8. magnet, magnetic domain

Vocabulary Review

Using Vocabulary

1. A generator produces an electric current; a transformer can change the voltage of that current.
2. A magnetic field is the space in which a magnetic force acts.
3. Alternating current changes direction while direct current does not.
4. Electric current induces magnetism in an electromagnet.
5. A motor changes electrical energy to kinetic energy, while a generator reverses the process to change kinetic energy to electrical energy.
6. Moving electrons cause magnetism.
7. Charged particles from the Sun are deflected to the poles by Earth's magnetosphere. There they cause atoms in Earth's atmosphere to emit light that is seen as the aurora.
8. Magnetic domains are the collection of atoms with aligned magnetic poles that are present in magnets.

IDENTIFYING ▷ Misconceptions

Assess

Use the assessment as follow-up to page 652F after students have completed the chapter.

Materials bar magnets on which the N and S labels have been covered with masking tape, compasses

Procedure Use the compasses to determine which end of each magnet is the north pole and which end is the south pole. Write the labels N and S on the tape, exchange magnets with another student, and determine if the other magnet is labeled correctly. Tell the other student what you think and return the magnet. Take off the tape to see which end is actually N and which is S.

Expected Outcome The north end of a compass needle points toward a magnet's south pole.

Checking Concepts

1. A
2. D
3. C
4. B
5. B
6. B
7. A
8. B
9. D
10. A

Thinking Critically

11. The magnetic force acting on the bar magnet is not strong enough to overcome the forces of gravity and static friction that are acting on the magnet.

12. Use another magnet that is already marked to see which end is attracted and which is repelled by a given pole.

13. A south pole; because the nail's field is aligned with the bar magnet's field, the head is a north pole and the point is a south pole.

14. Stronger; each coil adds its magnetic field to the field of the other coils. If the current increases, the magnet gets stronger.

15. Moving electrons; you can show this by holding a compass near a wire carrying direct current. The current will deflect the needle of the compass.

Chapter 22 Assessment

Checking Concepts

Choose the word or phrase that best answers the question.

1. What can iron filings be used to show?
   A) magnetic field
   C) gravitational field
   B) electric field
   D) none of these

2. Why does the needle of a compass point to magnetic north?
   A) Earth's north pole is strongest.
   B) Earth's north pole is closest.
   C) Only the north pole attracts compasses.
   D) The compass needle aligns itself with Earth's magnetic field.

3. What will the north poles of two bar magnets do when brought together?
   A) attract
   B) create an electric current
   C) repel
   D) not interact

4. How many poles do all magnets have?
   A) one
   C) three
   B) two
   D) one or two

5. When a current-carrying wire is wrapped around an iron core, what can it create?
   A) an aurora
   C) a generator
   B) a magnet
   D) a motor

6. What does a transformer between utility wires and your house do?
   A) increases voltage
   B) decreases voltage
   C) leaves voltage the same
   D) changes DC to AC

7. Which energy transformation occurs in an electric motor?
   A) electrical to kinetic
   B) electrical to thermal
   C) potential to kinetic
   D) kinetic to electrical

8. What prevents most charged particles from the Sun from hitting Earth?
   A) the aurora
   B) Earth's magnetic field
   C) high-altitude electric fields
   D) Earth's atmosphere

9. Which of these objects do magnetic fields NOT interact with?
   A) magnets
   C) current
   B) steel
   D) paper

10. Which energy transformation occurs in an electric generator?
    A) electrical to kinetic
    B) electrical to thermal
    C) potential to kinetic
    D) kinetic to electrical

Thinking Critically

11. Why don't ordinary bar magnets line themselves up with Earth's magnetic field when you set them on a table?

12. If you were given a magnet with unmarked poles, how could you determine which pole was which?

13. A nail is magnetized by holding the south pole of a magnet against the head of the nail. Is the point of the nail a north or a south pole? Sketch your explanation.

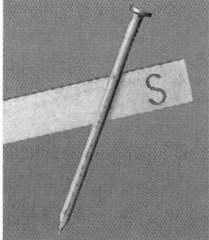

14. If you add more coils to an electromagnet, does the magnet get stronger or weaker? Why? What happens if the current increases?

15. What are the sources of magnetic fields? How can you demonstrate this?

Chapter ✔Assessment Planner

Portfolio Encourage students to place in their portfolios one or two items of what they consider to be their best work. Examples include:
- Assessment, p. 658
- Cultural Diversity, p. 665

Performance Additional performance assessments, Performance Task Assessment Lists, and rubrics for evaluating these activities can be found in Glencoe's **Performance Assessment in the Science Classroom.**

Developing Skills

16. Identifying and Manipulating Variables and Controls How could you test and compare the strength of two different magnets?

17. Forming Operational Definitions Give an operational definition of an electromagnet.

18. Concept Mapping Explain how a doorbell uses an electromagnet by placing the following phrases in the cycle concept map: *circuit open, circuit closed, electromagnet turned on, electromagnet turned off, hammer attracted to magnet and strikes bell,* and *hammer pulled back by a spring.*

```
electromagnet
turned on
          →  hammer
              attracted to magnet
              and strikes bell
circuit closed                    circuit open
hammer pulled
back by a spring
          electromagnet
          turned off
```

Performance Assessment

19. Multimedia Presentation Prepare a multimedia presentation to inform your classmates on the future uses of magnets and magnetism.

TECHNOLOGY

Go to the Glencoe Science Web site at **science.glencoe.com** or use the **Glencoe Science CD-ROM** for additional chapter assessment.

THE PRINCETON REVIEW — Test Practice

Magnetism affects all aspects of modern life. The table below lists some examples of processes involving magnetic fields.

Processes Involving Magnetic Fields

Example	Process	Result
Motor	Converts electrical energy into kinetic	Used in electric fans
Generator	Converts mechanical energy into electrical	Produce light
Charged particles from Sun	Trapped in Earth's magnetosphere	Aurora
Transformer	Change voltage through power lines	Deliver current to homes

Study the table and answer the following questions.

1. According to this information, which process most likely occurs naturally?
  A) conversion of electrical energy into kinetic
  B) conversion of mechanical energy into electric energy
  C) trapped charged particles in Earth's magnetosphere
  D) voltage changes through power lines

2. Hydroelectric power plants use the gravitational potential energy of water to turn generators, which then produce electricity. According to the table above, which process is this an example of?
  F) motor   **H)** charged particles
  G) generator   **J)** transformer

THE PRINCETON REVIEW — Test Practice

The Test-Taking Tip was written by The Princeton Review, the nation's leader in test preparation.
1. C
2. G

Developing Skills

16. Record how many uniform objects, such as paper clips, each could move or pick up.
17. An electromagnet is a device in which a magnetic field is generated by passing current through a wire coil.
18. See student page.

Performance Assessment

19. Ask students to note the sources of their information. Use **PASC**, p. 149.

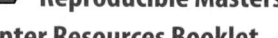

Assessment Resources

📁 Reproducible Masters

Chapter Resources Booklet
  Chapter Review, pp. 31–32
  Chapter Tests, pp. 33–36
  Assessment Transparency Activity, p. 43

Glencoe Science Web site
  Interactive Tutor
  Chapter Quizzes

Glencoe Technology

  Assessment Transparency
  Interactive CD-ROM Chapter Quizzes
  ExamView Pro Test Bank
  Vocabulary PuzzleMaker Software
  MindJogger Videoquiz

QUESTION 1: B

Students need to reread the passage in order to identify the best summary.

- **Choice A** No; this is not supported by information in the passage.
- **Choice B** Yes; this is a summary of the information in the passage.
- **Choice C** No; this is not supported by information in the passage.
- **Choice D** No; this is a detail from the passage.

QUESTION 2: F

Students must determine the meaning of the underlined word *conventional* using context clues.

THE PRINCETON REVIEW

All questions written and validated by The Princeton Review.

Read the passage. Then read each question that follows the passage. Decide which is the best answer to each question.

Magnetic Levitation Train

One of the first things people learn about magnets is that like magnetic poles repel each other. This is the basic principle behind the Magnetic Levitation Train, or Maglev.

Maglev is a high-speed train. It uses high-strength magnets to lift and propel the train to incredible speeds as it hovers only a few centimeters above the track. This helps the train to reach higher speeds than conventional trains. A full-size Maglev in Japan achieved a speed of over 500 km/h! Its electromagnetic motor can be precisely controlled to provide smooth acceleration and braking between stops. The magnetic field prevents the train from drifting away from the center of the guideway.

Because there is no friction between wheels and rails, Maglevs eliminate the principal limitation of <u>conventional</u> trains, which is the high cost of maintaining the tracks to avoid excessive vibration and wear that can cause dangerous derailments. Critics point out that Maglevs require enormous amounts of energy. However, studies have shown that Maglevs use 30 percent less energy than other high-speed trains traveling at the same speed. Others worry about the dangers from magnetic fields; however, measurements show that humans are exposed to magnetic fields no stronger than those from toasters or hair dryers.

This year in Japan a series of Maglevs will be tested on a 43-km demonstration line. Perhaps someday Maglevs will carry commuters to and from work and school in the United States.

Test-Taking Tip After you read the passage, write a one-sentence summary of the main idea for each paragraph.

This is a Maglev test train in Japan.

1. Which of the following statements best summarizes this passage?
   A) Maglev transportation is currently in use in Germany and Japan.
   B) Maglev might be a high-speed transport system of the future.
   C) Maglevs use more energy than conventional high-speed trains.
   D) Maglevs expose passengers to strong magnetic fields.

2. In this passage, the word <u>conventional</u> means _____.
   F) customary
   G) innovative
   H) political
   J) unusual

Reasoning and Skills

Read each question and choose the best answer.

1. Voltage increases when the output coil in a transformer has more turns of wire than the input coil. Which of the following increases voltage the most?

A)

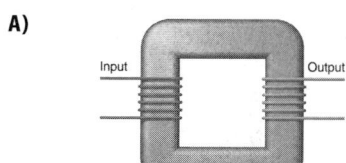
Input   Output

B)

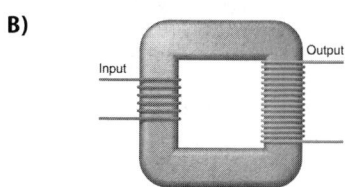
Output   Input

C)

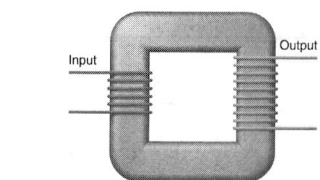
Input   Output

D)

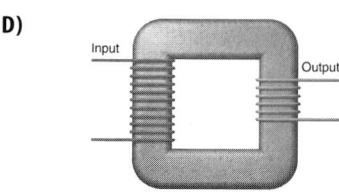
Input   Output

Test-Taking Tip   Use the information provided in the question to closely consider each answer choice.

2. Which of the following materials would make a good conductor?
F) plastic
G) wood
H) glass
J) copper

Test-Taking Tip   Remember that electrons move easily through conductors.

3. Shahid wanted to pick up pieces of metal with a magnet. Which of the following statements describes a situation in which the magnet would NOT pick up the pieces of metal?
A) The metal pieces were too close to the magnet.
B) The magnet was brand new.
C) The metal pieces were made out of aluminum foil.
D) The metal pieces and the magnet have the same magnetic poles.

Test-Taking Tip   Review what you have learned about magnetic materials.

Consider this question carefully before writing your answer on a separate sheet of paper.

4. Recall what you know about the production of electric current. Explain the similarities and differences between direct current (DC) and alternating current (AC).

Test-Taking Tip   Use the clues *direct* and *alternating* to guide your answer.

Standardized Test Practice

Reasoning and Skills

QUESTION 1: B

Students must understand voltage and transformers and look carefully at the diagram to determine the correct answer choice. Choice B has the greatest ratio of output turns of wire to input turns of wire.

QUESTION 2: J

Students must understand that metals are better conductors than nonmetals.

QUESTION 3: C

Students must know that magnets can only pick up objects that are made of iron, cobalt, or nickel.

QUESTION 4: Answers will vary.

Answers should include that electrons are moving in both an alternating current and a direct current, and both types of current carry electrical energy. Direct current flows in only one direction and alternating current changes direction many times each second.

Student Resources

Student Resources

About the Field Guide

- This field guide contains representative descriptions and photos of ten insect orders that enable the user to classify some insects.
- In using a field guide, students will apply steps of a scientific method as they observe, investigate, and draw conclusions.
- This field guide applies nationally; local and regional field guides are usually available for more specific local use.
- Encourage students to use this field guide outside the classroom.

Tie to Prior Knowledge

List responses on the board as students name insects they have seen or with which they are familiar. **Are some of these insects related? Explain.** Students may mention that some are anatomically similar. Other students may recognize that some similar insects have common ancestors.

 **Field Activity**

Have students work in small groups to classify the insects on the list into orders. Then have students work as a class to draw or find pictures of each insect and group them into their respective orders on a bulletin-board display.
Logical-Mathematical and Visual-Spatial

It's brown and creepy, and it has wings and six legs. If you call it a bug, you might be correct, but if you call it an insect, you are definitely correct. Insects belong to a large group of animals called arthropods. They are related to shrimp, spiders, lobsters, and centipedes. More insect species exist than all other animal species on Earth. Insects are found from the tropics to the tundra. Some live in water all or part of their lives, and some insects even live inside other animals. Insects play important roles in the environment. Many are helpful, but others are destructive.

How Insects Are Classified

An insect's body is divided into three parts—head, thorax, and abdomen. The head has a pair of antennae and eyes and paired mouthparts. Three pairs of jointed legs and, sometimes, wings are attached to the thorax. The abdomen has neither wings nor legs. Insects have a hard covering over their entire body. They shed this covering, then replace it as they grow. Insects are classified into smaller groups called orders. By observing an insect and recognizing certain features, you can identify the order it belongs to. This field guide presents ten insect orders.

Insects

Insect Orders

Convergent ladybug beetle

Coleoptera

Beetles

This is the largest order of insects. Many sizes, shapes, and colors of beetles can be found. All beetles have a pair of thick, leathery wings that meet in a straight line and cover another pair of wings, the thorax, and all or most of the abdomen. Some beetles are considered to be serious pests. Other beetles feed on insects or eat dead and decaying organisms. Not all beetles are called beetles. For example, fireflies, June bugs, and weevils are types of beetles.

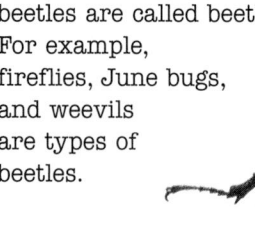

Male stag beetle

 **Field Activity**

For a week, use this field guide to help identify insect orders. Look for insects in different places and at different times. Visit the Glencoe Science Web site at **science.glencoe.com** to view other insects that might not be found in your city. In your Science Journal, record the order of insect found, along with the date, time, and place.

Resources for Teachers and Students

The Audubon Society Field Guide to North American Insects and Spiders, by Lorus Johnson Milne and Margery Milne, Alfred A. Knopf, 1980.

Insects: The Little Things That Run the World, Smithsonian Institution, Unipix Consumer Products, 1995. (Video)

Bugs: Insects, Spiders, Centipedes, Millipedes and Other Closely Related Arthropods, by Frank W. Lowenstein and Sheryl Lechner, Black Dog and Levanthal, 1999.

Dermaptera

Earwigs

The feature that quickly identifies this brown, beetlelike insect is the pair of pincerlike structures that extend from the end of the abdomen. Earwigs usually are active at night and hide under litter or in any dark, protected place during the day. They can damage plants.

Earwig

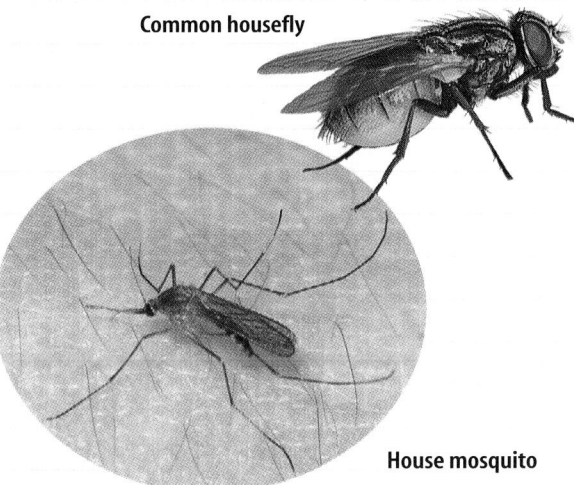

Common housefly

House mosquito

Diptera

Flies and Mosquitoes

These are small insects with large eyes. They have two pair of wings but only one pair can be seen when the insect is at rest and the wings are folded. Their mouths are adapted for piercing and sucking, or scraping and lapping. Many of these insects are food for larger animals. Some spread diseases, others are pests, and some eat dead and decaying organisms. They are found in many different environments.

Odonata

Dragonflies and Damselflies

These insects have two pairs of transparent, multi-veined wings that are nearly equal in size and cannot be folded against the insect's body. The head has a pair of large eyes on it, and the abdomen is long and thin. These insects are usually seen near bodies of water. Most members of this group hunt during flight and catch small insects, such as mosquitoes.

Dragonfly

Visual Learning

Explain to students that the photographs included with the description of each order illustrate the major characteristics of the order. Insects they observe may have characteristics slightly different from those shown in the photos.
IS Visual-Spatial

Teacher FYI

Nearly 100,000 of the estimated 1.5 million species of insects live in North America. Many insects provide valuable commercial products; others serve as the primary pollinators of flowers. Some insects harm plants or animals or damage their products.

Extension

Some students may wish to make an insect collection. Instruct them to use reference materials to find information about proper preservation and display. Have these students share their collections with the class. **IS Kinesthetic**

Activity

Have students work in small groups to write a poem describing the insects in a particular order. Encourage groups to share their poems with the class. **IS Interpersonal and Auditory-Musical**

Curriculum Connection

Math Have each student make a bar graph of the number of insects they find for each of the ten orders. Remind students to label both axes and provide a descriptive title for their graphs.
IS Logical-Mathematical

Quick Demo

Bring in several examples of ants and termites along with a hand lens, or enlarged pictures of ants and termites. Show students the small differences between the structure of the thorax and abdomen of an ant and the thorax and abdomen of a termite.

LS Visual-Spatial

Fun Fact

When taken all together, the termites on Earth are estimated to weigh more than the humans on Earth.

Make A Model

Divide the class into small groups. Direct each group to create a fictitious insect belonging to one of the ten orders. Depending on available resources, the fictitious insects may be drawings, construction paper, three-dimensional models, or computer designed. Each model should show the characteristics of the order it represents. These characteristics should be clearly labeled.

COOP LEARN **LS Kinesthetic**

Field GUIDE

Isoptera

Termites

Adult termites are small, dark brown or black, and can have wings. Immature forms of this insect are small, soft bodied, pale yellow or white, and wingless. The adults are sometimes confused with ants. The thorax and abdomen of a termite look like one body part, but a thin waist separates the thorax and abdomen of an ant. Termites live in colonies in the ground or in wood.

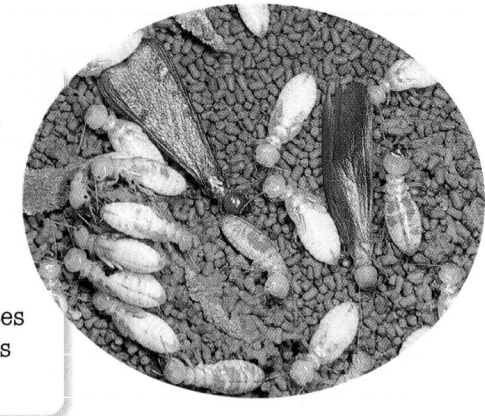

Pacific coast termites

Dictyoptera

Cockroaches and Mantises

These insects have long, thin antennae on the head. In species with wings, the back wings are thin and fanlike when they are opened and are larger than the front wings. In the mantis, the front legs are adapted for grasping. The other two pairs of legs are similar to those of a cockroach. Praying mantises are beneficial because they eat other, often harmful, insects. Most cockroaches are pests.

American cockroach

Carolina praying mantis

Paper wasp

Hymenoptera

Ants, Bees, and Wasps

Members of this order can be so small that they're visible only with a magnifier. Others may be nearly 35 mm long. These insects have two pairs of transparent wings, if present. They are found in many different environments, in colonies or alone. They are important because they pollinate flowers, and some prey on harmful insects. Honeybees make honey and wax.

American bumblebee

Black carpenter ant

684   STUDENT RESOURCES

SCIENCE Online
Internet Addresses

_____

_____

_____

Explore the Glencoe Science Web site at **science.glencoe.com** to find out more about topics in this field guide.

Lepidoptera

Butterflies and Moths

Butterflies and moths have two pairs of wings with colorful patterns created by thousands of tiny scales. The antennae of most moths are feathery. A butterfly's antennae are thin, and each has a small knob on the tip. Adult's mouthparts are adapted as a long, coiled tube for drinking nectar. Most moths are active at night, but some tropical moths are active during the day.

Yellow woolly bear moth

Buckeye butterfly

Periodic cicada

Water boatman

Hemiptera

Bugs

The prefix of this order, "Hemi-", means "half" and describes the front pair of wings. Near the insect's head, the front wings are thick and leathery, and are thin at the tip. Wing tips usually overlap when they are folded over the insect's back and cover a smaller pair of thin wings. Some bugs live on land and others are aquatic.

Orthoptera

Grasshoppers, Crickets, and Katydids

These insects have large hind legs adapted for leaping. They usually have two pairs of wings. The outer pair is hard and covers a transparent pair. Many of these insects make singing noises by rubbing one body part against another. Males generally make these sounds. Many of these insects are considered pests because swarms of them can destroy a farmer's crops in a few days.

Field cricket

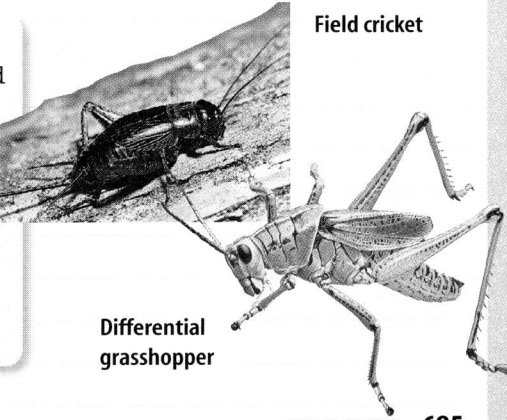

Differential grasshopper

FIELD GUIDE   685

Discussion

Why are some insects active only during daylight hours, and others are active only at night? Possible answer: By being active at different times, there is less competition for resources. This is also a way for some insects to avoid predators.

Extension

Have interested students interview an entomologist from a university, a specialist from a pest control business, a speaker from a natural history museum, or a consultant for an agricultural extension service. Students can write down the questions and answers in an interview format and share the interview with the class. **IS Interpersonal**

Teacher **FYI**

The classification of insects is an evolving process. As scientists learn more about the DNA of insects, new orders are suggested and insects are moved from one order to another. Not all scientists agree on a single classification system.

Curriculum Connection

Language Arts The names of orders that include winged insects all end with -ptera except for the order Odonata. Wingless insect orders have different endings. Have students find the roots for one of the ten orders in the field guide and report their findings to the class. **IS Linguistic**

Inclusion Strategies

Visually Impaired Many insects make distinctive sounds. Suggest that students research these sounds and make an audio presentation to the class. **IS Auditory-Musical**

Field Guides

About the Field Guide

- This field guide contains a key that enables the user to classify or identify some biomes.
- This field guide applies globally; local and regional resources are available for more specific local use. Several sources of information are listed below.
- In using a field guide, students will apply steps of a scientific method as they observe, investigate, and draw conclusions.
- Encourage students to use this field guide outside the classroom.

Tie to Prior Knowledge

Students will probably be familiar with your local biome. However, they may not be aware of the diversity of organisms present. Have students list as many plants and animals as they can think of that they have seen in your local biome.

Field Activity

Student answers should be based on information obtained from a local weather station or newspaper. Student graphs will not be identical to the graphs in the field guide but should resemble one closely enough to draw conclusions. The types of organisms found will vary depending on the biome in which you live.

Why don't you find polar bears in Florida or palm trees in Alaska? Organisms are limited to certain areas where they can live and survive due to factors such as temperature, amount of rainfall, and type of soil that is found in a region. A biome's boundaries are determined by climate more than anything else. Climate is a way of categorizing temperature extremes and yearly precipitation patterns. Use this field guide to identify some of the world's biomes and to determine which biome you live in.

Key
☐ Temperature range (°C)
▨ Precipitation (cm)

Interpreting Land Biome Climates

The following graphs represent typical climates in seven different biomes. To read each biome graph, use the following information in the key above. Note how each graph displays temperature range, precipitation levels, and the variation between months.

Biomes

Tundra

Winters in the tundra are long and harsh, and summers are short. There is little precipitation. In the tundra, you can find mosses, lichens, grasses, and sedges. The tundra supports weasels, arctic foxes, artic hares, snowy owls, and hawks.

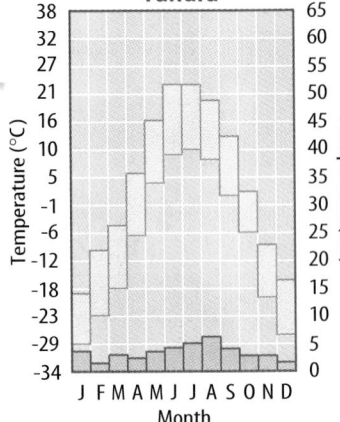

Tundra

Field Activity

Research to find last year's monthly averages for rainfall, high temperature, and low temperature for your area or a nearby city. For further help on last year's averages, visit the Glencoe Science Web site at **science. glencoe.com.** Prepare a graph of data using the example above. Based on your findings, which biome graph most closely matches your data? What biome do you live in? What type of plant and animal life do you expect to find in your biome?

Resources for Teachers and Students

Biomes of the World, Volumes 1–9, by Michael Allaby, Grolier Educational, 1999.

The Natural History of North America, by Edward Ricciuti, Random House, Cresent, 1995.

SCIENCE Online
Internet Addresses

_____

_____

_____

Explore the Glencoe Science Web site at **science.glencoe.com** to find out more about topics in this field guide.

Taiga

Winters in the taiga are cold and severe with much snow. Growing seasons are short. Conifers such as spruces, firs, and larches are common. In the taiga, you find caribou, wolves, moose, bear, ducks, loons, owls, and other birds.

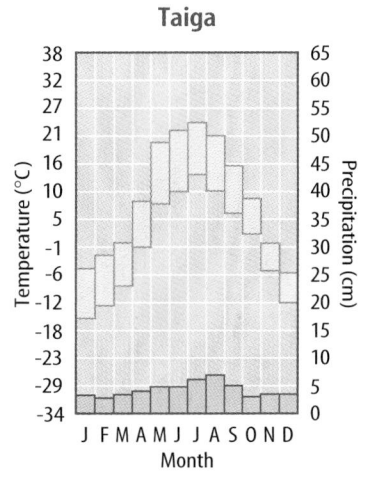

Taiga

Temperate Deciduous Forest

The temperate deciduous forest has cold winters, hot summers, and moderate precipitation. In a temperate deciduous forest, you can see trees such as oak, hickory, and beech, which lose their leaves every autumn. Wolves, deer, bears, small mammals, and many species of birds are common in a temperate deciduous forest.

Temperate Deciduous Forest

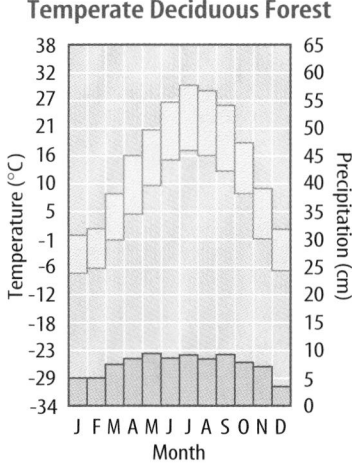

FIELD GUIDE 687

Discussion

Lead students in a discussion about plants and animals of the biome in which you live. **Why might you not be able to observe the expected types of plants and animals in your biome?** Many plants and animals live only in certain areas of a given biome. For example, pink ladies slipper orchids are found in temperate forests, but only in certain soils. Therefore, you could live in a temperate region and never see a pink ladies slipper.

Teacher FYI

The taiga is forest that lies south of the tundra. Most trees that grow in the taiga are conifers. Usually these areas are too cold and have soil that is too poor to support the growth of tall trees. The taiga is home to many species of birds, including several species of woodpeckers and owls. Mammals that live in the taiga biome include elk, lynx and snowshoe hares.

Using Science Words

Word Meaning Have students investigate the meaning of the word *deciduous*, which is derived from Latin. The word *deciduous* means "to fall off" and describes the seasonal shedding of leaves by trees. Trees that shed their leaves each year are called deciduous trees.

Curriculum Connection

Geography The Grand Canyon has starkly different climate zones that are arranged vertically instead of horizontally. The floor of the canyon has a hot, dry climate and vegetation similar to that of the Sonoran Desert. The rim of the canyon has piñon pines, which are typical of mid-altitude mountain slopes. Explain to students that the rim of the canyon is far above its floor, accounting for its major climatic differences. Have students locate the Grand Canyon on a map of the United States and determine in which biome it is located. **LS Visual-Spatial**

Quick Demo

Obtain a map of the United States. Use the information in the field guide to show students how the United States is divided into biomes. **IS Visual-Spatial**

Extension

Explain to students that biomes are not static, permanent divisions. The biome of a particular area can change over time. Have students research an area that has been classified into different biomes in different time periods throughout history. Have them report their findings to the class. **IS Logical-Mathematical**

Discussion

What are some adaptations that grasslands organisms might have? Explain. Possible answers: These organisms must be adapted to living without much water in the summer and winter. The organisms must also be able to withstand hot summers and cold winters, or be able to migrate.

Field GUIDE

Temperate Rain Forest

Temperate Rain Forest

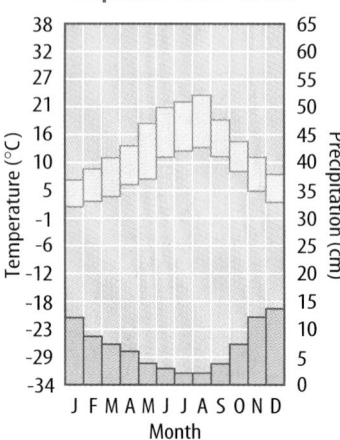

Temperature (°C) / Precipitation (cm)
Month: J F M A M J J A S O N D

The summers and the winters in the temperate rain forest are mild. Temperatures rarely fall below freezing. The temperate rain forest has heavy precipitation and high humidity. Trees with needlelike leaves, mosses, and ferns are common. Many organisms including salamanders, frogs, black bears, cougars, pileated woodpeckers, and owls live in the temperate rain forest.

Grassland

There is little precipitation during the grassland's cold winters and hot summers. The plants in the grassland are predominantly grasses although there are also a few trees. The grassland supports grazing animals, wolves, prairies dogs, foxes, ferrets, snakes, lizards, and insects.

Grassland

Temperature (°C) / Precipitation (cm)
Month: J F M A M J J A S O N D

Science Journal

Transitional Biome The grasslands are a transitional biome. This means that if amounts of average precipitation change, the area will become a different biome. Have students write a paragraph in their Science Journals that describes what they think would happen if a grassland biome received either more or less precipitation. **IS Linguistic**

Desert

Deserts are warm to hot in the daytime and cool in the evening. They receive sparse precipitation throughout the year. Cacti, yuccas, Joshua trees, and bunchgrasses grow in the desert. Small rodents, jackrabbits, birds of prey, and snakes are common in the desert.

Desert

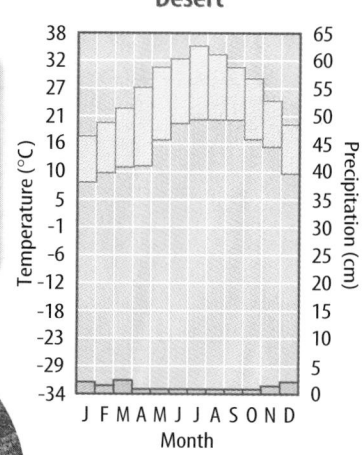

Content Background

Deserts are known for venomous species of spiders and scorpions. However, only a few of the many species of spiders and scorpions are venomous enough to endanger humans. For example, the tarantula and giant hairy scorpion look fierce, but they are not deadly to humans.

Fun Fact

Many students think deserts are large expanses of sand that have little or no life. In fact, most deserts contain a large variety of plants and animals that are specially adapted to living in desert environments.

Visual Learning

Tropical Rain Forest As students study the illustration, have them note the canopy, or heavy layer of growth at the top level of the forest. In many parts of the rain forest, this canopy allows little light to penetrate to the forest floor. Many plants have adaptations that allow them to grow close to the top of the canopy in order to receive light. **What can you infer light levels are like in the understory, which is below the canopy?** Light levels are low here, and plants grow in the shade.

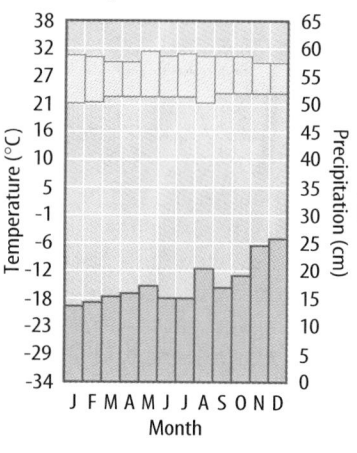

Tropical Rain Forest

The tropical rain forest is hot all year with precipitation almost every day. A great diversity of plant species grow in the tropical rain forest. It provides homes for birds, reptiles, insects, monkeys, and sloths.

FIELD GUIDE 689

Inclusion Strategies

Learning Disabled Have students make "biome boxes" using shoe boxes. Direct them to label their boxes with a particular biome name. They should then cut out or draw pictures that represent the plant and animal life found in that biome and arrange them in the biome box.

Field GUIDE

About the Field Guide

- This field guide contains information that enables the user to identify how the laws of motion apply to amusement park rides and to classify the rides according to their movements.

- In using a field guide, students will apply steps of a scientific method as they observe, investigate, and draw conclusions.

- This field guide provides general information about several types of amusement park rides. Information about specific rides often can be obtained locally.

- Encourage students to use this field guide to analyze rides they see at an amusement park or playground.

Tie to Prior Knowledge

Have students name their favorite amusement park rides. Record their responses. **How did you feel when you were on the rides?** Students may describe feeling "weightless" or feeling a strong tendency to move in various directions.

Field Activity

After students have completed this activity, have several volunteers show their drawings to the class and explain the movement of the ride. Allow class time for an open discussion of the forces involved.

Field GUIDE

I f you like smooth, gentle rides, don't expect to get one at an amusement park. Amusement park rides are designed to provide thrills—plummeting down hills at 160 km/h, whizzing around curves so fast you think you'll fall out of your seat, zooming upside down, plunging over waterfalls, dropping so fast and far that you feel weightless. It's all part of the fun.

May the Force Be with You

What you might not realize as you're screaming with delight is that amusement park rides are lessons in physics. You can apply Newton's laws of motion to everything from the water slide and the bumper cars to the roller coasters. Amusement park ride designers know how to use the laws of motion to jolt, bump, and jostle you enough to make you scream, while still keeping you safe from harm. They don't just plan how the laws of motion cause these rides to move, they also plan how you will move when you are on the rides. These designers also use Newton's law of motion when they design and build the rides to make the structures safe and lasting. Look at the forces at work on some popular amusement park rides.

Amusement Park Rides

Free-fall ride

Free Fall

Slowly you rise up, up, up. Gravity is pulling you downward, but your seat exerts an upward force on you. Then, in an instant, you're plummeting toward the ground at speeds of more than 100 km/h. When you fall, your seat falls at the same rate and no longer exerts a force on you. Because you don't feel your seat pushing upward, you have the feeling of being weightless—at least for a few seconds.

Field Activity

The next time you're at an amusement park, watch the rides. When you return home, make drawings of the rides using arrows to show how they move. Group the rides according to their movements. Compare your drawings and observations to the information in this field guide.

Resources for Teachers and Students

Amusement Park Physics, by Nathan A. Unterman, J. Weston Walch Publishers, 1999.

Roller Coaster: Wooden and Steel Coasters, Twisters and Corkscrews, by David Bennett, Book Sales, Inc., 1998.

Roller Coaster Science, by Jim Wiese, John Wiley & Sons, 1994.

"Amusement Park Physics," by Carole Escobar, *The Physics Teacher*, Volume 28, No. 7, pp. 446–453, October 1990.

"The Amateur Scientist," by Jearl Walker, *Scientific American*, Volume 249, No. 4, pp. 162–169, October 1983.

Roller Coaster: Design

The biggest coasters—some as tall as a 40-story building—are made of steel. Steel roller coasters are stronger and sway less than wooden roller coasters. This allows for more looping, more hills, and faster speeds.

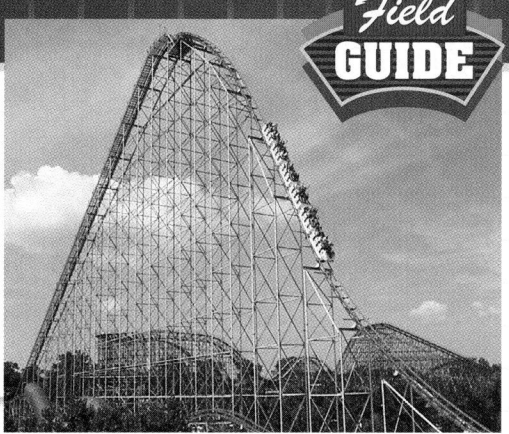

Roller coaster

Roller Coaster: The Coaster's Motion

Roller coasters are gravity-powered trains. Some coasters have motor-driven chains that move the cars to the top of the first hill. Then, gravity keeps it going.

The first hill is the highest point on the track. As the coaster rolls down the first hill, it converts potential energy to kinetic energy that sends it up the next hill. With each hill it climbs, it loses a little energy due to friction. That is why each hill is generally lower than the one before it.

Roller Coaster: Your Ride

Inertia is at work when you sweep around curves on a roller coaster. Inertia is the tendency for a body that's moving in a certain direction to keep moving in the same direction. For example, when the coaster swings right, inertia tries to keep you going in a straight line at a constant speed. As a result, you are pushed to the left side of your car.

Inertia tends to keep bodies moving in a straight line.

FIELD GUIDE 691

Discussion

How is your weight affected during freefall? Your weight is unchanged because the force of gravity is unchanged. You feel "weightless" because your downward acceleration is about the same as the acceleration resulting from gravity.

Activity

On the board, draw a sketch of a typical roller coaster track. Ask students to describe the forces and movement of a car at the top of a hill, along a straight part of the track, and at various places on a loop. At the top of a hill, the car moves slowly, and gravity accelerates it rapidly down the hill. On straight parts of the track, the car moves at its highest rate of speed. As it climbs a loop, gravity slows the car down, but it bends tightly around the top of the loop. Although the car slows down near the top, the passengers feel a strong deceleration. The car speeds up again coming down the other side of the loop.
L2 **LS Visual-Spatial**

Fun Fact

The first true roller coaster constructed in the United States was the *Gravity Pleasure Switchback Railway*. It was built in 1884 at Coney Island in Brooklyn, New York.

Teacher FYI

Most vertical loops in roller coasters are elliptical rather than circular. This shape, called a clothoid loop, has a greater height than width. This shape causes the cars to travel faster at the top of the loop so that they don't fall away from the track. It also prevents the cars from traveling out of the loop too fast.

Curriculum Connection

Geography Have students work with a partner to research a popular roller coaster in the United States. Pairs should collaborate on making a poster that shows the location of the roller coaster on an outline map of the United States. Posters should also include a drawing of the coaster and statistics such as how high it is and its maximum speed. L2 **LS Interpersonal**

Bumper Cars: Your Ride

Explain to students that the electricity used to power bumper cars flows from a wire grid above the cars down the metal poles attached to the back of each car. **Why do you think this method of powering the cars is used?**

Possible answers: It allows the cars freedom of movement around the floor; using electricity avoids the use of batteries that would constantly have to be recharged; having the electricity flow from the ceiling is safer for people who must walk across the enclosed floor.

Activity

Explain to students that a bumper car's momentum is the product of its mass (including the mass of the passenger) and its velocity. Allow students to use momentum carts to demonstrate that the speed and direction of cars after a collision is determined by conservation of momentum. Suggest that they vary the mass in the carts as well as the speed at which the carts approach one another. L2
Kinesthetic

Use Science Words

Word Usage Ask students to write definitions for the word *inertia*, first as it is used in science and then as it is used in everyday life. For each definition, have students write a sentence using the word. In science, inertia refers to the tendency of an object to remain at rest or to remain in motion at a constant speed unless acted upon by a force. In everyday life, inertia refers to the tendency to avoid changes in condition.

Field Guide

Bumper Cars: The Car's Motion

You control your bumper car's acceleration with the accelerator pedal. When the car you're in bumps head-on into another car, your car comes to an abrupt stop. The big rubber bumper around the bottom of the car diffuses the force of the collision by prolonging the impact.

Bumper Cars: Your Ride

When you first accelerate in a bumper car, you feel as though you are being pushed back in your seat. This sensation and the jolt you feel when you hit another car are due to inertia. On impact, your car stops, but your inertia makes you continue to move forward. It's the same jolt you feel in a car when someone slams on the brakes.

In a bumper-car collision, inertia keeps each rider moving forward.

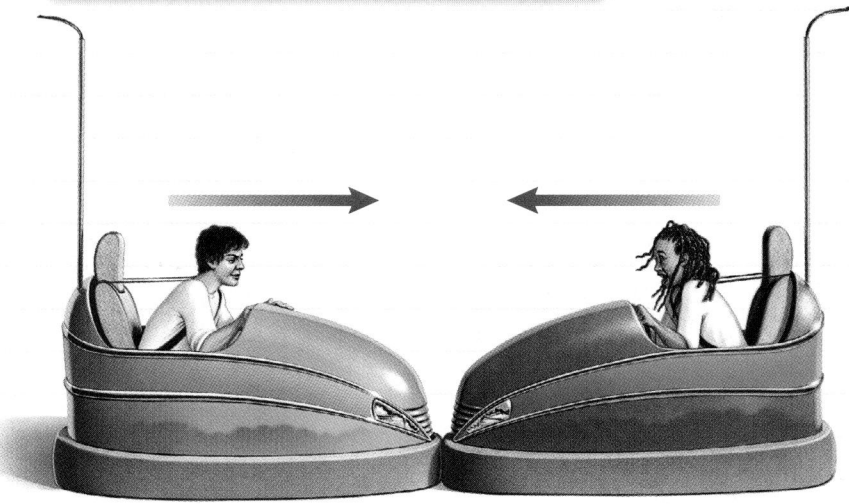

Science Journal

Experiences at Amusement Parks Have students write short stories about a time when they visited an amusement park. If they have never visited an amusement park, their stories can be fictional. Encourage students to describe the different rides they went on and the motion they experienced during the ride. **Linguistic**

SCIENCE Online
Internet Addresses

Explore the Glencoe Science Web site at **science.glencoe.com** to find out more about topics in this field guide.

Quick Demo

Demonstrate how the swing ride works by attaching a string to a one-hole rubber stopper and swinging it in a circle beside you. Show students that the stopper swings higher and with a larger radius if you increase its speed. When the speed is decreased, the stopper again swings lower and with a smaller radius. Help students understand that the vertical component of the string's tension balances the gravitational force. **IS Visual-Spatial**

Extension

Ask students to make a drawing that explains why swings can never go higher than a horizontal plane. Drawings should include arrows that show the gravitational force and the tension in the chain. Above the horizontal plane, the net force would be downward and the swing would become unstable.

Make a Model

Have students work in small groups to make a small model of a new amusement park ride. Each group should give a presentation demonstrating how the ride works. All members of the group should be prepared to answer questions from the class about the forces involved in the ride's movement. L2 COOP LEARN
IS Interpersonal

Swing Ride: Design

Some of the more powerful swing rides make about eight revolutions around the central pole each minute. These swing rides are capable of moving their riders at speeds of close to 50 km/h.

Swing Ride: Forces

As the swings rotate, your inertia wants to fling you outward, but the chain that connects your seat to the ride's central pole prevents you from being flung into the air. You can see the changes in force as the swing ride changes speeds. As the ride speeds up and the forces exerted on the chain increase, your swing rises, moves outward, and travels almost parallel to the ground. As the ride slows, these forces on the chains decrease, returning the swings slowly to their original position.

The arrows show the forces at work in a swing ride.

Teacher FYI

Some amusement park rides, including roller coasters and swing rides, have a circular motion that makes you feel as if you are being forced outward from the circle. You have this feeling not as the result of an outward force, but because your tendency to move in a line tangential to the circle is opposed by the centripetal acceleration pointing inward.

Inclusion Strategies

Learning Disabled When students are making the amusement park ride models, have them draw clear designs on paper before they begin construction. Encourage them to draw arrows showing the direction of the normal force and the gravitational force. Some students may need help understanding the forces involved in the movement. L1 IS **Visual-Spatial**

Field Guides

About the Field Guide
- This field guide contains representative descriptions and photos of different types of lightning. These illustrations enable the user to identify different types of lightning.
- In using a field guide, students will apply steps of a scientific method as they observe, investigate, and draw conclusions.
- Encourage students to use this field guide outside the classroom.

Tie to Prior Knowledge
Have students discuss any past observations they have made of lightning. **Under what circumstances did the lightning occur? Was it accompanied by thunder? At what times of day and during which seasons did the lightning occur? Did any damage occur as a result of the lightning?**

 **Field Activity**

Have students use a stopwatch to determine the length of time between the lightning bolt and the sound of thunder. Explain that the sound of thunder travels 1.6 km every 5 seconds. Then have students compute the distance of the source of the lightning from their location.

When storm clouds form, the particles in clouds collide with one another, removing electrons from some and adding them to others. Positive charges accumulate at the top of the cloud, leaving the negative ones at the bottom. These negative charges repel electrons in the ground below. As a result, the ground beneath the cloud becomes positively charged. The negative charges in the cloud are attracted toward the positively charged ground. They move downward in a zigzag path called a stepped leader. As the leader approaches the ground, a streamer of positive charges rises to meet it. When they meet, a return stroke—an electric spark called lightning—blasts up to the cloud.

The cycle of leader and return strokes can repeat many times in less than a second to comprise a single flash of lightning that you see.

Common Types of Lightning
The most common type of lightning strikes from one part of a cloud to another part of the same cloud. This type of lightning can occur ten times more often than lightning from a cloud to the ground. Other forms include strikes from one cloud to a different cloud, and from a cloud to the surrounding air.

694 STUDENT RESOURCES

Lightning

Cloud-to-Ground Lightning

This type of lightning is characterized by a single streak of light connecting the cloud and the ground or a streak with one or more forks in it. Occasionally, a tall object on Earth will initiate the leader strike, causing what is known as cloud-to-ground lightning.

Cloud-to-ground lightning

Field Activity

During a thunderstorm, observe lightning from a safe location in your home or school. Using this field guide, identify and record in your Science Journal the types of lightning you saw. Also, note the date and time of the thunderstorm in your Science Journal.

Resources for Teachers and Students

Lightning: Sheets, Streaks, Beads, and Balls, by Suzanne Harper, Franklin Watts, 1997.

Raging Planet: Lighting, Videotape, Discovery Communications, 1997.

Lightning, by Seymour Simon, Morrow Junior Books, 1997.

How the Weather Works, by Michael Allaby, Dorling Kindersley Limited, 1995.

Cloud-to-Cloud Lightning

Cloud-to-cloud lightning is the most common type of lightning. It can occur between clouds (intercloud lightning) or within a cloud (intracloud lightning). The lightning is often hidden by the clouds, such that the clouds themselves seem to be glowing flashes of light.

Cloud-to-Air Lightning

When a lightning stroke ends in midair above a cloud or forks off the main stroke of cloud-to-ground lightning, it causes what is known as cloud-to-air lightning. This type of lightning is usually not as powerful or as bright as cloud-to-ground lightning.

Cloud-to-air lightning

Content Background

Lightning can heat the air around it up to 30,000°C. Temperatures this high force air molecules to separate instantaneously. The sound wave caused by the explosion of air molecules is thunder.

Aside from being associated with thunderstorms, lightning can also occur among the ash clouds from a volcanic eruption. The static electricity that builds up among particles released by the volcano can cause cloud-to-cloud lightning as well as cloud-to-ground lightning.

Despite the detrimental effects lightning strikes can have on people or property, forest fires caused by lightning strikes are part of the natural process of forest regeneration. A form of nitrogen usable by plants is released from the atmosphere as lightning heats the air it travels through. In its new form this nitrogen reaches plants as rainwater is absorbed from the soil.

Use Science Words

Word Meaning Have students find the meaning of the word *fulgurite*. **How does this word relate to the subject of lightning?** Possible answer: Fulgurites are little tubes of glassy rock that have been fused from all other sorts of rocks by lightning strikes. Fulgurites are especially frequent in exposed crags on mountain tops. Fulgurite comes from the Latin root *fulgur* which means "lightning."

FIELD GUIDE 695

SCIENCE Online
Internet Addresses
_____
_____
_____
_____

Explore the Glencoe Science Web site at **science.glencoe.com** to find out more about topics in this field guide.

All Lightning Photographs
Have students examine pictures of lightning in other books. Challenge them to use this field guide to determine the type of lightning shown in each photo. Have the students explain their reasons for their classifications.
IS **Visual-Spatial**

Discussion

Have the class discuss lightning safety. **What should a person do (or not do) when lightning occurs?** Expand the discussion to include different settings such as at home, outside, at a pool, or on a boat when the lightning occurs. Possible answers: At home: Do not touch electrical appliances or stand near open windows, doors, or fireplaces. Outside: Do not take cover under a tree. In an open area such as a field or a beach, crouch down into a ball and balance on the balls of your feet. Near water: Exit the area as quickly as possible.

Extension

Have students formally research lightning safety. Suggest that they present their findings on a poster entitled "Lightning Safety Tips." Challenge students to relate the tips to the science of lightning. For example, crouching in a ball and balancing on the balls of the feet reduces contact with the ground, which can carry an electrical charge. This position also can help protect internal organs if a person is struck by lightning. L3 IS **Logical-Mathematical**

Field GUIDE

Field Guide

Some forms of lightning differ in appearance from the forked flashes commonly considered to be lightning. However, the discharge in the cloud occurs for the same reason—to neutralize the accumulation of charge.

Sheet lightning

Sheet Lightning

Sheet lightning appears to fill a large section of the sky. Its appearance is caused by light reflecting off the water droplets in the clouds. The actual strokes of lightning are far away or hidden by the clouds. When the lightning is so far away that no thunder is heard, it is often called heat lightning and usually can be seen during summer nights.

Ribbon Lightning

Ribbon lightning is a thicker flash than ordinary cloud-to-ground lightning. In this case, wind blows the channel that is created by the return stroke sideways. Because each return stroke follows this channel, each is moved slightly to the side of the last stroke, making each return stroke of the flash visible, and thus a wider, ribbonlike band of light is produced.

Ribbon lightning

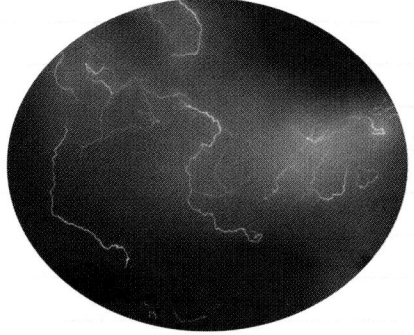

Bead lightning

Chain Lightning

Chain lightning, also called bead lightning, is distinguished by a dotted line of light as it fades. The cause is still uncertain, but it might be due to the observer's position relative to lightning or to parts of the flash being hidden by clouds or rain.

Cultural Diversity

Lightening Tales   Have students research how ancient civilizations such as the Greeks, the Romans, the Chinese, or Native Americans explained the occurrence of lighting. Students can record what they discover in their Science Journals. IS **Linguistic**

Some forms of lightning are rare or poorly understood and have different appearances than the previously described forms.

Sprites

Sprites are red or blue flashes of light that are sometimes cone shaped and occur high above a thundercloud, 60 to 100 km above Earth. The flashes are associated with thunderstorms that cover a vast area. Sprites are estimated to occur in about 1 percent of all lightning strokes.

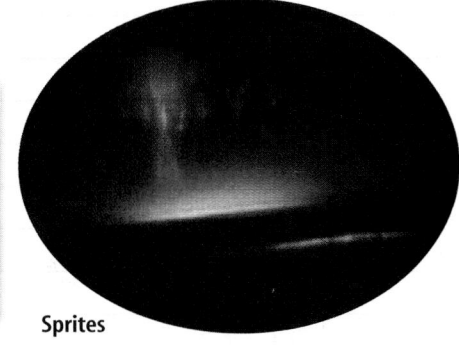

Sprites

Ball Lightning

There have been numerous eyewitness accounts of the existence of ball lightning, which appears as a sphere of red, yellow, orange or white light, usually between 1 cm to 1 m in size. Ball lightning seems to occur during thunderstorms, and appears within a few meters of the ground. The ball may move horizontally at a speed of a few meters per second, or may float in the air. Ball lightning usually lasts for several seconds and may vanish either quietly or explosively. Unlike other forms of lightning which can be seen by many observers at large distances, the small size of ball lightning and its random occurrence make it difficult to study. As a result, the causes of ball lightning still are not known, and even its existence is disputed.

St. Elmo's Fire

St. Elmo's Fire is a bluish-green glowing light that sometimes appears during thunderstorms around tall, pointed objects like the masts of ships and lightning rods. It also occurs around the wings and propellers of airplanes flying through thunderstorms. A sizzling or crackling noise often accompanies the glow. St. Elmo's Fire is caused by the strong electric field between the bottom of a thundercloud and the ground. This electric field is strongest around pointed objects. If this field is strong enough, it can pull electrons from atoms in the air. The glow is produced when these electrons collide with other atoms and molecules in the air.

FIELD GUIDE 697

Curriculum Connection

History Benjamin Franklin invented the lightning rod. Lightning rods are still used today to protect buildings and high structures such as the space shuttle launching platform from the effects of lightning strikes. A lighting rod is mounted on the top of a structure and is grounded some distance away from the structure. When lighting strikes, it is attracted to the rod, which then safely distributes the charge of electricity away from the structure itself. Have students research other lightning-related discoveries made by Benjamin Franklin. L2 LS **Linguistic**

As you study science, you will make many observations and conduct investigations and experiments. You will also research information that is available from many sources. These activities will involve organizing and recording data. The quality of the data you collect and the way you organize it will determine how well others can understand and use it. In **Figure 1,** the student is obtaining and recording information using a thermometer.

Putting your observations in writing is an important way of communicating to others the information you have found and the results of your investigations and experiments.

Researching Information

Scientists work to build on and add to human knowledge of the world. Before moving in a new direction, it is important to gather the information that already is known about a subject. You will look for such information in various reference sources. Follow these steps to research information on a scientific subject:

Step 1 Determine exactly what you need to know about the subject. For instance, you might want to find out what happened when Mount St. Helens erupted in 1980.

Step 2 Make a list of questions, such as: When did the eruption begin? How long did it last? What kind of material was expelled and how much?

Step 3 Use multiple sources such as textbooks, encyclopedias, government documents, professional journals, science magazines, and the Internet.

Step 4 List where you found the sources. Make sure the sources you use are reliable and the most current available.

Figure 1
Collecting data is one way to gather information directly.

Evaluating Print and Nonprint Sources

Not all sources of information are reliable. Evaluate the sources you use for information, and use only those you know to be dependable. For example, suppose you live in an area where earthquakes are common and you want to know what to do to keep safe. You might find two Web sites on earthquake safety. One Web site contains "Earthquake Tips" written by a company that sells metal scrapings to help secure your hot-water tank to the wall. The other is a Web page on "Earthquake Safety" written by the U.S. Geological Survey. You would choose the second Web site as the more reliable source of information.

In science, information can change rapidly. Always consult the most current sources. A 1985 source about the Moon would not reflect the most recent research and findings.

Interpreting Scientific Illustrations

As you research a science topic, you will see drawings, diagrams, and photographs. Illustrations help you understand what you read. Some illustrations are included to help you understand an idea that you can't see easily by yourself. For instance, you can't see the layers of Earth, but you can look at a diagram of Earth's layers, as labeled in **Figure 2,** that helps you understand what the layers are and where they are located. Visualizing a drawing helps many people remember details more easily. Illustrations also provide examples that clarify difficult concepts or give additional information about the topic you are studying.

Most illustrations have a label or caption. A label or caption identifies the illustration or provides additional information to better explain it. Can you find the caption or labels in **Figure 2?**

Figure 2
This cross section shows a slice through Earth's interior and the positions of its layers.

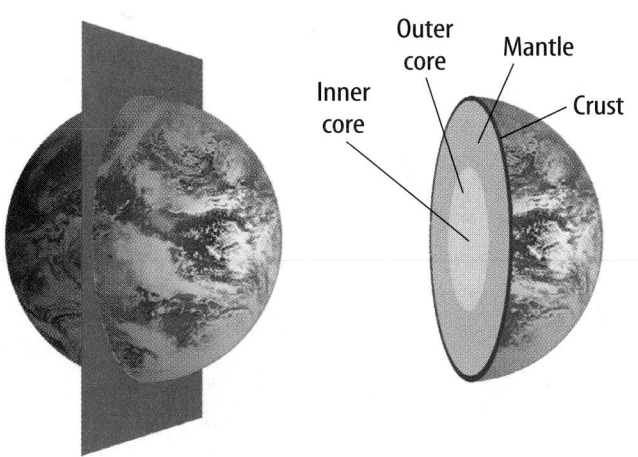

Venn Diagram

A Venn diagram illustrates how two subjects compare and contrast. In other words, you can see the characteristics that the subjects have in common and those that they do not.

The Venn diagram in **Figure 3** shows the relationship between two types of rocks made from the same basic chemical. Both rocks share the chemical calcium carbonate. However, due to the way they are formed, one rock is the sedimentary rock limestone, and the other is the metamorphic rock marble.

Concept Mapping

If you were taking a car trip, you might take some sort of road map. By using a map, you begin to learn where you are in relation to other places on the map.

A concept map is similar to a road map, but a concept map shows relationships among ideas (or concepts) rather than places. It is a diagram that visually shows how concepts are related. Because a concept map shows relationships among ideas, it can make the meanings of ideas and terms clear and help you understand what you are studying.

Overall, concept maps are useful for breaking large concepts down into smaller parts, making learning easier.

Figure 3
A Venn diagram shows how objects or concepts are alike and how they are different.

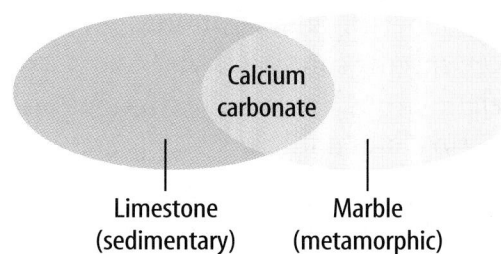

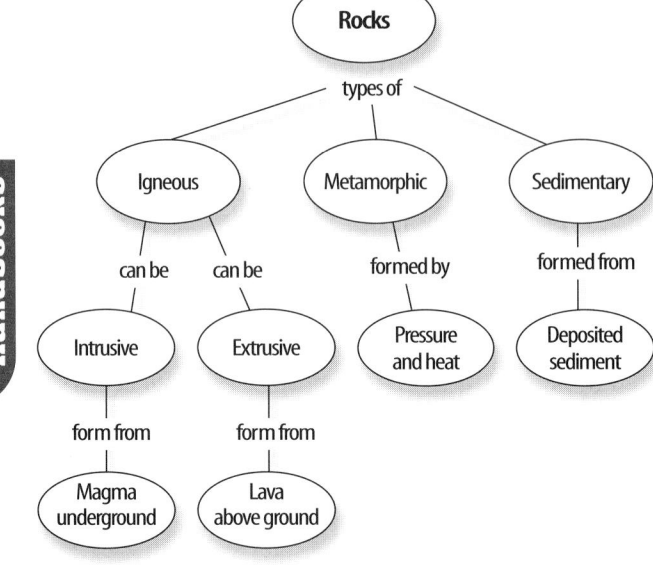

Figure 4
A network tree shows how concepts or objects are related.

Network Tree Look at the network tree in **Figure 4,** that shows the three main types of rock. A network tree is a kind of concept map. Notice how some words are in ovals while others are written across connecting lines. The words inside the ovals are science terms or concepts. The words written on the connecting lines describe the relationships between the concepts.

When constructing a network tree, write the topic on a note card or piece of paper. Write the major concepts related to that topic on separate note cards or pieces of paper. Then arrange them in order from general to specific. Branch the related concepts from the major concept and describe the relationships on the connecting lines. Continue branching to more specific concepts. If necessary, write the relationships between the concepts on the connecting lines until all concepts are mapped. Then examine the network tree for relationships that cross branches, and add them to the network tree.

Events Chain An events chain is another type of concept map. It models the order, or sequence, of items. In science, an events chain can be used to describe a sequence of events, the steps in a procedure, or the stages of a process.

When making an events chain, first find the one event that starts the chain. This event is called the initiating event. Then, find the next event in the chain and continue until you reach an outcome. Suppose you are asked to describe why and how a sound might make an echo. You might draw an events chain such as the one in **Figure 5.** Notice that connecting words are not necessary in an events chain.

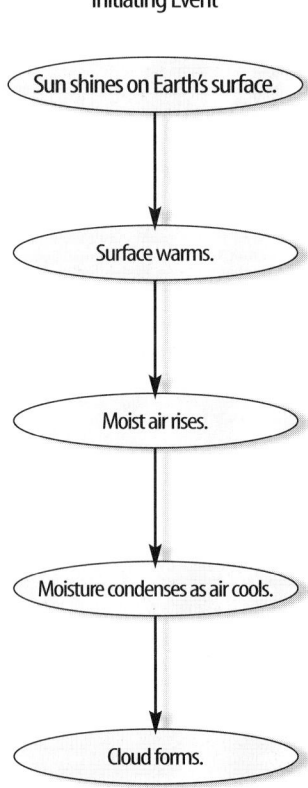

Figure 5
Events chains show the order of steps in a process or event.

Cycle Map A cycle concept map is a specific type of events chain map. In a cycle concept map, the series of events does not produce a final outcome. Instead, the last event in the chain relates back to the beginning event.

You first decide what event will be used as the beginning event. Once that is decided, you list events in order that occur after it. Words are written between events that describe what happens from one event to the next. The last event in a cycle concept map relates back to the beginning event. The number of events in a cycle concept varies but is usually three or more. Look at the cycle map shown in **Figure 6.**

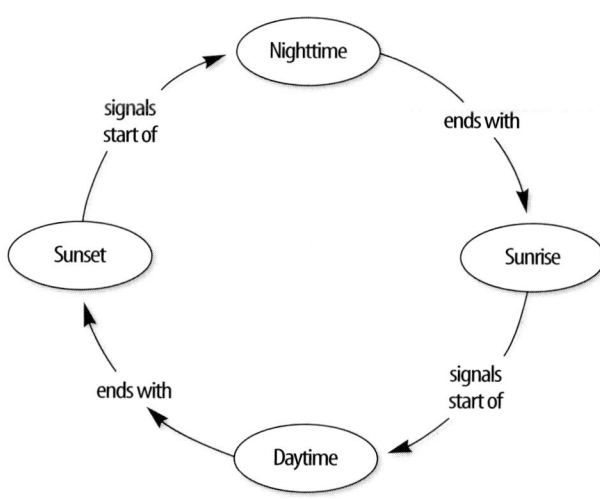

Figure 6
A cycle map shows events that occur in a cycle.

Spider Map A type of concept map that you can use for brainstorming is the spider map. When you have a central idea, you might find you have a jumble of ideas that relate to it but are not necessarily clearly related to each other. The spider map on mining in **Figure 7** shows that if you write these ideas outside the main concept, then you can begin to separate and group un-related terms so they become more useful.

Figure 7
A spider map allows you to list ideas that relate to a central topic but not necessarily to one another.

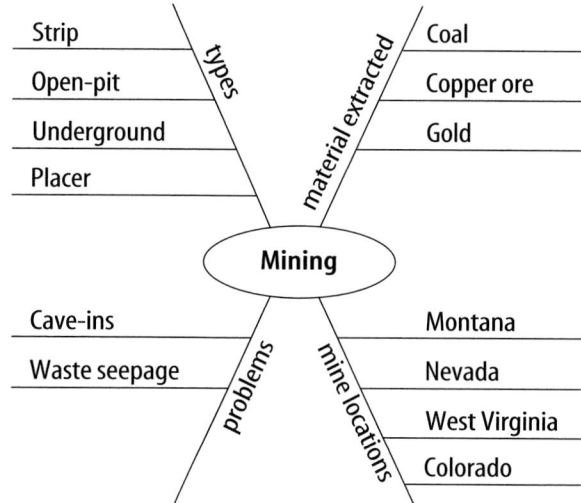

Writing a Paper

You will write papers often when researching science topics or reporting the results of investigations or experiments. Scientists frequently write papers to share their data and conclusions with other scientists and the public. When writing a paper, use these steps.

Step 1 Assemble your data by using graphs, tables, or a concept map. Create an outline.

Step 2 Start with an introduction that contains a clear statement of purpose and what you intend to discuss or prove.

Step 3 Organize the body into paragraphs. Each paragraph should start with a topic sentence, and the remaining sentences in that paragraph should support your point.

Step 4 Position data to help support your points.

Step 5 Summarize the main points and finish with a conclusion statement.

Step 6 Use tables, graphs, charts, and illustrations whenever possible.

Skill Handbooks

You might say the work of a scientist is to solve problems. When you decide to find out why one corner of your yard is always soggy, you are problem solving, too. You might observe that the corner is lower than the surrounding area and has less vegetation growing in it. You might decide to see whether planting some grass will keep the corner drier.

Scientists use orderly approaches to solve problems. The methods scientists use include identifying a question, making observations, forming a hypothesis, testing a hypothesis, analyzing results, and drawing conclusions.

Scientific investigations involve careful observation under controlled conditions. Such observation of an object or a process can suggest new and interesting questions about it. These questions sometimes lead to the formation of a hypothesis. Scientific investigations are designed to test a hypothesis.

Identifying a Question

The first step in a scientific investigation or experiment is to identify a question to be answered or a problem to be solved. You might be interested in knowing why a rock like the one in **Figure 8** looks the way it does.

Figure 8
When you find a rock, you might ask yourself, "How did this rock form?"

Forming Hypotheses

Hypotheses are based on observations that have been made. A hypothesis is a possible explanation based on previous knowledge and observations.

Perhaps a scientist has observed that thunderstorms happen more often on hot days than on cooler days. Based on these observations, the scientist can make a statement that he or she can test. The statement is a hypothesis. The hypothesis could be: *Warm temperatures cause thunderstorms.* A hypothesis has to be something you can test by using an investigation. A testable hypothesis is a valid hypothesis.

Predicting

When you apply a hypothesis to a specific situation, you predict something about that situation. First, you must identify which hypothesis fits the situation you are considering. People use predictions to make everyday decisions. Based on previous observations and experiences, you might form a prediction that if warm temperatures cause thunderstorms, then more thunderstorms will occur in summer months than in spring months. Someone could use these predictions to plan when to take a camping trip or when to schedule an outdoor activity.

Testing a Hypothesis

To test a hypothesis, you need a procedure. A procedure is the plan you follow in your experiment. A procedure tells you what materials to use, as well as how and in what order to use them. When you follow a procedure, data are generated that support or do not support the original hypothesis statement.

For example, premium gasoline costs more than regular gasoline. Does premium gasoline increase the efficiency or fuel mileage of your family car? You decide to test the hypothesis: "If premium gasoline is more efficient, then it should increase the fuel mileage of my family's car." Then you write the procedure shown in **Figure 9** for your experiment and generate the data presented in the table below.

Figure 9
A procedure tells you what to do step by step.

Procedure

1. Use regular gasoline for two weeks.
2. Record the number of kilometers between fill-ups and the amount of gasoline used.
3. Switch to premium gasoline for two weeks.
4. Record the number of kilometers between fill-ups and the amount of gasoline used.

Gasoline Data			
Type of Gasoline	Kilometers Traveled	Liters Used	Liters per Kilometer
Regular	762	45.34	0.059
Premium	661	42.30	0.064

These data show that premium gasoline is less efficient than regular gasoline in one particular car. It took more gasoline to travel 1 km (0.064) using premium gasoline than it did to travel 1 km using regular gasoline (0.059). This conclusion does not support the hypothesis.

Are all investigations alike? Keep in mind as you perform investigations in science that a hypothesis can be tested in many ways. Not every investigation makes use of all the ways that are described on these pages, and not all hypotheses are tested by investigations. Scientists encounter many variations in the methods that are used when they perform experiments. The skills in this handbook are here for you to use and practice.

Identifying and Manipulating Variables and Controls

In any experiment, it is important to keep everything the same except for the item you are testing. The one factor you change is called the independent variable. The factor that changes as a result of the independent variable is called the dependent variable. Always make sure you have only one independent variable. If you allow more than one, you will not know what causes the changes you observe in the dependent variable. Many experiments also have controls—individual instances or experimental subjects for which the independent variable is not changed. You can then compare the test results to the control results.

For example, in the fuel-mileage experiment, you made everything the same except the type of gasoline that was used. The driver, the type of automobile, and the type of driving were the same throughout. In this way, you could be sure that any mileage differences were caused by the type of fuel—the independent variable. The fuel mileage was the dependent variable.

If you could repeat the experiment using several automobiles of the same type on a standard driving track with the same driver, you could make one automobile a control by using regular gasoline over the four-week period.

Collecting Data

Whether you are carrying out an investigation or a short observational experiment, you will collect data, or information. Scientists collect data accurately as numbers and descriptions and organize it in specific ways.

Observing Scientists observe items and events, then record what they see. When they use only words to describe an observation, it is called qualitative data. For example, a scientist might describe the color, texture, or odor of a substance produced in a chemical reaction. Scientists' observations also can describe how much there is of something. These observations use numbers, as well as words, in the description and are called quantitative data. For example, if a sample of the element gold is described as being "shiny and very dense," the data are clearly qualitative. Quantitative data on this sample of gold might include "a mass of 30 g and a density of 19.3 g/cm^3." Quantitative data often are organized into tables. Then, from information in the table, a graph can be drawn. Graphs can reveal relationships that exist in experimental data.

When you make observations in science, you should examine the entire object or situation first, then look carefully for details. If you're looking at a rock sample, for instance, check the general color and pattern of the rock before using a hand lens to examine the small mineral grains that make up its underlying structure. Remember to record accurately everything you see.

Scientists try to make careful and accurate observations. When possible, they use instruments such as microscopes, metric rulers, graduated cylinders, thermometers, and balances. Measurements provide numerical data that can be repeated and checked.

Sampling When working with large numbers of objects or a large population, scientists usually cannot observe or study every one of them. Instead, they use a sample or a portion of the total number. To *sample* is to take a small, representative portion of the objects or organisms of a population for research. By making careful observations or manipulating variables within a portion of a group, information is discovered and conclusions are drawn that might apply to the whole population.

Estimating Scientific work also involves estimating. To *estimate* is to make a judgment about the amount or the number of something without measuring every part of an object or counting every member of a population. Scientists first measure or count the amount or number in a small sample. A chemist, for example, might remove a 10-g piece of a large rock that is rich in copper ore, such as the one shown in **Figure 10.** Then the chemist can determine the percentage of copper by mass and multiply that percentage by the mass of the rock to get an estimate of the total mass of copper in the rock.

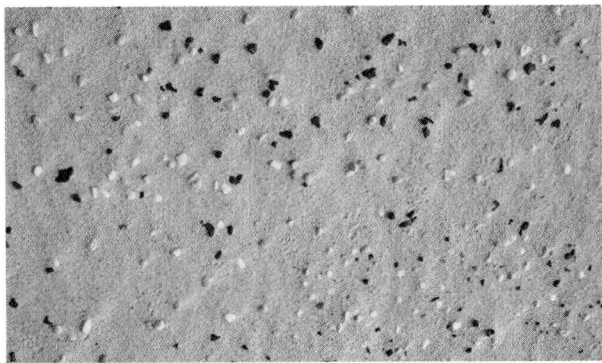

Figure 10
In a 1-meter frame positioned on a beach, count the pebbles that are longer than 2.5 cm. Multiply this number by the area of the beach. This will give you an estimate for the total number of pebbles on the beach.

Measuring in SI

The metric system of measurement was developed in 1795. A modern form of the metric system, called the International System, or SI, was adopted in 1960. SI provides standard measurements that all scientists around the world can understand.

The metric system is convenient because unit sizes vary by multiples of 10. When changing from smaller units to larger units, divide by a multiple of 10. When changing from larger units to smaller, multiply by a multiple of 10. To convert millimeters to centimeters, divide the millimeters by 10. To convert 30 mm to centimeters, divide 30 by 10 (30 mm equal 3 cm).

Prefixes are used to name units. Look at the table below for some common metric prefixes and their meanings. Do you see how the prefix *kilo-* attached to the unit *gram* is *kilogram*, or 1,000 g?

Metric Prefixes			
Prefix	Symbol	Meaning	
kilo-	k	1,000	thousand
hecto-	h	100	hundred
deka-	da	10	ten
deci-	d	0.1	tenth
centi-	c	0.01	hundredth
milli-	m	0.001	thousandth

Now look at the metric ruler shown in **Figure 11.** The centimeter lines are the long, numbered lines, and the shorter lines are millimeter lines.

When using a metric ruler, line up the 0-cm mark with the end of the object being measured, and read the number of the unit where the object ends. In this instance, it would be 4.50 cm.

Figure 11
This metric ruler shows centimeters and millimeter divisions.

Liquid Volume In some science activities, you will measure liquids. The unit that is used to measure liquids is the liter. A liter has the volume of 1,000 cm³. The prefix *milli-* means "thousandth (0.001)." A milliliter is one thousandth of 1 L, and 1 L has the volume of 1,000 mL. One milliliter of liquid completely fills a cube measuring 1 cm on each side. Therefore, 1 mL equals 1 cm³.

You will use beakers and graduated cylinders to measure liquid volume. A graduated cylinder, as illustrated in **Figure 12,** is marked from bottom to top in milliliters. This one contains 79 mL of a liquid.

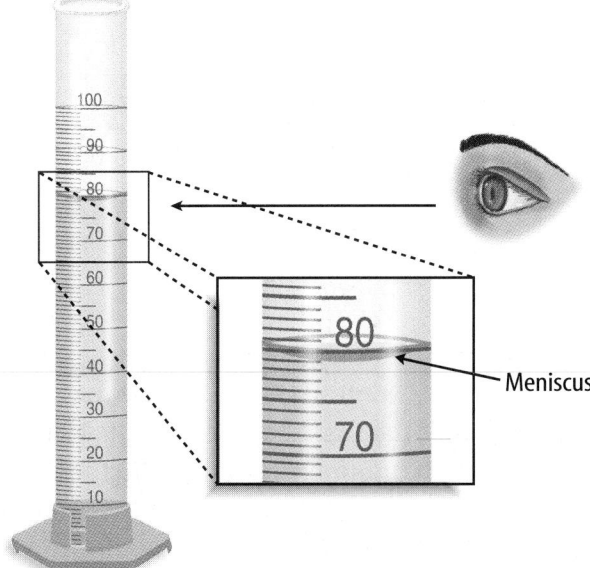

Meniscus

Figure 12
Graduated cylinders measure liquid volume.

Mass Scientists measure mass in grams. You might use a beam balance similar to the one shown in **Figure 13.** The balance has a pan on one side and a set of beams on the other side. Each beam has a rider that slides on the beam.

Before you find the mass of an object, slide all the riders back to the zero point. Check the pointer on the right to make sure it swings an equal distance above and below the zero point. If the swing is unequal, find and turn the adjusting screw until you have an equal swing.

Place an object on the pan. Slide the largest rider along its beam until the pointer drops below zero. Then move it back one notch. Repeat the process on each beam until the pointer swings an equal distance above and below the zero point. Sum the masses on each beam to find the mass of the object. Move all riders back to zero when finished.

Figure 13
A triple beam balance is used to determine the mass of an object.

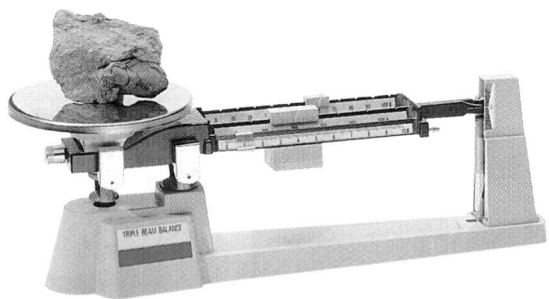

You should never place a hot object on the pan or pour chemicals directly onto the pan. Instead, find the mass of a clean container. Remove the container from the pan, then place the chemicals in the container. Find the mass of the container with the chemicals in it. To find the mass of the chemicals, subtract the mass of the empty container from the mass of the filled container.

Making and Using Tables

Browse through your textbook and you will see tables in the text and in the activities. In a table, data, or information, are arranged so that they are easier to understand. Activity tables help organize the data you collect during an activity so results can be interpreted.

Making Tables To make a table, list the items to be compared in the first column and the characteristics to be compared in the first row. The title should clearly indicate the content of the table, and the column or row heads should tell the reader what information is found in there. The table below lists materials collected for recycling on three weekly pick-up days. The inclusion of kilograms in parentheses also identifies for the reader that the figures are mass units.

Recyclable Materials Collected During Week			
Day of Week	**Paper (kg)**	**Aluminum (kg)**	**Glass (kg)**
Monday	5.0	4.0	12.0
Wednesday	4.0	1.0	10.0
Friday	2.5	2.0	10.0

Using Tables How much paper, in kilograms, is being recycled on Wednesday? Locate the column labeled "Paper (kg)" and the row "Wednesday." The information in the box where the column and row intersect is the answer. Did you answer "4.0"? How much aluminum, in kilograms, is being recycled on Friday? If you answered "2.0," you understand how to read the table. How much glass is collected for recycling each week? Locate the column labeled "Glass (kg)" and add the figures for all three rows. If you answered "32.0," then you know how to locate and use the data provided in the table.

Recording Data

To be useful, the data you collect must be recorded carefully. Accuracy is key. A well-thought-out experiment includes a way to record procedures, observations, and results accurately. Data tables are one way to organize and record results. Set up the tables you will need ahead of time so you can record the data right away.

Record information properly and neatly. Never put unidentified data on scraps of paper. Instead, data should be written in a notebook like the one in **Figure 14.** Write in pencil so information isn't lost if your data get wet. At each point in the experiment, record your information and label it. That way, your data will be accurate and you will not have to determine what the figures mean when you look at your notes later.

Figure 14
Record data neatly and clearly so they are easy to understand.

Recording Observations

It is important to record observations accurately and completely. That is why you always should record observations in your notes immediately as you make them. It is easy to miss details or make mistakes when recording results from memory. Do not include your personal thoughts when you record your data. Record only what you observe to eliminate bias. For example, when you record the time required for five students to climb the same set of stairs, you would note which student took the longest time. However, you would not refer to that student's time as "the worst time of all the students in the group."

Making Models

You can organize the observations and other data you collect and record in many ways. Making models is one way to help you better understand the parts of a structure you have been observing or the way a process for which you have been taking various measurements works.

Models often show things that are too large or too small for normal viewing. For example, you normally won't see the inside of an atom. However, you can understand the structure of the atom better by making a three-dimensional model of an atom. The relative sizes, the positions, and the movements of protons, neutrons, and electrons can be explained in words. An atomic model made of a plastic-ball nucleus and pipe-cleaner electron shells can help you visualize how the parts of the atom relate to each other.

Other models can be devised on a computer. Some models, such as those that illustrate the chemical combinations of different elements, are mathematical and are represented by equations.

Making and Using Graphs

After scientists organize data in tables, they might display the data in a graph that shows the relationship of one variable to another. A graph makes interpretation and analysis of data easier. Three types of graphs are the line graph, the bar graph, and the circle graph.

Line Graphs A line graph like in **Figure 15** is used to show the relationship between two variables. The variables being compared go on two axes of the graph. For data from an experiment, the independent variable always goes on the horizontal axis, called the *x*-axis. The dependent variable always goes on the vertical axis, called the *y*-axis. After drawing your axes, label each with a scale. Next, plot the data points.

A data point is the intersection of the recorded value of the dependent variable for each tested value of the independent variable. After all the points are plotted, connect them.

Bar Graphs Bar graphs compare data that do not change continuously. Vertical bars show the relationships among data.

To make a bar graph, set up the *y*-axis as you did for the line graph. Draw vertical bars of equal size from the *x*-axis up to the point on the *y*-axis that represents the value of *x*.

Figure 16
The amount of aluminum collected for recycling during one week can be shown as a bar graph or circle graph.

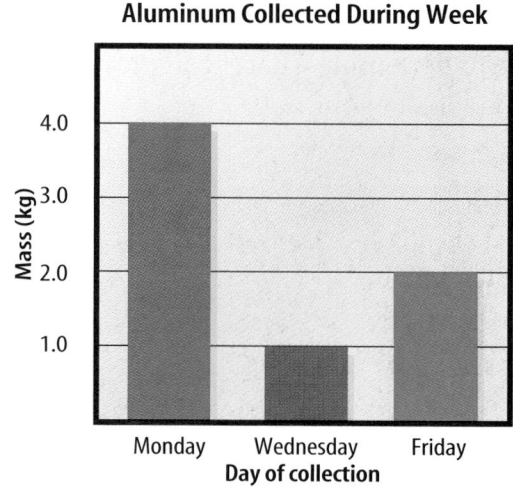

Circle Graphs A circle graph uses a circle divided into sections to display data as parts (fractions or percentages) of a whole. The size of each section corresponds to the fraction or percentage of the data that the section represents. So, the entire circle represents 100 percent, one-half represents 50 percent, one-fifth represents 20 percent, and so on.

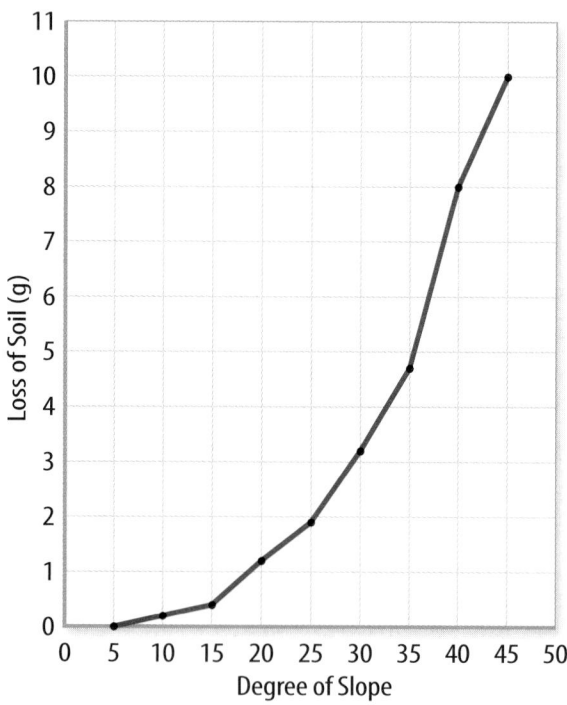

Figure 15
This line graph shows the relationship between degree of slope and the loss of soil in grams from a container during an experiment.

Analyzing Results

To determine the meaning of your observations and investigation results, you will need to look for patterns in the data. You can organize your information in several of the ways that are discussed in this handbook. Then you must think critically to determine what the data mean. Scientists use several approaches when they analyze the data they have collected and recorded. Each approach is useful for identifying specific patterns in the data.

Forming Operational Definitions

An operational definition defines an object by showing how it functions, works, or behaves. Such definitions are written in terms of how an object works or how it can be used; that is, they describe its job or purpose.

For example, a ruler can be defined as a tool that measures the length of an object (how it can be used). A ruler also can be defined as something that contains a series of marks that can be used as a standard when measuring (how it works).

Classifying

Classifying is the process of sorting objects or events into groups based on common features. When classifying, first observe the objects or events to be classified. Then select one feature that is shared by some members in the group but not by all. Place those members that share that feature into a subgroup. You can classify members into smaller and smaller subgroups based on characteristics.

How might you classify a group of rocks? You might first classify them by color, putting all of the black, white, and red rocks into separate groups. Within each group, you could then look for another common feature to classify further, such as size or whether the rocks have sharp or smooth edges.

Remember that when you classify, you are grouping objects or events for a purpose. For example, classifying rocks can be the first step in identifying them. You might know that obsidian is a black, shiny rock with sharp edges. To find it in a large group of rocks, you might start with the classification scheme mentioned. You'll locate obsidian within the group of black, sharp-edged rocks that you separate from the rest. Pumice could be located by its white color and by the fact that it contains many small holes called vesicles. Keep your purpose in mind as you select the features to form groups and subgroups.

Figure 17
Color is one of many characteristics that are used to classify rocks.

Comparing and Contrasting

Observations can be analyzed by noting the similarities and differences between two or more objects or events that you observe. When you look at objects or events to see how they are similar, you are comparing them. Contrasting is looking for differences in objects or events. The table below compares and contrasts the characteristics of two minerals.

Mineral Characteristics		
Mineral	Graphite	Gold
Color	black	bright yellow
Hardness	1–2	2.5–3
Luster	metallic	metallic
Uses	pencil "lead"	jewelry, electronics

Recognizing Cause and Effect

Have you ever heard a loud pop right before the power went out and then suggested that an electric transformer probably blew out? If so, you have observed an effect and inferred a cause. The event is the effect, and the reason for the event is the cause.

When scientists are unsure of the cause of a certain event, they design controlled experiments to determine what caused it.

Interpreting Data

The word *interpret* means "to explain the meaning of something." Look at the problem originally being explored in an experiment and figure out what the data show. Identify the control group and the test group so you can see whether or not changes in the independent variable have had an effect. Look for differences in the dependent variable between the control and test groups.

These differences you observe can be qualitative or quantitative. You would be able to describe a qualitative difference using only words, whereas you would measure a quantitative difference and describe it using numbers. If there are differences, the independent variable that is being tested could have had an effect. If no differences are found between the control and test groups, the variable that is being tested apparently had no effect.

For example, suppose that three beakers each contain 100 mL of water. The beakers are placed on hot plates, and two of the hot plates are turned on, but the third is left off for a period of 5 min. Suppose you are then asked to describe any differences in the water in the three beakers. A qualitative difference might be the appearance of bubbles rising to the top in the water that is being heated but no rising bubbles in the unheated water. A quantitative difference might be a difference in the amount of water that is present in the beakers.

Inferring Scientists often make inferences based on their observations. An inference is an attempt to explain, or interpret, observations or to indicate what caused what you observed. An inference is a type of conclusion.

When making an inference, be certain to use accurate data and accurately described observations. Analyze all of the data that you've collected. Then, based on everything you know, explain or interpret what you've observed.

Drawing Conclusions

When scientists have analyzed the data they collected, they proceed to draw conclusions about what the data mean. These conclusions are sometimes stated using words similar to those found in the hypothesis formed earlier in the process.

Conclusions To analyze your data, you must review all of the observations and measurements that you made and recorded. Recheck all data for accuracy. After your data are rechecked and organized, you are almost ready to draw a conclusion such as "salt water boils at a higher temperature than freshwater."

Before you can draw a conclusion, however, you must determine whether the data allow you to come to a conclusion that supports a hypothesis. Sometimes that will be the case; other times it will not.

If your data do not support a hypothesis, it does not mean that the hypothesis is wrong. It means only that the results of the investigation did not support the hypothesis. Maybe the experiment needs to be redesigned, but very likely, some of the initial observations on which the hypothesis was based were incomplete or biased. Perhaps more observation or research is needed to refine the hypothesis.

Avoiding Bias Sometimes drawing a conclusion involves making judgments. When you make a judgment, you form an opinion about what your data mean. It is important to be honest and to avoid reaching a conclusion if there is no supporting evidence for it or if it is based on a small sample. It also is important not to allow any expectations of results to bias your judgments. If possible, it is a good idea to collect additional data. Scientists do this all the time.

For example, the *Hubble Space Telescope* was sent into space in April, 1990, to provide scientists with clearer views of the universe. *Hubble* is the size of a school bus and has a 2.4-m-diameter mirror. *Hubble* helped scientists answer questions about the planet Pluto.

For many years, scientists had only been able to hypothesize about the surface of the planet Pluto. *Hubble* has now provided pictures of Pluto's surface that show a rough texture with light and dark regions on it. This might be the best information about Pluto scientists will have until they are able to send a space probe to it.

Evaluating Others' Data and Conclusions

Sometimes scientists have to use data that they did not collect themselves, or they have to rely on observations and conclusions drawn by other researchers. In cases such as these, the data must be evaluated carefully.

How were the data obtained? How was the investigation done? Was it carried out properly? Has it been duplicated by other researchers? Were they able to follow the exact procedure? Did they come up with the same results? Look at the conclusion, as well. Would you reach the same conclusion from these results? Only when you have confidence in the data of others can you believe it is true and feel comfortable using it.

Communicating

The communication of ideas is an important part of the work of scientists. A discovery that is not reported will not advance the scientific community's understanding or knowledge. Communication among scientists also is important as a way of improving their investigations.

Scientists communicate in many ways, from writing articles in journals and magazines that explain their investigations and experiments, to announcing important discoveries on television and radio, to sharing ideas with colleagues on the Internet or presenting them as lectures.

People who study science rely on computers to record and store data and to analyze results from investigations. Whether you work in a laboratory or just need to write a lab report with tables, good computer skills are a necessity.

Using a Word Processor

Suppose your teacher has assigned a written report. After you've completed your research and decided how you want to write the information, you need to put all that information on paper. The easiest way to do this is with a word processing application on a computer.

A computer application that allows you to type your information, change it as many times as you need to, and then print it out so that it looks neat and clean is called a word processing application. You also can use this type of application to create tables and columns, add bullets or cartoon art to your page, include page numbers, and check your spelling.

Helpful Hints

- If you aren't sure how to do something using your word processing program, look in the help menu. You will find a list of topics there to click on for help. After you locate the help topic you need, just follow the step-by-step instructions you see on your screen.
- Just because you've spell checked your report doesn't mean that the spelling is perfect. The spell check feature can't catch misspelled words that look like other words. If you've accidentally typed *mind* instead of *mine*, the spell checker won't know the difference. Always reread your report to make sure you didn't miss any mistakes.

Figure 18
You can use computer programs to make graphs and tables.

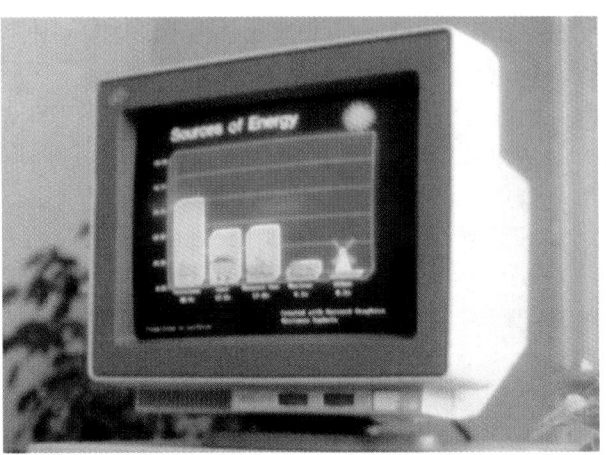

Using a Database

Imagine you're in the middle of a research project, busily gathering facts and information. You soon realize that it's becoming more difficult to organize and keep track of all the information. The tool to use to solve information overload is a database. Just as a file cabinet organizes paper records, a database organizes computer records. However, a database is more powerful than a simple file cabinet because at the click of a mouse, the contents can be reshuffled and reorganized. At computer-quick speeds, databases can sort information by any characteristics and filter data into multiple categories.

Helpful Hints

- Before setting up a database, take some time to learn the features of your database software by practicing with established database software.
- Periodically save your database as you enter data. That way, if something happens such as your computer malfunctions or the power goes off, you won't lose all of your work.

Doing a Database Search

When searching for information in a database, use the following search strategies to get the best results. These are the same search methods used for searching internet databases.

- Place the word *and* between two words in your search if you want the database to look for any entries that have both the words. For example, "Earth *and* Mars" would give you information that mentions both Earth and Mars.
- Place the word *or* between two words if you want the database to show entries that have at least one of the words. For example "Earth *or* Mars" would show you information that mentions either Earth or Mars.
- Place the word *not* between two words if you want the database to look for entries that have the first word but do not have the second word. For example, "Moon *not* phases" would show you information that mentions the Moon but does not mention its phases.

In summary, databases can be used to store large amounts of information about a particular subject. Databases allow biologists, Earth scientists, and physical scientists to search for information quickly and accurately.

Using an Electronic Spreadsheet

Your science fair experiment has produced lots of numbers. How do you keep track of all the data, and how can you easily work out all the calculations needed? You can use a computer program called a spreadsheet to record data that involve numbers. A spreadsheet is an electronic mathematical worksheet.

Type your data in rows and columns, just as they would look in a data table on a sheet of paper. A spreadsheet uses simple math to do data calculations. For example, you could add, subtract, divide, or multiply any of the values in the spreadsheet by another number. You also could set up a series of math steps you want to apply to the data. If you want to add 12 to all the numbers and then multiply all the numbers by 10, the computer does all the calculations for you in the spreadsheet. Below is an example of a spreadsheet that records weather data.

Helpful Hints

- Before you set up the spreadsheet, identify how you want to organize the data. Include any formulas you will need to use.
- Make sure you have entered the correct data into the correct rows and columns.
- You also can display your results in a graph. Pick the style of graph that best represents the data with which you are working.

Figure 19
A spreadsheet allows you to display large amounts of data and do calculations automatically.

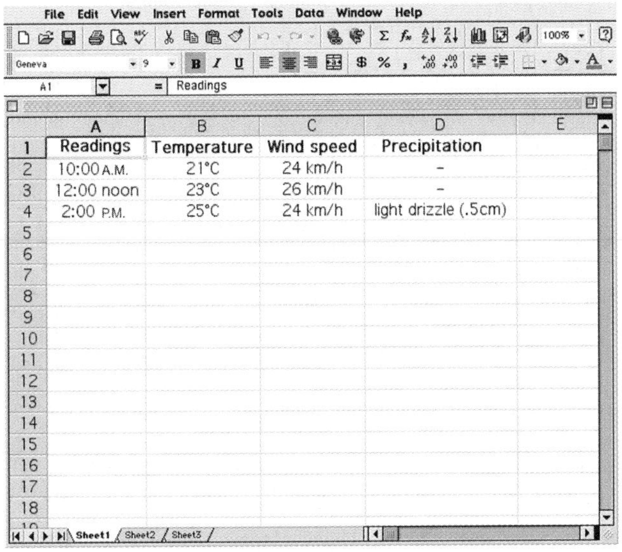

	A	B	C	D
1	Readings	Temperature	Wind speed	Precipitation
2	10:00 A.M.	21°C	24 km/h	-
3	12:00 noon	23°C	26 km/h	-
4	2:00 P.M.	25°C	24 km/h	light drizzle (.5cm)

Skill Handbooks

Using a Computerized Card Catalog

When you have a report or paper to research, you probably go to the library. To find the information you need in the library, you might have to use a computerized card catalog. This type of card catalog allows you to search for information by subject, by title, or by author. The computer then will display all the holdings the library has on the subject, title, or author requested.

A library's holdings can include books, magazines, databases, videos, and audio materials. When you have chosen something from this list, the computer will show whether an item is available and where in the library to find it.

Helpful Hints

■ Remember that you can use the computer to search by subject, author, or title. If you know a book's author but not the title, you can search for all the books the library has by that author.

■ When searching by subject, it's often most helpful to narrow your search by using specific search terms, such as *and, or,* and *not*. If you don't find enough sources, you can broaden your search.

■ Pay attention to the type of materials found in your search. If you need a book, you can eliminate any videos or other resources that come up in your search.

■ Knowing how your library is arranged can save you a lot of time. If you need help, the librarian will show you where certain types of materials are kept and how to find specific items.

Using Graphics Software

Are you having trouble finding that exact piece of art you're looking for? Do you have a picture in your mind of what you want but can't seem to find the right graphic to represent your ideas? To solve these problems, you can use graphics software. Graphics software allows you to create and change images and diagrams in almost unlimited ways. Typical uses for graphics software include arranging clip art, changing scanned images, and constructing pictures from scratch. Most graphics software applications work in similar ways. They use the same basic tools and functions. Once you master one graphics application, you can use other graphics applications.

Figure 20
Graphics software can use your data to draw bar graphs.

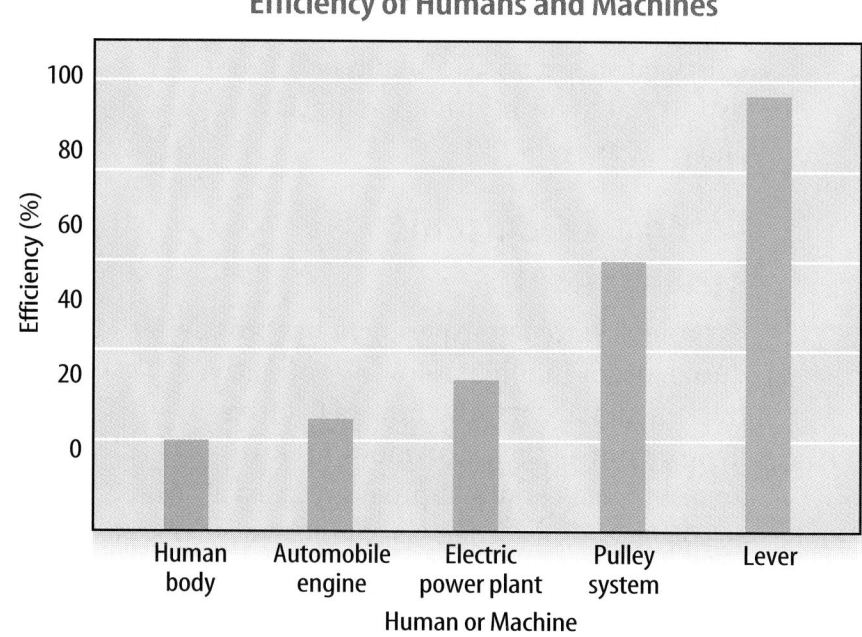

Figure 21

You can use this circle graph to find the names of the major gases that make up Earth's atmosphere.

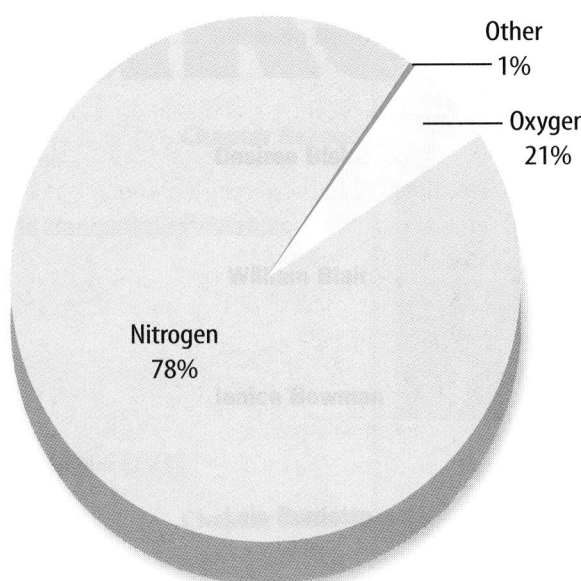

Other 1%

Oxygen 21%

Nitrogen 78%

Helpful Hints

- As with any method of drawing, the more you practice using the graphics software, the better your results will be.
- Start by using the software to manipulate existing drawings. Once you master this, making your own illustrations will be easier.
- Clip art is available on CD-ROMs and the Internet. With these resources, finding a piece of clip art to suit your purposes is simple.
- As you work on a drawing, save it often.

Developing Multimedia Presentations

It's your turn—you have to present your science report to the entire class. How do you do it? You can use many different sources of information to get the class excited about your presentation. Posters, videos, photographs, sound, computers, and the Internet can help show your ideas.

First, determine what important points you want to make in your presentation. Then, write an outline of what materials and types of media would best illustrate those points. Maybe you could start with an outline on an overhead projector, then show a video, followed by something from the Internet or a slide show accompanied by music or recorded voices. You might choose to use a presentation builder computer application that can combine all these elements into one presentation. Make sure the presentation is well constructed to make the most impact on the audience.

Figure 22

Multimedia presentations use many types of print and electronic materials.

Helpful Hints

- Carefully consider what media will best communicate the point you are trying to make.
- Make sure you know how to use any equipment you will be using in your presentation.
- Practice the presentation several times.
- If possible, set up all of the equipment ahead of time. Make sure everything is working correctly.

Math Skill Handbook

Use this Math Skill Handbook to help solve problems you are given in this text. You might find it useful to review topics in this Math Skill Handbook first.

Skill Handbooks

Converting Units

In science, quantities such as length, mass, and time sometimes are measured using different units. Suppose you want to know how many miles are in 12.7 km.

Conversion factors are used to change from one unit of measure to another. A conversion factor is a ratio that is equal to one. For example, there are 1,000 mL in 1 L, so 1,000 mL equals 1 L, or:

$$1{,}000 \text{ mL} = 1 \text{ L}$$

If both sides are divided by 1 L, this equation becomes:

$$\frac{1{,}000 \text{ mL}}{1 \text{ L}} = 1$$

The **ratio** on the left side of this equation is equal to 1 and is a conversion factor. You can make another conversion factor by dividing both sides of the top equation by 1,000 mL:

$$1 = \frac{1 \text{ L}}{1{,}000 \text{ mL}}$$

To **convert units,** you multiply by the appropriate conversion factor. For example, how many milliliters are in 1.255 L? To convert 1.255 L to milliliters, multiply 1.255 L by a conversion factor.

Use the **conversion factor** with new units (mL) in the numerator and the old units (L) in the denominator.

$$1.255 \text{ Ł} \times \frac{1{,}000 \text{ mL}}{1 \text{ Ł}} = 1{,}255 \text{ mL}$$

The unit L divides in this equation, just as if it were a number.

Example 1 There are 2.54 cm in 1 inch. If a meterstick has a length of 100 cm, how long is the meterstick in inches?

Step 1 Decide which conversion factor to use. You know the length of the meterstick in centimeters, so centimeters are the old units. You want to find the length in inches, so inch is the new unit.

Step 2 Form the conversion factor. Start with the relationship between the old and new units.

$$2.54 \text{ cm} = 1 \text{ inch}$$

Step 3 Form the conversion factor with the old unit (centimeter) on the bottom by dividing both sides by 2.54 cm.

$$1 = \frac{2.54 \text{ cm}}{2.54 \text{ cm}} = \frac{1 \text{ inch}}{2.54 \text{ cm}}$$

Step 4 Multiply the old measurement by the conversion factor.

$$100 \text{ cm} \times \frac{1 \text{ inch}}{2.54 \text{ cm}} = 39.37 \text{ inches}$$

The meterstick is 39.37 inches long.

Example 2 There are 365 days in one year. If a person is 14 years old, what is his or her age in days? (Ignore leap years).

Step 1 Decide which conversion factor to use. You want to convert years to days.

Step 2 Form the conversion factor. Start with the relation between the old and new units.

$$1 \text{ year} = 365 \text{ days}$$

Step 3 Form the conversion factor with the old unit (year) on the bottom by dividing both sides by 1 year.

$$1 = \frac{1 \text{ year}}{1 \text{ year}} = \frac{365 \text{ days}}{1 \text{ year}}$$

Step 4 Multiply the old measurement by the conversion factor:

$$14 \text{ years} \times \frac{365 \text{ days}}{1 \text{ year}} = 5{,}110 \text{ days}$$

The person's age is 5,110 days.

Practice Problem A book has a mass of 2.31 kg. If there are 1,000 g in 1 kg, what is the mass of the book in grams? 2310 g

Using Fractions

A **fraction** is a number that compares a part to the whole. For example, in the fraction $\frac{2}{3}$, the 2 represents the part and the 3 represents the whole. In the fraction $\frac{2}{3}$, the top number, 2, is called the numerator. The bottom number, 3, is called the denominator.

Sometimes fractions are not written in their simplest form. To determine a fraction's **simplest form,** you must find the greatest common factor (GCF) of the numerator and denominator. The greatest common factor is the largest common factor of all the factors the two numbers have in common.

For example, because the number 3 divides into 12 and 30 evenly, it is a common factor of 12 and 30. However, because the number 6 is the largest number that evenly divides into 12 and 30, it is the **greatest common factor.**

After you find the greatest common factor, you can write a fraction in its simplest form. Divide both the numerator and the denominator by the greatest common factor. The number that results is the fraction in its **simplest form.**

Example Twelve of the 20 peaks in a mountain range have elevations over 10,000 m. What fraction of the peaks in the mountain range are over 10,000 m? Write the fraction in simplest form.

Step 1 Write the fraction.

$$\frac{\text{part}}{\text{whole}} = \frac{12}{20}$$

Step 2 To find the GCF of the numerator and denominator, list all of the factors of each number.

Factors of 12: 1, 2, 3, 4, 6, 12 (the numbers that divide evenly into 12)

Factors of 20: 1, 2, 4, 5, 10, 20 (the numbers that divide evenly into 20)

Step 3 List the common factors.

1, 2, 4.

Step 4 Choose the greatest factor in the list of common factors.

The GCF of 12 and 20 is 4.

Step 5 Divide the numerator and denominator by the GCF.

$$\frac{12 \div 4}{20 \div 4} = \frac{3}{5}$$

In the mountain range, $\frac{3}{5}$ of the peaks are over 10,000 m.

Practice Problem There are 90 rides at an amusement park. Of those rides, 66 have a height restriction. What fraction of the rides has a height restriction? Write the fraction in simplest form. $\frac{11}{15}$

Skill Handbooks

Calculating Ratios

A **ratio** is a comparison of two numbers by division.

Ratios can be written 3 to 5 or 3:5. Ratios also can be written as fractions, such as $\frac{3}{5}$. Ratios, like fractions, can be written in simplest form. Recall that a fraction is in **simplest form** when the greatest common factor (GCF) of the numerator and denominator is 1.

Example A particular geologic sample contains 40 kg of shale and 64 kg of granite. What is the ratio of shale to granite as a fraction in simplest form?

Step 1 Write the ratio as a fraction. $\frac{\text{shale}}{\text{granite}} = \frac{40}{64}$

Step 2 Express the fraction in simplest form. The GCF of 40 and 64 is 8.

$$\frac{40}{64} = \frac{40 \div 8}{64 \div 8} = \frac{5}{8}$$

The ratio of shale to granite in the sample is $\frac{5}{8}$.

Practice Problem Two metal rods measure 100 cm and 144 cm in length. What is the ratio of their lengths in simplest fraction form? $\frac{25}{36}$

Using Decimals

A **decimal** is a fraction with a denominator of 10, 100, 1,000, or another power of 10. For example, 0.854 is the same as the fraction $\frac{854}{1,000}$.

In a decimal, the decimal point separates the ones place and the tenths place. For example, 0.27 means twenty-seven hundredths, or $\frac{27}{100}$, where 27 is the **number of units** out of 100 units. Any fraction can be written as a decimal using division.

Example Write $\frac{5}{8}$ as a decimal.

Step 1 Write a division problem with the numerator, 5, as the dividend and the denominator, 8, as the divisor. Write 5 as 5.000.

Step 2 Solve the problem.

$$
\begin{array}{r}
0.625 \\
8{\overline{\smash{\big)}\,5.000}} \\
\underline{4\,8} \\
20 \\
\underline{16} \\
40 \\
\underline{40} \\
0
\end{array}
$$

Therefore, $\frac{5}{8} = 0.625$.

Practice Problem Write $\frac{19}{25}$ as a decimal.

0.76

Using Percentages

The word *percent* means "out of one hundred." A **percent** is a ratio that compares a number to 100. Suppose you read that 77 percent of Earth's surface is covered by water. That is the same as reading that the fraction of Earth's surface covered by water is $\frac{77}{100}$. To express a fraction as a percent, first find an equivalent decimal for the fraction. Then, multiply the decimal by 100 and add the percent symbol. For example, $\frac{1}{2} = 1 \div 2 = 0.5$. Then $0.5 \cdot 100 = 50 = 50\%$.

Example Express $\frac{13}{20}$ as a percent.

Step 1 Find the equivalent decimal for the fraction.

$$
\begin{array}{r}
0.65 \\
20\overline{)13.00} \\
\underline{120} \\
100 \\
\underline{100} \\
0
\end{array}
$$

Step 2 Rewrite the fraction $\frac{13}{20}$ as 0.65.

Step 3 Multiply 0.65 by 100 and add the % sign.

$0.65 \cdot 100 = 65 = 65\%$

So, $\frac{13}{20} = 65\%$.

Practice Problem In one year, 73 of 365 days were rainy in one city. What percent of the days in that city were rainy?   20%

Using Precision and Significant Digits

When you make a **measurement,** the value you record depends on the precision of the measuring instrument. When adding or subtracting numbers with different precision, the answer is rounded to the smallest number of decimal places of any number in the sum or difference. When multiplying or dividing, the answer is rounded to the smallest number of significant figures of any number being multiplied or divided. When counting the number of **significant figures,** all digits are counted except zeros at the end of a number with no decimal such as 2,500, and zeros at the beginning of a decimal such as 0.03020.

Example The lengths 5.28 and 5.2 are measured in meters. Find the sum of these lengths and report the sum using the least precise measurement.

Step 1 Find the sum.

5.28 m	2 digits after the decimal
+ 5.2 m	1 digit after the decimal
10.48 m	

Step 2 Round to one digit after the decimal because the least number of digits after the decimal of the numbers being added is 1.

The sum is 10.5 m.

Practice Problem Multiply the numbers in the example using the rule for multiplying and dividing. Report the answer with the correct number of significant figures.   27 m

Solving One-Step Equations

An **equation** is a statement that two things are equal. For example, $A = B$ is an equation that states that A is equal to B.

Sometimes one side of the equation will contain a **variable** whose value is not known. In the equation $3x = 12$, the variable is x.

The equation is solved when the variable is replaced with a value that makes both sides of the equation equal to each other. For example, the solution of the equation $3x = 12$ is $x = 4$. If the x is replaced with 4, then the equation becomes $3 \cdot 4 = 12$, or $12 = 12$.

To solve an equation such as $8x = 40$, divide both sides of the equation by the number that multiplies the variable.

$$8x = 40$$
$$\frac{8x}{8} = \frac{40}{8}$$
$$x = 5$$

You can check your answer by replacing the variable with your solution and seeing if both sides of the equation are the same.

$$8x = 8 \cdot 5 = 40$$

The left and right sides of the equation are the same, so $x = 5$ is the solution.

Sometimes an equation is written in this way: $a = bc$. This also is called a **formula.** The letters can be replaced by numbers, but the numbers must still make both sides of the equation the same.

Example 1 Solve the equation $10x = 35$.

Step 1 Find the solution by dividing each side of the equation by 10.

$$10x = 35 \qquad \frac{10x}{10} = \frac{35}{10} \qquad x = 3.5$$

Step 2 Check the solution.

$$10x = 35 \qquad 10 \times 3.5 = 35 \qquad 35 = 35$$

Both sides of the equation are equal, so $x = 3.5$ is the solution to the equation.

Example 2 In the formula $a = bc$, find the value of c if $a = 20$ and $b = 2$.

Step 1 Rearrange the formula so the unknown value is by itself on one side of the equation by dividing both sides by b.

$$a = bc$$
$$\frac{a}{b} = \frac{bc}{b}$$
$$\frac{a}{b} = c$$

Step 2 Replace the variables a and b with the values that are given.

$$\frac{a}{b} = c$$
$$\frac{20}{2} = c$$
$$10 = c$$

Step 3 Check the solution.

$$a = bc$$
$$20 = 2 \times 10$$
$$20 = 20$$

Both sides of the equation are equal, so $c = 10$ is the solution when $a = 20$ and $b = 2$.

Practice Problem In the formula $h = gd$, find the value of d if $g = 12.3$ and $h = 17.4$. 1.41

Using Proportions

A **proportion** is an equation that shows that two ratios are equivalent. The ratios $\frac{2}{4}$ and $\frac{5}{10}$ are equivalent, so they can be written as $\frac{2}{4} = \frac{5}{10}$. This equation is an example of a proportion.

When two ratios form a proportion, the **cross products** are equal. To find the cross products in the proportion $\frac{2}{4} = \frac{5}{10}$, multiply the 2 and the 10, and the 4 and the 5. Therefore $2 \cdot 10 = 4 \cdot 5$, or $20 = 20$.

Because you know that both proportions are equal, you can use cross products to find a missing term in a proportion. This is known as **solving the proportion.** Solving a proportion is similar to solving an equation.

Example The heights of a tree and a pole are proportional to the lengths of their shadows. The tree casts a shadow of 24 m at the same time that a 6-m pole casts a shadow of 4 m. What is the height of the tree?

Step 1 Write a proportion.

$$\frac{\text{height of tree}}{\text{height of pole}} = \frac{\text{length of tree's shadow}}{\text{length of pole's shadow}}$$

Step 2 Substitute the known values into the proportion. Let h represent the unknown value, the height of the tree.

$$\frac{h}{6} = \frac{24}{4}$$

Step 3 Find the cross products.

$$h \cdot 4 = 6 \cdot 24$$

Step 4 Simplify the equation.

$$4h = 144$$

Step 5 Divide each side by 4.

$$\frac{4h}{4} = \frac{144}{4}$$

$$h = 36$$

The height of the tree is 36 m.

Practice Problem The ratios of the weights of two objects on the Moon and on Earth are in proportion. A rock weighing 3 N on the Moon weighs 18 N on Earth. How much would a rock that weighs 5 N on the Moon weigh on Earth? 30 N

Using Statistics

Statistics is the branch of mathematics that deals with collecting, analyzing, and presenting data. In statistics, there are three common ways to summarize the data with a single number—the mean, the median, and the mode.

The **mean** of a set of data is the arithmetic average. It is found by adding the numbers in the data set and dividing by the number of items in the set.

The **median** is the middle number in a set of data when the data are arranged in numerical order. If there were an even number of data points, the median would be the mean of the two middle numbers.

The **mode** of a set of data is the number or item that appears most often.

Another number that often is used to describe a set of data is the range. The **range** is the difference between the largest number and the smallest number in a set of data.

A **frequency table** shows how many times each piece of data occurs, usually in a survey. The frequency table below shows the results of a student survey on favorite color.

Color	Tally	Frequency
red	||||	4
blue	﷼	5
black	||	2
green	|||	3
purple	﷼ ||	7
yellow	﷼ |	6

Based on the frequency table data, which color is the favorite?

Example The high temperatures (in °C) on five consecutive days at a desert observation station are 39°, 37°, 44°, 36°, and 44°. Find the mean, median, mode, and range of this set.

To find the mean:

Step 1 Find the sum of the numbers.

$$39 + 37 + 44 + 36 + 44 = 200$$

Step 2 Divide the sum by the number of items, which is 5.

$$200 \div 5 = 40$$

The mean high temperature is 40°C.

To find the median:

Step 1 Arrange the temperatures from least to greatest.

$$36, \ 37, \ \underline{39}, \ 44, \ 44$$

Step 2 Determine the middle temperature.

The median high temperature is 39°C.

To find the mode:

Step 1 Group the numbers that are the same together.

$$44, 44, 36, 37, 39$$

Step 2 Determine the number that occurs most in the set.

$$\underline{44, 44}, 36, 37, 39$$

The mode measure is 44°C.

To find the range:

Step 1 Arrange the temperatures from largest to smallest.

$$44, 44, 39, 37, 36$$

Step 2 Determine the largest and smallest temperature in the set.

$$\underline{44}, 44, 39, 37, \underline{36}$$

Step 3 Find the difference between the largest and smallest temperatures.

$$44 - 36 = 8$$

The range is 8°C.

Practice Problem Find the mean, median, mode, and range for the data set 8, 4, 12, 8, 11, 14, 16.

mean, 10; median, 11; mode, 8; range, 12

Safety in the Science Classroom

1. Always obtain your teacher's permission to begin an investigation.

2. Study the procedure. If you have questions, ask your teacher. Be sure you understand any safety symbols shown on the page.

3. Use the safety equipment provided for you. Goggles and a safety apron should be worn during most investigations.

4. Always slant test tubes away from yourself and others when heating them or adding substances to them.

5. Never eat or drink in the lab, and never use lab glassware as food or drink containers. Never inhale chemicals. Do not taste any substances or draw any material into a tube with your mouth.

6. Report any spill, accident, or injury, no matter how small, immediately to your teacher, then follow his or her instructions.

7. Know the location and proper use of the fire extinguisher, safety shower, fire blanket, first aid kit, and fire alarm.

8. Keep all materials away from open flames. Tie back long hair and tie down loose clothing.

9. If your clothing should catch fire, smother it with the fire blanket, or get under a safety shower. NEVER RUN.

10. If a fire should occur, turn off the gas; then leave the room according to established procedures.

Follow these procedures as you clean up your work area

1. Turn off the water and gas. Disconnect electrical devices.

2. Clean all pieces of equipment and return all materials to their proper places.

3. Dispose of chemicals and other materials as directed by your teacher. Place broken glass and solid substances in the proper containers. Make sure never to discard materials in the sink.

4. Clean your work area. Wash your hands thoroughly after working in the laboratory.

First Aid	
Injury	**Safe Response ALWAYS NOTIFY YOUR TEACHER IMMEDIATELY**
Burns	Apply cold water.
Cuts and Bruises	Stop any bleeding by applying direct pressure. Cover cuts with a clean dressing. Apply ice packs or cold compresses to bruises.
Fainting	Leave the person lying down. Loosen any tight clothing and keep crowds away.
Foreign Matter in Eye	Flush with plenty of water. Use eyewash bottle or fountain.
Poisoning	Note the suspected poisoning agent.
Any Spills on Skin	Flush with large amounts of water or use safety shower.

SI—Metric/English, English/Metric Conversions

	When you want to convert:	To:	Multiply by:
Length	inches	centimeters	2.54
	centimeters	inches	0.39
	yards	meters	0.91
	meters	yards	1.09
	miles	kilometers	1.61
	kilometers	miles	0.62
Mass and Weight*	ounces	grams	28.35
	grams	ounces	0.04
	pounds	kilograms	0.45
	kilograms	pounds	2.2
	tons (short)	tonnes (metric tons)	0.91
	tonnes (metric tons)	tons (short)	1.10
	pounds	newtons	4.45
	newtons	pounds	0.22
Volume	cubic inches	cubic centimeters	16.39
	cubic centimeters	cubic inches	0.06
	liters	quarts	1.06
	quarts	liters	0.95
	gallons	liters	3.78
Area	square inches	square centimeters	6.45
	square centimeters	square inches	0.16
	square yards	square meters	0.83
	square meters	square yards	1.19
	square miles	square kilometers	2.59
	square kilometers	square miles	0.39
	hectares	acres	2.47
	acres	hectares	0.40
Temperature	To convert °Celsius to °Fahrenheit		°C $\times$ 9/5 + 32
	To convert °Fahrenheit to °Celsius		5/9 (°F $-$ 32)

*Weight is measured in standard Earth gravity.

Care and Use of a Microscope

Eyepiece Contains magnifying lenses you look through.

Arm Supports the body tube.

Low-power objective Contains the lens with the lowest power magnification.

Stage clips Hold the microscope slide in place.

Fine adjustment Sharpens the image under high magnification.

Coarse adjustment Focuses the image under low power.

Body tube Connects the eyepiece to the revolving nosepiece.

Revolving nosepiece Holds and turns the objectives into viewing position.

High-power objective Contains the lens with the highest magnification.

Stage Supports the microscope slide.

Light source Provides light that passes upward through the diaphragm, the specimen, and the lenses.

Base Provides support for the microscope.

Caring for a Microscope

1. Always carry the microscope holding the arm with one hand and supporting the base with the other hand.

2. Don't touch the lenses with your fingers.

3. The coarse adjustment knob is used only when looking through the lowest-power objective lens. The fine adjustment knob is used when the high-power objective is in place.

4. Cover the microscope when you store it.

Using a Microscope

1. Place the microscope on a flat surface that is clear of objects. The arm should be toward you.

2. Look through the eyepiece. Adjust the diaphragm so light comes through the opening in the stage.

3. Place a slide on the stage so the specimen is in the field of view. Hold it firmly in place by using the stage clips.

4. Always focus with the coarse adjustment and the low-power objective lens first. After the object is in focus on low power, turn the nosepiece until the high-power objective is in place. Use ONLY the fine adjustment to focus with the high-power objective lens.

Making a Wet-Mount Slide

1. Carefully place the item you want to look at in the center of a clean, glass slide. Make sure the sample is thin enough for light to pass through.

2. Use a dropper to place one or two drops of water on the sample.

3. Hold a clean coverslip by the edges and place it at one edge of the water. Slowly lower the coverslip onto the water until it lies flat.

4. If you have too much water or a lot of air bubbles, touch the edge of a paper towel to the edge of the coverslip to draw off extra water and draw out unwanted air.

Weather Map Symbols

Sample Station Model

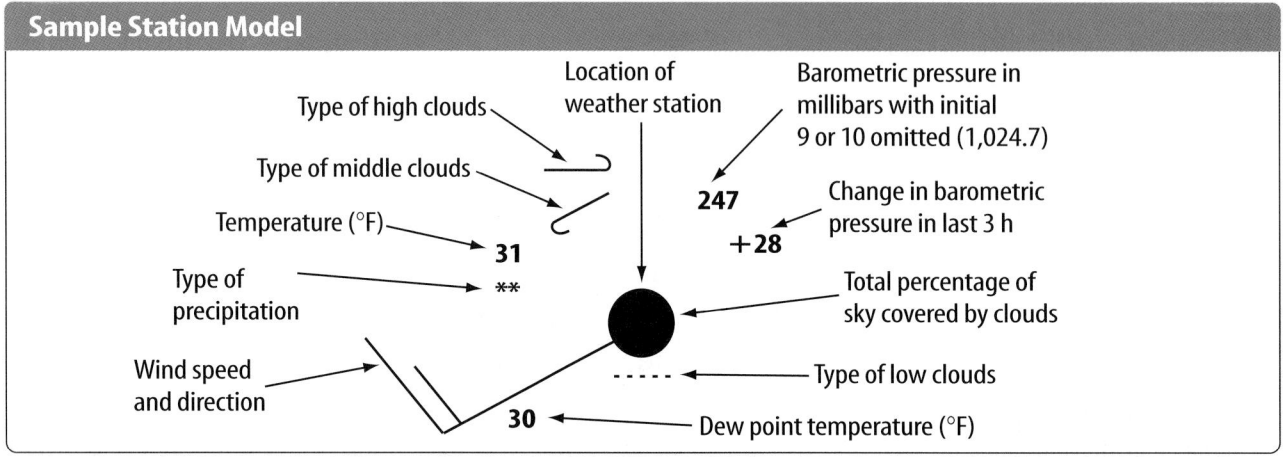

Type of high clouds

Type of middle clouds

Temperature (°F)

Type of precipitation

Wind speed and direction

Location of weather station

Barometric pressure in millibars with initial 9 or 10 omitted (1,024.7)
247

Change in barometric pressure in last 3 h
+28

Total percentage of sky covered by clouds

Type of low clouds

Dew point temperature (°F)
30

31

✱✱

Sample Plotted Report at Each Station

Precipitation		Wind Speed and Direction		Sky Coverage		Some Types of High Clouds	
☰	Fog	◯	0 calm	◯	No cover	⟍⟍	Scattered cirrus
★	Snow	╱	1-2 knots	◍	1/10 or less	⟍⟍	Dense cirrus in patches
●	Rain	╲	3-7 knots	◔	2/10 to 3/10	⟲⟍	Veil of cirrus covering entire sky
⊼	Thunderstorm	╲	8-12 knots	◑	4/10	⟍	Cirrus not covering entire sky
,	Drizzle	╲	13-17 knots	◑	–		
▽	Showers	╲	18-22 knots	◐	6/10		
		╲	23-27 knots	◕	7/10		
		╲	48-52 knots	◑	Overcast with openings		
		1 knot = 1.852 km/h		●	Completely overcast		

Some Types of Middle Clouds		Some Types of Low Clouds		Fronts and Pressure Systems	
∠	Thin altostratus layer	⌒	Cumulus of fair weather	(H) or High (L) or Low	Center of high- or low-pressure system
⫽	Thick altostratus layer	⌣	Stratocumulus	▲▲▲▲	Cold front
⟋	Thin altostratus in patches	- - - - -	Fractocumulus of bad weather	●●●●	Warm front
⟋	Thin altostratus in bands	——	Stratus of fair weather	▲●▲●	Occluded front
				▲⌒▲⌒	Stationary front

Reference Handbook

Topographic Map Symbols

▬▬▬▬	Primary highway, hard surface	⌒⌒	Index contour
▬▬▬▬	Secondary highway, hard surface	··········	Supplementary contour
═══════	Light-duty road, hard or improved surface	⌒⌒	Intermediate contour
=========	Unimproved road	⌒⊂⊃⌒	Depression contours
++++++	Railroad: single track		
╪╪╪╪	Railroad: multiple track	▬ ▬ ▬	Boundaries: national
╪┼╪┼╪	Railroads in juxtaposition	▬ ▬ ▬	State
		▬ ▬ ··	County, parish, municipal
▪▃▆▓	Buildings	▬ ▬ ▬	Civil township, precinct, town, barrio
♫⊞ cem	Schools, church, and cemetery	▬ ·· ▬	Incorporated city, village, town, hamlet
▫▭▨▨	Buildings (barn, warehouse, etc)	▬ · ▬ ··	Reservation, national or state
○ ○	Wells other than water (labeled as to type)	----------	Small park, cemetery, airport, etc.
●●●⊘	Tanks: oil, water, etc. (labeled only if water)	▬ ·· ▬	Land grant
⊙ ⚐	Located or landmark object; windmill	▬▬▬▬▬	Township or range line, U.S. land survey
⚔ ×	Open pit, mine, or quarry; prospect	▬ ▬ ▬ ▬	Township or range line, approximate location
[marsh symbol]	Marsh (swamp)		
[wooded marsh symbol]	Wooded marsh	⌒⌒⌒	Perennial streams
[woods symbol]	Woods or brushwood	→――←	Elevated aqueduct
[vineyard symbol]	Vineyard	○ ⌒	Water well and spring
[inundation symbol]	Land subject to controlled inundation	⌒×⌒	Small rapids
[submerged marsh symbol]	Submerged marsh	⌒≈⌒	Large rapids
[mangrove symbol]	Mangrove	[symbol]	Intermittent lake
[orchard symbol]	Orchard	⌒≈⌒	Intermittent stream
[scrub symbol]	Scrub	→=====←	Aqueduct tunnel
[urban area symbol]	Urban area	[symbol]	Glacier
		⌒↶⌒	Small falls
x7369	Spot elevation	[symbol]	Large falls
670	Water elevation	[symbol]	Dry lake bed

Rocks

Rock Type	Rock Name	Characteristics
Igneous (intrusive)	Granite	Large mineral grains of quartz, feldspar, hornblende, and mica. Usually light in color.
	Diorite	Large mineral grains of feldspar, hornblende, and mica. Less quartz than granite. Intermediate in color.
	Gabbro	Large mineral grains of feldspar, augite, and olivine. No quartz. Dark in color.
Igneous (extrusive)	Rhyolite	Small mineral grains of quartz, feldspar, hornblende, and mica, or no visible grains. Light in color.
	Andesite	Small mineral grains of feldspar, hornblende, and mica or no visible grains. Intermediate in color.
	Basalt	Small mineral grains of feldspar, augite, and olivine or no visible grains. No quartz. Dark in color.
	Obsidian	Glassy texture. No visible grains. Volcanic glass. Fracture looks like broken glass.
	Pumice	Frothy texture. Floats in water. Usually light in color.
Sedimentary (detrital)	Conglomerate	Coarse grained. Gravel or pebble size grains.
	Sandstone	Sand-sized grains 1/16 to 2 mm.
	Siltstone	Grains are smaller than sand but larger than clay.
	Shale	Smallest grains. Often dark in color. Usually platy.
Sedimentary (chemical or organic)	Limestone	Major mineral is calcite. Usually forms in oceans, lakes, and caves. Often contains fossils.
	Coal	Occurs in swampy areas. Compacted layers of organic material, mainly plant remains.
Sedimentary (chemical)	Rock Salt	Commonly forms by the evaporation of seawater.
Metamorphic (foliated)	Gneiss	Banding due to alternate layers of different minerals, of different colors. Parent rock often is granite.
	Schist	Parallel arrangement of sheetlike minerals, mainly micas. Forms from different parent rocks.
	Phyllite	Shiny or silky appearance. May look wrinkled. Common parent rocks are shale and slate.
	Slate	Harder, denser, and shinier than shale. Common parent rock is shale.
Metamorphic (non-foliated)	Marble	Calcite or dolomite. Common parent rock is limestone.
	Soapstone	Mainly of talc. Soft with greasy feel.
	Quartzite	Hard with interlocking quartz crystals. Common parent rock is sandstone.

Minerals

Mineral (formula)	Color	Streak	Hardness	Breakage Pattern	Uses and Other Properties
Graphite (C)	black to gray	black to gray	1–1.5	basal cleavage (scales)	pencil lead, lubricants for locks, rods to control some small nuclear reactions, battery poles
Galena (PbS)	gray	gray to black	2.5	cubic cleavage perfect	source of lead, used for pipes, shields for X rays, fishing equipment sinkers
Hematite (Fe_2O_3)	black or reddish-brown	reddish-brown	5.5–6.5	irregular fracture	source of iron; converted to pig iron, made into steel
Magnetite (Fe_3O_4)	black	black	6	conchoidal fracture	source of iron, attracts a magnet
Pyrite (FeS_2)	light, brassy, yellow	greenish-black	6–6.5	uneven fracture	fool's gold
Talc ($Mg_3 Si_4O_{10}$ $(OH)_2$)	white, greenish	white	1	cleavage in one direction	used for talcum powder, sculptures, paper, and tabletops
Gypsum ($CaSO_4 \cdot 2H_2O$)	colorless, gray, white, brown	white	2	basal cleavage	used in plaster of paris and dry wall for building construction
Sphalerite (ZnS)	brown, reddish-brown, greenish	light to dark brown	3.5–4	cleavage in six directions	main ore of zinc; used in paints, dyes, and medicine
Muscovite (KAl_3Si_3 $O_{10}(OH)_2$)	white, light gray, yellow, rose, green	colorless	2–2.5	basal cleavage	occurs in large, flexible plates; used as an insulator in electrical equipment, lubricant
Biotite ($K(Mg,Fe)_3$ $(AlSi_3O_{10})$ $(OH)_2$)	black to dark brown	colorless	2.5–3	basal cleavage	occurs in large, flexible plates
Halite (NaCl)	colorless, red, white, blue	colorless	2.5	cubic cleavage	salt; soluble in water; a preservative

Minerals

Mineral (formula)	Color	Streak	Hardness	Breakage Pattern	Uses and Other Properties
Calcite ($CaCO_3$)	colorless, white, pale blue	colorless, white	3	cleavage in three directions	fizzes when HCl is added; used in cements and other building materials
Dolomite ($CaMg(CO_3)_2$)	colorless, white, pink, green, gray, black	white	3.5–4	cleavage in three directions	concrete and cement; used as an ornamental building stone
Fluorite (CaF_2)	colorless, white, blue, green, red, yellow, purple	colorless	4	cleavage in four directions	used in the manufacture of optical equipment; glows under ultraviolet light
Hornblende ($(CaNa)_{2-3}(Mg,Al,Fe)_5-(Al,Si)_2 Si_6O_{22}(OH)_2$)	green to black	gray to white	5–6	cleavage in two directions	will transmit light on thin edges; 6-sided cross section
Feldspar ($KAlSi_3O_8$) ($NaAl Si_3O_8$), ($CaAl_2Si_2 O_8$)	colorless, white to gray, green	colorless	6	two cleavage planes meet at 90° angle	used in the manufacture of ceramics
Augite ($(Ca,Na)(Mg,Fe,Al)(Al,Si)_2 O_6$)	black	colorless	6	cleavage in two directions	square or 8-sided cross section
Olivine ($(Mg,Fe)_2 SiO_4$)	olive, green	none	6.5–7	conchoidal fracture	gemstones, refractory sand
Quartz (SiO_2)	colorless, various colors	none	7	conchoidal fracture	used in glass manufacture, electronic equipment, radios, computers, watches, gemstones

Reference Handbook

This glossary defines each key term that appears in bold type in the text. It also shows the chapter, section, and page number where you can find the word used.

A

abiotic (ay bi AH tihk) **factor:** any nonliving part of the environment, such as water, sunlight, temperature, and air. (Chap. 8, Sec. 1, p. 216)

abrasion: a form of erosion that can make pits in rocks and produce smooth, polished surfaces. (Chap. 16, Sec. 2, p. 478)

acceleration: change in velocity divided by the amount of time needed for the change to occur; takes place when an object speeds up, slows down, or changes direction. (Chap. 19, Sec. 1, p. 559)

acid rain: damaging rain or snow formed when gases released by burning oil and coal mix with water in the air. (Chap. 9, Sec. 1, p. 246)

aerobe (AY rohb): any organism that uses oxygen for respiration. (Chap. 3, Sec. 1, p. 62)

air mass: large body of air that has the same characteristics of temperature and moisture content as the part of Earth's surface over which it formed. (Chap. 11, Sec. 2, p. 318)

algae (AL jee): chlorophyll-containing, plantlike protists that produce oxygen as a result of photosynthesis. (Chap. 4, Sec. 1, p. 89)

alternating current (AC): electric current that changes its direction many times each second. (Chap. 22, Sec. 2, p. 666)

amniotic (am nee AH tihk) **egg:** behavioral adaptation of reptiles that allows them to reproduce on land; encloses the embryo within a moist environment protected by a leathery shell and has a yolk that supplies the embryo with food. (Chap. 7, Sec. 2, p. 191)

anaerobe (AN uh rohb): any organism that is able live without oxygen. (Chap. 3, Sec. 1, p. 62)

angiosperms: flowering vascular plants that produce a fruit containing one or more seeds; monocots and dicots. (Chap. 5, Sec. 3, p. 135)

antibiotics: chemicals produced by some bacteria that are used to limit the growth of other bacteria. (Chap. 3, Sec. 2, p. 67)

appendage (uh PEN dihj): structure such as a claw, leg, or antenna that grows from the body. (Chap. 6, Sec. 4, p. 164)

arthropod (AR thruh pahd): bilaterally symmetrical animal with jointed appendages, a protective exoskeleton, and a segmented body. (Chap. 6, Sec. 4, p. 164)

ascus (AS kus): saclike, spore-producing structure of sac fungi. (Chap. 4, Sec. 2, p. 102)

astronomical (as truh NAHM ih kul) **unit:** unit of measure that equals 150 million km, which is the mean distance from Earth to the Sun. (Chap. 17, Sec. 2, p. 499)

atmosphere: Earth's air, which is made up of a thin layer of gases, solids, and liquids; forms a protective layer around the planet and is divided into five distinct layers. (Chap. 10, Sec. 1, p. 282)

aurora: southern and northern lights that appear when charged particles trapped in the magnetosphere collide with Earth's atmosphere above the poles. (Chap. 22, Sec. 2, p. 665)

average speed: rate of motion calculated by dividing the distance traveled by the amount of time it takes to travel that distance. (Chap. 19, Sec. 1, p. 556)

English Glossary

B
---

bacteria: smallest organisms on Earth, each of which is made up of only one cell. (Chap. 2, Sec. 1, p. 39)

basidium (buh SIHD ee uhm): club-shaped, reproductive structure in which club fungi produce spores. (Chap. 4, Sec. 2, p. 102)

binomial nomenclature (bi NOH mee ul NOH mun klay chur): two-word naming system that gives all organisms their scientific name. (Chap. 1, Sec. 4, p. 24)

biogenesis (bi oh JEN uh suhs): theory that living things come only from other living things. (Chap. 1, Sec. 3, p. 19)

biosphere (BI uh sfihr): part of Earth that supports life—the top part of Earth's crust, all the waters covering Earth's surface, and the surrounding atmosphere; includes all biomes, ecosystems, communities, and populations. (Chap. 8, Sec. 1, p. 221)

biotic (bi AH tihk) **factor:** any living or once-living organism in the environment. (Chap. 8, Sec. 1, p. 216)

blizzard: winter storm that lasts at least three hours with temperatures of $-12°C$ or below, poor visibility, and winds of at least 51 km/h. (Chap. 11, Sec. 2, p. 325)

boiling point: temperature at which a substance in a liquid state becomes a gas. (Chap. 18, Sec. 1, p. 533)

budding: form of asexual reproduction in which a new, genetically-identical organism forms on the side of its parent. (Chap. 4, Sec. 2, p. 102)

C
---

cambium (KAM bee um): vascular tissue that produces xylem and phloem cells as a plant grows. (Chap. 5, Sec. 3, p. 133)

carnivore: meat-eating animal with sharp canine teeth specialized to rip and tear flesh. (Chap. 7, Sec. 4, p. 198)

cartilage (KAR tuhl ihj): tough, flexible tissue similar to bone but is softer and less brittle. (Chap. 7, Sec. 1, p. 184)

catalyst (KAT ul ust): substance that changes the rate of a chemical reaction without any change to its own structure. (Chap. 20, Sec. 3, p. 608)

cell: smallest unit of an organism that can carry on life functions. (Chap. 1, Sec. 2, p. 14)

cell membrane: flexible structure that holds a cell together, forms a boundary between the cell and its environment, and helps control what enters and leaves the cell. (Chap. 2, Sec. 1, p. 41)

cellulose (SEL yuh lohs): chemical compound made out of sugar; forms tangled fibers in the cell walls of many plants and provides structure and support. (Chap. 5, Sec. 1, p. 120)

cell wall: structure of plants, algae, fungi, and many types of bacteria that supports and protects the cell membrane. (Chap. 2, Sec. 1, p. 41)

chemical change: change in which the identity of a substance changes due to its chemical properties and forms a new substance or substances. (Chap. 18, Sec. 2, p. 541)

chemical property: any characteristic, such as the ability to burn, that allows a substance to undergo a change that results in a new substance. (Chap. 18, Sec. 2, p. 540)

chemical weathering: occurs when the chemical composition of a rock changes. (Chap. 16, Sec. 1, p.468)

chemosynthesis: process that occurs in deep ocean water where sunlight does not penetrate, in which bacteria make food from dissolved sulfur compounds. (Chap. 12, Sec. 4, p. 357)

chlorofluorocarbons (CFCs): group of chemical compounds used in refrigerators, air conditioners, foam packaging, and aerosol sprays that may enter the atmosphere and destroy ozone. (Chap. 10, Sec. 1, p. 288)

chloroplast (KLOR uh plast): green organelle in a plant's leaf cells where most photosynthesis takes place. (Chap. 2, Sec. 1, p. 43)

chordate (KOR dayt): animal that at some time in its development has a notochord, a nerve cord, and gill slits. (Chap. 7, Sec. 1, p. 182)

cilia (SIHL ee uh): short, threadlike structures that extend from the cell membrane of a ciliate and allow the organism to move quickly. (Chap. 4, Sec. 1, p. 93)

circuit: closed conducting loop through which electric current can flow. (Chap. 21, Sec. 2, p. 631)

closed circulatory system: a type of blood-circulation system in which blood is transported through blood vessels rather than surrounding the organs. (Chap. 6, Sec. 3, p. 160)

cnidarian (NIH dar ee un): radially symmetrical, hollow-bodied animal with two cell layers organized into tissues. (Chap. 6, Sec. 2, p. 154)

comet: large body of frozen ice and rock that travels toward the center of the solar system; may originate in the Oort Cloud, and develops a bright, glowing tail as it approaches the Sun. (Chap. 17, Sec. 2, p. 504)

community: all of the populations of different species in a given area that interact in some way and depend on one another for food, shelter, and other needs. (Chap. 8, Sec. 1, p. 220)

compound machine: a combination of simple machines. (Chap. 19, Sec. 3, p. 572)

condensation: process in which water vapor changes to a liquid. (Chap. 10, Sec. 2, p. 293)

conduction (kun DUK shun): transfer of energy by collisions between the atoms in a material. (Chap. 10, Sec. 2, p. 292) (Chap. 20, Sec. 2, p. 600)

conductor: material, such as copper or silver, through which electrons can easily move. (Chap. 21, Sec. 1, p. 628)

conic projection: map made by projecting points and lines from a globe onto a cone. (Chap. 15, Sec. 3, p. 449)

conservation: careful use of resources so that damage to the environment is reduced. (Chap. 9, Sec. 4, p. 265)

conservation of mass: states that the mass of the products of a chemical change is always the same as the mass of what you started with. (Chap. 18, Sec. 2, p. 545)

constellation (kahn stuh LAY shun): group of stars that forms a pattern in the sky and can be named after a real or imaginary animal, object, or person. (Chap. 17, Sec. 3, p. 506)

consumer: organism that gets its energy from eating producers. (Chap. 12, Sec. 4, p. 357)

contour feather: strong, lightweight feather that gives a bird its shape and coloring and can help the bird steer, attract a mate, and avoid predators. (Chap. 7, Sec. 3, p. 195)

contour line: line on a map that connects points of equal elevation. (Chap. 15, Sec. 3, p. 450)

control: standard to which the outcome of a test is compared. (Chap. 1, Sec. 1, p. 9)

convection (kun VEK shun): transfer of heat that occurs when particles move between objects or areas of different temperature. (Chap. 10, Sec. 2, p. 292) (Chap. 20, Sec. 2, p. 602)

Coriolis (kohr ee OH lus) **effect:** causes moving air and water to turn left in the southern hemisphere and turn right in the northern hemisphere due to Earth's rotation. (Chap. 10, Sec. 3, p. 296)

creep: the name for a process in which sediment move slowly downhill. (Chap. 16, Sec. 2, p. 475)

crystal: solid material with atoms arranged in a repeating pattern. (Chap. 13, Sec. 1, p. 378)

cuticle (KYEWT ih kul): waxy, protective layer that covers the stems, leaves, and flowers of many plants and helps prevent water loss. (Chap. 5, Sec. 1, p. 120)

cytoplasm (SI tuh pla zum): gelatinlike substance inside the cell membrane that contains water, chemicals, and cell parts. (Chap. 2, Sec. 1, p. 41)

D

decomposer: organism that breaks down tissue and releases nutrients and carbon dioxide back into the ecosystem. (Chap. 12, Sec. 4, p. 357)

deflation: erosion of the land by wind. (Chap. 16, Sec. 2, p. 478)

density: measurable physical property that can be found by dividing the mass of an object by its volume. (Chap. 18, Sec. 1, p. 530)

density current: forms when more dense seawater sinks beneath less dense seawater. (Chap. 12, Sec. 2, p. 348)

dew point: temperature at which air is saturated and condensation forms. (Chap. 11, Sec. 1, p. 313)

dicot: angiosperm with two cotyledons inside its seed, flower parts in multiples of four or five, and vascular bundles in rings. (Chap. 5, Sec. 3, p. 136)

down feather: fluffy feather that traps and keeps air warm against a bird's body. (Chap. 7, Sec. 3, p. 195)

E

earthquake: vibrations produced when rocks break along a fault. (Chap. 14, Sec. 1, p. 409)

eclipse (ih KLIHPS): event that occurs when the Moon moves between the Sun and Earth (solar eclipse), or when Earth moves between the Sun and the Moon (lunar eclipse), and casts a shadow. (Chap. 17, Sec. 1, p. 495)

ecology: study of all the interactions among organisms and their environment. (Chap. 8, Sec. 1, p. 216)

ecosystem: all of the communities in a given area and the abiotic factors that affect them. (Chap. 8, Sec. 1, p. 220) (Chap. 12, Sec. 4, p. 357)

ectotherm (EK tuh thurm): cold-blooded animal whose body temperature changes with the temperature of its surrounding environment. (Chap. 7, Sec. 1, p. 183)

electric current: flow of charge—either flowing electrons or flowing ions—through a conductor. (Chap. 21, Sec. 2, p. 631)

electric discharge: rapid movement of excess charge from one place to another. (Chap. 21, Sec. 1, p. 629)

electric field: field through which electric charges exert a force on each other. (Chap. 21, Sec. 1, p. 627)

electric force: attractive or repulsive force exerted by all charged objects on each other. (Chap. 21, Sec. 1, p. 627)

electric power: rate at which an electric appliance converts electrical energy into another form of energy; usage is measured by electric meters in kWh. (Chap. 21, Sec. 3, p. 640)

electromagnet: magnet created by wrapping a current-carrying wire around an iron core. (Chap. 22, Sec. 2, p. 661)

endospore: thick-walled, protective structure produced by a pathogen when conditions are unfavorable for survival. (Chap. 3, Sec. 2, p. 71)

endotherm (EN duh thurm): warm-blooded animal whose body temperature does not change with its surrounding environment. (Chap. 7, Sec. 1, p. 183)

endothermic (en duh THUR mihk) **reaction:** chemical reaction that absorbs energy. (Chap. 20, Sec. 3, p. 606)

energy: ability to cause change; can change the speed, direction, shape, or temperature of an object. (Chap. 20, Sec. 1, p. 588)

epicenter (EP ih sen tur): point on Earth's surface directly above an earthquake's focus. (Chap. 14, Sec. 2, p. 413)

equator: imaginary line that wraps around Earth at 0° latitude, halfway between the north and south poles. (Chap. 15, Sec. 2, p. 444)

erosion: the wearing away and removal of rock material. (Chap. 16, Sec. 2, p. 473)

estivation (es tuh VAY shun): period of hot, dry weather inactivity; in amphibians, involves moving to cooler, more humid areas underground. (Chap. 7, Sec. 2, p. 187)

exoskeleton: rigid, protective body covering of an arthropod that supports the body and reduces water loss. (Chap. 6, Sec. 4, p. 164)

exothermic (ek soh THUR mihk) **reaction:** chemical reaction that releases energy. (Chap. 20, Sec. 3, p. 607)

extrusive (ehk STREW sihv): igneous rocks that form when melted rock cools quickly on Earth's surface. (Chap. 13, Sec. 2, p. 385)

F

fault: surface along which rocks move when they pass their elastic limit and break. (Chap. 14, Sec. 1, p. 408)

fault-block mountains: mountains formed from huge, tilted blocks of rock that are separated from surrounding rocks by faults. (Chap. 15, Sec. 1, p. 442)

fission: simplest form of asexual reproduction in which two new cells are produced with genetic material identical to each other and identical to the previous cell. (Chap. 3, Sec. 1, p. 62)

flagella: whiplike tails of many bacteria that help them move around in moist conditions. (Chap. 3, Sec. 1, p. 61)

flagellum: long, thin, whiplike structure of some protists that helps them move through moist or wet surroundings. (Chap. 4, Sec. 1, p. 90)

focus: in an earthquake, the point below Earth's surface where energy is released in the form of seismic waves. (Chap. 14, Sec. 2, p. 412)

fog: a stratus cloud that forms when air is cooled to its dew point near the ground. (Chap. 11, Sec. 1, p. 315)

folded mountains: mountains formed when horizontal rock layers are squeezed from opposite sides, causing them to buckle and fold. (Chap. 15, Sec. 1, p. 441)

foliated (FOH lee ay tud): metamorphic rocks with visible layers of minerals. (Chap. 13, Sec. 3, p. 394)

food chain: model that describes how energy in the form of food passes from one organism to another. (Chap. 8, Sec. 3, p. 228) (Chap. 12, Sec. 4, p. 358)

food web: model that describes how energy in the form of food moves through a community; a series of overlapping food chains. (Chap. 8, Sec. 3, p. 230)

force: a push or a pull; SI unit is the newton. (Chap. 19, Sec. 2, p. 562)

fossil fuel: nonrenewable energy resource, such as coal, oil, and gas, formed from the remains of ancient plants and animals. (Chap. 9, Sec. 1, p. 244)

friction: force that resists motion between two touching surfaces and always acts opposite to the direction of motion. (Chap. 19, Sec. 2, p. 565)

front: boundary between two air masses with different temperatures, density, or moisture; can be cold, warm, occluded, and stationary. (Chap. 11, Sec. 2, p. 319)

G

galaxy (GA luk see): group of stars, gas, and dust held together by gravity. (Chap. 17, Sec. 3, p. 509)

gem: rare, valuable mineral that can be cut and polished. (Chap. 13, Sec. 1, p. 382)

generator: device that uses a magnetic field to turn kinetic energy into electrical energy and can produce direct current and alternating current. (Chap. 22, Sec. 2, p. 666)

genus: first word of the two-word scientific name used to identify a group of similar species. (Chap. 1, Sec. 4, p. 24)

geothermal energy: heat energy from below Earth's surface that can be used to generate electricity. (Chap. 9, Sec. 2, p. 254)

gill: organ that allows a water-dwelling animal to exchange carbon dioxide for dissolved oxygen in the water. (Chap. 6, Sec. 3, p. 158)

groundwater: water that soaks into the ground and collects in small spaces between bits of soil and rock. (Chap. 9, Sec. 3, p. 258)

guard cells: pairs of cells that surround stomata and control their opening and closing. (Chap. 5, Sec. 3, p. 131)

gymnosperms: vascular plants that do not flower, generally have needlelike or scalelike leaves, and produce seeds that are not protected by fruit; conifers, cycads, ginkgoes, and gnetophytes. (Chap. 5, Sec. 3, p. 134)

H
---

habitat: place where an organism lives. (Chap. 8, Sec. 2, p. 227)

heat: transfer of energy from one object to another due to a difference in temperature; flows from warmer objects to cooler objects. (Chap. 20, Sec. 2, p. 599)

herbivore: plant-eating mammal with incisors specialized to cut vegetation and large, flat molars to grind it. (Chap. 7, Sec. 4, p. 198)

hibernation: period of cold weather inactivity; in amphibians, involves burying themselves in mud or leaves. (Chap. 7, Sec. 2, p. 187)

homeostasis: ability of an organism to keep proper internal conditions no matter what external stimuli are occurring. (Chap. 1, Sec. 2, p. 15)

humidity: amount of water vapor held in the air. (Chap. 11, Sec. 1, p. 312)

hurricane: large, severe storm that forms over tropical oceans, has winds of at least 120 km/h, and loses power when it reaches land. (Chap. 11, Sec. 2, p. 324)

hydroelectric power: electricity produced from moving water. (Chap. 9, Sec. 2, p. 253)

hydrosphere: all the water on Earth's surface. (Chap. 10, Sec. 2, p. 293)

hyphae (HI fee): mass of many-celled, threadlike tubes forming the body of a fungus. (Chap. 4, Sec. 2, p. 100)

hypothesis: prediction that can be tested. (Chap. 1, Sec. 1, p. 8)

I
---

igneous (IHG nee us) **rock:** intrusive or extrusive rock that is produced when melted rock from inside Earth cools and hardens. (Chap. 13, Sec. 2, p. 385)

inclined plane: a sloped surface. (Chap. 19, Sec. 3, p. 575)

inertia: tendency to resist a change in motion. (Chap. 19, Sec. 2, p. 565)

instantaneous speed: speed of an object at any given time. (Chap. 19, Sec. 1, p. 557)

insulator: material, such as wood or glass, through which electrons cannot easily move. (Chap. 21, Sec. 1, p. 628)

intrusive (ihn TREW sihv): igneous rocks that form when melted rock cools slowly and hardens underneath Earth's surface. (Chap. 13, Sec. 2, p. 385)

invertebrate (ihn VUR tuh brayt): an animal without a backbone. (Chap. 6, Sec. 1, p. 152)

ion (I ahn): a positively or negatively charged atom. (Chap. 21, Sec. 1, p. 624)

ionosphere (i AHN uh sfir): layer of electrically-charged particles in the thermosphere that absorbs AM radio waves during the day and reflects them back at night. (Chap. 10, Sec. 1, p. 285)

isobars: lines drawn on a weather map that connect points having equal atmospheric pressure; also indicate the location of high-pressure and low-pressure areas and can show wind speed. (Chap. 11, Sec. 3, p. 327)

isotherm (I suh thurm): line drawn on a weather map that connects points having equal temperature. (Chap. 11, Sec. 3, p. 327)

J

jet stream: narrow belt of strong winds that blows near the top of the troposphere. (Chap. 10, Sec. 3, p. 298)

K

kinetic (kih NET ihk) **energy:** energy an object has due to its motion. (Chap. 20, Sec. 1, p. 590)

kingdom: first and largest category used to classify organisms. (Chap. 1, Sec. 4, p. 23)

L

land breeze: movement of air from land to sea at night, created when cool, dense air from the land forces warm air up over the sea. (Chap. 10, Sec. 3, p. 299)

latitude: distance in degrees north or south of the equator. (Chap. 15, Sec. 2, p. 444)

law: statement about how things work in nature that seems to be true all the time. (Chap. 1, Sec. 1, p. 10)

law of conservation of energy: states that energy cannot be created or destroyed, but can only be transformed from one form into another. (Chap. 20, Sec. 1, p. 594)

lever: a rod or plank that pivots about a fixed point. (Chap. 19, Sec. 3, p. 574)

lichen (LI kun): organism made up of a fungus and a green alga or a cyanobacterium. (Chap. 4, Sec. 2, p. 104)

light-year: about 9.5 million km—the distance that light travels in one year—which is used to measure large distances between stars or galaxies. (Chap. 17, Sec. 3, p. 512)

limiting factor: any biotic or abiotic factor that limits the number of individuals in a population. (Chap. 8, Sec. 2, p. 225)

liquefaction: occurs when wet soil acts more like a liquid during an earthquake. (Chap. 14, Sec. 3, p. 423)

longitude: distance in degrees east or west of the prime meridian. (Chap. 15, Sec. 2, p. 445)

M

magnetic domain: group of atoms whose fields point in the same direction. (Chap. 22, Sec. 1, p. 656)

magnetic field: area surrounding a magnet through which magnetic force is exerted and that extends between a magnet's north and south poles. (Chap. 22, Sec. 1, p. 655)

magnetosphere (mag NEH tuh sfir): magnetic field surrounding Earth that deflects most of the charged particles flowing from the Sun. (Chap. 22, Sec. 1, p. 657)

magnitude: measure of the energy released during an earthquake. (Chap. 14, Sec. 3, p. 422)

mantle: thin layer of tissue that covers a mollusk's body and that can secrete a shell. (Chap. 6, Sec. 3, p. 158)

map legend: explains the meaning of symbols used on a map. (Chap. 15, Sec. 3, p. 452)

map scale: relationship between distances on a map and distances on Earth's surface that can be represented as a ratio or as a small bar divided into sections. (Chap. 15, Sec. 3, p. 452)

marsupial: mammal that gives birth to incompletely developed young that finish developing in their mother's pouch. (Chap. 7, Sec. 4, p. 200)

mass movement: when gravity alone causes rock or sediment to move down a slope. (Chap. 16, Sec. 2, p. 473)

matter: anything that has mass and takes up space. (Chap. 18, Sec. 1, p. 529)

mechanical advantage: number of times a machine multiplies the effort force you apply to it. (Chap. 19, Sec. 3, p. 572)

mechanical weathering: breaks rocks into smaller pieces without changing them chemically. (Chap. 16, Sec. 1, p. 466)

medusa (mih DEW suh): free-swimming, bell-shaped body form in the life cycle of a cnidarian. (Chap. 6, Sec. 2, p. 155)

melting point: temperature at which a solid becomes a liquid. (Chap. 18, Sec. 1, p. 533)

metamorphic (me tuh MOR fihk) **rock:** new rock that forms when existing rock is heated or squeezed. (Chap. 13, Sec. 3, p. 393)

metamorphosis (me tuh MOR fuh sus): change of body form that can be complete (egg, larva, pupa, adult) or incomplete (egg, nymph, adult). (Chap. 6, Sec. 4, p. 165)

meteorite: any space fragment that survives its plunge through the atmosphere and lands on Earth's surface. (Chap. 17, Sec. 2, p. 505)

meteorologist (meet ee uh RAHL uh jist): studies weather and uses information from Doppler radar, weather satellites, computers and other instruments to make weather maps and provide forecasts. (Chap. 11, Sec. 3, p. 326)

mineral (MIHN uh ruhl): inorganic, solid material found in nature that always has the same chemical makeup, atoms arranged in an orderly pattern, and properties such as cleavage and fracture, color, hardness, and streak and luster. (Chap. 13, Sec. 1, p. 376)

mitochondria (mi tuh KAHN dree uh): cell organelles where cellular respiration takes place. (Chap. 2, Sec. 1, p. 42)

mollusk (MAH lusks): soft-bodied, bilaterally symmetrical invertebrate with a large, muscular foot, a mantle, and an open circulatory system; usually has a shell. (Chap. 6, Sec. 3, p. 158)

monocot: angiosperm with one cotyledon inside its seed, flower parts arranged in multiples of three, and vascular tissues in bundles scattered throughout the stem. (Chap. 5, Sec. 3, p. 136)

monotreme: mammal that lays eggs with tough, leathery shells instead of giving birth to live young. (Chap. 7, Sec. 4, p. 199)

motor: device that transforms electrical energy into kinetic energy. (Chap. 22, Sec. 2, p. 664)

mycorrhizae (mi kuh RI zee): network of hyphae and plant roots that helps plants absorb water and minerals from soil. (Chap. 4, Sec. 2, p. 104)

N

nekton: marine animals, such as fish and turtles, that actively swim in ocean waters. (Chap. 12, Sec. 4, p. 356)

niche (NICH): role of an organism in the ecosystem, including what it eats, how it interacts with other organisms, and how it gets its food. (Chap. 8, Sec. 2, p. 227)

nitrogen-fixing bacteria: bacteria that convert nitrogen in the air into forms that can be used by plants and animals. (Chap. 3, Sec. 2, p. 68)

nonfoliated: metamorphic rocks that lack distinct layers or bands. (Chap. 13, Sec. 3, p. 394)

nonpoint sources: pollution sources that come from many different places, such as industries, homes, and farms, and are difficult to trace to their origin. (Chap. 9, Sec. 3, p. 259)

nonrenewable: energy resources that cannot be replaced by natural processes in less than 100 years. (Chap. 9, Sec. 1, p. 248)

nonvascular plant: plant that absorbs water and other substances directly through its cell walls instead of through tubelike structures. (Chap. 5, Sec. 1, p. 123)

normal fault: break in rock caused by tension forces, where rock above the fault surface moves down relative to the rock below the fault surface. (Chap. 14, Sec. 1, p. 410)

nuclear energy: energy produced by splitting the nuclei of certain elements. (Chap. 9, Sec. 2, p. 255)

nucleus (NEW klee us): cell organelle that contains the hereditary material. (Chap. 2, Sec. 1, p. 42)

O

Ohm's law: relationship among voltage, current, and resistance in a circuit. (Chap. 21, Sec. 3, p. 637)

omnivore: plant-eating and meat-eating animal with incisors specialized to cut vegetables, premolars to chew meat, and molars to grind food. (Chap. 7, Sec. 4, p. 198)

open circulatory system: a type of blood-circulation system that lacks blood vessels and in which blood washes over the organs. (Chap. 6, Sec. 3, p. 159)

orbit: regular, curved path followed by Earth as it moves around the Sun. (Chap. 17, Sec. 1, p. 493)

ore: mineral resource that can be mined at a profit. (Chap. 9, Sec. 4, p. 266) (Chap. 13, Sec. 1, p. 383)

organ (OR gun): structure made of two or more different tissue types that work together to do a certain job. (Chap. 2, Sec. 2, p. 49)

organelles (or guh NELZ): specialized cell parts that perform a cell's activities. (Chap. 2, Sec. 1, p. 41)

organism: any living things that are made of cells, use energy, reproduce, respond, and grow and develop. (Chap. 1, Sec. 2, p. 14)

organ system: group of organs that work together to perform a certain job. (Chap. 2, Sec. 2, p. 49)

ozone layer: layer of the stratosphere with a high concentration of ozone; absorbs most of the Sun's harmful ultraviolet radiation. (Chap. 10, Sec. 1, p. 288)

P

parallel circuit: circuit that has more than one path for electric current to follow. (Chap. 21, Sec. 3, p. 639)

pathogen: disease-producing organism. (Chap. 3, Sec. 2, p. 71)

phloem (FLOH em): vascular tissue that forms tubes that transport dissolved sugar throughout a plant. (Chap. 5, Sec. 3, p. 133)

photosynthesis (foh toh SIHN thuh sus): process by which plants, algae, and many types of bacteria make their own food. (Chap. 2, Sec. 1, p. 43) (Chap. 12, Sec. 1, p. 343)

phylogeny (fi LAH juh nee): evolutionary history of an organism; used today to group organisms into six kingdoms. (Chap. 1, Sec. 4, p. 23)

physical change: change in which the properties of a substance change but the identity of the substance always remains the same. (Chap. 18, Sec. 1, p. 529)

physical property: any characteristic of a material, such as state, color, and volume, that can be observed or measured without changing or attempting to change the material. (Chap. 18, Sec. 1, p. 528)

pioneer species: first organisms to grow in new or disturbed areas; break down rock and build up decaying plant material so that other plants can grow. (Chap. 5, Sec. 2, p. 125)

placental: mammal whose young develops inside the female uterus until it is fully formed and ready to be born; has a placenta—a saclike organ—which supplies the embryo with food and oxygen and removes wastes. (Chap. 7, Sec. 4, p. 200)

plain: large, flat landform that often has thick, fertile soil and is usually found in the interior region of a continent. (Chap. 15, Sec. 1, p. 438)

plankton: tiny marine organisms, such as diatoms, that float in the surface waters of every ocean. (Chap. 12, Sec. 4, p. 355)

plateau (pla TOH): flat, raised landform made up of nearly horizontal rocks that have been uplifted. (Chap. 15, Sec. 1, p. 440)

point source: a single, identifiable source of pollution. (Chap. 9, Sec. 3, p. 259)

pollution: harmful waste products, chemicals, and substances in the environment. (Chap. 9, Sec. 1, p. 246)

polyp (PAH lup): vase-shaped, usually sessile body form in the life cycle of a cnidarian. (Chap. 6, Sec. 2, p. 155)

population: all of the members of one species that live in the same space at the same time. (Chap. 8, Sec. 1, p. 220)

population density: number of individuals in a population that occupies a definite area. (Chap. 8, Sec. 2, p. 224)

potential energy: energy that is stored due to position. (Chap. 20, Sec. 1, p. 592)

precipitation: water falling from clouds—including rain, snow, sleet, and hail—whose form is determined by air temperature. (Chap. 11, Sec. 1, p. 316)

primary wave: seismic wave that moves rock particles back and forth in the same direction that the wave travels. (Chap. 14, Sec. 2, p. 413)

prime meridian: imaginary line that represents 0° longitude and runs from the north pole through Greenwich, England, to the south pole. (Chap. 15, Sec. 2, p. 445)

producer: organism that can make its own food by photosynthesis or chemosynthesis. (Chap. 12, Sec. 4, p. 357)

protist: one-celled or many-celled eukaryotic organism that can be plantlike, animal-like, or funguslike. (Chap. 4, Sec. 1, p. 88)

protozoan: one-celled, animal-like protist that can live in water, soil, and living and dead organisms. (Chap. 4, Sec. 1, p. 93)

pseudopods (SEWD uh pahdz): temporary cytoplasmic extensions used by some protists to move about and trap food. (Chap. 4, Sec. 1, p. 94)

pulley: an object with a groove, like a wheel, with a rope or chain running through the groove. (Chap. 19, Sec. 3, p. 573)

R

radiation (ray dee AY shun): energy that is transferred by waves. (Chap. 10, Sec. 2, p. 292) (Chap. 20, Sec. 2, p. 603)

radula (RA juh luh): scratchy, tonguelike organ in many mollusks that has rows of teethlike projections used to scrape and grate food. (Chap. 6, Sec. 3, p. 159)

relative humidity: a measure of the amount of water vapor present in the air compared with the amount needed for saturation at a given temperature; can range from 0 percent to 100 percent. (Chap. 11, Sec. 1, p. 312)

renewable: energy resource that can be recycled or replaced by natural processes in less than 100 years. (Chap. 9, Sec. 2, p. 249)

resistance: a measure of how difficult it is for electrons to flow through a material; unit is the ohm. (Chap. 21, Sec. 2, p. 634)

reverse fault: break in rock caused by compressive forces, where rock above the fault surface moves upward relative to the rock below the fault surface. (Chap. 14, Sec. 1, p. 410)

revolution (re vuh LEW shun): movement of Earth around the Sun, which takes a year to complete. (Chap. 17, Sec. 1, p. 493)

rhizoids (RI zoydz): threadlike structures that anchor nonvascular plants to the ground. (Chap. 5, Sec. 2, p. 124)

rock: solid, inorganic material that is usually made of two or more minerals and can be metamorphic, sedimentary, or igneous. (Chap. 13, Sec. 1, p. 376)

rock cycle: diagram that shows how rocks are related to one another and how they change from one type to another. (Chap. 13, Sec. 3, p. 395)

rotation (roh TAY shun): spinning of Earth on its axis, which occurs once every 24 h, produces day and night, and causes the planets and stars to appear to rise and set. (Chap. 17, Sec. 1, p. 492)

runoff: water that flows over Earth's surface. (Chap. 16, Sec. 2, p. 479)

S

salinity (say LIHN ut ee): measure of the amount of dissolved solids, or salts, in seawater. (Chap. 12, Sec. 1, p. 342)

saprophyte: organism that feeds on dead or decaying tissues of other organisms. (Chap. 3, Sec. 2, p. 68) (Chap. 4, Sec. 2, p. 100)

scientific methods: procedures used to solve problems and answer questions that can include stating the problem, gathering information, forming a hypothesis, testing the hypothesis with an experiment, analyzing data, and drawing conclusions. (Chap. 1, Sec. 1, p. 7)

sea breeze: movement of air from sea to land during the day when cooler air from above the water moves over the land, forcing the heated, less dense air above the land to rise. (Chap. 10, Sec. 3, p. 299)

secondary wave: seismic wave that moves rock particles at right angles to the direction of the wave. (Chap. 14, Sec. 2, p. 413)

sedimentary (sed uh MEN tuh ree) **rock:** a type of rock made from pieces of other rocks, dissolved minerals, or plant and animal matter that collect to form rock layers. (Chap. 13, Sec. 2, p. 389)

seismic (SIZE mihk) **wave:** wave generated by an earthquake that travels through Earth. (Chap. 14, Sec. 2, p. 412)

seismograph: instrument used to register earthquake waves and record the time that each arrived. (Chap. 14, Sec. 2, p. 415)

series circuit: circuit that has only one path for electric current to follow. (Chap. 21, Sec. 3, p. 638)

simple machine: device that makes work easier with only one movement; can change the size or direction of a force, and includes the wedge, screw, lever, wheel and axle, pulley, and inclined plane. (Chap. 19, Sec. 3, p. 572)

slump: occurs when a mass of rock or sediment moves downhill along a curved surface. (Chap. 16, Sec. 2, p. 475)

soil: a mixture of weathered rock, organic matter, water, and air that supports the growth of plant life. (Chap. 16, Sec. 1, p. 470)

solar energy: energy from the Sun that is nonpolluting, renewable, and abundant but is available only when the Sun is shining. (Chap. 9, Sec. 2, p. 249)

solar system: system of nine planets and numerous other objects that orbit the Sun, all held in place by the Sun's gravity. (Chap. 17, Sec. 2, p. 498)

spontaneous generation: idea that living things come from nonliving things. (Chap. 1, Sec. 3, p. 19)

sporangium (spuh RAN jee uhm): round spore case of a zygote fungus. (Chap. 4, Sec. 2, p. 103)

spore: waterproof reproductive cell of a fungus that can grow into a new organism. (Chap. 4, Sec. 2, p. 101)

state of matter: physical property that is dependent on both temperature and pressure and occurs in four forms—solid, liquid, gas, or plasma. (Chap. 18, Sec. 1, p. 531)

static charge: buildup of electric charge on an object. (Chap. 21, Sec. 1, p. 625)

station model: indicates weather conditions at a specific location, using a combination of symbols on a map. (Chap. 11, Sec. 3, p. 327)

stomata (STOH muh tuh): small openings in the surface of most plant leaves that allow carbon dioxide, water, and oxygen to enter and exit. (Chap. 5, Sec. 3, p. 131)

strike-slip fault: break in rock caused by shear forces where rocks move past each other without much vertical movement. (Chap. 14, Sec. 1, p. 411)

supernova: very bright explosion of the outer part of a supergiant that takes place after its core collapses. (Chap. 17, Sec. 3, p. 509)

surface current: ocean current that usually moves only the upper few hundred meters of seawater. (Chap. 12, Sec. 2, p. 346)

surface wave: seismic wave that moves rock particles up and down in a backward rolling motion and side to side in a swaying motion. (Chap. 14, Sec. 2, p. 413)

symbiosis (sihm bee OH sus): any close interaction among two or more different species, including mutualism, commensalism, and parasitism. (Chap. 8, Sec. 2, p. 226)

symmetry (SIH muh tree): arrangement of individual body parts; can be radial (arranged around a central point), bilateral (mirror-image parts), or asymmetrical (no definite body shape). (Chap. 6, Sec. 1, p. 151)

T

temperature: measure of the kinetic energy of the atoms of an object. (Chap. 20, Sec. 2, p. 597)

theory: explanation of things or events based on scientific knowledge resulting from many observations and experiments. (Chap. 1, Sec. 1, p. 10)

thermocline: layer of ocean water that begins at a depth of about 200 m and becomes progressively colder with increasing depth. (Chap. 12, Sec. 1, p. 344)

tide: rhythmic rise and fall in sea level created by the gravitational attraction of Earth and the Moon and Earth and the Sun. (Chap. 12, Sec. 3, p. 353)

tissue: group of similar cells that all do the same work. (Chap. 2, Sec. 2, p. 49)

topographic map: map that shows the changes in elevation of Earth's surface and indicates such features as roads and cities. (Chap. 15, Sec. 3, p. 450)

topography: surface features of an area which influence the types of soils that develop. (Chap. 16, Sec. 1, p.470)

tornado: violent, whirling wind that crosses land in a narrow path and can result from wind shears inside a thunderhead. (Chap. 11, Sec. 2, p. 322)

toxin: poisonous substance produced by some pathogens. (Chap. 3, Sec. 2, p. 71)

transformer: device that changes the voltage of an alternating current with little loss of energy. (Chap. 22, Sec. 2, p. 668)

troposphere: layer of Earth's atmosphere that is closest to the ground, contains 99 percent of the water vapor and 75 percent of the atmospheric gases, and is where clouds and weather occur. (Chap. 10, Sec. 1, p. 284)

tsunami (soo NAH mee): seismic sea wave that begins over an earthquake focus and can be highly destructive when it crashes on shore. (Chap. 14, Sec. 3, p. 424)

U

ultraviolet radiation: a type of energy that comes to Earth from the Sun, can damage skin and cause cancer, and is mostly absorbed by the ozone layer. (Chap. 10, Sec. 1, p. 288)

upwarped mountains: mountains formed when blocks of Earth's crust are pushed up by forces inside Earth. (Chap. 15, Sec. 1, p. 442)

upwelling: ocean current that moves cold, deep water to the ocean surface. (Chap. 12, Sec. 2, p. 350)

V

vaccine: preparation made from killed bacteria or damaged particles from bacterial cell walls that can prevent some bacterial diseases. (Chap. 3, Sec. 2, p. 73)

vacuole (VA kyuh wohl): balloonlike cell organelle in the cytoplasm that can store food, water, and other substances. (Chap. 2, Sec. 1, p. 42)

variable: something in an experiment that can change. (Chap. 1, Sec. 1, p. 9)

vascular plant: plant with tubelike structures that move minerals, water, and other substances throughout the plant. (Chap. 5, Sec. 1, p. 123)

velocity: speed of an object and its direction of motion; changes when speed changes, direction of motion changes, or both change. (Chap. 19, Sec. 1, p. 559)

volcanic mountains: mountains formed when molten material reaches Earth's surface through a weak crustal area and piles up into a cone-shaped structure. (Chap. 15, Sec. 1, p. 443)

voltage: a measure of how much electrical energy each electron of a battery has; measured in volts (V). (Chap. 21, Sec. 2, p. 632)

W

water cycle: continuous cycle of water molecules on Earth as they rise into the atmosphere, fall back to Earth as rain or other precipitation, and flow into rivers and oceans through the processes of evaporation, condensation, and precipitation. (Chap. 8, Sec. 3, p. 232)

wave: the rhythmic movement that carries energy through water. (Chap. 12, Sec. 3, p. 351)

weather: state of the atmosphere at a specific time and place, determined by factors including air pressure, amount of moisture in the air, temperature, and wind. (Chap. 11, Sec. 1, p. 310)

weathering: a natural process that causes rocks to change, breaks them down, and causes them to crumble. (Chap. 16, Sec. 1, p. 466)

work: done when an applied force causes an object to move in the direction of the force. (Chap. 19, Sec. 3, p. 570)

X

xylem (ZI lum): vascular tissue that forms hollow vessels that transport substances, other than sugar, throughout a plant. (Chap. 5, Sec. 3, p. 133)

Spanish Glossary

Este glossario define cada término clave que aparece en negrillas en el texto. También muestra el capítulo, la sección y el número de página en donde se usa dicho término.

A

abiotic factor / factor abiótico: cualquier parte inanimada o sin vida en un medio ambiente, como por ejemplo, el agua, la luz solar, la temperatura y el aire. (Cap. 8, Sec. 1, pág. 216)

abrasion / abrasión: una forma de erosión que puede abrir hoyos en las rocas y producir superficies lisas y pulidas. (Cap. 16, Sec. 2, pág. 478)

acceleration / aceleración: cambio en velocidad dividido entre la cantidad de tiempo que se necesita para que ocurra el cambio; se presenta cuando un cuerpo acelera, decelera o cambia de dirección. (Cap. 19, Sec. 1, pág. 559)

acid rain / lluvia ácida: lluvia o nieve dañina que se forma cuando los gases liberados por la quema de petróleo y carbón se mezclan con el agua y el aire. (Cap. 9, Sec. 1, pág. 246)

aerobe / aerobio: cualquier organismo que usa oxígeno para la respiración. (Cap. 3, Sec. 1, pág. 62)

air mass / masa de aire: flujo enorme de aire que tiene las mismas características de temperatura y contenido de humedad que la superficie terrestre sobre la cual se formó. (Cap. 11, Sec. 2, pág. 318)

algae / algas: protistas tipo plantas que producen oxígeno mediante la fotosíntesis. (Cap. 4, Sec. 1, pág. 89)

alternating current (AC) / corriente alterna (CA): corriente eléctrica que cambia de dirección muchas veces cada segundo. (Cap. 22, Sec. 2, pág. 666)

amniotic egg / huevo amniótico: adaptación de comportamiento de los reptiles que les permite reproducirse en tierra; encierra al embrión dentro de un entorno húmedo, protegido por una cáscara correosa y contiene una yema que alimenta al embrión. (Cap. 7, Sec. 2, pág. 191)

anaerobe / anaerobio: cualquier organismo que puede vivir sin oxígeno. (Cap. 3, Sec. 1, pág. 62)

angiosperms / angiospermas: plantas vasculares con flores que producen un fruto que contiene una o más semillas; monocotiledóneas y dicotiledóneas. (Cap. 5, Sec. 3, pág. 135)

antibiotics / antibióticos: sustancias químicas producidas por algunas bacterias que se usan para limitar el crecimiento de otras bacterias. (Cap. 3, Sec. 2, pág. 67)

appendage / apéndice: estructura como una garra, pierna o antena que crece del cuerpo. (Cap. 6, Sec. 4, pág. 164)

arthropod / artrópodo: animal con simetría bilateral, apéndices articulados, un exoesqueleto protector y un cuerpo segmentado. (Cap. 6, Sec. 4, pág. 164)

ascus / asco: estructura productora de esporas, en forma de saco, en los hongos ascomicetos. (Cap. 4, Sec. 2, pág. 102)

astronomical unit / unidad astronómica: unidad de medida equivalente a 150 millones de kilómetros, lo cual es la distancia promedio de la Tierra al Sol. (Cap. 17, Sec. 2, pág. 499)

atmosphere / atmósfera: el aire de la Tierra, el cual está compuesto por una capa tenue de gases, sólidos y líquidos; forma una capa protectora alrededor del planeta y está dividida en cinco capas distintivas. (Cap. 10, Sec. 1, pág. 282)

aurora / aurora: luces boreales y australes que parecen cambiar cuando las partículas atrapadas en la magnetosfera chocan con la atmósfera de la Tierra por encima de los polos. (Cap. 22, Sec. 2, pág. 665)

average speed / velocidad media: tasa de movimiento que se calcula dividiendo la distancia recorrida entre la cantidad de tiempo que se tarda en recorrer esa distancia. (Cap. 19, Sec. 1, pág. 557)

B

bacteria / bacterias: los organismos más pequeños sobre la Tierra, los cuales están hechos de una sola célula. (Cap. 2, Sec. 1, pág. 39)

basidium / basidio: estructura reproductora en forma de bastón, en la cual los hongos producen esporas. (Cap. 4, Sec. 2, pág. 102)

binomial nomenclature / nomenclatura binaria: es un sistema de dos palabras que da el nombre científico a todos los organismos. (Cap. 1, Sec. 4, pág. 24)

biogenesis / biogénesis: teoría que establece que todo ser vivo proviene de otros seres vivos. (Cap. 1, Sec. 3, pág. 19)

biosphere / biosfera: parte de la Tierra que sustenta la vida: la parte superior de la corteza terrestre, toda el agua que cubre la superficie de la Tierra y la atmósfera circundante; incluye todos los biomas, ecosistemas, comunidades y poblaciones. (Cap. 8, Sec. 1, pág. 221)

biotic factor / factor biótico: cualquier organismo vivo o que alguna vez vivió en el medio ambiente. (Cap. 8, Sec. 1, pág. 216)

blizzard / ventisca: tormenta invernal que dura por lo menos tres horas, con temperaturas de –12°C o más bajas, poca visibilidad y vientos de por lo menos 51 km/h. (Cap. 11, Sec. 2, pág. 325)

boiling point / punto de ebullición: temperatura a la cual una sustancia en estado líquido se transforma en un gas. (Cap. 18, sec. 1, pág. 533)

budding / gemación: forma de reproducción sexual en que un organismo nuevo y genéticamente idéntico crece de un lado del organismo progenitor . (Cap. 4, Sec. 2, pág. 102)

C

cambium / cámbium: tejido vascular que produce células de xilema y floema a medida que crece la planta. (Cap. 5, Sec. 3, pág. 133)

carnivore / carnívoro: animal que se alimenta de carne y que posee colmillos afilados y especializados para desgarrar y romper la carne. (Cap. 7, Sec. 4, pág. 198)

cartilage / cartílago: tejido resistente y elástico semejante al hueso, pero que es más blando y menos frágil. (Cap. 7, Sec. 1, pág. 184)

catalyst / catalizador: sustancia que cambia la velocidad de una reacción química sin alterar su propia estructura. (Cap. 20, Sec. 3, pág. 608)

cell / célula: es la unidad más pequeña de cualquier ser vivo y que puede realizar las funciones vitales del organismo. (Cap. 1, Sec. 2, pág. 14)

cell membrane / membrana celular: estructura flexible que encierra la célula, forma una barrera entre la célula y su ambiente y ayuda a controlar lo que entra y sale de la célula. (Cap. 2, Sec. 1, pág. 41)

cellulose / celulosa: compuesto químico hecho de azúcares; forma fibras enredadas en las paredes celulares de muchas plantas y provee estructura y apoyo. (Cap. 5, Sec. 1, pág. 120)

cell wall / pared celular: estructura de plantas, algas, hongos y muchos tipos de bacterias que apoya y protege la membrana celular. (Cap. 2, Sec. 1, pág. 41)

chemical change / cambio químico: cambio en el cual la identidad de una sustancia cambia debido a sus propiedades químicas y forma una nueva sustancia o sustancias. (Cap. 18, Sec. 2, pág. 541)

chemical property / propiedad química: cualquier característica, como la capacidad de quemarse, que permite que una sustancia sufra un cambio, el cual da como resultado una nueva sustancia. (Cap. 18, Sec. 2, pág. 538)

chemical weathering / meteorización química: ocurre cuando cambia la composición química de las rocas. (Cap. 16, Sec. 1, pág. 468)

chemosynthesis / quimiosíntesis: proceso que ocurre en las aguas profundas del océano, donde no penetra la luz solar, en el cual las bacterias elaboran alimento a partir de compuestos sulfúricos disueltos. (Cap. 12, Sec. 4, pág. 357)

chlorofluorocarbons (CFCs)/ clorofluorocarbonos (CFC): grupo de compuestos químicos que se utilizan en refrigeradores, acondicionadores de aire, empaques de espuma y rociadores de aerosol; estos compuestos químicos pueden penetrar en la atmósfera y destruir el ozono. (Cap. 10, Sec. 1, pág. 288)

chloroplast / cloroplasto: organelo verde en las células de la hoja de una planta en donde se lleva a cabo la mayor parte de la fotosíntesis. (Cap. 2, Sec. 1, pág. 43)

chordate / cordado: animal que en algún momento de su desarrollo posee un notocordio y hendiduras branquiales. (Cap. 7, Sec. 1, pág. 182)

cilia / cilios: estructuras cortas filamentosas que se extienden de la membrana celular de un ciliado y que le permiten moverse rápidamente. (Cap. 4, Sec. 1, pág. 93)

circuit / circuito: bucle conductor cerrado por donde puede fluir la corriente eléctrica. (Cap. 21, Sec. 2, pág. 631)

closed circulatory system / sistema circulatorio cerrado: sistema circulatorio en que la sangre es transportada a través de vasos sanguíneos, en vez de bañar los órganos. (Cap. 6, Sec. 3, pág. 160)

cnidarian / cnidario: animal de cuerpo hueco con simetría radial y dos capas de células organizadas en tejidos. (Cap. 6, Sec. 2, pág. 154)

comet / cometa: astro extenso formado por hielo congelado y roca que viaja hacia el centro del sistema solar es posible que provenga de la nube de Oort y desarrolla una cola brillante e incandescente a medida que se acerca al Sol. (Cap. 17, Sec. 2, pág. 504)

community / comunidad: todas las poblaciones de diferentes especies en un área dada que interactúan de alguna manera y que dependen entre sí para obtener alimento, refugio y otras necesidades. (Cap. 8, Sec. 1, pág. 220)

compound machine / máquina compuesta: una combinación de máquinas simples. (Cap. 19, Sec. 3, pág. 572)

condensation / condensación: proceso en el cual el vapor de agua se transforma en un líquido. (Cap. 10, Sec. 2, pág. 293)

conduction / conducción: transferencia de calor mediante colisiones entre los átomos de un material. (Cap. 10, Sec. 2, pág. 292; Cap. 20, Sec. 2, pág. 600)

conductor / conductor: material, como el cobre o la plata, a través del cual los electrones se pueden desplazar fácilmente. (Cap. 21, Sec. 1, pág. 628)

conic projection / proyección cónica: mapa que se hace proyectando puntos y líneas de un globo terráqueo a un cono. (Cap. 15, Sec. 3, pág. 449)

conservation / conservación: uso cuidadoso de los recursos con el fin de reducir los daños al ambiente. (Cap. 9, Sec. 4, pág. 265)

conservation of mass / conservación de la masa: establece que la masa de los productos de un cambio químico es siempre la misma que la masa con que se empezó. (Cap. 18, Sec. 2, pág. 545)

constellation / constelación: grupo de estrellas que forma un patrón en el firmamento y puede recibir su nombre de un animal, una persona o un objeto real o imaginario. (Cap. 17, Sec. 3, pág. 506)

consumer / consumidor: organismo que obtiene su energía al consumir otros organismos. (Cap. 12, Sec. 4, pág. 357)

contour feather / pluma de contorno: pluma liviana pero resistente que les da a las aves su forma y colorido y les ayuda a maniobrar el vuelo, a atraer un compañero o una compañera y a evitar depredadores. (Cap. 7, Sec. 3, pág. 195)

contour line / curva de nivel: línea en un mapa que conecta puntos con igual elevación. (Cap. 15, Sec. 3, pág. 450)

control / control: el estándar que sirve para comparar los resultados obtenidos en un experimento. (Cap. 1, Sec. 1, pág. 9)

convection / convección: transferencia de calor que ocurre cuando las partículas se mueven entre cuerpos o áreas con distintas temperaturas. (Cap. 10, Sec. 2, pág. 292; Cap. 20, Sec. 2, pág. 602)

Coriolis effect / efecto de Coriolis: es la causa de que el aire y el agua en movimiento giren a la izquierda en el hemisferio sur y a la derecha en el hemisferio norte, debido a la rotación de la Tierra. (Cap. 10, Sec. 3, pág. 296)

creep: tipo de movimiento de masas en el cual los sedimentos se mueven cuesta abajo paulatinamente. (Cap. 16, Sec. 2, pág. 475)

crystal / cristal: material sólido cuyos átomos están ordenados en un patrón repetitivo. (Cap. 13, Sec. 1, pág. 378)

cuticle / cutícula: capa protectora y cerosa que cubre los tallos, hojas y flores de muchas plantas y que les ayuda a prevenir la pérdida de agua. (Cap. 5, Sec. 1, pág. 120)

cytoplasm / citoplasma: sustancia gelatinosa dentro de la membrana celular que contiene agua, sustancias químicas y partes celulares. (Cap. 2, Sec. 1, pág. 41)

D

decomposer / descomponedor: organismo que descompone tejidos y libera nutrientes y dióxido de carbono de regreso al ecosistema. (Cap. 12, Sec. 4, pág. 357)

deflation / deflación: erosión del suelo causada por el viento. (Cap. 16, Sec. 2, pág. 478)

density / densidad: propiedad física que se puede calcular dividiendo la masa de un cuerpo entre su volumen. (Cap. 18, Sec. 1, pág. 530)

density current / corriente de densidad: se forma cuando el agua salada más densa se hunde debajo del agua salada menos densa. (Cap. 12, Sec. 2, pág. 348)

dew point / punto de condensación: temperatura a la cual el aire se satura y se forma la condensación. (Cap. 11, Sec. 1, pág. 313)

dicot / dicotiledónea: angiosperma con dos cotiledones dentro de la semilla, partes florales en múltiples de cuatro o cinco y bultos vasculares en forma de anillos. (Cap. 5, Sec. 3, pág. 136)

down feather / plumón: pluma esponjosa que atrapa y guarda el aire cálido contra el cuerpo de un ave. (Cap. 7, Sec. 3, pág. 195)

E

earthquake / terremoto: vibraciones producidas cuando las rocas se rompen a lo largo de una falla. (Cap. 14, Sec. 1, pág. 409)

eclipse / eclipse: fenómeno que ocurre cuando la Luna se interpone entre el Sol y la Tierra (eclipse solar) o cuando la Tierra se mueve entre el Sol y la Luna (eclipse lunar) y el astro proyecta una sombra. (Cap. 17, Sec. 1, pág. 495)

ecology / ecología: estudio de todas las interacciones entre los organismos y su ambiente. (Cap. 8, Sec. 1, pág. 216)

ecosystem / ecosistema: todas las comunidades en un área dada y los factores abióticos que las afectan. (Cap. 8, Sec. 1, pág. 220; Cap. 12, Sec. 4 pág. 357)

ectotherm / de sangre fría: dícese del animal cuya temperatura corporal cambia con la temperatura de su entorno. (Cap. 7, Sec. 1, pág. 183)

electric current / corriente eléctrica: flujo de corriente, ya sea un flujo de electrones o de iones, a través de un conductor. (Cap. 21, Sec. 2, pág. 631)

electric discharge / descarga eléctrica: movimiento rápido del exceso de carga de un lugar a otro. (Cap. 21, Sec. 1, pág. 629)

electric field / campo eléctrico: campo a través del cual las cargas eléctricas ejercen una fuerza mutua. (Cap. 21, Sec. 1, pág. 627)

electric force / fuerza eléctrica: fuerza de atracción o de repulsión que ejercen todos los cuerpos con carga. (Cap. 21, Sec. 1, pág. 627)

electric power / potencia eléctrica: tasa a la cual un artefacto eléctrico convierte la energía eléctrica en otra forma de energía; su uso se mide en kilovatios-hora con contadores de electricidad. (Cap. 21, Sec. 3, pág. 640)

electromagnet / electroimán: imán creado al enrollar un alambre que conduce corriente alrededor de un núcleo de hierro. (Cap. 22, Sec. 2, pág. 661)

endospore / endóspora: estructura protectora de paredes gruesas que producen los patógenos cuando las condiciones son desfavorables para la sobrevivencia. (Cap. 3, Sec. 2, pág. 71)

endotherm / de sangre caliente: dícese del animal cuya temperatura corporal no cambia con la de su entorno. (Cap. 7, Sec. 1, pág. 183)

endothermic reaction / reacción endotérmica: reacción química que absorbe energía. (Cap. 20, Sec. 3, pág. 606)

energy / energía: capacidad de producir cambios; puede cambiar la rapidez, dirección, forma o temperatura de un cuerpo. (Cap. 20, Sec. 1, pág. 588)

epicenter / epicentro: punto sobre la superficie terrestre directamente sobre el foco de un terremoto. (Cap. 14, Sec. 2, pág. 413)

equator / ecuador: línea imaginaria que rodea la Tierra alrededor de 0° de latitud, equidistante del polo norte y el polo sur. (Cap. 15, Sec. 2, pág. 444)

erosion / erosión: desgaste y eliminación de material rocoso. (Cap. 16, Sec. 2, pág. 473)

estivation / estivación: período de inactividad durante temporadas calientes y secas; en los anfibios, implica el trasladarse a zonas más frescas y húmedas bajo tierra. (Cap. 7, Sec. 2, pág. 187)

exoskeleton / exoesqueleto: cubierta corporal protectora y rígida de un artrópodo, la cual le da apoyo al cuerpo y disminuye la pérdida de agua. (Cap. 6, Sec. 4, pág. 164)

exothermic reaction / reacción exotérmica: reacción química que libera energía. (Cap. 20, Sec. 3, pág. 607)

extrusive / extrusivas: rocas ígneas con o sin cristales que se forman cuando la roca fundida se enfría rápidamente en la superficie terrestre. (Cap. 13, Sec. 2, pág. 385)

F

---

fault / falla: superficie a lo largo de la cual se mueven y se rompen las rocas cuando exceden su límite de elasticidad. (Cap. 14, Sec. 1, pág. 408)

fault-block mountains / montañas de bloques de falla: montañas que se forman de enormes bloques rocosos inclinados, pero separados de las rocas circundantes por fallas. (Cap. 15, Sec. 1, pág. 442)

fission / fisión: la forma más sencilla de reproducción asexual en la cual se producen dos células nuevas con material genético idéntico al de la célula original. (Cap. 3, Sec. 1, pág. 62)

flagella / flagelos: filamentos móviles de muchas bacterias que les facilitan la locomoción en condiciones húmedas. (Cap. 3, Sec. 1, pág. 61)

flagellum / flagelo: estructura larga y delgada en forma de látigo de algunos protistas que les facilita el movimiento a través de medios mojados o húmedos. (Cap. 4, Sec. 1, pág. 90)

focus / foco: en un terremoto, es el punto sobre la superficie terrestre donde se libera la energía en forma de ondas sísmicas. (Cap. 14, Sec. 2, pág. 412)

fog / neblina: una nube estrato que se forma cuando el aire se enfría hasta su punto de rocío, cerca de la superficie terrestre. (Cap. 11, Sec. 1, pág. 315)

folded mountains / montañas plegadas: montañas que se forman cuando las capas rocosas horizontales se comprimen desde lados opuestos, lo que hace que se encorven y se doblen. (Cap. 15, Sec. 1, pág. 441)

foliated / foliadas: rocas metamórficas que poseen capas visibles de minerales. (Cap. 13, Sec. 3, pág. 394)

food chain / cadena alimenticia: un modelo que describe la manera en que la energía pasa de un organismo a otro en forma de alimento. (Cap. 8, Sec. 3, pág. 228; Cap. 12, Sec. 4, pág. 358)

food web / red alimenticia: modelo que describe la manera en que la energía (en forma de alimento) se mueve por una comunidad; una serie de cadenas alimenticias superpuestas. (Cap. 8, Sec. 3, pág. 230)

force / fuerza: un empuje o un jalón; el newton es la unidad SI. (Cap. 19, Sec. 2, pág. 562)

fossil fuel / combustible fósil: recurso energético no renovable que se formó de los restos de plantas y animales antiguos; por ejemplo, el carbón, el petróleo y el gas. (Cap. 9, Sec. 1, pág. 244)

friction / fricción: fuerza resistente al movimiento entre dos superficies que se tocan y que siempre actúa opuesta a la dirección del movimiento. (Cap. 19, Sec. 2, pág. 565)

front / frente: límite entre dos masas de aire que poseen diferentes temperaturas, densidad o humedad; puede ser frío, cálido, ocluido y estacionario. (Cap. 11, Sec. 2, pág. 319)

G

galaxy / galaxia: grupo de estrellas, gases y polvo que se mantienen unidos gracias a la gravedad. (Cap. 17, Sec. 3, pág. 509)

gem / gema: mineral precioso y valioso que se puede cortar y pulir. (Cap. 13, Sec. 1, pág. 382)

generator / generador: dispositivo que utiliza un campo magnético para convertir la energía cinética en energía eléctrica y el cual produce corriente directa y corriente alterna. (Cap. 22, Sec. 2, pág. 666)

genus / género: primera palabra del nombre científico de dos palabras, que se usa para identificar grupos de especies similares. (Cap. 1, Sec. 4, pág. 24)

geothermal energy / energía geotérmica: energía térmica que se encuentra debajo de la superficie terrestre y la cual se puede usar para generar electricidad. (Cap. 9, Sec. 2, pág. 254)

gill / branquia: órgano que le permite a un animal que mora en el agua el intercambio de dióxido de carbono por el oxígeno disuelto en el agua. (Cap. 6, Sec. 3, pág. 158)

groundwater / agua subterránea: agua que se infiltra por el suelo y se acumula en los pequeños espacios entre los trocitos de tierra y roca. (Cap. 9, Sec. 3, pág. 258)

guard cells / células guardianas: pares de células que rodean los estomas y controlan su apertura y cierre. (Cap. 5, Sec. 3, pág. 131)

gymnosperms / gimnospermas: plantas vasculares que no florecen; generalmente tienen hojas en forma de agujas o de escamas y producen semillas que no están protegidas por el fruto; coníferas cicadáceas, ginkgoes y gnetofitas. (Cap. 5, Sec. 3, pág. 134)

habitat / hábitat: morada de un organismo. (Cap. 8, Sec. 2, pág. 227)

heat / calor: transferencia de energía de un cuerpo a otro debido a diferencias en temperatura; fluye de cuerpos más calientes a cuerpos más fríos. (Cap. 20, Sec. 2, pág. 599)

herbivore / herbívoro: mamífero que se alimenta de plantas, cuyos incisivos están especializados para cortar la vegetación y sus molares, grandes y aplanados, sirven para molerla. (Cap. 7, Sec. 4, pág. 198)

hibernation / hibernación: período de inactividad durante temporadas frías; en los anfibios, implica el enterrarse en el lodo o en las hojas. (Cap. 7, Sec. 2, pág. 187)

homeostasis / homeostasis: característica de los seres vivos que les permite mantener las condiciones internas adecuadas, a pesar de los cambios en su ambiente. (Cap. 1, Sec. 2, pág. 15)

humidity / humedad: cantidad de vapor de agua que sostiene el aire. (Cap. 11, Sec. 1, pág. 312)

hurricane / huracán: tipo de tormenta extensa y severa que se forma sobre los océanos tropicales, con vientos de por lo menos 120 km/h y que pierde fuerza al llegar a tierra firme. (Cap. 11, Sec. 2, pág. 324)

hydroelectric power / potencia hidroeléctrica: electricidad producida de la fuerza del agua en movimiento. (Cap. 9, Sec. 2, pág. 253)

hydrosphere / hidrosfera: toda el agua de la superficie terrestre. (Cap. 10, Sec. 2, pág. 293)

hyphae / hifa: masa de tubos multicelulares filamentosos que forman el cuerpo de un hongo. (Cap. 4, Sec. 2, pág. 100)

hypothesis / hipótesis: predicción que se puede poner a prueba. (Cap. 1, Sec. 1, pág. 8)

igneous rock / roca ígnea: roca intrusiva o extrusiva que se produce cuando la roca fundida del interior de la Tierra se enfría y se endurece. (Cap. 13, Sec. 2, pág. 385)

inclined plane / plano inclinado: una superficie inclinada. (Cap. 19, Sec. 3, pág. 575)

inertia / inercia: tendencia a resistir un cambio en movimiento. (Cap. 19, Sec. 2, pág. 565)

instantaneous speed / rapidez instantánea: rapidez de un cuerpo en cualquier momento dado. (Cap. 19, Sec. 1, pág. 557)

insulator / aislador: material a través del cual no pueden fluir los electrones fácilmente; por ejemplo, la madera o el vidrio. (Cap. 21, Sec. 1, pág. 628)

intrusive / intrusivas: rocas ígneas que poseen cristales grandes y las cuales se forman cuando la roca fundida se enfría lentamente y se endurece debajo de la superficie terrestre. (Cap. 13, Sec. 2, pág. 385)

invertebrate / invertebrado: animal sin columna vertebral. (Cap. 6, Sec. 1, pág. 152)

ion / ion: átomo con carga positiva o negativa. (Cap. 21, Sec. 1, pág. 624)

ionosphere / ionosfera: capa de partículas cargadas eléctricamente en la termosfera que absorbe las ondas radiales AM durante el día y las vuelve a reflejar durante la noche. (Cap. 10, Sec. 1, pág. 285)

isobars / isobaras: líneas que se trazan en un mapa meteorológico conectando puntos que tienen la misma presión atmosférica; también indican la ubicación de las áreas de alta y de baja presión y pueden mostrar la velocidad del viento. (Cap. 11, Sec. 3, pág. 327)

isotherm / isoterma: línea que se traza en un mapa meteorológico conectando puntos que tienen la misma temperatura. (Cap. 11, Sec. 3, pág. 327)

J

jet stream / corriente de chorro: franja estrecha de vientos fuertes que sopla cerca de la troposfera. (Cap. 10, Sec. 3, pág. 298)

K

kinetic energy / energía cinética: energía que posee un cuerpo debido a su movimiento. (Cap. 20, Sec. 1, pág. 590)

kingdom / reino: la primera categoría y la más grande del sistema de clasificación de los organismos. (Cap. 1, Sec. 4, pág. 23)

L

land breeze / brisa terrestre: movimiento de aire nocturno desde la tierra hacia el mar y que se forma cuando el aire más frío y denso proveniente de la tierra fuerza el aire más cálido a ascender sobre el mar. (Cap. 10, Sec. 3, pág. 299)

latitude / latitud: distancia en grados al norte o al sur del ecuador. (Cap. 15, Sec. 2, pág. 444)

law / ley: un enunciado científico que describe cómo ocurren ciertos fenómenos en la naturaleza y que parece ser cierto consistentemente. (Cap. 1, Sec. 1, pág. 10)

law of conservation of energy / ley de conservación de la energía: establece que la energía no se crea ni se destruye, sólo se transforma. (Cap. 20, Sec. 1, pág. 594)

lever / palanca: barra o tablón que gira sobre un punto fijo. (Cap. 19, Sec. 3, pág. 574)

lichen / liquen: organismo compuesto de un hongo y un alga verde o una cianobacteria. (Cap. 4, Sec. 2, pág. 104)

light-year / año luz: aproximadamente 9.5 millones de km, o sea, la distancia que la luz viaja en un año. El año luz se utiliza para medir grandes distancias entre estrellas o galaxias. (Cap. 17, Sec. 3, pág. 512)

limiting factor / factor limitativo: cualquier factor biótico o abiótico que limita el número de individuos en una población. (Cap. 8, Sec. 2, pág. 225)

liquefaction / liquefacción: ocurre cuando el suelo mojado actúa como un líquido durante un terremoto. (Cap. 14, Sec. 3, pág. 423)

longitude / longitud: distancia en grados al este o al oeste del primer meridiano. (Cap. 15, Sec. 2, pág. 445)

M

magnetic domain / dominio magnético: grupo de átomos cuyos campos magnéticos apuntan en la misma dirección. (Cap. 22, Sec. 1, pág. 656)

magnetic field / campo magnético: área que rodea un imán a través de la cual se ejerce la fuerza magnética y que se extiende entre el polo norte del imán y el polo sur. (Cap. 22, Sec. 1, pág. 655)

magnetosphere / magnetosfera: campo magnético que rodea la Tierra y el cual desvía la mayor parte de las partículas cargadas provenientes del Sol. (Cap. 22, Sec. 1, pág. 657)

magnitude / magnitud: medida de la energía liberada durante un movimiento sísmico. (Cap. 14, Sec. 3, pág. 422)

mantle / manto: capa de tejido delgada que cubre el cuerpo de un molusco y que puede secretar una concha. (Cap. 6, Sec. 3, pág. 158)

map legend / leyenda de mapa: explica los símbolos que se usan en un mapa. (Cap. 15, Sec. 3, pág. 452)

map scale / escala de un mapa: relación entre la distancia en un mapa y la distancia real sobre la superficie terrestre, la cual se puede representar como una razón o como una pequeña barra dividida en secciones. (Cap. 15, Sec. 3, pág. 452)

marsupial / marsupial: mamífero que da a luz una cría no desarrollada completamente, la cual termina su desarrollo en la bolsa ventral de la madre. (Cap. 7, Sec. 4, pág. 200)

mass movement / movimiento de masa: cuando sólo la gravedad hace que las rocas o el sedimento se muevan cuesta abajo. (Cap. 16, Sec. 2, pág. 473)

matter / materia: cualquier cosa que posee masa y ocupa espacio. (Cap. 18, Sec. 1, pág. 529)

mechanical advantage / ventaja mecánica: número de veces que una máquina multiplica la fuerza de esfuerzo que se le aplica. (Cap. 19, Sec. 3, pág. 572)

mechanical weathering / meteorización mecánica: rompe las rocas en trozos pequeños sin cambiarla químicamente. (Cap. 16, Sec. 1, pág. 466)

medusa / medusa: forma corporal acampanada de vida libre en el ciclo de vida de un cnidario. (Cap. 6, Sec. 2, pág. 155)

melting point / punto de fusión: temperatura a la cual un sólido se convierte en un líquido. (Cap. 18, Sec. 1, pág. 533)

metamorphic rock / roca metamórfica: roca nueva que se forma cuando la roca existente se calienta o se comprime. (Cap. 13, Sec. 3, pág. 393)

metamorphosis / metamorfosis: cambio de forma corporal; puede ser completa (huevo, larva, pupa, adulto) o incompleta (huevo, ninfa, adulto). (Cap. 6, Sec. 4, pág. 165)

meteorite / meteorito: cualquier fragmento espacial que sobrevive su caída a través de la atmósfera y que llega a la superficie terrestre. (Cap. 17, Sec. 2, pág. 505)

meteorologist / meteorólogo: persona que estudia el tiempo y usa información del radar Doppler, de los satélites meteorológicos, computadoras y otros instrumentos para hacer mapas meteorológicos y pronósticos del tiempo. (Cap. 11, Sec. 3, pág. 329)

mineral / mineral: material sólido inorgánico que se halla en la naturaleza y que siempre posee la misma composición química: átomos arreglados en un patrón ordenado y propiedades como crucero, fractura, color, dureza y veta y brillo. (Cap. 13, Sec. 1, pág. 376)

mitochondria / mitocondria: organelo celular donde tiene lugar la respiración. (Cap. 2, Sec. 1, pág. 42)

mollusk / molusco: invertebrado con simetría bilateral de cuerpo blando, con una pata muscular, un manto y un sistema circulatorio abierto; por lo general tiene una concha. (Cap. 6, Sec. 3, pág. 158)

monocot / monocotiledónea: angiosperma con un cotiledón dentro de la semilla; las partes de la flor están arregladas en múltiplos de tres y los tejidos vasculares se encuentran esparcidos a lo largo del tallo formando bultos. (Cap. 5, Sec. 3, pág. 136)

monotreme / monotrema: mamífero que pone huevos con cáscaras resistentes y correosas, en lugar de dar a luz una cría viva. (Cap. 7, Sec. 4, pág. 199)

motor / motor: dispositivo que puede transformar la energía eléctrica en energía cinética. (Cap. 22, Sec. 2, pág. 664)

mycorrhizae / micorriza: red de hifas y raíces vegetales que ayudan a las plantas a absorber agua y minerales del suelo. (Cap. 4, Sec. 2, pág. 104)

N

nekton / necton: animales marinos, como los peces y las tortugas de mar, que nadan de forma activa en las aguas oceánicas. (Cap. 12, Sec. 4, pág. 356)

niche / nicho: papel que tiene un organismo en el ecosistema en el cual se incluye lo que come, su manera de interactuar con otros organismos y de conseguir alimento. (Cap. 8, Sec. 2, pág. 227)

nitrogen-fixing bacteria / bacterias nitrificantes: bacteria que convierte el nitrógeno del aire en formas que pueden usar las plantas y los animales. (Cap. 3, Sec. 2, pág. 68)

nonfoliated / no foliadas: rocas metamórficas que carecen de capas o bandas distintivas. (Cap. 13, Sec. 3, pág. 394)

nonpoint sources / fuentes no puntuales: fuentes de contaminación que se originan en distintos lugares, como las industrias, los hogares y las fincas y cuyo origen es difícil rastrear. (Cap. 9, Sec. 3, pág. 259)

nonrenewable / no renovable: recurso energético que los procesos naturales no pueden reemplazar en menos de 100 años. (Cap. 9, Sec. 1, pág. 248)

nonvascular plant / plantas no vasculares: planta que absorbe el agua y otras sustancias directamente a través de sus paredes celulares en lugar de estructuras en forma de tubo. (Cap. 5, Sec. 1, pág. 123)

normal fault / falla normal: ruptura en la roca causada por las fuerzas de tensión, en donde la roca sobre la superficie de la falla se mueve hacia abajo en relación con la roca debajo de la falla. (Cap. 14, Sec. 1, pág. 410)

nuclear energy / energía nuclear: energía que se produce al dividirse los núcleos de ciertos elementos. (Cap. 9, Sec. 2, pág. 255)

nucleus / núcleo: organelo celular que contiene el material hereditario. (Cap. 2, Sec. 1, pág. 42)

O

Ohm's law / ley de Ohm: relación entre el voltaje, la corriente y la resistencia en un circuito. (Cap. 21, Sec. 3, pág. 637)

omnivore / omnívoro: animal que se alimenta tanto de carne como de plantas y que posee incisivos especializados para cortar vegetales, premolares para masticar carne y molares para moler el alimento. (Cap. 7, Sec. 4, pág. 198)

open circulatory system / sistema circulatorio abierto: un tipo de sistema circulatorio de la sangre que carece de vasos sanguíneos y en el cual la sangre baña los órganos. (Cap. 6, Sec. 3, pág. 159)

orbit / órbita: trayectoria curva y regular que sigue la Tierra a medida que se mueve alrededor del Sol. (Cap. 17, Sec. 1, pág. 493)

ore / mena: recurso mineral que se pueda minar y vender con fines de lucro. (Cap. 9, Sec. 4, pág. 266; Cap. 13, Sec. 1, pág. 383)

organ / órgano: estructura compuesta de dos o más tipos diferentes de tejido que funcionan juntos para llevar a cabo una tarea en particular. (Cap. 2, Sec. 2, pág. 49)

organelles / organelos: partes celulares especializadas que llevan a cabo las actividades de la célula. (Cap. 2, Sec. 1, pág. 41)

organism / organismo: cualquier ser vivo; usa energía, está formado por células, se reproduce, responde a estímulos, crece y se desarrollan. (Cap. 1, Sec. 2, pág. 14)

organ system / sistema de órganos: grupo de órganos que trabajan juntos para realizar cierta función . (Cap. 2, Sec. 2, pág. 49)

ozone layer / capa de ozono: capa de la estratosfera con una alta concentración de ozono; absorbe la mayor parte de la radiación ultravioleta dañina proveniente del Sol. (Cap. 10, Sec. 1, pág. 288)

P

parallel circuit / circuito paralelo: circuito que tiene más de una trayectoria para el flujo de la corriente eléctrica. (Cap. 21, Sec. 3, pág. 639)

pathogen / patógeno: organismo que causa enfermedad. (Cap. 3, Sec. 2, pág. 71)

phloem / floema: tejido vascular que forma tubos que transportan azúcares disueltos por toda la planta. (Cap. 5, Sec. 3, pág. 133)

photosynthesis / fotosíntesis: proceso que utilizan las plantas, las algas y muchos tipos de bacterias para elaborar su alimento. (Cap. 2, Sec. 1, pág. 43; Cap. 12, Sec. 1, pág. 343)

phylogeny / filogenia: historia evolutiva de un organismo, sirve para que los científicos puedan clasificar los organismos en reinos. (Cap. 1, Sec. 4, pág. 23)

physical change / cambio físico: cambio en el cual las propiedades de una sustancia cambian pero la identidad de la sustancia permanece siempre igual. (Cap. 18, Sec. 1, pág. 529)

physical property / propiedad física: cualquier característica de un material, como el estado, el color y el volumen, que se puede observar o medir sin alterar o intentar alterar el material. (Cap. 18, Sec. 1, pág. 528)

pioneer species / especie pionera: los primeros organismos que crecen en áreas nuevas o que han sido perturbadas; desintegran las rocas y acumulan material en descomposición para que otras plantas puedan crecer en el lugar. (Cap. 5, Sec. 2, pág. 125)

placental / placentario: mamífero cuyas crías se desarrollan dentro del útero materno hasta que se forman completamente y están listas para nacer; posee una placenta (órgano en forma de saco), la cual suministra al embrión alimento y oxígeno y elimina sus residuos. (Cap. 7, Sec. 4, pág. 200)

plain / llanura: relieve enorme y plano que con frecuencia posee suelos gruesos y fértiles; por lo general se encuentra en las regiones interiores de un continente. (Cap. 15, Sec. 1, pág. 438)

plankton / plancton: organismos marinos minúsculos, como las diatomeas, que están a la deriva en las aguas superficiales de todos los océanos. (Cap. 12, Sec. 4, pág. 355)

plateau / meseta: relieve levantado y plano formado principalmente por rocas casi horizontales que han sido levantadas. (Cap. 15, Sec. 1, pág. 440)

point source / fuente puntual: una sola fuente identificable de contaminación. (Cap. 9, Sec. 3, pág. 259)

pollution / contaminación: introducción de productos de desecho, sustancias químicas y otras sustancias dañinos al ambiente . (Cap. 9, Sec. 1, pág. 246)

polyp / pólipo: forma corporal con forma de jarra, generalmente sésil, en el ciclo de vida de un cnidario. (Cap. 6, Sec. 2, pág. 155)

population / población: todos los individuos de una especie que viven en el mismo espacio al mismo tiempo. (Cap. 8, Sec. 1, pág. 220)

population density / densidad demográfica: número de individuos en una población que ocupan un área de tamaño limitado. (Cap. 8, Sec. 2, pág. 224)

potential energy / energía potencial: energía almacenada debido a la posición. (Cap. 20, Sec. 1, pág. 592)

precipitation / precipitación: agua que cae de las nubes; incluye la lluvia, la nieve, la cellisca y el granizo, y cuya forma la determina la temperatura del aire. (Cap. 11, Sec. 1, pág. 316)

primary wave / onda primaria: onda sísmica que mueve las partículas rocosas en un movimiento oscilatorio en la misma dirección en que viaja la onda. (Cap. 14, Sec. 2, pág. 413)

prime meridian / primer meridiano: línea imaginaria que representa 0° de longitud y corre desde el polo norte, atravesando Greenwich, Inglaterra, hasta el polo sur. (Cap. 15, Sec. 2, pág. 445)

producer / productor: organismo que puede elaborar su propio alimento mediante la fotosíntesis o la quimiosíntesis. (Cap. 12, Sec. 4, pág. 357)

protist / protista: organismo eucariota unicelular o multicelular que puede parecerse a las plantas, a los animales o a los hongos. (Cap. 4, Sec. 1, pág. 88)

protozoan / protozoario: protista unicelular que parece un animal y que puede vivir en el agua, en la tierra y en organismos vivos o muertos. (Cap. 4, Sec. 1, pág. 93)

pseudopods / seudópodos: extensión citoplásmica temporal que usan algunos protistas para la locomoción y para atrapar alimentos. (Cap. 4, Sec. 1, pág. 94)

pulley / palanca: objeto acanalado, como una rueda, por el cual se pasa una cuerda. (Cap. 19, Sec. 3, pág. 573)

R

radiation / radiación: energía que transmiten las ondas. (Cap. 10, Sec.2, pág. 292; Cap. 20, Sec. 2, pág. 603)

radula / rádula: órgano punzante de muchos moluscos parecido a una lengua, que tiene proyecciones parecidas a dientes que se usan para raspar y rallar el alimento. (Cap. 6, Sec. 3, pág. 159)

relative humidity / humedad relativa: medida de la cantidad de humedad que sostiene el aire, comparada con la cantidad de humedad que el aire puede sostener a una temperatura dada; puede variar de 0 por ciento a 100 por ciento. (Cap. 11, Sec. 1, pág. 312)

renewable / renovable: recurso energético que los procesos naturales pueden reciclar o reemplazar en menos de 100 años. (Cap. 9, Sec. 2, pág. 249)

resistance / resistencia: una medida del grado de dificultad con que los electrones pueden fluir a través de un material; la unidad de medida es el omnio (Ω). (Cap. 21, Sec. 2, pág. 634)

reverse fault / falla invertida: ruptura en la roca causada por las fuerzas de compresión, en que la roca sobre la superficie de la falla se mueve hacia arriba en relación con la roca debajo de la falla. (Cap. 14, Sec. 1, pág. 410)

revolution / revolución: movimiento de la Tierra alrededor del Sol, el cual se demora un año en completarse. (Cap. 17, Sec. 1, pág. 493)

rhizoids / rizoides: estructuras parecidas a hilos que anclan las plantas no vasculares al suelo. (Cap. 5, Sec. 2, pág. 124)

rock / roca: material sólido inorgánico que por lo general está compuesto de dos o más minerales; puede ser metamórfica, sedimentaria o ígnea. (Cap. 13, Sec. 1, pág. 376)

rock cycle / ciclo de las rocas: diagrama que muestra el proceso lento y continuo de las rocas en el cual éstas cambian de un tipo a otro. (Cap. 13, Sec. 3, pág. 395)

rotation / rotación: movimiento giratorio de la Tierra alrededor de su eje, el cual ocurre una vez cada 24 horas, produciendo el día y la noche y hace aparecer los planetas y estrellas como si saliesen y se pusiesen. (Cap. 17, Sec. 1, pág. 492)

runoff / escorrentía: agua que fluye sobre la superficie terrestre. (Cap. 18, Sec. 2, pág. 479)

S

salinity / salinidad: medida de sólidos disueltos (sales) en las aguas marinas. (Cap. 12. Sec. 1, pág. 342)

saprophyte / saprofito: organismo que se alimenta de los tejidos de otros organismos muertos o en proceso de descomposición. (Cap. 3, Sec.2, pág. 68; Cap. 4, Sec. 2, pág. 100)

scientific method / método científico: técnicas para solucionar problemas y responder preguntas que puede incluir los siguientes pasos: reconocer un problema, recoger información, formular y poner a prueba una hipótesis, analizar datos y sacar conclusiones. (Cap. 1, Sec. 1, pág. 7)

sea breeze / brisa marina: movimiento de aire diurno desde el mar hacia la tierra; se forma cuando el aire más frío sobre el agua se mueve hacia el interior forzando el ascenso del aire calentado y menos denso sobre la tierra. (Cap. 10, Sec. 3, pág. 299)

secondary wave / onda secundaria: onda sísmica que al moverse hace que las partículas rocosas vibren formando un ángulo recto a la dirección del movimiento de la onda. (Cap. 14, Sec. 2, pág. 413)

sedimentary rock / roca sedimentaria: un tipo de roca formada por fragmentos de otras rocas, minerales disueltos o materia vegetal y animal que se congregan para formar capas rocosas. (Cap. 13, Sec. 2, pág. 389)

seismic wave / onda sísmica: onda generada por un movimiento sísmico. (Cap. 14, Sec. 2, pág. 412)

seismograph / sismógrafo: instrumento que registra las ondas sísmicas y anota el momento de llegada de cada onda. (Cap. 14, Sec. 2, pág. 415)

series circuit / circuito en serie: circuito con una sola trayectoria a través de la cual puede fluir la corriente eléctrica. (Cap. 21, Sec. 3, pág. 638)

simple machine / máquina simple: dispositivo que facilita el trabajo con un movimiento solamente; puede cambiar el tamaño o la dirección de una fuerza; entre este tipo de máquina se incluyen la cuña, el tornillo, la palanca, la rueda y eje, la polea y el plano inclinado. (Cap. 19, Sec. 3, pág. 572)

slump / desprendimiento: ocurre cuando una masa de roca o sedimento se mueve cuesta abajo sobre una superficie curva. (Cap. 16, Sec. 2, pág. 475)

soil / suelo: mezcla de roca meteorizada, materia orgánica y aire que sustenta el crecimiento de plantas. (Cap. 16, Sec. 1, pág. 470)

solar energy / energía solar: energía proveniente del Sol que es renovable, no contamina y es abundante, pero que sólo funciona cuando brilla el Sol. (Cap. 9, Sec. 2, pág. 249)

solar system / sistema solar: compuesto por nueve planetas y numerosos otros objetos que giran alrededor de nuestro Sol y que se mantienen unidos gracias a la gravedad solar. (Cap. 17, Sec. 2, pág. 498)

spontaneous generation / generación espontánea: teoría que dice que los seres vivos pueden originarse a partir de la materia inerte. (Cap. 1, Sec. 3, pág. 19)

sporangium / esporangio: cápsula de espora redonda de un hongo cigote. (Cap. 4, Sec. 2, pág. 103)

spore / espora: célula reproductora impermeable de los hongos; puede crecer en un nuevo organismo. (Cap. 4, Sec. 2, pág. 101)

state of matter / estado de la materia: propiedad física que depende tanto de la temperatura como de la presión y que se presenta en cuatro formas: sólido, líquido, gas o plasma. (Cap. 18, Sec. 1, pág. 531)

static charge / carga estática: acumulación de cargas eléctricas en un objeto. (Cap. 21, Sec. 1, pág. 625)

station model / código meteorológico: indica las condiciones del tiempo en un lugar específico, mediante el uso de símbolos en un mapa. (Cap. 11, Sec. 3, pág. 327)

stomata / estomas: pequeñas aperturas en la superficie de la mayoría de las hojas de las plantas que permiten la entrada y salida del dióxido de carbono, del agua y del oxígeno. (Cap. 5, Sec. 3, pág. 131)

strike-slip fault / falla transformante: lugar donde las fuerzas de cizallamiento han ocasionado el rompimiento de las rocas, las cuales se deslizan una al lado de la otra en direcciones opuestas, pero sin mucho movimiento vertical. (Cap. 14, Sec. 1, pág. 411)

supernova / supernova: explosión muy brillante de la parte externa de una supergigante que se lleva a cabo después del colapso de su núcleo. (Cap. 17, Sec. 3, pág. 509)

surface current / corriente superficial: corriente oceánica que por lo general sólo desplaza unos cuantos cientos de metros del nivel superior de agua marina. (Cap. 12, Sec. 2, pág. 346)

surface wave / onda de superficie: onda sísmica que mueve las partículas rocosas de arriba hacia abajo en un movimiento rotatorio y de lado a lado en un movimiento de vaivén. (Cap. 14, Sec. 2, pág. 413)

symbiosis / simbiosis: cualquier interacción estrecha entre dos o más especies diferentes; incluye el mutualismo, el comensalismo y el parasitismo. (Cap. 8, Sec. 2, pág. 226)

symmetry / simetría: distribución de las partes corporales; puede ser radial (arreglada alrededor de un punto central), bilateral (con partes especulares) o asimétrica (sin forma corporal definida). (Cap. 6, Sec. 1, pág. 151)

T

temperature / temperatura: medida de la energía cinética de los átomos de un cuerpo. (Cap. 20, Sec. 2, pág. 597)

theory / teoría: explicación de fenómenos o cosas basada en el conocimiento científico generado a partir de múltiples observaciones y pruebas. (Cap. 1, Sec. 1, pág. 10)

thermocline / termoclina: capa de agua oceánica que comienza a una profundidad de unos 200 m y cuya temperatura disminuye progresivamente con la profundidad. (Cap. 12, Sec. 1, pág. 344)

tide / marea: ascenso y caída rítmicos del nivel del mar causados por la atracción gravitatoria de la Tierra y la Luna y la Tierra y el Sol. (Cap. 12, Sec. 3, pág. 353)

tissue / tejido: grupo de células similares que realizan la misma función. (Cap. 2, Sec. 2, pág. 49)

topographic map / mapa topográfico: mapa que muestra los cambios en elevación en la superficie terrestre e indica rasgos como caminos y ciudades. (Cap. 15, Sec. 3, pág. 450)

topography / topografía: relieves superficiales de un área que influyen en el tipo de suelo que se desarrolla en la región. (Cap. 8, Sec. 3, pág. 230)

tornado / tornado: tormenta de viento violento y arremolinado que se mueve sobre una estrecha trayectoria sobre la tierra y que puede ser resultado de los vientos laterales dentro de una tormenta eléctrica. (Cap. 11, Sec. 2, pág. 322)

toxin / toxina: sustancia venenosa que producen algunos patógenos. (Cap. 3, Sec. 2, pág. 71)

transformer / transformador: dispositivo que se usa para aumentar o rebajar el voltaje de una corriente alterna y el cual produce poca pérdida de energía. (Cap. 22, Sec. 2, pág. 668)

troposphere / troposfera: capa de la atmósfera terrestre más próxima a la tierra, contiene un 99 por ciento de vapor de agua y un 75 por ciento de los gases atmosféricos; es la región donde se forman las nubes y ocurre el estado del tiempo. (Cap. 10, Sec. 1, pág. 284)

tsunami / tsunami: onda marina sísmica que comienza sobre el foco de un terremoto y la cual puede ser muy destructiva cuando llega al litoral. (Cap. 14, Sec. 3, pág. 424)

U

ultraviolet radiation / radiación ultravioleta: energía que llega a la Tierra proveniente del Sol; puede causar daños a la piel y ocasionar cáncer; gran parte de esta radiación es absorbida por la capa de ozono. (Cap. 10, Sec. 1, pág. 288

upwarped mountains / montañas plegadas anticlinales: montañas que se forman cuando los bloques de corteza terrestre son forzados a ascender por fuerzas internas de la Tierra. (Cap. 15, Sec. 1, pág. 442)

upwelling / corriente resurgente: corriente oceánica que mueve las aguas frías y profundas hacia la superficie oceánica. (Cap. 12, Sec. 2, pág. 350)

V

vaccine / vacuna: preparación que se elabora a partir de bacterias muertas o partículas dañadas de las paredes celulares de bacterias; se usa para prevenir algunas enfermedades. (Cap. 3, Sec. 2, pág. 73)

vacuole / vacuola: organelo celular en forma de globo en el citoplasma que almacena alimento, agua y otras sustancias. (Cap. 2, Sec. 1, pág. 42)

variable / variable: cada una de las condiciones que pueden cambiar durante el curso de un experimento. (Cap. 1, Sec. 1, pág. 9)

vascular plant / planta vascular: planta con estructuras tubulares por donde se mueven los minerales, el agua y otras sustancias por toda la planta. (Cap. 5, Sec. 1, pág. 123)

velocity / velocidad: rapidez de un cuerpo y su dirección de movimiento; cambia cuando cambia la rapidez, cuando cambia la dirección del movimiento o cuando las dos cambian. (Cap. 19, Sec. 1, pág. 559)

volcanic mountains / montañas volcánicas: montañas que se forman cuando el material fundido llega a la superficie terrestre a través de partes debilitadas de la corteza y se amontona en una estructura que tiene forma de cono. (Cap. 15, Sec. 1, pág. 443)

voltage / voltaje: una medida de la cantidad de energía eléctrica que tiene cada electrón en una batería; se mide en voltios (V). (Cap. 21, Sec. 2, pág. 632)

W
---

water cycle / ciclo del agua: ciclo continuo de moléculas de agua en la Tierra, que ascienden en la atmósfera, regresan a la Tierra como lluvia u otro tipo de precipitación y fluyen hacia ríos y océanos a través de los procesos de evaporación, condensación y precipitación. (Cap. 8, Sec. 3, pág. 232)

wave / ola: en el océano, el movimiento rítmico que transporta energía a través del agua. (Cap. 12, Sec. 3, pág. 351)

weather / tiempo: estado de la atmósfera en un momento y lugar específicos, determinado por factores que incluyen la presión atmosférica, la cantidad de humedad en el aire, la temperatura y el viento. (Cap. 11, Sec. 1, pág. 310)

weathering / meteorización: proceso natural que rompe y desintegra las rocas. (Cap. 16, Sec. 1, pág. 466)

work / trabajo: se lleva a cabo cuando una fuerza aplicada causa el movimiento de un cuerpo en la dirección de la fuerza. (Cap. 19, Sec. 3, pág. 570)

X
---

xylem / xilema: tejido vascular que forma vasos huecos que transportan sustancias, excluyendo los azúcares, por toda la planta. (Cap. 5, Sec. 3, pág. 133)

The index for *Glencoe Science* will help you locate major topics in the book quickly and easily. Each entry in the index is followed by the number of the pages on which the entry is discussed. A page number given in boldfaced type indicates the page on which that entry is defined. A page number given in italic type indicates a page on which the entry is used in an illustration or photograph. The abbreviation *act.* indicates a page on which the entry is used in an activity.

A

Abiotic factors, 216–218, *217, 218;* air, 218, *218;* light, 217, *217;* soil, 218, *218;* temperature, 217; water, 217, *217*

Abrasion, 478

Acceleration, 559–561, *559;* calculating, 560; force and, 562, *562;* velocity and, 561, *561*

Acid(s): natural, 468–469, *469;* weathering and, 468–469, *469*

Acid rain, 246

Activities, 27, 28–29, 44, 50–51, 66, 74–75, 99, 108–109, 139, 140–141, 171, 172–173, 192, 202–203, 222, 234–235, 262, 268–269, 290, 300–301, 329, 330–331, 345, 362–363, 397, 398–399, 420, 428–429, 455, 456–457, 472, 482–483, 497, 514–515, 547, 548–549, 577, 578–579, 609, 610–611, 643, 644–645, 660, 670–671

Adaptations: of amphibians, 187, *187;* for flight, 194, *194;* of reptiles, 191, *191*

Adirondack Mountains, 442

Aerobe, 62, *62*

Agriculture, *242;* fungi in, 106, *106*

Air: heated, 295, *295;* movement of, 295–299, *296, 297;* oxygen in, 282–283, *283*

Air mass, 318, *318*

Air pollution, 246–247, *247, 267, 267;* environment and, 218, *218;* ozone depletion, 288–289, *288, 289;* smog, 283

Air temperature, 311, *311,* 327

Albatross, *193*

Algae, 89–92, *89, 91, 92, act.* 99; green, *act.* 44, 120, *120,* 217; oxygen production by, 288

Alligator, 190, *190*

Alternating current (AC), 666, 667

Alternative resources, 249–256; geothermal energy, **254,** *254;* hydroelectric power, **253,** *253;* nuclear energy, **255**–256, *255, 256;* solar energy, **249**–251, *249, 250, 251;* wind energy, 252, *252*

Altitude: and atmospheric pressure, 218, 286, *286*

Altostratus clouds, 315

Alveoli, 198

Amniotic egg, 191, *191*

Amoeba, 94, *94,* 96

Amphibians, 187–189, *187, 188, 189*

Anaerobe, 62, *62,* 65

Anemometer, 311

Angiosperms, 135–137, *135, 137,* 138

Anglerfish, 356, *356*

Animal(s). *see also* Invertebrate animals; Vertebrate animals; bottom-dwelling, 356, *356;* characteristics of, 150–152, *150, 151;* chordates, **182**–183, *183;* classifying, *act.* 149, 152, *152;* competition among, 225, *225;* habitats of, 227; hibernation of, 187; identifying, 535; reproduction of. *see* Reproduction; symmetry in, 151, *151;* weathering and, 467

Animal cell, *39, 40,* 45, *45*

Animal-like protists, 89, 93–96, *93, 94, 95, act.* 99

Annelids (segmented worms), 160–163, *161, 162, 163*

Annuals, 137, *137*

Antarctica: food webs in, 230, *230;* ozone hole in, 289, *289*

Anteater, 199, *199*

Anthracite coal, 245

Antibiotics, 67, 73, *73,* 107

Anticyclone, 319

Ant(s), 164, *164*

Apatite, 377, 380

Appalachian Mountains, 441

Apparent magnitude, 507

Appendages, 164

Appendices. *see* Reference Handbook

Aquatic ecosystems: freshwater, 217

Arachnids, 178, *178*

Archaebacteria, 65, *65*

Aristotle, 22

Arthropods, 164–169, *164, 165, 166–167, 168*

Ascus, 102

Asexual reproduction, 95, *95,* 155, *155*

Ash, 540, 541–545

Asteroid, 502, *502*

Index

Index

42; observing, *act.* 37; organization of, 47–49; plant, *39, 41,* 46, *46;* special functions of, 45–46, *45, 46;* solar, 251; structure of, 40–42, *40, 41*

Cell membrane, *40,* **41**

Cell theory, 38

Cellular respiration, 42, *42*

Cellulose, 120, 121, *121*

Cell wall(s), 41, *41,* 119, 120, 121

Celsius scale, 599

Centipedes, 168, *168*

Cephalopods, 160, *160*

Chalk, 390, 391, 468

Changes. *see* Chemical changes; Physical changes

Charge: electric, 624–630, *624, 625, 627, 628;* flow of, 631–633, *632, 633;* induced, 629, *629;* static, **625,** *625*

Charon (moon of Pluto), 504

Cheese: and bacteria, 70, *70*

Chemical bonds, 605

Chemical changes, 540, 541–542, *540, 541, act.* 548–549

Chemical energy, 588, 604–608, *604, 605, 606, 608,* 633, *633*

Chemical properties, 540–546; of building materials, 544; classifying according to, 544; common, 541–542, *541;* examples of, *540*

Chemical reactions, 604

Chemical rocks, 390, *390*

Chemical weathering, 468–469, *468, 469*

Chemistry Integration, 41, 70, 120, 154, 231, 348, 633

Chemosynthesis, 357

Chlorofluorocarbons (CFCs), 288, *288*

Chlorophyll, 62, 63, 89, 91, 101, 119, 357

Chloroplasts, *41, 43, 43, act.* 44, 119

Chordates, 182–183, *182*

Chromosome(s), 40, 42

Cilia, 93, *93*

Ciliates, 93, *93*

Circuit, 631, 636–645; electric energy in, 632, *632;* parallel, **639,** *639, act.* 643; protecting, 639, *639;* resistance in, 634–635, *634, 635, 636;* series, **638,** *638;* simple, 631, *631*

Circuit breakers, 639, *639*

Circulatory system: closed, **160;** open, **159**

Cirques, 477, *477*

Cirrostratus clouds, 315, *315*

Cirrus clouds, 315

Classification, 4, *act.* 5, 22–27; according to chemical properties, 542; of animals, *act.* 149, 152, *152;* of coins, *act.* 527; dichotomous key for, 26; field guides for, 25; history of, 22–23; of igneous rock, 385; of minerals, 381, *act.* 398–399; modern, 23, *23;* of plants, *122,* 123, *123;* of protists, 88, 89; scientific names in, 24–25, 123, *123;* of seeds, *act.* 27; of soils, *act.* 472; of vertebrate animals, 182, *183*

Clean Water Act, 260

Clear-cutting, 265, *265*

Cleavage, 378, *378*

Climate: change of, 349; ocean currents and, 348, *348,* 349, 350; soil formation and, 470

Clouds, 293, 314–316, *314, 315,* 321, *321*

Club fungi, 102, *102*

Club mosses, 128, *128*

Cnidarians, 154–155, *155*

Coal, *244*–245, 245, 248, *248,* 390

Coastal plains, 439, *439*

Cocci, 61, *60*

Coelum, 160

Coins: classifying, *act.* 527

Cold front, 319, *320*

Colony: space, *act.* 514–515

Color: of minerals, 379, *379;* as physical property, 529, *529*

Colorado Plateau, 440, *440*

Columbus, Christopher, 296

Comets, 504, *504*

Communities, *219,* **220;** symbiosis in, **226**

Compass, 654, 659, *659, act.* 660

Composting, *act.* 74–75

Compound Machine, 572

Compression forces, 410, *410*

Conch, 159, *159*

Conclusions, 9

Condensation, 293, *293,* 312, *312*

Conduction, 292, *292,* **600**–601, *601*

Conductor, 628, *628*

Conductors, 601

Cone-bearing plants, 119, 134, *134*

Conglomerate, *389,* 390, *395*

Conic projection, 449, *449*

Conifers, 134, *134,* 138, *act.* 139

Conservation, 265–266, *265;* of energy, 594–595, *595;* of mass, 544–546, **545,** 546

Constant speed, 558

Constellation, 506, *506,* 507

Consumers, 62, 64, 228, **357**

Continental glaciers, 476, *476*

Contour feathers, 195, *195*

Contour lines, 450

Contractile vacuole, 93, *93*

Control, 9

Convection, 292–293, *292,* **602**–603, *603*

Copper, 383, *383, 384;* ductility of, 534; reaction with oxygen, *541*

Copper wire, 628, 634, *634*

Index

Index

U

Credits

Art Credits

Glencoe would like to acknowledge the artists and agencies who participated in illustrating this program: Absolute Science Illustration; Andrew Evansen; Argosy; Articulate Graphics; Craig Attebery represented by Frank & Jeff Lavaty; CHK America; Gagliano Graphics; Pedro Julio Gonzalez represented by Melissa Turk & The Artist Network; Robert Hynes represented by Mendola Ltd.; Morgan Cain & Associates; JTH Illustration; Laurie O'Keefe; Matthew Pippin represented by Beranbaum Artist's Representative; Precision Graphics; Publisher's Art; Rolin Graphics, Inc.; Wendy Smith represented by Melissa Turk & The Artist Network; Kevin Torline represented by Berendsen and Associates, Inc.; WILDlife ART; Phil Wilson represented by Cliff Knecht Artist Representative; Zoo Botanica.

Photo Credits

Abbreviation Key: AA=Animals Animals; AH=Aaron Haupt; AMP=Amanita Pictures; BC=Bruce Coleman, Inc.; CB=CORBIS; DM=Doug Martin; DRK=DRK Photo; ES=Earth Scenes; FP=Fundamental Photographs; GH=Grant Heilman Photography; IC=Icon Images; KS=KS Studios; LA=Liaison Agency; MB=Mark Burnett; MM=Matt Meadows; PE=PhotoEdit; PD=PhotoDisc; PQ=PictureQuest; PR=Photo Researchers; SB=Stock Boston; TSA=Tom Stack & Associates; TSM=The Stock Market; VU=Visuals Unlimited.

Cover (l)Daniel J. Cox/Stone, (r)Photodisc, (bkgd)Corbis; **xiv** Zig Leszczynski/AA; **x** James H. Robinson; **xi** C.C. Lockwood/DDB Stock Photo; **xiii** James H. Robinson; **xix** Simon Fraser/Science Photo Library/PR; **xv** Robert Holmes/CB; **xvi** Philip Dowell/DK Images; **xvii** Gary W. Carter/VU; **xx** Michael P. Gadomski/PR; **xxiii** John Lemker/ES; **2–3** Diane Scullion Littler; **3** (l)Jonathan Eisenback/PhotoTake NYC/PQ, (r)Janice M. Sheldon/Picture 20-20/PQ; **4** Mickey Gibson/AA; **4–5** A. Witte & C. Mahaney/Stone; **5** Joanne Huemoeller/AA; **6** Kjell B. Sandved/VU; **8–9** MB; **11** Tek Image/Science Photo Library/PR; **12–13** MB; **14** (tl)Michael Abbey/Science Source/PR, (bl)AH, (r)VU/Michael Delannoy; **15** MB; **16** (tl tcl bcl)Dwight Kuhn, (tcr)A. Glauberman/PR, (tr)MB, (others)Runk/Schoenberger from GH; **17** (t)Bill Beaty/AA, (bl)Tom & Therisa Stack/TSA, (br)Michael Fogden/ES; **18** AH; **19** Geoff Butler; **20** (tl)Dover Pictorial Archive, (b)Johnny Autrey, (others)Janet Dell Russell Johnson; **22** (t)Arthur C. Smith III from GH, (bl)Hal Beral/VU, (br)Larry L. Miller/PR; **23** Doug Perrine/Innerspace Visions; **24** (l)Brandon D. Cole, (r)Gregory Ochocki/PR; **25** (l)R. Andrew Odum/Peter Arnold, Inc., (r)Zig Leszczynski/AA; **26** Alvin E. Staffan; **27** Geoff Butler; **28** (t)Jan Hinsch/Science Photo Library/PR, (b)MB; **29** MB; **32** (tl)Jeff Greenberg/Rainbow, (tr)Hans Pfletschinger/Peter Arnold, (bl)Peter B. Kaplan/PR, (bc)John T. Fowler, (br)Milton Rand/TSA; **33** MB; **36** Manfred Kage/Peter Arnold, Inc.; **36–37** LEGOLAND California; **37** MM; **38** The Science Museum, London; **39** (t)David M. Phillips/VU, (c)Richard Shiell/ES, (bl)Michael Keller/TSM, (bc)Zig Leszczynski/AA, (br)Reed/Williams/AA; **43** Gabe Palmer/TSM; **46** (tl)R. Kessel & G. Shih/VU, (tc)DM, (tr)Carolina Biological Supply Co./ES, (b)Bruce Iverson; **47** Ed Reschke/Peter Arnold, Inc.; **48** Norbert Wu/Peter Arnold, Inc.; **50** (t)Envision/George Mattei, (b)Morrison Photography; **51** DM; **52** Sam Ogden/Science Photo Library/PR; **53** (l)Custom Medical Stock Photo, Inc., (r)Sam Ogden/Science Photo Library/PR; **54** (tl)Michael Abbey/PR, (tr)J.L. Carson/Custom Medical Stock Photo, (bl)Paul Silver/BC, (br)Newcomb & Wergin/Stone; **55** (l)Kevin Collins/VU, (r)David M. Phillips/VU; **58** M. Cobos/M. Yokoyama; **58–59** David Matherly/VU; **59** AH; **62** Dr. L. Caro/Science Photo Library/PR; **63** (tl)Dr. Dennis Kunkel/Phototake, (tc)David M. Phillips/VU, (tr)R. Kessel & G. Shih/VU, (bl)Ann Siegleman/VU, (br)SCIMAT/PR; **64** (t)T.E. Adams/VU, (b)Manfred Kage/Peter Arnold, Inc.; **65** R. Kessel & G. Shih/VU; **66** T.E. Adams/VU; **67** (tl)M. Abbey Photo/PR, (tc)Oliver Meckes/Eye of Science/PR, (tr)S. Lowry/University of Ulster/Stone,

(bl)Richard J. Green/PR, (br)A.B. Dowsett/Science Photo Library/PR; **68** Ray Pfortner/Peter Arnold, Inc.; **70** (l)Paul Almasy/CB, (r)Joe Munroe/PR; **71** (t)Terry Wild Studio, (b)J.R. Adams/VU; **73** John Durham/Science Photo Library/PR; **74** (t)KS, (b)John Evans; **75** John Evans; **76** (tl)P Canumette/VU, (tr)John Evans, (b)Ken Graham/BC; **76–77** Dr. Philippa Uwins, The University of Queensland; **77** Heide Schulx/Max Planck Institute of Science; **78** (t)David Woodfall/DRK, (b)Argus Fotoarchiv/Peter Arnold, Inc.; **84** Stephen St. John/National Geographic Image Collection; **84–85** Glenn W. Elison; **86** Volker Steger/Peter Arnold, Inc.; **86–87** Art Wolfe; **87** (t)AMP, (b)Jana R. Jirak/VU; **89** (l)Jean Claude Revy/PhotoTake NYC, (r)Anne Hubbard/PR; **90** (tl) NHMPL/Tony Stone, (tr)Microfield Scientific Ltd./Science Photo Library/PR, (bl)David M. Phillips/PR, (br)M.I. Walker/Science Source/PR; **91** (l)Pat & Tom Leeson/PR, (r)Jeffrey L. Rotman/Peter Arnold, Inc.; **92** Walter H. Hodge/Peter Arnold, Inc.; **93** Eric V. Grave/PR; **94** (t) Kerry B. Clark, (b)Astrid & Hanns Frieder-Michler/Science Photo Library/PR; **96** (l)Ray Simons/PR, (c)MM/Peter Arnold, Inc., (r)Gregory G. Dimijian/PR; **97** (t)Dwight Kuhn, (b)AMP; **98** Richard Calentine/VU; **99** Biophoto Associates/Science Source/PR; **100** (l)Joe McDonald/BC, (r)James W. Richardson/VU; **101** Carolina Biological Supply Co./PhotoTake NYC; **102** (tl)file photo, (tr)Ken Wagner/VU, (b)Dennis Kunkel; **103** (l)Science VU/VU, (r)J.W. Richardson/VU; **104** (tl)Frank Orel/Stone, (tc)Charles Kingery/PhotoTake NYC, (tr)Bill Bachman/PR, (b)Nancy Rotenberg/ES; **105** (tl c)Stephen Sharnoff, (tr)Biophoto Associates/PR, (bl)L. West/PR, (br)Larry Lee Photography/CB; **106** (l)Nigel Cattlin/Holt Studios International/PR, (r)Michael Fogden/ES; **107** Ray Elliott/ Stone; **108** (t)Ken Wagner/VU, (b)AMP; **109** AMP; **110** (l)Walter Sanders/Time Pix, (r)Alvarode Leiva/LA; **111** Courtesy Beltsville Agricultural Research Center West/USDA; **112** (t)Andrew J. Martinez/PR, (c)Dennis Kunkel, (b)Nigel Cattlin/Holt Studios/PR; **113** (l)Michael Delaney/ VU, (r)AMP; **114** Nigel Cattlin/Holt Studios/PR; **116** Harry N. Darrow/BC; **116–117** Tom Bean/DRK; **117** MB; **118** TSA; **119** Laat-Siluur; **120** (t)Kim Taylor/BC, (b)William E. Ferguson; **121** (tl br)AMP, (tr)Ken Eward/PR, (bl)PR; **122** (tl)Douglas Peebles/CB, (tcl)Edward S. Ross, (tc)Gerald & Buff Corsi/VU, (tcr)Philip Dowell/DK Images, (tr)Dan McCoy from Rainbow, (c)Martha McBride/Unicorn Stock Photos, (bl)Gerald & Buff Corsi/VU, (bcl)Mack Henley/VU, (bc)Steve Callahan/VU, (bcr)David Sieren/VU, (br)Kevin & Betty Collins/VU; **123** (t)Gail Jankus/PR, (b)Michael P. Fogden/BC; **124** (l)Larry West/BC, (c)Scott Camazine/PR, (r)Kathy Merrifield/PR; **125** Michael P. Gadomski/PR; **127** (t)Farrell Grehan/PR, (bl)Steve Solum/BC, (bc)R. Van Nostrand, (br)Inga Spence/VU; **128** (t)Joy Spurr/BC, (b)W.H. Black/BC; **129** Farrell Grehan/PR; **130** AMP; **131** (l)Nigel Cattlin/PR, (c)Doug Sokell/TSA, (r)Charles D. Winters/PR; **132** Bill Beatty/VU; **134** (t)Robert C. Hermes, (cl)Doug Sokell/TSA, (cr)Bill Beatty/VU, (b)David M. Schleser/PR; **135** (t)E. Valentin/PR, (cl)Joy Spurr/PR, (cr)Dia Lein/PR, (c br)Eva Wallander, (bl)Wardene Weisser/BC; **137** (l)Dwight Kuhn, (c)Joy Spurr/BC, (r)John D. Cunningham/VU; **138** (l)J. Lotter/TSA, (r)J.C. Carton/BC; **140** (t)Inga Spence/VU, (b)Jim Steinberg/PR; **141** David Sieren/VU; **142** Michael Rose/Frank Lane Picture Agency/CB; **143** (l)Dr. Jeremy Burgess/Science Photo Library/PR, (r)Ron Levy/LA; **144** (t) Robert Hitchman/BC, (c)Stephen P. Parker/PR, (b)Milton Rand/ TSA; **145** (l)Adam Jones/PR, (r)William J. Weber; **148** Bill Beatty/ VU; **148–149** Jim Zipp/PR; **149** file photo; **150** (l)Fred Bravendam/Minden Pictures, (c)Scott Smith/AA, (r)Fritz Prenzel/AA; **153** Runk/Schoenberger from GH; **155** Carolina Biological Supply Co./PhotoTake NYC; **156** Oliver Meckes/PR; **157** Renee Stockdale/AA; **158** Anne Wertheim/AA; **159** (l)David Hall/PR, (r)Andrew J. Martinez/PR; **160** Alex Kerstitch/KERST/BC; **161** Robert Maier/AA; **162** James M. Robinson; **163** (l)Chris McLaughlin/AA, (c)Nancy Sefton, (r)A. Flowers & L. Newman/PR; **164** SuperStock; **166** (t)Joe McDonald/CB, (cl)Peter Johnson/CB; (c)F. Stuart Westmorland/CB, (cr)Natural History Museum, London, (b)Joseph S. Rychetnik; **167** (tl)John Shaw, (tr)Scott T. Smith/CB, (cl br)Brian Gordon Green, (cr)Richard T. Nowitz/CB, (bl)PhotoTake NYC; **168** (tl tr)SuperStock, (tc)Donald Specker/AA, (bl)John Fowler, (br)John Shaw/TSA; **169** (l)Alex Kerstitch/BC, (c)Nancy Sefton, (r)Scott Johnson/AA; **170** Richard Mariscal/BC; **171** MM; **172** (t)Super-Stock, (b)MM; **173** MM; **174** (t)Mike Severns/TSA, (c)Runk/Schoenberger from GH, (b)Kim Reisenbichler MBARI; **176** (t)Alex Kerstitch/VU, (c)Donald Specker, (b)Atkinson/AA; **180** Dave Roberts/Science Photo Library/PR; **180–181** Tom & Pat Leeson; **181** AMP; **185** (tl)F. Stuart Westmorland/Stone, (tc)Gerard Lacz/AA, (tr)Joyce & Frank Burek/AA, (cl)D. Fleetham/OSF/AA, (c)Tom McHugh/PR, (cr)Mickey Gibson/AA, (bl)Amos Nachoum/CB, (bc)D. Fox/OSF/AA, (br)Brandon D. Cole/CB; **186** (l)Science VU/VU, (r)Runk/Schoenberger from GH; **187** S.R. Maglione/PR; **188** Runk/Schoenberger from GH; **189** (t)VU, (bl)Runk/Schoenberger from GH, (br)George H. Harrison from GH; **190** (t)Robert J. Erwin/PR, (c)Wendell D. Metzen/ BC, (bl)PR, (br)Dan Suzio/PR; **192** Stephen Dalton/PR; **193** (l)PR, (cl)Jane McAlonen/VU, (cr)Erwin C. Nielson/VU, (r)Fritz Polking/VU; **194** (l)Jeff Lepore/PR, (r)Arthur R. Hill/VU; **195** (t)Tom & Pat Leeson/PR, (c)Andrew Syred/Science Photo Library/PR, (bl)Crown Studios, (br)Marcia Griffen/AA; **196** VU; **197** (l)Gerard Fuehrer/VU, (c)Richard Thom/VU, (r)Francois Gohier/PR; **199** (t) Dave Watts/TSA, (b)James L. Amos/CB; **200** (tl)S.R. Maglione/PR, (tr)SuperStock, (b)Carolina Biological Supply Co./PhotoTake NYC; **201** Ted Kerasote/PR; **202** (t)Mark Newman/PR, (b)Alan Carey; **203** Mella Panzella/AA; **204** Ressmeyer/ Wheeler Pictures/TimePix; **204–205** Barry Rosenthal/FPG; **205** Mark Garlick/Science Photo Library/PR; **206** (t)Fritz Polking/VU, (c)Dave B. Fleetham/VU, (b)David R. Frazier/PR; **207** (l)Alvin E. Staffan/PR, (r)John Cancalosi/DRK; **210** Christopher Hallowell; **212–213** Roger Garwood & Trish Ainslie/CB; **213** MB; **214** P. Parks/ OSF/AA; **214–215** Sanford/Agliolo /TSM; **215** AH; **216** Wm. J. Jahoda/PR; **217** (t)F. Stuart Westmorland/PR, (c)Michael P. Gadomski/ES, (b)George Bernard/ES; **218** Francis Lepine/ES; **220** (l)Roland Seitre-Bios/Peter Arnold, Inc., (c)Robert C. Gildart/ Peter Arnold, Inc., (r)Carr Clifton/Minden Pictures; **222** Bob Daemmrich; **224** Dan Suzio/PR; **225** (l)Arthur Gloor/AA, (r)Tim Davis/PR; **226** Gilbert Grant/PR; **227** John Gerlach/AA; **228** Michael P. Gadomski/PR; **229** (t)Joe McDonald/CB, (c)David A. Northcott/CB, (bl)Michael Boys/CB, (bc)Dennis Johnson/Papilio/CB, (br)Kevin Jackson/AA, (bkgd)Michael Boys/CB; **231** (t)Ray Richardson/AA, (tc)Suzanne L. Collins/PR, (bc)William E. Grenfell Jr./VU, (b)Zig Leszczynski/ES; **234** (t)Geoff Butler, (b)KS; **235** KS; **236** Allen Russell/Index Stock; **237** Courtesy Dave Garza DVM; **238** Gerard Fuehrer/VU; **239** (l)Richard Reid/ES, (r)Helga Lade/Peter Arnold, Inc.; **242** Paul Harris/Stone; **242–243** Richard H. Johnston/FPG; **243** DM; **247** Argus Fotoarchiv/P. Frischmuth/Peter Arnold, Inc.; **249** Tony Craddock/ PR; **250** (l tr)Joe Flores/DOE/NREL, (br)James Pacheco; **251** (l)Martin Bond/Science Photo Library/PR, (r)William J. Weber/VU; **252** Doug Sokell/VU; **254** Simon Fraser/Science Photo Library/PR; **257** Tom Van Sant, Geosphere Project/Planetary Visions/Science Photo Library/PR; **259** (l)Simon Fraser/Science Photo Library/PR, (r)The Telegraph Colour Library/FPG; **263** Kent Knudson/SB; **264** (tl)Lynn M. Stone, (bl)Lily Solmssem/PR, (r)Larry Miller/PR; **265** (t)J.P. Jackson/PR, (b)Christiana Dittman from Rainbow; **266** (t)Michael Simpson/FPG, (c)Ron Whitby/FPG, (b)Geoff Butler; **267** C.G. Randall/FPG; **268** (t)Yann Arthus-Bertrand/CB, (b)Morrison Photography; **269** Steve McCutcheon/VU; **270** Jerry Bauer; **271** Courtesy Tamara Ledley; **272** (tl)James Martin/Stone, (tr)Ken Graham/Stone, (bl)Leonard L.T. Rhodes/ES, (br)CB; **273** (l)Jim McDonald/CB, (r)Jeremy Hardie/Stone; **274** Geri Murphy; **278–279** Henry Diltz/CB; **279** Granger Collection, New York; **280** Lester V. Bergman/CB; **280–281** David Keaton/TSM; **281** MB; **282** NASA; **283** (t)David S. Addison/VU, (bl)Frank Rossotto/TSM, (br)Larry Lee/CB; **286** Laurence Fordyce/CB; **288** DM; **289** NASA/GSFC; **290** Michael Newman/PE; **292** Larry Fisher/Masterfile; **295** (t)Dan Guravich/PR, (b)Bill Brooks/Masterfile; **297** (t)Gene Moore/PhotoTake NYC/PQ, (cl)Phil Schermeister/CB, (cr)Stephen R. Wagner, (bl)Joel W. Rogers, (br)Kevin Schafer/CB; **298** Bill Brooks/Masterfile; **300–301** David Young-Wolff/PE; **302** Bob Rowan/CB; **303** Cour-

tesy The Weather Channel; **304** (l)J.A. Kraulis/Masterfile, (r)CB; **305** (l)Tom Bean/DRK, (r)Keith Kent/Science Photo Library/PR; **308** NASA; **308–309** Michael S. Yamashita/CB; **309** KS; **310** Kevin Horgan/Stone; **311** Fabio Colombini/ES; **315** (l)Joyce Photographics/PR, (r)Charles O'Rear/CB; 316 (l)Roy Morsch/TSM, (r)Mark McDermott/Stone; **317** (l)Mark E. Gibson/VU, (r)EPI Nancy Adams/TSA; **319** Van Bucher/Science Source/PR; **321** Jeffrey Howe/VU; **322** Roy Johnson/TSA; **323** (l)Warren Faidley/Weatherstock, (r)Robert Hynes; **324** NASA/ Science Photo Library/PR; **325** Fritz Pölking/Peter Arnold, Inc.; **326** Howard Bluestein/Science Source/PR; **329** MB; **330** (t)Marc Epstein/DRK, (b)Timothy Fuller; **332–333** Erik Rank/ Photonica; **333** Courtesy Weather Modification Inc.; **334** (l)Peter Miller/Science Source/PR, (r)Gary Williams/LA; **335** (l)George D. Lepp/PR, (r)Janet Foster/Masterfile; **336** Bob Daemmrich; **338** Manfred Kage/Peter Arnold, Inc.; **338–339** F. Stuart Westmorland; **339** Timothy Fuller; **340** (l)Laurie Evans/Stone, (c)Michele Westmorland, (r)Kevin Schafer/Peter Arnold, Inc.; **343** F. Stuart Westmorland; **345** MB; **347** TSADO/GSFC/TSA; **348** Tibor Bognar/TSM; **354** Gary Vestal/Stone; **355** (tl)Norbert Wu/DRK, (bl)Fred Bavendam/Minden Pictures, (r)Darlyne Murawski/National Geographic Image Collection; **356** (t)Norbert Wu/Peter Arnold, Inc., (bl)Fred Bavendam/Minden Pictures, (br)Tom & Therisa Stack/TSA; **357** (l)Tom & Therisa Stack/TSA, (r)Dwight Kuhn/DRK; **359** (clockwise from top) (1)Pieter Folkens, (2)Galen Rowell/CB, (3)Jeffrey L. Rotman/CB, (4)Douglas P. Wilson/Frank Lane Picture Agency/CB, (5)Deneb Karentz, (6)Flip Nicklin, (7)Rick & Nora Bowers/VU, (8)G.L. Kooyman/AA, (9)Peter Johnson/CB, (10)British Antarctic Survey, (b)Professor N. Russell/Science Photo Library/PR; **361** Mike Severns/Stone; **362** KS; **363** Betsy R. Strasser/VU; **365** NASA/Science Source/PR; **366** (l)Chris Huxley/Masterfile, (tr)Clyde H. Smith/Peter Arnold, Inc., (br)M.C. Chamberlain/DRK; **367** (tl)M.C. Chamberlain/DRK, (bl)Tom & Therisa Stack/TSA, (r)W. Wayne Lockwood/CB; **368** William Jorgensen/VU; **370** NASA; **371** Donna McWilliam/ AP/Wide World Photos; **372–373** Mike Zens/CB; **373** Mark A. Schneider/VU; **374** Carr Clifton/Minden Pictures; **374–375** David Muench/CB; **375** MB; **376** (l)DM, (r)MB; **377** Mark A. Schneider/VU; **378** (t)Manuel Sanchis Calvete/CB, (c)José Manuel Sanchis Calvete/CB, (bl)DM, (br)Mark A. Schneider/VU; **379** (l)Albert J. Copley/VU, (r)FP; **380** Tim Courlas; **382** (tl)Ryan McVay/PD, (tr)Lester V. Bergman/CB, (b)Margaret Courtney-Clarke/PR; **383** (l)Walter H. Hodge/Peter Arnold, Inc., (r)Craig Aurness/CB; **384** KS; **385** Kyodo/AP/Wide World Photos; **386** (l)Stephen J. Krasemann/DRK, (r)Brent P. Kent/ES; **387** (l)Breck P. Kent/ES, (r)Brent Turner/BLT Productions; **388** (t)Steve Kaufman/CB, (c)Galen Rowell/Mountain Light, (bl)Martin Miller, (br)David Muench/CB; **389** (t)John D. Cunningham/VU, (others)Morrison Photography; **390** Jeff Foott/DRK; **391** (l)Yann Arthus-Bertrand/CB, (r)Alfred Pasieka/Science Photo Library/PR; **392** NASA/CB; **393** (tl)Brent Turner/BLT Productions, (tr bl)Breck P. Kent/ES, (cl)Andrew J. Martinez/PR, (cr)Tom Pantages/PhotoTake NYC/PQ, (bl)Runk/Schoenberger from GH; **394** (tr)Peter Arnold/Peter Arnold, Inc., (tl)Stephen J. Krasemann/DRK, (bl)Christian Sarramon/CB, (b)M. Angelo/CB; **395** (t)Breck P. Kent/ES, (bl)DM, (br)Andrew J. Martinez/PR; **396** Bernhard Edmaier/Science Photo Library/PR; **397** Andrew J. Martinez/PR; **398** (t)Cliff Leight/Outside Images/PQ, (b)MM; **400** (t)Archive Photos, (bl)Stock Montage, (br)Brown Brothers; **401** (l)Arne Hodalic/CB, (r)Herbert Gehr/Timepix; **402** (t)Stephen J. Krasemann/DRK, (c)Michael Dalton/FP, (b)Tui De Roy/Minden Pictures; **403** (l)A.J. Copley/VU, (c)Barry L. Runk from GH, (r)Breck P. Kent/ES; **404** Breck P. Kent/ES; **406** Bettmann/CB; **406–407** Paras Shah/AP/Wide World Photo; **407** MB; **408** Tom & Therisa Stack/TSA; **410** (t)Tom Bean/DRK, (b)Lysbeth Corsi/VU; **411** David Parker/PR; **412** Tom & Therisa Stack/TSA; **414** Robert W. Tope/Natural Science Illustrations; **421** (l)Steven D. Starr/SB, (r)Berkeley Seismological Laboratory; **422** AP Photo/HURRIYET; **423** David J. Cross/Peter Arnold, Inc.; **426** James L. Stanfield/National Geographic Society; **427** Courtesy Safe-T-Proof; **428** (l)Ben Simmons/TSM, (r)Reuters NewMedia Inc./CB;

430 (l)Bettmann/CB, (r)RO-MA Stock/Index Stock; 431 Richard Cummins/CB; 432 (l)Reuters/STR/Archive Photos, (r)Russell D. Curtis/PR; 433 (l)Science VU/VU, (r)Peter Menzel/SB; 434 Vince Streano/CB; 436 David Weintraub/SB; 436–437 GSFC/NASA; 437 Dominic Oldershaw; 439 (l)Alan Maichrowicz/Peter Arnold, Inc., (tr)Carr Clifton/Minden Pictures, (br)Stephen G. Maka/DRK; 440 (t)Tom Bean/DRK, (b)CB; 441 John Lemker/ ES; 442 (t)John Kieffer/Peter Arnold, Inc., (b)Carr Clifton/Minden Pictures; 443 David Muench/CB; 446 Dominic Oldershaw; 451 (t)Rob & Ann Simpson, (c)Robert E. Pratt, (b)courtesy Maps a la Carte, Inc. and TopoZone.com; 456 John Evans; 457 Layne Kennedy/CB; 458 (l)Culver Pictures, (r)Photodisk; 459 (t)PD, (bl)William Manning/TSM, (br)Kunio Owaki/TSM; 460 (l)William J. Weber, (r)AH; 461 (l)Tom Bean/DRK, (r)Marc Muench; 464 Tom McHugh/PR; 464–465 Doug Menuez/SB/PQ; 465 KS; 466 Jonathan Blair/CB; 467 R. & E. Thane/ES; 468 (l)DM, (r)DM; 469 (t)AH, (bl)Layne Kennedy/CB, (br)Richard Cummins/CB; 472 KS; 473 USGS; 474 (t)Martin Miller, (c)D.P. Schwert/North Dakota State University, (b)Jeff Foott/BC, (bkgd) Roger Ressmeyer/CB; 476 (l)Chris Rainier/CB, (r)Glenn M. Oliver/VU; 477 (tl)John Lemker/ES, (tr)Francois Gohier/PR, (b)Paul A. Souders/CB; 478 (t)Gerald & Buff Corsi/VU, (b)Dean Conger/CB; 479 (t)KS, (b)Tess & David Young/TSA; 480 (l)Vanessa Vick/PR, (r)Gerard Lacz/ES; 481 Martin G. Miller/ VU; 482 Dominic Oldershaw; 483 MB; 484 (l)Will & Deni McIntyre/PR, (r)Robert Nickelsberg/Time Inc.; 484–485 Morton Beebe, SF/CB; 486 (t)Leonard Lee Rue III/PR, (cl)Layne Kennedy/ CB, (cr)C.C. Lockwood/ES, (b)Jonathan Blair/CB; 487 (l)Martin G. Miller/VU, (r)James P. Rowan/DRK; 488 Johnny Johnson/AA; 490 David Parker/Science Photo Library/PR; 490–491 David Nunek/Science Photo Library/PR; 491 Morrison Photography; 494 Lick Observatory; 495 Francois Gohier/PR; 496 Jerry Lodriguss/PR; 497 DM; 500 (l)USGS/Science Photo Library/PR, (r)NASA/Science Source/PR; 501 (t)CB, (bl)NASA, (br)USGS/ TSADO/TSA; 502 (t)JPL/TSADO/TSA, (b)CB; 503 (t)ASP/ Science Source/PR, (b)NASA/JPL/Tom Stack and Associates; 504 (t)NASA/JPL, (b)Dr. R. Albrecht, ESA/ESO Space Telescope European Coordinating Facility/NASA; 505 AP/Wide World Photos; 507 Dominic Oldershaw; 509 Palomar Observatory; 510 (c)Royal Observatory, Edinburgh/Science Photo Library/PR, (others)Anglo-Australian Observatory; 511 Frank Zullo/PR; 513 R. Williams/NASA; 514 (l)Movie Still Archives, (r)NASA; 515 MB; 516 (l)Pictor, (r)Pierce/Halser/NASA/Goddard Space Flight Center; 516–517 NASA; 517 NASA; 518 (t)Dr. Fred Espenak/PR, (b)Dr. R. Albrecht, ESA/ESO Space Telescope European Coordinating Facility/NASA; 519 (l)NASA, (r)National Optical Astronomy Observatories; 520 Rich Brommer; 522 William E. Ferguson; 523 Jeff Foott/DRK; 523 (l)Joyce Photographics/PR, (r)M. Deeble/Stone/OSF/ES; 524–525 Douglas Peebles/CB; 525 Henry Ford Museum & Greenfield Village; 526 Michael Newman; 526–527 AP Photo/Steve Nutt; 527 MB; 528–530 MM; 531 AH; 533 David Taylor/Science Photo Library/PR; 534 (t)SuperStock, (b)Ray Pfortner/Peter Arnold, Inc.; 535 AMP; 536 (l)Steve Kaufman/CB, (tr)Tom McHugh/PR, (br)Fred Bavendam/Minden Pictures; 537 Don Tremain/PD; 538 MB; 539 (t)Kenneth Mengay/LA, (c)file photo; (b)Mark Thayer; 540 (l)Richard Megna/FP, (cl)John Lund/Stone, (cr)Richard Pasley/SB, (r)T.J. Florian/Rainbow/PQ; 541 (l)Philippe Colombi/PD, (c)Michael Newman/PE, (r)Roger K. Burnard; 542 MM; 543 (t)Ralph Cowan/FPG, (bl br)AH; 545 Jeff Daly/VU; 546 Timothy Fuller; 548 (t)AH, (b)MM; 549 (l r)John A. Rizzo/PD, (c)AH; 550 (tl)SuperStock, (tr)S. Solum/Photolinks/PD, (bl)AMP, (br)Pat Lacroix/Image Bank; 551 (tl)file photo, (tr c)Siede Preis/PD, (bl)John Evans, (br) AH; 552 Elaine Shay; 554 ©1993 University of Wisconsin, Madison; 554–555 Ron Chapple/FPG International/PQ; 555 MB; 556 Dennis O'Clair/Stone; 557 Charles D. Winters/PR; 561 Gettyone; 562 Runk/Schoenberger from GH; 564 Lew Long/ TSM; 565 (l)MB, (r)Bob Daemmrich; 567 (tl tr)Bob Daemmrich, (b)Gregg Otto/VU; 568 (l)CB, (r)NASA, (bkgd)Roger Ressmeyer/ CB; 569 Stephen Simpson/FPG; 570 KS; 572 DM; 574 (l)Tom Pantages, (c)MB, (r)Bob Daemmrich/SB/PQ; 575 Bob Daemmrich; 576 (t)Tom McHugh/PR, (b)R.J. Erwin/PR; 577 KS; 578 (t)Helmut Gritscher/Peter Arnold, Inc., (b)Jonathan Nourok/PE; 579 Mary M. Steinbacher/PE; 580 (t)Adam Woolfitt/CB, (c)Daniel J. Cox/Stone, (b)Franck Seguin, TempSport/PQ; 580–581 Tom Brakefield/CB; 581 (t)Michael S. Yamashita/CB, (b)Walter Geiersperger/Index Stock/PQ; 582 (t)CB, (c)Joseph P. Sinnot/FP, (b)NASA; 583 (l) Ryan McVay/PD, (r)David Young-Wolff/PE; 586 Ezio Geneletti/The Image Bank; 586–587 Reuters New Media Inc./CB; 587 Bruno Herdt/PD; 588 Kennan Ward/TSM; 589 (tl)Michael Kevin Daly/TSM, (tr)Quest/Science Photo Library/ PR, (b)David Young-Wolff/PE; 590 Alan Thornton/Stone; 591 (t)W. Cody/CB, (cl)from The Extinction of the Dinosaurs by Eleanor Kish, reproduced by permission of the Canadian Museum of Nature, Ottawa, Canada, (cr)William Swartz/Index Stock/PQ, (bl)Duomo/ CB, (br)CB; 592 Paul Avis/LA; 594 (l)Jim Wark/Peter Arnold, Inc., (r)Lester Lefkowitz/TSM; 595 (l c)Jim Cummins/FPG, (r)David Young-Wolff/PE; 599 (t)MB, (b)Paul Barton/TSM; 600 (l)David Higgs/ TSM, (r)José Fuste Raga/TSM; 601 Thinsulate is a trademark of 3M, photo courtesy 3M; 604 (l)GH, (r)Laura Riley/BC/PQ; 607 Tony Freeman/PE; 610 (t)MB, (b)KS; 611 MB; 612 TSM; 613 Barkley Thieleman, The Paducah Sun/AP/Wide World Photos; 614 (t)Charlie Westerman/LA; (c)Steve Cole/PD, (b)Index Stock; 620 Layne Kennedy/CB; 620–621 (bkgd)Richard Pasley/SB/ PQ; 621 MB; 622 H. David Seawall/CB; 622–623 Peter Menzel/SB/PQ; 623 Geoff Butler; 625 (t) Richard Hutchings, (b)KS; 626 Stephen R. Wagner; 630 J. Tinning/ PR; 638 DM; 639 (t)DM, (b)Geoff Butler; 641 Bonnie Freer/ PR; 643 MM; 644–645 Richard Hutchings; 646–647 Tom & Pat Leeson/PR; 647 William Munoz/PR; 648 (t)DM, (c)AP Photo/ Matt York, (b)IC; 650 DM; 652 (t)John Evans, (b)Thomas Slorian/ Index Stock; 652–653 Argus Fotoarchiv/Peter Arnold, Inc.; 653 (t)Brown Brothers, (b)U.S. Dept. of the Interior/National Park Service/Edison National Historic Site; 655 Richard Megna/FP; 656 AMP; 658 PD; 659 John Evans; 661 (l)Kodansha, (c)Manfred Kage/Peter Arnold, Inc., (r)DM; 663 (t)Takeshi Takahara/PR, (b)Slim Films; 665 Bjorn Backe Papilio/CB; 667 Norbert Schafer/TSM; 669 Michael Newman/PE; 670 (t)file photo, (b)AH; 671 AH; 673 Courtesy France Ann Cordova; 674 (tl)IC, (tr)Digital Vision/ PQ, (bl)StockTrek/PD, (br)Spencer Grant/PE; 675 (l)SIU/Peter Arnold, Inc., (r)Latent Image; 676 file photo; 678 Fujifotos/The Image Works; 680–681 PD; 682 (t)PR, (b)David M. Dennis; 683 (t)Roy Morsch/TSM, (cl)Harry Rogers/PR, (cr)Donald Specker/AA, (b)Roger K. Burnard; 684 (tl)Tom McHugh/PR, (tr b)Donald Specker/AA, (cl)Harry Rogers/PR, (c)Carroll W. Perkins/ AA, (cr)Patti Murray/AA; 685 (tl)Harry Rogers/PR, (tr)Ken Brate/PR, (cl)James H. Robinson/ PR, (cr)Linda Bailey/AA, (bl)Ed Reschke/Peter Arnold, Inc., (br)MM; 686 Greg Probst/Stone; 687 (l)GH, (r)George Ranalli/PR; 688 (t)AH, (b)Tom Bean/Stone; 689 (t)Tom Bean/DRK, (b)Gary Braasch/Stone; 690 file photo; 691 (t)Dan Feicht, (b)VU; 692 José Carrillo/PE; 693 (t)AH, (b)Michael J. Howell/Rainbow/PQ; 694 CB; 695 (t)Bill Vaine/CB, (b)John Dudak/PhotoTake NYC/PQ; 696 (t)NOAA Photo Library/Central Library, OAR/ERL/National Severe Storms Laboratory (NSSL), (c)Richard Hamilton Smith/CB, (b)Jeffry W. Myers/CB; 697 AP Photo/ Geophysical Institute, University of Alaska, Fairbanks via RE/MAX; 698 Mitchell D. Bridwell/PE; 702 David Young-Wolff/PE; 704 Kaz Chiba/PD; 705 Dominic Oldershaw; 706 StudiOhio; 707 MM; 709 (bl)Elaine Shay, (br)Brent Turner/ BLT Productions, (others)AMP; 712 Paul Barton/TSM; 715 AH; 725 MM.

Acknowledgments

"Friends, Foes, and Working Animals," from The Solace of Open Spaces by Gretel Ehrlich, copyright © 1985 by Gretel Ehrlich. Used by permission of Viking Penguin, a division of Penguin Putnam Inc. From Hiroshima by Laurence Yep. Copyright © 1985 by Laurence Yep. Reprinted by permission of Scholastic, Inc. "Song of the Sky Loom" from Wearing the Morning Star. Reprinted by permission Brian Swann

PERIODIC TABLE OF THE ELEMENTS

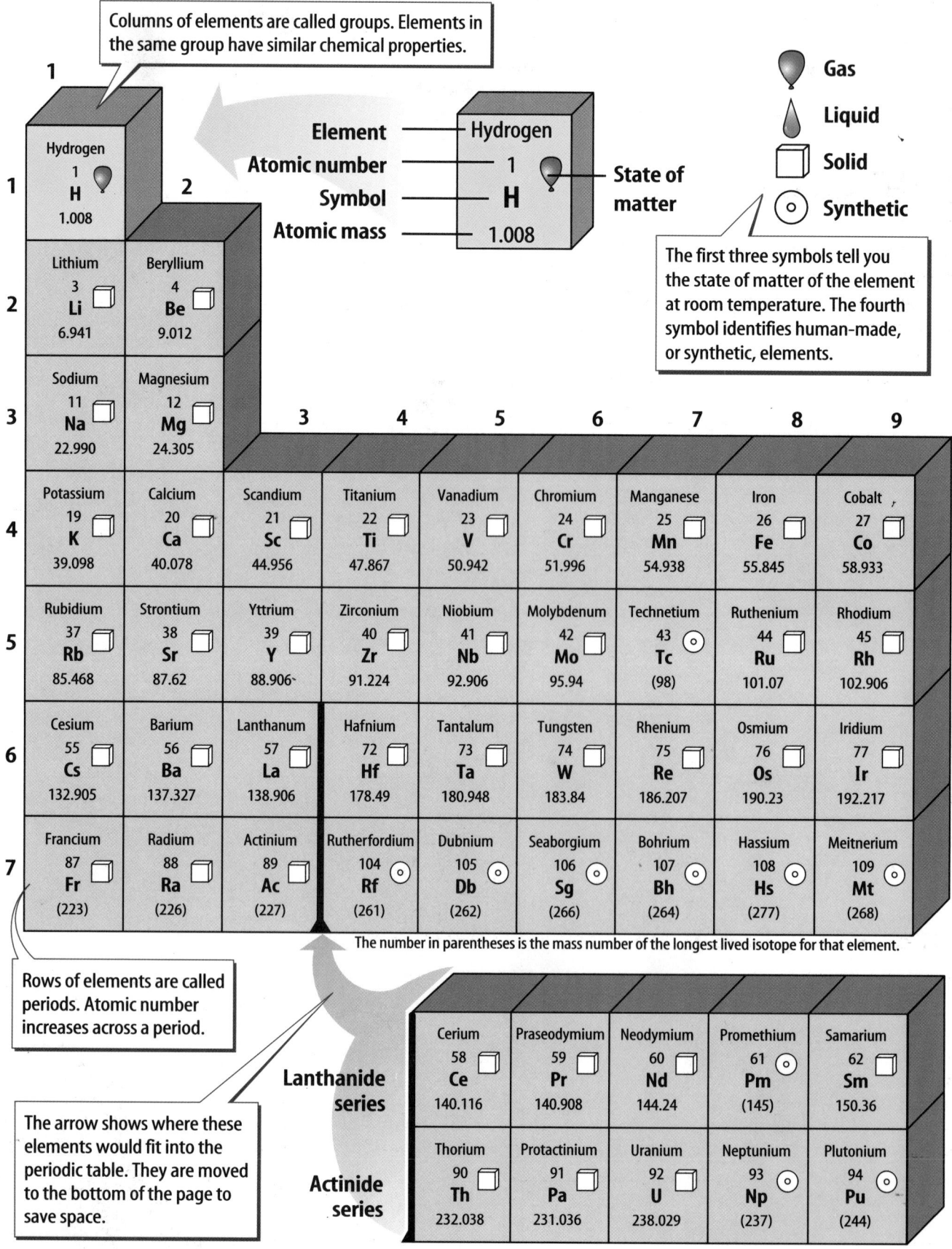

Columns of elements are called groups. Elements in the same group have similar chemical properties.

Element — Hydrogen
Atomic number — 1
Symbol — H
Atomic mass — 1.008

State of matter

- Gas
- Liquid
- Solid
- Synthetic

The first three symbols tell you the state of matter of the element at room temperature. The fourth symbol identifies human-made, or synthetic, elements.

1

1	Hydrogen 1 **H** 1.008

2	Lithium 3 **Li** 6.941	Beryllium 4 **Be** 9.012

3	Sodium 11 **Na** 22.990	Magnesium 12 **Mg** 24.305

	3	**4**	**5**	**6**	**7**	**8**	**9**
4	Scandium 21 **Sc** 44.956	Titanium 22 **Ti** 47.867	Vanadium 23 **V** 50.942	Chromium 24 **Cr** 51.996	Manganese 25 **Mn** 54.938	Iron 26 **Fe** 55.845	Cobalt 27 **Co** 58.933
5	Yttrium 39 **Y** 88.906	Zirconium 40 **Zr** 91.224	Niobium 41 **Nb** 92.906	Molybdenum 42 **Mo** 95.94	Technetium 43 **Tc** (98)	Ruthenium 44 **Ru** 101.07	Rhodium 45 **Rh** 102.906
6	Lanthanum 57 **La** 138.906	Hafnium 72 **Hf** 178.49	Tantalum 73 **Ta** 180.948	Tungsten 74 **W** 183.84	Rhenium 75 **Re** 186.207	Osmium 76 **Os** 190.23	Iridium 77 **Ir** 192.217
7	Actinium 89 **Ac** (227)	Rutherfordium 104 **Rf** (261)	Dubnium 105 **Db** (262)	Seaborgium 106 **Sg** (266)	Bohrium 107 **Bh** (264)	Hassium 108 **Hs** (277)	Meitnerium 109 **Mt** (268)

Potassium 19 **K** 39.098 | Calcium 20 **Ca** 40.078
Rubidium 37 **Rb** 85.468 | Strontium 38 **Sr** 87.62
Cesium 55 **Cs** 132.905 | Barium 56 **Ba** 137.327
Francium 87 **Fr** (223) | Radium 88 **Ra** (226)

The number in parentheses is the mass number of the longest lived isotope for that element.

Rows of elements are called periods. Atomic number increases across a period.

The arrow shows where these elements would fit into the periodic table. They are moved to the bottom of the page to save space.

Lanthanide series

Cerium 58 **Ce** 140.116	Praseodymium 59 **Pr** 140.908	Neodymium 60 **Nd** 144.24	Promethium 61 **Pm** (145)	Samarium 62 **Sm** 150.36

Actinide series

Thorium 90 **Th** 232.038	Protactinium 91 **Pa** 231.036	Uranium 92 **U** 238.029	Neptunium 93 **Np** (237)	Plutonium 94 **Pu** (244)